THE SOVIET UNION: WHAT LIES AHEAD?

Military-Political Affairs in the 1980s

Edited by
Major Kenneth M. Currie
and
Major Gregory Varhall

Published under the auspices of the
United States Air Force

Publication of this compendium does not constitute approval by any U. S. Government organization of inferences, findings, and conclusions contained therein. Publication is solely for the exchange and stimulation of ideas.

STUDIES IN COMMUNIST AFFAIRS
VOLUME 6

For sale by the Superintendent of Documents, U.S. Government Printing Office
Washington, D.C. 20402

Contents

i

Introduction

From 25 to 27 September 1980, nearly one thousand Soviet specialists from government, the military, and academia gathered in Reston, Virginia, for a conference sponsored by the Assistant Chief of Staff, Intelligence (ACS/I), United States Air Force. Their discussion of the topic "The Soviet Union: What Lies Ahead? Military-Political Affairs in the 1980s" constituted a truly comprehensive examination of all aspects of the problems of Soviet military power. This compendium of articles is the product of that conference.

Against the backdrop of the many changes that had taken place on the international scene, Major General James L. Brown, ACS/I, issued an invitation to the top scholars and other notable experts in the field of Soviet studies. Representatives of many shades of the political spectrum were invited to come to Reston for two days of panel discussions and for the presentation of new ideas and approaches as well as old ideas which perhaps had not been heard. Major General John B. Marks later replaced General Brown as ACS/I, and the enthusiastic support for the idea continued.

Originally, we had estimated that between 400 and 450 people might attend. Reservations poured in up to the final day of the conference, and, after the paper had settled, we found that 982 individuals had traveled from as far away as the Middle East to attend some or all of the conference. Panelists prepared papers which were then divided among 24 general subject areas all dealing with Soviet military-political affairs in the 1980s . . . a total of 96 articles were presented, discussed, critiqued, and questioned.

The conference achieved, and surpassed, its goals. The interchange of ideas among the leading government and academic experts on the Soviet Union and the fact that such an august body of specialists had focused on the most crucial challenge which faces the United States made the conference more than worth the effort.

This book is an attempt to present but some of the ideas which were expressed at the conference. Only about half of the articles could be presented because of space limitations. Other articles, at least as worthy of publication, could not be presented here because of their length or other factors such as copyright release. The articles have been subdivided into general headings; however, in many cases their scope is such that they have applicability to several areas of the field. They are and should be viewed as original contributions to the field of Soviet studies.

We should make two final points about the editing. First, we have standardized the use of abbreviations so that all Soviet terms appear in italics, and Soviet abbreviations have been used in preference to English abbreviations. Hopefully, this will serve to increase our understanding of Soviet practice and reduce confusion as to Soviet terminology. Second, we have had to make the usual editorial changes—shortening, imposing our own idiosyncrasies—to most of the articles herein. We take responsibility for these changes and for the readability of this volume. The final product, regardless of where the commas fall, makes a vital contribution to our understanding of US-Soviet relations.

*   *   *   *   *   *   *

Finally, the editors would be remiss were we not to make several acknowledgments. The original idea for the conference came from Lieutenant Colonel Robert E. Berls, Jr., formerly Chief of the Soviet Studies Branch, now of the National Defense University. The conference would not have succeeded without the herculean efforts of two other individuals: Master Sergeant Patricia A. Holloway, who—although new to the office—put together the myriad of administrative details into something that actually worked; and Paul M. Kozar, who kept the registrations, finances, and security arrangements straight and (tried to) handle VIPs. Lieutenant Colonel Phillip D. Gardner, currently Chief of the Soviet Studies Branch, took on himself the task of "scrubbing" the manuscript for those troublesome little "typos" and quirks of language which haunt an effort such as this right up to the end. We, of course, are culpable for any such problems which remain. Finally, our sincere thanks to all 96 panelists and contributors, but even more to the 900 other experts who challenged our minds and hopefully helped forge new solutions to many of the problems of Soviet military-political affairs confronting us today.

g.v
k.m.c.

Postscript   *April 23, 1984*

By the time this book reaches its audience, four years will have passed since the conference in Reston. Quite a bit has happened in those four years, and I must apologize to both our readers and, especially, our contributors for the delay. Nonetheless, after completely re-reading the material I feel it is as important now as when it was written. Very few points in the articles have been "overcome by events," and the insight of the authors is even more apparent in retrospect. I do ask, however, that our readers remember these articles were written in the middle of 1980 and, hence, do not have the benefit of four years' hindsight.

Finally, both Ken Currie and I owe a deep debt of thanks to Sergey Gordeyev for his reviewing and proofing the Russian citations. Sergey caught many things we were totally unaware of, and his knowledgeable comments, suggestions, and corrections were instrumental in improving the quality of our final product.

g.v.

Part I

The Soviet Military–Political Environment

Introduction

One of the basic shortcomings in many Western studies of Soviet military-political affairs has been a failure to appreciate the crucial differences between the Soviet and Western approaches to military strategy. The most common manifestation of this problem—"mirror imaging"—refers to the unfortunate tendency to view Soviet developments in Western terms or to use Western concepts to define Soviet decision-making on military-political matters. The former argument that the USSR accepted the US concept of "mutual assured destruction" serves as a case in point.

The articles in Part I examine the internal milieu in which Soviet military-political decisions are reached. The result is an attempt to view the questions of strategy and doctrine through Soviet eyes. It is almost certainly a truism that only by following such an approach can the West hope to acquire an accurate understanding of the Soviet challenge.

Richard Porter approaches his subject—Soviet military decision-making—using a cognitive processes methodology. He argues that Soviet military policy is the product of two dominant frameworks: the political and the military. The political framework provides overall decision-making guidance, while the military framework is concerned with the technical aspects of reaching decisions. Soviet military science and doctrine serve as the buffers between the two frameworks, shielding ideology from challenges to its infallibility and the military from excessive ideological dogma. The result is an exceptionally stable relationship. Porter argues that military doctrine, the "glue" in this relationship, implies the existence of a "compact" between the Party and the military.

David Jones and Daniel Hannaway are concerned with what can be termed the USSR's "military culture." Jones examines the "permanently operating factors" which shape Soviet strategic considerations and the military's role and attitudes in relation to the State and the Party. Despite the Russian Revolution, important prerevolutionary considerations remain strong: 1) the desire for stable frontiers, 2) support for a strong national government, 3) commitment to technological

4

progress, 4) the creation of institutions for mobilizing the state for defense, and 5) unity of the multinational state. The retention of attitudes and structures reminiscent of the past ensures continuity in foreign policy and in the military's relations with the existing regime. Daniel Hannaway is interested in the quality of Soviet military leaders. He examines the factors which the Soviet believe contribute to the formation of a good military leader. He concludes that ideological conviction and patriotism, initiative and independence, and pedagogical expertise are the most sought after qualities in the new generations of Soviet military officers.

Finally, Howard Frost explores an issue that has been the source of considerable controversy: the study of Soviet military-political relations in the USSR. Frost argues that much analysis has assumed the existence of endemic institutional conflict between the Party and the military, but he notes that analysis of the relationship should focus on the predominant elements of cooperation between the two leadership elites. While the Party is responsible for doctrine and the military for the formulation of military science, each group responds to the needs of the other so that military policy is the result of a highly coordinated process. Supporting the argument for a close working relationship are the presence of military leaders on Party bodies and the high percentage of Soviet officers who are Party members. Frost concedes that while there may well be potential sources of friction between the two institutions, these do not appear to threaten the close coordination between them. His conclusion: the Party–military relationship continues to be very strong.

Soviet Military Decisionmaking: A Framework for Analysis

Richard E. Porter

Introduction

This article seeks to aid those interested in the long-term directions of Soviet military policy. Consequently, it explores the realm of Soviet military decisionmaking from a different perspective and introduces a methodology derived from an analysis of cognitive processes.

I will begin by looking at some problems associated with analyzing Soviet military affairs and why a cognitive approach is worth exploring. The methodology described below exploits a simple cognitive construct common to all types of decisionmaking. Applied to the Soviet literature, it first permits the identification of two conceptual paradigms essential to Soviet military decisionmaking and, second, suggests the existence of two institutional frameworks which help these paradigms project themselves into the reality of contemporary decisionmaking. Finally, the two frameworks are tied together in a way which offers some novel insights into Soviet military decisionmaking.

Analytical Issues

The empirical evidence on Soviet decisionmaking is massive and yet hopelessly incomplete. The Soviets deny us some of the most basic information about their decisionmaking activity. That which does seep out is often fragmented and, in some cases, intentionally distorted.[1]

Our task of understanding is further complicated by the cultural differences between the Soviets and ourselves. The Soviets' unique historical experience is only part of the problem; their Marxist–Leninist philosophy gives them their own particular way of looking at the world. Differences in perspective alter the meaning of words and concepts, further aggravating the problem of understanding. For example, the concept of "war" in the West carries the connotation of intrawar bargaining and restraint absent from the Soviet's concept. To them, war is a destructive, annihilating affair dominated by nuclear weapons.

Despite its fragmentary character, we must still tie the evidence together if we are to understand the reality from which it comes. But the raw data give us few clues as to how to begin. Of the several possible approaches which have been proposed, one asserts national decisionmaking can be analyzed as if it were that of a rational individual decisionmaker. A second regards national decisionmaking as the product of internal bargaining among interest groups or bureaucratic entities. A third combines elements of the two in a single approach.[2]

The disadvantage of these approaches (and others like them) is that they generally focus on particular types of decisionmaking—bureaucratic, economic, political, military. In doing this, they arbitrarily exclude certain kinds of evidence which may be crucial to an overall understanding. These approaches also demonstrate a limited capability to look forward and thus offer little insight into long-term directions of Soviet military policy.

Methodology

An approach based on the decisionmaking process itself appears appropriate. First, decisionmaking is a fundamental responsibility of the leadership. Secondly, it is justifiable to assume that whatever its form, decisionmaking will reflect and be compatible with its underlying cognitive processes. A careful look at how individuals, groups, and institutions make decisions, in fact, reveals a construct common to all three processes.[3] This construct, or "decisionmaking framework," has three components: a "conceptual paradigm or cognitive model," an "objective or external reality," and "logical axioms" which bridge the gap between them.[4] The conceptual paradigm or cognitive model of external reality is essential to all decisionmaking because it permits the practitioner to deal with what would otherwise be an incoherent mass of evidence.

The logical axioms are an extension of the paradigm and reflect its basic values. They add the dimension of experience and help the paradigm project itself into the external world. Objective or external reality represents the world not as the paradigm sees it but as it truly exists. It encompasses both the totality of available empirical evidence and all the situational pressures which affect the decisionmaker. As a historical snapshot, its character continually changes. While it plays a major role in interpreting the present and immediate past, its dependence on empirical data and pressures of the moment limits its ability to look into the future.

In this approach, decisionmaking is the continual reconciliation of a conceptual paradigm with an objective reality. As a methodology, it is particularly attractive to those concerned with the long-term direction of Soviet military policy because it focuses on the aspect of decisionmaking which is more stable and historically consistent—the paradigm and its logical axioms. Also, it is symmetrical with the Soviet concept of dialectical unity which reconciles a "theoretical vision" to a similar objective reality. The Soviets call this reconciliation the "basic contradiction," or chief lever, of creativity and mental progress.[5] This symmetry is not surprising since the concept of a dialectic (which Marx borrowed from the German philosopher Hegel) was originally

7

formulated as an intellectual construct.

An inherent characteristic of all paradigms is their exceptional stability. Any restructuring impacts throughout the paradigm, generating psychological discomfort for individuals and organizations alike.[6] Group paradigms are more a consensus of shared images, values, and attitudes which serve to identify the group and define the nature of its activity. Because groups must consider the beliefs of all their members, modifying their paradigms is inherently more difficult than for individuals. Institutional paradigms, with their formally established structures, are the most difficult of all.

Once an organizational paradigm loses its utility or becomes discredited, it generates considerable internal stress within itself and eventually must be modified or replaced with a new paradigm. This often requires major changes to the organization's basic outlook and structure, which in turn severely test its ability to adapt and survive. If an organizational paradigm is based on an ideology which professes to be infallible, the option of giving way to new paradigms may not exist.[7] This phenomenon becomes clearer when we look at paradigms which claim to be the source of all "truth."

The existence of multiple operative paradigms complicates a paradigm analysis of decisionmaking. Consequently, the key concern of any such analysis is the "location" of truth.[8] In individual decisionmaking, the center of truth varies within the framework depending on the individual and the issue being addressed. Because of this variability, attempts to structure this type of decisionmaking are not practical without a deep insight into the personal beliefs of the individual and the situational factors influencing his actions.

This does not hold, however, for groups and institutions which have a dominant paradigm requiring truth eventually to reside within it. Soviet decisionmaking, for example, manifests a paradigm which is ideologically based (Marxism–Leninism) and professes to be the source of all truth. The political legitimacy of the regime is tied irrevocably to this ideological assertion. While other paradigms may initiate the decisionmaking process and offer recommended solutions, the truth on which action is taken must eventually fit within the ideological paradigm in order to preserve the party's political legitimacy.[9]

Should the party shed its ideological paradigm, it would also forfeit its political birth certificate. Thus, intellectual challenges to this paradigm tend to be perceived as challenges to the party's legitimacy. This partially explains the Soviets' sensitivity to ideological issues and why their task of reinterpretation is so difficult and painful. Accordingly, the ability to track the activity within this paradigm promises a good insight into the long-term directions of Soviet military policy. To do this, however, we must first know something about the nature and content of the operative paradigms which guide military decisionmaking.

Political Paradigm

The historical literature strongly indicates that Soviet decisionmaking is guided by a political and military paradigm. The political paradigm is based conceptually on Marxism, later "enriched" by Lenin to serve his revolutionary ambitions; the military paradigm remains controversial. The Party ideologues vehemently deny its existence because it suggests a source of truth outside Marxism–Leninism. There is adequate evidence in the Soviet literature, however, to confirm its presence. Conceptually, it is based on Western military thought (as codified by Clausewitz) modified to meet the social requirements of the Soviet state. Since paradigms inherently resist change, it is appropriate to begin our investigation of these two paradigms with the Russian Revolution and the formative years immediately following.

Philosophically, Marxism completely breaks with traditional Western thought and its metaphysical premises. By placing the source of all truth in the material world, it puts man's destiny outside the boundaries of human fallibility. To enable man to discover truth, Marx provided the concept of the dialectic—an ideological "porthole" through which to perceive and understand.[10] The dialectic had additional utility because it also described the "scientific" process by which the world moved toward its predetermined end. Marx ingeniously correlated the irregular pattern of this progression to historical stages of economic and social development. By defining the next historical stage as communism and giving it utopian qualities, he "scientifically" explained both the past and present and then linked them to an appealing future.

Marxism provided the professional revolutionary with two essential elements for his craft—a new source of legitimacy and a promise of inevitable victory. Its universal scope and utopian end greatly appealed to intellectuals such as Lenin who were disenchanted with the existing state of the world and wanted to change it.

Marx left a prophecy but no timetable for its fulfillment. Lenin and his associates were too impatient to wait for the "mole of history" to do its work and decided to give history a push toward its predetermined end. They asserted that the "conditions" of revolution could be created by an enlightened elite as well as by historical forces.

This assertion had a monumental impact on the subsequent course of Soviet decisionmaking because it gave truth a dual residence—within the material world and within the consciousness of a Bolshevik elite. Where Marx had turned Hegel's concept of the dialectic upside down to suit his purposes, Lenin righted it again to suit his. This dual residence of truth created deep within the political paradigm a basic contradiction in logic which was of great practical benefit because it greatly expanded decisionmaking flexibility. Communism became at the same time an international movement driven by economic laws and a national movement fostered by the ambitions of a well-organized elite. Such ideological "enrichment," however, could not be justified by words alone; it required a successful revolution.

Marxism provided the revolution with its philosophical base, but the struggle itself was driven by a logic unique to the revolutionary process and the events of the moment. Lenin's role was much like that of a military commander—meticulously calculating the strength of the enemy and then taking appropriate actions. Decisionmaking had to be opportunistic and tactical in nature;[11] an accurate assessment of the balance of power was absolutely essential. To confront the state at an inopportune time could destroy the movement, whereas to pass up a suitable opportunity could break the revolution's momentum and undermine its chances of success.

In light of these realities, it is not surprising the axioms which emerged to guide Soviet decisionmaking were military in nature. Some of the most discernible are:

- Priority of power
- Ends justify means
- Deceit and camouflage
- Seize the initiative
- Offense over defense
- Necessity of violence.

These axioms in various forms are still operative in the political paradigm today. The obsession with power and the meticulous calculation of its sufficiency is endemic to contemporary Soviet decisionmaking. The Soviets rarely just stumble into things—they carefully explore all the ramifications of major policy decisions.[12] Deceit and camouflage are an essential part of the revolutionary art, and few movements achieve power without mastering their use. Seizing the initiative and sustaining the momentum are paramount because they enhance control over events and increase the chances of success. Offensive action keeps the opponent off balance and intensifies morale and dedication. And the axiom that violence must accompany major social change ensures military considerations will weigh heavily in any efforts to advance socialism.[13]

The Bolsheviks achieved power against incredible odds and in the process acquired an unshakable faith in the correctness of their cause and its inevitable triumph. The revolutionary experience provided the crucible in which Marxism was bonded to its logical axioms and forged into a paradigm for political decisionmaking. Marxist doctrine legitimized the revolution, and the revolution legitimized the "enrichments" to the doctrine. These "enrichments" rightfully earned Lenin an honored place next to Marx. In its new form, Marxism–Leninism represented something quite different. Philosophically, it established an alternate source of truth and combined the inherent optimism of Marx with the tactical opportunism of Lenin. Doctrinally, it imparted to Soviet decisionmaking the necessary pragmatism and flexibility.

The revolution demonstrated that the advancement of socialism could be accelerated. In addition to the acceptance of Marxism, this acceleration required innovative decisionmaking based on accurate "scientific" analysis. The Bolsheviks' political legitimacy lies here—in their proved ability to read the pulse of history and act accordingly. Unfortunately, this legitimacy is conditional and depends on the party's continued ability to advance the socialist cause. The revolution marches on, led by the Party and buttressed by the full powers of the Soviet state. The political paradigm provides this trinity with a vision of its eventual destination and some general prescriptions on how to get there.

Military Paradigm

The military paradigm's emergence was not as dramatic as that of its political counterpart. Conceptually based on Western military thought, its fundamental tenets were established well before the revolution. Its major concern was not the validity of its content but whether or not it could survive the onslaught of a radically new political philosophy. The Party's recognition of its existence raised uncomfortable ideological issues. It suggested decisionmaking responsibility in a modern state was necessarily divisible. To explore the conceptual basis for Soviet military decisionmaking, it is appropriate to begin with Clausewitz's role in Soviet military thought.

It is difficult to separate Clausewitz's contributions to Soviet military thought from those of Lenin because they both shared a similar outlook on war. Lenin was an avid reader of military history and Clausewitz. As noted earlier, his role as a revolutionary leader approximated that of a military commander. Clausewitz's ideas about wars were particularly applicable because they reflected his experiences as a member of the Russian General Staff during the Napoleonic campaign in 1812.

Party theorists strongly reject the suggestion Clausewitz provides the conceptual basis for Soviet military thought.[14] They rightfully acknowledge his foresight in seeing war as the continuation of politics by other means. They fault him, however, for his failure to recognize the crucial importance of the class struggle from which all manifestations of war must emerge. Indirect challenges to this assertion exist—from Clausewitz and from the Soviets themselves.

Clausewitz established the special nature of military operations when he wrote that war has its own grammar. To him, it was a part of politics and at the same time separate from it. He used the analogy of the womb and the fetus. Politics, as the womb, nurtures the fetus and defines its nature. The fetus, however, although a part of the womb is an entity in its own right.[15] Prior to the revolution, the Marxist community recognized war as an art governed by its own imperatives. Engels' writings are often quoted by military writers to underline its

11

"unique" nature. In *Military Strategy,* Sokolovskiy echoes the theme: ". . . once the military movements on land and sea have been started, they are no longer subject to the desires and plans of diplomacy, but rather to their own laws which cannot be violated without endangering the entire expedition."[16] To establish the origin of a military paradigm, one needs to look beneath the polemics of the ideological rhetoric to the fundamental perceptions which guide military decisionmaking. Here, the difference between Lenin and Clausewitz is more discernible. Lenin's outlook reflects the basic optimism of Marx—later confirmed by triumphant revolution. Clausewitz's beliefs about war were the product of considerable personal experience—strongly colored by great defeats rather than great victories. Consequently, his outlook is inherently conservative and skeptical and reflects the primordial passions and brutality of the Napoleonic battlefield. To Clausewitz, war was an antiscience filled with imponderables.

The issue of a military paradigm was settled pragmatically by the exigencies of the times. The initial seizure of power confronted the party with a new responsibility for defending the state instead of destroying it. This task was beyond the capability of the Party's small, ill-equipped paramilitary units. The "primacy of power" axiom dictated a reversal of policy, and the Party attempted to reconstitute the Tsar's old army. Tsarist officers were invited to return and serve the new state. Those who accepted brought with them a familiarity with large-scale military operations and a schooled knowledge of Clausewitzian warfare.

This resurrection of the old soon embraced all state bureaucracies. Lenin and his associates had blundered seriously in their perception of the level of technical decisionmaking required (even in backward Russia) to run a large state. Prior to the revolution, Lenin wrote little which looked beyond the seizure of power. What he did write was shaped largely by ideology and not by any appreciation of practical realities.[17] Lenin never held a bureaucratic position; he naively believed bureaucratic decisionmaking was relatively simple and could be assumed easily by the "workers." The folly of this conviction became readily apparent when the entire bureaucracy ground to a halt in the civil war following the revolution.

Objective reality substantially altered the party's intended role in state decisionmaking. Marxism–Leninism was ill-suited to resolve the host of technical problems which confronted the new state. It was as if a small group of commandos had taken over General Motors: they were experts in seizing control but knew nothing about making automobiles. Consequently, the Party quickly confined its activities to defining institutional goals and pushing hard for their fulfillment—leaving the responsibility for technical decisionmaking to the qualified experts.

This pragmatic adjustment represented a significant ideological accommodation because it formally recognized the existence of other paradigms and other sources of truth. Dominance of the political paradigm was still essential for legitimacy, so the Party's new challenge was to ensure the technical sufficiency of state decisionmaking yet keep it within prescribed Marxist–Leninist boundaries.

The adaptation of Western military thought to the Soviet state took place in the period between the Russian civil war and the Great Patriotic War. The Party initially found itself strongly divided over the type of military establishment it needed. The issue had major political implications and ultimately became entangled in the power struggle to succeed Lenin. The emergence of Stalin brought a commitment to a large defense establishment, and the Party launched a major industrialization program to achieve it.

The Red Army was firmly established by the outbreak of war in 1939. Most doctrinal questions were resolved, but doubts persisted because there still had not been a "real" test of the new concepts in a major conflict. This occurred in the Great Patriotic War, and it was this experience which solidified Soviet military thought. The logical axioms which guided military decisionmaking became clearly discernible:

- Retain a high state of readiness
- Seek surprise
- Seize the initiative
- Sustain momentum
- Maintain maximum strength
- Attain total victory.

These axioms consistently are reflected today in the Soviet military literature. They project a strong predeliction for preemption. The ingredients for a decisive campaign are to be first off the mark, seize the initiative, build momentum, and crush the enemy with massive firepower.

The military paradigm emerged from the Great Patriotic War as a proved commodity. Its overriding concern is not the triumph of world socialism but the defense of the state and victory on the battlefield. It projects the same deep conservatism and skepticism which permeated Clausewitz's writings. War is filled with the unexpected, and the unexpected can determine its outcome. Consequently, the prudent are compelled to study war in its smallest detail—testing and retesting all plans, equipment, and personnel. Security is paramount; the slightest indiscretion eventually may lead to a major defeat.

Political Decisionmaking

The political paradigm serves as the conceptual basis for all state decisionmaking. As with all bureaucratic paradigms, it also provides a means of organizational control. In the Soviet case, this occurs with the help of a discernible cognitive structure which guides the institutional projection of the political paradigm. This structure is an external, institutional counterpart to the logical axioms.[18]

For the political paradigm, it introduces the concepts of the correlation of forces (COF) and centralized planning. The COF is a continuous calculation of the relationship of forces between socialism and capitalism. It is similar to a balance of power computation but encompasses every aspect of state policy. The Soviets divide it into four major categories: political, economic, military, and international. (The "political" provides the basis for foreign policy while the "international" addresses the world socialist movement.) The COF is an extension of the party's revolutionary decisionmaking, where making a "scientific" analysis was the first step toward tasking an appropriate action.

The COF is a "navigational fix", not a trend analysis. Measured within prescribed historical periods, it gives the Soviets "real world" flexibility and makes policy reversals like Brest–Litovsk and peaceful coexistence doctrinally possible. It imparts to Soviet decisionmaking a connotation of optimism and assurance by saying that the directed course of action is the "scientifically" correct one. Additionally, it provides a useful means of integrating the formulation and implementation of state policy.

While the COF focuses on conceptualization, centralized planning deals with implementation. Centralized planning is the Soviets' substitute for the West's free market system; it is an essential part of a nationalized economy. Its true attractiveness, however, lies not with its false claims of superior efficiency but its proved ability to control decisionmaking and marshal state resources toward specified goals. It does this better than any other system.[19]

For discussion, it is convenient to address centralized planning as long-term (5 years and beyond) and short-term (less than 5 years). The political paradigm affects long-term planning the most because it provides the vision of the Party's long-range goals. Unfortunately, it is this area of planning about which we know the least. The little we do know comes from information released about planning in the civilian sector. The Soviets appear to do scientific-technical forecasting which looks ahead 20 years, and they claim to write "perspective" plans which reach out 15 years. It is doubtful, however, that there is much specificity beyond the established Five–Year Plans.[20]

The objective reality dominates short-term planning. Its major considerations are more concrete—the availability of resources, the suitability of current technology, bureaucratic imperatives, and other national priorities. Much of this decisionmaking is technical. The Party functions more as an overseer, ensuring the system does not get bogged down and production quotas are met.

It is from this area of short-term planning that we get some of our best insights as to what the Soviets are about. The implementation of policies into hardware produces fragments of physical evidence. When properly tied together by skilled analysts, these fragments either can confirm old policy directions or suggest new ones. For Western defense planners, however, these insights often come too late to contribute to their own efforts.[21]

Military Decisionmaking

A similar framework exists for military decisionmaking. Its institutional form is centered in the concept of "military art," divided further into "strategy," "operational art" and "tactics." The Soviets' concept of tactics is somewhat similar to our own and concerns actions at the division level and below. Their concept of operational art, however, is unique. It addresses actions at the operational level between division and theater.[22]

Strategy is the highest form of military art. It unifies the objective requirements identified within tactics and operational art to ensure military operations will be both conceptually and organizationally integrated.[23] In the formulation of strategy, Soviet military thought gets its first substantive political guidance. Strategy is the first instrument of politics but still retains its unique "grammar" and fundamental concerns. It is operationally oriented—based on the realities of the battlefield and the primacy of victory—and contains few of the political-military concepts necessary to support strategies such as flexible response or mutual assured destruction.

A considerable amount of the activity within military art is directed at technology and its impact on the changing nature of war. In Soviet decisionmaking, theory seldom lags behind technology. In many instances, it is because they see new technologies first in the West. But regardless of their source—external or internal—all new technologies require a doctrinal screening. The military has this responsibility and ensures newly proposed systems will be compatible with current military thought and will be properly integrated into the current force structure. While the cognitive structure of military decisionmaking is somewhat rigid, its response to the demands of external reality is flexible and dynamic.

Decisionmaking frameworks, as is the case with their paradigms, manifest considerable conceptual stability. The "revolution in military affairs" offers a good insight into this phenomenon because it indicates what happens in the Soviet system when paradigms become noticeably out of step with their objective realities.[24] The introduction of nuclear weapons and their supporting systems into warfare challenged some of the fundamental tenets of the political and military paradigms. For example, the political paradigm proclaimed all great social change must necessarily be accompanied by violence. If this violence, however, meant the destruction of most of the Soviets' major cities and much of their economic base in a nuclear war, it was no longer an acceptable consequence. The military paradigm asserted future war would begin at the frontier and be decided by an accumulation of tactical and theater victories. But the nuclear age suggested war might begin with deep strikes into the heart of a nation, destroying its ability to wage war without the traditional land engagement.

What emerged from this debate was not (as one would expect) a fundamental restructuring of the two paradigms but their convenient expansion to accommodate a dramatically altered reality.[25] The political paradigm now held that violence still might accompany great social change but added that other means existed—such as peaceful coexistence—by which socialism could prove its superiority over capitalism. In similar fashion, the military paradigm claimed war could begin at the frontier or with deep nuclear strikes, either of which could decide its final outcome. The military suggested the nuclear age required larger rather than smaller conventional forces.

This pattern repeated itself organizationally and conceptually throughout the military establishment. For example, the Soviets created a nuclear capability but did not truly integrate it (in the sense we use the word "integrate") into their conventional force structure. They formed special units to employ nuclear munitions but attached them as separate entities to the existing organization. At the strategic level, they established the Strategic Rocket Forces as an independent command. At the tactical level, they placed their special units next to their conventional counterparts but kept their operational functions and chain of command separate.

Conceptually, the tested principles of military thought also changed little. What changed significantly was the nature of their application. For example, prior to the debate, the principle of "readiness" was the primary concern of the armed forces. The possibility of deep nuclear strikes, however, made it an urgent concern of the entire state and fostered a massive commitment to civil defense.

Political–Military Decisionmaking

The existence of two decisionmaking frameworks requires the Soviets to link them together suitably. It is imperative this linking ensure the dominance of the political paradigm and safeguard its ideological content.

Theoretically, this is easily accomplished by establishing the political framework as the guiding paradigm and the military framework as its complementary objective reality. This structural "realignment" is justifiable because successful revolutions automatically legitimize all previous actions. If such actions were not "scientifically" correct, then the revolution would have failed. But this solution is only partially

16

acceptable because it does not provide for an important third consideration—effective decisionmaking within the military framework. The military paradigm must be allowed to function unencumbered by excessive ideological dogma.

The Soviets accommodated this third consideration by integrating the decisionmaking process and not the individual paradigms.[26] They overlaid both frameworks with a network of objective laws, principles, and rules. Between the frameworks, they positioned two institutional buffers—"military science" and "military doctrine." These two buffers ensure the dominance and security of the political paradigm while permitting the military paradigm to function with relative efficiency.

Military science provides the institutional forum for the further development of military thought. The Soviets state that it addresses the

> . . . aggregate of diverse material and psychological phenomena of armed combat being studied and analyzed for the purpose of *elaborating practical recommendations* for the *achievement of victory* in war . . . .[27]

This definition clearly makes military science a primary concern of the military. It authorizes them to study any phenomenon which promises to enhance military capability. The call for "practical recommendations" strongly suggests the "objective laws of war" and the "laws of armed conflict" come from the military paradigm with its direct concern for battlefield effectiveness. The study, within military art, of the changing nature of war appears to produce the majority of these recommendations. They are then staffed up the organizational chain to confirm their validity and appropriateness. The truly important ones are then tossed into the forum of military science for Party consideration and approval. Those approved are linked subsequently in some unknown way to the objective laws of war and the laws of armed conflict; in turn, this links them to both decisionmaking frameworks.[28]

The actual linkage of these laws is a great mystery. The Soviets say they "closely interact, intertwine, and penetrate each other mutually, each within its own system as well as between systems."[29] Such complexity obviously requires considerable study to sort out. This built-in delay is a major benefit of the process because it protects the political paradigm against any unwanted surprises.

If the Party finds a recommendation to be noncontroversial and worthy of acceptance, it is approved, "linked" (?) and canonized as official decisionmaking guidance. If the Party determines a recommendation to be unacceptable, then it easily ejects it from military science before it becomes part of the official decisionmaking guidance. It is the recommendation which is both controversial and necessary that makes extended debate within military science so essential. The military science "buffer" holds the controversial recommendation until the political paradigm can be properly reinterpreted to accommodate it.[30]

Military doctrine also functions as a buffer between the two frameworks. Its basic concern is implementation. The Soviets define doctrine as the

> . . . *state's system of views and instructions* on the nature of war under specific historical conditions, the *definition of the military tasks of the state and armed forces* and the principles of their development . . . .[31]

Military doctrine belongs to the Party. It provides the military with its overall guidance. It outlines the nature of future war, who the enemies will be, and what general capabilities will be necessary. With guidance, the military determines the appropriate military strategy and force structure which it then recommends to the Party for approval. Doctrine is the institutional form in which these recommendations are debated. The Party reviews and then reconciles them against a host of other national concerns. The remnants of this process are then submitted as "scientifically" determined directives to the various state agencies for immediate implementation.

While the Party always has the last word, underlying the concept of military doctrine is a fundamental issue of political control versus military efficiency. The central question is not organizational authority but decisionmaking responsibility. When the Party placed political officers" throughout the military estabishment to monitor its activities, it placed, in effect, two operative paradigms at each organizational level. Two decisionmaking paradigms cannot function side-by-side at the same bureaucratic level without a definite network of laws, principles, and rules to govern their activity. Without such a network, one paradigm inherently asserts itself over the other, eventually undermining (possibly even destroying) its effectiveness.[32] This is essentially what happened in the 1930s. The Party, in an effort to consolidate its control, excessively interfered with military decisionmaking and extensively purged the officer corps. While these actions enhanced Party control, they also contributed significantly to the country's near defeat by Germany in 1941. It was a painful lesson both the political and military leaderships still remember. As a result, doctrine today represents an *implied compact* between the party and the military. It assures the Party that military decisionmaking will stay within prescribed ideological boundaries and ultimately serve state ends; it assures the military the decisionmaking freedom necessary to prepare effectively the nation's defense and support the Party's ambitious political goals.

Conclusions

For those interested in the long-term direction of Soviet military policy, the doctrinal literature serves as a good indicator. Practical recommendations and doctrinal positions—once taken—are "scientifically" correct and obligatory norms to which all Soviet decisionmakers must conform. Soviet military decisionmaking is presently founded on a highly stable political-military relationship which is unlikely to change drastically in the years ahead. Doctrine, buttressed by a well-institutionalized cognitive structure, is the glue which holds this relationship together. As a consequence, the transition to a generation of new leaders may cause perturbations, but little more.

Notes

1. The Party leadership purposely restricts the flow of information both within and from the Soviet Union. In military affairs, considerable information is compartmentalized within the military establishment and available only to the very senior political leadership.
2. For a more detailed description of these approaches, see Karl Spielmann's *Analyzing Soviet Strategic Arms Decisions* (Boulder: Westview Press, 1978).
3. The scientific community was used for the group analysis because its character is readily identifiable and its paradigm characteristics have been well analyzed. See Thomas Kuhn, *The Structure of Scientific Revolutions,* 2d ed. (Chicago: University of Chicago Press, 1970). The institutional analysis looked mostly at the Soviets since they are the subject of this study.
4. To go deeper into cognitive processes only serves to overshadow what we do know with a mountain of controversy over what we don't know. The crucial issue is whether or not this framework can function adequately at the level of specificity adequate for the empirical data it addresses. In this study, the construct appears more than adequate. To determine at what level of specificity it might lose its utility requires further cuts through the material at ever increasing depths.
5. See V. V. Druzhinin and D. S. Kontorov, *Concept, Algorithm, Decision* (Moscow: Military Publishing House, 1972), pp. 17–42.
6. This discomfort is called technically "cognitive dissonance."
7. An excellent insight into the nature of paradigm change is offered in Thomas Kuhn, op. cit.
8. Truth is a relative phenomenon. What concerns us is its center of gravity ("center"), not the delineation of its ultimate boundaries.
9. Most Soviet decisionmaking does, in fact, begin in other paradigms. Despite its claims of universality, Marxism–Leninism offers only limited substantive insight into the complex technical problems which abound in a modern state.
10. The mechanics of the dialectic entail a unity of opposites: a perpetual progression by which the conflict between a thesis and an antithesis results in a higher order synthesis. Hegel had originally proposed this concept as a cognitive construct. When Marx adopted it to describe the process of social change, he never really reformulated its basic assumption. Thus, the dialectic's claim of "scientific correctness" and infallibility is not based on empirical observation, as Marx suggests, but on Hegel's original laws of logic.
11. Revolutionary decisionmaking has few of the strategic considerations which drive conventional military operations because it has no requirement to defend territory or a state bureaucracy.
12. This is not to imply they don't occasionally misjudge; they obviously do. The old nemesis of human fallibility occasionally obscures their vision through the "porthole."
13. The necessity of violence has been modified due to the appearance of nuclear weapons. See the discussion of the "revolution in military affairs" in note 24 and in

19

the text above.

14. The Soviets are quite sensitive on this issue. See B. Byely, et al., *Marxism–Leninism On War and Army* (Moscow: Progress Publishers, 1972), pp. 523.
15. See Karl von Clausewitz, *On War*, ed. and trans. Michael Howard and Peter Paret (Princeton: Princeton University Press, 1976), p. 149.
16. See V. D. Sokolovskiy, *Soviet Military Strategy*, ed. Harriet F. Scott, 3rd ed. (New York: Crane, Russak and Company, 1975), p. 19.
17. See V. I. Lenin, "The State and Revolution," in Irving Howe, ed., *Essential Works of Socialism* (New York: Bantam Books, 1971).
18. It is important not to confuse this structure with organizational structure. It is cognitive and lies beneath the formally delineated bureaucratic decisionmaking process.
19. Lenin had not foreseen the need for a centrally planned economy. In 1917, there was no Russian word to describe this concept. Lenin believed the role of the state would decline after the seizure of power. See V. I. Lenin, op. cit., pp. 300–318.
20. Like us, the Soviets have not unraveled the mysteries of long range planning. They still seem to rely heavily on the collective judgements of "experts" although the emphasis on trend projection and futuristic modeling appears to be increasing.
21. One of the most comprehensive yet succinct discussions of this aspect of decisionmaking is Arthur Alexander, "*Decision–Making in Soviet Weapon Procurement*," Adelphi Paper No. 147 (London: Institute for Strategic Studies, Winter 1978–1979).
22. The Soviets' use of the word "doctrine" is quite different from ours and should not be substituted within the boundaries of "military art." The Soviet concept of doctrine will be discussed later.
23. The Soviets reject our contention that integrated military action can be achieved effectively by combining different operational doctrines under a unified command structure.
24. "The revolution in military affairs" is the slogan the Soviets attached to the institutional debate over the impact of nuclear warfare on state policy. The debate was suppressed during Stalin's lifetime and didn't formally begin until 1956, over 10 years after Nagasaki and Hiroshima. The sensitivity of the issues raised and the concurrent struggle within the Party for the reins of power perpetuated the debate well into the sixties.
25. Lenin first introduced this technique in his "enrichment" of basic Marxism over 60 years ago. It has served the Soviets well ever since.
26. The integration of paradigms is more typical of Western decisionmaking. It is not an alternative for the Soviets because it gives decisionmaking too loose a rein and doesn't ensure that truth will ultimately reside in the political paradigm. The overriding concern of all ideologically based paradigms is that they avoid crises and take every precaution to ensure decisionmaking gravitates toward established doctrine rather than away from it.
27. S. N. Kozlov, *The Officer's Handbook*, trans. under the auspices of the US Air Force (Washington: Government Printing Office, 1977), pp. 47–57, emphasis added.
28. To the Soviets, a law is that "which is continually repeated and reproduced in a phenomemon." The objective laws of war deal with issues at the national strategic level, while the laws of armed conflict concern those of the battlefield. For a further explanation of these laws, see V. Ye. Savkin, *The Basic Principles of Operational Art and Tactics* (Moscow: Military Publishing House, 1971), pp. 52–152.
29. Ibid., p. 87.
30. The forum of military science is additionally useful because it forces military thinkers continually to rephrase their thoughts in Marxist–Leninist language and thus stay conceptually close to Party doctrine.
31. Kozlov, op. cit., p. 62, emphasis added.
32. The ability to function effectively on the borders of different decisionmaking frameworks requires considerable skill. Individuals who have this skill usually have a much better chance of reaching positions of high responsibility than those who do not.

Russian Military Traditions and the Soviet Military Establishment

David R. Jones

The attitudes and preconceptions of Soviet military men have long been a subject of lively interest for Western soldiers, statesmen, and scholars. The views taken on this issue necessarily affect our perceptions of the probable advice given Soviet leaders by their military men and of the very nature of Soviet society itself. To date, most historical interpretations have ended with the somewhat abstract conclusions that the communist one-party state and Soviet "expansionism" are merely a continuation of Tsarist autocracy and "Great Russian imperialism" under a new guise. Such writings often make much of the Russian's alleged historically inbred taste for dictatorship, dreams of world conquest or pan–Slavist empire, supposed "urge to the sea," lust for warm water ports, and so on. And if they are frequently stimulating and occasionally informative beyond the level of generalities, most have little to say about the specific issue of the Soviet military's attitudes and place in its society.[1] As for Western studies that do treat these more general subjects, they for the most part concentrate on the problems believed to haunt the relationship between the Party and the armed forces. In so doing, they more often than not assume the existence of basic areas of possible civil-military antagonism within the Soviet system. Yet, with a few notable exceptions, this group of Western specialists largely ignores the impact of pre–1917 Russian influences on existing Soviet attitudes and practices.[2] To cite but one example, T. Colton's otherwise excellent study of "the structure of military politics" in the USSR mentions the Imperial Army only five times and then only in passing.[3] So if the analyses of the first group of scholars often suffer from the historicism inherent in their approach, the conclusions of the other just as frequently demonstrate a seeming lack of any comprehension of Russian history before Lenin.

What is remarkable about the approach of this second group is that it illustrates the extent to which even anti-communist writers believe in the reality of revolutionary change. As part of the more general European revolutionary tradition, Russian Marxist–Leninists have little trouble arguing that their October Revolution of 1917 opened a qualitatively new era in Russian and world history.[4] Even more than European revolutionary idealists, Russian rebels long held as an article of faith that the "revolution" would bring a transformation of both society and human nature. This view was well summed up by the great anarchist, Prince Petr Kropotkin, who stated that true revolutionaries seek to overthrow "everything" and then take upon themselves "the task of universal reconstruction in the course of a few years . . . like the work of cosmic forces dissolving and recreating the world."[5] While almost all non–Marxist writers agree in rejecting the possibility of such a complete break with the past, those scholars just mentioned unconsciously and implicitly still seem in practice to accept the validity of Soviet claims that 1917 marked just such a rupture. It is the purpose of this paper to demonstrate the very real strength of continuity in numerous areas of Soviet military life and thought. On this basis, I will then suggest some implications this may have for our understanding of the existing military establishment's strategic conerns and its own view of its place in Soviet society.

A "New Type" of Army

According to Soviet writers, their revolution of 1917 gave Russia a "new type" of armed forces to match their new socialist society. Yet, it is at least if not more difficult to discern the novel features of today's Soviet Army. Take, for example, the attributes ascribed to it in 1974 by the late Marshal A. A. Grechko. These comprised, he wrote,

> . . . the leadership of the Communist Party in all [aspects of] military building; the unity of political, economic and military leadership; the class character of the Armed Forces; the inviolable unity of the Armed Forces with the people; the regular [form of] organization of the army and fleet; the centralization of leadership and the principle of one-man command [rather than a system of dual commanders, one political and one military]; strong and conscious military discipline; the development of a spirit of Soviet patriotism and proletarian internationalism in the troops; and continual readiness on the part of both the country and the Soviet Armed Forces to repel aggression.[6]

Stripped of ideological flourishes like Party leadership, alleged "class" characteristics, and proletarian internationalism, there is little remarkable in the above list. Indeed, with a slightly different formulation, it could serve to describe most capitalist armed forces. However, contemporary communist claims of novelty depend rather on the essential Marxist–Leninist maxim that "at all times and in every country the army is created as an instrument of the ruling and possessing classes, and it is, therefore, destined to preserve and defend the profits of these classes."[7] Moreover, since the revolution abolished exploitation and raised the "toilers" to power, its forces quite "naturally" became transformed into "an army of the revolutionary people 'who know why they are fighting'—intended for the defense of the new social order of

22

socialism."[8]   To put it differently, for the communist, the mere fact of the October Revolution means ipso facto that the Soviet army is of a "new type," regardless of its outward forms and appearances.

If a Western observer is more skeptical, he can take comfort in the fact that the majority of the Red Army's original founders would not recognize their offspring. For in creating the Workers' and Peasants' Red Army (*RKKA—Raboche–Krest'yanskaya Krasnaya Armiya*), they drew on the long revolutionary liberal and socialist tradition that condemned regular standing forces and demanded their replacement by "universally armed peoples" in a "popular militia." Thus, the decree creating the *RKKA* on 15 (28) January 1918 announced confidently that it would serve "at present (as) the bulwark of Soviet power and a basis for replacing the standing army with the people in arms, and in the future will also be a support for the approaching socialist revolution in Europe."[9]   The "Oath of the Red Warrior" adopted on 22 April 1918 and retained until 1939 was imbued with similar sentiments. Swearing both as "a citizen of the Soviet Republic" and "a son of the toiling people," the soldier promised "before the laboring classes of Russia and the whole world . . . to defend the Soviet Republic," to die if necessary "for socialism and the brotherhood of man," and to serve continually "the great ideal of liberating the toilers of the world."[10]   In the meantime, the revolutionary wave had washed away almost completely the principles, forms, decorations, insignia, and traditions of the *RKKA*'s Imperial predecessor. The sweep was so complete that even the word "officers" (*ofitsery*)—once described by Lenin as "the spoiled and darling sons of the capitalists"—disappeared from the official Soviet vocabulary until 1943.[11]

The fate of these—like so many of the other—ideals of 1917 is self-evident from the characteristics listed by Grechko above, from even a brief glance at today's Soviet forces, and from the oath taken by their personnel. Now, a Soviet Russian soldier swears simply as "a citizen of the Union of Soviet Socialist Republics" to serve "my people, my Soviet Homeland, and the Soviet Government" and to die for "the achievement of complete victory" over their enemies. As for the earlier commitment to liberate the world's toilers, this has been replaced by a vague obligation merely to aid other "socialist nations" and "struggling peoples."[12]   The Soviet soldier now serves in a conscript army with a core of cadre troops that resembles that established by D. A. Milyutin in 1874 rather than the dreams of the Marxist revolutionaries of 1917. Despite continuing claims to the contrary, the present Soviet Army is anything but "new" in terms of its organizational forms and practices.

Retreat From the Ideal

In fact, the military ideals of 1917 collapsed very rapidly in the fires of civil war. By March 1918, Leon Trotsky had begun building a professionally officered regular army, and by that summer the new communist regime had undertaken its own mobilizations. For in practice, a militia army had shown itself to be incapable of defeating the Germans before Pskov, the combined forces of Generals A. I. Denikin and P. N. Krasnov in the south, and the Czechoslovak Legion in the east. The same dictates of military expediency brought about the defeat of the "Military Opposition," who opposed these policies, at the Eighth Party Congress of March 1919. Although this body only gave "provisional" approval to Trotsky's policies, on 16 December 1920 the Soviet government resolved to retain the conventionally organized and disciplined Red Army as the core of the new state's defenses. True, advocates of a militia remained numerous throughout the 1920s, but if their dreams at first were kept alive by the existence of a territorial militia and a program of universal military training, the Party in 1927 decisively relegated their visions to the far distant future. In the years that followed, Stalin's policies removed the militia idea from even the status of a pious hope.[13]

In itself, this process is not remarkable. After all, one can argue easily that certain hierarchical forms of organization are more or less inevitable for the maintenance of any effective military machine. Moreover, R. D. Garthoff's suggestion that the restoration of a rigid hierarchy and discipline within the armed services only reflects the trends prevalent throughout all areas of Stalinist society has much to recommend it.[14] What remains curious, however, is the restoration of so many social customs, institutions, and forms specifically resembling those of the Tsarist army in the armed forces of a state that otherwise has promoted so consciously its revolutionary, Marxist internationalist credentials. While similar characteristics may be found in most armies, many specific details of the Soviet military's procedures and social attitudes clearly are drawn directly from Tsarist precedents.

For example, the Soviet Army again uses decorations named after Imperial military heroes, the ribbons that once identified members of the Knights of St. George, the title "guards" for its elite regiments, the basic ranks (since 1935) originally adopted by Peter I, military schools modeled on those of the pre–1917 period, and discipline and drill that would have won applause from Paul I. Additionally, the political officers combine functions inherited from both the Emperor's chaplains and the gendarme officers General V. A. Sukhomlinov placed on unit staffs as political watchdogs. Soviet officers, as in the Tsar's army, find their everyday lives focused on a regimental club and largely governed by opinions of a regimental "family." While this body's powers are more limited than those of its Imperial predecessor, its approval of an officer's proposed bride is an important factor in his obtaining the unit commander's permission for the ceremony. Furthermore, the bride more frequently than not is an officer's daughter, the married couple will live in officers' housing, and their sons may well be educated in new cadet corps—now renamed Suvorov (army) or Nakhimov (navy)—schools. Most striking of all is the revival of an institution once specifically condemned by the Marxists as a "caste" and "feudal" institution: the officers' "courts of honor" (*ofitserskiye sudy chesti*). In other words, like their Imperial predecessors, Soviet officers have a legally instituted, corporate, judicial institution to settle "family" disputes and other matters touching "military honor." Its status is described in detail in most Soviet military-legal texts, and it has few parallels among the "class" armies of the Western imperialists.[15]

This list could be extended much further, and a full explanation of such a revival of Imperial forms obviously must go far beyond the simple needs of any military organization or of a hierarchical, industrializing society. Explanations such as Michel Garder's supposed synthesis of Russian "spiritualism" and Marxist "materialism" which in the end depend on some rather mystical view of the "Russian soul" are equally unconvincing.[16] In part, of course, one may attribute their reemergence to a revival of traditional (Great) Russian patriotism under the guise of "Soviet patriotism." Even so, whatever one concludes about their steadfastness in the face of a foreign invasion, it is difficult to argue that Russian workers and peasants ever had any special fondness for military service, the Tsar's military system, or its representatives.[17] In fact, only one section in Soviet society really would have hankered for a revival of the prerevolutionary military's corporate privileges and status. This group comprised the 50,000 ex-officers who entered the *RKKA* as "military specialists" during the civil war and the even more numerous former NCOs. While the former remained dominant until the early 1920s, the latter—in the persons of G. K. Zhukov, R. Ya. Malinovskiy, S. M. Budenny, S. K. Timoshenko, and many others—later stamped their personalities on the service and remained the military's foremost representatives right up until the 1970s. Together, these professionals formed a direct link between the Imperial and Soviet armies, a link that may go far to explain the restoration of Imperial norms. After all, in building the *RKKA* they could only be expected to draw from their experience in the one army they had known—that of Nicholas II.[18]

Permanently Operating Factors

Despite their lukewarm attitude toward the realities of routine military service, Russian and Soviet citizens have not been deaf to the calls of patriotism in times of crisis. As a perceptive British observer noted in early 1920, the *RKKA*'s morale largely was "drawn from its patriotism, and whatever Government were in power, provided it showed itself true to the People and able for defense, it would make no difference to the soldiers if the enemy were thundering at the gate."[19]

This was particularly true of old Imperial officers like A. A. Brusilov and his fellows, who responded to the Polish offensive of 1920 by throwing their full support enthusiastically behind Lenin's government.[20] That such feelings had deeper roots is indicated by the response of the Soviet Union's citizenry during the terrible years of the Great Patriotic War (1941–1945). Despite their suffering during Stalin's drive for collectivization and industrialization, the overwhelming majority steadfastly supported the dictator's efforts to repel the invader. Although this struggle saw the final return of past military traditions (in the revival of the term "officer," the establishment of Orders of Alexander Nevskiy, Suvorov, Nakhimov, and so on), neither this nor the numerous German atrocities fully explain this phenomenon. It seems, rather, to have sprung from the same sources as the stubborn resistance encountered by Napoleon in 1812 or the Poles during the Time of Troubles (1605–1613).

Such outbursts of dogged patriotism are only one symptom of the objective conditions that have brought about Russia's rise and existence as a national state. Western analysts tend to ignore the full implications of its vulnerability. Lacking clear-cut and easily defensible borders, its inhabitants learned early the cruel costs of political disunity and military weakness. According to the historian S. M. Solov'yev, the Kievan *Rus* and *Muscovy* suffered 245 external attacks between 1055 and 1462 and some 200 assaults during the more limited period 1240–1426. During the 528 years from 1365 to 1893, the Russian state was at war a total of 305.[21] The record during the present century, which has witnessed the German invasions of 1915–1918 and 1941–1944 as well as the gruesome civil war (1918–1922), is hardly more conducive to a sense of security. So while some chronicle a history of Great Russian expansionism, it seems equally plausible to interpret the facts as indicating their search for more stable and easily defensible frontiers, be it in the Ukraine, Poland, or Central Asia. The actual motives of expansion, of course, have varied with time and place. Nonetheless, the question of frontier security was almost always a major concern, and explanations stressing the dictates of defense usually are put forward quite sincerely by most Russian military men. If one cites instead the Manchurian adventure of 1904–1905 or the Turkish wars of the 1800s, most of them would point out that responsible soldiers opposed the first while they would justify the second as attempts to defend oppressed fellow Orthodox Slavs from a decadent Ottoman despotism.[22]

It is not necessary here to make a final adjudication between these two diametrically opposed views of this military past. Suffice it to say that national defense always has been a pressing concern for any Russian government. This does much to explain the prominence and respect won by the professional military in Russian society; the succession of strong, centralized, and autocratic regimes; and the latter's repeated attempts to strengthen and modernize the armed force. As R.

A. Woff recently pointed out, the strategic concerns raised by the geographic factor have changed remarkably little over the last century. In his words,

> . . . the problem of the security of the Russian heartland may be compared to a defensive triangle, the three sides of which are the defense and survival of the Russian heartland, the maintenance of Russian hegemony in Central and Eastern Europe, and control of the vast, porous Central Asian 'underbelly' that forms the southern borderland of Russia.[23]

Woff adds that in the late 1960s and 1970s, this "traditional triangle has been squared by the inevitable reemergence of the threat to the Soviet Far East for China." These long, vulnerable borders obviously go far to explain why Russians usually have sought to maintain a strong standing army and to use it to gain more secure frontiers when the occasion arose. Yet, if the latter meant the absorption of many non–Slavic areas into the Tsar's empire, on other occasions Russia's political and military leaders instead willingly have settled for a neutral—preferably friendly—buffer. From 1839 to the 1970s, Afghanistan, for instance, served as just that. In fact, many Soviet leaders today, given the costs of their intervention, may well wish they had left it in that role.[24]

There are other major implications of geography for Russian defense policy. With the arrival of the Tatars in the 1220s–1230s and the simultaneous rise of western enemies (Swedes, crusading knights, Poles, and Lithuanians), landlocked Muscovy became isolated from the rest of Europe. This cut the Russians off from Western intellectual and, more important militarily, technological advances. Historian Werner Philipp argues that overall this isolation forced the Russians to turn inward, transforming their country into "a distinct historical entity" that belonged neither to "East" nor "West." As this entity relied almost solely on tradition, it "became the conservative country *par excellence* in Europe."[25] Even so, military practice and technology was one area that could not he left only to the rule of traditions, however hallowed. For this reason, Muscovite rulers began restructuring and rearming their forces; first to defeat the Mongols, then their more advanced western neighbors. Indeed, the fact that Russian rulers from Dmitriy Donskoy through Stalin have had to play "catch-up ball" in the military-technological area lies behind many of the social innovations they have forced on their unwilling people. In addition, the same imperative has meant that the military themselves frequently have been found most prominent among those advocating further modernization. For whatever his ingrained respect for tradition, the professional soldier often recognized that a technological edge could give his possible opponents a dangerous advantage in any future conflict.[26] If they cannot gain the new weaponry for themselves, Russian soldiers sometimes

480-900 O - 85 - 2

seek to deprive assumed enemies of its advantages by joining the advocates of measures for arms control. Many argue that it was precisely this motive that brought about Russian agreement to the ABM treaty of 1972, but scholars have ascribed in part the same motives—in this case because of the costs of new field artillery systems—to Nicholas II's call for an international conference in 1898 to end the arms race.[27]

In part, a combination of geographical isolation, active enemies, and the need to match the latter technologically explains Muscovy's first westward moves of expansion. *Cordons sanitaires* did not enter Russian history after 1917 merely in an effort to quarantine the young Soviet regime. In the 1500s, Russia's enemies—especially the Hanse cities, the Poles and Livonians—"firmly adopted the practice of passing across the border neither the people who could 'civilize' Russia nor the goods that could increase the military might of the Muscovite sovereign."[28] So the problem of blocked "technology transfers" is one Russians have faced before. Further, their drive for the Baltic coast—for a "window on the world"—had as one practical aim the opening up of a channel for such transfers as well as a channel to the benefits of European trade and culture in general.[29] So here, motives other but no less militarily compelling than the mere desire to remove enemy threats (such as the Tatar hordes) or prevent future areas of danger (like disintegrating Poland, the Ukraine, and the Caucasus) have played a major role. Nonetheless, perceived military security remained an important element throughout.

Another aspect of this geographical factor is the fact that the overwhelming mass of the nearly landlocked Russian state's expansion and military interventions have taken place along its immediate periphery. This also same explains why no serious Russian fleet appeared before Peter I, and why even today the Soviet Navy yields pride of place to the ground forces. Even so, Western analysts should remember two major truths from the Russian past. Firstly, Admiral S. G. Gorshkov is not the first of his country's naval leaders to build a powerful naval force. In fact, one can even identify an article by young naval officers that appeared in *Vremya* (Time) in March 1863 as a forerunner of Gorshkov's own famous pieces in *Morskoy sbornik* (Naval Digest). From a different perspective, by the late 1890s, British experts like Fred Jane seriously worried that the rapidly expanding Russian Imperial Fleet posed a threat to their nation's supremacy. The parallels with many recent alarms need not be mentioned further, but on the former occasion the threat collapsed beneath Japanese guns at Tsushima in 1905 while the Kaiser rapidly replaced the Tsar as naval "Public Enemy Number One."[30]

A second truth deserving stress is that Russian interventions in the Mediterranean, Near East, and Africa—quite apart from the Middle and Far East—are anything but a novelty. Further, in most cases, these have occurred at times of expanding naval potency. For example, many forget that by 1800, Russia occupied Corfu as a base for the support of subsequent active naval and land operations in Southern Italy, along the Adriatic's eastern coast, and in the Adriatic proper. Additionally, St. Petersburg's interest in Egypt began in 1784, the Russians enjoyed considerable influence in Ethiopia in the 1880–1890s, and Russian volunteers gave active support to the Boers during 1899–1900. Such far-flung adventures frequently enjoyed the support of naval men who otherwise faced a prospect of seeing their warships shot up like "fish in a barrel." Thus, they sought base facilities at Villafranca in Piedmont in 1859 and Port Arthur in 1896 and sent squadrons to New York and San Francisco in 1863. So, while Imperial and Soviet interventions in Persia/Iran have fitted the model of land-based expansion along the periphery, those further afield have had naval backing. Even so, until the last decade at least, such initiatives remained sporadic. Yet, they do demonstrate that naval men, in spite of their state's necessary dependence on the might of its land forces, have not been blind to the wider political and military benefits of a powerful fleet in war and peace.[31]

The Imperial Army and Russian Society

Apart from the immediate needs of defense from outside enemies, in Russia the modern standing army has brought the state numerous other political and social benefits. To begin with, Muscovite–Russian expansion resulted in a multinational empire. Within this entity, the Imperial army became a supranational institution which, like the bureaucracy, did much to tie the various peoples together. It did so first by mixing recruits within units and by assigning them to places of service distant from their homes. In addition, under Milyutin's term as war minister (1861–1881), many in the army began to see it as serving in the role of a "national university." Here, young peasant and non-Russian conscripts might learn the rudiments of literacy in Russian and Imperial patriotism. At the same time, their experiences in the far-flung corners of the empire hopefully would give them some sense of the meaning of Russian citizenship. In this manner, the military served both as means of "Russification" as well as of modernization, for, as already noted, the practical demands of warfare often forced the most conservative of military leaders to become advocates of modern technology. In this last regard, one might recall that under Milyutin, the military's own schools (the so-called military gymnasiums) became the most progressive in the empire. Again, in 1910, the usually denigrated Grand Duke Aleksandr Mikhaylovich gave a major impetus to the creation of an air force, a service which was the second most powerful in the world by August 1914. And at the same time, another war minister—the hated V. A. Sukhomlinov—carried out major reforms which technologically overhauled the land forces and, in retrospect, did much to counter his later reputation as the "Minister of Defeat."[32]

The long-term results of the army's internal mixing of nationalities, training in patriotism, and advocacy of technology were as important as its contribution to the more practical and prosaic task of maintaining domestic order. Although the soldiers—both officers and men—disliked acting as gendarmes, by 1905 they had a long tradition of actively supporting the civil authorities' repression of strikes, outbreaks of peasant discontent, and nationalist rebellions. However, by then this struggle with the "internal enemy" had done much to split the military man from his civilian fellows and frequently blood relations in educated society. Many therefore placed the restoration of "national unity," on the German and Japanese models, as a primary objective during the last decade before World War I. In part, this explains the sincere cooperation of military men with the leaders of the Third *Duma,* Russia's new parliament. At a broader level, however, the most impressive measure was the army's promotion of nationalist youth movements. In 1909–1910, the soldiers first helped create the *Potesh–nyye,* or "Play Soldier," movement. This provided paramilitary training and sought to supply "the loyalty and discipline which is said to be lacking in Russian school life." But by 1911, attention had switched instead to a Russian form of the Boy Scouts. Founded by an officer of the Semenovskiy Guards, this organization had the direct backing of Nicholas II and Sukhomlinov. It still is recognized as the direct ancestor of the Pioneers but less generally as another nationalist forerunner of today's *DOSAAF.*[33]

As might be expected, the characteristics generally ascribed to the military establishment as a whole are specifically applicable to the officer corps. Like the bureaucracy and gentry (*dvoryanstvo*), it served as a supranational institution that offered careers to almost all races and creeds. In the latter category, Jews were the exception. The bar against them, however, was religious not racial: baptism removed almost all impediments to their advancement. Otherwise, the multinational composition of the command cadres is indicated by figures for the 15th Artillery Brigade stationed in Odessa. Between 1911 and 1914, its officers included 19 Great Russians, 9 Poles, 6 Baltic Germans, 1 Tatar, 1 Bulgarian, and 2 each of French and Greek ancestry. Similarly, Peter I's table of ranks opened up promotion on the basis of merit and education to all classes; with promotion, the successful gained entry to the gentry/nobility. Thus, the majority of professional officers were not the gold-shouldered aristocrats pictured in Bolshevik and Soviet propaganda. Sukhomlinov, in his search for officers, had removed exceptions which kept members of the "radical" intellectual professions (lawyers, doctors, and teachers) out of positions of command. More significant yet, by 1914, 40 percent of all officers below the rank of colonel were, by birth, members of the peasantry or lower urban classes, and many of their comrades—including the White leader

A. I. Denikin—were only a generation removed from such origins. In other words, as an institution the army was a means by which many intelligent natural leaders of the lower classes and subject nationalities could find advancement, simultaneously being absorbed into the existing social system and, if necessary, Russianized. In this manner, it long served as an important pillar of the Imperial regime.[34]

One other feature particularly distinguished the Imperial *ofitserstvo* from most of their European counterparts. With its founding under Peter I, the modern Russian army became a major vehicle for providing the basics of a Western education to the groups administering this Tsar's reorganized state. The officers therefore became an important element of Russia's educated upper classes and, as transfers to the civil bureaucracy had been deliberately facilitated by Peter's system of ranks, very frequently held major civilian positions. Even after 1850, when a new critical intelligentsia appeared, the career of the professional officer still attracted educated youths. Indeed, one-time representatives of the Russian armed services made major contributions to their country's culture. This is evident from writers like Mikhail Lermontov, Lev Tolstoy and Aleksandr Kuprin; or composers like Modest Mussorgskiy and Nikolay Rimskiy–Korsakov. Indeed, as late as 1917, officers still considered themselves members of a "military intelligentsia," and they filled the military press with their poems and short stories. At times, some even regarded themselves as the true heirs to the revolutionary populists of the 1870s since it was they, not the civilians, who taught the peasantry through the military's "national university." Of course, not all officers participated in such activities and attitudes. Even so, the military's self-image was not that of the "silly soldier man," and they were frequently less isolated or backward than has been claimed.[35]

But if a Russian officer could continue to consider himself to be an *intelligent (intellectual)*, it was as one devoted to the nation rather than to a particular political creed or party. While political, even revolutionary, commitments among some sections of the officer corps were common before 1880, they became progressively less so (but never entirely absent) after that date. Instead, the professional soldier tended to adopt a position of nationalist disinterest to party politics which was often summed up somewhat simplistically by the formula of "Faith, Tsar, and Fatherland." Although Imperial Russia was never "militarized" in the sense the term is used of Germany, rulers from Ryurik to Nicholas II, and later Stalin and "Marshal" L. I. Brezhnev, have made military titles and prowess—the attributes of a *vozhd'*—an essential part of their power myths.[36] While this in part merely reflects the significance of defense among their other concerns, after 1860 it probably also represented the ruler's desire to tie the growing nationalist sentiment to his own person and position. Even so, the average officer doubtlessly reserved his main commitment for the trinity's third element—the Fatherland—and there is little reason to assume he was any more or less "apolitical," in the sense of disinterest or ignorance of politics, than were many of his civilian fellows. Thus, the majority of the officers continued to support the Emperor as the embodiment of national honor until the nation-wide crises of morale of 1916–1917. Then, convinced by past defeats, stories of the alleged influence of Rasputin, and the claims of the opposition, the professional soldiers desperately sought to avoid civil war by abandoning a discredited Nicholas II in favor of the *Duma*. When this weak reed broke, some in desperation joined the Reds, Whites, or various nationalist movements. But the view of the majority was best expressed by General Brusilov. Asked for advice, he remarked that Russia survived while governments came and went, and, when possible, officers should stand aloof from civil conflict until a new regime appeared which again allowed them honorably to serve the nation against its external foes.[37]

Continuing Influences

An opportunity to follow this counsel came with the Russo–Polish War of 1920 and the Soviets' subsequent decision to maintain their own regular army. With the failure of the expected European (let alone world) revolution, the restoration of this institution had more than purely *military* significance. Faced with the old problems of external threats and widespread worker, peasant, and nationalist discontent, Lenin's government soon recognized the *political* benefits that this institution had brought their predecessors. With the ruling Party's control ensured by the network of political organizations and the presence of commissars (later deputy commanders for political affairs), the new conscript army could serve the new regime in a similar manner. Once again, it acted as a force preserving the existing, now supposedly socialist, social order from the assaults of internal enemies; as a school for teaching millions of recruits literacy and Soviet patriotism; and, along with the "All Union" government and Party machines, as a supranational institution binding the federated republics in a new union dominated by the Great Russians. In the context of the early 1920s, it was seen as particularly useful as a means for maintaining "proletarian" control over a largely peasant state while simultaneously promoting the celebrated merger, or *smychka,* of worker and peasant.[38]

In this manner, the old nationalist professionals' willingness to serve the new regime paralleled the latter's need for such services. Together, these factors converted the new Red Army into a relatively efficient, combat-ready standing force. For only these "military specialists" had the competence, training, and experience needed to recruit, organize, and train a regular force; to provide it with a doctrine; and to educate new command cadres. The demand for such skills was so great that at first even former Whites were used in the military schools to train the new proletarian, communist commanders.[39] True, the civil war had provided the ruling Party with its own crop of military heroes in the persons of M. V. Frunze, I. E. Yakir, K. E. Voroshilov, and others. But while they often received the public honors, beside them stood their ex–Tsarist colleagues like A. A. Svechin, B. M. Shaposhnikov, I. I. Vatsetis, A. E. Gutor, M. N. Tukhachevskiy, S. S. Kamenev, and so on. To a large extent, men of this latter category took responsibility for incorporating the general theoretical views of Marx and Engels—along with Lenin's precepts on armed conflict, his vision of Clausewitz, and the lessons drawn by Frunze and company from the civil conflict—into practical tactical and strategic doctrines based on older Russian practices. The extent of their influence is indicated by the fact that out of the 100 authors of the Field Regulations of 1929, 79 had served under Nicholas II. In that same year, another survey of 243 leading military writers demonstrated that 198 were ex-officers. Meanwhile, once the Soviet Union gave up its active pursuit of world revolution in favor of the more limited goal of "Socialism in One Country," these officers must have had little difficulty in finally replacing "Faith, Tsar and Fatherland" with a new trinitarian creed—that of "Communist Party, Soviet Government, and the People."[40]

The result was indeed a *smychka*, though not precisely the one anticipated by Lenin's government in 1920. Rather than the old officers becoming proletarian in outlook, the new "Red Commanders" increasingly came to resemble their Tsarist predecessors and present teachers. As early as 1923, Leon Trotsky, the Red Army's great founder, already deplored the reappearance of old forms and regimental histories, the latter being a literature used by "reactionary" regimes to foster the military's sense of heroic separateness from the rest of society.[41] By the mid–1930s, the rhetoric of revolutionary egalitarianism only thinly veiled the existence of such "proletarian" innovations as sharp pay differentials, special officers' stores and messes, the use of batmen, and even classes in ballroom dancing at the War Academy. The full extent of this restoration of former customs has been suggested above; one might note without exaggeration that only the return of dueling is needed to complete the process. With regard to the new commanders' supposed political consciousness, it seems clear that beneath the mask of communist ideology they mainly had absorbed the basic nationalist loyalties of their ex–Imperial instructors. In fact, during the 1920s, the main result of the Soviet government's efforts to create politically engaged command cadres in the Red Army seems to have been the extension of the Party's internecine struggles to it. As the purges of 1936-1938 so aptly demonstrate, by that date the loyalty of the overwhelming majority of officers could be taken for granted despite the armed forces intimate and fatal involvement in their state's internal politics—even if this brought quite different results from those its founders had intended.[42]

The Soviet officer corps also has inherited the traditional respect for artistic and intellectual endeavor. In part, this reflects the Marxist desire for a citizen-officer with a well-rounded education. So, while Soviet military education does not neglect professional specialist training, the military establishment simultaneously openly promotes other activities. These include the Red Army—later the Soviet Army—Chorus and Dance Ensemble and various ballet tours. More striking, however, is the regularity with which short stories and even poetry find their way into military periodicals and newspapers. In addition, the Soviet Ministry of Defense publishes novels and books of military verse quite apart from the memoirs and more usual military reading fare and even has issued two volumes of conference papers under the title *The Army and Literature.* So, the fact that no less a figure than Marshal R. Ya. Malinovskiy has authored a novel is fully within his service's tradition. This, along with the military's continuing interest in promoting modern technology—be it in the area of missiles, cybernetics, or beam weapons—suggests that the Soviet officer still has a right to see himself as a contributing member of his state's intellectual elite. In this respect, he can enjoy a self-confidence that some of his Western counterparts whose service traditions are more overtly and professionally narrow might well envy.[43]

The adaptation of the Imperial past for use by the Soviet present, of course, goes far beyond the realm of social and intellectual conventions. At the military administrative and institutional levels, the comparisons are just as persuasive. Here, the role of the Ministry of Defense, presiding over a network of military districts which preserves the basic structure adopted by Milyutin in 1862, first comes to mind. True, the ministry is now a combined services institution that unites all five branches of the Soviet Armed Forces: the Strategic Rocket Forces, Ground Forces, Air Defense Forces, Air Forces, and Navy. Nonetheless, many of the procedures followed, as well as the structures of subordinate bodies—like the General Staff—are consciously patterned on models from the Imperial past. Further, the overall system of decisionmaking in defense—which involves a Defense Council, a Military–Industrial Commission, and possibly an operational *Stavka,* or General Headquarters—has evolved to take on a form very similar to that adopted in 1915 by Nicholas II for waging World War I. Together with the military attitudes struck by Stalin, Khrushchev, and Brezhnev, such developments reflect both the strength of historical continuity and the fact that there may be a particular style and organizational structure suitable for ruling this sprawling, vulnerable Eurasian land empire.[44]

Similar signs of direct continuity or restorations could be catalogued for many other areas of Soviet military life. But here, one more will suffice. An English writer who has examined contemporary Soviet tactical and operational practices in the light of those in use in 1914

34

recently remarked that "although horses have been replaced with tanks and groups on foot by APCs, the Russian Army of 1912 looked remarkably like its modern counterpart." He reaches this conclusion on the basis of a number of examples, including a close comparison of the principles of war as detailed by V. E. Savkin in 1972 and the Imperial Field Service Regulations of 1912. While admitting that such general principles are not in themselves particularly Russian, this author argues for their distinctiveness in terms of "the strict order of priority in which they are placed and in particular forms of expression and attitudes." He ends by noting the persistence of these "70-year-old patterns of behavior" which are unlikely to be altered basically by any new technology. Therefore, today's emphasis on attack helicopters, new main battle tanks, laser-guided artillery shells, and so on stem from the fact that such weapons merely strengthen their long-held conception of the offensive by adding "more mobility, more speed, more punch."[45]

Implications

Having indicated the impact of past traditions on today's Soviet military establishment, we must return to consider once again the permanent effects of the Bolshevik military ideals of 1917. In the long run, these seem to have been minimal with regard to the style and position of the armed forces as an institution in Russian—now Soviet—society. After the brief, bleak period that followed the October Revolution of 1917, the profession of arms quickly regained general respect if not popularity. Regardless of their dislike of standing armies and fears of "Bonapartism" (or military coups), the communists themselves had resorted to the very institutions they once had condemned. So, in spite of his Marxist–Leninist vocabulary, today's Soviet officer has assumed a social position and adopted a self-image remarkably similar to those once possessed by his Imperial forebears. Since the service offers opportunities for social advancement, his outlook usually is basically conservative in spite of the fact that he may regard himself as technologically progressive and intellectually *au courant.* Like the Tsars before them, the Soviet leaders are encouraging such attitudes by offering social and material rewards as well as by carefully cultivating the services' traditions and esprit de corps. In return, the officers remain overwhelmingly loyal to both state and Party. Regardless of their origins, only a few individuals like General Grigorenko are likely to heed the calls of either political, religious, or nationalist dissidents. In other words, the officers in particular and the armed forces in general seem destined to remain a stabilizing force for integrating the USSR's numerous nationalities. They are as powerful a pillar of the existing system, despite its Great Russian bias, as they proved to be for the empire. Only a crisis of the proportions of 1916–1917, in which both the Party and the Soviet government lose all credibility, would change this situation.

Even in the turmoil of 1917–1918, the army did not aspire to seize power for itself. Unlike the military establishments of many developing countries, the Russian military consistently has viewed itself as the nationalist servant of the state's political rulers. To be sure, the military leadership expects to be consulted in areas touching upon its concerns. But in spite of the palace coups of old, the confused, abortive "Kornilov Affair" of 1917, and the victorious Bolsheviks' fears of a strong military leadership, the modern Russian armed forces have no tradition of direct political intervention. Of course, conflicts over particular policies and between personalities—as in the case of Khrushchev and Marshal Zhukov—may occur in the future. Yet, there is no basic danger of the military establishment seriously challenging the political leadership. This basic truth was well illustrated during the terrible purges of 1937–1939, and it should not be forgotten by those who study the frictions, real or otherwise, that so frequently are identified as existing in Party–military relations.[46]

The officers' acceptance of the supremacy of the political leadership obviously is strengthened still further by Marxist–Leninist indoctrination. Even so, the impact of this ideology seemingly is of much more practical significance at the levels of military doctrine and strategic policy. Given its obvious importance, this topic deservedly has received considerable attention in the West. While all the details of the development of this doctrine need not concern us here, a few points do need specific comment.[47]

To begin with, Marxism–Leninism has provided Soviet military men with a philosophical outlook, or world view, on warfare based on the allegedly "scientific" principles of the ruling ideology. At times, this may have hindered the adoption of certain technological advances (such as cybernetics), but on the whole, practice has proved itself to be relatively functional. For example, after World War I demonstrated the need for all strategists to expand their views beyond the purely military so as to include social and economic factors, few modern theorists chose to ignore these factors. Nonetheless, the stress placed by Marxism–Leninism on these elements helped ensure Soviet thinkers would devote considerable attention to the general context of modern war. But if the "immutable" laws of history have since been bent to allow the possibility of "peaceful coexistence," they do yet permit the conclusion that war, nuclear or otherwise, is impossible. For the Soviet world view argues that as long as classes exist, the struggle between capitalism-imperialism and socialism-communism will continue and so threaten an armed conflict. This possibility, combined with a continuing fear of a more fatal recurrence of the surprise scored by the Germans in June 1941, goes far to explain why Soviet military and civilian leaders are unconvinced by Western theories of the efficacy of mutually assured destruction (MAD). Consequently, they go on pursuing what, in their view, are prudent measures aimed at ensuring the USSR's survival under any circumstances and increasing its warfighting capabilities for any eventuality. At the same time, they do recognize fully that a nuclear conflict would be an unprecedented catastrophe for mankind. So Brezhnev and company still remain ideologically bound to insist their state would emerge victorious, if only at a fearful cost. Given some Western interpretations of these views, this may well be the most significant (as well as the purest) practical Marxist influence on existing Soviet doctrine.[48]

Meanwhile, the Soviets' own preconceptions may equally distort their view of Western policies. Imperial military men were no strangers to the great military thinker Karl von Clausewitz and his prescription that war must be subordinated rigidly to political goals. But thanks to the respect shown this German's work by Marx, Engels, and Lenin, it has become part of the dogma that informs all Soviet military thinking.[49] In practice, all these influences combine in a mode of "scientific" analysis of the "correlation of forces" likely to exist in any conflict. In accordance with the dictates of Marxism–Leninism, such an equation must comprise numerous factors above and beyond qualitative and quantitative military considerations. That such calculations are extremely complex is obvious. Similarly, the ever-changing and often uncertain or obscure nature of some elements is likely to induce caution in even the boldest practitioners of this art. Here, the recent invasion of Afghanistan may well have taught them a salutory lesson: while the initial military operations as such went as planned, it is almost certain that those responsible miscalculated both the strength of Afghan resistance and the nature of Western reaction. In any case, Soviet military men undoubtedly remain suspicious of the seemingly simplistic pragmatic ease with which their Western counterparts play war games and build scenarios based largely on technological considerations.[50]

Having admitted these aspects of the ideological heritage, it is time to return to the question of Russian traditions. For in spite of the fears of many, in practice it is very difficult to argue that the Soviet Union remains a revolutionary state dedicated seriously to spreading "world revolution." While still seeing this goal as desirable, its leaders have consigned its triumph in practice to the "inevitable" historical process. True, the USSR may be willing to help this process along as part of its "proletarian internationalist" duty to peoples struggling for "national liberation." Nonetheless, the Soviet leaders, devoted as they are first and foremost to defense of the "socialist commonwealth," are not likely to risk consciously a major conflict for this purpose. Mistaken commitments are, of course, always possible. But a cynic might well conclude that the Soviet "internationalist" soldier of today is a direct descendant of the Imperial Army's "Christian warrior" who on occasion shed his blood for his Orthodox and Slavic "brothers." After all, governments always invoke ideals higher than simple patriotism to justify operations beyond their immediate frontiers. More important still, such internationalism also has considerable utility in smoothing over nationalist differences *within* the Soviet Union, and it also justifies maintaining stability in the strategically vital East European bulwark.[51]

After all, given the resurgence of traditional Russian influences in the other aspects of Soviet military life, one might well expect a similar trend in the practical application of the new doctrine. This is especially the case since the professionals who incorporated the Bolsheviks' ideological imperatives into military theory were largely the ex-Tsarist officers noted above. Indeed, the English writer Christopher Bellamy has gone so far as to suggest that the Red Army's search for a "unified military doctrine" in the early 1920s in some ways only continued the efforts of Sukhomlinov and his supporters on the eve of World War I.[52] It is not surprising that the same influences and factors that had determined Imperial defense policies rapidly dominated those of the allegedly new state that occupied the identical geographical position, had the same resources, and so on. True, since that time scientific and technological advances—such as nuclear weapons and missiles—have had to be accommodated within both the military establishment's theory and structure as the Strategic Rocket Forces and Air Defense Forces. But if anything, its basic rationale has become even more narrowly focused on providing security for the Motherland.[53] For these reasons, past Russian strategic perceptions provide a useful commentary on current policy decisions.

One clear instance of such continuity is the Soviets' maintenance of massive, well-armed troop concentrations—prepared to take the offensive at a moment's notice—along their frontiers and in Eastern Europe. Rejecting such "alternative explanations" as paranoia, bureaucratic momentum, a desire for superpower status, or a determination to wage war on someone else's soil, one commentator insisted that "the strength of the Soviet Union, in the context of its known doctrines and policies, poses a real and growing threat to Western security."[54] But all these arguments ignore the simple fact that Russia, given its traditionally slow processes of mobilization, has always retained exceptionally large—by Western standards—forces along her Western frontiers. Similarly, such forces very often have been concentrated most heavily along the northeastern invasion routes through East Germany and Poland. Witness, for instance, the concentration of Nicholas I's forces on Warsaw.[55] Finally, given the superiority enjoyed by offensive concepts in both Russian and Soviet military thought over the last 70 years, the offensive posture assumed today is hardly surprising. Indeed, many of the comments heard so repeatedly about present Soviet deployments might have seemed equally applicable to those adopted by June 1941; nevertheless, few would now argue that Stalin was planning to attack Hitler.[56]

38

In other words, a belief in both mass and the necessity of an offensive posture has been commonplace in Russian military thought—facts that deserve attention in any assessment of Soviet intentions. Similar considerations touch on their perceived new willingness since 1970 to intervene in favor of "national liberation movements" and Soviet political interests abroad. Most, of course, agree in relating this development to the growing power of Admiral S. G. Gorshkov's Soviet Navy. Yet, the precise cause of this growth itself is still a matter of some dispute.[57] Here again, however, the lessons of Russia's past may shed some light. As noted above, this is not the first time Western naval powers have had to face the fact the bear has learned to swim. Further, on each occasion since the rule of Catherine II (1762–1796), a fleet developed primarily for the immediate purposes of defense has ended by being employed in upholding "state interests" further afield in the Mediterranean, Africa, the Far East, or in all three. From this, one might well conclude that although energetic Russian naval leaders justify their naval building programs in terms of direct concrete problems of security, before long they and their political masters perceive the more general political advantages to be gained by a strong fleet in the sphere of great power politics. Or to put it differently, once they possess a navy, the Russians usually have given in to the temptation to employ it for purposes other than those originally envisaged. Yet, despite its pretensions, this service has always held the junior position within the Russian and Soviet armed forces. In addition, its ability to conduct sustained interventions has never been more than highly limited at best. With regard to the situation today, recent studies demonstrate that the Soviet Union's reach remains similarly constrained—and this even with their Cuban "Gurkhas."[58]

Conclusions

Although other instances could be cited of the influence of Russian military traditions on the Soviet military establishment, enough has been said to demonstrate their impact on the latter's social attitudes and military thought. In part, this naturally results from the influence of the "permanently operating factors" as outlined above, but in part it seems to have risen from a more or less conscious—and probably natural—resurgence of Imperial patterns of behavior. In spite of its initial revolutionary impetus, Marxist–Leninist doctrine—with its complex analysis of "the correlation of forces"—has only reinforced the defensive conservatism that was ingrained in past Russian strategic (as opposed to tactical and operational) ideas. At the same time, however, Russian rulers have always taken seriously their state's rights as a great power. Even when a strong navy has been available, they have still been cautious about interventions and sustained commitments abroad. In this regard, Cuba is a major and very costly exception. Even so, large-scale interventions initiated directly by the Soviet leaders probably will continue to occur mainly on the Soviet periphery. If and when they believe their political and/or strategic security is threatened on their doorstep—as in Hungary, Czechoslovakia (perhaps Poland?), and probably Afghanistan—they will employ force with the military's willing support. The soldiers who still dominate the Ministry of Defense, however, can be expected to be much less enthusiastic about adventures abroad and to counsel withdrawal in the face of serious resistance, so long as this can be achieved without a disastrous loss of national prestige.

Unfortunately, Western policymakers can draw no easy prescriptions for action from the above discussion. Decisions in international politics always will be complex and contain some elements of uncertainty. Nonetheless, it is important that we work to understand both our own and our opponent's attitudes, fears, and paranoia. Meanwhile, an acceptance of the fact Soviet military planners remain basically conservative in the realm of foreign policy, are conscious of the USSR and the Warsaw Pact's many internal weaknesses, and will be cautious about overseas commitments does not necessarily mean we should be complacent about our own military posture. Like other great powers, the Soviet Union will be tempted to act in its interests when it can do so with minimal risks. Even so, it is a truism that decisions on Western military policies can only be effective if they are based on both a realistic assessment of Western needs *and* a proper perception of Soviet attitudes. And here, the Soviet military leaders' basic caution and conservatism should not be forgotten at a time when glib phrases of "Russian expansionism" and Communist "dreams of world empire" come so easily to the lips of many politicians. Such men too often forget that the world is not born anew every half decade and that it can be destroyed in a few short hours.

Notes

1. A debate on the relevance of the Russian past for the Soviet Union was recently reignited by Aleksandr Solzhenitsyn's article "Misconceptions About Russia Are a Threat to America," *Foreign Affairs*, Spring 1980, pp. 797–834. He maintains that it "is inappropriate to apply the word 'Russian' to the present authorities in the U.S.S.R., to its army or to its future military successes and regimes of occupation throughout the world," (p. 798) as this despotic, communist expansionist state has little or no relation to the pre–1917 Russian state. This provoked fierce rejoinders, published in the same journal's summer and autumn issues for 1980 and in the British journal *Encounter*, including the debate between Richard Pipes and Wladislaw G. Krasnow, "Anti–Soviet or Anti–Russian" (April 1980), and an interview with Lezek Kolakowski (January 1981). The most sophisticated defense of the continuity thesis is Pipes' *Russia Under the Old Regime* (New York, 1974). For his brief comments on Russian expansionism, see pp. 79–84. For arguments connecting this with Soviet imperialism, see V. S. Mamatery, *Soviet Russian Imperialism* (Anvil Books, 1964), the popular study by Virginia Cowles, *The Russian Dagger: Cold War in the Days of the Czar* (New York, 1969), and the thoughtful article by David Fromkin, "The Great

Game in Asia," *Foreign Affairs*, Spring 1980, pp. 936–951.

2. The most influential such study is probably Roman Kolkowicz, *The Soviet Military and the Communist Party* (Princeton, 1967). Among the works which give attention to continuity should be mentioned John Erickson's *The Soviet High Command, 1918–1941* (London, 1962); Raymond L. Garthoff's two studies, *How Russia Makes War: Soviet Military Doctrine* (London, 1954) and *Soviet Military Policy: An Historical Analysis* (London, 1966); and the articles of Christopher Bellamy and R. A. Woff cited below.

3. T. S. Colton, *Commissars, Commanders and Civilian Authority: The Structure of Soviet Military Politics* (Cambridge, Massachusetts, 1979).

4. So somewhat surprisingly on this point, Solzhenitsyn finds himself in a way agreeing with such Soviet writers as G. M. Sorokin, ed., *Velikaya Oktyabr'skaya Sotsialisticheskaya revolyutsiya i mirovaya sotsialisticheskaya sistema* [The Great October Socialist Revolution and the World Socialist System] (Moscow, 1969); S. I. Tyul'panov, ed. *Velikaya Oktyabr'skaya Sotsialisticheskaya revolyutsiya, korennoy perelom v istorii chelovechestva* [The Great October Socialist Revolution, A Fundamental Break in the History of Mankind] (Leningrad, 1969).

5. Peter Kropotkin, *The Great French Revolution, 1789–1793*, trans. N. F. Dryhurst (New York, 1927), Vol. 1, p. v.

6. A. A. Grechko, "Rukovodyashchaya rol' KPSS v stroitel'stve armii razvitogo sotsialisticheskogo obshchestva" [The Leading Role of the CPSU in the Building of the Army of the Developing Socialist Society], *Voprosy istorii KPSS* [Problems of History of the CPSU], May 1974, p. 30.

7. H. Bergmann, J. Smilga, and L. Trotsky, *Die russische sozialistische Rote Armee* [The Russian Socialist Red Army] (Zurich, 1920), pp. 5–6

8. G. V. Kuz'min, et al., *Imeni Lenina, Kratkiy istoricheskiy ocherk o voyenno-politicheskoy ordena Lenina Krasnoznamennoy Akademii imeni V. I. Lenina* [In the Name of Lenin, A Short Historical Sketch about the Military–Political Order of Lenin of the V. I. Lenin Red Banner Academy] (Moscow, 1966); see also, G. K. Zhukov, *Vospominaniya i razmyshleniya* [Reminiscences and Reflections] (Moscow, 1971), p. 68.

9. *Dekrety Sovetskoy vlasti* [Decrees of the Soviet Government] (Moscow, 1957), Vol. 1, p. 356. For discussions of the revolutionary Marxist military tradition, see R. Hohn, *Sozialismus und Herr* [Socialism and Man], 3 vols. (Zurich, 1959–1961); Gerhard Ritter, *Das Kommunemodell und die Begrundung der Roten Armee in Jahre 1918* [The Communist Model and the Establishment of the Red Army in 1918] (Berlin, 1965); S. M. Kliatskin, *Na zashchitiye Oktyabrya—Organizatsiya regulyarnoy armii i militsionnoye stroitel'stvo v Sovetskoy respublike, 1917–1920* [In Defense of October—The Organization of the Regular Army and Militia Construction in the Soviet Republic, 1917–1920] (Moscow, 1965); the abstract of this writer's conference paper, "The Rise and Fall of the Bolshevik Military Program, 1917–1920," in *Sbornik of the 1917 Study Group* (Leeds, 1976), Vol. 2, pp. 17–18; and my "Armies and Revolution: Trotsky's Pre-1917 Military Thought," *Naval War College Review*, July–August 1974, pp. 90–98.

10. *Dekrety Sovetskoy vlasti* (Moscow, 1959), Vol. 2, pp. 156–157; J. B. White, *Red Russia Arms* (London, 1932), pp. 124–125.

11. V. I. Lenin, *Collected Works*, 4th ed. (Moscow, 1965), Vol.28, p. 195; S. N. Kozlov, et al., *Spravochnik ofitsera* [Officer's Handbook] (Moscow, 1971), p. 171. On the use of the word officer, see the entry "Administrative Personnel" in David R. Jones, ed., *The Military–Naval Encyclopedia of Russia and the Soviet Union* (hereafter cited as *MERSU*) (Academic International, 1978), Vol. 1, pp. 27–31.

12. This oath was adopted on 10 June 1947; for its text, see A. I. Odintsov, *Uchebnoye posobiye po nachal'noy voyennoy podgotovke* [Teaching Aid for Beginning Military Training], 3rd ed. (Moscow, 1971), pp. 4–5.

13. This process is outlined in Kliatskin; Jones, "Rise and Fall . . . ."; John Erickson's articles, "The Origins of the Red Army," in R. Pipes, ed., *Revolutionary Russia*

(Cambridge, Massachusetts, 1968), pp. 224–258, and Some Military and Political Aspects of the Militia Army Controversy, 1919–1920," in C. Abramsky, ed., *Essays in Honour of E. H. Carr* (London, 1974), pp. 204–228; for the Comintern's views in 1927, see A. A. Geronimus and V. Orlov, *VKP(b) i voyennoye delo* [The All–Union Communist Party (Bolsheviks) and Military Affairs] (Moscow, 1928), pp. 223–224.

14. Garthoff, *Soviet Military Policy,* pp. 40–41.

15. The social position and customs of Imperial officers is outlined in E. Messner, et al., *Rossiyskiye ofitsery* [Russian Officers] (Buenos Aires, 1959); Hans–Peter Stein, "Der Offizier des russischen Heeres im Zeitabschnitt zwischen Reform und Revolution (1861–1905)" [The Officer of the Russian Army in the Period between Reform and Revolution (1861–1905)], in *Forschugen zur osteuropaischen Geschichte* [Research into East European History], Vol. 13 (Berlin, 1967), pp. 346–507; and Peter Kenez, "A Profile of the Prerevolutionary Officer Corps," in *California Slavic Studies* (Berkeley, 1973), Vol. 7, pp. 121–158. On those of their Soviet counterparts, see L. B. Ely, "The Officer Corps," in B. H. Liddell Hart, ed., *The Soviet Army* (London, 1956), pp. 395–402; Michel Carder, *A History of the Soviet Army* (London, 1966), pp 185–197; Kozlov, pp. 178–195; and A. I. Lepeshkin, ed., *Osnovy sovetskogo voyennogo zakonodatel'stva* [Fundamental Soviet Military Legislation] (Moscow, 1973). Direct comparisons between the two establishments also are drawn by Garthoff (*Soviet Military Policy,* pp. 29–41) and Erickson in his "The Soviet Military System: Doctrine, Technology and 'Style,'" in J. Erickson and E. J. Feuchtwanger, eds., *Soviet Military Power and Performance* (Hamden, 1979), pp. 38–40. One might note the same similarities in the realms of discipline, complaints about drunkenness among both officers and men, strict forms of drill, and so on.

16. Garder, pp. 49–55. A similar argument is put forward by S. Andolenko, *Histoire de l'Armee russe* [History of the Russian Army] (Paris, 1967), pp. 423–431, while Garthoff (*Soviet Military Policy,* p. 38) and Kolkowicz (pp. 18–22) make their argument of hierarchy, and no less a person than Trotsky agrees; see Trotsky, *The Revolution Betrayed* (New York, n.d.), pp. 86–104.

17. J. S. Curtiss, "The Peasant and the Army," in W. S. Vucinich, ed., *The Peasant in Nineteenth Century Russia* (Stanford, 1968), pp. 108–132; A. N. Drew, *Russia: A Study* (London, 1918), pp. 107–109; and H. Goldhamer, *The Soviet Soldier: Soviet Military Management at the Troop Level* (New York, 1975), pp. 23–35.

18. D. R. Jones, "Continuity and Change in the Russian Military Tradition," *RUSI Journal,* June 1975, pp. 30–31; C. Bellamy, "Seventy Years On: Similarities Between the Modern Soviet Army and Its Tsarist Predecessor," *RUSI Journal,* September 1979, pp. 33–35.

19. Mrs. P. Snowden, *Through Bolshevik Russia* (London, 1920), p. 87.

20. This process is described in D. R. Jones, "The Officers and the Soviets, 1917–1920: A Study in Motives," in *Sbornik of the 1917 Study Group* (Leeds, 1976) Vol. 2, pp. 21–33.

21. Cited in V. I. Shayditskiy, ed., *Na sluzhbe Otechestva* [In the Service of the Fatherland] (San Francisco, 1963), p. 516.

22. On the military and expansion, see Garthoff, *Soviet Military Policy,* pp. 3–28 and T. Hunczak, ed., *Russian Imperialism from Ivan the Great to the Revolution* (New Brunswick, New Jersey, 1974). Typical Soviet military treatments of this history are V. V. Kargalov, *Narod–bogatyr'* [The People—The Hero] (Moscow, 1971); P. A. Rotmistrov, *Istoriya voyennogo iskusstva* [The History of Military Art], 2 vols. (Moscow, 1963); and works such as V. I. Vinogradov, *Russko–turetskaya voyna 1877–1878 gg. i osvobozhdeniye Bolgarii* [The Russo–Turkish War of 1877–1878 and the Liberation of Bulgaria] (Moscow, 1978).

23. R. A. Woff, "Ground Forces," in D. R. Jones, ed., *Soviet Armed Forces Review Annual IV: 1980* [hereafter cited as *SAFRA*] (Academic International Press, 1980), pp. 77–78.

24. R. R. Rader, "The Russian Military and Afghanistan: A Historical Prespective," in ibid., pp. 308–328.

25. W. Philipp, "Russia's Position in Medieval Europe," in L. H. Legters, ed., *Russia: Essays in History and Literature* (Leiden, 1972), pp. 36–37.

26. For an outline of Russia's efforts in this regard, see this writer's "Central Military Administrative System and Policy Making Process (Before 1917)," in *MERSU,* Vol. 2, pp. 34–169.

27. S. I. Vitte, *The Memoirs of Count Witte,* trans. A. Yarmolinsky (New York, 1921), pp. 96–97; T. K. Ford, "The Genesis of the First Hague Peace Conference," *Political Science Quarterly,* Vol. 51, 1936, p. 364; on this interpretation of the ABM Treaty, see C. G. Jacobsen, "Ballistic Missile Defense: The Evolution of Soviet Concepts, Research and Deployment," in *SAFRA I: 1977,* pp. 169–172.

28. S. F. Platonov, *Moscow and the West,* trans. J. L. Weiczynski (Academic International Press, 1972), p. 5.

29. R. M. Hatton, "Russia and the Baltic," in Hunczak, pp. 106–120, details Russian problems and actions in this area up to Peter I.

30. See J. W. Kipp's "Russian Naval Reformers and Imperial Expansion, 1856–1863," in *SAFRA I: 1977,* pp. 127–128, and "Sergey Gorshkov and Naval Advocacy: The Tsarist Heritage," in *SAFRA III: 1979,* pp. 225–238; F. Jane, *The Imperial Russian Navy: Its Past, Its Present, and Its Future* (London, 1899).

31. Russian interests in the Mediterranean are discussed in E. V. Tarle, *Tri ekspeditsii russkogo flota* [Three Expeditions of the Russian Fleet] (Moscow, 1956); V. N. Alekseyev, ed., *Russkiye i sovetskiye moryaki na Sredizemnom more* [Russian and Soviet Sailors on the Mediterranean Sea] (Moscow, 1976); N. E. Saul, *Russia and the Mediterranean, 1797–1807* (Chicago, 1970); B. M. Dantsig, *Blizhniy Vostok v russkoy nauke i literature* [The Near East in Russian Science and Literature] (Moscow, 1973); and D. Hopwood, *The Russian Presence in Syria and Palestine, 1843–1914. Church and Politics in the Near East* (Oxford, 1969). Representative works on Africa are C. Jesman, *The Russians in Ethiopia. An Essay in Futility* (London, 1958) and S. Izedinova, *A Few Months With the Boers. The War Reminiscences of a Russian Nursing Sister* (Johannesburg, 1977). Their activities are reviewed briefly by E. Sarkisyanz, "Russian Imperialism Reconsidered," in Hunczak, pp. 59–60, along with their penetration of Persia (pp. 60–63). For more on Africa, see P. J. Rollins, "Russian Interest in Africa," in J. L. Weiczynski, ed., *Modern Encyclopedia of Russian and Soviet History* (Academic International Press, 1976), Vol. 1, pp. 50–55. It is also interesting that Imperial Russia even had some involvement in Latin America; see L. A. Shur, *Rossiya i Latinskaya Amerika* [Russia and Latin America] (Moscow, 1964); N. V. Kordev, *Yuzhnaya Amerika i Rossiya (1890–1917 gg.)* [South America and Russia (1890–1917)] (Kishinev, 1972); and L. Yu. Slezkin, *Rossiya i voyna za nezavisimost' v Ispanskoy Amerike* [Russia and the War for Independence in Spanish America] (Moscow, 1964). For other regions, see the relevant sections of Hunczak.

32. On the Imperial Army in its various aspects during the latter 1800s–early 1900s, see L. G. Beskrovnyy, *Russkaya armiya i Flot v XIX veke. Voyenno–ekonomicheskiy potentsial Rossii* [The Russian Army and Navy in the 19th Century. The Military–Economic Potential of Russia] (Moscow, 1973); F. A. Miller, *Dmitriy Milyutin and the Reform Era in Russia* (Vanderbilt University Press, 1968); P. A. Zayonchkovskiy, *Voyennoye reformy 1860–1870 godov v Rossii* [Military Reform in 1860–1870 in Russia] (Moscow, 1952); P. A. Zayochkovskiy, *Samoderzhaviye i russkaya armiya na rubezhe XIX–XX stoletii, 1881–1903 gg.* [Self–Government and the Russian Army at the Turn of the Twentieth Century, 1881–1903]; and N. Stone, *The Eastern Front, 1914–1917* (London, 1975). For specific comments on the army's role as an educational experience for conscripts, see N. N., "Narodnyy universitet v armii" [The People's University in the Army], *Ofitserskaya zhizn'* [Officer's Life] (Warsaw), 3/16 February 1907; "Atom," "Narodnyy universitet v armii," *Ofitserskaya zhizn',* 2/15 May 1909; and I. Bilyavskiy, "Ofitser i dyad'ka" [Officer and Uncle], *Ofitserskaya zhizn',* 19/26 June–2/9 July 1910.

33. On the army as a force for internal order, see V. A. Petrov, "Tsarskaya armiya v bor'be s massovym revolyutsionnym dvizheniyem v nachale XX veka" [The Tsarist

Army in the Struggle with the Mass Revolutionary Movement at the Beginning of the 20th Century], *Istoricheskiye zapiski* [Historical Notes] (Moscow, 1950), No. 34, pp. 321–332. The officers' reaction to this, and desire for national unity, is discussed in A. I. Denikin, *Staraya armiya* [The Old Army] (Paris, 1929), Vol. 1, pp. 94–95, 123–124; an article signed "Citizen," "Obshchestvo i armiya" [Society and Army], in *Voyna i mir, Zhurnal Voyenno–obshchestvennoy* [War and Peace, Military–Social Journal] (Moscow, 1906), Nos. 3 and 4; E. I. Martynov, *Iz pechal'nogo opyta russko–yaponskoy vovny* [From the Mournful Experience of the Russo–Japanese War] (St. Petersburg, 1906), p. 9, among other works. *Ofitserskaya zhizn'*, 8/21 May 1906, even published Maksim Lipkin's ode "Po povodu otkritiya Gosudarstvennoy dumy" [On the Occasion of the Opening of the State Duma] to greet the First Duma. On the military's relations with the Third Duma, see J. D. Walz, "State Defense and Russian Politics Under the Last Tsar" (unpublished PhD dissertation, Syracuse University, 1967). As for the youth movements, see Bellamy, p. 37; O. Pantyukhov, *O dnyakh by bylykh. Semeynaya Khronika Pantyukhovykh* [About Days Gone By. The Family Chronicle of the Pantyukhovs] (Maplewood, New Jersey, 1969), pp. 210–127; *Russkiye Skauty, 1909–1969* [Russian Scouts, 1909–1969] (San Francisco, 1969); and on the Air Forces, D. R. Jones, "The Birth of the Russian Air Weapon 1909–1914," *Aerospace Historian,* No. 3, 1974, pp. 169–171; R. Higham and J. W. Kipp, eds., *Soviet Aviation and Air Power: A Historical View* (Boulder, 1977), pp. 15–20.

34. M. Grulev, *Zapiski generala–yevreya* [Notes of a Jewish General] (Paris, 1939); Messner, pp. 4–17; Bellamy, pp. 35–36; Stein, pp. 374–420, 457–467; Kenez, pp. 128–150; B. M. Kochakov, "Sostav Petrogradskogo garnizona v 1917 g." [Personnel of the Petrograd Garrison in 1917], *Uchenyye zapiski LGU, Seriya istoricheskikh nauk* [Scholarly Notes of the LGU. Historical Science Series], No. 205 (Leningrad, 1956), p. 80.

35. Historians generally have accepted that late Imperial officers were "apolitical," narrow in outlook, and anti-intellectual, views supported by Denikin, *Staraya,* Vol. 2, p. 38; A. A. Kersnovskiy, *Istoriya russkoy armii* [History of the Russian Army] (Belgrade, 1935), Vol. 3, pp. 588 and 618; O. A. Ray, "The Imperial Russian Army Officer," *Political Science Quarterly,* December 1961, p. 584; Stein, pp. 457–487; and Kenez's section, "The Russian Military Mind" (pp. 150–158). Soviet historians do not disagree, though all admit the participation of numerous military men in political movements before 1881. That the above description, in practice, describes many officers (and civilians) is undoubted. Yet, the army also contained numerous other professionals with lively political and social interests, though not necessarily party affiliations, through the 1905 revolution right up to 1917. All the evidence cannot be cited here, but apart from the contemporary articles cited in notes 32 and 33, see L. K. Erman, *Intelligentsiya v pervoy russkoy revolyutsii* [The Intelligentsia in the First Russian Revolution] (Moscow, 1966), pp. 14–15, 217–223; L. T. Senchakova, *Revo–lyutsionnoye dvizheniye v russkoy armii v kontse XIX–nachale XX v. (1879–1904)* [The Revolutionary Movement in the Russian Army at the End of the 19th and the Beginning of the 20th Centuries (1879–1904)] (Moscow, 1929), p. 14–34; A. Mgebrov, *Vospominaniya artilleriyskogo ofitsera* [Recollections of an Artillery Officer] (Moscow, 1929), p. 13; L. Deich, "Voyennyye vo vremya pervoy nashey revoluyutsii" [Soldiers in the Time of Our First Revolution], *Byloye* [The Past], June 1918, p. 217; S. D. Mstislavskiy (Maslovskiy), "Otryvki o pyatom gode" [Passages about 1905], *Katorga i ssylka* [Imprisonment and Exile] (Moscow, 1928), No. 2 (29), pp. 7–36, and "Iz istorii voyennogo dvizheniya" [From the History of the Military Movement], *Katorga i ssylka,* No. 55, 1930, pp. 7–31; M. Baring, *A Year in Russia* (London, 1907), pp. 298–299; and so on. With regard to the view of the officer as an heir to the revolutionary populists of the 1870s in terms of educating the populace, see the article, "Militarizatsiya shkol'noy molodezhi" [The Militarization of School Children], *Ofitserskaya zhizn',* 10/23 July 1910, which urges them to "so to speak, 'go to the people'." This writer at present is preparing a large study of this question. As for the average officer's literary pretensions, see, for example, the almanac by L. V. Yevdokimov, ed., *Dosugi Marsa, Sbornik trudov ofitserov (Nauki–literatura–Khronika)*

[The Leisure of Mars. A Digest of the Works of Officers (Sciences-Literature–News)], No. 3 (Saratov, 1890).

36. *MERSU,* Vol. 2, pp. 37–41. Brezhnev's aspirations to military prowess are discussed in R. A. Woff's unpublished paper, "Marshal of the Soviet Union L. I. Brezhnev: A Portrait of a Military Career." This hopefully will appear in a later volume of *SAFRA.*

37. On the collapse of the Imperial Army, see the bibliography in A. K. Wildman's recent *The End of the Russian Imperial Army. The Old Army and the Soldier's Revolt (March–April 1917)* (Princeton, 1980). Brusilov's attitudes are discussed in Jones, "Officers and Soviets," pp. 22, 25–26; Bellamy, pp. 33–34; while one of many expressions of his advice is attested to in A. Levitskiy, "General Brusilov," *Voyennaya byl'* [Military Fact] (Paris, 1968), No. 89, p. 34.

38. For the details of this process, see Jones, "Continuity and Change," pp. 32–35.

39. Ibid. A typical discussion of the use of *voyenspetsy* is L. Spirin, "V. I. Lenin i sozdaniye sovetskikh komandnykh kadrov" [V. I. Lenin and the Creation of Soviet Command Cadres], *Voyenno–istoricheskiy zhurnal* [Military–Historical Journal], No. 4, 1965, pp. 3–16. For the use of the army as an institution of national unity, see *Armiya bratstva narodov* [Army of the Brotherhood of the Peoples] (Moscow, 1972) and T. Rakowska–Harmstone, "The Soviet Army as the Instrument of National Integration," in Erickson and Feuchtwanger, pp. 129–154. The use of ex–Whites in military schools is discussed in K. Karkov, "Povtornyye-kursy dlya komsostava VUZ" [Follow-on Courses for Communist Personnel of Higher Educational Institutions], *Voyennyye znaniya* [Military Knowledge], No. 11 (18), October 1921, p. 39.

40. St. Ivanovich (V. I. Talin), *Krasnaya armiya* [Red Army] (Paris, 1931), p. 33; Garthoff, *How Russia Makes War,* p. 45. A good impression of their influence can be gained by leafing through two recent Soviet contributions to their interwar writings: *Voprosy strategii i operativnogo iskusstva v Sovetskikh voyennykh trudakh (1917–1940 gg.)* [Questions of Strategy and Operational Art in Soviet Military Works (1917–1940)] (Moscow, 1970). Again, A. A. Svechin's *Strategiya* [Strategy], 2nd ed. (Moscow, 1927) was not replaced by a similar work until V. D. Sokolovskiy's *Voyennaya strategiya* appeared in 1962. With regard to a reworked trinity, it is interesting that Odintsov (p. 28) calls on Soviet servicemen to demonstrate "selfless dedication to the Soviet Homeland, Communist Party and the People."

41. L. Trotsky, *The New Course* (Ann Arbor, 1965), pp. 99–105.

42. On both the restoration of Tsarist forms and the purges, see my "Motives and Consequences of the Red Army Purges, 1937–1938," *SAFRA III: 1979,* pp. 256–264; D. F. Fedotoff–White, *The Growth of the Red Army* (Princeton, 1944), and E. Wollenberg's disillusioned *The Red Army. A Study in the Growth of Soviet Imperialism* (London, 1938).

43. The extensive network of existing military educational institutions and their programs is reviewed in H. Fast Scott and W. F. Scott, *The Armed Forces of the USSR* (Boulder, 1979), pp. 331–374, and the various editions of the official Soviet publication *Voyennyye akademii i uchilishcha. Dlya tekh, kto khochet v nikh uchit'siya. Spravki, sovety* [Military Academies and Schools. For Those Who Want to Study in Them. Information and Advice]. For the military's own view of its service, see such typical works as V. S. Staritsyn, ed., *Sovetskiy ofitser* [Soviet Officer] (Moscow, 1970) and I. Babenko, *Soviet Officers* (Moscow, 1976). As for their interest in literature, see the two volumes entitled *Armiya i literatura. Sbornik literaturno-kriticheskikh statey* [Army and Literature. A Digest of Literary–Critical Articles], published in Moscow in 1971 and 1978; Malinovskiy's novel *Soldaty Rossii* [Soldiers of Russia] (Moscow, 1969); as well as such typical works as A. E. Lukovnikov, ed., *Druz'ya odnopolchane. O pesnyakh rozhdennykh voyn* [Friends in the Same Unit. Songs Born in War] (Moscow, 1975); I. Strel'bitskiy, *Uragan. Dokumental'naya povest'* [Hurricane, A Documentary Story] (Moscow, 1977); and V. N. Orlov, ed., *Sovetskiye poety, pavshive na Velikoy Otechestvennoy voyne* [Soviet Poets Killed in the Great Patriotic War] (Moscow, 1965). All but the last were publications of the

Ministry of Defense.
44. This is outlined in *MERSU*, Vol. 2, pp. 142–165; see also, Bellamy, pp. 35–36. For the existing Soviet system, see H. Fast Scott and W. H. Scott, pp. 97–130, 173–225, and J. McDonnell, "Central Military Administrative System and Policy–Making Process (Post 1917)," in *MERSU*, Vol. 2, pp. 169–200.
45. Bellamy, pp. 29–33, 37. For his comparison, he uses text from V. Ye. Savkin, *Basic Principles of Operational Art and Tactics* (Moscow, 1972), trans. under the auspices of the US Air Force (Washington: Government Printing Office, 1973).
46. For the officers' attitudes and refusal to take long-term political responsibility in 1917–1920, see R. Luchett, *The White Generals: The White Movement and the Russian Civil War* (London, 1971), and many of the other works cited above. The Zhukov–Khrushchev dispute and other aspects of the history of Party-military relations are outlined by Kolkowicz and Colton, among others.
47. For a standard Soviet assessment, see *Marxism–Leninism on War and the Army* (Moscow, 1972), pub. under the auspices of the US Air Force (Washington: Government Printing Office, 1976).
48. For the overall impact of Marxism–Leninism on the development of Russian/Soviet military literature, see "Science of Military Administration" in *MERSU*, Vol. 2, pp. 1–15; P. H. Vigor, *The Soviet View of War, Peace, and Neutrality* (London, 1975); Garthoff's *How Russia Makes War* and his *Soviet Strategy in the Nuclear Age* (New York, 1958), among numerous other works. The issue of Soviet attitudes to MAD and nuclear war in particular recently has been discussed by D. S. Papp, "Nuclear Weapons and the Soviet Worldview," in *SAFRA IV: 1980*, pp. 337–351; R. Kennedy, "The Strategic Balance in Transition: Interpreting Changes in US/USSR Weapons Levels," in ibid., pp. 352–373; and R. L. Arnett, "Soviet Attitudes Towards Nuclear War: Do They Really Think They Can Win? *Journal of Strategic Studies*, September 1979, pp. 172–191.
49. For the text of Lenin's comments on Clausewitz and their place, see D. E. Davis and W. S. G. Kohn, "Lenin's Notebook on Clausewitz," in *SAFRA I: 1977*, pp. 188–222, and the same authors' "Bibliographic Notes on Marxist and Leninist Military Theory," ibid., pp. 222–229.
50. On the "correlation of forces" and the difficulties of its calculation, see A. A. Myer, "The Balance in Central Europe: Reflections Through the Soviet Prism," *Naval War College Review*, November–December 1980, pp. 15–43. On Soviet suspicions of American strategic approaches, see Kennedy, pp. 356–385, and F. W. Ermarth, "Contrasts in American and Soviet Strategic Thought," *International Security*, Fall 1978, pp. 140–143.
51. For example, General M. I. Dragomirov taught the Tsarist conscript that he was "a soldier of Christ," a theme officially reiterated in the Field Service Regulations of 1912; M. I. Dragomirov, *Moments du Soldat* [Moments of the Soldier] (Paris, 1889), p. 9. As such, the Soviet soldier naturally aided his Orthodox Slavic brothers against first Turkish and then German–Austrian aggression in a manner similar to how his Soviet successor is bound to protect the "socialist commonwealth" from the assaults of "imperialism" and, at least theoretically, aid others in "national-liberation struggles." For expressions of these Soviet imperatives, see I. I. Yakubovskiy, ed., *Boyevoye sodruzhestvo bratskikh narodov i armiy* [The Combat Cooperation of the Fraternal Peoples and Armies] (Moscow, 1975), and N. A. Butsko, et al., *Sovetskiy soldat—patriot, internatsionalist* [The Soviet Soldier—Patriot, Internationalist] (Kiev, 1978).
52. Bellamy, p. 36.
53. All Soviet authors place security of the motherland as the armed forces' first responsibility. For less well-known variants of this patriotic theme, see Odintsov's trinity in note 40; A. A. Yepishev's *Kommunisty armii i flota* [Communists of the Army and Navy] (Moscow, 1971), in which he calls on Party members "to do everything . . . so that within the Soviet Armed Forces is developed the valiant warrior, the staunch patriot, and the ardent citizen of our great, socialist power" (p. 94). And despite

glorification of volunteers who fought in Spain and China in the 1930s, writers like Kozlov (p. 12) and Odintsov (pp. 17–18) stress the use of internationalism as a source for internal unity, a theme more fully developed in V. F. Samoylenko, *Druzhba narodov—istochnik mogushchestva Sovetskikh Vooruzhennykh Sil* [Friendship of the Peoples—The Source of the Might of the Soviet Armed Forces] (Moscow, 1972).

54. A. Chalfont, "Arguing About War and Peace," *Encounter*, January 1981, p. 81.

55. J. S. Curtiss, *The Russian Army Under Nicholas I, 1825–1855* (Durham, 1965), p. 107. On the Soviet belief in mass, see Garthoff, *How Russia Makes War*, pp. 121–126, and J. Record, *Sizing Up the Soviet Army* (Washington, 1975), pp. 41–42.

56. For the Soviets' view of the importance of the offensive, see A. A. Sidorenko, *The Offensive* (Moscow, 1970), trans. under the auspices of the US Air Force (Washington, 1972); Savkin, p. 167 ff; and Bellamy, p. 37. On the attitudes and deployments in 1941, see A. M. Nekrich's comments in V. Petrov, *June 22, 1941. Soviet Historians and the German Invasion* (New York, 1968), pp. 124–129, and J. Erickson, *The Road to Stalingrad* (London, 1975), pp. 13–98. The same emphasis on offensive tactics and operations is evident in Imperial texts; see K. A. Vitsnuda, et al, *Polevaya spravochnaya knizhka ofitsera* (Officer's Field Handbook), 6th ed. (Odessa, 1913), p. 114 ff. Also, see Garthoff, *How Russia Makes War*, p. 65 ff., and Record, pp. 33–37.

57. This debate has provoked a number of recent works, including M. MccGwire, ed., *Soviet Naval Developments. Capability and Context* (New York, 1973); M. MccGwire, K. Booth, and J. McDonnell, eds., *Soviet Naval Policy. Objectives and Constraints* (New York, 1975); M. MccGwire and J. McDonnell, eds., *Soviet Naval Influence. Domestic and Foreign Dimensions* (New York, 1977): P. Murphy, ed., *Naval Power in Soviet Policy* (Washington, 1978); and B. Dismukes and J. M. McConnell, *Soviet Naval Diplomacy* (New York, 1979).

58. This conclusion is largely confirmed by recent studies of the Soviets' distant interventionary capability; see, for example, C. G. Jacobsen, "Angola and the Evolution of Soviet Theory and Capability for Intervention in Distant Areas," in *SAFRA II: 1978*, pp. 351–363; P. H. Vigor, "The 'Forward Reach' of the Soviet Armed Forces: Seaborne and Airborne Landings," in Erickson and Feuchtwanger, pp. 183–221; K. A. Dunn, "Power Projection of Influence: Soviet Capabilities for the 1980s," *Naval War College Review*, September–October 1980, pp. 31–47.

Principles of Soviet Military Leadership

Daniel Hannaway

Throughout history the effectiveness of a military force has been closely linked with the quality of leadership in that force. Thus, by examining what high-ranking Soviet military officers say about leadership, we may be able to gain some insight into the effectiveness of the Soviet Armed Forces. In doing so, we run the risk of being unable to distinguish theory from practice or propaganda from reality; yet, this approach does permit us to see what the Soviets themselves consider to be important.

Among the most authoritative statements on leadership in recent years is that from the accountability report of the Central Committee of the Communist Party of the Soviet Union (CPSU) to the 25th Party Congress:

> A modern leader should organically combine party loyalty with profound competence, discipline with initiative and a creative approach to the job. At the same time, in any area the leader must also take into account the sociopolitical and indoctrinizing aspects, be sensitive to people, their needs and requests, and serve as an example in work and in everyday life.[1]

While this pronouncement does not mention specifically the military leader, it does highlight the principal qualities mentioned by Soviet military writers discussing military leadership in the USSR.

With rare exception, the first-mentioned quality for effective military leadership is devotion to the Communist Party of the Soviet Union and the communist cause and love for the Soviet Union and its people. Today, approximately 90 percent of the Soviet officer corps belong to the CPSU or the Communist Youth League (*Komsomol*).[2] Unlike the separation of political affiliation from military service required in this country, the officer corps of the USSR rests on foundations of the inseparability of the two. One writer, addressing the political qualities of a military leader in a volume of the important Soviet *Officer's Library*,[3] states, "A leader who possesses the necessary professional qualities (a knowledge of the job and administrative capabilities), but who does not have sufficient political-moral qualities *cannot and does not have the moral right to lead* a collective."[4] This requirement for absolute loyalty and total devotion to the CPSU has accompanied the apparent fruition of "one-man command," a phrase which describes the embodiment in one person, the commander, of the authority and responsibility for insuring that all military actions and decisions are founded on a communist socio-political outlook. During the early years of Soviet rule, the position of political commissar was established, and the military was run by using "two-man command;" every order of the commander had to be countersigned by the political commissar, who was in theory regarded as the commander's coequal but who was in reality more powerful. This practice was abandoned during World War II when it proved to be too unwieldy during combat, but the role of the political officer as the unit ideologue continues undiminished to this day. The repeated references in Soviet military writing to "one-man command" are a clear indication of the importance placed on the political awareness and trustworthiness of commanders, and they also indicate recognition of a continuing need to insure the commander's authority is not diluted by overly zealous political officers who remain active and powerful even today.

The political qualities of leadership directly proceed from a true Marxist–Leninist outlook. Because of the communist belief in the existence of objective laws of social development which are explained in terms of dialectical reasoning, the Soviet military leadership seeks answers for effective leadership in terms of objectivity and science. Thus, the phrase "scientific leadership" has become quite popular. As the British scholar David Holloway very aptly observed, the "technocratization" of the Soviet military and the attendant use of cybernetics and quantitative analysis in decisionmaking have "stimulated disagreement about the relationship between leadership, with its emphasis on vision, determination and the ability to inspire others, and management, which stresses expertise, technique and efficient organization."[5] Holloway also observes that this "technocratization," a matter which will be discussed more fully below, has been marked by a reluctance among highly trained technical specialists to concern themselves with political training,[6] something which, as noted above, is of particular importance to the leadership.

What currently appears to be the most widely accepted "formula" for leadership comes from former Minister of Defense, Marshal of the Soviet Union A. A. Grechko. In his book *Armed Forces of the Soviet State,* Marshal Grechko set forth six requirements for effective military leadership:

1. Communist conviction and utter dedication to the Party and people;
2. High discipline and execution;
3. Initiative and independence;
4. Commander's will and organizational abilities;
5. High professional training and general and military-technical culture of officer cadres;
6. Ability to train and educate subordinates.[7]

Using these six requirements as a point of departure, let us examine what various Soviet military writers have to say about each, all the while keeping in mind they are essentially playing "Variations on a Theme by Grechko."

The first and foremost quality has already been discussed, yet it cannot be overemphasized just how much communist ideology totally permeates every other quality. It and it alone is what puts everything in the acceptable frame of reference for the Soviet officer.

A profound knowledge of Marxism–Leninism makes it possible for an officer to analyze the present-day military political situation in the world from class positions, to draw correct conclusions from it, to clearly understand the tasks posed by the party for the Soviet Armed Forces, and to realize his role in the defense of the Soviet motherland and the other nations of the socialist commonwealth.[8]

It is interesting to note that Grechko and others include dedication to the people and the homeland in this requirement. Thus, the deep and natural sense of patriotism is invariably linked with a less natural devotion to the Party as the foremost requirement of Soviet officers. Of course, Grechko himself is quick to point out that Soviet patriotism is not divorced from "proletarian internationalism, a sense of friendship of peoples and social humanism."[9] Nonetheless, one gets the distinct impression that the interests of the Motherland definitely transcend feelings of proletarian internationalism.

Grechko's second requirement, high discipline and execution, refers to the self-discipline needed to carry out orders from above despite the difficulties of the situation. Included in this general requirement are the qualities of honesty, truthfulness, accuracy, and timeliness. There seems to be a great deal of similarity between this, the second general requirement, and the fourth, *viz:* a leader should possess a commander's will and organizational abilities. The qualities of high discipline and execution required of the leader himself are the same qualities the leader must demand from his subordinates. The leader must be firm in his decisions and resolute in his desire to see the mission is accomplished despite difficulties and obstacles. The fact he has the organizational abilities needed for "rationally assigning men and equipment, and thoroughly coordinating and thoroughly providing for the actions of the troops"[10] is expected to insure the commander's decisions will be carried out successfully.

The third general requirement consists of initiative and independence. Since there is often a thin line between the execution of an order and the exercise of initiative and independence, it might be well to dwell on these qualities for a moment. In the Soviet system—which is founded on disciplined unity of thought and direction—there would appear to be little tolerance for initiative and independence. The very

fact that three of the four general requirements listed thus far are centered on obedience (i.e., obedience to the party, obedience to superiors,
and the will to demand obedience from subordinates) would seem to
relegate initiative and independence to an inconsequential role in the
overall list of desired qualities in a Soviet military leader. However,
Soviet writings repeatedly single out initiative as one of the most
important qualities a commander can have. For example, Major General A. Zyryanov of the Soviet Tank Troops, writing in the widely circulated *Soviet Military Review,* states: "But as not a single battle resembles another, the manuals contain only general instructions, leaving vast
possibilities for a commander or staff to display initiative and resource-
fulness."[11] He further cautions, however, that a "commander's initiative can be displayed fully only if it rests on a thorough knowledge of
the manuals, modern weapons, and the probable enemy's actions."[12]
Along the same lines, Colonel L. Yeremeyev writes: "The
commander's ability to act independently is an important quality based
on his self-confidence, the ability to analyze and critically estimate his
own activity, on his persistence in achieving a set goal and *readiness to
accept full responsibility for his actions."*[13] Some western observers discern a general lack in Soviet society of this "readiness to accept full
responsibility" as one of the reasons initiative has not been evident in
the Soviet military.[14] One could well understand why initiative and
independent action might be lacking in a society where obedience is
relatively riskless and initiative is often fraught with ill consequences.
Perhaps for this reason, Grechko himself recognized that "the military
educational institutions . . . play an important role in developing these
most valuable qualities (initiative, boldness, and independence in decision making) in future officers."[15] He also notes that senior officers
share in this responsibility and cautions them to avoid the extremes,
since a lack of control is just as harmful as "petty tutelage." A similar
observation is made by Colonel M. I. Galkin who writes: "Initiative
and activeness . . . depend greatly upon the nature of the relationship
between superiors and subordinates. Petty interference gives rise to
irresponsibility and inertia."[16] Yet, no sooner is this said than the
author talks of the need for continuous control over the activities of
personnel to insure victory! Judging from their writings, high-ranking
Soviet officers are apparently in favor of developing initiative and
independence in their subordinates; yet, it is also apparent they have
attached certain caveats to their words of encouragement. Thus, the
question remains: just how much initiative and independence is the
Soviet officer allowed to exhibit in what can only be described as a
very tightly controlled environment?

The final two requirements listed by Marshal Grechko bear directly
on this development of initiative and independence. The requirement
for high professional training has been of particular concern in recent
years as the complexity of modern weaponry has increased at an

astonishing rate. Over a decade ago, Roman Kolkowicz noted the image of the traditional officer was being changed by "technocratization"—the rapid influx of highly trained technical officers into the Soviet military.[17] According to Soviet sources, 16.3 percent of the officer corps in 1940 was composed of engineers and technical personnel. By 1954, the figure had jumped to 28.4 percent; today, nearly one of every two Soviet officers is an engineer or technician.[18] Indicative of the trend was the creation in 1972 of two new[19] ranks—warrant officer and ensign—designed, among other things, to help retain technicians beyond their original service obligation. This was especially true for those serving in the Strategic Rocket Forces, Air Defense Forces, and the Air Forces.[20] The overall educational level of the Soviet officer corps—and for that matter, the Soviet Armed Forces as a whole—is also on the upswing. Reportedly, close to 100 percent of the officers filling positions of brigade commander and higher, all ship commanders of first and second rank, and over 90 percent of regimental commanders have a higher military education.[21] At the beginning of the 1970s, 60 percent of the enlisted personnel possessed a secondary or higher education and 90 percent had some kind of technical specialization.[22] Today, almost 100 percent of all draftees have at least eight years education and about 80 percent have completed a full ten years.[23] What all this means in terms of leadership is perhaps best summed up by Colonel M. I. Galkin:

> While in the wars of the past the commander, in a number of instances, could successfully carry out the mission relying on personal experience and empirical knowledge, under present conditions this is clearly insufficient. Without theoretical knowledge and without mastering the most recent achievements of military science, a commander is now unable to successfully carry out his duties.[24]

Much has been written about the new demands placed on the Soviet officer as a result of the technological revolution in modern warfare. Most insist that in this era of fast-paced technological development, every officer—and especially commanders—must be engaged continually in self-education. Grechko himself notes: "Education does not end with the completion of a military school or academy or with the receipt of a diploma."[25] Because of the growth in specialization and despite all the efforts of conscientious military leaders to keep abreast with current developments, it is impossible for commanders to have an in-depth knowledge of all specialties. This has created new challenges for the Soviet military leadership, challenges which have not gone unrecognized. One officer, for example, writes that a commander "must recognize others (subordinates) have a superior knowledge in certain areas and have the right to an independent view."[26] Nonetheless, the commander remains the principal authority; thus, a potential area of conflict is apparent as technology advances at an ever-increasing rate. As the Deputy Chief of the Frunze Military Academy, Lieutenant General Reznichenko, points out: "An all-arms (combined arms—Ed.) commander must have good technical knowledge so as to be able to use the combat equipment and weapons of all arms of the service and special forces competently without 'prompting' by specialists."[27]

The concern with self-improvement and education leads us finally to Grechko's sixth general requirement for military leadership, the commander's role as an educator. There is an extraordinary emphasis in Soviet military writings on this particular subject, perhaps partially reflecting Soviet communism's self-appointed role as model and educator for the world. Then, too, there are very practical reasons. With the revision of the Military Service Obligation Law in 1967, the term of service for all conscripts except those serving in the Navy was reduced from three years to two because of the increased number of available 18-year-olds in the Soviet Union. This made the effectiveness of the junior officer as an educator more important than ever before because of the diminished amount of time available for unit training. According to Lieutenant General L. Kuznetsov: "The Soviet officer is not merely a military expert in the narrow sense of the word. He is a pedagogue and educator [sic] at the same time."[28] This role of "pedagogue and educator" bears directly on the officer's effectiveness as a leader. In examining the "making of a soldier," one writer comments there is more involved than intuition, and for that reason: "What is really needed is a scientific approach. That is why the Soviet Armed Forces attach exceptional importance to improving the pedagogical skill of the commanders."[29] By scientific approach, the writer means "to introduce all the latest, most advanced and progressive achievements secured by pedagogical science, and to discard all that is old and outdated."[30] It is worth noting in this regard that cadets in military schools are given courses in pedagogy to more successfully carry out their duties as officers."[31]

In discussing the officer's role as an educator, Soviet military writers use certain key words which are worthy of mention. Especially prevalent are "exactingness," "persuasion," "encouragement," and "prestige." Exactingness is nothing more than demanding obedience from subordinates and following up to see orders are carried out, advice is heeded, and so on. Obviously, there is an overlap between the exactingness demanded by the commander as an educator and the discipline inherent in Grechko's fourth requirement noted above, "the commander's will and organizational abilities." There is nothing particularly surprising in this since there is considerable interaction among all the requirements, and the isolation of leadership qualities for purposes of observation and analysis is really quite artificial since in reality it is the harmonious interplay of qualities which results in the effectiveness of a leader. The leader must maintain constant contact with his subordinates. He must know his subordinates well yet avoid undue familiarity which will destroy his ability to command. Familiarity and its direct opposite, coarseness, are unacceptable qualities for a Soviet officer. Colonel S. Titov observes: "It is impossible to ensure firm discipline and order in a military collective without making strict but reasonable demands on the men."[32] He further states that "the principle method of promoting discipline is persuasion, *i.e.*, explaining to the fighting man the particular demands of the service."[33] The question is, however, how does the leader persuade his men? One writer expresses the belief that the officer-educator must encourage and praise his subordinates publicly.[34] Another recognizes that while compulsion in the form of disciplinary punishment, admonition, warning, prohibition, and so on, are sometimes necessary, it is the true leader who teaches by encouragement and makes the encouragement more effective by insuring it is timely and public.[35] The final quality grouped under the commander's skill to educate is prestige. Colonel A. Barabanshchikov writes: "An officer who wishes to master the skills of training and education and become a master in this field should win prestige with the men."[36] He believes that a commander should gain the respect of his men by exhibiting political qualities (firm ideological conviction and national patriotic interest), professional qualities (knowledge of tactics, equipment, and regulations; boldness; initiative; personal courage), and moral qualities (displaying high moral standards).[37] Yet another writer equates the prestige of a commander with his power to influence people and believes that he achieves this prestige by being strict (exacting) in a fatherly way and showing concern for his men.[38]

From what has been presented, it is quite obvious certain aspects of the Soviet perception of leadership stand out in sharp relief. Paramount is the complete dominance and pervasiveness of the ideological/patriotic basis for leadership. In a country where there is only one political party, a party which claims it and it alone has the correct interpretation of the course of history and social progress, it would be foolish *not* to expect military leaders to be party members with firm political convictions. In the Soviet scheme, military force is a true extension of politics; thus, the leaders of that military force must be fully cognizant of that relationship and, more importantly, capable of explaining that role to subordinates. A fighting force which is convinced of the righteousness of its actions and the inevitability of its victory according to the so-called scientific laws of social progress can be formidable indeed. The cultivation of this conviction in every Soviet fighting man is the primary duty of the Soviet officer, and for him to be a believable model and true leader, he himself must be totally dedicated.

The role of the leader as an educator, the second of the desired qualities of leadership, is closely connected with the requirement that a military leader be dedicated to communism, for ideological education is one of his prime responsibilities in view of the principle of "one-man command." As the officer is instructed in *The Officer's Handbook*: "Ideological education and training are inseparably linked and there is constant interaction between them. The former imparts ideological direction to training and increases its effectiveness."[39] From a practical standpoint, the need for a leader to be an educator is extremely important; by properly teaching his subordinates, the leader is insuring they will later follow his example and try to emulate him. Thus, the terms "persuasion," "encouragement," and "prestige" take on considerable meaning if by a leader we mean someone who is followed by others because they *want to* and not because they *have to*.

The final quality which stands out is initiative. This is also the quality which creates the greatest interest not only for those outside the Soviet system looking in but also for those within the system itself. There can be little doubt Soviet military leaders recognize the need to foster initiative and independent thinking among their subordinates. They readily acknowledge that in future conflicts, especially nuclear conflicts, the need for initiative and independent thinking becomes critical with any breakdown in command and control since the employment and effects of modern weapons are measured in seconds and minutes, thereby allowing little or no time for hesitation. Thus, one general officer states:

> Under present conditions owing to the radical changes in the character of battle, the initiative and self-dependence of the commander and others participating in control of units and subunits acquires incomparably greater significance. It is impossible to foresee everything in advance. Rapid and frequent changes in the situation will demand alterations to a previously taken decision. If one waits for instructions from above one may lose time and this will lead to still greater complications in conditions of battle.[40]

Despite such a pronouncement, it must be remembered that the entire social and political system is built on the principle that orders must be strictly followed and deviation from the norm is unacceptable. Perhaps for this reason, General of the Army Tretyak qualifies initiative by calling for "reasonable initiative."[41] Moreover, initiative is clearly restricted to the means of accomplishing a mission and not the alteration of the mission itself:

> The superior commander's decision is an indisputable law for those who have to put it into effect. In this connection one may ask: "How then can one display initiative?" The answer is simple: the decision of a higher authority is directed precisely at developing a commander's creative thought. Having been assigned concrete missions, he

decides how to fulfill them.[42]

While this in itself is a rather radical departure from the blind obedience to established tactical procedures which we normally ascribe to Soviet military operations, the fact of the matter is that Soviet military leaders of today are faced with a dilemma. How do they promote initiative and demand absolute obedience at the same time? It is a question not easily answered and one with which they will struggle for some time to come.

Notes

1. A. M. Iovlev, *Deyatel'nost' KPSS po podgotovke voyennykh kadrov* (Activities of the CPSU in Training Military Personnel) (Moscow: Voyenizdat, 1976), excerpted in Joint Publications Research Service *Translations on the USSR Military Affairs*, 25 January 1978, p. 58.
2. Marshal A. A. Grechko, *The Armed Forces of the Soviet State* (Moscow: Voyenizdat, 1975) translated under the auspices of the US Air Force (Washington: Goverment Printing Office, 1977), p. 187.
3. Many of the works in this *Officer's Library* have been translated under the auspices of the United States Air Force and appear in the "Soviet Military Thought Series" available from the Superintendent of Documents, Washington, DC.
4. Colonel M. I. Galkin, "The Revolution in Military Affairs and the Increased Role of Science in Troop Leadership," in Colonel General N. A. Lomov, ed., *Scientific–Technical Progress and the Revolution in Military Affairs* (Moscow: Voyenizdat, 1973), translated under the auspices of the US Air Force (Washington: Government Printing Office, 1974), p. 233, emphasis added.
5. David Holloway, "Technology, Management and the Soviet Military Establishment," *Adelphi Papers*, No. 76 (London: Institute for Strategic Studies, 1971), p. 2.
6. Ibid., p. 3.
7. Grechko, op. cit., pp 188–189.
8. Iovlev, op. cit., p. 59.
9. Grechko, op. cit., p. 292.
10. Ibid., p. 189.
11. Major General A. Zyryanov, "The Regulations and Commander's Initiative," *Soviet Military Review*, February 1976, p. 26.
12. Ibid., p. 27.
13. Colonel L. Yeremeyev, "Commander's Independent Actions," *Soviet Military Review*, October 1976, p. 34, emphasis added.
14. See especially Major Timothy Felker, *Initiative: A Leadership Trait of the Soviet Officer* student research report (Garmisch: US Army Institute for Advanced Russian and East European Studies, 1976).
15. Grechko, op. cit., p. 193.
16. Galkin, op. cit., p 231.
17. Roman Kolkowicz, *The Soviet Military and the Communist Party* (Princeton: Princeton University Press, 1976). See especially Chapter IX.
18. Captain First Rank V. Drozdov, "The Soviet Officer Corps," *Soviet Military Review*, February 1977, p. 8.
19. Actually, the ranks of *praporshchik* (warrant officer) and *michman* (ensign) were used as far back as the 18th century in the Russian Army and Navy, respectively.
20. For further information, see John Erickson, "New Warrant Officers for the Soviet Armed Forces," *Journal of the Royal United States Institute for Defence Studies*, June 1973, pp. 47–51.

21. Drozdov, op. cit., p. 8.
22. John Erickson, "The Training of the Soviet Soldier," *Journal of the Royal United Service Institute for Defence Studies,* December 1971, p. 45.
23. Colonel General M. Sobolev, "Educational Role of the Soviet Armed Forces," *Soviet Military Review,* June 1980, p. 2.
24. Galkin, op. cit., p. 219.
25. Grechko, op. cit., p. 190.
26. Lieutenant Colonel A. Kitov, "The Commander's Prestige," *Soviet Military Review,* September 1970, p. 14.
27. Lieutenant General V. Reznichenko, "Modern Weapons and Troop Control," *Soviet Military Review,* December 1978, p. 12.
28. Lieutenant General L. Kuznetsov, "Competence in Method," *Soviet Military Review,* November 1976, p. 17.
29. Captain Second Rank P. Gorodov, "The Making of a Soldier," *Soviet Military Review,* December 1975, p. 28.
30. Ibid., p. 29.
31. Colonel A. Barabanshchikov, "The Officer's Pedagogical Skill," *Soviet Military Review,* May 1970, p. 44.
32. Colonel S. Titov, "Discipline in the Soviet Army," *Soviet Military Review,* August 1970, p. 8.
33. Ibid., p. 8.
34. Colonel K. Amirov, "Encouragement—An Important Method in Education," *Soviet Military Review,* July 1975, p. 37.
35. Colonel N. Federenko, "Methods Used in Educating Soviet Soldiers," *Soviet Military Review,* November 1976, p. 36.
36. Barabanshchikov, op. cit., p. 43.
37. Ibid., p. 43.
38. Titov, op. cit., p. 11.
39. Major General Ye F. Sulimov, "The Foundations and Principles of Soviet Military Development," in Major General S. N. Kozlov, ed., *The Officer's Handbook* (Moscow: Voyenizdat, 1971), translated under the auspices of the US Air Force (Washington: Government Printing Office, 1977), p. 87.
40. Lieutenant General G. Chuyko, "Initiative in Troop Control," *Soviet Military Review,* December 1980, p. 12.
41. General of the Army I. Tretyak, "The Commander's Creative Activity," *Soviet Military Review,* August 1980, p. 19.
42. Colonel I. Tikhonov, "Initiative in Battle," *Soviet Military Review,* June 1980, p. 21.

Soviet Party–Military Relations in Strategic Decisionmaking

Howard Frost

The views expressed here are the author's and do not necessarily reflect those of the Central Intelligence Agency. The author wishes to thank Karl Spielmann, Anthony Williams, and Mary Dunham for their comments on the draft. The author, however, takes sole responsibility for the contents and conclusion herein.

Relations between the Communist Party of the Soviet Union and the USSR Armed Forces have been a subject of significant controversy for Western scholars. According to the conventional wisdom, these relations are tense because of the independence from the Party military officers seek.[1] According to this view, the Party and the military are two distinct bodies in competition with each other; their conflicts can and do impair the formulation of military policy. Recent analyses, however, have focused on elements of cooperation between the groups with the resultant conclusion that military policy is more a product of coordination than competition between them.

Careful consideration of the decisionmaking process and the framework of its operation leads to the conclusion that the second view more accurately represents Soviet political-military relations; i.e., cooperative, not competitive, behavior predominates among the pertinent decisionmaking bodies. The analysis presented here concludes that, while tensions do exist between the Soviet political and military leaders, these tensions do not impair significantly the formulation of military strategic policy.*

Soviet sources are not explicit concerning the coordination that occurs among the higher party and military decisionmaking bodies in particular cases. They suggest, however, that strategic decisionmaking takes place within a framework in which the two groups have different responsibilities. Hence, the general nature of the interaction of these bodies can be understood from the distinctions the Soviets themselves make among the formal responsibilities of military field officers, theorists, and scientists, and those of political officers and top party leaders. After an examination of the formal and informal relationships between the two groups, I will offer some conclusions concerning the current

---

*For the purposes of this discussion, political and military leaders are presented as comprising different "groups" of society, though actually such delineation is much less clear.

dynamics of the party-military relationship.

The Soviets are very discriminating about the terminology they use to address different aspects of military thought. Take, for example, the fundamental distinction in Soviet military thought between military doctrine and military policy. For the Soviets, each term has conceptual as well as organizational implications for the proper development and conduct of military activities. According to the *Dictionary of Basic Military Terms* of the Voroshilov Academy of the General Staff, military doctrine has two aspects: political and military-technical. Military doctrine comprises the beliefs held and actions taken regarding military policy by the most powerful authority in the Soviet Union—the Politburo. Although its individual facets may be formulated by a diverse group of lower officials, military doctrine as it is formulated by the Politburo is the sum of authoritative concepts of military policy.[2] The distinction drawn here is that military doctrine comprises the policymakers' most fundamental perspectives and guidelines in the area of military affairs, while military policy is comprised of decisions formulated in response to specific situations. Military doctrine, based upon a military-political calculus, has by its nature more continuity and authority in strategic decisionmaking than military policy, which is based almost completely on a political calculus and designed in response to specific situations. Military policy may be based on military doctrine and may in turn contribute to it, but military policy never assumes the preeminence of military doctrine in decisionmaking. It is important to note, therefore, that it is a formal body composed primarily of political, not military, leaders which has the greatest impact on the formulation of military doctrine.

Another important facet of military thought is military science. Military science—which is clearly subordinate to military doctrine—is the system of knowledge from which the military-technical aspects of doctrine are derived. Concerned with the study of operations, military science includes a number of different approaches regarding the preparation of the state and its armed forces for war. Military science comprises not only military art, but also military-historical research, the physical and natural sciences (e.g., physics and aerodynamics), Marxist–Leninist methodologies, and other approaches considered useful in the study of military operations.[3]

Military art, the most important of these elements, comprises military strategy, operational art, and tactics. Military strategy "develops and studies concrete problems bearing on the nature of war."[4] Examining and determining the means for the direction of war, military strategy involves the study of

> the conditions and factors that determine, at any given historical moment, the nature of a future war, the distribution of military and political forces, the quality and quantity of

480-900 0 - 85 - 3

the means of waging war, the military and economic potential, the probable composition and strength of the opposing coalitions and their geographical arrangement.[5]

Operational art, on the other hand, concerns the direction of large units on the front, while tactics involves the movement of smaller combat units on the battlefield.[6] Generally, while the tenets of military art are scientifically based, developmental guidelines for military art research and design are formulated in response to the requirements of military doctrine. Military art, as well as the other aspects of military science, contributes to military doctrine in a type of "feedback" mechanism, enabling the adaptive evolution of doctrinal concepts.[7]

While military science is the tool employed by officers and institutions involved with military R&D programs to provide input into military doctrine, it is just one of several tools used by high-level political bodies in the development of military doctrine. Just as military science includes a variety of components, so also does military doctrine. When the party formulates military doctrine, it relies not only on military science but also on economic, political, and moral bases, all of which coalesce into a "dialectic approach"—a combination of analyses of the nature of future military conflicts, the resources and capabilities of the opposing sides, and the current military posture of the opponent.[8] The party's primacy in the formulation of military doctrine (e.g., the decision to commit military forces) is never questioned, but the relative weights to be given to the components of military policy, such as military as opposed to nonmilitary (economic or sociological) factors or past military practice as opposed to future projections on the nature of war, have been an area of some debate within decisionmaking circles. For example, arguments in military journals that focus on the importance of taking into consideration new technological developments in the formulation of modern doctrine indicate there has been disagreement on the relevance of World War II experiences as they would relate to a nuclear conflict.[9] Likewise, discussions on the number of tanks to be used in military forces, as opposed to motorized rifle divisions, reveal another disagreement on the factors of doctrine, as do discussions on the value of lessons learned from military conflicts in the Third World.

While one might think, given these well-defined categories, that party officials are the sole authors of military doctrine while military officials exercise their authority solely in the management of military science, such is not the case. Given the interpenetration of the party and the military, one finds military representatives in the most important party decisionmaking bodies and vice versa. In applying this theoretical framework to the actual decisionmaking process, one easily can conclude that the military has a strong voice in the formulation of supervisory input into military operations and research. An examination of the membership and option of the most important party and military decisionmaking bodies will clearly indicate the mutually supportive roles of these organizations.

Party–Military Interaction in High–Level Decisionmaking Bodies

To examine the relationship, I will first present the interraction of these two groups as it occurs in the main political and military decisionmaking bodies and then discuss several conflictual issues on which judgments can be made regarding this interaction.

As mentioned before, the party is accepted as the ultimate arbiter on military doctrine. Minister of Defense Dmitriy Ustinov stated in a 1979 speech:

> In accordance with the changes in the military-political situation in the world and with regard to the USSR's continually growing economic potential, (the party) determines the content and the basic directions of development of Soviet military doctrine.[10]

The Soviet *Officer's Handbook* states that questions of military defense, theory, and practice are decided

> in exact accordance with the ideology and policy of the party, on the basis of the directives and instructions formulated in the resolutions of congresses, of plenums of the Central Committee, and of the Politburo . . . .[11]

Quite obviously, the congresses are unsuitable for military policymaking not only because of the number who attend but also because of their lack of expertise in military affairs. It is well-known that these bodies listen to and approve policies presented by the country's leaders. The Central Committee plenums are somewhat more suitable. Ustinov comments:

> There is no area of military affairs which does not feel the constant wholesome influence of the party, its Central Committee, the Central Committee Politburo, and Marshal of the Soviet Union L. I. Brezhnev, General Secretary of the CPSU Central Committee . . . .[12]

Since Central Committee members nearly all have important fulltime jobs, live outside Moscow, and only convene for several days two or three times annually, it is apparent that little substantial military policymaking occurs in the plenums. Many members are unfamiliar with military matters, and senior command personnel in the armed forces usually have comprised 8 to 10 percent of the membership since the early 1960s. In fact, there have been relatively few plenums that have dealt specifically with military affairs.* Generally, plenums are concerned with ratifying Politburo decisions on military policy.[14]

In spite of the generally limited military policy role of the Central Committee, the presence of important officers in this elite body provides the armed forces with continuous institutional representation there. This presence serves as a "visible manifestation of the party's concern for the military establishment."[15] Most of the Central Committee military members owe their election to the post they hold in the Soviet Armed Forces. These officials have included the minister and first deputy ministers of defense, the service commanders in chief, the chief of the Main Political Administration, the chief of the Rear Services, the main inspector, and various service chiefs. While the percentage of military representatives on the Central Committee has not kept pace with the growth of that institution since the mid-1960s, it is clear that the military representation in this organization does serve an important function.[16]

The Central Committee's Secretariat is particularly important in military policy implementation because of its day-to-day supervisory responsibilities. Although there is not a specific department dealing with general military policy, there are four departments dealing with military affairs. These are the Departments of Defense Industries, Machine Construction, and Administrative Organs, and the Main Political Administration of the Soviet Army and Navy.[17] The first two departments supervise the nine defense industrial ministries (the Ministries of Defense Industry, Aviation Industry, Shipbuilding Industry, Communications, Radio Industry, Electronics Industry, General Machine Building, Medium Machine Building, and Machine Building).[18] The Department of Administrative Organs supervises military affairs, along with police and judicial activities, and its First Military Section in particular acts as a civilian organization which verifies military fulfillment of party instructions.[19] The Central Committee's fourth body with military supervisory functions, the important Main Political Administration (*GlavPU*), is headed by Army General A. A. Yepishev. This organization will be discussed in greater depth later, but suffice it here to say its main functions are to oversee the party-political apparatus within the Ministry of Defense (MOD). Specifically, *GlavPU* "is accountable to the Central Committee of the CPSU and the Defense Council, and reports to the Ministry of Defense on troop conditions and political work in the Army and Navy."[20] While checking on the execution of party policy, the *GlavPU* also serves as a coordinating body for party and Komsomol activities in the armed forces and as a supporting organization in military training to increase combat

---

*John McDonnell speculates that plenums dealing particularly with military matters were held in February 1955, October 1957, December 1958, December 1966, April 1967, June 1967, and December 1969.[13]

readiness and strengthen military discipline. In addition, because of its responsibility for the political education of military personnel, it organizes and manages the military's cultural and recreational organizations and conducts military sociological research. Finally, *GlavPU* also edits a number of service journals.[21]

In addition to the control over the military exercised by the Secretariat, the Central Committee occasionally establishes ad hoc committees which may have input into military decisionmaking or into party control over the military. These committees are usually organized to manage particularly complex foreign policy or defense issues such as those involved in the SALT negotiations.[22]

Clearly the nucleus of military policymaking is the Politburo and its subgroup on national defense, whose members are probably L. I. Brezhnev, N. A. Tikhonov, D. F. Ustinov, A. A. Gromyko, Yu. A. Andropov, and A. P. Kirilenko.* The Politburo is concerned generally with such matters as economic resource allocations for defense, overall manpower strength of the armed forces, decisions on major uses of Soviet troops abroad, and approval of SALT agreements. Although there are only three Politburo members with military rank (Brezhnev, Ustinov, and Andropov), the military establishment has a significant input into the routine military decisions of the Politburo. In April 1973, Minister of Defense and Marshal of the Soviet Union Andrey Grechko, as well as Minister of Foreign Affairs Anatoliy Gromyko and *KGB* head Yuriy Andropov, were made full members of the Politburo. The institutionalization of these ministry heads as full Politburo members reflects the importance of their ministerial positions for military policymaking and suggests that there was significant accord between these officials and Brezhnev on important military matters. In addition, there has been extensive support in the Politburo for military preparedness, a trend which likely will not diminish. Furthermore, professional soldiers and military intellectuals are invited to present their views to the Politburo and thereby enjoy significant access to this body.[23]

The main group responsible for military policy and the formulation of military doctrine is the Defense Council (*Sovet oborony*). This body, technically attached to the Council of Ministers and the Central Committee, carries significant authority since the majority of its members serve on the Politburo. The principal members of the Defense Council probably include all of the above-mentioned members of the Politburo's subgroup on national defense, plus Marshal N. V. Ogarkov. Brezhnev, Tikhonov, and Kirilenko probably hold their positions because of their rank on the Politburo and Ustinov because of his rank on the Politburo as well as his ministerial responsibilities and earlier involvement with weapons research and development and procurement.[24] (Suslov was probably a member because of his earlier membership in a predecessor

---

*The late Mikhail Suslov was a member as well.

63

organization to the Defense Council, the Supreme Military Council (*Vysshiy voyennyy sovet.*)[25] Ogarkov is likely a member because of his positions as First Deputy Minister of Defense and Chief of the General Staff. Other officials who may be called to attend meetings of the Defense Council are Marshal V. C. Kulikov, First Deputy Minister of Defense and Commander in Chief of the Warsaw Pact Forces, and Army General and Minister of Internal Affairs N. A. Shchelokov.[26] This body, therefore, includes the highest ranking party and military officers among its members and consultants. The integration of party and military elites in this body serves to facilitate cooperation between the two institutions. As Ustinov commented in a 1979 article which examines party-military cooperation during World War II, integration of military and party elites at the highest decisionmaking levels insures "the complete unity of party, state, and military leadership and (makes) it possible to develop the most expedient decisions and effectively implement them."[27]

Functions of the Defense Council are numerous. The Council examines

> the preparation of the country, the economy, and the people for war. It ensures that plans are in being for mobilizing industry, transport, and manpower for the possibility for war at various levels of intensity. It has the power to form new or abolish old military districts. The Council examines proposals, makes judgments, and issues decrees that have the effect of law.[28]

The Defense Council probably also has responsibility for defense budget plans, major weapons programs, and major shifts in military doctrine. It may monitor the status of defense programs initiated by the full Politburo as well as approve lesser defense policy questions such as the conduct of major training exercises or noncrisis force deployments.[29]

In wartime, this body probably would perform functions similar to those of the World War II State Defense Committee (*Gosudarstvennyy komitet oborony—GKO*). The *GKO*, during its existence from 1937 to 1945, controlled and directed military planning during the war. As Marshal V. D. Sokolovskiy notes:

> All leadership of the country and the armed forces during wartime will be carried out by the Central Committee of the Communist Party of the Soviet Union with the possible organization of a higher agency of leadership of the country and the Armed Forces. This higher agency may be given the same powers as the State Committee of Defense during the Great Patriotic War.[31]

The second highest decisionmaking body concerned with military affairs in the government's structure is the Military-Industrial Commission (*Voyenno–promyshlennaya komissiya—VPK*). Essentially a working commission of the Council of Ministers, this body serves to coordinate requirements of the Ministry of Defense with defense production industries. It also is thought to coordinate defense research and production activities which cut across individual ministerial lines, determine whether existing technologies are adequate to support particular programs, and distribute resources among defense programs.[32]

Since the Council of Ministers per se never meets, the *VPK* is essentially subordinate to the Presidium of the Council of Ministers and its chairman, Nikolay Tikhonov. Because of its responsibility to Tikhonov, the Commission probably makes its influence felt on the Politburo through his participation.

The *VPK* is chaired by Deputy Chairman of the Council of Ministers L. V. Smirnov. Other possible members of the *VPK* are I. F. Dmitriyev, Chief of the Central Committee's Defense Industries Department; M. K. Shkabardnya, Minister of Instrument Making, Automation Equipment, and Control Systems; K. M. Gerasimov, a Collegium member of *Gosplan;* and other officials of the Ministry of Defense, the nine key defense ministries, the Academy of Sciences, and the State Committee for Science and Technology. The *VPK,* therefore, is important because of the experience and expertise of its ministries and its well-balanced organizational representation. In fact, almost all the major "interest groups" of the defense industrial sector are found on this commission.[33]

Within the military branch of the chain of command, the organization directly subordinate to the Defense Council is the General Staff (*General'nyy shtab*). Originally modeled after the pre-World War I German General Staff, the Soviet General Staff is composed of First Deputy Minister of Defense Marshal N. V. Ogarkov and officers from the various services and branches. These officers are graduates of the Academy of the General Staff who have served an apprenticeship in a major military command. Upon finishing their service on the General Staff, they often return to the Academy of the General Staff to become faculty members.[34] The General Staff, which serves as the executive body for both the MOD and Defense Council, is a powerful body in its own right. Not only are the officials of the organization full party members and important decisionmakers in high-level military bodies, they are also in charge of various branches of the Soviet Armed Forces, military districts, and operational forces, and therefore exert a significant amount of control through the organizations they head.[35] As members of the General Staff Service by virtue of their graduation from the Academy, these officials report to the General Staff as well as to the Ministry of Defense. Even though its officers come from various branches of the armed forces, the General Staff is not in competition with the five Soviet services; it allocates roles and missions to these services, but its officers do not represent service interests.[36]

Broadly, the responsibility of the General Staff is to develop a "unified military strategy" based upon military doctrine—the military policy of the CPSU established by the Defense Council and Politburo. The General Staff

> thoroughly analyzes and appraises developing military-political conditions, determines the tendencies of development of the means of waging war and the methods of their application, organizes the training of Armed Forces, and implements the necessary measures to guarantee their high combat readiness to repulse any possible aggression.[37]

The General Staff in addition directs military operations, develops strategic concepts, targeting, and war plans, and assists in the formulation of general military policy by providing advice to the MOD Collegium and the Defense Council.[38] The General Staff is charged with coordinating the activities of the main staffs of the Armed Forces, the Rear Services, and the Civil Defense forces of the USSR as well as superintending the military districts, Soviet forces abroad, and the air defense fleets. Because of its responsibilities for the service branches, the General Staff is a focal point for the resolution of interservice rivalries. As the largest of the three primary bodies of the Soviet High Command and as an experienced group of military professionals, then, the General Staff is a very important link in the decisionmaking chain.[39]

Next in importance in the military chain of command is the Collegium of the Ministry of Defense. The organization has as its main responsibility the strategic direction and leadership of the Soviet Armed Forces during peacetime.[40] Minister of Defense Ustinov probably chairs this body, whose principal members are the deputy ministers of defense. This body probably also includes the chief of the *GlavPU*, the commanders in chief of the five armed services, and the chiefs of the Rear Services and Civil Defense.[41] Regardless of the exact composition of the Collegium, however, it is safe to assume that all its members are also members of the party, since virtually without exception military officers above the level of colonel are party members.

The functions of the Collegium are to assist in developing the armed forces, handle professional matters of ministry-wide significance, and provide recommendations on such issues as the allocation of manpower and financial and material resources. This body probably also advises the Minister of Defense and develops unified military positions on issues to be reviewed by the Defense Council and Politburo.[42] Although it has no decisionmaking authority, its recommendations may be issued as decrees through the Minister of Defense for the General Staff, which serves the Collegium as a type of secretariat. In addition, this body also has been said to be the organization in which are resolved latent rivalries between the General Staff and the Ministry of Defense concerning which organization has more authority in the direction of the armed forces.[43]

The Decisionmaking Process

To explain the operation of these groups in the policy process, Matthew Gallagher and Thomas Wolfe offer similar frameworks. Gallagher suggests strategic goals are first established in the Politburo or Defense Council, then specific military commitments are determined by these bodies as well as the General Staff and Ministry of Defense Collegium. Directives regarding military policies which originate in the second-level bodies would be channeled for implementation to the Ministry of Defense. Similarly, directives concerning military production would be channeled from the *VPK* to the nine defense industry ministries.[44]

Wolfe suggests Politburo members may question the economic feasibility of a policy alternative, its technological practicality, and the extent of the nation's need for it. He remarks that the first two of these questions can usually be answered by civilian researchers, but, if the issue is a military one, the Politburo decisionmaker usually has no alternative but to consult military colleagues, usually those in the General Staff, for the answer to the third.[45] Therefore, while the party elite may have the ultimate authority in the formulation of major military policy, it relies heavily on the military for advice. As the party has recognized military science as a state science, the legitimacy of the military's expertise is beyond question.

Furthermore, the military is very important for policy implementation. A sort of division of labor is created involving high-level policymaking bodies and subordinate military organizations, principally because of the implementation factor and the lack of alternate sources for consultation in the area of security policy analysis. This dynamic essentially means those whose advice is sought are those who have the greatest institutional interests at stake in strategic decisionmaking. It also signifies the system is weighted toward the views of the military professionals and their colleagues in the defense industry ministries.[46]

Even in this current period of economic difficulties for the Soviet Union, when a one to two percent GNP growth rate exacerbates difficulties in resource allocation decisionmaking, the military remains in an influential position. Its long-standing priority in allocations planning, its monopoly on military-technical information, and the important political positions of its chief representatives all combine to give it a continually strong voice in the decisionmaking process.

Additional Informal Ties

Having established the basic conceptual framework for the development of military policy, an examination can be made of some of the more subtle dynamics of the decisionmaking process. Initially, it is clear a preoccupation with military superiority is a major factor affecting Soviet decisionmaking. While nonmilitary factors are important in the development and execution of foreign policy, it appears, as Thomas Wolfe notes, a "psychology involving something more than a refined calculus of utilities and disutilities of military power helps to shape the attitudes of the Soviet leadership toward its accumulation." He observes furthermore that Soviet leaders simply have left open-ended the question of how much military power is "enough," finding it easier to reserve this issue for some indefinite date in the future than to try to resolve it in the present.[47] Therefore, the control of military decisionmakers over such a destructive force as the Soviet military endows them with significant prestige.

Furthermore, the argument for defense appropriations commands a very favorable response in Soviet decisionmaking bodies because of the importance of the armed forces in policy execution and because of the world prestige a strong military has brought the Soviet Union.[48] This awareness of the necessity and usefulness of a strong military is shared by both political and military decisionmakers, thus creating an environment particularly receptive to the interests of the military.

Likewise, it is clear the party and military elite are interpenetrated, and, at the very top levels of decisionmaking, party and military decisionmakers are often one and the same.[49] Given the overall concern for a strong military, the integration of political and military decisionmakers in the higher policymaking bodies, and the monopoly of information the military often has concerning weapons systems, it is apparent the military has significant authority in decisionmaking and strong channels for the representation of its views in the highest levels of policymaking.

In addition to the fact there are many political decisionmakers with military experience and even more with sensitivity to military concerns, one should also note many of the military officers holding important policymaking posts have had significant experience working in the political milieu of decisionmaking and in looking after their own interests. In fact, the current ministers of the nine defense ministries have a combined total of over 250 years experience in their fields, a figure which indicates these officials have had ample opportunity to learn to use the system to their advantage.[50] In addition, these officials and their deputies realize party officials in the Politburo and the Central Committee have control over their appointments; to avoid higher officials and risk losing their jobs, they are certainly circumspect about voicing very strong pro-military positions when such positions are not shared by many others.[51]

Acknowledging, then, that there are numerous channels for cooperation among party and military decisionmakers, what is the source and nature of conflict between the two groups? It is difficult to tell with certainty how much and how often the two have irreconcilable views; there is simply not enough open-source material to do so. To answer this question, I will discuss briefly a few issues where conflict has been known to occur and, from these issues, infer why antagonism occurs between the two. The issues here included are the Zhukov affair, Khrushchev's plan to reduce theater forces, and the use of the *KGB* and *GlavPU* to preserve political discipline and education within the armed forces. Although there has been significant conflict between the Party and military since the inception of the Soviet state, recent conflicts have occurred for the most part only when the Party has intruded too extensively into the military's own spheres of activity.[52]

The evidence from the Zhukov case indicates that he was dismissed not for being too assertive in military policymaking but for trying to reduce the influence of the Party on military life by such means as forbidding political deputy commanders in the Soviet Army from speaking with Central Committee members and diminishing the amount of required political work in the armed forces. Criticism of these initiatives was reflected in the decree which dismissed him. Resistance by many officers to Khrushchev's plan to reduce conventional forces in favor of ballistic missiles frequently was manifested in military writings in the early 1960s. The Khrushchev initiative disturbed members of some branches of the services more than others and was a major contributing factor to his demise. In addition, although it was not an issue involving a Party attempt to acquire more authority in military life, it did evoke a strong response from commanders who thought their jobs were threatened because of poor planning by the Party.[53]

Two potential institutional sources of conflict in Party-military relations are created by the presence of the *KGB* and *GlavPU* in military life. The Third Directorate of the *KGB* has responsibility in the military units for guarding against subversion and espionage in the armed forces. This organization allegedly recruits agents and informers within the military at virtually every level. While there is a certain conjunction of interest between the unit commanders and the *KGB* representatives to ensure discipline and security among the troops, available evidence indicates there is still some friction because of this presence.[54] The other institution for party control is the Main Political Administration. In the performance of its duties of political socialization of the Soviet solider, *GlavPU* often has been said to conflict with the role or prerogatives of the unit commander. Recent studies on the role of *GlavPU* have revised this perspective, focusing on such shared interests of the *zampolit* (deputy commander for political affairs) and the military officers as improving the efficiency of the armed forces in general, increasing the consideration given to military interests in high-level decisionmaking, and stressing the importance for advancement of a good political record to a military officer.[55] Considering many *zampolit* are recruited from the enlisted ranks, trained in service-related *GlavPU* academies, and continue to be very much a part of the professional military establishment, it is apparent that few major conflicts develop between the military and the *GlavPU*. If, as Edward Warner suggests, the main area of current Party-military conflict concerns the amount of time soldiers should spend in political as opposed to military training, it is clear that the *GlavPU*–military relationship does not create a major obstacle to Party-military relations in general.[56]

Conclusions and Projections for the 1980s

Comparing these potential sources of conflict with the demonstrated channels for cooperation, the obvious conclusion is that the areas of cooperation are qualitatively and quantitatively more extensive than those of conflict. It is patent the mutually beneficial interaction of Party and military officials in high-level policymaking bodies remains strong. Indeed, the question of Party-military conflict currently seems an irrelevant one to pose.

To make this assertion, however, is not to contend the symbiotic partnership of these two groups attenuates all potential conflicts. Because this examination has focused at a macroanalytical level upon organizational interactions, discussions of less obvious yet potentially important personality differences between Party and military leaders has been foregone. As we suggested earlier, personality and organizational clashes involving Party and military leaders have been and will continue to be sources of conflict, but these problems are not likely to affect seriously the institutional cooperation between the two groups.

In an effort to define more precisely the current relative importance of the Party and the military in strategic decisionmaking, some analysts have attempted to demonstrate that the Party has reasserted its control over the military since the mid-1970s. They contend that Ustinov's accession to the position of Minister of Defense in April 1976—instead of Kulikov—indicates the "Party's candidate" was chosen over the "military's candidate." Furthermore, they note the fact Ustinov's promotion was announced within 3 days of Grechko's death, while Grechko's promotion was not announced until 13 days after Malinovskiy's death; consequently, they suggest the Party had a much easier time having Ustinov appointed to the position in 1976 than it did in 1967 when Ustinov lost to the military's "candidate" Grechko after lengthy debate within the leadership. These analysts also assert Brezhnev's promotion to General of the Army in April 1975, his acceptance of the marshal's star several weeks later, and his appointment as Supreme Commander in Chief of the Armed Forces by at least October 1977 indicate he has "moved forthrightly to assert his absolute control over the decisionmaking apparatus."[57] Finally, these analysts cite the recent failure to create Soviet marshals among the senior commanders (with the exceptions of the Chief of Staff and Warsaw Pact Commander in Chief) as further evidence of the Party's move to assert its primacy over the military.[58]

Whether these points cumulatively make a case, however, is open to debate. Even if the argument can be proved cogent, Brezhnev's tenure is likely to be brought to a close by death or incapacitation, and the succession developments will necessitate a reevaluation of intra-Party and Party-military dynamics. It is clear, though, the post-Brezhnev period will continue to witness the continuity in Party-military relations observed thus far. As indicated earlier, a strong military continues to be an important factor in the calculus of Soviet foreign policy formulation. While perspectives on the use of the military in foreign policy execution may vary depending on the views of the next General Secretary, it is unlikely—given traditional predispositions and the nature of collective leadership politics in the Politburo—these perspectives are likely to vary significantly from those of other Politburo members or to result in major new directions in military policy. It is clear, for example, the burden of maintaining forces in Afghanistan and on the Chinese and Polish borders will remain and manpower shortages in the coming years will continue to have a strong influence in resource allocations. Therefore, it is safe to assume any changes which do occur in the style of military leadership and policy formulation are not likely to have a significant impact upon the broader dynamics informing strategic policymaking and Party-military relations.

The same approach to questions of military leadership and Party-military relations in the post-Brezhnev succession period can be applied as well to the Ustinov succession. Ogarkov has been suggested as the most likely candidate to succeed Ustinov, just as Kirilenko frequently has been proposed as Brezhnev's heir. Other factors have figured prominently in this speculation, such as how the successions will be affected if Brezhnev or Ustinov dies first. Here again, though, one is drawn to the conclusion that potential differences in leadership style between Ustinov's successor and other Politburo members are not likely to affect general Party-military relations, at least not in the early years of the succession period. Furthermore, the diversity of factors involved in these successions virtually precludes careful speculation on such issues as military leadership style. Therefore, given the current dynamics of Party-military relations, it is clear elements of cooperation deserve more weight than elements of conflict in arriving at an accurate assessment of future Party-military relations.

Notes

1. See works by Roman Kolkowicz and Abdurakham Avtorkhanov. For additional

articles which treat the tensions between these groups, see David Albright's research note, "A Comparative Conceptualization of Civil Military Relations," *World Politics,* Vol. 32, No. 4 (1980), pp. 557–563.

2. Marshal V. D. Sokolovskiy, *Voyennaya strategiya* [Military Strategy], 3rd ed. rev. (Moscow: Voyenizdat, 1968), pp. 62–63 (hereafter cited as Sokolovskiy); Colonel General A. I. Radziyeskiy, ed., *Slovar' osnovnykh voyennykh terminov* [Dictionary of Basic Military Terms] (Moscow: Voyenizdat, 1965), p. 41 (hereafter cited as Radziyevskiy); and Major General Zemskov, "Vazhnyy faktor pobedy v voyne" [The Important Factor for Victory in War], *Krasnaya zvezda* [Red Star], 5 January 1967, pp. 2–3.

3. Radziyevskiy, p. 42; Sokolovskiy, pp. 287–288; and Edward L. Warner, *The Military in Contemporary Soviet Politics* (New York: Praeger, 1977), p. 120 (hereafter cited as Warner).

4. Radziyevskiy, p. 44; and Sokolovskiy, p. 15.

5. Sokolovskiy, p. 18.

6. Radziyevskiy, pp. 145, 150, 224.

7. Colonel S. A. Tyushkevich, Major General N. A. Shushko, and Colonel Ya. S. Dzyuba, *Marksizm–Leninizm o voyne i armii* [Marxism–Leninism on war and the army], 5th ed. (Moscow: Voyenizdat, 1968), p. 357; and Major General S. N. Kozlov, "Voyennaya doktrina i voyennaya nauka" [Military Doctrine and Military Science], in *Metodologicheskiye problemy voyennoy teoriy i praktiki* [Methodological Problems of Military Theory and Practice], Major General N. Ya. Shushko and Lieutenant Colonel T. R. Kondratkov, eds. (Moscow: Voyenizdat, 1966), p. 91.

8. Colonel M. P. Skirdo, *Narod, Armiya, Polkovodets* [The People, The Army, The Commander] (Moscow: Voyenizdat, 1970), pp. 105, 123 (hereafter cited as Skirdo). For a good explanation of the interrelationships of military doctrine and the various components of military science, see A. A. Grechko, *Vooruzhennyye Sily Sovetskogo Gosudarstva* [Armed Forces of the Soviet State] (Moscow: Voyenizdat, 1974), pp. 288–302.

9. See Marshal D. F. Ustinov's comments in "Bezzavetno sluzhit' partii, rodine narodu" [Selflessly Serving the Party, the Motherland, and the People], *Krasnaya zvezda,* 30 June 1979, pp. 2–3; and Marshal N. V. Ogarkov, "Voyennaya nauka i zashchita sotsi-alisticheskogo otechestva" [Military Science and Defense of the Socialist Fatherland], *Kommunist* [Communist], No. 7, 1978, pp. 112–118.

10. Marshal D. F. Ustinov "Rukovodyashchaya rol' KPSS v stroitel'stve Sovetskikh Vooruzhennykh Sil" [The Leading Role of the CPSU in Building the Soviet Armed Forces], *Voprosy istorii KPSS* [Problems of History of the CPSU], No. 2, 1979, p. 29 (hereafter cited as Ustinov).

11. Major General S. N. Kozlov, ed., *Spravochnik ofitsera* [Officer's Handbook] (Moscow: Voyenizdat, 1971), p. 20.

12. Ustinov, p. 29.

13. John McDonnell, "The Organization of Soviet Defense and Military Policy Making," in *Soviet Naval Policy,* Michael MccGwire, Ken Booth, and John McDonnell, eds., (New York: Praeger, 1975), pp. 64–65 (hereafter cited as McDonnell).

14. Ibid.; and Vice-Admiral Sir Louis Le Bailly, et al., *The Strategic Intentions of the Soviet Union* (London: Institute for the Study of Conflict, 1978), p. 17 (hereafter Le Bailly). Kozlov, op cit, (pp. 20–21), states that the Central Committee resolves such issues as guidelines for weapons development and the evolution of military doctrine. It does so, however, primarily in its approval of Politburo decisions on these issues.

15. Warner, p. 43.

16. Le Bailly, et al., p. 17. For an interesting note on military representation on the Central Committee as a function of contemporary crises, see C. C. Jacobsen, *Soviet Strategy—Soviet Foreign Policy* (Glasgow, Scotland: Robert Maclehose & Company, 1972), p. 176. In addition, if a succession crisis occurs similar to the one in 1957, it is likely the Central Committee could indeed exercise an important policymaking role.

17. Abdurakhman Avtortkhanov, *The Communist Party Apparatus* (New York: Meridian

Books, 1966), p. 203.

18. Karl Spielmann, "Defense Industrialists in the USSR," *Problems of Communism,* September–October 1976, pp. 54–55. The Ministries of Tractor and Agricultural Machine Building; Chemical Industry; and Instrument Making, Automation Equipment and Control Systems are also sometimes included in the group.

19. Warner, p. 48.

20. C. V. Sredin, "Politicheskiye organy" [Political organs], *Sovetskaya Voyennaya Entsiklopediya* [Soviet Military Encyclopedia], Vol. 6, p. 420.

21. Ellen Jones, "The Role of the Soviet Political Officer," Defense Intelligence Report DDB–2610–29–79 (Washington: Defense Intelligence Agency, 1979), p. 1 (hereafter cited as Jones.)

22. Thomas Wolfe, "The Military Dimension in the Making of Soviet Foreign and Defense Policy," Report P–6024 (Santa Monica: The Rand Corporation, October 1977) (hereafter cited as Wolfe); and Warner, pp. 49–50.

23. Warner, pp. 44–55, 133, 169–170; and Wolfe, pp. 9–10. See also Marshal V. D. Sokolovskiy and Major General Cherednichenko, "O sovremennoy voyennoy strategii" [On contemporary military strategy], *Kommunist Vooruzhennykh Sil* [Communist of the Armed Forces], No. 7, 1966, pp. 61–65; and Marshal A. A. Grechko, "25 let tomu nazad" [25 years ago], *Voyenno–istoricheskiy zhurnal* [Military–Historical Journal], No. 6, 1966, pp. 7–15.

24. Warner, p. 46; Elizabeth Teague, "The Soviet Defense Council—Modern Successor to the Wartime GKO," Radio Free Europe/Radio Liberty Research Paper RL 246/81 (Washington, 1981).

25. Dale Pafenberg, ed., *Military Decision Making in the Soviet Union* (Washington: US Air Force, 1975), pp. 13–16 (hereafter cited as Pafenberg).

26. Ibid., pp. 15–16; and Harriet Fast Scott, "The Soviet High Command," *Air Force Magazine,* March 1977, p. 53 (hereafter cited as Scott).

27. Ustinov, p. 23.

28. Scott, p. 53.

29. Warner, pp. 46–47; and Pafenberg, pp. 12–13.

30. Ustinov, pp. 23–25; and Skirdo, pp. 137–139.

31. Sokolovskiy, p. 434.

32. Pafenberg, p. 18; and Wolfe, pp. 17–18.

33. Pafenberg, pp. 18 and 20; and interview with Harriet Scott, (McLean, Virginia, 2 December 1977).

34. William Spahr, "The Emergence of the Soviet General Staff During the Brezhnev Era," paper prepared for the 4–5 May 1979 conference of the Washington, DC chapter of the AAASS, pp. i–iii and 10; and Skirdo, p. 155.

35. Wolfe, p. 20.

36. Warner, p. 25; and Scott, p. 55.

37. Marshal V. G. Kulikov, "General'nyy stab" [General Staff], *Sovetskaya Voyennaya Entsiklopediya* [Soviet Military Encyclopedia], Vol. 2, p. 513.

38. Warner, p. 25. See also Harriet Fast Scott and William Scott, *The Armed Forces of the USSR* (Boulder: Westview Press, 1979), pp. 102–113 (hereafter cited as Scott and Scott).

39. Scott, pp. 54–56; and Warner, p. 25.

40. McDonnell, p. 83.

41. Scott, p. 53; interview with Scott, 2 December 1977. The Collegium is probably the successor to the Main Military Council (*Glavnyy voyennyy sovet*), which existed from 1953 until possibly as late as 1967. In wartime, many of the Collegium's members would comprise the *Stavka* of the Supreme High Command (*Stavka verkhovnogo glavnogo komandovaniya*). In many Western analyses of Soviet military policy, "Main Military Council" is often used interchangeably with Collegium.

42. McDonnell, p. 84; and Wolfe, p. 21.

43. Ibid. On the Main Military Council's functions and development, see also M. V. Zakharov, et al., eds., *50 let Vooruzhennykh Sil SSR* [50 Years of the Armed Forces

of the USSR] (Moscow: Voyenizdat, 1968), pp. 267–268, 478; "Glavnyy voyennyy sovet" [Main Military Council], *Sovetskaya Voyennaya Entsiklopediya* [Soviet Military Encyclopedia] Vol. 2, pp. 566–567; "Kollegiya ministerstva oborony SSSR" [Collegium of the Ministry of Defense of the USSR], Vol. 4, pp. 235–236; *Sovetskaya Voyennaya Entsiklopediya;* Kozlov, *Spravochnik ofitsera,* pp. 127–128; and A. S. Zheltov, ed., *V. I. Lenin i Sovetskiye Vooruzhennyye Sily* [V. I. Lenin and the Soviet Armed Forces] (Moscow: Voyenizdat, 1967), p. 146.

44. See Matthew Gallagher, "The Military Role in Soviet Decisionmaking," in McDonnell, op. cit., p. 48; and Malcolm Mackintosh, "The Soviet Military's Influence on Foreign Policy," ibid., p. 27.

45. Thomas Wolfe, *Military Power and Soviet Policy* (Santa Monica: the Rand Corporation, 1975), pp. 16–17 (hereafter cited as Wolfe). Civilian scientists may be involved in research on military-related projects, but on the level of military policy formulation, input by civilian researchers is slight if not nonexistent. Academicians working with such organizations as the institute for the Study of the USA and Canada and the Institute of World Economics and International Relations may provide papers on military and foreign policy, but these researchers have negligible say in the development of strategy or doctrine.

46. Ibid., p. 33.

47. Ibid., pp. 11–14.

48. Ibid., pp. 18–19; and Matthew Gallagher and Karl Spielmann, *Soviet Decision–Making for Defense* (New York: Praeger, 1972), p. 33.

49. See calculations on the number of party members in the military in Scott and Scott, pp. 116–117; and Thomas Wolfe, "The Military," in *Prospects for Soviet Society,* Allen Kassof, ed. (New York: Praeger, 1968), p. 126.

50. Wolfe, *Military Power,* p. 24.

51. Le Bailly, p. 15.

52. Ibid., p. 16.

53. Ibid; and Warner, pp. 99, 140, 145. For other veiled military criticism of party intrusion in military affairs, see General I. Pliyev, "Novaya tekhnika i voprosy ukrepleniya distsipliny" [The New Technology and Questions of Strengthening Discipline], *Kommunist Vooruzhennykh Sil,* No. 2, 1962, pp. 23–28; Colonel General V. Tolubko, "Otlichno znat' strategicheskoye oruzhiye" [Know Strategic Weapons Perfectly], *Krasnaya zvezda,* 8 January 1963, p. 2; Lieutenant Colonel P. Baranov, "Na obochine" [At the Roadside], *Krasnava zvezda,,* 20 March 1963, p. 3; and Colonel General A. L. Getman, "Bol'shoye serdtse komandira" [The Sympathetic Commander], *Krasnaya zvezda,* 29 March 1963, p. 2.

54. Le Bailly, pp. 15–17; and Warner, pp. 98–99.

55. Jones, p. 39.

56. Warner, pp. 74–75; and Timothy Colton, *Commissars, Commanders, and Civilian Authority* (Cambridge: Harvard University Press, 1979), pp. 201–217.

57. Le Bailly, p. 17; Michael Deane, "Political Control and Contemporary Soviet Military Development," paper presented at the Ninth Annual Convention of the American Association for the Advancement of Slavic Studies, Washington, DC, October 1977, pp. 8–11, 32; and Christian Duevel, "Brezhnev Named Supreme Commander–in–Chief of the Soviet Armed Forces," Radio Free Europe–Radio Liberty Research Paper RL 260/77 (Washington, 1977).

58. Le Bailly, p. 17.

Part II

The USSR as a Global Power

Introduction

The contributors to Part II are all concerned with a subject of vital importance to the West: the USSR's expanding global interests and its conduct as a major actor in international affairs. While these articles cover a broad range of issue areas—Soviet–European relations, Soviet activities in the Third World, and Sino–Soviet and Soviet–Japanese relations—the scope of their subjects demonstrates an ineluctable fact of international life: Moscow's determination to prove the validity of its assertion that there is no international issue that can be addressed without the involvement of the USSR.

Lincoln Landis presents the argument that current Soviet motives and the leadership's perception of a Western lack of will—rather than Marxian strategy and Leninist tactics—explain the USSR's foreign policy. The West should consider carefully the probable impact upon Soviet perceptions of its inaction in the face of previous Soviet uses of force. Landis contends that there is a certain irony in the USSR's growing international confidence: while the West has oversemphasized the role of ideology in legitimizing the Soviets' international behavior, the USSR is probably aware that it has passed along a mantle of illegitimacy ever since the October Revolution. Soviet confidence is not so much the product of historical assurance as it is the result of Western diffidence in the face of Moscow's uses of military power.

Vojtech Mastny argues that Europe always has been the Soviet measure of foreign policy success or failure and that Germany has been the critical country in Europe. The European order, Mastny contends, is the Soviets' most important ingredient in the international order which they seek to create. Despite this, there have been sharp fluctuations in Soviet perceptions of what constitutes the desirable European order. He believes that East–West tensions can be explained in terms of Europe: when the Soviets possess a clear European policy, tensions are of low order; when the Soviets' European policies produce disappointment, however, unpredictability and tension ensue until a satisfactory new framework is developed.

The next three articles in Part II are concerned with the Soviet Union's approach to arms control issues. Eugenia Osgood notes that disarmament—the idea if not the substance—has been a central feature of Soviet foreign policy since the revolution. There continue to be divergences of opinion within the Soviet leadership over the questions of deterrence, nuclear war, parity, and superiority. These differences reflect the interest groups from which they originate. Continued Soviet interest in strategic arms control, she asserts, will depend on the "delicate balance" between military and civilian interests, the direction of Soviet power projection, and US military and political behavior. George Kolt examines the differing Soviet and US attitudes toward arms control. Using Fred Ikle's negotiation classification scheme, he argues that while the US pursues innovation, the USSR variously seeks redistribution of burdens and effects, extension of the status quo, or side effects such as propaganda. He urges a wider appreciation for these differences; the result will be to lessen US impatience with slow results and increase the prospects for sound agreements. General Rowny, writing from his experience as the US Military Representative to SALT II, argues that the US must face certain facts when negotiating arms control with the Soviet Union: mutually beneficial treaties only result when the US and the USSR share a common objective, and the two superpowers do not share a common approach to arms control negotiations. He maintains that the absence of a common cultural heritage and a common objective has blunted US attempts to achieve a mutually advantageous treaty with the USSR.

The Soviet Union's extensive political and military activities in the Third World are the subject of the next six articles in Part II. Rajan Menon explores US and Soviet arms trade activities in the Third World in terms of the ability of these activities to win clients for either superpower. Menon concludes that despite sometimes high hopes, arms sales do not result automatically in substantive political benefits for the supplier. Richard Bissell addresses Soviet military aid activities in Africa, an area of increasing Soviet involvement over the past decade. The USSR has been successful in securing access to base facilities in the continent as a result of its military assistance. He also explores the various political reasons for Moscow's successes in establishing relations with a number of African states. Michael Boll examines a question of some importance, given the expanding activities of East European countries in the Third World: the role of the USSR's Warsaw Pact allies as agents of Moscow's foreign policy designs. Boll notes that it is often the East European presence that serves as the measure of the dimensions and targets of overall Soviet strategy. In his study of Bulgarian activities in the Third World, Boll analyzes the apparent "division of labor" between Moscow and the East European countries in the efforts to win the newly independent states for the Marxist–Leninist cause. Robert Donaldson examines the changes which have occurred in Soviet strategies toward the Third World, noting that the Brezhnev leadership has been more cautious than its predecessor in terms of expectations of results. He contends that the Third World still remains an area of secondary importance to the Soviets, and that the USSR's record there is characterized by both successes and failures. He urges US policymakers not to overestimate the appeal of the USSR in the Third World—given the region's intense nationalism and Moscow's limited economic resources—and to concentrate on economic and political, as well as military, issues. Bruce Porter asserts that a significant upsurge in Soviet military intervention in the Third World took place in the decade of the 70s. This trend was the result of Soviet nuclear parity with the US, advances in Soviet military mobility, growing Soviet confidence, and the US' post–Vietnam isolation. Porter contends that the only way to prevent a continuation of this trend is to effect a substantive change in US foreign policy. Finally, Robert Clute investigates the subject of Soviet objectives in Africa. He believes that the USSR is committed to the creation of Marxist–Leninist states on the continent; however, there apparently is no grand design for attaining that goal. Clute argues that Moscow's African policy has remained flexible and pragmatic, with the USSR concentrating on strategic rather than economic factors.

The remaining articles in Part II probe the area of Soviet relations with China and Japan—a subject that has assumed great significance in the wake of the normalization of Sino–US relations and Moscow's reactions thereto. Ray Cline argues that the primary strategic interest of the US should be the stabilization of the Beijing–Moscow–Washington triangle. He urges the US to avoid involvement in an Asian land war, to encourage Chinese cooperation with the non-communist countries of Asia, to avoid giving Beijing a reason either to provoke a war or reach accommodation with the USSR, and to maintain the stability of the triangle by avoiding tipping towards either country. Lyman Miller takes a look at the potential for changes in Sino–Soviet relations based on factions within the Chinese leadership. He maintains that two factions exist within the leadership in Beijing. One, promoted by Deng Xiaoping, has pressed for rapid modernization and drastic party reform, increasingly close ties with the US, and a confrontational posture toward the USSR. This is set against a group which favors more gradual modernization and reform, restraint in Sino–US relations, and a degree of detente in the relationship with the USSR. A proposal for unconditional negotiations put forward at the behest of the latter group was undermined by Soviet suspicions and Moscow's invasion of Afghanistan. Stuart Goldman discusses an issue of growing importance: Soviet–Japanese relations. He argues that the major issues in the relationship are primarily political and economic; military issues are of secondary importance. He asserts that Japan, with its technological base and shortage of natural resources, is a natural economic partner for a resource rich but technologically poor Soviet Union. Political factors, however, cloud this economic partnership. Disputes over the

"Northern Territories," Tokyo's normalization of ties with Beijing, the Korean issue, and the Japanese conception of a Pacific Community all cause political tension between the two countries. Militarily, each side is suspicious of the other's intentions. Taking all these considerations into account, Goldman explores several alternative futures for Soviet–Japanese relations in the 1980s.

Motives and Perceptions in the USSR's Global Outreach

Lincoln Landis©

Soviet motives and perceptions are the key to overcoming a tendency that is all too prevalent—the practice of changing appraisals of Soviet purposes to conform with fashion. We need to examine circumstances affecting the growth of Soviet power rather than just the consequences of the exercise of that power.

To begin, we should consider evidence for the basis of Soviet strategy. A dwindling number in the West would argue, after Afghanistan and the Polish situation, that Kremlin leaders are driven by a sincere desire for peaceful coexistence. The predominant current view basking in the apparent shambles of detente is that the Soviet Union's intentions are based on a Marxian drive for world dominance. Yet. I would propose a third explanation for the underpinnings of Soviet strategy: *hard-headed judgments by Russian leaders on how to preserve the Soviet system by exploiting the West.* An analysis of Soviet motives and perceptions, rather than mirror imaging, supports this latter view.

This "motives and perceptions approach" differs from Western assessments of the Soviet leaders' belief that "world revolution" conforms to history, thus "assuring inevitable socialist victory." If the so-called revolution and its modern version, "the world correlation of forces," are perceived as certain to bring victory for the USSR, why has the Kremlin attempted to surpass the West in strategic missiles and to develop an offensive capability in Europe? And, if history is bound to favor communism, why does the Soviet Union support insurgencies and intervene outside its borders, risking confrontation and wasting lives in the name of "liberation" and the "defense of socialism"? Why not let history take its course? In fact, General Secretary Brezhnev and his colleagues probably know all too well the crux of the so-called struggle between capitalism and socialism: the best hope of saving the Communist Party for future generations lies in destroying its greatest threat—the persisting idea of successful self-government in the free nations.

Emphasis upon the study of motives and perceptions challenges "a Soviet grand plan" theory in another important respect; instead of viewing the "threat" solely as a result of foreign forces, we should recognize that key elements of the Soviet challenge have originated here in our own minds and instincts which waver between urges for conciliation and defiance. Soviet motives and perceptions indicate that, for the West, being tough is not enough; we not only must be resolute but also more clever than the Soviet leaders. However, we cannot hope to be more clever if we don't fully understand what they are up to. It is ironic that untrammeled Western thinking could fail to take the measure of minds nurtured in a totalitarian environment.

Finally, an understanding of Soviet motives and perceptions permits us to challenge so-called grand strategy appraisals in a constructive respect, affording a note of optimism: since our behavior affects Soviet perceptions, we have the potential capacity to influence Soviet intentions and encourage Kremlin policies less dangerous to our interests.

For too many years we have focused on Soviet capabilities. The main result has been perhaps also the least expected—erosion of the West's superiority. Furthermore, in stressing capabilities, we have bypassed the most important Soviet capability of all—the power to persuade Western nations into a self-deception which views the USSR as a competitor or mere traditional rival, thereby slighting intentions as a legitimate subject of inquiry.

In neglecting intentions, we do not seem to have appreciated the need to signal our resolve to Soviet leaders. Instead, we have chosen to rely upon supposedly shared aspirations for peace and the idea that our restraint would be mirrored in Soviet actions. In negotiations, we seem to have finessed the ugliness of the underlying conflict, hoping instead for reciprocity in arms control and technical cooperation.

There are specific examples of Western self-deception. The architect of detente readily acknowledged his mistakes in gauging Soviet intentions a few years ago. Several former diplomats to the Soviet Union have supported detente apparently without feeling the necessity to enumerate the distinctions between their own expectations and those of prominent Soviet spokesmen. One advocate of detente reacted to news of the invasion of Afghanistan with disillusionment, declaring: "I feel betrayed . . . they ran out on us." This is the comment of another: "It just baffles me why the Soviets these past few years behaved as they have." A European leader was depressed about events in Poland which compelled him to postpone his summit plans in the East.

Even Western research proves to be counterproductive in assessing Soviet attitudes when it is biased from the beginning, as in the case of a recent prominent study built upon an astonishing assumption about Kremlin incompetence: Soviet leaders "fall to understand American policies." In suggesting that Soviet expansion somehow is hastily conceived and irrational, such thinking represents a failure to realize the USSR's regional and global perspectives are not mirror images of our own. In the Soviet setting, peaceful overtures which alternate with military initiatives frequently make sense and yield the desired results.

In fact, Kremlin leaders, intelligent and rational in pursuit of their aims, probably have been aware of the mantle of illegitimacy which has been passed along through the years, from Lenin's successful coup against serious Russian efforts at democracy in 1917 to Brezhnev's campaign for capitalist technology and grain in hopes of bolstering a sagging socialist economy. If there is indeed a sense of encirclement in the USSR, as is often stated, it is not likely to be triggered by Western alliances but by historically viable capitalist economies.

Soviet strategy is primarily a result of anxiety about popularly supported, market-oriented, successful Western societies. Soviet tactics consist of Leninist tools of manipulation applied against perceived Western weaknesses. Instead of a "grand plan strategy" resting on theory, Soviet strategy and tactics are combined in a pragmatic formula which is flexible, universal, and geared to subjugating the free world. It proclaims, however, several dignified concepts: "wars of national liberation," "global scientific-technical revolution," "world socialist planned economy," "world energy delivery system," and "world correlation of forces." These theories go in and out of fashion and often receive undeserved and earnest academic attention in the West. What we ought to observe, for example, is that—with public evidence of a one-way technology flow to the East—"the global scientific-technical revolution" as an idea begs for credibility and has been temporarily shelved. Moreover, with the invasion of Afghanistan and uncertainties concerning Soviet tolerance of events in Poland, other concepts damaged in the process—"wars of national liberation" and "the shift in the world correlation of forces inevitably in the direction of socialism"— begin to accumulate dust. What clearly does not change, however, is the Soviet leaders' full realization that any success in promoting these theories is dependent upon Western acquiescence or cooperation.

In reality, the current Soviet leadership seems intent on undermining Free World nations, not expeditiously but in a patient, systematic manner. Pragmatism rather than theory is the essence of Soviet strategy. Just as motives provide a clue to strategy, so an awareness of perceptions helps to clarify Soviet tactics. We are witnessing a convergence of sorts—that between Western diffidence and Soviet opportunism. On the one hand, our attitude appears to betray a frustrated idealism about our world role. On the other, Soviet tactics of opportunity have emerged from a calculated design for the survival of the party-state, a design resulting from fear and disdain for societies based on pluralism and individual rights.

Western behavior during the Cold War probably has been perceived as passive containment and then, under detente, a change to active accommodation, albeit with some risk to the USSR, as indicated by events in Poland. Soviet subversion and penetration seek to weaken the unity of the Western alliance and its ties to developing countries, exploiting Western acceptance of the earlier Soviet uses of military power at approximately 12–year intervals: first, Eastern Europe at the end of World War II; then Hungary in 1956; and, finally, Czechoslovakia in 1968.

Perceptions of Western weakness, I suggest, have tended to build the USSR's confidence in its ability to exploit Western military and political restraint. Such exploitation serves as an enabling mechanism with which to threaten Western interests and achieve the less than "inevitable" Marxist–Leninist goals. It is likely the West is seen by Moscow as squandering its psychological, political, economic, technical and military advantages. Soviet propaganda has translated this Western failure into a "shift in the world correlation of forces." The Kremlin likely is aware that detente, rather than "historical certainty," has provided openings for global outreach through diplomacy, trade, insurgency, and military action. The stage is patiently being set for ultimate Soviet victory by subverting and, if need be, subduing the primary source of Soviet discomfiture—successful nonsocialist states.

Some have predicted a diminishing Soviet global posture amid impressions Eastern Europe is coming apart and Afghanistan is turning into a "Russian Vietnam." In reality, Kremlin confidence continues to grow, and time may soon be running out for the West to provide a united front in Soviet perceptions. Motives and perceptions are not just platitudes—knowledge of them can enable us to act decisively to slow the growth of Soviet self-assurance while strengthening our own self-esteem and the Alliance's cohesion.

It is imperative that the West soon signal an improved military readiness and take steps to communicate effective public and individual attitudes to Soviet audiences. Our Russian area specialists should play a more influential role in planning and conducting Western strategy. Certainly, senior American officials would do well to eschew reliance upon Soviet interpreters. Greater activity by our specialists will tend to place in the proper perspective the efforts of Messrs. Dobrynin, Arbatov, Romanov, and others to to build an official congeniality which distracts attention from basic differences between our systems.

A necessary, frank dialogue can develop only if the Soviet side is aware that the West understands not only Soviet purposes but also its own vital interests. Mutual understanding is likely to develop only if we find a way to engage in "give and take" exchanges on an intellectual level.

Communication can also be served through a display of Western confidence which would permit, for example, weighty topics of mutual concern occasionally and appropriately to be spiced with both spontaneous and purposeful humor. It is possible to convey clearly the fact that we know "where the Soviet side is coming from." There are several steps we can take to demonstrate this:

> • avoid use of the inappropriate Western colloquial noun "Soviets" in referring to citizens of the USSR and reflect an awareness of such linguistic pitfalls as the careless translation

of the Russian equivalent of "energy question or issue" into the erroneous "energy problem or crisis";

• show disapproval of such Soviet anti–Western propaganda as that which alleges a NATO threat to the Warsaw Pact and Western plans to use force in the Middle East;

• show appreciation for the many sides of Russian culture, including colorful and instructive Russian anecdotes and proverbs;

• publicize critiques of the Soviets by West European communists—often suggested by Leonard Schapiro—to illustrate the gap between Soviet theory and practice, as in the treatment of dissidents;

• question the bizarre behavior of Soviet officials, such as former Premier Kosygin's intemperate response to Senator Ribicoff's delegation seeking a dialogue on SALT II; and

• ask for clarification of Soviet doctrine; for example, in view of the alleged "shift in the world correlation of forces," why was it appropriate to send Soviet troops into Afghanistan?

It is just as important to be able to communicate clearly "where our side is coming from." Again, there are several measures we can take:

• accord our ambassador to Moscow as prominent a role in East–West affairs as that enjoyed routinely by the permanent Soviet ambassador to Washington;

• convey the difficulty of selling the idea of "mutual trust" in the face of Soviet commitments to "victory over the West;"

• forcefully reject military intervention and subversion against sovereign states; and

• acknowledge that antagonisms existing between the United States and the Soviet Union frankly rule out so-called changes in relations from "warm" to "cool" and back again in periods of days, weeks, or years.

In summary, Western misunderstanding of Soviet motives and perceptions has been a self-inflicted wound which has obscured the potential for Western influence over the USSR's decisions to reach out beyond its borders. Kremlin leaders—inherently more pragmatic than ideological and more self-conscious than self-assured—habitually have gauged likely Western reactions before threatening the interests of the United States, Western Europe, and Japan. In this respect, Alliance members unwittingly have acted as indirect participants in the Politburo's military decisions. Relations with the USSR seem most stable if Soviet leaders have a healthy regard for Western unity as they confront typical domestic socialist headaches in their country.

Studying Soviet motives and perceptions will inform us why the

Kremlin works overtime to achieve what leaders of the USSR insist is historically assured. In fact, Soviet planners, aware that the Party flies false colors, are trying diligently to guarantee a sound future. The perceived conflict is not with capitalism—which they readily accept in controlled doses such as incentive pay and private garden plots—but with free nations possessing economic power and technical innovation. In Soviet perceptions, goals are ultimately achieved through state compulsion at home and subversion or military power abroad. In the latter case, acquiescence of the West is considered essential.

The main Soviet motive is to destroy the viability of Western societies as we know them through an interim phase of "peaceful coexistence on Soviet terms" yet to be revealed. Fear and hatred of the West support an urge to preserve a Soviet system which enjoys neither a mandate nor legitimacy. Since World War II, the West—even while enjoying clear nuclear superiority—has appeared to avoid confrontation, beginning with its massive drawdown of occupation forces within months of victory in Europe. This negative perception has served to build up Soviet confidence, despite distractions caused by domestic uncertainties and unrest within the socialist bloc.

A new Western momentum based on a knowledge of motives and perceptions could emerge. This momentum not only would call for improved military readiness and greater Alliance unity but also for more effective communication in public and official relations with the Soviet Union. It would then be reasonable to expect that the Kremlin, facing technical and agricultural deficiencies once again, might decide to make ideological concessions to those nations capable of providing antidotes to those ills. Future Soviet leaders might even begin to feel an urge to experiment with greater participation by ordinary citizens of the USSR in the economic life of the country. Whatever these leaders should choose to do on the domestic scene is likely to remain their own prerogative; however, what they choose to do in those areas which concern the Free World demands well-planned responses based on a thorough understanding of Soviet objectives.

The Soviet Union and European Order

Vojtech Mastny

The evanescence of detente has put in doubt the permanence of Europe's established international order. Has the "enduring balance"[1] which has kept peace on the continent for so long been damaged, perhaps irreparably? Or is the crisis a harbinger of a more durable new order which would emerge from the travails of the old? The widening range of possibilities is indicative of the instability. On the one hand, the relentless growth of Soviet military power seems to have increased the likelihood of Western Europe's falling sooner or later under the USSR's sway; on the other, the recent upheaval in Poland has also made eventual disintegration of the Soviets' own empire in Eastern Europe no less plausible. Whatever the probable course of events, Moscow maintains its crucial role as a determinant of the European order.

Regardless of their growing global involvement, Europe remains for the Soviets a critical yardstick of their international performance, for they have never ceased to consider themselves Europeans first. The acquisition of a European empire was, after all, the landmark event in their country's rise to superpower status. Even today, their economic relations with Europe as a whole far exceed those with the rest of the world. And the concentration of their military might on the old continent reflects a sound conviction that the key to the entire East–West balance is there.

Yet despite Europe's preeminence . . . or for that reason . . . Soviet notions of its desirable order have been elusive. Only superficially has Moscow's professed commitment to Marxism, with its assumption of the ultimate triumph of Communism, implied a clear and constant vision of such an order. Actual Soviet behavior has been explicable less by the constancy of its declaratory aims than by the change of its operational ones. And ever since the inception of the Soviet state, the frequency of that change has been suggestive both of a readiness to adapt the aims to the possibilities and a variable success in coping with a truly difficult problem.

At their best, Soviet statesmen, like any statesmen, have tried not only to respond to opportunities but also to shape them. At their worst, they have missed opportunities and have fallen victim to developments they could not control. What have been the objectives of their European policies at different times? How have the results compared with the expectations? What lessons could they draw from their successes and failures? Has there been a pattern of past behavior which

85

could facilitate prediction of future conduct?

The initial Bolshevik concept of European order—or disorder—was straightforward, simple, and inspiring. It envisaged an imminent seizure of power by Europe's revolutionary proletariat which would toss into the dustbin of history the imperialist system of nation-states dominated by the great powers and, ultimately, the institution of the state itself. In pondering the ways and means, Lenin was first attracted to the idea of a "United States of Europe" which would supersede the bankrupt international system. But on second thought, he rejected the formula because he suspected it would facilitate the preservation of imperialism's economic base. His conclusion, enshrined in a seminal article published in 1915, has continued to inspire his disciples' idiosyncratic view of any form of European integration.[2]

Even before the Bolsheviks took control in Russia, they regarded Germany as central to their design for revolutionizing Europe. For both ideological and geographical reasons, they saw it as the pivot. It is idle to speculate how they actually would have organized the continent had their design succeeded, for its chances of success were minimal. But there can be little doubt about the sincerity of their dedication to the idea of a loose association of congenial and coequal communist states which would gradually dissolve into the supranational entity postulated by their common ideology. Certainly, Lenin and Trotsky were sufficiently impervious to nationalism to abhor attempts at hegemony by any nation, especially including their own.

Germany did not lose its prominence in the Soviet scheme of things after the revolutionary hopes had receded. It remained critical to Moscow's strategy of breaking the perceived capitalist encirclement by disrupting the international system established at Versailles. The attempt to detach Germany from the system by means of the 1922 Rapallo treaty did not succeed, although it enabled the Soviet Union to develop a "special relationship" with Berlin which entailed mutually beneficial military collaboration and extensive trade. But this did not dissuade the Moscow operators from trying even harder in Germany than elsewhere to undermine national stability through the subversive activities of the Communist International.

Despite the consolidation of capitalist Europe, the Soviet leaders did not relinquish their hope that, beginning in Germany, it would ultimately collapse. It was the strength—and weakness—of the Marxist–Leninist doctrine they espoused that it could readily justify retreats as merely tactical and victories as strategic. In practice, however, Stalin's adoption of the policy of "socialism in one country," which he somewhat speciously justified by invoking Lenin's repudiation of the "United States of Europe," implied abandonment of any operational vision of European order.

The Soviet Union viewed with understandable dismay any signs of international stabilization, decrying especially the 1925 treaties of

Locarno. According to Stalin, the "spirit of war" was the principal content of the "spirit of Locarno."[3] He and his cohorts were still mesmerized by the vision of the united capitalist powers crusading against his "Fatherland of Socialism," a nightmare which never materialized. It was ironic, though otherwise only too consistent with Soviet premises, that Moscow's perception of danger mounted at the very time when Europe experienced its relatively most promising period of peace and prosperity.

The Soviet feeling of insecurity toward the end of the 1920s did not generate substantive interest in upholding the status quo, despite the occasional appearance of such interest. At that time, Moscow concluded nonaggression treaties with several of its East European neighbors—mainly in an effort to weaken France's putative *cordon sanitaire,* whose efficacy Moscow greatly exaggerated. Soviet membership in the League of Nations' special commission on European unification served little more constructive a purpose than to monitor better any capitalist attempts to close ranks. From 1931 on, the Soviets also participated in the Geneva disarmament conferences—but only to insist stubbornly on total disarmament. Had this ever materialized, all nations would have been militarily exposed; however, the Soviet Union presumably would triumph because of its exclusive access to what it considered to be the decisive weapon of international Communism.

Weakness bred a mixture of opportunism and wishful thinking which underlay Soviet policies. It was a stark and frustrating fact of life in those days for the ambitious leaders in Moscow that whatever scheme they contrived could make but marginal difference to the rest of Europe. The real threat to European order eventually came not from communism but from fascism—something the Soviets had not planned, but—given their *politique de pire*—something they had done little to prevent. Only Hitler's rise to power impressed on them—albeit gradually—that what was at stake was the future not only of the Versailles system but also very much their own.

Moscow's subsequent advocacy of collective security conveyed a clear preference for the familiar international order over the unknown perils of a fascist-dominated Europe . . . but not an unequivocal commitment to defend that order alongside the Western democracies. The policy rather aimed at encouraging the latter to assume more readily the considerable risks involved in taking the stand. For however much Stalin preferred the more benign French and British capitalists to the malevolent Nazi variety, he could not be certain—in view of the established Soviet record of troublemaking—whether *they* would prefer *him* to a German leader whose record at that time was not yet so bad.

Therefore, for his own reasons rather than because of anything the West could do, Stalin never ruled out accommodation with Germany, whose importance to Europe's order he continued to value above that of France or Britain. He could even be reasonably suspected of a sneaking admiration for the ease with which Hitler demolished the legacy of Versailles and the daring he displayed in challenging the peacemakers' work in Europe as a whole. Should push come to shove, it was improbable the Nazis would want to come to terms with the Moscow communists rather than with the Paris and London capitalists. But thanks to the deficiencies of Western statesmanship, the improbable came to pass, leading to the August 1939 Nazi–Soviet pact and, finally, the war which swept away what remained of the old order. Stalin must have concluded by then that a Europe dominated jointly by the two dictators might be to his liking after all; he certainly behaved accordingly.

The concept of European order in Stalin's pact with Hitler was alien to the Soviet tradition but consistent with that of Russian imperialism; it was also congenial with Stalin's personal penchant for power politics. It envisaged a continent divided into two spheres of influence in which the two aspirants for hegemony claimed both extra territory and a cluster of dependencies. Stalin did not regard the arrangement to be incompatible with the Nazi notion of the "New Order," as he embarrassingly proved in June 1941 by refusing to believe his German counterpart could possibly see any advantage in violating the pact. Even after Hitler's attack graphically had demonstrated spheres of influence offered little guarantee of security, Stalin retained his faith in their efficacy.

The vision of European order the Soviet leader proceeded to impress upon his new Western allies did not differ in kind from the one Hitler had denied him. In his revealing conversation with British Foreign Secretary Anthony Eden in December 1941, he insisted on keeping the territorial gains he had made as Hitler's accomplice. He demanded additional privileges—particularly military bases—which would have reduced much of Eastern Europe to a Soviet preserve, and he invited the British to do likewise with Western Europe. His uncompromising attitude in regard to former Polish territories—which he knew no Polish government could relinquish without appearing to its own people as Moscow's vassal—was calculated to induce the emergence of precisely such a subservient (though preferably noncommunist) government in the country which Stalin regarded as the centerpiece of his security system.

Although Germany was Stalin's foremost concern, he saw the answer to Russia's security problem in the solution of the Polish question, a matter which he could control better than the German problem. It was significant, though not sufficiently noticed at the time, that Stalin was evading commitment to any particular settlement in Germany, the source of some of the most painful Soviet miscalculations in the past. On various occasions, he floated ideas about what might be done with the Germans in order to probe his allies' intentions. Keeping his own options open, Stalin as late as 1943 did not shun exploring the possible renewal of a Soviet–German condominium in Europe, provided the conditions for a separate peace were right.[4] It was Hitler's doing, not his, that they never were.

Stalin's disposition to explore different options stemmed from Britain's rejection—under American pressure—of his initial bid for spheres of influence. The Russians never tried again. In August 1943, Ambassador Ivan M. Mayskiy told Eden that the East and the West either could "agree each to have a sphere of interest . . . or admit the right of the other to an interest in all parts of Europe," but he stressed his superiors' preference for the latter.[5] At the conference of foreign ministers later that year, the Soviet Union joined its allies in foreswearing any quest for spheres of influence, although it refused a formal undertaking to that effect. It argued disingenuously that this could "give rise to the belief that there had been some such intention on the part of one of the three countries here represented."[6]

By then, however, the opening prospect of a Soviet military advance into Europe had made spheres of influence a topical subject of public discussion in the West. Although the British and American governments did not officially endorse the idea, neither did they effectively discourage the favorable publicity it received, thus creating the impression of approving of or at least tolerating it. As far as the Soviet leadership was concerned, it did not take a position until after its advance beyond what it regarded as its home territory actually began on a large scale in the summer of 1944, and even then only in response to Churchill's initiative. It was the British Prime Minister who on 9 October played into Stalin's hands by suggesting the curious agreement on percentages spelling out the extent of the respective Western and Soviet influence in different countries. The supposed understanding, however, concerned only southeast Europe, and its exact meaning remained obscure.

With the defeat of Germany assured, Stalin's vision of the future had become both more sweeping and more vague than any arithmetic could express. Rather than a continent strictly partitioned by agreement, he envisioned one so enfeebled he could exercise undisputed control in one part while competing for influence on favorable terms in the other. Already in 1944, the Soviet government took exception to British encouragement of the effort by small Western European states to overcome their weakness by forming a larger integrated entity. Meanwhile, the Red Army's conquest of Eastern Europe was laying the foundations of a similar entity under the Soviets' own auspices. But so long as the war lasted and the exact location of the respective armies at its end remained uncertain, the nature of Moscow's control in the east and the extent of its influence in the west, as well as the geographical limits of either, remained problematic.

As hostilities drew to a close, Stalin evidently did not assume that competition for power and influence made conflict with the United

States and Great Britain inevitable, let alone desirable; his behavior showed that he chose to believe—despite growing signs to the contrary—that his allies would acquiesce to whatever form of control he would eventually decide to impose upon Eastern Europe . . . just as the latter chose to believe, despite growing signs to the contrary, that he would abstain from imposing upon Eastern Europe any form they loathed. An exceedingly equivocal understanding rather than any clear agreement on the partition of Europe was what really transpired during the later, much misrepresented conference at Yalta in February 1945.

The aftermath of the conference soon revealed the abyss which separated Soviet and Western notions of the postwar order, thus sealing the fate of the alliance. The West rightly judged Stalin's arbitrary behavior in Eastern Europe as the principal irritant responsible for the growing tension. But the Soviet leader, ever loath to admit he had erred, did not subscribe readily to the inevitability of confrontation between his exhausted country and powerful America. As late as May 1945, he implored of Harry Hopkins "whether the United States wished it or not, it was a world power and would have to accept worldwide interests."[7] He meant especially the supposed interest in underwriting his puppet regimes in Poland and elsewhere in his evolving sphere of influence. At that time, it was still not clear what the American interests in Europe were, but what they were not was sufficiently clear to prevent a meeting of minds.

The achievement of a mutually acceptable postwar settlement in Europe had been made difficult by Stalin's excessive security aspirations. It had been kept unlikely by the uncertainty he maintained about the limits of those aspirations. Finally, it became impossible because of his growing disposition to test the limits of Western tolerance. The resultant rising tensions eventually led to confrontation over a continent split into two hostile blocs . . . not a settlement he had bargained for. Germany emerged partitioned rather than intact, but diminished and exposed to predominant Soviet influence—the ideal solution indicated in the policies the Soviets had finally put into effect in the spring of 1945. But the unresolved German question was only a symptom, not the cause, of the incipient Cold War which determined the alternative order.

Thus, by default rather than design, the postwar order emerged once it became evident that nothing short of outright imposition of Soviet-style communist regimes could insure in Eastern Europe the measure of control Stalin craved but could not attain by means less damaging to his relations with the West. Moreover, the prospect of a prostrate Western Europe—the other premise of his original design—proved equally elusive as soon as the postwar recovery began. The inherent strength of West European democratic societies was merely mobilized, not created, by the change in American policy which culminated in the 1947 Marshall plan. In an important sense, it was not the difference in

Western policies but rather the difference between the performance of the Western and Eastern polities which exposed the fallacy of Stalin's preferred European order.

The demonstrated divergence of the two systems found its expression in the mutually shared notion of two irreconcilable power blocs fighting each other for total stakes by any means short of open warfare—the essence of the Cold War. For the Soviet Union and the West as well, this ideological belief replaced their more pragmatic concept of the postwar order, a concept which had gone wrong. By accentuating the basic conflict of values, the belief inspired a competition in which every gain by one side was viewed as a loss by the other—the "zero-sum game" which made the Cold War so difficult to win.

Although neither side achieved all it wanted, Stalin—by wanting more—achieved less. He had set himself an impossible task by attempting to impose uniformity in Eastern Europe . . . something the Americans never undertook in Western Europe. Nor could he hamper effectively Western Europe's political and economic recovery; in fact, he gratuitously added a military dimension by instituting the 1948 Berlin blockade and—even more so—by abetting the 1950 attack on South Korea. It was this latter aggression which clinched the American decision to rearm West Germany, thus aggravating immensely the German problem in the Soviet eyes.

Stalin rightly regarded West Germany as critical to Europe's resurgence and the German desire for reunification as dangerous to the integrity of his empire, but he distorted the threat by interpreting it in military terms and exaggerated it out of proportion by making the prevention of West German rearmament the ultima ratio of his European policies. Because of his fixation on a development he both misunderstood and could not control, he was inhibited from embracing a concept of international order more consonant with the evolving realities. As a result, he was courting yet another disappointment in a country where so many Soviet hopes already lay buried.

Nearer the end of his life, Stalin may have realized the futility of resisting the irresistible and begun moving toward accommodation.[8] In March 1952, he made his tantalizing proposal for the neutralization of a united Germany. This proposal possibly was more than merely another maneuver to abort Germany's dreaded rearmament, as it envisaged allowing Germany to keep its own army. It is more likely, however, that any desire for accommodation, especially one that would have entailed sacrificing the Soviet positions in East Germany, originated with the dictator's increasingly apprehensive entourage. We still do not know whether his security chief, Lavrenti P. Beriya, or anyone else in the entourage precipitated his death in order to change the course of Soviet policy, but if this indeed happened—and the circumstantial evidence is growing[9]—Stalin's mismanagement of the German question

480-900 O – 85 – 4

could have provided one of many possible motives.

Stalin was both the architect and victim of the postwar settlement he had so prominently, albeit unwittingly, brought about. Unable to come to grips with the requirements of a truly peaceful order, he failed to avert a confrontation with the United States which jeopardized Soviet security. Although he had led his country to replace Germany as Europe's strongest power, he had not disposed of but rather kept alive the German threat as he understood it. He left his successors an empire—the presumed rock on which his country's security would rest—but without any certainty that this anachronism would not eventually turn into the main source of its insecurity.

No sooner was Stalin buried than his successors began to act as if his death had removed a stumbling block to a European settlement. Premier Georgiy M. Malenkov insisted publicly there were no problems between the East and West which could not be resolved peacefully. An authoritative *Pravda* editorial seconded Malenkov by commenting favorably on Churchill's proposal to start solving outstanding problems by convening a high-level conference to negotiate mutual security guarantees. It only took exception to his suggestion of the 1925 Treaty of Locarno as a model (a bad word in the Soviet vocabulary) and invoked instead the more congenial spirit of the World War II alliance.[10] At a time when most Western statesmen other than Churchill still regarded the Cold War division of Europe as insuperable, their Moscow counterparts showed greater imagination. Even if the Soviet position entailed no new concept of the international order, it was at least suggestive of an effort to explore new ways toward attaining what had eluded Stalin.

How well did Stalin's heirs succeed where he had failed? They hardly had begun their exploration when the June 1953 uprising in East Germany set them back. It revealed the pitfalls of even a tentative consideration of relaxing Moscow's grip over any of its possessions— the policy reportedly associated with Beriya which probably contributed to his subsequent downfall. The investment the Soviets made in the survival of the East Berlin regime by crushing the revolt inhibited their freedom of maneuver. In early 1954, for the first time, they coupled a solution in Germany with an overall European settlement—a linkage which made attainment of both more difficult.

The linkage was part and parcel of Foreign Minister Vyacheslav M. Molotov's call for an all–European conference to establish a system of collective security. This echoed the Soviet bid for Western cooperation in containing German expansionism in the 1930s; indeed, it betrayed a similar concern. As the decision to rearm West Germany neared its implementation, Moscow watched with both anguish and impotence, best evident in its bizarre proposal in March 1954 for its own admission into NATO. Without substantive Soviet concessions, however, there was little chance of moving beyond the Cold War stalemate at a time when the West's solidarity was at its highest.

That seemed to change with the August 1954 rejection by the French National Assembly of the European Defense Community project. It provided the Russians with the gratifying spectacle of Western disunity. However, the prompt substitution of the doomed project with the Paris agreements—which envisaged bringing West Germany into NATO by May 1955—set a time limit within which any Soviet hopes either would have to be fulfilled or dashed. It was during this critical period that Moscow developed initiatives suggestive of a radical reassessment of its premises of the desirable European order.

The staging in November 1954 in the Soviet capital of a "European" security conference—which only Moscow's allies attended—conveyed a propensity for dramatic but ineffectual gestures. However, the conferees' announced intention to form their own counterpart to NATO should the Paris accords come into effect already presaged something different, however. The February 1955 resignation of Malenkov, who had been most closely associated with the false starts of the post–Stalin policies, confirmed Nikita S. Khrushchev's rise to supreme power. An outburst of Soviet diplomatic activity ensued.

The creation on 14 May of the Warsaw pact preceded by one day the neutralization of Austria by Soviet consent. Adding the multilateral Warsaw Pact alliance to the already existing system of bilateral pacts linking Moscow with its client states did not alter the military balance in Europe. Nor did the Soviet Army's withdrawal from Austria have that effect, for it was matched by the evacuation of Western armed forces. The true significance of the two events was political, and their coincidence provided the clue.

By underwriting the Austrian State Treaty, the Soviets rendered neutrality respectable, thus repudiating Stalin's notion of a world inhabited solely by friends and foes. At the same time, the formalization of the Soviet bloc through the Warsaw pact impressed on its members the fact that the enviable status granted Austria was not to be theirs. In another few days, however, Khrushchev signified his approval of the nonalignment practiced by neighboring Yugoslavia by his sensational reconciliation with Tito. He proceeded to foster nonalignment outside Europe as well by supplying Egypt with arms and making friends with other ex-colonial nations which Stalin had disparaged as capitalist puppets.

The common denominator of Khrushchev's moves was disengagement. He further promoted the concept at the July 1955 Geneva summit when the Soviet Union abandoned its policy of linkage between the European and the German settlements. The Soviets submitted a draft security pact at Geneva while concurrently pursuing accommodation with Bonn. Having indicated a willingness to establish diplomatic ties, they established them shortly after the conference. Meanwhile, another purpose of the Warsaw Pact became clearer in the Soviet offer to dispose of this still empty shell in return for the West's agreeing to do the same with NATO's full one. Throughout the fall, Moscow pursued the initiative by offering three more drafts of the security pact, the last with a plan for a zone of reduced armaments in middle Europe.

The motives behind the 1955 Soviet diplomatic offensive are still awaiting the thorough evaluation they deserve, but they must have extended beyond the mere desire to hinder Western unity and the impending West German contribution to it: the offensive gained momentum, as well as coherence, *after* the developments Moscow had been trying to prevent most had already materialized. Not only did the Soviet Union acquiesce, but it proceeded delivering genuine concessions, sometimes without anything in return—as was the case with the evacuation of the Porkkala naval base in Finland. The thrust of Khrushchev's policy suggests he was—or thought he was—ready to negotiate a military disengagement in Europe in order to pursue the competition with the West through primarily political means.

Khrushchev's dynamic concept of international order—compared to Stalin's static one—stemmed from a greater confidence in the Soviet ability eventually to prevail through competition rather than confrontation. That confidence rested on the dual premises of successful de–Stalinization and accelerated technological progress. The former would assist Soviet diplomacy by enhancing the image of "socialism" abroad; the latter would enable Moscow to rely for its security more on advanced weaponry than on the possession of land, thus justifying the military disengagement.

The 1956 upheaval in Eastern Europe which climaxed in the Hungarian uprising shattered that premise. When Hungary tried to follow the Austrian example by claiming neutrality, and the Soviet Union intervened by force to deny the claim, the sequence of events exposed not only the trap of disengagement but also the limits of de-Stalinization. In its own way, the intervention also highlighted the continued importance of land as a security factor, for the absence of Western troops in neutralized Austria reduced appreciably, perhaps critically, the Soviet risk in the operation. All of these unexpected developments cast doubt on the wisdom of Khrushchev's tampering with the old order and even prompted an attempt by Molotov and other stalwarts of that order to unseat him the following year.

Having mastered this challenge to his personal power and having restored a measure of stability in Eastern Europe by following Stalin's methods, Khrushchev had less incentive to resume his quest for negotiated disengagement and less prospect of success. He gave but lukewarm support to Polish Foreign Minister Adam Rapacki's proposal for a European nuclear-free zone which would have consisted of the two Germanies, Poland, and Czechoslovakia. In effect, the proposal had more to offer the Poles than the Soviet Union: their becoming wards of a major East–West agreement inevitably would have loosened their exclusive dependence on Moscow. In any case, Khrushchev killed the Rapacki plan by initiating the second Berlin crisis in November 1958. Unlike 1955, the Soviet Union now acted from a position of strength. The crisis evolved against the background of spectacular Russian technological advances (particularly in missiles) and impressive economic growth. Khrushchev's attempt to make West Berlin a "free city" by threatening to terminate the Allied rights of access amounted to a bid to substitute "forced" for negotiated dissengagement, the latter having been put in doubt by the crises in Eastern Europe. The Soviet Union further pressed for a ban on nuclear arms in all of Germany but not in Poland or Czechoslovakia. As a trade-off, it hinted at a possible denuclearized zone in the Far East, especially China.

The implications of the scheme were alarming. While the proposed arrangement in Germany would not have hindered Soviet supremacy in its eastern part, retreat from Berlin under pressure would have weakened the United States' position in Europe sufficiently to initiate the disintegration of NATO and Soviet ascendancy over its scattered remnants. The denial of nuclear arms to Moscow's increasingly difficult Chinese ally would have facilitated that ascendancy in Asia as well. Not only the reordering of Europe but also the reordering of a much larger part of the world now depended on the decision in Germany.

The design was too clever to be credible. The Berlin crisis strengthened rather than weakened Western solidarity and delayed in particular France's separation from NATO. The proposed Far Eastern nuclear ban plan precipitated China's open break with Moscow. In the end, the uncertainty Khrushchev created about the future of Berlin turned against him; it prompted so many East Germans to "vote with their feet" that it thus jeopardized the very survival of the regime they had left behind. In the last analysis, Khrushchev's design—like Stalin's before him—faltered because of the basic difference in policies the policies could only accentuate but not alter.

The irony of the situation was that it left the Soviet Union little choice but to insulate its part of Germany by erecting the Berlin Wall, thus wiping out the one enclave of disengagement which had survived even Stalin's lowering of the Iron Curtain. The result in 1961 was the worst war scare in Europe since Stalin's time. But the Wall, outrageous though it was, reinforced rather than challenged the balance from which Europe derived its stability. More ominously, the very futility of Khrushchev's attempt to alter that balance inspired him to try altering it on a global scale by spiriting his missiles to Cuba the following year.

It is still uncertain exactly what the Soviet leader wanted to accomplish by creating the missile threat or by offering to solve it at a time of his choice. But the magnitude of the threat was indicative of the magnitude of the design, a design in which Europe figured prominently. The importance of Khrushchev's European strategy may be gleaned from Moscow's departure from Lenin's dictum against European integration. Khrushchev—in a public statement and at a special conference of experts which seconded him—hinted for the first time that the Soviets no longer considered the Common Market to be a moribund capitalist ploy but the manifestation of a potentially hopeful trend.[11] They reasoned that the trend might serve Soviet interests by promoting European–American economic rivalry and painted the picture of a future economic rapprochement between the two parts of Europe. While secretly targeting their Cuban missiles on the United States, the Soviets were outlining a vision of a European "co-prosperity sphere" which would emerge after the Soviets, through their Cuban scheme, deprived Western Europe of American protection.

Whatever the specifics of the putative design—and they need not have been decided in advance—the ensuing fiasco did not immediately yield a substitute. Like Stalin when faced with the failure of his scheme after World War II, Khrushchev merely proceeded playing on the discord in the enemy camp without any apparent master plan. Taking advantage of de Gaulle's separate way, he cultivated France in an effort to isolate West Germany. But unlike Stalin, he tried at the same time to decrease rather than increase the overall East–West tension, thus helping to create the atmosphere which eventually made detente possible. Even in theory, the introduction into Soviet analyses of the very term "international system" was symptomatic of the change.[12] This did not necessarily entail any greater belief in the long-term compatibility of interests, but it did indicate an incipient appreciation that Soviet interests might be served better by stability than by disruption.

The process was too slow to enable Khrushchev to restore his tarnished leadership credentials. In any case, there was little promise in rapprochement with a France bent on reconciliation and intimate cooperation with West Germany. But Khrushchev—unlike Stalin— never lacked the courage to discard a misconceived policy and the imagination to find an alternative. By mid-1964, he seemed ready to initiate accommodation with Bonn during his planned visit there. He was overthrown before he could act . . . and in all probability, he was overthrown to prevent him from acting.[13] But if Germany again proved a Soviet leader's undoing, this was less because Khrushchev's nascent design was wrong than because it was premature—as its later resurrection by the very men who toppled him would show.

Even if Khrushchev's aborted German venture were the straw which broke the camel's back, the deeper reason for his downfall lay in his inability to manage an orderly transformation of the Soviet empire. Apart from his presiding over the momentous split with China, he had to tolerate Romania's partial and Albania's total defection from Moscow's fold and his inability to bring Yugoslavia back into it. He plausibly could be accused of having made matters worse by his "harebrained" scheming: Romania, for example, issued its most daring declaration of independence in foreign policy while Khrushchev suffered his Cuban embarrassment. Not surprisingly, therefore, the new leadership of Brezhnev and Kosygin seemed to attach higher priority to achieving order in their own backyard than to devising ambitious new schemes aimed at altering Europe's established power relationships. By that time, however, the roles had been reversed as initiatives in that direction emanated increasingly from the West.

Having shed their rigid notions about the immutability of Europe's partition, Western statesmen were more inclined than their Soviet counterparts could dare to press for movement. De Gaulle challenged the integrity of the two blocs by his vision of a Europe of sovereign states, especially luring Poland to assert its separate identity in the East much as France was doing in the West. The successive West German governments gradually began to promote in Eastern Europe "change through rapprochement." The American effort at "bridge building" aimed at achieving the same through "peaceful engagement."

The Soviet leaders did not readily rise up to the challenge. As with Stalin's heirs a decade before, Khrushchev's successors tended to pursue—only more cautiously—the course their predecessor had followed before he abandoned it by moving in a dangerous direction. They continued cultivating de Gaulle's France, closing their eyes to the threat his "Europe from the Atlantic to the Urals" implied for the integrity of their empire and indeed Russia proper. The notion was too vague and extravagant to be worrisome; there was more reason for concern in the more modest and pragmatic ways the West Germans and Americans were ready to use to pry open Eastern Europe. For nearly five more years, the Soviet Union belabored the menace Bonn's presumed revanchism and the United States' presence on the continent supposedly posed to its peaceful order.

These were initially the main themes of the campaign for a European security conference which Moscow resumed in 1966 after a 12-year interval. They pervaded the Warsaw Pact's Bucharest declaration urging unconditional acceptance of Germany's permanent division, withdrawal of foreign troops within national boundaries, and dissolution of both military blocs—all to be signed and delivered at the proposed conference . . . to which the United States would not be invited. If implemented, the proposal would have made Europe's security rest on the thin foundation of nonaggression pledges by the Europeans themselves and the Soviet Union, without any more effective safeguards against violation than mutual good will. This was not a very promising scheme, and the Russians hardly expected it to succeed. Rather than being designed to bring about the birth of a new order in Europe, their beating of the dead horse of German militarism served mainly to prop up the old order in Eastern Europe, an order which Romania's intended establishment of diplomatic relations with Bonn most immediately threatened to upset.

With the proposal for the security conference predictably stalled, the Soviet Union proceeded to reassert its authority in Eastern Europe by trying to shape the Warsaw Pact into a more effective instrument of regional integration.[14] While playing down the importance of the southern members of the alliance, the Soviets—at apparent Polish initiative[15]—sought to integrate the "northern tier" of countries most exposed to the Western peril—Poland, East Germany, and Czechoslovakia—through a greater measure of partnership. Moscow's need for greater cohesion among it diverse allies—rather than any greater willingness to engage in substantive discussions on European security—was also behind the next Soviet-sponsored declaration on the subject. Adopted at a gathering of party rather than government representatives (in the notable absence of the Romanians), this militant ideological pronouncement at Karlovy Vary in 1967 merely reiterated the old formulas in a more intransigent form. But the subsequent emergence of the Czechoslovak "socialism with a human face" challenged the cohesion of the bloc and particularly its northern tier more than ever before.

The Czechoslovak "heresy" and its suppression by Soviet tanks in August 1968 introduced a new chapter in Moscow's quest for European order. The intervention first prompted the enunciation of the "Brezhnev doctrine" which truculently asserted the Soviet Union's right to uphold the order of its choice in Eastern Europe by any means including force. But by March 1969, the Russians spoke a more conciliatory language, renewing their appeal for the security conference. The Warsaw Pact declaration issued that month in Budapest still listed the familiar demands for the acceptance of the German status quo, withdrawal of foreign military forces, and dissolution of the alliances—but only as topics for discussion. It showed a readiness to compromise.

It has been argued that stabilization in Eastern Europe was the prerequisite for Moscow's taking a more accommodating attitude toward the West.[16] But the Brezhnev doctrine, far from recording a stability restored, merely emphasized an intent to restore it. Nor had the vaunted "normalization" in Czechoslovakia as yet materialized by the time of the Budapest declaration. What had materialized was an alarming deterioriation of the Sino–Soviet conflict which suddenly threatened to grow into a war as a result of the Ussuri river clashes. Besides, the declaration itself apparently was not a simple Soviet *diktat* but rather the product of genuine consultations which the Soviets felt compelled to conduct with their allies.[17] Under such circumstances, it is fair to say Moscow developed its interest in a European settlement not because its imperial problems had been solved but because their solution was getting more difficult.

The decision to seek a negotiated settlement with the West could not have been easy for the Soviet leaders, for it involved risks which they previously had tried to avoid. It particularly entailed allowing for the transformation of West Germany from the bogeyman they conjured up to justify their clients' need for Soviet protection into the actual linchpin of the future peaceful order. At issue was the legitimation of access into Eastern Europe by West Germany, a nation whose historic experience and interests in the area rivaled most closely the Soviets'.[18]

Talks about the twin issues of the security conference and relations with West Germany thus began in late 1969 and continued—albeit in fits and starts—even though the problems of Soviet domination in Eastern Europe remained unresolved. During secret Moscow consultations in January 1970, for example, several of the Warsaw Pact allies balked at Soviet efforts to monopolize preparations for the conference. Later that year, riots forced the downfall of the government in Poland though, significantly, not another Soviet intervention which would have wrecked the prospects for accommodation with the West. Indeed, the trouble in Poland most likely gave the Russians the necessary incentive to speed up the process, thus leading to the conclusion of the network of the "eastern treaties" with Bonn and the quadripartite agreement on Berlin.

Even though this "solution" to the German question did not satisfy anyone fully, it gave all the parties—with the possible exception of East Berlin—instant gains and the promise of more to come. The Western powers acquired guarantees of access to Berlin, and the West Germans—by normalizing their relations with eastern Europe—gained the opportunity to influence its development. To contain the latter, potentially disruptive influence, the Soviet Union and its clients acquired less tangible but no less coveted West German recognition of the post-World War II boundaries. The evolving accommodation in Europe, though originally prodded by Soviet weaknesses, promised to help Moscow cope better with those weaknesses.

The settlement in Germany opened the road to the security conference. With its long cherished goal in sight, the Soviet Union even agreed reluctantly that each nation should participate as a sovereign entity rather that as a member of a bloc. It also accepted the American condition to advance simultaneously the Vienna discussions on the reciprocal reduction of conventional forces in Europe. The Soviets were willing to risk more but only because the West was also having its problems. As Marshall Shulman correctly stated, their campaign for the security conference served to "turn the instabilities of Western Europe to advantage while coping with those of Eastern Europe."[19] But more permanently, the success of this undertaking depended upon the outcome of what Pierre Hassner termed the "competitive decadence" of two systems each plagued by its own instabilities.[20]

That outcome remained uncertain when the Conference on Security and Cooperation in Europe finally convened at Helsinki in 1975. The great publicity its Final Act received in the Soviet media and the obvious self-satisfaction the Soviet leaders displayed on the occasion left little doubt they believed they had at last accomplished what they had so long sought. For them, Helsinki was *the* European settlement—something that had eluded Khrushchev and Stalin, not to mention Lenin and Trotsky. Nor was the supposed accomplishment diminished by its having been achieved without war and without revolution. It was the sweet fruit of the Soviet Union's having attained approximate military parity with the United States—the precondition and guarantee of detente as the Soviets understood it.

The Helsinki settlement, with its emphasis on general principles rather than on specific undertakings, depended more than most international agreements upon the materialization of certain trends anticipated by the signatories. For the Soviets, the foremost concern was the stabilization of the order they maintained in Eastern Europe as a result of their conquest of the area in World War II. This was to be achieved by the general acceptance at Helsinki of the existing frontiers and the renunciation of force in any international disputes. It is true the United States and its allies had long before given proof of their aversion to contesting forcibly Soviet gains. But the Soviets still valued the formality as a means to dispel persisting doubts about the legitimacy of the *internal* order they maintained; regardless of the stability of the *external* one—safeguarded by the East–West balance—those doubts were the deeper reason for their insecurity. To dispel these doubts once and for all, Soviet endorsement of the apparent platitudes of "Basket Three"— with its elevation of human rights to an indispensable attribute of a truly safe international environment—seemed a negligible price to pay for helping the West save face.

Another vital consideration was the sagging performance of the Soviet economy. To reverse the trend, the institutionalization of detente achieved at Helsinki promised easier access to badly needed Western technology without a political price. With skill and luck, that political price might be imposed instead on the West Europeans by making them more dependent on a Soviet–controlled supply of energy and raw materials. Never before had Moscow allowed its economy to become so enmeshed with the capitalist one. But never before had it been in a better position to control the terms of the relationship.

The ability of the Soviets to control those terms hinged on their third, and potentially most important, expectation from Helsinki. In positioning themselves as arbiters of the European order, they sought to manipulate the security *process* but not to allow any security *structure* to be erected as a shield against the manipulation.[21] They originally were the ones to insist on holding periodic follow-up conferences to help them shape the process without endangering any structure. If this could be done, the international order could be kept both relatively stable and steered gradually but irreversibly to Soviet advantage.

Such a concept of European order marked a significant departure

100

from the conventional Soviet wisdom that the greater the disruption in the West the greater the benefits for the East. This differed from Stalin's inconclusive Cold War of positions or Khrushchev's similarly deficient cold war of movement and combined elements of both in concurrently aiming at internal retrenchment and external accommodation—the happy marriage Khrushchev unsuccessfully had sought to contract toward the end of his tenure. Unlike the quintessential optimist Khrushchev, his gloomier successors could no longer aspire realistically to "burying" capitalism through more vigorous economic performance and growing attractiveness around the globe. But they still could hope to succeed where he had failed by managing the "competitive decadence" better than the West.

Nevertheless, Soviet relations with the West took a turn for the worse almost immediately after Helsinki—a change comparable to the aftermath of Yalta. To be sure, many symptoms of deterioration can be cited which antedated the conference. There were also developments outside Europe more conducive to conflict than any on the continent, but, from the Soviet point of view, Europe—and especially its eastern part—had been the focus of sufficient events of such magnitude as to account for the evanescence of detente and the rising specter of another Cold War.

In particular, the stabilization of the Soviet part of Europe has not taken place. The ink had hardly dried on the Helsinki Final Act when its seemingly innocuous "Basket Three" assumed political substance by giving new impetus to dissent in Eastern Europe and the Soviet Union itself. The acceptance of the principle that the shortcomings of the internal order in each signatory state were a legitimate object of scrutiny for all of them had been nothing short of a revolutionary development in international relations. Since then, repression has decimated the opposition in some parts of the Soviet empire but not in others. In Poland, new riots flared up in 1976; four years later, individual dissent by intellectuals merged for the first time with mass worker discontent shaking this cornerstone of the empire to its foundations.

Nor has the infusion of Western technology facilitated by detente succeeded in reversing the declining growth rates and falling productivity of the Soviet Union and its dependencies. Rather, the closer symbiosis with the stronger capitalist economies has made their weaker systems more vulnerable to disturbances in the world market. With few exceptions, the rate of inflation has increased, and the standard of living has declined. Further, Moscow could draw little comfort from the West's having to cope with many of the same problems, for this has only demonstrated the latter's better capacity to do so. In the crucial Polish case, massive foreign indebtedness has not only failed to forestall but actually has precipitated the crisis by exposing the regime's signal incompetence in putting the borrowed money to productive use. As a result, economic change forced political change for the first time anywhere in the Soviet bloc—an ominous development for its Marxist chiefs.

Faced with a worsening internal situation, the Soviets also have come nowhere near establishing themselves as the arbiters of Europe. For all their apparent deftness, they have been unable to capitalize on the persisting dissension within the Western alliance. They have failed to gain new footholds in Western Europe, as their abortive attempt to exploit the revolutionary turmoil in Portugal especially showed. To most Europeans, the Soviet relapse into internal repression has generated revulsion rather than respect. Already at the first follow-up conference in Belgrade, Moscow found itself uncomfortably isolated, having to defend furtively its dubious human rights record rather than self-assuredly imposing its preferred notions of security. The second conference in Madrid gave the USSR more reason to wonder about the fate of its original Helsinki scheme.

More than mere miscalculation altered the outcome of the settlement the Soviet leaders believed they had achieved in 1975. The baffling turn of events called into question the most subtle and promising design for international order they have yet devised. They could not fairly blame the Western governments; in determining the outcome, policies again mattered less than polities. As at the onset of the Cold War, the relative merits of the Soviet polity have been weighed and found wanting, thus casting doubt on its ability to afford detente. But this time the altered military balance—along with the decline of ideology as a driving force of policy—created a situation with the makings more of a real, rather than cold, war.

As the prospects for achieving its objectives by detente waned, so have Moscow's incentives to reduce its reliance on military might. Even without a decision to arm beyond the level of parity, the absence of a decision to the contrary sufficed to produce the same effect . . . continued growth with its own momentum, thereby further undermining the stability it was meant to foster. For this reason, it is immaterial (though of absorbing interest) whether the Russians actually have decided to strive for military superiority; the problem is really that of a runaway military machine in search of a purpose.

In managing this unprecedented situation, the Brezhnev leadership has so far shown less circumspection than Stalin and less imagination than Khrushchev. While acting aggressively outside Europe—from Angola to Afghanistan—it apparently has been unable to develop an alternative to the concept of European order which detente's eclipse has put in question. But the widespread belief—whether correct or not—that the military balance is shifting in their favor provides the Soviet leaders with a new temptation and its corresponding new risks. The temptation is to envisage a European order built solely on their reputed military superiority. The risk is that the attempt to implement it can produce a conflagration spelling the end of all order, but especially their own.

What does the record of past Soviet thought and action presage for Europe? In the Soviet leaders' tortuous and inconclusive quest for a desirable order, periods of hopeful anticipation have alternated with periods of disappointment. All this time, the Soviet behavior has been more predictable (though not necessarily more accommodating) when the policies reflected a clear concept of the ideal order. But whenever disillusioned leaders were groping for a new working concept, their conduct posed the greater danger of unpredictability. We are experiencing such a period now.

In theory, the tilting military balance currently imperiling Europe can be redressed easily enough by the West's applying its superior resources. Although the goal of redressing the balance is a necessary precondition to stability, it does not alone bring it about and can lead to the opposite result by imposing on the Soviets a timetable during which their putative military edge would have to be exploited lest it be forfeit. The challenge to Western statesmanship is in acting to restore the balance without putting such a timetable into effect. It is encouraging that over the years the prevailing Soviet record has been that of prudence rather than recklessness. But regardless of their calculating disposition, the Soviets have also been prone to grievous miscalculation.

At this critical juncture, the Polish upheaval has provided a respite by immobilizing a country vital to any Soviet forward strategy in Europe. The imposition of a military regime there after the authority of the communist party had collapsed opened a new chapter in the evolution and devolution of Soviet power. In an unprecedented departure from the principle of party supremacy over the army, the military has been called upon to solve problems that civilians had proved incapable of handling. If they succeed, the precedent will favor the militarization of policies in the Soviet Union as well by fostering reliance on the one and only resource the otherwise decaying Soviet system has been capable of exploiting well. But if they fail, then the whole array of unsolved and worsening problems that prompted their intervention in the first place will call for a transformation of the whole system in a manner ultimately conducive to an international order based on the values of pluralism rather than totalitarianism.

The widening range of outcomes which can ensue from the present crises highlights the need and the opportunity to deflect the unavoidable East–West competition from potentially lethal military rivalry toward more rewarding nonmilitary pursuits. Even in the heyday of detente, Soviet leaders asserted their brand of detente did not preclude but necessitated more vigorous political and ideological struggle.[22] As its terms have turned increasingly against them, the struggle may indeed worsen before the conditions for true detente as the West understands it improve. For this reason, the short-term outlook for stability is not as bright as most Europeans and Americans would wish. But neither is the long-term outlook as dim as some of them fear. Barring a military catastrophe, the chances of attaining the higher level of stability resulting from an international order both more peaceful and more just than the present one actually have improved.

Notes

1. As argued in A. W. Deporte, *Europe between the Superpowers: The Enduring Balance* (New Haven: Yale University Press, 1979).
2. "On the Slogan for a United States of Europe," reprinted in Robert C. Tucker, ed., *The Lenin Anthology* (New York: Norton, 1975), pp. 200–203.
3. "Political Report of the Central Committee at the Fifteenth Congress of the CPSU," December 1927, cited in Alvin Z. Rubinstein, ed., *The Foreign Policy of the Soviet Union* (New York: Random House, 1966), p. 106.
4. The evidence is assessed in Vojtech Mastny, "Stalin and the Prospects of a Separate Peace in World War II," *American Historical Review,* No. 77, 1972, pp. 1365–88.
5. Quoted in Vojtech Mastny, *Russia's Road to the Cold War: Diplomacy, Warfare, and the Politics of Communism, 1941–1945* (New York: Columbia University Press, 1979), p. 107.
6. Ibid., p. 120.
7. Memorandum by Bohlen on Hopkins–Stalin conversation, 27 May 1945, *Foreign Relations of the United States, The Conference of Berlin,* Vol. 1 (Washington: Government Printing Office, 1960), p. 39.
8. The thesis of Marshall D. Shulman, *Stalin's Foreign Policy Reappraised* (Cambridge: Harvard University Press, 1963).
9. It is used effectively in Abdurakhman Avtorkhanov, *Zagadka smerti Stalina: Zagovor Beriya* [The Riddle of Stalin's Death: The Beria Plot] (Frankfurt: Posev, 1976).
10. "K sovremennomu mezhdunarodnomu polozheniyu" [Concerning the Present International Situation], *Pravda,* 24 May 1953.
11. For details about this little known episode, see Rolf Sannwald, "Die Sowjetunion and die westeuropaische Integrationspolitik," in Erik Boettcher, ed., *Ostblock, EWG and Entwicklungslander* (Stuttgart: Kohlhammer, 1964), pp. 93–108.
12. William Zimmerman, *Soviet Perspectives on International Relations, 1956–1967* (Princeton: Princeton University Press, 1969), pp. 242–51.
13. The fragmentary evidence is best interpreted by Thomas W. Wolfe in his *Soviet Power and Europe, 1945–1970* (Baltimore: The John Hopkins Press, 1970), pp. 117–27.
14. For details, see Fritz Ermarth, "International Security, and Legitimacy: The Challenge to Soviet Interests in East Europe, 1964–1968," Memorandum RM–5909–PR (Santa Monica: The Rand Corporation, March 1969), pp. 33–52.
15. Wladyslaw Tykoczinski, "Poland's Plan for the 'Northern Tier,'" *East Europe,* Vol. 15, No. 11 (1966), pp. 9–16.
16. As suggested, for example, by Stephen F. Larabee, "The Politics of Reconciliation: Soviet Policy towards West Germany 1964–1972" (unpublished PhD dissertation, Columbia University, 1978), p. 156.
17. A. Ross Johnson, "The Warsaw Pact's Campaign for 'European Security,'" Memorandum R–565–PR (Santa Monica: The Rand Corporation, November 1970), pp. 21–23.
18. The implications are best accounted for in William E. Griffith, *The Ostpolitk of the Federal Republic of Germany* (Cambridge: MIT Press, 1978), pp. 200–209.
19. Marshall D. Shulman, "European Security Conference," *Survival,* No. 11, 1969, p. 373.
20. Pierre Hassner, "Cold War to Hot Peace," *New York Times,* 16 October 1973.
21. The distinction is Robert Legvold's, made in his "The Soviet Union and Western

Europe," in William E. Griffith, ed., *The Soviet Empire: Expansion and Detente* (Lexington, Massachusetts: Heath, 1976), pp. 243–44.

22. Brezhnev in *Pravda,* 28 June 1972, as quoted in Thomas W. Wolfe, "The Role of the Warsaw Pact in Soviet Policy," Memorandum P–4973 (Santa Monica: The Rand Corporation, March 1973), p. 13.

Soviet Perceptions of Arms Control

Eugenia V. Osgood

Introduction

"Exactly what grievances and ambitions, what fears and nightmares, are harbored by the Soviets, we do not know."

Harold Brown, *Department of Defense Annual Report,* Fiscal Year 1981.

When we consider perceptions, views, attitudes, and intentions, we are no longer in the realm of hard facts which can be measured with a yardstick and comfortably integrated into a quantitative construct but in the realm of human feelings. There is something comfortingly rational and solid about the quantitative frame of reference where graphs and statistics provide the underpinnings of certainty. At the same time, the uncharted morass of intentions and perceptions is usually approached with suspicion and misgiving. In the final analysis, however, both exclusive reliance on the factual and disavowal of the perceptual are faulty and misleading. It is a well-known fact that purely quantitative comparisons of force levels and weapons, while important, do not present an accurate picture of capabilities since they hide the qualitative dimension. On the other hand, perceptions and intentions, although not as easily ascertained as facts, also are vital components of reality, for it is in these "soft" and amorphous regions that "hard" decisions coalesce.

In his recent article on "Principles of Deterrence,"[1] John Collins went so far as to say that an opponent's intentions rather than his capabilities are the main target of deterrence. Thus, arms control should keep the capabilities in check while a credible military threat or successful political persuasion—or both—should deter and influence intentions.

In this article, based mainly on content analysis of Soviet open press pronouncements during the 1960s and 1970s, I shall try to give an overview of Soviet perceptions of the strategic environment (including American military policy and strategy) and Soviet views of deterrence and parity and their impact on Soviet attitudes toward strategic arms control.

The issues treated here are controversial, and other analysts may disagree with the conclusions drawn. Short of being able to read the minds of the Kremlin leaders or being present at secret Politburo meetings, however, there is no foolproof method to achieve absolute certainty about Soviet motivations and their effect on actions. But a careful analysis of Soviet statements, as well as a circumspect interpretation of Soviet "signals" to the West, may dispel some of the fog surrounding the Soviet "enigma."

Even though the findings presented here are incomplete due to time and space limitations, it is my hope that in a modest way this article will contribute to a better understanding of Soviet feelings and thoughts about war and peace and about the control of what they like to call "weapons of mass destruction." I intend to address the topic more fully in a monograph on Soviet perceptions of arms control to be completed by the end of 1982.

Disarmament and the Army Between the Two World Wars

While the idea of arms control did not come into its own in the Soviet Union until sometime in the 1960s, the idea, if not the substance, of disarmament has been the mainstay of Soviet foreign policy since the very inception of the Soviet state. It was then that Lenin issued his "Decree on Peace," a communist counterpart to Wilson's Fourteen Points. Lenin's immediate goal was to wage diplomatic and psychological warfare against the Germans, to launch a "peace offensive," and to make peace an instrument of policy, at least during the "breathing period" needed to strengthen the new state internally. The Brest–Litovsk Treaty convinced him, however, that without a strong army, it was impossible to negotiate an equitable peace. As a result, Lenin sought a viable defense capacity to "repel imperialist aggression."

Brest–Litovsk still haunts Soviet military and political leaders. They distinguish not only between a "just" and "unjust" war but also between a "just" peace and an "unjust," humiliating, and militarily repressive peace—epitomized by Brest–Litovsk.[2] Still, even an imperfect peace was a boon to a new state with practically no resources for the creation of a viable defense base and with highly unstable internal conditions. Under the circumstances, Lenin countered the arguments of Trotsky and others by asserting that "peace will advance our cause an infinity of times better than war" for "peace will open the way to our influence a hundred times better and wider."[3] However, this peace was not synonymous with disarmament—at any rate not unilateral Soviet disarmament. The Soviet Union perceived itself as encircled, threatened, and resented—if not hated—by most of its neighbors, and it definitely needed an army to defend itself and to survive.

Disarmament became a slogan, something to be achieved in the far-distant future after the proletariat has disarmed the bourgeoisie.[4] "When the communist order (*kommunisticheskiye otnosheniya*) has won a victory in the entire world, eternal peace will be established," conclude the authors of a recent monograph on *Philosophy and Military History;*[5] then and only then will "military history cease to exist as a social phenomenon."

In view of the above, one certainly could call the Soviet attitude toward disarmament ambivalent. On the one hand, there may be the desire for a "just" peace offering the chance to build a viable economy and to advance the cause of socialism by peaceful means; on the other, there has been the fear or simply the lack of desire to disarm before the other side. The recent upsurge in Soviet military power has compounded the problem; now disarmament would be tantamount to stripping a large and powerful sector of the Soviet government apparatus of its prerogatives. It would involve a major overhaul of the economy, the retraining of millions of indivduals, and—worse than anything else—the surrender of a really remarkable achievement of which the USSR can boast: its weapons and its well-trained armed forces.

Throughout the years, Soviet disarmament efforts have been viewed in the West as pure propaganda. Nevertheless, disarmament proposals have been an integral and not unimportant part of Soviet foreign policy. "Universal and complete disarmament" is now formulated in Article 28 of the USSR Constitution as one of the primary aims of the Soviet state. Official Soviet textbooks and publications customarily tend to picture the entire diplomatic history of the Soviet Union as one long "struggle for disarmament."[6]

The most notable Soviet disarmament effort before World War II was the proposal for "general disarmament" submitted to the League of Nations first in 1927 and again in 1932. Soviet opinion portrays the proposal as the most comprehensive and "realistic" of all proposals submitted and complains it was not given consideration and was "buried" in paperwork because it originated in the USSR.[7] As a rule, so the Soviet reasoning goes, Western governments refuse to consider Soviet disarmament proposals today because of their "fear of the military might of the USSR." Why then, they ask, did the West not accept the Soviet plan of 1927–1932 when the Soviet Union was militarily weak. Their answer: because neither disarmament nor collective security were ever seriously considered by members of the "Robbers' League" (as the League was known in the USSR), concerned as they were with national interests and national security. (And so, undoubtedly, was the USSR.)

This was probably the last time in history that a real opportunity for disarmament presented itself to the world. Soon, all disarmament plans had to be shelved under the impact of the crises of the 1930s. The signing of the "Anti-*Komintern* Pact" by Germany and Japan in 1936 was a threatening political gesture aimed directly at the USSR. Strangely enough, however, Stalin and Foreign Minister Litvinov's efforts to revive the moribund League (of which the Soviet Union was now a member) continued.

While going through the motions of defending the USSR through collective security, Stalin actually was pursuing a very practical "Realpolitik" of building "socialism in one country" while proclaiming solidarity with the international goals of the Comintern. The "territorial militia" principle along which the Red Army had been organized by France placed little strain on the Soviet economy, but it proved impractical in the long run. While it allowed for short-term mobilization of eight million soldiers, there were only 560,000 professionally trained "cadres."[8] The system perpetuated technological backwardness, and Stalin realized that change was imperative. In his oft-quoted 1931 speech he pledged not to allow Russia ever to be "beaten" again because of backwardness and military weakness.

An ambitious R&D program already had begun in the late 1920s. In the 1930s, the Soviets produced large quantities of weapons, some of them of very high quality (e.g., the T–34 tank, the *Il–2 Shturmovik,* and the *Katyusha* rocket artillery, all later successfully used in the war with Germany).[9] The territorial principle was abandoned and the armed forces trained in the use of the new weapons. After the near disaster of World War II, Stalin continued to stress military research and development while paying lip service to traditional Soviet concerns with "peace and disarmament."

Disarmament, Arms Control, and the Nuclear Dimensions

In a bipolar world with a drastically altered "correlation of forces" and with a new nuclear dimension, the Soviet Union faced a dilemma. Although a world power with a newly acquired empire of satellite states and the undisputed head of the "socialist bloc," the USSR's security was diminished and its vulnerability increased. Although the Soviet army was still strong, the other power had the atomic bomb and was not averse to using it as a tool of foreign policy. The US atomic bombings of Japan were seen as the first steps in a "diplomacy of force," coercive measures designed to make the Soviets realize that cooperation with the United States was to be on American terms.

Soviet accounts of the Cold War make the West appear as the villain. Churchill's "Fulton speech" in 1946 is said to have inaugurated a long series of Western "threats and acts of intimidation." The old pre-World War II phantom of "capitalist encirclement" returned, reinforced by the Truman doctrine, "containment," "rollback," the creation of NATO, the fear of German rearmament, and US "atomic diplomacy" with veiled and not so veiled atomic threats against Russia. Ironically, in the words of a historian, in 1947–48 when the Russians "lived in the greatest fear of a preventive attack by the West to forestall their acquisition of a nuclear armament, the West lived in fear of a preventive attack by the Red Army to forestall its own rearmament . . . ."[10] Such was the distortion of mutual perceptions caused by suspicion and a breakdown in communications, to be followed by worst-case analyses on both sides.

During the Cold War, disarmament was used as a defensive propaganda weapon. From the day the UN was created, the USSR used it as a forum for introducing various "peace," disarmament, and arms reduction proposals. In 1949–50, the Soviet–sponsored Peace Movement collected "hundreds of millions" of signatures for their appeal to ban nuclear weapons. Billed as a "desperate struggle for peace by the forces of communism," the Peace Offensive coincided with the first Soviet atomic explosion and with the beginning of a new buildup in the Soviet Armed Forces.[11] The latter was variously interpreted in the West as either deterrence against "capitalist attack" or a smokescreen for an aggressive military buildup.

There was no doubt in Stalin's mind that the USSR badly needed the bomb to end the US atomic monopoly.[12] The first Soviet atomic explosion in 1949 became one of the most important events on the Soviet scene. While it terminated the American monopoly and improved the Soviet strategic posture, it also started the first spiral in the atomic race into which the Soviet Union was now inexorably drawn.

In 1946–1947, at the first meeting of the UN Atomic Energy Commission, the United States presented the Baruch Plan for the prohibition of the manufacture of atomic bombs and for placing all phases of the development and use of atomic energy under an international authority. The USSR presented its own program and vetoed the Baruch Plan because it contained "almost unlimited rights of intervention" in the "economic life" of the Soviet Union. An impartial observer, the Swedish Minister for Disarmament, Alva Myrdal, agreed the Soviet objections to the plan were not unjustified.[13]

The pattern of atomic disarmament negotiation was thus established: both sides would present proposals which contained provisions the other side could not accept. The US would be concerned particularly with verification; the Soviets would be obsessed with secrecy and security. These two mutually exclusive requirements have bedeviled both disarmament and arms control negotiations ever since. As Alva Myrdal sees it, the last opportunity to bring nuclear weapons under international control was lost forever, and the superpower "game of nuclear disarmament" began.[14]

It is anybody's guess whether either the USSR or the US was in earnest about its respective plans at the 1947 UN meeting: the Soviets were hard at work on the bomb, and the US conducted the first postwar atomic test on Bikini Atoll 17 days after the presentation of the Baruch Plan to the technical commission. Perhaps this was the wrong time to think seriously of disarmament; the cold war was on and the international atmosphere was tense and hostile. The Cominform, created in 1947 as a successor to the Comintern, appeared to reaffirm the unity of the Soviet bloc. Also in 1947, the Truman doctrine and the Marshall Plan spelled out in no uncertain terms America's decision to preserve the political, military, and economic cohesion of the West.

Only after Stalin's death did East–West tensions subside somewhat. This was mainly the work of Khrushchev, whose unorthodox behavior, imagination, and ebullience were unprecedented and isolated phenomena among the dour Soviet bureaucratic elite. Stalin's reign of terror was exposed and the destalinization process begun. The "technical revolution" in military affairs brought about a reorientation of the entire Soviet military effort towards nuclear weapons, a reduction in the size of the standing army (billed as "first steps towards disarmament"), and a new nuclear age military doctrine.

Although world war with the "imperialists" previously was considered inevitable, the 20th Congress of the CPSU in 1956 came to the conclusion that it was, after all, possible to *avert* world war. Khrushchev's disbanding of the Cominform lent some credence to his assurances of the Soviet Union's peaceful intentions, which were reaffirmed at the 21st Party Congress in 1959 (all this after the Soviet Union built its first ICBM and launched the *Sputnik*). The 21st Congress even decided to amend one of Lenin's precepts by declaring that world war could be eliminated even *before* the complete victory of socialism on earth.[15] During his years in office, Khrushchev passed from an initial fascination with nuclear weapons to the full realization of their catastrophic potential as well as their deterrent value and he denounced nuclear war as "madness."

In 1961, the 22nd Congress of the CPSU again endorsed a peace program stressing peaceful coexistence and asking for peaceful settlement of international disputes. The drive for peaceful coexistence continued through the 1960s parallel to the Soviet missile buildup. The latter, justified by the danger of capitalist surprise attack, continued at a steady pace until a rough parity with the US was reached and arms control came of age. In the meantime, some measures to limit the spread of nuclear weapons had been agreed upon. In 1963, a partial ban on nuclear testing was signed in Moscow, and in 1968 the Nuclear Nonproliferation Treaty was negotiated.

It is doubtful whether either the Soviet Union or the United States has ever been sincere in its efforts toward nuclear disarmament. But Soviet disarmament proposals are being submitted regularly to the UN and are doggedly pursued on a multilateral, collective security level. While their concrete results are nonexistent, their propaganda value is high. Now more than ever, the Soviet leadership wants to project a "peaceful" image abroad and to reassure its own people of its concern for "peaceful coexistence;" should an armed conflict develop the "militant imperialist circles" will inevitably take all the blame, thus absolving the Soviet government of any guilt.

Although disarmament and arms control have been moving farther and farther apart, one should, for the sake of completeness—and to put things in perspective—mention some typical recent disarmament initiatives. In stark contrast to American media which hardly ever publicize disarmament proposals, the Soviet press publicizes them extensively while also grossly exaggerating their importance. The Soviet token withdrawal of another group of tank units from East Germany on 12 May 1980 was hailed as a sincere show of goodwill and an important "unilateral reduction" of Soviet troops in Central Europe; a first step toward "military detente" which the Soviets advocate as a desirable corollary to political detente.[16] Ironically, on the threshold of the great military buildup of the 1980s, the UN Disarmament Committee began drafting a resolution proclaiming the 1980s as the second disarmament decade. In his letter to Secretary General Waldheim, Soviet Foreign Minister Gromyko defined the main task of the new decade as the preservation and consolidation of "everything positive that was achieved in the sphere of arms control in the seventies . . . ."[17] In May 1980 alone, the following events took place: the Warsaw Pact celebrated its 25th anniversary with all manner of peace-minded declarations on the nonuse of force, the International Seminar on Disarmament was held in Norway, and the World Peace Council met in Budapest. Naturally, the Soviet press said nothing about the objections that may have arisen at these meetings to the Soviet use of force in Afghanistan since it had been officially justified as legitimate defense of a friendly socialist regime, the real "aggressors" being the "militant imperialist circles" allegedly supplying the rebels with arms.

Soviet Perceptions of the American Threat

Before discussing Soviet attitudes towards strategic arms control, one should consider some of the factors in the strategic environment shaping these attitudes. Since the arms in question are mainly nuclear, two of the most important factors to weigh would be (1) Soviet views of American strategic doctrine and warfighting posture in the nuclear age (i.e., Soviet perceptions of the "American Threat") and (2) Soviet indigenous views of nuclear war, nuclear strategy, deterrence, parity, and superiority as they apply to the superpower relationship.

The first of these factors is even more difficult to assess than the second one. The expressions of Soviet views available to us are either in the open press or in the somewhat restricted circulation journal *Military Thought*, although the differences between the two are negligible. While there is always a coherent party line in the USSR, some divergences of opinion, some "variants" of the party line, are permissible. There is a difference between what the party leadership will say to the Soviet civilian and what the military leadership will tell the rank-and-file of the army (which again differs from what is written in military journals for the military elite). Then there are the writings by civilian professionals mainly for civilian professionals: ideologically "correct" but perceptive and well-documented analyses of US attitudes by "Americanologists" and other foreign specialists at the Institute for the Study of the USA and Canada and at *IMEMO* (Institute for World Economics and International Affairs). Only a careful comparison of what is said at various levels minus the inevitable rhetoric can bring us a little closer to what is really thought and felt in the Soviet Union, especially on such "loaded" issues as the American military stance.

On the other hand, Soviet analysts and all those in the USSR who come into contact with Western open sources are probably overwhelmed by the wealth of material available, by the multiplicity of views both official and private and by the differences and fluctuations of opinions. Especially when it comes to foreign policy and military strategy, they can take their pick from the whole gamut of pronouncements by "hawk" and "dove," moderate, conservative, and liberal, and the right and left "lunatic fringe." Their choices either reflect what they believe to be actual American attitudes or what seems to support the current party line. Unfortunately, the latter is often the case. As a result, we find some very biased accounts of conditions in the United States, although fairly objective studies are being done from time to time by the USA Institute and by *IMEMO.*

Certain issues such as the use of force by the US as an instrument of foreign policy, US declaratory strategic doctrine (which, according to the Soviets, includes surprise attack and preemption), and American views on nuclear war as a means toward the attainment of political ends have spawned a veritable flood of commentary in the Soviet press. The number of statements and the intensity of feelings expressed attest to the grave concern these issues have for the Soviet leadership and the various interest groups likely to contribute to the shaping of policy.

On the whole, Soviet commentators agree that force or the threat of force has been traditionally used by the United States as the main instrument of foreign policy.[18] The favorite American expression quoted in this context is Dean Acheson's "from a position of strength." The most widespread American belief is said to be that almost any foreign policy problem can be solved either through the threat of force or, if necessary, through direct application of force, including its nuclear dimension. Americanologists from the USA Institute have argued that this has changed, since first use of nuclear weapons could now prove suicidal to the US, and that currently the US concentrates on the political and psychological parameters of military power in its global strategy.[19] A 1978 statement by a Vice Admiral of the Soviet Navy, however, reiterates the typically unidimensional, conservative military view: "American military doctrine invariably has been determined by the goal of world supremacy, in which force is recognized is the sole means of achieving it. Nuclear warfare is considered to be the basic means for resolving contradictions and disputes in international relations."[20]

Such intransigence is common in propaganda articles for the political indoctrination of the armed forces.[21] Since 1967, when A. I. Yepishev, Chief of the Main Political Administration, began his campaign for increased emphasis on the "moral/political" factor, soldiers have been taught to "hate the enemy passionately" and to have confidence in their eventual victory over imperialism even under the trying conditions of nuclear combat. The enemy has been made to appear as a monster: cruel, ruthless, bent on the destruction of communism by force of arms, ready to unleash a thermonuclear war.[22] Clearly, such statements are difficult to reconcile with the pro-detente pronouncements of the political leadership, and it is doubtful whether they reflect the real views of the better informed upper echelons of the military.

Whether or not the Soviets believe that the use of force by the US will involve nuclear weapons, the consensus of opinion is that the most important goal of American global strategy has been and still is the preservation of the American political system and the deterrence and eventual destruction, or internal erosion, of communism—i.e., "containment" (*sderzhivaniye*) and even "rollback" (*otbrasyvaniye*). It is recognized that the strategic plans of the "imperialist struggle" against the "world socialist system" also provide for the extensive utilization of peaceful means, both ideological and economic, including an attempt to slow down the economic development of the "socialists" by "saddling them with a heavy burden of armaments."[23]

As far as the direct use of military force in a war—especially a nuclear war—is concerned, the Soviets have always viewed the West as emphasizing not "deterrence" but "intimidation" through superior military power.[24] The Russian expression for strategic deterrence (*sderzhivanive putem ustrasheniya*) itself suggests intimidation (*ustrasheniye*). Sometimes *ustrasheniye* alone is used to denote deterrence (especially by hardliners), while the use of the word *sderzhivaniye* (which also means containment) for deterrence is common in the writings of "Americanologists" and other "moderates."

For years, innumerable articles have been published in the Soviet press on the aggressive and offensive nature of US strategic doctrine. Its official "deterrence" label consistently has been described as a "cover-up" for its true, warwaging nature. In a 1975 article, the well-known analysts of the USA Institute, M. A. Mil'shteyn and L. S. Semeyko, recapitulated the history of US strategic doctrine up to 1974.[25] Their views are not far removed from those expressed in Sokolovskiy's *Military Strategy* and from those of many other writers on the issue.

According to Mil'shteyn and Semeyko, the US believed in general nuclear war as a legitimate instrument of policy at least until the early 1960s. (According to more conservative writers, it has always believed in it and still does.) They distinguish an early period during which preventive nuclear war against the USSR was advocated; followed by the one-weapon "massive retaliation" doctrine (according to them, an offensive, first-strike capability and strategy derived from Douhet's ideas of strategic air supremacy); then by "flexible response" and "assured destruction"; and finally not to forget the unattainable first-strike counterforce and its more modest variant of "selective targeting." All are alleged to originate in striving to find a way to use nuclear weapons to "allow the US to survive and win a nuclear confrontation."[26] While the American rationale for the formulation of the flexible response strategy was the recognition of the fact that retaliation by total destruction could only deter total wars and thus a lower-level response for lesser threats was indicated, the Soviets have generally condemned flexible response as an attempt to "legitimize the use of nuclear weapons and to lower the nuclear threshold."[27]

Throughout the years, preemptive strike (*uprezhdayushchiy udar*) has been widely discussed as a viable Western option, and counterforce has been treated as synonymous with a first-strike capability and with the achievement of surprise by dealing a sudden disarming blow. A particularly dim view of counterforce was taken by Genrikh Trofimenko, head of the Foreign Relations Department at the USA Institute, in a 1970 article and later in his 1976 monograph *The USA: Politics, War, Ideology* where he elaborated on the provocative nature of counterforce strategy which "provokes the other side to strike first."[28] While he grudgingly acknowledged the US had arrived at a stage where mutual deterrence became a necessity, he went on to say this happened only because it failed to develop a first-strike capability in the 1960s. In his article, he predicted that the US would go back to counterforce sometime in the 1970s, even though counterforce is extremely destabilizing to mutual deterrence (*vzaimosderzhivaniye*).

While there was thus some official ackowledgement of the existence of mutual deterrence after the achievement of parity, analysts continued harping on the theme of aggressiveness in American doctrine. In a 1971 article, Lieutenant General Mil'shteyn quoted an unidentified US Air Force manual as proof that American officers still had to prepare both for the first and second strike.[29] His conclusion: even under conditions of "realistic deterrence," first strike is a viable US military option. Not surprisingly, the prevailing Soviet view of "assured destruction" and of the principle of "strategic sufficiency" in American doctrine has been that it is used to justify the acquisition of a *sufficient* capability for the *assured destruction* of the military and economic potential of the USSR in a first strike.

There has been widespread criticism of the "selective targeting" option, described as the 1970s' somewhat less ambitious edition of counterforce. Mil'shteyn and Semeyko, among others, have called it "just another attempt to force nuclear war into the rigid framework of a game, as if one could really count on the opponent's 'playing by the rules.'" They expressed the prevailing Soviet view of nuclear war;

namely, once it starts, escalation is inevitable.[30] Any attempt to "limit the use of nuclear weapons only increases the likelihood of war."[31] Also, since it calls for greater warhead precision, it encourages a qualitative arms race and raises suspicions that the US is trying to acquire a first-strike capability which, presumably, increases the likelihood of preemption by the Soviet side.[32]

Frequent Soviet references in the 1960s to a possible preventive strike by the US may be related to the introduction of the "counterforce" concept by then Secretary of Defense Robert McNamara who actually implied that a first use of nuclear weapons on military targets in response to a nonnuclear attack was a possibility. Counterforce thus became a successor to "massive retaliation" as far as nuclear response to a nonnuclear attack was concerned.[33] A whole literature developed in the 1960s on "surprise nuclear attacks" from the West, seen as the "blitzkrieg variant" of preventive war. Some commentators asserted that even the new "assured destruction" concept was based on the idea of a preventive or preemptive attack.[34]

The Soviets were not alone in their fear of being attacked. A Western analyst attending a discussion on arms control and disarmament in Moscow in the early 1960s was struck by the "symmetry of fears on either side." According to him, "it was as plausible that the Western powers might launch a surprise attack on the Soviet Union to forestall a surprise attack that they feared the Soviet Union was on the point of unleashing against them, as was the reverse occurrence, with the Soviet Union as aggressor."[35]

Only after the signing of the 1972 SALT I agreement did the stream of accusations of US "first strike intentions" either stop or become more muted. But not for long. As early as 1974, there was a reference to the "Pentagon theoretician" Colin Gray and his article dealing with the "long-term legalization of the arms race" and with "first-strike capabilities."[36] In the second half of the 1970s, "Atlantic strategists" were said to be exploring "first-strike options" in Europe, and the US Navy was supposed to be adopting an "ocean strategy" concentrating on SLBMs and aiming at "world supremacy" through sea supremacy (*gospodstvo na more*).[37] New military programs, tactical nuclear weapons, cruise missiles, the neutron bomb, Eurostrategic systems in the weapons sector; "trilateralism," the "China card," and the "Pacific doctrine" in the political sector again appear to have reinforced Soviet apprehensions. Americans were again "striving for military superiority through the open pursuit of counterforce capabilities" in spite of SALT I and detente.[38]

Of course , these discussions of the "threat from the West" would be deprived of much of their urgency if the Soviets knew exactly what the real attitude of the US is toward nuclear warfare. Wide divergences of Soviet opinion still exist on this issue. Among the military the view is still commonly professed—and probably held—that the US will use any weapon to combat communism. This has been a traditional Soviet perception. The "Neo-Clausewitzians" (B. Brodie, W. Kintner, V. Schramm, H. Kahn, T. Shelling, and S. Possony) have been accused of attempting to legitimize nuclear war as an instrument of policy.[39] The Soviets have thus consistently portrayed the West as striving to legalize nuclear war, to minimize its impact, and to utilize it as a tool for the achievement of political ends.

However, better informed and more moderate circles in the Soviet professional establishment, mainly *IMEMO* and the USA Institute, have been aware for a long time of the many divergent trends in Western thinking on the subject of nuclear war. For example, the *IMEMO* journal reported as early as 1960 on a "more realistic and flexible thinking among US politicians who are beginning to doubt whether a global war could be used as final means towards achieving foreign policy goals."[40] Later in 1966, it reported two tendencies in the West: "sober-thinking" politicians and military leaders who understood that nuclear war could not serve as a instrument of policy, and the "others," the aggressive militarists, who regrettably were still determining the main direction of military-political thought in the "capitalist world." Especially after the signing of SALT I, statements that the West may have reevaluated its nuclear policy and crossed off nuclear war altogether as a viable option became more common. In 1974, Mil'shteyn and Semeyko stated the US had realized what widespread destruction would be wrought by total war and concluded that "leading circles in the West do not want a nuclear holocaust and see only one alternative: peaceful coexistence."[41]

But Soviet fears of the American nuclear threat are not easily allayed. Frequent references to the "zigzag foreign and military policy of American imperialism" attest to the insecurity they feel in the face of the frequent changes which take place in American leadership, foreign and domestic policy orientation, and declaratory strategic doctrine. In short, they are afraid of us, and they do not trust us. No matter what improvement in international relations may have taken place as a result of detente and arms control, they are always on the lookout for a "hardening" in the US position, a return to a policy "from a position of force," and a return to a search for a first-strike capability.

In the later 1970s, both the *Amerikanisty* and the policymakers in the civilian leadership expressed concern about the progressive deterioration of Soviet–American relations. There was much discussion of a new US and NATO buildup. The 1978 NATO decision to increase military budgets and the 1979 decision to deploy new medium-range missiles in Europe especially have been scored as a "grave threat to world stability."[42] Both *IMEMO* and USA Institute analysts have commented on Western plans for a "qualitative leap" in the arms race in the 1980s and for the achievement of military superiority in Europe,

117

beginning with the installation of Eurostrategic missile systems.[43] Apprehensions have also been voiced in the Soviet press that the new technology may be welcomed by the West Germans as a means toward acquiring their own nuclear option; a development which the Soviets have always dreaded and opposed.[44] The Euromissiles decision also has been viewed as NATO's attempt to divert Soviet attention and capabilities from the Sino–Soviet border and to engage the USSR in a new Warsaw Pact/NATO arms race. All in all, from the Soviet perspective, it appears to have been one of the most unpopular NATO undertakings to date. According to a news item in the London *Observer,* it may have served as the emotional "last straw" in terms of the Soviet decision to invade Afghanistan. (NATO voted to deploy the missiles at its 12 December meeting, and the crucial meeting of the Politburo at which Brezhnev was apparently overruled on Afghanistan came on 19 December 1979.)[45]

The Soviets have been justifying the presence of *their* missiles in Europe by the existence of West European systems. Several Soviet analysts, both civilian and military, have alleged that NATO plans to modernize and install Pershing II missiles in Europe go back to 1974–75. They maintained that the development of the SS–20 was a reaction and not a unilateral rearmament measure. In this connection, Leonid Brezhnev said that during the last ten years the number of nuclear weapons in the Soviet Eurostrategic arsenal "has not been increased by one missile, by one airplane," and the number of launchers has actually been reduced."[46] While the statistics published in the annual *Military Balance* confirm that the number of the systems has remained the same, there is an important qualitative difference: the old, vulnerable IRBMs and MRBMs are being replaced by very different systems . . . mobile missiles equipped with three independently targetable, highly accurate nuclear warheads.

The Soviets currently portray the US as having abandoned the inconvenient principle of parity in order to attain unambiguous predominance through the acquisition of highly destabilizing weapons systems. Both of the alleged goals—unilateral superiority and deliberate destabilization—violate the "spirit" of SALT. Two important pieces of writing deal with this issue: Colonel General M. Mil'shteyn's May 1980 article in *SShA* (USA) and Aleksey Arbatov's (Georgiy Arbatov's son) 1980 monograph *Security in the Nuclear Age and Washington's Policy* (an analysis of American national security policy in the 1960s and 1970s).[47] Both authors deplore the movement away from the stability offered by assured destruction; are unhappy about the official US endorsement of a "countervailing" strategy which reintroduces the ideas of nuclear warfighting and escalation dominance; and quote 1980 and 1981 Department of Defense reports in support of their assertion that the new strategy is aiming, if not at unequivocal superiority, then at least at some kind of counterforce parity at a higher level of technology and on a massive scale, thereby necessitating a much higher outlay for defense on both sides.

Although the US strategy has been pegged officially as deterrence through a "warwaging and warwinning strategy" (not far from what is widely held to be the Soviet deterrence concept, sometimes described as "deterrence through intimidation"), the Soviets say it could evolve into a first-strike strategy with more precise and invulnerable mobile systems such as the MX. Already in July 1978, Lieutenant General Mil'shteyn described the MX as a "new, destabilizing, and dangerous strategic weapons system."[48] Both Arbatov and Mil'shteyn have stressed the dangers inherent in counterforce with its search for "surgical precision." They also frown on what they perceive as the current American acceptance of nuclear war as an instrument of policy and the belief in victory in such a war.

It almost looks as if, after much ideological soul-searching, but mainly in the interest of survival, the Soviet leadership not only rejected nuclear war as a viable tool of foreign policy but also grudgingly accepted mutual assured destruction (MAD)—although it contradicted their view of history—because of the stability it offered for power projection and for economic growth in the civilian sector. At the same time, the maintenance of a strong defense posture and the necessity to nurture the belief in possible victory among the armed forces and in the populace put them in the uncomfortable position of having their cake and eating it—and not being able to convince the world of their essentially peaceful intentions (at least on the nuclear level). Now, to their dismay, they realize the time has come when the Americans find MAD wanting, even when complemented by flexible response at a lower level, and were going back to a counterforce strategy which necessitated a whole new panoply of precision weapons "in order to be able to fight and win a nuclear war."

The American nuclear posture is somewhat analogous. There always has been a warfighting element in assured destruction allowing for other military options. Both "massive retaliation" and "flexible response" have been viewed as basically warwaging strategies. The Soviets are aware of our SIOP and of the various contingency plans (counterparts of which undoubtedly exist on the Soviet side).[49] One of the American plans, "Dropshot" (of massive retaliation vintage), recently declassified, has been widely publicized in military journals as tangible proof the US intended to wage preventive war against the USSR in 1957. Thus, although the principal mission of the US strategic forces has been deterrence, the US also has been unable to convey a purely deterrent message to its prospective opponent.

The "new American strategy" is viewed quite correctly by the Soviets as not entirely new, being basically a return to McNamara's counterforce of the 1960s and representing a further elaboration of strategic flexibility. Some sophisticated Soviet analysts (such as M. A.

Mil'shteyn, Aleksey Arbatov, and Genrikh Trofimenko) express the belief that this strategy will be used mainly as a "bargaining chip" in negotiations and to exert pressure on the Soviet Union rather than to seize the strategic initiative. But they and other more hardline, mainly military, analysts are aware of its explosive potential.[50] Since land-based Soviet ICBM systems represent 85 percent of Soviet nuclear forces (against 26 percent for the US), the acquisition of a true counter-force capability would make it possible for the US to knock out the greater part of Soviet retaliatory force in a first strike, thus virtually disarming the Soviet Union and, possibly, deterring retaliation by the remaining missiles through a threat to destroy Soviet cities. The Soviets may be envisaging the following standard scenario: the Americans destroy their military targets and the political leadership with one well-aimed counterforce strike and deter the Russian deterrent (i.e., deter the Russians from striking at American cities) because Soviet cities are still being held hostage. Or the Soviets, with their newly beefed up hard target kill capability, decide to execute an identical strike, annihilating American military targets and, perhaps, also the American leadership and deterring *our* deterrent. Or both plans fall through, escalation control is not exercised, the "rules of the game" are not adhered to, the deterrent is used, and universal devastation follows: i.e., the war "tends toward the absolute . . . ."[51] This, in fact, is what most Soviet analysts envision as the almost inevitable outcome of *any* nuclear engagement. Although it is obviously mentioned for deter-rence purposes, unlimited escalation may not be an empty threat. Because of the geographic proximity of the Soviet land-based strategic forces to population centers, the collateral damage which would accompany even a pure "counterforce" strike on Soviet targets may provoke an all-out response.[52]

In this context, the following prophetic statement by Bernard Brodie comes to mind. Formulated in 1959, it provides a vivid description of the situation we will be facing increasingly in the 1980s:

> Technological progress could . . . push us rapidly toward a position of almost intolerable mutual menace. Unless some-thing is done *politically* [emphasis added] to alter the environment, each side before many years will have thousands of missiles accurately pointed at targets in the other's territory, ready to be fired at a moment's notice. Whether or not we call it "pushbutton war" is a matter of our taste in phraseology, but there is no telling ourselves that the time for it is remote.[53]

While the writings of Soviet strategic analysts reflect their conviction that a tense, hair-trigger situation as described above—with crisis stabil-ity at an all-time low—could in fact develop through a counterforce arms race, they do not offer satisfactory explanations why this may come about. Their reasoning impresses us as one-sided and incomplete. Even such highly intelligent and well informed specialists on strategy and arms control as Lieutenant General M. A. Mil'shteyn and Aleksey Arbatov have never made it clear that the USSR *also* has a counter-force capability which has contributed to the American decision to invest in counterforce to maintain "essential equivalence" with the Soviet Union. On the contrary, Genrikh Trofimenko has claimed (in a paper which may have never been published in the Soviet Union) that "all systems of strategic arms suited for counterforce options were adopted by the Soviet Union *only after* they had been procured and deployed by the United States."[54]

To date, Aleksey Arbatov is one of the few Soviet analysts to have elaborated on the vulnerability of the US Minuteman force (see pp. 264–65 of his monograph). While he acknowledges the possibility that such vulnerability may in fact exist either now or at some time in the future, he underplays its importance since it would affect only 26 percent of the US nuclear potential, leaving the entire sea-based force intact and capable of retaliation. His conclusion: American worries are exaggerated, especially since SALT will help to preserve the military balance.

American "grand strategy," always an important part of the "American threat," has been viewed lately as veering towards a greater emphasis on "containment" of the Soviet Union not only militarily but also through political and economic means. Since President Ford's "Pacific Doctrine" replaced the "Guam Doctrine," the US has been actively engaged in maintaining a "balance of power" in the Pacific and attempting to "militarize" further the Indian Ocean. "Containment" and "encirclement" of the USSR on the seas, the China connection, and possible Japan/US/China military alliance all appear to the Soviet as particularly disturbing elements of US foreign policy. On the one hand, they have pointed out that the China–US rapprochement is precarious and even dangerous for the US. "It is not known who will milk whom: the Americans the Chinese goat or the Chinese the American cow," quipped a Soviet observer.[55] Some day, the Soviets warn, after having extracted all it needs from the US, China may attack its partner and benefactor. On the other hand, there is a strong underlying fear both of a substantial buildup of Chinese military strength with American help and of a US–USSR confrontation, perhaps instigated by China. As perceived by the Soviets, this is a long-standing Chinese dream, crystallized as early as 1958–59 in the slogan: "to sit on the mountain and watch the two tigers struggle."[56]

In spite of some strongly worded criticism of American foreign policy in the Soviet media there has been a universal acclamation of political detente as "the only alternative open to mankind" as well as persistent calls for "military detente." An editorial in the January 1980 issue of the authoritative navy journal *Morskoy sbornik* contains an impassioned and, for this journal, unprecedented plea for "military detente," for the limitation and gradual reduction of armaments, and for a "military balance," stressing the responsibility of the two superpowers to avoid global armed conflict.[57] Criticism of American "detractors of detente" has been widespread. Several articles and interviews with Georgiy Arbatov contain probably the most eloquent criticism of the "anti-detente" elements to date. He views them as destructive, irresponsible, and prone to equating patriotism with militancy.[58]

Soviet Nuclear Strategy and Views of Nuclear War and Deterrence

Soviet military doctrine has been viewed in the West as determined largely by Soviet military capabilities and the leadership's perceptions of future wars. Soviet doctrine is also said to stress a counterforce, first-strike, and warfighting ability for a massive, all-out nuclear war effort.[59] Bleak views of Soviet intentions, coupled with somber estimates of growing nuclear Soviet capabilities, and reinforced by the Soviet admission that their nuclear strategy is offensive, have resulted in a high threat perception in the West. The conclusion is frequently drawn that a warfighting doctrine and an offensive strategy make the initiation of nuclear war likely if not imminent. However, this line of reasoning omits a very important factor in the formation of Soviet doctrine and strategy: the historical conditioning of a nation's mentality and the convergence of this mentality with a new set of military options.

There has been a "war mentality" in the USSR from the very beginning and the concept of the offensive traditionally has been emphasized by both Russian and Soviet strategists. Suvorov's much-quoted *Science of Victory* (*Nauka pobezhdat'*) extols the primacy of the offensive. In the 1920s, Frunze saw the offensive as superior to the defensive for it was "good for the morale of the army." He believed the basic tactical and strategic concepts of the Red Army should be based on the offensive. Lenin said that "the offensive and not the defense should become the slogan of the masses."[60] Trotsky spoke of the "political offensive," quite consistent with the "strategic defensive." Marshal Tukhachevskiy believed that the offensive was the only strategy that could lead to victory. Last, but not least, Stalin also seems to have been convinced that the offensive alone could bring victory. The irony of it is that while the Red Army evolved a fairly coherent and predominantly offensive military strategy prior to World War II, what saved it from defeat in the war was its contingency doctrine based on the Clausewitzian concept of defense in depth. The German campaign with its deep thrust into Russian territory, the Russian defense, and the subsequent offensive seem to have been lifted out of Clausewitz's book *On War.*

The political side of Soviet war doctrine, expressed in Sokolovskiy's

Military Strategy and reiterated in the 1977 edition of the Soviet *Military Encyclopedia* with a disclaimer by Brezhnev of any intention to "wage aggressive war," is basically defensive.[61] It reflects the changes it has undergone from the thesis of the inevitability of a global war to one more in accord with Marxist "historic optimism" which states that the goals of socialism can be accomplished without a world war. However, the deeply entrenched concept of the "strategic offensive" for defense purposes, expressing the doctrine's "military-technical" side, is in both sources termed "decisive for the outcome of military action."

The convergence of tradition and innovation in the realm of strategy took place when the familiar concept of the "offensive"—with a good deal of help from Clausewitz—was applied to the new strategic missile weapons. No grander scenario was ever drawn up for the delectation and intoxication of military minds than a future nuclear world war which would encompass all continents; be waged on the ground, on the seas, in the air, and in space; where the "incredible spatial expansion of combat action" would kill hundreds of millions of people and bring "simultaneous defeat and destruction of the economic potential and armed forces throughout enemy territory."[62]

Such a war would be the embodiment of Clausewitz's dream of "absolute war"—impossible in the prenuclear age—which, "untrammeled by any conventional restraints," would break loose "in all its elemental fury."[63] It would be a triumph of pure strategy, accomplishing all in one single sweep without any "friction" and without the intermediaries of operational art and tactics. This was heady stuff, and it undoubtedly appealed to many military men. Many of them viewed nuclear weapons as simply the highest achievement in firepower and manuever: two of the "main elements in the combat might of the troops." Now the firepower of the nuclear explosion, coupled with the mobility of the rocket, became a powerful strategic factor which could determine the outcome of the war.[64] Admiral Gorshkov said that nuclear weapons work even better than conventional ones on a tactical level when used by fleets in a sea battle to annihilate the adversary.[65] What a disappointment it must have been when the civilian leadership decreed that offensive nuclear weapons existed only for deterrence and defense.

Although Soviet offensive strategy emphasizes the advantages of initiative and surprise, the declaratory doctrine (i.e., the view of the type of war likely to be waged by the Soviet Union) agrees with Clausewitz's affirmation that "the defense is a stronger form of war than the offensive." The Soviets also seem to have adopted another Clausewitzian maxim: "a defensive campaign can be fought with offensive battles, and in a defensive battle we can employ our divisions offensively."[66]

The scope of this paper does not allow for a discussion of the "preemptive strike" option which some analysts view as the basis of

480-900 O - 85 - 5

Soviet nuclear strategy. Naturally, the Soviet always have been aware of the advantages and dangers of preemption and of launch-on-warning, but so have we. One only has to read NSC–68 (1950) which points out the "military advantages of landing the first blow" and of "striking with our full weight as soon as we are attacked, and if possible, before the Soviet blow is actually delivered."[67] It can be safely assumed that both sides would have considered, or perhaps would now consider, preemption if faced with incontrovertible evidence that an attack is about to be launched.

But the likelihood of deliberate initiation of nuclear war by the USSR is remote. A world nuclear war would not only destroy all the "achievements" of socialism but would constitute a worldwide economic and environmental disaster. This is the official view of the Soviet civilian and military leadership today; it is very unlikely that the leadership could swing suddenly over to embracing a nuclear holocaust as an instrument of policy.

Time does not permit a discussion of the evolution of the Soviet views of nuclear war. In the 1950s, the "orthodox" Marxist–Leninsist line then existed side-by-side with the outright condemnation of nuclear war which was made by General Talenskiy and others.[68] The debate between traditionalists and "progressives" continued until 1967 when an unsigned editorial in *Krasnaya zvezda*[69] put an end to the dispute by repudiating the orthodox position on the viability of nuclear war as an instrument of policy and quoted the CPSU program to that effect. A recent article in the *Journal of Strategic Studies* presents a convincing and well-documented recapitulation of Soviet attitudes towards nuclear warfighting up to the late 1970s. The author argues that both civilian and military leaders now largely discount war as a viable means for achieving foreign policy goals and no longer view it as a zero-sum game ending in a meaningful victory.[70] "Only madmen and adventurists can assert that a brighter civilization will arise out of the radioactive ashes of a nuclear war," concludes a commentator in a 1979 article in the Soviet journal *International Affairs.*[71]

These attitudes should generate a strong concern with deterrence. In 1962, in his book *War and the Soviet Union,* Herbert Dinerstein said the following about deterrence: "A theoretical distinction, never precise, has long been made between a military posture that will deter the enemy from undertaking war and one designed to bring war on the enemy, destroy his forces, and occupy his territory."[72] Given this definition and Soviet leadership commentary about the catastrophic consequences of nuclear war, it appears the Soviet Union definitely should favor deterrence over warfighting. According to Sokolovskiy's *Military Strategy* and hundreds of Soviet commentators, it does; as they put it, "the only alternatives offered by history are peaceful coexistence or catastrophic war." But does the Soviet view of peaceful coexistence include a deterrence relationship as it is envisaged in the West?

The Soviets do not like to speak of deterrence (professing to be more interested in the "friendlier" condition of "military detente"), and their attitude towards it tends to be ambivalent. Neither *sderzhivaniye* nor *ustrasheniye* (the two Russian terms for "deterrence") made it into the *Soviet Military Encyclopedia*. But there is a thorough understanding of deterrence among their more enlightened analysts.[73] On the other hand, some critical commentary has been directed at the *precariousness* of deterrence. Writers on disarmament especially have viewed deterrence as a very insecure foundation of peace and even incompatible with detente.[74] There is no such thing as "stable deterrence," according to Professor Pokrovskiy, who wrote that "nuclear weapons cannot play the role of peace preservers. Experts know only too well that the stockpiling of atomic weapons does not diminish but greatly increases the danger of another war." Thus, peace cannot be assured through deterrence alone.[75]

Still, deterrence has been a well-known concept in Soviet political and military circles at least since the time of Khrushchev. He even made the heroic though unsuccessful effort to restructure the Soviet armed forces in accordance with a one-weapon, "more bang for the ruble" deterrence strategy relying on the massive retaliatory capacity of nuclear missiles.

Although a de facto deterrence relationship existed in the 1960s and was later made official by SALT I, its acceptance—especially by the Soviet military establishment—has been a slow and painful process. A debate flared up in 1973 after the signing of SALT I. Again, as in the previous debates, it focused on the viability of nuclear war and the possibility of a meaningful victory. The "moderates"—the champions of detente from the USA Institute—underscored the futility of further arms competition, viewed victory in a nuclear war as Pyrrhic, and pointed to the economic benefits of arms control and stable deterrence. On the other hand, the writers of the military-political establishment still thought a meaningful victory in a nuclear war possible and advocated a warfighting capability to counter the growing threat of "imperialist aggression." They criticized the "quantifiers" who placed too much stress on the material damage which would result from a nuclear war and discounted the "moral superiority" of the communist spirit. However, the military view was not unanimous: some military writers considered nuclear war unacceptable because of the massive destruction involved. Lieutenant General Zhilin, the Chief of the Institute of Military History of the Ministry of Defense, even professed a belief in mutual destruction when he spoke of a "situation where both combatants not only can destroy each other, but can also considerably undermine the conditions of existence of mankind."[76]

Statements on "mutual assured destruction" are few and far between in the Soviet open press, at least in part for ideological reasons, for mutual destruction is not seen as part of the Marxist–Leninist historical process, but the victory of socialism is. However, statements on the destructive, "suicidal," and "catastrophic" effects of nuclear war (which *imply* belief in assured destruction) are frequent in all quarters, both civilian and military. If anything, they have been becoming more common in the last three to four years. Leonid Brezhnev especially is known for his many statements describing nuclear war as the ultimate tragedy for all humanity and expressing the apprehension that this final "ideological dispute"—should it ever arise—could end as a catastrophe for both camps (not just for the capitalists). He also argues it would result in the "death of ideologies," for—along with millions of people—"their views, so they say," will also perish."

A 1977 monograph, *Voyna i armiya,* produced by faculty members of the Lenin Political Academy (the usually conservative D. A. Volkogonov, Z. S. Milovidov, S. A. Tyushkevich), attests to a shift to a pro-deterrence and pro-detente orientation, at least among the military-political establishment (as distinguished from the usually more hard-line General Staff coterie). The group takes a dim view of nuclear war as an instrument of policy for the USSR for it would not be conducive to the achievement of communism's political goals. They reiterate Lenin's saying that "any peace will open better and wider the way to our influence" than war, and that a peaceful policy will "increase the propaganda value of the revolution a hundred fold."[77]

Thus, it seems clear that although the Soviets do not speak in terms of assured destruction, they actually believe in it; that is, they believe the US has the capacity to inflict unacceptable damage on the Soviet homeland and they know that they have the capacity to do likewise, either in a retaliatory or a preemptive strike. Since even counterforce preemption will not deprive the US of the capacity to deliver a crushing retaliatory blow to Soviet objectives, it is highly debatable whether their much advertised "warfighting capability" (basically their version of our flexible response) will enable them to achieve anything but a Pyrrhic victory.

Since assured destruction, realistic deterrence, and essential equivalence are based on a rough parity of strategic forces, do the Soviets believe in parity as a viable objective of stability? Imperfect as deterrence is, both in the practical and in the ideological frame of things, the Soviets view it, together with their hard-won nuclear parity, as a stabilizing asset in the same league as detente, East–West trade, and other benefits of peaceful coexistence. Additionally, the *amerikanisty* have said the maintenance of strategic parity is an essential prerequisite for the continuation of detente.

On 18 January 1977, in his speech in Tula, Leonid Brezhnev denied explicitly for the first time that the USSR sought military superiority. In statements during the next year, he accepted parity as a basis for the US–USSR relationship. This disavowal of a search for superiority was soon echoed by other Soviet leaders.[78]

However, the Soviet concept of "parity" differs from what is meant in the US. Parity for the Soviets is related not only to military but also to political equality—i.e., to being accepted by the US as an equal and not being dealt with or negotiated with "from a position of strength." It means being accepted on their own terms and having their interests recognized as legitimate. They are extremely sensitive on this issue and are easily hurt if they feel that they are being dealt with as politically, culturally, or socially inferior. (These psychological determinants of behavior are largely discounted in the West, but their importance is growing; sometimes "style" is almost as important as "substance" in our dealings with the Soviet Union.)

Unfortunately, some of the Soviet's legitimate "needs" are incompatible with traditional American "needs" and place the United States in a position where it feels both its prestige and its security are threatened. It is a well-known fact the Soviets resent the American stereotyping of them as a "land power," a mold they have been trying to break for years in order to achieve some kind of "naval parity" with the US. For them, parity on the seas is synonymous with equality and with "equal rights" to power projection around the world. In a 1979 article in *Morskoy sbornik*, Admiral V. Gulin discussed naval parity and concluded that it was incompatible with US "sea supremacy." Quoting Brezhnev, he noted that "Washington see(s) a threat (in) the presence of Soviet ships in the Mediterranean, in the Indian Ocean, in other seas . . . . But . . . it . . . sees as normal and natural that the US 6th Fleet is constantly in the Mediterranean, and the 7th Fleet—near China and Indonesia . . . ."[79]

Speaking of political parity, the Soviets particularly resent being coerced into doing things "the American way." This applies to the "limited nuclear war scenario," construed as another unwelcome American proposal to make them play "according to Pentagon rules." Why, the Soviets ask indignantly, should the US have the right to "lecture" a sovereign state (and a superpower, at that)?

As relations with the US worsen, the USSR has been resorting more and more to a "language of confrontation"; not a new trend, for verbal abuse directed at the West for years has been one of the standbys of Soviet propaganda. However, while the Soviets have been excoriating the "capitalist West" for its evils, the implication usually has been these evils are the fault of the system, not the people. The language used by Western analysts and commentators, on the other hand, often has expressed not only disdain for a politically inferior system but also veiled or manifest cultural prejudice.[80] References to Soviet armies itching to overrun civilization like the Mongolian hordes of olden times abound in Western writings. There is a widely propagated belief that the Soviets are capable of all kinds of unethical actions and devious practices from which we, thanks to our cultural heritage, are exempt. One does not have to go far to find an example. A recent official report contains the following, not very felicitously phrased, passage: "If the Soviets should decide to commit the ultimate barbarity and destroy Western Europe, they could do it just as they could at any time destroy a large part of the United States . . . . It is not possible to design against such madness, we can only deter it."[81] Obviously, the implication is the Soviets are barbarians who may also be *mad* enough actually to commit the ultimate barbarity by destroying the seat of real culture: Western Europe and the United States.

If the Soviets are so committed to deterrence and parity, one might ask, why are they continuing their military buildup? Why are they developing new weapons above and beyond what, in our perception, they need for deterrence? Why do their military men constantly talk about capitalist aggression and the need for strengthening and improving their combat capabilities? Partly because they believe that they need more for deterrence "through intimidation" of the adversary than *we* believe necessary for "deterrence through punishment," but also because among their military there has always been a drive for superiority. The armed forces are viewed not only as a "bulwark of peace" but also as one of the greatest achievements of the state, a great source of national pride. Although both civilian and military leaders now talk about parity and disclaim interest in superiority, the same leaders, when making speeches on Armed Forces Day on February 23, will glory in the "increasing defense capability" of the fatherland, in the fact that the Soviet Army is "stronger than ever before" and that the "striking power, firepower, and mobility" of the Soviet Armed Forces have "increased immeasurably."[82]

The concept of superiority is definitely not alien to the Soviet political and military scene. In the third edition of Sokolovskiy's *Military Strategy* (1968)—in what seems to be a carryover of the Khrushchevian bluff of the first and second editions—Soviet superiority in nuclear weapons is taken for granted. To wit: "Our superiority in nuclear weapons we consider as indisputable. According to competent American specialists, our superiority in total nuclear might and strategic nuclear weapons is considerable" (p. 232). And according to an entry in the *Soviet Military Encyclopedia* (Vol. 2, p. 253), the strengthening of the defense capability of the USSR requires the ensuring of military technical superiority over the military forces of "aggressive blocs." Such claims are often made by the Soviet military to convince the Party leadership of the need for more weapons, more R&D funds, and, perhaps, the need for the USSR actually to acquire clear-cut military superiority "in the interest of peace" or to "repel aggression."

Soviet attitudes towards deterrence, parity, and superiority are neither homogeneous nor stable. They are determined by many factors, one of the most important being American intentions and capabilities, usually seen "through a glass darkly." As a consequence, "worst case analysis" flourishes in the Soviet military establishment—as it does in ours—and it contributes to making arms control negotiations a veritable tug-of-war.

Soviet Attitudes Toward Strategic Arms Control

Since disarmament efforts have never yielded any tangible results, apart from engaging friend and foe in the peaceful process of negotiations, one would have expected the Soviet Union—if at all interested in arms reduction—to become receptive to the more realistic idea of arms control introduced by the West. The fact is, however, that this initiative—like most Western proposals—was met with distrust and subjected to a good deal of criticism before it was finally accepted. The "so-called arms control"—according to a Soviet commentator—first aroused interest in the West in the early 1960s as a means to stabilize the arms race and create a more stable international climate. The official Soviet position at that time was that arms control was a compromise which did not ensure the solution of disarmament problems but instead made an arms race "harmless." Suspicions were also expressed regarding the motives of the Western powers: perhaps arms control with its verification clauses "would be used for the collection of military intelligence" by the Western intelligence agencies.[83]

The following factors may have been involved in the leadership's decision to negotiate a limit on strategic arms:

1. The desire to keep the American threat from reaching the dangerous "first-strike" level;

2. In the absence of any interest in fighting a general nuclear war, the opportunity to invest in power projection and in a "political offensive;"

3. The hope to maintain strategic parity and, if possible, improve strategic posture through a buildup in permissible areas;

4. The possibility to help the ailing Soviet economy and satisfy some urgent consumer demands;

5. The prospect of keeping the military happy and busy by involving it in arms control decisionmaking, thus achieving a greater civilian-military cohesion at the higher levels of government. (The latter would obviously be out of the question in any serious disarmament effort.)

These objectives—especially the first—are still valid and are probably considered an integral, although unofficial, part of SALT II. Recent changes in American foreign policy and nuclear strategy, if anything, have intensified the urgency of the Soviet appeal for an arms control agreement.

A possible sixth factor may have been the much touted Soviet Peace Program promulgated at the 24th Party Congress and endorsed by the

Central Committee in May 1972, just before the signing of SALT I. The program had been widely publicized in Eastern Bloc countries as an unprecedented "state strategy of peace"; it is quite possible that its signing was timed so subsequent Moscow agreements would reinforce its effect and lend it some credence on a military-strategic level. The program foreshadowed the 1975 Helsinki Conference on Security and Cooperation in Europe. Although it only restated in rather general terms what had been said many times before, it was billed officially as a great landmark of the Soviet "Leninist policy of peace" and of peaceful coexistence.[84]

How did the USSR react to the signing of the SALT I interim agreement? With the exception of the more conservative military circles, the industrial military managers, and the hardliners of the Party *apparat,* the Soviets reacted with jubilation and enthusiasm. All documents were published triumphantly in the press. There was much optimism concerning the forthcoming economic and cultural exchanges. It was also hoped there would be gains on the strategic level: a stabilization of the arms race and eventual arms reduction. As Genrikh Trofimenko, senior US foreign policy analyst at the USA Institute put it:

> The extraordinary importance of the SALT agreements signed in Moscow consists first of all in the fact that they concern the very foundation of the US and USSR's military might: their strategic weapons; thus, they are unprecedented in the history of relations between states with diametrically opposed social and economic systems. While they do not entirely remove the danger of nuclear war, they can help to avert it while, at the same time, helping to maintain the defense capability of the USSR and its allies.[85]

Analysts with technical expertise did point out the shortcomings of SALT I; e.g., the fact that it did not block all channels of the strategic arms race and allowed qualitative improvements. They were aware of the difficulties involved in determining "parity" or "strategic sufficiency." Geographic asymmetry, different basing of strategic forces, and problems with determining the relative strategic value of various components of the "strategic balance" were cited as complicating factors in the negotiations. But they expressed the hope that in spite of "almost insurmountable difficulties," final agreement would be reached in the future and would eventually lead to arms reduction.[86]

The one really complicating factor on the Soviet side was their determination to base negotiations on "equal security" rather than mutual vulnerability (the latter expression never appears in Soviet writings). While the strategic parity under SALT involved them in an "assured destruction" relationship, they still seem to espouse the philosophy of damage limitation and survival; in other words: security.

Their civil defense program probably has been built up for that purpose rather than because of any secret first-strike intentions. Their investment in a disproportinately large number of land-based ICBMs and improvement in their hard target kill capability may derive from similar considerations: a search for invulnerability rather than for offensive options. The hardening of their land-based ICBM silos and improvement in their hard target kill capability may derive from similar considerations: a search for invulnerability rather than for offensive options. Western analysts often have commented on the Soviet "obsession" with security; Soviet efforts do look like a prime example of their irrational drive to achieve the impossible, even in the extreme circumstances of a nuclear confrontation.

In the subsequent four years, SALT—supplemented by detente—became a "meaningful relationship" between East and West. It provided a platform for "thrashing out" military-political problems and helped involve the political leaders of both countries in strategic planning. Even though the military still exerts a strong conservative influence in arms control matters, the "correlation of forces" in this sector points to a change for the better if the detente orientation persists among the next generation of leaders and there are no unexpected international developments.

While the SALT process proved satisfactory to the Soviets as far as permissible improvement and buildup of their strategic potential was concerned, it has been deemed unsatisfactory in limiting the other side's quantitative and qualitative strategic arms expansion. Thus, at least from the Russian point of view, we are at a dangerous juncture in the SALT process. The controlled arms race seems to have gotten out of hand as far as US capabilities go and is again threatening them with the specter of "counterforce" and "surprise strike." Since the Soviets are concerned about their security and also would like to retain all the prerogatives that "superpower" status has conferred on them, they have to remain militarily equal—if not superior—to the US and cannot opt out of the arms race. On the other hand, their policy interests in the Third World and within the socialist bloc are supported better by conventional rather than nuclear forces, and they would be better off with many fewer nuclear weapons if only the American threat did not exist . . . .

But the Soviet leadership *wants* SALT, and it condemned former President Carter's proposal to postpone its consideration by the Senate. In his speech at the Paris meeting of European Communist and Workers' Parties, Boris Ponomarev, the Party secretary in charge of relations with nonruling Communist parties, quoted Carter's statement that "if the US, having signed the SALT Treaty then refused to ratify it, it would find itself in the role of an instigator of war who had refused to take part in the joint attempt to limit the spread of the most destructive weapons known to mankind."[87] Since an arms control agreement seems to be in the interest of both sides, the Soviets say they do not understand why they have to "pay a price for SALT II."

Although for a long time the official US position was that SALT II was in the interest of both sides, the Soviets seem to want it more than we do. Why? SALT not only may blunt sufficiently the American buildup and remove the danger of American acquisition of a first-strike capability, it could provide stability in military and political relations. Such stability would facilitate further Soviet power projection abroad and, at the same time, would be conducive to a better functioning of the Soviet economy. Helping an ailing economy and satisfying urgent consumer demands may have been one of the factors considered when negotiating SALT I, and the situation remains unchanged under SALT II. According to some Western analysts, the economic benefits of arms control so far have been negligible for both sides. But an uncontrolled weapons competition and the accompanying international tensions may curtail severely international trade and nip in the bud any intitiatives by the Soviets to raise industrial production in the civilian sector. As of now—and probably for many years to come—the Soviet economy is ailing, and consumer demands, now more urgent than ever, are still unsatisfied. It is not surprising that several Soviet analysts comment angrily on the "economic exhaustion" (ekonomicheskoye izmatyvaniye) the US wants to inflict on the Soviet Union by involving it in a costly arms race while trying to solve its own problems of inflation, recession, and unemployment through a new wave of military spending.[88]

The Soviets have been extremely defensive about the Afghanistan intervention. They will not admit it could have been a good reason for the postponement of SALT II, having been perceived in the West as a change in Soviet grand strategy and as escalation to a higher rung of risk taking. Brezhnev has argued that since Afghanistan was "vital" to Soviet security, it had to be "saved" from becoming an "imperialist bridgehead" on the Soviet border and falling prey to American and/or Chinese interests.[89]

Perhaps as a justification for Afghanistan, the "internationalist duty" of the Soviet Army has been seen as "expanding and deepening,"[90] although there has been no radical departure from the accepted party line of support to national liberation movements. Since military stability, reinforced by arms control, may be essential for continued USSR support to such movements, "military detente" at the strategic level has been acclaimed widely both by civilians and the military, as a desirable complement of political detente.

At the same time, according to all available accounts, at least part of the Soviet military leadership is not averse to the pursuit of strategic superiority, often caring more for their own vested interests than for the foreign and domestic policy interest of the country as a whole. Talk of "military detente" may go against the grain of many a conservative member of the military establishment whose main concern is "strengthening the defensive might of the motherland." Although the primacy of civilian leadership in the Soviet Union is indisputable, the military manage to exert a strong conservative influence on national security policies, including arms control.[91]

How and through what channels, one might ask, will these hard-line military elements exert pressure on the civilian leadership? This brings us to the structure of the Soviet "arms control apparat," which is by no means unified although centrally controlled. There actually appears to be a deliberate scattering of both civilian and military groups at all levels, with the final decisions on SALT reached in a subgroup of the Politburo at top leadership level.

The Central Committee Secretariat—especially its Cadres Abroad, International Affairs, and Defense Industry Departments—furnish some inputs to the Politburo, and interaction between the political and military leadership takes place in the Defense Council. The International Organizations Division of the Ministry of Foreign Affairs may be the Soviet counterpart to our ACDA, but the real technical expertise on SALT can be found in the military establishment: in the General Staff's Arms Control Section. It is believed that the military position on SALT, arrived at in the Arms Control Section, tends to be conservative and that the military also directly influences the SALT negotiations through its representatives on the negotiating team.

Another important civilian body, the Academy of Sciences and its institutes (the Institute for the Study of the USA and Canada and *IMEMO*) provide a counterweight to the hard-line military. Senior specialists from these institutes have personal access to the political leadership. Although they still rely on services of retired military officers (such as M. A. Mil'shteyn and L. Semeyko) for technical expertise, new cadres of civilian specialists are being trained. However, the influence of the military is still considerable at the present time, and it may continue to tilt arms control proposals toward positions favorable to defense interests for some time to come.[92]

Soviet Military R & D: Implications for Arms Control

Although the main elements in the Soviet weapon acquisition process, the Ministry of Defense and the nine defense industry ministries are dominated by the military, the final approval of the plans and the establishment of defense spending priorities lies with the Politburo[93] and is thus controlled by the Party leadership. While the Ministry of Defense places orders, supervises development and production, and assimilates the final results, the nine defense industries control plants, research institutes, and design bureaus where the actual R&D work is done. The Defense Council and Military Industrial Commission (*VPK— Voyenno–promyshlennaya komissiya*) exercise control over the activities of the main elements.[94]

Soviet R&D is usually viewed as evolutionary and incremental, for innovation is inhibited by bureaucratic structure and the traditional tendency not to discard anything old but to add and improve. With the exception of ICBMs, where a drive for major technical advances has been noticed, and some new weapons based on the laser and particle beam, the evolutionary trend appears to be typical of Soviet R&D. However, Soviet leaders have been known to intervene personally to advance a weapons development proposal.[95]

Since the late 1920s, the slogan of Soviet R&D has been to "catch up and overtake" (*dognat' i peregnat'*) the capitalists. So far, they have succeeded mainly in the military sector. Soviet military R&D is estimated to represent 40 percent to 80 percent of total Soviet R&D. This has spawned an R&D bureaucracy and a number of institutions with a stake in the continuation of the effort. It can be assumed safely that any attempts at reduction will be met with stubborn resistance, while any increases in the scope and volume of the R&D effort will add another "spiral" to the R&D bureaucracy and make future reductions difficult if not impossible.

While Soviet R&D appears to be mainly evolutionary, it is also capable of extreme concentration of effort on a single goal. From the point of view of arms control, it would be desirable if such initiatives could be discouraged or regulated and limited under the terms of an arms control treaty. It is a known fact that major technological changes have resulted in major changes in military doctrine and strategy. Such breakthroughs, should they occur in the future, would make the control of armaments and the avoidance of armed conflict on a strategic scale even more difficult than they are now.

Conclusion

Practically since its inception, the USSR has integrated a "peace offensive" into its foreign policy while paying close attention to its military effort, its concern with security apparently overriding all other concerns. The West consistently has met the "peace offensive" with disbelief, the Soviet military buildup with alarm, and Soviet intentions in the political and military spheres with distrust.

Under conditions of parity and mutual deterrence, Soviet views of arms control reflect the moderate or conservative orientation of the various elements furnishing inputs into the making of policy. Thus, arms control—specifically SALT—has been perceived variously as:

1. the first step toward disarmament or, at least, arms reduction;

2. a nuisance, limiting the development of a particularly cherished weapons program, restricting the sphere of influence of a particular armed forces component, and

generally restricting the influence of the military;

3. a good chance to develop and build new weapons not limited by the treaty and to increase the stockpile of permissible weapons to new ceilings;

4. imperfect because it does not limit bilateral buildup;

5. imperfect because it allows the US to "violate its spirit" by creating new systems.

Disarmament propaganda aside, in their many messages to the West, the Soviets have made it quite clear that they want political detente supplemented by "military detente"; parity, both political and military; and SALT II or an equivalent agreement (which may be part of "military detente"). Conversely, they would rather not be confronted with the new US "countervailing strategy," a NATO-Warsaw Pact missile race, and the attendant tension on the European continent. They profess not to be interested in the dubious and expensive advantages of counterforce superiority and in the dangerous dynamics of an uncontrolled arms competition. However, they have not denied their interest in power projection and in rendering military aid to socialist regimes. But they have also stressed the two superpowers' responsibility to preserve the world from a global nuclear war.[96]

Continued Soviet interest in SALT and perhaps in eventual strategic arms reduction will depend on internal conditions in the USSR, especially on the delicate balance between civilian interests (mostly economic and thus potentially benefitting the population of the country) and military interests (partly parochial, partly expressing legitimate concern with the defense of the state). It will depend on the direction the Soviet policy of "power projection" will take (the more daring the projection, the greater may be the need for a qualitative edge to ensure political leverage). To a very considerable extent, Soviet interest in arms control will depend on the American "balancing act" in the political and military sector. An American foreign policy which is firm but receptive to dialogue and a strong but not too threatening military posture may send the right signals to the Soviets and further both our national interests and international stability.

Notes

1. John M. Collins, "Principles of Deterrence," *Air University Review,* November–December 1979, pp. 17–26.

2. S. A. Tyushkevich, *Filosofiya i voyennaya teoriya* [Philosophy and Military Theory] (Moscow: Nauka, 1975), pp. 17–26.

3. Quoted in E. I. Rybkin, et al., *Filosofiya i voyennaya istoriya* [Philosophy and Military History] (Moscow: Nauka, 1979), p. 308.

4. See "Voyennaya programma proletarskoy revolyutsii" [The Military Programme of Proletarian Revolution], in V. I. Lenin, *O voyne, armii i voyennoy nauke* [On War, the Army, and Military Science] (Moscow: Voyenizdat, 1965), p. 304.

5. *Filosofiya i voyennaya istoriya*, p. 309.

6. See, for instance:

    B. Ponomarev, A. Gromyko, eds., *History of Soviet Foreign Policy,* Vols. I & II (Moscow: Progress Publishers, 1973);

    I. S. Kremer, A. O. Chubaryan, *Ocherk istorii vneshney politiki SSR* [History of Soviet Foreign Policy] (Moscow: Prosveshcheniye, 1964);

    Authors' collective, including former UN Ambassador Arkadiy N. Shevchenko. Edited by V. A. Zorin, *Bor'ba Sovetskogo Soyuza za razoruzheniye, 1946–1960* [The USSR's Struggle for Peace, 1946–1960] (Moscow: Mezhdunarodnyye otnosheniya, 1961);

    Authors' collective headed by Academician V. G. Trukhanovskiy, *Ot dekreta o mire do programmy mira, 1917–1975* [From the Peace Decree to the Peace Program, 1917–1975] (Moscow: Politizdat, 1975);

    Professors N. I. Lebedev and N. M. Nikol'skiy, eds., *Vneshnyaya politika Sovetskogo Soyuza (aktual'nyye problemy)* [Soviet Foreign Policy (Current Problems)] (Moscow: Mezhdunarodnyye otnosheniya, 1976).

    V. Mamontov, *Disarmament—The Command of the Times,* (Moscow: Progress Publishers, 1970).

7. Kremer, Chubaryan, op. cit., p. 73. On the other hand, Alva Myrdal, in *The Game of Disarmament* (New York: Pantheon, 1978), views the American "Hoover Plan" as the most comprehensive disarmament plan submitted to the Conference for the Reduction and Limitation of Armaments.

8. According to General Petr Grigorenko (interviewed in October 1979), the territorial army was not only technologically backwards but also unreliable and could not be counted on to carry out forced collectivization measures when the soldiers were called upon to put down unrest in their own villages.

9. David Holloway, "The Soviet Style of Military R&D," paper presented at the May 1979 Symposium of the AAASS, Washington, DC Chapter.

10. Louis J. Halle, *The Cold War as History* (New York: Harper and Row, 1975), p. 188.

11. Andrzej Korbowski, "Eastern Europe and the Soviet Threat," in *The Soviet Threat: Myths and Realities,* Grayson Kirk, ed. (New York: The Academy of Political Science, 1978), pp. 66–76.

12. An interesting and illuminating account of the success of the Soviet atomic project is given by David Holloway in "Entering the Nuclear Arms Race: The Soviet Decision to Build the Atomic Bomb, 1939–1945," Working Paper (No. 9) of the International Security Studies Program (Washington, DC: The Wilson Center, 1979).

13. Myrdal, op. cit., pp. 73–75.

14. Ibid., p. 77.

15. Kremer, Chubaryan, op. cit., pp. 180–190.

16. Moscow World Service in English, 12 May 1980.

17. Moscow *TASS* in English, 13 May 1980.

18. For a recent Soviet recapitulation of the history of American use of force as an instrument of policy, see V. I. Bogachev, "Vooruzhennaya interventsiya kak instrument vneshney politiki SShA" [Military Intervention as an Instrument of US Foreign Policy], in *SShA* [USA], No. 6, June 1980, pp. 120–127. The article makes extensive use of information provided by Barry Blechman and Stephen Kaplan in *Force Without War* (Washington: Brookings Institution, 1978).

19. M. A. Mil'shteyn and L. Semeyko, "Problema nedopustimosti yadernogo konflikta (o novykh podkhodakh SShA)" [The Problem of the Inadmissibility of Nuclear Conflict (On New US Approaches)], *SShA,* November 74, p. 3.

20. Vice Admiral A. Gontayev, "American Military Doctrine," *Morskoy sbornik* [Naval Digest] No. 2, 1978, pp. 110–117.

21. E.g., see Colonel I. Pavlov, "V. I. Lenin, KPSS ob agressivnoy prirode imperializma i neobkhodimosti vysokoy bditel'nosti sovetskikh ludey, voinov armii i flota" [V. I. Lenin and the CPSU on the Aggressive Nature of Imperialism and the Need for High Alertness on the Part of Soviet People and Army and Navy Soldiers], *Kommunist Vooruzhennykh Sil* [Communist of the Armed Forces], No. 20, October 1978,

pp. 79–86.

22. Ibid.

23. I. M. Puzin and M. A. Balanchuk, *Mezhdunarodnyye svyazi NATO: Voyenno–ekonomicheskiy aspekt* [The International Links of NATO: The Military–Economic Aspect] (Moscow: Mezhdunarodnyye otnosheniya, 1979), p. 224. Also see note 87.

24. As seen by Genrikh Trofimenko, perhaps the greatest Soviet authority on American doctrine and strategy, the American perception of deterrence always has been based on superiority rather than parity. Thus, deterrence has been "containment of the adversary through intimidation, from a position of unequivocal superiority" (*sderzhivanive protivnika putem ustrasheniya s pozitsii bezuslovno prevoskhodyashchey sily*). *SShA: politika, voyna, ideologiya* [The USA: Policy, War, Ideology] (Moscow: Mysl', 1976), p. 111.

25. "Problema nedopustimosti yadernogo konflikta," p. 3.

26. Marshal of the Soviet Union V. D. Sokolovskiy, ed., *Voyennaya strategiya* [Military Strategy] (Moscow: Voyenizdat, 1968), p. 78.

27. With the exception of Genrikh Trofimenko, who in his monograph *SShA, Politika, Voyna, Ideologiya,* p. 336, welcomed the American adoption of "flexible response" as a wise move away from the "strategic bluff" of massive retaliation and a return to more "realistic" strategic pluralism.

28. "Nekotoryye aspekty voyenno-politicheskoy strategii SShA" [Some Aspects of the American Military–Political Strategy], *SShA,* October 1970, pp. 14–17. Also see the discussion of counterforce on pp. 75–80 of *Voyennaya strategiya.*

29. "Amerikanskiye voyennyye doktriny: preyemstvennost' i modifikatsiya" [American Military Doctrines: Continuity and Change], *ME i MO,* August 1971, pp. 30–39.

30. "Problema nedopustimosti yadernogo konflikta," *SShA,* November 1974.

31. At the same time, the Soviet armed forces were reported to have adopted some very similar strategies, "limiting" and diversifying the utilization of nuclear weapons in the Soviet variant of a "flexible response" and, possibly, even their equivalent of a "selective targeting option." (For the latter hypothesis, see Joseph D. Douglass and Amoretta M. Hoeber, "The Nuclear Warfighting Dimensions of the Soviet Threat to Europe," *The Journal of Social and Political Studies,* Vol. 3, No. 2, p. 107. For a Soviet monograph which seems to corroborate their findings, see Stepan Il'yin, *Moral'nyy faktor v sovremennykh voynakh,* 3rd ed. (Moscow: Voyenizdat, 1979), where on pp. 65, 105, and 174 "strategic strikes on military targets of the adversary" are envisioned as a "most important" and "essential" method of military action in a future war, although strikes on industrial objectives and other economic targets are not excluded. However, the official Soviet position on retaliatory strikes is still one of a massive response, combining counterforce and countervalue elements in what has been called a "countercenter" strategy.

32. While Soviet commentators habitually complain of American "aggressiveness" in international relations as well as in the American doctrine, their frequent use of such expressions as "strategic balance," "parity," "military balance," "essential equivalance," "stability," (*strategicheskoye ravnovesiye, paritet, voyennoye ravnovesiye, ravenstvo po sushchestvu, stabil'nost'*) suggests an underlying belief, or at least strong interest in, an essentially deterrent relationship.

33. See "Commencement Address", University of Michigan, 16 June 1962, *Survival,* September–October 1962, p. 194–196.

34. E.g., Gen. Kurochkin in *Krasnaya zvezda* [Red Star] (hereafter abbreviated as *KZ*), 9 July 65; Colonel General Povaliy in *KZ,* 8 October 1964; Cherednichenko in *Life Abroad,* No. 23, June 1965; P. F. Batitskiy, interview in *Pravda,* 6 February 1968; Major General K. Bochkarev, *Sovetskaya Kirgiziya,* 25 August 1970.

35. John Polanyi, "Armaments Policies for the Sixties," *Survival,* March–April 1962, Vol. 4, No. 2 p. 76.

36. *ME i MO,* November 1974, pp. 3–19.

37. G. A. Vorontsov, *SShA i Zapadnaya Yevropa, novyy etap otnosheniy* [The US and Western Europe – A New Stage] (Moscow: Mezhdunarodnyye Otnosheniya, 1979),

pp. 50–51.

38. On US naval superiority, see "The Future of US Sea Power," in *Proceedings*, 1979. The Soviets are displeased with our striving for "maritime supremacy", a "sine qua non" of our naval stance, according to Admiral Thomas B. Hayward. Admiral S. G. Gorshkov, Commander of the Soviet Navy, views it as a growing "threat" of encirclement on the seas, to be countered by a buildup of the Soviet Navy. See his *Morskaya moshch' gosudarstva* [Sea Power of the State] (Moscow: Voyenizdat, 1976), pp. 460–462.

For a discussion of the current desirability of counterforce and first strike, see Carl H. Builder, "Why Not First–Strike Counterforce Capabilities," *Strategic Review*, Spring 1979, pp. 32–39.

39. Among others, T. Kondratkov in "XXV S'yezd i problema mira i voyny" [The XXVth Congress and the Problem of War and Peace], *Voyenno–istoricheskiy zhurnal* [Military–Historical Journal], No. 7, 1976, pp. 3–10.

40. "*Aktual'nyye problemy mirovoy politiki*" [Current Problems of World Politics], *ME i MO*, No. 1, January 1960, pp. 3–33.

41. "Problema nedopustimosti yadernogo konflikta," *SShA*, November 1974, p. 3.

42. A typical argument is presented in a recent volume, authored by what appears to be a team of junior researchers from the USA Institute: *SShA i NATO, istochniki voyennoy ugrozy* [US and NATO, Two Sources of the Threat of War] (Moscow: Voyenizdat, 1979).

43. Daniil Proektor, "At a Turning Point: Questions of War and Peace in Present-Day Conditions," *Novoye Vremya* [New Times] No. 46, 9 November 1979, pp. 4–6.

44. *FBIS. Special Memorandum. Soviet Views of European Arms Issues and the NATO Council's December Decision* (3 December 1979, FB79–10029). For a much more strident commentary on the NATO decision, see especially Army General M. Kozlov, "Bloc of Aggression and War: The Offensive Nature of NATO Armed Forces Groupings," *KZ*, 20 November 79, pp. 2–3; Major General R. Simonyan, "The NATO Eurostrategists' Dangerous Concepts," *KZ*, 28 December 1979, p. 3; Major I. Sidel'nikov, "Komu i dlya chego nuzhno yadernoye prevoskhodstvo" [Military Superiority—Who Needs it and Why?], *KZ*, 15 January 1980, pp. 2–3.

45. The Observer (London), 13 January 1980, p. 1. However, Harold Brown, the former Secretary of Defense, when asked at the July 1980 National Security Affairs Conference whether he believed in the possibility of "linkage" between the two decisions, replied that he saw the two events as contiguous but not connected.

46. E.g., see V. S. Shein, "Za fasadom yadernoy modernizatsii" [Behind the Facade of Nuclear Modernization], *SShA*, No. 3, March 1980, pp. 6–16.

47. M. A. Mil'shteyn, "Nekotoryye kharakternyye cherty sovremennoy doktriny SShA" [Some Typical Tendencies of the Current US Doctrine], *SShA*, No. 5, May 1980, pp. 9–18.

48. M. A. Mil'shteyn, "Kuda natseleny amerikanskiye rakety" [Where American Missiles are Targeted], *Izvestiya*, 19 July 1978, p. 3. This, by the way, is also what Senator Moynihan said in his 19 November 1979 *New Yorker* article, where he deplored the creation of a tense counterforce environment through our deployment of the MX missile—"an offensive first-strike weapon"—which, he thought, the Russians might try to counter by abandoning the fractionation limits on warheads and going to as many as 30 warheads per missile.

49. *Bezopasnost' v yadernyy vek*, p. 28.

50. E.g., see *KZ*, 5 June 1980, p. 1–2, for speech by N. V. Ogarkov, Chief of the Soviet General Staff, who referred to a "countervailing strategy" as a "massive retaliation strategy in a new guise" created for dealing a preventive blow with strategic means. Also, see Lev Semeyko, "Stavka na potentsial pervogo udara" [A Stance Based on a First Strike Potential], *KZ*, 8 August 1980, 3.

51. See Robert Jervis, "Why Nuclear Superiority Does Not Matter," *Political Science Quarterly*, Winter 1979–80, pp. 617–633.

52. See Desmond Ball, "Soviet ICBM Deployment," *Survival*, July–August 1980, pp.

167–170.
53. Bernard Brodie, *Strategy in the Missile Age* (Princeton: Princeton University Press, 1959), p. 304.
54. See his "Changing Attitudes Toward Deterrence," ACIS Working Paper, No. 25, July 1980, p. 24.
55. *FBIS Daily Report, Soviet Union*, FBIS–SOV–80, 7 January 1980.
56. O. B. Borisov and B. T. Koloskov, *Soviet–Chinese Relations 1945–1970, (Translation)* (Bloomington: Indiana University Press, 1975), p. 155.
57. "Bor'ba SSSR za voyennuyu razryadku" [The USSR's Struggle for Military Detente], *Morskoy sbornik*, No. 11, November 1979, pp. 78–85.
58. See Zorin and Falin's interview with Georgiy Arbatov on Moscow Domestic Service, March 1980. Also, see G. Arbatov, "Vneshnyaya Politika SshA na poroge 80-kh godov" [US Foreign Policy on the Threshold of the 80s], *SShA*, No. 4, April 1980, pp. 43–54. The same article appeared in *Pravda*, 3 March 1980, p. 6.
59. The following monographs include a Soviet first-strike counterforce attack among the options the Soviet leadership may be seriously considering:
    Joseph D. Douglass and Amoretta M. Hoeber, *Soviet Strategy for Nuclear War* (Stanford: Hoover Institution Press, 1979);
    Harriet Fast Scott and William F. Scott, *The Armed Forces of the USSR* (Boulder: Westview Press, 1979);
    Soviet Armed Forces Review Annual, David R. Jones, ed., Vol. 2 (Gulf Breeze, Florida: Academic International Press, 1978), p. 51;
    Leon Goure, Foy D. Kohler, and Mose L. Harvey, *The Role of Nuclear Forces in Current Soviet Strategy* (Coral Gables, Florida: University of Miami Press, 1974).
60. "Napadeniye, a ne zashchita dolzhno stat' lozungom mass" [The offense, not defense, must become the slogan of the masses], in V. I. Lenin, *Polnoye sobraniye sochineniy* [Complete Collected Works] (Moscow: Gosizdat, 1960), Vol. 13, pp. 376–377; also see M. V. Frunze, "Yedinaya voyennaya doktrina i Krasnaya Armiya" [A Unified Military Doctrine and the Red Army], in *Izbrannyye proizvedeniya* [Selected Works] (Moscow: Voyenizdat, 1977), pp. 29–46.
61. *Sovetskaya Voyennaya Entsiklopediya*, Vol. 3 (Moscow: Voyenizdat, 1977), pp. 225–229.
62. See Sokolovskiy, op. cit., p. 11; and Colonel General S. M. Shtemenko, "Nauchno-tekhnicheskiy progress i yego vliyaniye na razvitiye voyennogo dela" [Military–Technical Progress and Its Influence on the Development of Military Affairs], in *Problemy revolyutsii v voyennom dele. Sbornik statey* [Problems of Revolution in Military Affairs Digest of Articles], compiled by P. M. Derevyanko (Moscow: Voyenizdat, 1965), pp. 70–86.
63. Karl von Clausewitz, On War (Princeton: Princeton University Press, 1976), p. 593.
64. S. A. Tyushkevich, et al., eds. *Marksizm–Leninizm o voyne i armii* (Moscow: Voyenizdat, 1968).
65. Gorshkov, op. cit., p. 367.
66. Clausewitz, op. cit., pp. 351–359.
67. "NSC–68. April 14, 1950," in *Containment: Documents on American Policy and Strategy, 1945–1950*, Thomas H. Etzold and John Lewis Gaddis, eds. (New York: Columbia University Press, 1978), p. 432.
68. Major General N. Talenskiy, "Reflecting on the Last War," *International Affairs* (Moscow), May 1965, p. 23.
69. "Theory, Politics, Ideology: On the Essence of War," 24 January 1967.
70. Robert L. Arnett, "Soviet Attitudes Towards Nuclear War, 1972–1977," *Journal of Strategic Studies*, September 1979, pp. 172–191. Also see Raymond Garthoff, "Strategic Deterrence and Arms Limitation in Soviet Policy," *International Security*, Summer 1978.
71. I. Glagolev, "Disarmament and Economic Development," *International Affairs*, May 1979, pp. 94–106.
72. Herbert Dinerstein, *War and the Soviet Union* (New York: Praeger, 1962), p. 18.

139

73. See, for example, G. Trofimenko, "Voyenno-strategicheskiye aspekty. . . ." Also see a detailed discussion of deterrence in his monograph *SShA: politika, voyna, ideologiya,* pp. 111–114, 166–80.

74. V. Kelin, "Razryadka—put' k prochnomu miru" [Detente—A Road to Stable Peace], *ME i MO,* March 1977, p. 4–14; and N. Podol'skiy, "Disarmament—Road to Lasting Peace," in *International Affairs,* February 1978, pp. 25–26.

75. "Atomic Deadlock," *News* (Moscow), No. 6, 1956, pp. 13–14.

76. "Characteristics of Current World Development," *Mezhdunarodnaya zhizn'* [International Affairs] No. 11, November 1973, pp. 31–34.

77. *Voyna i armiya* (Moscow: Voyenizdat, 1977), p. 130.

78. See Ustinov's speech commemorating 60 years of the Soviet Armed Forces, *Kommunist Vooruzhennykh Sil,* No. 5, March 78, pp. 1124; Colonel Ye. Rybkin in *Voyenno–istoricheskiy zhurnal,* No. 1, 1977, pp. 3–9; Major General Rair Simonyan in *Pravda,* 14 June 1977, p. 4.

79. Vice Admiral V. Gulin, *Morskoy sbornik,* No. 11, November 1979, pp. 78–85.

80. See, for example, Colin Gray, "Strategic Stability Reconsidered," pp. 13 and 40, paper presented at the 7th National Security Affairs Conference, 21–23 July 1980, National Defense University, Washington, DC, where he argues that because of the Soviet leadership's callous disregard for the life of its citizens, retaliation against Soviet cities would be ineffectual, for "societal destruction . . . may be insufficiently unacceptable to Soviet politicians" who take an instrumental view of the lives of their citizens.

81. Department of Defense Annual Report Fiscal Year 1980, p. 85.

82. "Nadezhnyy shchit Rodiny" [The Reliable Shield of the Motherland], *KZ,* 23 February 1975, pp. 1–2; Army General V. Kulikov (then Chief of USSR Armed Forces General Staff), "Armiya zashchity Oktyabrya" [The Army of the Defense of October], *Komsomol'skaya Pravda,* 23 February 1975, pp. 1–2.

83. I. G. Usachev, *Sovetskiy Soyuz i problema razoruzheniya* [The Soviet Union and the Problem of Disarmament] (Moscow: Mezhdunarodnyye Otnosheniya, 1976), pp. 58–60.

84. A. Gavrilov, "Programma bor'by za mir i bezopasnost'" [A Program for a Struggle for Peace and Security], *ME i MO,* July 1971.

85. G. A. Trofimenko, "Sovetsko–Amerikanskiye soglasheniya ob ogranichenii strategicheskikh vooruzheniy" [Soviet–American Agreements on the Limitations of Strategic Armaments], *SShA,* September 1972, pp. 3–16.

86. M. A. Mil'shteyn, L. S. Semeyko, "Ogranicheniye strategicheskikh vooruzheniy: problemy i perspektivy" [Limitation of Strategic Armaments: Problems and Outlook], *SShA,* December 1973, pp. 3–12.

87. *Pravda,* 29 April 1980, p. 4.

88. E.g., Yuriy V. Kastasonov, "Voyenno-politicheskaya strategiya SShA na rubezhe 70–80kh godov" [The Military Political Strategy of the USA on the Threshold of the 80's], *SShA,* No. 2, February 1980, pp. 9–12; also, Captain I. Gorshechnikov, "Avanturisticheskiye doktriny apologetov gonki vooruzheniy [The Adventurist Doctrines of the Apologists of the Arms Race], *Kommunist Vooruzhennykh Sil,* No. 8, April 1980, pp. 88–87. Similar sentiments were expressed by Valentin Falin, Deputy of the International Information Department of the Central Committee, in an interview with *Der Spiegel,* 5 November 1979, and by the commentator V. Nekrasov in *"Mif vzdornyy no opasnyy,"* *Kommunist,* No. 12, August 79, pp. 91–102.

89. *Pravda,* 13 January 1980, p. 1.

90. In a short *Krasnaya zvezda* editorial of 15 March 1980, p. 1, discussing the duties of the Red Army, the words "international" and "internationalism" occur ten times. For more emphasis on "internationalism," see "Vneshnyaya politika KPSS – internatsializm v deystvii" [The Foreign Policy of the CPSU—Internationalism in Action], *Morskoy sbornik,* December 1979, pp. 3–7; and the article by Colonel Ya. Kirshin and Major V. Popov, "Leninskoye ucheniye o voyne i armii i sovremennost'" [Lenin's Teachings on War and the Army and the Contemporary Period], *Morskoy sbornik,*

February 1980.

91. Edward L. Warner, III, *The Military in Contemporary Soviet Society: An Institutional Analysis* (New York: Praeger, 1977), p. 239.

92. See Thomas Wolfe, *The SALT Experience: Its Impact on US and Soviet Decisionmaking* (Santa Monica: The Rand Corporation, September 1975).

93. Warner, op. cit., p. 176.

94. For an excellent discussion of Soviet R&D, see David Holloway, "Soviet Style of Military R&D," AAASS paper, May 1979.

95. Ibid.

96. For a high-level formulation of Soviet declaratory policy on essential equivalance, parity, military balance, the principle of equal security (*"primernoye ravenstvo," "paritet," "voyennoye ravnovesiye," "printsip ravnoy bezopasnosti"*) and for the official denial of a striving after military superiority (*"voyennoye prevoskhodstvo"*) and first-strike potential (*"potentsial'nost' pervogo udara"*), see Andrey Gromyko "Razoruzheniye—nasushchnaya problema sovremennosti" [Disarmament—An Urgent Problem of Our Time], *Kommunist,* No. 11, July 1980, pp. 6–23.

Soviet and American Perceptions of Arms Control

George Kolt

In a recent article on the SALT process, Senator Moynihan noted that "if the familiar man from Mars were to be presented with a chart showing the rise of Soviet weaponry of the past three decades and told that somewhere during that period an arms limitation agreement was signed with the United States, the visitor would be quite unable to pick out the year."[1] Can there be any doubt that our outside observer would be equally puzzled by the contrast between the last decade's proliferation of arms control negotiatons on a variety of issues (such as armed forces in Europe, chemical weapons, antisatellite weapons, and conventional arms transfers) and the simultaneous growth in the activities that these negotiations were supposed to control? Indeed, the results have been so paltry that even a proponent of arms control could only portray it as having "essentially failed"[2] while a very vocal advocate of reductions in military spending has characterized SALT as "an exercise in joint arms management."[3]

If failure in establishing effective or adequate arms control is so widely acknowledged, what are the reasons for it? A number of explanations have been advanced, ranging from the perfidy of Soviet negotiators coupled with the incompetence of their Western counterparts to the irreconcilability of Soviet and American strategic aims. In this article, I would like to explore one facet of that last explanation: namely, the possibility that Soviet and American statesmen approach negotiations from widely differing perspectives. I believe such an exploration can help us not only to understand the history of arms control but also to assess the frequently cited argument that even if negotiations yield meager results, it is still helpful to maintain the negotiating *process*. The exploration I am suggesting should help us decide whether the two sides are engaged in the same process and, if not, whether the process nevertheless can acquire value which transcends the differing interpretations of the two sides.

As a basis for my investigations, I will use Ikle's categorization of negotiations by objective which appeared in his seminal 1954 study. Ikle advanced five contrasting motivations which bring nations to the bargaining table:

(1) Extension: the desire to prolong an existing agreement or to codify an existing situation;

(2) Normalization: the perception of a situation as being unstable or abnormal and the desire to change it

(conferences to end war, sign peace treaties, and establish diplomatic relations are the best examples of this type of negotiation);

(3) Redistribution: the situation in which there is clearly an offensive side which demands the existing state of affairs be changed in its favor and a defensive side which must decide how to react to the demand; if the defensive side either refuses to negotiate or adopts a rigid negotiating position, the offensive side must choose between giving up its goal, using coercion to gain its aim, or postponing the realization of it while simultaneously strengthening its coercive capabilities;

(4) Innovation: the mutually shared objective is to create a new and better relationship between the parties (examples are trade agreements or the creation of new organizations; for example, the North Atlantic Treaty Organization or the European Economic Community).

(5) Side Effects: a situation in which either or both parties are motivated not by the publicly announced purpose of the negotiations but by the desire to use the negotiations for concealed purposes. These concealed purposes could be to prolong a situation which is becoming increasingly untenable for the other party (e.g., the North Vietnamese use of the Paris negotiations), to gather intelligence about an opponent (such as his true aims, his relationship with his allies, his domestic situation, his vulnerabilities), to gain time (either to strengthen one's own position or to deter the other party from using his coercive powers to the full), to conduct a propaganda campaign, or to make gains elsewhere (e.g., to affect third parties or to use the one set of negotiations in order to gain strategic advantages in another set of negotiations or simply in a related situation).[4]

As Ikle points out, negotiations rarely fit into the pure types outlined. Still, one set of objectives will often predominate, and—what is more pertinent for our purposes—the dominant objectives of the two parties are seldom the same. What has been the case in the arms control negotiations of the last decade?

With the exception of the UN–sponsored Conference on Disarmament (where I will let the reader decide the dominant objectives of the parties), it is the US which has taken the initiative to convene negotiations on such various topics as strategic arms limitations, a complete and comprehensive test ban, chemical warfare, antisatellite testing, and conventional arms transfers. I do not believe it necessary to go into each of these talks in detail to suggest that the primary US objective has been the desire to create a new and mutually beneficial relationship between the parties—or, put in Ikle's terms, innovation. This objective stands out most clearly in the case of SALT where the US sought to persuade the Soviet Union mutual vulnerability meant stability, negated—at least greatly diminished—the need for further weapons acquisition, and made an explicit recognition of this fact feasible and desirable so as to decrease the chance of nuclear war. It is unlikely the Soviet Union initially accepted this proferred US objective at face value. After all, in the late 1960s and early 1970s, the US still held the lead in most indices of strategic power and thus could be logically expected to seek to codify the existing balance; that is, to carry out extension negotiations. For the Soviet Union, then, the purpose of the negotiations had to be buy time to build up its own forces (it will be remembered that the momentum was clearly on the Soviet side) and eventually to codify a *redistribution* of strategic power in the negotiations.

It may be objected that I have skipped too quickly from the Soviet rejection of extension negotiations to redistrubtion negotiations, thereby leaving out the possible Soviet acceptance of the US aim of innovation. Could the Soviets have espoused the goal of creating strategic stability which, in the US definition, meant neither side—either now or later through the construction of new systems—could credibly hope to attack the other without risking its own destruction? Could the Soviets have agreed strategic superiority was an outdated concept?

Unfortunately, the US approach was completely foreign to Soviet thinking. On the historical plane, it sought to replace the dynamics of inevitable historical evolution—which is the main tenet of the Marxist–Leninist world view—with an artificially created, and therefore illusory, stability. On the military plane, it placed the emphasis on the technological while downplaying if not ignoring the psychosociological element which is an essential part of Soviet strategic thinking. Finally, on the very pragmatic political level, the US approach advanced a kind of stability which was foreign to the Soviet experience. It was a stability based on the acceptance of some common ground rules (the law, if you will) and equality, whereas the Soviet concept of stability entailed a hierarchical order, with the person or nation at the top of the pecking order controlling the actions of those below and thus introducing order into the social dynamic of history.

This historical Soviet view made it unlikely the USSR would accept the US strategic objective either at face value when the US still had strategic superiority or as a long-range mutual goal. In keeping with that view, the first Soviet aim had to be foiling the suspected US goal of extension and pursuing redistribution. This has been the general Soviet approach to SALT; the question underlying the entire SALT debate in the US is whether the Soviets have succeeded in using the negotiations for that redistribution of power.

Although I have concentrated on SALT because it is the most prominent example of the different US and Soviet approaches, an examination of other negotiations would reveal similar contrasts. In the talks on chemical warfare, for instance, the US has been driven not only by its idealistic desire for innovation but also by its realization of weakness. Conversely, the Soviet Union is quite satisfied with the current imbalance, does not wish to jeopardize it, and does not currently need an agreement to protect it; nevertheless, it does see the necessity of negotiating for the propaganda side effects such negotiation permits. In the area of conventional arms transfers, the Soviet Union—having ascertained but not subscribed to the US desire to be innovative—sought to use the talks to promote its geopolitical goals; it thereby helped make the talks moribund.

An even more interesting example of contrasting aims can be found in the talks on Mutual and Balanced Force Reductions in Europe (MBFR), for these are negotiations which both the US and USSR entered without great enthusiasm. The US proposed the talks mainly to show the NATO policy of defense and detente really meant what it said, to complement the Conference on Security and Cooperation in Europe (CSCE) with a conference which would deal with genuine military issues, and to demonstrate the undesirability of unilateral US troop reductions. For its part, the Soviet Union accepted MBFR—minus the B—as a quid pro quo for US acquiescence to CSCE.

Once the negotiations began, however, the two sides rapidly moved from the original, mutually held side effects objective to a more traditional pattern. The US easily fell back on its traditional attitude of idealism and generally came to view the talks as another opportunity to be innovative by creating greater stability at a lower force level, with great stress on numbers. But unlike SALT, it was the USSR which would have to agree to a certain redistribution of military power. While rejecting this Western goal—and incidentally the data which supported it—the Soviet Union, having obtained a flawed but nevertheless spectacular CSCE agreement, now discovered actual and potential benefits in MBFR. In the short run, there was the opportunity to probe the Western position and sometimes exacerbate differences among the NATO allies. In the long run, the talks had the potential not only of codifying the military balance in favor of the Warsaw Pact (thus, the extension objective as against the NATO redistribution objective) but also of beginning a political redistribution in Europe in which the Soviet Union would acquire the right to participate in the defense decisionmaking process of those countries located in the reduction area—with the FRG naturally being the focus of Soviet efforts. In MBFR, this danger became known as the *droit de regard* and explains why the West German government has been most leery of this particular Soviet aim while, nevertheless, remaining committed to the negotiations for other reasons.

Since this article is not devoted to the German view of arms control negotiations, I will leave the explanation of German aims to others and instead probe US motivations. Why, after the irreconcilability of Western and Soviet aims had become apparent, has the US remained the prime mover behind MBFR, even at the cost of sometimes irritating its allies?

To explain this phenomenon, I think it would be helpful to turn to Henry Kissinger's characterization of American diplomatic practice. Criticizing that practice, Kissinger described it as being grounded in three traditions—the idealistic, the pragmatic, and the legalistic—but lacking the geopolitical tradition.[5] In MBFR as well as in other negotiations, I think these three traditions have tended to reinforce and merge with one another—the idealistic bringing the US to the bargaining table and keeping it there while shaping some of the US positions and policies; the pragmatic producing the desire to solve the problem at hand by achieving a result through an agreement; and the legalistic leading to concentration on the specifics at the expense of the larger world view. In MBFR, this combination of traditions sometimes resulted in the data discussion's being viewed by some as pretrial discovery proceedings to be followed by a search by two well-meaning opponents for a settlement which incorporates their shared ideals. Overall, then, the three traditions create the danger of making unwarranted assumptions about the long-range aims of the Soviet Union and ignoring the side effects of US positions and of the negotiations themselves.

For their part, the Soviets—unhampered by the three US traditions and steeped in the geopolitical approach—have found it relatively easy to negotiate for side effects and not to let a desire for agreement endanger the potential long-run redistribution benefits which Western idealism, impatience, or simply lassitude could someday produce.

Such a result, of course, is not preordained. After all, the MBFR talks have been going on for some seven years without producing the prize sought by the Soviets, while over a decade of other arms control negotiation has produced more controversy than disastrous consequences for the West. The avoidance of disaster means, on the whole, the United States has been mesmerized by the innovative objectives it initially sought, the idealistic-pragmatic-legalistic traditions have not had the field to themselves, and strategic and geopolitical considerations have generally prevailed in the end. The consequence has been few negotiations have culminated in an agreement.

This paucity of results has caused, on the one hand, deep pessimism about arms control in the future and, on the other hand, justifications of negotiations on the basis of process alone. I think the root causes of this pessimism and almost desperate defense of arms control are one and the same; namely, exaggerated, idealistic, innovative expectations. The most promising remedy to this predicament seems to be simply not to expect too much from arms control. Within the context of this paper, this means not to attribute your own intentions to the other party but rather to realize two parties can enter a negotiation with different objectives; to recognize an important aspect of the negotiations is to identify the objectives of the other side with greater precision than could be done beforehand; and to be aware that in some cases parties with different objectives can still emerge with an agreement satisfactory to both.

The best example of such a development—and, therefore, of the potential value of some arms control—is the partial test ban treaty. The initial US aim was indeed innovative and idealistic, but the United States did not let this goal become so urgent as to lead it to sign a lopsided agreement. For its part, the Soviet Union alternated between negotiating for propaganda side effects and for an advantageously unverifiable treaty. But when it became interested in another side effect—the improvement of relations with the United States in an effort to gain maneuvering room in its dispute with China—the USSR was ready to move. The result was a high-level conference and an agreement. Granted, the agreement came after massive Soviet testing and probably after both sides realized they could do without further aboveground testing. Still, the cessation of that type of testing did decrease fallout and benefit mankind. The act of signing an agreement allayed fears the other side might begin testing again at any time, made both sides more confident, and thus discouraged the planning for contingency testing.

Putting those negotiations in the context of this paper, one can draw three conclusions: (1) events external to the negotiations and not the vaunted negotiation process led to a breakthrough; (2) the dominant objectives of the two sides still differed, but there was enough congruence to produce an agreement without subscribing to the illusion both sides were now governed by innovative, idealistic objectives; and (3) it is essential to assess continually the objectives of all negotiating parties, to mark time in a low-key unpublicized manner as long as the objectives remain irreconcilable and as long as there is some hope of movement without the creation of adverse side effects, and to seize the opportunities when the objectives become reconcilable even if still not identical.

Notes

1. Daniel Patrick Moynihan, "Reflections: The SALT Process," *The New Yorker,* 19 November 1979, pp. 104–180 and p. 142.
2. Leslie H. Gelb, "A Glass Half Full," *Foreign Policy,* No. 36, Fall 1979, pp. 21–30.
3. Richard J. Barnett. cited in Moynihan, loc. cit.
4. Fred Charles Ikle, *How Nations Negotiate* (New York: Harper & Row, 1954), pp. 26–42.
5. Henry A. Kissinger, *The White House Years* (Boston: Little, Brown, and Company, 1979), pp. 55–65.

The Soviets Are Still Russians

Edward L. Rowny

It has become fashionable to say we must face the facts about negotiating arms controls with the Soviets. The problem is, which facts?
There are so many of them. What I intend to do here is, first, present
the facts I believe we must face in negotiating arms control with the
USSR, and second—perhaps more importantly—describe how I believe
we must face these facts.

I spent six and one-half years as the US military representative to the
SALT II talks in Geneva. In that time, I discovered principal differences between the Soviet and American objectives and approaches
to arms control. First, the superpowers can negotiate a mutually
beneficial treaty under only one set of circumstances: when we both
share a common objective. Second, the US and the USSR do not
share a common approach to arms control negotiations. The US nego-
tiates for the sake of negotiating; we put more emphasis on reaching an
agreement than we do on the agreement's substance. The Soviets,
however, see negotiations as a tool—as a means to an end rather than
as an end themselves. Consequently, they are vigilant about the substance of an arms control agreement.

The lack of a common arms control objective between the two
superpowers is due mainly to a lack of a common sociopolitical background. The path of development of the Greco–Roman heritage and
liberal-democratic tradition in the West seldom intersected the path
transversed by the Byzantine culture in the East—either historically or
philosophically. In short, Russians and Americans are more unalike
than alike.

The following will describe how the absence of a common heritage
and a common objective have stifled US attempts to achieve a mutually
beneficial treaty on arms control with the Soviet Union. The conclusion will indicate how I believe the United States must face the facts
on negotiating with the Soviets.

The facts did not surface all at once; the American side learned them
gradually during SALT II's three separate phases. Between spring
1973 and the Vladivostok Accords in November 1974, US negotiators
were imbued with an optimism which produced great expectations.
The facts which manifested themselves during the first phase—although
they had high nuisance value—did not appear to be inimical to US
national security interests.

First, there was the inevitable "administrivia" with which we had to
deal. It seemed somehow beneath the dignity of the US side to bother

with picayune details. For our counterparts, however, nothing was too insignificant to ignore. The Soviets—true to form—sought to manipulate administrative arrangements and to control the agenda in order to influence the eventual outcome of the negotiations.

Another fact of life was our discovery the Soviets and Americans have no common points of reference with regard to security. Despite the absence of common borders (other than in the Bering Strait) and US assurances that we harbored no aggressive intentions, the Soviets were never convinced they possessed adequate defenses. Fear of "capitalist encirclement"—though a smoke screen—was invoked whenever the Soviets sought to justify their larger arsenals.

Establishing rapport during the initial phase of the negotiations was hampered by a third fact: Soviet secrecy. Westerners instinctively seek to divulge enough information to facilitate negotiations, stopping short only when it would hurt our national security. The Soviets seek to divulge nothing—even if it means the bargaining process becomes stalemated. At times, this was carried to ridiculous extremes. For example, I once attempted to make "small talk" with the newly arrived wife of a Soviet negotiator. I asked her, in Russian, how many children she had. She became quite agitated. Sidling over to one of their known KGB operatives, she asked if it were permissible for her to divulge such information.

Finally, the entire Western negotiating experience hinges on compromise. Because negotiators of each generation have inculcated this concept in their successors, compromise has become an American institution. Compromise, however, is not part of the Russian culture and language. In fact, the Soviets use the word in a pejorative sense: only "weak" entities compromise. Perhaps not surprisingly, in the period prior to the Vladivostok Accords—and throughout SALT II—genuine compromise was conspicuous by its absence.

Following the opening phase of the negotiations, facts ceased being mere annoyances; they were transformed into genuinely threatening propositions. With the exception of the hopeful March 1977 Carter initiatives, the entire two and one-half years were beset with frustrations.

The first fact encountered during the second phase of negotiations was that divine intervention—or something like it—would be required to translate the abstract Vladivostok aidememoire into concrete treaty language. Westerners are impatient, especially if progress is impeded. The Soviets have patience—or, if your prefer, obstinance. This meant they would not budge from their interpretation of the Ford–Brezhnev Accord. Every time the United States sought to define the treaty in specific terms, the Soviets simply reiterated their previous generalizations.

A related—and more depressing—fact which came to the fore during SALT II's second phase consisted of semantic distortion. For Westerners, words—and the context in which they are used—have precise, unequivocal connotations. For the Soviets, words mean—as they did to Alice in Wonderland—whatever they want them to mean. For example, on one occasion I thought I was about to achieve a breakthrough because a Soviet general had agreed to discuss the "characteristics" of the BACKFIRE bomber. (I should note the Soviets would never address themselves to the capabilities of Soviet systems, arguing that to do so would reveal military secrets.) Referring to some charts in *Interavia,* a Swiss magazine, I proceeded to show the general—in objective terms—that the BACKFIRE possessed intercontinental capabilities. "No," the Soviet general said, "you have not presented objective arguments but only engineer's estimates. Figures lie and liars figure. Therefore, your arguments are subjective. But Leonid Brezhnev has said that the USSR will never use the BACKFIRE against the United States. And that is the objective truth." His remarks left me incredulous and speechless.

Self-image is a crucial factor in international affairs—just as it is in interpersonal relations. I believe the United States entered into SALT II with a realistic self-image; we were cognizant of both our assets and liabilities. In contrast, the Soviets often displayed a serious inferiority complex. On one occassion, a Soviet general told me it would be equitable if the Soviets were permitted greater numbers of weapons because the United States possessed better technology. Later, when I alluded to US technological advantages, the Soviet general was highly incensed: "Whatever the US can do, the USSR can do," he maintained.

Finally, the Soviets gave some indications during this second phase that they had begun to formulate a conception of compromise. Unfortunately, it was not a quid pro quo exchange; rather, compromise to the Soviets meant "What's mine is mine; what's yours is negotiable."

The final two years and three months of negotiating SALT II were a period of great disillusionment. During this last phase, the United States was smarting from the Kremlin's rejection of our March 1977 proposals. Sensing our vulnerability, the Soviets pressed us to the utmost. The types of agreements we were reaching with the Soviets were indeed injurious to our national security.

One constraint under which we labored was time. Successive US administrations had told us we could not let time pass without some "progress" to show for it. The Soviets seemed to have time on their hands and made progress just by using the calendar. When the United States made a proposal, it wanted closure with the Soviets in the shortest possible time. If we could not achieve this "progress," we became nervous and made yet another proposal before the first was resolved. Consequently, the Soviets were able to "pick the raisins from the cake." That is, they took what they liked from each of our successive proposals without regard for what we expected of them. Thus, the Soviets took the raisins and left us holding the dough.

Another Soviet technique was to suggest continually that we reach agreement "in principle" and let the lower echelons work out the details. The September 1978 Carter–Gromyko conference was an example; the Soviets pocketed all points favorable to them and insisted points advantageous to the United States be renegotiated from scratch. The result was predictable: agreement could be reached only if we compromised halfway between their new position and ours. In other words, we met them three-quarters of the way toward the original Soviet position.

The Soviet "red herring" technique became an all too familiar negotiating fact of life. The United States tried to resolve disputed issues by dealing with the specifics; the Soviets sought to resolve all issues in their favor by introducing new, often extraneous, elements into the argument. Both sides expended great amounts of time and energy debating the merits of the new elements. Eventually, the Soviets would drop these points, and we would feel we had triumphed. It was, of course, a Pyrrhic victory; we often would settle on the previous Soviet terms without having budged them from their original position.

*   *   *   *   *   *   *

These were the negotiating facts I believe we faced in SALT II. As a result of them, the United States was presented with an unequal treaty injurious to our national security. It gave the Soviets a unilateral right to 308 heavy missile launchers; the US was given no way of compensating for such an important asymmetry. It gave the Soviets the right to exclude 375 intercontinental range-capable BACKFIRE bombers from their totals. It did not provide for equal levels of strategic forces as called for by the Public Law 92–448, the Jackson Amendment.

Moreover, SALT II—as initialed by Presidents Carter and Brezhnev in June 1979—was unverifiable. One cannot verify what cannot be defined. The SALT II treaty did not adequately define the systems being limited, notably MIRVed missile launchers and cruise missiles. Also, it gave the Soviets the right to encrypt telemetry, thereby permitting them to test more than one new type of ICBM.

Moreover, SALT II undermined NATO cohesion—a sure weakness the Soviets would seek to exploit. Prior to SALT II, our allies could rely upon US strategic power to provide the "umbrella" in the event of an outbreak and escalation of hostilities in Europe. Now that it has become clear to European military and strategic analysts that a SALT II agreement would codify a situation locking the United States into a strategically inferior position vis-a-vis the USSR, the Allies saw the need to improve both their conventional and theater nuclear forces.

For these reasons, I informed the Joint Chiefs of Staff on 21 May 1979 that I could not support the Administration's position; I tendered my resignation from my SALT II post and my Army commission.

*   *   *   *   *   *   *

In conclusion, it may well be that SALT I was an experiment; consequently, one should not judge too harshly the imprudent hopes attached to it. As one observer of strategic affairs has noted:

> SALT I did not establish arms control nor has it imposed strategically relevant arms limitations on the Soviet Union. It permitted the Soviet Union to do what it intended to do anyway: Soviet economic and technological weaknesses were the only constraining factors. The United States, by contrast, accepted numerical inferiority and was lulled into complacency about this situation.

But SALT I is past, and we now must face the present. And just as surely, we must face the future—a time when we will certainly be negotiating arms control with the Soviet Union. We must embark upon that future and upon arms control negotiations keeping in mind the words of Edward Gibbon. In his celebrated work *The Decline and Fall of the Roman Empire,* Gibbon noted:

> The savage nations of the globe are the common enemies of civilized society; and we may enquire with anxious curiosity, whether Europe is still threatened with a repetition of those calamities which formerly oppressed the arms and institutions of Rome.

It is clear the US public was ahead of its previous leadership in the realization the United States needed to improve its defense posture and do so rapidly. We not only need to spend more; we also need to spend it in the right places and in accordance with a long-range strategic plan.

It also is clear the·United States must put negotiations in their proper place. Unlike us, the Soviets first establish goals and objectives. Only as a third priority did they enter into negotiations on their strategic arms. The United States, on the other hand, has had its priorities reversed. First, it decided to negotiate; then it allowed negotiations to influence its design and deployment of forces; only last did it look around to see what could be achieved with its truncated forces. It is high time the United States put its priorities in the proper order.

Finally, we must recognize the Soviets have a long-range objective of promoting wars of liberation in order to spread "good socialism" at the expense of "bad capitalism". We need to be on guard to counter the Soviet tactic of insisting on a "normalization" and revival of detente, a tactic which is certain to follow consolidation of their gains in Afghanistan. They will simply use this ploy to assist them in their drive towards warm water ports and control over Middle Eastern oil.

Inevitably, we have returned to negotiating arms control with the Soviets. We have done so because it is in the interest of both superpowers. Hopefully, we will be able to negotiate from a position of strength. We will—if we have learned anything from our experience—have lost our naivete concerning Soviet objectives and motivations. We will—if we employ good common sense—recognize how the Soviets negotiate and thus prevent—or at least minimize—losses at the negotiating table.

It is toward this end I have presented these facts.

The Soviet Union, the Arms Trade, and the Third World

Rajan Menon©

The value of arms purchased by developing countries between 1968 and 1978 rose from $4 billion to $16 billion.[1] Accompanying this proliferation of weapons has been a growth in the literature devoted to assessing its causes, effects, and prospects for control. The topics that have been explored include the motives of the major suppliers, the extent to which they have been able to use arms transfers to fulfill foreign policy goals, the impact on stability in troubled regions, and the relationship between economic development and the acquisition of arms. This analysis is concerned with the Soviet Union, the second largest supplier of weapons to the Third World. It addresses a number of related issues concerning the Soviet military sales program: its scale, scope, and nature; the political and economic motives underlying it; and its utility as means for the pursuit of external objectives.

The Dynamics of the Arms Trade

While the adverse consequences of the "creeping militarization"[2] created in the Third World by the arms trade have been commented upon extensively, few serious observers expect that a greater awareness of its dangers will restrain either buyers or sellers. The pessimism about the prospects for slowing the worldwide transfer of arms is, for a variety of reasons, well founded.

The international system lacks strong executive, legislative, and judicial institutions and as a result is bereft of centralization, predictability, and institutional mechanisms for orderly change. International organizations and law do provide for a modicum of order, but they lack legitimacy and consequently are not comparable in their efficacy to the institutions and body of law found in stable domestic systems. Also lacking is a set of widely accepted norms concerning appropriate political means and ends. Instead, there is contention—frequently outside an institutional setting—based upon discordant ideologies, conflicting economic claims, and divergent perceptions of an acceptable status quo. Since the characteristics of the international system create an environment in which the possession of military power is vital, it is clear why those states unable to produce a wide range of weapons must, and will,

---

buy them.

Aside from being quasi-anarchic, the international system is also characterized by interdependence; the security and economic welfare of a state is linked to the actions of others. Since the technology to manufacture an array of modern weapons is unevenly distributed, and given the importance of military power in the international system, it is not surprising that arms transfers have been regarded by those able to export weapons as a major instrument that can be used to shape the policies of other states. In East/West competition, arms transfers have been, and will continue to be, used to compete for influence in the Third World; in the North/South arena, they will be used to coopt influential Southern states. Arms sales will also be stimulated by the purchasing power petrodollars give to oil-producing states.

The future spread of weapons in the less developed countries will also depend on the capacities of Third World armament industries. Between 1965 and 1975, 31 countries in Asia, Africa, and Latin America began to manufacture weapons through a combination of licensed production and indigenous development. In this quest for self-sufficiency, a minority composed of India, Israel, South Africa, and Brazil led the others, having begun the production of aircraft, missiles, armored vehicles, naval ships, small arms, electronics, and aeronautical engines.[3] Future efforts towards self-sufficiency in arms by several developing countries will continue, and the transfer of weapons technology—as opposed to the weapons themselves—will be an even more important part of the global arms trade than it is presently. But it will continue to be the transfer of arms—not growing production in developing countries—which accounts for most of the increase in Third World armaments.

Although the rate of generational change in weaponry was faster in the interwar period than it has been in the postwar years, the time and expense involved in research and development (R&D) and the costs of production have increased steeply.[4] Given the financial constraints with which developing countries must contend, they will be hard-pressed to meet all their defense needs through their own industries. Even in India and Israel, where indigenous production is relatively advanced, imports continue to be sizable, while in licensed manufacture, despite a steady increase in the percentage of locally made parts, critical components continue to be imported. Further, R&D expenditures are small (in India less than two percent of total defense expenditure between 1969 and 1978), and the defense industries of even the most advanced weapons producers in the developing world will be unable to keep up with rapid changes in future weapons technology.[5]

Recent developments in weapons technology also caution against optimism regarding the prospects for any marked and sustained decline in the global arms trade. Although the effect that precision-guided munitions (PGMs) will have on the mode of warfare is disputed,[6] it is

155

generally agreed that they will increase the rate of attrition of armor and aircraft and contribute to the growth of the arms trade by increasing the importance of greater forces, a larger inventory, and the availability of suppliers who are both able and willing to replace stocks depleted in battle. The Soviet Union's relatively cheap and less complicated armaments may be attractive to buyers confronting the prospect of high attrition rates and financial costs in a weapons milieu in which the PGM has gained acceptance.

Moscow, the Arms Trade, and the Third World

A significant development in the global arms trade has been the emergence of the Soviet Union as a major supplier. Although it had the second largest gross national product (GNP) during the 1930s, the Soviet share of the market in major weapons was negligible. From 1930–1945, it accounted for less than six percent of the market in combat aircraft and tanks and for ten percent in armored personnel carriers. By 1968, the situation had changed decisively; the USSR now was responsible for almost 30 percent of the combat aircraft, helicopters, tanks, and submarines sold.[7]

Several developments account for this growth in Soviet military sales. The rise in defense production during the Second World War and the subsequent progress made in economic reconstruction provided the means to enter the arms market. The favorable context to do so was supplied by the economic losses suffered during the war by Britain, France, and Italy, and the consequent reduction of their global role in general and their role as weapons suppliers in particular. The opportunity was afforded by the steady pace of decolonization in the 1950s and 1960s which witnessed the birth of several new nations who viewed the acquisition of military power and the transition from weakness to strength as an integral part of the overall objective of development. With the abandonment of Stalin's Eurocentric strategy and the adoption of a global foreign policy under Khrushchev and Brezhnev,[8] arms transfers became major instrument for competition with the United States in the Third World.

But it is not the expanding Soviet military sales program that has been responsible for the decline in the American position in the international arms market. As Table 1 indicates, although the United States continued to be the largest exporter of arms in 1968 and 1977, its market share declined from 50.3 percent to 39.2 percent. The share of its major competitor, the Soviet Union, also fell, although only slightly. What accounts for the diminishing US role in the global arms trade is not a surge in Soviet weapons transfer but the reemergence of some of the major suppliers of the interwar period—Britain, France, and Germany. Thus, between 1968 and 1977, while all major arms suppliers increased the absolute value of their exports, France's went up by 42 percent, West Germany's by 35 percent, and Britain's by 28 percent. In contrast, the Soviet Union and the United States expanded the value of their transfers by a relatively smaller 13 percent and 6 percent, respectively.[9] Another, more recent, trend not reflected in Table 1 is the emerging role in the arms trade—either through direct sales or retransfers—of 14 developing countries whose contribution to total sales was 6 percent in 1976 and 4 percent in 1977.[10]

Table 1:   Market Shares of Major Arms Exporters

(percentage of total deliveries)

	1968		1977
US	50.3	US	39.2
USSR	29.8	USSR	29.5
France	3.4	France	7.4
United Kingdom	3.0	United Kingdom	4.7
Poland	2.8	West Germany	4.5
China	2.6	Czechoslovakia	2.7
Others	8.1	Others	12.0

Note: Total arms exports were $8,670 million in 1968, and $16,700 million in 1977.

Source: US Arms Control and Disarmament Agency, *World Military Expenditures and Arms Transfers 1968–1977* (Washington: Arms Control and Disarmament Agency 1979), Table D, p. 18.

Owing to the surge in oil prices since 1973, regional rivalries and conflicts in the Middle East, the Horn of Africa, and South Asia, and superpower competition, the majority of arms exports went to the developing world—68 percent in 1968 and 78 percent in 1977.[11] As Table 2 shows, on the supply side, the pattern which emerges in total arms sales reappears in transfers to the developing countries as a whole and to OPEC as a subset. Between 1973 and 1977, the US and the USSR accounted for over 65 percent of the weapons exported to these two groups, with the United States being the largest supplier.

Of the 117 developing countries listed in the Arms Control and Disarmament Agency's data, the Soviets exported to 41 while the United States supplied arms to 58. Because of the proximity and strategic importance of the regions, the Soviet arms transfer program is focused on the Middle East and South Asia. From 1973 through 1977, sales to Egypt, Iraq, Syria, India, and Libya accounted for 59.4 percent of all Soviet transfers to the developing world.

While the United States has led the Soviet Union in exports to the Third World, Table 3 shows that within the communist system, the Soviets are the major exporters by far, having easily overshadowed their archrival, China. Chinese transfers amounted to a mere 3.8 percent of Soviet deliveries between 1954–1968 and fell to 2.8 percent over the 1969–1978 period. In addition, if one assumes that—with the

157

partial exception of Romania—the external activity of the Warsaw Pact nations generally complements Soviet objectives, it is significant that Chinese arms sales were exceeded sizably by Eastern Europe in every year since 1972.

Table 2: Sources and Diversion of Conventional Arms Exports 1973-77

| | (Millions Current Dollars) | | | | | | |
	Total	US	USSR	France	UK	W. Germany	Other
World	71,320	27,010	23,370	4,490	3,235	2,225	10,990
Total		(37.9)	(32.8)	(6.3)	(4.5)	(3.1)	(15.4)
Developing	52,334	21,614	16,495	3,360	2,465	1,925	6,475
	(73.4)a	(41.3)	(31.5)	(6.4)	(4.7)	(3.7)	(12.4)
OPEC	18,118	6,823	5,360	1,385	1,215	950	2,385
	(25.4)b	(37.7)	(29.6)	(7.6)	(6.7)	(5.2)	(13.2)
	(34.6)c						

Note: Figures within parentheses are rounded percentage shares.
a = % of World total; b = % of World total;
c = % of total transfers to developing countries

Source: Based on US Arms Control and Disarmament Agency, *World Military Expenditures and Arms Transfers 1968–1977*, Table IV, p. 155.

Table 3. Soviet, East European, and Chinese Military Relations with Developing Countries: Arms Agreement and Deliveries

(Millions of Dollars)

| | Agreements | | | | Deliveries | | | |
	Total	USSR	E. Europe	China	Total	USSR	E. Europe	China
Total	33,815	29,655	3,260	910	28,675	25,310	2,570	760
1955-68	6,555	5,495	810	250	5,505	4,585	745	175
1969	485	360	125	NEGL	555	450	80	25
1970	1,265	1,150	50	65	1,105	995	80	30
1971	1,790	1,590	120	80	1,045	865	120	60
1972	1,865	1,635	150	80	1,360	1,215	70	75
1973	2,965	2,810	130	25	3,330	3,130	120	80
1974	4,840	4,225	530	85	2,500	2,310	165	25
1975	2,290	2,035	215	40	2,190	1,845	225	85
1976	3,730	3,375	215	145	2,970	2,575	315	80
1977	5,710	5,215	450	50	3,910	3,515	325	70
1978	2,320	1,765	465	90	4,205	3,825	325	55

Note: 1) NEGL = Less than $500,000; 2) Yearly figures have been rounded.

Source: US Central Intelligence Agency, National Foreign Assessment Center, *Communist Aid Activities in Non–Communist Less Developed Countries*, ER 79-10412U, September 1979, p. 2.

Since the Soviet arms transfer program got underway in 1955, it has undergone some important changes. While in the 1950s and early 1960s the value of Soviet military exports and economic aid to developing countries was roughly comparable, since 1968 the ratio has been about 2.5 to 1 in favor of arms.[12] Clearly, arms transfers have become an increasingly important instrument of Soviet diplomacy.

The program has also become more flexible since the mid-1960s. Until then, arms were provided exclusively to nonaligned states who could not be considered pro-Western. While supplies to such customers were maintained in the succeeding years (except where bilateral relations deteriorated—as in Egypt, Somalia, and Indonesia), conservative states with traditionally strong ties to the West also received Soviet arms—Iran in 1967 and 1973, Pakistan in 1968, and Kuwait in 1977.

The terms of supply have also shifted since 1973. Prior to that year, Soviet arms were usually provided on credit at 2.5 percent interest with a 10–12 year amortization period. Repayments were made in local currency which the Soviets then used to finance imports from the recipient. While this arrangement built up Soviet economic ties with the developing country and supplied the USSR with a flow of raw materials, the political objectives of forging cordial relations and countering Western influence outweighed considerations of economic gain. Although the political rationale for arms exports has by no means dissipated, in recent years Moscow has concluded major arms deals with Algeria, Iraq, and Libya in exchange for hard cash, while other countries—such as Egypt and Syria—received financing from oil-producing states for imports on similar terms.[13] While the commercial facet of Soviet military sales will be discussed in the next section, it should be emphasized that the financial considerations behind Soviet arms transfers have not pushed the political motives to the background. As the $1.7 billion Indo–Soviet arms accord announced in May 1980 shows, Moscow is still prepared to supply arms on lenient terms for political reasons.[14]

The final change involves the types of weapons being exported. In the 1950s and 1960s, transfers to the developing world primarily consisted of obsolete, second-line equipment being phased out as the postwar modernization of the Soviet Armed Forces proceeded. An examination of recent Soviet transfers shows that this practice now has been superseded by a willingness to supply the latest equipment, some of which is still being introduced into the Warsaw Pact forces. For example, recent supplies to Algeria, Libya, Iraq, Syria, and India have included *MiG–23BN* and *MiG–25* aircraft, *T–72* tanks, *BMP* armored personnel carriers, and SA–9 surface-to-air missiles.[15] While the reasons underlying this shift are not clear, in the case of the Arab states, the importance of the purchasing power of petrodollars cannot be dismissed.

Except in India, this large influx of sophisticated weaponry has led to the presence of a sizable number of Soviet military advisers and technicians in these countries. Of the 12,070 Soviet and East European personnel stationed in noncommunist less developed countries in 1978, 6530—or 54 percent—were in Algeria, Libya, Syria, and Iraq.[16] This reliance on Soviet technocrats is likely to continue into the forseeable future; although the oil revenues available to these states—indirectly, in the Syrian case—will enable them to request advanced weaponry, they lack the infrastructure and skilled manpower pool to undertake the tasks of maintenance, repair, and training on an independent basis.[17]

The Economics of Arms Transfers

Although several studies allude to the possibility Soviet arms transfers are shaped not only by political considerations but by economic ones as well, few have pursued the matter much further. The neglect of the economic aspects of Soviet arms transfers has many causes. Most scholars have felt the political gains Moscow makes from its arms exports are more relevant and significant. Also, although data on the value, direction, and content of Soviet military exports are available from a number of sources, the information available on the economic reasons behind them is both inadequate and unreliable. The insufficient attention given to this aspect of arms exports must also be viewed as a reflection of the dominant tendency to "blackbox" the internal workings of the Soviet political process and to explain Soviet foreign policy as primarily a continuing response to changing external threats and opportunities perceived by the Kremlin leadership.

When Soviet arms transfers to the developing world began, the motives were primarily political. Khrushchev had decided to abandon Stalin's hostile posture toward noncommunist Third World nations and to respond to Dulles' strategy of containment by forging ties with the newly independent states. Apart from this, Khrushchev was quick to realize, in view of the vastness of the area and the changes taking place there, the developing world would be a major venue of Soviet–American competition. He was equally quick to understand that the export of arms to the developing countries would be a major means with which to pursue Soviet objectives.

As noted earlier, the terms under which the USSR provided weapons to developing nations in the 1950s and 1960s were fairly liberal—the interest rates were low, and repayment was to be made in local currency over a fairly long period. That the conditions were not more stringent was due to many reasons, among them the financial constraints—particularly the shortage of hard currency—under which developing countries operated, the eagerness of the Soviets to establish a presence in the Third World, and the willingness of the US at this time to supply arms free or on easy terms of credit.

160

Even during this period, however, the Soviets were not oblivious to economic considerations. Grants accounted for an insignificant share of their arms transfers and a provision was made that the outstanding balance on a loan would be cleared with convertible currency in the event depressed world market price levels made it impossible for the developing country to liquidate its debts through the export of commodities.[18] It is also clear that the repayment provisions governing Soviet arms supplies assured the Soviet economy a reliable supply of goods for which convertible currency did not have to be spent. There were also periodic allegations the Soviets, as well as the East Europeans, were reselling these commodities—made up primarily of raw materials and some consumer goods—to the West for hard currency at concessional prices, thereby making inroads into the export markets of the developing countries.

Yet, it is unwarranted to conclude that in this period Soviet arms transfers were economically motivated to any significant degree; any commercial benefits derived were incidential to their main purpose, which was political. For the developing countries, repayment in exports was clearly preferable to the expenditure of scarce convertible currency, and there were no instances in which the Soviets refused to reschedule debts and proceeded to exercise their contractual right to collect payment in hard currency.

In recent years, interest in the economic rationale for Soviet arms exports has been kindled by reports Moscow has been spurred by the bonanza accumulated by oil-rich Algeria, Libya, and Iraq to move toward hard currency as the medium of payment. A 1977 Central Intelligence Agency report maintained the Soviets had earned $1.5 billion in hard currency from arms sales in that year, and a CIA publication which appeared in the following year asserted "Almost all the arms for commodities trade of earlier years has given way to payments in hard currency."[19]

The Soviet Union's need for hard currency is indisputable. The "extensive" growth strategy under which it attained rapid rates of growth by progressively increasing labor and capital investments is becoming less appropriate under present conditions.[20] The demographic effect of World War II, the decline in the birth rate, and the utilization of available surplus rural labor have combined to create a situation in which the number of new entrants into the work force will drop in the future. Further, the rising aspirations of the consumer may make it difficult to reinvest increasing amounts of current output. Soviet planners realize the slowdown in growth rates since the mid–1950s necessitates the adoption of an "intensive" strategy which— by increasing incentives, labor productivity, and the level of technology in the economy—seeks to expand the output per composite unit of labor and capital invested.[21]

In the course of making the "intensive" approach an integral part of the Soviet growth model, hard currency will play a major role in a number of ways. In an effort to upgrade the technological level of their economy, the Soviets have increased sharply their imports of industrial machinery and equipment from the West; these purchases rose from $510 million in 1965 to about $5 billion 10 years later.[22] Given their petroleum and raw material commitments to Eastern Europe and Cuba, the periodic large-scale purchases of grain from abroad, and the noncompetitive nature of many of their industrial goods, technology imports have been financed to a large extent by Western credits and the issue of promissory notes. As a result—and despite the hard currency earned by exports, gold sales, tourism, and arms sales—the Soviets owed the West between $13.5 and $15 billion at the end of 1978.[23] Sizable imports are likely to continue since a steady process of transfer is needed to keep pace with the rapid changes in modern technology. In addition, the Soviet ability to increase oil exports to the West—which presently account for almost 50 percent of their hard currency earnings—will depend on the access to the drilling technology to tap the oil reserves of Siberia and expand their presently limited off-shore drilling efforts.[24]

Against this background, the suggestion the Soviets have a clear incentive to expand their export of arms for hard currency and to reconsider the commodity repayment scheme appears plausible. Yet, this conclusion should be weighed against some other facts. Between 1968 and 1977, exports never exceeded 4.7 percent of the Soviet gross national product in any year, and arms exports as a percentage of total exports averaged 13 percent over the same period (greater than the average for the US, France, Britain, and Germany). This does not support that the conclusion weapons exports are a major source of Soviet earnings abroad.[25]

However, since the major portion of Soviet trade is conducted with socialist and developing countries and does not—for the most part—involve hard currency, it is still necessary to examine whether arms sales abroad account for a significant portion of total Soviet hard currency receipts. Data pertaining to this question are presented in Table 4. It is apparent that since 1972, the importance of arms sales as a contributor to the hard currency chest has increased. Nevertheless, while absolute earnings from this source generally have risen steadily from 1970 to 1978, their share of overall hard currency income has remained fairly static since 1973. With the exception of 1973, arms sales have never provided more than nine percent of all hard currency earned, and nonmilitary exports play a far greater role in this regard.

In view of the important Soviet economic stake in acquiring convertible currency, there is still the question of whether they will step up future deliveries of arms to the oil-rich Middle East. For Algeria, Libya, and Iraq—short of a major war in the region—the need to absorb the large orders already placed with the Soviet Union will work

Table 4:   Sources of Soviet Hard Currency Earnings

(Millions of Dollars)

	1970	1971	1972	1973	1974	1975	1976	1977	1978
Exports (f.o.b.)	2,201	2,630	2,801	4,790	7,470	7,835	9,721	11,345	13,157
Gold Sales	0	79	38	900	1,178	725	1,369	1,618	2,673
Arms Sales	100	87	122	1,345	1,000	793	1,108	1,500	1,644
	(3.5)	(2.6)	(3.5)	(16.3)	(9.0)	(7.5)	(8.1)	(9.4)	(8.4)
Tourism (net)	43	45	53	116	117	136	150	175	200
Merchandise freight	400	260	250	640	640	520	640	710	700
Other Transporta-tion (net)	120	110	120	230	330	330	390	390	410
Interest from Assets in Western Banks	NA	87	110	252	405	234	288	292	685
Income from Direct Investments Abroad	0	0	0	0	1	2	8	2	3
Total	2,864	3,298	3,494	8,273	11,141	10,575	13,674	16,032	19,472

Note: The figures in parentheses have been rounded and denote earnings from arms sales as a percentage of total hard curreny income.

Source: Paul G. Ericson and Ronald S. Miller, "Soviet Economic Behavior: A Balance of Payments Perspective" in US Congress, Joint Economic Committee, *Soviet Economy in a Time of Change,* Vol. 2, 96th Congress, 1st session, 10 October 1979, Table I, p.212.

against any steady and big increases in demand for some years. In addition, the massive acquisitions from the USSR since 1973 may well lead these states to use the bargaining power conferred on them by their cash reserves to diversify future sources of supply for political reasons. Iraq, for instance, may turn to suppliers other than, or in addition to, the USSR to restock its inventory following the war with Iran. Algeria, Libya, and Iraq, while purchasing large amounts of Soviet weaponry, carefully have avoided relying on a single supplier. From 1968 to 1977, Libya bought $490 million from Western European sources, Iraq—$370 million, and Algeria—$240 million.[26] Even if future demand from these Arab states were to increase markedly, the Soviets would have to take into account the effect the prolonged export of large quantities of front-line equipment would have on the needs of both their own forces as well as those of the other Warsaw Pact members. Finally, whatever the incentive to resort increasingly to the sale of arms on a hard cash basis, it will have to be balanced against the abiding interest which Moscow has in continuing to supply politically important and strategically located non-OPEC states such as Afghanistan, India, Ethiopia, and Vietnam whose hard currency reserves are limited.

Thus, arms sales presently account for only a small portion of the Soviet Union's annual hard currency income, and there is little reason to expect their future potential to be significantly greater. This is not to suggest the USSR will not receive such payments from its oil-producing customers. Indeed, it would be strange if the Soviets—given their crucial need for hard currency—were to accept soft currency from the Algerians, Iraqis, and Libyans, whose foreign exchange holdings are so vast. In fact, far from being onerous, such an arrangement may well be preferred by these states for it infuses two critical elements into the donor-recipient relationship: an element of equality, and an implied willingness to shop elsewhere if any hesitance is shown in meeting the demand for front-line hardware.

Arms and Influence

As noted in the first section, interdependence and competition in contemporary international politics create the need for means that can be used to shape the behavior of others. Along with economic aid and cultural diplomacy, arms transfers represent a salient instrument for this purpose; as a result, most studies on arms exports have been concerned with their effectiveness for acquiring influence. Although any effort to gauge the relationship between arms transfers and influence presupposes a clarification of what is meant by the latter term, few analyses devote much time to this conceptual chore.[27]

Influence is a means through which one state induces another to do or not to do something. In attempting to exert influence, a variety of resources can be employed, of which arms transfers constitute one. Three considerations must be kept in mind when assessing the degree of influence which state A has over state B. First, if A prevails upon B to act in a desired manner despite the high costs (political or economic) incurred by B, then A's influence is higher than would be the case if no significant costs were involved for B. Second, influence can manifest itself both when A gets B to take an action B otherwise would not and in cases when A makes it possible for B to so something which is mutually beneficial. In the former instance, there is a coercive dimension in the relationship; thus, A's influence is higher than in the latter situation. Third, a clear distinction must be drawn between presence and influence. The economic aid and arms provide a presence; the question of whether this ultimately yields influence should not be prejudged.

It is paradoxical that despite vast deliveries to their major customers, neither the US nor the Soviet Union has been able to exercise much control over how and when their weapons are used. Not only were American arms used in Turkey's invasion and occupation of Cyprus, the US arms embargo failed to bring about a withdrawal of forces and ultimately was lifted in 1978 to facilitate US access to intelligence facilities and to prevent any loosening of Turkey's ties with NATO.[28]

The Soviets have had similar experiences. During the Bangladesh crisis of 1971, despite repeated Soviet pleas for a negotiated settlement which would respond to Bengali grievances while maintaining the unity of Pakistan,[29] the Soviets—who since the 1960s had been concerned by the growth of Sino–Pakistani amity—were unable to prevent the Indian government from concluding by the end of the year that it would have to act militarily in order to rid itself of the refugee burden created by the exodus of people fleeing battle-stricken East Pakistan. In fact, when war broke out, the Soviets moved to supply arms to India and to provide diplomatic support for Indian operations in East Pakistan by vetoing Security Council ceasefire resolutions favored by Beijing and Washington.

In Egypt, where Anwar Sadat declared 1971 "the year of decision" and repeatedly sought advanced Soviet weapons, Cairo's heavy and longstanding dependence on Soviet weapons failed to provide Moscow with reliable leverage. Despite their desire to avoid a major war in the region at a time when US–Soviet detente was delicately being welded together, and their pessimism regarding the prospects of a good showing by the Arabs, the Soviets proved to have little influence. Sadat's autobiography makes it clear the Soviets paid a price for trying to head off precipitous Egyptian military action by stalling his insistent requests for arms. Sadat's resentment of what he viewed as an imperious effort to tie his hands built up to the point where, in July 1971, the Soviet military personnel stationed in Egypt were ordered to leave and access to the onshore facilities crucial to the operations of the Soviet Mediterranean fleet was terminated.[30] Although it is true the Soviets received advanced notification about the Yom Kippur war of 1973, it was not a request for Soviet permission but a fait accompli.[31] Once the war broke out—given the stake they had built up in Egypt over the years—the Soviets quickly were drawn into the crisis; they airlifted large supplies of arms to Egypt and Syria and even threatened to intervene when Israeli forces moved farther across the West Bank of the Suez Canal after the breakdown of the 22 October ceasefire.

The Soviet–Egyptian relationship also reveals a feature of arms sales which limits a supplier's influence: the weapons transferred are retained by a recipient and used in ways deemed appropriate even after political ties between buyer and seller go sour. After Soviet–Egyptian relations turned hostile, the Soviets could do little to prevent Sadat from selling Soviet-supplied arms to the Afghan guerrillas.

Other cases point to a similar Soviet inability to control the end use of the weapons they supply to developing countries. In May 1976, the Soviets were unable to prevent Syrian President Hafez al-Assad from intervening in the Lebanese civil war against the Moslem–PLO forces despite their clear opposition to his move. The fact the Syrian army was equipped with Soviet weapons did little to deter Assad or enhance Moscow's influence.[32] Apart from press reports critical of Syria's actions, Moscow failed to resort to any punitive actions that might have provoked indignation and defiance from Damascus.

Similarly, a year later, the Soviets wanted to avoid a choice between their existing ties with Somalia and the relationship they were forging with the radical Ethiopian military regime which had emerged after the September 1974 ouster of Haile Sellasie. However, their past arms transfers to Somalia proved useless in preventing Siad Barre from invading the Ogaden region of Ethiopia in August 1977—in support of Somali irredentist claims—and they were forced to make such a choice. The decision to back Ethiopia led to the abrogation of the Soviet-Somali friendship treaty and the loss of access to the ports and shore-based facilities which had enabled the Soviets to expand markedly the on-station time of their naval deployment in the Indian Ocean.[33]

This does not mean that no relationship exists between arms transfers and influence. In India, for example, the $1.1 billion in arms provided by the Soviets between 1973 and 1977—plus the links New Delhi perceives between Indo–Soviet relations and India's security concerns vis-a-vis China—have made for a stable relationship which has weathered intermittent uncertainties.[34] Further, as demonstrated by its tepid response to the Soviet invasions of Czechoslovakia (August 1968) and Afghanistan (December 1979) and its recognition of the Vietnamese-backed Heng Samrin government of Kampuchea in July 1980,[35] India has been willing to take Soviet foreign policy interests into account in instances where the cost is low. Similarly, the radical Arab states have acquired an incentive to maintain close ties with the Soviets because of the importance of Soviet weaponry and Soviet support for their objectives in the Middle East, while Angola values the Soviet–Cuban presence and the availability of Soviet arms as a form of insurance against South Africa (which mounted large-scale offensives in June 1980 and August 1981 against Angola-based SWAPO guerillas) and the dogged UNITA guerillas of Jonas Savimbi.

The USSR thus has been able to employ arms transfers to create a stable presence in a number of countries by supporting their security goals and to evoke responsiveness toward Soviet interests when the recipient views the costs as tolerable. The Soviets, however, have not been able to induce their major arms customers to make costly adjustments in policy to propitiate the USSR. Iraq's Baathist government, despite large weapons acquisitions from the Soviet Union, has taken a number of steps at variance with Soviet preferences. Soviet displeasure did not prevent the execution of 20 soldiers—and the incarceration of others—in May 1978 on charges of setting up pro-Soviet cells. In March 1979, Iraq—together with Syria—remained neutral and sought to mediate a ceasefire in the war between the two Yemens, despite Soviet support for South Yemen. More recently, the Iraqis have strongly criticized the Soviet invasion of Afghanistan.[36] In Angola, a Soviet presence has been established through economic aid, arms supplies, and 1300 military advisers from Eastern Europe and the USSR. Although this has created a durable relationship, the Angolans insist it does not prevent Angola, as an independent and sovereign nonaligned state, from developing its relations with capitalist countries."[37] As a demonstration of this intent, Angola has worked in a pragmatic spirit with several Western banks and corporations.[38]

For countries which have received the bulk of their military equipment from the Soviet Union, a sharp deterioration in bilateral relations undoubtedly would pose the problem of finding an alternate supplier and acquiring the spare parts needed to keep the existing inventory operative. When Sadat turned to China for *MiG* engines after Soviet–Egyptian relations soured in the years following the Yom Kippur war, Moscow pointedly reminded him that the Chinese would never be able to supply the required quantity.[39] The Soviets also forbade India—which produces Soviet aircraft under license—from meeting an Egyptian request for spare parts.[40] Nonetheless, a heavy dependence on Soviet weaponry has not deterred states from turning away from the USSR when they felt close ties with the Soviet Union were no longer in their interests. Sadat annulled the Soviet–Egyptian treaty in 1976, blocked further Soviet access to Egyptian ports, and, in the years which followed, looked to the United States for arms.[41] More recently, Somali has followed this example, giving the US access to ports and airfields—once used by the Soviets—in exchange for arms.

If the Soviet Union, as in the case of the United States, has acquired only a limited and specific type of influence through its arms transfers, there are three explanations for this. First, the global arms trade presently is characterized by multiple sources of supply. A developing country can thus obtain its weapons from more than one source, thereby guarding against the political implication of excessive dependence on a single supplier. Or, in cases where the major portion of its inventory has come from one country, it can in the long run turn elsewhere. Second, it is *prima facie* true that a state which provides the bulk of another's weapon needs should gain the potential for leverage. Yet, the recipient's bargaining power is enhanced once it realizes arms supplies are an expression of the importance the supplier attaches to it. Third, the use of force to discipline a recalcitrant arms client is an option fraught with hazards. It would open the possibility of a confrontation with the other superpower and damage the ties and image of the Soviet Union in the Third World, a constituency to which

Moscow attaches a great deal of importance.

The fuzziness which characterizes the definition of influence in studies on Soviet arms transfers is encountered in the case of another term as well. While most observers point out that the quest for overseas bases is one major motive underlying Soviet arms transfers, there is a tendency not to define what constitutes a "base." It is used interchangeably with "facility," or "base facility," and little effort is made to discuss what specific rights the Soviets enjoy and under what conditions.[42] A base is an installation or location which supports and serves as the point of origin for the operations of a military force. The right of use is guaranteed by treaty, and the lessee possesses means for internal communications and is responsible for security. A distinction may be drawn between port privileges and the use of land-based facilities; in the latter case, there exists a visibly greater degree of access.[43] In the context of naval operations and deployments, a base may be used for a variety of support functions: the storage of supplies and ammunition, repair, replenishment, reconnaissance, and communications.

The quest for conceptual clarity in political science undoubtedly has generated quibbling over picayune details from time to time. However, if the term "base"—like "influence"—is used without specificity, vague and misleading conclusions about Soviet arms transfers can result. If the definition just offered is employed, it is apparent that since the evacuation of Port Arthur (China) and Porkalla (Finland) in the 1950s, the Soviet Navy has not had an overseas base. The Soviet Union has been able to negotiate access to facilities in a number of states to whom weapons have been supplied—Guinea, Egypt, Somalia, South Yemen, and Syria. In Egypt and Somalia, the Soviets gained de facto bases, succeeded in getting access to onshore facilities, and were able to expand the length of Mediterranean and Indian Ocean deployments as a result. In both cases, however, these benefits abruptly came to an end when the Soviet Union's relations with the host country soured. Elsewhere, the degree of access varies. While the Soviets have utilized some facilities for reconnaissance (Conakry), offshore repairs (Latakia), and supplying friendly states (Aden for arms deliveries to Ethiopia, and Algerian airfields for airlifts to Angola), these activities were permitted because the host country viewed them as being consonant with its own interests.

The USSR does not have naval facilities in the Third World comparable to those of the US at Subic Bay, Diego Garcia, and Yokosuka. It legitimately may be argued even in the case of facilities where a presence is secured by treaty, prolonged and reliable access still depends on the state of relations between the user and the host states. This merely underscores the constraints under which both superpowers operate; it does not make any more persuasive the contention the Soviets have a secure network of bases in the Third World which can be used in combat or conflict-related operations.

Conclusion: The Outlook

The inability of suppliers to control the use of arms by recipients, the rapid growth in the number of weapons in the developing world, and the possibility local crises may escalate through superpower involvement all point toward the need to control the global arms trade; nevertheless, the prospects for any effective agreement are dim. Although five countries-the US, USSR, France, Britain, and West Germany—account for 85 percent of the value of the weapons sold worldwide, the emergence of any accord is made unlikely by the fact each has important political and economic reasons to continue transferring arms.

For the Soviet Union, the driving force behind arms transfers will continue to be political. Though the export of weapons has provided the Soviets with only limited influence in the developing world, it has provided them with a visible presence. This, together with the realization that some influence is better than none, will ensure Moscow's continued heavy reliance on this instrument of diplomacy.

Nevertheless, the Soviets will have to guard against certain consequences which may stem from their decision to rely on arms sales, as opposed to economic aid, as the major instrument of their Third World diplomacy. The Soviet Union's decision to remain neutral in the war between Iran and Iraq and its decision not to back Iraq's military efforts through arms shipments may weaken the Soviet position in that country. This reveals a special burden for arms suppliers: key recipients are certain to expect political backing and further supplies of materiel in times of war; the war, however, may be one in which the supplier's wider interests necessitate neutrality. Another possible consequence is illustrated by Soviet–Libyan relations. Here, massive shipments of Soviet weaponry have increased both the ambition and the power Qaddafi has to pursue his regional objectives. These shipments, however, have not necessarily increased Soviet influence to the point where the USSR can assure itself the goals chosen by Libya—and the means used to pursue them—are compatible with Soviet interests. The Soviet Union cannot ignore the possibility that an attack by Soviet-equipped Libya on US–backed Egypt will raise the specter of superpower involvement and perhaps confrontation.

Because of their geopolitical importance for the USSR, the Middle East and South Asia will continue to be major destinations for Soviet arms exports. In the Middle East, arms sales—in addition to being a source of hard currency—will be a major means by which the Soviet Union maintains its ties with the radical Arab states opposed to the uncertain Camp David peace process and to growing American ties to Egypt, the Sudan, Somalia, and Oman. As the most important source for these Arabs states which reject the Camp David approach, the Soviet Union is in a position to influence the viability and permanence of any agreement on the Arab–Israeli dispute. Indeed, it is doubtful if a lasting Middle East settlement can be achieved if it does not provide for Soviet participation in the negotiations.

In South Asia, arms supplies will continue to be used to complicate China's security by building up rival India as a counterweight and to bolster the embattled Karmal regime in Afghanistan. The loss of important facilities in Somalia, the development of a major American naval facility at Diego Garcia, and US access to military facilities in Egypt, Kenya, Somalia, and Oman will lead the USSR to use arms sales to gain access to naval and air facilities in the northwest portion of the Indian Ocean.

Notes

1. Ruth Leger Sivard, *World Military and Social Expenditures 1978* (Leesburg, Virginia: WMSE Publications, 1978), Table 1, p. 20.
2. Idem, ibid, 1978, p. 9.
3. Michael Moodie, "Defense Industries in the Third World: Problems and Promises," in Stephanie Neuman and Robert Harkavy, eds., *Arms Transfers in the Modern World* (New York: Praeger, 1980), Table 17.1, pp. 296–297.
4. Robert Harkavy, *The Arms Trade and International Systems* (Cambridge, Massachusetts: Ballinger, 1975), pp. 41–47.
5. On defense production in India and Israel, see Moodie, pp. 300–302, and Rajan Menon, "The Military and Security Dimension of Indo–Soviet Relations," in Robert H. Donaldson, ed., *The Soviet Union and the Third World: Success and Failure* (Boulder: Westview, 1981), pp. 232–247.
6. Cf. James L. Foster, "New Conventional Weapons Technologies: Implications for the Third World," in Uri Ra'anan, Robert L. Pfaltzgraff, Jr., and Geoffrey Kemp, eds., *Arms Transfers to the Third World: The Military Buildup in Less Industrial Countries* (Boulder: Westview, 1978), pp. 65–84; and James F. Digby, *Precision–Guided Munitions: New Chances to Deal With Old Dangers,* Report P–5384, (Santa Monica: The Rand Corporation, March 1975).
7. Harkavy, pp. 60–78.
8. See Roger E. Kanet and Rajan Menon, "Soviet Policy Toward the Third World," in Donald R. Kelley, ed., *Soviet Politics in the Brezhnev Era* (New York: Praeger, 1980), pp. 235–247.
9. US Arms Control and Disarmament Agency, *World Military Expenditures and Arms Transfer 1968–1977* (Washington: ACDA, 1979), p. 10.
10. Ibid., Figure 16, p. 10; US Arms Control and Disarmament Agency, *World Military Expenditures and Arms Transfers 1967–1976* (Washington: ACDA, 1978), Figure 14, p. 10.
11. US Arms Control and Disarmament Agency, *World Military Expenditures and Arms Transfers 1968–1977,* p. 16.
12. Orah Cooper and Carol Fogarty, "Soviet Economic and Military Aid to Less Developed Countries, 1954–78," in US Congress, Joint Economic Committee, *Soviet Economy in a Time of Change,* Vol. 2, 96th Congress, 1st session, 10 October 1979, p. 694.
13. This shift in supply terms of Soviet arms has been noted in a number of sources: US Congress, House of Representatives, Committee on International Relations, *The Soviet Union and the Third World: A Watershed in Great Power Policy?,* 95th Congress, 1st session, 8 May 1977, p. 71; US Central Intelligence Agency, National Foreign Assessment Center, *Communist Aid Activities in Non–Communist Less Developed*

Countries 1978, ER79–10412U, September 1979, p. 3; Cooper and Fogarty, p. 654. It should be noted that since the early 1970s, the US has introduced a commercial element into its arms transfer program by shifting from grants and sales overwhelmingly to sales. See Anne Hessing Cahn and Joseph J. Kruzel, "Arms Trade in the 1980s," in Cahn, et al., *Controlling Future Arms Trade* (New York: McGraw–Hill, 1977), p. 35. Economic considerations have also been the single most important factor in the case of French arms exports and an important factor in the case of Britain as well.

14. See Mohan Ram, "Indo–Soviet Arms Deal," *Economic and Political Weekly* (Bombay), 31 May 1980, pp. 953–954; *Statesman* (Calcutta), 28 May 1980; *Times of India* (Bombay), 28 May 1980. Indian news reports maintained the agreement was concluded on the "most favorable terms." The loan bears an annual interest of 2.5 percent and is repayable over a 17–year period. Another example of the willingness to subordinate economic considerations to political goals is the Soviet-Peruvian arms deal involving the sale to Peru of *Su*–22 fighter-bombers for $250 million on easy credit terms and favorable prices.

15. See International Institute for Strategic Studies, *The Military Balance, 1978–9*, pp, 105, 106, 40; and *New York Times*, 29 August 1979; 5 September 1979; 2 November 1979; and 14 March 1980.

16. US Central Intelligence Agency, *Communist Aid Activities*, Table 3, p. 4.

17. It should be noted that the importance of advisory personnel has also been characteristic of US arms sales to high cash-low skill countries like Iran and Saudi Arabia. Training and technical services play a much bigger role in US arms transfers than in the case of the Soviet Union. See US Central Intelligence Agency, National Foreign Assessment Center, *Arms Flows to LDCs: US, Soviet Comparisons, 1974–77*, ER 78–10 49U, November 1978, p. 5.

18. Uri Ra'anan, "Soviet Arms Transfer and the Problem of Political Leverage," in Ra'anan, et al., *Arms Transfers to the Third World*, p. 134.

19. US Central Intelligence Agency, *Communist Aid to Less Developed Countries of the Free World, 1977*, pp. 1–2; and *Communist Aid Activities in Non–Communist Less Developed Countries 1978*, p. 3.

20. See US Congress, Joint Economic Committee, Subcommittee on Priorities and Economy in Government, *Soviet Economic Problems and Prospects*, 95th Congress, 1st session, 8 August 1977, pp. 1–6.

21. John P. Hardt, "Soviet Economic Capabilities and Defense Resources," in Grayson Kirk and Nils H. Wessell, eds., *The Soviet Threat: Myth and Realities* (New York: Academy of Political Science, 1978), pp. 123–129.

22. US Congress, Joint Economic Committee, *Soviet Economic Problems and Prospects*, p. 3.

23. Paul G. Ericson and Ronald S. Miller, "Soviet Economic Behavior: A Balance of Payments Perspective," in US Congress, Joint Economic Committee, *Soviet Economy in a Time of Change*, Vol. 2, p. 217.

24. The shift to Siberia is a consequence of the diminishing output from the oil fields in the Urals–Volga region. The need for Western technology stems from the inhospitable climate and terrain of Siberia and the Soviet lag in drilling technology.

25. US Arms Control and Disarmament Agency, *World Military Expenditures and Arms Transfers 1968–1977*, Table I, p. 61, and Table III, pp. 128, 129, 147, 151.

26. Ibid., Table IV, pp. 156–157.

27. For a discussion of the concept of influence, see Alvin Z. Rubinstein's excellent introductory chapter in Rubinstein, ed., *Chinese and Soviet Influence in the Third World* (New York: Praeger, 1975); and Idem, *Red Star on the Nile: The Soviet–Egyptian Influence Relationship since the June War* (Princeton: Princeton University Press, 1977). Also see Rajan Menon, "India and the Soviet Union: A Case Study of Inter–Nation Influence" (PhD dissertation, University of Illinois at Urbana–Champaign, 1979), Chapter I.

28. See William H. Lewis, "Political Influence: the Diminished Capacity" in Neuman and Harkavy, eds., *Arms Transfer in the Modern World*, pp. 185–186.

29. This is well documented in Vijay Sen Budhraj, "Moscow and the Birth of Bangladesh," *Asian Survey*, Vol. 13, No. 5 (May 1973), pp. 482–495.

30. Anwar al-Sadat, *In Search of Identity* (New York: Harper and Row, 1977), pp. 215–247, 287.

31. Ibid., p. 247. Sadat maintains that after the outbreak of war, the Soviets tried to persuade him to accept a ceasefire on four occasions. This suggests that while airlifting arms to Egypt and Syria, Moscow did not want to see a prolonged confrontation despite the initially favorable showing of the Arab states.

32. In fact, the Syrians launched their operations while Kosygin was on an aircraft bound for Damascus in an effort to mediate Iraqi–Syrian differences on the Lebanese situation. Robert O. Freedman, *Soviet Policy Toward the Middle East Since 1970*, rev. ed. (New York: Praeger, 1978), pp. 241–242.

33. In Somalia, the Soviets had unrestricted access to the port of Berbera, utilized Somali airfields for reconnaissance flights, and constructed a missile handling and storage facility ashore. See *USSR and Third World*, Vol. 5, No. 5 (13 May–6 July 1975), pp. 218, 255–257.

34. Thus, despite expectations to the contrary, the Janata government elected in March 1977 continued India's policy of maintaining close ties with the USSR. See Rajan Menon, "India and the Soviet Union: A New Stage in Relations?", *Asian Survey*, Vol. 18, No. 7 (July 1978), pp. 731–750.

35. Although India's decision has been linked—most notably by the Chinese—to the large Indo–Soviet arms agreement concluded in the previous month, it should be noted that Mrs. Gandhi—who was returned to office in January 1980 after a 3–year interregnum—had included a commitment to recognize the Heng Samrin government in her party's election manifesto.

36. On the Iraqi government crackdown against allegedly pro–Soviet military personnel, see the editorial note in *Current Digest of the Soviet Press*, Vol. 30, No. 31 (30 August 1978), p. 5. On Iraq's attitude toward the Yemeni civil war and the Soviet intervention in Afghanistan, see the dispatches by Marvin Howe, in *New York Times*, 3 March 1979 and 18 January 1980.

37. Interview of Angolan foreign Minister Paulo Texeira Jorge with Vladimir Obrubov and Sergey Sarkisyan, *New Times* (Moscow), No. 31, July 1979, p. 23.

38. Gerald Bender, "Angola: Left, Right, or Wrong," *Foreign Policy*, No. 43, Summer 1981, p. 66.

39. In the words of a commentator on Radio Moscow's Arabic service: "Press reports say that 30 engines for Soviet–made military aircraft used by the Egyptian army are being shipped from China . . . I cannot judge whether or not these engines are suitable for modern warplanes . . . but without a doubt, 30 engines are not sufficient for the hundreds of planes which Egypt obtained from the USSR." Cited in *USSR and Third World*, Vol. 6, Nos. 2–3 (1 April–31 July 1976), p. 128.

40. Sadat, *In Search of Identity*, p. 212.

41. According to a 28 July 1980 report in *Time:* "During the next five years, Washington plans to send more than $4 billion worth of arms to Egypt to replace antiquated Soviet equipment."

42. E.g., Robert E. Harkavy, "The New Geopolitics: Arms Transfers and the Major Powers' Competition for Overseas Bases," in Neuman and Harkavy, *Arms Transfers in the Modern World*, pp. 131–148.

43. Richard B. Remnek, "The Politics of Soviet Access to Naval Support Facilities in the Mediterranean," in Bradford Dismukes and James McConnell, eds., *Soviet Naval Diplomacy* (New York: Pergamon, 1979), pp. 357–403.

Soviet Aid to Africa

Richard E. Bissell

> Just how is it possible to construct the usage of a military trade or art [sic] by means of the Marxist method? This is the same thing as trying to construct a theory of architecture or a textbook on veterinary medicine with the aid of the Marxist method . . .
> To play chess 'according to Marx' is altogether impossible, just as it is impossible to wage war 'according to Marx.'

> (Leon Trotsky, 1922)

The principal issue which must be confronted with regard to Soviet military aid to Africa is not statistical but political. The philosophies behind the actions of any military institution rely heavily upon its historical experience; for that reason, one can gain much from the views of the "father of the Red Army," Leon Trotsky. That creator of modern Soviet military thought, his historians reliably report, turned not to the German Marx for inspiration but to the other German, Karl von Clausewitz.[1] Soviet military behavior in Africa, then, becomes far more understandable—in the context of Clausewitz's philosphy—as politics carried on through other means.

Soviet military aid to Africa necessarily has quantitative dimensions. These are summarized in the appendices of this article in terms of aid commitments, deliveries, and inventories of Soviet weapons in Africa after two decades of African independence. Each of these figures has a political implication which needs to be explored.

Of greater overall importance, however, are several questions about the Soviet Union in Africa which must be answered: (1) What is the nature of the change in Soviet military aid policy since the Angolan and Ethiopian interventions? (2) In what sense is the emergence of such a change a function of altered political circumstances in the African region? (3) Can military aid policies be said to presage a new role for the Soviet Union in African politics in the 1980s? In contrast to the other studies of this subject, all of Africa will be included in this analysis, given the important interconnections between Soviet military policy in North and sub-Saharan Africa.

Until five years ago, reasonably clear historical patterns of Soviet arms transfers to Africa could be discerned.[2] In effect, sub-Saharan Africa was at the end of the pipeline and received the oldest weapons available. The Middle East had far higher priority, a pattern not broken even with the massive arming of Somalia after the 1969 coup—if one considers Somalia to be part of the Middle East/Indian Ocean military theater. Certainly, the North African states obtained highly sophisticated weapons; such sales and the consequent political alliances which they engendered were meant to balance the NATO presence in the Mediterranean. The arming of Algeria and Egypt had no counterpart in sub-Saharan Africa until the 1970s (in statistics, such a differentiation is obscured by the inclusion of Somalia in sub-Saharan Africa). It could be argued that only after gaining a foothold in Somalia and being badgered by the African states for allying with expansionist Somali aims, did the Soviet Union consider carefully its military role in sub-Saharan Africa.

The Soviet military role in non-Arab Africa before the Portuguese revolution of 1974 was confined largely to competition with the Chinese for influence among the anti-colonialist guerrilla groups. A new doctrine for the projection of conventional military power certainly was emerging in the early 1970s—as seen in the extension of Soviet naval influence—and it is thus hazardous to suggest Soviet expansion into central and southern Africa was "caused" by the Portuguese revolution and the related decolonization. Quite clearly, though, the Soviets had a new capability and doctrine for the escalation of military arms aid to Africa when the opportunities in Angola, Mozambique, and Ethiopia appeared. Thus, we viewed the surge of a Soviet military presence in southern Africa and the transfer of clients in the Horn of Africa as a tide which seemed to come from nowhere.[3] That the United States was preoccupied elsewhere during this transitional period of Soviet policy is undeniable. We are now realizing the costs of this distraction were substantial, given the growth of Soviet influence in Africa.

In the 1974–1977 period, the Soviet Union began to rationalize its military presence in sub-Saharan Africa by relating such activities to Soviet political strategy. Limited arms transfers to Guinea in 1969–1970 made possible the establishment of base rights for both air and sea operations by the Soviets in the Atlantic Ocean. The deployment of longrange Tu–95/BEAR D reconnaissance planes to Guinea, however, did not occur until 1973, and the principal role of the air capability appears to have been directed more at the entrance of the Mediterranean than anywhere else. Only in 1975 did the Soviets begin regular air patrols in the Gulf of Guinea and the southeast Atlantic.[4] Guinea accumulated a sizable inventory of Soviet weaponry in the process, as indicated in Appendix B. Soviet operations have been restricted by Conakry, but insurance was obtained in Mali by the exchange of military aid for access to an airbase constructed by Soviet advisors.

If there is one country which can be excluded from the zero-sum Soviet–American conflict in Africa, it would have to be Nigeria. Clearly, the Soviets would prefer to have an active role in Nigeria, the cockpit of West Africa. Simply by making themselves available as needed, the Soviets have become the principal supplier of the Nigerian Air Force. Nevertheless, the Nigerian experience has been difficult for the Soviet Union, particularly because of the transparent Soviet desire to weave a network of comprehensive ties and the evident Nigerian ability to evade such a trap. The Soviets established a special position during the Nigerian civil war through the ready supply between 1966 and 1969 of arms to the federal government. Yet, in the wake of the civil war, the Soviets have squandered almost entirely the advantage gained. As one Nigerian scholar recently commented, "Nigerian-Soviet relations have been in crisis since the end of the Nigerian Civil War."[5] Although the principal Nigerian unhappiness with the Soviets actually evolved from the repeated delays in construction of a steel mill promised in 1968, the growing disrepute of the Soviet Union has caused other problems: some stories relate to Soviet mismanagement of supplies to Nigeria during the civil war, and others involve the deliberate Soviet snubbing of Nigeria during the USSR's arms airlift to Angola in 1975–1976. The Soviet diplomatic style is frequently offensive, as pointed out by the Director–General of the Nigerian Institute of International Affairs: "In dealing with the Soviet Union, one gets the impression of being asked to find one's place in a set design. In dealing with the United States, one gets the impression of dealing with a state that is prepared to consider several options."[6] It seems unlikely Soviet military influence beyond the existing air force ties will be allowed to prosper any time soon.

The Soviets adhere to a similar pattern in the rest of Africa. In central Africa, the Soviet Union is seeking entree to the core state, Zaire, expressing interest in whatever ties President Mobutu might allow (none so far),[7] while in the meantime settling for military links with the willing states of the region: the Congo Republic and, until recently, Equatorial Guinea.

In the south, the prize is obviously South Africa. Until a systemic revolution in South Africa can be developed, however, the Soviet Union is seeking to build up a range of military ties with the so-called Front-Line States to the the north: Angola, Zambia, Mozambique, and Madagascar. The ties to these key states are not uniform due to the varied means through which the Soviet Union came to have a presence.

In east Africa, the Soviet Union lost a political liability by severing ties with Somalia and gained access to the headquarters of the Organization of African Unity (OAU) in Addis Ababa. Moscow also succeeded in defusing some of Kenya's antagonism toward the Soviet Union. Kenya, it is sometimes forgotten, has a treaty of friendship with Ethiopia which was renewed in February 1979.

In North Africa, the recent emphasis has been on Algeria and Libya, both fortuitously interested in influencing trends in the Third World, particularly in the rest of Africa. Thus, they are important repositories for military stores which can be transferred south of the Sahara. The Libyans appear to have a special goal of reducing French influence in Africa, as evidenced by the direct intervention of Libyan forces and arms transfers to pro-Libyan factions in the civil war in Chad. Other little noticed erosions of the French position have occurred: the second session of the Beninese–Libyan Joint Commission was held in August 1980; subsequent sessions are scheduled every 6 months.[8] Certainly, Beninese military procurement patterns have not been altered substantially yet—although Benin did purchase two *An-26* transports in 1978—but every sale increases the Soviet presence in a region which possesses such small military forces.

The Soviet efforts to create a new security structure in Africa can be best understood in the context of the Angolan and Ethiopian crises of 1974–1977. The immediate need in both crises was the transfer of men and material by continuous, assured sea and air transport in order to establish pro-Soviet governments which otherwise would have perished quickly in civil war. The fact the Soviet Union was able to accomplish its aims in both cases implies the existence of far more than merely a military capability: the countries in the region which provided transit for Soviet transport activity also were willing to commit themselves politically to Soviet regional goals. In that sense, Soviet influence in Africa is stronger than the ties which bind NATO (as illustrated by European attitudes towards American resupply operations in Israel in recent years). The Soviet Union clearly has learned much in the 20 years since it was unable to resupply Patrice Lumumba in his bid to retain power in the Congo. The Soviet Union, particularly in the Angolan crisis, has demonstrated a political capability without which its military means would be largely ineffectual.

There also has been change in the composition of aid since the Angolan and Ethiopian interventions which is not reflected in the statistics covering the monetary value of aid. A significant part of the military aid now being transferred consists of personnel who have two missions: (1) to operate and maintain increasingly sophisticated weaponry, and (2) to maintain regimes in power that would otherwise fall from internal opposition. Each of these manpower purposes is new, at least in importance. The use of *MiG-23s* in Algeria, Libya, and Ethiopia raised the level of air power technology to new heights in Africa and resulted in a new degree of complexity in maintenance, thus virtually ensuring the involvement of Soviet (or Cuban) Air Forces personnel. On the naval front, the Soviets generally have chosen simply to use Soviet ships to carry out necessary missions rather than transfer high technology equipment to clients.[9] Examples are the evacuation of the routed Ethiopian army from Massawa in January 1980 and the protection of the sea supply lanes to Angola in 1976. The Soviets also have established shore facilities to support their naval operations: the use of Somalia's port of Berbera was allowed under the terms of a 1972 arms agreement.

The use of Soviet bloc personnel to maintain regimes in power has been the most dramatic new task. The use of Cuban infantry— sometimes working in tandem with officers of the Soviet General Staff—to reverse the political tide in Angola and Ethiopia has surprised and impressed many observers. Previous Soviet practice appeared to be to support regimes reasonably firmly in place, but there were few resources the Soviet Union could throw into a battle to save a shaky regime which lacked the domestic support or coercive power to survive. Thus, the Soviets meekly departed after the fall of Kwame Nkrumah in 1966 and did not seem unduly disturbed by Modobo Keita's demise in Mali in 1968. In the wake of such setbacks, one informed observer could say accurately that the Soviet Union seemed "to be trying to free the process of 'influence-building' from the vicissitudes of local politics."[10] In a rather sudden switch in the mid–1970s, however, the Soviets apparently decided that in particular cases, intense involvement in "local politics" was the answer—thus, their response in Ethiopia and Angola. Nevertheless, this does not warrant the conclusion Moscow can no longer walk away from difficult situations: in 1980, the Soviets experienced a temporary loss of friends in Uganda and Equatorial Guinea, but even the Soviets must have realized the inhumane regimes in each case were not worthy of saving for whatever strategic purposes.

The third aspect of Soviet military aid in the 1970s which has changed, as noted by other observers, is the increasing use of military equipment transfers to raise hard currency. Even in a region as poor as Africa, countries such as Angola, Nigeria, and Zambia have been buying weapons systems for cash on the barrelhead or at commercial-level interest rates.[11] Such purchases have been made possible by the rising value of particular resources—especially oil—as well as by the lowered political expectations of the local populations, thus allowing greater percentages of national budgets to be devoted to arms purchases. The centralization of power in Zambia, for instance, has allowed President Kaunda to spend $85 million on Soviet arms at a time of falling copper prices and insufficient maize supplies. Such purchases can create a vicious cycle: scarce resources spent on arms can arouse public resentment, thus necessitating greater purchases of arms to suppress domestic dissent. Given Soviet long-term goals, however, the creation of such a cycle is generally in Moscow's interest since it tends to inhibit the willingness of the United States to sell arms in order to avoid fostering further societal instability and dissent.[12]

The African Political Milieu

Soviet military aid in Africa is not merely the result of some grand design; it also clearly came about as a result of the growing receptivity of African states to military involvement with the Soviet Union. In the latter respect, there are a number of changes in the African environment which have facilitated Soviet involvement and should cause concern about future levels and sources of arms in the African region.

The realignment of Soviet allies in Africa in the 1970s has placed the Soviet Union squarely with the political majority of the OAU. Radio Moscow's rhetoric in condemning South Africa, deploring the "imperialist designs" behind Somali expansionism, supporting a "new international economic order" which would loosen the "shackles of neo-imperialism," and opposing "Zionist imperialism" in the Middle East all reflect the USSR's willingness to establish political solidarity with the international concerns of the African majority. Even in those states which do not purchase arms from the Soviet Union—or purchase only a few, as in the Nigerian case—there is a willingness to believe the Soviet political line. Thus, even when rational minds could see reason to oppose the Soviet Union and condemn the Soviet invasion of Afghanistan, several African states in the UN voted with the Soviet Union and a large number abstained. One of the principal themes played by the Soviets to gain support among African states is the Western "neo-imperialist" presence. While independence has arrived for Africa, freedom and prosperity are not also present; as a result, the Soviets encourage the Africans to take out their resentment on the Western states. In this atmosphere, the Africans are encourage to break as many bonds as possible with the West, beginning with military ties.

The termination of the decolonization process has also changed the military emphasis in Africa. Previously, the struggle in the former Portugese territories and in Rhodesia, for instance, involved relatively small-scale covert assistance to the liberation groups fighting white rule. The conflicts which now face African states are at a higher magnitude of violence. The establishment of armies in newly independent states readily gives rise to regional arms races. This dynamic could be seen in the initial Soviet arming of Somalia followed by the Soviet arming of Ethiopia. The second conflict, not yet joined, is the potential fight between South Africa and its neighbors to the north. A stimulus of this nature was certainly at work in the Zambian purchase of Soviet arms in 1980; if tensions rise between South Africa and its neighbors, the highly sophisticated weaponry of South Africa could easily cause

178

its antagonists to bargain with the Soviets for very advanced weapons. The final stages of the decolonization process may still provoke widespread arming and bloodshed, whether over Namibia's future or the final disposition of the former Spanish Sahara. Soviet arms already are engaged in both issues.

The dissolution of the "Third World bloc" has changed considerably the international outlook for African states. All African states need international alignments to avoid the loneliness of poverty and powerlessness. In the years since independence, the problem of international alignments has grown more acute as more capable elites have found particular avenues to international prominence. The sense of pan-African solidarity so common in the 1960s faded, and, by the late 1970s, the Third World groupings were dissolving as well. At this point, there is a great need for individual African states to find a sense of security. For the Francophone states, there always have been forms of close association with France, including that intangible type of cultural entanglement which explains so much of France's continuing presence in Africa.[13] The emergence of a Soviet conception of a "socialist commonwealth" has been reassuring to those states willing to accommodate themselves to the Soviet scheme of the universe; with those political links comes an assurance of security in the form of arms and advisers. The network of Soviet ties which frequently accompanies military aid is a rich one spanning all aspects of society: the treaties of friendship and cooperation frequently include military support agreements on trade and technology issues and, in the case of Angola, even a party-to-party agreement which places the MPLA in the category of an Eastern European communist party.

Despite the fact military aid agreements are generally negotiated within the framework of overall treaties of friendship and cooperation, the experience of most African states has been that the military and political ties specified in such treaties flourish far better than the economic and technological bonds.[14] As a result, superficially absurd situations arise: the continued operations of Gulf Oil in Angola with the installations guarded by Cuban troops, or the operation of Mozambique's harbors and railways by South Africans, while Maputo infiltrates guerrillas armed with AK–47s into South Africa. The relative weight given to each form of aid, however, can be deduced in one case from the behavior of the Ethiopian government. The Provisional Military Administrative Council (PMAC) survives as a result of Soviet/Cuban military aid and enormous allotments of American Public Law 480 food aid. In July 1980, the Ethiopians showed their appreciation for each by welcoming Fleet Admiral of the Soviet Union Sergey Gorshkov (member of the CPSU Central Committee and Commander in Chief of the Soviet Navy) for a week-long red carpet visit and expelling the American Ambassador to Ethiopia, Frederic Chapin. Military aid obviously can be effective in obtaining political aims.

What is extraordinary is the present weakening of the African faith the West can offer some form of solidarity to counter effectively the attraction of Soviet ties. Britain has lost the influence which might be expected of a former colonial power; its willing withdrawal from the region east of the Suez and its dismal record in solving the Zimbabwe–Rhodesian dilemma severely damaged its African position. The United States seems unable to offer a consistent vision which might serve as a rallying point for an international African coalition. France retains a measure of influence, as already mentioned, but has been unable to extend it beyond the Francophone countries, thereby denying it a role as an African rallying point. The most recent attempt to develop a non-Soviet sense of solidarity with Western Europe—that of Olaf Palme and the Second International—shows few signs of being any more successful. The emergence of the Soviet Union as a global military superpower reinforces, at a minimum, its prestige as a focus of African solidarity.

One reason for the loss of African solidarity has been the continent's clear evolution since independence into the "haves" and the "have nots," a division which is focused primarily upon the existence of resource reserves valuable enough to earn development funds from the industrial states. As the value of these resources has risen, so has the interest of the Soviet Union and other outside powers in providing political/military resources to control them. On occasion, such aid will involve defending the resources—as the 2000 Cuban soldiers in Cabinda are doing for Angola and Gulf Oil—or it may involve attempting to gain control of the resources, as allegedly happened in the arming of the two invasions of Shaba Province in Zaire in the late 1970s. The calculation of the future value of the resources in southern Africa simply raises further the likely military price which will be paid by the Soviet Union in that subregion.

The "have nots" have their own peculiar problems as well, particularly instability, which derive from the poverty of their position. The instability arising from sheer poverty—whether in Liberia, Ghana, or Somalia—is a challenge established governments will necessarily try to resist. Thus, they will seek out those governments which are willing to provide the military material necessary to insure domestic tranquility. The repression required to maintain order in an atmosphere of declining standards of living frequently has deterred the United States from providing military aid. The Soviet Union appears to have been rather more forthcoming; a dictatorship can always be rationalized as a "dictatorship of the proletariat."

Most importantly, the Soviet Union appears to be willing to intervene militarily where a systemic revolution has just occurred. Such was the case in both Angola and Ethiopia. The implications of such interventions are worth exploring.

The Soviet historical experience draws them into such revolutionary situations. The Soviet experience in 1917 is not an example Moscow wants aspiring members of the socialist commonwealth to repeat: the disintegration of the army, the suing for peace (with the painful result of Brest–Litovsk), and years of civil warfare combined with the compromise of the revolution.[15] It is reasonably inevitable that in such a systemic revolution the army would disintegrate; nevertheless, the Soviet Union apparently decided that in countries such as Angola and Ethiopia (and later, Afghanistan), it was willing to provide armed forces sufficient to maintain national integrity while the revolution continued. The unprecedented deployment of Cuban forces to both countries and the Soviet army leadership and equipment provided can only be considered a reflection of the collapse of the indigenous armed forces. It has been observed elsewhere that the greatest loss brought about by the disintegration of the armed forces in a revolution is the scattering of noncommissioned officers whose technical talents are essential to operating an army.[16] It is thus not surprising that foreign personnel seem to be maintaining and sometimes operating the mechanized equipment in African armies. The energies of the leadership in such regimes are not going into military questions but rather into the intricacies of a political organization (sometimes simply eliminating opponents as in Ethiopia) which eventually may yield a new army politically loyal to the Soviet-oriented government.

Implications for Future Soviet Military Aid Policies

The changes in Soviet global activity and the African political scene point in only one direction: increased Soviet military activity in Africa. As long as the Soviet Union seeks to increase its access to base facilities throughout Africa, the principal tool for obtaining such access will be military aid and sales. There are several African dimensions, too, which point to an increased Soviet role.

First, the projected conflict with South Africa cannot be sustained by the black African states alone. The evident capability of South Africa to produce nuclear weapons and its clear superiority in conventional weapons indicate that the states in southern Africa, at least, eventually will desire some form of security umbrella which might diminish the likelihood of South African retaliation against their provocations. Nevertheless, an extensive security guarantee by the Soviet Union is unlikely to appear soon, given the opportunities afforded for increased Soviet penetration by continuing the tensions in southern Africa.

The record of expanding Soviet influence in Africa in recent years is not one of moving beyond current Soviet capabilities. The recent buildup of military ties in the arc of states north of South Africa has proceeded gradually: in Angola and Mozambique, it has stemmed from support for the revolutionary phase of their current governments; in Zambia, it is a spin-off of support for the Rhodesian ZAPU movement,

181

and the inclusion of Zimbabwe in Soviet military planning would be the next logical step. On the east coast, the Soviet military planners have made a number of overtures to Madagascar—some of them successful—in an effort to supplant French influence. In the recent purchase of *MiG*–21s by Madagascar, for instance, the Soviets were reported by sources in Antananarivo to have offered very attractive terms: out of the 15 *MiG*–21s, 3 were sold at "full price," 9 others were sold at a 50 percent discount, and 3 were provided free.[17] Only with the completion of the military containment of South Africa would the Soviet Union move forward to provide the guarantees—whether in the form of security pacts or a nuclear umbrella—which would permit a major conflict in southern Africa.

The extension of Soviet military personnel into Africa under the Brezhnev regime has been a cautious process clearly dependent upon the establishment of a congenial political environment in which to take military risks. Even then, in the major cases of Angola and Ethiopia, Soviet personnel have not been principally at risk, for thousands of Cuban legionnaires have manned the front lines in the battles to bring unpopular regimes to power. The future of such personnel aid policies is not clear-cut. The Soviet leadership will be undergoing a change, probably to a generation who did not experience World War II as adults; their sense of caution may be of a different magnitude. The second imponderable will be the lessons learned by the Soviet leadership in Afghanistan. If the Soviets judge the use of their military power in Afghanistan (clearly part of the Third World) to have been worth the cost, it will be used to bring other countries into the socialist commonwealth.

Finally, a distinction needs to be drawn between the various forms of Soviet military aid and their likely use in Africa. The Chinese, among the most experienced of Soviet observers, have said:

> By forming military blocs, concluding friendship and cooperation treaties and offering lavish economic and military 'aid,' they (the Soviets) try hard to control and enslave not only the Third World countries but also those of the Second World. When they fail to achieve their ends by 'peaceful' means, they resort to military coup d'etat, subversion and even direct armed intervention and aggression.[18]

What the Chinese pointed out in 1976 remains largely true today, particularly in the preference of Soviet military policy to obtain hegemony by "peaceful means." In the context of aid, the peaceful approach is exemplified by the provision of arms accompanied by advisers and political support if requested by a securely independent government. If the Soviet-supported elite faces armed hostility, however, troops will be provided from some source. The key to the 1980s is the new capability of the Soviet Union to fine tune its military aid elements in

Africa, whether of a "peaceful" or "active" nature. Whether that capability will be used may depend not only on events in Africa but also on the Soviet experience in using this capability elsewhere in the Middle East and Asia.

Notes

1. Baruch Knei–Paz, *The Social and Political Thought of Leon Trotsky* (Oxford: Clarendon Press, 1978), p. 253.
2. See Wynfred Joshua and S. P. Gibert, *Arms for the Third World: Soviet Military Aid Diplomacy* (Baltimore: The John Hopkins University Press, 1969), and Uri Ra'anan, *The USSR Arms the Third World* (Cambridge: MIT Press, 1969).
3. For historical analyses of the changes in Soviet doctrine in Africa, see my "Union of Soviet Socialist Republics," in Thomas H. Henriksen, ed., *The Communist States and Sub–Saharan Africa* (Stanford: Hoover Institution, 1981), and Stanley H. Kober, "Soviet Policy Towards Southern Africa," *Radio Liberty Research,* RL 123/79, 18 April 1979.
4. Charles C. Petersen, "Trends in Soviet Naval Operations," in Bradford Dismukes and James M. McConnell, eds., *Soviet Naval Diplomacy* (New York: Pergamon Press, 1979), pp. 57, 77–78.
5. Ray Ofoegbu, "Foreign Policy and Military Rule," in Oyeleye Oyediran, ed., *Nigerian Government and Politics under Military Rule, 1966–79* (New York: St. Martins Press, 1979), p. 138.
6. Bolaji Akinyemi, "Mohammed/Obasanjo Foreign Policy," in ibid., p. 167.
7. See "Zaire's Difficult Decades," *Sovetskaya Rossiya* [Soviet Russia], 1 July 1980, p. 3, in Foreign Broadcast Information Service (FBIS) *Daily Report: Soviet Union,* 8 July 1980, p. J1. In 1979, Zaire did restore diplomatic relations with Cuba and the German Democratic Republic.
8. Cotonou Domestic Service in French, 6 August 1980, in FBIS *Daily Report: Mideast/Africa,* 7 August 1980, p. T1.
9. For the pre–1976 naval transfers, see Michael L. Squires and Ann R. Patterson, "Soviet Naval Transfers to Developing Countries, 1956–1975," in Michael MccGwire and John McDonnell, eds., *Soviet Naval Influence: Domestic and Foreign Influences* (New York: Praeger, 1977), pp. 530–538.
10. Robert Legvold, "Soviet and Chinese Influence in Black Africa," in Alvin Z. Rubinstein, ed., *Soviet and Chinese Influence in the Third World* (New York: Praeger, 1975), p. 172.
11. The terms of the Zambian deal were spelled out in "Zambia Buys Soviet Arms Valued at $85 Million," *Washington Post,* 8 February 1980, p. 22.
12. On the US case, see Charles F. Doran, "U.S. Foreign Aid and the Unstable Polity: A Regional Case Study," *Orbis,* Vol. 22, No. 2 (Summer 1978), esp. pp. 448–450.
13. Legvold, op. cit., p. 173.
14. The texts of such treaties of friendship and cooperation are remarkably detailed recitations of Soviet influence; for the Angolan treaty, for example, see *Pravda,* 9 October 1976, or USSR Ministry of Foreign Affairs, *Sbornik deystvuyushchikh dogovorov, soglasheniy i konventsiy zaklyuchennykh SSSR s inostrannymi gosudarstvami* [Digest of Current Treaties, Agreements and Conventions Concluded by the USSR with Foreign Governments] (Moscow: Mezhdunarodnyye otnosheniya, 1978), Vol. 32, pp. 27–28.
15. Katharine Chorley, *Armies and the Art of Revolution* (Boston: Beacon Press, 1973), p. 196.
16. Ibid., p. 192.
17. Paris AFP, 27 June 1980, in FBIS *Daily Report: Sub–Saharan Africa,* 1 July 1980, p. U3.

18. "Naked Exposure of Soviet Revisionists' Colonial Expansion," *People's Daily,* 4 February 1976, in FBIS *Daily Report: People's Republic of China,* 4 February 1976, p. A4.

Appendix A

Military Inventories Supplied by the Soviets

Algeria
500 *T*–54/–55/–62 med tanks
450 *BTR*–40/–50/–60/–152 APCs
FROG–4 SSM
SAGGER ATGW
SA–7 SAM

6 ex–Soviet *S*01 large patrol craft
16 ex–Soviet FAC(M) with STYX SSM
10 ex–Soviet *P*–6 FAC(T)
2 ex–Sov *T*43 ocean minesweepers
1 ex–Sov *Polnocny* LCT

24 *Il*–28
90 *MiG*–21
30 *Su*–20
30 *MiG*–17
40 *MiG*–23
6 *MiG*–23R
20 *MiG*–15
8 *An*–12, 5 *An*–24
4 *Mi*–6, 42 *Mi*–42, 12 *Mi*–8
SA–2/–6 SAM

Angola
85 *T*–34, 150 *T*–54, 50 *PT*–76 tanks
200 *BRDM*–2
150 *BTR*–50/–60/–152
SAGGER ATGW
SA–7 SAM

2 ex–Sov *Shershen* FAC(T)
1 ex–Sov *Zhuk* patrol craft
1 ex–Sov *Polnocny* LCT
15 *MiG*–17, 12 *MiG*–21
5 *An*–26
19 *Mi*–8
3 *MiG*–15*UTI*

Benin
2 *An*–2

Congo
T–59 medium tanks
3 *PT*–73 light tanks
10 *BRDM*–1
44 *BTR*–152

10 *MiG*–15/–17
4 *An*–24
5 *Il*–14

Egypt
850 *TP*–54/–55, 750 *T*–62 medium tanks
80 *PT*–76 light tanks
300 *BRDM*–1/–2
200 *BMP*–76–PB MICV
2500 *OT*–62/–64, *BTR*–40/–50/–60/–152 APC
200 *SU*–100/*JSU*–152 SP guns
SA–7/–9 SAM, SA–2/–3/–6

12 ex–Sov submarines (6 W–, 6 R–class)
4 ex–Sov *Skoriy* destroyers
12 ex–Sov large patrol craft
10 ex–Sov FAC(M) with STYX SSM
26 ex–Sov FAC(T)
4 ex–Sov *Shershen* FAC(G)
14 ex–Sov minesweepers
4 ex–Sov LCT
14 ex–Sov LCU

23 –*Tu*–16
100 *MiG*–21
120 *Su*–7*BMK,* 46 Su–20
108 *MiG*–21*MV/U,* 24 *MiG*–23S, 6 *MiG*–23*U*
26 *Il*–14, 16 *An*–12
20 *Mi*–4, 32 *Mi*–6, 55 *Mi*–8

Ethiopia
100 *T*–34, 500 *T*–54/–55
? *BRDM*–2 scout cars
500 *BTR*–40/–60/–152 APC
SAGGER ATGW
SA–2/–3/–7 SAM

186

2 ex-Sov *Osa* II FAC(M) with STYX SSM
2 ex-Sov *Mol* FAC(T)

17 *MiG*–17, 50 *MiG*–21, 20 *MiG*–23
8 *An*–12, 4 *An*–22, 1 *Il*–14
25 *Mi*–8/–6

Guinea
30 *T*–54/–55
10 *PT*–76
40 *BTR*–40/–152 APC

2 ex-Sov *P*–6 FAC(T)
3 ex-Sov *Poluchat* costal patrol craft

10 *MiG*–17, 3 *MiG*–21
4 *Il*–14/–18, 4 *An*–4
2 *MiG*–15*UTI*

Guinea–Bissau
T–34 medium tanks
BTR–152 APC
1 ex-Sov *P6* FAC(T)

Libya
2000 *T*–54/–55/–62
200 *BMP* MICV
400 *BTR*–40/–50/–60, 140 *OT*–62/–64 APC
SAGGER ATGW
SA–7 SAM

3 ex-Sov F–class submarines
6 ex-Sov *Osa*–II FAC(M) with STYX SSM
1 ex-Sov *Polnocny* LCT

24 *Tu*–22/BLINDER A
24 *MiG*–23
5 *MiG*–25R/*U* (Soviet-crewed)
5 *MiG*–23*U*
12 *Mi*–8/–24
SA–2/–3/–6 SAM

Madagascar
8 *MiG*–21*FL*
2 *Mi*–8

480-900 O - 85 - 7

Mali
20 *T*–34 medium tanks
20 *BRDM*–2 APC
10 *BTR*–40/–152 APC

8 *MiG*–17
3 *An*–2, 2 *An*–24, 2 *Il*–14
2 *Mi*–4, 1 *Mi*–8

Morocco
40 T–54 medium tanks
SA–7 SAM

Mozambique
240 *T*–54/–55/*PT*–76
BTR–40, *BRDM* Armored cars
BTR–40/–152 APC
SAGGER ATGW
SA–6/–7 SAM

1 ex–Sov *Poluchat* large patrol craft

Nigeria
3 *MiG*–17, 18 *MiG*–21*MF*
2 *MiG*–15*UTI*, 2 *MiG*–21*U*

Somalia
80 *T*–34/–54/–55
50 *BTR*–40/–50/–60, 100 *BTR*–152 APC
SA–2/–3 SAM

3 ex–Sov *Osa*–II FAC(M) with STYX SSM
8 ex–Sov FAC(T)
1 ex–Sov *Poluchat* large patrol craft
6 ex–Sov *P02* coastal patrol craft
1 ex–Sov *Polnocny* LCT, 2 ex–Sov *T*4 LCM

3 *Il*–28
15 *MiG*–17
7 *MiG*–21*MF*
3 *An*–2, 3 *An*–24/–26
6 *Mi*–4, 4 *Mi*–8
4 *MiG*–15*UTI*

Sudan
70 *T*–54, 60 *T*–55 medium tanks

100 *BTR*–40/–50/–152 APC

12 *MiG*–17*F*
5 *An*–24
10 *Mi*–8

Tanzania
40 *T*–59/–60/–62
SA–3/–6 SAM

4 ex–Sov *P*4 FAC(T)
1 ex–Sov *Poluchat* large patrol craft

Uganda
10 *T*–34, 15 *T*–54/–55
120 *BTR*–40/–152 APC
SAGGER ATGW
SA–7 SAM

21 *MiG*–21, 10 *MiG*–17
2 *MiG*–15*UTI*

Zambia
30 *T*–54 medium tanks
6 *Mi*–6

Sources:
International Institute for Strategic Studies, *The Military Balance, 1979–1980* (London, 1979).
SIPRI, *World Armaments and Disarmament: SIPRI Yearbook 1980* (Stockholm, 1980).

Appendix B

Arms Commitments and Deliveries to the African Region by the Soviet Union

($ million)

Commitments

	1956-73	1974	1975	1976	1977	1978
North Africa	490	1825	535	----	18000	315
Sub-Saharan Africa	330	365	145	800	1415	845
Total	820	2190	680	800	3215	1165

Deliveries

North Africa	435	150	380	810	925	1175
Sub-Saharan	275	90	255	325	585	1220
Total	710	240	635	1135	1510	2395

Source: CIA, *Communist Aid Activities in Non–Communist Less Developed Countries, 1978,* September 1979, p. 3.

The "Division of Labor" Within the Soviet Penetration of the Third World: The Role of Bulgaria

Michael M. Boll

Introduction

Growing concern over increased Soviet influence in the Third World, especially in Africa and along the vital Red Sea, has given rise to numerous recent studies of Soviet strategy and successes. In 1978, Avigdor Haselkorn provided a framework for understanding Soviet motivations, arguing that Moscow's primary goal involved creation of a collective security system along the Soviet periphery which, *inter alia*, would allow use of Third World facilities and perhaps troops in future military engagements. In its minimal form, such a collective arrangement would insure the denial of Third World assistance to the US and her Western allies.[1] The same year, W. Scott Thompson gave detailed evidence of augmented Soviet penetration in Africa which confirmed the growing Soviet drive to achieve effective projection of power far from the Russian heartland.[2] The growing military entanglements were discussed once again by Nimrod Novik in 1979. Particularly disturbing to Novik was the massive November 1977 Soviet airlift to Ethiopia of fighter-bombers, *T*–34 tanks, and antiaircraft missiles. Proof that the USSR had modified its military doctrine to fit large-scale supply operations was the presence of empty cargo planes in the Ethiopian operation, a test scenario for even larger power projections in the future.[3]

While such studies are important in relating details of a concerted Soviet penetration of the Third World, they have, to date, focused too narrowly upon the most visible and disturbing aspects of Moscow's strategy. The Soviet–South Yemeni and Soviet–Angolan Friendship Treaties, as well as the recent massive airlift to the Horn of Africa, are but the obvious results of a protracted and carefully planned drive to enhance socialist influence in all areas of this vital region. More importantly, exclusive scrutiny of the tangible and visible Soviet successes obscures the more complex involvement of Soviet and East European personnel in support of a domestic African socialist base. While it is the presence of Soviet and/or Cuban advisers and troops which indicates the success of a particular penetration effort, often it is the existence of East European economic and technical advisers which reveals both the dimensions and the selected targets of the overall

Soviet strategy. It is this "allied" activity which has escaped Western attention; allied efforts which suggest a division of labor within the socialist camp in a concerted and far-reaching drive to win the newly independent states for the Marxist cause.

It is difficult to account for the lack of Western studies examining East European efforts in the grand Soviet strategy.[4] To be sure, analysts carefully have noted Cuban troop activities in Ethiopia and Angola and have mentioned the role of East Germany in providing military and security force supervision both north and south of the Sahara.[5] But the more fundamental political and economic efforts of Moscow's Warsaw Pact allies rarely merit discussion, despite compelling evidence indicating their key importance within the general penetration strategy. In its recent report on communist aid to the Third World, the CIA concluded that East European credits and grants to sub–Saharan African greatly exceeded Soviet assistance; $517 million to a mere $11 million in 1978 alone, with the most important recipients being two key Soviet client states—Ethiopia and Angola.[6] This disparity is likely to grow in the coming years because of Moscow's preference for allocating large aid grants to two or three developing states.[7] While the CIA report fails to distinguish between Soviet and East European personnel working in Third World states—lumping them together under a single entry—the presence of nearly 10,000 Bulgarian technicians in Libya alone accounts for almost one-third of the total Soviet and East European commitment in North Africa.[8] Bulgarian contributions to the training of Third World cadre and specialists is equally important, as this author can testify from his own studies at the G. A. Nasser Foreign Institute in Bulgaria during the summer of 1979.

Bulgaria's Role in the Socialist Penetration of Africa

An analysis of Bulgaria's growing importance in the penetration of key Third World states sheds considerable light upon overall socialist policy, including the previously mentioned efforts to establish a socialist collective security system. The evidence from Sofia offers convincing proof that a "division of labor" now exists which allocates to Bulgaria a role in Third World relations of nearly equal importance to the military role accorded Havana. It is likely this sharing of tasks is a direct result of an important, if neglected, Eastern Bloc conference on Africa held in Budapest in November 1976. Attended by African specialists from the socialist states, the conference posited as its main goal the coordination of the heretofore unsystematic socialist activities on the African continent. As the Hungarian journal *Kulpolitika* reported:

> It was decided at the conference that it should be proposed to the governmental organizations responsible for international economic relations and also to the Comecon

Secretariat that economic relations with the developing countries and the drawing up of joint agreements should be coordinated more precisely. The participants considered it would be expedient to expand the relevant part of the Comecon Comprehensive Program . . . and to lay down the general outlines of their common principles: to itemize programs for individual developing countries; to elucidate the special interests of the different socialist countries; and to outline the system for implementation of the detailed program.[9]

While this final report focuses primarily upon economic aid and trade, it now is clear the recommendations for the specific tasks of each East European state included political, party, and military concerns. Bulgaria's role in the coordinated socialist plan currently involves four different, yet integrated, goals: (1) projection of the merits of socialist economic organization as the preferred means of rapid Third World modernization, (2) allocation of trained specialists to assist state-directed enterprises in the Third World with the aim of the eventual predominance of the public over the private sector, (3) expansion and strengthening of the "denial" clauses in the numerous collective security agreements linking Africa and Eastern Europe, and (4) the education, advising, and training of Third World revolutionaries in the "correct" methods of social, economic, political, and party development. Goals 2 and 3 are shared with other East European states, although Bulgaria has taken the lead in selected African states. Goals 1 and 4 are the most important tasks assigned to Sofia.

The Bulgarian Modernization Model: An Example to Emulate

It has often been noted that what separates an American from a Marxist view of reality is the heavy stress accorded by the former to what is—the status quo—in sharp contrast to the Marxist perception of change, of the dynamic inherent in any apparently stable situation. And so it is with regard to perceptions of Bulgaria. To most Americans, this nation remains a little-known entity which is rarely visited and which represents the territorial and cultural backwaters of the European continent. Its population of less than 9 million is not large by American standards, and the estimated per capita income of slightly less than $3,000 a year compares unfavorably even with figures available for other East European states.[10] What is neglected in such appraisals is the dramatic changes which have occurred in Bulgaria since the socialist revolution of 1944. These changes attract great attention among the poorer Third World states just beginning their own drives for rapid modernization. Equally important, the history of Bulgaria prior to 1944 contains significant parallels with the experiences of former colonial states—parallels not found in any other East European socialist nation. As the Bulgarian press ceaselessly reiterates, Sofia also experienced centuries of domination by a foreign power—Turkey—holding alien values—a period which sharply limited Bulgaria's economic and political development. Only with the advent of socialism could rapid and planned modernization take place, the results of which are evident to anyone who has spent time visiting Bulgarian cities and industrial installations. In short, Bulgaria's historic legacy and consistent tempo of economic development since 1944 make her a unique model for the smaller Third World states to follow. As a young African intellectual confided to this author in the summer of 1979 in Sofia: "To achieve the standards of West Germany in the near future is beyond our wildest dreams. But to do what Bulgaria has done—ah, that is a different matter."

In August 1979, the foreign language monthly *Bulgaria Today* devoted a special issue to the economic achievements of the previous four decades. Energy production was 1,000 times that of 1939, ferrous metal output was up 800 times, output of the products of mechanical engineering up 900 times, and per capita income was 4 times the prewar level. Today, the journal proudly noted, Bulgarian industry turned out in five days what required an entire year in 1939! With only one-third the manpower, agricultural production was three times the 1939 level. Production of nitrogen fertilizers exceeded that of West Germany, France, and Britain on a per capita basis, and Bulgaria ranked first in per capita energy production in the Balkans despite a dearth of natural power resources.

> Today Bulgaria is an industrial-cum-agrarian country—an advanced socialist state with developed up-to-date industry, large mechanized agricultural and a constantly growing national revenue.[11]

Similar glowing reports of successful, rapid modernization fill Bulgarian journals in an attempt to impress others with the viability of the Bulgarian model. The theoretical journal of the Bulgarian military, *Armeyski Kommunist,* reported that Bulgaria has sustained an average growth rate in national income of 8.8 percent between 1951 and 1977, industrial production had increased over 12 percent per year, and foreign trade expanded at 14 percent a year in the same period.[12] The dimensions of social and demographic change attending this period of socialist construction are indicated by statistics which show agriculture contributing 59 percent to the value of the social product in 1939, but industry only 19 percent; by 1977, industry contributed 66 percent and agriculture a mere 12 percent.[13] For an observer from the Third World, Bulgaria indeed has devised a successful method for emerging from economic backwardness.

Journalistic reports on achievements are but one method of attracting the attention of social reformers in the Third World. More important are the numerous tours and inspections of Bulgarian industry and agriculture arranged for increasing numbers of Third World guests. The ultimate purpose of these demonstrations was made clear by Bulgarian Party Chief Zhivkov at the 33rd Congress of the Bulgarian Agricultural People's Union (*BZNS*) in December 1976. Billed as a celebration of the great successes of Bulgarian development, Sofia extended invitations to a wide array of agricultural and economic experts from the Third World. Delegations from 80 parties and movements representing 62 states attended. In the keynote speech, Zhivkov stressed Bulgaria's own history of backwardness—a legacy rectified through rapid socialist modernization—and dwelt upon Bulgaria's unique capacity to understand similar problems in contemporary Third World states. The most feasible path to progress, Zhivkov intoned, was the route Bulgaria herself had followed, including acceptance of socialist aid.

> Bulgaria has passed along this path. Thirty years ago the Bulgarian people too lived in poverty, in great poverty. The land was parcelled out, technology was primitive, and the productivity of labor was extremely low. Industry was very weakly developed. We were the second most backward state in Europe, behind us was only Albania . . . . As you yourself can affirm, Bulgaria today is a developed industrial-agrarian state with a stable tempo of growth for her productive forces. As to the peoples' living standards, we are on the path of overtaking the more developed socialist and capitalist states in the not far future.[14]

In addition to the modernization model, Zhivkov emphasized the natural moral ties Bulgaria possessed with the newly liberated states—moral ties woven in Bulgaria's refusal to take part in the evils of colonialism and neocolonialism. Following completion of the congress, Third World leaders began individual tours of Bulgaria's economic achievements.

Even prior to the December 1976 congress, Bulgaria had invited leaders of key African states to examine firsthand the results of her modernization model. In October 1976, Agostino Neto, Chairman of the Popular Movement for the Liberation of Angola (*MPLA*)—an important socialist target—arrived in Sofia for a five–day visit. As Zhivkov remarked in his welcoming speech:

> Your visit will give you the possibility to familarize yourself with the successes of the Bulgarian people in socialist construction. *And we are prepared to share with you our experience in socio–economic reorganization which transformed Bulgaria from a backward agrarian state into a state with developed modern industry, with large mechanized farms, with flowing science, education and culture.*[15]

During his visit, Neto undertook an extensive tour of agricultural complexes, hydroelectric stations, automobile factories, and other installations in four Bulgarian cities. Upon completion, Neto confirmed his intention to modernize Angola through a similar socialist reorganization:

> It is the decision of the Angolan people to travel the socialist path, a path which passes through the construction of organs of popular power and through reorganization in the economic sphere, including collectivization of agriculture.[16]

A series of important Bulgarian–Angolan accords for economic assistance were concluded prior to Neto's departure.

One year later, in September 1977, Pedro de Kastro Vandisnem, Chairman of the Angolan People's Republic, began his tour of Bulgaria. Once again, Sofia's leaders stressed the importance of the Bulgarian model and their willingness to aid Third World states in socialist modernization. This time, Bulgarian Prime Minister Stanko Todorov took the lead, promising that:

> Our state will share the experiences accumulated in the construction of socialism and will render assistance with specialists, machines, technology, and the preparation of cadres in the areas of agriculture, pharmaceuticals, food-processing plants and the use of mineral resources.[17]

That same year, high-level officials arrived from Mali, Libya, and Tanzania, and Prime Minister Todorov accentuated Bulgaria's achievements during an extensive tour of East Africa.[18] In June 1978, Libyan strongman Qaddafi—in the company of his ministers for agriculture, trade, and industry, and the deputy ministers of transport and the Central Libyan Bank—visited Sofia for economic discussions and inspections.[19] Later that fall, Zhivkov undertook a protracted tour of Angola, Mozambique, Ethiopia, Nigeria, and South Yemen and brought home new economic accords. 1979 witnessed high-level visits by party and state leaders from South Yemen, as well as Mozambique and several other important African states. Perhaps the parting remarks of Ali Nassur Mohammed, Prime Minister of South Yemen best capture the intentions and successes of his Bulgarian hosts:

> The experience of the Bulgarian people in the construction of socialism makes a forceful impression. We are studying the revolutionary experience of the Bulgarian people![20]

Bulgarian's Economic Penetration of the Third World

The rapid expansion of Bulgaria's economic ties with Africa is, in part, a natural result of her concerted effort to proselytize on behalf of her modernization model. Yet these ties serve an additional function within the overall strategy of influencing target states to move towards the socialist world. Since 1975, Bulgaria has formed joint economic committees with various African and Middle Eastern states including Angola, the People's Republic of the Congo, Ethiopia, Ghana, Guinea, Libya, Mozambique, Tanzania, Zambia, and South Yemen. A mere listing, however, sheds little light upon the significance of these new relations.

In October 1976, upon completion of Angolan party leader Neto's Sofia visit, a series of accords were approved which offer insight into the depth of Bulgaria's Third World economic penetration. Included in these agreements was an understanding on scientific and technological cooperation which promised interstate assistance in joint scientific investigation, construction of Angolan production facilities, exchange of documentation, cooperation in land reclamation, the building of agrarian and industrial installations and mines, and the exchange of specialists and teachers.[21] A trade agreement provided for most favored nation status, as well as for Bulgarian exports of metal cutters, road-building equipment, textiles, agricultural machines, and other industrial goods for the depressed Angolan economy. Given the withdrawal of Portuguese technicians in the wake of the *MPLA* victory—a withdrawal whose deleterious effects were prominently discussed in the major Bulgarian journals prior to Neto's visit[22]—the accords provided proof of Bulgaria's desire to protect the image of the *MPLA* as an effective agent of economic and social change. During his 1978 return visit to Angola, Zhivkov approved a 13–point Treaty of Friendship and Cooperation which identified further areas for Bulgarian assistance.[23] According to a report of the Bulgarian Telegraph Agency (*BTA*) of 19 October 1978, 500 Bulgarian specialists already were active in various branches of the Angolan economy. During his tour, Zhivkov took pains to meet with his fellow countrymen, noting for local press consumption that their efforts had produced a modern agricultural economy in the province of Uila, complete with exemplary production levels of corn, vegetables, and fruits. In the district of Kasinga, Zhivkov boasted, Bulgarian and East German experts had constructed agricultural cooperatives—showcases for the surrounding villages.[24]

Relations with Mozambique are equally impressive. In the period since 1975, Mozambique and Bulgaria signed agreements for scientific-technological assistance, economic cooperation, trade, and mutual assistance in the areas of agriculture and food processing. At the suggestion of Bulgarian specialists, Mozambique, in 1977, drafted a general plan—scheduled to run until the year 2000—for the rational use of water resources in the key Limpopo River Basin. Soviet and Bulgarian specialists are to share in this task. Bulgaria also has contracted for construction of the important Massinger and Mapai Dams and will erect a 40–megawatt power plant at Massinger. Sofia also will build the Maputo–Cabo Delgado Highway.[25] In August 1979, Bulgaria provided Mozambique with a long-term grant exceeding $200 million to be disbursed through the year 2000.[26]

One could cite similar economic accords and the presence of Bulgarian specialists for nearly all the African nations with whom Bulgaria has formed joint economic commissions. The most impressive ties, however, are those with Libya. Those ties were initiated carefully during Zhivkov's 1976 visit to Tripoli. At this meeting, the two states— through a general treaty on Development of Friendship and Cooperation—approved an extended list of projects in diverse economic areas. Bulgarian specialists today take credit for construction of the Tripoli airport, a large brick factory, over 3000 apartments, an airfield in Seba, expansion of the harbor at Zaviia, numerous hospitals, sports centers, and other facilities too numerous to mention.[27] According to a recent CIA report, Bulgaria now maintains 10,000 technical experts in Libya, a number which accounts for nearly one-third of all Soviet and East European technical personnel in North Africa.[28]

The Bulgarian government stresses the unselfish, nonexploitative nature of her economic ties with the Third World, a theme which has some validity when compared to traditional Western investments.[29] In no case are assets acquired by Bulgarian assistance teams, and even the oft-suggested motive of expanding Bulgaria's trade with nations that pay in badly needed hard currency finds little support in existing trade figures. According to the most recent Bulgarian statistical handbook, trade with most of the key African states is still too minimal to be included. Libya, as expected, dominated the statistics but accounted for a mere 3.3 percent of Bulgaria's exports in 1977 and only 0.5 percent of imports. The few remaining African states listed—Nigeria, Guinea, and the Sudan—added only fractional amounts.[30] What, then, justifies this intense Bulgarian effort to expand her economic connections?

One motive—rarely, if ever, mentioned—is the atavistic nature of some segments of the Bulgarian population. As defined and described by authors such as Joseph Schumpter and Hannah Arendt (in a different context to be sure), atavistic characteristics are traits possessed by diverse groups in a population which relate to goals and methods of an earlier socical formation. Thus, war for Schumpter and imperialism for Arendt reflected a precaptialistic, feudal grouping of traits which remained in nascent capitalistic society—traits which found fulfillment in social and political endeavors inconsistent with the needs of the new society. It is not too farfetched to identify a similar pattern in Bulgaria: technical assistance and on-the-spot aid allow some members of Bulgarian society a freedom and sense of personal responsibility impossible within the rigidly controlled domestic atmosphere. This author has met many Bulgarians who display traits typical of the more self-reliant

Westerner—a great sense of daring and freedom. These are men and women who have spent time as specialists and diplomats in Africa and the Gulf states. Such individuals possess extensive libraries of "forbidden books" and maintain contacts with foreigners which are unthinkable for the average citizen. Perhaps Bulgaria's "export" of her more restless specialists offers an escape valve for the individuals holding traits more compatible with the pre–1944 period of an individual-centered, pluralistic society. Important as this escape valve may be, it figures little in the official explanations for expanded contact with the Third World.

The *raison d'etre* for Bulgaria's "selfless" engagement within Africa must be sought within the more general Soviet and East European penetration strategy. Soviet studies of this activity are numerous, but a recent essay by Anatoliy Gromyko capsulizes the main themes in the socialist perspective. To Moscow, African states have the ability to achieve high rates of economic growth, provided they spurn capitalistic institutions and values. While creation of a dedicated Marxist–Leninist leadership is deemed vital—a topic to be discussed shortly—emphasis is placed upon continuing struggle between the public and private sectors in the emerging African states. Successful socialist construction requires

> . . . consolidating and expanding the public sector in in the economy on an anticapitalistic basis, subordinating the various types of economic activity to the development of the leading one, that of a socialist nature, and creating the social and economic conditions for it to prevail.[31]

Assistance in the relentless struggle between the public and private sectors is the major goal of Bulgarian and East European efforts.

The rapid expansion of Bulgarian economic aid has been accompanied by numerous theoretical studies in Bulgarian journals which stress the creation of state economic institutions as a required stage for a socialist victory in Third World states. As theorist Anton Getsov notes:

> The economic aid of the socialist states is directed above all to advancing the key branches in the economy of the developing states. Aid from the socialist states is directed chiefly to the development and strengthening of the state sector in strategic branches. And the presence of a broad, stable state sector is the required basis for achieving rapid progress in economic reorganization upon which the economic independence of the state is built.[32]

Such a pattern of development creates sharpening contradictions between the growing state-directed proletariat and the remnants of the native bourgeoise.

The deepening of the national liberation movement and its development into a national democratic revolution necessarily leads to an intensification of the class contradictions.[33]

With each expansion of the state sector, the "forces of progress" grow. Thus, in Tanzania, through augmentation of state economic direction aided by East European assistance, the working class increased by 50 percent.[34]

The success of the concentrated and coordinated socialist effort to promote the dominance of the state sector, coupled with the emerging collective security system, is the most tangible evidence of East European achievement. According to Soviet authors, a wide belt of African states with a "socialist orientation" now exists, accounting for 30 percent of all African territory and 25 percent of the population.[35] It is this fundamental social and political reorientation upon which the more visible and alarming expansion of Soviet military and diplomatic connections rests. Bulgaria continues to play a vital role in this awesome development.

Bulgaria and the "Denial" Aspects of the Collective Security System

If the expansion of economic arrangements with Third World states forms the positive aspect of socialist strategy towards Africa, crucial "denial" clauses in recent interstate agreements are the negative aspect. While predicting the eventual completion of the socialist reorientation of targeted African states, the USSR and her East European allies limit carefully the possibilities for any future Western military ties through the inclusion of key clauses in numerous friendship treaties. Such clauses restrict possible African temptations to abandon their socialist connections in response to growing Western efforts to combat spreading Soviet influence. As expected, the USSR has taken the lead in this area, although Bulgaria is becoming an important participant in such restrictive agreements.

In October 1976, the Soviet Union initiated the first of the "denial" agreements in a lengthy Friendship Treaty with Angola. Chapter 11, the key, stated:

> Both of the contracting states testify that they will not enter into alliances or accept participation in any grouping of states, or likewise in activities or measures directed against the high contracting party.[36]

The seriousness of this pledge was reaffirmed in Chapter 12 which asserted that neither nation possessed understandings with any nation which might contradict this solemn pledge. Treaties with identical or similar clauses now exist between the Soviet Union and Mozambique,

Ethiopia, and South Yemen.[37] As one might expect, the Soviet example has been followed by other Warsaw Pact allies and by Cuba, with the most recent successes coming as a result of the lengthy visit of East German Party Chief Honecker to East Africa and South Yemen in the fall of 1979.[38] Bulgaria also has not been idle, concentrating on the target states of Angola and Mozambique.

In October 1978, Zhivkov's tour of sub-Saharan Africa produced a series of new Friendship Treaties and Agreements. The treaty with Angola contained an identical "denial" clause. The Bulgarian proudly noted that only Moscow had preceded Sofia in such an understanding with Luanda.[39] That same week, the same clause found its way into a new Bulgarian–Mozambican accord.[40] Bulgaria possesses more limited accords with other key states such as Ethopia, Libya, and South Yemen, although the future may well find their upgrading to include this important pledge.

The extent of active Bulgarian military assistance to the new client states remains unclear. The most visible military presence remains Cuban, with more than 20,000 troops and advisers in Angola and an estimated force of 17,000 in Ethiopia.[41] East German contributions are estimated at about 1,700 troops and advisers in Africa, with an additional 2,000 in South Yemen. The visits of East German Defense Minister Hoffmann and Party leader Honecker suggest some expansion of force allocations.[42] By these standards, Bulgaria's role pales. This is a clear indication such assistance is assigned to other socialist states. Nevertheless, Bulgarian military personnel reportedly are stationed in Ethiopia,[43] and the Bulgarian–Mozambican accord noted above contains a clause on active military cooperation. During his visits to Angola and Mozambique, Zhivkov was hailed as a leader who had provided vital military help during the recent periods of civil war. Frequent visits to Bulgaria by African military specialists and defense ministers are regularly noted in the Bulgarian press. Nevertheless, active military aid to client states is secondary in importance in Bulgaria's efforts to expand the belt of African states with a "socialist orientation."

Bulgaria and the Development of a Marxist–Leninist Leadership in the Third World

Despite evident successes, the Soviet penetration strategy remains tentative, constantly exposed to possible reverses and defections. "Denial" clauses, expansion of the public sector, and the presence of thousands of socialist military and economic personnel insure the desired reorientation of targeted states only to the degree the local political leadership remains steadfast in its pursuit of socialist goals. The Soviet and East European boasts of an emerging belt of African states with a "socialist orientation" conceal deep anxieties over the failure of such states to create the Marxist–Leninist leadership which is seen as crucial for comprehensive socialist reorientation. Therefore, the political reeducation and training of Africa's revolutionary cadre assume a central role in the socialist penetration of the third world. As Gromyko stated in his contribution to *International Affairs:*

> The African countries developing in a socialist way have not completely extricated themselves from the capitalist world's economic fold and are still tied to it by many economic tethers. *The social and economic reforms underway in Algeria, The People's Republic of the Congo, Guinea, Tanzania, Angola, Mozambique, Benin, and Madagascar are not being implemented under a working–class dictatorship and the leadership of Marxist–Leninist parties.* The leadership here is often provided by revolutionary democrats whose advanced sections often go over to scientific socialism.[44]

In the required "reeducation" drive, Bulgaria plays a role which is not even inferior to that of Moscow.

The dimensions of Bulgaria's contribution to the training of Marxist–Leninist Third World cadre reflect several important aspects of the comtemporary "realpolitik." First, in Third World affairs, the presence of Bulgarian party workers produces much less local backlash than a visible Soviet effort. Also important are the similarities between Bulgaria and the newly independent African states with respect to size, economic potential, and the long years of foreign bondage. Finally, the reliability of the Bulgarian leadership in the eyes of Moscow is a record unmatched by other East European parties.

In the past half decade, Bulgarian theorists have devoted time and effort to analyzing the needs of the contemporary liberation movements.[45] A recent study, however, merits detailed scrutiny since it reflects the general socialist strategy for a successful scenario of Marxist development in the Third World which posits the emergence of a firm Marxist–Leninist cadre as a sine qua non.

> The success of further revolutionary reorganization in those states with a progressive orientation depends upon the presence of a revolutionary organization which perceives the construction of socialism as its final goal. In the course of reorganization, such an organization is created or else the existing, gradual evolution towards communism produces . . . [such a party].[46]

Even in the most advanced "socialist" African states, such an organization has yet to emerge.

> Undoubtedly, this is a temporary and historically transient phenomenon. The continuing socio-economic development of these states . . . will unavoidably give rise to a communist

movement (providing) leadership for the socio-political developments.[47]

The emergence of a "revolutionary-democratic party, inspired by the ideals of scientific socialism" is viewed as a natural historical occurrence once the revolutionary successes of the initial national liberation movement have stabilized.

> These revolutionary-democratic parties formed after the gaining of national independence, after power has been taken into the hands of the patriotic-progressive forces, have a different character. They are more homogeneous (than the earlier national liberation movements) as to social composition and with respect to their ideological-political positions.[48]

Typical of such parties in the author's opinion are the contemporary South Yemeni Socialist Party which replaced the Yemeni United Organization of the Political Front, the *MPLA* of Angola, *FRELIMO* in Mozambique, and the ruling parties in Benin and the Congo. The sole thread linking these groups is recognition of scientific socialism as the preferred basis for socio-economic reorganization. And yet, further party development is essential if initial gains are not to be aborted. For Mashkov, even the reformed *MPLA* falls short of gaining the status required for an avant-garde, Marxist–Leninist party. Time and, most important, outside assistance are still needed.

> For the continuing development of the class struggle which the *MPLA* began more than 20 years ago, an avant-garde party is necessary which, led by the scientific ideology of the proletariat, Marxism–Leninism, organizes and leads the working class and other revolutionary classes in the struggle for the overthrow of capitalism and construction of socialism.

> This party will develop from the *MPLA;* the conversion into a Marxist–Leninist Party![49]

While many factors influence the emergence of this third and final stage of revolutionary party development, among the most important is the "unselfish, comprehensive assistance of the States of the Socialist Commonwealth led by the Soviet Union."[50]

In fulfillment of her duty to provide "comprehensive assistance" to the developing avant-garde parties, Bulgaria has negotiated an extensive series of party agreements, exchanges, and training sessions with important members of key African revolutionary parties. In Angola, Bulgaria has cooperated closely with the USSR in offering the *MPLA* the accumulated knowledge of party development. While the details of the numerous Bulgarian Communist Party–*MPLA* accords have not been published (four were signed in October 1978 alone), a TASS release covering a similar Soviet–*MPLA* agreement provides some insight. The Soviet understanding, signed in October 1976, lists six key areas of interparty cooperation: (1) broadening of interparty ties at all levels and the exchange of experience, (2) regular exchange of party delegations, (3) cooperation in preparation of party cadre, (4) strengthening of contacts between organs of mass communications, (5) expansion of ties between social organizations, and (6) yearly meetings to review existing efforts aimed at specific programs of cooperation.[51] The importance of Eastern European guidance was emphasized again by Bulgarian politburo member Takov at the 1977 reorganizational meeting of the *MPLA*.

> The communists and all workers of Bulgaria greet the revolutionary conquests of the Angolan people which affirm anew the power of our era: the world socialist community, the international proletariat, and the national liberation movement of the people.[52]

In nearby Mozambique, Bulgaria's efforts to promote inter-party relations appear to exceed those of the USSR. Referring to an interparty protocol signed in October 1978, the Bulgarian press stated:

> This agreement-protocol for 1979–1980 reflects the mutual desire to strengthen and deepen party ties on the basis of Marxism–Leninism, proletarian internationalism, and the unity of the revolutionary struggle. In this regard, the two parties will exchange working groups to study their experiences in party work in organizational areas, preparation of cadre, and mass organizations. They will study party work in socialist reconstruction of industry and agriculture, and party leadership in socio-economic activities, and in propaganda and ideological work. The two will bring about cooperation between socio-political organizations, will exchange informational documents and publications on internal and external policies, and will facilitate cooperation between central press organs. The two parties will exchange delegations at congresses, national conferences, and other important celebrations. The Central Committee of the Bulgarian Party will reserve stipends for training cadre in the academies for social science (majors) and social administrators, and will send lecturers in the fields of party construction, party leadership, economics, education, and culture.[53]

Possibilities for even broader contacts were anticipated:

> The people of Mozambique under the leadership of *FRELIMO* declared at their third conference (in 1977) their decision to create a Marxist–Leninist Party which will direct the construction of a socialist society in Mozambique.[54]

204

Similar party agreements, some less extensive in nature, now exist between Bulgaria and the African states of Benin, Libya, and Zambia. In each case, Bulgarian efforts to influence party development are insured. The most concerted attempt in this direction, however, currently is in a state on the African periphery, South Yemen. While the enhanced importance of this region has grown due to the continuing oil crisis—witness the October 1979 South Yemeni Friendship Treaty[55]—Bulgaria has maintained close ties with Aden since the late 1970s. Under an agreement signed in 1978, the Yemeni Socialist Party and the Bulgarian Communist Party arranged for exchanges of numerous working groups to examine party experiences and ideological developments. Bulgaria has tendered invitations for party congresses, symposia, seminars, and theoretical conferences. Party documents and publications are regularly exchanged, and Bulgaria has pledged to dispatch lecturers and to train Yemeni party cadre.[56] In a recent interview granted to the Bulgarian Party newspaper *Rabotnichesko Delo,* General Secretary of the Yemeni Socialist Party and President of the Republic Abdul Ismail confirmed the priority of future party development:

> The chief task of our Party at this stage of development is defined . . . by the ideology of our Party and the course of the revolution. *And this is why we consider the ideological preparation of the working class in our state to be the most important means for the realization of the aims of the revolution.*
> We highly value the support and assistance which the Party and the Government of the People's Democracy of Bulgaria render us. This strengthens our fighting unity against the imperialistic and reactionary forces, provides us with the possibility to achieve the goals of our revolution in the name of progress, socialism, and peace. Such aid is an expression of true proletarian internationalism.[57]

It is apparent the expanded military aid granted South Yemen by East Germany and the USSR continues to be supplemented by the equally important and, in the long term, more decisive assistance devoted to insuring the proper evolution of the ruling socialist party.

The significance of Bulgaria in the ideological "gleichschaltung" of Third World revolutionary cadre was confirmed anew in December 1978 through the selection of Sofia as host for the Worldwide Congress of Communist and Workers Parties. Attended by high-ranking representatives from 73 revolutionary parties in Africa, Asia, Europe, and the Americas, this conference reemphasized the major tenets of the penetration strategy. Eschewing the more complex debates as to role of parties in the advanced states, the meeting focused upon the needs of the Third World. As *Armeyski Kommunist* reported:

> The international theoretical conference reviewed several

important aspects of the successes and perspectives of the revolutionary struggle in the states of Africa, Asia, and Latin America.[58]

The most important theme stressed was precisely the one forming the basis of existing Bulgarian-Third World interparty agreements:

> The intense process of forming a revolutionary party which has the ability to mature into an avant-garde and guiding political force, into a party of a Marxist–Leninist type.[59]

In the weeks following the conference, *Rabotnichesko Delo* carried extensive interviews with the participants. Perhaps the strongest praise for past and present Bulgarian efforts came from Mozambique's *FRELIMO* representative:

> The delegate from *FRELIMO* stressed the significance of the great revolutionary legacy of (Communist Bulgaria's founder) Georgi Dimitrov. From him we learned the method for determining the chief tasks at every stage of the historical process, the means of winning all progressive forces for our cause.[60]

Bulgaria and Mexico: A New Stage in the Penetration Strategy

In the fall of 1979, Western analysts were stunned by the announcement from Mexico City of future Soviet assistance in the training of Mexican military cadre. Once again, the evident results of a carefully planned penetration strategy eclipsed examination of the step-by-step process of creating confidence measures between Mexico and the East Bloc which had resulted in the announcement itself. Once again, little Bulgaria—unobserved—had played a dominant role.

Relations between Bulgaria and Mexico are a recent thing, a fact which makes the results to date even more impressive. Diplomatic recognition was extended only in 1974; the exhange of ambassadors was deferred until the following year. In 1975, Mexico signed a cooperation accord with the East European Council of Mutual Assistance (COMECON), followed by the formation of a Mexican–COMECON joint economic commission in 1976. That same year, the first Mexican–Bulgarian trade agreement was approved. In March 1978, a Bulgarian–Mexican intergovernmental commission negotiated a series of understandings on economic cooperation.[61] These initial ties, however, gave only the slightest hint of the role Bulgaria was to play in the economic life of America's neighbor.

In May 1978, Mexican President Portillo, his wife, and a group of high cabinet officals arrived for a five-day visit in Sofia. From the moment of his first public speech, it was apparent Portillo was deeply impressed with the Bulgarian modernization model and expected both theoretical and practical assistance in Mexico's own economic development:

> Bulgaria is able to show impressive achievement in the production of food. Its quick transition from a traditional to a highly developed agricultural economy is a model. The new conceptions for agrarian-industrial development offer rich possibilities for the exchange of experiences, and we have already determined the specific areas of cooperation. This cooperation must embrace every step in agricultural production.[62]

In the following three days, Portillo took the road already well-traveled by Third World leaders by visiting agro-industrial plants in four Bulgarian cities. On 29 May, the results were announced. An unprecedented total of 13 economic accords had been signed which pledged Bulgarian assistance in agriculture, food processing, joint industrial production, exchange of technical documentation, joint seminars, cooperation in banking, and the exchange of specialists.[63] The Bulgarian model clearly made a deep impression, as Portillo himself stated:

> . . . for Mexico, the high achievements of Bulgaria in the efficient organization of agriculture are extraordinarily (*izvunredno*) suitable, especially in the areas of the organization of production, in distribution of the fruits of labor and in the creation of large agrarian-industrial complexes.[64]

Even more startling were the high political compliments Portillo paid his Bulgarian hosts:

> I wish to stress before the Bulgarian people the exceptional impression which that great politician who is the president, Zhivkov, left with me. He has the problems of the state and the world at his fingertips, he knows everything (*znae vischko*), is familiar with everything, and this gave me the strongest impression that he is a man who is not satisfied with what has been done and what is being done. He speaks of future projects with a confidence that inspires awe.[65]

Hints that the discussions had touched upon the more sensitive issue of Mexico's possible drift towards socialistic organization were also forthcoming. Referring to Bulgaria's form of rural collectivization, Portillo remarked:

> This is one of the models which will be useful for us because, as I said already, you have decided one of the most important problems confronting us at the moment—

ownership. It is not only important who possesses the land, but how, for whom, and for what it is cultivated.[66]

In April 1979, Zhivkov returned Portillo's visit, receiving the keys to Mexico City and signing a new series of economic agreements. The friendly tone of this new meeting was set by Portillo:

> . . . for Mexico, the production of food is of primary significance. In this area, Mexico can and must learn from the intensive system of production of your great state in which we see many *similarities with the Mexican nation.*[67]

Now it was Zhivkov's turn to review Mexico's economic progress, concentrating upon those areas in which Bulgaria was directly involved. Most interesting were two large agro-industrial complexes in the Mexican state of Guerrero where 24 Bulgarian specialists had been employed for some time.[68] The new agreements signed will expand this direct technical assistance even further. Phase one of the penetration strategy was again in process.

Conclusion

As Soviet analysts glance back at the decade just ended, they must take heart in the expanding belt of Third World states with a "socialist orientation" which constitute further evidence of the "irreversible" world drift towards Marxism. Yet when the accolades are disbursed in Moscow, others too must gain praise for their intense labors aimed at the essential, if less visible, structural changes in the targeted less developed states. Bulgaria's contributions continue to form a basic part of the overall penetration strategy, a strategy which proves its feasibility with each new success. Recent activities in Mexico confirm the importance of the Bulgarian connection.

The present study began with the suggestion that concentration upon the more evident military ties between the USSR/Cuba and the Third World often conceals the more fundamental step-by-step implementation of the penetration strategy itself. In this respect, the much overused American slogan of "small is beautiful" retains some validity. Examination of the policy objectives and implementing activities of Moscow's smaller allies contributes a fresh and often central insight into the general policy of the socialist commonwealth. Frequently, these allies lack the subtleties of diplomacy characteristic of a superpower, allowing the observers to more easily grasp the main dimensions of policy. One must wonder what information might be gained from an examination of East German or Czechoslovak motives and strategy on behalf of their military assistance to the Third World. More partial studies, in conjunction with a continuing examination of Soviet policy, might lead to a comprehensive understanding of the penetration strategy as a whole. In December 1979, the complex intertwining of socialist and client states took on a new dimension: Ethopia and South Yemen negotiated their own friendship treaty with provisions for military cooperation. It appears the ongoing Soviet penetration drive—in all its phases—offers ample room for extensive Western research.

Notes

1. Avigdor Haselkorn, *The Evolution of Soviet Security Strategy, 1965–1975* (New York: Crane, Russak and Company, 1978).
2. W. Scott Thompson, *Power Projection: A Net Assessment of U.S. and Soviet Capabilities* (New York: National Strategy Information Center, 1978).
3. Nimrod Novik, *On the Shores of Bab Al–Mandab: Soviet Diplomacy and Regional Dynamics* (Philadelphia: Foreign Policy Research Institute, 1979).
4. The best studies of Eastern European aid to Africa remain the series of six Radio Free Europe Research Reports which appeared between 1 March and 21 June 1979. Although filled with details, these reports fail to discern a coordinated effort.
5. For East Germany, see the extensive coverage of Erich Honecker's November 1979 visit to Ethiopia in *Neues Deutchland,* 14 November 1979 See also Robert M. Bigler, "Role of Surrogate Forces in Soviet Penetration of Africa," *Africa Institute Bulletin,* Vol. 16, Nos. 16 and 17 (1978), pp. 251–255.
6. National Foreign Assessment Center, *Communist Aid Activities in Non–Communist Less Developed Countries, 1978* (Washington: Central Intelligence Agency, 1979), pp. 7–8.
7. In 1978, large-scale economic credits to 2 states—Morocco and Turkey—accounted for 90 percent of Soviet assistance. For an assessment of rising Soviet aid to Turkey, see Michael M. Boll, "Turkey between East and West: The Regional Alternative," *The World Today,* September 1979, pp. 360–368, and Michael M. Boll, "Turkey's New National Security Concept: What It Means for NATO," *Orbis,* Fall 1979, pp. 609–631.
8. *Communist Aid Activities in Non–Communist Less Developed Countries, 1978,* pp. 14 and 20.
9. *Kulpolitika* [World Politics] (Journal of the Hungarian Institute of Foreign Affairs, Budapest), No. 1, 1977, p. 132, as translated in Aurel Bereznai, "Hungary's Presence in Black Africa," *Radio Free Europe Research Report,* 2 April 1979.
10. While statistical accounts of East European per capita income vary, I have used in this study those offered in *The Military Balance, 1979–1980* (London: The International Institute for Strategic Studies, 1979).
11. *Bulgaria Today* (Sofia), No. 8, 1979, pp. 35–41.
12. G. Mirov, "The International Economic Authority of Bulgaria," *Armeyski Kommunist* [Army Communist], No. 8, 1979, pp. 35–41.
13. See *Statisticheski Godishnik na Narodna Republika Bulgariia* [Statistical Yearbook for the Bulgarian People's Republic] (Sofia, 1978), p. 12.
14. *Rabotnichesko Delo* [Workers Affairs] (Sofia), 2 August 1977 (hereafter referred to as *RD*).
15. Ibid., emphasis added.
16. *RD,* 14 October 1976.
17. Welcoming speech by Bulgarian Prime Minister Todorov, RD, 27 September 1977.
18. See *RD,* 26 January 1977, 4 May 1977, and 9–12 May 1977.
19. *RD,* 18 and 21 June 1978.
20. *RD,* 13 April 1979.
21. *RD,* 17 October 1976.

22. See *RD*, 21 January 1976.
23. *RD*, 22 October 1978.
24. *RD*, 21 October 1978.
25. See *RD*, 25 June 1978, 23–26 October 1978, and *Communist Aid Activities in Non–Communist Less Developed Countries*, 1978, p. 23.
26. *AF Press Clips*, 7 September 1979, p. 17.
27. *RD*, 22–25 December 1976, 31 August 1977, 10–12 May 1977, and 21 June 1978.
28. *Communist Aid Activities in Non–Communist Less Developed Countries, 1978*, pp. 14 and 20. These figures strike this author as a bit too high. See *RD*, 17 June 1978 for Bulgarian estimates.
29. For a Bulgarian discussion of "selfless" motives, see R. Ulyanovskiy "The USSR and the National Liberation Movement," *RD*, 18 November 1976.
30. *Statisticheski Godishnik na Narodna Republika Bulgariia*, pp. 361–362
31. Anatoliy Gromyko, "Socialist Orientation in Africa," *International Affairs* (Moscow), September 1979, p. 97.
32. A. Getsov, "Real and Selfless Aid," *RD*, 24 September 1976.
33. V. Martinov, "Basic Tendencies in the Development of the Third World," *Politicheska Agitatsiya* [Political Agitation], No. 12, June 1978, p. 63.
34. I. Khlebarova, "Africa, the Working Class Gathers Strength," *RD*, 24 July 1977.
35. Gromyko, p. 95.
36. *Pravda*, 9 October 1976.
37. See *Pravda*, 3 April 1977, 21 November 1978, and 26 October 1979.
38. See the "denial" clauses in the East German–Ethiopian Friendship Agreement and in the East German–South Yemeni agreememt, *Neues Deutschland*, 16 and 19 November 1979.
39. *RD*, 22 October 1978.
40. *RD*, 25 October 1978.
41. See the estimates in *Newsweek*, 3 December 1979, and *UPI*, 15 May 1979.
42. See William F. Robinson, "Eastern Europe's Presence in Black Africa," *Radio Free Europe Research Report*, 21 June 1979, and *Neues Deutschland*, 14–19 November 1979.
43. *Washington Post*, 4 July 1978.
44. Gromyko, p. 97, emphasis added.
45. See L. Entin, "Africa, The Actual Problems of Socialist Orientation, *RD*, 21 August 1978, as well as Khlebarova and Marinov.
46. Khristo Mashhkov, "The Formation of a Revolutionary Avant–Garde Party in the Developing States," *Polititicheska Agitatsiya*, No. 23, December 1978, p. 73.
47. Ibid.
48. Ibid., p 74.
49. Ibid., p. 76.
50. Ibid., p. 77.
51. *TASS* (in Russian), 14 October 1976.
52. *RD*, 9 December 1977.
53. *RD*, 25 October 1978.
54. Ibid.
55. For this treaty, see *Pravda*, 26 October 1979.
56. *RD*, 30 October 1978.
57. *RD*, 13 October 1979, emphasis added.
58. Todor Ganchev, "International Unity on a Marxist–Leninst Foundation," *Armeyski Kommunist*, No. 3, 1979, p. 79.
59. Ibid., pp. 79–80.
60. Interview with Serge Vieira of *FRELIMO*, *RD*, 14 December 1978.
61. For a review of Bulgarian–Mexican economic and diplomatic developments, see Valeri Natan, "Equal Rights and Mutual Profit," *RD*, 29 March 1979.
62. *RD*, 26 May 1978.
63. *RD*, 29 May 1978.

64. *Ibid.*
65. Interview with President Portillo, *RD,* 29 May 1979.
66. Ibid.
67. See Portillo's toast to Zhivkov, *RD,* 15 April 1979, emphasis added.
68. *RD,* 6 April 1979.

The USSR in the Third World: Opportunities, Obstacles, and Objectives

Robert H. Donaldson

Although the swirl of current events in Indochina, Southeast Asia, the Middle East, or Africa provides ample occasion for discussion of Soviet intentions and activities in several "hot spots" of the Third World, I have chosen in this article to take a longer range perspective. Precisely because the attention of the public and policymakers lately has been focused so intensely on Soviet activity in areas of crisis and possible superpower confrontation, an assessment of the USSR's goals and behavior in the larger context is vitally needed. While the burden of such an exercise is toward discerning trends which might prevail in Soviet policy through the 1980s, the search for Moscow's objectives and for patterns in its activities necessarily must begin with the Bolshevik forerunners of the current regime.

Indeed, from the very beginning of the Bolshevik movement in Russia, its leaders avowed an appreciation for the importance of the "East" to the world revolutionary cause. Although Lenin and his colleagues in the years immediately following the October Revolution concentrated their attention in foreign policy on problems relating to the industrially advanced countries of Europe, they remained sensitive to the role the "toiling masses of the East" could play in assisting the proletariat to achieve its victory over the world imperialist system. Still, it remained for the heirs of Stalin to make—as probably their most important foreign policy achievement—the first substantial and continuing Soviet investments in the area now commonly known as the "Third World." (The term is used here to refer to the less developed noncommunist countries of Asia, Africa, and Latin America. This area currently comprises two-thirds of the world's states and almost half its population.)

During the first years of the century, Lenin saw—in the context of his theory of imperialism—the value of a temporary tactical alliance between communist forces and the "national liberation movement" in the East. Writing in 1916, he argued the proletariat must give "determined support to the more revolutionary elements in the bourgeois-democratic movements" in their agitation for national liberation.[1] Such bourgeois-led movements were deemed worthy of support not only because they created the internal conditions necessary for capitalist (and then socialist) development, but also because they were directed against the imperialist powers. Their success thus weakened the system of imperialism itself. This Leninist position, worked out before 1917, has continued to occupy a central place in Soviet policymakers' analyses in the contemporary era. It was only after the death of Stalin that a shift in Soviet policy could be discerned, however. The initial thrust of the active Soviet reentry into the countries of the East came in seeming response to the policies of Moscow's American rival and the new Soviet ally in Beijing. Washington's efforts in 1954–55 to enlarge the ring of containment by enlisting allies on the Soviet Union's southern periphery (Pakistan, Iraq, Iran) alarmed the Soviets, and the hostile reaction to the American policy on the part of the emerging "neutralist" nations encouraged Moscow to counterattack. Moreover, Zhou Enlai's success in capitalizing on the antiimperialist mood at the Bandung Conference of Asian and African States held in Indonesia in 1955 demonstrated anew the possibilities for a communist-nationalist alliance against the imperialists' designs.

Thus, by 1955, there was in Moscow a reawakened appreciation of the importance of the Third World as the vital "strategic reserve" of imperialism and as an arena in which the Soviets could wage the bipolar struggle with solid prospects of success (but at lower level of risk than would be posed by a direct challenge in the "main arena" of confrontation). The year's significant events foreshadowed the Soviet priorities and techniques in this new arena: Moscow's entry into the Middle East by means of the arms deal with Nasser's Egypt; the visit to Moscow of India's Prime Minister Nehru and the return trip to India, Burma, and Afghanistan by Khrushchev and Bulganin; and the dramatic announcement the Soviets would finance and construct a giant steel mill at Bhilai in India. These early targets of Soviet activity were chosen for their strategic importance in the struggle with the West rather than for any particular features of their internal development, and the Soviets soon set about—with great optimism but little sophisticated knowledge of the domestic affairs of the Third World states—to revise the doctrinal bases of their new policy.

Clearly then, Lenin prepared the ideological foundations for the communist alliance with the forces of national liberation; in its early years, however, the besieged Soviet state lacked the resources for an operational commitment in the East. Stalin had more resources at his command, but his own experiences and attitudes had blunted and distorted the Leninist perception of strategic opportunity in the imperialist reserve. It took the new Soviet leadership—at the helm of the world's second mightiest state and eager to demonstrate the continued revolutionary vitality of its ideology—to provide the fresh doctrinal approach to undergird the new operational initiatives in the Third World.

Like Lenin, Khrushchev sensed that as long as the brunt of the independence movement was aimed at the imperialist West, it would serve the interests of the communist East. There was a sufficient community of interest to provide the basis for a temporary alliance against the common enemy—a new "Zone of Peace," he called it. As for the future, it was Khrushchev's confident assertion that aid from the socialist bloc could allow the Third World countries to break away from the imperialist economic grip and launch their plans for industrialized and truly independent national economies. The inevitable result of this process would be the emergence of a class-conscious proletariat ready to respond to the political program of its communist vanguard and—once the "national bourgeoisie" had revealed the compromising side of its dual nature—to assume political power, even by peaceful means.

But (to paraphrase a remark Soviet writers would later aim at Third World leaders) to proclaim the prospects for socialism is easier than to achieve them. Only a few years after their initial plunge into Asia and Africa, the Soviets were discovering that their initial optimism concerning the enlargement of the camp of socialism was misplaced. With only rare exceptions (such as Indonesia), the communist parties in these regions were either still nonexistent, weak, or persecuted by the new nationalist allies of the Soviet Union. Some Afro–Asian communist leaders were bold enough to voice their frustration at this state of affairs. But the primary problem was the unwillingness of the nationalist and revolutionary elites in the new nations to adhere to Marxism–Leninism or "scientific socialism" or to proclaim their willingness to establish "people's democracies" in their countries. The fiercely nationalistic leaders of Asia and Africa had their own goals for political and economic progress, and, though many of them were influenced by Marxist thought and "socialist" ideals, they were loath to accept the Soviet approach and model. Needless to say, those leaders who spurned formal communist affiliation were uncomfortable with a Soviet policy which proclaimed their inevitable removal from power.

At the root of this dilemma was a woeful ignorance on the part of Soviet politicians and their advisers of the actual social and economic conditions prevailing in the Third World. Khrushchev's initial proclamation of the "Zone of Peace" strategy had asserted as the sole criterion for Soviet support of the new regimes the degree of anti-imperialist content in their foreign policies, but—as the Soviets and the nationalist leaders themselves increasingly turned their attention to the problems of development—the artificiality of the orthodox Soviet approach became even more evident. It was not until the 20th Party Congress freed Soviet analysis from the sterile formulas of Stalin that scholars were able to do the research necessary to provide a more sophisticated understanding of the internal politics and economies of Third World countries.

The Soviet Union's approach to the Third World has truly been opportunistic, not only in its willingness to modify the Marxist–Leninist doctrine to fit a variety of circumstances but also in its use of a wide range of instrumentalities for establishing its presence and extending its influence. Often based in bilateral agreements of variable duration,

214

Moscow's relations with the nations of the Third World are spread broadly in the political, economic, military, and cultural spheres. They reach beyond government-to-government dealings and include relationships with both communist and noncommunist parties; contacts and exchanges among trade union, student, scientific, artistic, and other groups (both directly through the Soviet counterpart organization and through various international communist-front organizations); the massive dissemination of both printed material and radio propaganda; the on-the-scene activities of tens of thousands of Soviet technicians and advisers, both civilian and military; and so forth.

Taken as a whole, the Soviet contacts with Third World countries fully exemplify the techniques of what Andrew Scott has termed "informal penetration"—"means by which the agents or instruments of one country gain access to the population (or parts of it) or processes of another country" and in which "the special nature of cold warfare must be sought."[2] As Scott analyzes it, this phenomenon has increased in frequency and importance for several reasons, among which are the greater role of public opinion in many nations, the development of ideological struggle, the technological revolution in communication and transportation, the increased destructiveness of full-scale warfare, and the emergence of a large number of new nations in the postwar era. Although they are also employed by the United States (as well as by China and a number of smaller countries, including Egypt and Cuba), the Soviet Union's utilization of these techniques of informal penetration has been—by virtue of its Leninist ideology and the totalitarian structure of its own state system—more coordinated and massive than any rival effort.

In recent years, the spectacular aid projects Khrushchev favored have been abandoned, and Soviet aid and trade agreements are being cast in a long-range framework, institutionalized through bilateral economic commissions and allowing for greater integration with the Soviet and East European plans for development. In a growing number of cases, imports from the less developed countries have been utilized as alternatives to domestic investment in the exploitation of raw materials. Extravagant claims regarding the accomplishments of foreign aid have been dropped, replaced by an emphasis on the limitations of what can be accomplished by Soviet resources. As Foreign Minister Gromyko put it:

> It is natural, however, that the Soviet Union's potential for rendering economic assistance is not infinite. Of course, the Soviet state cannot fail to be concerned for the well being of its own people. The Soviet Union . . . allocated funds to render the developing countries economic and technical assistance on the basis of its own capabilities.[3]

Increasingly, the motivations for Soviet aid and trade have been expressed in terms of mutual economic benefit, including the joint exploration and production of raw materials (for example, oil and natural gas) with repayment provided through shipments of the product itself. Prime Minister Kosygin described this to the 24th Party Congress in 1971:

> Our trade and economic cooperation with many [Third World countries] is entering a stage at which one can begin to speak of stably founded, mutually advantageous economic relations. Our cooperation with them is based on the principles of equality and respect for mutual interests . . . and is acquiring the characteristics of a stable distribution of labor . . . . At the same time, by expanding trade with the developing countries, the Soviet Union will gain the oppportunity of satisfying more fully the requirements of its own national economy.[4]

In the opinion of one respected Western observer of the Soviet scene, this new emphasis on creating firm and beneficial ties between the economies of the developing countries and the USSR amounts to an effort to fight imperialism by adopting imperialists techniques—a strategy which he has labeled "counterimperialism."[5]

Soviet aid and trade relations remain concentrated in a few areas, but there is little doubt these are chosen according to considerations of strategic benefit rather than by criteria of "progressiveness" alone. Even in cases where radical pro-Soviet regimes have been replaced by more moderate and less friendly governments, the Soviets have demonstrated a concern for protecting their considerable investments by maintaining "businesslike relations." In addition to economic factors such as debt repayment, the acquisition of new markets, or access to raw materials, the Soviets consider such factors as the degree of Chinese or Western interest in a country, its importance to Soviet security, or its ability to provide support facilities—including airports, harbors, or sites for communication stations—for Soviet military activities.

These latter factors have assumed greater importance in recent years as the Soviet Union has deployed a substantial naval force in the oceans and seas surrounding the Third World, and as it has sought to use this new capability not merely for military defense but for the political purpose of "protecting state interests in time of peace." Prior to the Second World War, the Soviet Union (and Russia before it) played the role of a "land power" and lacked a significant naval capability. But in the postwar period, Moscow has invested heavily in a large navy whose mission has been essentially defensive in nature. The post-Stalin development of Soviet surface and submarine vessels armed with tactical cruise missiles has been designed primarily to neutralize the perceived threat posed first by US aircraft carriers and, more recently, by the American strategic missile submarine force which the USSR has sought to counter through a massive antisubmarine warfare effort while adding a formidable sea-based attack capability of its own.

In addition to these purposes of defense and strategic deterrence, the Soviets have also in the last decade deployed their navy in such a way as to support foreign policy objectives, most notably in the Third World. In both the Mediterranean Sea and the Indian Ocean, they have sought to establish a peacetime naval "presence" featuring frequent port calls in the littoral countries, both to demonstrate their interest in these areas and to signal their resolve in times of crisis.

An interesting and significant illustration of this evolving purpose has been provided in the last decade by the Soviet naval presence in the Indian Ocean. First manifested with the appearance of two vessels in 1968, the Soviet deployment has slowly but steadily increased in both size and visibility. In recent years, the Soviets have maintained a permanent squadron of 15 to 20 vessels, with occasional "surges" in times of crisis to a squadron of more than 30. The original Soviet deployment was based on a combination of factors: a military-strategic concern over a potential submarine threat from the United States and the internal bureaucratic needs and organizational routines of the Soviet Navy.

Once established, however, the Soviets found the naval presence useful both as a means of safeguarding their growing commerce and as an instrument in the heightening political competition with Washington and Beijing. Thus, for most of the period, the primary purpose of Soviet naval activity has been the building and maintaining of political and economic influence in the littoral states. At times, this activity has focused on particularly strategic countries as the Soviets have sought to solidify their relations and express a commitment without provoking an overt military reaction from their global rivals. Moreover, the Soviets have on occasion utilized this capability for dramatic demonstrations of their resolve to back up their own and their clients' interests in times of crisis (e.g., the Bangladesh war of 1971, the Iraq–Kuwait conflict of 1973, and the period following the 1973 Middle East War).[6]

In utilizing its expanded naval capability for the purpose of "showing the flag" and supporting its foreign policy objectives, the Soviet leadership seems to be following the examples of the "imperialist" British and American navies and the teachings of their 19th century mentor, Admiral Alfred Thayer Mahan. Their activities demonstrate they have mastered the principle that subjective *perception* of strength and relative superiority weighs heavily in the competition for influence. Admiral Stansfield Turner, in an article published just prior to his appointment as Director of the US Central Intelligence Agency, expressed the point well:

> . . . though the United States can wield the presence tool more effectively, the Soviets have been playing the game well. Realizing that they are dealing with perceptions, they

are gaining maximum advantage from the fact that any change is news . . . . And as our Navy constricts and draws back from traditional deployment patterns, the Soviet Navy has been demonstrating increasingly imaginative and frequent global deployment of forces in response to developments in international politics—as in Angola, Mozambique, the Indian Ocean and West Africa. It seems a confirmation of the claim that we are a declining sea power and that they are a growing and restive one. The invalidity of that claim is academic if it is universally believed.[7]

Addressing the naval balance, Admiral Turner proceeded to demonstrate that in terms of specific objectives and missions, the US Navy remains adequate to the task. The Soviet Navy has achieved wide-ranging capabilities in strategic deterrence and naval presence, but it remains inferior in its mission of sea control—capable of denial only and not of assertion—and in its ability to project power ashore through amphibious and tactical air capabilities.[8] Nevertheless, the expansion of the Soviet Navy in the Brezhnev era has signaled Moscow's determination to achieve the status of a global superpower—not confined to the Eurasian landmass, but capable of projecting its power far beyond its own borders. In pursuit of this objective, the Soviets have given renewed importance to the achievement of a strong position in strategic areas of the Third World.

In two decades of active involvement, the Soviet Union has acquired a considerable stake in the Third World. However, we should not make the mistake of assuming this large investment implies the Third World is an objective of the highest priority for the Soviet leaders; the Soviets also have vital interests elsewhere. The compatibility of one of them—the relationship with the United States—with the active promotion of the "national liberation struggle" in southern Africa has been challenged by the US ever since the closing months of the Ford administration. The Soviets, however, have denied a conflict exists between their obligations under detente and their commitment to the "liberation struggle." As Secretary Brezhnev put it at the 25th Party Congress in 1976:

> Detente does not in the slightest way abolish, and cannot abolish or change the laws of the class struggle. We do not conceal the fact we see detente as a way to create more *favorable* conditions for peaceful socialist and communist construction.[9]

Indeed, he might have added that support of Third World "liberation" movements remains for the Soviets a primary means of demonstrating—at a time when they are under heavy challenge—their continuing ideological bona fides and loyalty to revolution. We do not have to accept at face value Brezhnev's bald claim that this is the only

Soviet motivation: "The Soviet Union is not looking for any benefits for itself, is not hunting for concessions, is not trying to gain political supremacy and is not seeking any military bases. We are acting as our revolutionary conscience and our communist convictions permit us."[10]

In fact, the Brezhnev-era approach seems much more attuned to precisely such factors as the satisfaction of Soviet military and economic interests, just as it has lowered the expectation Third World regimes are viable candidates for the rapid transformation to socialism. The Soviet timetable is longer and the style more cautious than it was in Khrushchev's time, and—in addition to such general and long-standing objectives as increasing Moscow's own influence—there are now more immediate goals such as gaining access to key resources, support facilities for naval expeditions, or trade routes. For these objectives and the supporting range of tactics, the term "counterimperialism" indeed seems most appropriate. And this complex of interests, much more than revolutionary impulse or ideological affinity, seems to provide Moscow's major criterion for the concentration of its energies and resources in the Third World.

In fact, the assumptions underlying the "revolutionary conscience" and "communist convictions" of the Soviet leaders have been under constant challenge in the Third World, and the wells of "creative Marxism–Leninism" seem to have run dry in the effort to salvage them. Socio-economic change occurs in the Third World in ways quite different from Soviet expectations; political change has been notoriously resistant to the neat categorizations of Marxist analysis.

Ironically, states which are judged most "progressive" by one set of measures may still prove to be very reluctant to follow the ideological prescriptions or policy advice of the Soviet Union. The record of Soviet relations with such states as Egypt, India, Indonesia, and Ghana is replete with instances of Moscow's inability to influence its supposed friends and clients. When the issue is of marginal importance to it, a state might be disposed to follow its patron's lead; in cases where its vital interests diverge from those of its great power friend, the Third World state frequently will pursue an independent course. Given its own stake in the region and its fear of being displaced by a great power rival, the patron usually is unable or unwilling to dictate. As a recent study of Soviet and Chinese influence in the Third World concluded, "Soviet and Chinese policies seem to have been adjustments to the needs of Third World countries more often than the latters' decisions have yielded to the preference of the Communist courters."[11]

The powerful force of nationalism thus has been a major obstacle to Moscow's efforts to enlist the resources and support of the countries of the Third World for achieving its own vital objectives. Moreover, the Third World's growing determination to exert full political and economic sovereignty has recently underscored the large degree of incompatibility between its own purposes and preferences and those of

219

the industrialized "great powers." At the United Nations and in special settings such as the May 1976 UN Conference on Trade and Development (UNCTAD IV) or the August 1976 Colombo Conference of Nonaligned Nations, the USSR has been finding itself in the uncomfortable position of being lumped together with other developed countries (the "North") and forced by the Third World (the "South") into a defensive position regarding its policies and tactics.

In response to this challenge, Moscow has sought to emphasize its own economic strength and developmental experience as resources freely available to the less developed countries and to reinforce the notion there is a natural community of interests between the USSR and the Third World. The problems of underdevelopment—food scarcity, overpopulation, illiteracy, mass underemployment—are all portrayed as consequences of the "crisis of capitalism" and the neocolonialist policies of the Western imperialists. To the extent the program for a "New International Economic Order" (NIEO) attacks the policies and practices of the West, the Soviets are willing to give it their full support. And yet its sponsors (the "Group of 77," which included 111 countries at the time of UNCTAD IV) have also included in their platform demands for changes in the policies and behavior of the USSR and its East European allies. The barter system of trade, the nonconvertibility of communist bloc currencies, and the refusal of the bloc to grant trade preferences to Third World products have been particular objects of Third World dissatisfaction. The efforts of Soviet representatives to deny the USSR bears any specific "obligation" or shares any collective responsibility for the worsening economic plight of the Third World are increasingly resented by spokesmen for the latter.

In the realm of trade with the Third World, Soviet practices are in fact far from the model of good behavior Moscow projects at international fora. The volume of Soviet trade with the developing countries did indeed rise during the 1970s, but the latter's share of total Soviet imports and exports actually fell. Only about 5 percent of Third World trade is with the USSR, whereas 75 percent is with the developed capitalist countries. Moreover, Third World trade with the Soviet Union is increasingly unbalanced, to the extent Moscow's trade surplus with the Third World countries has been increasingly important in helping to compensate for its trade deficit with the West. Nor does the Soviet Union by any means provide a favored market for the manufactured products of the developing countries; the capitalist West, in fact, imports a larger share of manufactures from the Third World than does the USSR.

Soviet pricing practices also have come under increasing fire from Third World sources. It is said to be common to find the prices of Soviet products sold to developing countries to be 15 to 25 percent higher than prices of the same products sold by the West, while Third World exports to the USSR often receive 10 to 15 percent less than world prices.[12]

Asia, Africa, and Latin America have become important sources of raw materials for the Soviet Union. This includes not only foodstuffs but critical industrial raw materials as well. In 1975, 20 percent of Soviet imports from the Third World consisted of petroleum products; Western estimates project that the Eastern bloc will be importing substantially more oil and gas by the mid–1980s. The Soviet and East European aluminum industries are increasingly reliant on foreign sources of bauxite and aluminum. Eastern bloc tin imports, principally from Southeast Asia, are increasing; the bloc already is entirely dependent on Third World supplies of natural rubber and sheet mica.[13]

In describing the economic benefits of trade between the socialist and developing countries, Soviet spokesmen neglect to mention weapons constitute over half the USSR's exports to the Third World. The arms trade is an important source of hard currency for the Soviet Union; as a result, it proves economically as well as politically beneficial to Moscow. Nevertheless, the harsh reality of this side of Moscow's cooperative relationship with the developing countries appears to give the Soviets a vested interest in Third World turmoil and contrasts sharply with the USSR's protestations in favor of detente, disarmament, and the reduction of military spending.

The Soviet Union's claims regarding its economic assistance program have been considerably scaled down since the mid-1960s; as we saw above, Moscow now stresses the limitations on its ability to provide credits but professes to be helping to the greatest extent possible. The reality is that the USSR's average annual aid contribution amounts to about 0.05 percent of its GNP, compared to about 0.33 percent for the Western countries (and 0.70 percent targeted by the NIEO platform). Moreover, of the $11 billion in aid pledged by the USSR in the first 2 decades of its assistance program, only about $6 billion was ever actually delivered. Deliveries often lag about seven years behind commitments. The Soviets contribute only tiny amounts to multilateral foreign assistance programs such as the UN Development Program, and even these amounts are often unused because they are provided in nonconvertible currency.

For most of the Third World nations, Soviet economic assistance is virtually nonexistent; Moscow's aid program has been highly concentrated, especially when compared to the American program. The bulk of Soviet aid has gone to countries in the Middle East and South Asia; in fact, two countries—India and Egypt—have received almost 30 percent of the total amount extended since 1955. Contrary to an impression often conveyed by Soviet propaganda, Soviet economic aid has not been in the form of grants—grants actually comprised less than five percent of the total—but primarily in the form of long-term credits at varying amounts of interest. Nor is Soviet aid extended to the less developed countries for the free purchase of needed commodities; it is strictly "tied" to Soviet goods, and then usually in the context of approved projects.

Prospects for the Future

To put in perspective the Soviet relationship with the Third World, it is worth recalling how far Moscow has progressed in its presence and influence compared with its almost total isolation only 25 years ago. The examples and trends we have cited are not intended to deny the fact the USSR carries substantial weight in Asia, Africa, and even Latin America; rather, they suggest Moscow's economic policies in particular may have reached a point of diminishing returns.

The Soviet Union's relationship with the Third World on issues relating to the NIEO appears to be increasingly frayed. As in the fairy tale of the emperor's new clothes, some voices at the edge of the crowd are beginning to shout out in anger and frustration at the nakedness they really see in Soviet policies. Or, to cite Roger Hansen's use of a different metaphor to illustrate the same conclusion:

> The Soviet Union's days as a Southern cheerleader without responsibilities would appear to be numbered . . . . Already the developing countries, viewing the Soviet Union as a "have" power, are increasing their criticism of Soviet trade and aid policies that are negligible in their efforts to assist Southern economic development.[14]

What is happening to the USSR's position in the Third World is an apt illustration of the handicaps Moscow suffers as a result of its limited international economic capabilities. The Soviets have been able to gain footholds in a number of strategic Third World locations, particularly on the periphery of the Indian Ocean, by virtue of their political and military support of leftist movements, backed up with ample supplies of Soviet arms and frequently with Cuban troops. Yet, they have found it exceedingly difficult to sustain their influence or to prop up their client regimes through military means alone. Conversely, in areas where the USSR has not established a military supply relationship, it hardly has any influence at all. To put it another way, the Soviets' expanding political ambitions in the Third World, initially boosted by their military instrumentalities, are in the long run subject to being undermined by Moscow's limited economic capabilities.

Apart from the implications this has for the long-term success or failure of Soviet policies in the Third World, the Soviet overreliance on military instrumentalities of influence has profound consequences for both East-West and North-South relations. In the former case, the wave of initial Soviet successes in Africa and the Middle East, even prior to the invasion of Afghanistan, aroused American anxieties to the point of threatening to reverse progress in arms limitation talks and the overall detente relationship—and perhaps even to the point of provoking American military countermeasures in the Persian Gulf–Indian Ocean area. The costs of this likely setback to East–West relations and the revival of US–Soviet zero-sum competition in the Third World are compounded by the danger domestic stability and prospects for progress toward development in the Third World will be disrupted even further. As the states of the South have clearly perceived, the heating up of the East–West competition may well doom the North–South dialogue and the prospects for agreement on the New International Economic Order.

One possible conclusion is that this is precisely what the Soviets have sought to achieve—by refusing to engage seriously in the North–South dialogue and by pursuing their own destabilizing bilateral relationships in the Third World, the Soviet policymakers have consciously promoted a breakdown of the North–South negotiations on the NIEO. If this is the case, the Soviets would seem to have opted for a policy which threatens them with several adverse consequences. The major spokesmen for the Group of 77 are not likely to regard the Soviets as blameless in the case of such a breakdown, and, assuming the South remains unified, it is difficult to see how Moscow could recoup sufficient prestige or display sufficient economic generosity to allow her to build a viable East–South alliance. To the extent an embittered South (including the OPEC nations) seeks to take retaliatory measures against the recalcitrant North—for example, further hikes in raw material prices, new embargoes, unilateral defaulting on debts, nationalization of joint enterprises—the Soviet Union likely would not be immune from harmful economic consequences. Even apart from the costs to its own economy which might follow economic warfare or economic collapse in the South, the Soviet Union is by now sufficiently dependent on the Western capitalist economies to be vulnerable economically to disruptions which might occur in the West.

These trends suggest that as the "South" collectively mobilizes its strength and resources in order to pursue its platform of demands against the industrialized "North," the Soviet leaders may find it increasingly difficult to define their interests in a way compatible with those of the Third World states. Despite their efforts to distance themselves from the "imperialist" West, the Soviets are increasingly associated with "the other superpower" in the eyes of the world's "have-nots." The major challenge to Soviet policy in the coming decade may lie in Moscow's ability to adjust its doctrine and strategy to take into account this growing North–South conflict. Whether and how the Soviets accomplish this may well determine if that conflict envolves into constructive dialogue or destructive confrontation.

By way of conclusion, I would reassert that Soviet influence in the Third World at the beginning of the 1980s remains limited, in part by the strong impulses toward autonomy and national self-determination in the Third World countries. Many of Moscow's biggest "victories" have resulted from events over which it had little or no control. Thus, US policymakers should not overestimate the appeal of the Soviet Union in the Third World or its prospects for success there. Moreover, the US, in its own choice of policy instruments in these regions in the coming decade, should give as much or more careful attention to the promotion of economic development and political institutionalization as to the military aspects of enhancing security.

Notes

1. V. I. Lenin, "The Socialist Revolution and the Right of Nations to Self–Determination," in *The National–Liberation Movement in the East* (Moscow, 1957), p. 109. For a further discussion of the Leninist legacy, see Robert H. Donaldson, *Soviet Policy toward India: Ideology and Strategy* (Cambridge: Harvard University Press, 1974), Chapter 1.
2. Andrew M. Scott, *The Revolution in Statecraft: Informal Penetration* (New York: Random House, 1965), especially Chapter 1.
3. *Pravda,* 5 October 1976, p. 4.
4. *Pravda,* 7 April 1971, p. 6.
5. Richard Lowenthal, "Soviet Counterimperialism," *Problems of Communism,* Vol. 25, No. 6 (November–December 1976), pp. 52–63.
6. For a more detailed explication of this view of Soviet activity in the Indian Ocean, see Geoffrey Jukes, *The Indian Ocean in Soviet Naval Policy,* Adelphi Papers, No. 87 (London: IISS, May 1972); Oles Smolanski, "Soviet Policy in the Persian Gulf," in Michael MccGwire, Ken Booth, and John McDonnell, eds., *Soviet Naval Policy: Objectives and Restraints* (New York: Praeger, 1975), pp. 278–286; and James McConnell, "The Soviet Navy in the Indian Ocean," in Michael MccGwire, ed., *Soviet Naval Developments: Capability and Context* (New York: Praeger, 1973), pp. 389–406.
7. Admiral Stansfield Turner, "The Naval Balance: Not Just a Numbers Game," *Foreign Affairs,* Vol. 55, No. 2 (January 1977), p. 346.
8. Ibid., especially pp. 342–344.
9. In *Documents and Resolutions: XXVth Congress of the CPSU* (Moscow: Novosti, 1976), p. 39.
10. Ibid., p. 16.
11. Alvin Z. Rubinstein, ed., *Soviet and Chinese Influence in the Third World* (New York: Praeger, 1975), p. 223.
12. Alexander Wolynski, "Soviet Aid to the Third World: Strategy before Economics," *Conflict Studies,* No. 90, December 1977. See also, "How Soviet Revisionism Plunders the Third World Economically," *Peking Review,* No. 17, 1974, p. 23.
13. Arthur D. Little, Incorporated, *Dependence of the Soviet Union and Eastern Europe on Essential Imported Materials Year 2000,* Study for Navy Project 2000, September 1977, pp. 13–19.
14. Roger Hansen, *Beyond the North–South Stalemate* (New York: McGraw–Hill, 1979), p. 6.

The USSR in Third World Conflicts

Bruce D. Porter

As the 1970s progressed, the problem of Soviet involvement in Third World conflicts rose steadily in priority on the US foreign policy agenda. The USSR intervened by means of arms shipments, advisers, and sometimes troops in at least eight local conflicts during the decade: the Indo–Pakistani War, the October War, the War in Vietnam, the Angolan civil war, the Ogaden War, the intracommunist clashes in Indochina (Vietnam's invasion of Cambodia and China's response), South Yemen's clash with Yemen, and the civil war in Afghanistan. The Soviet Union had intervened in local conflicts before, of course, but the magnitude, scope, and apparent success of its efforts in the 1970s were perhaps without precedent.

In the 1950s and 1960s, the Kremlin's involvement in local conflicts, though often noisy, generally took place on a quite modest scale with respect to the actual quantities of military equipment delivered to clients at war. The principal exceptions were the arms delivered to North Korea and North Vietnam; even in those cases, however, the Soviet Union took care to maintain a safe enough distance from the actual vortex of conflict so as to make a collision with the United States a fairly remote possibility. Though Moscow transferred massive quantities of arms to Egypt, Syria, Indonesia, and India, and lesser volumes to over 20 additional nations, the shipments usually preceded or followed any actual outbreak of hostilities; the Soviet leaders displayed their penchant for caution by refraining in most instances from large-scale arms shipments to regimes concurrently embroiled in conflict, particularly noncommunist regimes, and by minimizing the participation of Soviet personnel in combat or combat support.

Commencing with the War of Attrition in the Middle East (1969–70), the Soviet Union's historical restraint in this regard eroded markedly. In that conflict, over 10,000 Soviet military advisers engaged in a wide range of combat support, Soviet soldiers flew fighter planes and manned SAM installations, and Moscow transferred thousands of tons of weaponry to the Arabs. It was the USSR's first large-scale military effort on behalf of a noncommunist client at war since its effort to support the Kuomintang in the 1920s. Events in the following decade proved the War of Attrition was not an anomaly. The 1970s witnessed three massive Soviet air- and sealifts of arms to client regimes at war, the deployment in combat of over 40,000 Soviet-armed Cuban troops in Africa, and the outright invasion and occupation of a Third World country by the USSR—all phenomena unheard of during the seemingly

225

stormier years of the "Cold War."

The USSR's military activities in the Third World were a cause for growing concern on the part of the Nixon, Ford, and Carter administrations; the sense of alarm derived not only from the quantum leap in the magnitude and boldness of Soviet efforts but also from the simple reality that Moscow was more successful at the game than it had been in earlier decades. Though the War of Attrition ground to a halt in 1970 in a tactical defeat for the Arabs, throughout the remainder of the decade not a single Third World ally of the USSR suffered a *military* defeat—five of the conflicts mentioned earlier ended following a military victory by the Soviet-backed side; two of the conflicts ended in stalemate; and one, the Afghan civil war, is still disputed. The Soviet Union deserves only partial credit for the military success of its Third World allies, of course, since indigenous and regional factors also weighed heavily in the outcome of each conflict; but the cumulative effect of a series of Soviet-backed military victories was to engender an almost worldwide perception of rising Soviet power and momentum.

The picture appears rather less bleak when it is remembered the military success of Soviet allies in the Third World did not always mean a favorable diplomatic outcome for Moscow. Though the USSR managed to salvage from the Yom Kippur War a military stalemate and a moral victory for the Arab side, it experienced soon after a rapid and virtually total loss of influence in Egypt. Soviet military assistance to Ethiopia triggered Siad Barre's expulsion of nearly 2000 Russian advisers from Somalia in November 1977, and it meant the loss of the largest Soviet military base outside the Warsaw Pact. The invasion of Afghanistan may yet preserve communist rule in Kabul, but Moscow incurred high costs in terms of its relations with the West and with the the Moslem world. Undeniably, the Soviet Union suffered a number of considerable setbacks during the 1970s, and any discussion of Soviet success during the decade needs to be balanced by a recognition of this.

The USSR's achievements were substantial, nevertheless, particularly compared with its foreign policy performance in the Third World in previous decades: Pakistan, an important Asian ally of both China and the United States, was dismembered by the Indo–Pakistani War; the US suffered a deeply demoralizing defeat in Indochina and not long thereafter endured the embarrassing fiasco of the Angolan crisis; Ethiopia, a former US ally and influential African nation, became a virtual Soviet satellite; the Pol Pot regime, allied with China, was toppled by Hanoi's army; Soviet troops moved 500 miles nearer to the Persian Gulf. The virtual flood tide of pro-Soviet regime changes that began with the fall of Saigon was particularly notable—between 1975 and 1980, seven pro-Soviet communist or radical leftist regimes came to power by armed force, most of them as the result of civil wars or coups in which Soviet-supplied weaponry played a prominent role.

The events of the decade also were propitious for the Soviet Union in another sense: they contributed to the growing disillusionment of many Third World leaders with the United States, convinced a number of those leaders that the future of the world lay with the East rather than with the West, and in this manner paved the way for close Soviet ties to several previously aloof African and Asian states. In the long run, these largely immeasurable effects may be of considerable significance. It is true, perhaps, that the entry of such weak and under-developed countries as Angola, Ethiopia, Cambodia, and Afghanistan into the Soviet "camp" does not amount to more than a slight shift in the global balance—not even if the collective weight of those countries in world affairs is considered. But widespread perceptions of Soviet strength and American weakness affect the decisionmaking of hundreds of statesmen and diplomats around the world—and not in a way favor-able to American interests. It would be self-delusion on the part of the West to suppose a cumulative series of setbacks is without significance.

As the 1970s progressed, the Soviet Union found it difficult to main-tain the untenable position of seeking normal and even cooperative relations with the Western powers while at the same time supporting the maximalist demands of the most implacable anti-Western regimes with military aid and diplomatic succor. Inevitably, concern that the Russians were running rampant in the Third World served to erode public support for detente in the US, solidified support for increased military spending, and hastened the momentum of the Sino–American rapprochement. During the Yom Kippur War and again during the Angolan crisis, Henry Kissinger warned that Moscow's actions imperiled the entire Soviet–American relationship and undermined the prospects for a stable international order. Shortly after the Ogaden conflict, Dimitri K. Simes observed that "the new pattern of Soviet imperial gunboat diplomacy threatens to modify the rules of the inter-national game." By 1979, Robert Legvold could write that turmoil in the Third World had overwhelmed all other considerations in the superpower rivalry "save the growth and increased projection of Soviet military power whose menace it serves to accentuate." Jimmy Carter's State of the Union address in January 1980, shortly following the invasion of Afghanistan, identified "the steady growth and increased projection of Soviet military power beyond its own borders" as one of three principal challenges facing the United States.[1]

At this point, a double caveat is in order. Though there was a rising trend of Soviet military involvement in the Third World during the 1970s, the USSR was not an actor, and certainly not a principal actor, in every Third World conflict which took place. A number of local conflicts during the decade, as well as during earlier decades, passed without any significant involvement by either Moscow or Washington. For the most part, the Kremlin was prudent in choosing to become involved only in those conflicts where the USSR had considerable tac-tical and strategic advantages and where the probability of a confrontation with the US was small. Likewise, it would be erroneous to assume the Soviet Union is in some way able to instigate local conflicts and then orchestrate their unfolding. Though the USSR occasionally has armed and encouraged clients to resort to hostilities, such as it apparently did in the Indo–Pakistani War of 1970–71, it can only do so when the existing pressures toward conflict are already enormous. The USSR has also attempted on occasion, not always with success, to restrain overeager clients—its effort to pressure Egypt and Syria into an early cease-fire during the October War is an example. But perhaps the most typical scenario is when the Soviet Union simply exploits or seeks to influence the course of a conflict which breaks out independently of Soviet or American pressures. The Kremlin is opportunistic but not omniscient; tenacious but far from omnipotent.

Yet, if it is fallacious to disregard the manifest limitations on Moscow's power, it is equally spurious to deny that there has been an upsurge in the last decade in Soviet interventionary behavior or to assert that the USSR's military activities in the Third World pose no problem for the US and should be overlooked as irrelevant or even benign and stabilizing. The problem does exist, and it has become serious. Were the United States simply to allow the Soviet Union unchallenged latitude of action throughout the Third World, untoward consequences would follow: a sharp decline in American influence abroad and the wholesale defection of numerous Third World regimes to the security afforded by alliance with Moscow. In the long run, the US will probably have but little choice to contest in some manner Soviet military initiatives in the Third World; the real challenge will be to shape policies which can cope effectively with the Soviet effort while yet contributing to preservation of the general peace.

The shaping of an effective American approach toward the problem of Soviet military involvement in Third World conflicts will require, among other things, an understanding of the fundamental causes underlying the USSR's extraordinary activism in the Third World during the 1970s. This article will not attempt to set forth policy prescriptions— which are only meaningful within the framework of an entire and integral foreign policy—but it will attempt to examine some of the historical trends which culminated in the extraordinary events of the 1970s. It will also consider the possible implications of past trends for the decade which lies ahead.

Four historical trends converged in the 1970s to make possible the exceptional upsurge in the USSR's military involvement in the Third World. In ascending order of significance, they were as follows: (1) the USSR's achievement of a large and survivable second-strike nuclear capability; (2) advances in Soviet mobility forces; (3) the rising confidence of the Soviet leadership; and (4) the post-Vietnam isolationist retreat of the United States. None of these factors alone was decisive, but their cumulative effect was profound.

First, *the USSR's achievement of a large and survivable second–strike nuclear capability.* From 1945 until the middle or late 1960s, Washington enjoyed meaningful superiority over Moscow in the area of strategic nuclear weapons. The crux of this superiority lay in the US capability to destroy with a first strike Soviet nuclear delivery vehicles in sufficient number to blunt the effect of any all-out retaliatory strike. Though the Soviet Union in any exchange would have retained enough residual forces to damage US interests seriously, it could have retaliated against an American first strike only at the risk of inviting the wholesale destruction of its cities and a destruction far worse than the US would have suffered. Any calculation of the ultimate outcome doubtlessly counseled prudence to the Kremlin. Stated differently, the risks and potential costs of escalation to the nuclear level were much higher for the USSR during this early period than they were for the US.

American's nuclear superiority exerted a tacit but pervasive influence on diplomatic and military developments around the world—it counterbalanced the Soviet advantage in conventional ground forces in Europe and it deterred Moscow from making overt, military challenges to US interests in the Third World. The latter consequence came about because of the risks of escalation implicit in any crisis or local conflict in which both the United States and the Soviet Union were involved. Washington's nuclear advantage was by no means a tractable instrument, however—it could not prevent the USSR from putting pressure on Berlin nor could it prevent Moscow from undertaking indirect and cautious support of revolutionary movements around the world; above all, it was an insufficient factor in the total diplomatic equation for guaranteeing political outcomes favorable to the West if other factors were missing.[2] But US nuclear superiority did result in a dampening effect on Soviet assertiveness and latitude of action in the Third World and elsewhere.

As the 1960s progressed, the political advantages conferred on the United States by virtue of its nuclear superiority began to erode as a consequence of the USSR's buildup of its sea-based nuclear forces, the manifold expansion of its ICBM forces, and the hardening of its missile silos. Robert McNamara in January 1968 declared the USSR "had achieved, and most likely will maintain over the foreseeable future, an actual and credible second strike capability . . . ."[3] That same year, the Soviet Union deployed for the first time a medium-range ballistic missile (the SS–N–6) aboard a nuclear-powered submarine; there followed the rapid deployment of nuclear-powered submarines carrying medium- and (in 1974) long-range missiles. The existence of this fleet made the security of the Soviet second-strike force virtually unassailable throughout the 1970s. Long before the US Minuteman force became significantly vulnerable to a first strike by the USSR, Soviet ICBM and SLBM *invulnerability* had radically altered the nuclear equation. By greatly reducing the utility of an American first strike, it lowered the threshold of risk for Moscow in local conflicts. The Soviet achievement, in effect, gave it a kind of protective umbrella behind which it could exploit its conventional advantages and its ties with revolutionary regimes and parties in the Third World.

Soviet thinkers readily recognized the consequences of the USSR's achievement of nuclear parity. One Soviet scholar, V. V. Zhurkin, in a work on American behavior in local crises and conflicts, asserts that as a result of the Soviet attainment of nuclear parity, "the hopes of the USA for employing nuclear blackmail as a means of obtaining its goals in international crises were exploded."[4] A number of Soviet writers have identified the year 1970—when the USSR is said to have achieved nuclear parity—as the beginning of a new phase in international relations, one more favorable to the Soviet Union.[5] It seems to be no accident the USSR's more openly offensive approach toward conflict and revolution in the Third World after 1970 correlated with its achievement of effective nuclear parity. By itself alone this shift from imbalance to parity would not have sufficed to make possible the Kremlin's more activist foreign policy, but it was a necessary condition, and it was coupled with other equally significant developments.

Second, *Soviet advances in mobility or interventionary forces.* A global diplomacy cannot be conducted without the requisite military capabilities to support and sustain distant initiatives. Grouped under the rubric "mobility forces," such capabilities include naval combat power, sealift capacity, airlift capacity and distant assault forces (both amphibious and airborne.) It is sometimes said the USSR lacked the capability to project military power much beyond its borders prior to the 1970s. This is only partially correct—as early as the Spanish civil war (1936–38), the Kremlin managed to muster sufficient sealift to furnish the Loyalists with massive quantities of weaponry, and this capacity grew substantially in the 1950s and 1960s.[6] However, until the 1970s, Moscow lacked the necessary airlift capacity for rapid and versatile actions abroad, the assault forces required for direct military intervention outside the Warsaw Pact, and the naval combat power essential for extending political influence overseas and for discouraging foreign interference in a distant military operation.

The Soviet Union's drive to expand its mobility forces was in full swing by the end of Khrushchev's decade in power; it continued with accelerated momentum under Brezhnev. The growth in naval combat power was particularly impressive—from 1961 to 1979, the USSR deployed 3 new classes of escort ships, 5 classes of destroyer/ASW vessels, 4 classes of cruisers, and 2 classes of small carriers; the total number of new, large warships deployed was over 200. In effect, the Russians constructed an entire blue water navy in two decades, an achievement in some ways reminiscent of Imperial Germany's naval buildup prior to World War I. The USSR established a permanent naval presence in the Mediterranean and Indian oceans for the first time in its history, and, in 1964, it inaugurated an extensive, ongoing program of port visits by Soviet warships to Third World ports;[7] the Soviet fleet also began to play a significant diplomatic and deterrent role in local crises and conflicts.[8]

In sealift, though the USSR already possessed adequate capacity for most military contingencies, the deadweight tonnage of the Soviet maritime fleet more than doubled from 1965 to 1979, and its logistical competence improved considerably. Most of this expansion was probably for commercial reasons; however, many of the newer transport vessels are easily adaptable for military purposes, and the officers of the maritime fleet are believed to be naval reservists ultimately responsible to a military command line.

The Soviet Union also made rapid strides in airlift: the aggregate lift capacity of Soviet Military Transport Aviation (*VTA*) in millions of ton-miles grew from 11.4 in 1965 to 26.4 in 1977; it is still increasing steadily because of continuing deployment of new *Il*–76 transport planes.[9] The ratio of long-range to short-range transports in *VTA* also rose significantly during this period.

In the area of assault forces, the USSR further strengthened and refined its most potent strike force; namely, the seven highly trained and well-equipped airborne divisions which fall under a special directorate in the Ministry of Defense. The range to which this force can be projected is still limited by available air transport, but, within a roughly 2,000–mile radius from the Soviet border, the USSR can perhaps match or exceed any airborne deployment by the United States, except in Europe. The utility of the airborne divisions for influencing the course of local conflicts or for intervening directly abroad has been demonstrated in the past. All seven divisions were placed on a high alert during the October War, a move which did much to shape American decisionmaking during the crisis; the 105th Airborne Guards Division spearheaded the Soviet invasion of Afghanistan, and airborne forces also played a key role in the Soviet intervention in Czechoslovakia in 1968. Progress in amphibious assault capabilities has been much more moderate—the USSR reactivated the "naval infantry" (marines) in 1964, and it has since grown to about 15,000 troops (compared with roughly 180,000 US Marines). The USSR also procured three new classes of tank landing ships between 1962 and 1979, including the modern, highly armed *Ivan Rogov*–class, deployments of which are continuing.[10]

Though the Soviet Union rightfully might have been considered a superpower following its recovery from World War II, it did not become a truly global power until the 1970s, when these investments began to yield significant fruit. Russia's newfound military reach

---

VTA—Voyenno–transportnaya aviatsiya—Eds.

greatly facilitated its massive interventions in the October War, the Angolan civil war, the Ogaden War, and the civil war in Afghanistan. While interventions on that order might have been conceivable in the 1960s, they only could have taken place at relatively inhibited speeds and with much higher risks and more formidable logistical difficulties for the Soviet military.

By 1980, despite these impressive advances, the USSR's overall standing with respect to mobility forces remained clearly inferior vis-a-vis the United States. It had attained nuclear parity but not nuclear superiority. Therefore, though the growing military power of the USSR was an important factor in making possible its growing involvement in Third World conflicts, it cannot alone explain why Moscow more often than not dominated Washington in Third World crises from 1970–80. In order to understand what happened, it is necessary to consider two additional elements of a more political nature.

Third, *the growing confidence of the Soviet leadership.* In the United States, it has become customary to speak of the "lessons of Vietnam" a phrase which usually connotes the declining utility of military power in the modern world. Overlooked is the fact the Soviet leadership also learned lessons from Vietnam—lessons not about the limitations of military power but about its manifest political utility. The Politburo learned military power *can* be employed to sustain a client regime, and involvement in a local conflict *can* yield significant political and strategic benefits. Since 1975, some Soviet writers have referred to the fall of Saigon and the *MPLA*'s victory in Angola shortly thereafter as together constituting a crucial turning point, a turn toward Soviet ascendancy.

Throughout the 1970s, Soviet leaders and spokesmen repeatedly stressed the overall balance of forces in the world was shifting in favor of the socialist community and "a fundamental restructuring" of international relations was underway.[11] Regarding Soviet advances in the Third World during the decade, A. Iskenderov in December 1978 wrote:

> ". . . one thing is indisputable: on the whole the national liberation movement is on the ascent . . . . This is confirmed by the historic victories of the heroic Vietnamese people, the emergence in the course of revolutionary struggle of progressive states like Angola, Mozambique, Guinea–Bissau, and the Cape Verde Islands, the successful course of the revolution in Ethiopia, the revolution in Afghanistan and other revolutionary changes in Asia and Africa."[12]

Boris Ponomarev of the Central Committee Secretariat observed in January 1980 that the past decade had been marked by the continuing unfolding and deepening of the national liberation process and by the erosion of capitalist strength. He added to Iskenderov's list of successes the overthrow of the Pol Pot regime in Cambodia, the Iranian revolution, and the rising revolutionary ferment in Latin America. Echoing Gromyko's words at the 24th Party Congress, Ponomarev declared the strength of the socialist community had reached such proportions that no serious international problem would or could be resolved without its cooperation.[13]

The increasing self-assurance of the top Soviet leadership flowed both from the reality of the changing military balance and from the decade's succession of Soviet-backed military victories in the Third World. A kind of self-feeding mechanism was in operation—each successful intervention abroad increased the assurance and decisiveness with which the Kremlin acted in the next crisis; confidence in turn contributed to successful implementation.

The invasion of Afghanistan demonstrated the newfound confidence of the Soviet leadership perhaps more than any other event in the decade. Attempts by some Western observers to portray it as an act of Soviet desperation are unconvincing—the Kremlin acted swiftly and decisively, pursuing its purposes without apparent hesitation even after the full extent of the international uproar became evident. The significance of the move is underscored by an anecdote Chiang Kai-shek tells about a visit he had with Lenin in the early 1920s. Sun Yat-sen had sent Chiang to Moscow to seek Soviet backing for the Kuomintang's struggle for power in China. Lenin readily agreed to supply the Nationalists with ammunition, arms, provisions, instructors, and advisers, but he laid down a firm caveat: absolutely no Russian soldiers would engage in combat. Lenin explained that following the Red Army's disastrous losses in the Polish campaign of 1920, he had issued a new directive regarding the future policy of world revolution. It ruled Soviet Russia should render the utmost material and moral support to wars of national liberation but "should never again employ Soviet troops in direct participation."[14]

Though Soviet pilots flew combat missions in the War of Attrition and Soviet advisers regularly undertook a broad variety of combat support missions, it is worth noting that during the six decades following the Red Army's debacle on the Vistula in 1920, regular Soviet ground troops did not once engage in combat in the Third World. When Moscow intervened in local conflicts, it did so with arms shipments, advisers, and the "proxy" troops of Cuba, but never until Afghanistan did it intervene with Soviet troops. The invasion of Afghanistan therefore marked the crossing of a threshold of considerable historical significance. It is inconceivable that a regime which has conducted its foreign policy steadfastly according to the Leninist principle of retreating where weak and advancing only where victory was assured would have gone into Afghanistan without a high measure of confidence in the ultimate outcome and in the reality of a new world military and political balance.

Fourth, *the post-Vietnam isolationism of the United States.* The USSR's growing military power and rising confidence only made feasible what was first made possible by the drift and uncertainty of US diplomacy after Vietnam. Postwar history suggests the Politburo is finely attuned to shifts and nuances in American foreign policy and to the high risks associated with actions which might arouse Washington to a military response; it was only natural, therefore, that Moscow take advantage of the opportunities opened to it by America's turn inward in the 1970s.

Already by 1970, the seeming interminability of the war in Vietnam had evoked an unprecedented degree of isolationist sentiment among influential circles in the United States. Pressures to end the war quickly were tremendous and contributed in part to the "seige" mentality of the Nixon White House. Nevertheless, from 1970 to 1975, Washington persisted in conducting a foreign policy which seriously attempted to deter or delimit Soviet military activities around the world. The US responded to the USSR's arming of India in 1970 with passive deployments of its own forces and diplomatic demarches that hinted at the possibility of American intervention on behalf of Pakistan. Additionally, in 1973, Washington alerted its military forces when it appeared the USSR was prepared to intervene in the Middle East with its airborne divisions.

The fall of Saigon in April 1975 deepened the isolationist mood of the nation, affecting even many who had supported the fundamental purposes of the war effort. The collapse of the South seemed to confirm the claim of those who had declared the war effort was futile and US military power could not prevent an inevitable communist revolution in South Vietnam. From then until the end of the decade, the US assumed more or less the role of a spectator, instead of an actor, in the international system.

The depth of the American plunge into what has been termed "neo-isolationism" revealed itself plainly but six months after Saigon fell; that is, at the time of the Angolan crisis. Colombian novelist Gabriel Garcia Marquez, a confidant of Fidel Castro, claims that prior to making a major commitment of troops to Angola, the Cuban cabinet made a "rapid analysis" of whether or not the United States would intervene openly. It concluded the fall of Saigon, as well as the weakening of the presidency in the Watergate affair, made a major intervention by Washington unthinkable.[15] The Kremlin probably made a similar assessment. The Cuban analysis was vindicated on 19 December 1975 when the US Senate voted 54 to 22 in favor of the Tunney amendment to a defense appropriation bill, cutting off all American aid to Angolan nationalist groups and effectively ending a small CIA operation in support of *FNLA* and *UNITA*. Though the wisdom of the Ford administration's decision to undertake the covert operation may be questioned, it is doubtful the USSR would have dared to undertake its own intervention—violating as it did so many of the unwritten rules of Soviet-American relations—without a high degree of confidence it would not be obstructed by external impediments.

When the Ogaden War took place in 1977–78, it was the first time in postwar history the Soviet Union undertook a large-scale military operation outside Eastern Europe without the United States becoming involved militarily. America's neo-isolationism persisted throughout the decade and was perhaps the principal reason the Soviet leadership so readily abandoned its traditional prudence with respect to the use of military instruments abroad. Adam Ulam observed in 1978 that "no Soviet move or ruse has undercut the effectiveness of U.S. foreign policy as much as what the Americans have done to themselves in the wake of Vietnam and Watergate."[16]

The first two of the four elements discussed above are almost certain to persist well into the 1980s; the outlook for the third and fourth is rather more uncertain.

Barring revolutionary technological developments in the West, the Soviet Union should not lose its long-sought nuclear parity at any time during the decade. The invulnerability of its land-based forces may decline somewhat if and when the MX missile is deployed by the United States, but the USSR's basic nuclear umbrella—a secure second-strike force—will remain intact, much of it under the oceans. The credibility of either power launching a first strike against the other will be quite low, unless circumstances arise where one side concludes the cost of a general war is warranted and where one side badly miscalculates the intentions of the other. The strategic nuclear balance, therefore, will exert no more inhibiting influence on Soviet behavior in the Third World during the 1980s than it did during the 1970s; conventional forces, particularly mobility forces, will thus be enhanced in importance.

Moscow will continue the effort to expand and improve its mobility forces, seeking to close further the gap which now exists between its own capability to project power and that of the United States. It even may strive to attain a kind of "parity" in this area to match its earlier achievement of strategic parity. Admiral Gorshkov's announcement in December 1979 that the USSR's first nuclear-powered, large-deck carrier was under construction indicates the seriousness of the Soviet effort; most Western analysts have argued the Soviets would never build heavy carriers because of their high cost, increasing vulnerability, and low utility for a traditional land power.[17] The principal value of the new carrier or carriers will be in projecting Soviet political influence and military power overseas. The new carrier is only the most dramatic product of an intensive shipbuilding program which would seem to portend a decade of increasing strength and perhaps assertiveness on the part of the Soviet fleet. As of 1980, the USSR was constructing four new classes of nuclear-powered cruisers, including a number of 32,000–ton battle cruisers with heavy guns for shore bombardment; such guns are of little utility against a modern, missile-equipped fleet, but they might have a telling impact in certain local crises, even if only passively deployed. The USSR is also constructing the new *Berezina*–class of heavily armed, 40,000–ton logistics craft apparently designed for replenishing warships on the high seas; this should reduce the navy's dependence on foreign port facilities. The most telling indicator of Moscow's naval ambitions, however, consists of the large capital investments currently being made in the expansion and refurbishment of Soviet shipyards, a policy which suggests Soviet naval construction is slated to accelerate further in the 1980s as the USSR bids to close the gap in the area of its most manifest military inferiority.[18]

Soviet air transport capabilities also will expand substantially during the decade as a result of continuing developments of the *Il*–76 long-range transport and of a new plane being developed, the *An*–40, expected to have a larger capacity than the American C-5.[19] This growing airlift capacity will enhance directly the combat potential of the Soviet airborne divisions; the naval infantry's assault capabilities will also improve somewhat as further deployments of the new *Ivan Rogov* tank landing ship continue.

Thus, as the decade progresses, Moscow's overall capability to sustain distant military operations will increase steadily and significantly. Whether or not its relative capability vis-a-vis the United States will also increase depends, of course, on what measures are taken by Washington. There is much evidence to suggest the Soviet leaders would like to narrow the US lead, though they may never achieve "parity" in mobility forces simply because their military requirements are so different from those of the United States.

Turning now to the third category discussed earlier—that of the Soviet leadership's increasing confidence—the picture of what lies ahead becomes more obscured. To some extent, the newfound confidence of the Kremlin's leaders is based on what Soviet ideologists might call "objective factors"; namely, the changing military balance. Viewed in historical perspective, however, Russia's present confidence in its external affairs is a fairly new phenomenon, and it may well be quite fragile. There exists the possibility the USSR will become bogged down and politically chastened in Afghanistan, Poland, or elsewhere. It is also thinkable that a succession struggle or pressing economic troubles might place a damper on the Soviet Union's recent activism abroad. A series of diplomatic reversals or bungled military interventions abroad might also cause the Soviet leadership to turn inward for a period of internal reform and development, much as happened in the late 1920s and early to mid–1930s. Certainly, US policymakers would do well to keep in mind the possibility that appropriate diplomatic steps might in the right circumstances encourage a certain reassertion of prudence and caution on the part of the Soviet leadership.

The United States, however, cannot rely on the 1980s' bringing any turnabout in Soviet attitudes or activism, not even if the war in Afghanistan continues interminably or if the USSR's troubled economy stagnates even worse. Internal difficulties can have the effect of encouraging foreign policy activism, as desperate leaders undertake foreign initiatives in the hope either of enhancing their own political power and standing at home or uniting a fragmented polity. An internal succession struggle following Brezhnev's death or retirement might lead to an extended pause in Soviet endeavors abroad, or it might lead to greater activism—Khrushchev's rise to power resulted simultaneously in gestures of rapprochement to the West and in a much more vigorous policy of wooing Third World regimes away from the former colonial powers by means of economic and military aid; the transition to Brezhnev took place abruptly and without evident crisis, yet Soviet foreign policy became somewhat more hard-line and activist as a result, particularly with respect to supporting wars of national liberation in the Third World. The United States cannot afford to stake its own security on the assumption of yet unevidenced internal developments in the USSR leading to a new Soviet moderation abroad; the West will be fortunate enough if the historical pull of centuries of Russian military inferiority and extreme caution suffices to render Soviet foreign policy no more belligerent or activist than it now is.

Assuming the Soviet leaders continue to act with a measure of self-assurance in their foreign affairs, the above three elements alone point toward a decade of heavy Soviet involvement in local conflicts, one likely to be all too reminiscent of the latter 1970s. It seems probable the USSR will continue to arm local clients—occasionally encouraging them to resolve their disputes by military force—but in any event always striving to take advantage of any hostilities which do occur whenever political and strategic gains seem attainable. Moscow probably will continue to support and to exploit revolutionary tendencies in the Third World, seek to establish itself more firmly as the "natural ally" of leftist regimes, and strive to damage the stability and security of countries with friendly ties to the United States. Quite possibly, further massive air- and sealifts of Soviet arms to Third World regimes will take place, and the troops of Third World allies of the USSR again may be deployed in combat in a manner which will serve Soviet interests. The relative contribution of Cuba to the Soviet effort in the Third World will probably decline, however, at least as far as Havana's military contribution is concerned. This is because Castro still has nearly 40,000 troops in Angola and Ethiopia alone, as well as a few thousand in other countries, and he cannot keep sending more abroad indefinitely. Perhaps other "proxies"—Ethiopian, South Yemeni, Vietnamese, or even East German troops—will take their place. Since the

USSR has crossed the threshold of employing its own troops in combat in the Third World, there may be a somewhat greater probability Soviet soldiers will be sent abroad again in the 1980s. The Kremlin is likely to use this particular instrument with great caution and, due to logistical limitations, only in regions near the USSR.

In the face of such eventualities, the future direction of US foreign policy becomes a critical variable. Of the four elements which contributed to Soviet success in the Third World during the 1970s, it is the one most under American control and most subject to change by the decisions and leadership of American statesmen. The United States cannot control the outbreak of local conflicts or determine the course of events in the Third World any more than can the Soviet Union, nor can Washington prevent Moscow from providing military assistance to client regimes which seek it; to state these limitations is but to acknowledge the verities of international diplomacy in the nuclear age. But if the United States does not control events in the Third World, it can influence them, sometimes decisively. If it cannot prevent the Soviet Union from intervening abroad, it can often dissuade or deter it; if it intervenes nonetheless, the United States can affect the costs and benefits of Soviet actions. Certainly, many of Moscow's interventions in the 1970s and at least some of the resulting military and political successes would have occurred even if American diplomacy had responded with perfect acumen, but US isolationism and the consequent failure of the White House to formulate an effective American policy contributed to the acuteness of the problem.

This essay is not a policy brief but only a diagnosis of some of the events which occurred in the 1970s and a brief prognosis of what may lie ahead. In conclusion, let it simply be observed that America's most crying need in its foreign policy—in the Third World and elsewhere—is a restoration of national confidence, sense of purpose, and esprit de corps. Although the nation suffered a cumulative series of setbacks in the Third World during the 1970s, many of them as the result of superior Soviet diplomacy, the events of the decade did not even come close to irretrievably compromising US security or even US standing in the Third World. It is pointless and self-defeating to dwell on the past mistakes of American foreign policy; it is imperative to realize the United States still possesses numerous advantages over the Soviet Union, not the least of which is the free and democratic system of government which continues to appeal powerfully to the world's peoples. The United States needs to shed its post-Vietnam self-effacement and neo-isolationism—not forgetting the lessons of that war but also not focusing on them to the exclusion of all other considerations—for only a purposeful and resolute American diplomacy will be capable of meeting successfully the challenges which lie ahead in the 1980s.

Notes

1. *Department of State Bulletin (DOSB)* Vol. 69, 29 October 1973; p. 528, and *DOSB*, Vol. 72, 23 February 1976, p. 209; Dimitri K. Simes, "Detente, Russian Style," *Foreign Policy*, No. 32, Fall 1978: P. 54; Robert Legvold, "The Super Rivals: Conflict in the Third World," *Foreign Affairs*, No. 57, Spring 1979, p. 755; *Presidential Documents*, Vol. 16, 28 January 1980, p. 195.
2. Barry M. Blechman and Stephen S. Kaplan, *Force Without War: U.S. Armed Forces as a Political Instrument* (Washington: The Brookings Institution, 1979), pp. 127–29, argue the strategic weapons balance did not influence the outcome of crisis incidents in which both the United States and the Soviet Union were involved. The argument is based principally on a statistical breakdown of the *outcome* of incidents which occurred during various eras of the strategic balance; the study, however, does not (and perhaps could not) separate out all the other factors which came to bear in each situation. Nor is it possible to measure or know how many times the USSR refrained from taking action (i.e., times when no incident occurred) precisely because of its leaders' perceptions of the strategic balance.
3. *Statement Before the Senate Armed Services Committee on the FY 1969–73 Defense Program and the 1969 Defense Budget*, 22 January 1968, pp. 46–7.
4. V. V. Zhurkin, *SShA i mezhdunarodno–politicheskiye Krizisy* [The USA and International Political Crises] (Moscow: Nauka, 1975), p. 49.
5. See, for example, G. A. Trofimenko, "Vneshnyaya politika SSha v 70-e gody: deklaratsii i praktika" [The Foreign Policy of the USA in the 1970s: Declarations and Practice], *SShA* [USA]; December 1976, p. 15; G. A. Trofimenko, "Sovetsko–Amerikanskiye soglasheniya ob ogranichenii strategicheskikh vooruzheniy" [Soviet–American Agreements on the Limitation of Strategic Arms], *SShA*, September 1972, p. 7; K. M. Georgiyev and M. O. Kolosev, "Sovetsko-amerikanskiye otnosheniya na novom etape" [Soviet–American Relations in a New Stage], *SShA*, March 1973, p. 13.
6. Office of the Chief of Naval Operations, Department of the Navy, *Understanding Soviet Naval Developments* (Washington: Government Printing Office, 1975), p. 39; Richard Ackley, "The Merchant Fleet" in Michael MccGwire and John McDonnell, eds., *Soviet Naval Influence: Domestic and Foreign Dimensions* (New York: Praeger, 1977), p. 298.
7. Anne M. Kelly, "Port Visits and the 'Internationalist Mission' of the Soviet Navy," in *Soviet Naval Influence*. pp. 510–29; Michael MccGwire *et al.*, eds., *Soviet Naval Policy: Objectives and Restraints* (New York: Praeger, 1975), pp. 389–418.
8. An extensive study of the diplomatic role played in recent years by the Soviet fleet is Bradford Dismukes, ed., *Soviet Naval Diplomacy* (London: Pergamon Press, 1979).
9. Robert P. Berman, *Soviet Air Power in Transition* (Washington: The Brookings Institution, 1978), p. 36; Peter Borgart, "The Soviet Transport Air Force," *International Defense Review*, No. 6, 1979, pp. 948–50.
10. *Strategic Survey*, 1979, p. 45; *Defense Daily*, 21 March 1980, p. 118; *Jane's Fighting Ships 1979–80* (New York: Franklin Watts, 1979), pp. 548–50.
11. For numerous examples of this, see R. Judson Mitchell, "A New Brezhnev Doctrine: The Restructuring of International Relations," *World Politics*, Vol. 30, April 1978, pp. 366–90.
12. A. Iskenderov, "Yedinstvo trex revolyutsionnykh potokov—vazhneyshaya predposylka sokhraneniya i uprocheniya mira" [The Unity of Three Revolutionary Currents—A Major Precondition for the Preservation and Strengthening of Peace], *Mezhdunarodnaya zhizn'* [International Life], November 1978, p. 73.
13. Boris Ponomarev, "Neodolimost' osvoboditel'nogo dvizheniya" [The Invincibility of the Liberation Movement], *Kommunist* [Communist], No. 1173, January 1980, p. 11.
14. Chiang Kai–shek, *Soviet Russia in China: A Summing–up at Seventy* (New York: Farrar, Strauss and Cudahy, 1957), p. 22.

15. *Washington Post,* 12 January 1977, which is an excerpt in translation from the original by Gabriel Garcia Marque, *"Cuba en Angola: Operacion Carlota"* [Cuba in Angola: Operation Carlota], *Proceso* [Process], January 1977, pp. 6–15.

16. Adam Ulam, "U.S.–Soviet Relations: Unhappy Coexistence," *Foreign Affairs,* Year-end issue, 1978, p. 567.

17. See, for example, Robert Waring Herrick, *Soviet Naval Strategy* (Annapolis: US Naval Institute Press, 1968), p. 155.

18. Drew Middleton, *New York Times,* 10 and 17 December 1979.

19. Borgart, pp. 948–50.

The Soviet Presence in Africa

Robert Clute

The purpose of this article is not to analyze the historical background of Soviet foreign policy in Africa but to examine the current Soviet presence on that continent and the American response thereto. There can be little doubt the long term Soviet ideological objective is the creation of Marxist–Leninist states in Africa under Soviet hegemony. However, the Soviet Union appears to have no grand design to attain this goal[1] or any expectation for its realization in the near future.[2] Soviet policy has remained fluid and pragmatic with a heavier emphasis on strategic or military rather than economic factors and on perceived Soviet national needs relatively uninhibited by ideological constraints. This explains Soviet support of such rulers as Idi Amin of Uganda and Emperor Haile Selassie of Ethiopia. Although Soviet policy was relatively successful in Africa during the 1950s and 1960s, it still did not prove to be a great threat to the Western world— with the possible exception of Soviet activities in Egypt—and the US enjoyed a rather strong diplomatic position on the continent. Portugal and South Africa had managed to maintain control in southern Africa, and Soviet influence in this area was minimized.

However, the 1970s present an entirely different picture. Africa had not been very important to the US from a strategic standpoint in the earlier period, but by the 1970s, the continent was increasingly important to the US as a source of oil and minerals. Beginning with the oil embargo of 1973, the US also faced a deteriorating situation in the Middle East which was complicated by the fact the major trade routes to Africa and the Middle East were threatened by a strong Soviet presence in the Horn of Africa. The Soviet Union also had established a strong military presence in southern Africa, a region which is a principal source of minerals for the United States. The Soviet Union emerged as a first-rate military power able to engage in quick strikes and rapidly move huge quantities of war materials over vast distances. Moscow also evidenced a willingness to engage in military intervention. The US had difficulty in responding adequately to the changed Soviet presence. The US suffered from the post-Vietnam unpopularity of intervention abroad, had curtailed its military assistance to Africa, and did not fare well in either foreign aid or trade with Africa. In recent months, this has forced the US to reexamine completely its African foreign policy in general.

Soviet interest in Africa really did not begin until after the Bandung Conference of Asian and African States in 1955. Soviet policy was conspicuously unsuccessful during this period as evidenced by the failure of Soviet-backed Premier Patrice Lumumba in the Congo Crisis of 1960–61 and the overthrow of a number of heads of state with which Moscow had close ties—such as Bella of Algeria in 1965, Nkrumah of Ghana in 1966, and Keita of Mali in 1968. However, the Soviet Union could also point to a number of successes. It had established rather wide diplomatic relations on the continent and had developed close ties with a number of client states—such as Algeria, Egypt, Guinea, and Sudan—which provided the USSR with naval and air facilities.

Soviet aid to Africa from 1954–69 was only $1,995 million, or 30 percent of its total aid to less developed countries. Aid was given to relatively few African countries, with Algeria and Egypt receiving 11.6 percent and 50.2 percent of Soviet aid for the entire continent.[3] African assistance from developed market economies and multilateral agencies during 1961–1969 was $14,978 million! It is worthy of note that 52.3 percent of all communist aid to Africa during the 1954–69 period was in the northern tier of Africa where the Soviet Union was most active, with distribution as follows: Algeria—10.4 percent, Ethiopia—4.1 percent, Egypt—23.1 percent, Mali—3.4 percent, Somalia—2.9 percent, Sudan—5.5 percent, and Tunisia—2.9 percent.[4] Soviet aid was not large when compared to that of the developed economies of the free world, but the USSR consistently devoted a large portion of its total Third World aid to Africa. Soviet projects such as the Aswan Dam also established an awareness of the Soviet economic presence in Africa. Likewise, the Soviet Union increased its good will in the northern tier of Africa, an area of strategic importance due to Soviet interests in the Mediterranean, the Red Sea, the Gulf of Aden, and the Indian Ocean.

Soviet military aid to Africa showed significant gains during the 1960s. As will be noted in Table 1, the Western powers were still the major suppliers of arms to North Africa, with the exception of Egypt. As illustrated by Table 2, although the UK was the largest supplier of arms to sub-Saharan Africa in the 1950s, it declined considerably in the 1960s. The US supplied slightly more arms to sub-Saharan Africa than did the Soviet Union in the 1960s, but the Soviet Union had become the principal supplier by the last half of the decade.

During the 1960s, the Soviet Union was also building up its navy. By 1964, the Soviet Union had deployed surface combat ships in the Mediterranean.[5] In 1967, Great Britain announced it would withdraw its naval forces from the Indian Ocean and the Persian Gulf; in 1968, the Soviet Union began to show the flag in the Indian Ocean. In 1969,

Table 1.   Pattern of Major Weapon Supplies to North Africa, 1950-1969

Country	Supplier	1950	1951	1952	1953	1954	1955	1956	1957	1958	1959	1960	1961	1962	1963	1964	1965	1966	1967	1968	1969
Algeria	USA																				
	France														1	1					
	USSR													2	2	1	2	2	2		
	Other													1	1	1					
Egypt	USA	2			1	2	1														
	UK		1	1	1	1	1	1	1					1							
	France					1	1														
	USSR						2	3	3	3	2	2	4	4		3	3	2	3	4	44
	Other				2	1	1	1													
Morocco	USA										1					1		2	2		
	UK																				
	France							2	1	1	1	1	1	1	1	1	1			1	
	USSR											1	1		1	1	1		1		
	Other												1						1	1	
Tunisia	USA										1	1	1	1	1	1	1	1	1		
	France								1		1	1			1	1	1	1			1
	Other											1	1	1							

1 = less than $10 million; 2 = $10-50 million; 3 = $50-100 million; 4 = more than $100 million.

Source: Stockholm International Peace Research Institute (SIPRI), *The Arms Trade with the Third World* (1971), pp.507, 582.

Table 2. Sub-Saharan Africa: Supplies of Major Weapons, by Supplier

(US $million, at constant (1968) prices)

	1950-1954		1955-1959		1960-1964		1965-1969		1950-1969	
	$Million annual average	%	$Million annual average	%	$Million annual average	%	$Million annual average	%	$Million total	% total
USA	2	28.6	1	10.0	7	21.9	5	13.2	71	16.7
UK	5	71.4	8	80.0	7	21.9	6	15.8	128	30.2
France					4	12.5	6	15.8	47	11.1
USSR					5	15.6	8	21.1	64	15.1
Other		2.9	1	10.0	9	28.1	13	34.7	114	26.9
Total	7	100.0 [sic]	10	100.0	32	100.0	38	100.0 [sic]	424	100.0

Source: SIPRI, *The Arms Trade with the Third World* (1971), p. 608.

during joint maneuvers and normal operations of the Pacific and Black Sea fleets in the Indian Ocean,[6] the Soviet Navy accumulated 1,670 ship days in the Indian Ocean; by 1970, the figure reached 2,387. The highest number of ship days the US recorded from 1967–1973 was 1,410 in 1973.[7]

Thus, by the end of the 1960s, the Soviet Union had established an increasing number of client states and wide diplomatic representation in Africa. The Soviet Union had become the major arms supplier to Africa, and its navy was becoming a growing influence in African waters. Although Soviet influence in the northern tier of Africa was strong, it still had not established its presence in southern Africa, the major source of US mineral imports from that continent. Soviet aid to Nigeria during the Biafran War had also established closer ties with that country, whereas US–Nigerian relations had cooled considerably; this proved to be a problem for the US in the 1970s.

The Escalation of Soviet Power

The Soviet naval buildup increased in the 1970s. It is estimated that within eight years of Great Britain's announcement of withdrawal from the Indian Ocean and Persian Gulf, Soviet naval forces in these areas had quadrupled. In the early 1970s, the average number of Soviet warships in the Indian Ocean at any given time was estimated to be between 18 and 22.[8] During the Yom Kippur War of 1973, the US Sixth Fleet with 60 ships in the Mediterranean faced a Soviet fleet of 95 ships. After 1966, the Soviet Union also began construction of the *Alligator*–class tank landing ship which could carry an entire marine battalion and 25 to 30 tanks.[9]

The USSR also built up its merchant marine and received considerable experience in providing military supplies over long distances to North Vietnam. Prior to the closing of the Suez Canal, it was estimated that 47 Soviet cargo vessels unloaded in the port of Haiphong per month. Even after the route had been lengthened by the closing of the canal, an estimated 22 to 25 vessels arrived per month.[10] By the end of 1972, the Soviet Union had 2,140 active merchant ships as compared to the United Kingdom's 1,762, Liberia's 2,139, Japan's 2,210, West Germany's 797, and the United States' 680. As of 1974, Norman Polmar reported the USSR had more active mine sweepers, patrol torpedo craft, all-gun cruisers, amphibious vessels (of 250 feet or larger), and a larger diesel-propelled submarine attack force than the United States, the United Kingdom, and France combined.[11] The Soviet Union also had more escort ships and frigates than the United States. The latter, however, had twice as many nuclear-propelled submarines in its attack fleet.

Although the Soviet Union had not acquired actual bases in Africa, it enjoyed the use of air and naval facilities in Iraq on the Persian Gulf;

Algeria, Egypt, and Libya on the Mediterranean; Sudan on the Red Sea; South Yemen; the port of Berbera, Somalia (which controlled the entrance to the Red Sea) and other ports of Somalia on the Indian Ocean; Fernando Po and Conakry on the west coast of Africa; and Port Louis in Mauritius. In the early 1970s, the Soviets were also expanding naval facilities in Somalia as indicated by the fact that in 1971, 32 of 54 Soviet visits to East African ports were to Somali ports.[12] In 1974 after the military coups in Ethiopia, the Soviet Union hastened to increase its ties with that country in order to strengthen the Soviet position on the Red Sea.

By the late 1960s and early 1970s, the Soviet Union had begun to cut down considerably on its economic aid to Africa. From 1954–1965, Africa received $1,746 million, or 46 percent of all Soviet foreign aid to Third World countries. Sub-Saharan Africa received $390 million, or 9.8 percent. During this period, Egypt received $1,002 million, Algeria $231 million, and Ethiopia $102 million,[13] leaving little for the rest of Africa. As will be noted in Table 3, the Soviet Union had concentrated its economic aid in the northern tier of Africa; i.e, that portion which is strategically important to the Middle East. The African portion of Soviet aid to the Third World during the first half of the 1970s had dropped to 13 percent and sub-Saharan Africa received only 1.8 percent. It is also worthy of note that many of the countries which provided air and naval facilities to the Soviet Union were among the leading recipients of Soviet economic aid.

Soviet military aid to the Third World from 1971–76 was $13,850 million, according to Pentagon estimates. Africa received $2,201 million, or 15.9 percent of total Third World military assistance aid;[14] however, $656 million, or almost 30 percent of the continent's military assistance from the Soviet Union, had gone to Egypt; in 1974, the USSR concluded a one billion arms agreement with Libya. In contrast, United States military assistance to Africa from 1962–1976 was only $590.9 million.[15]

Since 1975, there has been a marked increase in Soviet military activity in Africa. In that year, Moscow gave full support to the Popular Movement for the Liberation of Angola (*MPLA*). After the Portuguese withdrawal in November 1975, the Soviet Union supplied the *MPLA* with large amounts of arms, and Cuba sent a sizable combat force to assist in defeating the rival groups of the *MPLA* in Angola. A massive sea and airlift aided by Cuban, East European, and Algerian pilots delivered $300 million in arms to Angola, compared to a total of $54 million in arms which the Soviet Union had supplied to the *MPLA* in the previous 14 years.[16] The cooperation which the Soviet Union received from African states was truly amazing. Soviet and Cuban air transports stopped over in Guinea and Guinea–Bissau, military equipment was reportedly being sent to Tanzania for transport to Angola, Congo–Brazzaville served as a staging area for two squadrons of Soviet

MiG–21s,[17] and Cuban vessels landed at Pointe Noire.[18] Dictator Macias of Equatorial Guinea permitted the Soviet "fishing depot" on the Island of Bioko to be used as a staging area for the Cuban troops.[19]

Table 3. Soviet Economic Aid to Africa 1954–1975

(in millions of dollars)

	1954-1975	1970	1971	1972	1973	1973	1975
Total Third World	10,850	194	862	581	657	575	1264
Total Aid to Africa	2,735	51	388	---	10	17	73
Algeria	425		189				
Cameroon	8						
Central African Republic	2						
Chad	10				1		9
Congo	14				4		
Equatorial Guinea	1						
Ethiopia	104				1		1
Ghana	93						
Guinea	200					2	
Guinea-Bissau	1						
Kenya	48						
Mali	86					12	
Mauritania	4				1		
Morocco		98	44				
Niger	2				1	1	
Nigeria	7						
Rwanda	1				1		
Senegal	9				1	1	
Sierra Leone	28						
Somalia	153						62
Sudan	64						
Tanzania	20						
Tunisia	34						
Uganda	16						
Upper Volta	1				1		
Zambia	6						
Egypt	1,300	196					
Other		3					

Compiled from Orah Cooper, "Soviet Economic Aid to the Third World," in Joint Economic Committee, Congress of the United States, *Soviet Economy in a New Perspective,* 1976, p. 194; and Leo Tansky, "Soviet Foreign Aid: Scope, Direction, and Trends," in Joint Economic Committee, Congress of the United States, *Soviet Economic Prospects for the Seventies,* 1978, p. 775.

The Soviet military operation in Angola was of immense importance. It illustrated that the Soviet Union was a superpower able rapidly to sustain large-scale military operations almost anywhere in the world. It heralded the beginning of the "proxy wars" using Cuban troops. The unwillingness of the United States Congress to continue American support to the *MPLA* opposition was mute evidence that the post-Vietnam reluctance to engage in foreign intervention would give the Soviet

Union a relatively free hand in military adventures in Africa. Former Secretary of State Kissinger wrote of the Angola situation:

> We were determined to resist Soviet aggressiveness, but we thought the chances better if our policy also gave expression to hope. It remains to be seen whether, given our historical experience and the bitterness of our recent past, it is possible to walk the narrow path, whether we are doomed to oscillate erratically between excessive conciliation and excessive bellicosity.[20]

When Angola became a Soviet client state, it also gave the USSR its first stronghold for intervention in southern Africa, particularly mineral rich Zaire, Zambia, Botswana, and Namibia. The Soviet Navy and Air Forces also had facilities for extending their activities down the entire west coast of Africa. Finally, as Vanneman and James have noted, "the new Soviet 4,900–mile missile aboard a Soviet submarine, operating from Angola would offer significant new strategic possibilities."[21]

The Soviet Union also had established close ties with Mozambique. It is reported to have supplied $12 million in military aid to Maputo between 1971–1975.[22] In 1976, the Soviets established closer ties with the new *FRELIMO* (Front for the Liberation of Mozambique) government of Mozambique. In April 1977, the Soviet Union and Mozbique signed a Treaty of Friendship and Commerce. Although the country has a radical socialist government, it is debatable whether it could be considered a Soviet client state.[23] It certainly does not provide the Soviet Union the same support as does Angola. However, it is generally viewed as a potentially dangerous spot in southern Africa where the Soviet Union might radically improve its position.

The Soviet Union's thorniest problem was the Horn of Africa. The Soviet Union had given considerable aid to Ethiopia under Haile Selassie's reign but had at the same time supported the Eritrean rebels struggling for freedom from Ethiopia. The USSR had also supplied aid to Somalia since 1962 and had developed a huge naval complex at Berbera which included a deep water port, fuel storage facilities, an airfield, facilities for storing tactical missiles,[24] and a communication system; SAM missiles were installed to defend the port.[25] After the 1974 military coups in Ethiopia, the Soviet Union attempted to establish closer ties with the Mengistu government and, in 1975, greatly increased arms shipments to Ethiopia.[26] The Ogaden dispute between Somalia and Ethiopia led to war between the two countries in 1977 and resulted in a change in Soviet policy.

The Soviet Union continued to supply aid to Ethiopia but refused to aid Somalia. As a result, the Soviets were expelled from Somalia and relations between the two countries were severed. During 1977, with the worsening of Soviet–Somali relations, the US became more active in Somalia but withdrew after the Somali invasion of the Ogaden; once again, the Soviet Union could be assured the American government would not intervene. The Soviet decision to support Ethiopia seems to have been calculated, a fact which would explain why one of the most important installations in Somalia—a floating drydock—was towed across the Gulf of Aden prior to the actual break in Somali–Soviet relations.[27]

In late November 1977, the Soviet Union began a massive airlift to Ethiopia. In 1978, the US Department of State estimated Soviet arms transfers to Africa were $1.2 billion, with the major portion going to Ethiopia;[28] other estimates for the 1978 period have been as high as $2 billion, however. There was also a massive influx of Soviet technicians and Cuban troops. The Somali invasion was defeated in March by a ground strategy planned by three Soviet generals;[29] in January 1978, a military conference in Addis Ababa included General Koliyako, Soviet Chief of Staff in Libya, and Cuban defense Minister Raul Castro.[30] After the defeat of Somalia in the Ogaden in March, the Soviet Union moved to suppress the guerrilla forces in Eritrea. Although Cuban advisors participated in Eritrea, the Cuban troops were left in the Ogaden to face Somali guerrillas who continued to fight after the Somalia defeat. Despite massive investments in arms and personnel, the Soviet Union and Cuba still face a vigorous guerrilla opposition in both Eritrea and the Ogaden.

The presence of communist "economic technicians" in sub-Saharan Africa in 1978 was estimated to be 37,255, of which the USSR and Eastern Europe provided 70; Cuba—10,970; and China—18,615.[31] The presence of communist military personnel in sub-Saharan Africa had increased markedly after the Angolan operations, as illustrated by Table 4. Note the sizable communist military presence in southern Africa. Obviously, it was a low risk operation for Soviet personnel, with the bulk of the burden being assumed by Cuba.

This is not meant to be an exhaustive, but an illustrative, treatment of Soviet activities in Africa. For instance, Soviet support of guerrilla activities in Namibia, Zimbabwe, and elsewhere is not covered. It is sufficient to establish the enormous drive and growth of Soviet power and the pragmatic, opportunistic nature of such growth. Such a policy must of necessity be for short-term power objectives and may in the long run lead to enormous unpopularity in Africa. Thus, it results in numerous failures. Soviet action in Ethiopia and Libya has made Sudan a bitter enemy; Soviet action in Algeria has alienated Morocco; enormous investments in Egypt and Somalia have been lost; the fighting still continues in Eritrea, the Ogaden, and Angola despite massive Soviet and Cuban aid, and these areas could become "Soviet Vietnams." Soviet aid to discredited regimes—such as Uganda and the Central African Empire—which have later fallen—also have not enhanced the Soviet image. Obviously, Soviet aims were tactical, not ideological.

Table 4. Communist Military Personnel in Sub-Saharan Africa, 1978

Country	Total	E. Europe*	USSR & Cuba	China
Angola	20,300	1,300	19,000	
Equatorial Guinea	290	40	150	100
Ethiopia	17,900	1,400	16,500	
Guinea	330	100	200	30
Guinea-Bissau	205	65	140	
Mali	195	180		15
Mozambique	1,130	230	800	100
Other	1,330	500	485	345
Total	41,680	3,815	37,275	590

Source: Under Secretary of State for Political Affairs David Newsom, in *U.S. Interests in Africa*, note 1, below, p. 47.
*More than half Soviets, nearly 1000 believed to be East Germans.

The steady growth of Soviet power has presented a real challenge to the United States and the other Western nations due to the increasing importance of Africa to the West during the past decade. As a result of the oil embargo of 1973, deteriorating relations with the Middle East during the 1970s, and the fall of the Shah in Iran, Africa has become extremely important as a source of petroleum products, as illustrated in Table 5. Since 1977, Gulf Oil has been operating in Angola to increase its oil production which in 1976 provided 60 percent of that country's governmental revenues.[32]

Table 5. Oil Production and Exports, African Countries, 1977

(In Thousands of Barrels Daily)

Country	Production	Exports	Exports to US	Exports to the US as percent of: Total Exports	Exports to the US as percent of: Total US Imports
Nigeria	2097	2030	1130	55.7	13.2
Libya	2064	1943	704	36.2	8.2
Algeria	1123	1008	544	54.0	6.3
Gabon	222	202	35	17.3	*
Egypt	413	103	36	3.5	*
Angola	171	150	0	0	0
Tunisia	89	61	0	0	0
Zaire	23	17	0	0	0

*Less than 1/2%.
Source: Professor Morris Adelman, prepared statement in *U.S. Interests in Africa.* Cited in note 1, below, p. 224. Imports include crude oil and petroleum products.

It is worthy of note that the Soviet Union has very strong influence in Libya and Algeria and is on excellent terms with Nigeria. In 1977, the US imported 1,304,000 barrels of crude petroleum per day from North Africa and 972,000 from West Africa. By 1978, the US imported 1,188,000 barrels per day of crude petroleum from West Africa and 1,313,000 from North Africa. However, the greatest threat to Western oil supplies may come from growing Soviet strength in African and Middle Eastern waters. In 1977, the US and Western Europe received 2,016,000 and 7,891,000 barrels of crude petroleum respectively from the Middle East via the Cape of Good Hope. This represents 84.7 percent of the crude petroleum being brought around the Cape. The Suez Canal lacks the capacity to handle large tankers and has become inconsequential in transporting Middle Eastern oil. In 1978, the US and Western Europe imported 2,094,000 and 7,565,000 barrels per day respectively from the Middle East via the Cape, an amount which represented 85.5 percent of the Middle Eastern oil being transported around the Cape.[33]

African minerals—especially cobalt, chromium and copper— also have become increasingly important to the United States. These minerals are found mostly in southern Africa. Table 6 indicates the enormous portion of the world's mineral reserves which are located in Africa. The Soviet Union could greatly endanger such supplies. Angola is a client state which could prove to be a threat to Zaire, the Congo, Botswana, and Zambia. If the Soviet Union strengthens its relations with Mozambique, it could serve as a threat to Zambia and Zimbabwe. If the present government of South Africa fell and pro-Soviet elements took over in Namibia, the mineral rich area could fall into the Soviet sphere, and a major source of minerals for the United States might be lost.

This does not present a very glowing picture of the African situation. Overall, the Soviet Union has made major gains. Fortunately, it still has not established a truly Marxist–Leninist state under the leadership of a communist party. It also never has applied the Brezhnev Doctrine to Africa and has withdrawn from host states at their request. However, if countries such as Ethiopia and Angola reach the stage of being truly Marxist–Leninist states, it will be interesting to see if the Soviet Union will choose to apply the Brezhnev Doctrine. Such a choice would change completely the Soviets' position in the eyes of most African states. Hopefully, before that time—if it were to come—the United States would have developed a better response to the Soviet presence in Africa. About the only direct American military response has been during the second Shaba invasion of Zaire from Angola in May of 1978. The US and France supplied logistical support to and the US ferried French and Belgian troops to Zaire, thereby helping to defeat the invaders.[34]

480-900 0 - 85 - 9

Table 6. African Minerals.

(25 percent or more of world production or reserves)

Mineral	Percent of estimated 1978 world production	Percent of world reserve
Arsenic	8.0	25.0
Asbestos (crocidolite)	100.0	100.0
Bauxite	15.0	30.0
Cesium		30.0
Chromium	40.0	97.0
Cobalt	66.0	40.0
Corundum	85.0	75.0
Diamond	65.0	90.0
Fluorspar	13.5	32.5
Gem stones	75.0	65.0
Germanium	30.0	22.0
Gold	57.0	48.0
Kyanite	35.0	5.0
Manganese	31.0	50.0
Phosphate		25.0
Platinum group	45.0	72.5
Tantalum	22.0	70.0
Uranium	29.0	32.0
Vanadium	41.0	49.0
Vermiculite	40.0	40.0

Source: Charles Eddy, Deputy Assistant Secretary, Department of Interior, in *U.S. Interests In Africa,* cited in note 1, below, p. 215.

American Response During the Carter Administration

It would not be fair to place the blame for the lack of an adequate American response entirely on the Carter administration. A goodly portion of the American apathy could be attributed to the general malaise of the public and Congress as an aftermath of Vietnam. Early in his administration, the President announced the US would not become involved in foreign conflicts simply because the Soviets were present. The administration also aimed to cut down on its arms shipments to the Third World; however, this did not actually occur. Military assistance to Africa from 1977 to 1979 was $1,838 million, of which Egypt received $1,500 million. From 1962–76, the United States had spent only $591 million on military assistance in Africa.[35] The problem was the United States had not increased such expenditures enough to meet the new Soviet military challenge.

The major thrust of African policy under Andrew Young and the Carter administration was to stress economic and social development by building lasting long-term relations with African states. The Carter administration also continued and expanded the Ford administration's policy of supporting majority rule in southern Africa. As a matter of fact, the administration was quite successful, with an active policy in southern Africa which will probably pay dividends in Zimbabwe, Namibia, and southern Africa in general.

The Carter administration's stand was well presented in October 1979 by Under Secretary of State David Newsom in testimony before the Subcommittee on Africa of the Committee on Foreign Affairs of the House of Representatives. Mr. Newsom noted:

> The Soviet Union is not well equipped to contribute importantly to economic development, the fundamental long term goal in Africa . . . . While we provide military equipment within limits, we prefer to compete where we face comparative advantage, in support of economic and social development.[36]

This is a noble statement, and it would be admirable if it were carried out; there have been no signs of any great economic successes of the United States government in Africa, however. A glance at Table 7 reveals the USSR has as meager an assistance program as the United States. Furthermore, American policy does not seem to have been able to respond to exigencies. For instance, President Nyerere requested $375 million in financial assistance in 1979 to assist the Tanzanian economy in recovering from its war to liberate Uganda from Idi Amin. War-torn Uganda was also badly in need of aid.[37] Somalia also had enormous refugee problems and an economy in desperate straits. In 1979, Uganda received a paltry $3 million in economic assistance, and Tanzania received $1.2 million less than she had received in 1978! The US did, however, respond to Somalia; aid increased from $800,000 in 1977 to $28.9 million by 1979.[38]

The United States does not have an impressive record of trade with Africa either, as indicated by Table 8. In truth, the former colonies built up preferences for goods from the colonial powers, and trade channels were not well established with the United States. These patterns have persisted. It is the Europeans who are economically important in Africa. As a matter of fact, the United States is in considerable difficulty, principally because of its oil imports from Nigeria. Abraham Katz, former Deputy Assistant Secretary of Commerce for Internal Economic Policy, testified that Nigerian imports from the US had dropped from $985 million in 1978 to $550 million in 1979.[39] Andrew Young noted in a Congressional hearing during 1979:

253

Table 7. Development Aid to Africa 1970s

(In Millions of Dollars and % of Total African Aid)

Source	1970	%	1971	%	1972	%	1973	%	1974	%	1975	%	1976	%	1977	%	1978*	%
OPEC									904	20	471	10	823	16	1000	16	950	14
US									270	6	294	6	353	7	371	6	470	7
France									62	12	715	16	617	12	697	10	620	9
West Germany									344	7	393	9	313	6	398	6	4115	6
USSR	51		388				10		17	**	73	2	26	1	21	**	10	**
Western European Countries									2027	44	2188	48	2413	48	3157	50	3320	50

*Estimate
**Less than 1/2%.

Sources: Compiled from *U.S. Interests In Africa*, cited in note 1, below, pp. 92-93; *Soviet Economic Prospects for the Seventies*, cited in note 3, below, p. 775.

Table 8. Selected African Trade Figures, 1970–1977

(In Millions of Dollars)

Year	1970	1974	1975	1976	1977
US Exports to Africa	1,560	3,590	44,870	5,120	5,440
% of world exports to Africa	10.1	9.0	9.8	10.1	9.1
US Imports from Africa	900	5,885	7,020	10,140	16,020
% of world imports from Africa	6.3	13.8	18.2	21.9	29.7
EEF/CEE Exports to Africa	7,330	14,630	23,750	23,920	29,170
% of world exports to Africa	47.6	36.6	48.0	47.3	49.1
EEF/CEE Imports from Africa	8,530	22,630	18,170	21,970	22,800
% of world imports from Africa	59.4	53.0	47.2	47.6	42.3
Japan's Exports to Africa	1,070	3,880	4,590	5,040	5,720
% of world exports to Africa	6.9	9.7	10.0	9.6	
Japan's Imports from Africa	775	2,330	1,790	1,970	1,920
% of world imports from Africa	5.4	5.5	4.6	4.2	3.2
USSR Exports to Africa	580	840	800	730	870
% of world exports to Africa	3.8	2.1	1.6	1.6	1.5
USSR Imports from Africa	600	1,400	2,920	2,670	3,060
% of world imports from Africa	4.2	3.3	7.6	5.8	5.7
US Exports to South Africa	570	1,160	1,300	1,360	1,080
% of world exports to Africa	3.7	2.9	2.6	2.7	1.8
US Imports from South Africa	Not Available.				

Source: Compiled from United Nations, *Statistical Yearbook, 1978*, pp. 450–455.

. . . I mean right now we are buying $6 billion worth of oil from Nigeria, and they are giving all of the money to build their expressways to Germany. The consumer market is run by the British. The Italians are developing apartments and housing, and the Israelis are doing water projects.[40]

Perhaps the most embarrassing part of American relations with Africa is the fact the Republic of South Africa offers the strongest military establishment, has minerals which we badly need, and is a major importer of United States goods.

Except for the initiative in southern Africa, the Carter policy was an incremental one with rather parsimonious financing and little new initiative. In the spring of 1978, the United States announced it would supply arms to Somalia if it were reinvaded by Ethiopia on the condition that Somalia would renounce any territorial aspirations in Kenya and Ethiopia. The Soviet Union was warned by National Security Advisor Zbigniew Brzezinksi that increased Soviet–Cuban activities would jeopardize the SALT agreements. In May of 1978, when Shaba insurgents invaded Zaire from Angola, the United States ferried French and Belgian troops to Zaire.[41] These actions all represented a stiffening of American posture but no great policy change. However, from 1978 onward, there was speculation as to whether the African policy espoused by Secretary of State Vance and former Ambassador Young would continue, or whether the "globalists" led by Brzezinski would prevail.

In 1979, the Center for Strategic Studies of Georgetown University conducted a study for the Department of Defense which stated that Western interests were threatened by Soviet expansion and advocated a more forceful policy in Africa with greater resources to support such a policy.[42] The fall of the Shah, the taking of the American hostages in Iran, and the invasion of Afghanistan by the Soviet Union during the year built up pressures to which the administration had to respond. President Carter announced the new "Carter Doctrine" in his State of the Union Address of 23 January 1980. He noted:

> . . . Any attempt by an outside force to gain control of the Persian Gulf region will be regarded as an assault on the vital interests of the United States of America and such an assault will be repelled by any means necessary including military force.

The President also announced arrangements were being made for "key naval and air facilities to be used by our forces in the region of Northeast Africa and the Persian Gulf."[43]

The old policy of stressing economic and social development has not been abandoned, but the globalists obviously have prevailed in military matters. This may have its pitfalls for long-term relations, as the Soviets already have learned. Two possible problems emerged immediately—Morocco and Somalia. The Carter administration backed the sale of arms to Morocco. These arms undoubtedly have been used by Morocco in its conflict with the Algerian-backed *Polisario* insurgents who oppose the former's claims to the Spanish Sahara. The Organization of African Unity (OAU) at its Monrovia meeting of July 1979 called for a referendum in this area. Undoubtedly, any large-scale military support of Morocco against the Polisario would not meet with OAU approval; however, King Hassan is a long-time supporter of the

United States, and such aid is supported by Egypt and Saudi Arabia.[44]

Somalia also has long coveted the Ogaden in Ethiopia and northern Kenya, both of which contain large populations of ethnic Somali origin. There is a real danger armaments sent to Somalia might be used against Kenya and Ethiopia. The United States has been unwilling to provide arms unless Somalia would renounce their use against Kenya and Ethiopia. The United States for a time also refused to meet the conditions of President Barre for use of the Berbera base in Somalia.

Both Morocco and Somalia represent the sort of situation in which the Soviets became involved; it is a situation the United States would be wise to avoid. The United States, however, has acquired the use of naval and air facilities in Egypt, Kenya, Somalia, and Oman which should bolster the American position in those areas. The United States seems to have moved to a new military posture vis-a-vis the Soviets; however, it remains to be seen whether the administration and Congress will provide the necessary financial support to carry out this posture effectively.

No really new posture has emerged in regard to economic and social development. The administration's request for African aid for Fiscal Year 1981 was up considerably from funds for 1977–1979; however, such funds would not be sufficient for any significant or innovative breakthrough in the area of development. Seventy percent of African countries had a lower per capita growth rate in the 1970s than in the 1960s.[45] The United Nations Economic Commission for Africa has called attention to the deterioration of economic conditions for most African countries and has predicted a continental crisis if steps are not taken to reverse these trends.[46] In order to strengthen its position in Africa, the United States will need a completely new and more vigorous approach to African social and economic development, something which does not seem to be in the offing at the moment but which will be necessary to build long-term, lasting relations and political stability in sub-Saharan Africa.

Conclusions

The Soviet Union gradually built up its military potential and African diplomatic bases during the 1960s. Soviet military successes in Africa during the 1970s—when that continent had become very strategic to the West because of the oil routes to the Middle East and a greater dependence on African oil and minerals—caused a complete upset of the power balance. Africa now seems to be caught in the East–West conflict, and the United States has moved to a globalist posture vis-a-vis the Soviet Union in that area.

Soviet policy in Africa has been risky and has not always been successful. The instability of many of the African regimes does not provide much permanency for the foreign interventionist . . . as the USSR already has discovered. Nationalism is also a serious factor in African policy, as the Soviets learned when they lost their enormous military investments in Egypt and Somalia. If the United States pursues a globalist policy in Africa, it must be a good deal more careful in choosing its allies than the USSR. The United States must also build up its military strength, particularly in the area of rapid deployment forces, in order to back up a globalist policy in Africa. The United States will also need to adopt more imaginative developmental policies and to supply a great deal more economic aid than has been the case in the past. As a corollary, a much more vigorous trade policy must be adopted which will increase exports to African states on equitable terms, thereby reducing the one-sided trade relationship which now exists. Finally, the United States must also realize the Western European countries have considerable influence in Africa; therefore, it would be wise to work more closely with them in foreign policy formulation than has been the case in the past.

It is difficult to predict what the position of the Reagan administration will be; few statements were made during the campaign directed specifically to Africa.[47] The Reagan administration has placed great stress on economizing, a fact which may prove to be an impediment to any expansion of economic aid to Africa. The Reagan administration may also seek closer ties with the Republic of South Africa, a development which would have serious consequences for relations with other African countries. There can, however, be little doubt the Reagan administration will advocate a stiffer defense policy and most foreign policy questions will be interpreted within the framework of East–West confrontation. One would thus expect the new administration to put greater stress on a globalist posture in African affairs.

Notes

1. See David E. Albright, "Soviet Policy," *Problems in Communism,* Vol. 27, 1978, p. 28 ff.; statement of M. Crawford Young in US Congress, House Committee on Foreign Affairs, Subcommittee on Africa, *US Interests in Africa,* Hearings, 96th Congress, 1st session (Washington: Government Printing Office, 1979), p. 82.
2. See Anatoliy Gromyko, "Socialist Orientation in Africa," *International Affairs* (Moscow), No. 9, 1979, pp. 96–98, 102; and Albright, op. cit., pp. 24–25.
3. Leo Transky, "Soviet Foreign Aid: Scope, Direction, and Trends," in Joint Economic Committee, Congress of the United States, *Soviet Economic Prospects for the Seventies,* (Washington: Government Printing Office, 1973), p. 775.
4. Compiled from United Nations, *Statistical Yearbook* (1966), pp. 684–686; (1969) pp. 642, 670; (1970) p. 708; (1971) pp. 708–710; (1973) p. 715.
5. Albright, op. cit., p. 29.
6. Alvin J. Cottrell and R. M. Burrell, "The Soviet Navy and the Indian Ocean," *Strategic Review,* Vol. 2, 1974, p. 28.
7. Senator James McClure, "The Decline of the West in Africa: Is it Irreversible?" in Roger C. Pearson, ed., *Sino–Soviet Intervention In Africa* (Washington: Council on American Affairs, 1977), pp. 91–92.
8. Ian Greig, *The Communist Challenge to Africa* (New York, 1977), p. 29.

9. N. Polmar, *Soviet Naval Power: Challenge for 1970s* (1974), p. 67.
10. Greig, op. cit., p. 33.
11. Polmar, op. cit., p. 114.
12. Christopher Stevens, *The Soviet Union and Black Africa* (New York: Holmes and Meier, 1976), p. 174.
13. Compiled from Transky, op. cit., p. 775.
14. Greig, op. cit., p. 110.
15. Office of Planning and Budgeting, Bureau for Program and Policy Coordination, Agency for International Development, *U.S. Overseas Loans and Grants, July 1, 1945–September 30, 1979*, p. 87.
16. Peter Vanneman and Martin James, "The Soviet Intervention in Angola: Intentions and Implications" *Strategic Review*, Vol.4, 1976, p. 93.
17. Ibid., p. 95.
18. Greig, op. cit., p. 255.
19. David Ottaway, "Africa: U.S. Policy Eclipse" *Foreign Affairs*, Vol. 58, 1979, p. 651.
20. Henry Kissinger, *White House Years* (Boston: Little, Brown and Company, 1979), p. 157.
21. Vanneman and James, op. cit., p. 97.
22. Walter F. Hahn and Alvin J. Cottrell, *Soviet Shadow Over Africa* (Coral Gables, Florida: Advanced International Studies Institute, 1976), p.58.
23. See US Congress, House Committee on International Relations, Subcommittee on Africa, *Foreign Assistance Legislation for Fiscal Year 1979*, Part 3, 95th Congress, 2nd Session, Hearings (Washington: Government Printing Office, 1979), pp. 23–24.
24. Albright, op. cit., p. 30.
25. Cottrell and Burrell, op. cit., p. 31.
26. Albright, op. cit., p. 32.
27. Richard Bissell, "Soviet Policies in Africa," *Current History*, Vol. 47, 1979, pp. 126–127.
28. Under Secretary of State for Political Affairs David D. Newsom, in *U.S. Interests in Africa*, p. 61.
29. Colin Legum, "The African Crisis," *Foreign Affairs*, Vol. 57, 1979, p. 634.
30. Bissell, op. cit., p. 127.
31. Newsom, op. cit., p. 47.
32. Jennifer C. War, "U.S. Policy in Southern Africa," in Joint Economic Committee of the Congress of the United States, *The U.S. Role in a Changing Political Economy: Major Issues for the 96th Congress*, 96th Congress, 1st Session, 1979, p. 591.
33. Compiled from data in United States Department of Energy, *International Petroleum Annual*, 1978, p. 23.
34. Legum, op. cit., pp. 634, 636.
35. *U.S. Overseas Loans and Grants*, pp. 14, 87.
36. *U.S. Interests in Africa*, p. 54.
37. Ottaway, loc. cit., p. 65.
38. *U.S. Overseas Loans and Grants*, pp. 15, 130, 133.
39. *U.S. Interests in Africa*, p. 53.
40. Ibid., p. 26.
41. Legum, op. cit., p. 636.
42. See "Implications of Soviet and Cuban Activities for U.S. Policy" and "Caesar's Planners Look at Africa," *Africa Report*, January–February 1980, pp. 49–53.
43. For text of speech, see *Congressional Quarterly Weekly Report*, Vol. 38, 1980, pp. 200–202.
44. *African Recorder*, Vol. 19, 1980, p. 337.
45. "$707 million Request for Economic and Security Assistance," *United States Department of State Bulletin*, Vol. 80, 1980, p. 27.
46. Ottaway, op. cit., p. 638.
47. For a detailed discussion of Ronald Reagan's views on Africa, see Richard Deutsch, "Reagan's African Perspectives," *Africa Report*, July–August 1980, pp. 4–7.

Stabilizing the Beijing–Moscow–Washington Triangle

Ray S. Cline

Ten days before Christmas in 1978, President Jimmy Carter proudly announced to the world that the United States and the People's Republic of China (PRC) had agreed to establish full diplomatic relations on the first day of the New Year. He had no other purpose, he said, than "the advancement of peace."

The President's message, nevertheless, knocked the delicately poised Beijing–Moscow–Washington triangle off balance, at least temporarily. The resulting imbalance has not yet been restored. The tilt toward Beijing, sponsored mainly by Assistant to the President for National Security Affairs Zbigniew Brzezinski, became more and more pronounced in 1979 and 1980. "Few actions," Brzezinski said, "will contribute more to the security and stability of our important positions around the rim of Asia . . . than a constructive involvement with China." The prospects for an "equilibrium" and a "stable system of independent nations in Asia" which Secretary of State Cyrus Vance promised have not yet appeared. Instead, Secretary Vance has disappeared.

The reason for doubts, indeed pessimism, about US policy is the view in Moscow that the United States finally and formally has combined forces with the Soviet Union's bitterest antagonist, the PRC, to form a "united front" against the USSR. For the 20 years since Sino–Soviet antagonism broke out into a definitive split in the early 1960s, the USSR's hostility toward its giant neighbor has deepened. Approximately 45 Soviet army divisions guard the 4500–mile communal border. It is no wonder Soviet President Leonid Brezhnev reacted with strong reservations about US intentions when Carter moved abruptly to end the 30–year US policy of not formally recognizing the mainland regime which had fought a bloody war in Korea against US forces and provided indispensable logistic support to Hanoi during the Vietnam war.

Soviet leaders immediately charged that the United States hoped to push China into a war with the USSR and that the United States would use China as a tactical diplomatic tool for exerting greater leverage to obtain concessions from the USSR in global conflicts of interest. *Izvestiya,* on 9 January 1979, warned: "Naturally our country will draw appropriate conclusions to its defense in the face of actions threatening peace."

The Soviet leaders lost no time in staging aggressive moves world-wide, continuing to take steps toward what they call an "irreversible gain in the correlation of forces"—a decisive shift of world power away from China and the United States and its allies. Soviet naval and air forces immediately began using the elaborate former US base facilities at Cam Ranh Bay in Vietnam and provided extensive logistic support to the Vietnamese armies in the defensive battles against the PRC attack early in 1979, as well as for the massive invasion and military occupation of Kampuchea. In a sense, this Soviet move encircled China while threatening the sea lanes throughout the West Pacific.

Then, at the end of December 1979, in defiance of global opinion, an estimated 10,000 Soviet Army troops marched into Afghanistan. With modern, heavy equipment, they callously assaulted the fiercely resisting Afghan people and took command of all aspects of Afghan government policy under the thin facade of local communist puppet rulers. This aggression was condemned as a blatant violation of international law—as the Kremlin must have expected—by more than 100 nations (including the United States, China, West Europe, and the whole Moslem world) who demanded the removal of all foreign troops from Afghanistan. In the roll call vote at a remarkable General Assembly meeting of the United Nations on 14 January 1980, most of the non-aligned countries sided with the United States against the Soviet Union—an unprecedented linking of support.

The Kremlin leaders paid little, if any, attention. Since 1975, they have been carrying on what Moscow terms "national wars of liberation" in a number of regional conflicts. Their ultimate goal is to establish a Marxist–Leninist system of Soviet-model governments which eventually, according to Soviet strategic doctrine, would spread across the face of the earth. As a major element in this worldwide strategy, the USSR is building on the Eurasian continent a formidable pro-Soviet military alliance of states to the south and south-west of China.

The Soviet Union now enjoys more power and causes more fear in Asia than ever before. These regional moves to incorporate large slices of the area into the Soviet political, economic, and strategic sphere have been supplemented by a substantial buildup of the USSR's Pacific naval and air forces in the Vladivostok–Petropavlovsk region of the Soviet maritime provinces and by the deployment of an equivalent of a division of ground forces on the disputed "northern island" adjacent to Hokkaido. The tremors of Asian concern about the USSR and its ally, Vietnam, run from Japan and South Korea through the Strait of Malacca, to Indonesia, Malaysia, and Singapore, and on down to Australia and New Zealand, as well as across to Thailand.

In the meantime, Soviet leaders have been dispatching weapons, intelligence officers, military advisers, and terrorist training teams to all of the trouble spots in the Mideast and Africa. The Soviet occupation of Afghanistan has gained a foothold for the forces of the USSR in due course, if the political conditions are right, to take two more prizes: Iran and Pakistan. The first will become available if Khomeini's revolutionary government totally tears apart the thin social fabric of that society; the second is already directly in danger along the Afghan border.

The pattern of Soviet indirect aggression had already been well established by a series of military interventions (usually with Cuban troops in front of Soviet advisers and logisticians) in Angola, Shaba (Zaire), Ethiopia, and South Yemen. Afghanistan simply added organized Soviet military forces to the mix, yet this extra ingredient provided the shock which finally focused world attention on Soviet policy. As these menacing moves have unfolded, Soviet leaders have not only brought about a major change in the patterns of stability everywhere but also have thwarted long-standing Chinese attempts to accumulate influence in Third World nations.

On the second side of the strategic triangle, China, a nation which throughout its long history has always considered itself the "central kingdom," still holds to the political philosophy that it is potentially and by right the greatest power on earth. The Chinese communists now in control in Beijing have grafted Marxist–Leninist dialectics onto this traditional Chinese cultural attitude. Ritual incantations of Maoist doctrine have fallen away sharply since the death of the former head of state, Mao Zedong.

The Constitution of the Chinese Communist Party, adopted under Premier Hua Guofeng and approved unanimously on 18 August 1977, is still in force pending approval of a new one slated for this year [1980]. The 1977 Constitution proclaims that the Party "unites with the proletariat, the oppressed people and nations of the world and fights shoulder to shoulder with them to oppose the hegemonism of the two superpowers, the Soviet Union and the United States, to overthrow imperialism, modern revisionism, and all reaction." By 1978, the PRC's dominant leader, Vice Premier Deng Xiaoping, plainly had adopted the maxim of Lenin and Mao favoring a policy of joining ranks with the weaker of the two enemies to bring down the other. Hence, Deng's joyful greeting of Carter and his skillful implication of the United States in the PRC's military attack on Vietnam.

To reiterate its stand on hegemonism and to make certain the USSR completely understands the shift in strategic emphasis, the Chinese communists insisted the joint communique establishing diplomatic relations with the United States make clear "each is opposed to efforts by any country or group of countries to establish . . . hegemony in the Asia–Pacific region or in any other region of the world." Beijing could not have been disappointed by Moscow's fiery response that the hegemony concept was an excuse for "creating an anti-Soviet alliance." Whether or not Washington knew what was happening, the impression such an alliance was being formed was exactly what Vice

Premier Deng had in mind.

President Carter and Dr. Brzezinski were so pleased to get kind words from Deng, they extracted no concessions from the PRC for the US recognition of Beijing and placidly allowed him to "play the American card" against the USSR. When Deng came to Washington, he obviously sought to bolster the sagging economy of China by holding out the prospects of a vast Western economic and military aid program in direct defiance of the Soviet Union's hostility to the PRC. He put aside, for the time being at least, his long-term requirements of "liberating" Taiwan (the Republic of China)—having extracted some extraordinary promises from President Carter to reduce drastically American relations with Taiwan—and gambled he could consolidate his own domestic political power base and protect China from the Soviet Union by fashioning a period of cooperation with the United States. His aim was to borrow billions of capitalist dollars and import modern technology for China's industry and military forces. In this way, he deftly spread the notion he had enlisted the aid of the United States against what he considered the more powerful enemy, the Soviet Union. While not much actual trade or aid has yet resulted from this maneuver, the greater cordiality in Washington–Beijing relations has indeed startled other Asian nations as well as the USSR. After all, Brzezinski has argued he was "playing the China card" against the USSR rather than the other way around.

At present, the capabilities the PRC leaders have to act either for or against the USSR or the United States are extremely limited by poverty and overpopulation. The Chinese regime has a billion people it can barely feed and clothe. Its greatest strategic strength lies simply in the fact no nation would want to get bogged down trying to conquer it. Border skirmishes and limited nuclear exchanges are feasible, but an Afghan-style invasion of China is unthinkable. The PRC leaders intend to expand their influence in the world, however, whenever it is possible and safe to do so. They know the weakness and backwardness of their society are their chief handicaps, but they are trying to "modernize" while working within their means to frustrate the Soviet moves in Asia by highlighting parallel interests with the United States.

In the fall of 1978, Premier Hua took an extended trip to Yugoslavia, Romania, and Iran to urge resistance to pressures from the USSR, even within the Soviet bloc, and to explain the need for curbing Soviet military expansion. In the wake of this trip, the USSR affirmed its support for the Teheran revolutionaries. Soon after, in March 1979, Beijing denounced the long moribund Sino–Soviet Alliance of 1950. Neither capital has yet accepted the text of an agreement for the continuation of friendly Sino–Soviet state-to-state relations. Communist Party relations have been suspended for many years, but international relations never were broken off completely until last year. *Pravda,* the official Soviet organ, placed all the blame for the present antagonisms on

Beijing, portraying the USSR as the aggrieved party. *Pravda's* argument was based on the fact China had laid down certain unrealistic requirements for "normalizing" relations with Moscow. These were reported to include the termination of Soviet military assistance to Vietnam and the withdrawal of Soviet troops from Mongolia as well as Afghanistan.

In all of these current maneuverings, the Chinese communists have not forgotten one of Mao's teachings which persisted even after his demise and the stripping of his mantle of infallibility. The ultimate Chinese wisdom behind Mao's instructions to unite with the weaker enemy was aimed at provoking war between the two enemies . . . in this era, the two superpowers—the United States and the Soviet Union. Chinese policy today probably, at bottom, is based on the old proverb, "We will sit on the mountain and watch the two tigers fight." Four years after Mao's death, Beijing still seems to hold to his thought that even if China is a victim of a conventional or thermonuclear exchange between the superpowers, the PRC will be the final victor. "If the imperialists unleash war on us, we may lose more than 300 million. So what?" he asked Khrushchev 20 years ago in urging him to start military hostilities against West Europe.

The United States is faced with two sides of the Beijing-Moscow–Washington triangle thrusting in opposite directions. China, a regional power, has set out on a course to increase its strength and prestige at home, relying on the United States to further its interests. The USSR, a global power, is making every effort to enhance its influence abroad, striking at weak spots such as the Mideast and South Asia as well as East Asia. The United States, placing itself between the two, has much to lose and little apparent to gain in the short term by too close a strategic linkage with the PRC. On the surface, the Soviet Union appears to want to relax tensions with the United States, but its words calling for the US Congress to ratify the SALT II Treaty and resume the more genial climate of diplomacy of the pre-Afghanistan era do not coincide with Soviet deeds in threatening US interests around the rim of Eurasia, especially in the Persian Gulf.

Following the US opening of full diplomatic relations with Beijing, Moscow doubled its financial support to Cuba—exceeding $3 billion during 1979—in addition to providing sophisticated military weapons, including aircraft, free of charge. At the same time, the Soviet Union expanded its military presence—naval, ground, and air—in Cuba while guaranteeing Fidel Castro against US wrath as he overtly and covertly intervenes in political or revolutionary conflicts in the Caribbean and in Central America—notably Jamaica, Nicaragua, and El Salvador. As this Soviet–Cuban cooperation solidifies, the Kremlin stands ready to exploit targets of opportunity in the Western Hemisphere as well as in American home waters.

In Latin America, on the African continent, and in Eurasia, Soviet aggressions have disrupted the patterns of political stability and turned many nations away from the United States and the West. In these areas, already 1.5 billion people, or 25 percent of the earth's population, live under communist one-party dictatorships. In economic terms, these Soviet advances are jeopardizing the access of the United States and its allies to Mideast oil and to the nonfuel minerals of southern Africa which are vital to the prosperity and functioning of all the advanced industrial nations.

No area, not even West Europe, is more important to the well-being of the United States and its allies than Asia and the Pacific where geographical proximity makes the rivalry between the two communist giants potentially disruptive and explosive. US trade with nations of the Pacific Basin amounts to 40 percent of US world trade or more than the total of trade with the European community. Canada, Japan, South Korea, China/Taiwan, Hong Kong, and Australia lead the list of Pacific partners in the international trading world.

For its part, the primary strategic interest of the United States is to restabilize the Beijing–Moscow–Washington triangle. American power and prestige must be deployed more deftly to guard against either a movement by Beijing toward rapprochement with the USSR or by Moscow toward war. Either rapprochement or war between the USSR and the PRC would be disastrous for the security of the United States and its allies, especially in Asia. At present, both of these eventualities are distinct possibilities as a result of the Carter–Brzezinski tilt toward the PRC, a tilt which has antagonized the Kremlin without providing any certain accretion of military strength which could operate against the USSR.

The United States should therefore keep a flexible position not too close to either of the communist giants, lest one of them be startled into a drastic policy realignment. Instead, the United States should give first priority to its central strategic goal of maintaining cooperative relations with its true friends whose national objectives lean toward the political, social, and economic processes of the open, pluralist societies. In the global community of noncommunist nations, the key element in the survival of the free world as it now exists is US strategic leadership in mobilizing a strong voluntary alliance of seafaring, international trading states to resist Soviet domination and protect the movement of commerce and defensive military forces as needed among its members. The United States cannot shirk this role. The PRC, if it remains basically anti-Soviet, can be a strategic asset in this effort simply by cooperating with the western nations rather than accommodating to Soviet imperialistic policy aims.

Above all, the United States must preserve a strategic posture guaranteeing a balance of power with the Soviet Union no worse—and preferably better—than the present balance. To this end, it should refrain from forging a military alliance with the PRC, for even the suspicion of such an alliance invites bolder reactions from the USSR. Moscow might feel compelled to strike one or the other of the partners—probably the weaker, the PRC—before it becomes too late or, on the other hand, to buy off some ambitious political element in Beijing with generous military and economic aid to be used at the expense of American interests in Asia.

After all, during the many years modernization will require under the most optimistic assumptions, the "China card" will be, in terms of military strength compared with the USSR, only a "deuce." The United States cannot rely on gambling with such uncertain assets. It must build its strategy on the bedrock of its own military strength linked with key allies on the shores of all the world's oceans from Great Britain, France, West Germany, and Italy on the Atlantic-Mediterranean side to Japan and Australia along the vital sea lanes of the vast Pacific–Indian Ocean region.

In summary, the United States should aim at (a) avoiding involvement in a land war in Asia, either on the Sino–Soviet border or in South and Southeast Asia; (b) encouraging the PRC to move toward cooperation, not conflict, with noncommunist Asian nations, including Taiwan; (c) giving no ground for the PRC either to provoke war with the Soviet Union or to reach an accommodation with Moscow for some regional advantage; and (d) stabilizing the triangle, not tilting it either way, by recognizing America's own frontiers are at the most distant edges of the oceans where security and prosperity go hand in hand.

Chinese Foreign Policy Coalitions
and Soviet Options in China

H. Lyman Miller

In the mid–1970s, in the years before Mao Zedong's death, Moscow's best hopes for a favorable turn in relations with China seemed to rest on the possibility a post–Mao Chinese leadership might seek to end the years of unrelenting hostility toward the USSR. Although before Mao's death the Soviet press occasionally expressed faint optimism over the presence of "healthy forces" on the Chinese political scene and perfunctorily insisted the fraternal friendship of the Soviet and Chinese peoples endured, Soviet commentary on China under Moa exuded a resigned and overwhelming pessimism over the prospects for improvement in Sino–Soviet relations. The rigidity of Mao's ideological and geopolitical views on the Soviet Union, together with his personal antagonism toward the Soviet leadership, gave Moscow little grounds for optimism as long as he lived.

In 1976, on the eve of Mao's death, Soviet pessimism was underscored frequently and authoritatively. Brezhnev's report to the 25th CPSU Congress on 24 February, for example, reviewed the futility of past Soviet efforts to initiate conciliation with Beijing and stressed the impetus for change would have to come from Beijing. "It is up to the Chinese side," Brezhnev declared, stating that if China "returns to a policy which is really based on Marxism–Leninism, abandons a course which is hostile to the socialist countries, and embarks on a path of cooperation and solidarity with the socialist world," Moscow would respond in an "appropriate" manner.[1] *Pravda* articles on China in January and April written by the quasi-authoritative pseudonymous author "I. Aleksandrov"—one discussing the death of Premier Zhou Enlai and the other the Chinese political scene following the second purge of Deng Xiaoping—fleshed out the pessimistic Soviet approach to China encapsulated in Brezhnev's party congress statements and portrayed Mao as the most bitterly anti–Soviet member of a Chinese leadership dominated by elements committed to anti–Sovietism.[2]

Immediately upon Mao's death in September 1976, Moscow acted on the presumption a post–Mao leadership might be less committed to unrelenting anti–Sovietism. The CPSU sent a condolence message to the CCP even though party relations had been broken since 1966. The Soviet media quickly dropped their usual program of negative commentary on China and began to carry long reminiscences on the warmth and benefits of Sino–Soviet cooperation in the 1950s.

Undoubtedly at Moscow's initiative, Soviet negotiator L. I. Il'yichev returned to Beijing at the end of November to reopen the Sino–Soviet border talks which had been dormant since 1975.[3]

Beijing, for its part, remained unyielding. The CPSU condolence message was rejected outright. Although the Soviet media showed restraint in commentary on China in the last months of 1976, the Chinese media showed no hint of moderating their polemics against Moscow. Moreover, although Beijing agreed to Il'yichev's return, Vice Premier Li Xiannian made it clear on the eve of the resumption of the talks that Beijing was not ready to compromise and accused Moscow of "wishful thinking and daydreaming" in its attempts to give the world "false impressions" about prospective improvements in Sino–Soviet relations.[4]

By early 1977, having explored the views of the post–Mao leadership in the border talks and continuing to be confronted by public Chinese hostility, the Soviet leadership evidently concluded Mao's death had done nothing, at least in the near term, to alter long-standing Chinese attitudes on relations with the Soviet Union. In February 1977, Soviet media polemics against China resumed and Il'yichev returned to Moscow.[5] An "I. Aleksandrov" article in *Pravda* on 14 May and a speech by Leonid Brezhnev on 30 May—the first comment by the Soviet leader on China since the cessation of Soviet polemics the preceding fall—attacked China as a major threat to world peace and provided an authoritative capstone to the failure of Soviet efforts to explore the possibility of improving relations with post–Mao China.[6] A long summary report on an earlier forum of Soviet specialists on China which appeared in the Soviet academic journal *Problems of the Far East* soon thereafter seemed designed to ensure adherence to the pessimistic official Soviet line which had emerged over the preceding spring.[7] Events over the next year and a half—most notably the solidification of Beijing's ties with Japan and the United States and the Chinese punitive attack on northern Vietnam—only served to solidify Soviet pessimism.[8]

The depth of Moscow's pessimism and frustration over prospects for its relations with post-Mao China are difficult to measure. It seems clear in retrospect, however, that Moscow's frustration at the failure of its initial efforts to improve relations with China after Mao's death, together with traditional Soviet caution and suspicion in dealing with China, contributed to Moscow's failure to explore fully the potential for improved relations when an important opportunity to do so finally emerged on the Chinese political scene in 1979. This article attempts to demonstrate that the Chinese offer of talks with Moscow in April 1979 was a product of the momentary ascendancy in Beijing of a coalition of party leaders who believed China's domestic and foreign policy interests required a degree of detente in Sino–Soviet relations. The article argues further that, because of important tactical considerations regarding Soviet options in Vietnam and innate Soviet suspicion and caution in responding to the Chinese offer, Moscow effectively contributed to the demise of the Chinese proposal. How significant Moscow's missed chance in China turns out to be in the long run, of course, can be estimated only by placing the 1979 episode within the context of subsequent events over a broad span of time. In the short run, however, a number of factors on the Chinese scene suggest the combination of strategic interests and political considerations which prompted the Chinese offer for talks in 1979 are not likely to reemerge soon.

Origins of the Chinese Proposal

The Chinese proposal to open new political talks with Moscow, made on 3 April 1979 in the course of denouncing the 1950 Sino–Soviet treaty of alliance, marked a fundamental departure from the approach Beijing consistently had employed since 1969 in negotiations with the Soviet Union. Since the opening of the border talks in Beijing in 1969, the Chinese rigidly had insisted implementation of the "Zhou–Kosygin understanding" on resolving border tension between the two countries precede progress in all other aspects of bilateral relations. The "understanding"—which Beijing insisted was achieved by Premiers Zhou Enlai and Aleksey Kosygin during the latter's stopover at Beijing airport on 11 September 1969—had provided, according to the Chinese, for agreement on maintenance of the status quo on the border, prevention of future armed clashes, and withdrawal of both sides' armed forces from the disputed border areas. Beijing's rigorous and tireless insistence on implementation of this alleged "understanding," despite Moscow's equally steadfast denial of its existence and attempts to promote progress in other areas of Sino–Soviet relations, had stalemated Sino–Soviet relations since 1969.

Beijing's proposal for new talks, however, appeared to be without conditions. As reported in Xinhua's dispatch on the National People's Congress Standing Committee's decision to abrogate the 1950 treaty on 3 April—and presumably as conveyed to Soviet Ambassador Shcherbakov on the same day—the Chinese offer simply declared Beijing's readiness to "resolve outstanding issues and to improve relations" between the two countries. In contrast to every Chinese public statement since the early 1970s prescribing the basis for improvement in bilateral relations, the new Chinese proposal omitted any mention of the long-standing precondition that both sides implement the 1969 "understanding." Moreover, after a skeptical memorandum from Soviet Foreign Minister Gromyko sought clarification of exactly what Beijing had in mind, the Chinese elaborated their proposal in a manner which more unambigously showed the contrast between their present approach and their past negotiating stance. A 5 May PRC Foreign Ministry memorandum thus called for new talks to set down fundamental principles governing relations between the two countries and to promote commercial, scientific and technical, and cultural contacts between them. Negotiation of the border issues—for ten years the focus of the Chinese negotiating position—might be relegated to separate concurrent sessions of the border talks, according to the Chinese note.[9]

The new Chinese tack thus fundamentally inverted longstanding Chinese negotiating priorities. In doing so, it conformed to the general approach Beijing traditionally had employed in bilateral negotiations in which it hoped to make significant progress—i.e., to seek improvement in the cosmetic aspects of bilateral relations not in dispute while setting aside contentious issues, hoping that in the long run the improved atmosphere of trust between the two sides would contribute to the eventual resolution of disputed issues.[10] At the same time, the new Chinese approach also conformed to the negotiating approach Moscow had preferred toward Beijing since the early 1970s.

The origins and intentions of this remarkable break in the continuity of Beijing's approach to relations with the Soviet Union are to be found in the Chinese leadership debate over domestic and foreign policy problems which occurred in the wake of the CCP's landmark Third Plenum in December 1978 and Beijing's "counterattack" against Vietnam in February 1979. The Chinese offer of new Sino–Soviet talks thus coincided with the apparent resolution of several other important issues which had up until that time sharply divided the Chinese leadership. Aside from Vietnam, these other issues included the problem of reassessing the party's history under the last two decades of Mao Zedong's leadership and the need for further party rectification; the blossoming of the dissident "democracy movement" in Beijing and the breakdown of social order in several Chinese cities; the growing realization of the extent and seriousness of imbalances and gaps in the national economy; and resurgent leftist attacks on the decisions of the Third Plenum.

Positions adopted at party meetings in late March and early April to resolve debate over these issues uniformly reflected the views and concerns of one coalition of leaders in particular within the Chinese leadership. Led by CCP Chairman Hua Guofeng and Vice Chairmen Ye Jianying and Li Xiannian, this group of "moderate" or "centrist" leaders had up to that time pressed the importance of maintaining domestic stability and political unity for the sake of pursuing China's "four modernizations" development programs. They were opposed by another coalition of party leaders led by party Vice Chairman Deng Xiaoping who advocated drastic political reform for the sake of the "four modernizations." The various decisions reached in late March and early April were important political setbacks for the latter group. Consistent in timing and compatible in objective with the other decisions emerging at the same time on the domestic front in China, the offer of political talks with Moscow thus seems to have been promoted by the coalition of moderate party leaders led by Hua Guofeng and Ye Jianying, as the following summary discussion of the separate issues involved attempts to show.[11]

Party History and Rectification

Although the top party leadership had been united over the broad direction of China's "four modernization" plans since Mao's death, the leadership divided sharply over the issue of how the party organization needed to be reformed and its membership purged in order to make it a suitable instrument to guide China's modernization. The CCP's membership doubled during the decade spanning the Cultural Revolution—more than 36 million members in 1977, compared to 18 million members in 1966. As the post-Mao leadership endorsed policies intended to promote rapid modernization, the criteria for recruiting cadres and evaluating their performance accordingly demanded more and more emphasis on technical and administrative expertise rather than the highly politicized criteria which were used to recruit and evaluate cadres during the Cultural Revolution. The reliability and disposition of the cadres who joined the party during the Cultural Revolution therefore emerged as an issue of growing contention among the party's top leaders.

One group of leaders, closely associated with Deng Xiaoping, consistently pressed after 1977 for a more thorough purge of the party's ranks to remove cadres who, because of divergent ideological conviction or political interest, could not be counted on to implement the leadership's rapid modernization policies. Deng and his political supporters similarly pressed for a more critical evaluation of Mao Zedong's leadership of the CCP after 1957, particularly during the Cultural Revolution, in order to discredit the ideological legitimacy of the leftist cause. Failure to press party rectification and reassessment of certain questions in the party's history, as press commentary linked to Deng stressed, would in the long run endanger the success of the "four modernizations."

Another group of leaders, led by Hua Guofeng and Ye Jianying, urged a more gradual approach to the leftist cadre problem. Stressing the necessity of maintaining "stability and unity" for the sake of the success of the "four modernizations," these leaders argued that leftist cadres in the lower ranks of the party and state organizations should be given an opportunity to implement the modernization programs, being removed only when they actively resisted them. Issues such as reevaluation of Mao's leadership and the Cultural Revolution, these leaders believed, presently were too sensitive. Attempts now to carry too far party rectification and historical reassessment, they stressed, would create greater political disruption and impede the modernization effort early on.

The party's Third Plenum, held on 18–22 December 1978, ratified compromise decisions on these issues. The plenum communique thus acknowledged an important gain for Deng by recognizing in a circuitous but nevertheless unprecedented manner Mao Zedong's fallibility, noting that "it would not be Marxist to demand that a revolutionary leader be free from all shortcomings and errors." The communique also put a "high evaluation" on Deng Xiaoping's controversial campaign to take "practice as the sole criterion for truth," an effort to break the shackles of Maoist doctrine on policy formulation. At the same time, the plenum upheld the moderates' cautious view on reevaluating the Cultural Revolution; the communique stated that "shelving" the issue would not hinder the party from concentrating on efforts to achieve the "four modernizations." The plenum also declared a "successful conclusion" to the nationwide campaign to criticize the "gang of four" and expose their followers, although it observed the rectification movement should continue in a "small number" of local areas where the campaign was "less developed."[12]

Although moderate leaders undoubtedly viewed the plenum's decisions as reflecting a party consensus which ought to stand for a long period of time, it rapidly became clear that Deng viewed the plenum only as consolidating political gains he had achieved thus far; he continued to press for endorsement of his view on party reform beyond the plenum consensus. Immediately after the plenum, the Beijing press again began to carry articles on themes Deng had advanced before the plenum as essential to the success of the modernization programs. Arguments began to appear in late January, for example, for a redefinition of the line of Lin Biao and the "gang of four" as "ultraleftist" rather than "ultrarightist," a view for which Deng did appear to win leadership endorsement by March. Commentary associated with Deng similarly renewed efforts to reassess controversial questions in the party's history; an early March *People's Daily* article in particular went blatantly farther than any previous press commentary in specifying some of Mao's errors.[13] Meanwhile, moderate arguments against reopening such questions and for preserving the Third Plenum consensus countered arguments put forward on behalf of Deng and his supporters in the Chinese press.

By late March, however, coincident with evident leadership meetings in the capital, commentary in the Beijing press overwhelmingly endorsed the "stability and unity" position of the party moderates; comment advocating Deng Xiaoping's views dropped out of the media completely. The trade union newspaper *Workers' Daily* on 21 March, for example, stressed that "impetuosity" in pursuit of resolution of controversial issues such as the Cultural Revolution is "not good for China's cause" and labeled "groundless" the view that resolution of such issues is indispensable to the success of the "four modernizations."[14] The *People's Daily* declared on 1 April that resolution of internal party matters like the Cultural Revolution would need "several years of practice and understanding" and called on the party to "postpone for the time being the solution of certain problems and concentrate on the future, on unity and on construction."[15] Clearly, those among the leadership attempting to uphold the compromise resolutions of the Third Plenum had, at least for the moment, successfully defended against efforts by Deng to alter the party's authoritative line on such questions.

Dissidence and Urban Disorder

What blossomed during the winter months of late 1978 and early 1979 into Beijing's "democracy movement" began as a typical wall poster campaign in the capital. The November wall poster campaign gained explicit support from Deng Xiaoping, however, who defended it publicly and provided it tacit justification in his arguments that stronger democracy in intraparty debate and in Chinese society at large was essential to Chinese modernization.[16] In the absence of a clear-cut official line against public expression of dissent, the wall poster campaign gradually escalated well beyond the scope of previous campaigns as a wide variety of underground publications flourished in Beijing and several other major Chinese cities.[17]

Some in the leadership possibly associated the burgeoning "democracy movement" with the outbreak of serious urban disorder in some cities. Problems in Shanghai appear to have been the worst; youth home from the country for the Spring Festival refused to return to the countryside, and other strains of discontent supplemented the ranks of the dissident movement there. According to Shanghai media accounts, local order was disturbed frequently in some parts of the city; at one point, rail traffic was momentarily disrupted. These problems led Shanghai party chief Peng Chong and the municipal government to issue on 6 March a strict public security notice banning many of the activities associated with the "democracy movement." Heretofore a staunch supporter of many of Deng Xiaoping's views on political issues, Peng apparently took this action on his own authority and in the absence of clear central guidance.[18]

The same late March party meetings which produced a moratorium on efforts by Deng and his supporters to reopen sensitive questions in the party's history and to press for more thorough rectification of the party's ranks also evidently succeeded in suppressing the "democracy movement" in the name of "stability and unity." In the last two weeks of March, the capital press began to call for limits on the dissident movement, ending a long period of ambiguous central press treatment of the issue. The *Beijing Daily* on 18 March, for example, warned that "we certainly cannot appease or indulge counterrevolutionaries" who "sabotage our stability and unity" by "waving signboards of democracy," by "gathering crowds and creating disturbances," and by "sabotaging" social order and interfering with economic production.[19] Once the capital press began to attack the "democracy movement," public security notices modeled after the Shanghai decree were quickly issued in several cities and provinces. The moderate group of leaders undoubtedly prompted a notice banning such activities in Beijing, and a *People's Daily* editorial on 5 April—ostensibly marking the third anniversary of the 1976 Tiananmen rioting—proclaimed the need to maintain "stability and unity" at all costs and to protect the "four fundamental principles"—the superiority of the socialist road, the necessity of the dictatorship of the proletariat, the need to uphold Marxist-Leninist–Mao Zedong Thought, and the need to maintain CCP hegemony—evidently in anticipation the anniversary might provide an occasion for an even greater outpouring of dissident sentiment.[20]

Economic Readjustment

Serious difficulties in orientation, coordination, and planning of the national economy as set down at the Fifth National People's Congress in February 1978 were acknowledged in passing at the party's Third Plenum in December 1978. The plenum communique observed that "there are still quite a few problems in the national economy, some major imbalances have not been completely changed, and some disorder in production, construction, circulation and distribution has not been fully eliminated."[21]

The extent and seriousness of the economic imbalances and difficulties did not become apparent publicly, however, until late March or early April, when press commentary—presumably reflecting ongoing leadership discussions of the economy—announced a three–year program to "readjust, reform, consolidate, and improve" the national economy. Modeled on the readjustment program announced in 1961 in an effort to overcome China's "three bitter years" of economic problems following the Great Leap Forward, the 1979 program called for major cutbacks in capital construction projects, stronger emphasis on agriculture and light industry, and less stress on heavy industrial development.[22]

The necessity to uphold social stability and political unity while inaugurating this economic readjustment effort was underscored by the *People's Daily* on 2 April. Pointing out the harm a pursuit of personal political ambitions and causes and an excessive toleration of anarchism and "ultra-democracy" would bring to the "four modernizations," an authoritative commentary in the party paper that day emphasized that "especially at a time when our economy faces many difficulties and needs a series of readjustments," it is "even more necessary to stress the principle that the interests of the individual are subordinate to those of the collective."[23] The need to overcome serious problems in the national economy thus appears to have lent support to those in the leadership who had been stressing "stability and unity" above all else.

Vietnam

Whatever the various factors weighing in Beijing's decision to launch a punitive strike against Vietnam, there do not seem to have been serious leadership differences over the eventual decision to do so. Of all the top Chinese leaders, Deng Xiaoping does indeed seem to have been the most vigorous in declaring the need to teach Hanoi "a lesson." But in the period from 25 December—when a *People's Daily* editorial gave Hanoi "clear warning" a "counterattack" against alleged SRV border provocations was possible—until 17 February—when Chinese troops actually began to cross into Vietnam—other Chinese leaders—including Hua Guofeng and Li Xiannian—joined Deng in warning Hanoi.

However strongly the leadership may have been united behind the decision to attack, there was clear evidence in the Beijing press the Chinese leadership consensus had dissolved by the time Chinese troops were withdrawn in early March. Although exactly how much Beijing had hoped to achieve in launching the punitive strike is not clear, the impact of the Chinese action on Vietnam's efforts to consolidate its position in Cambodia was ostensibly less than dramatic, and intimations of Chinese disappointment with the performance of the PLA itself surfaced obliquely in the press in the following months.[24]

It seems clear from the defensive tone of authoritative press commentary that the results of the punitive attack on northern Vietnam became a contentious leadership issue in the late March–early April period. Two editorials on 26 March—one in the *People's Daily* and the other in the *Liberation Army Daily*—thus sharply defended the need for the attack. The *Liberation Army Daily* in particular called the "counterattack" a "just war" and declared "it would not do if we had not fought it."[25]

The source of criticism of the decision to intervene may well have been the resurgent leftist leaders in the Chinese leadership. Such leaders, who had apparently lost active power in the leadership after the Third Plenum, probably saw the mixed results of the Vietnam "counterattack"—together with the array of domestic problems the leadership was debating at the end of March—as an opportunity to reassert themselves and regain some of the standing they had lost at the plenum. Press commentary appearing several weeks after the late March-early April period thus recalled that in late March, a "left erroneous trend" reemerged which attacked the decisions of the Third Plenum as "revisionist" efforts at "chopping down Chairman Mao's banner" and made "provocative statements" alleging China's current situation was a "mess." Later referred to in antagonistic press commentary as the "two whatevers" faction, these resurgent leftist critics undoubtedly included Wang Dongxing, a party vice chairman and Mao's former bodyguard who reappeared in public in late March for the first time in several weeks.

Leadership moderates such as Hua Guofeng and Ye Jianying, to judge by the 26 March *People's Daily* editorial, continued to defend the necessity of the Vietnam strike; however, they now cited the uncertain regional environment in the aftermath of the attack as yet another situation demanding "stability and unity" at home. In assaying China's domestic tasks in light of the Vietnam situation, the 26 March editorial observed that China may not expect its borders to be tranquil and "free from incidents." In such a context, it noted that "only by achieving stability and unity and the four modernizations can we . . . caution the hegemonists against acting recklessly." This conclusion was termed the "common understanding that we have achieved through our counter-attack against Vietnam."[26]

In sum, the variety of major decisions emerging from party leader-ship meetings in late March and early April all point to the reascend-ancy of moderate elements in the Chinese leadership who stressed the necessity of upholding political stability and unity against challenges from both the right—and Deng Xiaoping in his efforts to extend party reform beyond the Third Plenum consensus—and against challenges from a newly assertive left. It seems reasonable to presume on the basis of timing alone that the decision to offer new political talks to the Soviet Union was a product of the same, reascendant moderate seg-ment of the Chinese leadership.

This presumption is strengthened in light of press commentary from the late March-early April period which suggests a concern for stabiliz-ing China's international environment for the sake of the "four modern-izations," a concern closely paralleling that of the moderates for domes-tic political "stability and unity." Although Chinese media previously had occasionally mentioned the need to do so, the media theme of "building a stable international environment of prolonged peace" became particularly prominent after the late March period. More strik-ingly, the trade union paper *Workers' Daily* carried on 5 April—two days after the offer of talks to Moscow—a long reminiscence on the career of former CCP Secretary Wang Jiaxiang which defended Wang's 1961 proposal for "three liquidations and one reduction" (*sanhe yishao*). That proposal had suggested an overall "liquidation" of ten-sions with the USSR, the United States, and the West in general while China attempted to cope with domestic difficulties arising from the Great Leap Forward.[27] Finally, a long article in the April issue of the academic journal *Philosophy Studies* defended the concept of "two com-bines into one"—an idea associated with former CCP party school chief Yang Xianzhen and attacked during the Cultural Revolution as an ideological justification for the "three liquidations and one reduction." Inviting parallels with China's current situation, the article cited as a paradigmatic example of Yang's principle Lenin's conclusion of the Treaty of Brest–Litovsk in 1919 to provide the newly founded Soviet state a "breathing space" from international pressure and tension.[28]

Motivated by an overriding concern to reduce tensions on China's

Soviet and Vietnamese frontiers to ensure a "peaceful international environment for concentrated pursuit of the modernization drive," the aim of the moderates' proposal for talks with the Soviet Union was thus clearly tactical and not strategic—i.e., derived not from a fundamental reconsideration of the Soviet Union and the nature of its role in world affairs itself but from an alternate way of dealing with the Soviet menace to China. The Chinese punitive strike on Vietnam had served only to harden Soviet–Vietnamese solidarity against Beijing; although Chinese media had given no hint of concern over Soviet pressure during the military operation itself, Chinese anxieties may be inferred from subsequent media comment. During the Chinese strike, Beijing's press ignored both Soviet leadership warnings to stop "before it is too late" and the inauguration of what Western press accounts have described as an unusually large Soviet Far Eastern military exercise.[29] On 10 April, however—well after Chinese troops were out of Vietnam and after the end of the Soviet exercise—Xinhua reported the Soviet exercise as an attempt at "sabre-rattling," citing foreign press observations that it had been "mounted ahead of schedule."[30]

In calling for talks with Moscow, therefore, the moderate leadership in Beijing hoped to appeal to Moscow's overwhelming national interest in improving relations with China and induce a moderation of Soviet antagonism toward China and a measure of restraint in Soviet support for Hanoi against Beijing. In discussing a different point in another context, in fact, the *Liberation Army Daily* on 30 March—just preceding the Chinese offer to the Soviets—alluded to the essence of Beijing's tactical approach:

> Facts have shown that the big hegemonists (the USSR) and the small hegemonists (Vietnam), while collaborating with each other, are also using each other, each having its own goals. Their actions all start from their own self-interests. To regard things in the world as coming from a monolithic bloc is being unrealistic.[31]

However tactical Beijing's motivations were, the Chinese offer of new talks allowed for the possibility of genuine progress in Sino–Soviet bilateral relations in expanding the noncontentious aspects of the relationship. Differences in principle undoubtedly would continue to divide both sides, as Beijing's unending media polemic against Soviet foreign policy suggested at the time. The proposal nevertheless offered Moscow a foothold on the Chinese scene which the Chinese persistently had denied the Soviets for more than a decade, an opportunity to establish the germ of Sino–Soviet detente which Moscow might hope to nurture into a more solid relationship in the future.

After reacting initially with surprise and suspicion to the unconditional Chinese offer for new bilateral talks, Moscow's eventual authoritative response suggested the Kremlin perceived the tactical aims of the offer and sought to preserve its options regarding China should the bilateral talks lead nowhere. Beijing, seeing that Soviet conditions on accepting the proposal for talks undercut its goals in offering them, sought unsuccessfully to induce Soviet flexibility on its demands; eventually—coincident with Deng Xiaoping's resurgence domestically—the Chinese shifted their approach to the talks altogether.

Initial Soviet surprise at and suspicion of the 3 April Chinese proposal was evident in Moscow's initial authoritiative reaction to the Chinese decision to denounce the 1950 treaty. A Soviet government statement on 4 April scored Beijing's long anticipated announcement of its decision—which the proposal for talks accompanied—as an action hostile to the interests of both the Soviet and Chinese peoples. Reflecting Soviet uncertainty, however, the statement made no reference to Beijing's offer of talks. After two weeks' deliberation, Soviet Foreign Minister Gromyko presented a note to the Chinese ambassador in Moscow skeptically pointing out that Beijing had intransigently rejected all Soviet gestures to China over the years and calling on Beijing to "present its views on the subject and aims of the talks."[32]

After Beijing outlined its offer on 5 May to open talks on the broader range of areas of Sino–Soviet contacts and to relegate negotiation of border problems to separate talks, Moscow finally accepted the Chinese proposal, but on specific terms. On 4 June, a Soviet Foreign Ministry memorandum passed by Gromyko to the Chinese charge d'affaires in Moscow declared Moscow's readiness to open negotiations with Beijing to formulate a document not only committing both sides to the five principles of peaceful coexistence in governing their mutual relations—as Beijing itself had urged—but also recording both sides' commitment against "hegemony in world affairs." The memorandum specified further that the talks would open in Moscow at the deputy foreign minister level in July or August.[33]

Moscow's insistence on the inclusion of the antihegemony issue in the Sino–Soviet talks clearly implied the Kremlin understood Beijing's tactical motivation in making the 3 April proposal. The public emergence of serious Sino–Vietnamese differences in the years after 1975 had had important advantages for Soviet policy toward an implacably hostile China, and Soviet–Vietnamese cooperation blossomed in the context of shared antagonism toward Beijing. Particularly in the wake of Beijing's attack on Vietnam, Moscow could not realistically undertake negotiations to improve relations with China without the real prospect of weakening ties with Hanoi, an unacceptable loss should talks with China prove as fruitless as previous Sino–Soviet negotiations had over the previous decade. By insisting Beijing agree to a common commitment to opposing "hegemony," however, Moscow could proceed to explore the possibility of improved relations with China in the newly proposed talks and yet preserve its options in Hanoi.

The fact Soviet concerns over maintaining its relationship with Vietnam as an important asset in its policy toward China underlay Moscow's response to the Chinese proposal for talks was made clear in authoritative Soviet statements around the same time. Speaking in Budapest on 1 June, Brezhnev declared Moscow was ready to approach the proposed talks "positively and in earnest" but, "of course, not at the expense of the interests of their countries."[34] Later in the same vein, on 11 July, a *Pravda* article by "I. Aleksandrov" insisted the "subject and aim of the talks and their principal content be clearly designated." Noting that speculations the Chinese hoped to use the proposed Sino–Soviet talks "to bring pressure to bear" on Vietnam "in particular" are "not denied in Beijing," Aleksandrov warned that "calculations of this kind have no chance of success." The USSR naturally hoped for improved relations with China, the article observed, but added that "it has never sought cooperation with anyone at a price of rejecting principles or damaging the interests of its friends or allies." To underscore the point further, Aleksandrov quoted Brezhnev's statements in Budapest.[35]

Beijing's reaction to Moscow's insistence the issue of opposing hegemony be the focus of the proposed talks was openly pessimistic. Effectively responding to the Soviet terms for the proposed talks' agenda as conveyed in the 4 June memorandum, Hua Guofeng expressed doubt over prospects for progress in the talks if the hegemony issue were included. Speaking on Sino–Soviet relations on 18 June in his work report to the second session of the Fifth National People's Congress, Hua questioned Moscow's readiness to include the hegemony issue in the talks' agenda in light of the Soviet Union's consistently hegemonistic behavior in world affairs. "Prospects for the Sino–Soviet negotiations," Hua concluded, "depend on whether the Soviet Government makes a substantive change in its position."[36]

Beijing's pessimism regarding inclusion of the antihegemony issue in the talks is comprehensible in view of the aims the Chinese entertained in proposing the negotiations. Moscow's insistence on addressing the issue obstructed Beijing's hopes of improving the broader cosmetic aspects of Sino–Soviet relations while setting aside the central contentious issues which had stalemated relations over the years and thereby undermined the tactical purposes of the proposal. According to Western press accounts of statements made by Chinese leaders to foreign visitors in Beijing in the weeks thereafter, the Chinese accordingly began to express doubt about prospects for the talks as restricted by the proposed Soviet agenda.[37]

By midsummer, however, the Chinese appeared to shift tactics on the problem of convening the talks and their agenda. An exchange of Soviet and Chinese notes in August—reported by the foreign press but not by either Soviet or Chinese media—concluded agreement on opening the talks in Moscow in September.[38] In reporting Chinese Vice Foreign Minister and chief negotiator Wang Youping's departure for Moscow for the talks, moreover, *Xinhua* recounted the contentiousness between the two sides through the summer over the talks' agenda. Although Chinese spokesmen in June had expressed pessimism on the outcome of the talks if the hegemony issue were included, *Xinhua* now declared the question of "judging a state by whether it promotes or combats hegemonism in world affairs" should "naturally be placed on the agenda of the talks." In preparing for the talks, moreover, *Xinhua* charged Moscow with attempting "unilaterally to set a host of limits" on the negotiations. These limits, *Xinhua* added, included both the demand the talks not address "any issue relating to a third country" (*Xinhua* explaining by "a third country" Moscow "naturally means the country used by the Soviet Union to threaten China") and the condition the talks not discuss problems connected with the withdrawal of troops from the Sino–Soviet border area or from Mongolia.[39] While Beijing in April had appeared to offer talks aimed at improving the noncontentious aspects of Sino–Soviet relations, the Chinese in September seemed poised to confront Moscow squarely on the issue of hegemonism in the talks.

Accordingly, Chinese and Soviet negotiators in Moscow continued to dispute the agenda of the talks; however, the issue now was not whether the question of opposing hegemony should or should not be included but the scope of the discussion of the question. The two sides finally agreed to proceed to open formal sessions of the talks after five preliminary sessions had failed to resolve the agenda problem. In the formal sessions themselves, which opened on 17 October, Beijing evidently addressed the hegemony question in terms of the full range of Soviet foreign policy behavior. Throughout the talks, Chinese media revealed nothing of the substance of the negotiating positions.[40] Nevertheless, a scathing *People's Daily* article by the virulently anti-Soviet commentator Ren Cuping on 15 October—the first article by that author in two years—probably reflected Beijing's broad negotiating approach of attacking a wide range of Soviet "hegemonistic" actions and policies throughout the world, including unusual references to Soviet "hegemonic" threats toward China itself on the Sino–Soviet border and in Mongolia.[41] A long *Pravda* article by "I. Aleksandrov" on 8 December, after the close of the talks, implicitly confirmed the thrust of Chinese discussion of the hegemony question in the talks by rebutting virtually the same allegations against Soviet behavior the Ren Guping article had raised.[42]

Beijing's midsummer transition to a more confrontational approach to the negotiations thus completely contradicted the premises on which the initial offer of talks had been founded and marked a reversion to the former hardline approach the Chinese had employed in dealings with Moscow over the previous decade. This reversion simply may have been the product of a Chinese reassessment of the value of the talks in the face of persistent Soviet inflexibility on the talks' agenda. Unable to back easily out of negotiations which they had proposed, the Chinese may have decided to turn the talks into yet another forum from which to denounce Moscow and its foreign policy.

A more fundamental reason for the change in Beijing's approach to the negotiations, however, is suggested by its coincidence with the domestic political resurgence of Deng Xiaoping through the summer of 1979. While Deng had been the object of the political leftists' attacks on the broad range of policies associated with him earlier in the spring, Deng rapidly counterattacked against his radical antagonists despite continuing efforts by leadership moderates to restrain new political conflict in the name of "stability and unity" and the "four fundamental principles." By July and August, Deng appeared to be regaining ground on several domestic issues lost earlier in the year; by September, he won clear-cut leadership endorsement of several of his views well beyond the consensus prevailing at the Third Plenum the previous December. Therefore, the confrontational approach to the talks with Moscow may have reflected the views on the Soviet Union of a politically resurgent Deng Xiaoping.

Deng's political counterattack against his spring critics began within weeks after his setbacks in the late March-early April period. As reflected first in newspapers in provinces where the local party leaderships previously had remained sympathetic to Deng and his views and then in central press organs which frequently reflected his views, Deng and his political supporters began an effort to discredit his radical leftist critics as a "left erroneous trend" which had wrongly attacked the policies of the Third Plenum and remained a serious impediment to implementation of the "four modernizations." Typical of such press commentary advancing Deng's viewpoint was a long commentary in the *Guangming Daily* on 11 May. Ostensibly marking the first anniversary of the inauguration of the campaign to "take practice as the sole criterion of truth," the article observed that the "practice" discussion proved to be a "struggle between two ideological lines" within the party and that the "erroneous tendency" of some members of the party to persist in applying Mao Zedong Thought rigidly as a type of "dogmatic Marxism" was disrupting the "four modernizations" and causing "rampant factional activities which undermine stability and unity." The article insisted the policies and decisions of the Third Plenum, as modifications of the party line adopted at the 11th Party Congress in 1977, were "completely normal" and in accordance with the necessities of the current situation. The effort to reassess the party's past, the article added, including its "defeats and errors," is indispensable to the party's effort to ensure the success of the modernization drive.[43] By late June and early July, several provinces where the leadership remained sympathetic to Deng began to discuss the need to "make up the missed lesson" in the campaign to take practice as the "sole criterion" of Marxist truth.

Press commentary through the same period reflecting moderate leadership views insisted on maintaining the "four fundamental principles" enunciated in late March—when Deng had been hurt politically—and avoiding an endorsement of Deng's political themes. One of the more revealing episodes in the continuing divergence between the party moderates and Deng centered on the celebrations of the 60th anniversary of the 4 May movement. In a long speech, Deng supporter Zhou Yang grouped the 4 May movement with the 1942–1943 Yanan rectification campaign and the previous year's "practice" campaign as the three great ideological transformations in modern Chinese history aimed at "emancipating the mind." While acknowledging the damage to current Chinese causes from a "right erroneous trend" in society—the Beijing "democracy movement"—Zhou singled out the "left erroneous trend" in the party as the "main force opposing our efforts to realize socialist modernization."[44]

By contrast, in marking the same occasion in a speech on the following day, Hua Guofeng acknowledged the necessity of integrating the "basic principles" of Marxist–Leninst–Mao Zedong Thought with the concrete practice of present-day China and avoiding making them an "unchallengeable dogma"; at the same time, however, he declined to endorse Deng's campaign to take practice as the "sole criterion" of truth. Instead of recognizing the threat of the "left erroneous trend" to the modernization effort, as Zhou Yang had done, Hua defended the "four fundamental principles" which had been the keynote of the late March-early April effort to rein in the "democracy movement" in Beijing.[45]

Despite moderate efforts to restrain both leftist attacks on Deng and Deng's efforts to counterattack the left and renew his political campaigns, Deng's gains by midsummer were unmistakable. Commentary marking the party anniversary on 1 July, for example, renewed authoritative discussion on the need for a more extensive party rectification drive, even though the Third Plenum had called for an end to such a campaign in most areas of China.[46] In August, moderates in the leadership who previously had refrained from endorsing Deng Xiaoping's campaign on "practice" began to do so publicly, signaling a new leadership consensus on the issue and an important victory for Deng on the party's ideological line. A nationwide movement to "make up the missed lesson" in the "practice" discussion—already underway in provinces sympathetic to Deng—began simultaneously.[47] Most telling of all, the major speech marking the 30th anniversary of the founding of the PRC, delivered on 30 September by Ye Jianying, offered the most critical examination of the Cultural Revolution to appear in Chinese media thus far; in addition, it endorsed Deng's "practice" campaign and cited the need for further party rectification.[48] Only on the issue of increasing democracy within the party and society at large was the domestic scene in the fall of 1979 evolving in a direction not clearly favorable to Deng.[49]

Although it cannot be proved conclusively that Deng Xiaoping actively opposed the April offer to the Soviet Union for new political talks, the proposal nevertheless emerged at a time when Deng's political fortunes over vital domestic issues were at a low ebb; it therefore seems reasonable to suspect Deng at least did not originate the proposal. Confidence in the speculation Deng not only did not support the proposal but actually actively opposed it is strengthened by the observation that Beijing's shift to a more confrontational approach to the agenda of the Sino–Soviet talks coincided with the success of Deng's efforts to counter his critics among the leadership and press ahead once again with the party reforms and policy revisions he had advanced previously.

Afghanistan and the Suspension of the Talks

Both Soviet and Chinese media reported the close of the first round of talks in a straightforward manner, leaving the impression that, despite the talks' failure to do anything more than provide a new forum for both sides to air familiar differences, further rounds of the talks would be convened without undue delay. *Xinhua* thus stated simply that during the first round of talks, both sides had "expounded their respective stands on the relations between the two countries;" Chinese media thereafter declined to offer any comment on the talks themselves.[50] *TASS* summed up the first round of talks on 5 December by noting the Soviet side had put forward a draft proposal on the principles to govern bilateral relations between the two countries and both sides had "come forward with substantiations" of their respective stands. A long *Pravda* article three days later by "I. Aleksandrov" rebutted specific views which the Chinese presumably had advanced during the talks and reasserted Moscow's original demand that the talks center on the formulation of a document incorporating a commitment against hegemonism. Despite Beijing's obstinacy, the article declared, the talks nevertheless would "be continued in Beijing on the agreed date."[51]

Since the close of the first round of talks, however, the negotiations have yet to reconvene in the Chinese capital and remain suspended indefinitely by Beijing in the wake of Moscow's intervention in Afghanistan. If Soviet caution and inflexibility regarding the terms for holding the opening round of talks contributed to their eventual barrenness, Moscow's decision to commit Soviet troops directly in Afghani-

480-900 O - 85 - 10

stan completely undercut the underlying political support for the talks in Beijing.

Whatever factors inherent in the Afghan situation itself and in Soviet relations with the West figured into Moscow's decision to intervene in Afghanistan, the Kremlin leadership undoubtedly weighed the impact such an action might have on relations with China. Moscow's appraisal of the course of the recently closed first round of Sino–Soviet talks certainly played a major part in that assessment. If the pessimistic appraisal of Beijing's attitudes and foreign policy orientation contained in the 8 December *Pravda* article in fact reflected a consensus among the Soviet leadership on the prospects for change in China's views, the Kremlin may well have concluded that talks or not, there was little to be lost in relations with China in undertaking the intervention in Afghanistan.

While Moscow may thus have anticipated a predictably harsh Chinese reaction to the Soviet move into Afghanistan, the depth and stamina of Chinese hostility subsequently may have surprised and dismayed the Soviets. Beijing's response in late December was authoritative and bitter. On 30 December, Beijing issued a government statement—an official vehicle which Beijing normally reserves for events or actions which the Chinese regard as seriously threatening China's security or encroaching on PRC sovereignty—which stated that Moscow's actions in Afghanistan prove "the Soviet hegemonists are the most truculent and adventuristic" and Moscow's "aggressive ambitions are unlimited." Warning that such Soviet aggression must be stopped, the government statement pledged the PRC and the Chinese people to "work tirelessly with all countries and peoples" to frustrate Soviet expansion.[52] To underscore the impact of Moscow's action on Sino–Soviet relations themselves, PRC Vice Foreign Minister for Soviet and bloc affairs Zhang Haifeng summoned the Soviet ambassador in Beijing on 31 December to denounce Moscow's intervention as "a threat to China's security" which "cannot but arouse the grave concern of the Chinese people themselves."[53]

Thereafter, Chinese media went out of their way to publicize harsh denunciations of the Soviet action made by the Chinese leadership during conversations with visiting foreigners in the capital. A torrent of press commentary poured forth, calling the Soviet move a "new stage" in Moscow's progress toward implementing its grand design for world domination and appealing for concerted world efforts to compel a Soviet withdrawal from Afghanistan. Finally, and evidently after being convinced by Secretary of Defense Brown's anti-Soviet rhetoric during his 6–10 February visit to Beijing that a firm US response to the Soviet action was forthcoming, *Xinhua* reported the Sino–Soviet talks were suspended indefinitely. Inasmuch as the Soviet intervention "menaces world peace and the security of China" and "creates new obstacles for the normalization" of Sino–Soviet relations, further sessions of the talks would be "inappropriate" under present circumstances.[54]

The resolution and urgency with which the Chinese have persisted in condemning the Soviet move into Afghanistan have shown not the slightest signs of moderating. Authoritative Chinese statements and press commentary continue to stress the ominous global implications of the Soviet action and persist in pressing for close international collaboration—particularly among the United States, Western Europe, and Japan—in meeting the Soviet strategic challenge. Although Chinese commentary has not continued to underscore explicity the imputed threat of the Soviet intervention in Afghanistan to China itself, regular Chinese efforts to link the Soviet action in Afghanistan to Moscow's support for Hanoi's attempts to consolidate its hold over all of Indochina implicitly reflect Chinese concerns. These concerns focus on Soviet encirclement of China as much as the global strategic import of the Soviet intervention.

Beijing has persisted in this regard despite a clear-cut, serious Soviet effort in the spring of 1980 to induce Chinese moderation by attempting to improve bilateral relations. On 7 April, just 4 days before the final expiration of the 1950 Sino–Soviet treaty, a long "I. Aleksandrov" article in *Pravda* urged that "every opportunity and practical channel"— including the suspended political talks—be pursued to normalize relations between the two countries. Earlier, on 20–28 March, according to Western press reports, Soviet Foreign Ministry China specialist Mikhail Kapitsa made an unannounced visit to Beijing which neither the Chinese nor the Soviet media reported. And on 14 February, the 30th anniversary of the signing of the 1950 treaty—and a day traditionally marked before the Cultural Revolution as Sino–Soviet friendship day—Moscow released a Chinese veterinarian taken captive by Soviet border guards in July 1979.[55]

Both in response to the Soviet gestures and in an effort to reassure the international community to whom Beijing was continuing to appeal for unity against Moscow that China itself was contemplating no departure from its anti-Soviet course, Chinese media publicized a flurry of sharply anti-Soviet remarks made by the Chinese leadership.[56]

Conclusion: Chinese Foreign Policy Coalitions

The preceding examination of the origins of the Chinese proposal for new political talks with Moscow in 1979—as a major break in the continuity of China's negotiating stance toward the USSR—and the course of events leading to the talks' present limbo leads to two conclusions. One concerns the existence of foreign policy differences among the Chinese leadership and the other concerns the nature of the Soviet response. The chain of events after April 1979 first of all suggests two major differing viewpoints on policy toward the Soviet Union competed among the Chinese leadership during that period, and, for a brief time, Beijing was receptive to significant improvements in relations with Moscow. Second, the preceding analysis suggests Moscow's exceedingly cautious, dilatory, and restrictive demands in response to the Chinese offer in the end obfuscated early progress in the prospective talks and delayed their opening beyond the time domestic political support in Beijing for such talks remained ascendant. In the end, Moscow's willingness to accept the predictably negative consequences for Sino–Soviet relations of its decision to intervene in Afghanistan effectively undermined the very assumptions on which the original offer of talks had been made by Beijing.

Divergent views among the Chinese leadership on how to deal with the Soviet Union appear to proceed from differing evaluations of the requirements of Chinese modernization in an uncertain international environment; both viewpoints are related to other evident variations in leadership opinion on other aspects of PRC foreign policy. One such viewpoint, associated most prominently with Deng Xiaoping, appears to emphasize China's backwardness in a dangerous international setting threatened most immediately by an implacably aggressive Soviet Union. Domestically, according to this viewpoint, Chinese survival requires rapid, all-out modernization and drastic political reform. Deng Xiaoping's aggressive campaigns to remove policy formulation from the constraints of Maoist dogma, his efforts to purge cadres irrevocably committed to Mao's doctrines and to promote cadres of a more managerial stamp, his efforts to implement drastic economic reforms stressing production at the expense of formerly paramount political principles, and his attempts to implant a rigorous legal framework to stabilize Chinese politics and society as China modernizes all seem based on these assessed requirements.

Deng's views of China's domestic needs and his assessment of China's international environment lead him to specific positions on China's foreign policy. No Chinese leader, judging by his statements to foreign visitors as reported by *Xinhua* and the Western media, appeared to be more ready to point out the relentless and global character of the threat of Soviet expansionism and the need for concerted international action to meet it. Pressing for a foreign policy which stresses the need to confront Soviet influence actively and aggressively throughout the world, Deng accordingly appears to be the foremost proponent among the leadership for maintaining Beijing's traditional hardline toward Moscow; consequently, as this article has argued, Deng probably was responsible for the change in Beijing's approach to the Sino–Soviet talks in the summer of 1979.

By the same token, Deng Xiaoping also appears to be the foremost proponent for closer ties with the West, particularly with the United States. Deng's views on this score stem not only from the strategic importance of the West in counterbalancing the Soviet Union but also from his belief the West offers the greatest possibilities for support in

286

China's modernization needs; consequently, Deng regularly stresses the "long-term strategic" aspects of such relationships.

Deng's views on the value of close ties with the United States seem particularly clear-cut in this regard. No leader has appeared to be more at the center of efforts to promote Sino–American cooperation and to foster collaboration against the Soviet Union than Deng. Perhaps the most blatant example in this regard was *Xinhua's* account of Deng's conversation with Secretary of Defense Harold Brown in Beijing on 8 January 1980. Calling on China and the United States to "do something in a down-to-earth way" to deal with Soviet hegemonism in the wake of Moscow's intervention in Afghanistan, Deng— according to *Xinhua's* English transmission only—called for "an alliance" of all countries to "counter the Soviet Union's policy of global expansionism." An extraordinary and unprecedented advance over China's consistent call for a less formal "united front" against Soviet aggression, *Xinhua* only belatedly corrected Deng's remark to the actual Chinese wording Deng had used; that is, all countries should "unite" (*lianhe gilai*).[57]

The other major view among the Chinese leadership on relations with the Soviet Union is associated with leaders whom this article has described, according to their domestic political views, as moderates. These leaders acknowledge China's backwardness relative to the most developed countries of the world and the dangerous nature of China's international environment. Accordingly, such leaders support the general overall thrust of the "four modernizations" programs. But either out of ideological reservations or concern for the potential political effects and their own political interests, these leaders cannot endorse the program of rapid domestic policy revision and party reform promoted by leaders like Deng Xiaoping; instead, they urge a more gradual approach to such issues in the interest of "stability and unity."

In foreign policy, moderate leaders appear to take positions in keeping with the same priorities they uphold on domestic issues. Just as China, in this view, cannot afford the political disruption that unduly hasty policy revision and party rectification may entail, China likewise cannot afford to exacerbate its regional international environment by antagonizing an aggressive Soviet Union. Such leaders are therefore willing to introduce a degree of detente into Sino–Soviet relations— stopping well short of rapprochement, but at least allowing a measure of flexibility in those relations. These leaders, this article has suggested, were the architects of the April 1979 proposal for unconditional talks with Moscow.

With regard to the United States, moderate leaders appear to have significant reservations and have not gone as far as Deng Xiaoping in pressing for closer Sino–American cooperation. Where *Xinhua* had committed an extraordinary, undoubtedly intentional, slip in translating Deng's call for "unity" against Moscow into a call for "alliance" during

Secretary Brown's visit and had reported Deng's conversation with Brown at some length, the news agency's report on Hua Guofeng's talk with Brown merely noted that Hua and Brown had "exchanged views on issues of common concern and discussed in detail the situation in Afghanistan."[58]

If the preceding delineation of the two major viewpoints on China's current situation and its consequent interrelated foreign and domestic policy needs is accurate, then prospects for significant change in Sino–Soviet relations in the foreseeable future rest heavily on the evolution of domestic politics in China. The emergence of the Chinese proposal for new talks with the Soviet Union, as this article has argued, was the product of one such episode in the continuing process of political contention within the post-Mao leadership. It was also an opportunity whose domestic political ramifications Moscow evidently failed to perceive.

Soviet press evaluations of the evolution of domestic politics in post-Mao China—to the extent they reflect Soviet leadership views on China—have been overwhelmingly negative in weighing the implications for Sino–Soviet relations. In condemning the April 1979 decision to denounce the 1950 Sino–Soviet treaty in particular, Soviet commentary denounced Deng Xiaoping and Hua Guofeng equally, displaying no apparent perception of possible divergences between such leaders over foreign policy.

Moreover, commentary during the same period which saw positive developments in China which might eventually bear hopeful implications for improved Sino–Soviet relations was clearly the result of misplaced Soviet optimism. Comments by prominent *Izvestiya* commentator Aleksandr Bovin and CPSU Central Committee consultant Nikolay Shishlin, for example, which saw potential for positive change in the reorientation of Chinese economic planning toward production of consumer goods and the reevaluation of the role of class struggle in socialist society in accordance with the line of the 8th CCP Congress 1956 clearly were cases of sowing seed on barren ground, as each of these internal Chinese developments has been promoted above all else by Deng Xiaoping.[59] The reevaluation of the role of class struggle in socialist society represents Deng's effort to counter only the domestic implications of Mao Zedong's thesis of "continuing the revolution under the dictatorship of the proletariat" put forward in the early 1960s as the ideological basis of his critique both of the Soviet Union under Khrushchev and his domestic political opponents, a thesis which culminated in the Cultural Revolution. Ironically, as much as Deng Xiaoping has revised Mao Zedong's domestic policies, he remains Mao's outstanding heir with regard to policy toward the Soviet Union.

In apparently failing to appreciate the tenuous political balance which prevailed at the moment of the Chinese proposal for new talks with no preconditions, Moscow therefore miscalculated its response to the Chinese offer. Temporizing and intransigence over the agenda of the talks—however necessary from considerations of caution with regard to Hanoi—permitted time for the domestic political situation in Beijing to evolve in a direction unfavorable to potentially substantive negotiations, whereas a more flexible negotiating approach in response to the Chinese offer early on might have permitted the talks to open and establish a momentum of their own and a status less immediately susceptible to change from domestic political change on the Chinese side. The decision to intervene in Afghanistan directly ultimately made it politically untenable for a leader in Beijing to assert realistically that accommodation with Moscow could reliably lessen Soviet pressures on China.

Inasmuch as Deng Xiaoping's views on the Soviet Union seem rooted in his overall assessment of China's domestic and international situation, a major shift in his views on dealing with Moscow seems unlikely short of an enormous alteration of Moscow's own policies or a catastrophic breakdown in the reliability of the West, both strategically and as a source of support for Chinese development. As long as Deng and his political supporters maintain their hegemony among the Chinese leadership—and the results of the CCP's Fifth Plenum in February 1980 and the third session of the Fifth National People's Congress in August 1980 strongly suggest they will, at least in the near term—Soviet options in China appear to be diminishing rapidly. If that is the case, then the opening to Moscow in April 1979 will turn out to have been a major opportunity for Moscow to facilitate change in China's policies during a rare juncture of flexibility and transition in China; Sino–Soviet relations will have already turned a decisive corner for several years to come, just as they did in the early 1960s.

Notes

1. *Pravda,* 25 February 1976; Foreign Broadcast Information Service, *USSR: Daily Report* (hereafter cited as FBIS–USSR), 25 February 1976, supplement on proceedings of the 25th CPSU Congress.
2. *Pravda,* 16 January 1976, in FBIS–USSR, 19 January 1976; and *Pravda,* 28 April 1976, in FBIS–USSR, 29 April 1976.
3. The CPSU condolence message to the CCP was carried by *TASS* on 9 September 1976, and is published in FBIS–USSR, 10 September 1976. Moscow reported Il'yichev's return to Beijing on 28 November 1976, in FBIS–USSR, 29 November 1976.
4. *Xinhua,* in English, 15 November 1976, as reported in Foreign Broadcast Information Service, *PRC: Daily Report* (hereafter cited as FBIS–PRC), 16 November 1976.
5. On the resumption of Soviet polemics, see, for example, the *Pravda* "Observer" article, 10 February 1977; a partial translation appears in FBIS–USSR, 10 February 1977. *TASS* reported Il'yichev's departure from Beijing on 28 February 1977; FBIS–USSR, 28 February 1977.
6. *Pravda,* 14 May 1977, in FBIS–USSR, 16 May 1977. *TASS* reported Brezhnev's comments on China, contained in a speech welcoming Bulgarian party leader Todor Zhivkov to Moscow, on 30 May 1977; FBIS–USSR, 31 May 1977.

7. *Problemy dal'nego vostoka,* [Problems of The Far East] No. 4, 1977, pp. 45–72. An English translation appears in Joint Publications Research Service publication, No. 70613, 9 February 1978, pp. 34–44.

8. A revealing account of Sino–Soviet relations under the 1950 treaty, and particularly in the post-Mao period—including comments on the significance of Chinese attitudes toward the United States and Vietnam for them—appeared in *Problemy dal'nego vostoka,* No. 11, 1980, pp. 13–30.

9. *Xinhua* in English, 3 April 19–9, in FBIS–PRC, 3 April 1979. The 5 May memorandum was never released by Chinese media themselves, although several foreign news media have reported its contents. An evidently authentic near-text version of it appeared in *Le Monde,* 11 May 1979, pp. 1 and 3.

10. This, for example, characterizes Beijing's current approach to improving relations with India. See the commentary by *Xinhua* correspondent Zhou Cipu, *Xinhua,* in English, 24 June 1980, in FBIS–PRC, 25 June 1980.

11. This section of the present article summarized the argument presented at length and in much greater detail in a article by the same author entitled "From the Third Plenum to the April Adverse Current: The Domestic Politics of Sino–Soviet Detente," presented to the New England Regional Conference of the Asian Studies Association, 20 October 1979, publication pending.

12. "Communique of the Third Plenary Session of the 11th Central Committee of the CCP," *Xinhua,* in English, 23 December 1978, in FBIS–PRC, 26 December 1978; *Renmin ribao,* 24 December 1978.

13. Article By Lu Dingyi, *Renmin ribao,* 8 March 1979; FBIS–PRC, 16 March 1979.

14. *Gongren ribao,* 21 March 1979; *Xinhua,* in English, 21 March 1979.

15. *Renmin ribao,* 1 April 1979; FBIS–PRC, 2 April 1979.

16. *Xinhua* report on Deng Xiaoping comments to visiting Japanese Democratic Socialist Party leader Sasaki, in FBIS–PRC, 28 November 1978.

17. *Chengming,* a left-wing journal on Chinese affairs published in Hong Kong, described several such underground publications in its March 1979 issue, pp. 28–32.

18. Shanghai *Wen hui bao,* 8 March 1979, according to Shanghai radio, 8 March 1979, in FBIS–PRC, 9 March 1979.

19. *Beijing ribao,* 18 march 1979; FBIS–PRC, 26 March 1979.

20. *Renmin ribao,* 5 April 1979; FBIS–PRC, 5 April 1979.

21. *Renmin ribao,* 24 December 1978.

22. See, for example, *Renmin ribao* article by He Jianzhang, "The Readjustment Policies Are Completely Correct," 3 April 1979.

23. *Renmin ribao,* 2 April 1979; FBIS–PRC, 3 April 1979.

24. A *Jiefangjun bao* editorial on 18 March 1979, for example, observed that the "counterattack" against Vietnam had provided "a very good review of our frontier defense and our economic construction and national defense as a whole." See FBIS–PRC, 20 March 1979. A long review of national defense priorities by Minister of National Defense Xu Xiangqian in the October 1979 *Hongqi* stressed the need for upgrading the PLA's logistical capabilities, a priority that probably emerged from the punitive attack on Vietnam.

25. *Renmin ribao,* 26 March 1979, and *Jiefangjun bao* on the same day, as reported in FBIS–PRC, 27 March 1979.

26. Ibid.

27. *Gongren ribao,* 5 April 1979; FBIS–PRC, 4 May 1979.

28. Wu Quiwen, "Zemeyang 'zai duilimian de tongyi bawo duilimian'" [How Do We 'Grasp the Opposites in the Unity of Opposites'?], *Zhexue yanjiu,* No. 4, April 1979, pp. 21–26.

29. See the election speeches of Leonid Brezhnev and Aleksey Kosygin in FBIS–USSR, 5 March and 2 March 1979, respectively.

30. *Xinhua,* in English, 10 April 1979, in FBIS–PRC, 11 April 1979.

31. *Jiefangjun bao,* 30 March 1979, as reported by *Xinhua* Chinese service, 30 March 1979, in FBIS–PRC, 2 April 1979.

32. *Pravda,* 18 April 1979; FBIS–USSR, 19 April 1979.
33. FBIS–USSR, 5 June 1979.
34. Brezhnev speech on Hungarian television, as reported by *TASS,* 1 June 1979; in FBIS–USSR, 4 June 1979.
35. *Pravda,* 11 July 1979; FBIS–USSR, 11 July 1979.
36. *Renmin ribao,* 26 June 1979; FBIS–PRC, 2 July 1979 "Supplement."
37. Interestingly enough, the long review of Sino–Soviet relations carried in the journal *Problemy dal'nego vostoka* (cited above, note 8) recalled that in a memorandum to the Chinese on 23 June 1979, "the Soviet side, with due account to the proposals of the Chinese side, agreed to include as a subject of negotiations the extension of trade, scientific and technical contacts and cultural exchanges" to supplement the 4 June Soviet note's insistence that the talks discuss the central issue of opposition to hegemony. Soviet media had not previously mentioned the existence of a 23 June memorandum.
38. *Kyodo,* in English, 29 August 1979, in FBIS–PRC, 30 August 1979.
39. *Xinhua,* in English, 22 September 1979, in FBIS–PRC, 24 September 1979.
40. In contrast to their complete silence on sessions of the former Sino–Soviet border talks, Chinese media routinely and briefly reported each preliminary and formal session of the talks, identified the members of its negotiating delegation, and carried occasional *Xinhua* commentary on the talks' progress.
41. *Renmin ribao,* 15 October 1979; FBIS–PRC, 16 October 1979.
42. *Pravda,* 8 December 1979; FBIS–USSR, 10 December 1979.
43. *Guangming ribao,* 11 May 1979; FBIS–PRC, 14 May 1979.
44. *Renmin ribao,* 7 May 1979; FBIS–PRC, 11 May 1979.
45. *Renmin ribao,* 4 May 1979; FBIS–PRC, 4 May 1979.
46. See the *Renmin ribao* editorial on 30 June and the "contributing commentator" article in the same paper on the following day; FBIS–PRC, 3 and 8 July 1979.
47. An article in the September *Gongren ribao* by a Shanghai party secretary revealed that the CCP Central Committee had recently issued an eight-point circular stressing the need to launch new discussions of the idea that practice is the "sole criterion of truth" as an antidote to the "two whatevers" viewpoint.
48. *Renmin ribao,* 30 September 1979; FBIS–PRC, 1 October 1979.
49. Deng's position of the democracy movement by the fall of 1979 is not clear: although he had previously defended greater democracy within society at large, see his attacks, apparently on dissident writers like Wei Jingsheng, at the Fourth National Congress of Artists and Writers, in *Renmin ribao,* 31 October 1979, and also in FBIS–PRC, 1 November 1979.
50. *Xinhua,* in English, 30 November 1979; FBIS–PRC, 3 December 1979.
51. *TASS,* in English, 5 December 1979; FBIS–USSR, 11 December 1979.
52. *Renmin ribao,* 31 December 1979; FBIS–PRC, 31 December 1979.
53. *Renmin ribao,* 1 January 1980; FBIS–PRC, 31 December 1979.
54. *Xinhua,* in English, 20 January 1980; FBIS–PRC, 21 January 1980.
55. *Pravda,* 7 April 1980; FBIS–USSR, 8 April 1980. On Kapitsa, see FBIS–PRC, 28 April 1980. On the Soviet release of the Chinese veterinarian, see *Renmin ribao,* 2 May 1980; FBIS–PRC, 2 May 1980.
56. See, for example, Deng Xiaoping's comments to the Italian press corps accompanying PCI leader Enrico Berlinguer to Beijing, in FBIS–PRC, 17 April 1980; the remarks of Wang Bingnan on the 110th anniversary of Lenin's birth, in FBIS–PRC, 25 April 1980; and the remarks of Hua Guofeng on the eve of his visit to Japan, in FBIS–PRC, 22 April.
57. *Xinhua,* in English, 8 January 1980, in FBIS–PRC, 8 January 1980; and *Xinhua's* correction, in FBIS–PRC, 10 January 1980.
58. *Xinhua,* in English, 9 January 1980, in FBIS–PRC, 10 January 1980.
59. See, for example, the comments of Bovin and Shishlin on Moscow Radio on 17 July 1979, in FBIS–USSR, 18 July 1979.

291

Soviet–Japanese Relations and the Strategic Balance in Northeast Asia

Stuart D. Goldman

The Context of Soviet–Japanese Relations

The object of this article is to focus on Soviet–Japanese relations and the impact of these relations on the strategic balance in Northeast Asia.

Japan's role on the international stage is ambiguous. Economically, Japan is a global superpower by quantitative as well as qualitative measures. Japan's 1979 GNP of $1,013 billion ranks close behind that of the USSR ($1,261 billion) and surpasses Soviet economic performance in most qualitative indicators.

Militarily, Japan is a lightweight, possessing a modest home defense capability but virtually no power projection or force projection capability. Even Japan's ranking of ninth internationally in defense spending is somewhat artificial, since Japan's insistence on manufacturing its own military equipment results in extraordinarily high per-unit costs and highly inflated procurement costs relative to actual weapons procurement. While Japan's Self-Defense Forces (SDF) are not negligible and do possess some substantial capabilities such as antisubmarine warfare, overall the SDF is smaller and less well-armed than the South Korean or Taiwanese armed forces.

Japan's international political stature is difficult to evaluate. One crude assessment would be to call Japan's political stature moderate—"averaging" the product of her economic and military power. Such a calculation, however, is too crude to yield anything but the most superficial result. Perhaps a more useful approach would be to judge Japan's political stature on a case-by-case basis, noting that the results are highly scenario-dependent.

In contrast, the role of the Soviet Union on the international stage seems quite apparent. Militarily and politically, the USSR is a global superpower, albeit with economic feet of clay.

In comparing the Soviet Union and Japan, these asymmetries are strikingly apparent. They exert a powerful influence on relations between the two states. But there are a number of other factors which enter into the equation; most notably, the character of US–Soviet and Sino–Soviet relations and the regional power balances in East Asia and Northeast Asia. In addition, the role of historically conditioned perceptions should not be overlooked in assessing the present and future character of Soviet–Japanese relations.

292

Americans who sometimes imagine the Soviet Union's troublesome emergence as a Pacific Ocean power derives from the post-World War II era would do well to remember Russia crossed the northern tier of Eurasia and penetrated to the Pacific while the United States were still British colonies. Moreover, Russian explorers and fur traders crossed the North Pacific and established settlements in North America at a time when other American pioneers were still struggling to penetrate the Appalachian Mountain barrier from the opposite direction.

The ever-expanding Russian Empire, pushing southward from the Kamchatka Penninsula, encounted a Japanese presence in the Kurile Islands in the first years of the 19th century, resulting in some long-distance pushing and shoving between Tsarist Russian forces and those of Tokugawa Japan. A half-century later, Commodore Perry, who "opened" Japan for the United States in 1853, was preceded and followed by Russian naval squadrons bent on the same mission.

In 1858–61, Russia became a major East Asian power on the basis of enormous territorial acquisitions extorted from a moribund China. At the same time, Japan was throwing off her two and one-half centuries of self-imposed isolation and preparing to enter into her extraordinary process of modernization.

From the first, Russia and Japan perceived one another with suspicion and mistrust as competitors for power in Northeast Asia in the context of a decaying Chinese Empire. Russia's early advantages of size and superior military technology were offset by Japan's proximity to the contested region and the vigor and single-mindedness of her new government after 1868. In 1875, Russia and Japan resolved the disputed sovereignty of the northern islands lying between Hokkaido and Kamchatka in a treaty which granted Russia ownership of Sakhalin in exchange for Japanese sovereignty over the Kurile Islands. From that time to this, relations between the two states have been marked by continued suspicion and mistrust, highlighted by recurrent flareups of violence in 1904–5, 1918–22, 1937–39, and 1945.

In the Russo–Japanese War of 1904–5, Japan erased the contempt in which she was held by the Tsarist government and established herself as the dominant regional power by expelling Russian influence from Korea and Southern Manchuria. Additionally, the Japanese acquired control of southern Sakhalin as well as commercial fishing rights in the coastal waters of the Russian Maritime Province.

In 1918, as the Russian Empire seemed to disintegrate in the agony of world war, revolution, and civil war, Japanese forces intervened massively in an attempt to seize control of a large part of Russia's Far Eastern empire. The Japanese intervention came to naught but exacerbated the already bitter animosity between the two rivals for Northeast Asian dominance.

The late 1930s saw a series of relatively little-known and apparently obscure Soviet–Japanese conflicts at various points along the 3,000 mile frontier between the USSR (and its Outer Mongolian protectorate) and Japan's recently acquired puppet state of Manchukuo (Manchuria). The last and largest of these episodes reached the proportions of a small undeclared war in which the Japanese were defeated decisively.[1] Thereafter, the Japanese directed their attention southward and the Soviets westward, providing the basis for the Soviet–Japanese Neutrality Pact of April 1941. Tokyo and Moscow observed the provisions of the Neutrality Pact until the final days of the Second World War. But on 8 August 1945, in precise conformity with US–Soviet agreements reached earlier at Yalta, the Soviet Union entered the war against a nearly prostrate Japan.

The provisions of the Yalta Agreement and the success of the Soviets' August 1945 offensive had the effect of undoing a half-century of Japanese imperialism and expansion in Northeast Asia. In addition to being expelled from Manchuria and Korea, Japan was forced to retrocede southern Sakhalin to the USSR. Japan was also compelled to give up the Kurile Islands which were forcibly occupied by the Soviets. Japan was relegated to the four main home islands and minor offshore islands to be determined by the victorious allies. This verdict was confirmed by the San Francisco Peace Treaty of 1951, although because of emerging Cold War hostility, the Soviet Union was not a party to that treaty and has yet to conclude a peace treaty with Japan.

Although the military verdict of 1945 apparently ended the traditional Russian–Japanese power struggle with indisputable Soviet dominance, actually the contest for dominance of Northeast Asia continued, with the United States and a renascent China as major actors. With Japan under American occupation and tutelage, the age-old suspicion and antagonism between Moscow and Tokyo continued. The Soviet government saw postwar Japan first as a tool of, and later a co-conspirator with, US imperialism's attempt to encircle the USSR with a hostile and threatening ring of bases. For its part, Tokyo's traditional hostility toward Russian expansionism and communist subversion (nurtured by the American occupiers) assured that the Japanese government and people would continue to take a jaundiced view of Soviet intentions in the region.

These historically conditioned perceptions are still much in evidence in contemporary Soviet–Japanese relations and will probably continue to exert significant influence on bilateral relations for the foreseeable future. But, of course, Soviet–Japanese relations are profoundly affected by the dynamics of US–Soviet and Sino–Soviet relations, by US–Japanese and Sino–Japanese relations, and by events on the Korean Peninsula, in Taiwan, and elsewhere relevant to the balance in Northeast Asia.

The next section of this article will examine how these various factors impinge upon the major issues in contemporary Soviet–Japanese relations.

Major issues in Soviet–Japanese relations today are primarily economic, political, and, to a lesser degree, military. These issues are complex and interrelated. They can be listed separately, but discussion or action on one tends inevitably to spill over to the others.

Economic Issues. Japan and the Soviet Union constitute one of the greatest, most natural, and largely undeveloped economic partnerships in the world. No country is as bountifully endowed with so wide an array of natural resources as the Soviet Union. A large part of these riches—including huge deposits of coal, oil, and gas—are located in Soviet Asia far from the Soviet industrial heartland and population centers. Exploitation of these immense resources will require intensive, well-managed application of capital and technology. However, the USSR is perennially embarrassed by serious deficiencies in the requisite capital, technology, and management skills.

Japan, critically deficient in most of the natural resources so abundant in Soviet Asia, is an economic giant particularly strong in the areas of investment capital, technology, and management. Moreover, the geographical propinquity of Japan to many of the Soviet resource centers would facilitate further joint exploitation. The potential for a mutually rewarding partnership is enormous and seems almost foreordained by what the Soviets would call "objective material forces"—i.e., economic geography.

In the 10 years from 1968 to 1977, a number of major Soviet-Japanese joint development projects were initiated. These were based on Japanese financing and, in many instances, dependent upon Japanese technological assistance as well. (See Tables 1 and 2.) In that decade, Japan's Export–Import Bank granted credits of nearly $1.5 billion to the USSR in support of these joint development projects. In the same period, another $1.75 billion in Japanese credit was extended from their Export–Import Bank and from private banks for the export of 25 Japanese "turn-key" plants and for 1.2 million tons of special wide-diameter pipe for gas and oil pipelines through Siberia.[2]

Soviet repayment in the joint development projects was primarily in extracted raw materials: wood and wood products, coal, gas, and oil—commodities in high demand in the Japanese economy.

Despite the mutually beneficial character of many of these projects, the Japanese have shown considerable restraint and have not participated to anything near the degree sought by the Soviet government. Indeed, in describing the Japanese attitude toward further expanding trade ties with the USSR, the psychological term "approach-avoidance conflict" seems appropriate—a situation in which the subject is simultaneously attracted and repelled by the same object. The attractiveness of the object in this case is self-evident: Japan's appetite for raw

Table 1. Siberian Development Projects Approved by 31 July 1977

Date of Agreement	Purpose	Amount of Credit	Soviet Supply Commitments
July 1968	Exploitation of forest reserves in Amur Province	$133 million for technical assistance and machinery and $30 million for consumer goods	8.02 million cubic meters of sawed and processed wood from 1969-1973
December 1970	Construction of new port in Wrangel Bay	$80 million for purchase of equipment and materials	
December 1971	Development of wood chips	$45 million for equipment and $5 million for consumer goods	8.05 million cubic meters of wood chips and 4.7 million meters of industrial pulp for 10 years starting in 1972
June 1974	Exploitation of coking coal in south Yakutia	$450 million	104.4 million tons of coking coal from 1979-1984
July 1974	Second forest development project	$550 million for equipment, machinery, and consumer goods	18.4 million cubic of wood in 5 years from 1975-1979
January 1975	Prospecting for petroleum and natural gas on the continental shelf off Sakhalin	$100 million for ore exploration ships and oceanbed drilling equipment; $22.5 million for machinery, instruments, and computers for the ships; $30 million for workers' comsumers goods	50% of oil developed (gas amount determined separately) during the period when loan being repaid and for 10 years afterward
March 1976	Prospecting for natural gas in Yakutia	$25 million (US private banks also to supply $25 million	10 billion cubic meters of liquefied natural gas per year for 25 years (the same to the US)

Source: Peggy L. Falkenheim, "Some Determining Factors in Soviet-Japanese Relations," *Pacific Affairs*, Winter 1977–78, Vol. 50, pp. 615–16.

296

Table 2. Japan Export-Import Bank Credits for Plant Exports to the USSR

Date	Type of Plant	Amount in Billion Yen
July 1975	4 ammonia plants	71.4
February 1976	4 ammonia plants	71.4
March 1976	500,000 tons of large-caliber steel tube	48.5
May 1976	1 ammonia plant; 1 uric acid plant	27.8
May 1976	1 synthetic rubber plant	27.8
July 1976	1 liquefied petroleum gas plant	57.6
June 1977	10 ammonia plants; 3 compound fertilizer plants	85.4

Source: Peggy L. Falkenheim, "Some Determining Factors in Soviet-Japanese Relations," *Pacific Affairs,* Winter 1977–78, Vol. 50, pp. 615–16.

materials, especially fuels, is enormous. The "repulsion" perceived by Japanese political and business leaders has economic, political, and strategic components.

The economic obstacles to greatly expanded Soviet–Japanese economic cooperation center on Japanese concerns regarding profitability and assurance of repayment. Since the major joint-development projects generally call for very large Japanese investments "up front" to be repaid by Soviet deliveries of a percentage of the exploited resources over a period of years, the Japanese need to be sure the amount of exploitable resources (proved reserves) is large enough to justify the otherwise nonrecoverable investment in developing Soviet production capacity. This is not a problem in the forestry projects since the amount of timber is readily ascertainable. Such is not the case with oil and gas fields in Arctic or deep underwater locales.

Related to this is the question of precise rates of payment. The Soviet government wants to maximize Japanese participation in the development of Siberia but is leery of being exploited economically by Japanese capitalists. Soviet foreign trade negotiators are notoriously hard bargainers. For example, Soviet–Japanese negotiations concerning the Tyumen oil project (one of the most ambitious projects yet considered) broke down completely in October 1974 when the Soviets attempted to alter their original proposal by reducing the amount of oil to be supplied to Japan from 40 to 25 million tons per year.[3]

Of all the resources in the Siberian treasure trove, it is oil which would be sought most vigorously by Japan on purely economic grounds. Furthermore, the disappointingly poor Soviet performance in developing the Siberian oil fields underlines their need for outside help.

However, the rapid depletion of the USSR's older oil fields suggests that most—if not all—of the new Siberian production will be needed to satisfy domestic Soviet requirements and those of her East European allies, leaving little available for export to Japan.

There is another fear in Tokyo regarding Soviet repayment. What would happen if, after billions of dollars of Japanese investment in Soviet productive capacity, the Soviet government, perhaps responding to a changed international climate, refused to make delivery of promised raw materials? Some Japanese fear their country would have no effective recourse under such circumstances. This fear causes Japanese decisionmakers in government and industry to prefer projects which promise rapid pay off and little risk such as the forestry and coking coal deals in which repayment was scheduled to occur within three to five years.

For more ambitious, higher risk schemes such as development of the vast Tyumen oil fields where the *initial* Japanese investment was to have been in excess $1 billion with repayment stretching on for decades, Toyko sought insurance by trying to make it a trilateral US–Japanese–Soviet project. If Washington and Toyko were in the deal together, the reasoning went, neither would be likely to be left holding the bag, for Moscow would be obliged to honor its commitments. While this might be sound logic on one level, it makes agreement less likely by introducing another party with veto power into the negotiations. The Tyumen project discussed above ultimately collapsed when the United States lost interest and the Japanese chose not to go it alone.[4]

There are also political considerations which militate against greatly expanded Soviet–Japanese economic cooperation. As stated above, Soviet–Japanese relations are strongly influenced by US–Soviet and Sino–Soviet relations as well as by Japan's own bilateral relations with the United States and China.

The past few years have brought a progressive cooling of US–Soviet relations which, especially after the Soviet invasion of Afghanistan, have become confrontational. At the same time, relations between Toyko and Beijing have grown warmer, especially with the conclusion of the Sino–Japanese Peace and Friendship Treaty of August 1978. Given the seemingly implacable hostility between Beijing and Moscow, the growing tension between Washington and Moscow, and the US–Chinese rapprochement, it is only natural the influence of Washington and Beijing would militate against greatly increased Soviet-Japanese cooperation, as Toyko would not wish to antagonize the United States and China by greatly increasing economic cooperation with a nation presently perceived in Washington and Beijing as a relentless foe.

In addition, there is still the traditional, historically conditioned anti-Russian/anti-Soviet sentiment in Japan which would act as a drag on any attempt to greatly expand Soviet–Japanese cooperation. Naturally, such events as the Soviet invasion of Afghanistan tend to deepen this anti-Soviet sentiment in Japan, for many Japanese perceive their nation as a small, relatively weak country adjacent to the Soviet colossus and are alarmed by the Soviet invasion.

Another political obstacle to expanded Soviet–Japanese economic cooperation is the territorial dispute over the so-called Northern Territories, a group of islands north of Hokkaido which were seized by the USSR in 1945. The issues in this territorial dispute will be discussed later. At this point, it is relevant to note that the stubborn Soviet refusal to discuss the matter—indeed, their bland insistence there *is no* territorial dispute—is perceived by the Japanese public and government as arrogant and unreasonable and fouls the general atmosphere of Soviet–Japanese relations.

Still another economic issue in Soviet–Japanese relations is the fisheries question, a highly complex issue which has perennially clouded relations between the two nations throughout the 20th century. The Soviet Union and Japan are the world's two leading fishing nations, each employing huge, modern long-distance as well as intensive local offshore fishing fleets. While the two fishing powers share certain common interests vis-a-vis less aggressive fishing nations, closer to home each attempts jealously to guard the fishery resources in their own North Pacific coastal waters while seeking to maximize exploitation of the resources of the other. Since both governments feel it is vital to maintain and increase the caloric and protein contributions to the national diet provided by the fishing industry, this rivalry has overtones which transcend cold economic statistics.

The activities of each nation's long-distance fishing fleet in the other's coastal waters is regulated by a bilateral fisheries agreement stipulating annual aggregate quotas as well as limits for certain species of fish. Periodic renegotiation of the fisheries agreement is often an occasion for tense and emotional high-level diplomacy. The most recent fisheries agreement, concluded in 1977, was preceded by Moscow's abrupt and unilateral declaration of a 200–mile offshore economic zone. The ensuing negotiations have been characterized almost universally as the most bitter and prolonged since the Second World War.[5] The specific issues need not concern us here. It is probably true both sides adopted inflexible attitudes and were insensitive to the other's interests. That these negotiations, which dragged on acrimoniously for three months, left bitter feeling on both sides is generally conceded. The chief Japanese negotiator was the little-known Minister of Agriculture and Forestry, Zenko Suzuki. This same Zenko Suzuki succeeded Masayoshi Ohira as Prime Minister of Japan in mid–1980.

Political Issues. The major political issues in contemporary Soviet–Japanese relations include: (a) a World War II peace treaty; (b) competing visions of a new Asian international order; (c) Japan's policy of "equidistance" between the USSR and China; and (d) the Northern Territories dispute.

The Soviet Union and Japan have yet to conclude a formal peace treaty ending the Second World War. This has not prevented them from conducting normal diplomatic relations, but it is an unfinished piece of business which, as long as it remains outstanding, symbolizes a certain lack of concordance between them. Both sides would like to conclude a treaty—on their own terms. It is the Northern Territories dispute more than any other issue which stands in the way. So far, neither side seems willing to compromise on this territorial issue. Moscow has attempted to finesse the peace treaty question by proposing a bilateral treaty of good neighborliness and cooperation. For its part, Tokyo is willing to consider such a treaty—provided it addresses the Northern Territories issue, which Moscow flatly refuses to do; ergo, impasse.

Beyond the treaties question, the Soviet Union's intense and bitter struggle with China for political/military dominance in Asia conflicts with Japan's drive for a stable East Asian order with herself as the economically dominant force. These divergent long-term regional interests have given rise to two competing visions of a new East Asian international order.

From time to time since 1969, the Brezhnev regime has suggested the need for some sort of Asian collective security arrangement. One of the distinguishing characteristics of the proposal, which Moscow has reiterated at intervals through the 1970s, is its vagueness. The plan apparently is conceived as a loose association of states without a binding military alliance.[6] It is perceived by most non-Soviet observers as an attempt to isolate China and rally diplomatic support for the USSR in Sino–Soviet competition for influence in Asia and as an attempt to facilitate the expulsion of "Western imperialism"—i.e., US influence—from Asia.

Partly in response to Western—especially American—suggestions Japan move beyond its very low profile "omnidirectional" foreign policy (which has been called nonpolicy by critics), the Japanese government of former Prime Minister Ohira began to articulate its own vision of a new East Asian international order. The Japanese concept, labeled the "Pacific Community," is scarcely less vague than Moscow's Asian collective security scheme. The central idea is an association of Pacific Basin nations joined harmoniously in economic—and perhaps political—cooperation. What is most notable about this plan is the prospective membership: Japan, the five ASEAN states, South Korea, Taiwan, Australia, New Zealand, the United States, and Canada. China is frequently mentioned by Japanese spokesmen as a *probable* member. The Soviet Union is excluded, although Japanese spokesmen occasionally allude to the possibility of the USSR joining the Pacific

Community at some indefinite point in the future, well after the Community is established and its character and policies set.

Predictably, this Japanese vision of a Pacific Community elicits no enthusiasm but considerable suspicion in Moscow, particularly the variant which explicitly includes China and excludes the USSR.[7] In a recent private conversation with a Soviet diplomat, the latter was at pains to elicit my opinion as to whether this Pacific Community notion truly emanated from Toyko or from Washington. In any case, it is perceived in Moscow as inherently anti-Soviet, a perception which perhaps is not altogether groundless.

Throughout most of the 1970s, successive Japanese governments have stated their intention of maintaining equidistance in Japan's economic and political relations with the Soviet Union and China. This concept (which was translated into US foreign policy as "even-handedness") seemed to be a reasonable and prudent Japanese approach to Sino–Soviet hostility. However, international relations are rarely static, and precise equidistance is a very difficult position to maintain in the fluid conditions of a Sino–Soviet rivalry viewed by both Moscow and Beijing as a zero-sum conflict in which each begrudges every instance of Japanese cooperation with its arch rival.

Japanese economic planners seem to have concluded in 1978–79 that China might be a more fruitful source of petroleum products than the USSR. This may have been based on the belief the less developed Chinese economy will be able to spare a greater portion of its growing oil production for export to Japan and that China constitutes a better market than the USSR for the slumping Japanese steel industry. In any case, China has become an important source of oil for Japan. In 1978, Japan imported 53,638,000 bbls of oil from China compared to 414,000 bbls from the USSR. In 1979, 54,472,000 bbls came from China and 301,000 bbls from the USSR. For the first half of 1980, the figures show an increase of Chinese exports of 30,001,000 bbls and a drop in Soviet exports to a mere 25,000 bbls.[8]

Nonetheless, the most important single political issue in Soviet-Japanese relations today appears to be the Northern Territories. The disputed territory consists of three islands (Etorofu, Kunashiri and Shikotan Islands) and a small archipelago (the Habomai group) lying north and east of Hokkaido, the northernmost of the main Japanese home islands. These disputed islands, along with Sakhalin and the whole Kurile chain, were forcibly occupied by the USSR in 1945.

The Yalta Agreement between Roosevelt and Stalin provided for the Japanese cession of Sakhalin and the Kuriles to the Soviet Union. The 1951 San Francisco Peace Treaty which Japan signed confirmed her surrender of Sakhalin and the Kuriles, although the USSR, not a signatory to that Treaty, was not named as recipient of the Kuriles. The dispute resolves around conflicting definitions of the extent of the Kurile Islands. In the Soviet view, all 36 islands lying between the

Kamchatka Penninsula and Hokkaido are part of the Kurile chain belonging to the USSR as a result of the postwar settlement. The Japanese claim Etorofu, Kunashiri, Shikotan, and the Habomais are Japanese offshore islands and the Kuriles proper begin north of Etorofu. Both Toyko and Moscow buttress their claims with conflicting historical evidence and interpretations of international law.

The Kurile chain as a whole has major strategic significance for the USSR and is important economically as well. On 2 September 1945, the day Soviet forces occupied Shikotan and the Habomais, Stalin publicly declared, "Henceforth, the Kurile Islands shall not serve as a means to cut off the Soviet Union from the ocean or as a base for a[n] . . . attack upon our Far East, but as a means to link the Soviet Union with the ocean and as a defensive base . . . ."[9]

Indeed, since 1945, the USSR has used the Kuriles as a shield to turn the Sea of Okhotsk into a Soviet lake and as a springboard to project Soviet power into the Northern Pacific. The islands are studded with air installations for reconnoitering Japan's Pacific littoral and with electronic facilities for monitoring air and sea traffic and communications between Japan and North America. Nearby Buroton Bay on Shimushiru Island shelters a Soviet submarine base suitable for interdicting North Pacific sea lanes in the event of war. Etorofu itself possesses a fine deep water harbor which was used as a staging point for Japan's attack on Pearl Harbor.[10]

The Soviets also have invested heavily in the Kuriles, including the disputed islands, to maximize their considerable economic potential. Shikotan, in addition to possessing three crab canning plants, is the principal base for the Soviet Pacific whaling fleet. Etorofu boasts two whale processing plants and the largest salmon hatchery in the world. There is also mineral wealth: sulphur from Kunashiri and Etorofu used in Sakhalin's cellulose industry and titanium-magnetite from Etorofu used in aircraft and shipbuilding and in the chemical industry. In addition, the waters surrounding the Kuriles, including the disputed islands, are exceptionally rich and productive fishing grounds.[11]

The Japanese undoubtedly are alive to the strategic and economic significance of the disputed islands, but there is widespread agreement among knowledgeable observers that the driving force behind the Japanese claims is more politico-phychological than military or economic. Clearly, some of the disputed islands would seem to conform to the "common-sensical" definition of Japanese offshore islands. The westernmost of the Habomai group, for example, is scarcely two miles from Hokkaido. Although no Japanese presently live on the disputed islands (the 16,500 surviving Japanese residents of the Kuriles were repatriated when the Soviets occupied the islands), there is a general consensus in Japan that some of the islands seized by the USSR in 1945 rightfully belong to Japan and ought to be returned. In the Japanese view, lofty principles are involved, including international justice and the inalienability of national sovereignty. For many Japanese, the symbolism of the issue has not yet and is not likely ever to reach the level of feverish intensity throughout Japan which accompanied the campaign for the return of US-occupied Okinawa. (One million Japanese live on Okinawa.)

Yet the Japanese government's position on the Northern Territories, based on a working consensus among numerous groups and organizations centered mainly in Northern Japan, has remained consistent for three decades: "Etorofu, Kunashiri, Shikotan and the Habomais, called the Northern territories [sic] . . . are part of Japan's inherent territory, historically and juridically, and should naturally be under this country's sovereignty."[12] Thus speaks the ruling Liberal Democratic Party. Interestingly, *all* of the major opposition parties, including the Socialist and Communist Parties of Japan, not only endorse the government's position but exceed it, calling for the return of the *entire* Kurile chain.[13] In a recent step, the Japanese government designated 7 February as Northern Territories Day to be marked throughout Japan by rallies and demonstrations advocating return of those territories.

The Soviet position on this issue today is simple and unambiguous: there is nothing to discuss. But this has not always been the Soviet position.

The USSR, having boycotted the US–sponsored San Francisco Peace Treaty of 1951, established formal diplomatic relations with Japan in 1956. The two countries failed to conclude a peace treaty at that time because of the Soviet rejection of Toyko's demand for the return of all the Northern Territories. The two countries did, however, sign a Joint Peace Declaration in October 1956 in which the USSR pledged to return Shikotan and the Hamobais to Japan after the conclusion of a Soviet–Japanese Peace Treaty.[14]

But in 1960, after the renewal—and strengthening—of the US–Japan Security Agreement, Moscow altered its position on the Northern Territories, declaring there could be no retrocession of Shikotan and the Habomais, regardless of whether a peace treaty were concluded, unless the US–Japan Security Agreement was nullified and all American troops withdrawn from Japan. Since then, Moscow continually has stiffened its position: in 1968, stating its intention no longer to recognize even residual Japanese sovereignty in the Northern Territories; in 1976, stipulating Japanese could no longer visit their relatives' graves on Shikotan and the Hamobais without valid passports and Soviet visas; and in 1977, by the inclusion of all the Northern Territories in the Soviet 200–mile economic zone.[15] The somewhat undiplomatic statement of Soviet Ambassador Polyanskiy to a Japanese newspaper reporter in Tokyo in November 1978 that "the Soviet Union has no intention of transferring to Japan a single piece of stone, let alone an island"[16] nicely captures the spirit of the Soviet position on the Northern Territories.

That there is a connection between US–Japanese security ties and the stiffening Soviet position on the Northern Territories seems plausible. Why should we return these islands to Japan, the Soviets ask, only to have them turned into military bases directed against us? (Japanese suggestions of a pledge to keep the islands demilitarized if returned have elicited no interest in Moscow.)

But in all likelihood there is another factor of over-riding importance behind Moscow's uncompromising attitude: i.e., the implications of the Northern Territories issue for Sino–Soviet relations. From the founding of the People's Republic of China through the early 1960s, Beijing consistently supported the Soviet position on the Northern Territories. However, as Sino–Soviet relations began to deteriorate seriously, Beijing's attitude changed. The Chinese began to voice claims on huge chunks of Soviet territory acquired from China by Tsarist imperialism through "unequal treaties" and "extortion" in the 19th century. In July 1964, Mao Zedong startled a visiting delegation of Japanese Socialists (and the Soviet government as well) by announcing, "I approve of the Kuriles being returned to Japan. Russia already has taken too much land."[17]

The Chinese linkage of the two territorial issues was unmistakable. Even if Moscow were inclined to compromise with Toyko on the Northern Territories, that might embolden Beijing in its own territorial claims. The Chinese were viewed in Moscow as dangerous and utterly unpredictable. Their claims, if taken seriously, were a challenge to the territorial integrity of the USSR. This disease of questioning the post-World War II boundaries might even spread to the Soviets' western frontiers where Poles, Germans, Romanians, Lithuanians, Estonians, Latvians, and others had long historical memories and lingering "bourgeois nationalist" anti-Soviet sentiments. In the Soviet view, this was a Pandora's box which had to be kept tightly sealed at any cost, even if the cost in strained relations with Japan was high.

The linkage of Japanese and Chinese territorial claims against the Soviet Union dates back many years before the current Sino–Soviet dispute. In the 1930s, with Japan's seizure of Manchuria from China, Japan acquired a 3,000-mile frontier with the Soviet Empire, and with it innumerable border disputes and conflicting territorial claims. This led to a series of increasingly bloody border conflicts. For example, in the summer of 1938, Soviet and Japanese forces fought a pitched battle for two weeks over a disputed boundary ridgeline between Manchuria and the Soviet Maritime Province. Three full infantry divisions were engaged as well as artillery, tanks, and aircraft. Thousands of soldiers were killed before a negotiated settlement was reached. This battlefield is not far from the disputed island in the Ussuri River where Soviet and Chinese forces mauled each other in March 1969.

The territorial issue behind the Sino–Soviet battle of March 1969 centered on control of a tiny island in the Ussuri River. An interesting principle of international law was involved. This principle, called the *"thalweg* doctrine," stipulates that ordinarily the sovereignty of islands in a river which is an international boundary is determined by the relationship of the island to the river's main navigable channel. The main channel is defined as the international boundary. In a southward flowing river, such as the Ussuri, if the main channel passes east of an island, that island belongs to the country on the western side of the river, and vice versa. However, in fast-flowing rivers subject to freezing, thawing, and flooding, the actual main navigable channel can shift from one side of an island to the other, thus raising the question of whether or not the sovereignty of the island should change with the shifting of the main channel. International law, such as it is, is not clear on this point.

Just such a case arose at Damanskiy/Chenpiao Island in the Ussuri River where the main channel shifted from the western to the eastern side of the island, providing the opportunity for a Chinese claim to a previously Soviet-controlled island. The Soviets asserted ownership of the island, despite the shift of the main channel of the river, and, in March 1969, a clash between Chinese and Soviet border patrols grew into a pitched battle.

The disputed island is tiny, heavily wooded, uninhabited, and seemingly unimportant in and of itself. It was the principle that mattered. For Moscow, that principle has immediate practical application elsewhere. Further upstream, at the juncture of the Amur and Ussuri Rivers, stands Khabarovsk, a major Soviet urban, industrial, and administrative center and the headquarters of the Far Eastern Military District. Fronting Khabarovsk is a larger and much more important island which shields the city from the opposite (Chinese) shore. Here, too, nature had played the same trick, shifting the river's main channel from southwest to northeast of the island and opening a Chinese claim to the island.

If the Soviets accepted the principle of altering the sovereignty of islands according to shifts in the river channel, the Chinese would be able to fortify the island and bring artillery to bear point blank at the heart of Khabarovsk. This would be militarily and psychologically intolerable to the Soviets. Consequently, they always have resisted attempts to apply the principle of shifting sovereignty of river islands. The Soviets fought a battle against superior Japanese forces further up the Amur River in the summer of 1937 defending the same principle. Despite the Japanese sinking of several Soviet gunboats, Moscow refused to abandon the principle.

By far, the most serious of the Soviet–Japanese border conflicts of the 1930s occurred in 1939 over a boundary dispute between Manchuria and Outer Mongolia. The fighting rapidly escalated, reaching the level of a small undeclared war. Whole field armies totaling several hundred thousand troops, a thousand tanks, and a thousand aircraft were committed to battle. There were as many as 50,000 casualties in 4 months of intense fighting (May–September 1939).[18] In this case, the Soviets prevailed, effectively enforcing their interpretation of the boundary.

It is interesting to note that in each of the Soviet–Japanese border conflicts of the 1930s, the Chinese government consistently upheld the Japanese interpretation of the boundary—this despite the fact China and Japan were then engaged in a bloody, full-scale war and the USSR was rendering China valuable aid in its struggle against the Japanese invaders.

But the Chinese government (of Chiang Kai–shek, not Mao Zedong) also had a principle to uphold, for the Manchurian territory on which the Japanese faced the Soviets had, after all, been seized by Japan from China. It might again revert to China in the future (as it did in 1945). Therefore, the Chinese perceived that their own interests coincided with those of Japan when it came to boundary disputes with the USSR.

Thus, the Soviets, who also have long memories of these wartime experiences, will reach their own conclusions regarding the implications of linkage between the current Northern Territories dispute with Japan and China's irridentist ambitions. This is not to say a shift in the Soviet attitude toward the Northern Territories is impossible, but it seems unlikely except under extraordinary circumstances.

Military Issues. In view of the great disparity between Soviet and Japanese military power, the alignment of Japan with the Western security network, and the rising level of international tension, it is perhaps not surprising the Japanese government views the Soviet Union and its steadily growing military capability with some apprehension and the phrase "Soviet military threat" is heard more frequently in Japan, even from high-ranking government officials.

The Soviet Union regularly spends perhaps 20 times more on defense than Japan and possesses a military establishment of incomparably greater size and strength. Even if one counts only those Soviet forces deployed in East Asia, the asymmetry is still striking, particularly in view of the gradually declining American military presence in the Western Pacific. Naturally, Soviet Far Eastern forces are not deployed exclusively, nor even primarily, against Japan, but there are aspects of the Soviet deployment which seem particularly disturbing and threatening from the Japanese perspective.

One such highly publicized development was an announcement by the head of Japan's Self Defense Force (SDF) that the Soviet Union was greatly increasing its troop strength on islands in the disputed Northern Territories very close to Japan. The Soviet buildup reportedly amounts to roughly one division-equivalent, including tanks and artillery.[19] Since Japanese aggression against the USSR does not seem plausible, this Soviet buildup is widely believed in Japan to be aimed at exerting pressure or intimidation on Tokyo or perhaps something worse. Despite the publicity surrounding the Soviet buildup in the Northern Territories, there are other Soviet military deployments in East Asia of potentially greater military significance to Japan. The USSR has recently deployed SS–20 mobile MIRVed IRBMs and DELTA–class SSBNs in the Far East. While these strategic weapons are presumably directed mainly against China (and, in the case of the DELTA submarines, against the United States) their immense destructive power could be directed against Japan. BACKFIRE bombers also have been deployed recently in the Far East. In addition to their capability as strategic bombers which could easily strike Japan, these aircraft are believed to have a major role in Soviet plans for antishipping warfare should the need arise. Another deadly threat to Japan's vital sea lanes in the event of war is the Soviets' large and growing force of attack submarines based in the Northwestern Pacific. The Soviet Pacific Fleet has also been strengthened recently by the arrival of the new VTOL aircraft carrier *Minsk*, the large new amphibious assault ship *Ivan Rogov*, and the *Karaclass* guided missile cruiser *Petropavlovsk*. The operational capability of Soviet naval and naval air units also has been enhanced greatly by Vietnam's granting of base facilities at Cam Rahn Bay and Danang (granted during the Sino–Vietnamese conflict of February 1979), thereby placing Soviet forces athwart Japan's southern sea lanes and jeopardizing Japan's oil lifeline. Finally, the Soviet Sixth Airborne Division stationed at Khabarovsk has been brought up to full combat strength. Although clearly targeted primarily against China, this division made the politically telling demonstration of a parachute drop on Etorofu, the largest of the islands in the disputed Northern Territories.[20]

Given the abundant Soviet military capability vis-a-vis Japan and the rapid deterioration of East–West detente, it is not surprising the national security outlook of Japan's SDF is rather somber. What may be surprising is the Soviet Union's claim to be profoundly disturbed by its own national security outlook as viewed from Khabarovsk. Naturally, it is the United States and China rather than Japan which constitute the principle sources of concern. Yet, in the Soviet view, it is the threat of an alliance among the United States, China, and Japan which is most feared. If such an alliance came about and achieved maturity, the Soviets fear, the result could be a mighty America in concert with a remilitarized Japan, with both supplying modern weaponry to the Chinese hordes.

Clearly, it is in the Soviet interest (and presumably a high Soviet priority) to prevent the remilitarization of Japan in earnest. If so, Soviet actions seem not always to be in harmony with this goal. Soviet propaganda for years has been reiterating the charge that Japan already is being remilitarized and transformed into a powerful, dangerous, revanchist, militarist nation of neo-samurai. This seems rather disingenuous to most Japanese in view of the relentless Soviet military buildup concurrent with the Japanese government's holding of defense spending at or slightly below the level of 0.9 percent of GNP. Moscow replies that while the SDF's share of GNP may remain steady, the rapid growth of Japan's GNP provides the financial basis for a rapid military buildup in violation of the self-denying, antiwar, anti-armed force Article IX of Japan's Constitution.

Article IX is interpreted to limit not only the size of the SDF— although not precisely—but also the character of its weapons and missions; no nuclear weapons, of course. Also, no weapons with significant offensive power projection capability. (There was the episode when F–4 Phantom jets purchased from the United States by the Air SDF were obliged by the Japanese government to have their midair refueling probes removed, thus limiting their range and denying them tactical offensive capability.)

There can be little doubt successive Japanese governments have stretched their interpretation of Article IX far beyond the intent of its (American) drafters. This has been accomplished with the assistance of numerous high court rulings, with the support of a majority of the Japanese people, and at the urging of the United States government. The Soviet government, which is known internationally for its flagrant and cavalier disregard of many of the high-sounding provisions of its own constitution, is not likely to have much impact on Japanese decisionmaking by admonishing the decisionmakers for alleged violations of Japan's constitution. Also, many of those familiar with Japanese history and culture probably would agree the dual Soviet formula, in practice, of trying to intimidate the Japanese with demonstrations of awesome military might while steadfastly refusing even to discuss the Northern Territories issue (which most Japanese consider to be the most important political item on the agenda of Soviet–Japanese relations) is not a program well-calculated to secure Japanese acquiescence.

What Lies Ahead?

The final section of this article will sketch out three alternative possibilities for the evolution of Soviet–Japanese relations and the implications of each for the strategic balance in Northeast Asia and for US foreign policy and national security:

(1) Serious deterioration of Soviet–Japanese relations leading to vigorous Japanese participation in an anti-Soviet alliance with the United States, China, and NATO.

(2) Evolution of far-reaching Soviet–Japanese partnership based on economic cooperation, leading to the political

neutralization, or "Finlandization," of Japan.
(3) Continuation of the status quo, characterized by ambivalence in the bilateral relationship.

(A fourth possibility initially was considered: the emergence of Japan as a muscular, independent politico-military force; i.e., as a new superpower. Such an outcome conceivably could grow out of a scenario such as that suggested in number one above. It was rejected for this article because it seemed too improbable to evolve in the 1980s, the prescribed time frame for this study.)

Alternatives (1) or (2) imply radical departures from present patterns of Soviet–Japanese relations. The first implies Japan's emergence as a potent regional military power in order to help resist the threat of Soviet hegemonism. While the United States and China might desire this outcome, Japanese leaders are unlikely to see it as serving their nation's best interests. First, the economic burden of rapidly doubling or tripling the defense expenditures necessary for Japan to build a competitive regional military force would be severe. The effect on her balance of trade also would be highly adverse, to say nothing of the formidable political and constitutional obstacles. Furthermore, Japanese leaders are likely to conclude that as long as the United States is present as a protector of last resort, Japan's national security would lose more than it would gain by attempting to play an active role in confronting the Soviet Union in Northeast Asia. Also, as long as Moscow continued to offer the carrot of economic cooperation, Toyko would be loathe to cut itself off gratuitously from that highly rewarding trade, as it might have to do by actively participating in an anti–Soviet alliance.

The Soviets, for their part, would have no incentive willfully to push Japan into their enemies' arms. If their political and/or military actions in other parts of the world became so obnoxious as to risk profound alienation in Tokyo, they might counterbalance that by offering the Japanese opportunities to dip into the Siberian treasure trove on highly favorable terms, terms which for Moscow might be uneconomic but very politic.

The second alternative implies Japan's becoming a political client/ vassal of the Soviet Union in exchange for economic well-being. Such an outcome would fly in the face of Japan's traditional, historically conditioned distrust of the Soviet Union and seems improbable except as the result of a successful Soviet bid for global, or at least Eurasian, hegemony. If Japan were to adopt such a course merely on economic grounds, her realignment would likely tip the scales in favor of Soviet hegemony in Eurasia. After achieving a hegemonic position, however, Moscow would no longer *need* Japan as a partner and might be tempted to reduce her to the status of an economic and political vassal. Japan would have little leverage. Given the continued existence of a politically, economically, and militarily independent West, however, the USSR could not hope to supplant the West as Japan's principal economic partner.

It has been suggested Moscow might try to lure Japan into economic partnership via a favorable settlement of the Northern Territories question. But the political constraints (regarding China and Eastern Europe) on such a Soviet ploy are very great, and it seems unlikely the Northern Territories, per se, would be sufficient incentive for Japan to reorient itself fundamentally internationally.

It is conceivable a major aberration of US policy toward Japan could drive Tokyo into Moscow's arms, but it would have to be something drastic, such as an American neo-isolationist withdrawal from the Western Pacific or an all-out trade war shutting Japan out of the American market. As regards the former, it could be triggered by an American withdrawal from South Korea, followed by violent unification under Soviet–sponsored North Korean dominance. This would be traumatic for Japan (and China). In view of the unstable political evolution in South Korea in 1979–80, a precipitous and potentially catarophic chain of events can be imagined. But the advent of this Northeast Asian "domino theory" is easily avoidable, given a modicum of prudence in Seoul, Tokyo, and Washington. As for an all-out trade war, it would be so obviously self-destructive as to appear unlikely but not impossible.

In conclusion, it appears the most likely course for future Soviet–Japanese relations is a continuation of the status quo with its ambivalent balance between substantial economic cooperation and political/military antipathy.

Notes

1. This subject is treated in detail in Stuart D. Goldman, *The Forgotten War: Soviet–Japanese Conflict and the Outbreak of World War Two* (New York: Rawson and Wade, forthcoming).
2. Peggy L. Falkenheim, "Some Determining Factors in Soviet–Japanese Relations," *Pacific Affairs,* Vol. 50, Winter 1977–78, pp. 615–17.
3. Falkenheim, p. 617.
4. Ibid.
5. Hiroshi Kimura, "Soviet and Japanese Negotiating Behavior: The Spring 1977 Fisheries Talks," *Orbis,* Spring 1980, p. 43.
6. Rodger Swearingen, *The Soviet Union and Postwar Japan* (Stanford: The Hoover Institution Press, 1978), pp. 212–15.
7. A. Tselev, "'Pacific Community': Another Bloc?," *Soviet Military Review* (Moscow), September 1980, pp. 53–4.
8. Statistics furnished by officials of the Embassy of Japan, Washington, DC.
9. John J. Stephan, "The Kurile Islands: Japan Versus Russia," *Pacific Community,* Vol. 7, No. 3 (April 1976), p. 319.
10. Ibid.
11. Ibid.
12. Swearingen, p. 192.

13. Swearingen, pp. 192–3; and Stephan, pp. 323–4.
14. Falkenheim, p. 605.
15. Falkenheim, pp. 605–6.
16. *Asahi Shinbun* (Tokyo), 26 November 1978.
17. Stephan, p. 328.
18. Goldman, *The Forgotten War.*
19. William Chapman, "Japan Reports Soviet Buildup on Disputed Island," *Washington Post,* 27 September 1979, p. A23.
20. C. G. Jacobsen, "Sino–Soviet Crisis in Perspective," *Current History,* October 1979, p. 111.

Part III

Soviet Military Capabilities

The question of Soviet military capabilities has received a great deal of attention in the West as a consequence of the Soviet military buildup that has taken place since the mid–1960s. While the scope of and the intentions behind this buildup have been the source of considerable dispute, one fact seems inescapable: the increase in Soviet military capabilities has presented the USSR with a greatly enhanced ability to project its power overseas. Angola, Ethiopia, and South Yemen are just a few examples of the results this development has brought about. The articles presented in Part III examine several aspects of the question of Soviet military power.

Stanley Kober, citing Soviet sources, notes three purposes behind the growth in Soviet military power: the political effect which it produces in the event of war; the political effect it has upon the Western powers in peacetime—i.e., a moderation in their activities vis-a-vis the USSR; and the political effect it has upon the nonaligned states in terms of persuading these countries that the "prevailing wind blows from the East." Kober concludes that Soviet military power is not the result of an action-reaction phenomenon or an exaggeration of the Tsarist military legacy but the product of definite and relatively specific political goals.

Alan Smith examines the question of Soviet military manpower needs in the 1980s and the problems posed by a drop in the draft age number of young men which will occur in the coming decade. Smith notes that by 1990, one-third of each draft age cohort* will consist of Central Asian, Kazakh, and Transcaucasian peoples, thus exacerbating problems of cultural and linguistic assimilation for the Soviet Armed Forces. Unwilling to reduce the size of its military, the USSR likely will resolve its manpower shortages in several ways, including restricting military deferments and continuing a vigorous program of language training for the minorities.

Martha Brill Olcott explores a specific feature of the same question of Soviet manpower needs: the impact of the large Soviet Muslim minority. She outlines several of the problems which the "demographic explosion" of the Muslim populations has created for the Soviet military: projected changes in the Armed Forces' ethnic makeup; the mechanical difficulties caused by increased numbers of Muslim recruits;

---

*Kogorta or cohort is the word used by the Soviets to describe this pool of draftees.

312

the cultural problems posed by the Muslims; and the need to use the Armed Forces as a means of socialization, particularly with regard to the Muslim population.

Soviet military power cannot be viewed in isolation. An essential element of the Soviet military power equation in Europe is the Warsaw Pact. Ivan Volgyes examines the reliability of the non–Soviet Warsaw Pact allies. He contends that their reliability is in serious doubt because the East European military experience has focused on intra-alliance conflict (i.e., Czechoslovakia and Hungary). Volgyes probes the problem of Pact reliability using subsystem parameters—education, value formation, traditions, benefits, and fear—arguing that a knowledge of these parameters is mandatory for those decision-makers concerned with devising a strategy toward the USSR.

Robert Kennedy contrasts Soviet and US strategy in Europe and contends that the advent of strategic nuclear parity and the Soviet theater nuclear buildup have altered the political equation on the continent. The USSR and its Pact allies are prepared to wage combined arms warfare using all types of weapons (conventional, nuclear, and chemical), while the US and its NATO allies continue to focus on conventional forces and the planning for a conventional conflict. He advocates three broad actions be taken by NATO to redress the current imbalance: a shift in emphasis from conventional to conventional/nuclear/chemical warfare; a shift from short-range to long-range Eurostrategic systems; and a modernization of battlefield nuclear capabilities.

Gary Guertner also is concerned with Western strategy toward the Soviet Union. He asserts that US strategy has been dominated by technical variables. What is needed, he argues, is a move away from the pursuit of limited warfighting options to a broad strategic view based on the USSR's vulnerabilities in the geopolitical, ethnographic, economic, and historical realms. Viewing the USSR as a vulnerable multinational state, Guertner urges the US to adopt an ethnic-based, countercombatant, and counterindustrial targeting doctrine in order to strengthen prewar deterrence.

In the final contribution to Part III, Carl Reddel focuses on the continued Soviet attention to human resources in war, a factor which he argues receives very little attention in the West. He asserts that Russian history and Marxism–Leninism have been instrumental in the formulation of a view that is misunderstood in the US. This Western misunderstanding, he contends, is due to an underestimation of the importance of the role of ideology for the Soviet military and the failure to view war as only one dimension of the struggle between imperialism and socialism.

Causes of the Soviet Military Buildup

Stanley H. Kober

Throughout the tenure of the Brezhnev regime, the Soviet Union has been steadily building up its military power. Although the evidence of the buildup is so obvious it is no longer in dispute, Western observers are divided in their interpretations of the motivation behind it. In general, the explanations can be divided into four groups.

First, there is the argument the Kremlin is genuinely apprehensive about the threats confronting the USSR. Arrayed against the Soviet Union are the United States, Western Europe, Japan, and the People's Republic of China; allied with it are the countries of Eastern Europe, Cuba, and Vietnam. None of these countries can offer the Soviet Union much in the way of military support, and some of them are of doubtful political reliability. Given Russian history, in particular the tragedy of the Second World War, it is no wonder the Soviets feel insecure.

On the surface, this argument appears very reasonable, but there are several problems with it. In the first place, if the Soviets are so worried by the military threat to their country, why do they not upgrade the operational readiness of their strategic forces? Only about 15 percent of first-line Soviet nuclear submarines operate away from port at any given time, which means 85 percent can be destroyed in port in a surprise first strike; by comparison, the United States keeps over 50 percent of its SSBNs at sea.[1] Similarly, only about 25 percent of Soviet ICBMs are kept on alert status, able to respond to a "bolt from the blue," in contrast to more than 80 percent for the United States.[2]

Why do the Soviets assign such a low priority to the operational readiness of their strategic forces? It cannot be the consequence of some inability to maintain readiness. If the Soviets are worried their equipment will wear out faster at high levels of readiness, they could simply devote more of their military budget to operations and maintenance, or to the development of more reliable and durable components, and less to the development and procurement of new weapons systems. If the Soviets do not do so, it must be because they *choose* not to do so, which means they cannot be excessively worried about the threats which surround them.

The Soviets' negotiating record in SALT also casts doubt on this first explanation. For example, there is the curious absence of any Soviet effort to limit MIRV in SALT I. John Newhouse, who notes in his history of SALT I that "the Russians . . . never mentioned MIRV themselves," suggests "their attitude is better explained by technological lag; the United States was ahead in all or most qualitative aspects of offensive and defensive weapons, and the Soviet interest lay not in discussing America's advantages, but in canceling them by some other means."[3] But if this is the case, why did the Soviets insist on including cruise missiles in the SALT II limitations, something they had refused to do in SALT I, when the United States had not demonstrated any advanced capability in this technology?[4] Another explanation is that the Soviets, in SALT's early years, did not understand the importance of MIRV. This explanation, however, is not supported by the evidence. A 1971 Soviet text issued by a publishing house controlled by the Ministry of Foreign Affairs flatly states that "in creating the MIRV system, the US has established as its goal the destruction of Soviet intercontinental rockets of the retaliatory or, in the presently accepted terminology, 'second strike.'"[5]

What, then, explains Soviet behavior regarding MIRV? It is difficult to avoid the conclusion the Soviets were not interested in limiting MIRV. Consequently, one can only infer that the Soviets, instead of being concerned by the short-term advantage MIRV would confer on the United States because of its lead in the technology, were focusing on the long-term advantage MIRV would give them because of their greater missile throwweight. To get to the long term, however, one must first survive the short term. For the Soviets to have made this tradeoff, therefore, they could not have envisaged the United States as a particularly dangerous threat; otherwise, the risk simply would have been too great.

This conclusion is supported by other examples of Soviet behavior in SALT. According to Newhouse, the Soviets did not share the American concern with verification,[6] and Ambassador Gerard Smith, the former head of the US SALT delegation, has testified before Congress that "as a general matter, the Soviets resist specificity in agreements."[7] This, it hardly bears noting, is precisely the opposite of the behavior one would expect from a country supposedly obsessed with threats to its security. The evidence, in short, is overwhelming that the Soviet Union's military buildup cannot be explained by any sense of danger emanating from the international environment.

The second explanation of the Soviet military buildup is that it is the result of an action-reaction phenomenon initiated by the United States. Like the first explanation, this one is not without its supporting evidence. In 1960, for example, Khrushchev enunciated a defense posture which very explicitly reflected a conviction in the validity of minimum deterrence. Rockets, he said, "are not cucumbers . . . . You don't eat them, and only a certain number of them are required to repel aggression."[8] However, as the Kennedy administration began to increase expenditures on strategic weapons, Khrushchev reversed course and publicly urged the expansion of Soviet strategic forces to respond to the new threat.

315

Nevertheless, if one looks only at the Brezhnev era, the action-reaction thesis becomes more difficult to substantiate. Although American defense spending in real terms declined during much of this period—a fact acknowledged in the Soviet media, albeit rarely[9]—Soviet defense spending has increased steadily. Moreover, the Soviets have not merely followed the American lead in developing certain weapons but have initiated their own programs in areas ignored by the United States (e.g., ASAT, civil defense). Indeed, studies of the "arms race" between the United States and the USSR have concluded, to the evident surprise of some of the authors, that there is no arms race; instead of the United States' acting and the USSR's reacting, the Soviet military effort clearly exceeds that of the United States.[10]

The third hypothesis is that the Soviet military buildup is simply the reflection of a peculiarly Russian obsession with defense which dates back to Tsarist times. "Russian governments," George Kennan has emphasized, "at all times have maintained forces in being far greater than anybody else could see the reason for."[11] The implication is that the Soviet military buildup is simply the product of inertia, with no well-defined political goals.

This argument, like the others, has a certain initial appeal. It is, after all, indisputable that Tsarist regimes maintained very large armies. Nevertheless, this does not by itself demonstrate that the present Soviet leadership has no ideas concerning the utility of military power in the nuclear era. To prove this point, one must examine current Soviet literature and show that the Soviets do not define any purpose for their military power. Such an examination reveals, however, that the Soviets do define several purposes for their military power. These rationales, which constitute our fourth explanation, can be divided into four categories.

First, the Soviets believe military superiority enhances deterrence. As Ye. Tyazhelnikov, the present head of the Central Committee's Propaganda Department, told the Supreme Soviet in 1969, "the stronger the homeland, the quieter the enemy."[12] Unlike the Americans, the Soviets have no misgivings their strength might prove destabilizing. They have very little patience for the value-neutral Country A–Country B type of analysis which so dominated American strategic thinking in its attempt to transcend the Cold War.[13] Instead, the Soviets remain convinced wars result from value-laden political factors.[14] In other words, the Soviets believe countries initiate war when they think they can achieve a desired political result by so doing.[15] The best way to frustrate this kind of calculation is to make it as clear as possible no such kind of result can be anticipated. Hence, the Soviets believe the more military power they have, the safer they are. And, because they do not suffer from the *angst* which inspired American attempts at value-neutral analysis, they do not worry about entrusting *their* political leadership with ever greater military power.

Second, the Soviets believe all wars, including nuclear wars, have political results. As one Soviet military theoretician has put it: "In war, as a rule, one side conquers and the other suffers defeat."[16] Nor is this position held only by military theoreticians. Recently, Vadim Zagladin, First Deputy Chief of the Central Committee's International Department, forcefully expounded the same sentiment:

> War and peace are no more than two different forms of existence of the exploiting society, and as such they are closely interlinked. Let us recall Lenin's noteworthy statement that "war is the continuation through means of violence of the policy pursued by the ruling classes of the warring countries long before the war. Peace is the extension of that same policy, including changes in the ratio between opposing forces created through military operations. War in itself does not change the direction followed by the policy before the war, but merely accelerates this development." Therefore, the foundations of future peace are laid in the period of the war and its sociopolitical characteristics are defined. *The nature of the peace is definitively established by the outcome of the war.*[17]

None of this means the Soviet leadership wants war. On the contrary, Soviet authorities repeatedly emphasize that nuclear war cannot be a rational means of achieving any political goal, and there is no reason to believe they are insincere in this regard. Rather, it merely signifies that however convinced the Soviet leadership may be that peace is preferable to the Pyrrhic victory which would result from a nuclear war, a Pyrrhic victory is still preferable to defeat. In other words, they believe that if relations between East and West deteriorate to the point of war, it is foolhardy to base one's policy on the assumption the political leaders of the two sides—in the aftermath of unprecedented destruction—will resolve their differences in some agreeable compromise. If the political differences were so serious as to lead to nuclear war, it is unlikely indecisive nuclear exchanges will lead to their resolution. Instead, it is more reasonable to assume such deep differences will continue to frustrate attempts to terminate the war just as they frustrated efforts to preserve the peace; consequently, the war will end in the same manner in which previous total wars ended: with winners and losers.[18] And since the side which begins the war from a superior military position is more likely to prevail, the Soviets feel compelled in peacetime to achieve the greatest military advantage they can.

Third, the Soviets believe their growing military power, by changing the balance of power between East and West, inspires a more respectful and conciliatory attitude toward them on the part of the United States and the other Western powers.[19] The Soviets proceed from the premise that the differences between East and West, which arise from the different class interests of the two societies, are fundamentally irreconcilable. Although Soviet leaders recognize the existence of a "more moderate wing" in the West, they do not attribute this moderation to goodwill: the moderates, Brezhnev has explained, simply "assess the present correlation of forces in the world soberly."[20]

Underlying this hard-line, ideological interpretation is a realistic evaluation of the nature of politics. The Soviets believe objective factors—e.g., military and economic power—are more important than subjective factors—i.e., the inclinations of certain powerful individuals. This is because objective factors not only shape subjective ones—note Brezhnev's explanation of political moderation in the West—but also define the limits of action available to political leaders. In other words, capability is more important than intent. It does not matter if, say, an American president wants to do something so long as he cannot do it. On the other hand, there is cause for concern if an American president does not want to do something but still retains the capability, for he could always change his mind. Since objective factors are a more enduring basis for policy than subjective ones, and since they can be more directly influenced by Soviet activity, it is here the Soviets concentrate their effort.

Finally, the Soviets see their growing power favorably affecting the struggle for influence in the Third World. To understand this point, it is necessary, first of all, to recognize they view international politics as bipolar, divided along East-West lines.[21] Although they realize most of the Third World does not divide readily into these categories at this time, they are convinced Third World countries must become either capitalist or communist in the end; there is no third alternative. A critical factor determining the choice made by Third World countries will be the balance of power between East and West. Third World leaders, in their view, will want to be on the winning side in this global confrontation; consequently, they bend with the prevailing wind.

In addition, the growth of Soviet military power favorably affects Soviet goals with respect to the Third World by influencing the outcome of regional conflicts. Not only does it provide the Soviet Union with a greater capacity to affect the outcome of such conflicts, it also constrains Western options by raising the risk. As P. N. Fedoseyev, Vice President of the USSR Academy of Sciences, has succinctly put it: "Often the outcome of armed struggle in revolutionary war depends on the balance of the two main world forces."[22]

Nevertheless, it may still be objected that although the Soviets define specific goals for the buildup of their military power, their expectations are unrealistic. According to one school of thought, military superiority in the nuclear era can have no political utility. Thus, it does not matter what the Soviets think; their efforts are futile.

Are the Soviets, then, correct in believing their growing military power will have the effects they intend? With regard to their first objective—enhancing the effectiveness of their deterrent—it is difficult to dispute them. Of the two types of deterrence—the traditional type which identifies deterrence with an effective defensive capability and the more novel type which identifies it with the ability to inflict sufficient punishment on an adversary—the former, if attainable, is clearly preferable. It must be remembered the American theory of punitive deterrence emerged from the superiority of strategic offensive capabilities over strategic defensive capabilities, thereby making it impossible to base defense on traditional warfighting concepts. American strategic theoreticians, however, could not accept punitive deterrence as an imposed necessity; consequently, they transformed it into a desideratum. Deterrence, as a result, became not only distinct from defense but incompatible with it as American strategic thinking ultimately concluded the best security against nuclear attack lay in remaining vulnerable to it.

The Soviets have no patience with this kind of reasoning. Their reaction to the imposed necessity of a punitive deterrent has been to strive to replace it with something better, not to pretend it is better than it is. This is not to say they will be successful in their efforts, but we should recognize that if their efforts prove successful, their deterrent will be superior to America's. It should be self-evident that a capability both to defend one's territory and punish an aggressor is more effective than the capability merely to punish.

Similarly, it is difficult to quarrel with the Soviet contention that the side that wins the war will be in an advantageous position to determine the nature of the subsequent peace. The underlying question, though, is whether it is possible to win a nuclear war. If we assume that humanity as a whole is not destroyed, we can presume some people will emerge relatively better off than others and, in that limited sense, might be called "winners." Admittedly, however, this is more a semantic than substantive point. The real question, in terms of policy, is whether anybody could initiate nuclear war as a means of achieving political goals. On this point, the Soviets are unambiguous: nuclear war is not a rational means to this end, since the destruction visited upon the initiator certainly would exceed the benefits of victory, even assuming victory can be achieved. Consequently, nuclear war would be started only as an act of desperation. Nevertheless, the Soviets hasten to point out that this situation—the result of the superiority of strategic offense over strategic defense—probably is a temporary aberration that could be transformed with the advent of new technology. Marshal Ogarkov, the Chief of the Soviet General Staff, has been especially clear on this point:

> The experience of past wars convincingly demonstrates
> that the appearance of new means of attack always has led
> inevitably to the creation of corresponding means of

counter-action, and in the end to working out of means of conducting battles, engagements, operations, and wars as a whole . . . .

This also applies fully to rocket–nuclear weaponry, whose creation and rapid growth have forced military-technological thought and practice actively to work out means and measures of countering it. In its turn, the appearance of means of defense against weapons of mass destruction caused the perfection of rocket-nuclear means of attack. All of this confirms that the continuous opposition of means of attack and defense—that is, of weapons and military technology—is one of the leading sources of the development of military affairs as a whole.[23]

In other words, the Soviets believe that the domination of strategic offense over strategic defense is unlikely to endure forever. The clear implication of this is that, when strategic defense becomes feasible, it may be possible to win a nuclear war, since the initiation of nuclear war no longer would be suicidal.

With regard to the third objective—to moderate the attitude of the Western powers toward the Soviet Union—it is very apparent the Soviets have been successful. There can be no doubt American policy toward the Soviet Union has changed as Soviet power has increased. Nowhere is this more apparent than in the policy of detente adopted by the Nixon administration. Although he campaigned on a pledge of preserving American military superiority, Nixon reversed course and settled for sufficiency soon after he assumed office. In his turn, Henry Kissinger has explained that detente was designed "to manage the emergence of Soviet power without sacrificing vital interests."[24] Clearly, then, if Soviet power had not been emerging, there would have been no need for a policy of detente.

Finally, there is the question of the effect growing Soviet power has on the Third World. Here, it may be argued, the growth of Soviet power has not prevented serious reversals, such as the eviction of Soviet influence from Egypt. Nevertheless, even if the Soviet Union has not been successful everywhere, this does not mean it has been successful nowhere. If in the early 1960s the Soviet Union had to stand by helplessly while Western intervention determined the outcome of the Congo crisis, in the 1970s it was the United States which stood aside while Soviet and Cuban intervention decided the fate of Angola. Moreover, as Soviet calculations predicted, the success of the Soviet effort, far from alienating African countries, had the opposite effect. Kenneth Kaunda, who had denounced the Soviet Union as a "plundering tiger" during the course of the intervention and had called upon it to "leave the task of liberating Africa to Africans," reversed course after the Soviet-assisted victory of the Popular Movement for the Liberation of Angola *(MPLA).* Thus, when Soviet President Nikolay

Podgornyy came to visit in 1977, Kaunda publicly hailed the Soviets as "colleagues in the struggle" against white rule in southern Africa,[25] and the following year the government-owned *Zambia Daily Mail* even went so far as to suggest the Patriotic Front enlist Soviet and Cuban soldiers to fight in Zimbabwe.[26] Similarly, Samora Machel of Mozambique, who had previously leaned toward China, began to change his direction. Visiting Moscow in May 1976, he was enthusiastic in his praise for the Soviet Union; in March 1977, he signed a friendship treaty with the USSR. Shortly afterward, several hundred Cubans were reported to be in the country training the Mozambique Army and Rhodesian guerillas.[27]

In short, it would appear that here, too, the growth of Soviet military power is having its intended effect. Soviet military power is proving effective in deciding Third World conflicts, and, if the nonaligned conference in Havana was any indication, the change in the international balance of power is encouraging many Third World countries to take an increasingly anti–Western stance. Thus, even if the Soviets are not always successful in the Third World, the trend of developments would hardly seem comforting for the West.

In conclusion, therefore, it is clear the Soviet military buildup, far from being aimless or defensive, is designed to enhance Soviet political capabilities in the international arena. There can be no doubt it has been successful in this regard. Still, it must be pointed out that the additional benefit at times has been questionable, for the success of Soviet expansionism has produced further economic burdens for the USSR, which now finds itself obligated to support a host of insolvent foreign regimes. This is not to suggest the buildup of Soviet power does not threaten Western interests, but that some aspects of it are more threatening than others. Consequently, in formulating their policy for responding to the Soviet military· buildup, Western policymakers should concentrate on those aspects threatening Western security and not worry about temporary Soviet triumphs which, in the long term, increasingly are turning out to be liabilities.

Notes

1. General George Brown, *United States Military Posture for FY 1979* (Washington: Government Printing Office, 1978), p. 28.
2. Walter Pincus, "Debut of Soviet Missiles Could Color U.S., NATO Politics," *Washington Post,* 26 June 1980, p. A2.
3. John Newhouse, *Cold Dawn: The Story of SALT* (New York: Holt, Rinehart, and Winston, 1973), p. 174.
4. Testimony of Paul Nitze in the US Congress, House Committee on the Armed Services, *Full Committee Hearings on the Military Implications of the Strategic Arms Limitation Talks Agreements,* 92nd Congress, 2nd session, 1972, p. 15132.
5. Yu. N. Listvinov, *Pervyy udar* [First Strike] (Moscow: Izdatel'stvo "Mezhdunarodnyye otnosheniya," 1971), p. 197. For an explanation of the importance of the Listvinov book, see Kenneth A. Myers and Dimitri Simes, *Soviet*

Decision–Making, Strategic Policy, and SALT, ACDA/PAB–243, 1974, pp. 53–54.

6. Newhouse, op. cit.

7. US Congress, Senate Committee on the Armed Services, *Military Implications of the Treaty on the Limitation of Anti–Ballistic Missile Systems and the Interim Agreement on Limitations of Strategic Offensive Arms,* Hearings, 92nd Congress, 2nd session, 1972, p. 295.

8. *Pravda,* 29 May 1960, translated in *Current Digest of the Soviet Press,* 29 June 1960, p. 11.

9. See, for example, C. I. Svyatov "O stroitel'stve vooruzhennykh sil SSha v 70-e gody [Developments of the US Armed Forces in the '70s]," *SSha* [USA], No. 12, 1975, pp. 115–117; and I. Basova and S. Blagovolin, "Novyye yavleniya v deyatel'nosti voyenno-promyshlennykh kompleksov [New Phenomena in Activities of Military and Industrial Complexes]," *Mirovaya ekonomika i mezhdunarodnyye otnosheniya* [World Economy and International Relations], No. 9, 1979, p. 46.

10. See Albert Wohlstetter, "Is there a Strategic Arms Race?" *Foreign Policy,* No. 15, 1974, pp. 3–20, and "Rivals, but No 'Race'," *Foreign Policy,* No. 16, 1974, pp. 48–81. Also, see Jacek Kugler, A. F. K. Organski, and Daniel J. Fox, "Deterrence and the Arms Race; The Impotence of Power," *International Security,* No. 4, 1980, pp. 105–138.

11. Foy D. Kohler and Mose L. Harvey, eds., *The Soviet Union: Yesterday, Today, Tomorrow* (Coral Gables, Florida: University of Miami Center for Advanced International Studies, 1975), p. 124.

12. *Izvestiya,* 13 July 1969, translated in *Current Digest of the Soviet Press,* 6 August 1969, p. 12. At the time, Tyazhelnikov was head of the Young Communist League *(Komsomol).*

13. A good example of this is the abundant American literature on international systems which examines, among other things, whether bipolar or multipolar systems are more stable. To the Soviets, this definition of stability (i.e., peace) as a function of the *number* of "poles" in the international system to the utter exclusion of the *policies* followed by those "poles" is completely unacceptable.

14. "Wars always have been a continuation of the policies of one or another classes or states and will remain so until the social and national reasons giving rise to them disappear." *Metodologicheskiye problemy voyennoy teorii i praktiki* [Methodological Problems of Military Theory and Practice], 2nd ed. (Moscow: Voyenizdat, 1969), p. 80.

15. "Politics, from an evaluation of military and political factors, selects the most propitious moment to start a war, taking into account all the strategic considerations." V. D. Sokolovskiy, *Soviet Military Strategy,* trans. Harriet Fast Scott, 3rd ed. (New York: Crane, Russak and Company, 1975), p. 21.

16. P. Trifonenkov, "The Objective Laws of War and the Principles of Military Art," *Kommunist Vooruzhennykh Sil* [Communist of the Armed Forces], No. 1, 1966, translated in Joint Publications Research Service (JPRS) 34498, 10 March 1966, p. 17.

17. V. Zagladin, "Working Class, Socialism, and Peace," *Mirovaya ekonomika i mezhdunarodnyye otnosheniya,* No. 11, 1979, translated in JPRS 74904, 10 January 1980, p. 21, emphasis added.

18. "Every country participating in a war, regardless of whether it is attacking or defending, will stop at nothing to achieve victory and will not acknowledge defeat without having employed and without having expended the entire arsenal at its disposal." R. Simonyan, "US and NATO 'Nuclear Strategy,'" in *Zarubezhnoye voy–ennoye obozreniye* [Foreign Military Review], 1980, No. 6, trans. in Joint Publications Research Service (JPRS), *USSR Report: Military Affairs,* No. 76424, 12 September 1980, p. 39.

19. "The possibility of successful talks with the USA, the possibility of a normalization in Soviet–American relations, is an important result of the activity of the Communist Party, the Soviet state and the entire Soviet people in strengthening the country's

economic and defense might, in further consolidating the unity of Soviet society and in unifying the socialist commonwealth . . . . The change in the alignment of forces in favor of socialism . . . has served the strengthening of peace and international security. Evidence of this is provided by the improvement of the situation in Europe; further evidence is provided by the normalization of Soviet–American relations." G. Arbatov, "On Soviet–American Relations," *Kommunist,* No. 3, 1973, translated in *Current Digest of the Soviet Press,* 9 May 1973, p. 4.

20. L. I. Brezhnev, *Leninskim kursom* [Following Lenin's Course] (Moscow: Politizdat, 1970), Vol. 2, p. 412.

21. "As before, present-day international relations essentially reduce to a contest between the two social systems, though its [sic] forms inevitably undergo changes under the direct influence of shifts in the balance of world forces." Sh. P. Sanakoyev and N. I. Kapchenko, *Socialism: Foreign Policy in Theory and Practice,* trans. V. M. Sukhodrev (Moscow: Progress Publishers, 1976), pp. 85–86.

22. P. N. Fedoseyev, et al, *Leninist Theory of Socialist Revolution and the Contemporary World* (Moscow: Progress Publishers, 1975), p. 423.

23. N. V. Ogarkov, *Vsegda v gotovnosti k zashchite Otechestva* [Always Ready to Defend the Homeland] (Moscow: Voyenizdat, 1982), p. 36, emphasis added.

24. *Department of State Bulletin,* 19 January 1976, p. 70.

25. *Keesing's Contemporary Archives,* pp. 27663, 27779, and 28401.

26. *The Times* (London), 27 June 1978, p. 1.

27. *The Economist,* 7 May 1977, p. 13.

Military Manpower Supply and Demand in the Soviet Union

Alan B. Smith

Issues

Soviet military planners will face several issues in balancing manpower supply and demand during the 1980s. First, they will have difficulty in maintaining their forces at their current level of about five million men[1] unless they modify the system by which they obtain manpower. The armed forces depend on conscription to provide the bulk of their manpower, and the number of young men reaching draft age each year in the late 1980s will decline to the levels of the mid–1960s. Consequently, the net pool of draft-eligible young men will drop from about ten million in 1980 to less than seven million in 1989.

The changing ethnic composition of the USSR's population could further complicate the task of military manpower planners. People from the Central Asian, Kazakh, and Transcaucasian Republics will comprise almost one-third of each draft cohort by the end of the 1980s. As a result, ethnic minorities—who have weak command of the Russian language and cultural backgrounds different from those of the Slavic majority—will make up an increasingly large percentage of military manpower. Assimiliation of these peoples into the mainstream of the armed forces will pose an increasing burden on the Soviet military training system.

Regardless of the ethnic composition of the manpower pool, the Soviets will have to contend with the problem of maintaining the combat capabilities of a force composed largely of short-term conscripts while continuing to introduce more complex weapons systems. They must ensure their military units have enough skilled people to operate and maintain these systems effectively.

The decline in cohort size may also cause the Soviets to examine more closely how they allocate available manpower resources between the military and civilian sectors of the economy. The Soviets traditionally have relied on the addition of large numbers of new workers to their labor force to sustain growth in the economy. The anticipated combination of more people reaching retirement age and fewer reaching working age will cause annual increments to the Soviet population of able-bodied age to drop to about 0.5 million in the mid–1980s. (Through the 1970s, these increments averaged over 2.4 million.)[2] In the absence of significant improvements in labor productivity, these declines will reduce the current growth rate of the Soviet economy. A slowing rate of economic growth could cause Soviet planners to advocate military force reductions to compensate for sagging labor force growth in the civilian sector.

Manpower Supply

In the past, the number of men eligible for military service has been defined for computational simplicity as the conscription-eligible cohort.[3] This method suggests military manpower needs will be met only by 18–year-olds, ignoring 19– through 26–year-old deferees in the draft pool. Because recent cohorts have been close in size to the annual demand for military manpower, this narrow definition of manpower supply has dramatized the potential impact on the military of short-term variations in cohort size.

A less constrained manpower supply picture emerges, however, if the Soviet concept of the draft pool is used to calculate the number of people available for military service. The estimated annual demands for conscripts from each cohort can be calculated by assuming males are conscripted at varying rates throughout their entire period of eligibility for military service (ages 18 through 26). Subtracting this annual demand from the net manpower pool indicates the numbers of men not conscripted each year. These numbers can be used to estimate the overall size of the draft pool. Draft pool calculations are discussed further in the annex to this article and the results are summarized in Figure 1.

Demand for Manpower

The Soviet armed forces require regular additions to their officer, career enlisted, and conscript ranks. Conscript accessions, however, place the only significant burden on the draft pool. Officer replacements come primarily from a system of full-time, three- to five-year higher military schools; the remainder are commissioned from the warrant officer ranks and from universities with reserve officer programs. Assuming that 20 percent of Soviet military personnel are officers[4] and that the average officer is on active duty for 20 years,[5] the annual requirement for officers can be calculated as 5 percent of 1,000,000, or roughly 50,000 men—a small burden on the draft pool. To meet this annual demand, however, the Soviets probably have nearly 200,000 men—approximately 4 percent of their military manpower—enrolled as cadets in military schools.

Career enlisted personnel are recruited from the ranks of conscripts who may opt for noncommissioned or warrant officer status toward the end of their mandatory service periods. Consequently, the NCO and

Military Manpower
Supply and Demand

Millions of men

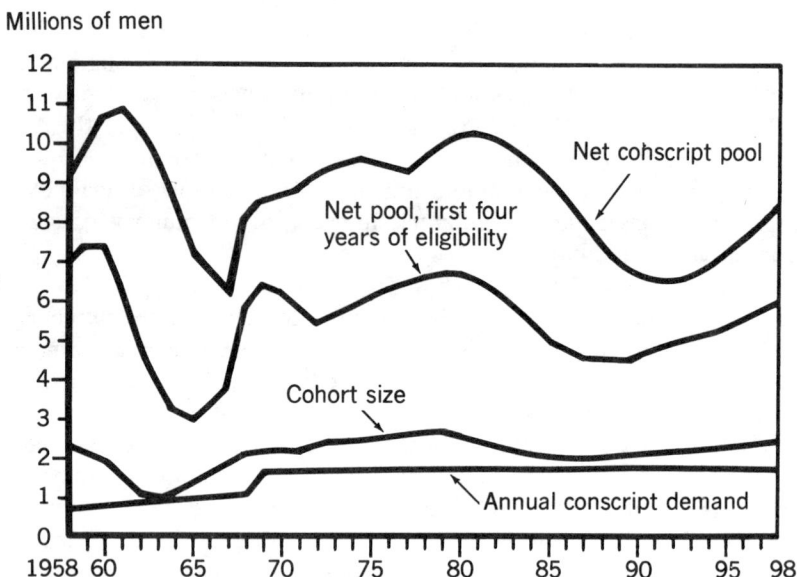

Note: The net conscript pool includes young men 18-26 (19-26 prior to 1968) who have not served on active duty. The rapid increase in annual conscript demand and the size of the net pool in the late 1960s reflect changes made to the draft law in 1967. These changes reduced the term of service from three years to two and lowered the initial age for conscription from 19 to 18.

Figure 1

warrant officer replacement process places no direct burden on the draft pool.

Annual requirements for conscripts are high because they comprise the bulk of the USSR's military manpower and have short terms of service. If 20 percent of Soviet military personnel are officers, 4 percent are cadets, and about 5 percent are career enlisted personnel, then approximately 70 percent—or some 3.5 million—are conscripts. Because the conscript's average term of service currently is 2 years, half, or nearly 1.8 million, must be replaced each year. The line labeled "annual conscript demand" in Figure 1 shows this estimate of annual demand.

Options

For the next two or three years, the Soviets can continue to balance military manpower supply and demand by varying the number of deferments granted yearly for pursuit of higher education and medical reasons. Simply drafting larger shares of the available young men to meet military requirements could result in unrealistically high rates of military service participation by cohorts of the mid-1980s, however. The calculations underlying Figure 1 (see Annex) indicate that if the Soviet military remains constant in size, over 85 percent of the cohorts becoming eligible for military service between 1985 and 1989 will have to serve. The Soviets probably will try to avoid letting the participation rate rise to these levels because it would cut too far into the ranks of the unfit and those obtaining educational deferments.

While simply drafting a larger percentage of available young men is not a realistic solution to the manpower problems facing the Soviet armed forces, a number of additional options would allow military planners to reduce strains on the conscript pool and maintain current force levels. These options include increasing the term of conscripted service, making greater use of military reservists recalled to active duty for short periods of time, retaining more extended servicemen, and increasing the use of women and civilians in the military. In all likelihood, the Soviets will implement some combination of these measures in addition to maintaining high cohort participation rates to ensure desired manning levels.

Increased Terms of Service. The most attractive option to the Soviets probably will be to increase the term of conscripted service. Extending the term of service by as little as 6 months would obviate the need for other changes in the draft system (see Figure 2). Manning levels could be maintained without significantly altering current patterns of conscription. This option would keep average cohort conscription rates at about 70 percent through the late 1980s. Moreover, the economic costs associated with this option probably would be less than those associated with some of the others because it would affect, in the main, relatively unskilled young people just out of secondary school. Although an increase in the term of service would be unpopular, concern about public reaction probably would not seriously constrain the political and military leadership from exercising this option.

Reservists. The draft law contains provisions which allow the military periodically to recall reservists for refresher training. Reservists can be recalled to active duty in peacetime for short periods which can total up to about 1½ years. They probably will consider greater use of this authority to provide a solution to short-term military manpower shortages. If used in routine tasks requiring minimal refresher training,

Effect of Longer Terms of Service
on Cohort Conscription Rates

Percentage of
cohort conscripted

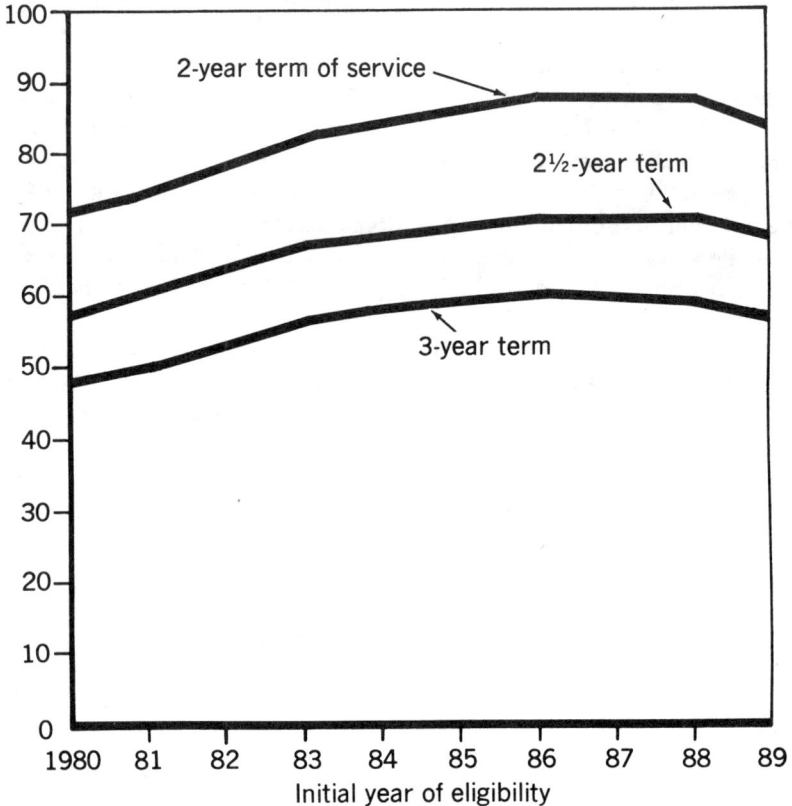

Figure 2

reservists could replace full-time personnel who, in turn, could be assigned to tasks more directly related to combat readiness.

Better Retention. The Soviets probably would like to retain more conscripts as extended servicemen. A modest increase in retention rates would make the military more professional and perhaps more effective by lessening the reliance on conscripts in junior leadership positions. Extended servicemen make up a small portion of the force, however, and it would be difficult to increase the retention rate sufficiently to have a worthwhile impact on conscription requirements. The number of extended servicemen would have to be at least doubled to reduce conscription requirements significantly. Increases in voluntary enlistments on this scale are unlikely, however, as long as civilian job opportunties for ex-servicemen remain abundant and Soviet military life continues to be relatively harsh.

Women. The introduction of mandatory military service for women or even expansion of the present voluntary recruitment program would enhance the USSR's ability to maintain military manning levels. At present, women play only a token role in the Soviet Armed Forces. A major change in thinking on the part of the Soviet leadership would be necessary for women to assume greater roles in the military.

Civilians. Putting more civilians into jobs currently held by uniformed personnel would also ease military pressures on the manpower pool, but—as in the case of increasing the role of women—it would require a shift in thinking by the leadership. The Soviet Armed Forces traditionally have put military personnel into defense-related positions whether or not they call for unique military skills. It appears unlikely the Soviets will change their civilian manning practices enough to affect significantly the demand for conscripts in the next decade.

Reduction in Force. Finally, the Soviet military could respond to declines in manpower supplies by reducing the size of the armed forces. Because the defense establishment historically has had a first claim on scarce resources, including manpower, and the Soviet leadership appears committed to maintaining a strong national defense, it is unlikely military manning levels will be affected significantly by restricted manpower supplies.

Changing Ethnic Mix

Unlike earlier problems of restricted manpower supplies, issues surrounding the changing ethnic composition of the cohort cannot be resolved by manipulating the manpower procurement system. Assimilation into the military of peoples whose cultural backgrounds are different from those of the Slavic majority will require more complex procedures.

In the past, ethnic minorities have been used extensively in the Construction, Transportation, and *MVD* Internal Security Troops.[6] By using minorities in these services, the Soviet leadership minimized the effects of their low educational attainment and general lack of Russian language proficiency. Men from the southern tier of republics, who made up less than 20 percent of the 1970 cohort, will comprise almost one-third of the 1989 cohort,[7] and, of necessity, increasing numbers of them will be placed in combat units.

The nature of the existing military systems for training conscripts and for operating military equipment should make it easier for the Soviet military to accept minorities into combat units. The military training system currently provides conscripts with only narrowly specialized practical skills. Limitations in these skills are compensated for by giving conscripts tightly defined, well-supervised tasks and relying on junior officers for many of the "hands on" technical chores which would be performed by enlisted men in the armed services of other countries.

The increased infusion of minorities into the military could lead occasionally to heightened racial tensions, but the Soviets should be able to deal with this problem successfully by the continued application of firm discipline to all members of the military. In addition, the Soviets probably which continue to shunt minorities into the many low-skill jobs which exist in the armed forces. Rigorous testing procedures and continuing racial distrust will keep sensitive enlisted positions and membership in the officer corps, for the most part, reserved for the Slavic majority.

Manpower Cuts?

The demographic problems facing the Soviets through the next decade will almost certainly contribute to a slowdown in economic growth. This could lead the Soviets to consider reductions in the size of the armed forces to alleviate manpower shortfalls in the civilian economy. To measure the economic benefits of military manpower reductions, I postulated a reduction by one million men in the size of the armed forces phased over several years. I measured the benefits of this reduction in terms of the additional manpower which would be made available to the civilian economy.

Such a reduction in the size of the armed forces would allow only marginal improvements in the growth of the population available to the civilian economy. Uniformed military men make up only about three percent of the Soviet working-age population. Thus, even massive reductions in the size of the armed forces would not significantly change the slowing trend in new labor resources (see figure 3). Consequently, manpower cuts would have a negligible impact on the Soviet economy.

Effect of a Military Manpower Reduction on the Incremental Growth of the Civilian Population of Able-Bodied Age

Thousands
of people

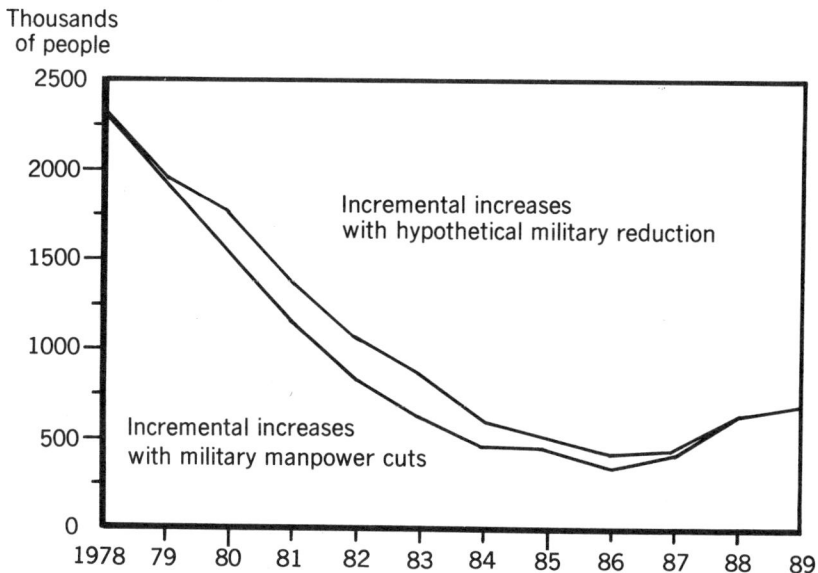

Figure 3

Annex

Method for Estimating Rates of Conscription

To show the effects of distributing the burden of military conscription on males between the ages of 18 and 27 rather than on 18–year-olds exclusively, I developed a matrix (Table A) showing the distribution of Soviet males by age group. Assuming the total annual requirements for manpower *and* the percentage of the requirement for each age group both remain constant (Table B), I was able to subtract from Table A and produce a matrix (Table C) which showed the numbers of Soviet males not conscripted in each year. This third matrix provided the data needed to estimate the size of the draft pool and the military participation rate of each cohort during its entire period of eligibility for military service.

Table A. Soviet Males by Age Group

(Thousands)

Year	Age								
	18	19	20	21	22	23	24	25	26
72	2292	2208	2231	2184	2123	2051	1871	1635	1372
73	2439	2288	2204	2227	2179	2118	2046	1866	1631
74	2467	2435	2284	2199	2222	2174	2113	2041	1861
75	2496	2463	2430	2279	2194	2216	2168	2107	2035
76	2560	2491	2457	2424	2273	2187	2209	2161	2100
77	2606	2555	2485	2451	2418	2266	2181	2202	2154
78	2647	2601	2549	2479	2444	2411	2259	2174	2195
79	2638	2642	2596	2543	2472	2437	2403	2252	2167
80	2542	2633	2636	2589	2536	2465	2430	2396	2245
81	2433	2538	2627	2630	2582	2529	2458	2423	2389
82	2309	2429	2532	2621	2623	2575	2521	2450	2415
83	2173	2305	2424	2526	2614	2615	2567	2514	2443
84	2107	2170	2300	2418	2520	2607	2608	2560	2506
85	2063	2103	2165	2295	2411	2513	2599	2600	2552
86	2020	2059	2099	2160	2289	2405	2505	2592	2592
87	2011	2016	2055	2094	2154	2282	2398	2498	2584
88	2031	2008	2012	2050	2088	2149	2276	2391	2491
89	2092	2028	2004	2008	2045	2083	2143	2270	2384
90	2135	2088	2024	1999	2003	2040	2077	2137	2263
91	2138	2132	2084	2019	1994	1997	2034	2071	2130
92	2168	2134	2128	2080	2014	1989	1992	2028	2065
93	2219	2164	2130	2123	2075	2009	1984	1986	2023
94	2260	2215	2160	2125	2118	2069	2004	1978	1981

Table A (Continued)

(Thousands)

Year	Age								
	18	19	20	21	22	23	24	25	26
95	2311	2256	2211	2156	2120	2112	2064	1998	1973
96	2363	2308	2252	2206	2150	2115	2107	2058	1993
97	2415	2359	2303	2247	2201	2145	2109	2101	2053
98	2464	2451	2355	2298	2242	2195	2139	2104	2095
99	2508	2460	2407	2350	2293	2236	2190	2134	2098
00	2544	2504	2456	2402	2344	2287	2231	2184	2128

Note: Data in this table were compiled from unpublished information provided by the United States Department of Commerce, Foreign Demographic Analysis Division.

Table B

Age

	18	19	20	21	22	23	24	25	26
Percentage of Annual Cohort	45	30	10	5	5	2	1	1	1
Number of Draftees (1000s)	787	525	175	87	87	35	17	17	17

Table C. Males Not Conscripted

(Thousands)

Year	Age									Total
	18	19	20	21	22	23	24	25	26	
1972:	1505									
1973:	1652	976								
1974:	1680	1123	797							
1975:	1709	1151	943	705						
1976:	1773	1179	970	850	612					
1977:	1819	1243	998	877	757	570				
1978:	1860	1289	1062	905	783	715	546			
1979:	1851	1330	1109	969	811	741	690	522		
1980:	1755	1321	1149	1015	875	769	717	666	498	8765

Table C (Continued)

(Thousands)

Year	Age									Total
	18	19	20	21	22	23	24	25	26	
1981:	1646	1226	1140	1056	921	833	745	693	642	8902
1982:	1522	1117	1045	1047	962	879	808	720	668	8768
1983:	1386	993	937	952	953	919	854	784	696	8474
1984:	1320	858	813	844	859	911	895	830	759	8089
1985:	1276	791	678	721	750	817	886	870	805	7594
1986:	1233	747	612	586	628	709	792	862	845	7014
1987:	1224	704	568	520	493	586	685	768	837	6385
1988:	1244	696	525	476	427	453	563	661	744	5789
1989:	1305	716	517	434	384	387	430	540	637	5350
1990:	1348	776	537	425	342	344	364	407	516	5059
1991:	1351	820	597	445	333	301	321	341	383	4892
1992:	1381	822	641	506	353	293	279	298	318	4891
1993:	1432	852	643	549	414	313	271	256	276	5006
1994:	1473	903	673	551	457	373	291	248	234	5203
1995:	1524	944	724	582	459	416	351	268	226	5494
1996:	1576	996	765	632	489	419	394	328	246	5845
1997:	1628	1047	816	673	540	449	396	371	306	6226
1998:	1677	1139	868	724	581	499	426	374	348	6636
1999:	1721	1148	920	776	632	540	477	404	351	6969
2000:	1757	1192	969	828	638	591	518	454	381	7328

Note: These data do not include officer candidates. The horizontal totals at the right provide an indication of the size of the draft pool in each year.

Total conscription rates for each cohort were calculated by comparing the number of men not conscripted by the last year of their cohort's period of eligibility with the size of the cohort in that year. In 1988, for example, the cohort which becomes eligible for military service in 1980 will be 26 years old and number about 2,491,000 men. If the assumptions underlying Table B are valid, the number of men not conscripted from that cohort could be about 744,000. Under these conditions, the military conscription rate will be

$$\frac{2491 - 744}{2491} = 70 \text{ percent}$$

Using this method the following data can be calculated.

Table D

Percentage of Cohort Conscripted by Initial Year of Eligibility

1980	71	1987	89
1981	74	1988	88
1982	78	1989	85
1983	82	1990	84
1984	85	1991	84
1985	87	1992	82
1986	88		

Notes

1. The overall military manpower figure was cited in a CIA research paper entitled *Soviet and US Defense Activities, 1970–79: A Dollar Cost Comparison*, SR80-10005, January 1980, p. 7. The number includes uniformed members of the Ministry of Defense plus the Border Guards of the Committee for State Security and the Internal Security Troops of the Ministry of Internal Affairs—organizations which are manned by conscripts serving in accordance with the 1967 *Law on Universal Military Service*.
2. The Soviets define the population of able-bodied age as males between the ages of 16 and 59 and females between 16 and 54. Working age population data were provided by the Bureau of Economic Analysis, US Department of Commerce, and cited in a CIA research aid entitled *USSR: Some Implications of Demographic Trends for Economic Policies*, ER 77-10012, January 1977.
3. Murray Feshbach and Stephen Rapawy, "Soviet Population and Manpower Trends and Policies," *The Soviet Economy in a New Perspective* (Washington: Government Printing Office, 1976), p. 41.
4. John Erickson, *Soviet Military Power* (London: Royal United Services Institute for Defence Studies, 1971), p. 14.
5. *Reference Book of Laws for Officers of the Soviet Army and Navy* (Moscow: Military Publishing House, 1970), p. 60.
6. Jeremy Azrael, *Emergent Nationality Problems in the USSR*, Rand Corporation Report R-2172-AF, September 1977, p. 17.
7. Derived from unpublished data made available by the Foreign Demographic Analysis Division, US Department of Commerce.

335

Soviet Muslims and the Military

Martha Brill Olcott

In recent years, Western analysts have become increasingly aware of the myriad problems associated with the "demographic explosion" occurring in the Muslim regions of the Soviet Union.[1] This article will focus on one aspect of this problem: the challenges posed to the Soviet military by the changing ethnic makeup of the Soviet Armed Forces. The article briefly treats the projected changes in the ethnic makeup of the Soviet Armed Forces as well as the difficulties the increase in Muslim population in the services will cause. It then goes on to discuss the military as a means of socialization and the special problems posed by the Muslims. The discussion of these problems is intended to be thought-provoking rather than conclusive, as ethnic data for the Soviet Armed Forces are virtually nonexistent.

*   *   *   *   *   *   *

In the first two decades of Soviet rule, national principles were applied to the organization of the armed forces, and generally most nationalities were assigned to units and divisions composed exclusively or nearly exclusively of members of their own population group. However, when the Soviet Armed Forces were being organized at the time of the Civil War, the degree of resistance the Bolsheviks encountered in the Muslim territories made them wary of trusting these populations save under closely supervised situations. Thus, in Turkestan and the Caucasus, the "national" divisions were actually joint Russian-native ventures, and, in some areas—most particularly in Kazakhstan and the North Caucasus—the native population was not even made subject to the draft until 1928. Although throughout the 1920s and 1930s, the *korenizatsiya* principle—the introduction of non-Russian populations at all levels in all sectors of the economy, Party, and society—remained in effect and was applied to the territorial divisions of the all-union army.[2]

There is little evidence the ideals of *korenizatsiya* led to any sort of all-out effort to train and maintain a non-Russian officer corps. When in 1938 the national formations were replaced by *kadrovyy prinstsip*—placing new draftees into the first available military slots—there were very few national officers available to disperse throughout the army, and the armed forces remained commanded and dominated by Russians. The Russian language was the sole language of command, and admission to the various officer training schools—as well as promotion up through the ranks—became definitionally linked to Russian-language competency. This remains the situation even today. It was briefly departed from during World War II when two Kazakh divisions and one division each of Uzbeks, Tadzhiks, and Azeris were formed, allegedly to mobilize more quickly these populations to serve at the front. The actual motivation for this action seems to have been to increase the loyalty and dedication of the Muslim fighters who were led by noncommissioned officers of their own nationality, received commands in both Russian and their native languages, and were subjected to patriotic propaganda in their native languages.[3]

Shortly after the conclusion of World War II, these national brigades were disbanded and the army returned to the principle of assigning individual recruits to the first available spaces. Furthermore, in the post-World War II period there has been an increased emphasis on the army as a national ideological school. The army's role in the creation of Soviet patriotism is continually underscored in the Soviet press as well as in the military training literature. Of particular importance is the special role played by the army in the socialization of non-Russian nationalities. This role is constantly restated in the political literature, but probably the most succinct statement was made by Brezhnev himself in his speech marking the fiftieth anniversary of the Soviet federation:

> Our army is a special one. It is a school for international-
> ism, instilling sentiments of fraternity, solidarity, and mutual
> respect for all nations and nationalities of the Soviet Union.
> Our armed forces form a single family, the living embodi-
> ment of socialist internationalism.[4]

There are various reasons for the increased attention to political sociali- zation in recent years. Undoubtedly, one reason is the new role created for the Soviet Army by the emergence of Eastern Europe and the creation of the Warsaw Pact. This routinely places the Soviet Army outside the borders of the Soviet state and makes it a representa- tive of socialism for the more politically unstable populations of Eastern Europe. Yet another reason, of greater relevance to this arti- cle, consists of the deep reservoirs of nationalism which were revealed throughout the Soviet Union in the wake of Khrushchev's "thaw." The relaxation of tensions led the leadership to confront the widespread and pervasive nature of nationalist ties in the Baltic and the Ukraine. Recent evidence points to the conclusion that the Muslim nationalities are not as quiescent as previously understood but are in fact increasingly concerned with the preservation of their secular and religious traditions even when this means opposing the official Soviet ideology as stated by Moscow.[5]

Furthermore, the change in the conscription law in 1967 magnified the problems caused by the imperfect political socialization achieved by the national schools. The new draft law reaffirmed that military service should be accomplished in ethnically mixed units with Russian as the sole language of command and continued the charge to the Soviet Army that these units were to serve as the basis of political integration. However, this was to be accomplished in 2 years instead of the previous 3, and the age of military service was dropped to 18. To compensate for the reduced term of conscription, Soviet youths aged 16 through 18 were subjected to compulsory preinduction training in military rules and customs, the handling of small arms, cartography, and political propaganda work. This is carried out in some 300,000 branches of *DOSAAF* (the All-Union Voluntary Society for Assistance to the Army, Air Forces, and Navy). This places a great deal more responsibility in the hands of the national minority cadre not only to train the potential recruits in the Russian language but also to give them their major preparation for military service.

The role assigned to the *DOSAAF* schools, as well as the functioning of the entire socialization process, take on new importance when one considers the changing demographic structure of the Soviet Armed Forces. Estimates made in 1975 by demographer Dr. Murray Feshbach project that by the year 2000, approximately one-third of the new military conscriptees will come from the southern region of the Soviet Union; i.e., Central Asia, Kazakhstan, and the Caucasus.[6] In a more recent estimate, Dr. Feshbach further refines the earlier prediction and asserts that Central Asia and Kazakhstan will account for 19.5 percent of the 18–year-old male population in 1980, 23.7 percent in 1987, and 26.3 percent in the year 2000. He projects that in that same year, the Transcaucasus will account for 6.9 percent of the draft age population.[7] Over this period, however, the total manpower pool will grow smaller. Assuming the Soviets wish to keep the size of the armed forces constant at about 4 million people, they will have to go from drafting approximately 80 percent of the 18–year-olds to over 93 percent of the draft eligible population. This means that even if there were some desire to underrepresent selectively the Muslim population in the armed forces in an attempt to keep the tenor more Russian (and there are absolutely no data to support the assumption the Soviets have this intention), it would be nearly impossible for them to do so while keeping constant the total number of men under arms. Looking further into the twenty-first century, the percentage of draftees from Muslim national backgrounds will continue to grow at a rapid rate. Projections made from the 1970 census show the population from the 4 core republics of Central Asia (Uzbekistan, Tadzhikstan, Kirghizia, and Turkmenistan) more than doubling by the year 2000, and the total number of Muslims in the Soviet Union in the year 2000 has been estimated at 76.8 million, or 24.8 percent of the population.[8] Although preliminary figures from the 1979 census indicate some drop in the birthrate in the Muslim territories, the Muslim nationalities are still reproducing at a rate 3 to 5 times greater than their Slavic and Baltic counterparts; if earlier projections are slightly high, they still indicate the direction of things to come. In the immediate future the increased percentage of non-Russian conscripts in the armed forces places some rather severe strains on the system of military training as well as the actual functioning of the armed forces in potential combat situations. The most striking problem is Russian-language training. At the time of the 1970 census, only 24 percent of the non-Russian population in the Soviet Union were considered to be fluent in Russian; in Central Asia, only about 15 percent of the Uzbeks, Tadzhiks, and Turkmen were able to speak Russian fluently.[9] The entire decade of the 1970s has witnessed a virtually nonstop attack by the center on the weakness of Russian language training in the national regions. Of the Muslim national regions, Turkmenistan and Kirghizia have come in for special criticism.[10] Summary data published for the 1979 census reflect what must be a marked improvement in Russian language education in the national regions as they show 25–30 percent of the Tadzhik, Turkmen, and Kirghiz population reporting they speak Russian as a second language. The figures for Uzbekistan jump from 14.5 percent to 49.5 percent; this is so much greater than the advances made elsewhere, however, that I look on them with suspicion. Nonetheless, even the 1979 figures reflect what Soviet observers themselves report—the level of Russian language proficiency of the recruits from the national regions is insufficient. To quote from a 1978 article written by a teacher in the Ural State Pedagogical Institute: "Language preparation of students to serve in the Soviet Army is at the present time one of the gravest problems which confronts the national schools."[11] The author goes on to argue the "graduates of the national schools are unable for a long time to be given responsible tasks in the army and when possible they are assigned to the service divisions."[12] Western analysts have made mention of the problems of non-Russian officers not being able to understand commands in Russian and the general difficulty of doing political work among soldiers with a poor command of the language.[13] Still other Soviet sources claim that even Central Asian students who have completed high school do not know enough Russian to obtain specialized training or, more importantly, to master military regulations.[14] As the number of non-Russian soldiers in the army continues to grow, so does the seriousness of the threat implicit in the poor command of Russian by such recruits.

The recruits from the Muslim nationalities also enter the armed forces with less education on the average than do their Russian counterparts. Breakdowns by nationality are not yet available for data on education for the 1979 census, but the 1970 statistics report rather striking differences between the Russians and the Central Asians in particular.[15] In the case of the Russians, 534 of every 1,000 males over 10 years of age had some secondary or higher education; the figures for the Central Asians ranged from a high of 485 for the Turkmen to a low of 411 for the Uzbeks. The problems posed by the differences of educational achievement become even more acute when one first considers the language problem: the education completed by most members of the national minorities was in their own language and did not necessarily enable them to read or understand the technical vocabulary of the military training manuals, and the general educational quality of the rural schools in Central Asia is reputed to be considerably lower than those in the Russian regions. This poses severe problems for those in charge of manpower deployment for the armed forces; the traditional ploy of assigning new Central Asian recruits to service and construction brigades cannot work for a massively expanded Central Asian contingent. Some portion of the Muslim recruits have to be dispatched to combat divisions or technologically more advanced jobs or the jobs themselves must be scaled down as there are fewer skilled Russian recruits to fill them.

One of the most serious problems posed by the demographic changes in the Soviet army is the greater challenge to the political education network. The Soviets are quite explicit that "the military training of the Soviet Armed Forces runs parallel with their political education."[16] The armed forces exist, of course, primarily to defend and advance the military interests of the Soviet Union, but, because of the ideological nature of the Soviet Union and the fact there is universal male conscription, the military serves as the last opportunity for the state to be assured its future citizens have been socialized properly. As stated by a recent Soviet military historian, "Soviet military education and training lay emphasis on the formation among armed forces personnel of a Marxist–Leninist world outlook, political awareness, and a clear understanding of their duty to their country."[17] Every Soviet soldier is required to attend a two–hour political lecture twice a week. In recent years, the military press and professional journals have devoted a lot of coverage to the need to improve the quality and the amount of the propaganda work which has been done among the enlisted men.[18] Although much of this literature does not focus directly on the problems posed by the nationalities—the existence of a multinational army is applauded officially as a positive achievement—it would be difficult for the propaganda officers to single out national minority soldiers. However, it is hard to believe it is coincidental that the increased attention to problems of political education comes at the very time the Soviet Army is changing its ethnic complexion. Indeed, there are, in fact, some references in the literature, albeit unobtrusively placed, to the special problems of political socialization faced by the non-Russian soldiers. There is discussion of the difficulties of propaganda work among those nationalities, particularly the Central Asians, who do not understand the content of the talks. It is noted that these soldiers are often ostracized by their Russian counterparts because of their strange language and seemingly funny ways.[19] Furthermore, the problems of doing propaganda work among the minority nationalities are magnified by the low level of political education these recruits received in their local *DOSAAF* schools. One Soviet source complains that even when bilingual military reserve officers are present, all the teaching aids (texts and audio-visual materials) are in Russian—not even the most basic military dictionaries and lexicons have been translated into the national languages.[20]

One topic which is pointedly ignored in the Soviet literature is the suspicion with which the regime views many of the non-Russian recruits. It is quite apparent the Soviet authorities, recalling national minority opposition to Bolshevik rule, have not forgotten the long legacy of Russian–Muslim antagonism. During the Civil War, the majority of the Central Asians supported the Basmachi, a revolt by Turkestanis against Bolshevik rule which prevented the Soviets from taking effective control of this territory until 1924. There were widespread periodic outbursts of armed resistance in Turkestan for another decade, and a situation of near civil war existed during the period of collectivization.[21] Even at the time of the mobilization of non-Russians into the armed forces in 1942, some former Basmachi leaders led Tadzhik resistance to the draft.[22] There are also some reports of Basmachi resistance in Turkmenistan in the early 1950s during Stalin's final reassertion of political control. The history of Russian-Muslim relations in the North Caucasus is equally marred by periodic outbursts of anti-Russian violence; the Soviets were so convinced there had been substantial Muslim disloyalty during the Nazi occupation of the Caucasus and the Crimea, the entire Crimean Tatar people as well as several North Caucasian groups—including the Chechen, the Ingush, and the Khabardins—were deported *en masse* following the reconquest of their territories by the Red Army.[23] There has also been suspicion of the Muslims due to the defections to the Nazis of a number of non-Russian prisoners of war. Whether or not the incidents of collaboration and defection during World War II were appreciably greater among the Muslims than among other non-Russians (the Ukrainians, of course, come to mind in this regard) or the Russians themselves is of course open to question; the Soviets seem to have overreacted to the Muslim transgressions. In general, they view the problem of the socialization of these populations as a more difficult and necessary one if Muslim soldiers are to be assigned to positions of political sensitivity.

It is necessary at least to query whether the Soviet fears about the loyalty of the Muslim national minorites are well-founded; whether potential recruits from Central Asia and the Caucasus can be expected to be less loyal than their Russian counterparts. Of course, the complete absence of empirical data about the political beliefs of Soviet soldiers—or anyone else for that matter—makes it difficult to reach conclusive statements. However, it seems quite apparent to a student

of Soviet Islam that, although the Muslim minorities are not definitionally less loyal than their Russian counterparts, the loyalty they feel
to the Soviet Union is certainly quite different and still contains strong
elements of loyalty to their own national past. Official Soviet patriotism is infused with a sense of loyalty to Russia, a point which was
stressed throughout the Second World War when the sanctity of the
motherland had been violated by fascist invaders. But even today, this
is an important theme, and the leading role of the Russian people in the
building of communism is an implicit precept of Soviet patriotism
which poses a problem for all national minorities. As Brezhnev stated
in his speech celebrating the fiftieth anniversary of the Soviet federation:

> The party was aware that this line (i.e., economic, cultural
> and socio-economic development) could be implemented in
> practice only through great and all-round assistance to the
> once oppressed nations and nationalities by the more
> advanced parts of the country, above all, the Russian people
> and its working class.[24]

Officially, this thesis is endorsed by the leaders of the Central Asian
communist parties. As First Secretary of the Communist Party of
Uzbekistan Rashidov wrote in an article in the 23 May 1980 issue of
Pravda, the "forcible imposition" of Russian language and Russian culture upon the peoples of Central Asia is a myth perpetuated by anti-
communists. He goes on to argue:

> Every socialist nation selects from the culture of other
> peoples all the best features that it finds acceptable, absorbs
> them, and makes these good elements a component part of
> its national culture . . . . Can this be considered to be an
> 'infringement' of our national culture? Certainly not.
> Through their creative adoption of the forms and media of
> other peoples' culture, the Uzbek people have raised their
> culture to a new and higher level.[25]

How pervasive Rashidov's attitudes are among the leadership of the
Central Asian Republic Communist Party membership, let alone among
the nonparty population, is more difficult to know. However, even if
his thesis is accepted, it is clear from most other indications that the
party leadership of each of the national republics is committed to
preserving the record of its own national past—albeit in a form which
is consistent with the tenets of socialism—and many of the Central
Asian leaders have been rebuked by Moscow for refusing to give adequate credit to the leading role of Russia, Russian workers, and Russian
culture in the building of communism in their republics.[26] This is not
meant to imply the party leadership in Central Asia is disloyal or anti-
communist, but simply that some are uncomfortable with the heavily

Russo-centrist view of the official political ideology of which the military socialization literature is representative. If the political attitudes of the party elite are being called into question, what can we expect of the beliefs of youth, particularly those from the rural areas who are as influenced by Islam as they are by party teachings? Recent Soviet studies—the most striking of which is the 1978 book by T. Saydbayev, *Islam i obshchestvo* [Islam and Society]—portray Islam as a far more influential force in forming and influencing the attitudes of the Central Asian and Caucasian populations than we in the West previously believed. It is not clear whether this is an instance of religious revival or the realization by the Soviet authorities that in order to counter the authority and influence enjoyed by both official and illegal clergy, the problem of Islam must be addressed head on. According to Saydbayev, up to 50 percent of the rural population in various regions of Central Asia are willing to be identified as believers in Islam; he goes on to argue that Islam is a far more pervasive force among youth than is Christianity: 10–15 percent of the Muslim youth identify themselves as believers, whereas only 1–1.5 percent of Russian and Ukrainian youth are willing to be identified publicly with Orthodoxy.[27] There are other data to support these conclusions. A 1971 study in Kirghizia noted that about 20 percent of a sample of pedagogical institute students expressed ties to Islam; a 1973 study in Karakalpakia reported that over 50 percent of the population aged 18–30 surveyed had identified with Islam.[28] Finally, a more recent study of religion in Turkmenistan maintained that the rural population continued to retain strong ties to Islam even when relocated to an urban environment,[29] a finding which raises the question of whether the military experience is enough to undo previous socialization.

It seems evident the pattern of socialization to which Muslim youth are exposed is quite different from that of Russian youth. The educational experience may be similar, using what are at least purported to be standardized curricula, even while being conducted in a different language. Nevertheless, most other aspects of the socialization experience are certainly different. The official religious establishment of Central Asia and the Caucasus—the state-recognized muftiates or ecclesiastical administrations—try to maintain a very public presence and seek to influence the thoughts and actions of believers and nonbelievers alike. The doctrine they preach is undoubtedly too conciliatory for the most observant Muslims, hence the phenomena of illegal clergy and the persistence of Sufi orders in the countryside. However, while they accept the leadership of the Soviet Communist Party and the superiority of its ideology to that of any other secular force, their pronouncements are couched in religious terms and extol the virtue of Islam and the need to lead a religious life. Their goal is to merge the secular and the spiritual and to create a synthesis acceptable to both party and believer. A good example of this strategy is the speech by

Sheikh-ul-Islam Aliaga Suleiman-zade, former Chairman of the Ecclesiastical Administration of the Muslims of Transcaucasia, on the fiftieth anniversary of the founding of the Soviet federation:

> The 50 years of existence of our multinational state, with the permission of gracious and merciful Allah, have been years of the development of the national economy and the country's military might and of improvements in the population's well-being and culture. By the will of Allah, Soviet science has moved to the forefront of the development of human thought. Freedom, equality, fraternity, and friendship among nations and nationalities have triumphed. All this is in keeping with the holy Koran and is being accomplished with Allah's blessing.[30]

The official clergy seems to be following a twofold strategy. On an ideological level, they are determined to demonstrate the ways in which Soviet ideology and Koranic teachings are mutually supportive. On a more pragmatic level, they have sought to depict most Muslim rituals and observances of Muslim holidays as national customs. In the latter regard, they have been extremely successful. Throughout Central Asia, work stops during the celebrations of the Kurbanbairam and the Uraz-bairam, and Ramadan in Central Asia and Muharram in Azerbaijian are considered special periods when public manifestations of religious observance are commonplace. The mosques are filled and crowds of thousands have been reported in the streets.[31] Furthermore, the practice of the Muslim ritual of circumcision is universal for males and is truly understood as a national custom. More difficult to characterize, but equally widespread, is the practice of burial in consecrated soil.

It is thus rather easy to conclude that the political culture of the Muslim nationalities is distinct from that of the Russian and other European nationalities. They are not definitionally less loyal to the Soviet state; there is every reason to believe they strongly identify with it as their homeland. For the Muslims—practicing ones—loyalty to the Soviet Union is accompanied by loyalty to other Muslims and even to the tribe or subnationality. This does not make them anti-Russian or anti-Soviet, but it does make the Russo-centered political socialization engaged in by the armed forces a bit further from their experiential base, thus complicating the whole process of their socialization by professional propagandists.

It is also quite possible the difference in world views between Russians and Muslims makes the whole experience of service in the armed forces less attractive to the latter. The two years the Central Asian or Caucasian draftee gives up are years in which he is separated from his home, his culture, and his language. He receives a greater Russian language competency and quite possibly some technical training, and these skills increase his potential for mobility upon discharge both to cities within his own republic and to other parts of the Soviet Union as well. There is no evidence, however, that the Muslim nationalities are interested in acquiring this mobility. In fact, the little evidence available points to the opposite conclusion. The Central Asian nationalities have the lowest rate of urbanization of any group in the Soviet Union, and—in contrast to the situation in European Russia—Muslim youths are motivated to move to the cities only with difficulty. A 1975 study by Arutuyan showed that whereas 16 percent of the rural youth surveyed in Kaliningrad Oblast intended to move to the city in the near future, only 5.5 percent of rural Uzbek youth surveyed expressed a similar interest.[32] Nevertheless, while the Central Asian and Caucasian youth may not be eager to serve and may not gain particularly as a result of the experience, there is little evidence they resist military service.[33]

Despite all the Soviet rhetoric about the multinational quality of the armed forces, there is little actual data to support the conclusion the army serves as an effective means of integrating the national minorities into the official Russian-dominated political culture and ideology. Major cultural differences remain between Central Asians and Russians who have served together in the armed forces, and there is no evidence Russians and non-Russians in the same military units even associate. What scanty evidence does exist seems to point to exclusionary associational patterns against and by national minorities.[34] In a recent article, Professor Teresa Rakowska–Harmstone argues that the time served by Central Asians not only fails to increase Soviet patriotism but rather (by placing Tadzhiks, Turkmen, Kazakhs, Kirghiz, and Uzbeks in touch) fosters instead a stronger sense of Muslim solidarity. Certainly, the language training the Central Asians are exposed to, even within the armed forces, is not sufficient to permit the subsequent integration of Muslim youth.[35]

It is hard to know precisely why the military experience does not seem to be a particularly useful one in achieving the socialization and integration of the Muslim nationalities. One reason is probably the fact Muslims find it difficult to identify with the entire experience. The army is in virtually all respects a Russian institution. Russian is the sole language of command, and all instruction or materials Soviet soliders receive are in Russian, thus making comprehension difficult for most of the Central Asian and Azeri recruits. The new recruit is placed in a multinational unit, but Russians comprise the majority of the enlisted men and an overwhelming percentage of the officers. There is almost no published data on the ethnic composition of the officer corps, but the scanty evidence available supports the notion the upper ranks of the army—and certainly the Soviet General Staff—are predominantly Slavic. The non-European nationalities are more prevalent in the lower ranks and among the noncommissioned officers.[36] The low representation of national minorities in the officer corps can be explained at least partly on linguistic grounds: most non-Slavic high school graduates lack the Russian competency necessary to pass the entrance examinations to the various officer candidate schools, graduation from which is a prerequisite for professional military service. The absence of significant representation of Muslim nationals in the officer corps does not seem to impede the present functioning of the armed forces, but, as the Soviets themselves realize, it may have more serious implications for the future. The Soviets stress that the major political role of the officer is the example he sets for the enlisted men under him.[37] The absence of officer role models for the Central Asians and other Muslims will become more serious as the percentage of these nationalities in the enlisted ranks of the armed forces increases.

In the case of the Soviet invasion of Afghanistan, the potential advantages of Central Asian officers became readily apparent as the Uzbek and Tadzhik lieutenants and captains, serving as interpreters and advisers to the fraternal Afghan army, became natural intermediaries for the Russian senior officers. Their presence enabled the Soviets to portray the USSR as a multi-ethnic state, a nation which is part of Asia as well as Europe. With the level of opposition the Soviets encountered, it is difficult to ascertain whether or not any psychological advantage accrued to them because of this. The Afghan freedom fighters were quick to respond with allegations the Soviet Union was an oppressor of Muslims. The presence of Central Asians in the armed forces, however, certainly aided communications with the Afghan forces and the Afghan population in general.

Reports about the sympathies and performance of Central Asian enlisted men in Afghanistan are varied and contradictory. It seems that in the early days of the fighting—December 1979 and January 1980— local Category II and Category III divisions with large numbers of Central Asians were assigned to Afghanistan. They were indoctrinated to believe they were fighting to free their kinsmen (there are Uzbeks, Kirghiz, and a large Tadzhik community in Afghanistan) from an oppressive regime and that the new regime for which they were fighting was socialist and would defend the rights of Muslims— allegations which presumably would be viewed favorably by the Soviet Central Asians. However, after a few months of fighting, the Central Asian troops seem to have become less than committed to the Soviet cause; in February, the Western press was filled with reports of troop movements from Afghanistan and the replacement of Central Asians with troops from the Baltic republics and Western Russia. This can be explained in part by the fact the initial invasion force consisted of large numbers of reservists who had completed their 90–day tour of duty and were consequently replaced by regular forces. However, there seems to have been some dissatisfaction on the part of the Russian command with its Muslim troops for a variety of reasons: some Central Asians fell victim to anti-Turkish opposition on the part of the Pushtun; others found it difficult to fire on Uzbek or Tadzhik rebels or to raze their villages when ordered to do so; and still others, upon learning more about the internal situation in Afghanistan, decided they had greater sympathy for the Muslim rebels than for the socialist Afghan government.[38]

For their part, the Soviets went to great trouble in their own military press to refute as anti-communist propaganda charges that they were championing forces against Islam.[39] It is clear these articles were for internal Soviet consumption, but whether they were intended as motivation for the Muslim minorities is difficult to determine. If they were then the Soviets have introduced a dramatically new turn in their propaganda efforts. While they have previously gone to great lengths abroad to be seen as defenders of Islam, they have been reluctant at home to use religion as a source of motivation. Finally, the implications of the Soviet experience in Afghanistan for any future military incursions are unclear. The Soviets experienced mixed success in using Muslim soldiers in a Muslim nation; in Afghanistan, the Soviet Muslims clearly represented the "higher culture." It is difficult to predict how loyal Soviet Muslims would be if they were dispatched to fight in a Muslim country which had a comparable or nearly comparable level of economic development, particularly if such a country were revered as a center of Islam.

It is still too early to tell how the Soviets themselves evaluate the performance of the Muslim nationals in Afghanistan, what level of loyalty and support they expected, and whether they were disappointed by the mixed success they experienced. Nor is it possible to know what efforts will be made to improve the integration of the Central Asians and other Muslims within the armed forces within the future. From the vantage point of a foreign observer, the strategy the Soviets seem to be following is to place most of their hopes upon improved language training. In the past five years, there has been even more attention devoted to the problem of dual-language education. In 1975, a major conference was held to devise ways to improve Russian language training in the secondary and higher educational institutions in the national regions. Several new publications designed to aid Russian-language teachers in the national schools have sprung up. However, articles dealing with the problems of Russian-language education for future servicemen underscore the magnitude of the problem. As a language teacher from Kazakhstan wrote:

> Thus, there stands the question about the complex resolution of language preparation of students of the national schools for service in the ranks of the Soviet Army. Its resolution lies not only in lessons of Russian language and literature but also the process of the entire activity of the pedagogical collective of the school and upper division of the community.[40]

480-900 0 - 85 - 12

The solution he suggests would require the complete rethinking of the Russian language curricula to include military vocabulary and patriotic themes throughout. Furthermore, he recommends language classes be taught with the total submersion of the student in Russian. The goals of political education, he recommends, should also receive support throughout the student's educational program, and military themes should be integrated into the texts of other fields. Such a strategy would be extremely costly, and it is not clear whether the regime is willing or able to divert the necessary resources to achieve a truly bilingual society. Furthermore, even if bilingual education becomes a reality, the larger political goals of the Soviet Armed Forces might still fail to be achieved. The armed services would be functionally integrated—i.e., composed of enlisted men capable of understanding Russian language commands and executing most technical tasks—but, given the culturally diverse nature of the Soviet Union and particularly the pervasive qualities of Islam among the Muslim nationalities, I am less confident the Soviets could ever achieve the desired uniformity of political socialization. Hence, I believe such statements as that by the late Marshal Grechko which noted "in the course of socialist construction . . . in our country, there has occurred the most complete coming together of nations and peoples, and there has been formed a new historical grouping of people, the Soviet people" remain merely assertive of a goal unlikely to become a reality in the foreseeable future.[41] The question then remains: Will the Soviets change their strategy in order to create a "Soviet" consciousness, or will they simply accept the ethnic and cultural diversity of their population and be content with a less than perfect socialization process?

Notes

1. On the demographic problem, see Murray Feshbach and Stephen Rapawy, "Soviet Population and Manpower Trends and Policies," in *Soviet Economy in a New Perspective,* Joint Economic Committee US Congress, 14 October 1976, pp. 113–154 (hereafter cited as Feshbach and Rapawy); Murray Feshbach, "The Structure and Composition of the Soviet Industrial Force," NATO Directorate of Economic Affairs, 1980, pp. 59–69 (hereafter cited as Feshbach).
2. The army was so reorganized in 1924.
3. It is worth noting that the 4 May 1980 issue of *Krasnaya zvezda* [Red Star] recalled the positive impact of native language propaganda work during World War II.
4. Helene Carrere D'Encausse, *Decline of an Empire* (New York, 1979), p. 160 (hereafter cited as Carrere D'Encausse).
5. See Martha Brill Olcott, "The Development of Nationalism in Kazakhstan," unpublished paper.
6. Feshbach and Rapawy, p. 148.
7. Feshbach, p. 58.
8. Ibid., p. 58.
9. Feshbach and Rapawy, p. 148.
10. *Current Digest of the Soviet Press,* Vol. 24, No. 43 (1973), p. 23, and *Current Digest of the Soviet Press,* No. 51, p. 23.

11. R. A. Abuzyarov, "Yazykovya podgotovka uchashchikhsya v protsesse voyenno-patrioticheskogo vospitaniya [Language Preparation of Pupils in the Process of Military–Patriotic Education]," *Russkiy yazyk v natsional'noy shkole* [Russian Language in the National School], No. 4, 1978, p. 64, hereafter cited as Abuzyarov.
12. Ibid., p. 65.
13. Herbert Goldhamer, *The Soviet Soldier* (New York: Crane and Russak, 1975), p. 188 (hereafter cited as Goldhamer).
14. F. L. Subanova, "Chtoby svobodno vladet' russkoy rech'yu" [In Order to Speak Russian Fluently], *Russkiy yazyk v natsional'noy shkole*, No. 4, 1978, p. 54.
15. *Itogi vsesoyuznoy perepisi naseleniya 1970 goda, t. 4, Natsional'nyy sostav naseleniya SSSR* [Totals of the All-Union Census of Population for 1970, Vol. 4, National Structure of the Population of the USSR] (Moscow, 1973), pp. 393–405.
16. M. Ruban, *The Soviet School of Courage and Warcraft* (Moscow, 1976), p. 27, hereafter cited as Ruban.
17. Ibid., p. 13.
18. See 5 June 1980 issue of *Krasnaya zvezda* for the report of a recent conference on this theme.
19. Goldhamer, p. 188.
20. Abuzyarov, p. 166.
21. See Martha Brill Olcott, "The Basmachi or Freemen's Movement in Turkestan, 1918–1924," *Soviet Studies*, forthcoming, 1981.
22. N. Rutych, "Afganistan i Rossiya" [Afghanistan and Russia], *Posev* [Crops], No. 5, 1980, p. 48.
23. See Aleksandr Nekrich, *The Punished Peoples* (New York, 1978).
24. V. Shetsov, *Nations and Nationalities in Socialist Society* (Moscow, 1974), p. 125.
25. *Current Digest of the Soviet Press*, Vol. 32, No. 21, p. 3.
26. See *Current Digest of the Soviet Press*, Vol. 26, No. 26, p. 33, for some attacks against the official Kazakh literary establishment.
27. T. Saydbayev, *Islam i obshchestvo* [Islam and Society] (Moscow, 1978), pp. 180–181.
28. Zh. Bazarbayev, *Sekulyarizatsiya naseleniya sotsialisticheskoy karakalpakii* [The Secularization of the Population of Socialist Karakalpakia] (Nukus, 1973), p. 53.
29. N. Bayramsakhatov, *Novyy byt i islam* [The New Life and Islam] (Moscow, 1979), p. 17.
30. *Current Digest of the Soviet Press*, Vol. 31, No. 13, p. 9.
31. N. Ashirov, *Islam i natsii* [Islam and Nation] (Moscow, 1975), p. 65.
32. As quoted by Feshbach and Rapawy, p. 125.
33. Carrere D'Encausse, p. 160.
34. See V. Vladimirov, "Senior Lieutenant Askar Satarov," *Soviet Military Review*, No. 11, 1972, pp. 28–31, for a brief portrait of Central Asian associational patterns.
35. Teresa Rakowska–Harmstone, "The Soviet Army as the Instrument of National Integration," in John Erickson, ed., *Soviet Military Manpower and Performance* (Hamden, 1979), p. 148.
36. Ibid., pp. 143–144. Rakowska–Harmstone reports that in 1943, 90 percent of the officer corps was Russian; of the 59 generals appointed between 1940 and 1975, only two had Turkic last names.
37. See M. Sobolev, *Partiynaya organizatsiya v voinskom kollektive* [Party Organization in a Military Collective] (Moscow, 1977), where this theme is repeated throughout the first half of the book.
38. Alexandre Bennigsen, "Soviet Muslims and the World of Islam," *Problems of Communism*, March/April 1980, p. 47.
39. *Krasnaya zvezda*, 29 June 1980.
40. Abuzyarov, p. 69.
41. *Armiya bratstva narodov* [The Army Fraternity of Peoples] (Moscow, 1972), p. 21.

The Reliability of the Warsaw Pact Armies*

Ivan Volgyes

More than 6 decades have passed since the successful October Revolution led by the Bolsheviks created the first Soviet state in Russia, and more than 35 years have passed since the first communist states were created in the heart of Eastern Europe by the victorious Soviet armies. By any test of time, such historical periods are certainly adequate for impassioned historical analyses dealing with these communist systems and with the relationship of the military and society in Eastern Europe. Certainly, such a historical period seems to be sufficient to be able to discern the "uniqueness" or "peculiarities" of the relationship between politics and the military; this article attempts to accomplish this task in a brief form, constrained by space, time, and research limitations. The main purposes of this article, then, are

1. To examine the peculiarities of political-military relationships within the communist states of Eastern Europe;
2. To discuss the specificities of the role of the armed forces within the alliance known as the Warsaw Pact;
3. To discuss the reliability of these forces in domestic or international politics; and
4. To attempt to provide a framework for the future delineation of the concept of reliability as an operational category.

Peculiarities of Communist Military Politics

The armed forces of the communist states of Eastern Europe at first glance obviously fulfill the traditional roles played by armed forces everywhere: they provide the backbone of domestic defense of the regime against internal and external enemies. There is obviously nothing peculiar about such a role; the army of every state and every nation fulfills these same functions.[1] Moreover, the armies in the states under consideration, as elsewhere, are convincing interest groups constraining the regimes' ability to advance in areas other than military might, to agitate for an increase in military might, and to ally themselves with

---

*This is an updated version of several studies, including "Military Politics of the Warsaw Pact Armies," in Morris Janowitz, etc., *Civilian Military Relations: Regional Perspectives* (Beverly Hills: Sage, 1982) and several articles coauthored with Dale Herspring and appearing in *Armed Forces and Society* (Winter 1980; Spring 1977).

the "steel and coal" complexes for ever greater strengthening of the "commanding heights" of industry.[2] Furthermore, just as in many other developing states, in all of these states the armies are purposive social instruments whose roles in the transformation of the maintenance of social equilibrium are major contributions to the strength of the nation.[3] In all these traditional contributions, the armies of Eastern Europe fulfill traditional patterns which can be replicated in just about any society.

Lest we forget, however, there are certain things peculiar in the nature of communist states which determine the relationship of the military and the polity. The first aspect of these peculiarities lies in the nature of the allocation of power in communist states.[4] Although in many states—except in the so-called party-army or army-dominated states—the military and its powers are curtailed by "civilian" considerations, in communist states the role of the military, like the role of other instruments, is subordinated to the communist party in all its manifestations. Much has been said about the subordination of the military to the party through such traditional methods as the use of political officers, or the utilization of the main administration within the party *apparat,* or the double informing activities of the ever-present political spies. At this stage, perhaps, we should merely try to conceptualize this relationship as functionally determined, rather than engaging in futile controversy over the party-army relationship.[5]

The concept of functional determination allows us to view the party-army relationship in a variegated light.[6] In communist polities, to use somewhat outmoded systems analysis terminology, the party controls the input, the output, and the feedback mechanisms of society. The party, in other words, determines the bases on which decisions are made, makes the decisions, and manufactures support for the decisions reached. With respect to the army, however, the party always had—and during the last four decades certainly enlarged—a somewhat different role: it allows—and with some notable exceptions has always allowed—the army to play a role in the input process. I think today it is safe to say the input processes have been more open to army demands than to those of any other apparat, with the possible exception of the political police organs. It is clear, of course, that as the modernization of the technical levels of the armed forces has increased, input has become even greater; complexity has demanded technical expertise and secrecy, and the party has found itself even more reliant on the army which—when the chips are down—it has to trust on the input level.[7]

Remarkably, as the Soviet polity developed, the party also had to open up, to some extent, even the feedback loop of support to "spontaneous" expressions: the army had been genuinely involved in expressing support of or opposition to certain measures instituted by the Party which affected performance of the military as a whole. For example, such "minor" controversies as the percentage of recruit training time devoted to political instruction or the use of conscripts in the physical aspects of "building socialism" certainly have been clear instances where genuine feedback, though channeled, was used as the basis for altering decisions already set.

It is also true, however, that the output processes of decisionmaking have remained closed to the army and have been monopolized by the party *apparat*. The centralism of that process is well-known, and the decisions rendered leave no doubt the army must accept them. And yet, even this process has been refined and tuned during the last decades; today there are two mechanisms which make the process of subordination more palatable to the army as a whole.

The first of these mechanisms relates to the role of the leading personalities of the military complex. The party has been exceedingly careful to ensure military leaders are promoted not merely on the basis of their technical knowledge but also on the basis of their party loyalty. Consequently, a military decisionmaker, regardless of rank, is not placed in his position of authority because of his abilities but because of his Party connections: loyalties *coupled* with military ability. Though this can be said of any sphere of communist power relationships, it is especially true of Soviet and East European military-party power relationships. "Mistakes" of course, will occur: a Zhukov, a Moczar, or a Kiraly may step forward in periods of stress, but the Party has been remarkably successful in judging its military cadres.[8]

The second mechanism of output subordination-palatability refers to the peculiar nature of the Warsaw Pact alliance system within which multinational units are integrated. Here, independent national decisionmaking on military matters is subordinated not merely to national desiderata but also to cross-cutting cleavages within the alliance system.[9] In other words, local decisionmaking on what percentage of the national budget can be devoted to the armed forces is only one element of the process; the military leadership often receives additional "funds" or "equipment" and "training" or "exercise support" from the Warsaw Pact, more specifically from the USSR. Conversely, national-level decisions regarding the percentage of allocations for defense or army-related activities are frequently set at the Pact level rather than at the domestic level. In a sense, of course, this duality creates tensions within the domestic decisionmaking system—e.g., Romania, East Germany or Hungary—but it does lend a certain level of responsibility to the leaders of the armed forces which they otherwise would not possess.

A second aspect of this peculiarity lies in the fact that the armed forces, in general, are supposed to have grown out of the population and are supposed to represent the widest strata in the common national effort to defend the socialist fatherland(s). However, from the outset of the existence of communist power, a rather irrational fear—the fear of

Bonapartism—has plagued the communist leaders.[10] Trotsky's power as the head of the Red Army and Tukhachevskiy's and Zhukov's power combined with their powerful personalities capable of acting against the Party "proper"—e.g., against its leadership—were viewed with an alarm greater than necessary from the perspective of rationality. Nonetheless, this somewhat irrational fear of Bonapartism—based on the mistaken reading of incidents in European history from which incorrect "laws" were deduced, feared, and generalized by people who did not really understand history but wished to alter that which they understood so little—has led to the peculiarity that the Party created two instruments which are the duopolists of power: the army and the political police. The *KGB* and its separate organizations, indeed, are expected to act as checks on the power of the military; in the service of their mission to the Party, they are certainly expected to exercise at least a coequal function in system and subsystem maintenance activities.[11]

Some, of course, would argue this is not unique; Hitler's Germany was also characterized by similar dualities.[12] What is unique, however, in the Soviet and East European cases is that the *KGB* and its various local organs (a) successfully have penetrated and to a great extent control the various armies and (b) retain a cross-national network of control which is truly integrated under Soviet direction to a far greater extent than the control networks in the communist armies in general.[13]

A third important aspect of the peculiarity of the communist alliance system stems from the nature of ideology. Marxism, before the establishment of the Soviet state in 1917—and then internationally before the establishment of the East European communist states in 1945—was a prescriptive ideology; since then it has become descriptive, a tortuous zig-zag of "meaningless" phrases in search of justification for the existence and exercise of power. As the doctrine acquired body and the system territory and as communist encirclement replaced enforced isolation, the presence of the new "fraternal" states had to be justified in the ideology as well.[14] The cautious justification of instilling "socialist patriotism" in the citizenry of the member-states of the alliance systems, as this ideology developed "creatively," comes dangerously close to uncorking the specters of nationalism and the common enemy and—aside from the perspective of Bulgaria—such a possibility is not viewed by the USSR as beneficial to its own existence. Consequently, the USSR and the ruling parties have utilized two major, and more controllable, issues in order to ensure the mastering of the military subsystems: fostering cynicism on the one hand and instilling certain "socialist" values on the other.[15] The fostering of cynical attitudes is unique to Soviet-type systems only insofar as the scope of cynicism is concerned. In other systems, cynicism is an accepted part of the operation of society. Due to the all-comprehensive nature of communist ideology, however, cynicism—the operationalized concept of cognitive dissonance—is mandated for a whole array of human activities. It is, of course, true that for the efficient operation of the communist system, one must drift away from the prescriptive ideology which results from the gross misunderstanding of 19th century history; as the system develops, cynicism, fostered by reality and prophecies which are unfulfillable, must be stressed over idealism and becomes necessary for survival and system maintenance. What *is* unique, however, is that the adoption of cynicism becomes *expected* in all forms of sociopolitical existence, and behavior must conform to values already set in advance.

A concomitant desire to instill *certain* values through the process of socialization as a long-term goal, however, must reinforce the instilling of cynicism mentioned above. As far as the USSR is concerned, it is obvious the leaders care very little about a whole array of value socialization which takes place internally. They do not care if the internal systems in each of these states propagate a wide array of values with differing emphases. The parameters of tolerance relate to two values only: the unquestioned control of society by the party and the nonexistence of unbridled anti-Soviet nationalism. The *necessitas sine qua non,* therefore, which the Soviet elite must instill in the members of the alliance system lies in the socializing of *attitudes which require the army to follow the orders of the party and not act against the USSR and to be prepared to fight "traditional enemies" other than the Russians.* The USSR does not care if a political system in the Warsaw Pact stresses Stalinism or democracy, liberalism or centralism, private farming or state control, private initiative and profit or total socialist control; it only cares that the values of the allies not propel them toward loosening the reins held by the party or turning them away from the existing military-political alliance system. Consequently, with the help of the *KGB* and through benefits, training, and elite status extended to the military, the system must insure the loyalty and reliability of the professional armed forces.

The Warsaw Pact: Systemic Peculiarities

Excellent past studies have dealt with various aspects of the Warsaw Pact as a military alliance. Both classified and unclassified studies in the United States and in Europe have done an admirable job describing the physical dimensions of this impressive alliance system.[16] Based on these studies, intelligent observers certainly can delineate the physical size, organization, and even performance of the Pact. Suffice it to say the Warsaw Pact is composed primarily of armies of communist states whose physical locus is Eastern Europe, whose deployment as a force in action has taken place only in intra-systemic conflict, and whose development and deployment generally have been in accordance with the desires of the major actor of the alliance, the USSR.

Herein lies the first major conceptual problem in the discussion of the alliance system; namely, the problem of whether one can regard this system as a "genuine" alliance or one "imposed upon" the participating states. On the one hand, it should be noted that the very size of the USSR makes its weight in the system so great as to raise serious questions about the importance of such tiny allies as Bulgaria or Hungary. On the other hand, the dominance of the USSR and the distribution of global tasks among the various armies of the Pact (for example, the assignation of global political police training tasks to the East Germans) raises the point that it is a specific type of an alliance system with varied missions.

History, of course, is a limited source of predictive values. It is contradictory at best, and descriptive analyses of past events are useful only as visits of condolence. For history tells us the size of a preponderant ally renders its miniscule partners' role so subordinate, the "true" nature of an alliance becomes obsolete.[17] Although history assures us that such an aberration as the tail wagging the dog is possible, compatible size remains one of the operational concepts for "genuine" alliance systems. And yet the history of this alliance system shows remarkable divergences of opinion on various issues, regardless of actual size. Witness the vehemence of the demand on the part of such states as East Germany and Czechoslovakia for a speedy occupation of Hungary in 1956—far ahead of Soviet shifts in the policy toward occupation versus the divergent attitudes of the variously sized allies in 1968.

The genuineness of the alliance system has also been questioned because it is viewed as being imposed upon the member states. Certainly, there is a great deal of proof the Soviet forces, even after 35 years of presence in the region, are viewed as occupiers: 1956 and 1968 are outstanding examples to prove this point, although in the case of Czechoslovakia the true animosity toward the USSR occurred only *after* 21 August 1968. Some elements of support for the alliance—aside from sheer imposition—however, have come from within the native military establishments and from officers corps which have had continuous existences for more than a quarter of a century. The reason for their support of the system is relatively simple: they have been told the only alternatives to their participation would be retaliation by an angry populace; at best, a neutralization and abolition of the army as a potential defender of the historic nation; and a corresponding end to their power, prestige, and livelihood. Although we will be dealing with this subject later, it is safe to conclude the vast majority of the professional members of the armed forces prefer their present existence to an uncertain future.

It certainly would be unfair for us not to mention some aspects of the Warsaw Pact which are more positive from the communist perspective than the views implied above. Undoubtedly, from time immemorial, there has been a broad spectrum in which "alliances" tended to work; notwithstanding Machiavelli's advice to his prince, alliances have frequently been unipolar and concentrated around a particular actor.[18] Preponderant US or German strength has not brought the NATO alliance's genuineness into question. What brought the Warsaw Pact's genuineness into question has been the political reality of imposed rule upon Eastern Europe, *not* the nature of the military alliance which stemmed from the political imposition created by Soviet occupation. Nonetheless, we must mention that the USSR, in general, has been averse to the institutionalization of the alliance system; informal arrangements are more subject to manipulation by the dominant power. In this sense, though probably only in this sense, the Warsaw Pact can and should be viewed as a "victory" for the non-Soviet actors of the system.[19]

Curiously, there are other aspects of the Warsaw Pact which are "peculiar," though not necessarily counterproductive, from the systemic perspective. One of these is the fact the presence of the alliance system helps psychologically to mitigate the USSR's deep-seated feeling of "loneliness" as the "whipping boy of history." It is a symbolic function, to be sure, but being able to refer to an action undertaken by the "communist alliance system" or the "Warsaw Pact" is preferable to acting alone. Hence, unlike Hungary in 1956, the invasion of Czechoslovakia in 1968 was undertaken by the Warsaw Pact—even if Romania did not participate and the Soviets had to force Hungarian participation on Kadar, who wished to avoid being labeled an "invader" by the Czechoslovak population.[20] In fact, there is a great deal of evidence Bulgaria, East Germany, and Poland agitated *for* intervention *before* the Soviet Politburo was prepared to intervene.[21] Furthermore, the East German and Czechoslovak leaders also urged Soviet intervention in Poland long before Soviet patience finally ran out in December 1981.

Moreover, it is important to recall that the Warsaw Pact also can be regarded as a genuine system because of the great deal of mutual interaction which takes place every day. As mentioned above, the military in each of the member states derives not merely prestige but real, significant benefits from the system: besides plush officers' clubs and special stores, the benefits include the possession and use of the most modern military hardware intended to awe external *as well as* domestic audiences. The more modern and extensive the hardware, the greater the prestige of the domestic controllers of the use of violence. Conversely, the lack of such hardware—for example, antiaircraft or modern missile systems—implies a lack of prestige in the intraalliance scheme of things. In this respect, the USSR is regarded by the national military elites as the source of benefits as well as the source of tension: one gets what the USSR chooses to give, but the USSR does not give as much modern equipment to its allies as it does to some non-member states.

This alliance is also an important contributor to the national power and economic health of at least some of the member states. The allocation of responsibilities for military production—small arms, artillery, tanks, etc.—within the Pact has increased significantly the economic capabilities of such states as East Germany and Czechoslovakia; the net exports of arms produces hard currency or other external trade benefits. There is one more export item as important as hardware exports: military personnel. East Germany's "traditional" role of supplying the developing states—especially those in Africa—with security assistance is certainly far more ubiquitous today than was the past role of the United States. And—in a personal aside—it must be mentioned that the role played by the East German security forces makes CIA training of the *SAVAK* look like child's play in the international setting.

In short, the alliance in Eastern Europe is based on two contradictory elements: (1) imposed rule by a great power which determines both the political context of the domestic environment and the limits of its change, and (2) a system of mutualities and mutual benefits of military-economic relations. The tension existing between these not very creative contradictions comprises the dynamics upon which the alliance system must operate. Precisely for this reason, the management of the alliance system must be certain the values possessed by the individual actors will not contradict the goals of the alliance or the USSR. In other words, the management of the conduct of violence must insure the reliability of the means of violence. It is to this subject we must turn in the third section of this article.

The Concept of Reliability: An Assessment

It would be foolish to say that any one analyst can render a comprehensive judgment concerning the reliability of an ally in an alliance system or of an actor in the domestic environment. The reliability of Western armies in combat or internal political crises is subject to speculation. When we attempt to assess the "reliability" of members of competitive alliance systems, the analysts are constrained by (1) the *secrecy* relating to the Warsaw Pact forces; (2) the *interpretation* based on minimum levels of available information; and (3) the *coloring* of the interpreted findings, be it through the black lens of unwarranted gloom or the rosy hue of wishful thinking.

I should hasten to add that Western analysts are not the only ones constrained by such limitations. To my knowledge, only one major study on the reliability of the Eastern European armed forces in the 1970s has been commissioned for the Soviet General Staff; unfortunately, I have neither seen the study nor have knowledge of its findings. The only comment I have *heard* on it simply stated that the authors of this study also struggled with the notion of reliability and were unable to come up with hard, operationally useful terms.

Let me therefore suggest that the term "reliability" ought to be at least conceptually delimited.[22] Reliability—a "normative commitment to the regime"—in its simplest form can be defined as an *expectation* an actor *under given circumstances* is likely to undertake *or not* undertake certain actions.[23] Reliability, moreover, implies a certain actor can be *trusted* to act or not act *under certain circumstances* in a given manner. Hence, reliability is a symbolic dual set of actions: on the one hand, there is the *expectation* of a certain act by somebody other than the actor; on the other hand, there exists *the action itself.* Reliability, therefore, is predicated upon (1) *the set of values creating the expectation on the part of the groups or individuals that the actor will act in a certain manner* and (2) *the collection of values and attitudes possessed by the actor upon which behavior is based.* Of course, it is recognized that behavior also alters values or at least that alterations in behavior and values can occur simultaneouly in praxis; however, the fact they do occur simultaneously does not alter the duality of the concept in its applicability.[24]

The concept of reliability is also confusing as a result of constraints stemming from external or internal sources. External force can act as a constraint: for many, the force utilized by the USSR to compel its allies to act in a certain manner is sufficient, if applied consistently, to compel certain types of behavior. The type of reliability, however, which operated among the armed forces of the Warsaw Pact states, and which ought to be analyzed and to which reference is made in this article, is a result of value-based behavior on the part of the armed forces. This behavior is predicated upon a certain *choice* in both the domestic and the external environment. The cheapest method of insuring reliability lies in the socialization of behavioral values in the members of the professional military forces.

The meaning of the term "professional military forces" in Eastern Europe and the communist states in general, of course, is varied.[25] The degree of commitment *within* a system to survival of the system, policies pursued, and methods of pursuit also varies among the duopolists of force. For example, the secret police of Hungary, the *AVO,* were far more committed to the survival of the system and to the policies and the methods utilized in pursuing these policies than was the army in 1956. In 1968, in Czechoslovakia, the armed forces and the police were equally minimally committed to the survival of the system, but the interests diverged concerning the methods and the policy goals of the system. On still another level, the armed forces in Romania were opposed to intervention in Czechoslovakia, but there are strong indications the security forces of that state were far less ambivalent about participating in such an attack. And finally, in the case of the Polish crackdown of December 1981, while the "army" fulfilled only transport and traffic monitoring roles, the security forces were 100 percent utilized to break the back of the Polish workers' movement.

Consequently, any study of reliability must concentrate on two different subjects: (1) the expectations of the subsystemic actors at the national decisionmaking levels and the expectations of the decisionmakers at the international system levels; and (2) the behavior of the military on both subsystem and system levels. In other words, any study dealing with the reliability of the military must concentrate on (1) the values and expectations of the national-level decisionmakers; (2) the values and expectations of the Soviet and Warsaw Pact political elites; (3) the value-based behavior of the military and its subunits on the national level of conflict; and (4) the behavior of the military on the international level of conflict. Let me reemphasize that it is just as essential for analysts to concentrate on the expectations of the elite as on the actual or projected behavior of the military instruments. To offer just one example: the belief in the commitment of the army to the regime may impel the decisionmaker to adopt certain policies he may not adopt otherwise. If Ceausescu were not convinced the army would back him up against some "fraternal assistance," he would not risk the adoption of certain anti-Soviet policies. False expectations caused the downfall of Rakosi and Gero in Hungary in 1956 and of Gierek in 1980–1981.

The leadership, of course, is not a unitary category; within it one may find various beliefs, attachments to policies, and goals. Due to the fact that in communist states the principle of democratic centralism continues to obtain, we cannot say a party leadership which loses control over its population will be allowed to remain in power. Consequently, party leadership in this article refers only to an elite remaining in control of political events and following certain externally and internally constrained policies—presumably tolerated by or in accordance with the desires of the USSR.

As indicated above, within the communist elites, the expectations of the armed forces' commitment can be examined at three levels: (1) to the system, (2) to policies pursued, and (3) to methods of pursuit. Within each of these levels of commitment, one can discern two dimensions: national and international.

Commitment to the domestic system refers to the expectations of the elite that the armed forces will defend the system against "enemies of socialism." The elite's belief in a trust of the armed forces is essential in decisions directed toward solving domestic crises with high levels of tension. The perennial question, "What would happen if I called out the army to crush a food riot in, for example, Radom, and it refuses to move out of the barracks?" must have caused the Polish leadership continuous nightmares and acted as a major constraint on the use of the army though not of the security forces.

On the international level, the belief the army will or will not act in defense of the system must cause plenty of worries to the Soviet elite. Nevertheless, the elite has been quite successful in judging the expected behavior of the armed forces of the various Warsaw Pact states. Certainly, the belief in imminent conflict with the Polish armed forces, which place national values higher than "socialist commonwealth" values, has been one of the preponderant reasons for the USSR's continuous efforts during the last 3 to 5 years to bail the sick Polish economy out of its perennial bankruptcy, and the Soviet preference for using the Polish security forces rather than its own armed forces to destroy Solidarity and the democratic movement in 1981–1982 can be understood only in this light. Simultaneously, the expectation the Czechoslovak armed forces would not act in the defense of national over "systemic" values impelled the Soviet leadership in 1968 to put real teeth into the Brezhnev Doctrine by its cannibalistic invasion of Czechoslovakia.

Expectations of commitment on systemic levels rank hierarchically above expectations to back certain policies, although the end results of certain policy pursuits may be a systemic transformation, however unexpected. In general, on the national level the elite expects and can receive the support of its army for policies dictated by the center; however, notable exceptions abound. For example, the Polish armed forces cannot be expected to control effectively food riots by workers, and the Czechoslovak army cannot be expected to shoot at the demonstrators on Wenceslas Square if the latter were to demand the restoration of the "Czech Spring."

On the international level, Soviet leaders are also constrained in adopting policies whose backing would not be assured. The reintroduction of the 1950s practice of placing Soviet advisors all the way to battalion level, for example, would meet strong opposition; the sending of East European troops to Afghanistan would trigger defections; and similar policy adoptions would meet corresponding difficulties.

Finally, the methods of implementation, though hierarchically still on a lower level, are just as important in the eyes of the leadership as it formulates its expectations toward the armed forces. Kadar in 1957 could not have expected army support for his policies, as witnessed by the inordinately high rate of defections and the enormously low number of recruits who stayed on as noncommissioned officers in the Hungarian armed forces. On the other hand, the methods currently employed by the Hungarian leadership can be expected to receive the support of this miniscule force. Ceausescu's methods of control, on the contrary, have to be counterbalanced by a continuous wooing of the army, a task which is quite cumbersome in Romania today.

Internationally, Soviet methods for maintaining the internal status quo or pursuing policies are also causes for concern. While intrabloc conflicts have not come to the fore openly, dissatisfactions regarding the use of force in Afghanistan as a threat to detente have been noted not merely in Romania but also in Hungary and Poland. Although the USSR could count on continuous support for its allocation of specialized responsibilities, it could not expect support for such heavy-handed activities as the sudden increase in political education demanded of the

Warsaw Pact forces since the invasion of Afghanistan. Though the support for or commitment to the methods of implementation ranks the lowest in terms of importance—as in all alliance systems because of the large number of issues involved—this level cannot and should not be neglected if the smooth operation of the Pact is a desired goal.

The reliability of the armed forces when viewed as a behavioral consequence of values is an equally complex task for analysis. In other earlier studies with my good friend Dale Herspring, I already have attempted to outline the concept of behavioral reliability. Let me merely summarize our findings.[26]

Analytically, political reliability in the armed forces of Eastern Europe can be divided into four categories: internal-offensive, internal-defensive, external-defensive, and external-offensive. Before discussing each of these categories, a few caveats are in order. First, political reliability is an analytical ideal type; consequently, no armed forces will ever act completely in accordance with these categories in every situation. Furthermore, military units differ in their degree of reliability within each category; for example, it is possible for one armed forces unit to be highly reliable in the face of an external threat, while another is of only minimal utility to the party in such a situation. Second, internal-offensive reliability is a *sine qua non* for other types of political reliability. A military which is likely to overthrow its own government cannot be relied upon to defend or support the government's policies during a crisis situation. Third, there is nothing teleological or deterministic about these categories. Regression can and has occurred. Fourth, these categories are not necessarily interrelated. For historical and other reasons, it is possible for a country to be high in one category and low in another, while the opposite may be true for a different state.

Internal-offensive reliability refers to the probability significant segments of the professional officer corps will act against the party leadership by attempting a coup d'etat in the furtherance of military interests or will try to force such interests on an unwilling party leadership.

It is important to emphasize that attention is focused upon the professional officer corps; no one can assume the officer corps normally acts and thinks as a monolithic entity. Nor can it be assumed, as some writers have, that party-military relations are primarily characterized by institutional conflict.[27] In this category, the professional officer corps is particularly important; unlike the other three categories of reliability discussed here in which the actions of conscripts are vital, here they are of secondary importance. Officers give orders and engage in bureaucratic politics, and there is little likelihood of a coup if the professional officer corps opposes such a policy. Furthermore, in the normal course of bureaucratic politics, the armed forces in communist as well as noncommunist systems appear to be as divided by intragroup rivalries as are other bureaucratic organizations.[28] Only when either vital military interests are challenged by the party leadership or a serious variance in values develops between the officer corps and the party leadership does the professional military close ranks in acting against or opposing the party leadership; it is only then that serious institutional conflict may result.[29]

Internal-defensive reliability refers to the willingness of the armed forces to support the regime against an internal threat. Externally inspired threats—such as a fifth column—are excluded from this category. Since the military normally will not be called upon to defend the regime against an internal threat unless the situation has already deteriorated badly (when police and security forces have proved unable or unwilling to handle the situation), its response probably will be of vital importance. This is particularly true of an area as traditionally unstable as Eastern Europe.

The role of the conscript looms large in this category. Loyalty to the regime by officers—while vital—will not suffice. A few officers are not likely to dissuade a large, angry crowd of striking workers from attacking party headquarters. Assuming police and security forces are unable to handle the situation, only a large show of force by highly disciplined, well-armed military units is likely to have the desired effect.

The party is often able to enhance the loyalty of the officer corps by offering it rewards not available to the remainder of society, such as special stores and special housing. This is generally not the case with conscripts. In some cases, in an effort to gain conscript loyalty, it is possible to make appeals to patriotic symbols as General Jaruzelski consistently tried after imposition of martial law in 1981. This is not usually possible, however, with internal-defensive reliability. Conscripts come from society, and their loyalty to the regime will be influenced strongly by the dominant political culture (the values, beliefs, and attitudes toward existing political structures in society as a whole. Furthermore, there is an important distinction between the dominant political culture and the official political culture.[30] These young men may be asked to fire on their fellow countrymen—in some cases on their friends and relatives. The conscripts' "definition of the situation" therefore will be important. A regime defined by the populace as a surrogate for a foreign power or as working against the national interest will receive little support. On the other hand, if the populace views the government as its own, has a major stake in it, or feels an external threat demands internal stability, then the populace is likely to support it. Thus, the major question to be asked here is the degree to which the party's official policies coincide with the dominant political culture as evidenced by the conscripts' willingness to carry out party orders.

The non-Soviet Warsaw Pact governments have called on their armed forces on a number of occasions to put down internal disturbances. Unfortunately, from these governments' standpoints, the record over the past 30 years is a rather dismal one. In all seven cases when such disturbances have been noted, the armed forces consistently refused to support the regimes when confronted with a serious internal disturbance. These seven cases include:

Pilsen, 1953—The Czechoslovak army refused to put down the riots.[31]

East Berlin, 1953—Some East German military units reportedly refused to leave their barracks and march against the demonstrators.[32]

Poznan, 1956—Regular army troops refused to disperse rioters (and in some cases joined them), making it necessary to bring in special security forces from Warsaw.[33]

Budapest, 1956—Not only did the army refuse to support the regime when faced with attacks on secret police headquarters,[34] 80 percent of the officer corps refused to sign pledges to the Kadar regime after the Soviets intervened.[35]

Prague, 1969—57.8 percent of the officers under 30 years of age left the army at their own request after the Soviet invasion: the government was forced to rely on security and border troops rather than the regular army to put down anti-Soviet disturbances on the anniversary of the invasion.[36]

Gdansk, 1970—The army strongly resisted involvement in putting down the riots, and—according to one observer—disobeyed Kliszko's demand to use "overwhelming force to put down the demonstrations."[37]

Lodz and Warsaw, 1976—Then Defense Minister Jaruzelski, when asked about the possibility of using army troops to put down the riots, is reported to have stated: "Polish soldiers will not fire on Polish workers." This pattern of action was not broken in 1981–82.

While it is always possible one of the armies under consideration will support the regime in putting down internal disturbances in the future, they are likely to be of only limited utility. Furthermore, based on past experience and assuming the security and police forces are unable to cope with the situation, the regimes concerned appear to have two general choices: either they may call in Soviet troops, or—in those cases where the presence of the Soviet Army would serve only to exacerbate the situation—they may be forced to capitulate partially to the demands of the rioters. The latter was the course selected by the Polish government in 1976 when price rises were rescinded, and the same capitulation has been repeatedly observed in 1980. The governments of Eastern Europe have a long way to go to convince their own armed forces they are concerned primarily with the national interest in the internal sphere and are thus worthy of support against internal opponents; only when ambivalent positions are held by the army can such regimes as that of Jaruzelski's count on the army's passivity.

External-defensive reliability refers to the probability the armed forces will defend the state against external threats. As was the case with internal-defensive reliability, loyalty by the officer corps, while necessary, is not sufficient; the role of the conscript is also very important. Thus, in attempting to ascertain the probability of the armed forces' support for the party in this situation, the attitudes of society at large play a vital role. If the populace views the regime as defending the country's national interest in standing up to an external threat, the chances of military support will be considerably enhanced.

External-defensive actions in Eastern Europe can be divided into three major categories: defense against an attack by other non-Soviet Warsaw Pact neighbors, against an attack by the Soviet Union, and against an attack by NATO. The willingness of the armed forces to support the regimes under these circumstances will be influenced strongly by the nature of the enemy, the attitudes of the populace toward military resistance to external threats, the scenario utilized by the aggressor, and the degree of indigenous military organization and cooperation.

External-offensive reliability refers to the willingness of the military to support the regime in offensive campaigns against other countries. The role of the conscript also assumes critical importance here. Soldiers will be less likely to go voluntarily into battle for the sake of a government they perceive as repressive or as qualified in its defense of the national interests than they would be for one which is fighting for the nation's manifest destiny. For example, a population which perceives an offensive war involving Soviet interests as not in accord with their own could present problems for the Soviets in combat operations. One might argue, as some have suggested to me, that when led by competent officers and fired upon, any soldier will fight. We are not arguing that Eastern European forces will refuse to fight if called upon to engage in an offensive campaign which they feel is against their national interest. Nevertheless, their attitude toward the conflict will play an important, if not decisive, role. There are numerous cases in the past when armies have fought with varying degrees of intensity and initiative, primarily as a result of their perceptions of the relevance of the conflict. As a result, from Moscow's standpoint, to be highly reliable in an offensive campaign, the populations of the Eastern European countries involved would have to identify their own national interests closely with those of the USSR. And, as recent events in Eastern

Europe have shown, such a development is unlikely under most circumstances.

External-offensive operations can be divided into four categories: an attack on another non-Soviet Warsaw Pact country, an attack on a neutral country, an attack on the USSR, and an attack as a Warsaw Pact member on NATO. In addition to the factors which influence the performance of the armed forces in an external-defensive situation, the success or failure of an offensive, as well as its duration, will also play key roles. A popular war which is going well probably will maintain military support. A protracted war which is experiencing difficulty, however, could lead to passive resistance and, if the situation deteriorated badly, to defections.

All of the above points briefly stated in this section of this article, of course, are situational and country-specific, and we must emphasize this over and over, lest we forget its importance. Each conflict and each scenario will be different, and contingency studies should be and must be made for each separate scenario. Such operational plans, however, are not within the purview of this article, although their undertaking—in my view—is warranted both by security and academic considerations. Some generalizations on how the various Warsaw Pact states attempt to insure reliability by inculcating certain socialized values and adopting certain policies can be readily identified, and it is to this task we must now turn in the concluding section of this article.

Operationalizing Reliability as Behavior

Behavior, as the literature clearly indicates, can be of two types: spontaneous and premeditated.[38] Although both are the results of inculcated values, spontaneous behavior is more often the result of value transformation, rejections of previously accepted though not deeply held values, or events through which the praxis becomes a major value. Spontaneous value transformation—from our perspective—occurs, for example, when the armed forces face a rioting crowd and decide to join the crowd rather than shoot at it. Premeditated, or "predicate behavior," is based on inculcated values which have been socialized by the individuals and groups. There need not be a deep commitment to any single value or to a *belief* in the correctness of the ideology in order for the commitment to be maximum; rather, the individual subjects merely must be convinced of the *relative* merit of positions and values held in order to act on the expected bases. Thus, for example, the Romanian officer does not need to believe in Marxism and/or the Fatherland in order to be reliable as an instrument; he merely must be convinced Marxism is better than the alternatives available to him at that time or that the Romanian Fatherland has given him more benefits than otherwise would be availble to him, let us say, under Soviet occupation.[39]

Our evaluation of the reliability of the Warsaw Pact forces must also include one other element, especially in regard to external offensive or defensive operations. That element is a certain respect for past history, not as a predictive model, but as a model which hitherto has been followed. Included in this model are such considerations as the nature of the traditional enemy, the nature of the situation, and the opportunity for action. In cases of a conflict against traditional enemies, history clearly shows that the people of Eastern Europe have been willing to fight with far greater determination than they have against neutrals or former allies; history also teaches us that the nations of the East have always been opportunistic enough to jump ship as soon as defeat of the major ally of the alliance system to which they belonged seemed certain. Only Hungary—a country which with faultless historical hindsight has always chosen the losing side of a conflict and has attended all wars during the last 500 years and won none—stuck with Hitler until her total defeat in World War II.

Having said this, we should turn our attention to operationalizing elements of the concept of reliability. The liability of the armed forces of Eastern Europe can be viewed as based upon eight main components out of which composite indices may be created for the purposes of simple extrapolation. It must be emphasized that this index is simply a heuristic device; nonetheless, it can be a guide to an evaluation based on concrete rather than impressionistic grounds. In brief, here are the eight main components of the concept of reliability:

1. the extent of the co-option of the officers corps—the "Good Life";
2. the degree of control functions by party or political officers;
3. the educational process—value socialization;
4. subordination/integration—the extent and presence of Soviet control;
5. the fear of reprisals—both by the population and by the party;
6. the nature of the traditional enemy in conflict;
7. the situational element—both short- and long-range effects; and
8. the nature of the army's mission.

It must be emphasized that this examination focuses mainly on the projected behavior of the officer corps. In general, even in the Polish crisis of 1981–82, the officer corps will determine the behavior of the recruits or enlisted men. Unless the chasm between the officers and enlisted men is very wide and appears to widen, it generally can be predicted that the soldiers are likely to follow the leadership of the officers. The communist states always have been careful not to alienate

366

the soldiers to the extent "colonial"-type mutinies are expected to occur. With this caveat in mind, let us now turn to an examination of the main components of the concept of reliability.

The Co-option of the Officer Corps

This component is relatively stable and can be examined in great detail. It includes three major considerations:

    a. the prestige of the corps;

    b. the mobility factor; and

    c. relative levels of satisfaction.

The prestige of the officer corps is very important. In some cases, such as Poland or East Germany, the prestige factor is based on past history, and the projected heroic glory of the army as a defender of the nation is carried over from the past. In other states with miniscule armed forces or with a heritage which reflects negatively on the army—such as Hungary and Czechoslovakia—the prestige of the armed forces is considerably lower, and efforts to enhance it have not been noticeably successful.

The mobility factor of the officer corps is also very important. In the past, specifically during the early years of communist power, the army served as an instrument of upward mobility. It was especially important as a stepladder of mobility for peasant lads in the army and the security services, though in the latter case their percentages were estimated to have been smaller than in the armed forces. As the internal development of the state continued and interclass mobility came to a halt—a process rapidly taking shape in Eastern Europe—the army and the party remain the only major means for interclass mobility, much like the army and the clergy used to be in the prewar or feudal periods.[40] Nonetheless, here, too, one notices that the standards of the officers' schools are slowly being adjusted upward; once again, the "military tradition" has become a major reason for individual selection of the armed forces as a career.

Finally, the *relative* levels of material satisfaction are very important elements in our evaluation; again, this is quite measurable. Such considerations as basic pay, bonuses, housing, and special privileges are the basic components of material satisfaction. It must be emphasized, however, that one cannot and should not view income and pay in an absolute sense but in a manner of comparable actual earning potentials. Hence, in economies where earnings supplementing activities involving the second economy are considerable, even very high pay scales are not going to insure relative satisfaction; on the contrary, they would result in feelings of relative deprivation. On the other hand, in countries where the black market economy is miniscule in terms of income supplementing activities, high pay scales are usually more adequate to insure regime support.

Control Functions

The implementation and exercise of control functions by the party directly or by the political officers indirectly seems to be a double-edged sword in the party's continuous struggle to insure reliability. On the one hand, too great a control—giving equal or superior command positions to *politruks** of one sort or another—increases control by the party; on the other, it decreases technical efficiency and, as a direct result, almost always leads to the subsequent strengthening the non-party components of the command structure. Too little control, on the contrary, as a result of the constant fear of Bonapartism, is unthinkable; even in such cases as that of of General Moczar, the fear of his control over even the nonmilitary activities of the *ZBoWiD* created an unjustifiable institutional paranoia among the Polish party elite. And while it is true General Jaruzelski led a coup in 1981 forming a Military Council for National Salvation, the Polish junta was communist and pro-Moscow. Under the guise of military rule, the "principal bases of socialism" were preserved. As stated in the earlier section of this article, the best possible means for the party to combat this fear is the appointment of reliable party members to command positions. While this policy does not guarantee against the emergence of individuals like Colonel Maleter, it is still preferable to the other two options outlined above. The naming of responsible individuals with the proper *partiy–nost'* has been relatively successful at the upper levels of command and relatively unsuccessful at the lower levels, mostly because the party has little *real* knowledge of attitudes and values possessed by the subcommand officer corps. Consequently, what is measurable here is (a) the extent of party control and (b) the extent of involvement by political officers in command-level decisions. When the two are compared, the amount of party control provides an indication of trust or mistrust of the army by the party elite.

The Educational Process

The process of political socialization can and does offer enforce values desired by the regime. Socialization of values, however, is a long-term process exceedingly difficult to attain since contrary socializers abound. As far as the communist parties of the region are concerned, the creation of a "communist man" or a "communist officer" is a long way off, and I would submit that the political elite does not really care if *all* the values desired by the system are inculcated in the individual members of the armed services. In fact, the possession of certain minimal "noncommunist" values which are not contradictory to the military desiderata seems to be far more important than the generalized inculcation of "communist values." The "let's take Czechoslovakia" mentality is clearly preferred over the "accepting different

---

Politicheskiy rukovoditel' [Political Instructor]—Eds.

368

roads of strategy" mentality.

The curious problem with the socialization of the armed forces consists of the clear differences between subsystem and system desiderata. In other words, values to be inculcated according to the national interests of the elites of the individual states are not necessarily the same as those desired by the Soviet leadership. Although in such states as Romania, Poland, and even Hungary, "socialist patriotism" is emphasized as a positive value, support of the "interests of the socialist community" and the "Brezhnev Doctrine" is certainly a more preferable attitude from the Soviet Union's perspective.

One could ask whether the Soviet leadership actually cares if the attitudes possessed by the indigenous militaries are "communist" attitudes. One could wonder if the Soviet leaders really are not more interested in sowing a "little" not anti-Soviet but, let us say, anti-Romanian nationalism among the Hungarian armed forces. Certainly, the nonintegration of the individual units indicates an ambivalence toward the process of creating a truly international army. It also leaves open the real probability that the Soviet leadership would prefer functionally usable separate units to foster its interests, even if the units failed to possess "communist" characteristics. Similarly, the local leadership also possesses functional desiderata, but the two functionalities are far from being the same.

One must also emphasize that there is a distinct difference between the socialization of officers and enlisted men. I have analyzed that difference in another essay; here, it is important to mention only that the values to be inculcated tend toward far more specific value components among the officer training institutions than among recruits.[41] Although that results in recruits who are less socialized and less "communist" than officers, the larger number of recruits to be socialized has left the leadership little or no choice in selecting the number and type of messages or the audience.

At any rate, the extent and the messages of value socialization can be measured quite easily. Textbooks, criteria, curricula for both officer training institutions and for the recruits, books for the high school military education curricula, and the literature for the population and youngsters at large—a considerable source of information which should not be neglected!—are widely available. The extent of the success of these efforts may be more difficult to discern, although the specialized military periodicals are excellent sources for other information.

Subordination/Integration

This is one of the more technical components of the research on reliability. Due to the classified nature of most such information—both from the Soviet and from the American perspectives—we have the anomaly that independent researchers have a hard time assessing the extent or presence of Soviet control. Nonetheless, we can differentiate conceptually between the mere presence of the Soviet Armed Forces on the territory of member states and the integration of Soviet personnel *within* the native forces. The presence of Soviet forces may indicate the Soviet Union is not perfectly at ease in leaving the national units without supervision; however, their mere presence is a threat to both the population and to the leadership. In those cases where the visible presence of the Soviet forces would cause a greater threat to domestic peace than warranted—e.g., Hungary and Poland—the conditions of the visible Soviet presence are severely curtailed. In the Polish case, the numbers are actually quite small. The visible presence of Soviet forces in East Germany and Czechoslovakia is a demonstrative indicator, however, of Soviet unease.

The integration of Soviet personnel with units of the local forces has been altered radically since the 1950s. By the 1960s, the crudest forms of integration—the presence of Soviet "advisors" all the way down to the lowest units of command—had been replaced with less obtrusive "instruments"—"liaison officers" located mostly at division command levels and above. These officers, of course, are supplemented by *GRU–KGB* informers at all levels, but we have no certain method of assessing their presence and the extent of their integration with the armed forces.

Let me say a few words about the integration of the Soviet security forces with the political police of the various Eastern European states, since a part of these units are obviously also a part of the armed forces as a whole. Although practically no reliable literature exists on the subject, there can be no doubt these security services make up a system whose integration level greatly exceeds that of the armed forces. This integration extends to forcing the COMECON representatives to adopt uniform codes on what may or may not be sown in border zones—in an effort to limit escape from the East—and to create unified security systems for the exposed Western borders. The personnel of these units are likely to be interchangeable with their Soviet counterparts. Such interchangeability does not extend to cooperation on the level of integration with the other non-Soviet members of the Pact, however. Information—except perhaps between the USSR and Romania—is shared with Soviet counterparts regularly, although operational controls are probably kept within the national units. In spite of the difficulty of assessing the degree of integration from open sources, I believe ample documentation now exists from interviews and defectors to attest to these conclusions.

Fear of Reprisals

It seems to be clear that fear is as potent a source of behavior as any of the other sources outlined above, and the fear of the personal "what will happen if . . . ?" is a very important component of making these units reliable for regime purposes. On the one hand, there exists the fear in the armed forces—especially among those officers who are in the employ of the various security services—of what would happen in a *losing* situation or after the loss is experienced. The experience of Budapest in 1956 cannot help but shape the personalities and value systems of members of the security services. In this sense—and Poland amply demonstrates this point—this fear makes the security forces the most reliable component of regime support in cases of domestic defensive activities; in fact, the elites do not fail to use every opportunity to point out the brutal murder of *AVO* officers by the angry masses in 1956.

But the fear of the loss of prestige, position, and "perks" by the officer corps is also a real fear and impels most officers to come to the aid of the regime in domestic crises. Only in such instances and at such places where the army has a national existence either separate from or in contradistinction to the communist elite can it be presumed the army will be somewhat less than loyal in internal-defensive situations.

Let me hasten to add, however, that this fear is somewhat counterbalanced by another concern which also must nag at the minds of the individual officers: the fear of the party should the party—or the Soviet Union and the party—remain successful in defending its interests. The brutality and harshness meted out to those members of the armed forces who participated in the 1956 Hungarian revolt were designed specifically to discourage similar "defections" from the officer corps throughout the bloc. This fear is reinforced on both the system and subsystem levels and can be documented easily from the support materials used for socialization purposes. Consequently the notion of fear—however potent a part fear has in ensuring compliance—must be handled with extreme care.

The Nature of the Traditional Enemy

It takes only a cursory glance at the national histories of the East European states to realize how important the concept of the "traditional enemy" remains even today. Notwithstanding the nearly four-decades-old theme of the "socialist fraternal community," today Romanians hate Hungarians, Hungarians hate Romanians and just about everybody else, and the Poles hate the Germans. The list can be expanded practically without any upper limit. The trouble for the Soviet Union is—aside from the Bulgarians and, until 1968, the Czechs and Slovaks—the Russians have been everybody's common traditional foe. 1968 took care of Czechoslovak goodwill toward the USSR for many years to come. Nonetheless, the utilization of the armed forces of each country against a "traditional" enemy is far easier than against a "traditional" ally. For instance, the Polish troops joined the occupation of Czechoslovakia with some vigor and great willingness; their use against Hungary would have been met with some resistance. Similarly, the use of Hungarian troops against Romania would not meet the same resistance as was experienced in their deployment against Czechoslovakia or in the projected deployment against Poland.

From the systemic perspective, the USSR has been greatly concerned that integration in any form of subunit not take place *within* the alliance, lest that integration possibly assume an anti-Soviet tone. Early Soviet opposition to the proposed Balkan Federation or to the various Danubian Alliance schemes stems from Moscow's well-founded paranoia that the *only* traditional enemy of all of these states over the past century (except Bulgaria, of course!) has been Russia. Such opposition is manifested in the Pact's communication and command system, which involves a Soviet integrator in all cases and discourages otherwise normal contacts among the non-Soviet members.

The Situational Element

Perhaps in no instance is the old adage "everything depends on the situation and terrain" as important as in the case of analyzing the reliability of an ally. Simply put, everyone loves a victor. The question, however, which must be asked concerns the circumstances under which the leadership and the military elite can begin to raise concerns about the chances for victory. And here the conceptual handle which must be used is that of short-range or long-range situational elements. In General Hackett's unfortunately all too optimistic view, the US counteroffensive begins on D+13; shortly after, thought-provoking questions are raised in the minds of Eastern European leaders about their participation.[42] Such thoughts are based on their conviction of the superiority of Western technology and the mediocrity of Eastern, specifically Soviet, technology. Such convictions—however justly deserved in our own optimistic view of ourselves and pessimistic view of our opponents—at present are not backed up by fact, and the Soviet leadership seems to be aware of it. As a result of this awareness, the USSR has been hammering away at its own superiority *precisely with the aim of convincing first their own allies* and only secondarily with the aim of convincing the wary and underrated West. I believe this is a battle for the minds of these very leaders; whatever we can do to foster their positive views of us will decrease in the long run their reliability as purposive instruments . . . should we and they be granted the luxury of thinking in the long run.

The short-run problem offers an entirely different perspective. An external-offensive intrusion in Western Europe will utilize only East German, Polish, and perhaps Czech units in the short run; the situational factor will determine their participation or reliability far more than long-range considerations. These units, of course, will be given specific tasks, and their reliability will depend partially on the nature of the enemy (e.g., national makeup of the opposition forces) and on the strength with which the USSR puts their "backs to the wall" in compelling them to fight. The Soviets, of course, are also caught in a dilemma in utilizing "unwilling" allies to fight: the greater they force them to fight, the less likely will be their reliability. Strategic opportunities for the West to "wean" away these "reluctant" forces abound in such situations, provided proper methods can be used.

The Mission of the Various Armies

This is one of the components on which a relatively large amount of "hard" data is available. Obviously, the very mission of the army determines the extent of the Soviet military trust. The equipment, training, and mission goals of the various armies are fairly easy to discern. Thus, the Soviet failure to provide advanced air defense systems to the East German army and the relatively poor equipment given to the Hungarians reveal Soviet concern over the reliability of these forces. Moreover, the projected missions of the Polish forces as forward advance troops places them on the relatively Western reaches of Poland, thereby leaving the eastern part of Poland open to Soviet advances should such a move be viewed as necessary by the Soviet leadership. Examples abound, and while the mission does not directly indicate the value structure of the armed forces, it does indeed reveal a relatively clearly measurable component which must be evaluated as a part of the operational reliability of the non-Soviet Warsaw Pact forces.

Summary

In this article, an attempt has been made to discuss the "unique" in regards to the communist armies of Eastern Europe and to assess the alliance system within which these armies operate. Moreover, an attempt also has been made to discuss their reliability as purposive instruments and to operationalize the main components of this reliability. It must be emphasized, however, that such a study is merely a beginning, as the *analysis of these main components of reliability provides different results for each of the participating states.* For those who expected more concrete results, I can only add that this study—as well as the others I have undertaken by myself or with Dale Herspring—is a result of ongoing research. Perhaps sometime in the near future we will get closer to operational results. Let us hope it will not be too late.

Notes

1. J. C. Baynes, *The Soldier in Modern Society* (London, 1972).
2. F. D. Freeman, "The Army as a Social Structure," *Social Forces,* 27 (1948–1949); Vernon V. Aspaturian, "The Soviet Military–Industrial Complex: Does It Exist?" *Journal of International Affairs,* Spring–Summer 1972.
3. Samuel Huntington, *The Soldier and the State: Theory and Politics of Civil–Military*

Relations (Cambridge: Harvard University Press, 1957).

4. Dale Herspring and Ivan Volgyes, *Civil–Military Relations in Communist States* (Boulder: Westview, 1978).

5. David E. Albright, "A Comparative Conceptualization of Civil–Military Relations," *World Politics,* July 1980; pp. 553–576.

6. Timothy Colton, *Commissars, Commanders and Civilian Authority: Structure of Soviet Military Politics* (Cambridge: Harvard University Press, 1979); Michael Deane, *Political Control of the Soviet Armed Forces* (New York: Crane and Russak, 1977); Raymond A. Garthoff, "The Marshals and the Party: Soviet Civil–Military Relations in the Postwar Period," in Harry Coles, ed., *Total War and Cold War: Problems in Civilian Control of the Military* (Columbus: Ohio State University Press, 1962); Roman Kolkowicz, *The Soviet Military and the Communist Party* (Princeton: Princeton University Press, 1962); William E. Odom, *The Soviet Volunteers: Modernization and Bureaucracy in a Public Mass Organization* (Princeton: Princeton University Press, 1973); and Edward Warner, *The Military in Contemporary Soviet Politics* (New York: Praeger, 1977); as well as other works listed in the attached bibliography devote particular attention to this problem.

7. Zbigniew Brzezinski, *Political Controls in the Soviet Army* (New York: Columbia University Press, 1954); Dale Herspring, *East German Civil–Military Relations (1949–1972)* (New York: Praeger, 1973); Herspring, "Technology and the Changing Political Officer in the Armed Forces: The Polish and East German Cases," *Studies in Comparative Communism,* Autumn 1977; and David Holloway, *Technology, Management and the Soviet Military Establishment* (London: Institute for Strategic Studies, 1971).

8. Timothy Colton, "The Zhukov Affair Reconsidered," *Soviet Studies,* April 1977.

9. Lawrence Caldwell, "The Warsaw Pact: Directions of Change," *Problems of Communism,* September–October 1975; Walter Clemens, "The Changing Warsaw Pact," *East Europe,* June 1968; Curt Gasteyger, "Probleme und Reformen des Warschauer Pakts [Problems and Reform in the Warsaw Pact]," *Europa Archiv,* 10 January 1967; Patricia Haigh, *The World Today,* April 1968; and Hans Von Krannhals, "Command Integration within the Warsaw Pact," *Military Review,* May 1961.

10. Needless to say, the fear of Bonapartism or praetorianism has not been confined to the communist militaries. For a few classical studies dealing with the topic, see S. E. Finer, *The Man on Horseback* (London: Pall Mall Press, 1962) and Samuel Huntington's numerous works, including *Changing Patterns in Military Politics* (New York: Glencoe, 1962), and *Political Order in Changing Societies* (New Haven: Yale University Press, 1968), especially chapter 4.

11. John Barron, *The KGB* (New York: Readers Digest Press, 1974); Frederick G. Barghoorn, "The Security Police," in *Interest Groups in Soviet Politics* (Princeton: Princeton University Press, 1971); Robert Conquest, *The Soviet Police System* (New York: Praeger, 1968); Peter Deriabin, *Watchdogs of Terror* (New Rochelle, New York: Arlington House, 1972); and Simon Wolin and Robert M. Slusser, *The Soviet Secret Police* (New York: Praeger, 1957).

12. Bracher, Sauer, and Schultz, *Die Nationalsozialistische Machtbegreifung* [The National Socialist Power Concept] (Kohls: Westdeutsches Verlag, 1960).

13. Kent Brown, "Coalition Politics and Soviet Influence in Eastern Europe," in Jan F. Traska and Paul Cocks, eds., *Political Development in Eastern Europe* (New York: Praeger, 1977).

14. Colonel General P. I. Yefimov, *Boyevoy Soyuz Bratskikh Armiy* [The Combat Union of the Fraternal Armies] (Moscow: Voyenizdat, 1974) contains a good statement of these changes.

15. Ivan Volgyes, "The Military as an Agent of Political Socialization," in Herspring and Volgyes, *Civil–Military Relations in Communist Systems;* and Herspring and Volgyes, "The Military as an Agent of Political Socialization in Eastern Europe," *Armed Forces and Society,* February 1977.

16. Aside from the works already quoted above, see Peter Gosztony, *Zur Geschichte der*

Europaischen Volksarmeen [On the History of the European People's Armies] (Bonn: Hohwacht, 1977); Walter C. Clemens, "The Future of the Warsaw Pact," *Orbis,* Winter 1968; Michael Cxizmas, "Das militarische Bundnissystem in Osteuropa [The Military Alliance System in East Europe]," *Allgemeine Schweizerische Militarzeitschrift* [Swiss General Military Journal] October–November 1967; Michael Garder, "Der Warschauer Pakt [The Warsaw Pact]," *Europa Archiv,* 25 December 1966; and "Le Potentiale Militaire de Satellites de l'URSS [The Military Potential of the Satellites of the USSR]," *Revue Militaire Generale,* June 1965; Guedon, "Le Service Militaire dans les Pays du Bloc Sovietique [Military Service in the Countries of the Soviet Bloc]," *Revue de Defense Nationale*; April 1964; Eugene Hinterhoff, "Die Potentiale des War-schauer Paktes [The Potential of the Warsaw Pact]," *Aussenpolitik* [Foreign Policy], August 1965; and, by the same author, "The Warsaw Pact," *Military Review,* June 1962; Bela Kiraly, "Why the Soviets Need the Warsaw Pact," *East Europe,* April 1969; Roman Kolkowicz, "Spezifischer Funktionswandel des Warschauer Paktes [Specific Functional Activities of the Warsaw Pact]," *Aussenpolitik,* January 1969; and by the same author, "The Warsaw Pact: Entangling Alliance," *Survey,* Winter–Spring 1969; Andrzej Korbonski, "The Warsaw Pact," *International Concilia-tion,* May 1969; Malcolm Mackintosh, "The Warsaw Pact Today," *Survival,* May–June 1974; J. Pergent, "Le Pacte de Varsovie et l'Inventaire des Forces de l'Est [The Warsaw Pact and the Inventory of the Forces of the East]," *Est et Ouest* [East and West] July 1967; Robin Remington, *The Warsaw Pact* (Cambridge: MIT Press, 1971), and by the same author, "The Warsaw Pact: Communist Coalition Politics in Action," *Yearbook of World Affairs,* 1972; Paul R. Shirk, "The Warsaw Treaty Organization," *Military Review,* May 1969; Richard F. Staar, "The East European Alliance," *U.S. Naval Institute Proceedings,* September 1964; Thaddeus Von Paschta, "Das System der sowjetischen Militarberater in den Satellitenstaaten [The System of Soviet Military Advisers in the Satellite States]," *Wehrkunde* [Army Intelligence] September 1962; and Fritz Wiener, *Die Armeen der Warschauer Pakt–Staaten: Organi-sation, Taktik, Waffen und Gerate* [The Armies of the Warsaw Pact States: Organiza-tion, Tactics, Weapons, and Equipment] (Wien, 1974).

17. For a good statement on the problem, see Robert O. Keohane, "Lilliputian's Dilem-mas: Small States in International Politics," *International Organization,* Summer 1969.

18. On the general topic of alliances as "genuine" systems, see the following recent studies:

Basso, J. "La cooperation internationale [International Cooperation]," *Annuaire du Tiers Monde,* Vol. 1, 1974, pp. 447–462.

Brams, S. J. and Heilman, J. G., "When to join a coalition, and with how many others, depends on what you expect the outcome to be," *Public Choice,* Vol. 17, Spring 1974, pp. 11–25.

Bredow W. Von, "Intersystemare Kooperation und Abrustung [Intersystem Cooperation and Disarmament]," *Blatter fur deutsche und international Politik* [News-papers for German and International Politics], Vol. 19, No. 1 (1974), pp. 17–34.

Caplow, Theodore, "A Theory of Coalitions in the Triad," *American Sociological Review,* Vol. 21, 1956, pp. 489–493.

Caplow, Theodore, "Further Development of a Theory of Coalitions in the Triad," *American Journal of Sociology,* Vol. 64, 1959, pp. 488–493.

Day, H. R., "The resource comparison model of coalition formation," *Cornell Journal of Social Relations,* Vol. 10, No. 2 (Fall 1975), pp. 209–221.

Cassidy, R. Gordon and Neave, Edwin, "Dynamics of Coalition Formation, Prescription versus Reality," *Theory and Decision,* Vol. 8, No. 2 (April 1977), pp. 159–171.

Chertkoff, Jeff, "The Effects of Probability of Future Success on Coalition Forma-tion" *Journal of Experimental and Social Psychology,* Vol. 2, No. 3 (July 1966), pp. 265–277.

Deibel, Terry L., "A Guide to International Divorce," *Foreign Policy,* Spring 1978, pp. 17–35.

Dimitrijevic, V., "International Relations and the Existence of Regions," *International Problems* (Belgrade), No. 14, 1973, pp. 81–88.

Kann, R. A. "Alliances versus Ententes," *World Politics,* Vol. 28, No. 4 (July 1976), pp. 611–621.

19. For a good statement of the topic, see Frigyes Puja, *Miert van szukseg a Varsoi Szerzodesre?* [Why is There a Need For the Warsaw Pact?] (Budapest: Ziriniyi, 1970).

20. Jiri Valenta, *Soviet Intervention in Czechoslovakia: Anatomy of a Decision* (Baltimore: The Johns Hopkins University Press, 1979), p. 96.

21. Erwin Weit, *At the Red Summit* (New York: Macmillan, 1973), p. 201.

22. Much of the material contained in the following few pages is based upon an earlier study by Dale Herspring and myself and contained in *Armed Forces and Society,* Winter 1980, under the title "Political Reliability in the Eastern European Warsaw Pact Armies."

23. Gabriel Almond and Sidney Verba, *The Civic Culture* (Boston: Little, Brown, 1965).

24. The following section is condensed from our earlier study cited in note 22 above.

25. Herspring and Volgyes utilize the term "professional military force" to include all those with 10 years or more of active military position.

26. See note 22.

27. See, for example, Roman Kolkowicz, *The Soviet Military and the Communist Party* (Princeton: Princeton University Press, 1967), esp. chapters 2 and 4; Raymond Garthoff, *Soviet Military Policy* (New York: Praeger, 1966), esp. chapters 2 and 3; Herbert Goldhamer, *The Soviet Soldier: Soviet Military Management at the Troop Level,* esp. chapter 8; and Michael Deane, *Political Control of the Soviet Armed Forces.*

28. For a discussion of this situation in the United States, see Demetrios Caraley, *The Politics of Military Unification* (New York: Columbia University Press, 1966). For the USSR, see William E. Odom, "The Party Connection: A Critique," and Karl Spielmann, "Defense Industrialists in the USSR," in Herspring and Volgyes, eds., *Civil–Military Relations in Communist Systems* (Boulder: Westview, 1978).

29. Timothy J. Colton, "The Party–Military Connection: An Overview," in ibid.

30. Archie Brown, "Introduction," in Archie Brown and Jack Gray, eds., *Political Culture and Political Change in Communist States* (London: Macmillan Press, 1977), pp. 7–8.

31. A. Ross Johnson, "Soviet–East European Military Relations," in Herspring and Volgyes, eds., *Civil–Military Relations in Communist Systems.*

32. Heinz Godau, *Verfuhrter, Verfuhrer, Ich war Politoffizier der NVA* [Seduced, Seducer, I Was a Political Officer in the NPA] (Cologne: Markus Verlag, 1965), pp. 78–84.

33. Flora Lewis, *A Case History of Hope* (New York: Doubleday, 1958), p. 143; Richard Hiscocks, *Poland: Bridge for the Abyss?* (New York: Oxford University Press, 1963), p. 192.

34. Bela Kiraly, "Hungary's Army: Its Part in the Revolt," *East Europe,* Vol. 7, No. 6 (June 1958), pp. 8–10.

35. Ferenc A. Vali, *Rift and Revolution in Hungary* (Cambridge: Harvard University Press, 1961), p. 434.

36. Robert W. Dean, "The Political Consolidation of the Czechoslovak Army," *Radio Free Europe Research,* Czechoslovakia/14, 29 April 1971, pp. 16, 20.

37. Michael Costello, "The Party and the Military in Poland," *Radio Free Europe Research,* Poland/12, 26 April 1971, pp. 1–2.

38. Ivan Volgyes, "Political Socialization in Eastern Europe," in Ivan Volgyes, ed., *Political Socialization in Eastern Europe: A Comparative Framework* (New York: Praeger, 1976).

39. The Hungarian proverb, "That's what there is, that's what you have to like," expresses the widespread feeling of the population about the lack of alternatives available to them.

40. Walter Connor, *Socialism, Politics, and Equality* (New York: Columbia University Press, 1980).

41. Ivan Volgyes, "Political Socialization of the Military: the Case of Hungary," in

Herspring and Volgyes, eds., *Civil–Military Relations in Communist States.*

42. General Sir John Hackett, *The Third World War* (New York: Berkeley Publishers, 1980). It is instructive, however, that the Polish military regime in a broadcast on Polish television on 25 February 1982 used the Hackett book as "proof" of Western plans to "destabilize" Poland and Eastern Europe, thereby justifying ex post facto the previous imposition of martial law.

Soviet Strategic Vulnerability: Deterring a Multinational State©

Gary L. Guertner*

Introduction: Limitations in the Strategic Debate

The efforts to ratify both SALT treaties will be remembered above all else as a competition for shaping public and congressional percep- tions of the strategic balance. Nearly all critics have argued that the nuclear balance is delicate and that weapons symmetry is a requirement of strategic stability. Isolated variables (megatonnage and throw- weight, for example) have been cast in scenarios illustrating US ICBM vulnerability and Soviet first-strike incentives. Many of these argu- ments were incorporated in the Jackson Amendment to SALT I which mandated equal numerical ceilings in SALT II. Each Administration since 1972 has been bound by the Jackson Amendment but has rejected efforts to define precise qualitative balances between strategic forces or to rival every Soviet weapons system. Instead, the concept of essential equivalence has been substituted. Thus, weapons advantages enjoyed by the Soviets need not be matched so long as they are offset by other US advantages. Stability under this rubric requires equivalent but not equal capabilities across the technical spectrum.[1]

Like its critics armed with first-strike scenarios, the Carter admin- istration's concept of essential equivalence was limited to weapons characteristics. Both illustrate how the SALT process has been dom- inated by a wide range of technical "imperatives" pushing US strategic doctrine further in the development of limited nuclear warfighting options. It is this writer's contention that the stability of nuclear deter- rence must be viewed across a wider spectrum of variables if these trends are to be reversed and the arms competition they foster checked. The technical must be linked more precisely with the full range of threats faced by each country. These include the geopolitical, economic, ethnographic, and even historical factors that surely influence the calculus of Soviet strategic planning. This article exam- ines these variables, emphasizing the geopolitical/ethnographic vulnera- bilities unique to the Soviet state. Its central thesis is that Soviet sensi- tivity to these problems, particularly to the crisis loyalty of their

---

©*Political Science Quarterly*. Reprinted by permission.
*I would like to thank Dan Caldwell, Fred Neal, William Potter, Gregory Treverton, Enders Wimbush, and especially Don Schulz for their helpful comments on earlier drafts of this article.

"nationalities" in the union republics, introduces an element of doubt in Soviet strategy sufficient to strengthen the credibility of US strategic forces at levels considerably below the current SALT II ceilings, and without further development of counterforce or limited nuclear options in US strategic planning and force procurement policies.

Any assessment of the nuclear balance is partly a subjective comparison. Numbers alone may be misleading in the clues they offer about both intentions and capabilities. Our knowledge of all variables remains theoretical, since neither testing nor experience has confirmed the validity of rival strategic doctrines. It is now generally recognized that these gaps in our knowledge are a two-edged sword. On the one hand, they are highly desirable: certainly no sane person would want to confirm or disprove our strategic theories through experience (i.e., through nuclear war). By the same token, the very uncertainties of warfare contribute to the effectiveness and stability of deterrence. On the other hand, these ambiguities also have their negative side—especially for the prospects of arms control—for they promote force planning based on worst-case assessments of enemy capabilities.[2]

The difficulty with worst-case assessments is that they focus almost entirely on weapons symmetries or asymmetries. Yet, other considerations may well be equally important, if not more so. One of the least examined variables in the nuclear equation, for instance, involves geopolitical vulnerabilities to societal disruption and political fragmentation. US strategic literature treats the Soviet Union as a unitary state, powerful in its military and political potential to threaten the United States and its allies. Little has been done in unclassified sources to examine the multinational character of the Soviet state and its potential effect on the Soviet-American mutual deterrence relationship.[3]

Ethnic Russians soon will comprise only a minority of the Soviet population.[4] They are concentrated in the central areas of the USSR and are buffered from neighboring countries by union republics populated predominantly by non-Russian ethnic groups. Most importantly, many of these ethnic minorities have long histories of political independence. How Soviet leaders have managed pressures for autonomy or independence by these groups during periods of crisis or national stress tells us a great deal about Soviet perceptions and sensitivity towards these points of vulnerability. World War I and the Bolshevik revolution, for example, led to temporary independence for some ethnic groups which later had to be reintegrated forcibly by the Red Army. Similarly, during World War II, Stalin relocated entire ethnic populations to the interior of the country for fear they might collaborate with the Germans. Nor was this fear unwarranted. Many groups did defect in large numbers, taking up arms on the German side. As the German armies moved toward the Ukraine, the Baltic regions, and Belorussia, they were conquering regions that had been most cruelly hit by the forced collectivization of 1930–33, famine, and Stalin's

379

russification policies. Had the Germans been capable of humane and moderate treatment of Soviet nationalities in these areas, their occupation could have become a danger to the Soviet system even after the German retreat. One can only speculate as to what additional problems the Soviets would have encountered had Hitler in 1941 proclaimed the independence of the Ukraine, Belorussia, and the Baltic states. According to Adam Ulam, the continuous demands for a second front in Europe, even when the Germans could no longer win in the east, were prompted by the urgent necessity to reconquer Soviet territories as soon as possible before any form of anti-Soviet organization could take root.[5] As it was, pockets of anti-Soviet partisans in these areas resisted the Soviet Army for several years following the German surrender in 1945.[6]

More recently, the resurgence of Islam in combination with increased ethnic nationalism on or near the Soviet border has increased the possibility that the USSR's own Islamic and minority populations in the areas bordering Iran and Afghanistan may in the future press for autonomy. Once set in motion, the pressures of nationalism could start all of the Soviets' ethnic dominoes falling out of control. Parallels might, for example, be drawn between the Soviet invasions of Afghanistan and Czechoslovakia. Soviet sensitivity to events in Iran and Afghanistan is undoubtedly heightened by the potential impact of change in these areas upon Soviet Islamic citizens in Central Asia. A similar situation existed in Czechoslovakia where reforms had an unsettling effect on autonomy-minded Ukrainian nationalists.[7] The Ukraine had developed close cultural and economic links with Czechoslovakia. This, in combination with a small Ukrainian population in Slovakia (the number would be greater if Stalin had not annexed the Carpatho–Ukraine in 1945, thereby extending the Soviet border to Czechoslovakia and Hungary, facilitating the projection of military power into those countries, and minimizing future irredentist conflicts that might arise between Ukrainians and Eastern Europeans), resulted in Ukrainians being more exposed to the reformist and nationalistic ideas expressed in Czechoslovakia. This exposure, superimposed upon indigenous nationalism, resulted in a breakdown of the official Soviet monopoly of the means of public communication and political socialization. According to the "Ukrainian hypothesis," for Soviet officials no "mental frontier" separated the Czechoslovak crisis from the Ukrainian problem.[8] The nationality problem played a dominant role in shaping Soviet perceptions of the "Prague Spring," with the impetus to action coming from the inside to the outside. According to this thesis:

> Czechoslovakia would have appeared in the mind's eye of the Soviet leadership as a union republic in which the 'bourgeois nationalists' were actually getting away with what 'they' were trying to do in the Ukraine . . . . The definition

of and response to the Czechoslovak situation . . . would be considered from *this* perspective as a projection outward of a campaign underway already in the Ukraine and other national republics to combat local nationalism and anti-Russianism. The critical factor here would be the cognitive impact that Ukrainian dissent had presumably already made upon the Soviet leadership.[9]

The precise relationship between contemporary Soviet domestic and foreign policies cannot be stated without firsthand knowledge of decisionmaking. Whatever the linkage may prove to be, there is little doubt that Soviet domestic vulnerabilities are taken into account during times of crisis and play a role in Soviet assessments of both their conventional and strategic force requirements. The nationalities issue is especially significant in assessing Soviet vulnerability to nuclear war. Nuclear retaliation (or the threat of retaliation) concentrated in ethnic Russian areas would significantly increase Soviet vulnerabilities while allowing the US greater economy of nuclear force. To take a crucial example: most Soviet ICBMs have been concentrated along major west-east rail lines and several northern spurs, from an area north of Moscow to the east of Lake Baykal (see Maps 1 and 2). The outer perimeter of Soviet ICBM deployments enclose an area with the highest population density and the largest concentrations of Great Russian population in the USSR. Twenty of twenty-six Soviet ICBM fields cut through the heart of these concentrations. The majority of strategic bomber bases and over 60 percent of Soviet industrial production are also located within the perimeter of this belt.[10]

There are also important climatological conditions affecting Soviet vulnerability to nuclear attack. Prevailing ground winds would carry local fallout over the most densely populated areas of the country. From November to March, winds generally blow from the southern and western perimeters of the ICBM belt toward the major population centers (see Map 2). From April to October, they blow from the northern and western perimeters to the same centers (see Map 1). These patterns increase the possibility of high radiation exposure since large directional changes in the wind serve to concentrate fallout more locally. In short, prevailing wind patterns throughout the year ensure that early fallout (the most lethal) would cover areas with the highest population density and the highest concentration of ethnic Russians.

The implications are thus painfully clear: in the event of nuclear attack, Soviet minorities will have a far better chance of survival than ethnic Russians since there are fewer strategic and economic targets in their homelands. Even a limited nuclear attack on centers of Great Russian power could signal the political disintegration of the USSR. If the Soviet regime were not politically incapacitated and could deal effectively with nationalist or ethnic challenges to central authority,

Map 1

ICBM SITES ARE ALONG MAIN WEST-EAST RAIL LINES AND SEVERAL NORTHERN SPURS. OUTER PERIMETER ENCLOSES LARGEST POPULATION CONCENTRATIONS.

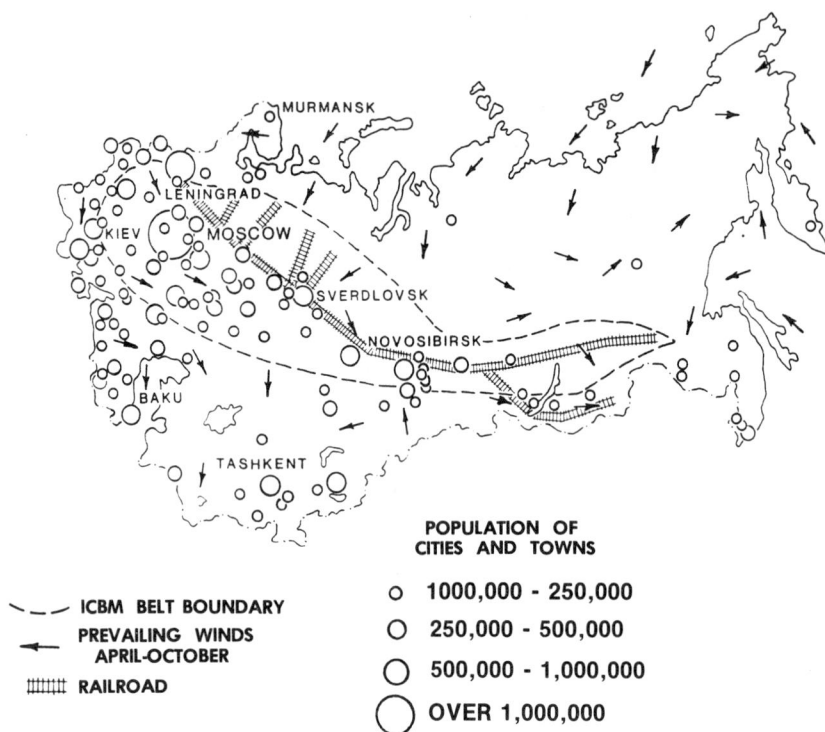

POPULATION OF
CITIES AND TOWNS

~ _ ~ ICBM BELT BOUNDARY

← PREVAILING WINDS
APRIL-OCTOBER

||||||| RAILROAD

O 1000,000 - 250,000

O 250,000 - 500,000

◯ 500,000 - 1,000,000

◯ OVER 1,000,000

SOURCES:
1. HAROLD FULLARD, SOVIET UNION IN MAPS
2. AIR FORCE MAGAZINE, MARCH 1978
3. JOHN COLLINS, AMERICAN AND SOVIET MILITARY TRENDS

what problems might it face from the Chinese or from its "allies" in Eastern Europe? These critical political questions are largely ignored by most American strategic analysts (and especially by SALT II critics), who have been preoccupied by technical issues and the allegedly delicate nuclear balance of power. At best, nuclear weapons are an imperfect means of compensating for the geopolitical liabilities unique to the Soviet state. These liabilities place serious constraints on the use of Soviet strategic power as a tool which can be employed in

MAP 2

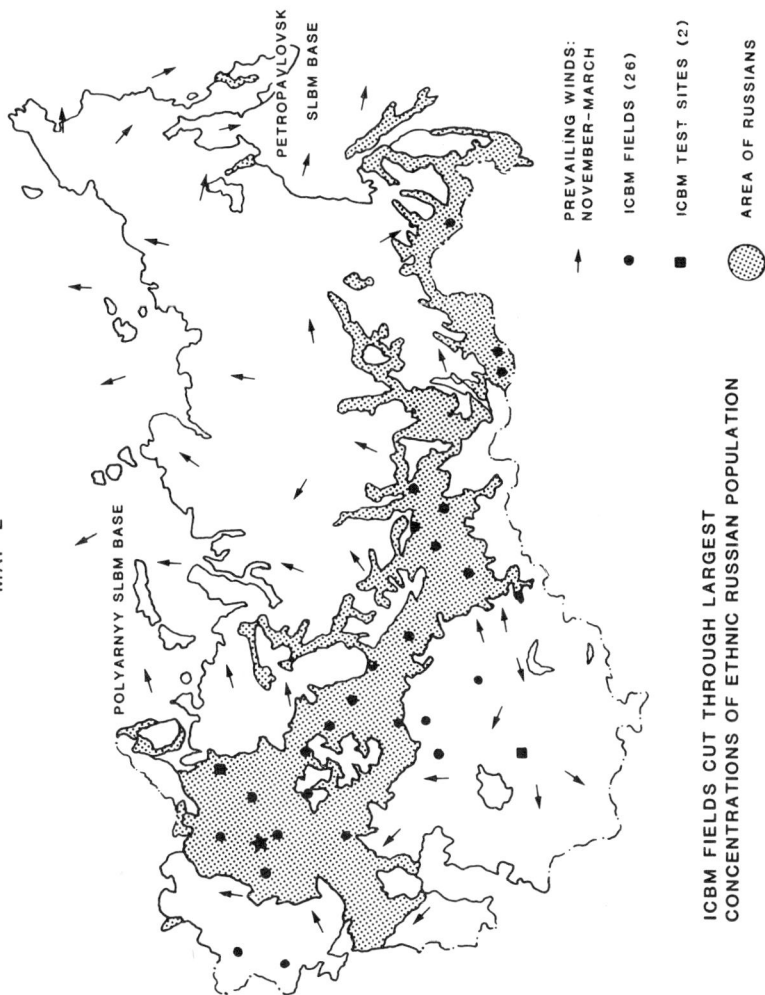

PETROPAVLOVSK SLBM BASE

POLYARNY SLBM BASE

PREVAILING WINDS:
NOVEMBER–MARCH

ICBM FIELDS (26)

ICBM TEST SITES (2)

AREA OF RUSSIANS

ICBM FIELDS CUT THROUGH LARGEST
CONCENTRATIONS OF ETHNIC RUSSIAN POPULATION

Source: 1. Harold Fullard, Soviet Union in Maps

2. Desmond Ball, SURVIVAL, August 1980

383

preplanned ways to coerce concessions from an adversary or which might tempt Soviet leaders to reckless and inflexible positions during crises.

Soviet Strategic Doctrine and Domestic Stability

Strategic doctrine in the United States has emphasized technical capabilities of weapons systems and their combined impact on the conduct of war if deterrence fails. Limited nuclear options, control of escalation, and nuclear "dueling" are regarded by Soviet observers as attempts to rationalize the use of nuclear weapons or to engage in political intimidation, especially during times of crisis.[11] The Soviets share with many of our European colleagues a sense that recent American doctrine has evolved from a purely technical milieu. Its models contain only one of the three broadly defined elements—operational activity, political motivation, and stability of the social and political structure—that Clausewitz defined as being intrinsic to war.[12] *Operational activity* dominates US warfighting scenarios, while references to *political motivation* and the stability of the *social structure*—our own as well as Soviet—are often absent. In contrast, Soviet strategic analysts have been far more attentive to the full continuum of possibilities ranging from politics to war. There is, admittedly, extensive and unsettling interest in the actual conduct of nuclear war. Preemption, combined arms, and counterforce emphasis, for example, are sinister and threatening aspects of Soviet doctrine singled out by many American analysts.[13] To conclude, however, that an emphasis on warfighting constitutes a rejection of deterrence is to engage in a very selective reading of Soviet doctrine. Soviet writings since the Malenkov-Khrushchev era are filled with references to the unprecedented devastation nuclear war would bring to both capitalist and socialist states. To argue, as Richard Pipes has done, that the Soviets believe they might be able to fight and "win" nuclear wars is to misread fundamentally the Soviets' frame of reference.[14] Both their ideology and history reinforce the sobering Russian experience of repeated invasions, attempts at diplomatic isolation, and encirclement by hostile forces. The question, then, is whether they see nuclear warfighting capabilities as credible instruments of policy (political motivation, in Clausewitz's terms) which might facilitate the achievement of specific and well-defined global objectives, or whether their emphasis on warfighting is a reaction to anticipated future aggression against the USSR. Clearly, in the Soviet strategic mind-set the latter is the case. Soviet doctrine repeatedly emphasizes that if nuclear war comes, it will be forced on the USSR, perhaps by a capitalist system caught in the death throes of its "final crisis" desperately seeking to reverse the inevitable course of history. This "anticipatory" view of future dangers, combined with the Soviets' own acute sense of vulnerability, has fostered strategic policies that are quite different from their US counterparts.[15] In the Soviet view, deterrence based on punishment through retaliatory second strikes—the basis of the US doctrine of assured destruction—may not be sufficient during the final and potentially aggressive period of capitalism. Thus, the final and potential adversaries must be convinced that there is no hope of achieving their goals through military means. Military forces must be in a position to deny victory if deterrence fails. This theme—the denial of victory in nuclear war—has remained a major and constant refrain in Soviet doctrine since Khrushchev's historic speech at the 20th Party Congress in which he reversed the classic Leninist dictum of the inevitability of war between capitalist and socialist states: "But war is not fatalistically inevitable. Today there are mighty social and political forces *possessing formidable means to prevent the imperialists from unleashing war . . . ."*[16]

The ability to deny victory to the enemy further strengthens deterrence but does not preempt its importance in Soviet doctrine. Soviet rejection of limited nuclear war and controlled escalation and the absence of references—even in abstract terms—to how a nuclear war would be terminated are evidence of a commitment to deterrence and delineate major differences between Soviet and American thinking about counterforce strategies.[17]

To argue that the Soviet strategic buildup and the emphasis on warfighting portends an era of Soviet assertiveness in the form of nuclear "Trotskyism" is to ignore the importance of social and political stability during periods of threat, crisis, or war which is emphasized in Soviet commentaries. Social-political cohesion may be as essential an element in Soviet calculations as survivable, second-strike capabilities are in US doctrine. The Soviets view war, including nuclear war, as being protracted in duration as compared with the short, spasmodic exchanges popularized in so much Western literature. The political significance of this is that the latter are fought and generally decided by existing forces, using resources which are immediately available. Although existing forces are also viewed as important in a long war, mobilization and support of the civilian sectors of the economy and political systems are as critical and are so emphasized in Soviet writings. Soviet military doctrine thus stresses the continued probability of a long war waged by large armies and conducted by combined force operations—strategic, tactical, and conventional—in which victory is described in terms of the destruction of enemy military potential, seizure of strategic areas, occupation of territory, installation of friendly governments, and, perhaps, ideological conversion.

It is important to remember that in the Soviet view, all of this is seen as a response to aggression, not as a policy choice in pursuit of preplanned Soviet objectives. Because of the unprecedented destructiveness of nuclear war, Soviet doctrine emphasizes both the importance of its prevention and the necessity of preparing for the possibility of its being waged. A major gap between theory and capabilities is the Soviet inability to occupy the United States. This, in turn, must certainly create doubts as to whether any first-strike capability could "eliminate" US military and economic capabilities while Soviet combined forces were engaging the remnants of the "imperalist coalition" in Western Europe and, at the same time, holding off certain "jackals" (China), controlling Eastern Europe,[18] subduing unrest among their own nationalities, and perhaps dealing with aroused and militant Third World elements on their borders during the "recovery period." Surely, any responsible leadership would harbor the gravest doubts as to the adequacy of Soviet strategic and conventional forces to underwrite the enormous wartime demands placed on them by Soviet doctrine. As Benjamin Lambeth has eloquently pointed out:

> Because obligations place open-ended demands on Soviet force availability, performance, and durability, the Soviet leaders can never feel so complacent about the adequacy of their preparedness efforts as to permit any prolonged resting on their strategic oars.[19]

Lambeth's observations are in sharp contrast to the often repeated belief that Soviet military preparedness goes far beyond legitimate defense requirements. If correct, Soviet notions of "sufficiency" are inevitably going to be more ambitious than their American counterparts. Combined threats to Soviet security—especially geopolitical and ethnic—may do more to enhance the credibility of US deterrence than any variant of military hardware or technical capability popularized by the SALT debate. To argue that the Soviet Union is planning to use its growing strategic power as an instrument of imperial expansion is to take enormous and speculative leaps beyond anything contained in Soviet published materials as well as to ignore the geopolitical restraint described above.[20]

Policy Implications for US Strategic Doctrine and Arms Control

There is little doubt the Soviet strategic buildup—or more accurately, catch-up—has contributed to major changes in US strategic doctrine. These changes can be seen in Secretary of Defense Harold Brown's Annual Defense Reports from 1979–81 in which he delineates the requirements for the stable deterrence on which the Carter administration based US strategic programs and SALT II. These can be summarized as:

Survivability
Assured destruction
Flexibility
Essential equivalence

386

SAFE (if the debate can tolerate yet another acronym) incorporates *survivability and assured destruction* from the Kennedy-Johnson and early Nixon years and refers to the required capability of the US retaliatory force to inflict an "unacceptable" level of damage to urban-industrial (and some military) and, more recently, "political power structure" targets in the Soviet Union even after absorbing a full-scale Soviet attack.[21]

Flexibility, or limited nuclear options, was given wide publicity by Secretary of Defense James Schlesinger in 1974. This latest variant of the counterforce strategy refers to the growing capability of US strategic forces to respond to a Soviet attack on a lower scale than all-out retaliation against Soviet cities and incorporates "limited" attacks against Soviet military targets, including missile silos and command and control centers. Secretary Brown has also described this as a "countervailing strategy"[22] in the sense that retaliation is selective and commensurate with the level of provocation. Thus, "countervailing" or limited nuclear options are initial responses, while the "assured destruction" capacity against Soviet cities and industrial complexes is held in reserve.[23] This limited, but potentially protracted, nuclear warfighting doctrine was reaffirmed and made more specific in Presidental Directive 59 signed by Carter during the summer of 1980.[24]

SAFE then, is a hybrid in the evolutionary process from a predominantly countervalue-based targeting doctrine to a greater emphasis on counterforce targeting. This process has dominated the strategic debate, dividing advocates of limited nuclear options and "strategic stabilizers" over the desirability of hard target, counterforce options.[25] The "warfighters" advocate strategies and force levels which reflect the traditional belief that strategic weapons and doctrine must be prepared to fight wars, not just deter them. Maintaining a warfighting capability is the other side of the deterrence coin. Deterrence, according to this view, cannot be maintained credibly in the absence of declared operational plans and capabilities. It is argued here that credible deterrence can be maintained, as it has in the past, independent of limited warfighting options. This can be accomplished by insuring survivable, second-strike forces assigned limited missions (e.g., retaliation in response to a direct attack on the United States or its NATO and Japanese allies) while maintaining credible conventional force levels to meet crises below the nuclear threshold.

Strategy and Deterrence

The most important measure of a nation's strategic deterrent is its ability to survive an initial attack and perform its assigned missions.[26] The size and characteristics of that deterrent should be determined not by the need for matching Soviet counterparts but by the requirements of destroying specific Soviet targets. What those missions or targets should be is at the heart of the strategic debate. One reasonable objective—presumably agreed on by all participants—is the erosion or elimination of Soviet confidence in military solutions to crisis. As Colin Gray has recently put it: "One of the essential tasks of the American defense community is to help ensure that in moments of acute crisis the Soviet General Staff cannot brief the Politburo with a plausible theory of victory."[27]

This study has attempted to demonstrate that a Soviet decision to go to war requires much more than the military confidence of the General Staff. The Soviet calculus requires political, social, and economic confidence as well. This presents US planners with a broad deterrence spectrum in targeting those interrelated values which most credibly will prevent Gray's "victory" briefing from becoming plausible. Alternative strategies could be based on the Soviet geopolitical vulnerabilities described above and on the requirements for denying Soviet forces what they, themselves, delineate as the prerequisites for "victory".

According to Soviet doctrine, "victory" includes combined conventional-strategic force coordination in wars of potentially long duration during which the economic, political, and social viability of Soviet and allied states are vital. Under such circumstances, what kinds of threat would have the most deterring effect on the Soviet leadership? It is the thesis of this article that the broad outlines of such a deterrent would include an ethnic-based countercombatant, counterindustrial targeting doctrine. Within this framework, declaratory policies and force procurement decisions would avoid hard target, counterforce or countervalue, "city-killing" strategies. In short, there are credible alternatives to both assured destruction and the current destabilizing counterforce options.

An Ethnic–Based Targeting Doctrine?

To a large extent, US targeting doctrine is ethnically based by default, since the majority of strategic and industrial targets are located in the central Great Russian republic (RSFSR). Amplifying the prospects for assured and concentrated retaliation by even a limited force against military and industrial targets in the ethnic Russian areas could strengthen the credibility of US deterrence. (The dangers and potential backlash from such a policy are discussed below.) This could be done through a declaratory policy that held out the prospect of limiting retaliatory attacks on non-Russian union republics (exceptions are described below).

Countercombatant and Counterindustrial Targets

The term "countercombatant" was first introduced in the strategic

388

debate by Bruce Russett.[28] In essence, Russett argued that the "rational" Russian leader would be deterred by the prospects of severe damage to the armed forces of the Soviet Union—forces that are heavily relied upon for the combined conventional-strategic force emphasis found in Soviet doctrine, as well as the maintenance of internal security and bloc cohesion. Their loss or degradation surely would be as unacceptable as the loss of cities. The concept is defined more narrowly here than by Russett, whose definition included all nuclear striking forces. Here, a more limited target acquisition process is advocated, with the emphasis on conventional force concentrations, their logistical support bases, transport and storage areas, air bases, and naval port facilities. Land-based missile silos would be specifically excluded. The object—if first-strike incentives are to be avoided—is not to *deny* the Soviets a credible nuclear retaliatory force; rather, the intent is (1) to reduce—but not eliminate—Soviet capacity for inflicting damage on the United States and, more importantly, (2) to reduce to unacceptable levels the capacity to defend themselves tactically at home, in Europe, and on the Chinese border. Surviving Soviet ICBMs have limited use in these latter conflicts where Soviet doctrine prescribes occupation by ground troops. Moreover, their employment against American cities could invite counterstrikes on Russian cities.

Soviet troop configurations lend themselves to such a strategy since first-line combat formations are predominantly ethnic Russian. Many are garrisoned at points distant from (or, at worst, adjacent to) population centers in both the Soviet Union and in Eastern Europe. Where they can be identified, non-Russian troop concentrations might be deliberately avoided. The object would not be the total destruction of the Soviet Army but the prospect of such substantial and assured degradation that combined threats to the Soviet state could not be met. Internal security forces, including the *KGB,* might also be targeted where they are concentrated.

Targeting the industrial potential of the Soviet Union has always been an integral part of the US strategy. The ability to destroy one-half to two-thirds of the Soviet industrial base was a major objective under the assured destruction doctrine of the 1960s and forms a major part of US doctrine—as delineated as recently as Secretary Brown's FY 1981 Annual Defense Report. There was a brief period during the Nixon years when the emphasis shifted to economic "recovery time." But early in the Carter administration, Secretary Brown moved away from this strategy on the grounds that anti-recovery concepts were too vague and could be used to justify increases in strategic forces.[29] (The same argument, of course, could also apply to the counterforce-limited nuclear options endorsed by Brown.) Indeed, this seemed to be very much the case, since Secretary Rumsfeld claimed that 8,500 warheads were required for adequate coverage of all targets, including those necessary for implementing the anti-recovery doctrine.[30] In any case, such figures are suspect, given the economic concentrations that characterize the centrally planned Soviet economy.

For a variety of reasons—historic, economic, and political—the Soviet Union, despite its geographic expansiveness, has concentrated its industry and population in less than a quarter of its total area. Key industrial complexes, clustered around major cities, are more concentrated than in the United States, and a limited number of facilities comprise the bulk of the productive capacity in many major industries.[31] A good example would be the controversial Kama River truck and auto facility, a giant complex the size of Manhattan where one-fifth of all Soviet vehicles are produced.[32] Similarly, the Office of Technology Assessment has shown that an attack on petroleum refineries in the USSR could, with 10 missiles (7 Poseidon and 3 Minuteman IIIs), destroy 73 percent of the refining capacity.[33] Electrical power, transportation, food processing, chemical plants, and steel are equally vulnerable. Clearly, Soviet planners have chosen industrial efficiency and typically Russian "massive" complexes over civil defense considerations. The centrally planned economy has such vulnerable choke points which, if destroyed, would curtail production in many other industries. Existing civil defense programs cannot confidently ensure a modern nation against the vulnerability of industrial interdependence. The degree of damage the US could inflict on unprotectable economic resources with only a fraction of its total forces would be so great that the Soviet Union could be effectively eliminated as a major industrial power.

For the Soviets, recovery would be complicated by the political problems they would confront in presumably less damaged non-Russian republics. Could the economically linked—but physically less damaged—zones be counted on for recovery assistance as in the case of other localized disaster recovery efforts? Or would scarcity and chaos further stimulate the centripetal forces of nationalism and separatism?[34] The lessons of World War II so often cited by American analysts alarmed by Soviet civil defense programs are not applicable in nuclear war scenarios.[35] Many of the outlying union republics served their buffer functions well in World War II, absorbing the initial damage and destruction of the German Army. In a nuclear war, the reverse would be true. The central Great Russian zone (RSFSR) would receive immediate and highly concentrated levels of damage. Recent studies conducted by the Congressional Budget Office conclude that the force requirements for a counterindustrial strategy would be closer to the 300–400 range of earlier McNamara estimates. Soviet vulnerability to limited nuclear attack, even after efforts to harden industrial complexes (construction of special canopies, foundations, and sandbagging), is extensive. Eleven "surviving" Poseidon submarines, for instance, could be expected to achieve 50 percent destruction of a hardened Soviet industrial base (85 percent with no hardening). The Trident I missiles currently being deployed (224 by the end of FY 1981) increase the estimated destruction of a hardened Soviet industrial base to 60 percent (assuming a total force of 240).[36]

US strategic bombers are even less affected by Soviet civil defense efforts. Of 380 bombers in the force, at least 100 could be expected to survive a first strike, assuming normal peacetime alert. These bombers could be expected to destroy 70 percent of the Soviet industrial base without hardening, or 65 percent if hardened. Twice as many weapons would be available if the bomber force were on a generated alert; under such circumstances, 80 percent of a hardened industrial base would be destroyed. Even more threatening, when cruise missiles are deployed, a surviving force of only 60 B–52s could be expected to destroy nearly 85 percent of the unprotected Soviet industrial base.[37]

Even these grim statistics may exaggerate force requirements, since credible deterrence may not demand the total destruction of Soviet industry. The destruction of essential choke points in a highly interdependent economic system effectively would shut down industrial production, even if many plants and industrial centers survived. Soviet sensitivity to threats aimed at the industrial infrastructure which supports its superpower status, combined with its strategic preceptions of long wars requiring a stable political and economic base, suggest that a countereconomic second-strike emphasis may be an effective (but, thus far, insufficiently explored) means for achieving both stable and credible deterrence and strategic arms reductions.

A Strategy for Deterrence or "Victory"?

The positions outlined here entertain no illusions that nuclear war can be closely and surgically controlled or that it could avoid killing millions of civilians by both the immediate and delayed effects of a nuclear exchange (regardless of what targets are included or excluded from strategic doctrines). *Above all, the arguments here are aimed at strengthening the credibility of prewar deterrence.* That, in turn, rests on the ability of both sides to maintain survivable second-strike forces against targets sufficiently valued by their adversary that threats against them will effectively deter a first strike. The Soviet military and economic targets discussed in this study meet these requirements since they are identified in Soviet military writings as vital prerequisites for victory. The fundamental question dividing strategic analysts in the United States—and perhaps in the Soviet Union as well—is precisely what these targets should be and what forces and technical capabilities should be arrayed against them.

One side advocates hard target, counterforce capabilities, gained only at the cost of increased crisis instability, including an enhanced possibility of preemptive attack. Soviet counterforce superiority would not be militarily feasible so long as the US retained survivable second-strike forces. Survivability can and must be independent of Soviet force characteristics. It does not require the time-urgent, hard target kill capabilities of the MX missile or the MK–12A warhead or the counter-force accuracy proposed for Trident II. Seeking survivability by preempting threatening systems does not create deterrence; rather, it leads to a runaway process since, under crisis conditions, options may become mandates for survival. Stability and survivability can coexist within the framework of a weapons acquisition strategy that emphasizes survivability rather than counterforce capabilities.

Rejecting hard target, counterforce options in US force procurement decisions and declaratory policies would be a major step requiring strong and determined leadership. Soviet vulnerabilities described here could be used effectively in the domestic debate required to allay fears in Congress, the press, and among the attentive public. The difficulties in developing a convincing strategic dialogue would be compounded by the dangers of a potential Soviet backlash. Soviet policymakers listen to what we tell ourselves. What we say in *Foreign Affairs,* in a State of the Union address, in a speech at West Point, or in a Senate debate provides the bulk of what they hear. Not infrequently, we fail to take into consideration the potential effect. If the domestic debate involved widespread discussion of Soviet vulnerabilities, especially references to the "nationalities," with no accompanying restraints in the deployment of counterforce systems, their heightened perceptions of US hostility could easily prompt countermeasures against what could appear to be the nuclear variant of the "captive nations" theme. The net result would be a major escalation of the arms race. An emphasis on Soviet vulnerabilities in official declaratory policies could be used effectively only in defense of major qualitative restraints and/or quanti-tative reductions in US strategic forces.

The feasibility and extent of strategic arms reductions under the tar-geting strategies proposed here would be contested bitterly. Ceilings proposed by analysts without access to classified targeting data may be arbitrary and imprecise. However, what is openly known about Soviet vulnerabilities suggests that a credible deterrent could be maintained at force levels considerably below the 8,500 warheads advocated by Rumsfeld and certainly well below (perhaps as much as 50 percent) current US force levels of 9,200.

Where is the balance between "prudence and paranoia?" It appears unlikely that we will ever have agreement. It would also seem that strategic arms competition, with or without SALT, is moving further in the direction of paranoia.

Notes

1. US Department of Defense, *Annual Report, Fiscal Year 1980,* p. 76.
2. A recent and detailed analysis of this is Stanley Sienkiewicz's "Observations on the

Impact of Uncertainty in Strategic Analysis," in *World Politics,* October 1979, pp. 90–110.

3. Russett and Gray briefly discuss the problem. See Bruce Russett, "Assured Destruction of What?" *Public Policy,* Spring 1974, pp. 121–138; and Colin Gray, "Nuclear Strategy: A Case for a Theory of Victory," *International Security,* Summer 1979, pp. 54–87. See also Bernard Albert, "Constructive Counterpower," *Orbis,* Summer 1976, pp. 343–66.

4. Some experts had predicted the 1980 census would show ethnic Russians to be a minority. The most recent issue of *Population of the USSR* claims ethnic Russians constitute 52.4 percent of the population. Quoted by Dan Fisher, *Los Angeles Times,* 23 February 1980, Part I–A, p. 1.

5. Adam Ulam, *Expansion and Coexistence: Soviet Foreign Policy 1917–73,* 2nd ed. (New York: Praeger, 1974), pp. 326–7.

6. Reported in *The New York Times,* 19 April 1946, p. 19; 15 May 1949, p. 1; 26 July 1949, p. 9; and 1 May 1950, p. 10.

7. For a more complete discussion of this situation, see Grey Hodnett and Peter Potichnyi, *The Ukraine and the Czechoslovak Crisis* (Canberra: Australian National University, 1970).

8. Ibid., pp. 121–5.

9. Ibid., pp. 124–5.

10. Kevin N. Lewis, "The Prompt and Delayed Effects of Nuclear War," *Scientific American,* July 1979, pp. 35–47.

11. See, for example, Georgiy Arbatov, "The Dangers of a New Cold War," *Bulletin of the Atomic Scientists,* March 1977, p. 38; Radomir Bogdanov and Lev Semeyko, "Soviet Military Might: A Soviet View," *Fortune,* 26 February 1979, pp. 46–52; and Robert Legvold, "Strategic 'Doctrine' and SALT: Soviet and American Views," *Survival,* January/February 1979.

12. Michael Howard, "The Forgotten Dimensions of Strategy," *Foreign Affairs,* Summer 1979, pp. 975–86; and Lawrence Freedman's review of Roger Speed, "Strategic Deterrence in the 1980s," in *Survival,* January/February 1980, p. 45.

13. For example, Joseph Douglass, Jr. and Amoretta Hoeber, *Soviet Strategy for Nuclear War* (Stanford: The Hoover Institution, 1979); Paul Nitze, "Deterring our Deterrent," *Foreign Policy,* Winter 1976–77, pp. 195–220; or William Van Cleave and Roger Barnett, "Strategic Adaptability," *Orbis,* Fall 1974, pp. 655–76.

14. Richard Pipes, "Why the Soviet Union Thinks It Could Fight and Win a Nuclear War," *Commentary,* July 1977, pp. 21–34.

15. Dennis Ross, "Rethinking Soviet Strategic Policy: Inputs and Implications," *ACIS Working Paper,* No. 5 (Los Angeles: Center for Arms Control and International Security, UCLA, 1977), especially pp. 5–13.

16. Leo Gruliow, ed., *Current Soviet Policies, II* (New York: Praeger, 1957), pp. 29–63, emphasis added.

17. Raymond Garthoff, "Soviet Views on the Interrelationship of Diplomacy and Military Strategy," *Political Science Quarterly,* Fall 1979, p. 404.

18. The Soviets fear that Western strategy includes efforts to break up the socialist community and to separate individual countries from its ranks. See ibid., p. 398.

19. Benjamin S. Lambeth, "The Political Potential of Soviet Equivalence," *International Security,* Fall 1979, p. 37.

20. This is the thesis of a recent book on Soviet strategic doctrine. See Douglass and Hoeber, op. cit., p. *ix.*

21. US Department of Defense, *Annual Report, Fiscal Year 1981,* p. 66. McNamara first defined "unacceptable damage" as destruction of 20–25 percent of the Soviet population and 50 percent of industry. Secretary Brown initally defined the same term as destruction of a minimum of 200 major cities but has avoided specifying numerical requirements in his reports for fiscal years 1980 or 1981.

22. Ibid., p. 65.

23. Ibid., p. 66.

24. See *The New York Times,* 6 August 1980, p. 1.
25. For the major points dividing "warfighters" and "stable balancers" see Leon Sigal, "Rethinking the Unthinkable," *Foreign Policy,* No. 34, Spring 1979, pp. 35–51.
26. A mission approach is discussed by General Maxwell Taylor in "What If SALT II Fails?" *AEI Defense Review,* Vol. 2, No. 4, p. 22.
27. Gray, op. cit., p. 56.
28. Russett, op. cit., pp. 124–125.
29. See Department of Defense, *Annual Report, Fiscal Year 1978 and 1979.*
30. US Department of Defense, *Annual Report, Fiscal Year 1978,* pp. 21 and 78.
31. Fred Kaplan, "The Soviet Civil Defense Myth," *Bulletin of Atomic Scientists,* April 1978. See also Geoffrey Kemp, *Nuclear Forces for Medium Powers,* Adelphi Paper No. 196 (London: International Institute for Strategic Studies, 1974).
32. US Congress, Office of Technology Assessments, *The Effects of Nuclear Weapons* (Washington: Government Printing Office, 1979), p. 54.
33. Ibid., p. 76.
34. For a historical examination of the problem, see J. Hirschleifer, *Disaster and Recovery: A Historical Survey,* Report RM–3079–PR (Santa Monica: The Rand Corporation April 1963).
35. For example, Leon Goure, *War Survival in Soviet Strategy* (Washington: Advanced International Studies Institute, 1976), and T. K. Jones, *Industrial Survival and Recovery After Nuclear Attack: A Report to the Joint Committee on Defense Production, US Congress* (Seattle: The Boeing Aerospace Company, November 1976).
36. US Congress, Congressional Budget Office, *Retaliatory Issues for the US Strategic Nuclear Forces* (Washington: Government Printing Office, 1978), pp. 25–27.
37. Ibid., p. 28.

Soviet Theater Nuclear Forces: Implications for NATO Defense*

Robert Kennedy

Since World War II, the principal focus of Western defense policies has centered on efforts designed to offset the preponderance of Soviet conventional power on the continent of Europe. To this end, NATO, over the years, generally has relied on US strategic and theater nuclear superiority to bring balance to the military equation in Europe. In a landmark speech delivered in London at the International Institute for Strategic Studies in October 1977, however, Helmut Schmidt, mindful of improving Soviet strategic and theater nuclear capabilities, expressed concern over the changing strategic conditions which now confront the Alliance. According to Schmidt, SALT had codified the Soviet-American strategic nuclear balance, thus neutralizing the strategic nuclear capabilities of the superpowers. As a result, he cautioned, the significance of the East–West balance of tactical nuclear and conventional weapons had been magnified.

The Federal German Chancellor went on to suggest that while the Soviets had apparently accepted parity at the strategic level, they had given no clear indication of a willingness to accept the principle of parity for Europe. In fact, he argued, "the Warsaw Pact has, if anything, increased the disparities in both conventional and tactical nuclear forces."[1] Since European and American defense specialists have long been aware of what generally has been perceived as a clear Soviet conventional advantage, Schmidt's remarks focused public attention on a series of issues which already were commanding high-level NATO interest and thus sparked an intensification of the debate over the nature of the Soviet theater nuclear buildup, over the implications of that buildup for deterrence and defense, and over the appropriate NATO response.

Soviet Theater Nuclear Force Improvements

During the last decade, NATO has signaled a willingness to reduce the number of nuclear weapons systems and warheads in the European theater and, indeed, during talks on Mutual and Balanced Forced

*This article was originally prepared for and presented at the Assistant Chief of Staff/Intelligence, USAF–sponsored conference, "The Soviet Union: What Lies Ahead?," in September 1980, and later reprinted in *Air Force Magazine,* Vol. 64, No. 3 (March 1981).

Reductions in Europe (MBFR) offered an option which included a reduction in theater nuclear forces and weapons. In contrast, the Soviet Union has been methodically improving its theater nuclear forces at all levels.

Tactical/Battlefield Systems (Rx = 5–100 NM)

On the tactical or battlefield level, NATO once possessed an overwhelming superiority in nuclear weapons systems and warheads. In some quarters, that superiority has been considered one of the primary pillars in the deterrence of the overwhelmingly superior Soviet conventional forces. Today, the Warsaw Pact has over 600 FROG and SCUD A missiles of which over 400 can be considered to have a nuclear mission. Moreover, they are now replacing their older FROG rockets with the SS–21. Although little data is currently available on the SS–21, it is reported to have a considerably greater range than the FROG and presumably has incorporated improvements in reaction time, missile reliability, accuracy, and handling characteristics.[2]

The Soviet Union is also now deploying dual-capable 203–mm and 240–mm artillery. According to the Secretary of Defense, nuclear-capable artillery are currently only deployed in the Soviet Union.[3] However, Soviet nuclear artillery easily could be moved to support nuclear operations against NATO.

While NATO still retains a relative overall advantage in short-range systems and warheads as a result of a substantial deployment of nuclear artillery, the gap between NATO and Warsaw Pact battlefield capabilities has narrowed considerably over the past decade and a half, and the overwhelming superiority once enjoyed by NATO has disappeared (see Table 1).

Battlefield Support Systems (Rx = 101–500 NM)

The Soviet Union also has been upgrading its medium-range battlefield support systems. Currently, the Soviets have deployed approximately 500 battlefield support missiles and over 1,200 tactical aircraft and are capable of delivering over 800 nuclear weapons with such systems. Moreover, they are now replacing their liquid-propelled SCUD B and SS–12/SCALEBOARD missiles with SS–23s and SS–22s and are rapidly improving the nuclear strike capabilities of their tactical air systems. The addition of the FITTER C and D aircraft and later versions of the MiG–21 aircraft with improved avionics and generally greater ranges than the older Soviet fighters suggests an improved capacity for low altitude penetration and attack.

In comparision, NATO fields 180 Pershing I missiles, approximately 255 medium-range battlefield support aircraft (of which only about 100 are likely to be reserved for nuclear missions), and about 300 nuclear warheads to support these systems. Such a comparison suggests a stark imbalance in medium-range systems in facor of the Warsaw Pact (see

Table 1. Tactical/Battlefield Nuclear Systems.

WARSAW PACT						NATO					
Artillery						Artillery					
Type	Deployed	PNM	RX	WHt	WHa	Type	Deployed	PNM	Rx	WHt	WHa
203–mm	na	150	16	300	270	155–mm	1654	827	10	1654	1489
240–mm	na	150	na	300	270	203–mm	258	129	11	258	232
TOTALS		300		600	540	TOTALS	1912	956		1912	1721
Tactical Missiles						Tactical Missiles					
Type	Deployed	PNM	Rx	WHt	WHa	Type	Deployed	PNM	Rx	WHt	WHa
FROG/ SS–21	375	250	40/60	250	200	Lance	97	97	60	97	87
SCUD A	251	168	45	168	134	Honest John	42	42	20	42	29
						Pluton	42	42	65	42	34
TOTALS	626	418		418	334		181	181		181	150

Source: Derived from information and data appearing in the *Department of Defense Annual Report Fiscal Year 1982, The Military Balance 1981–1982,* and Air Vice-Marshal Stewart W. B. Menaul, "The Shifting Theater Nuclear Balance in Europe," *Strategic Review,* Vol. 6, No. 4 (Fall 1978), pp. 34–45.

Key: Tactical/Battlefield Nuclear Systems: Those systems with a range of 5–100 NM.

Warsaw Pact: Includes all systems in Eastern Europe and in the western military districts of the Soviet Union.

NATO: Includes systems currently assigned or earmarked for the European theater.

PNM: Probable nuclear mission. The Secretary of Defense has indicated that some of the 203–mm and 240–mm artillery pieces now deployed by the USSR have been adapted to fire nuclear projectiles. Air Vice-Marshal Menaul has estimated that the Soviet Union now has 150 203–mm gun/howitzers with a nuclear capability. It is reasonable to assume that as a minimum, the Soviets have deployed an equal number of 240–mm gun/howitzers.

Rx: Approximate maximum range in nautical miles.

WHt: Total warheads estimated to be available in peacetime.

WHa: Warheads assumed to be available for delivery on wartime targets given probable system in-commission rates. For artillery and Lance missiles, the general wartime availability factor is assessed at 0.9. For Honest John, the factor has been assessed at 0.7. All other systems are assessed at 0.8.

Table 2). On the other hand, some of NATO's battlefield support requirements can be covered by tactical air assets drawn from those which, because of their range, are considered Eurostrategic (Table 3). However, tactical air assets so employed would reduce the total number of nuclear strikes likely to be available against Eurostrategic targets.

Eurostrategic Systems (Rx = 501–4000 NM)

Perhaps most significant, especially for US European allies, is the slow but methodical change in the balance of nuclear capabilities which is taking place at the Eurostrategic level. In the mid- and late 1960s, it was generally assumed that the West had a clear advantage in systems which recently have come to be called Eurostrategic. US Polaris submarines committed to SACEUR, NATO medium-range strike aircraft deployed on the continent or stationed offshore on carriers, the British bomber and Polaris submarine fleets, and the French Mirage IVA strike aircraft and their expanding ballistic missile submarine fleet were considered a more than adequate match for the medium bombers and the 750 or so MRBMs and IRBMs the Soviets had deployed to support long-range nuclear operations in Europe.

During the last decade and a half, however, the Soviets have made a determined effort to offset Western capabilities. With the introduction of the FENCER and FLOGGER aircraft, the Soviet Union has substantially improved the range, payload, avionics, and ECM capabilities of its European nuclear strike air arm. Admiral Thomas H. Moorer, then Chairman of the US Joint Chiefs of Staff, in early 1974 described the FENCER as "the first modern Soviet fighter to be developed specifically as a fighter-bomber." Its two-man crew (pilot and weapons system operator) suggests an increased ability to conduct night, all-weather, low altitude, precision nuclear missions into the heart of Western Europe. *Jane's* places the FENCER, which entered squadron service in 1974, in the same class as the USAF F–111. Today, the Soviets have deployed approximately 735 FENCER and FLOGGER B and D aircraft in the European theater.

Coupled with continued improvements in its high performance fighter aircraft, the Soviet Union also has begun deploying a new generation, variable-geometry, supersonic bomber known in the West by the NATO code name BACKFIRE. Manufactured by Tupolev, the BACKFIRE is reported to have a maximum speed at high altitude of Mach 2.5 and an "on the deck" supersonic penetration capability. It can carry a full range of free-fall/gravity weapons as well as the most technically advanced air-to-surface nuclear cruise missiles available in the Soviet inventory.[4] To date, the Soviets have deployed approximately 50 BACKFIRE bombers to the European theater. However, the Soviet Union is reported to be producing the BACKFIRE at a rate of 30 aircraft per year with an expected deployment of up to 300 aircraft.

Table 2. Medium–Range Battlefield Support Systems.

WARSAW PACT						NATO					
Battlefield Support Missiles						Battlefield Support Missiles					
Type	No. Deployed	PNM	Rx	WHt	WHa	Type	No. Deployed	PNM	Rx	WHt	WHa
SCUD B/ SS–X–23			160			Pershing I	180	180	390	180	162
SS–12/ SS–22	506	506		506	455						
	506	506		506	455						
Tactical Aircraft						Tactical Aircraft					
Type	No. Deployed	PNM	Rx	WHt	WHa		No. Deployed	PNM	Rx	WHt	WHa
Su–7 (FITTER A)	124	31	390	31	20	Jaguar	219	80	465	80	64
Su–17 (FITTER C/D)	525	181	390	262	210	Etendard	36	18	390	36	29
Su–20 (FITTER C)	30	8	390	16	13	TOTALS	255	98		116	93
MiG–21 (FISHBED J/K/L/N)	562	140	260	140	120						
TOTALS	1241	310		449	363						

Source: Derived from data appearing in *The Military Balance 1980–1981,* and *Jane's All the World's Aircraft 1979–1980.*

Key: Medium–Range Battlefield Support Systems: Those systems with a range of 101 NM to 500 NM.

PNM, Rx, WHt, and WHa: See Table 1. A general availability factor of 0.9 was used to determine WHa for all battlefield support missile systems except the SS–N–4 (SARK). A factor of 0.7 was used for SARK. The factor used for tactical aircraft was 0.8. It was assumed that ½ of the Etendards would be retained in a nuclear role. It was also assumed that two warheads would be available for all FITTER C and D Etendard aircraft. One warhead for each of those that remain. The range estimates (Rx) for tactical aircraft are the greater of the ranges indicated in the above-mentioned source documents assuming a hi-lo-hi combat mission profile. The FITTER C/D range was adjusted for a lighter bomb load than that indicated in *Jane's* and for the addition of external fuel tanks.

399

Table 3. Eurostrategic Systems.

WARSAW PACT

Mid-Range Missiles (MR/SLBMs)

Type	No. Deployed	PNM	Rx	WHt	WHa
SS-4 (SANDAL)	340	340	1000	340	306
SS-N-5(SERB)	57	57	600	57	40
TOTALS	397	397		397	346

Intermediate Range Missiles (IR/SLBMs)

Type	No. Deployed	PNM	Rx	WHt	WHa
SS-5 (SKEAN)	40	40	2200	40	36
SS-20*	154	154	2700	462	416
TOTALS	194	194		502	452

Aircraft

Type	No. Deployed	PNM	Rx	WHt	WHa
Su-19 (FENCER)	360	90	1000+	180	114
MiG-23/27 (FLOGGER B&D)	375	94	520	94	75
Tu-16 (BADGER)	232	116	1800	232	186
Tu-22 (BLINDER B)	94	47	1750+	94	75
Tu-26 (BACKFIRE B)	49	24	2500+	96	97
TOTALS	1110	371		696	597

NATO

Mid-Range Missiles (MR/SLBMs)

Type
NONE

Intermediate Range Missiles (IR/SLBMs)

Type	No. Deployed	RNM	Rx	WHt	WHa
SSBS-S-2/3	18	18	1600	18	16
Polaris*	64	64	2500	48	43
MSBS M2/M20*	80	80	2000	64	58
Poseidon	40	40	2400	400	360

Aircraft

Type	No. Deployed	RNM	Rx	WHt	WHa
Vulcan B-2	57	57	2000	114	91
Buccaneer	60	30	1000	60	48
Mirage IVA	33	33	1000	33	26
FB-111	156	78	1000*	156	125
F-4	364	121	600	121	97
Mirage IIIE	105	30	650	30	24
F-104	318	106	500+	106	85
A-6	20	10	1000+	20	16
A-7	40	20	1000+	40	32
TOTALS	1153	485		680	544

Table 3 (Continued)

AGGREGATE EUROSTRATEGIC CAPABILITIES

	No. Systems Deployed	PNM	WHt	WHa
NATO	1353	687	1210	1021
WP	1701	962	15595	1355

Source: Derived from information and data appearing in the *Department of Defense Annual Report Fiscal Year 1982, The Military Balance 1981–1982, Jane's All the World's Aircraft 1979–1980,* and *Jane's Weapon Systems 1979–1980.*

Key: Eurostrataegic Systems=systems with a maximum range of 501–4000+ NM. Mid–Range Missiles (MR/SLBMs)=systems with a maximum range of 1500–4000+ NM.

PNM, Rx, WHt, and WHa: See Table 1. A general availability factor of 0.9 was used to determine the warheads available (WHa) for Euro-strategic missions for ground launched missiles, 0.7 for Soviet SSBNs, 0.9 for NATO SSBNs, and 0.8 for all aircraft. The ranges (Rx) listed for aircraft are the greater of the ranges listed in the above source documents and assume a hi-lo-hi combat mission profile.

Notes* It is assumed that 27 SS–20 missile launchers are deployed in the European theater with 1 reload available per launcher and 3 MIRVs per missile. It is assumed that two British Polaris and three French submarines are on patrol during peacetime and an additional submarine could be readied by the British and French during time of crisis.

Of the new generations of systems currently being deployed by the Soviet Union in Europe, however, none has created as much concern and controversy as the deployment of the SS–20 IRBM. The SS–20 is a solid-fueled, two-stage, MIRVed, mobile missile which is currently replacing or supplementing the older, less accurate, less reliable SS–4s and SS–5s. One former senior Department of Defense civilian official now writing under the name Justin Galen has noted that the reliability, accuracy, reload, and retargeting capability of the SS–20 should permit its use "effectively in first strike, launch-on-warning, or second-strike attacks." Furthermore, he contends that with the deployment of the SS–20, the Soviet Union "could probably launch a reliable mass strike with such systems against virtually every NATO air base, weapons storage site, C³ [command, control, and communications] site, and fixed missile sites with negligible warning."[5] A more pointed illustration of the concern which has been raised by the SS–20 are the remarks made by French strategist Pierre Gallois. Gallois has suggested that with the addition of the SS–20, the USSR can now destroy NATO's entire inventory of nuclear weapons in 10 minutes.[6]

As a result of such improvements, the Soviet Union today fields a formidable array of Eurostrategic capabilities. They currently have deployed about 600 MR/IRBMs and SLBMs, over 1000 nuclear-capable aircraft, and nearly 1,600 warheads to support theater-wide nuclear operations. In comparison, the West (including French theater forces) has deployed approximately 200 IR/SLBMs, 1150 tactical/strike aircraft, and 1200 warheads to support theater-level nuclear operations. (See Table 3).

In Sum

The inherent "softness" of the data available on Soviet and Western nuclear capabilities makes precise measurements of the balance a captive of the many assumptions which have been made. Nevertheless, given the data at hand, the composite of theater nuclear capabilities now available to the Soviet Union suggests the NATO/Warsaw Pact balance of nuclear forces has shifted from one which once favored the West to one which now *appears* to favor the Soviet Union and its Warsaw Pact allies. While the West may retain an advantage at the tactical/battlefield level, the Soviets are clearly ahead in medium-range systems and now have what appears to be an aggregate numerical advantage in Eurostrategic systems. Moreover, with the addition of FENCER, FLOGGER, and BACKFIRE aircraft and SS–20 IRBMs, the technological superiority which once was thought clearly to favor NATO is now being seriously challenged.

This is not to suggest that the Soviet Union has as of yet achieved any meaningful overall quantitative or qualitative theater nuclear superiority. However, the data do support the contention that, at best, a kind of rough parity exists at the theater nuclear level. Furthermore, trends suggest the USSR has not decided to limit or reduce its efforts in the field of theater nuclear forces. On the contrary, the continued improvement of Soviet theater nuclear capabilities portends an increased nuclear threat to the West.

Soviet Doctrine

The Emphasis on Surprise and Offense

Soviet theater nuclear force improvements complement and are complemented by Soviet doctrine. Since the Khrushchev period, Soviet military writers have rejected the idea of adopting the strategic defense during the first phases of a conflict as had been done under Stalin in the early part of World War II.[7] Today, Soviet doctrine focuses on surprise and rapid offensive warfare. In this regard, the Soviet writers contend the Soviet emphasis on offensive warfare has nothing in common with the "aggressive and predatory content" of Western military doctrine.[8] Nevertheless, the Soviets increasingly have emphasized the importance of strategic and tactical surprise and rapid offensive combat operations as vital prescriptions for success should conflict occur.

While Soviet military writings do not support the notion the Soviets would launch a "bolt out of the blue,"[9] surprise is viewed as one of the most important principles of military art. Colonel Vasiliy Ye. Savkin, in one of the early and basic books of the "Officers Library" series produced by the Military Publishing House in Moscow and recommended for all officers and students in higher military schools, has written:

> outcome of war . . . depends primarily on the correlation of available, strictly military forces of the combatants at the beginning of the war . . . the beginning of a war can have a decisive effect on the outcome.[10]

According to Savkin:

> From this law come a number of the most important principles of military art, including the principle of surprise . . . .[11] Surprise has been a most important principle of military art since olden times.[12]

As a result, he contends:

> The desire for surprise has begun to permeate all decisions for the conduct of operations and battles.[13]

In another major work in the same series, Colonel A. A. Sidorenko has contended that the history of conflict itself has emphasized the value of surprise. He noted: "Extremely often the absence of surprise turned out to be the reason for the failure of an operation at its very beginning."[14]

Equally stressed by Soviet military theorists is the importance of rapid offensive combat operations. Indeed, Soviet military science considers the offensive as the main type of military combat action. Savkin writes: " . . . the offensive is the basic form of combat action, since only by a decisive offensive conducted at a high tempo and to a great depth is total defeat of the enemy achieved."[15] Similarly, Sidorenko in his seminal work on offensive warfare stressed the need for the "swift development of the breakthrough," the value of a rapid "offensive in depth," the importance of night operations in "striving to attain surprise and continuity in the offensive," the contribution of airborne and amphibious forces to increased attack rates and ultimately to "the successful conduct of offensive operations," and in general the importance of maneuver and shock action on the modern battlefield.[16] Likewise, Division Commander Colonel Lobachev has argued:

> A high tempo is not a goal in itself, but a means to achieving victory in combat. The speed of movement of the attackers denies the enemy the opportunity to freely maneuver with his forces and equipment, to utilize the reserve . . . and it neutralizes many of the strengths of the enemy defense.[17]

The Role of Nuclear Weapons

From the Soviet perspective, nuclear weapons enhance the importance of surprise and rapid offensive operations which, in turn, synergistically enhance the value of nuclear weapons in securing victory. In describing the relationship between nuclear warfare and Soviet doctrine and defense planning, Soviet writers have proclaimed the nuclear weapon as the "most important element of the battlefield," and "the basic means of destruction." They suggest that "the side which employs nuclear weapons with surprise can predetermine the outcome of battle in his favor." The late Minister of Defense Marshal Andrey Antonovich Grechko wrote: "Nuclear missiles will be the decisive means of armed conflict."[18] Likewise, Major General V. V. Voznenko concluded, "Decisive victory in an offensive is achieved by using the results of nuclear strikes . . . ."[19]

Concerning the synergistic relationship between nuclear weapons and rapid offensive warfare, Soviet writers contend that the high combat qualities of shock forces permit the exploitation of

> . . . the results of the employment of nuclear and other means of mass destruction [chemical] most effectively, overcoming the enemy's defense at a high rate, breaking through

into his deep rear swiftly, advancing over any terrain including that contaminated with radioactive substances, and inflicting powerful blows on the enemy.[20]

They maintain "nuclear weapons create an opportunity to quickly alter . . . the balance of forces of the sides" and "the high maneuverability and dynamism of warfare . . . [are] a result of equipping the troops with nuclear weapons and their complete motorization." They believe "nuclear weapons make it possible in the shortest period of time to cause great losses to the defending side, and to create breaches in its battle formations." They contend that "nuclear strikes can destroy the strongest centers and strong points in the enemy defense, his reserves, means of mass destruction, and other important objectives." As a result, Soviet military writers have concluded that through "the stunning effect of surprise attacks by nuclear and conventional weapons and decisive operations by troops, the enemy's capabilities are sharply lowered . . . the correlation of forces changes immediately . . . . He may panic and his morale will be crushed."[21]

There are many reasons the Soviets would seek to avoid conflict in Europe, especially nuclear conflict. However, their doctrine and the forces they have been building methodically suggest: (1) they believe *should* war occur in Europe, it is likely to involve the use of nuclear weapons; (2) they intend to be prepared for such a war should it occur; and (3) they believe that in conjunction with surprise and rapid offensive maneuver, the coordinated use of nuclear weapons will have a decisive effect on the outcome of the conflict.

Implications for NATO Defense

A Devalued Deterrent

To be sure, Soviet theater nuclear force improvements have not neutralized the ability of the West to deter conflict in Europe. Moscow is likely to harbor few illusions about the destructive potential of the West's theater, as well as strategic, nuclear arsenal—which by any standards remains formidable. Thus, Soviet leaders are not likely to set out deliberately on a course which they believe might well lead to a nuclear exchange.

Nevertheless, in a broader sense, improvements in Soviet theater nuclear capabilities have resulted in a depreciation of the deterrent effect of the West's nuclear arsenal. From a Western perspective, the deterrence once provided by Western nuclear superiority was never limited simply to the notion of deterring the deliberate initiation of conflict. Rather, an effective deterrent also was viewed as one which served to limit Soviet policy options in time of crisis and thus prevent a slow slide to nuclear war based on mutual miscalculation. In theory, although Soviet leaders could be expected to test Western resolve in any number of ways, ultimately they would be deterred not only from the deliberate initiation of conflict but also from specific actions which might lead to conflict and an ensuing escalation to levels at which they were at a clear relative disadvantage.

Today, in an age of strategic parity, the attainment by the Soviets of a rough equivalence at the theater nuclear level is likely to provide the Soviet Union with increased room for political maneuver in peacetime and during crises. Although Soviet leaders are basically conservative in outlook and well aware of the probable consequences of conflict in Europe, they are also keenly aware of Western European concerns over the potentially devastating effect of a nuclear war in Europe. In light of such concerns, Soviet leaders are now likely to believe that "sober" assessments by the West of the new balance of nuclear capabilities on the continent of Europe reduce the risk of war erupting from crises disputes. As a result, Soviet leaders are likely to feel somewhat more confident they can engage successfully in political coercion, crisis bargaining, and bluffing. Unfortunately, such confidence may well lead to more strident Soviet behavior, the concomitant potential for miscalculaton, and ultimately to the very conflict all sides seek to avoid.

A Decline in Western Self-Confidence

Perhaps as significant as the potential for Soviet miscalculation during crises is the debilitating effect knowledge of that potential is likely to have on Western European elites during peacetime. In 1960, in an attempt to answer what he considered to be the fundamental question confronting the alliance as it fashioned defense policies and strategies in an age of nuclear weapons—namely, can the West defend Europe without destroying it?—Liddel Hart concluded:

> The answer—if we are honest, and brave enough to face hard facts—can only be that, in the present conditions, effective defense is not possible. For defense in a real sense of the word, as defined in dictionaries, means to "preserve, protect, keep safe, or even to avoid attack." At present if nuclear weapons . . . are actually used no country can hope to keep safe, or even to avoid fatal destruction.[22]

The continued Soviet buildup of theater nuclear weapons and their development of a doctrine which emphasizes the integrated use of nuclear, chemical, and conventional weapons in Europe underscores this dilemma. As a result, a growing number of European elites are understandably uncomfortable with the current situation, uncertain as to the nature of security provided through the NATO link, unhappy with the inability of the United States to provide a "quick fix" even though the complexities of the environment may not admit to quick fixes, and increasingly may be willing to seek accommodation (although they certainly would not call it that) with the Soviet Union. In some respects, this is understandable. Moreover, as a way of forcing an exploration of new alternatives for improving Western security, such reaction can even prove to be beneficial. However, the dividing point between the constructive exploration of alternatives and condescension could well be difficult to define clearly. Thus, although the great subtleties of political maneuver have frequently taken place at this point, the hazards to the continued cohesion of NATO are great.

Increased Vunerabilities

In 1971, Marshal Andrey Grechko detailed Soviet targeting priorities for their longer range theater nuclear forces. At the top of the priority list were US Pershing missile bases, nuclear-capable NATO air force units, tanker bases, British and French nuclear submarines, tactical nuclear weapons storage sites, and US aircraft carriers. Such targets were then followed by major ports, military bases and barracks, nuclear reactors, command and control centers, and the transportation and supply net.[23] Thus, the West's nuclear forces and critical command, control, and supply nodes have been principal candidates for Soviet attack for over a decade. However, the addition of the SS–20 IRBM and the continued deployment of new generation tactical fighter/bomber aircraft such as the FENCER and BACKFIRE have increased significantly the vulnerability of Western defense capabilities.

The high accuracy of the SS–20 has reduced the number of warheads required to assure the destruction of a specific target, while the MIRVed warhead has increased substantially the potential number of targets which can be struck by a single missile. As a result, whereas in the past it would have been necessary for the Soviet Union to launch 2, perhaps 3, of their older SS–4 or SS–5 missiles in order to have a high confidence of destroying a specific target—thus rapidly exhausting their capabilities—today, it is theoretically possible for the Soviets to destroy with slightly over 100 SS–20 missiles the same number of targets it would have taken their entire force of SS–4s and SS–5s to destroy.

Likewise, older generation aircraft frequently lacked the avionics, electronic countermeasure range, and payload characteristics which make the new generation fighter-bombers and BACKFIREs a serious threat to the NATO deep rear.

Planning for the Wrong War

Despite dramatic improvements in Soviet theater nuclear capabilities and the corresponding development of a doctrine which focuses on the integrated use of nuclear, chemical, and conventional capabilities should war occur in Europe, the US bias for conventional forces and conventional planning which began during the Kennedy Administration persists. That bias was an outgrowth of an increasing concern among

Europeans[24] as well as Americans over the effects of a two-sided nuclear exchange in Europe which had been made possible as a result of the deployment by the Soviets in the late 1950s and early 1960s of a sizable theater nuclear capability. In light of Soviet deployments, the utility of a defense based on the near spasmodic nuclear response to a major Warsaw Pact conventional aggression—which seemingly characterized the era of "massive retaliation"—was seriously questioned. Capturing the essential thrust of Alliance concerns at the time, General Andre Beaufre has written:

> . . . as the Soviet nuclear threat developed, it became increasingly difficult to believe that recourse to a "nuclear exchange" would be made for any reason other than the defense of absolutely vital objectives. It seemed wise, therefore, to anticipate a more or less extended period of resistance before unleashing "massive retaliation."[25]

In response to such concerns, the Kennedy Administration began to refocus its efforts on improving capabilities for defense at the conventional level. The doctrine which issued from a number of studies and pronouncements became known as the doctrine of "flexible response." In theory old tripwire forces would be replaced by forces more adeqately prepared to meet a Soviet conventional thrust. This would give pause to the Soviets and permit them to reflect on the consequences of pursuing a conflict which might well escalate to levels at which they were at a clear disadvantage. Thus, Soviet conventional capabilities would be partially offset by an improved NATO conventional force posture. Moreover, through improvements in conventional force posture, the use of nuclear weapons might be forestalled, thus raising the nuclear threshold.

The practical effect, however, of this shift to a conventional strategy was all but to eliminate serious thinking about the conduct of operations on a nuclear battlefield and the psychological effect on friend and foe alike of being fully prepared for such conflict. According to a study by John P. Rose, 50 percent of the instruction and training at the Army's Command and General Staff College (C&GSC) in the mid–1950s was devoted to theater nuclear conflict. In 1957–1958, 614 regular course curriculum hours focused on the nuclear battlefield. Moreover, the weight of military writing during the period clearly indicated an emphasis on theater nuclear operations. In the 8–year period immediately preceding the Kennedy administration's emphasis on conventional defense, the Army's *Military Review* published 155 articles which dealt with theater nuclear warfare. In contrast, in the 8–year period from 1962 to 1969, only 26 articles were published by *Military Review* on the subject. By the late 1960s, C&GSC instruction on nuclear conflict had dropped to 16 hours.[26]

The continued improvement in Soviet strategic and theater nuclear capabilities over the last decade and a half has altered significantly the military environment on the continent of Europe. The United States and its NATO allies no longer can rely on an unquestioned Western nuclear superiority to deter all uses of nuclear weapons by the Soviets. As a result, the assumption the Allies and the Warsaw Pact might engage in a conflict in Europe with neither side resorting to nuclear weapons is simply unrealistic. Yet, the US emphasis on conventional forces and planning for conventional conflict remains.

This no doubt results partially from a recognition of a clear imbalance in favor of the Warsaw Pact in conventional weapons systems and force structures and a perceived need in some quarters to provide some relative balance of capabilities at all levels of potential conflict— especially as Soviet strategic and theater nuclear capabilities have improved. In part, the emphasis on conventional forces and planning may reflect the difficulty of planning for a nuclear war for which no previous conflict serves as a guide to potential requirements. Moreover, this emphasis may, to some degree, reflect the hope that the conventional nuclear "firebreak" would not be crossed. Almost certainly, the bias reflects a strong reluctance to broach a subject which has become extremely politically sensitive in Western Europe. On this latter point, Robert Lawrence has written:

> . . . there has been one possible kind of war that has been virtually impossible to discuss publicly in any reasoned and coherent manner. This is tactical nuclear war, the use of nuclear weapons for limited tactical military purposes, a subject that has taken on an almost leprous appearance and seems essentially unable to stir intellectual curiosity let alone serious consideration by students, pundits, or policy makers.[27]

Likewise, General Maxwell Taylor has said:

> The thought of using any kind of nuclear weapons is so repugnant to civil authorities as to preclude virtually any serious discussion of the possibilities or conditions under which these weapons might be used.[28]

As a result of this reluctance to face seriously the possibility—indeed, given improved Soviet capabilities and the implications of Soviet doctrine, the probability—that should war occur in Europe it would involve the use of nuclear weapons, US/NATO defense posture has failed to keep pace with the changing political and military environment in Europe. It was fashioned at a time when NATO had a significant preponderance of nuclear capabilities. That preponderance now has disappeared. Yet, when one strips the rhetoric from policy pronouncements and carefully examines NATO forces, doctrine, and training, one is forced to conclude, as William Van Cleave and Sam Cohen have, that there is "little more than confusion concerning the employment of tactical nuclear weapons."[29]

Today, strategic and theater nuclear parity mandates the United States and its NATO allies to be fully prepared for the full spectrum of conflict should war occur in Europe. Given Soviet capabilities and a Soviet doctrine which focuses on the intensive, coordinated use of nuclear as well as conventional and chemical munitions, what is now necessary is (1) a thorough review of Alliance forces, doctrine, and posture with the intent of improving NATO's ability to deter and, if necessary, defend against a combined Soviet conventional, chemical, nuclear offensive; and (2) the development of a NATO deterrent and defense strategy which would increase the probability of deterring a Soviet nuclear preemption during a severe crisis.

In Response

To the end of improving NATO's deterrent and defense posture, the following broad courses of action appear promising. First, NATO should shift the emphasis of its nuclear capabilities from short-range battlefield systems to long-range Eurostrategic systems. Today, the only area of nuclear deployments in which NATO has a clear advantage is at the battlefield level. Planned improvements in NATO's Eurostrategic capabilities through the addition of 572 cruise missiles and Pershing IIs are a step in the right direction—not simply as a response to Soviet deployments of the SS–20 but for the value of such long-range systems as a deterrent in their own right. Deterrence depends on the adversary's believing that the potential benefits of a conflict are outweighed by the costs. While current battlefield systems, if used, would clearly reduce the probability of a successful Soviet combined arms offensive in Central Europe, the effects of their use threaten the destruction of Western Europe; thus, they have an adverse psychological impact on Western Europe during peacetime and raise questions as to whether the Alliance would ever authorize the release of such weapons in Europe until perhaps it was already too late.

Acquisition, deployment, and employment policies which emphasize the use of long-range nuclear systems designed to attack Soviet forces, staging areas, command and control networks, and lines of communication in the western districts of the Soviet Union and in Eastern Europe would place the Soviet Union and its Eastern European allies on clear notice that, should the Soviets initiate a conflict in Europe, Warsaw Pact territories would not be spared from destruction—NATO does not intend to limit damage to Western Europe but rather intends to take the conflict directly to the enemy. Thus, the credibility of the West's nuclear deterrent would be enhanced. It is simply more credible to threaten to attack Soviet forces in the western military districts of the Soviet Union and in Eastern Europe with nuclear weapons than it is to threaten to destroy Western Europe in order to save it from Soviet aggression. Moreover, such an approach would further enhance deterrence by increasing the precalculable costs of aggression to the Soviets, by increasing the reluctance of the Soviet Union's Eastern European allies to participate in conflict preparations during severe crises, and by reducing the Soviet planners' confidence that a well-integrated, coordinated Warsaw Pact attack could be orchestrated without providing the kind of advanced warning to NATO which might reduce seriously the effectiveness of the Soviet forces during the critical early stages of conflict.

Emphasis on long-range systems might also be psychologically encouraging to the nations of Western Europe. Such an emphasis is likely to enhance, not diminish, the linkage between theater nuclear conflict in Europe and the US strategic nuclear deterrent. Europeans might reason that a Western focus on battlefield systems suggests a willingness to engage in a war limited to Central or perhaps even just Western Europe. An emphasis on the use of Eurostrategic systems might well suggest to many Europeans an early US intent to take those measures necessary to thwart a Soviet takeover of Western Europe, including nuclear strikes deep into the Soviet Union.

One principal concern, however, in emphasizing long-range systems is the impact of such a move on the arms race. However, a clear emphasis on Eurostrategic systems need not result in a spiraling nuclear arms race in Europe. NATO need not increase the absolute numbers of its nuclear weapons or systems. Rather, NATO might, as it modernizes its forces, emphasize those forces with a deep nuclear interdiction capability. No dramatic new programs need to be approved. Indeed, a subtle shift in emphasis is likely to serve better the politics of Western Europe. Moreover, efforts to cap the numbers of nuclear systems and warheads available to both sides should continue, and, if undertaken in conjunction with efforts to achieve parity at all levels, including the conventional level, could well contribute to a more stable military relationship in Europe.

Second, while deemphasizing battlefield nuclear capabilities, NATO should modernize those capabilities so it is better able to meet the political and military requirements for deterrence or defense against a possible Soviet combined conventional-chemical-nuclear thrust. Current battlefield weapons, if employed in Western Europe, would result in high levels of collateral damage. Thus, they exacerbate the Western dilemma of how to save Europe without destroying it. On the other hand, while the West has no control over the size of warheads likely to be employed by the Soviet Union or over Soviet targeting policy, it could reduce the absolute levels of collateral damage likely to be

480-900 O - 85 - 14

sustained as a result of the Allied use of nuclear weapons through the introduction of reduced blast/enhanced radiation (RB/ER) weapons. The controversy surrounding the planned introduction of the RB/ER weapon (the so-called neutron bomb) in the latter 1970s makes it politically difficult for the United States or its Western European allies to open debate on the subject. Nevertheless, the facts remain and, in my opinion, should be confronted directly. A one-kiloton (KT) RB/ER weapon essentially produces the same desired military effects as a 10–KT standard fission weapon. However, its use could reduce significantly the number of unintended casualties and collateral damage outside the immediate target area (see Table 4). Although current modernization programs for battlefield systems include improvements of warheads which offer the option for including RB/ER features with a relatively short lead time, in my opinion, failure to make the RB/ER features an integral part of the arsenal places an increased emphasis on the need for adequate warning and increases the burden on NATO decisionmakers during severe crises; it forces them to make decisions concerning the incorporation of the RB/ER feature just at the time they are seeking to reduce tensions and avoid conflict.[30]

Table 4. Radius of Effects (Meters).

	Tank Crew Incapacitation Yield	Unprotected From Radiation	Urban Destruction Casualties
1-KT ER	700	1000	400
10-KT Fission	700	1200	1200

Source: S. T. Cohen and Brigadier General Edwin F. Black, "The Neutron Bomb and the Defense of NATO," *Military Review,* Vol. 63, No. 5 (May 1978), page 59.

Finally, NATO must give equal emphasis to nuclear as well as conventional planning for conflict in Europe. As a result of Soviet theater nuclear force improvements, NATO must be prepared to conduct operations not only on a purely conventional battlefield but also in a fully integrated conventional-chemical-nuclear environment. Training, doctrine, force structures and dispositions, approaches to the prepositioning of equipment, the time-phasing of reinforcing combat troops, support forces, equipment, and so on, must now be optimized for operations in a nuclear as well as conventional environment. Such a posture would not run counter to NATO's primary goal of deterring conflict. Indeed, it would contribute to deterrence. Present force posture invites the Soviets to use nuclear weapons. As a result of nearly 20 years of conventional emphasis in planning, NATO today is highly vulnerable to a Soviet nuclear attack. Speaking about Soviet incentives for early use of nuclear weapons, Jeffrey Record has argued, "it would appear as if the Alliance has set out deliberately to tailor and deploy its forces so as to provide every conceivable incentive for the Soviet Union to strike first with nuclear weapons."[31] What is now necessary is not only an extension of current US/NATO efforts designed to reduce the vulnerabilities which have crept into our posture often as a result of our emphasis on planning for conventional conflict, but also a marked effort to train, equip, and deploy forces fully prepared to meet and defeat a Soviet combined arms, conventional-chemical-nuclear offensive. Such a posture not only would enhance deterrence but also would provide for an effective defense across the spectrum of conflict should deterrence fail.

Notes

1. Helmut Schmidt, "The 1977 Alastair Buchan Memorial Lecture," *Survival*, Vol. 19, November–December 1977, pp. 3–4.
2. Both the FROG and SCUD A missiles were reported to have poor reaction times, low reliability, poor operational accuracy, and a primitive manual interface with Soviet targeting and command and control systems. See John M. Collins and Anthony H. Cordesman, *Imbalance of Power: An Analysis of Shifting US–Soviet Military Strengths* (San Rafael, California: Presidio Press, 1978), p. 300.
3. Secretary of Defense Caspar W. Weinberger, *Soviet Military Power* (Washington: Government Printing Office, 1981), p. 30.
4. See John W. R. Taylor, ed., *Jane's All The World's Aircraft 1978–79* (London: MacDonald and Jane's Publishers Limited, 1978), pp. 201–202.
5. Justin Calen, "The Nuclear Balance, Part One: Recent Force Trends and Improvements," *Armed Forces Journal International.* December 1977, p. 30.
6. See Joseph Fitchett, "NATO Arms Talks Test US–Europe Ties," *The International Herald Tribune*, 30 April 1979, p. 1.
7. See Thomas W. Wolfe, *Soviet Power and Europe 1949–1970* (Baltimore: The Johns Hopkins University Press, 1979), p. 199.
8. See, for example, Lieutenant Colonel L. Korzun, "Defense in Modern Combat," *Krasnaya zvezda* [Red Star], 22 August 1964.
9. See Joseph D. Douglass, *The Soviet Theater Nuclear Offensive* (Washington: Government Printing Office, 1976), pp. 3–4.
10. V. Ye. Savkin, *Operativnoye iskusstvo i taktika* [Operational Art and Tactics] (Moscow: Military Publishing House, 1972), p. 89, henceforth referred to as Savkin.
11. Ibid., p. 90.
12. Ibid., p. 230.
13. Ibid., p. 234.
14. Colonel A. A. Sidorenko, *Nastupleniye* [The Offensive] (Moscow: Military Publishing House, 1970), p. 30, henceforth referred to as Sidorenko.
15. Savkin, p. 284.
16. Sidorenko, pp. 11–39.
17. Colonel Lobachev, "A High Tempo of Attack—The Indispensable Condition for Victory," *Voyennyy vestnik* [Military Herald], Vol. 5, No. 2 (February 1977), p. 44, quoted in Frederick C. Turner, *Comments on FM 100–5 From A Soviet Point of View* (Carlisle Barracks, Pennsylvania: US Army War College, 15 March 1978), p. 19.
18. Andrey A. Grechko, *On Guard for Peace and the Building of Communism* (Moscow, 1971), trans. Joint Publications Research Service (Springfield, Virginia: National Technical Information Service, 1972), p. 33.
19. Colonel Ceneral N. A. Lomov, ed., *Nauchno–tekhnicheskiy progress i revolyutsia v voyennom dele* [Scientific–Technical Progress and the Revolution in Military Affairs] (Moscow: Military Publishing House, 1973), p. 144, henceforth referred to as Lomov.

20. Sidorenko, p. 46.

21. For example, see Sidorenko, pp. 40–70 and 109–124; Savkin, pp. 232–233; and Lomov, pp. 40–41 and 143–156.

22. B. H. Liddell Hart, *Deterrent or Defense* (New York: Frederick A. Praeger, 1960), p. 47.

23. Andrey A. Grechko, *On Guard for Peace and the Building of Communism,* quoted in Hubertus Hoffman, "SS-20 Multiplies USSR's Nuclear Superiority," *NATO's Fifteen Nations,* December 1978–January 1979, p. 44.

24. The Europeans had been sensitized to the potential impact on Western Europe of a defense based on the use of nuclear weapons by the SHAPE war game "Carte Blanche" which had been held in West Germany, the Lowlands, and northeastern France in 1955. In that exercise, the simulated use of 355 atomic bombs resulted in an estimated 5.2 million prompt casualties, not to mention the residual casualties resulting from the impact of devastation and the longterm effects of nuclear radiation.

25. Andre Beaufre, *NATO and Europe* (New York: Alfred A. Knopf, 1966), pp. 57–58.

26. John P. Rose, "US Army Doctrinal Developments: The Nuclear Battlefield 1945–1977" (unpublished PhD dissertation, University of Southern California, 1977), Chapter 4. Quoted in William Van Cleave and S. T. Cohen, *Tactical Nuclear Weapons: An Examination of the Issues* (New York: Crane, Russak and Company, 1978), pp. 5–6, henceforth referred to as Van Cleave and Cohen.

27. Robert M. Lawrence, "On Tactical Nuclear War," *Revue Militaire Generale,* January 1971, p. 46.

28. General Maxwell D. Taylor, *Precarious Security* (New York: W. W. Norton, 1976), p. 14.

29. Van Cleave and Cohen, p. 9. See Brown, *DOD Annual Report FY 81.* p. 146.

30. For a further discussion of the author's views of the pros and cons of the RB/ER debate, see Robert Kennedy, "New Weapons Technologies: Implications for Defense Policy," *Parameters,* Vol. 19, No. 5 (September–October 1977), p. 208.

31. Jeffrey Record, "Theater Nuclear Weapons: Begging the Soviet Union to Preempt," *Survival,* Vol. 19, No. 5 (September–October 1977), p. 208.

414

The Soviet View of Human Resources in War

Carl W. Reddel

Introduction

The American military services clearly emphasize the critical importance of people as a resource in accomplishing their various tasks and
in fulfilling their responsibilities.[1] Their central role and significance in
the American military receive both verbal obeisance and the support of
administrative programs designed to improve their individual and collective lot. To say "people are important" approaches the level of
aphoristic truth. People are also important in the Soviet view of war,
but their central position in the Soviet view is not readily recognized
by Americans and is given less attention than factors such as the role of
nuclear weapons and the impact of a continually changing and improving Soviet military technology.[2]

Perhaps this results from an American focus only on people in the
uniformed services as resources for war and a neglect in theory and
practice of the potential or actual role of the general population in war.
How do people, the general population, become what the Soviets
describe as "human resources" (*lyudskiye resursy*)?[3] A number of
diverse influences have contributed to the development of the Soviet
view. Russian experience with war, especially in the 19th and 20th
centuries, and the ideology of Marxism–Leninism have been especially
influential in its formation. No single factor accounts for its evolution,
but its centrality in the Soviet view is so basic it readily may become
an unstated assumption affecting other discussions. Similarly, the
American belief that "people are important" in war may become an
unexamined assumption. The general population is not neglected in
American popular discourse on war; it receives much attention in the
American media.[4] But this attention is superficial insofar as it fails to
integrate the concept of people as human resources into a broader
understanding of modern warfare, especially from the viewpoint of
professional military thought. The enthnocentrism of this American
view may result not only in conceptual superficiality, but it may also be
dangerous in that the failure or the unwillingness to accept the central
position of people in the Soviet view risks the misunderstanding of
"human resources" as a vital element in the Soviet perception of
modern war.[5]

The Soviet view of people in war has assumed a larger importance in
recent times because of increasing problems in the United States concerning people in uniform and the relationship of the population at

large to its military services. The problems of the volunteer army, conscription, and the United States' lessening international influence—based on a diminishing capacity to project economic and military strength—have caused a broad reexamination of the American military services' role in American life[6] but not a reexamination of the strategic role of the general population in the general American view of war, especially in light of the Soviet military system and its guiding doctrine.[7]

However, Soviet success in projecting its military power has focused attention on Soviet strengths, as well as the weaknesses of which Americans are fond. Change in the various factors contributing to success in war and variations in their relative strength and weakness can cause a radical shift in which factor or factors assumes the critical, decisive role in modern warfare. The perspective taken by American students of the Soviet military has to be affected by changes in the larger strategic context within which the projection of military power is judged. As Christoph Bertram, Director of the International Institute for Strategic Studies, stated in the introduction to papers delivered at a conference on "Prospects of Soviet Power in the 1980s:"

> It was one thing to live with Soviet power at a time of unquestioned American strategic superiority and internationalist determination—but quite another when the Soviet Union has reached parity in most of the indicators of military power and the United States' military effort is impeded by the need to come to terms with pressing domestic problems . . . .[8]

As the Soviets achieve parity or even superiority in war technology, the significance of the human factor grows in relative terms. American weaknesses and deficiencies in the ability to maintain effective fighting forces, in securing the support of its civilian population, and in the capability to mobilize for war are all accentuated in the context and relief of Soviet successes in dealing with these questions of human resources. Soviet capability and effectiveness in the use of people in warfare may not have changed significantly in absolute terms, but they may have changed to the Soviets' advantage relative to an American position of increasing difficulty. Even more important is the possibility that the relative significance of human resources in warfare—in the context of technological parity—eventually may have an unanticipated and unmeasured weight in the strategic balance.

This article does not measure the relative weight of human resources in the strategic balance; rather, it seeks an explanation for American reluctance to examine them more completely and suggests reasons why they are viewed differently by the Soviets. We misunderstand Soviet military programs for a number of reasons. John Erickson stated that one of the greatest impediments is "an overall lack of understanding of the Soviet military system," a deficiency which cannot be remedied by one article or one conference.[9] This article begins with an examination of two elements which the author believes contribute to American misunderstanding of the Soviet view of people in war: an underestimation of the significance of ideology in understanding the Soviet military, and a neglect of the breadth of the Soviet view of human conflict, a view in which war is only one dimension of the larger and more significant conflict between imperialism and socialism. A brief description of the Soviet view of people as "human resources" in war follows, and the article concludes with speculative comment on its meaning for the future.

Significance of Ideology

Ideology lives. In spite of all the arguments and statements to the contrary, ideology is not dead. It is alive, vital, and extraordinarily important in understanding the Soviet military, especially their professional concern: war. Of course, it is possible to become enamored with ideology to the exclusion of other relevant factors, as Americans have in the past; perhaps the extremity of that experience is partially responsible for the advocacy of such a view as the "end of ideology."[10] In any event, this may be nothing more than the failure of many Americans to understand the word in the broadest sense of its Western definition and a reluctance to accept the priority given to the subject in the Soviet hierarchy of values, particularly that of the Soviet military profession.[11]

Examining the etymology of the word may be the most immediately useful approach to understanding it in a generally acceptable Western context. Ideology was born of revolution, first appearing in English in 1796 as a direct translation of the new French word, *ideologie,* which was proposed that year by the French rationalist philosopher, Destutt de Tracy. Meaning at that time a "philosphy of mind" or "science of ideas," ideology's definition continued to evolve over the years.[12] Leaping to a contemporary standard English language definition, one finds the following: "the doctrines, opinions, or way of thinking of an individual, class, etc., specif., the body of ideas on which a particular political, economic, or social system is based."[13] (To this I would add, "on which a particular *military* system is based.") If one accepts this broad definition, it is difficult to see how ideology could have come to an "end" of its influence or be "dead."[14]

The advocates of the belief that ideology's influence had ended were no doubt attempting to redress an imbalance and to suggest that Marxim–Lenninism by itself was not a valid guide for *Westerners* in understanding the operation of the Soviet system. In turn, they were suggesting that factors of political and economic power, and traditional

Realpolitik, were better long-term guides.[15] But this is a false dichotomy because in the Soviet view these are not separable factors; rather, they are inextricably intertwined.[16] And within this intertwining, ideology is categorically essential and important because, in brief, it explains the world to the people living in it; it constitutes a "world view." Can anything be more important?

We can ask the question of Leonid Brezhnev.[17] Of Khrushchev.[18] And others. The consistency of their responses and their unwillingness to compromise on this issue should leave little doubt concerning the Soviet view of the importance of ideology. But more to the point of this discussion, how does it relate to war, the central subject of Soviet professional military development?

For the Soviets, ideology possesses great significance in at least two major dimensions. First, it determines the Soviet solider's view, as it does that of other Soviet citizens, of why war is a fact of life in the 20th century. Moreover, it determines his personal and societal identity in relationship to the phenomenon of war.[19] Second, it is an object of specific concern insofar as it assists the Soviet military professional in understanding his professional problems. At this point, ideology becomes—more practically in the professional sense—military doctrine, science, and art.

Because the Politburo determines the officially acceptable views for the country as a whole as well as for the military, no essential internal conflict exists between the civilian and military sectors of society in their views on war. Military doctrine constitutes the official views and positions on the broadest questions of war and peace. Military science is a very large umbrella for a number of professional concerns: military technical sciences, military history, military geography, military economics, development of the armed forces, and military art.[20] From the American viewpoint, the last may constitute the most professional dimension of military science to the extent it involves applications in the form of strategy, operational art, and tactics.[21]

Military art is the traditional professional concern of soldiers everywhere, but American military professionals are in error if they relegate other dimensions of Soviet military science to seriously diminished levels of significance. Marxism–Leninism has broadly defined the phenomenon of war for Soviet military professionals; their understanding of modern war's professional requirements is not limited to military art in the narrowest sense of military applications. World War I suggested to such leaders of Western democracies as Clemenceau that "war was too important an affair to leave solely to the generals";[22] in the 20th century, however, an understanding of the profound interrelationships of politics, economics, and society may have been absorbed best in the professional military sense by the Soviet military.

The failure to treat all dimensions of Soviet military science with judicious balance may be the most serious methodological error in the

Western attempt to understand Soviet military professionals.[23] The error is natural, understandable, and unforgivable, especially if it contributes to an unrealistic perception of a potential enemy's strength and weaknesses. All of us understand human behavior from the context of our own experiences, education, and personal development in the broadest and most specific sense. We delight in the musical comment which asks why women can't be more like men because we accept and enjoy the fact of basic differences. American military professionals are much more reluctant to accept as significant the basic differences between the Soviet and American military professionals, especially with regard to the role played by ideology.

Human Conflict

The Soviet perception of modern war is grounded in the larger Marxist–Leninist perception of human conflict. It therefore possesses apparent contradictions and paradoxes when first viewed by the American unfamiliar with Marxism–Leninism and may be dismissed too readily as nonsensical, or at least as "very strange."[24] These problems do not exist, however, for the Soviet soldier because he does not view war in isolation from other socio-political phenomena. Indeed, he understands it as a part of the economic woof and social warp of the fabric of mankind's political and historical evolution.

To consider war as existing on the same continuum of human conflict as peace is not unnatural in the Soviet view. Essentially, it constitutes a political extrapolation from the belief that absolute stasis in living organisms, whether political or biological, does not exist.[25] Peace may be a relatively static political condition between states, but movement is always occurring. This provides an interesting contrast to the generally held American view that war is the opposite of peace.

Even more striking to the American is the Soviet view of war as primarily important because of its political, not military, significance. This poses special problems for the American military professional who historically has viewed the separation of politics and professional military affairs as distinct and necessary. For the Soviet military professional, war is the most intense and final form of the political act and possesses ultimate significance in its political/military results.[26]

The comprehensive nature of the Soviet view of war is striking. All dimensions of political, social, and economic activity may have more or less direct professional relevance for the Soviet military. In any event, political, social, and economic considerations are not excluded from the conceptualization of war and are part of Soviet professional military education.[27]

The comprehensive view of war embodied in Marxism–Leninism is tied closely to the Soviet conviction that modern war is revolutionary in its comprehensive impact.[28] Modern war is viewed as having an impact in all the dimensions in which man lives individually and socially. War affects man not only politically, socially, and economically, but also culturally. This view is due to at least two major factors, one of which is the nature of modern war itself as a gargantuan, all-encompassing phenomenon with a life of its own. The other is rooted in the indirect nature of Marx and Engels' study of war. They were not primarily students of military history or of strategic military problems. Rather, they were attempting to design and construct a theory which would explain comprehensively the world in which they lived.[29] War was therefore primarily understandable within the context of political, social, and economic relationships; not solely in military terms.

The Soviets endorse Marx's view of war as contributing to revolution, especially with regard to its effect upon the defeated nation. Although war is not sought as a precondition for revolution, waging war can be seen as advancing the cause of revolution, a political consequence constituting a touchstone for measuring the validity of the results of military actions and events.[30] This also provides military endeavors with a larger moral purpose and justification. For Soviet soldiers to be conscious of their contribution to the triumph of the just cause in the larger workings of the historical process is considered very important.[31] To know with certainty that their sacrifices contribute to the cause of revolution may be a major contribution to the morale of Soviet soldiers.[32]

Marx was a humanist.[33] From this fact emerges the basis of much of Soviet thought on many questions, including war. Marx's goal was liberation of the human being from the political, social, and economic fetters which bind men individually and socially. In the historical process of seeking that liberation, human beings became a resource and a tool, a means to achieve a greater end. The search became the end, and the "temporary" use of human beings became habitual. The result was dehumanizing, but the central focus remains the same: man or mankind.

The humanist focus of Marxism has been carried over into the Marxist–Leninist view of war. People are in the final Soviet analysis the single most important factor in the winning of war, "since it is precisely on the people's attitude and the general populace's participation that the course and outcome of a modern war depend."[34] Furthermore, for the Soviets, "under contemporary conditions, this proposition acquires the force of a law."[35] This conclusion is reinforced by Soviet military experience in the 20th century, by wars of attrition and bloodletting outside the ken of American experience.[36] It is only with great reluctance that Americans accept this, for they are habituated to a view which emphasizes what the Soviets do *to* people rather than what they do *for* people.[37] Also, Americans carry out of their own revolutionary past, dim and fogbound as it now is, the conviction they have progressed beyond other societies in their dedication to affairs of human spirit. This sometimes self-righteous attitude does not promote an objective frame of mind towards the Marxist-Leninst view; as a result, essential elements concerning the role of people in war escape consideration.

Popularly speaking, the Soviets are condemned to an essentially materialistic view of life, while Americans for all their faults are said to remain the final champions of the human spirit. Focusing on this question has prevented consideration of how the Soviets have developed a pragmatic appreciation for the role of human resources and the human spirit in modern war. Ironically, American industrial advance has made Americans champions of the materialistic and technological base in war and has relegated questions of human resources and human spirit to a lesser role. In contrast, the Soviets believe the final victory will be one of the human spirit wherein the Soviet military professional will surmount all difficulties and obstacles, not only because of his nation's technological advances but—in the final, possibly dangerously equal, contest—because of a Soviet advantage in purely mental and spiritual qualities.[38]

If this qualitative superiority is to constitute the vital difference in winning a war, the Soviets mean to have it; but they also consider people quantitatively as a basic means to success in modern war. Closely related to the comprehensive view of war which is an integral part of Marxism–Leninism is the view that people are significant in every dimension with regard to war. The Soviets clearly understand that the political, economic, and social dimensions of war and military operations are meaningless without people. This means modern war cannot be waged successfully without the support of a whole society.

The ideological basis for the role of people in modern war was reinforced by Russian historical experience with 20th-century war and its unparalleled loss of life. The human losses in World War I were appalling to all and led to widespread rejection of the leaders who permitted and guided the slaughter. In Russia, it was a major cause in the removal of the 300–year-old Romanov dynasty and those, such as Aleksandr Kerenskiy, who attempted to sustain a war effort beyond the people's will or means. Similarly, Lenin's understanding of this central human fact was a major contribution to the Bolshevik victory. For those Russians who survived the First World War, the Second was even more undiscriminating in the ferocity of its impact—given the technological military advances of the interwar period—upon all members of Russian society. The sheer *survival* of people was absolutely critical to defeating the Germans, who paid with an exceptional blood-letting of their own on the Eastern Front. The Russian will to endure became an extraordinary human factor in the winning of the war. Given this direct historical experience with the human factor in modern war and the specific attention paid by the Soviets to the continually evolving scientific and technological means of waging war—which in turn have the broadest possible societal impact—the Soviets find it incomprehensible that future wars would not involve every dimension of their society.

Human Resources

The term "human resources" (*lyudskiye resursy*) possesses broad and comprehensive meaning in the Soviet military view.[39] The term includes people in the nation's productive life and military services, including those who can be called upon to reinforce the armed services, the various branches of the economy, and civil defense. They constitute a significant part of the military potential of a country, insofar as they are an integral part of the economic base which determines the overall strength and capacity of a country for waging modern war. Most critical in the Soviet view of people in war is the advantage in mobilizing, controlling, and directing human resources in war provided by the socialist state's organizational structure. This advantage also is perceived to be the result of a greater social consciousness and discipline than found in capitalist countries and of the ability of the Soviet leadership to apply human resources more effectively to the tasks most essential for achieving the goals necessary for victory in war.

With such breadth in definition, the Soviet view that "people are important in war" approximates the American view in its aphoristic qualities. However, the Soviet view is based on a much more specific and carefully delineated official view of a nation's military potential than that possessed by the American leadership.[40] The foundation of a nation's military potential is the economic potential which underlies and makes possible its development. This military potential is in turn expressed in the military and combat power (*voyennaya i boyevaya moshch'*) of the state. Clearly, people are an inseparable part of both the economic and military potential of the state; in the Soviet view, their significance and weight as a component of a country's military potential cannot be determined accurately apart from all other constituent factors. A Soviet list of the factors constituting military potential includes the following:

(1) the quantity and quality of arms and military equipment;
(2) the degree of availability to the troops of the necessary material support for the conduct of modern war;
(3) the number of personnel; their moral-political, psychological, general educational, military, and military-technical preparation; and their field, sea, and aerial training;
(4) the availability of reserves trained and ready for mobilization;

(5) the structure of the armed forces, the ratio of military equipment to people, and the correspondence of organizational forms to the requirements of modern war;
(6) the level of study of military doctrine and theory and the degree of their correspondence to the practical realities and demands of military practices;
(7) the degree of preparedness of command personnel and their skill in troop command and control;
(8) the level of combat readiness of the armed forces;
(9) the mobilization capabilities of the state.[41]

The intertwining of these factors and the need to relate them to each other in determining their relative efficacy in war suggests a very complex task. Moreover, in the Soviet view, focusing on one of these factors to the exclusion of others is artificial and fraught with the risk of misperception. Nonetheless, focusing on the human dimension of war as viewed by the Soviets may be useful and revealing for Americans. One Soviet work on the subject flatly states that human resources are "the most important indicator of states' military potential."[42]

As suggested earlier, the Soviet view of the significance of people in war has roots in ideology and Russian historical experience, but Western theory and practice of war has also been influential. Soviet military theorists did not originate the concept of mobilizing a state's entire resources for war. Niccolo Machiavelli (1469–1527) not only "encompassed the whole complex of military problems and realized that an inner connection exists between technical military detail and the general purpose of war, between military institutions and political organizations,"[43] but he also possessed the view that "war should be waged with the entire resources, particularly the human resources of the state . . . ."[44] In more recent times, events and developments in Western Europe such as the French and Industrial Revolutions have given the state's population at large increasing significance in the waging of war. The principle of the "nation-in-arms" was proclaimed in the French Revolution; with the Industrial Revolution came the capability to exploit more fully both human and material resources. In various, ways Russia was tied to these developments down to World War I and possessed no "theory or concept of war which differentiated it from what we now, by convention, call the West."[45]

Perhaps the most distinctive feature of Russian military theory in the Soviet period, apart from its cohesiveness and lack of diversity, is its subordination to political and social theory.[46] Marxist social theory was formed into a theory of war by Marx, Engels, Lenin, Stalin, and others. The crux of the Soviet view is the belief that "war . . . is a sociohistorical phenomenon arising at a definite stage in the development of class society."[47] With the disappearance of class, the basis for war's existence is removed. As Julian Lider summarized, "When there is no class, there can be no state, no politics, nor any war."[48] Meanwhile, Soviet thinking about war retains a distinct and continuing consciousness of it as a social phenomenon. As a result, the significance of people in war as "human resources" has a basic primacy which may be overlooked with the advance of Soviet military technology and the American search for the appropriate technological responses, "quick fixes," or breakthroughs necessary to deal with the successes of Soviet military technology.

As noted above, Russian experience with war in the twentieth century was devastating for the population at large and resulted in a direct link between the populace and the national experience of the state with war; this simultaneously reinforced the view of war as a social and political phenomenon. The huge numbers of people mobilized, the creation of large reserves, and the tremendous losses of World War I were dimensions of a social experience with war which were further amplified in World War II. The Soviet conclusion is straightforward: "The necessity for mass armies and timely preparation of huge mobilized reserves remains a general regularity of military development in our time."[49]

A key institution in the mobilization of the Russian masses and in the maintenance of large reserves is the Soviet military district system, an institutional structure which grew out of the Russian historical experience with war as well as out of Soviet military theory. The failure to study this central institution in the Soviet military system before the ground-breaking work begun under John Erickson's leadership in 1977, and the tremendous work remaining on the subject, may reflect the Western misunderstanding of the significance of human resources in the Soviet view.[50] A detailed and comprehensive knowledge of the military districts should provide a notable indicator of the Soviet capacity to wage war because of its institutional continuity with Russia's historical evolution as a garrison state and the manner in which it satisfies the bureaucratic and administrative requirements growing out of efforts to implement Soviet military theory. The Soviet military district survives both peace and war, a fact consistent with the blurring of the distinctions between war and peace which sometimes appears confusing to the Western eye. The comprehensiveness of its role and purpose was best stated in a summary report on a workshop of Soviet military districts:

> Partly by historical legacy and tradition and partly by design, the Soviet military district serves both as an administrative organization in peacetime and as the framework within which Soviet military forces and civilian enterprises transit from a peacetime to a wartime status. The military district therefore retains all of the elements necessary to the process of creating and supporting the military power of the Soviet state. Although the development of the prerequisite

combat capabilities is the primary business of the military district, the military district may be viewed as a primary instrument for strengthening and implementing the Marxist–Leninist precept of the unity of the Armed Forces and proletariat. This ideal of harmonious and productive civilian-military relations in peacetime fosters another Soviet wartime ideal—the unity of the front and the rear.[51]

No theoretical concept reinforces the basic importance of human resources in the Soviet military view more than that of the "rear" (*tyl*). According to one Soviet author, human resources will be used in three fundamental ways in war: ". . . military service in the armed forces (as well as reserve personnel in case the latter are called up), service in civil defense units from the moment war begins, and work in the nation's economy."[52] Considering that in the broad sense the term "rear" during wartime means "the entire territory of the country with its population, economy, state and political structure,"[53] the role of human resources is basic to the Soviet consideration of war. The concept of the rear is additionally delineated to include those units and installations which provide the direct and indirect supporting links to the military units themselves, including operational and close support units.[54] In the final analysis, the "stability of the rear determines the course and outcome of war," a condition which is essentially arrived at by "the political and state leadership of the country and not by the military command."[55]

The Soviet view of modern war as a changing and dynamic phenomenon incorporates a consciousness of the need for more rather than fewer people in waging war. If the war is conventional, more people will be required than in World War I or World War II, given the evidence that modern war involves ever-increasing numbers of casualties and an ever larger percentage of the whole population; if the war is nuclear, immense casualties will be suffered by both the military services and the civilian population. Although the scientific-technical revolution has increased labor productivity, it also has increased the scope of the Soviet Armed Forces' material requirements, complicated military technology and its production, and increased the likelihood of large human losses in the course of military operations. The need for trained and qualified specialists in the armed forces, the military economy, and civilian defense has grown, not diminished. The experience of World War II reinforced the belief that the general population must be called upon to support and supplement the labor resources of the nation, thereby freeing males for the military forces. The potential sources for meeting the human resource needs of modern war include the full male and female able-bodied population, pensioners, and secondary school students in the higher grades. As effectively summarized in a Soviet article on the subject, "one must assume that the entire population will work to one degree or another, with the exception of infants, the sick and disabled."[56] In short, nothing in the Soviet view of war, or in the Russian experience with war in this century, suggests that fewer rather than more people will be involved in the wars of the future.

Comment

Recent Western comment on the Soviet population and its relationship to war includes both demographic and cultural analysis.[57] This combined appproach is extremely valuable if one accepts the view that "war is a cultural phenomenon."[58] However, the Soviet Union's severe demographic problems may appear different to various observers when put into the context of Russian historical development. For example, the Soviet use of manpower in Central Asia for military purposes might be viewed in light of the fact that when the Russian Empire entered World War I, "the population of Central Asia . . . was not liable for compulsory military service in Imperial Russia."[59] In this perspective, the Soviet Union has experienced relative success in the integration of its non-Russian population into the military institutions of the state; socialism has provided the means for organizing and rationalizing the tremendous resources of the Russian Empire, a garrison state long—but inefficiently—organized for war.[60]

Apart from the relative success in integrating non-Russian nationalities into the military institutions of the state, the Soviet Union possesses extraordinary experience in manipulating its human resources. Although it continues to face tremendous problems with "the adequate distribution and supply of labor resources for maximum economic production,"[61] the Soviet Union also believes it has "the capability of thoroughly and completely mobilizing all the resources of the state" for waging modern war.[62] Whatever the problems of Soviet population resources, the belief exists that those resources available can be focused more rapidly and effectively on meeting the needs of the socialist state at war than they can in the nonsocialist states. In the economy at large, for example, the conditions for war may indicate that "the most radical means of effectively utilizing the able-bodied population in the economy will be its organized redistribution among branches of industry, with primary channeling to enterprises in the war industry."[63]

The arbitrariness of such actions suggests human costs in terms of personal sacrifice and loss of personal freedom foreign to the experience of most Americans. The willingness of Soviet leaders to have their people bear such costs provides an advantage relative to Western societies because the experience of Russians with war in the 20th century indicates their leaders know whereof they speak. From the professional Soviet military viewpoint, there may also be a distinct advantage in being able to view human resources in terms of military effectiveness rather than in terms of the criteron of efficiency which is used in the American organization of military forces.

For the future, the Soviet *view* of human resources in war may be more important than the *numbers* involved, especially if it is buttressed by a will to execute. The Soviet view correctly posits modern war as dynamic, continually changing, and comprehensive in impact; furthermore, it requires the support of the general population and demands that professional military officers understand war in its fullest political, economic, and social context. Moreover, Americans should not view the will of the Soviet leadership—as expressed in its military policies—as something which requires the support of the general population in the manner Americans understand to be necessary for the support of military policies in the United States.

Perhaps more significant for the future is the need not to dehumanize the Soviet military and its view of war. In the long run, an American focus on the technological dimension of war, neglect of the professional insights derived from the study of military history, concentration on demographic as opposed to cultural analysis of human resources, and misinterpretation of the materialist bias in socialism may lead to an underestimation of the degree to which socialism can use its human resources for military purposes. This may not prove injurious or fatal to Americans in the short run of events, but Marxism–Leninism is notable for its historical perspective, using the whole of mankind's past and all of its future for its contribution to the identity and role of the Soviet military professional. This perspective might eventually provide a strategic advantage of its own to the Soviets, making it possible to outflank or outrun those with a shorter perspective in time and a narrower definition of the demands of modern war.

Notes

1. Harold Brown stated, "The overriding Defense manpower objective is to increase the combat effectiveness of the Armed Forces. In that effort the most important factor, often taken for granted in discussions of sophisticated equipment, is attracting and retaining capable, motivated people . . . ." (*Annual Report of Secretary of Defense: FY 1981 Budget, FY 1982 Authorization Request and FY 1981–1985 Defense Programs* (Washington, 29 January 1980), p. 262.
2. Ibid. A case in point is the excellent series, "Soviet Aerospace Almanac," published by *Air Force Magazine* since 1975. Also see Donald M. Bishop, "The Tragic Triumph of Material Thinking," *Air Force Magazine,* June 1980, p. 91.
3. As defined by P. V. Sokolov in the article *"Lyudskiye resursy," Sovetskaya Voyennaya Entsiklopediya* [Soviet Military Encyclopedia], (Moscow, 1978), Vol. 5, pp. 55–56.
4. See cover story in *Time,* "Who'll fight for America?", 9 June 1980.
5. Ken Booth points out in *Strategy and Ethnocentrism* (New York, 1979) that Americans can be as "culture-bound" (p. 15) as others and that "strategic opinion in the West has been based overwhelmingly on the assumption that doctrine as it has evolved in the United States has been both right and best" (p. 41). He further argues that this causes serious problems for our understanding of the Soviet Union and its military strategy (pp. 100–104).

6. See the range of works listed by Tomma N. Pastorett in "The All–Volunteer Armed Forces," *Special Bibliography,* No. 245, Air University Library, Maxwell AFB, Alabama, September 1978. The volume edited by Peter Karsten, *The Military in America* (New York, 1980), is also pertinent in this regard.

7. Volumes such as *Human Resources for National Strength* (Washington, 1972) by Eston J. White and *Defense Manpower* (Washington, 1974) by Stanley F. Falk, E. M. Gershater, and Glen L. Simpson are largely descriptive and do not examine human resources as they relate to questions of military doctrine and strategy.

8. *Adelphi Paper,* No. 151 (London, 1979), p. 1.

9. "Soviet Military Capabilities," *Current History,* October 1976, p. 78.

10. Daniel Bell, *The End of Ideology,* 2nd rev. ed. (New York, 1962).

11. G. V. Sredin wrote, "It is impossible to imagine a single area of military activity, combat studies, alert duty, measures for strengthening military discipline and organization, cultural leisure and the daily routine of the soldier outside the realm of ideological influence." "Ideologicheskaya rabota" [Ideological Work], *Sovetskaya Voyennaya Entsiklopediya* (Moscow, 1977), Vol. 3, p. 495. *The Officer's Handbook,* translated and published under the auspices of of the US Air Force (Washington, 1977), pp. 3–4, describes "Marxism–Leninism and its teaching on war and the army" as a "foundation of military development."

12. Raymond Wilson provides an excellent survey of this evolution in *Keywords: A Vocabulary of Culture and Society* (Glasgow, 1976), pp. 126–130.

13. *Webster's New World Dictionary,* 2nd College Edition (New York, 1970).

14. This is also the view and definition of George C. Lodge, who wrote, "Ideology is thus a living structure, a bridge by which values are given specific meaning in various cultures at different points in space and time conveyed into the life of the community." *The New American Ideology* (New York, 1975), p. 8. This is not to deny the limits on ideology's influence "as a force of conviction," as Flora Lewis noted during her recent travels to the Soviet Union and Eastern Europe (*New York Times,* 8 August 1980).

15. The relative value of ideology and *Realpolitik* in understanding the Soviet system was discussed long ago in "Ideology and Power Politics: A Symposium," *Problems of Communism,* Vol. 7, No. 2 (March–April 1958), pp. 10–35.

16. This view is based upon materialist dialectics. See the section on the "universal connection of phenomena" in the *Fundamentals of Marxism–Leninism: Manual,* 2nd rev. ed. (Moscow, 1963), pp. 62–70. A good short discussion of the confusion in Western discussions on "The end of ideology?" is found in the article by Edward Shils, "The Concept and Function of Ideology," *International Encyclopedia of Social Sciences* (New York, 1968), Vol. 7, p. 66.

17. Brezhnev has asserted that military and economic detente would not mean an end to the struggle between ideologies. See Christopher Wren, "Soviet Is Adamant Against Detente in Struggle of Ideas," *New York Times,* 26 November 1975, p. 3. At the 25th Party Congress he stated, "We Soviet Communists consider defense of proletarian internationalism the sacred duty of every Marxist–Leninist. Some bourgeois leaders affect surprise and raise a howl over the solidarity of Soviet Communists, the Soviet people, with the struggle of other peoples for freedom and progress. This is either outright naiveness or more likely a deliberate befuddling of mind." *New York Times,* 25 February 1976, p. 14.

18. N. S. Khrushchev said, "It would be a betrayal of our Party's first principles to believe that there can be peaceful coexistence between Marxist–Leninist ideology on the one hand and bourgeois ideology on the other. We have always said this." *Khrushchev Remembers* (Boston, 1970), p. 512.

19. As General A. A. Yepishev wrote, "The world outlook is a system of man's views about nature, society, thinking and his own place in public affairs." *Some Aspects of Party–Political Work in the Soviet Armed Forces* (Moscow, 1975), p. 220.

20. A. A. Grechko, *"Voyennaya nauka"* [Military Science], in *Sovetskaya Voyennaya Entsiklopediya* (Moscow, 1976), Vol. 2, pp. 183–188.

21. S. P. Ivanov and A. I. Yevseyev, *"Voyennoye iskusstvo"* [Military Art], in *Sovetskaya Voennaya Entisklopediya* (Moscow, 1976), Vol. 4, p. 211.

22. Harvey A. De Weerd, "Churchill, Lloyd George, Clemenceau: The Emergence of the Civilian," in Edward M. Earle, ed., *Makers of Modern Strategy* (Princton, 1971), p. 303.

23. If all dimensions of Soviet military science were treated seriously, we would be following what John Erickson described as "the first theroem governing research into the Soviet military system: *always follow the Soviet lead*, do what they are doing, for they pursue such programmes with a deliberate purpose and a sense of history which is closely aligned with their operational commitments and perceptions." *On Investigating Soviet Military Institutions* (Maxwell AFB, November 1975), p. 2.

24. P. H. Vigor, author of the single best book on the Soviet view of war, wrote, "Many strands of the Marxist theory of war, and of the Soviet practice of that theory, are very strange to the ordinary reader." *The Soviet View of War, Peace and Neutrality* (London, 1975), p. 5. Popular American misunderstanding of the meaning of detente for the Soviets is an example of the confusion which arises out of the failure to understand the Marxist–Leninst view of human conflict.

25. "Nature and society do not know absolute rest, immobility, immutability. The world presents a picture of constant motion and change," *Fundamentals of Marxism–Leninism,* p. 31. Marx and Engels' effort to integrate contemporary biological findings into their political and social analysis is described by Lewis S. Feuer, "Marx and Engels as Sociobiolgists," *Survey,* Vol. 22, No 4 (Autumn 1978), pp. 109–136.

26. See the section on "War is the tool of policy," in Vigor, *Soviet View of War,* pp. 86–89.

27. In a published letter (6 December 1976), Major General George J. Keegan, then Assistant Chief of Staff for Intelligence and Director of the Air Force Intelligence Service, wrote to Lieutenant General Raymond B. Furlong, then Commander of Air University, that the *Soviet Military Thought* series published by the United States Air Force from the Soviet "Officers' Library" series "deals with the entire broad issue of of human conflict, as does no other literature in the world." *Education Journal,* No. 1, Fall 1977, p. 29.

28. A conviction which has its origins, according to Bertram D. Wolfe, in Lenin's attribution of "a positive role to war as the mother of revolutions," in "War is the Womb of Revolution: Lenin 'Consults' Hegel," *The Antioch Review,* Vol. 16, No. 2 (June 1956), p. 192.

29. According to Lyman H. Legters, "the Marxian view of war springs not from the study of military history but from the theoretical constant designed to explain the economic, social, and political world in which the two men, Marx and Engels, lived." "Marxism and War," L. L. Farrar, Jr. ed., in *Political and Social Study* (Santa Barbara, 1978), pp.72–73.

30. "Historical experience shows that wars—especially those that acquire great scope—intensify the contradictions of capitalism, increase the distress of the masses, awaken political consciousness in the people, and create conditions under which the working peope rise to the struggle against the bourgeois system. In this sense, war has a definite connection with revolution, which was most characteristically manifested in World War I and World War II." M. I. Galkin and P. I. Trifonenkov, "War," in *Great Soviet Encyclopedia,* trans. of 3rd ed. (New York, 1974), Vol. 5, p. 649.

31. Colonel General K. Ambaryan, "Officer Training," *Soviet Military Review,* No. 5, May 1971, p. 9; Major General S. K. Il'in, *Moral'nyy faktor v sovremennykh voynakh* (Moscow, 1979), p. 105.

32. Major General F. M. Richardson, *Fighting Spirit: A Study of Psychological Factors in War* (New York, 1978), pp. 137–138.

33. I use this in the sense that Marx sought human self-development and self-perfection and used "the whole of human history" as the stage for his life. Jerrold Seigel *Marx's Fate: The Shape of a Life* (Princeton, 1978), p. 387.

429

34. M. P. Skirdo, *The People, the Army, the Commander*, translated under the auspices of the US Air Force (Washington: Government Printing Office, 1978), p. 38.
35. Ibid.
36. The Soviets believe this to be true to the extent they entitled a series of documentary films for American audiences on World War II as "The Unknown War." For a review of the film and Harrison Salisbury's book version of the film, see Joshua Rubenstein's review in "World War II—Soviet Style," *Commentary*, May 1979, pp. 65–67.
37. Robert Conquest, *The Human Cost of Soviet Communism* (Washington, 1971), Senate Document No. 92–36.
38. According to N. A. Lomov, "The political, moral, and psychological potential caused by the attitude of the people to a war determines the ability of the troops to endure the harshness of war and achieve victory. 'In any war,' said V. I. Lenin, 'victory ultimately is determined by the morale of those masses who shed their blood on the battlefield.'" *Scientific and Technical Progress and the Revolution in Military Affairs* (Moscow, 1973), pp. 277–278.
39. The term is concisely defined in the encyclopedia article by P. V. Sokolov cited above. This summary paragraph is also based on the more detailed examination contained in his book, *Voyna i lyudskiye resursy* [War and Human Resources] (Moscow, 1961).
40. S. A. Tyushkevich, "Potentsial voyennyy" [Military Potential], in *Sovetskaya Voyennaya Entsiklopediya* (Moscow, 1978), Vol. 6, pp. 473–474.
41. Ibid.
42. Sokolov, *Voyna i lyudskiye resursy*, p. 2.
43. Felix Gilbert, "Machiavelli: The Renaissance of the Art of War," in Edward M. Earle, ed., *Makers of Modern Strategy* (Princeton, 1971), pp. 22–23.
44. Norman H. Gibbs "The Western Theory of War," in C. D. Kerning ed., *Marxism, Communism and Western Society* (New York, 1973), Vol. 8, p. 299.
45. Gibbs, "Western Theory of War," p. 305.
46. Thomas N. Wolfe, "The Communist Theory of War," in *Marxism, Communism and Western Society*, Vol. 8, p. 308.
47. V. D. Sokolovskiy, *Soviet Military Strategy*, 3rd ed., trans. and ed. Harriet Fast Scott (New York, 1975), p. 173.
48. Julian Lider, *On the Nature of War* (Westmead, Farnborough, Hants, England, 1977), p. 212.
49. Sokolov, "*Lyudskiye resursy,*" p. 55.
50. Workshop conducted in Washington, DC on 28 January 1977.
51. Lieutenant Colonel Lynn Hansen and Rex D. Minckler, *The Soviet Military District in Peace and War: Manpower, Manning, and Mobilization* (Washington, 1979), p. ii.
52. Major General K. H. Dzhelaukhov, "Human Resources in Modern Warfare," *Voyennaya mysl'* [Military Thought], No. 1, January 1969, p. 24.
53. As given in the *Tolkovyy slovar' voyennykh terminov* [Explanatory Dictionary of Military Terms] (Moscow, 1966) and cited in the translator's note in the article by Colonel General K. Abramov and Major General M. Ivanov, "Leninist Ideas Concerning the Role of the Rear in Warfare." *Voyennaya mysl'*, No. 9, September 1971, p. 25.
54. Ibid.
55. Colonel I. Zhernosek, "On Theoretical Bases for the Development of Principles and Systems of Rear Support," *Voyennaya mysl'*, No. 4, April 1965, p. 1.
56. Dzhelaukhov, "Human Resources in Modern Warfare," p. 27.
57. Murray Feshbach, "Soviet Demographic Trends and Possible Implications for Soviet Defense Manpower Planning," in Rex D. Minckler, et al., *Soviet Defense Manpower*, GE–TEMPO Report (GE TMP–18, 14 July 1977), pp. E1–16; Michael Rywkin, "Central Asia and Soviet Manpower," *Problems of Communism*, Vol. 28, No. 1 (January–February 1979), pp. 1–13; Alexandre Bennigsen, "Soviet Muslims and the World of Islam," *Problems of Communism*, Vol. 29, No. 2 (March–April 1980), pp.

38–51.

58. Booth, *Strategy and Ethnocentrism,* p. 144.

59. Nikolay Galay, "The Geopolitical and Strategy Significance of Soviet Central Asia," *Studies on the Soviet Union,* Vol. 4, 1968, p. 46.

60. Richard Pipes wrote, "Even more than the western monarchies of the early modern age, Moscow was organized for warfare . . . . The principal resources of the empire were channeled into military purposes," in *Russia Under the Old Regime* (New York, 1974), p. 115. Richard Hellie also described the Russian state as a "garrison state" in "The Structure of Modern Russian History: Toward a Dynamic Model," *Russian History,* Vol. 4, No. 1 (1977), p. 3.

61. Jeff Chinn, *Manipulating Soviet Population Resources* (New York, 1977), p. 124.

62. Colonel A. Lagovskiy, *Strategiya i ekonomika* [Strategy and Economics] (Moscow, 1957), p. 51.

63. Dzhelaukhov, "Human Resources in Modern Warfare," p. 26.

Part IV

The Soviet Military Economy

How does the USSR support its massive military establishment? What role does the military economy play vis-a-vis the civilian economy in the Soviet Union? How extensive is the Soviet military economy, or—to put it differently—does a Soviet military-industrial complex really exist? The articles in Part IV are devoted to an investigation of these and other questions concerning the economic impact of the Soviet military effort.

What percentage of Soviet industrial output is represented by the Soviet military machine? Norbert Michaud argues that the rapid growth in the defense machinery sector of the Soviet economy has far exceeded the growth of Soviet industry as a whole or of the entire economy and likely constitutes 14–16 percent of total industrial output. He maintains that defense procurement underlies the growth in the Soviet machine industries.

Lee Morgan claims that the Soviet defense industry—specifically the aviation industry—offers a promising model for attaining increased effectiveness in the rest of the Soviet industrial base. According to Morgan, the aviation industry ministries have been successful in adapting complex, evolving technology to improving product performance. The methods employed by these materials in achieving this success have potential application to the other non-defense industries.

Rebecca Strode compares US and Soviet aircraft design approaches, arguing that while the US emphasizes versatility and technological sophistication, the USSR has stressed simplicity, commonality, prototype modeling, incrementalism, and reliance on foreign technology. The Soviet approach has been very much the result of an R&D community plagued by irrationality, bureaucratic ossification, and negative historical experience. Despite these drawbacks, she maintains that the US has little reason to take comfort; we should expect future Soviet aircraft to represent the most sophisticated technology the Soviets can produce.

Robert O'Connell takes a look at the tank and its continued importance in Soviet concepts of land warfare. He compares the tank's evolving role on the land battlefield to that of the battleship in naval warfare and notes the doubtfulness of the tank's utility as the cornerstone of Soviet offensive doctrine. Despite expected countermeasures, the tank will continue to be vulnerable; O'Connell urges a US ground forces weapons acquisition strategy based on these vulnerabilities.

432

John Skipper considers one aspect of a larger problem that has been the source of considerable disagreement within the US: methods for costing Soviet weapons systems. Noting that the Soviet penchant for secrecy prevents the publication of figures on individual weapons systems, he presents a methodology and some cost estimates for individual Soviet navy units. He then shows how the costs of ships have varied on a year-to-year basis and presents some total cost estimates for Soviet naval unit construction.

Kelly Scheimberg is concerned with the problem of improving US forecasts of Soviet weapons developments. He asserts that commonly held beliefs on Soviet design preferences—simplicity, commonality, and incrementalism—are belied by the occasional indications of complex, technologically sophisticated, and revolutionary design concepts. Scheimberg advocates a cybernetic approach to understanding the Soviet design process, arguing that conventional decisionmaking theories and models have been unable to recognize and address the "adaptive" aspects of the process.

Finally, Richard Thomas focuses on the activities of Soviet military R&D agencies. He notes that the Soviets have upgraded the faculties of military academies and enlisted the support of the Ministry of Defense research establishments in order to increase Soviet R&D capabilities. The Soviets are striving actively to expand the scientific background of young military officers so that they may better understand the relationship between research and weapons development. The potential results: more efficient management of the R&D system and decreasing dependence on foreign—particularly Western—R&D results.

An Epagoge for an Increasing
Soviet Defense Share, 1965–1979

Norbert Michaud

Introduction

The present intelligence community estimate of the share of Soviet defense outlays in the gross national product for 1965–1979 is 11–13 percent. This implies the defense sector grew at a rate which was only about as fast as the rate of growth of the economy as a whole. Published Soviet statistics, however, can be interpreted as clearly indicating an increase in the defense share during this period.

According to the Soviet data, the machinery sector is growing at a faster rate than Soviet industry as a whole as its share of industry increased from 20 percent in 1970 to 29 percent in 1978.[1] Even if the defense machinery industry grew only as fast as the entire machinery sector, it still would represent a growing share of industry as a whole. However, it can be surmised from Soviet statistics that the defense sector actually is growing faster than the machinery sector and constitutes a growing proportion of Soviet industry.

In the absence of Soviet statistics on the nine defense ministries, a residual approach was developed to measure the output, employment, profits, and capital investment for these industries. These 9 ministries are part of a machinery industry which also includes 11 nondefense machinery ministries.[2] Statistics on the entire machinery industry are published in official statistical handbooks as well as books and periodicals. These sources also provide limited data on the nondefense ministries. By summing up the data available on the nondefense machinery industries and deducting this from the totals for the machinery industry, a series of residuals can be derived.

The totals—and, in effect, the residuals—have been adjusted to remove the value of output of nonmachinery ministries included in the output of total machinery on an establishment basis.[3] The value of output for the nondefense ministries does not include enterprises not subordinated to them. Deducting the statistics on the nondefense ministries from an adjusted total would overstate the residuals.

Size of the Soviet Defense Machinery Sector

The size of the defense machinery sector represented by the nine defense ministries was measured in three ways: by the gross value of output (GVO), by employment, and by capital investment. (See Appendix B for the development of these estimates.) Although different sets of information were used to derive the three estimates for the defense ministries, the results are fairly consistent in indicating the share for the defense ministries is large (see Table 1). Though somewhat varied, the percentages were not expected to be equal because the ratio of output to employment or investment differs from plant to plant and industry to industry. For these reasons, the differences in the percentages are not a good basis for projecting the growth in the shares over time.

Table 1. Indications of Defense Machinery Shares.

	GVO (1975) (billions of rubles)	Employment (1967) (millions of employees)	Capital Investment (1971) (billions of rubles)
Machinery Industry	137.6	9.9	5.94
Less: Civil Ministries	64.0	4.8	3.20
Equals: Defense Ministries	73.6	5.1	2.74
Defense Ministries as Percent of Machinery Industry	53.5*	51.5*	46.1*

*One adjustment of this share would recognize the double counting; that is, the components which are interchanged between the defense and nondefense sectors and in the net would most likely favor the defense sector and raise its share.

While the large size of the defense ministries' share is important, the growth of the defense ministries and defense output is of greater interest. Assuming the present estimate of defense procurement for 1970 (expressed in 1970 prices) is generally accurate, a rate of growth in the defense machinery ministries since 1970 in excess of the present estimate of 3–4 percent[4] would imply even higher growth than the 4 percent now estimated for total defense outlays.

Growth of the Defense Machinery Sector

The defense ministries grew at a faster rate than the nondefense ministries whether measured by GVO or employment. During 1965-1966, the GVO of just 3 of the 9 nondefense ministries grew faster than the GVO of the entire machinery industry; by 1978–1979, only 1 of 11 (2 new ministries were introduced in the meantime) nondefense ministries were able to achieve such a rate of growth. (See Appendix C, Table

435

C-1.) The same can be said of employment; the growth rates for employment in the nondefense ministries—derived from published data—indicate none of these ministries had a higher rate of increase in employment than the average for the entire machine industry. (See Appendix C, Table C-2.) So the defense ministries as a group must have had a higher GVO growth rate than the 8 percent achieved by the machinery industry as a whole in 1978–1979—which is, of course, a weighted average rate for nondefense and defense ministries—and a faster employment growth rate than the 3 percent which characterized the machinery industry as a whole.

The GVO growth rate for the 9 nondefense ministries as a group specifically is cited by one Soviet author as 10.1 percent during 1966–1970 and 10.0 percent during 1971–1975.[5] He also cited the machinery industry growth as being 11.8 percent during 1966–1970 and 11.5 percent during 1971–1975. This clearly implies the other, uncited, ministries were growing at an even faster rate. How much faster can be calculated by developing a GVO estimate for several years on the basis of a few GVO values, their allocations among the ministries, and their growth rates. (See Table 2.)

Table 2. Growth of the Machinery GVO.

	1965	1970	1975	1979
Machinery Industry*	44.6	77.5	137.6	193.2**
Less: Civil Ministries***	23.5	37.5	64.0	82.2**
Equals: Defense Ministries	21.1	40.0	73.6	111.0
Defense Ministries as Percent of Machinery Industry	47.3	51.6	53.5	57.5
Average Annual Growth Rates for Defense Machinery		13.6	13.0	10.8

*The machinery GVO figures published in the NKs [Naradnoye Khozyaystvo: "National Economy," a yearly report. Ed.] are adjusted per the factors listed in Appendix A.
**Even though the price base has since been changed to 1975 prices, the 1976 price series was extended by using the announced growth rates.
***See Appendix D.

On the basis of these derived GVO values for the defense ministries, the growth of these ministries during 1970–1979 was 11.9 percent. This exceeds the machinery industry rate of 10.6 percent and the 6.5 percent rate of growth for all industries during 1970–1978.[6] It therefore can be concluded on the basis of published Soviet statistics that the defense ministries represent an increasing part of Soviet industry. While this general conclusion can be made categorically, there are a number of refinements necessary before the precise shares and growth rates can be

436

ascertained with very high levels of confidence.

Basis for the Rapid Growth in the Machinery Industry

The major cause of the rapid rise in machinery value statistics probably is not due to inflation or increases in output. For example, physical output in the automobile industry is increasing about 3 percent a year; however, the GVO is increasing at about 10 percent per year. Price increases on resource inputs or on finished products would have to be occurring at a high annual rate to explain the continued rise in the GVO.

Resource prices for materials generally have declined. The wholesale price index for ferrous metallurgical and for chemical and petrochemical products indicates little change in prices between 1970 and 1978.[7] Average wages have continued to increase about 3 percent, and much of this may have been due to upgrading rather than arbitrary wage increases.

Prices on final products apparently have not increased rapidly either. The official price index for machinery during 1970–1978 indicates 20 percent deflation, not inflation. Furthermore, the profitability rate in the machinery sector remained stable, or declined, until the late 1970s. Such a situation normally occurs when final product prices do not increase faster than unit costs or when prices decline faster than costs. By 1974, eight of the nine nondefense ministries were showing lower profit rates than in 1970. (See Appendix E.) The defense sector also experienced declining profitability rates. This suggestion of noninflationary pricing is supported by a study of inflation in the machinery industry.[8]

If there had been considerable inflation or deflation in either the general economy or in the defense sector, it would follow that the price base for the defense estimates should be updated. The defense share would change if inflation were uneven between defense and the rest of the economy; inflation does not appear to be the primary cause of the rapid GVO growth, however. The cause of the rapid rise in GVO can be attributed more easily to increases in resource outputs. According to the changes in the cost structure of the machinery industry, the major cause of the cost increases would have to be materials.[9] Yet, material prices have not increased enough; thus, the increase in material costs can be attributed only to greater material utilization. This could occur as a result of either increased sophistication or increased inefficiency. In either case, this respresents an increase in the costs of resources devoted to machinery output.

Labor utilization has not increased at a particularly rapid rate. Labor growth in the machinery industry has been only about 3 percent per year, and labor costs—along with energy costs—have not kept pace with the growth in the production costs. Only amortization and other

437

overhead costs such as rent have grown faster than overall production costs, but these are relatively small accounts.

Measuring the Commitment of Resources to Defense

Normally, a constant price series is the best way to measure the real growth in a value series such as the GVO. Where the objective is to measure relative resource commitment, however, a current price series may be preferable—especially if there is little or no inflation or deflation but large changes in resource utilization rates.

One way of developing a current price series is to adjust the Soviet "comparable," or constant, price series of machinery GVO.[10] This series already includes prices on new products presumably reflecting high resource requirements. To reintroduce price reductions on older products, the official price index was applied to the comparable price series. These price reductions are reintroduced on the grounds they represent efficiencies or a reduction in resource requirements.

The present procurement estimate is a current price series in that it takes into account the reductions in resource requirements due to the learning effect. However, inefficiencies may be overlooked because the price increases on new systems may not incorporate the increases in costs other than those anticipated in US cost models.

A smaller GVO growth rate is indicated in current prices. The machinery industry growth was about 9 percent during 1970–1978, compared to 12 percent in "comparable" prices. (See Appendix G.) Despite a larger price adjustment for the defense sector, the growth rate for the defense ministries remained higher than the growth rate for the entire machinery industry. In the current price GVO series, the growth rate for the defense sector is 10.2 percent, compared to 13.6 percent in the comparable price series.

Implications

The rapid growth of the Soviet machinery sector—particularly the defense machinery sector—indicates an increase by 1978 in the share of industry devoted to defense. (See Appendix H.) If the relative position of the defense sector has grown as a result of "real" increase, then the defense burden has been increasing since 1970. If the defense sector has grown more rapidly than industry because of inflation, the defense share measured in today's prices would be higher throughout the entire period. In either case, the defense share in 1978 and beyond would be much higher than the presently estimated 11–13 percent.[11] (See Line I in Figure 1.)

If the civil machinery sector has increased 7–8 percent since 1970, it is very likely the cost of defense programs has increased just as quickly if not more so. Defense activities obviously have taken priority and most likely have received greater increases in resources than nondefense machinery production. The growth of the defense machinery ministries strongly suggests the increase in the cost of the defense programs exceeds that of the nondefense machinery industries and comprises a larger, and growing, share of the machinery industry. This is in sharp contrast to the present estimates of a 3–4 percent growth and a declining share of machinery output.

A real growth rate in the defense machinery sector of 10 percent would mean that between 1970 and 1978, defense procurement was growing as quickly if not more quickly than other defense resource categories; total defense outlays were increasing by at least 7–8 percent annually and total defense outlays increased as a share of GNP from 11–13 percent in 1970 to 14–16 percent in 1978 (Lines I and II in Figure 1). This contrasts not only with the 11–13 percent now estimated for the entire period but also with the presently estimated decreasing share of total machinery production represented by defense procurement.

In the unlikely event the 10 percent growth in defense machinery output is due primarily to inflation (Line III in Figure 1), the burden calculation—based on a more recent price base—would be much higher. An inflation rate of 10 percent would exceed that of the economy as a whole by 8 percent or more. With a shift in the price base from 1970 to a later base year—e.g., 1978—the defense outlays would become relatively more significant than before. Instead of a defense share of 11–13 percent measured in 1970 prices, the burden for the entire period would be 14–16 percent.

The most likely cause of the rapid growth in defense machinery is a combination of real and inflationary factors (Line IV in Figure 1). Splitting the 10 percent growth between the two would still mean a 14–16 percent burden in 1978, but the burden share would have been increasing gradually since 1970.

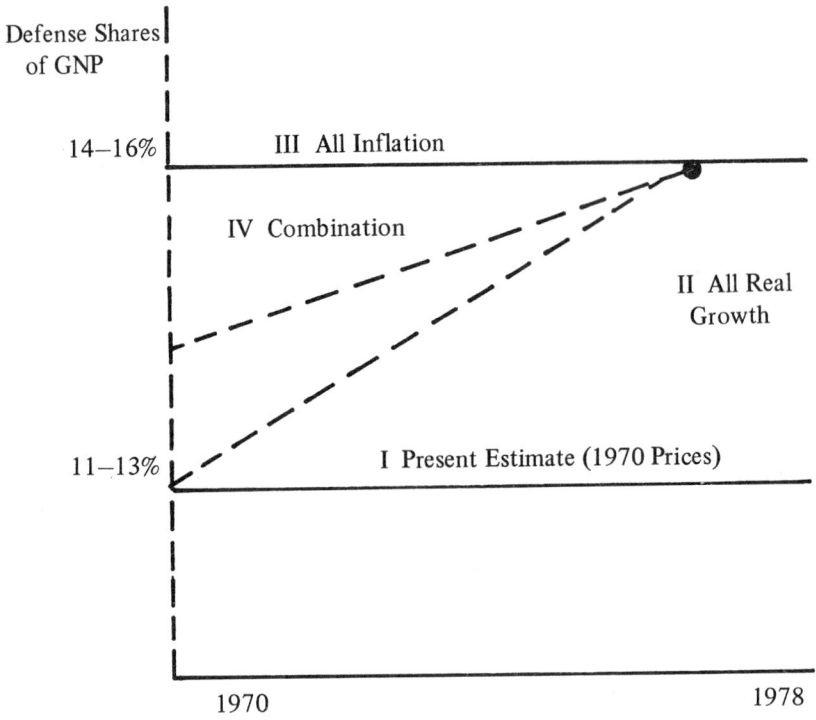

Figure 1. Alternative Implications of 10 Percent Growth in Defense Machinery.

440

Appendix A

It is likely the smaller size of the ministerial GVO, compared to the established GVO,* is due entirely to the omission of enterprises from the nondefense ministries. If so, their addition would augment both the total machinery GVO and total nondefense machinery GVO; consequently, the size and growth of the residual—or defense ministries—would not change. However, the latter's share of the total would decrease; thus, it might be argued the defense shares cited in this study are slightly overstated. On the other hand, the adjustments made for later years were assumed to be the same as for 1975 and may be excessive; there could be a trend for more enterprises to be absorbed into the ministries and for total machinery GVO to need less adjustment.

Table A–1. Adjustment of Established GVO to Derive Ministerial GVO.*

	1965	1970	1975	1979
Factor	1.089	1.089*	1.064*	1.064

*These factors would apply to the employment and capital investment data as well.

---

*T. V. Voyekova, *Model' "dokhod–tovary" i balans narodnogo khozyaystva* [The "Income-Commodity" Model and the National Economic Balance] (Moscow, 1978), p. 119.

Appendix B

A. *Gross Value of Output:* The GVO of the nondefense machinery industries can be calculated on the basis of information on the Ministry of Light Equipment. In 1975, its output was 3.2 billion rubles[*] and represented 5.0 percent of the total machinery output of the nondefense ministries[†] (which, by inference, is 64 billion rubles).[‡] The total GVO for the machinery industry was 146.4 billion rubles,[§] or 137.6 billion rubles when adjusted to obtain only ministerial GVO. Deducting 64 billion from the latter leaves 73.6 billion rubles for the defense ministries.

B. *Employment:* The employment in the nondefense ministries was derived on the basis of information in a science monograph.[*] The relationship of inventors to employment was provided along with the number of inventors in each nondefense ministry. The number of inventors in some defense ministries was also provided, but not the ratios of inventors to employees and using the nondefense ratios would provide unreliable estimates. The total employment for the nondefense ministries was 4.8 million out of the 10.8 million employed in the machinery industry (or 9.9 million in the machinery ministries).

C. *Capital Investment:* The capital investment in 8 of the 9 nondefense ministries in 1971 amounted to 3.1 billion rubles.[**] Figures for the

---

[*]*Vestnik mashinostroyeniya* [Engineering Industry Herald], No. 10, 1977, p. 17, listed 1.2 billion rubles for 1965 and 3.26 billion for 1975. *Ekonomika i organizatsiya promyshlennogo proizvodstva* [Economics and Organization of Industrial Production], No. 5, 1978, p. 57, gave the GVO figures for 1965 as 1.2 billion and 3.8 billion for 1978 and specifically associated the data with the Ministry of Light Equipment.

[†]The institute of Hamburg is cited as the source of the nondefense industry allocations for 1965, 1970, and 1975. *The Market for Machine Tools in the Soviet Union Through 1980* (New York: Chase World Information Corporation, 1977). The percentage allocations were cited by Yu. Kozlov in *Razvitiye i razmeshcheniye mashinostroyeniya SSSR* [Development and Location of the Engineering Industry of the USSR] (Moscow, 1977).

[‡]General confirmation of this estimate was obtained using the 1973 GVO for the automotive ministry updated to 12.7 billion rubles for 1975. This represents 21.9 percent of the total of nondefense machinery output.

[§]The Soviet statistical annual *Narodnoye khozyaystvo* publishes the annual GVO for industry and provides the percentage allocation by industry, including the machinery industry.

[*]Tsentral'nyy Sovet VOIRa, *Sravnitel'nyye pokazateli po izobretatel'stvu i ratsionalizatsii ministersty i vedomstv SSSR za 1966−67 gg. (po dannym statotchetnosti po forme 4MT* [Comparative Invention and Rationalization Indices for USSR Ministries and Departments for 1966–67 (According to Current Statistical Reporting by Form 4–MT] (Moscow, 1968), p. 3. Three alternative sets of estimates are possible; the range of the estimates is reasonably small for individual ministries, and it is probably less than five percent for the total—with a very high confidence level in that estimate. (Also, see John Mertens, "Comparing Ministerial and Branch Labor Force Data from 1967" (unpublished working paper, US Department of Commerce).

[**]P. N. Zhevtyak and V. I. Kolesnikov, *Pribyl' v sotsialisticheskom rasshirennom vosproiz−vodstve* [Profit in Expanded Socialist Reproduction] (Moscow: Finansy, 1976), p. 157.

smallest ministry, the Light Machinery Ministry, were not listed, presumably because it had little or no capital investment or else it did not support the author's thesis. In either case, this is the smallest ministry, and it is not apt to have much capital investment. An additional 100 million rubles are assumed for this ministry, bringing the nondefense total to 3.2 million. Total capital investment in the machinery industry was 6.469 rubles.* Adjusting the total to derive the sum of the ministerial investment leaves 5.940 million rubles and a residual of 2.74 million (5.94 − 3.20).

Table B-1. 1967 Employment Estimates.

Civil Ministries	Inventors (thousands)	Ratio to Employees	Total Employees (thousands)
Heavy Machinery	75.5	.10	755
Agricultural Machinery	65.5	.10	655
Electrical Equipment	69.1	.111	767
Machine Tool	40.1	.111	445
Chemical Machinery	32.2	.111	357
Construction Machinery	23.7	.111	263
Instruments	33.5	.125	418
Light Equipment	27.0	.125	337
Automotive	65.1	.125	814*
Total			4811

*Employment in the automotive industry was 901.8 million in 1972. *Planovove khozyaystvo* (The Planned Economy), No. 1, 1975, p. 111.

*Narodnoye khozyaystvo, p. 480.

443

Appendix C

Table C-1. GVO Growth Rates (By Percent of Base Year).*

	1965-1966	1978-1979
Nondefense Ministries		
Automotive Equipment	115**	107
Chemical Equipment	111	106
Construction Equipment	115**	104
Electrical Equipment	110	103
Heavy Equipment	111	100.8
Instruments	115**	109**
Light Equipment	109	104
Tools	110	107
Agricultural Equipment	110	104
Animal Husbandry Equipment	-	107
Power Machinery	-	104
Machinery Industry	112	108

*Published in *Ekonomicheskaya gazeta* [Economic Journal] for each year and in various Soviet publications.
**Exceeded the machinery industry growth.

Table C-2. Employment Growth Rates (By Perecent of Base Year).*

	1977-1978
Nondefense Ministries	
Automotive Equipment	102
Chemical Equipment	101 ·
Construction Equipment	100
Electrical Equipment	101
Heavy Equipment	101
Instruments	101
Light Equipment	101
Tools	102
Agricultural Equipment	100
Animal Husbandry Equipment	102
Power Machinery	102
Machinery Industry	103

*Derived on the basis of indexes of GVO growth and labor productivity published periodically in *Pravda* and other Soviet publications. The labor productivity index is based on increases in the GVO per worker.

Appendix D

Nondefense Ministries GVO:

1975:   See Table 1

1970:   The automotive industry GVO was 9.175 billion rubles in 1972.*
             This was adjusted using growth rates for the ministry back to 1970.
             Similarly, the Light Equipment Ministry GVO for 1975 was adjusted
             back to 1970 using that ministry's growth rates:

Automotive Industry: Total GVO:

7.0 billion GVO divided by 19.7%** =   35.5

Light Equipment Ministry:

1975: 3.2 billion rubles (3.2 divided
      by 1.56; growth rate factor =
      2.1);

1970: 2.1 billion rubles; 21 divided by   5.6% =   37.5

1965:
             Light Equipment Ministry:

             1.2 billion GVO divided by 5.1%* =   23.5

_____

*Planovoye khozyaystvo, No. 1, 1975, p. 111.
**Kozlov, p. 31.

445

Appendix E

Table E-1. Profitability Rates (In Percent of Production Costs).

	1965*	1970*	1972*	1974**
Ministries				
Heavy Equipment	17.5	20.4	20.9	17.7
Electrical Equipment	24.0	23.4	21.3	14.4
Chemical Equipment	22.3	20.4	19.8	14.1
Tools	18.6	25.4	26.9	19.9
Instruments	32.4	33.4	32.3	34.0
Automotive Equipment	18.8	14.1	16.1	15.9
Tractor	15.4	11.9	11.7	11.4
Construction Equipment	22.4	21.5	21.4	18.8
Light Equipment	26.4	22.1	25.6	17.6
WT Average***	20.5	19.9	19.8	17.1
Machinery Industry	18.1	21.5	20.0	15.2
Defense Sector***	16.0	23.0	20.0	13.0

*E. M. Karlik, *Ekonomika mashinostroyeniya* [Economics of the Machine Industry] (Leningrad, 1977), p. 296.
**A. A. Koshuta and L. E. Rosenova, *Kachestvo i Tsena* [Quality and Price] (Moscow, 1976), p. 146.
***Weighted on the basis of GVO values.

Appendix F

Table F-1. Production Cost Structure in the Machinery Industry.*

	1965	1970	1975	1978
TOTAL	100	100	100	100
Materials	57.1	62.4	61.9	61.8
Labor	30.2	25.6	23.6	23.1
Energy	3.5	3.6	3.2	3.2
Amortization	4.8	4.6	5.5	6.2
Other	4.4	3.8	5.8	5.7

Narodnoye khozyaystvo, various years.

447

Appendix G

Table G-1. Growth of Machinery GVO (In Billions of Rubles).

	1970	1975	1978	1970-1978 Average Growth
Machinery (Ministerial) GVO				
Comparable 1967 Prices	77.5	137.6	193.2	12.0%
Current Prices*	75.6	113.1	149.7	8.9%
Defense Machinery GVO				
1967 Prices	40.0	74.7	110.0	13.6%
Current Prices	39.0**	61.8***	86.1****	10.2%

*Applying official price index for machinery industry.
**Official index 1967 = 100; 1970 = 97.5.
***Based on a price index of 118 for 1970-1975.
****The index for 1975 was extended to 1978 using the official machinery price index.

Machinery Price Reductions for 1970-1975

	Planned	Actual
Machinery Industry	12%	15.4%
Nondefense Ministries	9%	
Defense (Residual) Ministries	14.5%	(18.0%)

Source: Yakovets and Karlik

Table G-2. Employment Estimate (In Millions)

	Total Industry	Machinery Industry	Machinery Ministries	Nondefense Ministries	Defense Ministries	Defense Ministries % of Total
1965	27.5	9.90	9.09	4.61	4.48	16.3
1970	31.59	12.02	11.03	5.10	5.93	18.8
1975	34.05	13.82	12.99	5.65	7.34	21.6
1978	36.0	14.62	13.74	5.84	7.90	21.9

Appendix H

Table H-1. Machinery Shares of Industrial Output

(Based on 1967 Prices)

	1965	1970	1975	1979
Industry*	100%	100%	100%	100%
Machinery Industry**	18%	20%	25%	29%
Nondefense Ministries**	9%	10%	11%	12%
Defense Ministries**	9%	10%	14%	17%
Defense Ministries (Based on Current Prices)	10%	11%	12%	14%

*Published in various editions of *Narodnoye khozyaystvo* (extrapolated for 1979 based on recently announced growth rates).
**Based on data developed early in this study.

The level of employment and industrial share of the defense sector can be estimated for each year. The growth of employment for the nondefense ministries can be derived for each year based on the Soviet statistics on output per worker. Combining these growth factors with the employment figures for 1967 results in estimates of the level of employment for the nondefense ministries for each year. Deducting these estimates from the machinery industry total provides estimates of employment in the defense sector. Defense employment has been increasing as a share of industrial employment.

Calculation of the Burden Rates for 1978

Based on the calculations, the defense burden for 1978 should be three percentage points higher than in 1970. This is the case regardless of whether the 10 percent growth in defense machinery is due to inflation (and the price base is changed to 1978) or to real growth. Instead of an 11–13 percent burden rate in 1978, it should be in the 14–16 percent range.

I. Assuming no change in the price base, all of the 10 percent growth in machinery is real and machinery represents 50 percent of total defense.

	1970 Estimate	Inflation Factor (annual)	Growth Factor (annual)	1978 Estimate (factored)	1978 Estimate (normalized)
GNP	100%		3.6%**	133.2%	100.0%
Machinery	6%*		10.0%***	12.9%	9.6%
Other Defense	6%*		5.0%****	8.9%	6.6%
Total Defense	12%				15.2%

II. Assuming a change in the price base to 1978, that all 10 percent of the growth is due to inflation, and that machinery is 50 percent of defense outlays.

	1970 Estimate	Inflation	Growth Factor	1978 Estimate (factored)	1978 Estimate (normalized)
GNP	100%	2%	3.6%	155.2%	100.0%
Machinery	6%*	10%***	-	12.8%	8.3%
Other Defense	6%*	2%****	5.0%****	10.4%	6.7%
Total Defense	12%				15.0%

*This represents the midpoint of the 11-13 percent range.
**This is the average real GNP growth estimated by CIA for 1976-1978.
***This is the average rate of defense machinery growth estimated in this study.
****Other defense accounts grew at least as fast as total defense outlays.

Notes

1. *Narodnoye khozyaystvo SSR* [National Economy of the USSR], 1978, p. 131.
2. For more information, see *Level and Trend of the Gross Value Output in the Soviet Defense Machinery Ministries,* Report DDB–1910–4–79 (Washington: Defense Intelligence Agency, 1979).
3. This was brought to my attention by Dr. Robert Abbott. A recent Soviet book by T. V. Voyekova indicates the ratio of establishment to ministerial GVO for Soviet machinery was 1.089 in 1979 and 1.064 in 1975. See Appendix A for further discussion.
4. *Soviet Spending for Defense: Trends Since 1965 and the Outlook for the 1980s* (Washington: Central Intelligence Agency, October 1979). The investment account is estimated to be increasing more slowly than the total defense outlays of 4 to 5 percent.
5. V. Fal'tsman, "Intensification of the Development of the Production System," *Voprosy Ekonomiki* [Economic Questions], No. 1, January 1978, pp. 25–36.
6. *Narodnoye khozyaystvo,* 1978.
7. Ibid., p. 138.
8. J. Steiner, *Inflation in Soviet Industry and Machine Building and Metal Working (MBMW), 1960–1975* (unpublished working paper, Central Intelligence Agency), pp. 42–52.
9. Materials remained at a fairly high, stable proportion of total costs and therefore must have induced the increases which occurred in total costs. See Appendix F.
10. A current price series also was developed by R. Abbott in *Estimating Soviet Spending for Military Hardware from Machine Building and Metal Working Statistics,* Report SR M 79–10078 (Washington: Central Intelligence Agency, June 1979). This series is higher, but the growth rate is only slightly lower for the 1970–1975 period than indicated by the series developed herein.
11. According to the *Handbook of Economic Statistics,* 1979, Report ER 79–10274 (Washington: Central Intelligence Agency, 1979).

USSR Aircraft Industry: Will Transfer of Work Practices To Nondefense Industries Promote Future Economic Growth?

W. L. Morgan

The problem is posed:

> Will the successful work practices of the USSR military product industrial sector be assimilated as a practical model for realizing increased effectiveness in the USSR's nondefense industrial base?

References to the work practices and outlooks of the USSR aviation industry reflect, in part, the fortuitous availability of public information. As a mature, successful industrial ministry dealing routinely with complex and rapidly advancing technology, the USSR Ministry of the Aviation Industry is a suitable representative of the military product industrial sector. All of the ministries in the industrial sector for military products traditionally have been accorded high priority; this in turn has resulted in considerable product achievements and the securing of a major role in the creation of assets which have facilitated the attainment of national goals.

The secondary product lines of production enterprises in the military product industrial sector also make direct contributions to the civilian national economy. A part of the aviation industry's support for agriculture was demonstrated to Western journalists who visited the supersonic transport production line; they were shown a secondary production line for aluminum chicken incubators.[1] The nature of the assistance by the aviation industry to the lagging elements of the nondefense industrial base to be addressed in this article, however, concerns the adaptation of techniques and procedures for moving technology into production for the purpose of generating improved economic performance. In turn, this improved performance generates additional investment resources. These resources form a large national pool with an increased capacity for meeting the acceleration of resource demand associated with continuity of support to the development and production of military products—the accelerating demand reflecting increased complexity and cost of weapons. The direct linkage among (1) the performance of the nondefense industrial sector of the USSR national economy (2) the pace of weapon development and (3) the reflection of technology accomplishment in the production of weapons is demonstrated in the following (paraphrased) statement by Minister of Defense Dmitriy Fedorovich Ustinov: the directions and development of military doctrine are linked to the state of the economic potential of the national economy; there exists a direct dependency of weapon development potential on the level of development of the economy.[2] The statement—by a Minister of Defense who climbed the career ladder as a civilian manager in the defense industrial sphere and who rose to the upper strata of the Politburo as the Party's tsar of the military product industrial base—reflects the emphasis on the idea that the essence, character, and methods of conducting war are influenced significantly by the nation's economic pulse. The military product industrial sector needs concomitant improvement in the performance of the overall economy in order to accommodate its continually spiraling demand for increased resource allocations.

It is of interest to review briefly the history of the actions which had an impact on science and industry in the 1950s and 1960s; these actions resulted in conditioned resistance to economic reform among USSR S&T (scientific and technical) personnel as well as the ingraining of what are still operative perceptions. Also during this time, the indirect influence of the aviation industry could be discerned in the activities of highly capable scientists who were moving out of the industry into positions of responsibility in the national science base. These scientists—with their established vision of the function of a scientific research institute—contributed to aviation industry outlooks and created a legacy of significance for the current efforts at industrial reform.

The late 1950s and 1960s were certainly turbulent for scientists in fundamental research institutes and difficult as well for the hierarchy of industrial ministries and managers of production enterprises. The Soviet Party and government made aggressive moves to change the status quo. These moves were motivated by the need to improve the performance of the national economy. As a result, the traditional cherished independence and aloofness of the fundamental scientist was vigorously assailed. In the industrial base, the purview of all ministers over production was curtailed sharply.

Prior to the formal initiation of reform in 1966, system inertia dictated, in part, the invulnerability of the scientist imbued with the quest for fundamental knowledge and the production enterprise manager who resisted change. Both of these types were able to function without substantial modification of their work environments.

The scientist rode out the buffeting which accompanied organizational change, budget gyrations, and constant haranguing with a great deal of reinforcement from the elite peer group. This resistance included peer group rejection of many of the initiatives of the Party-supported science leadership. The scientist could keep his ideals intact if his institute director was similarly disposed; e.g., manpower cuts decreed early in a year usually were reversed before the year was over.

The factory manager (more often than not educated as an engineer and not necessarily sympathetic to the underlying macroeconomic arguments) survived by devoting appropriate energy to meeting long-standing norms and accommodating change—but only change the resident special design bureau could accommodate with existing floorspace, tooling, manpower competence, and supply flow without adverse impact on its centrally planned production goals. The Party officials of the responsible oblast apparatus privately were inclined to be just as obdurate as the factory manager regarding change which threatened the oblast's plan fulfillment. Production goals were more likely to be met if production line upheaval was averted. Motivation to incorporate new technology into products was apparently missing, and sincere, widespread motivation was essential to attain even a modicum of success, given the fact the central authorities' demands represented the antithesis of the preferred choices at the working level.

The Party's apparent obsession to assert its authority over the science faction once and for all continues to lurk in the background. This goal is not necessarily consistent with improving technology flow into product design. The flaw is the lack of interest in or talent for engineering design possessed by the fundamental research scientist.

The experiment which started late in the 1950s at the Novosibirsk Science City addressed the science-to-engineering gap. This experiment was unique in several respects: 1) the diversity of collocated research activities; 2) the concentration of capital investment; and 3) the leadership, which consisted of implanted industrial talent. The original Science City hierarchy included senior scientists from the Central Aerohydrodynamic Institute (*TsAGI—Tsentral'nyy aerogidrodina-micheskiy institut*) of the aviation industry—scientist-administrators who were all experienced in shaping research accomplishments to fit applications and in planning the shifting of concepts from the laboratory to the design bureau to the production enterprise. One of these scientists, Sergey Alekseyevich Khristyanovich, organized the Institute of Theoretical and Applied Mechanics in Novosibirsk. During his tenure, a substantial amount of the institute's research responded to industry-funded contracts, providing research results with an applicational bent which were verified by extensive experimental support from the institute's test facilities. The rather large investment in test facilities was a manifestation of aviation industry philosophy. Of equal interest was Khristyanovich's influence on the revitalization of Novosibirsk State University. The curriculum was very reminiscent of the Moscow Physical Technical Institute—a higher education institute influenced by Khristyanovich in the 1950s which became a source of well-educated cadre for *TsAGI*.

Khristyanovich's successor was Vladimir Vasil'yevich Struminskiy, an important researcher from the Central Aerohydrodynamic Institute. He continued actively to foster advances in technology with potential application to advanced aerodynamic system design. Subsequent replacements did not come from *TsAGI* but possessed the same orientation. Mikhail Alekseyevich Lavrentev, also of *TsAGI*, organized the Hydrodynamics Institute and functioned as the overall Director of the Novosibirsk Science City. He oriented the environment toward good science; that is, science conceived in a research plan which eventually would be coupled with good engineering. The Science City's experimental fabrication installation facilitated the performance of applied research which complemented the technology accomplishments of the scientific research institutes of the complex. Innovations created by this experimental fabrication laboratory were presented directly to production enterprises—allowing the engineers who had worked with the scientific researchers to interact directly with the enterprises' special design bureau engineers in solving floor space and technological problems associated with planning and implementing product improvements or process modifications.

This is powerful medicine for slowing industrial growth. Instead of flogging scientists into line to perform practical works—a concept foreign to many—a Science City is created which is remote, to a helpful degree, from the prejudices of the industrial core centered in Moscow. The lessons learned in the effective exploitation of science have helped the Siberian region in the short and long run and have provided a much needed example for national reform.

Another *TsAGI* scientist, Mstislav Vsevolodovich Keldysh, President of the USSR Academy of Sciences from 1961 through 1975, exerted influence on the superstructure of the national science faction. The increased number of industry people elected to the science academy and the redesignation of Academy of Sciences departments provided better representation for industry accomplishments and created improved opportunity for influencing Politburo judgments on the directions and philosophy of research. This development can be credited to Keldysh. Some scientists acquired a greater interest in science application through the involvement of the academy's scientific research institutes in the space program. Keldysh's personal achievements at the Laboratory of Applied Mathematics of the academy's Institute of Mathematics and the scale of the practical work he fostered at the laboratory were examples to other directors of research institutes.

Additional examples in the national academy are Anatoliy Alekseyevich Dorodnitsyn and Oleg Mikhailovich Belotserkovskiy, also scientists from *TsAGI*. These pragmatic scientists are exerting important influence on the research activities of the national academy's institutes in their respective roles as Director and Deputy Director of the Computer Center of the USSR Academy of Sciences. They are setting positive examples for their fellow institute administrators through their promotion of the in-depth involvement of the Computer Center in contracted industry support work.

The transfusion of the experience of the scientist-administrators is not the only element of the aviation industry's historical contributions to economic reform. The strong, well-endowed, centralized research institutes of the aviation industry—with their firm grasp of the technologies pertinent to product design and their partnership with the design bureaus in solving design problems—could not be duplicated throughout the national economy, but the functional form can be synthesized in an organizational concept based on the research institutes and design bureaus of the aviation industry. The research institutes and design bureaus of the aviation industry were models for the electronic industries of the military product sector and the latter's use of a combined research-design organizational form that personified effective coupling of function and involvement. This has become the general model in the national economy for the "product association"—a key organizational structure fostered in the current reform and suggested by the functional organization in the military product sector.

The technical standards historically enforced throughout the aviation industry assured assimilation of prototype fabrication experience acquired at the design bureau by the production enterprise. Few industries outside the military product sector enjoyed the routine enforcement of standards which assured the transfer of experience from developer to producer. A single system of design documentation was created and implemented in the USSR from 1968 through 1973. The core standard—the Unified System of Design Documentation—dates from 1970, and the overall system of standards has the force of law in application at the national economic level.[3] External support has been improved.

The potential for additional transfer of successful experience from the aviation industry to other industries in the national economy is apparent in certain features of the development process as prescribed for all industries by the Unified System of Design Documentation. The following information on flight vehicle development is taken from a 1978 Russian-language document. The author, V. I. Tikhomirov, is a senior professor of industrial economics at the Moscow Aviation Institute. In the document, he addressed the organization, planning, and administration of the production of flight vehicles. Tikhomirov related in some detail the nature of the customer tasking communicated by the "technical assignment."[*] Significantly, the customer, the lead design bureau for the project, and the entire register of scientific research institutes of the aviation industry previously have interacted for a considerable period of time in addressing the realizable goals of the develop-

---

[*]"Technical assignment" is the initial event in the development cycle defined by the Unified System of Design Documentation. The event is triggered by government approval of the flight vehicle development project, accompanied by the allocation of resources for the accomplishment of the project.

ment project.

Initially, industry-customer interaction begins with the scientific research institute undertaking conceptual investigations which might form the nucleus of understanding for defining a potential new or improved product goal. If the goal under investigation demands a departure from the evolutionary expansion of the supporting technology base, considerable time and resources are devoted over and above the routine continuous process. When knowledge is sufficient, a preliminary design is supplied to the customer—a design which represents a negotiated compromise between the customer's demands and the industry's consensual judgment of what can be done. The customer uses this preliminary design to define the formal requirements for a new product when seeking Party and government approval. During the time required for approval from the Party and government, the industry research institutes continue to perform applied research—that is, tailoring of verified research accomplishments to the proposed design application—in order to establish the overall system design bureau and the subsystem and component design bureaus necessary to give the desired controlled-risk response to the "technical assignment."

Tikhomirov states that the aviation industry's policy in regard to the degree of acceptable risk demands that a minimum of two-thirds of the applied research accomplishments required to support the development be on-hand before accepting developmental responsibility. The scientific and technical council of the lead design bureau prepares the draft of the government resolution describing the intended development project and the associated resource allocations. Therefore, the details of the description of the development goals tasked in the "technical assignment" are never a surprise and are never unrepresentative of industry guidelines. A controlled flow of technology is guaranteed— something which is never too upsetting to production enterprises.4

In this description of the routine process of defining new products, the role of customer demand and customer 'clout' is evident. The current reforms deal with the latter via contract negotiation and the customer's ability to withhold all payment until the contract is satisfied on time in the desired amount and quality.

The prescribed use of test facilities to support every major step of the development process leading to the official development qualification is also important. The thoroughness and confidence of the test data at each step in development is the key to the quality and timeliness of the development. The capital investment required to follow such a development philosophy is very large since the test facilities needed to simulate authentically the operational environment and diagnose the performance of complicated developments are quite complex. The demand for test support throughout the national economy would not be expected to approach that of the aerospace industries, but the role of test facilities and the emphasis on an authentic testing regimen to ensure suitable R&D progress are analagous if the work practices of the military product industrial sector are to be emulated.

The reforms potentially may permit some copying of the success experienced in the military product sector. However, the unfavorable inertia generated by standard operating procedures must be defeated. Certainly, the opportunity for labor intensive solutions is not substantial, considering the results of recently conducted demographic studies. In 1979, the head of the State Planning Committee, in addressing the Supreme Soviet, emphasized the need for limiting new construction and according priority to the completion of unfinished construction.[5] To the degree the reforms focus on the reproduction of the military product sector's development and production procedures, there will be a discernible emphasis on the completion of test support and experimental fabrication resources in the nondefense industrial sector.

The circumstantial evidence suppports a general surmise that the reforms in the national economy reflect considerably the work procedures of the military product industrial sector. The use of profits by lagging industries to improve their ability for test support of development will indicate further application of the defense sector model. The degree of success will be discernible in the level of enforcement of the customer's right to withhold payment for R&D services not performed or performed unsatisfactorily.

The military product sector's influence in national circles continues to accelerate. Keldysh's replacement is from the nuclear energy industry, thereby maintaining the influence of the military product industrial sector on the science faction. Furthermore, the creation of a new section in the Academy of Sciences for "Applied Problems" has the beneficial effect of grouping together the academy research institutes with the greatest potential for industrial support.

Improved performance of the unsatisfactory components of the national economy's industrial base is linked directly to satisfaction of the spiraling demand for complex weapon development and production resources. The potential exists for a reopening of the 24th Party Congress' discussion of resource reapportionment in order to spur the laggards. The 11th Five Year Plan could well contain the weighting of capital investment which will best prepare the substandard performers to contribute in an improved manner.

Notes

1. "Reports of a Group of European Aviation Writers Touring the USSR Aviation Industry," *Aviation Magazine* (France), No. 441, April 1966.
2. D. F. Ustinov, "Rukovodyashchaya rol' KPSS v stroitel'stve Sovetskikh Vooruzhennykh Sil [The Leading Role of the CPSU in the Building of the Soviet Armed Forces], "*Voprosy istorii KPSS* [Problems of History of the CPSU], No. 2, February 1979, pp. 14–34; and "Strazh mirnogo truda, oplot vseobshchego mira [Guarding Peaceful Labor, the Bulwark of Universal Peace], "*Kommunist,* No. 3, February

1977, pp. 11–22.

3. R. A. Yegoshin, et al, *Handbook on the Single System of Design Documentation* (Khar'kov: Prapor Publishing House, 1975), unedited machine translation, FTD–ID(RS)T–0554–77, Foreign Technology Division, Air Force Systems Command, Wright-Patterson AFB, Ohio, 22 April 1977.

4. V. I. Tikhomirov, *Organization, Planning, and Administration of the Production of Flight Vehicles* (Moscow: Mashinostroyeniye Publishing House, 1978), unedited machine translation, FTD–ID(RS)T–2081–78, 22 January 1979.

5. N. Baybakov, "Rech' na vtoroy sessii Verkhovonogo Soveta SSSR [Speech to the Second Session of the Supreme Soviet of the USSR], *"Ekonomicheskaya gazeta* [Economic Gazette], November 1979.

Soviet Design Policy and Its Implications
For US Combat Aircraft Procurement

Rebecca V. Strode

The prices of US tactical aircraft have increased enormously over the past three decades, to the point that severe budgetary pressures now constrain the nation's efforts to procure aircraft in the quantity required to maintain its accustomed defense capabilities. The most expensive tactical aircraft currently under production, the Navy's F–14, is 50 times more costly measured in constant dollars than the most expensive World War II fighter.[1] If the postwar trend continues, the unit cost (u.c.) of a hypothetical "F–1985" might well exceed 50 million dollars, or almost three times the price of the F–14. The consequence of higher procurement prices is fewer purchases; as a result, the US/Soviet numerical balance in tactical aircraft shifted over the decade 1965–1975 from a 78 percent US advantage to a 7 percent US deficit (see Table 1).

Table 1. US/Soviet Balance in Tactical Aircraft

1965			1975		
US	USSR	Ratio US:USSR	US	USSR	Ratio US:USSR
5800	3250	1.78	5000	5350	0.93

Source: John M. Collins and Anthony H. Cordesman, *United States/Soviet Military Balance: A Frame of Reference for Congress* (Washington, DC: Government Printing Office, 1976), p. 45.

Quantity, of course, is not the only measure of military capability; quality plays an equally important role, and it is precisely the high performance characteristics of recent US aircraft that have been largely responsible for the escalation in price. High performance and high costs both derive from two basic aspects of US fighter aircraft design: versatility and technological sophistication. American aircraft have consistently embodied systems and components which have marked the bounds of the technologically feasible at the time of their construction. This trend in US design was clearly endorsed by Rear Admiral T. R. McClellan, Chief of the Navy's Air Systems Command, in testimony before the Senate Armed Services Committee. Asked why the Navy chose the Grumman F–14 over McDonnell Douglas' less expensive aircraft, Admiral McClellan replied, "In a fighter aircraft, sir, we try to get the maximum design we can."[2]

The second aspect of US design, versatility, enables a single fighter to carry out a variety of missions: close support, air superiority, interception, and interdiction. Close support constitutes the tactical air forces' most immediate contribution to the battlefield outcome by striking directly at the enemy's deployed forces while they are engaged against friendly ground units. It requires the ability to fly at very low altitudes under heavy fire. Air superiority is achieved by destroying enemy air power on the ground and by maintaining air-to-air combat dominance in the sky. This mission puts a premium on energy-maneuverability, particularly the ability to turn inside an opponent and bear high load factors, since air battles are generally not fought at maximum speed but in an "envelope" ranging from Mach 0.6 at 10,000 feet to Mach 1.4 at 17,000 feet. The interception of enemy bombers and other aircraft demands speed, maneuverability, and range. Finally, modern, multirole combat aircraft (MRCA) are designed to accomplish missions of interdiction; that is, to conduct deep penetration of heavily defended areas in order to attack well-guarded targets. Because this mission pits the pilot against a numerous array of enemy radar, missile, and other air defense systems, interdiction requires great range and payload, low-altitude capability at Mach 0.8–0.9, sophisticated avionics and navigational equipment, powerful ECM/ECCM equipment, and efficient fire control systems—all of which translate into larger and more expensive aircraft than would be necessary for fighters not required to operate deep over hostile territory.[3]

Interdiction is the most controversial of tactical air missions because its risks and costs are high while its outcome—the reduction of enemy logistical support—constrains the opponent's military initiatives only in the long run and with debatable effectiveness. Yet, it has played a major role in US combat experience. During World War II, interdiction accounted for 51 percent of US sorties in the European theater. During the Pacific Leyte campaign, despite the fact that air superiority had not yet been achieved, almost 20 percent of the sorties involved interdiction. In the Korean War, the share was 55 percent, and, while precise figures are not available for the war in Southeast Asia, it is likely that interdiction strikes accounted for 75–79 percent of all US sorties.[4] Should the United States become involved in an air war in the next decade or so, multirole fighters would probably spend between one-sixth and one-third of their flight time on interdiction missions.[5]

While the versatility typically built into US fighters may drive up their unit costs, less versatile aircraft would not necessarily be less expensive. Multirole aircraft provide several program, as opposed to unit, cost savings, including:

- developmental savings (it is easier to design one aircraft than several),
- production economies of scale, and
- maintenance savings through standardization.

Multirole aircraft also offer the important combat advantage of flexibility. Since aircraft are not lost in equal or predictable proportions in time of war, it is beneficial to have at one's disposal aircraft which can perform a variety of missions and hence can be shifted about as necessity dictates. The disadvantage of multirole aircraft is a certain loss of cost-efficiency due to the requirement each possess the capability to fulfill several missions even though performing only one at a time. Consequently, on any given assignment, a multirole aircraft is equipped with a number of systems which are superfluous to the accomplishment of its mission.

The advantages and disadvantages of mission-specific aircraft are the converse of those enumerated for multirole fighters. On the one hand, single-mission aircraft appear to be more effective since they need not embody "superfluous" capabilities. On the other hand, such aircraft do not provide the economies of scale and standardization offered by MRCAs. As for combat, the advocates of more specialized aircraft argue that no multirole fighter can perform any single mission as proficiently as one specially designed for the task. However, those who favor MRCAs point to the loss of flexibility which a mission-specific force structure entails and contend that it is preferable to perform several missions reasonably well than one superbly and others not at all.[6]

Further examination of this debate lies beyond the scope of this article. Suffice it to say that there exists a growing number of critics of US procurement policy who feel MRCAs place an inordinate fiscal burden on tactical air forces. It should be noted, however, that the argument of many of these critics does not stop at challenging the value of multimission fighters but goes on to question the need for maximum technologies in general, be they incorporated in multirole or mission-specific aircraft. The F–111, for example, is mission-specific (for deep penetration) but at the same time very expensive (unit cost = $15 million) due to sophisticated capabilities. Now it is clear the use of state-of-the-art technology increases cost as well as capability, and, insofar as there are budgetary constraints, there will be a tradeoff between quality and quantity. The task, then, reduces to determining the extent to which combat advantages accrue to technologically superior aircraft.

Advanced American fighters have confronted inferior Soviet aircraft on several occasions, and it is instructive to examine the results. In the "MiG Alley" of Korea, the F–86 Sabre was pitted against the MiG–15 deep over hostile territory, a condition which favored the North

Korean, Chinese, and Soviet pilots. Yet the American aircraft—larger, more complex, and the most expensive fighter the United States had yet built—achieved a remarkable kill ratio against its Soviet opposite and thus proved to be clearly cost-effective. But the results of more recent battles have been more ambiguous. The currently deployed F–4 Phantom and MiG–21, for example, have met over both Vietnam and the Middle East; although the American plane again proved to be the better fighter, its margin of superiority was not always so great as to justify its cost in the unequivocal manner of the F–86. The exact combat ratio between the F–4 and MiG–21 in the Vietnam War remains classified, but William White of the Brookings Institution has estimated it to be about 2 or 3 : 1 in favor of the Phantom. During the summer of 1972, air-to-air combat resulted in the loss of 12 MiG–21s, 4 MiG–17/19s, and 11 F–4s, yielding a kill ratio of about 1.5 MiGs for every Phantom shot down.[7] In the October 1973 war, Israel's 550 combat aircraft—127 of which were F–4 Phantoms—were highly effective in air-to-air combat against Soviet-built MiGs but proved vulnerable to the Egyptian Army's SAMs.[8]

Where national security is at stake, cost-efficiency analyses alone are hardly persuasive, and it must again be stressed that the F–4 did win the battle for the sky in both Vietnam and the Middle East. But to the extent that cost-efficiency criteria are valid considerations in determining force structure, the F–4's performance might be seen as somewhat disappointing. Almost three times as heavy as the MiG–21 and with a 38 percent greater combat radius, it costs about three times more to produce measured in dollar terms.[9] But is it three times more effective, or do technological improvements at some point become subject to diminishing returns?

Critics of current US force structure believe the latter to be the case and contend that savings could be realized without significant loss of combat effectiveness by limiting the missions and capabilities of tactical aircraft. Proponents of this policy frequently look to the Soviet Union for an example of an alternative procurement policy and claim the USSR has secured its defense at lower cost by restricting its tactical air forces to air superiority and ground attack missions with little regard to interdiction, by building simple mission-specific aircraft rather than MRCAs, and by resisting the temptation always to push technology to the limit when designing new aircraft opting instead for quantity over quality. A closer inspection, however, reveals this analysis to be seriously flawed. First, it is not at all clear Soviet tactical air forces truly "cost less" than their American counterparts. Second, the argument confuses past capabilities with current policy and then unjustifiably projects that policy into the future. The purpose of this article is to provide a more accurate understanding of Soviet design policy and to suggest the implications that policy holds for future combat aircraft production.

It is true the USSR's Frontal Aviation forces generally have not undertaken deep interdiction missions and the service's aircraft are primarily designed for air superiority or ground attack. They are also more mission-specific than the major US fighters. The *MiG*–21 and –23 are designed for air superiority, the *Su*–7 and –17 for close support, and the *Su*–19 for penetrating ground attack against hardened targets. Within the *PVO*, aircraft also are designed for specific, limited roles. Pilot training, for example, concentrates on ground control interception, not free air combat; and the *MiG*–25, while performing high-altitude, high-speed interception ably, is far less capable in other regimes. The *Su*–9 was designed as a point defense interceptor; the *Yak*–28 as a low-altitude interceptor. The *Tu*–28 was built specifically for long-range interception.[10] None possess the multirole capabilities of US fighters.

It is also true Soviet aircraft do not exhibit the same level of technology as US aircraft. But one should not underestimate Soviet equipment, for in some areas it performs very well. The USSR's electro-optical and laser systems are highly capable, as are its ECM and infrared equipment. But overall, Soviet designers do not build into their aircraft the high performance characteristics typical of US forces. Their onboard computers are less sophisticated, and they fall far short of the United States in the use of composites and miniaturized avionics.[11] Indeed, the *MiG*–25 in which Viktor Belenko defected in 1976 did not even make extensive use of advanced metals. The aircraft was constructed primarily of steel, with titanium found only in structures subject to extreme heating such as the wing leading-edges. The resultant weight penalty reduced the amount of equipment which could be carried; this constraint was further exacerbated by the aircraft's use of vacuum tubes rather than solid-state circuitry in its electronics. A comparative examination of climb, acceleration, turn radius, and radar capability reveals the superiority of the F–15 and F–16 to late model *MiG*–21s and the *MiG*–25; even the older F–4 compares favorably.[12]

Underlying the differences between US and Soviet aircraft are divergent approaches to aircraft design. The United States has emphasized complexity, versatility, and technological sophistication and has been willing to sacrifice a certain amount of quantity in exchange for higher quality. Within the Soviet Union, however, radically different practices were fostered among the R&D community during Stalin's rule and have remained persistent features of Soviet design policy to this day. The five most prominent of these recurrent patterns are

- simplicity,
- commonality,
- prototype modeling,
- incrementalism, and

• reliance on foreign technology.

The simplicity of Soviet designs relates to their modest performance specifications which are just sufficient to allow completion of the minimum tasks required and no more. Simplicity is evident in the designs as a whole, in the utilization of conventional, readily available construction materials, and in the lack of detailed finishing.

Commonality refers to the use of standardized parts and assemblies on various types of aircraft whenever possible. Alternatively, an entire aircraft series may, upon reaching obsolescence in its original role, be modified to fulfill some new system requirement. (This is not, however, the multirole principle found in NATO designs; Soviet aircraft usually have not been designed with more than one function in mind. It is only after an aircraft no longer can perform the specific mission for which it was originally created, or when an unforeseen requirement has arisen for which no aircraft yet exists, that an attempt is made to find a new use for the older series.) The *ASh*–82 engine, for example, was used to outfit the World War II–vintage *La*–5 fighter, the *Tu*–2 frontal bomber, and the *Pe*–8 long range bomber. Indeed, 20 years later, it was still in service on the *Il*–14 passenger carrier and the *Mi*–4 helicopter.[13] Similarly, the *Su*–9 interceptor and the *Su*–7 ground attack fighter, although fitted with different wings, armament, and equipment to suit their particular roles, nevertheless possess identical fuselages and tails.[14] To take another example in a somewhat different vein, the *M*–4/BISON, though currently being phased out of its bomber role, is being modified to serve as a tanker, and a version of the old *Tu*–95/BEAR has been developed to operate in an ASW capacity.[15]

The third feature of the USSR's design process, prototype modeling, specifies the purpose to which research, development, testing, an evaluation are being directed. In the Soviet Union, newly designed aircraft fall into two categories: "test" (*opytnyye*) and "experimental" (*eksperimental'nyye*). Test models are designed to serve as prototypes of forthcoming series production aircraft, and the emphasis is placed on feasibility and existing technologies. Experimental aircraft, on the other hand, are not intended for series production but are built to test a particular new technology or flight characteristic—record-breaking speed, new maneuvers, a new design principle, and so on.[16] Prototype modeling, then, provides a link between the static traits of Soviet design policy (simplicity and commonality in series production aircraft) and the dynamic features which foster innovation (incrementalism and foreign input).

The conservatism of Soviet aircraft design policy is nowhere better exemplified than in its stress on innovation through incremental improvement. The approach blends well with the nation's predilection for commonality, since when only modest, step-by-step changes are introduced to upgrade performance, follow-on aircraft are left with many of the same features as their predecessors. Although experimental prototypes (*I* and *Ye* series) occasionally introduce major improvements in technology, the predominant pattern has been gradual upgrading. Even what appear to be discontinuous advances in the performance characteristics of deployed aircraft have in fact been achieved little by little through prototype testing. The transition from the *MiG*–9 to the delta-wing *MiG*–21, for example, involved five intervening prototypes: (1) the *Ye*–50, a swept-wing aircraft with an upgrade *MiG*–19 engine; (2) the *Ye*–2A, a swept-wing model equipped with the future *MiG*–21 production engine; (3) the *Ye*–5, a delta-wing prototype with the same fuselage and engine as the *Ye*–2A; (4) the *Ye*–6, preproduction series very similar to the *Ye*–5; and, finally, (5) the production version, the *MiG*–21F/FISHBED C. This model itself has undergone extensive upgrading since its introduction in 1960; as a result, the most recent version has twice the range and payload of the original.[17]

The other major avenue to qualitative improvement employed by the Soviets is to borrow from Western technology and experience. Numerous examples could be given, from jet engines to integrated circuitry. Such innovation may take the form of partial borrowing or complete replication (*bez otsebyatiny*). As A. Fedoseyev, an applied scientist who recently emigrated from the Soviet Union, explains: "The themes of new military developments are taken from foreign technical journals and intelligence information on foreign equipment, and often arise as a result of obtaining actual examples of the equipment from abroad."[18]

Source of Soviet Design Policy

Conservatism and simplicity are evident in all aspects of Soviet design, but the reasons for their prominence are not so easily identified. Do they result from the free choice of the nation's leaders in light of various cost-benefit analyses? Or do they reflect the limited options available to a country plagued by economic irrationality, bureaucratic ossification, and negative historical experience? Those who see in Soviet force structure an alternative to the escalating costs of defense procurements generally accept the former explanation, and the Soviets do claim to find in their approach practical advantages which do not inhere in the United States' more complex designs. However, there is strong evidence that the deeper source of the conservatism and technological modesty found in Soviet aircraft designs lies in the systemic inadequacies of the Soviet policy.

Certain benefits do accrue to the Soviet design policy outlined above. Aircraft can be completed more quickly, for instance, if they are unencumbered by nonessential accessories and are derived from previous models.[19] In addition, simplicity facilitates pilot training and eases the pilot's task under the difficult conditions of combat. World War II in particular drove this lesson home to the Soviets. As former test pilot M. Gallay explains:

A plane does not live by speed alone! Consequently, all our efforts were directed toward getting the new fighters 'off,' with the goal of making them reliable and accessible to any pilot of average qualifications. (In a major war, you won't get very far on aces alone!)[21]

With this in mind, the Soviets not only designed simplicity into their *MiG*–3 but, upon receiving American lend-lease aircraft, straightway stripped them of nonessential equipment such as extra fuel lines and gauges.[22]

Commonality, too, makes good sense. It reduces the logistics problems associated with providing spare parts, saves time and resources, and makes it easier for pilots to switch from one type of aircraft to another.[23] Prototype testing minimizes uncertainty and avoids the problems which can arise when one attempts to manufacture unproved designs. Through prototype testing, costs, and performance can be scrutinized before substantial commitments to a project have been made.[24]

Like simplicity and commonality, incremental innovation can facilitate pilot training and performance. For example, a *MiG*–21 was modified in the 1960s to provide an experimental analog to the *Tu*–144 supersonic transport then in development. The analog *MiG* had its tailplane removed; it was then fitted with a scaled-down version of the *Tu*–144's ogival wing in order to accustom the test pilots to the wing's aerodynamic effects before they took the larger plane into the air.[25] But far more important is the impact of the incremental approach on quantitative measures of military power. Once again, the USSR's wartime experience played a crucial role:

The fact is that any measure—even the most effective—is not suitable if its realization would hold up the output of combat aircraft from the assembly line for even a few days. The front can't wait! Over the field of battle in those days our aircraft were already fewer in number than the enemy's. This gap had to be reduced, or at least not increased. Therefore, in the course of designing aircraft, the necessary results had to be obtained with relatively few means—only those which could be incorporated without holding up production.

This was a good school! The ability to achieve improved tactical-technical characteristics without having to turn the whole aircraft design upside down became one of the most important elements in the work style of our aeronautical engineers and scientists, even in relatively calm times, when there was no special need for it.[26]

The Soviets do not like to discuss their reliance on foreign technology, but one can surmise that this method of innovation reduces R&D outlays not only on individual projects but on applied science as a whole. Thus, when the technology, materials, and equipment needed to replicate a Western aircraft or other weapon have been lacking, entire new branches of industry have been created. According to Fedoseyev, the government believes this to be an infallible method of determining how best to allocate the nation's research funds and order investment priorities.[27]

But for all the advantages of Soviet design practices, there are costs as well. Overreliance on foreign technology, for instance, may bring short-term savings on R&D, but it exacts a tremendous toll over the long run by inhibiting domestic experimentation and ultimately weakening the nation's scientific base. That the USSR spends some 40 percent more on R&D than does the United States yet continues to exhibit inferior technology is a clear manifestation of this dilemma.[28] Moreover, while incremental innovation can provide steady, gradual improvements in aircraft capabilities, it inhibits the realization of major advances and thereby exposes the Soviet Union to the risk of sudden obsolescence due to technological breakthroughs in the United States.

Logistics savings provided by commonality and interchangeability of parts may not be sufficient to offset the logistics burden of servicing faulty equipment. Here an instructive illustration may be taken from civil aviation about which information is more accessible. When the USSR entered the export market for jumbo jet liners, it priced its *Tu*–154 at only half the cost of the Boeing 747 in order to compensate for the aircraft's marked technological inferiority. Several sales were made to developing nations but, within six months, these buyers had canceled all contracts. Even with its much lower purchase price, the *Tu*–154 could not justify its operational costs: time between overhauls, for instance, was but 600 hours compared to 3000 for the 747.[29] Commonality of parts constantly in need of repair is hardly a positive characteristic.

Finally, although the relative simplicity of Soviet aircraft would seem to translate into lower unit costs than those in the United States, this may not be the case. Dollar cost comparisons estimate only what it would cost to replicate Soviet equipment in the US; they do not indicate the true cost of that equipment to the USSR. Given the vast differences between the two countries' economic systems, resource endowments, labor productivity and industrial-technical capabilities, these two costs may vary widely even in fiscal terms, not to mention the more complex issue of opportunity costs. It may be that the Soviets build unsophisticated aircraft because that is all they are capable of producing, and even such as they build are extremely expensive in terms of human and material resources consumed (and denied to the economy as a whole). Certainly this would be the conclusion suggested by the performance of the civilian industrial sector.

There are, however, important distinctions between military and civilian production processes in the USSR which partially mitigate the impact of overall inefficiency on armament production. To an extent not true of the civilian sector, something akin to consumer sovereignty may be discerned in military production; the consumer being, of course, the Soviet government. Weapons producers respond to the demands of the Ministry of Defense which delineates detailed specifications the new equipment must satisfy. Quality control standards are more demanding and inspection commissions less susceptible to supplier pressure. In the civilian sector, quality control is the responsibility of the Department of Technical Control (*Otdel tekhnicheskogo kontrolya*, or *OTK*), but, since *OTK* inspectors receive bonuses from the enterprise and therefore benefit when the plant does well, they can usually be persuaded to accept defective products if correction would so disrupt the production schedule as to jeopardize plan fulfillment. Where weapons systems are produced, however, the *OTK* inspection is followed by a special military inspection. The *voyenpredy* (military representatives) who conduct this examination are permanently attached to a particular enterprise but completely independent from its management. Their wages are paid by the Ministry of Defense, not the enterprise, and hence they have no vested interest in the enterprise's bonus system. The *voyenpredy* are instructed to pay no heed to production delays which might result from the rejection of defective output. While this presumably improves product quality, rejections are reportedly quite frequent, a fact which must drive up costs.[30]

Perhaps the feature which most distinguishes military production in general, and aircraft production in particular, from the civilian production process is the existence of competition among military design bureaus. Competitive designing has been the rule in the aviation industry since 1930–40, when over 20 designers were instructed to come up with 2 or 3 basic types of aircraft. Competition occurs in all aviation projects, civil and military, at the initial, preproduction stage (when broad, tentative ideas are put forward); however, for military aircraft, it continues among two or three bureaus all the way down to the prototype testing phase. Although competition remains an important feature of aircraft research and development, there is some evidence (admittedly incomplete) that it has abated over the years. In 1945–49, 37 percent of identified prototypes were put into production; in 1950–54, 44 percent; in 1955–59, 57 percent; and 1960–65, 50 percent.[31] Unfortunately, more recent data is not available, but it may be that rising R&D costs have made it increasingly difficult to shelve designs on which considerable resources already have been expended. Occasionally, both competing prototypes are accepted for series production.[32]

Despite these departures from nonmilitary practice, military industrial production—especially in such high technology fields as aircraft development—remains hampered by many of the same scarcities, irrationalities, and disincentives which plague the civilian sector. The design philosophy which has emerged from these circumstances has attempted simply to make the best out of a bad situation. Quantity is not chosen *over* quality . . . it is accepted for lack of any other option. For reasons to be explained below, the Soviet R&D community simply has been unable to produce the sort of sophisticated equipment found in Western air forces and has hence been obliged to make a virtue of necessity. The interpretation was summarized trenchantly by the famous designer A. N. Tupolev:

> The country needs aircraft like it needs black bread. Of course, you can imagine pralines, tortes, etc., but to no purpose—we haven't the ingredients to make them. From this it follows:
>
> (a) that we must develop a doctrine concerning the missions which aviation is to perform, and that doctrine must be based on a realistic conception of the capabilities of projected aircraft;
>
> (b) that, on the basis of technology and production processes which already have been assimilated, we must turn out long production runs of those aircraft which correspond to that doctrine;
>
> (c) that if these aircraft fall somewhat behind those in the West in terms of technology—to hell with them; we'll get by on quantity; and
>
> (d) that, in order to prevent quality from falling *too* far behind quantity, the design bureau should (i) concentrate on the technology of constructing experimental aircraft, without being burdened with responsibility for series production, and (ii) work on two basic tasks: designing aircraft intended for production and designing purely experimental aircraft used to achieve technological breakthroughs.[33]

As indicated in this passage, Tupolev traced several aspects of Soviet design policy—the creation of simple, "black bread" aircraft in large quantities for limited missions by means of prototype modeling—to the short supply of materials and equipment apparently endemic to the planned economy. This situation is somewhat alleviated in the production of weapons due to the top priority enjoyed by the military sector. Nevertheless, problems remain. In order to accommodate the plan, researchers are required to specify at the beginning of the year all the supplies they will need throughout the entire 12–month period. Yet, a researcher cannot know in advance which materials he will require for experiments he has not yet conceived. As Fedoseyev notes:

> I never could comprehend why they would entrust me

with millions in the plan system (and sometimes even wastefully), yet not trust me to spend literally a few rubles to encourage people, to raise their interest in their work, or to purchase an instrument or some material directly from a store. After all, *I* knew how to make my planned work less expensive.[34]

One response of Soviet industrial officials to the problems of supply has been to keep the production process as much as possible within their own organization, be it the enterprise or the ministry. Consequently, the aviation industry is highly concentrated at both the development and the manufacturing level. The number of design bureaus are few and of the thousands of components that make up an aircraft, 90–95 percent are produced by the Ministry of Aviation Industry.[35] But such ministerial "empire-building" creates its own set of problems. Transportation costs, for example, will often be needlessly high as parts are procured from a plant within the same ministry perhaps several hundred miles away rather than from a plant producing identical components, but for a different ministry, right in the same city. Moreover, as military equipment grows more complex, it becomes more and more difficult, even in the face of ministerial protectionism, to insulate weapons production from the deficiencies of the rest of the economy. Thus, Brezhnev, at the 25th Party Congress, insisted that planners and producers take greater cognizance of the interdependencies which exist among branches of the economy, and Major General M. Cherednichenko soon responded that the defense industries had taken the General Secretary's admonition to heart and would act upon it.[36] To what extent procedures have changed, however, remains unknown.

The role of the Party at the operational (as opposed to the declaratory) level is itself ambivalent. Within the civilian economy, one of the chief functions of *obkom* and *raykom* officials is to overcome supply bottlenecks, primarily by authorizing violations of the plan.[37] Presumably, the same holds true for defense industries. But such has not always been the case, and while recent evidence is lacking, past experience indicates that on occasion the Party may even obstruct the flow of supplies. Yakovlev recounts in his memoirs that for more than 5 months in 1946 no progress was made toward constructing a design bureau called for in the plan. Neither materials nor workers had been provided, the Minister of the Aviation Industry, Mikhail Khrunichev, complained to Stalin, and

> . . . the local organs not only do not help, but even hinder
> . . . . You see, the Obkom Secretary has been detaining the
> construction workers sent to us there, figuring that they are
> more useful in reconstruction work.[38]

This episode, coming soon after the war, may be atypical, but the reconciling of conflicting claims on scarce supplies remains a major task of the Party *apparatchiki*, one they may not always be able to fulfill. As for the ministry itself, it does its best, as indicated by Khrunichev's appeal. But here, too, problems of supply are sometimes so severe that the government simply resigns itself to their inevitability and urges producers and scientists to do the same. Artem Mikoyan once complained to a group of Canadian industrialists, for instance, that the Ministry of the Aviation Industry would not allow him to use as much titanium in his designs as he would like, and engine designer Kuznetsov confirmed that he had met with the same difficulty.[39]

Even designs which have been approved for series production and hence presumably utilize only available materials remain jeopardized by unforeseen shortages. Gallay notes that demands from the production engineers "grab the designer by the throat" as costs and breaches of contract by "tens and hundreds of supplying plants" make the original design unworkable.[40] It may take an entire year to convert the design into a blueprint that can be produced,[41] and the process is far from orderly. Designer O. Antonov has remarked:

> It is common knowledge that the director of a plant engaged in series production and the chief designer who plans the machines or other items produced by the plant often get along like cats and dogs.
>
> It is common knowledge that the introduction of a new and better product, or even a proposal to improve and modernize an item already in production, sometimes meets a hostile reception by the director.[42]

Taut planning and short supplies not only result in production delays, they also slow the pace of modernization at the plant. In response to a recent appeal by O. Antonov for improved quality in the production of sophisticated equipment, the Novosibirsk aviation enterprise director G. Vanag replied that everyone recognized the need for innovation, but few results can be expected until resources are provided. Too often, Vanag complained, the enterprise is left "to fight one-on-one against difficulties which [the planners] themselves are simply unable to handle."[43]

While supply problems have placed limits on the sophistication the Soviets have been able to achieve thus far in their combat aircraft, such difficulties could conceivably be overcome by allocating a still greater share of the country's material resources to this sector at the expense of civilian consumption. There is, however, a deeper source of the simplicity (or, one might say, backwardness) characteristic of Soviet designs which is much less amenable to solution. Its roots go back to the early years of Soviet rule, particularly the 1930s. This is the network of disincentives to innovation which pervades the scientific and industrial communities and atrophies their performance potential. Reluctance to experiment with new methods and concepts has been ingrained through historical memory and current experience; through excessive bureaucratization and rigid planning; and, above all, through the basic distrust in which the scientific community is held by the Soviet government.

Obstacles to Innovation

Of the bureaucratic impediments to innovation, some arise from the ministerial system of organization and others from the planning mechanism. As noted previously, the industrial ministries have attempted to build self-contained "empires," partly in an effort to reduce supply difficulties, but perhaps more to consolidate and enhance the authority of their various agents, be they enterprise directors or government officials. Consequently, enterprises, research organizations, and individuals subordinated to one ministry often lack contact with their counterparts in others, and these communication barriers hinder the flow of information across ministerial lines.[44] The result is duplication of effort and slower progress. Ministries may hesitate to endorse technological drives which would necessitate reliance on organizations outside their control. The Minister of the Aviation Industry, for example, might be reluctant to force the pace of innovation if such a policy would depend for its success on input from the Academy of Science. A slower pace which remained within the capacities of the ministry's own research institutes and experimental design bureaus might seem preferable to dependency on nonsubordinates.[45]

Within the mechanism of central planning, the Soviets have been unable to define criteria of success which would guide economic units to optimum output. Early efforts at cost-efficiency calculations specified weight as the unit of account, the goal being greater weight at lower cost. The perniciousness of this standard in aircraft production soon made itself felt, for it removed the incentive to build aircraft with the lightweight materials needed to obtain high thrust-to-weight ratios.[46] But even when gross output targets were superseded by financial indicators in 1965, the defense industries may have used the newly instituted profitability norms to justify risk aversion and discourage innovation rather than to improve efficiency through technological advance.[47] Even tying bonuses directly to innovation has failed to produce the intended effect. The bonuses tend to lose their merit/incentive character over time and become an expected component of the researcher's salary. Moreover, there is a tendency toward artificial innovation wherein existing products are given but minor modifications and new names in order to meet innovation quotas.[48] When bonuses can be obtained by such simple measures, there is little incentive to undertake major innovation programs, particularly since they may require a temporary reduction in the other plan indices (gross output, profitability, etc.) by which success is measured.

The most important incentives encouraging innovation are prestige, financial benefit, and career advantages provided to designers whose prototypes are accepted for series production. But the process also encourages conservatism insofar as designers believe that their designs will have a greater chance for approval if they resemble aircraft accepted previously.[49]

Apart from the simplistic, often irrational, incentive structure developed by the central authorities, the plan framework and its bureaucratic accoutrements retard innovation through their inflexibility. Before beginning a project, a research team must draw up two documents: the "technical assignment" (*technicheskoye zadaniye,* or *TZ*) or the "tactical-technical requirements" (*taktiko–tekhnicheskiye trebovaniya,* or *TTT*), and Plan Form No. 4. The *TZ* or *TTT* defines the proposal and must be approved by (1) the director of the team's scientific-research institute, (2) its *voyenpred,* (3) a representative of the military client, (4) an agent of the Defense Ministry's coordinating organization for military research, and (5) the particular ministry to which the research group is subordinated. The procedure takes months at best and can draw out for as much as two years. The various authorities involved often have divergent interests and place incompatible demands on the project. Plan Form No. 4 is a cost estimate and time schedule for the proposals. It specifies the types and quantities of all materials and equipment which will be needed. It must be signed by the research group's ministry—and often by the minister himself—as well as by all concerned enterprises, suppliers, and planning organs.[50]

The *TZ, TTT,* and Plan Form No. 4 cannot be changed without permission of the ministry; such permission rarely is given. If, during the course of research, it becomes evident an anticipated procedure is no longer necessary, still it must be performed in order to fulfill the plan. "Thus," writes Fedoseyev, "having expended a tremendous amount of nerves, labor, and time on the *TZ* or *TTT* and Form No. 4, the researcher dons the cruelest corset, binding himself hand and foot."[51]

The plan framework into which defense contracts must fit and the rigidity of the approval process just described conspire to freeze aircraft designs at an early stage. The *MiG–25* high-altitude interceptor is a case in point. Designed to counter the B–70 high-altitude, supersonic bomber which the United States had under development in the early 1960s, the fighter would appear to have lost much of its raison d'etre when the B–70 program was cancelled. Yet production of the *MiG–25* has continued right up to the present; indeed, it did not even make its maiden flight until after the B–70 program had been dropped. While its high speed and ceiling grant it continued value in a reconnaissance role, its relatively poor performance in low altitude regimes at a time when the air threat to the Soviet Union has shifted decidedly toward low flying attackers (both aircraft and cruise missiles) has considerably degraded its effectiveness as an interceptor. It might have been wiser from the Soviet perspective to have canceled the *MiG*–25 altogether and to have undertaken the development of a new interceptor of radically different design, but the momentum of the program was apparently too great to overcome. Such are the costs of bureaucratic inertia, plan rigidity, and risk avoidance.[52] Thus, while much can be said for a steady state production process, its negative concomitants ought not to be ignored. The gradualist approach to design prevalent in the Soviet Union makes rapid adjustment to changing situations that much more difficult, especially when the new conditions call for major departures from previous designs.

The Communist Party leadership has at times sought to overcome excessive caution in the scientific community by exerting pressure for discontinuous leaps in technology. In this regard, design bureau chief O. Antonov has noted that it sometimes "takes a fight" to push through an innovation: "The Party has several times rolled up its sleeves, gone after one industry or another, and, dragging it out of the morass of gradualism, given it a powerful push in a direction that the country required."[53]

On the other hand, Party and government officials also on occasion have offered resistance to innovative proposals put forward by researchers. Gallay, for example, although generally endorsing the nation's incremental approach to force improvement, nonetheless criticizes the obstacles presented by the "conservatism" of the leadership and bureaucracy.[54] The problem is also described in Yakovlev's memoirs. In 1951, Stalin told Yakovlev to stop work on several new designs, explaining:

> We already have a good plane in the *MiG*–15, and there is no sense in building new fighters in the near future. Better just to modernize the *MiG*.[55]

This attitude disturbed Yakovlev for two reasons: first, cancellation might lose him the trust his designers had in his leadership abilities; and, second, he knew that:

> . . . if all experimental work were organized around modernizing existing series of aircraft and not on building new, more advanced ones, before long we would inevitably fall behind . . . .
> I felt it was necessary to create something qualitatively new.[56]

Yakovlev therefore began work in conjunction with the engine designer Mikulin on a fighter with an improved thrust-to-weight ratio, the *Yak*–25 reconnaissance aircraft. Stalin was impressed and ordered Artem Mikoyan to use the same engine on an interceptor. The result was the *MiG*–19, another illustration of incrementalism and commonality in Soviet aircraft design.[57]

480–900 O – 85 – 16

Party conservatism in matters of applied science derives in part from the leadership's lack of confidence in the abilities of Soviet scientists. Fedoseyev reveals that research engineers in the USSR frequently are ordered to copy Western equipment without modification and are not allowed to make improvements even if such are clearly needed. Later, no doubt, the United States or other originating country will correct the problem, but unless the USSR obtains an example of the improved model, no correction will be made on the Soviet copy.[58]

Ultimately, the leadership's lack of confidence in the skill of Soviet scientists probably derives less from past performance—the deficiencies of which largely can be attributed to the defects in the economic and incentive structures already discussed—than from the basic distrust the leadership feels toward all intellectual segments of the society. This distrust impacts negatively on the quality of Soviet science in a number of ways. First, it has fostered a censorship which weakens the country's scientific base by limiting the number of people to whom access to foreign scientific and technical materials is allowed.[59] This element has probably lessened somewhat with time and may continue to do so. But a more serious problem derives from the harsh sanctions imposed from failure and from the fear which the threat of such sanctions engenders among the scientific community.

The system of unlimited liability for failure reached its apex under Stalin who felt that the "epidemic of improvements" degraded weapon designs. He encouraged designers to resist demands for innovations from the military consumer, saying: "The designer shouldn't be at everyone's beck and call; he above all others answers for the machine, and if he is given unfounded, irresponsible demands, he must protest."[60] Stalin's advice often turned into an angry warning. At one confrontation, Yakovlev recalls:

> He pointed his finger at us and threatened, "Remember: a designer must be firm; he must protect his aircraft from irresponsible advisers. It's hard to make a good machine, but very easy to spoil it. And it's the designer who'll have to answer for it!"[61]

The sanction for errors included criminal prosecution under laws "on technological discipline" and punishment was extremely severe. A man could lose his job and see his career ruined even for petty mistakes and delays while significant failures could mean imprisonment or even death. Moreover, the system was arbitrary, with even the best designers being incarcerated in various *sharagi,* or special prison-laboratories, in which scientists and engineers were forced to do research. Such was the fate of the great designer Tupolev and many of his subordinates during the 1930s and 1940s.[62]

Such sanctions are no longer imposed for errors in design, but they still remain in the memory or historical cognizance of many scientists in the USSR today. The phenomenon was not unique to the Stalin period; even under Khrushchev, the aircraft designer A. A. Arkhangelskiy was imprisoned for his failure to produce a successful prototype of the Tu-110. And still today, not a chart is drawn, not a formula computed without someone's signature at the bottom. An error can still cause severe detriment to one's career, prestige, and living standard.[63] Given the price which failure may exact, combined with the quite comfortable life-style which moderate success will bring, it is not surprising that designers hesitate to contract into ambitious projects. Risk aversion is the salient characteristic of the Soviet aircraft R&D community. It is this which encourages design simplicity, modest, incremental innovation, and heavy reliance on proved foreign technology.

Those who see in the Soviet Air Forces an example of a limited cost force structure fail to appreciate the true cost which industrial inefficiency and economic irrationality impart to the USSR's defense programs. In addition, misinterpretations arise when the dearth of positive incentives and the existence of actual disincentives to innovate are equated with a deliberate cost-effectiveness decision. Past performance as well as current developments indicate that the relatively unsophisticated technological level of Soviet aircraft derives more from lack of ability than lack of desire. As the capabilities of the R&D community improve, therefore, one can expect Soviet designs to grow more complex.

This trend already can be observed in the recent, growing emphasis among the Frontal Aviation forces on deep interdiction missions, particularly with the deployment of the Su-19 and MiG-27. It can also be seen in the latest prototypes of Soviet tactical aircraft currently being tested at Ramenskoye Airfield. The "Ram-K," a variable geometry air superiority fighter believed designed as the follow-on to the MiG-25, appears to be a "close approximation" of the Grumman F-14, according to a Pentagon spokesman. The "Ram-L," a Sukhoy analog to the McDonnell Douglas/Northrop F-18, will be equipped with advanced medium range air-to-air missiles (AMRAAMs) of the type now in early development in the United States when the aircraft reaches full deployment in 1983. Finally, the "Ram-J" ground attack aircraft—which is already in production and whose deployment is imminent—resembles the Northrop A-9, the aircraft rejected by the United States Air Force in favor of the Fairchild A-10 close support aircraft.

All three prototypes are evidence of progress toward more complex, more expensive fighters, and the Ram-K and -L exhibit considerable multirole capability. The trend, then, seems to be away from the single-mission aircraft previously produced by the Soviet Union. Among the advanced systems now in evidence are terrain-avoidance radar; doppler navigational equipment; look-down, shoot-down and side-looking airborne radar; Gatling-type guns mounted in pods; laser-guided weapons; and real-time electro-optical surveillance equipment—precisely the sort of equipment which has escalated US fighter costs.[64]

Conclusion

The implication of this interpretation of Soviet aircraft design policy is that the USSR will produce aircraft of as high a quality as it is capable. Just what technological level will be reached is difficult to project as it depends on the extent to which the government can rationalize its economy and improve its incentive structure. As Stalinist repression fades into the more distant past and a new generation of researchers comes to the fore, the fear of innovation may subside somewhat. But unless deeper changes transpire in the leadership's attitude toward intellectual segments of society, it seems doubtful that risk aversion will disappear altogether. One might expect, therefore, to see a more rapid pace of technological advance in the future but one still somewhat behind that of which the United States is capable.

Even given this interpretation of Soviet policy toward aircraft design, it still might be the case that the United States should move toward cheaper aircraft in greater quantities. But in weighing this alternative, it is essential that Soviet trends not be ignored. Since technological inferiority is not the preferred Soviet strategy, one cannot assume the capabilities of Soviet aircraft will remain static. Consequently, if the United States opts to reduce unit costs by procuring less sophisticated aircraft, it must be willing to see its margin of qualitative superiority over the Soviet Air Forces gradually erode.

This is not necessarily an unacceptable situation since technological superiority does not always translate into greater combat effectiveness. For example, the short service life of Soviet equipment is less of a penalty in military than civilian aviation. Since civil aircraft are generally designed for approximately 30,000 hours of flight service while designers of combat aircraft aim for only 5,000, a component whose durability is far too low for civilian use may be perfectly satisfactory in military aircraft. To take another example, consider the *MiG*–21C captured by Israel during the 1967 war. Although gaps of up to one-eighth of an inch were found in the butt joints of the skin panels, the drag penalty of such shoddy finishing was minor. Faced with a choice between poor workmanship and delays on the production line, the Soviets, as one observer noted, "showed no hesitation in choosing the former and getting the hardware."[65] Choosing the proper balance among quality and quantity, technology sophistication, and cost reduction is thus an extraordinarily difficult task, but a correct decision cannot be made without due regard to the adversary aircraft with which one's own pilots would have to contend in the event of war. The nature of Soviet design policy suggests the USSR's fighters will be the most complex and capable aircraft the Soviets can produce.

Notes

1. Measured in constant 1975 dollars, the F-14's flyaway unit cost is approximately $17,000,000; that of the World War II F4U Corsair, $350,000. See William D. White, *U.S. Tactical Air Power: Missions, Forces, and Costs* (Washington: The Brookings Institution, 1974), pp. 47-48, hereinafter referred to as *U.S. Tactical Air Power.*

2. US Congress, Senate Committee on Armed Services, *Fiscal Year 1973 Authorization for Military Procurement, Research and Development, Construction Authorization for the Safeguard ABM, and Active Duty and Selected Reserve Strengths, Part 6: Bomber Defense, Tactical Air Power, and F-14. Hearings.* 92nd Congress, 2nd session, 1972, p. 3788.

3. White, *U.S. Tactical Air Power,* pp. 63 and 69.

4. The large number of interdiction flights during the Southeast Asian conflict is in part a reflection of the lack of strong air opposition by the North Vietnamese, a factor which reduced the need for counterair strikes. Thus, because the supply of US air power was abundant and the demand for alternate missions limited, the heavy reliance on interdiction during the Vietnam War may not be indicative of normal US tactical air doctrine. See ibid, p. 67.

5. Information provided by industrial specialist.

6. White, *U.S. Tactical Air Power,* pp. 56-58; and Bonner Day, "Pros and Cons of a Multimission Fighter Force," *Air Force Magazine,* Vol. 62, No. 4 (April 1979), pp. 60-61.

7. White, *U.S. Tactical Air Power,* pp. 45 and 65-66.

8. Of the 114 aircraft Israel lost, all but 20 were shot down by SAMs, whereas some 400 of the 500 Arab aircraft lost were shot down in air-to-air combat. See Nadav Safran, *Israel: The Embattled Ally* (Cambridge: Harvard University Press, 1978), pp. 275 and 311.

9. White, *U.S. Tactical Air Power,* p. 65. This estimate should be accepted only in conjunction with two caveats. First, the estimated dollar costs of Soviet aircraft are conjectural. White, for example, estimated the *MiG-21*'s price tag to be $1.3 million, while the Israelis believe it to be $2 million (1975 dollars). Secondly, and more importantly, dollar cost comparisons are often misleading in that they do not reflect the true burden which a weapon system places on the Soviet economy. A weapon which costs $2 million to replicate in the United States might be far more costly to the Soviets, in terms of resource allocation and opportunity cost, because of systemic industrial and research inefficiencies. That such inefficiencies do exist in Soviet aviation R&D is a point this study seeks to demonstrate.

10. US Air Force, *Soviet Aerospace Handbook* (Washington: Government Printing Office, 1978), pp. 40 and 45.

11. Composites are nonmetallic construction materials (such as graphite epoxy) which have higher strength-weight ratios than commonly used aircraft metals (aluminum, steel, titanium). With weight savings of 25-50 percent over conventional materials, they also provide high thrust-weight ratios. In addition, composites improve vibration damping, enhance resistance to fatigue, and retard environmental damage. Composite materials will not rust or corrode; hence, they extend vehicle durability and reduce operational costs. The United States began development of advanced composite materials for Air Force applications in 1963 and currently uses them on the F-111 horizontal stabilizer, F-5 fuselage, F-15 wing, F-16 forward fuselage, and B-1 horizontal and vertical stabilizers.

12. *Jane's All the World's Aircraft, 1975-76,* ed. John W. R. Taylor (London: Jane's Yearbooks, 1977), pp. 386-388 and 500-501; *Jane's All the World's Aircraft, 1976-77,* ed. John W. R. Taylor (London: Jane's Yearbooks, 1978), p. 445; and George Panyalev, "*MiG-21 bis* and F-16A Air Combat Potential: A Comparison," *International Defense Review,* No. 9, 1978, pp. 1431-1432.

13. M. Gallay, *Ispytano v nebe"* [Flight Tested], *Novyy mir* [New World], No. 4, 1963, p.

51.

14. Arthur J. Alexander, *R&D in Soviet Aviation,* Report R–589–PR (Santa Monica: The Rand Corporation, 1970), pp. 21–22.
15. *Soviet Aerospace Handbook,* pp. 50 and 92.
16. M. Gallay, *Tret'ye izmereniye* [The Third Dimension] (Moscow, 1973), p. 9.
17. Arthur J. Alexander, *Decision–Making in Soviet Weapons Procurement,* Adelphi Paper No. 147/148 (London: International Institute for Stategic Studies, 1978/79), pp. 34 and 49–52.
18. A. Fedoseyev, *Zapadnya: Chelovek i sotsializm* [The Trap: Man and Socialism] (Frankfurt/Main: Posev, 1976), pp. 115–117, hereinafter referred to as *Zapadnya.*
19. Arthur J. Alexander, *Weapons Acquisition in the Soviet Union, United States, and France* (Santa Monica: The Rand Corporation, 1973), p. 10, hereinafter referred to as *Weapons Acquisition.*
20. Gallay, *Tret'ye izmereniye,* pp. 32–33.
21. Gallay, *"Ispytano v nebe: Okonchaniye"* [Flight Tested: Conclusion], *Novyi mir,* No. 5, 1963, p. 86.
22. Alexander, *R&D in Soviet Aviation,* p. 23.
23. *Soviet Aerospace Handbook,* p. 93; and *Samolety Strany Sovetov* [Aircraft of the Land of the Soviets] (Moscow, 1974), p. 183.
24. Alexander, *Weapons Acquisition,* p. 11; and Alexander, *Decision–Making in Soviet Weapons Procurement,* p. 34.
25. *Samolety Strany Sovetov,* p. 234; and Heinz J. Nowarra and G. R. Duval, *Russian Civil and Military Aircraft, 1884–1969* (London: Fountain Press, 1970), p. 201.
26. Gallay, *Tret'ye izmereniye,* p. 33.
27. Fedoseyev, *Zapadnya,* pp. 115–116.
28. *Soviet Aerospace Handbook,* p. 94.
29. Information provided by industry specialist.
30. Hannes Adomeit and Mikhail Agursky, *The Soviet Military–Industrial Complex and its Internal Mechanism* (Kingston, Ontario: Center for International Relations, Queen's University, 1978), pp. 19–25.
31. Alexander, *R&D in Soviet Aviation,* pp. 22–25.
32. This was the case with the *Yak*–15 and *MiG*–9 fighters and the *An*–10 and *Il*–18 transports.
33. A. N. Tupolev, quoted in G. Ozerov, *Tupolevskaya sharaga* [Tupolev Construction Bureau], 2nd ed. (Frankfurt/Main: Posev, 1973), p. 57.
34. Fedoseyev, *Zapadnya,* p. 144.
35. D. P. Andrianov, M. Z. Gendel'man, et al, *Management, Planning, and Economics of Aircraft Production,* trans. by Translation Division, Foreign Technology Division, Wright-Patterson Air Force Base (1964), p. 97.
36. Major General M. Cherednichenko, *"Sovremennaya voyna i ekonomika"* [Contemporary War and Economics], *Kommunist Vooruzhennykh Sil* [Communist of the Armed Forces], No. 18, September 1971, pp. 25–26.
37. For a thorough study of this point, see Jerry F. Hough, *The Soviet Prefects: The Local Party Organs in Industrial Decision–Making* (Cambridge: Harvard University Press, 1969).
38. A. Yakovlev, *Tsel' zhizni: Zapiski aviakonstruktora* [Life's Goal: Notes of An Aircraft Designer], 2nd ed. (Moscow, 1970), p. 485.
39. Alexander, *R&D in Soviet Aviation,* p. 12.
40. Gallay, *Tret'ye izmereniye,* p. 271.
41. Alexander, *R&D in Soviet Aviation,* p. 16.
42. O. Antonov, "Why Does It Take a Fight to Modernize Output?" *Current Digest of the Soviet Press,* Vol. 9, No. 16 (29 May 1957), p. 6.
43. G. Vanag, *"Upravleniye kachestva"* [Quality Control], *Trud* [Labor], 6 January 1979, p. 2.
44. Alexander, *R&D in Soviet Aviation,* p. 16.
45. Karl F. Spielmann, "Defense Industrialists in the USSR," *Problems of Communism,*

Vol. 25, No. 5 (September–October 1976), p. 60.

46. See S. A. Sarkisian, "*Predvaritel'noye opredeleniye zatrat na proizvodstvo aviatsionnykh izdeliy—vazhnaya ekonomicheskaya problema*" [Preliminary Determination of Costs in the Production of Aviation Articles—An Important Economic Problem], in *Predvaritel'noye opredeleniye trudoyemkosti i sebestoymosti izgotovleniya aviatsionnykh izdeliy* [Preliminary Determination of Manpower Requirements and Costs of Production of Aviation Articles], ed. by D. P. Andrianov and S. A. Sarkisian (Moscow, 1962).

47. David Holloway, "Technology, Management, and the Soviet Military Establishment," Adelphi Paper No. 76 (London: International Institute for Strategic Studies, 1971), p. 6.

48. A good description of this process in the civilian economy may be found in Jospeh Berliner, *The Innovation Decision in Soviet Industry* (Cambridge: MIT Press, 1976), particularly Chapter 14.

49. Alexander, *Decision–Making in Soviet Weapons Procurement*, pp. 32–33.

50. Fedoseyev, *Zapadnya*, pp. 161–164.

51. Ibid., pp. 164–165.

52. Norman Friedman, "The Soviet Mobilization Base," *Air Force Magazine*, Vol. 62, No. 3 (March 1979), pp. 67–70; and William Schneider, "Trends in Soviet Frontal Aviation," *Air Force Magazine*, Vol. 62, No. 3 (March 1979), p. 81.

53. Antonov, "Why Does It Take a Fight to Modernize Output?" p. 6.

54. Gallay, *Tret'ye izmereniye*, p. 271.

55. Yakovlev, *Tsel' zhizni*, p. 491.

56. Ibid., pp. 491–492.

57. Ibid., p. 493.

58. Fedoseyev, *Zapadnya*, p. 116.

59. See also Adomeit and Agursky, "The Soviet Military and Industrial Complex and its Internal Mechanism," p. 31.

60. Joseph Stalin, quoted in Yakovlev, *Tsel' zhizni*, p. 347.

61. Joseph Stalin, quoted in Ibid., p. 348.

62. See Ozerov, *Tupolevskaya sharaga*, for an eyewitness account. See also Fedoseyev, *Zapadnya*, p. 117.

63. A graphic illustration of the pressures under which Soviet aircraft designers work was provided to a group of Canadians by Alexander Yakovlev when he said, "After considerable negotiations with the customer as to *what* will be produced, the designer signs the contract and symbolically hands over his testicles with the contract. When the aircraft is delivered as specified, he gets his testicles back." Quoted in Alexander, *Decision–Making in Soviet Weapons Procurement*, p. 60.

64. Clarence A. Robinson, Jr., "Soviets to Field Three New Fighters in Aviation Modernization Drive," *Aviation Week and Space Technology*, Vol. 110, No. 13 (26 March 1979), pp. 14–15.

65. William H. Gregory, "Soviet Union Seeks Balance in Technology," *Aviation Week and Space Technology*, Vol. 99, No. 12 (18 March 1968), p. 88.

The Soviet Tank and US Weapon Acquisition

Robert L. O'Connell

Scientific and technical intelligence analysts frequently have been criticized for what is perceived as a reluctance to integrate their findings into a larger policy context. With this criticism in mind, this article is intended to take what is now known about Soviet Ground Forces weapon acquisition and relate it to a larger historical framework with the hope such a structure might yield useful information on potential acquisition strategies.

Before this can be done, however, it is necessary to provide some background information. As with any military organization, each of the five Soviet services acquires weapons for a variety of reasons, the sum of which is unique to that particular service. In the case of the ground forces, a long-standing national policy to exert military pressure on Western Europe, combined with recent historical experience (World War II) and certain organizational tendencies, has led the Soviet Army to develop a coherent and highly articulated military doctrine emphasizing a massive and rapid armored assault westward. It is clear that land arms—both in terms of type and quantity—have been acquired largely to fulfill requirements generated by this doctrine. At the center of this procurement strategy and the military posture upon which it rests is the main battle tank. For this reason, the following paragraphs will emphasize the tank in an effort to draw conclusions about its future in the Soviet arsenal largely through historical analogy with a now obsolete weapon system, the armored battleship.*

My reasons for choosing the battleship are twofold: first, it constitutes recent history's only analogous experience to the development and use of armored vehicles; second, historical analysis indicates strongly that battleships survived in the fleets of the major naval powers for approximately two decades beyond the point when combat demonstrated them to be largely obsolete—at least for the purpose for which they were originally intended: mass fleet actions.

Nevertheless, historical comparison must be used cautiously; the battleship is hardly a perfect analogue to the tank. For one thing, battleships were high-value targets with no one fleet possessing more than 50 first-rate ships at one time. On the other hand, the Soviets have 40,000 tanks, each of which must be dealt with separately. Moreover, "obsolete" is a relative term. For a considerable period after the

---

*Note: This article was written several months before the current proposal to recommission four IOWA–class US battleships—Eds.

battleship had been shown to be outmoded as a strategic weapon, it demonstrated its usefulness in tactical shore bombardment. Similarly, arguments which tend to cast doubt upon the utility of the modern tank as an instrument of the offense do not necessarily reflect negatively on the tank's effectiveness in the defensive mode.

In spite of these qualifications, certain parallels between the tank and the battleship are extremely suggestive. Just as with contemporary tank designers, naval architects laying out battleships were forced to contend with the fact armor plate was relatively very heavy and therefore suitable primarily for protecting only the ship's vitals. Hence, after the turn of the 20th century, most battleships concentrated their armor in belts around the turrets, barbettes, and magazines; that is, armoring selectively in a fashion analogous to the modern tank's design emphasis on protecting the front portions of the turret and upper glacis. In other words, along certain planes of attack, both battleship and tank are inherently more vulnerable than along others.

In the case of the battleship, this condition ultimately would prove fatal. For during the latter portion of the 19th century, weapons developers from a variety of sources were beginning to explore the possibility of attacking naval vessels below the waterline. Their creations—basically the mine and torpedo—would revolutionize naval warfare. Not only did these weapons attain near invisibility by operating below the surface, they attacked the victim in its most vulnerable and least protected portions, thus directly threatening the vessel's watertight integrity. To make matters worse, these subsurface weapons proved from the beginning to be inherently small, inexpensive to produce, and capable of being employed by a wide variety of carriers including, eventually, the subsurface weapon par excellence, the submarine. Naval warfare would never be the same. Practically overnight, the once invincible capital ship found itself beset by a host of potential adversaries which all relied on stealth and were optimized to attack, quite literally, below the belt.

Now, within the last two decades, something similar has happened to the tank. Beginning with the introduction of first-generation antitank guided missiles (ATGM), weapon technology has moved steadily in the direction of what can be called unconventional tank killers. In general, these weapons also tend to be smaller and easier to produce than their targets, to rely heavily upon concealment, and to have a marked tendency to strike the victim in areas beyond its main zones of protection.

Of course, the mere appearance of a significant threat to a hitherto dominant weapon is seldom sufficient to drive that weapon into obsolescence. In the case of both the battleship and, more recently, the tank, the military organizations controlling them reacted promptly to create counters—some of them quite effective—to the new threat. What emerges, then, is a series of moves and countermoves, the course of which must be followed to see the ultimate effect on the original threat.

Often, it is this chain of events—spelled out in increasing cost, complexity, and circumscribed operational utility—rather than the original threat which seals the fate of an extant weapon system. For this reason, it is instructive to examine briefly the development of the battle fleet subsequent to the realization that subsurface weapons were indeed a significant threat.

First, the design of the battleship itself changed. In an effort to keep capital ships out of the reach of torpedoes, much longer ranges of engagement were emphasized—a trend which led directly to the creation of the so-called all-big-gun or dreadnought battleship. This resulted not only in a dramatic increase in battleship costs; the extension of artillery ranges had the unintended effect of rendering capital ship engagements inherently less decisive.

While there is no exact parallel in contemporary tank development, it is notable that the ranges of main guns have been increasing steadily. While other factors are involved in this development, certainly one strong motive is the urge to avoid being outranged by antitank guided missiles. In all major armies—including the Soviet—this increase in ranges has necessitated the development of increasingly sophisticated and expensive fire control mechanisms. This trend has reached the point where fire control may account for as much as one-third the cost of a modern tank—no small matter to an inefficient producer of electronics components such as the USSR. In any case, it is clear the new generation of Soviet tanks—the T–64 and T–72—constitutes a dramatic increase in cost and complexity over its immediate predecessor, the T–62. Moreover, while the long-range accuracy of all modern tanks has undoubtedly increased under normal and test conditions, there is some reason to believe the operation of sophisticated fire control might be degraded severely in the confusion and atmospheric obscuration of battle, especially at extreme ranges.

Yet, the impact of unconventional threats is hardly limited to their immediate objects. Even more significant than the changes to the battleship wrought by surface weaponry is the effect such weapons have had upon fleet auxiliaries. These ships had their origins in the "Age of Sail" when three-decked ships of the line, carrying more guns and about the same sail area, proved incapable of catching lesser classes. As a result, it became necessary to include one- and two-decked auxiliaries capable of bringing their opposite number to heel. Naval warfare was then a highly stylized affair with each auxiliary having its own offensive function leading up to the climactic clash of battle lines. Subsurface weaponry changed all that, however. Gradually, but inexorably, more and more fleet auxiliaries were drawn to the defensive task of screening and protecting battleships. Moreover, as the complexity of this task revealed itself, new auxiliaries were created to perform specialized functions. By the opening of World War I, the size and intricacy of the screen had grown to the point that just putting to sea became a major operation. Problems of command and control became nightmarish. Indeed, during the height of the Battle of Jutland—the only instance when the main bodies of the British and German fleets suceeded in coming into contact—Admiral Jellicoe was heard to mutter: "I wish somebody would tell me who is firing and what they're firing at." This was shortly before he broke the action off on the rumor of an impending torpedo attack.

Now, in this matter of auxiliaries, the parallels with the contemporary Soviet Ground Forces are clear. At the moment, the tank—especially when used in the offensive mode—has few pretensions to self-sufficiency upon the modern, high-intensity battlefield. Knowing this, the Soviets have fielded an even more complex family of specialized vehicles to support the tank. Hence, an advancing Soviet tank column can count on the aid of numerous *BMP* infantry combat vehicles to provide troop support; several types of self-propelled artillery dedicated to softening up long-range targets; and the *ZSU–23–4* mobile antiaircraft gun and several types of surface-to-air missile launchers to fight off enemy aircraft. Moreover, the numbers and types of vehicles are increasing constantly, with systems specifically dedicated to assaulting ATGM emplacements being only one of several recent acquisitions.

Plainly, the problems involved in coordinating such a land armada are growing, especially when the nature of Soviet Ground Forces doctrine is considered. A strategy which is so oriented toward the offensive and which places such emphasis on rapidity of advance and seizure of initiative is not necessarily complemented by such a complex mix of weaponry. During the 1973 Middle East War, for example, there were reports indicating extreme reluctance on the part of Egyptian tankers to move forward once their surface-to-air missiles were stripped from them. While Soviet troops are presumably better trained and motivated, the problem of their coordinating a variety of complementary functions under combat conditions is not to be taken lightly. Nevertheless, when the general question of the ATGM threat was considered during the mid-1970s in a broad-based intraservice debate, the consensus that emerged called for greater coordination and teamwork among armored vehicle types.

But if contradictions do appear to exist in Soviet armored doctrine, the Soviet Ground Forces have little choice but to live with them. Just as the naval world clung to the battleship, the Soviet Army will remain wedded to the tank for the forseeable future. Cumulatively, an enormous amount has been spent on tanks. Moreover, if tanks were to go, the vast array of auxiliaries would have little independent meaning and use.

Economic necessity demands the tank be protected. For this reason, we can expect the Soviet Ground Forces to field over the next decade a variety of guided projectile countermeasures—possibly including diversionary flares, radar attenuating smokes and aerosols, and even signal absorbing paint. Probably a number of these will be quite effective. Yet, it also seems probable the Soviets will tend to overrate their effectiveness. For psychologically, it seems the Soviet Ground Forces are ill-equipped to accept the demise of the tank as a prime instrument of the offensive. Besides, because of the loyalty engendered by its World War II heroics, the tank by its very nature demands the respect of its operators. Like the battleship, it is a large, loud, baleful looking machine . . . the very kind most men instinctively tend to equate with power. On the other hand, its enemies—just as with the enemies of the battleship—tend to be stealthier and less impressive; threats which, even in a time of considerable technological sophistication, tend to be underestimated. Therefore, on the basis of both objective analysis and psychological preference, it seems likely the tank is destined to retain a central place in Soviet military planning.

Nevertheless, both the weapon and the strategy which it suggests are vulnerable. Constraints in size, weight, and cost prevent the tank from being protected along all planes of attack. Moreover, when used offensively out in the open, the tank's mass, noise, and copious heat signature make it a substantial emitter which can be homed in on.

This has definite implications for US weapon acquisition. First, it should be emphasized that this line of reasoning applies primarily to the offensive uses of the tank and should not be taken as supportive of any changes in US tank acquisition strategy. The manner in which we plan to our tanks in Europe (defensively and often under cover) makes them considerably less vulnerable than their opposite Soviet numbers. On the other hand, the Soviet strategy is blatant. It calls for armored columns to race across hundreds of miles of enemy territory overcoming all obstacles in the process. By nature, it demands a great deal more of the tank. Under the circumstances, it makes sense to aim our weapon development programs directly at the Soviet tank: to strike it at its most vulnerable points and to drive it from its supporting vehicles.

Fortunately, in spite of considerable confusion and uncertainty, US research and development appears to be doing just this. Not only are a wide variety of promising alternatives being explored, but several already have been fielded. Two prime examples are the TOW/Cobra ATGM system and the A–10 fighter which mounts the GAU–8 30–mm armor-piercing cannon. Both weapons have been produced in the hundreds and employ aerial mobility to attack tanks and armored vehicles in their thinly protected upper portions. While the effectiveness of these systems can be expected to increase with the introduction of the Hellfire ATGM and the all-weather version of the A–10, more sophisticated tank killers are waiting in the wings. Both the Copperhead cannon-launched laser-guided projectile and the SADARM target sensing submunition are in advanced development and are aimed at providing traditional artillery with an indirect antiarmor capability, again based on top attack. Finally, both the Air Force's Wide Area Antitank Munition and the Army's Assault Breaker programs are developing wide area submunition packages to be delivered by plane or tactical missile and relying, once more, on top attack.

This is an incomplete list, but it should be sufficient to indicate US research and development is actively exploring a wide range of alternative means to exploit Soviet vulnerabilities. Of course, not all of these options will produce good weapons. Most, in fact, will fail. Moreover, if the history of innovation in warfare provides any guidance, the problems of separating the relatively few successes from the rather more numerous failures prior to actual combat will remain formidable.

This is particularly pertinent in the context of the threat. Soviet armored doctrine places great emphasis on a preponderance of numbers. This is the major reason their military planners are willing to accept some vulnerability in armored vehicles. They plan to overwhelm us with mass before we can react: even if the kill ratio of a particular US antitank weapon approaches one-to-one, it will fail if it is present on the battlefield in insignificant numbers. Fortunately, the spectrum of antitank options now being considered is—as a whole— reasonably cost-effective and can—with some exceptions—be produced more quickly and cheaply than an equal number of tanks. Under the circumstances, it makes sense to deploy a fairly wide range of alternatives and to insure each is present in numbers the Soviets cannot disregard. Undoubtedly, some will not live up to their expectations. Yet, in aggregate, the systems will provide a credible and effective defense, capitalizing on redundancy to minimize the chances any one countermeasure will checkmate the whole.

This is bound to be expensive. Yet, it makes more sense to channel most of the additional procurement money expected over the next decade in this direction rather than to parcel it out among all the ground forces-related programs ripening in the developmental cornucopia.

The Soviet tank is at the heart of Soviet strategy in Europe. Should war come, it is the prime weapon US and NATO troops would have to defeat. Yet, if it became apparent our ground forces' defenses had developed to the point the Soviet tank could no longer perform its intended offensive role, the chances of such an attack would be diminished. Moreover, it is just possible that, after spending perhaps 30 billion rubles on their land armada, the spectacle of its technological demise might provide the Soviets a graphic lesson in the futility of such buildups and the ultimate necessity for sincere arms control. Of course, there are still those who urge the resurrection of the battleship.*

---

*Note: Despite the return of the IOWA–class battleships after this article was penned, these arguments bear consideration and are used by critics of the battlewagon, even within the Navy.—Eds.

An Estimate of the International Market Value of the Soviet Navy

John W. Skipper

During the past several years, a number of individuals and almost all of the Western news media have sounded the alarm that the Soviet Union is building or has built a large and powerful navy. Cost estimates have been included in some of the warnings.

This article is a cost estimate. It attempts to show what the entire Soviet Navy would cost if built in Western shipyards. In other words, the international market value of the Soviet Navy, used in this analysis, is defined as the cost of building this fleet in noncommunist shipyards. The Russian/Soviet propensity for secrecy sparked this search because they do not publish the cost of separate units, and the amounts shown in the defense budget they publish is insufficient to build the units which have appeared.

There are many ways to estimate an unknown. But, in estimating the international market value of the Soviet Navy, two methods stand out. One is known as the "pie theory." This is a purely deductive process and determines the cost, for example, of a submarine in the following manner:

1. Total Soviet military expenditures for a given year are equal to 100 percent.
2. The naval slice of these expenditures is equal to (for example) 47 percent.
3. Naval ship construction is equal to (for example) 40 percent of the navy share.
4. Submarine construction is equal to (for example) 65 percent of the navy ship construction share.
5. The submarine construction share is divided into equal parts.
6. A large submarine is equal to one and one-half parts.

Many deductions and suppositions must be made to produce this answer, not the least of which is the total Soviet military expenditures for a given year.

A derivative of this theory follows the pattern partway, then divides the amount of expenditures by the total tonnage produced in a given year and multiplies the cost per ton by the submarine tonnage to produce a unit cost. This is an improvement over the pure "pie theory," but one must still be content with defining accurately the answer required in step one.

The second method commonly quoted is the "cost estimating relationship (CER)." This method attempts to estimate what it would cost in the *US* to produce the physical and performance characteristics of the Soviet unit. This method is better than the "pie theory." A variant of CER ("comparison shopping," using known *Western* costs as opposed to only US cost) was selected to produce the estimates in this article. These estimates have been termed "world market value estimates."

To accomplish this estimate, it is first necessary to establish a data base which shows the cost of building Western naval ships. This is then related to the age and type of Soviet ships. Other steps include the comparison of the Western and Soviet ships and the conversion of the costs to a common dollar base.

The estimates presented here were all computed using data bases, algorithms, and formulas designed specifically for this task. The data bases were compiled using only open source material. Consequently, the results may not always agree with the official government figures of any nation.

As in all statistical studies, there were some units which did not fit the norm. There were some Soviet ships with no Western counterpart or for which the cost of at least three Western counterparts were not available. To produce estimates for these units, average cost tables were compiled. These tables are the result of categorizing the known cost data to fit the Soviet ship types and then averaging the costs.

It is understood that a certain amount of error is inherent in any compilation of this type. A plus or minus 10 percent error is assigned to these estimates. Even if the error were one hundred percent, the trend would be the same.

Unless otherwise indicated, all estimates are compiled using 1979 dollars.

In order to show clearly the difference between "strategic and tactical submarines," the strategic—or ballistic missile—units and the tactical—or attack—units are presented separately. This separation of strategic and tactical submarines came about as a result of some differing opinions as to whether or not estimates of the strategic submarines should be included in the navy total. There is the possibility the Soviets consider them a part of the strategic forces, and their costs, therefore, may not be a part of the Soviet Navy's budget. However, it must be remembered no submarine puts to sea without the capability to fire torpedoes. While the "strategic missile submarine" may have a primary mission not requiring this capability, it must still be countered to prevent its use as a conventional, torpedo-firing submarine. In other words, a submarine is a submarine is a submarine.

I have estimated that in 1967, a Soviet ballistic missile submarine would have cost about $162 million in 1967 dollars. That is, the first of the YANKEE–class submarines probably cost at least that amount, less missiles. The 1974 price, in 1974 dollars, for this same class of submarine was probably about $266 million. The "valley" in Figure 1 for 1975 should not be taken to mean a drop in SSBN construction but only a drop in new units reported in the Western news media. This same rule is true for all figures.

Market Value Estimates of
Soviet Ballistic Missile Submarines

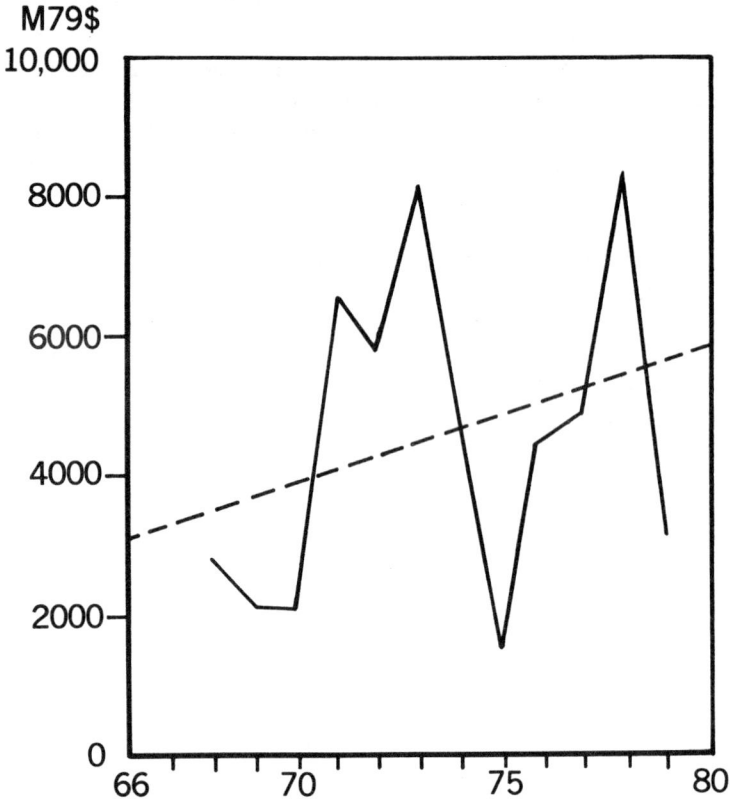

Figure 1

Figure 2 shows the yearly investment in Soviet attack submarines. This includes diesel- and nuclear-powered units. There is a vast difference in the estimated market value of these units depending on which power source is used. For example, it is estimated a diesel-powered FOXTROT–class submarine, constructed and priced in 1973, would have cost about $12 million; a nuclear-powered VICTOR-class submarine, built and priced in the same year, would have cost about

490

Market Value Estimates of
Soviet Attack Submarines

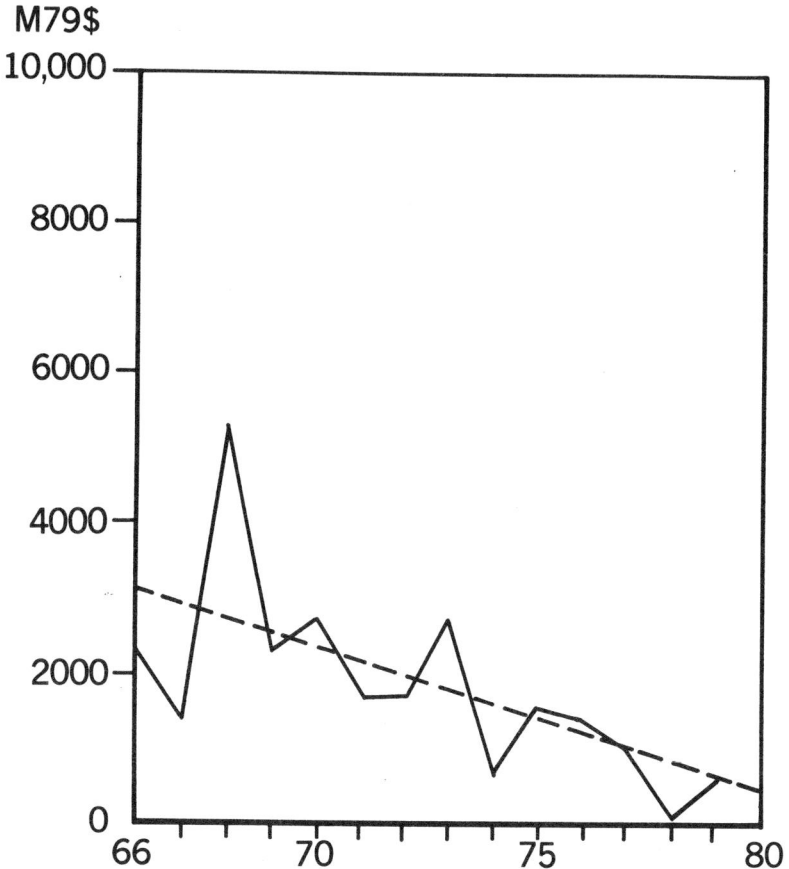

Figure 2

$94 million. It is not clear why the Soviets continue to build diesel-powered submarines. However, two possible explanations come to mind: (1) they are built for export, as a number have been, and (2) it has occurred to Party planners that a $12 million diesel submarine can just as well patrol the approaches to Mother Russia as can a $94 million nuclear-powered submarine.

Cruisers have found a new place in the Soviet Navy since the day in 1956 when Premier Khrushchev said they were fit only to transport diplomats on state visits. Figure 3 depicts a strong increase in investment in this type of ship. The 1975 estimated market value for a *Kresta* II–class cruiser, less missiles, is about $151 million in 1975 dollars. The new cruisers are not yet included in this estimate.

Destroyers are increasing in importance in the Soviet Navy as Figure

Market Value Estimates of Soviet Cruisers

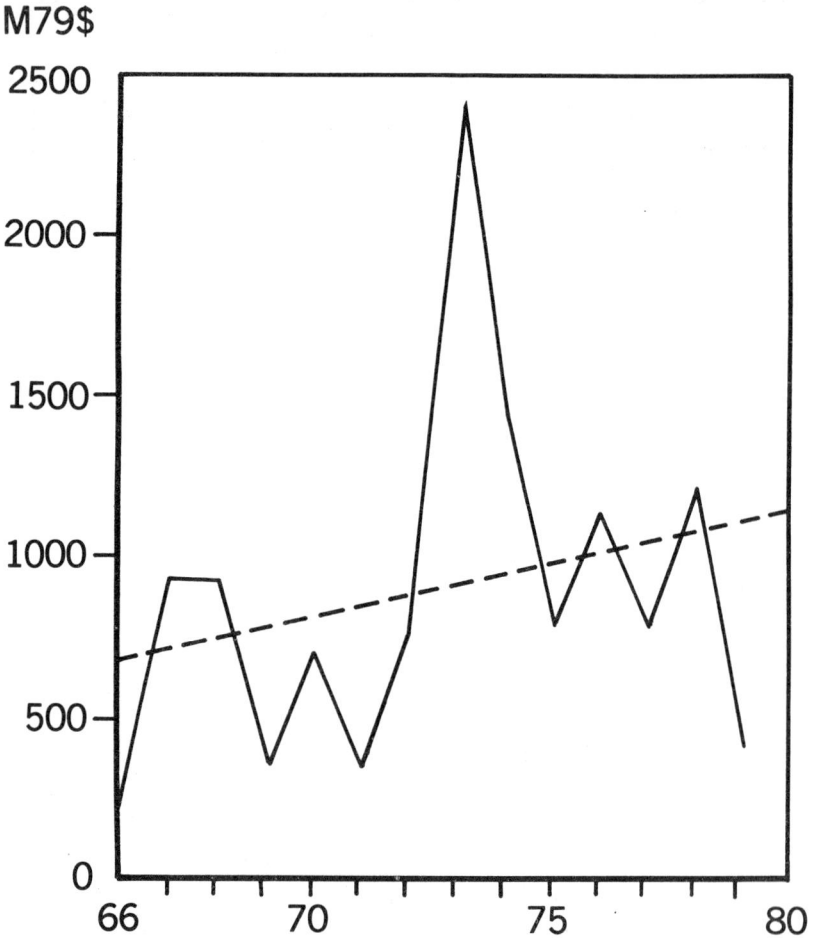

Figure 3

4 shows. At the beginning of the period (in 1966), a *Kashin*-class destroyer would have had an estimated market value in 1966 dollars of approximately $60 million; by 1976, when the *Krivak*-class destroyers

Market Value Estimates of Soviet Destroyers

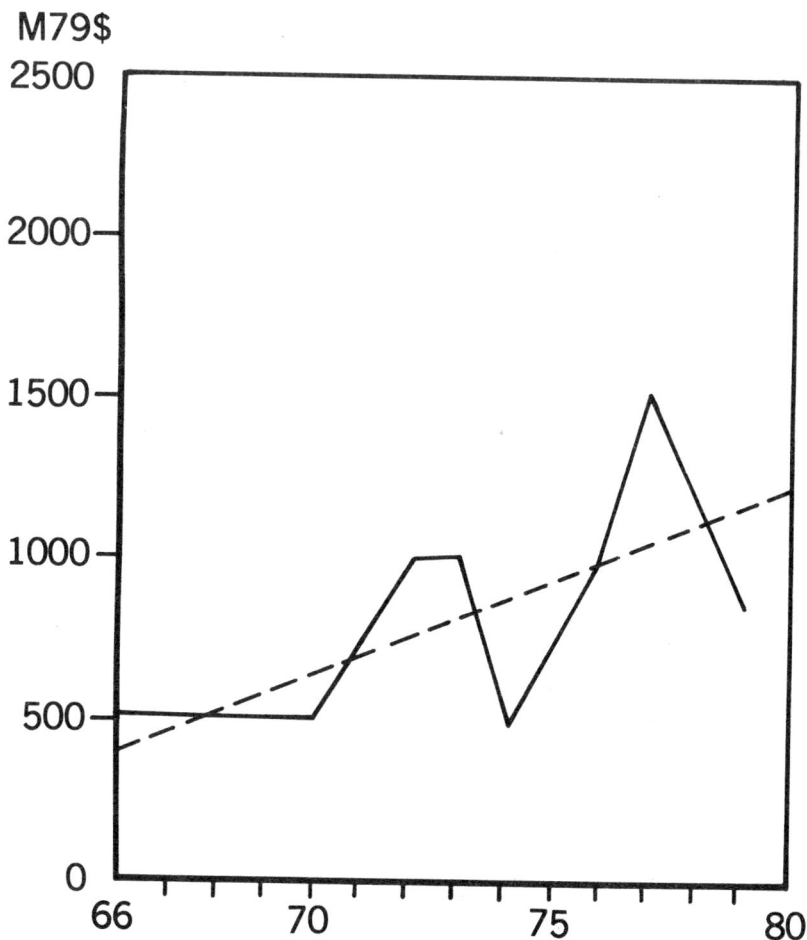

Figure 4

were being built, the estimated market value had risen to about $118 million each in 1976 dollars.

Figure 5 shows the market value estimates for Soviet major surface combatants, including the *Kiev*, cruisers, and destroyers. In this figure, the year 1973 stands out as a high year. This is partially attributable to the *Sverdlov* command cruisers. This was also the last year for construction of *Kashin*-class destroyers, while *Krivak*-class destroyers were

Market Value Estimates of Soviet Major Surface Combatants

M79$

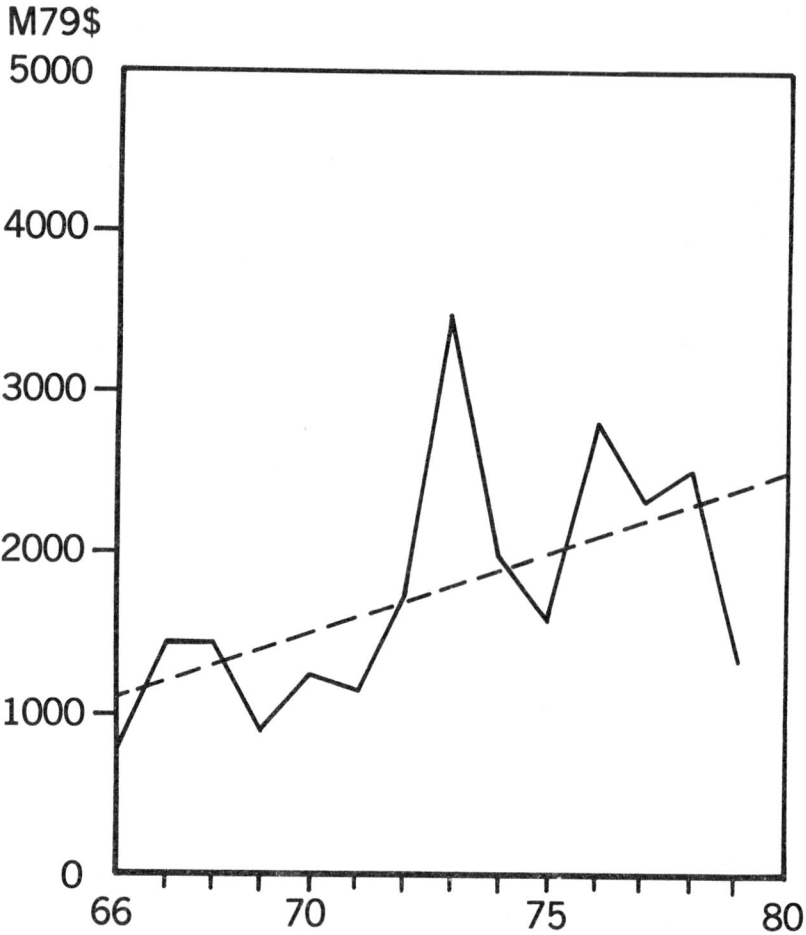

Figure 5

also being constructed. In short, it was a big year for major surface combatants.

Figure 6 indicates that until the last 3 years, there was a decline in emphasis in the Soviet Navy on the small ocean-going combatants. This could have come about for several reasons, but two things come to mind: (1) the increased cost and emphasis on major surface combatants, and (2) the increased cost of these small combatants. In 1966,

Market Value Estimates of
Soviet Small Ocean-going Combatants

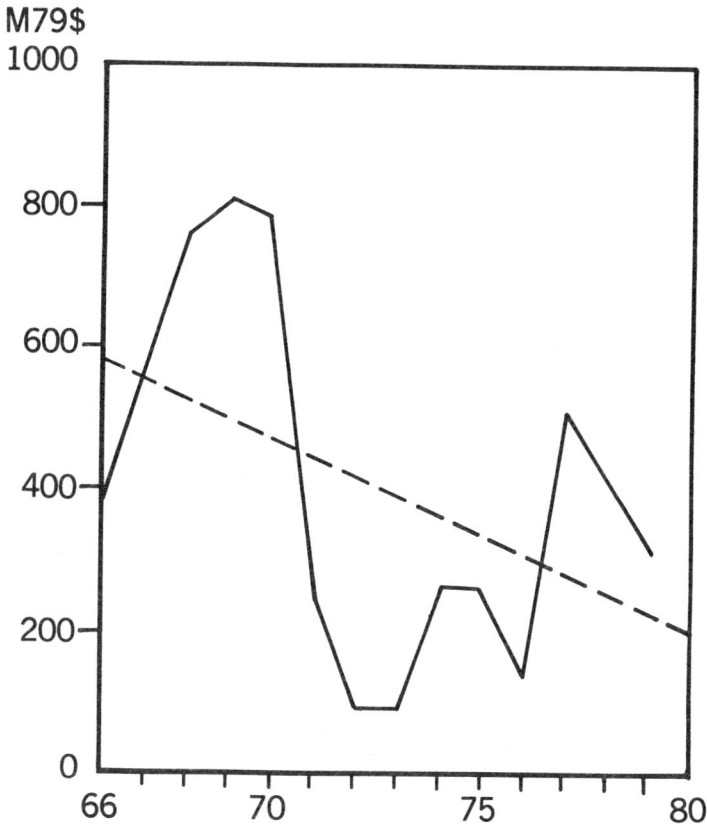

Figure 6

a *Mirka* I-class ship is estimated to have had a market value of about $6 million in 1966 dollars. It appears the Soviets stopped building the *Mirka* I–class about 1968 and the *Mirka* II-class about 1970. The possible replacement for the *Mirka*, the *Nanuchka*-class small missile ship, is estimated to have a 1976 market value, less missiles, in 1976 dollars of about $20 million per unit. These two things could have combined to bring about the temporary drop in investment in this type of ship.

Fast attack craft comprise another ship type which has had a sudden increase in investment in the last few years (Figure 7). The reasons given for the change in investment in small ocean-going combatants could also be advanced in this case. An example of the increase in unit cost can be found by examining the *Shershen*- and the *Turya*-classes. In 1966, a *Shershen* is estimated to have had a market value of only about $1 million in 1966 dollars. However, in 1976, a *Turya* is estimated to have had a 1976 dollar market value of about $16 million. This surely must say that, as with the rest of the world, the Soviets—in some cases—are spending more and getting less.

Mine warfare is traditionally a Russian art. So, too, is the practice of minesweeping. Figure 8 indicates a continuing interest but slightly declining investment. As new classes of minesweepers come to the attention of the Western media, the long-term trend may change.

With the introduction of the *Alligator*-class landing ships in 1966, the Soviet Naval Infantry was provided with large, long-legged support ships. Figure 9 shows a steadily increasing interest in this force.

One way to measure a navy and get some idea of its intended use is to gauge the support and repair ships it builds. A country which intends to operate in distant waters needs support ships, while a navy built only for coastal defense has no need for such ships. The fact the Soviets are building so many support ships must say something about how they plan to use their navy (Figure 10).

Total Soviet yearly construction estimates and this same information, less the estimates for ballistic missile firing submarines, are shown in Figure 11. This gives some idea where the Soviet Navy's money is going. Without the SSBNs, the yearly investment could have gone up very slowly.

These figures represent only what the Soviets have shown to the West; they do not include ships not yet reported in the Western media. The total construction estimates for these years do not include the tooling-up or shipyard construction necessary to produce this armada.

However it is viewed, the Soviet government is spending a large sum of money (a big percentage of Soviet GNP) on building a new, modern, powerful, and influential Navy. They have been doing this for a long time. They probably will continue on this course for several more years.

The growth of the "Russian" fleet is the fulfillment of Peter the Great's dreams of changing a land-oriented giant into a world power through the development of a large navy. Peter's children have achieved his dream. Whether they now choose to dominate the world or only exert a large influence on it will depend on the resistance they meet from their own citizenry and from the West. They must be convinced the saner course of peace is the more profitable.

Market Value Estimates of Soviet Fast Attack Craft

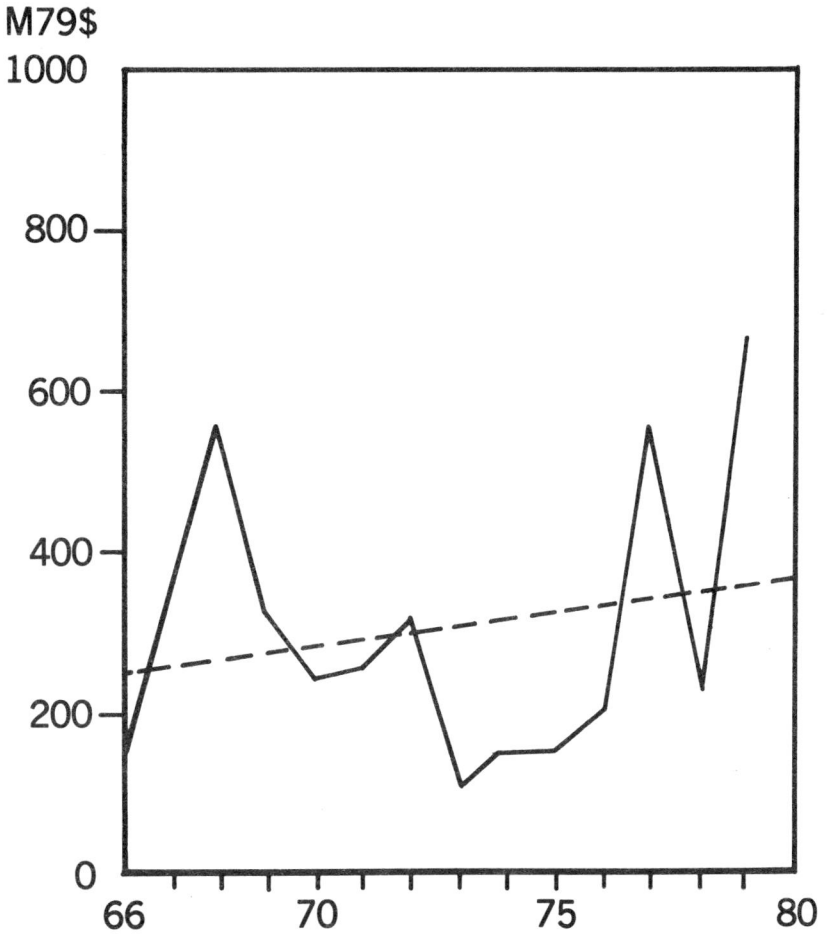

Figure 7

skipper figure 8

Market Value Estimates of
Soviet Mine Warfare Ships and Craft

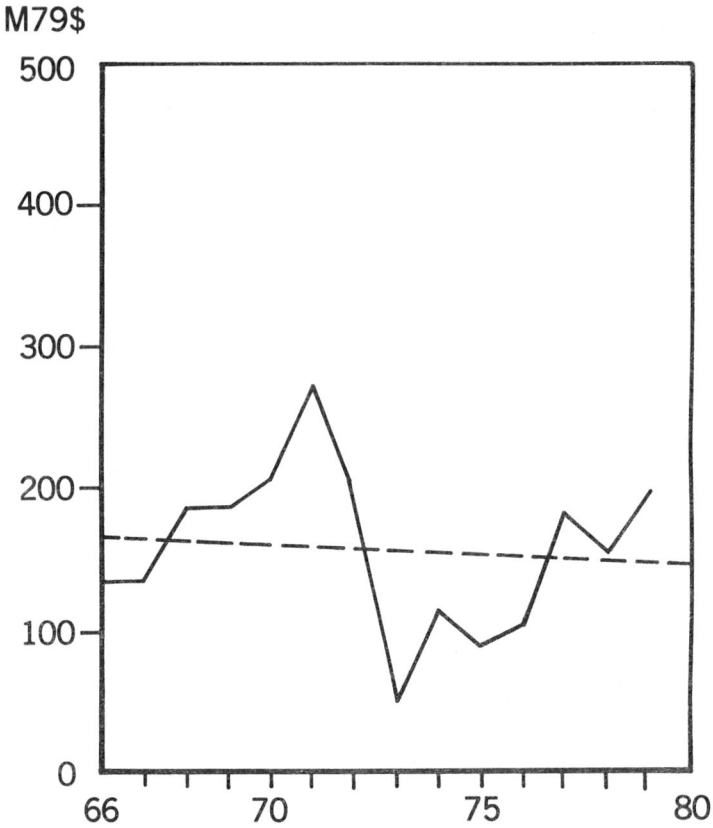

Figure 8

Market Value Estimates of Soviet Amphibious Force Ships and Craft

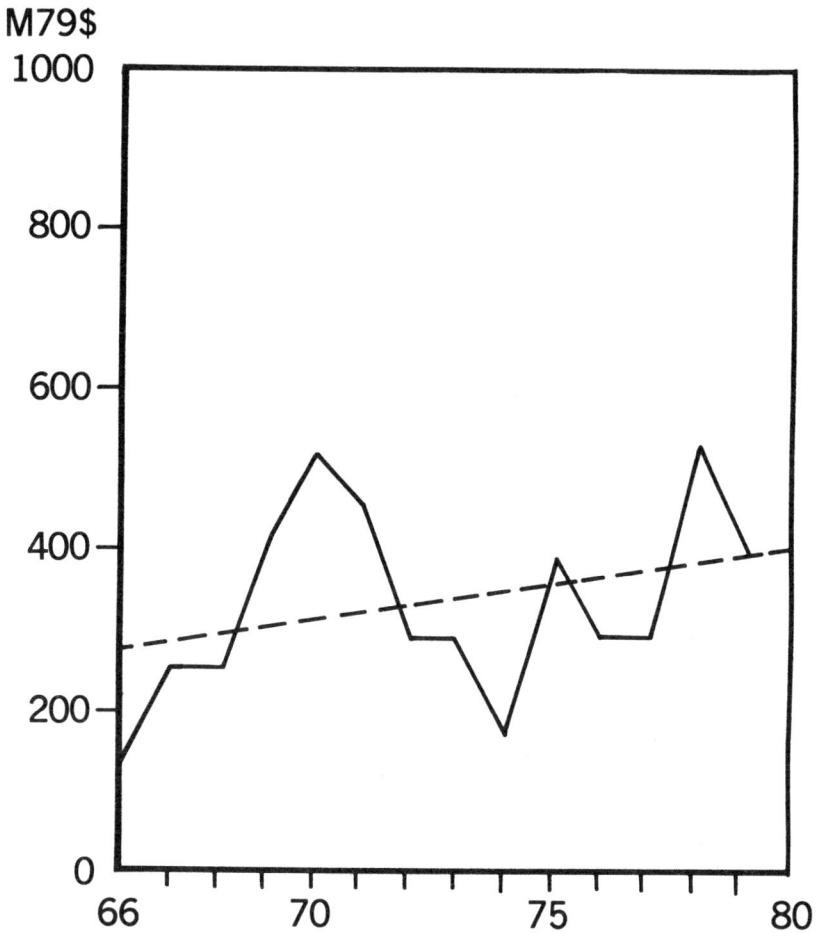

Figure 9

Market Value Estimates of Soviet Support Ships

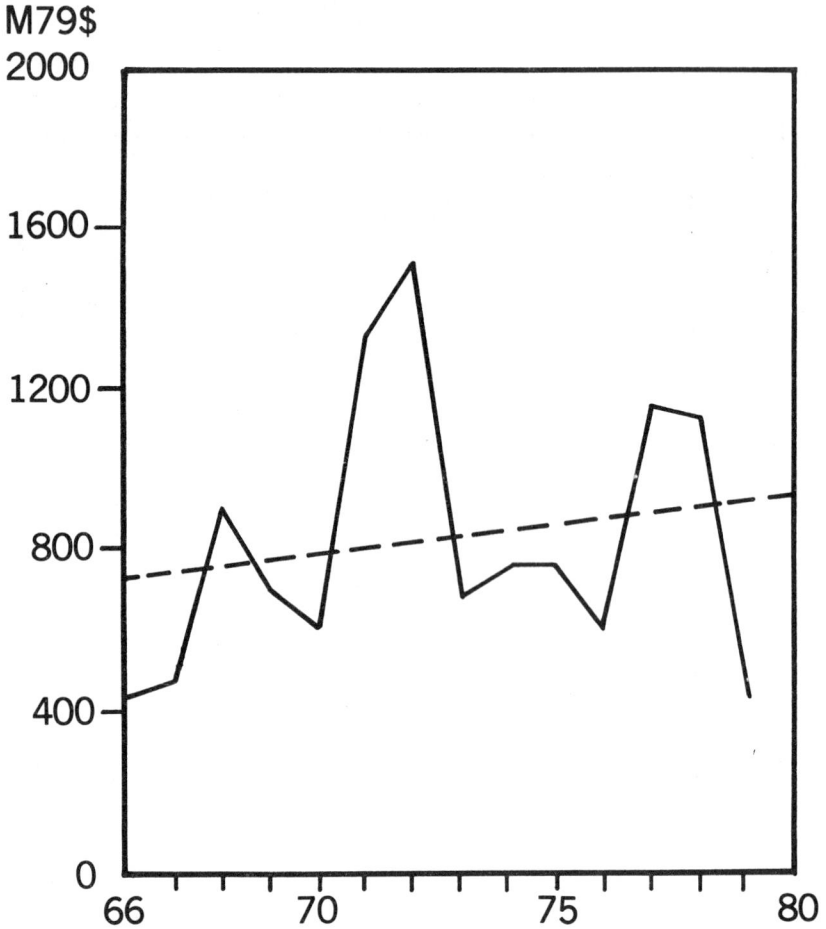

Figure 10

Market Value Estimates of Soviet Navy Shipbuilding

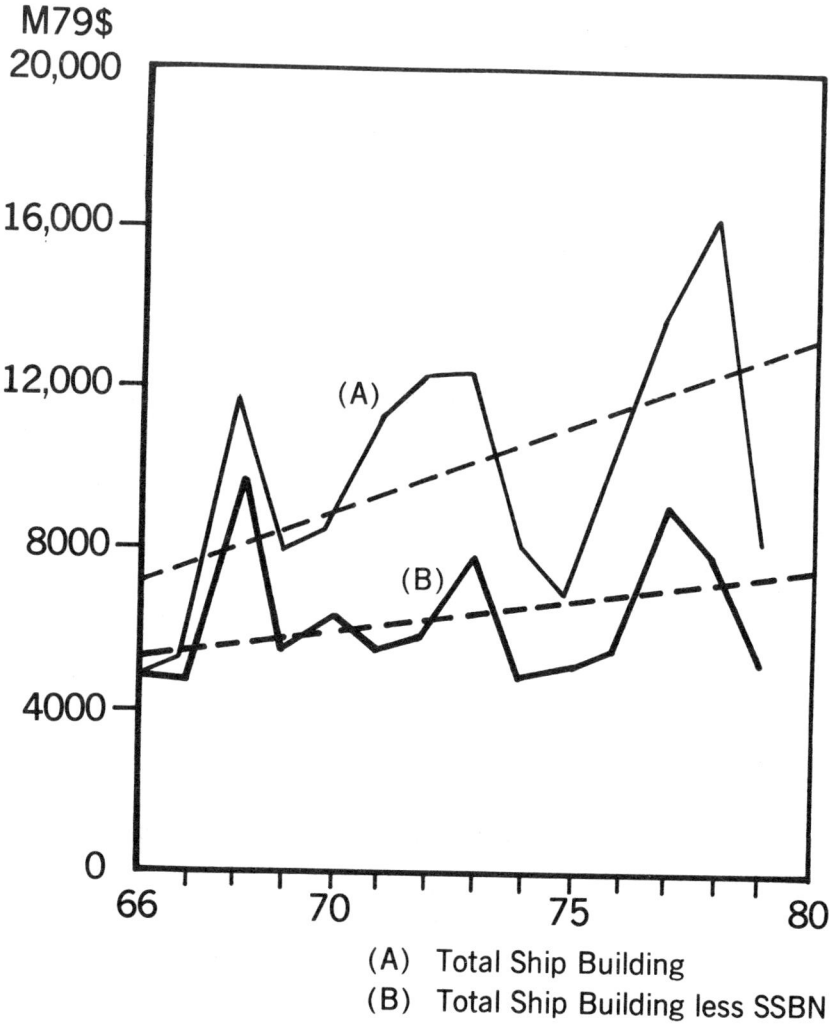

(A) Total Ship Building
(B) Total Ship Building less SSBN

Figure 11

A Cybernetic Approach to the Analysis of Soviet R&D Activity

Haskell R. Scheimberg

Introduction

Within the past three decades, Soviet military power has come to equal that of the United States. The Soviets' newly won "parity status" is based to a great extent on the ability of their Party, state, military, industrial, and scientific organizations to produce a wide variety of sophisticated weapons in large quantities. The bureaucracy developing and producing these weapons, the Soviet military R&D system, contributes to the increasing capacity of the USSR to influence the course of global events and to develop initiatives challenging Free World security.

Effective efforts to deter hostile Soviet initiatives depend, among other things, on the ability of US analysts to anticipate in sufficient detail the capabilities of future generations of Soviet weapons and prepare appropriate responses. Our ability to evaluate Soviet weapons development is a function of our understanding of Soviet decisionmaking processes. Decisions shape the transformation of inputs into outputs.

Attempts to forecast Soviet weapon system developments have led to differing specifications of inputs and outputs. Alexander, for example, proposes budgets, scientists, engineers, and technology as inputs to the Soviet military R&D system and performance, missions, and military value of weapons emanating from the system as output. He observes that:

> The counting of scientists and engineers, the enumeration of advanced or lagging technologies, the emphasis on specific weapons performance figures, are by themselves poor guides to military capabilities—now or in the future. There is at best only a loose connection between inputs and outputs, technology and value, especially in military R&D where so many other forces intervene.[1]

The loose connection between inputs and outputs may, as Alexander speculates, be attributable to "the processes and choices which determine how . . . resources are employed." Similarities in the design of Soviet weapons—which include simplicity, component commonality, and continuous adaptation of design—suggest to Alexander that these

502

processes and choices link inputs to outputs and are subject to "a common set of forces." These forces, according to Alexander,

> [arise] for the most part, from Soviet doctrine on the mass use of force, from pressures of the economy, and from a bureaucratic inertia supported by a general satisfaction with the process.[2]

The forces operating on the system are, I believe, more basic than those specified by Alexander. The process transforming inputs into outputs is more fundamental than decisionmaking. This is not to say decision processes do not play an important role in determining how R&D activities may culminate in weapons. Nor do I want to minimize the utility and merit of Alexander's insightful analyses of how doctrinal, economic, and bureaucratic forces mediate decision processes. What I suggest is an alternative formulation of the problem based on a different paradigm which may be capable of addressing such questions as: When is a decision called for? or What are the purposes of a particular weapon system?

Paradigms and Theories

The selective filter through which we observe our environment determines what issues and problems we find relevant. This filter, or paradigm, as Kuhn has referred to it,[3] is represented by a belief system which embraces a set of fundamental assumptions which give structure and meaning to the world around us. These assumptions are the foundations of theories and models used to explain the events we encounter. Problems are formulated and their solutions sought within the context of a paradigm. In much the same way that Euclidian geometry and Newtonian physics provide a foundation for inquiry in the fields of mathematics and physics, the "analytic" paradigm described by Steinbruner[4] can be used to organize the analysis of Soviet weapons development and acquisition activity.

While a paradigm serves to focus attention on a comprehensible portion of the incomprehensible totality of complex issues, it is the theory flowing from a paradigm which provides relationships between objects and events. Theories belonging to what Steinbruner has labeled the "analytic" paradigm focus attention on decision processes. These theories require examination of issues such as Soviet weapons development in terms of choices; i.e., alternative courses of action available to a decisionmaker attempting to attain a particular goal or objective. To the extent the behavior we seek to explain and ultimately to predict is a product of choice (the conscious and sometimes rational selection of one alternative from among many), explanation and prediction may indeed be possible. One should ask, however, when operating within this paradigm: Under what circumstances are decisions called for?

How are goals and the means of evaluating them established? What is the likelihood of change? Ambiguities which arise in answering these and other questions inherent in decisionmaking approaches to weapons issues tend to engender doubt. They leave us dissatisfied with our understanding of the situation.

We can—like Alexander, Allison, Spielmann and others—seek resolution of such questions within the analytic paradigm. Or, we can—like Steinbruner, Beer, and others—seek explanation within an alternative paradigm. I have opted to do the latter; that is, to examine Soviet weapon developments in terms of the purposive activities of a survival-oriented control system. Within this cybernetic framework, system behavior is judged to maintain survival variables within specific limits. Questions about system behavior are answered in terms of the interactions among three related categories of variables: environment, resources, and performance.[5] Before attempting to define the interactions among the sets of variables pertinent to Soviet weapons developments, however, the concepts of purposive behavior and control will be discussed.

Purposive Behavior

Purpose relates to the goal-directed, problem solving, error correcting behavior observed in many natural and artificial systems.[6] These systems share certain identifiable characteristics which enable us, in some cases, to infer the rules which govern their behavior. The nature of the homomorphisms characterizing purposive systems has been described by Howland:

> Although the systems are structually quite different, they are functionally similar. These functional similarities make it possible to develop general theory which can be used to describe and explain the behavior of a wide range of systems.[7]

Relatively few efforts have been made, however, to apply purposive concepts to complex societal problems. Beer[8] and Steinbruner are among the few who have defined the problem of controlling a national economy in purposive terms. Reluctance to apply purposive concepts to societal issues stems in part from the difficulty of establishing meaningful goals for societal activities. In addition, Miller claims "the concept of purpose has been made suspect to most scientists by teleological formulations which suggest that living systems strive for mystical ends which are not clearly formulated."[9]

Beer notes teleological formulations arise when an observer attempts to define behavior in terms of goals appropriate to his own purposes. What is being observed, however, is an entropic process:

504

Natural systems organize themselves over a period of time to be what they immanently are. To an observer, who determines the criteria by which the end result is called organized, this process looks like learning or, in general, adaption. In fact it is a process of entropy.[10]

It is, according to Beer, the "self organizing," entropic pressure upon "complex and richly interacting systems" which drive them from "a less to a more probable state," thus creating for the observer the perception of purpose.[11]

Beer suggests there is a natural mechanism, entropy, which explains purpose. The observer attributes purpose, or goals, to entropic processes.[12] If we are willing to recognize that purpose is attributed to systems by the observer as a means of explaining the system's behavior, we can proceed to examine in a meaningful manner the control aspects of behavior associated with the Soviet military R&D system.

System Modeling

In order to describe and model a real world entity, it is useful to abstract the real world as a set of variables, which we will call a system.[13] This system is a model of the real world entity. The set of variables used to describe relevant aspects of the real world entity and its behavior are limited only by the ingenuity and imagination of the observer. Depending on what we want to know about the real world entity, we select different sets of variables and generate different information. It is therefore essential that problems be formulated prior to system definition to ensure appropriate selection of variables.

A basic characteristic of an adaptive system is the ability to use resources to counter environmental disturbances and remain in desired states. Living organisms are entities which exhibit adaptive capability. They survive by virtue of their ability to maintain their internal states, the value of their essential variables, within genetically defined limits. Goals are defined as the states the system must assume in order to satisfy its purpose—survival in the case of a living entity.

Modeling is the process of selecting variables; i.e., identifying a system and inventing/discovering relationships between those variables. To the extent appropriate variables are selected and the specified relationships between variables are descriptive of aspects of the real world about which information is sought, the model generates useful information.

Cybernetic Models

Wiener[14] defines cybernetics as "the science of control and communication in the animal and the machine." Ashby, in slightly different terms, suggests that cybernetics is the study of how, in a given situation, certain entities, capable of producing a wide variety of behaviors, restrict their behaviors to those enabling them to achieve specific goal states.[15] Miller, drawing from both Wiener and Ashby, defines cybernetics as

> the study of methods of feedback control . . . . It has led to the recognition of formal identities among various sorts of nonliving and living systems. In complex systems, control is achieved by many finely adjusted interlocking processes involving transmission of matter—energy and information.[16]

Control, as defined by Wiener and Miller, combines two important processes which are differentiated in Ashby's view of cybernetics: regulation and control. Paraphrasing Ashby,[17] regulation is the process of blocking the effects of disturbances on essential variables. A good regulator is able to maintain the value of essential variables within desired limits. Control is the process of establishing appropriate reference values; i.e., goals and limits for essential system variables. "A form of behavior is adaptive if it maintains the essential variables within . . . limits."[18] Cybernetic concepts and models provide a useful means of describing adaptive behavior.

Ashby, Howland, and Miller have used cybernetic models to explain adaptive behavior. These models describe the regulatory process which maintain systems within survival states in the face of internal and external disturbances. Howland, for example, identifies a number of functions including regulation, control, monitor, comparator, and memory which enable systems to achieve a dynamic balance between environmental disturbances and survival states.[19]

In terms of the problem being addressed in this article—the proliferation of Soviet weapons—an analyst attempting to use a cybernetic model would begin by formulating the following questions:

1. What is the system most appropriate for analysis?
2. What are the system's goals; i.e., what variables are held in what limits?
3. How do weapons contribute to the achievement of these goals?
4. What is the role of R&D in the goal achievement process?

I will address these questions using a cybernetic approach.

The System and Its Goals

Earlier it was suggested that cybernetic models can generate information about time-dependent interactions among environmental,

Howland's Structural Model

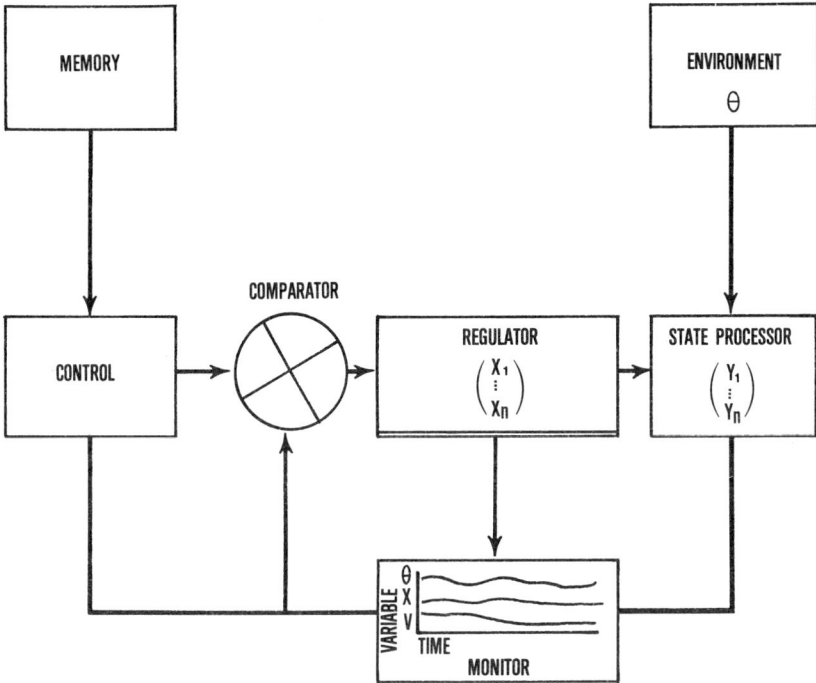

Figure 1

resource, and system performance variables. Meaningful system definition requires selection of essential variables in all three categories. Any model to be used for the analysis of weapons issues would have to include a much broader range of variables than those conventionally associated with the analysis of the Soviet military R&D system. Weapons issues must, of necessity, embrace issues of societal survival. It is, after all, Soviet society which ultimately pays for the design and development of weapons, and it is Soviet society the weapons are designed to serve. While the significance of the role played by the Soviet leadership and the vast bureaucracy it commands in shaping societal perception cannot be overlooked, it is society's demand for survival which allows the Soviet leadership to exercise its many powers.

What does societal survival demand of the Soviet leadership? Among other things, Soviet society requires access to food, fuel, and manpower.[20] In order to ensure the availability of these resources, some degree of control over the outcomes of global events is required. Consider, for example, situations which could be perceived by the

507

Soviet leadership as affecting their current or future resource availability. Failure to control these situations could jeopardize access to these critical resources. The goals the Soviets pursue, however, reflect interests which are not always consistent with societal survival. It must be remembered that leaderships strive to maintain their own favorable access to resources made possible by their position. System performance is measured with respect to its requirements, but—depending on the judge—the assessment of performance may differ.

Control, which in its broadest sense includes the concept of regulation, implies an ability to maintain system performance variables within survival—i.e., goal state—and limits. Every situation has a spatial and temporal dimension. That is, outcomes of situations in one place can affect situations in other places at other times. Perfect control is the ability to achieve favorable outcomes for events everywhere both now and in the future. The ability to regulate and control depends upon having appropriate resources in the right place at the right time as well as knowing how to employ the resources.

Regulation and control are achieved in the following manner: The memory provides the controller with estimates of how, when, and where a particular set of resources should be applied to accomplish a given set of goals. The monitor records the current system state while the comparator, based on data obtained from the monitor, detects discrepancies between the system's actual state and that specified by the controller. The regulator applies resources to reduce the difference between the actual and controller-specified state. Constant feedback of information from the monitor and comparator to the regulator about the current state of the system is required to ensure the system achieves its goals. Without appropriate resources or the skill to apply them, regulation and control are impossible.[21]

The Soviet Union, as an adaptive system, is in constant interaction with its environment. Regulation and control of system performance variables would be relatively simple were it not for disturbances generated by processes in the system's internal and external environment. The precise nature of disturbances acting upon a system are not usually understood. In fact, the only manifestation of a disturbance may be the errant behavior of performance variables.[22] An observer viewing the behavior of an adaptive system might not know the nature of the disturbance affecting the system. What is seen is the behavior of performance variables.

In order to deal with the variety of disturbances which could potentially impact upon the system, the system must have a variety of alternatives at its disposal. "Variety," the number of alternative states a system or the system's environment can assume, measures an important facet of a regulation and control problem. Howland reports:

> Variety is more than the spice of life, it is necessary for life. Homeostatic behavior is possible only if a system has

sufficient variety, i.e., has the resources to go to enough states to maintain its essential, (survival), variables within survival limits, given disturbances from its environment. Ashby's Law of Requisite Variety states that "only variety can destroy variety" (Ashby, 1957). This means that variety in the environment, the number of disturbances which can impinge on the essential variables of a system, must be countered by the variety in the system regulator.[23]

There are basic problems facing an adaptive system: (1) having sufficient regulatory variety to match the variety generated in its environment and (2) having the skill to use its regulatory variety effectively.

An observer wishing to describe and predict the behavior of an adaptive system must infer not only the nature of disturbances impacting on the system but also how the system assesses those impacts. This must be inferred from the system's reponse to disturbances. What an observer views—and in some cases only with considerable difficulty— are interactions between disturbances and resource allocations. These manifestations of activity, which include everything from machinery and equipment to art and literature, provide the only available data for inferring the goals pursued by their producers. Inferences we make about Soviet goals and how these goals are attained are made on the basis of such artifacts. The analytic method we use is, in many respects, similar to that of the archaeologist.

Weapons and the Regulatory Process

Weapons are a type of artifact which can be used to assess societal behavior. Alexander asks:

> Why does the Soviet Union acquire the number and sort of weapons she does? Why, for example, does she have more than 40,000 tanks, when 20,000 would be twice as many as any other country possesses? Why does she continue to produce new tanks at a rate of 4,000 per year—four times the American production rate?[24]

Alexander suggests that answers to the questions he poses can be found, partially, in Soviet decisionmaking processes. "Centralized authority, rigidly hierarchial organization, inflexible outlook and conservative reactions to change" are, in Alexander's view, the primary attributes of this process.[25] I do not argue with Alexander's basic thesis. In his view, "the best guide to what will happen tomorrow is what happened yesterday."[26] I do, however, question an implication which could be drawn from this logic—the Soviets build the number and sort of weapons they do because organizational process and bureaucratic inertia make change difficult. It should be pointed out that Alexander is careful not to draw this implication as some of his readers, it seems, have done. I suggest the Soviets behave in this way because such behavior promotes regulation and control of variables perceived as essential to their societal survival. The Soviets produce the number and sort of weapons they do because these weapons enable the Soviets to regulate the outcome of events perceived as vital to Soviet interests. The Soviets persist in this behavior and do not alter the institutional arrangements which produce it because it serves Soviet interests. Scott and Scott note, "Without military power, the Soviet Union today simply would be another developing nation."[27]

Earlier, the spatial and temporal dimensions of control were noted. Based on these considerations, different regulatory resources are required to maintain system performance variables within the limits established by a controller. Weapons, in their capacity as regulatory resources, must therefore be designed to meet the spatial and temporal requirements of the situations in which they will be used. The Soviets have opted to address the multiple requirements necessitated by varying space-time considerations in terms of a large number of different weapons systems. The success of these weapons systems, in the sense they make possible the achievement of societal goals, makes departure from this design philosophy unlikely.

We must not, however, become victims of our own analysis by believing these patterns will persist. They persist only as long as they serve their purpose. The weight of doctrine, the inertia of organizational process, and the trajectory of years of past experience may inhibit change, but they will not deter it in the face of disturbances perceived as threats to vital interests. R&D activity is the hedge against disturbances which may jeopardize national survival.

The Role of R&D

The role of R&D activity is to develop the scientific and technical capacity to meet future regulation and control requirements. Sheinin, a Soviet specialist in the organization and management of scientific activity, relates the basic objectives of Soviet scientific activity:

> The general line of science policy is control of the scientific and technical revolution, and this purpose is divided into subpurposes (with a diminishing generality) like ensuring equilibrium between society and the natural environment, between the given social system and its sociopolitical environment, within the given social system, notably, between science and the other sectors of social production, within science—between the various lines of research—and also between the individual categories (stages)

The purposive, control-oriented expression of Soviet science policy is evident in the selection of weapon-related research areas. While Sheinin does not address weapons issues specifically, it is clear he views the relationship between society and its environment in cybernetic terms similar to those described in this paper.

Sheinin's thesis is that there are two basic approaches to planning and organizing scientific activity in support of societal goals: centralization and decentralization. The decentralized approach "provides the flexibility needed to satisfy a number of here-and-now requirements, and also for taking account of unforeseen events."[29] He notes, however, that this approach is insensitive to long-range goals. In contrast, the centralized approach tends to be more sensitive to long-range needs and to

> make more efficient use of limited financial and personnel resources, thereby making the system as a whole more flexible and adaptive.[30]

Sheinin indicates the Soviets have organized their scientific and production resources so as to achieve a meaningful balance between these two approaches. According to Sheinin, scientific and production-oriented organizations within the USSR are arrayed in four types:

1. complex scientific and technical institutions concentrating research, design, development, and technological work within a developed experimental production area;
2. research institutes at major industrial enterprises or in production associations;
3. science-production associations which include research, design, development, and technological organizations and industrial enterprises; and
4. academic institutes including design offices and experimental production areas.

The activities of these organizational complexes are state-regulated by such means as subsidies, tax privileges, and depreciation allowances.[31] The "scientific network" of which these four complexes are a part "helps to accelerate the maturing of new ideas."

By giving the state both the means of regulating the thrust of scientific research and the authority to interpret societal goals, the Soviets are in a position to regulate and control the maturation of "new ideas." The ideas which would in this cybernetic view be given priority are those which are believed to have the highest probability of contributing to the development of the regulatory capability needed to maintain essential system variables within limits. If there is a link between the inputs and outputs of the Soviet military R&D systems as defined by Alexander, it is in the matching of R&D effect to the perceived control requirements of Soviet society.

Conclusions

In summary, it may be dangerous to ascribe the proliferation of Soviet weapons systems to bureaucratic inertia, organizational process, history, or doctrine without first assessing the regulation and control implications of these forces. It may be the observed proliferation is the result of a conscious Soviet policy to increase its regulatory variety relative to that of the US. If, as Scott and Scott suggest, only weapons systems keep the Soviets from being a "developing nation," it is clearly in their national interest to build weapons. Soviet weapon-building behavior can be explained in terms of the USSR's efforts to increase the variety of the disturbances with which the US must contend, thereby creating a relative control advantage for the Soviets. If this is the case, then we might benefit by viewing their efforts in a cybernetic frame of reference.

Notes

1. Alexander, Arthur J., *The Process of Soviet Weapons Decisions,* Report P–6137 (Santa Monica: The RAND Corporation, 1978), p. 3.
2. Ibid., p. 4.
3. Kuhn, T. S., *The Copernican Revolution* (New York: Vintage, 1959).
4. Steinbruner, J. D., *The Cybernetic Theory of Decision* (Princeton: Princeton University Press, 1974), p. 25.
5. Howland, D. and Colson, H. D., "Cybernetic Modeling of Large-Scale Systems," in T. I. Oren, ed., *Cybernetics and Modeling of Large–Scale Systems* (Naumer: International Association for Cybernetics, 1977), p. 12.
6. Ackoff, R. L. and Emery, F. E., *On Purposive Systems* (New York: Aldine Atherton, 1971); Gerard, R. W., "The Neurophysiology of Purposive Behavior," in H. Forester, D. White, L. J. Patterson, and J. K. Russell, eds., *Purposive Systems* (New York: Spartan, 1968).
7. Howland, D., Colson, H. D., and McLean, C., *The Analysis of Tactics,* RF Project 1643 Final Report (Columbus: The Ohio State University Research Foundation, 1973), p. 16.
8. Beer, S., *Fanfare for Effective Freedom,* The Third Richard Goodman Memorial Lecture, delivered at Brighton Polytechnic, Mouslecomb, England, 14 February 1973.
9. Miller, J. G., *Living Systems* (New York: McGraw–Hill, 1978), p. 40.
10. Beer, S., *Decision and Control* (New York: John Wiley, 1966), p. 359.
11. Ibid., p. 350.
12. Ibid., p. 357.
13. Ashby, W. R., *An Introduction to Cybernetics* (New York: John Wiley, 1957).
14. Wiener, N., *Cybernetics* (New York: John Wiley, 1948).
15. Ashby, op. cit., p. 3.
16. Miller, op. cit., p. 36.
17. Ashby, W. R., *Design for a Brain* (London: Chapman and Hall, 1960), p. 199.
18. Ashby, *An Introduction to Cybernetics,* p. 58.
19. Howland, op. cit.
20. Scheimberg, Haskell R., "A Cybernetic Model of Certain Aspects of Soviet Behavior" (unpublished PhD dissertation, Ohio State University, 1980).

21. Howland, "Cybernetic Modeling of Large-Scale Systems," p. 15.
22. Ashby, op. cit.
23. Howland, *Adaptive Information Systems for Decision and Control* (draft, 1980).
24. Alexander, Arthur J., "Decision-Making in Soviet Weapons Procurement," *Adelphi Papers* 147/8 (London: International Institute for Strategic Studies, 1979), p. 1.
25. Ibid., p. 2.
26. Ibid., p. 41.
27. Scott, Harriet Fast and Scott, William F., "The Future of the Soviet Union," draft of a paper to be presented at Hoover Institution Conference on "The Futures of the Soviet Union," 13–15 September 1978, p. 1.
28. Sheinin, Y., *Science Policy: Problems and Trends* (Moscow: Progress Publishers, 1978), pp. 323–324.
29. Ibid., p. 330.
30. Ibid.
31. Ibid., p. 324.

R&D in Soviet Military Academies

Richard E. Thomas

Introduction

There is little need to justify the study of Soviet military research and development agencies and activities—the increasing sophistication and capability of Soviet military technology are well-documented, and Soviet leaders appear to be not only aware of but willing to use the increased leverage which has been provided them by their intense and well-funded scientific and engineering research efforts.

Since the ability to make war now equates almost totally to the ability to develop weapons technologies out of scientific research, it is altogether appropriate to study the Soviet R&D system and examine its relationship to the Soviet military. In pursuit of this objective, open literature provides relatively little hard information, thereby leaving much to inference and rationalization. One must fervently avoid the problem which has, in the writer's opinion, plagued US studies of the Soviet Union for three decades. That problem is currently called the "mirror image syndrome" although it has gone by other names at other times and it has its roots in either or both of two views. Years ago, when US technology was supreme in the world, one heard comments which seemed to say, "Since we (the US) are the smartest people in the world, then everyone, including the Soviets, will do as we have done." That attitude persists in spite of repeated evidence of its invalidity.

The second and related view evolves from a lack of information coupled with an intense desire to produce a conclusion or a recommendation, however poorly based. The rationale is, "If we have no information on how the Soviets operate, let's assume they do it like we do." Having made that assumption, the doors are thereby opened to all manner of unjustified interpolation and extrapolation. Such efforts have done a disservice to the United States and are to be summarily rejected.

The words which follow are arrayed in a rather simple format. First, there is an attempt to establish an objective, to describe what we would like to know about Soviet military R&D. This is followed by a review of the information at hand and an analysis of that information. The principal concern of this article is an examination of the activities of Soviet military academies and their role in military research and development.

Statement of the Problem

Ideally, of course, it is desirable to know as much as possible about Soviet military R&D activities, including the lines of research currently being pursued and the resources being devoted to those pursuits. Given the secrecy which shrouds these activities, it is unlikely that such direct information would ever become available; therefore, one is left to study the information available on peripheral aspects of Soviet military R&D and to infer as much as one reasonably can concerning the central elements of those efforts.

One looks, then, for information on organizational structure, personnel budgeting, decisionmaking processes, and the like, information which may constitute pieces of the puzzle.

Information and Analysis

There are several groups of agencies involved in research in the USSR and, given the pervasive presence of the Soviet military, one must assume that any or all of them might be involved in military R&D. They include:

Soviet Academy of Sciences
Republic Academies of Science
Regional Institutes
Universities
Research Institutes of the Ministry of Defense
Military Academies
Research Institutes of Other Ministries
Enterprise Institutes
Production Association Institutes

There is surely some redundancy in this list. Enterprise institutes are no doubt largely or perhaps totally controlled by the associated ministry despite the fact that some funding may come from nonministerial resources. The activities of the republic academies of science are greatly influenced by the national Soviet Academy of Sciences. However, by accepting the redundancy, one begins to dissect the organizations and to learn, hopefully, how each functions as part of the whole.

There is a fair amount of information available on the organizational structure and leading personnel of the Academy of Sciences, the republic academies, and a few other research organizations.[1] Kruse-Vaucienne and Logsdon[2] have described some of the broader relationships which exist among the Academy of Sciences, the republic academies, the universities, and the ministerial institutes; however, they did not discuss the military academies. In an excellent work, Hutchings[3] relates past and current trends in Soviet science to their efforts to improve design capability and review the impact of defense-related

515

concerns.

Kassel[4] has studied the relationship between the "visible" element of the Soviet scientific establishment and the defense effort. He concludes that in military R&D projects, the Soviet Academy of Sciences retains technical control under the oversight of the State Committee for Science and Technology through which military cognizance is exerted. On the other hand, Hutchings holds the view that the State Committee had oversight power only from 1961 to 1963, at which time major control of research efforts was transferred back to the Academy. In any event, open literature reveals little about the way in which military R&D is conducted, but, as Kassel concludes, when one looks at the publications produced by elements of the Academy, there is little doubt that they are involved in military R&D.

In considering the Soviet military R&D system, one wonders about the role of military academies. With new technology being developed and more sophisticated weaponry being produced for Soviet forces, there are related demands for greater expertise among military officers. How is this need being met?

In addition to advanced course work, it might be possible to achieve this educational objective through the involvement of students of the military academies in military R&D programs. Moreover, it would appear that military R&D must be conducted in response to and under the control of military officers who identify needs and establish criteria for and monitor weapons development programs. Such activity would seem to demand that the military officers involved understand R&D processes, an understanding which would be enhanced by their own past involvement in R&D programs of the Soviet military.

Let us, therefore, examine some of the appropriate literature. Odom[5] describes the already large and growing military-educational complex in the USSR and points out that in 1976 there were 16 academies and 7 institutes offering advanced degrees to officer candidates of the Soviet military. They supervise research and, with oversight, grant degrees at the candidate of sciences and doctor of sciences levels, although Hutchings[6] states many of these degrees are granted in secret. Some officer candidates attend civilian universities for specialized work and actually may be employed by those institutions.

It is important to note many members of the Soviet military work in the Soviet Academy of Sciences, although there is no indication they belong to an organized military element within the Academy.

Based on papers written by Soviet officers and published in the Soviet journal *Voyennaya mysl'* [Military Thought], most of the research activities conducted in military academies have dealt with military theory and practice, although concern has been expressed for having advanced students involved more in investigations conducted by the research institutes. In 1964, Colonel V. Choporov[7] called for more involvement by the higher military academies and institutes in scientific research. He pointed out that research conducted at the military academies at that time dealt with "current problems in military affairs in the light of recent achievements of science and technology." However, he clearly believed the military educational institutions were capable of much more—using the vastly improved capabilities of the faculties—and noted how they might contribute "if more favorable conditions were created."

Choporov may have been echoing the call by Khrushchev for greater involvement by all higher educational institutions in research work. Later studies[8] indeed indicate such involvement is occurring. Choporov discussed the need to adjust teaching loads in order to accommodate research supervision by faculty; he also described opportunities for investigation of new teaching methods utilizing movies and television. The substantial improvement in experimental facilities at higher military schools would enhance, in his view, the prospects for participation in research efforts, although modern computing facilities were lacking at that time.

Interestingly, Choporov called for more cooperative activities between military educational institutions and scientific research establishments. He described not only the appointments but also the beneficial educational influence this would have on the officers/students. He confirmed the fact the more able graduates of military schools go into the research establishments when he described the recruiting advantages which accrued to research institutes working cooperatively with military academies. "A scientific establishment would have the best opportunities to select young associates from the ranks of the capable graduates of the higher military school . . . ." Finally, Choporov cited several models, including the Novosibirsk State University and other institutions.

Progress along the lines described by Choporov was slow, however, and most military research activities at the higher military schools emphasized military science studies and investigations related to "the needs of the troops." Those needs translate into improved political training and higher motivational skills on the part of the academy graduates.

A 1966 conference[9] dealt with the emphasis placed by the Soviet Communist Party on the role of science in military development. The education of troops and staff, the use of modern concepts of command and control, and the need for higher standards in military scientific research and writings were major themes of the conference.

Colonel Kuz'min described some of the research activities of the Lenin Military Political Academy faculty leading to the evolution of improved textbooks for the troops along with books on teaching and psychology. Kuz'min reviewed the accomplishments of researchers studying the Great Patriotic War.[10]

An important paper[11] written by Colonel General Shkadov, Chief of the Main Directorate of Military Educational Institutions of the USSR Ministry of Defense, appeared in 1971. It represented a high-level response to a debate conducted on the pages of *Voyennaya mysl'*, a debate triggered by an earlier paper by Major General Yegorov dealing with graduate study, degrees, and rank. Shkadov discussed the "planning" which governs graduate study in military educational institutions and the research establishments of the Ministry of Defense. Out of this planning effort, enrollment schedules are developed which describe the number of students to be admitted each year and the disciplines into which they will be directed.

The selection of those admitted is based on (1) research aptitude, (2) academic performance, and (3) competitive entrance examinations. Following a study program, an additional set of examinations—so-called candidate examinations—are administered. These examinations are keyed to the dissertation topic selected for the student.

Student research is supervised by doctors or professors who compose a kind of graduate faculty, and it is inferred that the staff of scientific research establishments participate in this function. The student is advised of his dissertation topic following its approval by a research council two or three months after the student begins his studies—this would tend to focus the student's interest and activity at an early stage. However, Shkadov recommended that, in addition to the student's specialty area, candidate examinations include sections on "mathematics, computer technology, and related sciences." That computer technology was viewed in 1971 as a general requirement for *all* candidates is important. The students are also required to obtain some teaching experience and must take courses in education and psychology.

Shkadov states that use is made "of leading scientists to work with these students." Therefore, it indeed appears closer cooperation with research and educational institutions has come about. Moreover, military educational institutions are being required to produce specialists at the doctor of science level, no doubt to staff the Ministry of Defense research establishments and for assignment in other agencies.

It appears the number of students involved in these advanced programs has risen rapidly, imposing severe quality control problems on administrators. Dissertations should contain "significant contributions" and "new scientific and practical conclusions," and their evaluation should be done in a competent and high-principled way. The research councils which control these activities are composed of representatives of educational institutions and the research establishments; therefore, the linkages between the two agencies occur at all levels. In considering a given piece of research, the leading organization determines its usefulness; as a result, the research establishment might in some cases control the student's research activities.

Conclusions

It appears that in the mid- to late 1960s, the Soviets recognized the need to increase graduate study opportunities for those students attending higher military educational institutions. They systematically have upgraded the faculties of military academies and have enlisted the support and involvement of the scientific research establishments which are part of the Ministry of Defense. Through this program, leading researchers in the USSR take part in the intellectual development of young military officers, and those officer graduates who demonstrate a high competence for research become members of the staffs of the research agencies.

This program no doubt will have effects beyond the increase in the technical competence of those military officers involved. One can conjecture that, as the officers advance through the ranks, the Soviet defense establishment increasingly will be populated by individuals who, because of their research background, will have a better understanding of the relationship of research to weapons development. Moreover, with that perspective, they might be able to manage better the entire research/development/production system. At the very least, one would expect the hand of military research to be strengthened, with a consequent acceleration in the rate of evolution of high technology weaponry springing from *Soviet* research; that is, with decreasing dependence on Western R&D results.

Notes

1. *The World of Learning,* Vol. II, 28th ed. (Europa Publications, 1978), and *Guide to World Science, Vol. II, USSR,* 2nd ed. (Francis Hodgson, 1976).
2. V. M. Kruse–Vaucienne and John M. Lodgson, *Science and Technology in the Soviet Union* (Washington: George Washington University Press, 1979).
3. Raymond Hutchings, *Soviet Science, Technology, and Design: Interaction and Convergence* (London: Oxford University Press, 1976).
4. S. Kassel, *The Relationship Between Science and the Military in the Soviet Union,* Report R–1457–DDRE/ARPA (Santa Monica: The Rand Corporation, 1974).
5. Dale R. Herspring and Ivan Volgyes, eds., *Civil–Military Relations in Communist Systems* (Boulder: Westview Press, 1978).
6. Hutchings, op. cit.
7. Colonel V. Choporov, "Increase the Role of Higher Military Educational Institutions in Scientific Research, *Voyennaya mysl'* [Military Thought], No. 10, 1964, pp. 51–61.
8. See Hutchings, op. cit., and Kassel, op. cit.
9. Colonel M. Vasilenkov and Colonel Ya. Stepnykh, "A Chronicle of Military–Scientific Work," *Voyennaya mysl',* No. 10, 1966, pp. 75–79.
10. Colonel G. Kuz'min, "The Experience of Scientific–Research Work in Academies," *Voyennaya mysl',* No. 8, 1967, pp. 49–58.
11. Colonel General I. Shkadov, "The Important Task of Higher Educational Institutions and Scientific Research Establishments," *Voyennaya mysl',* No. 6, 1971, pp. 76–85.

Part V

The Soviet Armed Forces:
Their Organization and Training

The articles included in Part V cover a variety of subjects related to the organization and training of the Soviet Armed Forces. Regrettably, not all five of the Soviet service arms—Strategic Rocket Forces, Ground Forces, Air Forces, Navy, and Air Defense Forces—and the several branches can be discussed due to space limitations, but the articles included here give an excellent idea of the scope of the Soviet military's activities. The first three articles deal with elements of Moscow's fighting forces: the Air Forces, Security Forces, and the Soviet Navy. The last two contributions in Part V examine a trend of some concern in the West which has become known as the "militarization of Soviet society." These two articles examine how the Soviets prepare the populace for the rigors of military duty and for continued service to the Soviet state once active military service is ended.

Lynn Hansen probes the role the Soviet Air Forces—specifically, the element of the Air Forces known as front aviation—play in the Soviet concept of combined arms warfare. He explores the changes in equipment and organization that have taken place in front aviation, pointing out that these do not portend a change in doctrine but rather a concerted effort to match technology and armament to the requirements of Soviet doctrine. Finally, he projects the changes in front aviation which we should look for in the coming decade: look-down, shoot-down capabilities for interceptors and advanced precision-guided munitions for fighter-bombers.

Jim Reitz explores an aspect of Soviet combat capability that all too often receives little attention in the West—the Soviet Security Forces, the *KGB* and the *MVD*. He emphasizes that these troops are considered to be integral parts of the Soviet Armed Forces with specific combat missions in wartime. Reitz traces the organization and activities of the security troops and discusses their World War II role with a view to projecting their likely missions in a future war. He argues that these forces cannot be ignored, for they provide a body of highly trained, politically motivated soldiery that is equal in size to, if not larger than, the entire United States Army.

Roger Barnett is concerned with what he considers to be a critical question in terms of abilities to wage future conflict: the role of strategic reserves in Soviet wartime strategy; particularly, the wartime mission of the USSR's ballistic missile submarines. He examines the Soviet concept of strategic reserve forces, the meaning and importance attached to them, their composition, and what forces (i.e., Soviet SSBNs) may be earmarked for such a reserve force.

Leon Goure opens the discussion of the role of the military in Soviet society with an analysis of the USSR's paramilitary training programs. He argues that the objective of these efforts is to strengthen the defense, warfighting, and war survival capabilities of the USSR. Goure examines the organization and activities of the paramilitary training programs. He avers that the objective of these efforts is to strengthen the defense, warfighting, and war survival capabilities of the USSR. Goure examines the organization and activities of the paramilitary organizations in Soviet schools—especially those of the DOSAAF, a youth organization whose activities include military sports "games" that are in reality military exercises. While noting that these programs sometimes fall short of their standards, he concludes that they clearly benefit the Soviet Armed Forces and Soviet civil defense through the training they offer.

Gregory Lathrop also discusses military socialization but within the confines of the Armed Forces themselves; that is, how the military is used to inculcate the desired values in the young, frequently non-Russian, recruit. He explores the roles of the military collective, the military sports program, and the omnipresent political indoctrination efforts in instilling the correct political and social values in the young soldier. He also discusses in detail the value of the Soviet Armed Forces in the assimilation—or Russification—of the non-Russian nationalities. He argues that the Armed Forces' use as a "national university" is intended to augment the other traditional agencies of socialization. The result of these activities may be a decrease in military effectiveness, but the leadership obviously feels this is a price worth paying.

Front Aviation in Soviet Combined Arms Warfare

Lynn M. Hansen

The role of the Air Force in armed combat is so important that no significant operation in a future war, and military operations as a whole in their various forms and manifestations, can occur without the active involvement of aviation which is able to carry out major and diverse missions both independently and in collaboration with the other services of the armed forces.[1]

The bright blue uniform tabs, epaulets, and insignia distinguish the Soviet airman from his colleagues who serve in the infantry, artillery, armor, or other specialist arms and branches in the Soviet Armed Forces. Yet, his uniform also bears the distinctive cyrillic letters on the epaulets denoting membership in the Soviet Army (*Sovetskaya Armiya*). This is not "army" in the sense most often understood in the West but the armed services of the Soviet state. The Soviet airman finds his place in one of the five combat services (Ground Forces, Navy, Air Forces, Air Defense Forces, and Strategic Rocket Forces) as a member of the Air Forces.* The Air Forces have a separate organizational hierarchy with their own commander in chief who is also a deputy minister of defense.

The identification of the Soviet airman as part of the Soviet Army and sometimes even the Soviet Army Air Forces should not lead to the assumption that he belongs to the ground forces in a manner reminiscent of the US Army Air Forces in World War II. Rather, it is indicative of the role the Soviet Air Forces play in the overall scope of Soviet combined arms warfare.

With the imprimatur of the highest levels of political and governmental leadership, Soviet military doctrine stipulates that a future war can only be won through the combined efforts of all services and arms of the Soviet Armed Forces. This principle pervades the whole of Soviet miliary art from strategy through operational art and tactics.

In general terms, combined arms involves the participation of subunits, units, and formations of all branches of troops and special troops interacting with aviation (and naval elements in coastal sectors) to achieve specific combat objectives. The combined arms army is the

---

*Voyenno–Vozdushnyye Sily (VVS) denotes military air forces and includes *dal'nyaya aviatsiya* (Long Range Aviation), *voyenno–transportnaya aviatsiya* (Military Transport Aviation), and *frontovaya aviatsiya* (Front Aviation).

most pronounced example of this concept providing the mechanism for the interactive process (*vzaimodeystviye*) between the various branches of arms subordinate to the ground force command. While this is most evident at the operational and tactical levels, it may also extend to the strategic level where the combined arms concept prescribes the interactive process between the five combat services and other major entities of the Soviet Ministry of Defense in the achievement of military tasks.

The importance of strategic combined arms warfare is becoming increasingly important in Soviet military art as military theoreticians and strategists recognize that strategic actions in a theater of military operations must be accomplished through the combined efforts of all services. Each service therefore acts in accordance with a single strategy defined by military science but in harmony with its own operational art. As the highest level of military art, strategy is realized largely through the successful application of the principles of operational art and tactics. Thus, each service may have its own mode of strategic operations, its own operational art, and its own organizational specifics, but all services interact in combined arms warfare to fulfill strategic requirements.[2]

The wartime organization into theaters of military operations (*teatr voyennykh deystviy—TVD*) provides the framework for the strategic direction of military operations which enhances the interactive process at the strategic and operational levels not only between the five branches of service but even between different fronts.[3] This means that assets can be detached from one front and applied to another for specific purposes. More importantly, however, the Strategic Rocket Forces, Long Range Aviation, Air Defense Forces, and elements of the Navy may be directed by the TVD leadership to interact with a front to perform strategic and operational tasks.

With a doctrinal foundation predating World War II, independent air operations conducted at the outset of a war to introduce a specific campaign or to achieve strategic goals may also be considered part of the interactive process of combined arms warfare. Indeed, air operations could be conducted in concert with the employment of weapons of mass destruction* by the Strategic Rocket Forces and/or Navy. An air operation would normally include elements of both Long Range Aviation and Front Aviation but may be conducted—depending upon the strategic/operational situation—by either force without support from the other.

In its original form, Front Aviation (*voyenno–vozdushnyye sily fronta*) had 55 to 60 percent of its aircraft subordinated directly to ground force commanders at the army/operational (*armeyskaya aviatsiya*) and tactical (*voyskovaya aviatsiya*) levels. This dispersal of air power made it difficult to employ the principle of mass in the early months of the

---

*A Soviet concept which includes chemical, biological, and radiological warfare in addition to the generally accepted effects of nuclear weapons.

Great Patriotic War and was the most debilitating feature of the operational art of the Red Army Air Forces. This situation was rectified when on 5 May 1942, Stalin signed an order creating the air army (*vozdushnaya armiya*) which ultimately placed all command and control authority for front aviation in the hands of an air army commander.* The precedent was thus established for a command and control structure which continues, in its most essential aspects, through the present. The air army commander was subordinated to the front commander at the operational level of military art and served under him as a deputy for aviation.[4]

The massing of air power can occur across two or more fronts and involve more than one air army in what is essentially a strategic action. The fact that Front Aviation participates in combined arms warfare at the strategic level of Soviet military art belies the oft stated premise that front aviation assets belongs to the front commanders. The command relationships are more complicated in that the air army commander must respond to operational/tactical requirements at the front level under the direction of the front staff† and commander and to strategic requirements at the *TVD* level under the direction of the General Staff and the *TVD* commander or his deputy for aviation. This becomes somewhat simpler, if one harkens back to the basic precept that the front aviation air army is a military component employed within the parameters of Soviet combined arms doctrine at the level of military art required by the situation. The front commander operates at the operational level as a combined arms commander and the air army at that level is a member of the combined arms team.

Air Army Organization

The air army is the largest operational and organizational entity in Front Aviation. Within the USSR, each military district is said to house its own air army and an additional four such armies support the groups of Soviet forces stationed outside the Soviet Union. Using that general formula, the possible peacetime deployment of the Front Aviation air armies can be consititued as follows:

> 16th—Group of Soviet Forces, Germany (GSFG)
> 37th—Northern Group of Forces, Poland
> —Central Group of Forces, Czechoslovakia

---

*It was not until nearly 18 months later, during the North African campaign, that the Allies learned the cost of having air support dispersed among army divisions: a resultant inability to mass air power. FM 100–20 in July 1943 declared that gaining air superiority was the first requirement for successful land operations, rejecting the principle of organic control and allowing the centralization of control required to gain maximum results from air power.

†The front staff also includes General Staff officers.

—Southern Group of Forces, Hungary
30th—Baltic Military District
1st—Belorussian Military District
57th—Carpathian Military District
17th—Kiev Military District
13th—Leningrad Military District
—Moscow Military District
5/15th—Odessa Military District[5]
34th—Transcaucasus Military District
6th—Turkestan Military District

Of these, the 16th Air Army headquarted at Zossen-Wuensdorf in the German Democratic Republic is the largest and most powerful of the Front Aviation air armies and has an air order of battle estimated by some as up to 900 combat aircraft.[6]

Although most air corps were disbanded after World War II, the 16th Air Army retains a Northen Fighter Corps with headquarters at Wittstock and a Southern Fighter Corps at Wittenberg. The major combat formation is, nevertheless, the air division. In the GSFG, there are five air divisions headquartered at Puetnitz, Rechlin, Zerbst, Grossenhain, and Merseburg.[7] Independent reconnaissance regiments, auxiliary units, and assault helicopter regiments complete the list of organizational components which fly the Front Aviation mission.

In line with their combat tasks and aircraft inventories, air divisions fall in the general categories of fighter-interceptor, fighter-bomber (ground attack), and light bomber.[8] The Puetnitz, Zerbst, and Merseburg divisions generally are considered to be fighter-interceptor formations, while those at Rechlin-Laerz and Grossenhain fall into the fighter-bomber category. Each division normally consists of three regiments; each regiment (*aviatsionnyy polk*) is equipped with a single aircraft type and its corresponding trainer versions. Each regiment within a division, however, could have different types of aircraft; thus, a fighter-bomber division could have one regiment of FITTER C, one of FITTER D, and one of FLOGGER D. (The FENCER A, *MiG-21*/FISHBED, and the venerable *MiG–17*/FRESCO could theoretically be substituted for the aforementioned aircraft in any given fighter-bomber regiment). Similarly, a fighter-interceptor division could be equipped with a regiment of FISHBED K, a regiment of FISHBED L/N, and a regiment of FLOGGER B/G—or a mix of the above, including a situation where all three regiments could have the same aircraft type.[9]

The most common air army regimental organization includes three squadrons. Each squadron (*aviatsionnaya eskadril'ya*) should have about 16 aircraft plus 2 to 4 trainers. Each of the three flights (*zveno*) which make up a squadron would have four aircraft, with additional aircraft possibly allotted to the squadron chief of staff, the political officer, deputy commander, and commander. These last four aircraft could also comprise an operational reserve.[10]

An Offensive Force

Soviet military doctrine and science consider the offensive the main and decisive form of combat operations. This is a fundamental principle which predates World War II; it was enunciated very early in the history of the Red Army, and Mikhail Frunze was one of its chief advocates. With its basic goal of destroying the enemy, the offensive is the most important aspect of military endeavor—defense is merely a state in which one prepares for the subsequent offensive.[11] The Soviet Army (including the Air Forces) is, therefore, an army equipped and geared for the offensive. Front Aviation must be understood as an offensive entity whose tasks are directly related to the support of the ground force offensive.

As is often the case, Soviet military-scientific analysis of World War II has shown that air force doctrine (more properly, operational art) has been fundamentally and consistently correct. As Major General Timokhovich puts it, "the experience of the Great Patriotic War confirmed the role and purpose of aviaton in the offensive operations at the front."[12] However, the Red Air Forces did not have the technology and equipment norms with which to implement fully and successfully its own doctrine.[13] Nowhere was this more evident than in Front Aviation during the first two and a half decades following the war. Moreover, the decisions taken under Khrushchev's leadership reflected an interlude characterized by an ill-placed reliance on strategic missile systems and an accompanying debilitating effect on the development and procurement of the aircraft technology required to execute doctrinal principles. Thus, Front Aviation in the 1950s and 1960s appeared to take on a defensive posture. That which is sometimes called the change in Soviet Air Forces doctrine in the mid–1960s—manifested in the offensive capabilities of third generation Soviet aircraft—was not a doctrinal change but a stage of development in operational art characterized by the matching of aircraft technology to doctrinal requirements. Between 1967 and 1977, for example, Soviet spending for the Air Forces increased much more rapidly than it did for any other military service and grew at over three times the rate of increase for defense spending as a whole from 1969 to 1973.[14] The Brezhnev regime's contribution to air power can therefore be couched in terms of a reorientation which has stressed the role of aviation in combined arms warfare with special emphasis on its contribution to the offensive.

Air Supremacy

Thorough analysis of military operations in the Great Patriotic War has convinced the theoreticians of Soviet military science that air supremacy (*gospodstvo v vozdukhe*) constitutes an essential condition for victory in any future conflict. If the battle for air supremacy is won by the attacker, it is claimed, then ground force operations—supported by air strikes—can develop successfully at the high speeds demanded by operational norms. If, however, air supremacy is not attained, the ground offensive will develop more slowly and be more complicated. The defense will have time to organize counteraction both in the air and on the ground, thus frustrating the achievement of offensive tasks. Hence, not a single offensive operation can end successfully without air supremacy.[15]

Even during the war, Soviet military art maintained that air supremacy was a combined arms responsibility. It was not a goal in itself but one of the most important conditions for final victory. It could only be gained by the united efforts of all branches and services of the armed forces. In actual fact, however, nearly all of the air supremacy requirements fell to the Air Forces. It is anticipated that the Air Forces will bear the major responsibility in a future conflict. Nevertheless, postwar developments in technology and armaments have since provided all services with the means to contribute to the achievements of air supremacy, and the extension of combined arms activity into the atmosphere is more than ever a reality. The overall direction of the campaign for air supremacy often will be exercised by the national strategic leadership; it will determine the degree of participation of each of the services and branches of the armed forces.

Consistent with the tenets of Soviet military science, air force operational art differentiates among strategic, operational, and tactical air supremacy. The fundamental concept which operates at all three levels is that hostile aircraft may be destroyed either on the ground (or on aircraft carriers) or in aerial combat.

Tactical Air Supremacy

At the tactical level, the organization of the interaction involved in the winning of air supremacy takes place at front and army level within an air defense entity comprised of both aviation and ground force air defense personnel (*PVO voysk*). Insofar as possible, an overall aerial battle plan is developed in advance and briefed to subordinate units. This plan may be reasonably well defined, or it may merely contain the major commander's combat concept. Subordinate commanders must comply with the latter while invoking the Soviet concept of initiative in conformity with the combat situation.[16] Fighter aircraft and ground antiaircraft systems are to work together closely. Their operations will be defined by zones, altitudes, and times of operations. Fighters normally operate at extended ranges within the limits of their operational radii along the main approaches used by enemy aircraft. Zones for surface-to-air missile (SAM) and antiaircraft artillery (AAA) systems are usually determined on the basis of the targets being defended, with due recognition given to range and altitudes of effective fire.[17]

The implementation and realization of the interactive process relative to the battle for air supremacy at the operational/tactical level has become a relatively complicated and sophisticated operation. The difficulty, in particular, of combating aircraft which approach at extremely low altitudes has led to further refinements in the methods for controlling the interaction between air defense forces and aviation. In addition to the warning provided by radar systems, information from specially designated air observers located at command posts and in all subunits is fed into the air defense network computers, to determine how much time is required to intercept the attackers with a particular type of weapon.[18] On the basis of the air defense operator's analysis of the situation, the commander chooses surface-to-air missiles, conventional AAA, or fighters. In the latter case, pertinent information is passed to aviation command posts; the latter use electronic data processing to determine aircraft target assignments as well as scramble and recovery airfields.[19]

Operational Air Supremacy

At the operational level (i.e., a front) aerial combat (*vozdushnyy boy*) assumes primary significance in the battle for air supremacy. Because of the increased aircraft survivability provided by hardened aircraft shelters and the difficulty in launching surprise massed attacks by aircraft against airfields, the importance of destroying aircraft in aerial engagements and battles (*vozdushnaya bitva*) is increasing in Soviet Air Forces operational art. It is anticipated that air battles will be fought both in the course of repelling hostile strikes and in launching offensive actions. In Soviet theory, the air battle is an aggregate of air engagements unified by a common operational concept and conducted simultaneously or sequentially by main groupings of aviation with the objective of destroying enemy aircraft in the air.

Battles for operational air supremacy are usually conducted in the interests of individual strategic or front operations. As part of the interactive process, operational air supremacy activities are undertaken, first of all, in the interests of the ground forces. This means that the battle for operational air supremacy will intensify as it synchronizes with the execution by the ground forces of their most important operational tasks. During the penetration of the defense by ground forces, the aerial battle is expected to become even more significant. The assumption of the main thrust of the attack by tank armies, assault crossings of water obstacles, and the retention of bridgeheads are other situations in which operational air supremacy operations will increase.[20]

The direct organizer of the operational air supremacy battle is the air army commander and his staff. In accordance with the front combined arms commander's operational concept, the air army commander will maneuver and mass his aircraft on the main axes of attack and ensure the availability of aircraft to support tactical as well as operational requirements.

Strategic Air Supremacy

The ultimate goal, of course, is neither tactical nor operational but overall superiority within the *TVD*: strategic air supremacy. The logic of Soviet military theory indicates that this can be the sum total of tactical and operational successes. (The relationship between operational and strategic air supremacy is particularly close.) Nevertheless, there are explicit strategic operations which aim at the achievement of air superiority at the strategic level. These may well be waged through the joint efforts of all the services but may also be restricted to aviation. In both cases, the overall campaign for air supremacy at the strategic level is planned and organized by the strategic leadership* at the national or *TVD* level and executed by the General Staff and/or Headquarters, Soviet Air Forces.[21]

The Navy's involvement in the battle for strategic air supremacy will center on the destruction of carrier-based aircraft through aerial battle, air-to-surface attacks, surface-to-surface actions, and submarine warfare—each with the express objective of destroying hostile naval aircraft and operating facilities within a specific maritime theater of military operations. Nevertheless, elements of Soviet Naval Aviation (*Aviatsiya Voyenno–Morskogo Flota*) may be placed temporarily under the strategic leadership of the *TVD* air commander and operationally subordinated to the air army commander in pursuit of strategic objectives. Amphibious landing operations involving coordinated interaction between naval forces and ground troops in order to secure aviation facilities or eliminate air defense on coastal axes may also become part of a combined effort to achieve strategic/operational air supremacy on a broad front.

The Strategic Rocket Forces also may contribute to the achievement of air supremacy by using intermediate and medium range ballistic missiles[22] to destroy aircraft and facilities on the ground. The likelihood of the Strategic Rocket Forces participating in the combined services combined arms struggle for air supremacy will depend upon a number of factors related to the level of conflict, particularly whether it is nuclear or nonnuclear. Nevertheless, the importance of air supremacy in modern warfare is so important to Soviet military art that conditions could require the utilization of the most expedient forms and modes for gaining and holding superiority in the air. This stems from a basic premise in combined arms doctrine which emphasizes that the

---

*In World War II, the *Stavka* (Headquarters, Supreme High Command).

distribution of weapons among the various services and branches of the armed forces exerts a direct influence on the correlation of forces (*sootnosheniye sil*). This being so, it follows that the correlation of forces after an attack (in this case, air forces) will be more advantageous to the Soviets if they use those forces which possess the greater probability of overcoming defenses.[23] In addition to nuclear weapons, such expedient forces could include attacks on airfields by chemical weapons delivered by the Strategic Rocket Forces as well as by aircraft.

Independent Air Operations

The most massive action by the Soviet Armed Forces in pursuit of air supremacy will be the independent air operation. Although it has often been suggested that nonnuclear hostilities in Europe more or less would commence automatically with *the air operation,*[24] it must be remembered that this is but one option in the Soviet game plan. Moreover, a war of any duration at all probably would include several air operations designed to assist in the task of gaining strategic air supremacy. Nevertheless, Soviet respect for Western air forces and the doctrinal requirement for air supremacy certainly would suggest that an intensive air operation at the outset of a full-scale nonnuclear conflict is a preferred Soviet option.

Senior Soviet Ground Forces commanders generally did not consider the independent air operations conducted by the Red Army Air Forces during World War II* to be too effective because of the lack of sufficient poststrike reconnaissance. Postwar analysis has convinced the Soviets that their original operational art was correct. In recent years, particularly since the mid–1960s, the concept of independent air operations has been strengthened; today, it is an integral part of Soviet military art and strategy. Consequently, the air operation does not represent a major change in the operational doctrine of the Soviet Air Forces. Rather, aircraft technology and the dedicated efforts of the Kremlin's defense planners have made the implementation of longstanding operational art a contemporary reality through the matching of armament norms to doctrinal requirements. Thus, the intensity and seriousness of a future conflict will be matched by the intensity of the air war, particularly in its early stages.

An independent air operation consists of a number of offensive actions planned and executed by the Soviet Air Forces staff and the General Staff on behalf of the Supreme High Command in the pursuit

---

*In late October or early November 1941, for, example, the *Stavka* ordered the Air Forces commander to conduct an air operation lasting from 5 to 8 November to destroy German aircraft at their airfields. Three hundred Russian aircraft were to make simultaneous strikes on 19 airfields. The operation was planned by the Air Forces staff with orders written by the Air Force Headquarters and signed by the General Staff.[25]

of operational or strategic goals in specific *TVDs* or maritime theaters of military operations.[26]Such operations cover the entire theater where hostile aircraft are based and are usually timed to coincide with the initiation of offensive operations. The basic aim is the destruction of enemy air power along a particular strategic axis or within an entire *TVD*.[27] Surprise, deception, camouflage, and secrecy are to be fully implemented as part of the operation.

Any surprise attack scenario therefore should include an initial independent air operation at the outset of hostilities. Nevertheless, independent air operations of various sizes and scope will be organized periodically throughout any extended war. Soviet military science explicitly categorizes the types of targets which must be attacked at the outset of a conflict or a major campaign. The top three priorities inevitably include the nuclear delivery means, airfields, and command and control systems. In 1977, Lieutenant General Gareyev, Chief of the Military Science Directorate of the Soviet General Staff, stated that the most important missions for the air forces were the destruction of fixed targets—such as enemy nuclear missiles on their launch pads and nuclear weapons aircraft at airfields—and mobile targets—such as airborne aircraft, battlefield missile forces, aircraft carriers, and guided missile warships at sea. Thus, an independent air operation—in addition to its role in gaining air supremacy—will have as its mission the destruction of operational-tactical and tactical nuclear weapons. The latter includes the so-called forward based systems and those aircraft assigned a nuclear delivery mission. Thus, the Soviet emphasis on attacks on airfields grows out of both nuclear and nonnuclear considerations.[28]

A massive air operation in support of the air supremacy requirement probably will include medium bombers assigned to Long Range Aviation and Naval Aviation working in close coordination with Front Aviation aircraft belonging to several air armies. If the experience of World War II is relevant to the current situation—and there are no demonstrated reasons to assume otherwise—fighter aviation (*istrebitel'naya aviatsiya*) belonging to the Air Defense Forces could also participate.

Such an air operation probably will be conducted around the clock and could last up to six days, although three days appears more likely.[29] Nevertheless, the greatest effectiveness is expected during the first massed strike. According to Soviet Air Force Commander in Chief Marshal of Aviation Kutakhov, the fundamental task of the operation is the neutralization of the main force of enemy aviation during the first day of hostilities.[30] This is in line with the Soviet experience in conducting air operations during the Great Patriotic War. Postwar analysis has shown that over 40 percent of the total enemy aircraft losses during air operations occurred during the first massed attack, 30 percent during the second, and 20 percent during the third.[31]

Although the air operation's major contribution to the air supremacy mission is the destruction of aircraft and means of nuclear attack, air-strikes would also be conducted against command and control centers, runways, fuel, ammunition, and other logistical depots. Additional targets include reserves (especially tank reserves), radar, communications, and radio-technical means.[32]

The operational art of the Soviet Air Force includes the principle that the neutralization of the enemy's air defense forces is a prerequisite for successful air operations. It follows that the destruction of ground air defense weapons would also be a major priority in the conduct of the independent air operation introducing a major offensive. Many of the early sorties flown by Front Aviation fighter-bombers are, therefore, most likely to be dedicated to that task.* FITTER C and D, FLOGGER D, and FENCER A aircraft equipped with precision guided munitions appear to be the most likely candidates for this mission.[33]

The importance of suppressing the various defensive systems is illustrated in the composition of a typical World War II aerial strike force: only 35 to 40 percent of the aircraft were bombers and attack aircraft with the mission of striking the primary target. Nearly two-thirds of the attacking force consisted of fighters, 30 to 38 percent of which flew cover while the remainder blocked and engaged those defensive fighters from other bases which might attempt to intercept the primary strike force.[34] The percentages would change in a future conflict, but the principle of neutralizing the air defense systems would remain in force.

Penetration of the air defense system would be planned closely and controlled tightly to ensure coordination among all the forces and weapons involved.† This places additional emphasis on the firmness, continuity, and security of the command and control system which will direct the activities of various aviation assets and other units/subunits in performing the penetration mission according to a specific timetable with minimum losses. The attacking forces will have modeled every predictable aspect of the penetration in advance. As pointed out by the commander of the 16th Air Army, Lieutenant General V. Korochkin, air force operational art has adopted the premise that modern combat is highly dynamic; therefore, under conditions of limited time, there will be no opportunity to make new calculations or design new approaches to the target once the pilots are airborne.[35]

---

*Dual capable fighter-interceptors such as FLOGGER B and G, FISHBED K, L, N and future variants of these airframes could also participate in anti–SAM activity, although their more likely mission would be counterair.

†Combined arms doctrine provides for the possibility of other services participating in the neutralization of air defenses. Heliborne raids by special subunits such as the *brigada osobogo nazhacheniya* [special purpose brigade] against specific systems are but one example of the actions which might complement the air operation.

The attacking forces also will attempt to achieve surprise by using various camouflage techniques, deception, disinformation, and general military cunning. Such activities will also include the widespread employment of electronic countermeasures (ECM). ECM will have to be coordinated among the attacking groups and their combat support during all phases of the mission.

Substantial numbers of fighter forces will accompany and support the attacking aircraft. In addition to close escort fighters intended to cut off enemy fighters, some air armies may form special maneuver groups whose mission will be to engage those enemy aircraft which have had sufficient time to take off and proceed to intercept position. Other fighters, perhaps even including those of the *PVO*, will be held in reserve to repel enemy air attacks on friendly airfields and facilities.

The increased range and effectiveness of the fighter-bombers and fighter-interceptors assigned to Front Aviation enables them not only to support penetration by aircraft belonging to Long Range Aviation but also to participate in attacks on enemy airfields in the full depth of the attack zone. (It should also be noted that Front Aviation aircraft are capable of delivering nuclear weapons.)[36] Such a mission is confirmed by the presence in East Germany of a complete replica of the USAF base at Bitburg, Federal Republic of Germany. 16th Air Army ground attack missions are regularly flown against this replica.[37]

A subcategory of conventional air operations probably includes the use of small groups performing nearly autonomously and tasked with sealing off airfields deep in the enemy's rear. This mode of attack will be particularly important in preventing the dispersal of aircraft to secondary or auxiliary airfields not under direct attack.

Despite the technological advances evident in the third generation aircraft currently in the Soviet inventory, it is common wisdom that they cannot match on a one-for-one basis the technical capabilities of such Western aircraft as the F–15. Thus, a prime prerequisite is numerical superiority in air-to-air fighters. This doctrinal tenet is more than a means to compensate for technological inferiority, however; it is derived from the Soviet historical experience. Even during the initial period of World War II when the Russians were being severely beaten, the Red Air Forces were able to mass their assets to achieve a quantitative superiority of three to one in fighters in order to drive off the attackers. Although the ratio varied slightly during subsequent major operations, no major offensive or counteroffensive operations were initiated by the Russians until they were assured of meeting the doctrinal requirement for superiority in numbers.[38]

Testimony to the importance of numerical superiority can be found in Soviet aircraft production figures. Currently, the USSR's aircraft industry outproduces the United States in fighter aircraft by a factor of about two. This amounts to approximately 1,000 new fighters and fighter-bombers (not counting helicopters) each year. A typical two–year production rate would equal all the US tactical fighters in Europe, all the fighter replacements (including the Air National Guard and Air Reserve), plus the remainder of the NATO Central Region fighter inventory.[39] Put another way, Soviet military aircraft production is sufficient to replace the entire front-line aircraft force of the Royal Air Force once every six months.[40]

Direct Support of the Ground Forces: Cover

While Soviet military science stresses that air supremacy is to be obtained in the interests of the Soviet Ground Forces, there are also four aspects of Soviet Air Forces operational art which relate to the direct support of ground operations: (1) cover, (2) air accompaniment, (3) [close] air support, and (4) reconnaissance.

The task of providing cover for ground force operations finds its most usual expression in the requirements for local or tactical air supremacy. In recent times, this has undergone a spatial expansion resulting from the application of modern antiair technology to the battlefield. *PVO voysk** units and subunits are now equipped with highly mobile SAM and gun systems[†] which are intended to keep defensive NATO air attackers off the backs of advancing ground forces. While the cover mission at river crossing and other specialized operations remains essentially as before, the addition of the *PVO voysk* antiaircraft system allows covering fighter-interceptors to extend the periphery of the defended area around the ground forces. Hence, current Soviet Air Forces training includes the interception of NATO aircraft before they can reach the likely surface-to-air missile launching zone.[41]

The extension of the area covered by Soviet fighters may occur under the preferred operational mode of strictly centralized control of aerial encounters by ground intercept controllers. Front Aviation pilots, however, may also function in an independent mode: identify targets, choose the closing direction, and make their own choices of weapon and firing sequence.[‡] In such conditions, each two-plane element and even each aircraft may maneuver independently and utilize

---

Protivovozhdushnaya oborona sukhoputnykh voysk (Air Defense of the Ground Forces).

[†]Major systems include the SA–4/GANEF, SA–6/GAINFUL, and SA–8/GECKO. The first two have a tracked vehicle outfitted with tracking and guidance radar and other tracked vehicles serving as transporter-erector-launchers (TELs). The SA–8 is a wheeled system capable of moving at higher road speeds with vehicle columns. Because each vehicle has its own missile *and* radar, it also represents a decrease in launcher readying time. Other systems include the handheld, infrared-guided SA–7/GRAIL, the SA–9/GASKIN, and the ZSU–23–4 which can fire its 23–mm antiaircraft cannons while on the move.

[‡]The idea that Soviet pilots may exercise initiative and independence in aerial combat is not univerally accepted. Nevertheless, Soviet tactical writings emphasize the require-

different combat methods.[42]

When flying this type of cover mission, flights and elements may be assigned particular sectors and required to fly certain search patterns to observe low flying, camouflaged targets against a wooded terrain background. A key objective is the attainment of surprise: to find and hit the attacker before he can take counteraction. Thus, radio silence and radio discipline are closely practiced.[43] This mode of operation, with or without radar control, is essentially a defensive fighter patrol basic to providing cover to the first echelon units of a front during heavy ground fighting. It extends the area of cover and leaves the air defense mission in the immediate proximity of forces in contact to the *PVO* SAM systems.

Closely allied to the defensive fighter patrol is the "free hunt" (*svobodnaya okhota*) which allocates certain hunting areas to fighter aircraft operating in combat pairs. They search out targets visually or with the aid of onboard avionics. This type of operation usually will involve only the most experienced and capable pilots because it represents, in Soviet eyes, the ultimate in independent combat operations.[44]

Autonomous or semiautonomous defensive cover operations by Soviet fighters generally have been hampered by the inability of airborne radars to acquire and attack hostile aircraft flying a low-altitude, high-speed ingress route. However, the Soviets now have completed testing of a look-down, shoot-down system for the *MiG–23/* FLOGGER and *MiG–25/*FOXBAT fighters. Deployment is expected in the early 1980s. When this technology is deployed and employed in the tactical arena, it will have serious implications for NATO's ability to maintain air superiority. It becomes even more threatening because of the capability simultaneously to track and fire at multiple targets.[45]

Recent Soviet exercises, such as *Neman,* indicate that air activity may be 3–tiered in some situations such as river crossings. Assault helicopters would operate at the lower tier, ground-attack aircraft in the middle, and fighters flying cover in the upper tier.[46] The tiered approach can also be found in those situations where ground-based *PVO* systems must cooperate with fighter-interceptors in providing cover. In such instances, the systems are assigned priorities according to zones, times, and altitudes in a scheme which is thought to be most compatible with operational contingencies.[47]

---

ment for pilots to be able to fly and fight in an independent mode. Soviet experience in World War II and that of their client in Southeast Asia have shown that over 75 percent of the aircraft they shot down were hit on the first controlled pass from aft angles of approach. When given the choice, this would obviously be their preferred tactic. However, despite the Soviet penchant for controlled combat, it is the author's conviction there is an ongoing evolution in Soviet fighter tactics which requires careful monitoring and analysis, particularly with regard to the USAF Red Flag and similar programs.

Depending upon the circumstances, interceptors may also fight within the surface-to-air missile belt and continue to harry attacking aircraft all the way to their targets. The Egyptians, for example, agreed that their aircraft losses from friendly missiles in the 1973 war were relatively so small that the tactics of using both interceptors and missiles in the same airspace was operationally sound and effective against enemy formations.

Regardless of the specific conditions under which the cover mission is flown, the underlying objective is to deny the enemy air force the possibility of interfering with the offensive actions of the ground forces. Thus, while it involves and is part of the struggle for air supremacy, the cover mission may be successful if it interferes with or disrupts the attacking aircraft and stops them from hitting their targets.

Reconnaissance

It is difficult to overstate the importance which Soviet military science attaches to reconnaissance. In some major World War II campaigns, for example, 25 to 30 percent of all aerial sorties were for reconnaissance purposes.[48]

Strategic reconnaissance is generally the province of Long Range Aviation and, one suspects, satellite systems. It is organized and directed by the Soviet General Staff and, where aircraft systems are employed, by Soviet Air Force Headquarters.[49] Despite the national level character of strategic reconnaissance, its results are usually available to the front commander and staff as well as to the front's air army commander.

Operational reconnaissance is conducted in the interests of the front command element and the air army. Its targets are to be the enemy's operational reserves, the rear logistical system, and airfields.[50] Although one cannot say so with precision, the MiG–25R appears to be the ideal platform for performing the operational reconnaissance mission at the frontal level. The FOXBAT B is equipped with five cameras in the nose section. This camera system is said to provide a 70 kilometer wide sector coverage.[51] In the FOXBAT D, the cameras have been replaced by a large side-looking airborne radar (SLAR) which probably enhances reconnaissance capabilty under adverse light and weather conditions.[52]

Approximately 70 percent of the reconnaissance missions flown by Front Aviation during World War II were tactical. The remainder were operational.[53] The enemy's defensive arrangements, command posts, artillery, force groupings, and immediate reserves were generally targets for tactical reconnaissance sorties. The same importance would probably be given to tactical reconnaissance in a future conflict. However, in World War II, regular combat units flew approximately 80 percent of all reconnaissance sorties; specialized reconnaissance units and subunits accounted for only 20 percent.[54] Advances in reconnaissance technology indicate this mission would be performed by specialized platforms in any future conflict. At the tactical level, the FOXBAT is complemented by the *MiG–21/FISHBED H*—which can carry a pod with cameras or other sensors—the *Yak–28/BREWER D*, and possibly the older *Yak–27/MANGROVE*—both with special camera mountings. Virtually all helicopters also have a reconnaissance capability, especially the smaller *Mi–2/HOPLITE* which has a special role as an artillery spotter.[55]

Command and Control

The success of combined arms warfare under contemporary conditions largely depends upon the efficiency of the command and control system. This is especially true as it pertains to the interaction between aviation and ground troops. Firmness, continuity, flexibility, and security of the command and control mechanism are prerequisites for success. To ensure these characteristics, the commander of the supporting air force unit or subunit (or his personal representative) personally interacts with ground force staffs and bears the major responsibility for the organization of cooperative methods and procedures (*vzaimodeystviya*).[56]

The mission assignments for aviation usually come from the front or army level with the air force staff and field headquarters responsible for planning the parameters and details of the supporting tactical air operation. Air army operations groups are present in auxiliary command posts (*vspomogatel'nyye punkty upravleniya—VPU*) with ground staffs in major sectors.[57] Such an operations group usually consists of eight to ten air force officers representing operations, intelligence, cryptography, communications, and meteorology.[58] Its tasks include (1) control of air force assets over the battlefield during interaction with the ground forces, (2) guidance and redirection of aircraft to priority targets, (3) direct air force influence over the outcome of the battle by determining the most decisive use of air, (4) ascertainment of new enemy tactics and development of countertactics, and (5) close coordination between the air force commander and the ground forces in whose interest aviation is being employed.[59]

Within this system, the air liaison officer (*aviapredstavitel'*) plays a critical role as the bridge between the ground support requirements and the air forces command and control network.[60] Second only to the air liaison officer in the control function are the forward air controllers (*aviavodchiki*) who are physically present with ground force elements. These are usually rated officers from the supporting air unit. They direct aircraft to targets on the battlefield and report changes in the battle situation to the air liaison officer.[61] In the interests of personal safety, the forward air controller probably will follow the World War II practice of wearing a ground force uniform without proper rank insignia. His equipment will be mounted on a mobile vehicle such as an armored personnel carrier in order to keep pace with the rapid combat tempo envisioned in Soviet military art.[62]

Air warning, guidance, and communications posts (*vozdushnoye nablyudeniye, opoveshcheniye i svyaz'—VNOS*) are established within a few kilometers of the forward edge of the battle area (FEBA) in order to facilitate the task of guiding ground attack aircraft or assault helicopters to their targets. Headed by a pilot from a unit operating in the sector, the *VNOS* post provides a link in the command and control communications systems and also serves as a navigational beacon to vector attacking aircraft and orient pilots toward their targets (see Figure 1).[63]

Air Accompaniment

The operational art of the Soviet Air Forces does not emphasize aerial interdiction per se but rather stresses air accompaniment as part of the interactive process so prevalent in Soviet combined arms doctrine. Interdiction, in US Air Force parlance, consists of air operations against the enemy's military potential at such a distance from friendly forces that the detailed integration of the air mission with the fire and movement of friendly forces is not required. Air accompaniment, on the other hand, is neither interdiction nor close air support but the utilization of aviation in the offensive to complement other means of fire. As indicated by the chief of the Frunze Academy, General A. Radziyevskiy, aviation assets are massed in a decisive number on the axes of the main attack throughout the entire operational depth.[64]

Although the basic concept of operations in depth (*glubokaya operatsiya*) has existed since the early days of the Red Army, it will be particularly significant in future warfare. Advances in modern military technology—particularly airframes and avionics—have enabled the Soviets to extend the parameters of the in-depth operation to strike deeper in enemy defenses. In essence, the "operations in depth" concept calls for three basic elements: (1) a breakthrough of the enemy's tactical defensive zone, thereby creating a breach in the entire defense system through the combined use of infantry, armor, artillery, and aviation; (2) the exploitation of the breakthrough by introducing mobile groups (including tactical airborne/heliborne landings) into and through the breach to transform tactical success into operational success; and (3) the development of operational success through operational pursuit until total defeat of the enemy grouping is achieved, thus providing a favorable position from which to initiate a new operation.[65]

The employment of air forces assets in operations in depth may resemble an independent air operation because the aircraft are maneuvered to provide massed airstrikes. These strikes are not strategic but tactical-operational and are performed in direct support of ground

Command and Control
of the Air Operation

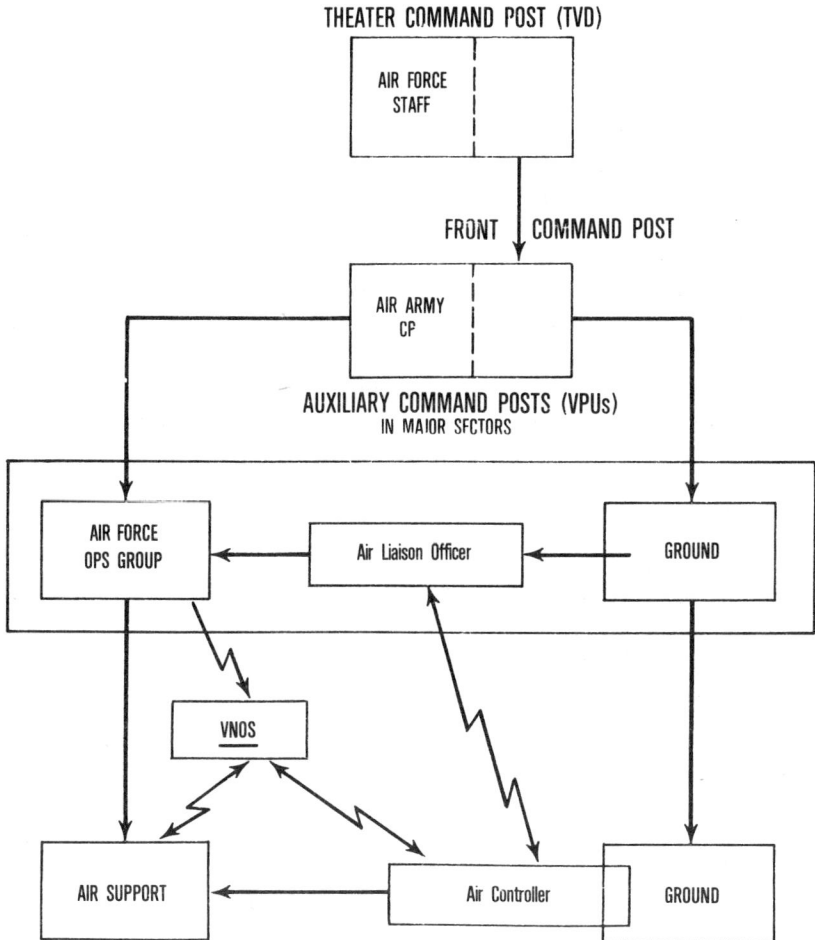

THEATER COMMAND POST (TVD)

```
┌──────────────┬────────┐
│  AIR FORCE   │        │
│    STAFF     │        │
│              │        │
└──────────────┴────────┘
```

FRONT │ COMMAND POST

```
┌──────────────┬────────┐
│   AIR ARMY   │        │
│     CP       │        │
└──────────────┴────────┘
```

AUXILIARY COMMAND POSTS (VPUs)
IN MAJOR SECTORS

```
┌──────────────────────────────────────────────────────┐
│  ┌──────────┐   ┌────────────────┐   ┌──────────┐     │
│  │ AIR FORCE│◄──│Air Liaison Officer│◄──│  GROUND  │   │
│  │ OPS GROUP│   └────────────────┘   └──────────┘     │
│  └──────────┘                                          │
└──────────────────────────────────────────────────────┘
```

VNOS

```
┌──────────┐   ┌────────────────┐   ┌──────────┐
│AIR SUPPORT│◄──│ Air Controller │   │  GROUND  │
└──────────┘   └────────────────┘   └──────────┘
```

Constructed according to information contained in
Colonel Ye. V. Koyander, Ya - Rubin, Prikazyvayu
(Moscow: Voyenizdat, 1978).

Figure 1

forces in their most important sectors. Because they are tactical-
operational, the front commander bears overall responsbility for the
operation; his deputy for aviation (the air army commander) is responsible for the actual conduct of aviation operations. Under the
latter's direction, the air army staff defines and resolves the problems of
cooperative interaction (*vzaimodeystviye*) with the commanders and
staffs of the ground force armies.

539

For normal fixed-wing tactical air strikes, the air army commander has a balanced variety of aircraft types at his disposal. The ground attack FLOGGER D and FITTER C and D would probably fly the bulk of the air accompaniment missions in support of breakthrough operations (complementing HIND and HIP assault helicopters). The highly optimized FENCER A would be available for deeper penetration missions to the full depth of the tactical zone. However, the counter-air FLOGGER and FISHBED fighters could also support the ground attack accompaniment mission by trading their air-to-air missiles for rocket pods and small bombs. In addition to the flexibility afforded by these fixed-wing aircraft, the combined arms commander can call upon assault helicopters to attack in wave formation approaching the target from below tree top level, climbing to firing altitude, delivering ordnance, then dropping back to low altitude to egress while four more helicopters appear.[66]

The stress on mobility, maneuverability, and mass in Soviet military art significantly enhances the role of the air forces in combined arms doctrine for a fast moving conflict in Central Europe. As Marshal Kutakhov has stated, aviation not only can switch attacks from one axis to another, it also can be shifted between various theaters of military operations.[67] At the direction of the strategic leadership, reserve formations can be flown from military districts in the USSR to areas near the battlefield in order to achieve the mass desired at any given point or axis of operations.

Maneuver can be accomplished by the deployment of aviation formations from the strategic reserve or from tactical operating bases to fields nearer the target sector or simply by exploiting the increased operational radii of contemporary third generation aircraft.* Moreover, FISHBED, FLOGGER, and FITTER aircraft can operate from auxiliary airfield and even sod strips.[68] In addition, there are specially prepared landing strips on most major freeways (*Autobahnen*) in East Germany and Poland which can serve as dispersal bases and could be used for recovery if main operating bases were knocked out of action.[69]

The air accompaniment mission may be divided into two phases: the preparatory attack and strikes flown in support of advancing infantry and armor after the actual operation has commenced. For the most part, air strikes during the preparatory attack will be coordinated closely with artillery barrages in order to extend laterally or vertically the range of fire. Principle targets are enemy artillery, operational reserves, and antitank weapons. Coordination is the responsibility of the air army staff working closely with the front artillery staff and ground force commanders. If artillery and air operate at the same time, aviation will strike targets farthest from the artillery batteries; the

---

*Such aircraft represent a twofold and threefold increase in operational range and up to four times the payload of such predecessors as the *MiG*–17/FRESCO and the *Su*–7/FITTER A.

latter will be directed against the closer targets.[70] If they operate at different times, both may be directed at the same objectives to increase fire saturation of the target area. Under some conditions, there may even be overlapping coverage which, as one may imagine, requires greater coordination. In any case, the time, place, and targets of each air strike must be planned in connection with the operations of the supporting artillery.

As the operation in depth proceeds, air accompaniment evolves from the preparatory attack to a range of air-to-ground missions. These may take the form of preplanned missions, strikes in response to a combined arms commander's requirements, or "free hunt" search and destroy missions.

In the second of these options, air forces units may be placed under the direct operational control of a ground army commander who establishes targets, objectives, and times of operations. This would be particularly true when the supported unit is active in the operational depth of the enemy defense. Under these circumstances, the air forces command would decide the tactics, weaponry, and size of the air component required to carry out the mission.[71]

In some instances, fighter-interceptors such as FISHBED and FLOGGER B and G flying cover for advancing ground units may be diverted from their counterair mission to attack ground targets with their onboard cannon.[72] As a general rule, however, tactical operations would be conducted by a strike group, approximately one-third of which would be counterair fighters flying cover for ground attack aircraft.[73]

"Free hunt" tactics would also be employed against mobile targets. This could involve a flight of two elements—each composed of two aircraft—with one element providing cover for the other, or it could consist of a single two-aircraft sortie.[74] The "free hunt" mission is akin to armed reconnaissance because the objective is to search out and destroy targets which threaten the ongoing offensive action. Chief among those targets would be nuclear delivery systems. Therefore, the importance of the "free hunt" mode could increase in the coming years in light of the 1979 NATO decision to modernize its tactical nuclear weapons delivery capabilities by deploying Pershing II and the ground-launched cruise missile (GLCM).

Close Air Support

In US terms, close air support consists of air attacks against hostile targets in close proximity to friendly forces. These air operations require detailed integration of each aerial mission with the fire and maneuver of the friendly forces.

Traditionally, Soviet ground forces have relied on tanks, artillery, and other means of direct fire to provide close support to troops in contact. Air support (*aviatsionnaya podderzhka*) has been a broader concept defined generally as combat operations conducted for the purpose of assisting ground forces to achieve their combat objectives. While this definition allowed the inclusion of close air support, it more properly meant the wide-ranging forms of air attack with less emphasis on providing direct support to ground commanders in close contact with the enemy. Nevertheless, the Soviet Air Forces do have a rich historical tradition of providing close support to ground operations. The *Il–2 Shturmovik* of World War II fame probably flew more missions in support of ground armies than any other single aircraft type. However, as the Soviet Air Forces made the transition to the jet age, there was no aircraft which unquestionably could fall heir to the *Shturmovik's* role and tradition.

The venerable *MiG–15* and its successor the *MiG–17/FRESCO* have won universal acclaim for their maneuverability and longevity. But neither possesses the ordnance carrying capability or range necessary to be a true ground attack aircraft. The *Su–7/FITTER A*, the *Il–28/BEAGLE*, and the *Yak–28/BREWER* were all designed to deliver ordnance in support of ground operations. None was an unqualified success. The technological advances evident in such third generation aircraft as the FITTER C, FITTER D, FLOGGER D, and FENCER A certainly improve the deep strike and interdiction capabilities of the Soviet Air Forces but appear less suited to the close air support mission.

The most likely heir to the legacy and, in some respects, the close air support role of the famous *Shturmovik* is the *Mi–24/HIND* helicopter. Although considerably slower than the *Il–2*, it is capable of carrying a greater assortment and load of armaments and can be more responsive to a ground force commander's support requirements than fixed-wing aircraft operating from fixed bases. As a Soviet writer has indicated, the time from request to actual airstrike diminishes substantially if available army aviation includes helicopter gunships capable of offering air support, even if limited in scope and depth. This meets the demands of ground force unit commanders to the greatest degree.[75] In fact, the requirement for an aviation force which can respond quickly to support requests when coupled with various references to army aviation (*armeyskaya aviatsiya*) lends credence to the theory that assault helicopter regiments—consisting of both *Mi–24/HIND* and *Mi–8/HIP E* helicopters—may be subordinated directly to individual army commanders for tactical purposes.[76]

As part of a combined arms commander's operational and tactical reserves, assault helicopters could utilize their superior maneuver capability to augment existing artillery or to compensate for its shortage. This would be particularly useful in a fast moving battle where towed artillery, in particular, would be disadvantaged. River crossings and the expansion of bridgeheads are other examples of situations where the attack helicopter would function at a great advantage above operating troops while fixed-wing aircraft carried the attack deeper into the defensive zone.

The short turning radius of helicopters and their slower airspeed and ability to fly nap-of-the-earth mission profiles provide substantial advantages over fixed-wing aircarft in supporting troops at or near the FEBA. Helicopters could approach their targets at extremely low level guided by forward air controllers, "pop up" to achieve the proper attack angle, and fire from the swoop or from the hover at a range of 1,000 to 3,000 meters. Such tactics greatly reduce exposure time to enemy aircraft systems and the attacking helicopters can turn and descend to low level to egress the battle area or take up position for a subsequent attack. The presence of a separate weapons system operator in the HIND and HIP also promises greater accuracy and effectiveness.[77]

Both the HIND A and D as well as the HIP E appear to be especially optimized for antiarmor warfare. Equipped with a large calibre 4–barrel machine gun (or machine cannon) under its nose, primary armament of 4 32–shot rocket pods (128 unguided 57–mm rockets), and 4 SPIRAL laser-guided antitank missiles, the HIND D may be the world's most formidable attack helicopter. Not far behind, the HIP E is less sophisticated but is more heavily armed with up to 192 57–mm rockets in 6 pods plus 4 antitank guided missiles.[*]

Into the 1980s

The theories and principles which delineate the Soviet art of warfare are not static nor have they ceased to develop. This fact is simple, straightforward, and relatively self-evident in light of the advances made in military technology since the Russian Revolution. Yet, one must differentiate between development and change. The basic principles of operational art and tactics (to use the title of Colonel Savkin's well-known tome) do develop, but they are unlikely to undergo radical change. In Soviet military science, these principles do not constitute the point of departure of an investigation but, rather, its final results.[78]

In considering Soviet aviation in its relationship to combined arms doctrine—whether it be past, present, or future—the tenets of Soviet operating doctrine and their relationship to overall strategy and military doctrine must continue to play a key role. The developments in Soviet operational-tactical aviation in the 1980s will reflect what the Politburo—with much advice from the General Staff—perceives is required to ensure the ability of the Air Forces to implement the prin-

---

[*]The East German version of the HIP E is even more heavily armed, having 6 (instead of 4) guided antitank missiles in addition to the 6 57–mm rocket pods and a machine gun which can be aimed.

ciples of their operational art. This is, of course, a reactive process; advances in Western capabilities are evaluated in the context of their impact on Soviet military operations. But equally so, it is a question of doctrine determining what technological capabilities and tactical innovations are necessary to carry out the Politburo's politico-military strategy.

The Soviet Union's own military-industrial complex has been particularly impressive in the 1970s in striving to fill the norms imposed upon it by defense planners. A simple list of aircraft deployed during the last decade—even without considering total production—is testimony to the efforts of the defense establishment to revitalize front aviation: FISHBED K, L, N; FOXBAT B, D; FLOGGER B, G; FENCER A, FLOGGER D; FITTER C, D; HIND A, D; and HIP E.

Following the deployment of these aircraft in the 1970s, the 1980s probably will witness a concerted effort to maximize their capabilities both technologically and tactically. According to a pattern established with the MiG–21/FISHBED, the aircraft of the 1970s will probably undergo a series of modifications in the 1980s. For example, FLOGGER Bs probably will disappear and be replaced by Js, Ks, Ls, etc. Each new variant will represent an optimization of an existing capability or the development of a new capability. Look-down, shoot-down radar is an example of what reasonably can be expected for fighter-interceptors. In the ground attack field, more and better precision guided weapons with greater stand-off range for the FENCER, FITTER, and FLOGGER aircraft appear probable. Special emphasis will be given to missiles for attacking such Western SAM systems as Roland II and Patriot. Attack helicopters will become more plentiful and increasingly sophisticated as close air support platforms and antiarmor hunter-killers. This proliferation of heavily armed helicopters could also include a model optimized to some degree for air-to-air combat against other helicopters or even fixed-wing aircraft.[79]

Although the Soviets conceive of innovation and intitiative in terms conditioned by Marxist–Leninist theory and their own historical and social experience, it is safe to predict rather revolutionary trends within the armed forces away from the traditional dependence on higher authority toward greater freedom at the tactical level. As technological capabilities expand the scope of possible actions and decisions, the Soviets will acknowledge the requirement for tactical flexibility at the lower echelons of command. This flexibility is possible only through the practice of individual initiative. This will be particularly true for Front Aviation air army pilots who function in a fluid and nonpredictable environment. Thus, the hints of tactical maneuver, dogfighting, and the freedom to decide the attack option which are now largely confined to the pages of military journals will begin to become realities in the early part of this decade. "Free hunt" operations, for example, will not be an aberration but a standard operational-tactical practice with special emphasis on NATO's mobile missile systems.

All this is not to suggest there will be no new aircraft systems entering service during the 1980s. Quite the contrary, existing systems probably will be augmented by two to three new specialized airframes, including a tankbuster analogous to the A-10 and some kind of air supremacy fighter. A new helicopter of innovative design would also appear to be a possibility for the future, although whether it would be a single-purpose or a dual role system remains unclear.[80]

What is certain is that aviation—both fixed-wing and rotary-wing—will continue to play a vital role in the prosecution of Soviet combined arms theory. Developments in the 1970s have provided a balanced, technically sound tactical air force which provides the basis upon which the Soviets can build and diversify in the 1980s.

Notes

1. Colonel General N. A. Lomov, ed., *Scientific–Technical Progress and the Revolution in Military Affairs* (Moscow: Voyenizdat, 1973), translated and published under the auspices of the US Air Force (Washington, DC: Government Printing Office, 1977), p. 110.

2. Colonel M. P. Skirdo, *The People, The Army, The Commander* (Moscow: Voyenizdat, 1970), translated and published under the auspices of the US Air Force (Washington DC: Government Printing Office, ND), p. 117.

3. Lieutenant Colonel Lynn M. Hansen, "The Soviet Command Structure: From Party to Military District," *The Soviet Military District in Peace and War: Manpower, Manning, and Mobilization* (Washington: GE TEMPO, 28 September 1979), Report GE79 TMPT–30, p L–12.

4. Lieutenant General M. Kiryan, "The Soviet Strategic Leadership During the War," *Soviet Military Review,* No. 6, 1979, pp. 2–5. Also, M. N. Kozhevnikov, *Komandovaniya i shtab VVS Sovestskoy Armii v Velikoy Otechestvennoy Voyne* [The Command and Staff of the Air Force of the Soviet Army in the Great Patriotic War] (Moscow: Nauka, 1977), p. 52; and "The Organization of Aviation Control during the Years of the Great Patriotic War," *Voyennaya mysl'* [Military Thought], No. 5, 1972.

5. Lieutenant Colonel Lynn M. Hansen, "The Resurgence of Frontal Aviation," *Strategic Review,* Fall 1978 p. 72. Also, John Erickson, "The Expansion of Soviet Airpower," *Airpower in the Next Generation* (London: Macmillan, 1979), p. 50.

6. Friedrich Wiener and William J. Lewis, *The Armies of the Warsaw Pact* (Vienna: Carl Ueberreuter, 1976), p. 95. Wiener credits the 16th Air Army with 1,400 aircraft. John Erickson, in "Some Developments in Soviet Tactical Aviation," *RUSI Journal,* September 1975 lists about 900 aircraft. In "The Expansion of Soviet Airpower," p. 51., Erickson provides the figure of 844 planes which can be topped quickly up to a war strength of 1,200 aircraft.

7. Hansen, "The Resurgence of Frontal Aviation," p. 73.

8. *Volksarmee* [People's Army], No. 11, 1978, p. 7.

9. Hansen, op. cit.

10. John Erickson, "The Expansion of Soviet Airpower," p. 52. Also, Colin S. Gray, "Soviet Tactical Airpower," *Air Force Magazine,* March 1977, p. 63.

11. Colonel V. Ye. Savkin, *The Basic Principles of Operational Art and Tactics* (Moscow: Voyenizdat, 1972), p. 249. See also, John Erickson, *The Soviet High Command* (London: Macmillan, 1962), pp. 120–130.

12. Timokhovich, *Operativnoye iskusstvo VVS v Velikoy Otechestvennoy voyne* [Operational

Art of the Air Forces in the Great Patriotic War] (Moscow: Voyenizdat, 1976), p. 106.

13. See John Erickson, "The Soviet Military System: Doctrine, Technology, and Style," in *Soviet Military Power and Performance* (London: Macmillan, 1979).
14. James H. Hansen, "The Development of Soviet Aviation Support," *International Defense Review,* No. 5, 1980, p. 683.
15. Timokhovich, op. cit., pp. 16ff. Also, Ye. A. Shilovski, *Voprosy strategii i operativnogo iskusstva v Sovetskikh voyennykh trudakh 1917–1940* [Problems of Strategy and Operational Art in Soviet Military Work 1917–1940] (Moscow: *Voyenizdat,* 1965), p. 516.
16. Major General L. Mikryukov, "Upravleniye istrebitelyami v vozdushnom boyu" [The Control of Fighters in Air Combat], *Voyenno–istoricheskiy zhurnal* [Military–Historical Journal], No. 9, 1977, pp. 42–48.
17. Major General M. I. Cherednichenko, "On Features in the Development of Military Art in the Postwar Period," *Voyenno–istoricheskiy zhurnal,* No. 6, 1975 pp. 19–30.
18. Lieutenant Colonel N. Molchanov, "Maneuvering Anti–Aircraft Artillery, "*Voyennyy Vestnik* [Military Herald], No. 6, 1975, pp. 84–86.
19. Mikryukov, op. cit.
20. Timokhovich, op. cit., p. 65.
21. Ibid., pp. 16–20.
22. Marshal V. D. Sokovlovskiy, ed., *Military Strategy,* 3rd ed., edited with analysis and commentary by Harriet Fast Scott (New York: Crane, Russak and Company, 1975), p. 246.
23. Colonel L. Semeyko, *Voyennaya mysl'* No. 8, 1968, quoted in Leon Goure and Michael J. Deane, *"The Soviet Strategic View,"* Strategic Review, No. 4, 1979, p. 89.
24. See, for example, Phillip A. Peterson, *Soviet Air Power and the Pursuit of New Military Options* (Washington, DC: Government Printing Office, nd), p. 7.
25. Kozhevnikov, op. cit., p. 56.
26. Timokhovich, op cit, p. 70.
27. Lomov, op cit, p. 150.
28. Lieutenant General M. Gareyev, "Vsegda na strazhe zavoyevaniy Oktyabrya" [Always on Guard over the Achievements of October], *Voyenno–istoricheskiy zhurnal,* No. 11, 1977, pp. 19–21.
29. Timokhovich, op. cit., p. 70.
30. Marshal of Aviation P. S. Kutakhov, "The Conduct of Independent Air Operations," *Voyenno–istoricheskiy zhurnal* No. 6, 1972, pp. 20–28, translated and published by the US Air Force in *Selected Soviet Military Writings, 1970–1975* (Washington, DC: Government Printing Office, 1977), p. 243.
31. Timokhovich, op. cit., p. 82.
32. Colonel A. A. Sidorenko, *The Offensive* (Moscow: Voyenizdat, 1970), translated and published under the auspices of the US Air Force (Washington, DC: Government Printing Office, 1976), p. 124.
33. Harold Brown, *Department of Defense Annual Report, FY1979,* p. 202.
34. Timokhovich, op. cit., p. 83.
35. Lieutenant General V. Korochkin, "Breakthrough to the Strike Target: New Weapons and Tactics, *Krasnaya zvedzda* [Red Star], 11 July 1979.
36. "Powerful Wings of the Motherland," *Kommunist Vooruzhennykh Sil* [Communist of the Armed Forces], No. 14, July 1979, pp. 28–33.
37. Charles Gilson and Dan Boyle, "F–15 and the Air Defense of Europe," *International Defense Review,* No. 5, 1978, p. 696.
38. Timokhovich, op. cit., pp. 63, 64.
39. Secretary John C. Stetson and General David C. Jones, "Statement to Accompany Presentation to the House Armed Services Committee," February 1978.
40. Air Chief Marshal Sir Andrew Humphrey, quoted in Charles Gilson, op. cit.
41. Major General N. Tuzov, "Searching for an Attacking Air Target," *Soviet Military Review,* No. 4, 1979, pp. 16–18.
42. Ibid.

43. Colonel V. A. Uryzhnikov, "In a Complex Situation," *Krasnaya zvezda,* 7 January 1977, p. 2.
44. Timokhovich, op. cit., p. 130.
45. *Aerospace Daily,* 5 November 1979, p. 18.
46. Colonel Yu. Bondarve, "In a Complex Situation," *Krasnaya zvezda,* 28 July 1979, p. 1.
47. Cherednichenko, op. cit.
48. Timokhovich, op. cit., p. 121.
49. Ibid., p. 124.
50. Ibid.
51. George Panyalev, "Underestimated in the West: The MiG–25 Foxbat Weapons System," *International Defense Review,* No. 2, 1977, p. 258.
52. John W. R. Taylor, "Gallery of Soviet Aerospace Weapons," *Air Force Magazine,* March 1980.
53. Timokhovich, op. cit., p. 14.
54. Ibid.
55. Major General I. Vorob'yev, "The Tactics of Fire and Maneuver," *Krasnaya zvezda,* 5 June 1979, p. 2.
56. Colonel Ye. V. Koyander, *Ya – Rubin, Prikazyvayu* [I Am Rubin, I Command] (Moscow: Voyenizdat, 1978), p. 105.
57. Colonel G. Bryukhovskiy, "Features of Employing Aviation in the Manchurian Operation," *Voyenno–istoricheskiy zhurnal,* No. 8, 1979, pp. 17–21.
58. Koyander, op. cit., p. 105.
59. Ibid., p. 202.
60. Ibid.
61. Ibid.
62. Ibid., also, Lieutenant Colonel Yu. Gudymenko, "Podderzhivaya Motostrelkov" [Supporting Motorized Rifle Troops], *Aviatsiya i Kosmonavtika* [Aviation and Cosmunautics], May 1978, pp. 6–7.
63. Ibid., p. 140.
64. General of the Army A. A. Radziyevskiy, "The Art of Gaining Victory," *Soviet Military Review,* June 1978, p. 26.
65. Savkin, op. cit., p. 45.
66. See Colonel V. Izgarshev, "Helicopter Crews," *Krasnaya zvezda,* 27 August 1979, p. 2.
67. Marshal of Aviation P. S. Kutakhov, *Pravda,* 18 August 1974.
68. *Soldat und Technik* [Soldier and Technology], February 1977, p. 110.
69. Lieutenant Colonel L. Chuyko, "Headed by The Commander," *Krasnaya zvezda,* 6 July 1976, p. 1. The former commander of the 16th Air Army, General Babeyev, is credited with landing his own aircraft on a highway strip in East Germany and then taking off again. See also Clarence A. Robinson, "Increasing Soviet Offensive Threat Spurs Strategic European Air Arm," *Aviation Week,* 1 August 1977, p. 46; and Colonel P. Korobkov, "Dispersed Basing of Aviation under Conditions of Waging a Modern War," *Voyennaya mysl',* No. 11. 1973.
70. Marshal of Aviation P. S. Kutakhov, "The Air Forces, Past and Present," *Voyennaya mysl';* No. 10, 1973. The Soviet Air Forces Commander writes that in combat operations with conventional weapons, tactical aviation will be the main means of destroying targets located outside the range of ground force weapons.
71. Timokhovich, op. cit., p. 170.
72. Major General L. Nosov, "Sudden Combat Task," *Krasnaya zvezda,* 27 May 1976, p. 2.
73. Colonel Ye. Veraksa, "Fighter Tactics," *Soviet Military Review,* March 1978, p. 37.
74. Timokhovich, op. cit., pp. 89–90.
75. P. Studenikin and D. Shnyukas, "Over the Neman", *Pravda,* 28 July 1979, p. 6. Also Captain Yu. Bondarev, op. cit.
76. This is basically my own theory which has evolved from extensive reading independ-

ent of firm or conclusive evidence. See, however, Colonel A. Drozhin, "Basic Trends in the Organizational Development and Employment of Army Aviation," *Voyennaya mysl'*, No. 9, 1979.

77. "Air Defense of Soviet Advance Forces," *Flight International*, 28 August 1976, p. 56. Also, L. Hansen, "Soviet Helicopter Operations," op. cit.

78. Colonel V. Chervonobab, "Principles of Military Art and their Development," *Voyennaya mysl'*, No. 11, 1971.

79. Colonel M. Belov, "How to Fight Helicopters," *Soviet Military Review*, September 1979, pp. 18–19.

80. Ibid.

The Soviet Security Troops—
The Kremlin's Other Armies

James T. Reitz

In the uneasy quiet which preceded the Soviet invasion of Afghanistan, the Armed Forces of the Soviet Ministry of Defense were estimated by a series of credible open US and other Western sources to consist of somewhere between 4 million and 4.5 million persons.[1]

At the same time, the same sources were paying varying degrees of lip service to two other highly trained, permanent, regular Soviet troop establishments: those of the Committee for State Security (*KGB*)—the best known and probably the most numerous of whom are the Border Troops—and the troops of the Ministry of Internal Affairs (*MVD*)—generally known as "Internal Troops." These units—generally lumped together in Western thinking as security troops when they are indeed thought of at all—were credited with 350,000 to 500,000 troops.

Other less institutionally trammeled analysts, among them myself, consider the figures for the MOD and security troops to be low. The Ministry of Defense (MOD) figures do not take into sufficient consideration railway construction and civil defense troops; the sprawling officers schooling system; the equally ramified system of the military commissariats; and the preinduction and reserve training system, among others. The Security Troop estimates are low because the community has not even identified and put manpower figures to all forms of these troops. For example, only Border Troop figures are considered in the open source *KGB* troop totals. No strength figures exist for such hazy elements as the Government Signal Troops and other very distinctively uniformed *KGB* troops.

While the maximum figure for the Border and Internal Troops slightly more than doubles the estimate of a decade ago, I suspect this reflects a belated correction of strength levels rather than any rapid actual growth. (At that point, DIA carried 175,000 Border Troops and 75,000 Internal Troops.) No drastic new factor in the Soviet system that I am aware of has occurred to cause this doubling. Currently, the conventional wisdom has increased the numbers of Border Troops by 10 percent and Internal Troops by 300 percent.[2] I suspect these changes represent the community's grudging giving in to pressure from a few enthusiastic, close students of the Security Troops rather than actual documentable increases.

Even so, this reassessment of numbers has not been accompanied by an acceptance of the Security Troops as bona fide, full-fledged members of the Soviet military establishment, even though legally they are considered by the Soviets to be components of the Soviet Armed Forces. In what I believe to be still another perceptual lag, the terms "militarized," "paramilitary," and "police" are subtly attached in order to present them as less than first-class, handpicked, highly motivated and trained soldiers who represent the last bulwark of the Soviet regime.

It is these non–MOD troop bodies with which this article is concerned—their organization; manpower; peacetime and combat history; legal status in the Soviet Armed Forces; selection; schooling; training; and their future military implications.

KGB Troops

The Border Troops are the largest component of the regular armed forces of the *KGB*. Another highly important but smaller body of *KGB* forces consists of the Government Signal Troops. The *KGB* troops about whom the least is known are the special guard forces who are charged with the overt security of the Kremlin, other top Party and government offices in and around Moscow, and perhaps other places of importance in the Soviet Union.

Western estimates of the Border Troops' strength have for years remained at 175,000–200,000; many good unofficial sources believe this figure to be too low.[3] The *KGB* Signal Troops are responsible for high-level communications between government (including military) and probably Party echelons in Moscow and their outlying headquarters. The only strength estimate available for these troops is a highly suspect WWII figure of 15,000. No known estimates exist for *KGB* guard troops. It is the author's opinion that *KGB* troop levels—counting Border Troops, Signal Troops, and other more vague troop elements—might easily reach over one-quarter million.[4] All these highly trained elite *KGB* troops, a huge aggregate of counter-intelligence and security operatives, and a large number of foreign intelligence operatives are combined under a large central *KGB* staff in Moscow and, to some extent, under *KGB* subordinate staffs. The various major *KGB* components may have some activities in common—such as schooling, procurement, and communications—as well as some autonomous capability in these areas.

An extremely simplified diagram of the top level organizations of the *KGB* showing its troops and other security elements is shown in Figure 1.

The very first element of Soviet military power encountered by a visitor to the Soviet Union consists of the *KGB* Border Troops. They have been described as constituting in fact the "Iron Curtain" and having the responsibility for physically checking every transient into or out of the country and apprehending illegal border crossers. They are a highly trained, well-armed, uniformed body of soldiery operating under the Chief of the Main Directorate of Border Troops, one of the several main directorates of the *KGB*.

KGB Troop and other
Security and Intelligence Elements

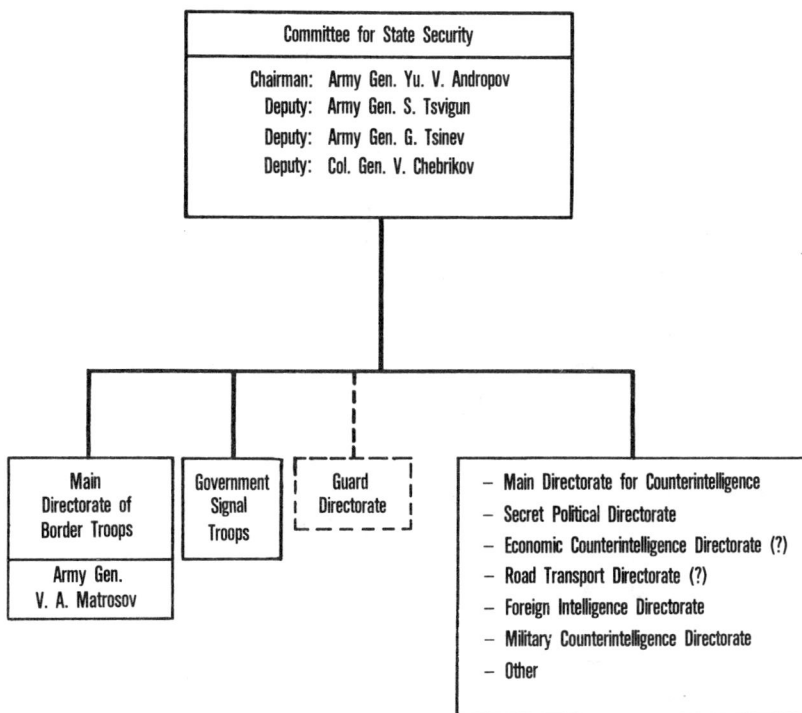

```
┌─────────────────────────────────────────┐
│        Committee for State Security       │
│                                           │
│  Chairman:  Army Gen. Yu. V. Andropov     │
│  Deputy:    Army Gen. S. Tsvigun          │
│  Deputy:    Army Gen. G. Tsinev           │
│  Deputy:    Col. Gen. V. Chebrikov        │
└─────────────────────────────────────────┘
```

Main Directorate of Border Troops	Government Signal Troops	Guard Directorate	– Main Directorate for Counterintelligence – Secret Political Directorate – Economic Counterintelligence Directorate (?) – Road Transport Directorate (?) – Foreign Intelligence Directorate – Military Counterintelligence Directorate – Other
Army Gen. V. A. Matrosov			

(?) Current Existence in doubt

Figure 1

Organization and Function

Border Troop Headquarters

The present Chief of the Main Directorate of Border Troops—also a deputy chairman of the *KGB*—is V. A. Matrosov, recently promoted to the rank of Army General (4 stars). (A veteran Border Troop officer who served many years as Chief of Staff of Border Troops, he succeeded Colonel General P. Zyryanov in 1972 as Chief of Border Troops and has since jumped in rank two grades from lieutenant general.)

At least five other general and flag officers have been identified in the open press in recent years as members of his staff:[5]

First Deputy Chief and Chief of Staff –
Lieutenant General V. F. Labanov

Chief of the Political Directorate –
Lieutenant General V. Gaponenko
Deputy Chief – Vice Admiral N. E. Dalmatov
Deputy Chief – Major General V. Vlasenko
Deputy Chief of the Political Directorate –
Major General I. Ivanchishin

While the list may well not be complete, it indicates a rather sizable Border Troop staff which probably consists of at least personnel, operations, communications, rear services, and political directorates, and probably intelligence/counter-intelligence and cryptographic elements as well. One or two open literature reports indicate the Moscow Border Troop headquarters may be an operational one which either controls, coordinates, or closely watches day-to-day activity along the extensive 60,000-km Soviet frontier.[6]

Districts

Organizationally, the Soviet Border Troops are distributed around the perimeter of the country in 9 border districts, each extending as far as 100–3,000 km along the border and 300–600 km into the interior.[7] Within the last year or so, at least eight general officers have been identified in Soviet media as Border Troop district commanders. Six are major generals (one star) and two are lieutenant generals (two stars). Other major generals are listed as district political deputies. (See Figure 2.)

Each border district has a sizable staff reflecting the makeup of the larger Border Troop staff in Moscow. As in the Soviet Army, the Border Troop staff has a chief of staff, a chief of rear services, and a chief of the political directorate, all of whom function as border district deputy commanders. The chief of staff supervises intelligence, operations, communications, and training. The rear service chief supervises logistics and procurement. The political deputy supervises the continuous political training which, if anything, is more intensive than that given MOD troops.

Much Border Troop personnel processing—call-up, discharge, and maintenance of possible reserve rosters—is done for the *KGB* by the Defense Ministry and its nationwide system of military commissariats. By the same token, procurement of common supply items seems to be largely handled for the Border Troops—and probably for other *KGB* and *MVD* troops and establishments—by MOD supply services.

General Organizational Structure of the Main Directorate of the KGB Border Troops

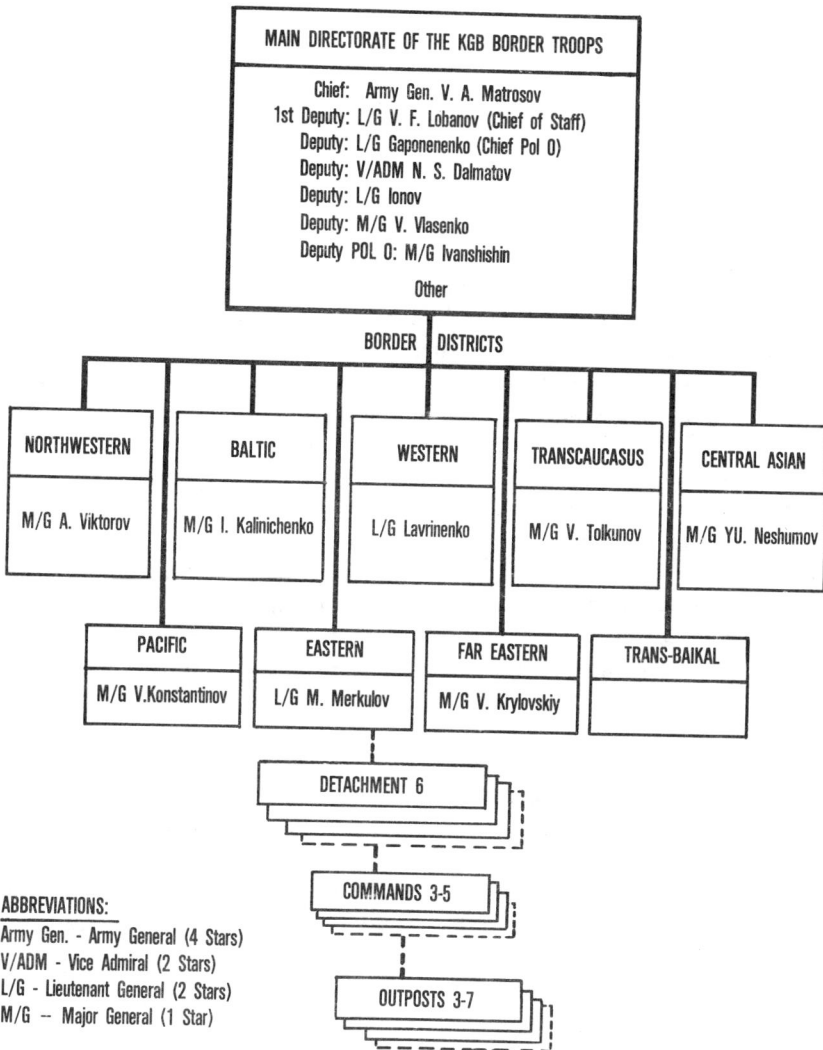

```
┌─────────────────────────────────────────────────┐
│     MAIN DIRECTORATE OF THE KGB BORDER TROOPS     │
├─────────────────────────────────────────────────┤
│         Chief:  Army Gen. V. A. Matrosov          │
│   1st Deputy: L/G V. F. Lobanov (Chief of Staff)  │
│     Deputy: L/G Gaponenenko (Chief Pol O)         │
│          Deputy: V/ADM N. S. Dalmatov             │
│              Deputy: L/G Ionov                    │
│             Deputy: M/G V. Vlasenko               │
│        Deputy POL O: M/G Ivanshishin              │
│                                                   │
│                     Other                         │
└─────────────────────────────────────────────────┘
```

BORDER DISTRICTS

NORTHWESTERN	BALTIC	WESTERN	TRANSCAUCASUS	CENTRAL ASIAN
M/G A. Viktorov	M/G I. Kalinichenko	L/G Lavrinenko	M/G V. Tolkunov	M/G YU. Neshumov

PACIFIC	EASTERN	FAR EASTERN	TRANS-BAIKAL
M/G V.Konstantinov	L/G M. Merkulov	M/G V. Krylovskiy	

DETACHMENT 6

COMMANDS 3-5

OUTPOSTS 3-7

ABBREVIATIONS:
Army Gen. - Army General (4 Stars)
V/ADM - Vice Admiral (2 Stars)
L/G - Lieutenant General (2 Stars)
M/G -- Major General (1 Star)

Figure 2

An attached *KGB* counterintelligence section functions nearly independently. As in the case of other elements of the armed forces, the *osobyy otdel* (Special Section) maintains an autonomous surveillance function over the Border Troops, although the latter are themselves a *KGB* troop unit.

Each district headquarters reportedly maintains a non-commissioned officer training school and some enlisted specialist training courses. District enlisted schools may have from 300 to 700 men in training.

District headquarters are normally located in a sizable city away from the border and apparently are connected to Border Troop[8] headquarters and Moscow by independent communication facilities.

Organization Below District Level

Subordinate to the districts are a number of border *otryady* (detachments) and possibly *komendatury* (independent commands), small air and sea elements where the district terrain warrants, plus some horse-mounted units in desert and other roadless wastelands. Each district may also have a separate signal battalion.[9]

Border Troop districts are thought normally to have at least six detachments. Border detachments reportedly have responsibility for land areas from 50 to 500 km along the border and 50 to 150 km deep, depending on terrain and other factors.[10] There is considerable disagreement as to the size of border detachments. Former Border Troop field officers put them at 1,200–2,500; a second source estimates 2,500–3,500 officers and men.[11] There seems to be general agreement that the detachments consist of three to five line commands (*komendatury*), plus a reserve or maneuver group.

Border *komendatury* strengths are believed to vary from 200–500 men.[12] A former *komendatura* commander estimates an average strength of between 350 and 400. Each command is thought to consist of three to seven *zastavy* (line outposts), a reserve, and a support outpost. The outposts average about 50 men and may cover an area as small as 5 km long by 3 km deep to as large as 20 km long by 15 km deep, depending on terrain.

Maritime and Air Elements

Organization and strength of the Border Troop maritime and air elements are much more obscure than those of the ground elements. Air units of light rotary- and fixed-wing aircraft are thought to be assigned to each district. These aircraft are used for reconnaissance, transport of supplies, and even operations.[13]

Border Troop maritime units are believed to be assigned directly to the headquarters of those districts with water areas. Most of them have light, armed fast cutters, many of which are hydrofoils. They enforce a 12–mile limit along the Soviet sea frontier and are in the major border lake areas as well. They escort shipping in and out of port and often maintain shipside watch during layovers. Shore elements also maintain shore and port security watches, and they sometimes maintain wharfside guard or even watch aboard a particular ship under surveillance.[14]

Other Materiel

Border Troop armament apparently consists of small arms up to and including light and heavy machine guns; some armored personnel carriers and possibly other armor, including light tanks; some light artillery and mortars; the previously mentioned air and naval craft; and radar. The Border Troops were described a decade ago as being fully motorized. In the appropriate terrain, they still use horse-mounted and ski patrols and even aerosleds.[15]

Physical Security

In maintaining the 24–hour security of the 60,000–km Soviet border zone, the Border Troops use integrated systems of surveillance, pass controls, hidden and open physical and electronic barriers, fixed and roving patrols, detection and alarm devices, explosives, tripwires, and observation posts. Fixed-wing and rotary-wing aircraft patrol vast stretches of difficult border terrain. Foot, horse-mounted, and vehicular patrols are used in other areas. Specially trained guard and patrol dogs are employed.[16] Small, fast, lightly armed patrol boats and cutters patrol border river, lake, and offshore ocean areas. A whole network of observation and warning devices and methods are used along the entire periphery. Occasionally, there are strong points, firing points, ambushes, trenches, ditches, and other works where the terrain and border situation warrant. Searchlights, electronic and infrared devices, telescopes, mines, dogs, fences, wire, ploughed areas, and numerous other measures are all coordinated in a huge, endless complex backed by human watchmen or patrolmen. The average restricted land area extends about 20 miles into the interior from the border.[17]

The pass control system, which tightens as the border is approached from inside the Soviet Union, limits the number and types of people living in the border zones. The immediate border area is completely forbidden to any inhabitants or traffic. The Border Troops also maintain a fairly limited number of legal entry-exit road and rail crossing points around the periphery of the country as well as all the international entry points at Soviet airports and seaports.

Other Intelligence and Security

The Soviet Border Troops also employ undercover counterintelligence operatives and informants to a considerable depth on both sides of the border. Border Troop intelligence officers reportedly cooperate with high *KGB* (non–Border Troop) headquarters in arranging two-way passage of Soviet agents and also cooperate with the intelligence personnel of other elements of the Soviet Armed Forces in the immediate vicinity. Interagency intelligence and counterintelligence of this sort are usually controlled at district headquarters or higher.[18]

In addition to Border Troop undercover operatives, the entire population of the border area, the civil police and auxiliary militia, and the local territorial *KGB* surveillance network work together to inform the Border Troops of the presence of strangers and untoward activity in border areas.[19]

Other Personnel Matters

As a constituent element of the Soviet Armed Forces, the *KGB* Border Troops wear the same basic uniform and insignia as do Soviet Army troops, except for the bright green enlisted shoulder board background and the distinctive all green service cap top. Maritime Border Troops wear the same uniform as the Soviet Navy except for the predominant Border Troops green of the officers' shoulder boards; seamen wear a broad green ribbon with the words "Naval Forces of the Border Troops" around the traditional Soviet sailor's hat.[20] Border Troop and Internal Troop officer specialists wear the same silver shoulder boards as do Soviet Army medical, veterinary, and administrative officers, and Border and Internal Troop line officers wear the same gold-backed shoulder boards as do Soviet Army combat arms officers.[21]

Call-ups

The *KGB* Border Troops, like the Soviet Army and the *MVD* Internal Troops, have a regular officer cadre with a small leavening of career enlisted men. Most Border Troop soldiers, however, like those of the other armed services, are conscripts called up in semiannual levies under the universal conscription law.

The semiannual call-ups are accomplished through the auspices of the local military commissariats of the Ministry of Defense on the basis of quotas levied on the Defense Ministry by the *KGB*. As in the case of the *MVD* troop conscripts, records of the incoming draftees have been thoroughly reviewed and culled and the young men interviewed by Border Guard representatives who, like their *MVD* counterparts, take only the most politically reliable of those best qualified mentally and physically.[22]

Possible Border Troop Reservists

A number of oblique references indicate the existence of a Border Troop reserve. One document refers to pre–WWII Soviet manuals that show sample blank reports entitled "Registration Report of Junior Commanders of the Reserve of the Red Army and the Border and Internal Troops of the *NKVD*." There are other references in the same publication to "Reservists of the Army, Navy, and *NKVD* listed on General and Special Registers."[23] A *Pravda* article (on the occasion of Border Troops Day in May 1968)[24] includes an accompanying photograph of two individuals: the "legendary" reserve Colonel N. F. Karatsupa, who for years has been mentioned in Border Troop exploits, and a reserve private, V. I. Ved. Another report of a Border Guard commanders' meeting on the Border Troops' 50th anniversary lists eight active Border Troop officers and a "major of the reserve M. D. Bryzgalov." A *TASS* broadcast described a medal being awarded all career officers and NCOs of the Army, Navy, Border, "and Security

Troops" on duty or to those who had been transferred to reserve or retired status after completion of 20 years' active duty.[25] Lastly, Mr. V. A. Artem'yev states separate Border Troop and Internal Troop reserve lists were kept by military commissariat officers; there were other lists in regular Soviet Army units in which Soviet Army personnel had been given security troop mobilization designations. These individuals were constantly under surveillance for reliability purposes and were transferred to Army reserve rolls if any political weakness was indicated.[26]

	KGB Border Troops	Only Joint Estimates Available	MVD Internal Troops
1945†		700	
1946–52		-	
1953†		400	
1954–57		-	
1958†		400	
1959		-	
1960		350	
1961–63		-	
1964		300	
1965		270	
1966–67		230	
1968		250	
1969–70†	175		75
1971		230	
1972–74	175		125
1976	180		130
1977	200		230
1978–80	200		250

†Data derived from official US publications; other years derived from the annual *Military Balance* series published by the International Institute for Strategic Studies, London.

Figure 3.   Various Western Estimates of Soviet Border and Internal Troop Strength (1945-1980) (in thousands).

Troop Privileges

Pay and allowance norms for Border Troops as well as for other *KGB* and *MVD* troops have been reported as both equal to and higher than those for MOD troops. There is hardship pay in the Soviet Armed Forces pay scale, and—since so many of the Border Troops are in greatly isolated, mountain, or desert area—this may be one reason for any differential.[27]

Security Troops are reportedly fed and clothed better than those in the Army, and most attaches would agree that they look considerably better turned out than the average Soviet Army conscript. Our two former Border Troop field grade personnel report that in their day, the Border Troops were fed better than the Soviet Army.[28]

The Border Troops have their own system of hospitals, polyclinics, and infirmaries. They also have access to other *KGB* sanatoria, rest homes, and health resorts in the Crimea, the Caucasus, and the Baltic areas.[29]

Schools and Training

Officers of the Border Troops are commissioned as lieutenants after training through a number of 4-year higher military schools (officer commissioning schools) of the Soviet Armed Forces whose policy and direction are the responsibility of the *KGB* and *MVD* rather than the MOD. There are:

- the Alma Ata Higher Border Troop Command School,
- the Moscow Higher Border Troop Command School, and
- the Golitsyno Higher Border Troop Military–Political School (near Moscow).

After stiff examination, these 3 schools accept selected civilian candidates from age 17 to 21, active Soviet servicemen to age 21 regardless of branch or military specialty, and reservists to age 23 who have already completed obligatory service. Graduates of the two command schools are certified as "combined arms officers." Those who finish the Moscow command school are also given the specialty description of "translator-foreign language specialist." Golitsyno graduates are listed as "officers with a higher military-political education."[30]

Border Troop officers reportedly receive further training at the Frunze Military Academy (a Ground Forces-run combined arms school roughly equating to a combination of the US Army Command and General Staff College and the Army War College). Some higher training for Border Troop Officers may also be given at the *MVD* Academy which opened in 1974.

Political Indoctrination and Surveillance

The Border Troops have a hierarchy of organic political officers as well as attached *KGB* counterintelligence personnel.[31] The political reliability and dedication of the Border (and other security) Troops to the regime should not be underestimated. According to one border district commander, almost 99 percent of the Border Troops are Party members or Young Communists.[32] Normally, Border Troop conscripts are chosen largely from the Slavic peoples (mostly Great Russian) from the interior areas of the country.

Auxiliary Support Organizations and Elements

Just as the Soviet Army, Navy, and Air Forces have the Voluntary Society for Cooperation with the Army, Aviation, and the Fleet

(*DOSAAF*) as a popular mass support and premilitary training organization on which to rely, the Soviet Border Troops have their own highly active "Young Friends of the Border Troops" organization. These pre-teenage and teenage boys and girls have Pioneer uniforms complete with green-striped shoulder boards and overseas caps. The size of this organization is unknown.[33]

Cooperation with Other Communist Countries

The Soviet Border Troops have had a long and extensive military aid and training program for satellite border troops. Daily operational cooperation between Soviet and satellite border troops is standard practice.[34]

> . . . the Soviet Border Troops, fulfilling their international duty, helped the brother Socialist countries to organize their borders and have shown and are showing them all possible help. At present, a close fighting comradeship has developed between the USSR Border Troops and the Border Troops of a series of other Socialist powers.[35]

A second Soviet article described coordinated Polish–Soviet Border Troop communications and operations and the interchange of Polish/Soviet Border Troop decorations.[36] In a third article in the same vein, Soviet Border Troop General Kishentsev wrote: "As the result of the joint skilled activities of the Border Troops of the Soviet Union, Czechoslovakia, Hungary, and Romania, hundreds of border violators have been apprehended."[37] A Bulgarian Border Troop article stated: "The Border Troops are our older brothers in combat."[38] Interestingly enough, among the very small handful of Soviet officers who were identified as having served in North Vietnam in the later 1960s were two Border Troop colonels who helped the North Vietnamese set up a border troop system.

Pre–WWII Operational Experience

According to Colonel General P. I. Zyryanov, Chief of the *KGB* Border Troops from 1952 to 1972 (and allegedly a Border Troop officer for more than 40 years), the Border Troops were given the responsibility of safeguarding the Soviet frontiers as early as the civil war. Border Troops initially were made up of special units "from the best battalions and regiments of the Red Army."[39]

Just prior to the Soviet entry into WWII, a considerable, positive transformaton of the Soviet Border Troops' mission, organization, and possibly strength took place. In a lengthly article, I. I. Petrov pointed out that, from the Soviet viewpoint, the international situation immediately before WWII was such that "the complicated situation required the systematic strengthening of the security of the borders."[40] He put the Border Troop numbers in just the border districts along the western Soviet boundaries at "about 100 thousand" in this prewar period (1939–1941). Colonel of the Reserve Shevchenko corroborates the 100,000 figure, which he lists as being assigned to 9 border districts under 9 general officers, possibly all Border Troop generals. He does indicate, however, that some backup Internal Troops might have been included in this number.[41] The authors of *The Soviet Secret Police* put the overall Border Guard strength before 1941 at 70 detachments in 14 districts.[42]

In the 2 years of not quite war, Petrov reports the Border Troops took part in over 560 skirmishes, allegedly killing or wounding over 2,000 and capturing 6,000 would-be border violators.[43]

Role In WWII

The first Soviet troops to bear the brunt of the German attack in June 1941 were the comparatively lightly armed Border Troops (apparently in some way reinforced by *NKVD* Internal Troops). "From the Barents to the Black Sea . . . the Germans first came up against Border and Internal Troops of the *NKVD*." In some cases, even Border Guard dependents fought in the actions.[44] The *NKVD* Border elements appear to have given a good account of themselves until they were relieved by reinforcing Army elements or, in many cases, until they were wiped out.[45] Shevchenko describes subsequent Border Troops activities:

> After the battles along the border, Border Troops carried out military responsibilities of the High Command in many sectors of land, sea, and river theaters of operation, at the front, in the rear of their own troops and of the enemy, on their own native land and beyond the borders. Border units of company to brigade and division size were attached to tank and other units of regular troops . . . . Whole armies were made up of Border Troops. . . . Combat ships of the naval Border Guard divisions fought through the whole war as part of the Black, Baltic, and Northern Fleets, in the river and lake squadrons . . . (either in support of or as part of the landings) Aviation units of the Border Troops fought in many air battles as part of the army air forces and fleet air arms.[46]

Border Troop units also fought in battles around Moscow, Kiev, Odessa, Sevastopol, and Pskov; on the Karelian Isthmus; around Murmansk; and later at Belgrade, Koenigsberg, Bucharest, Budapest, Warsaw, Prague, Sofia, and Vienna.

The sealing off of army rear areas seems to have been a task given over mostly to Border Troops units (with some Internal Troop participation). As early as June 1941, the top-level organization of Border Guard functions was shuffled. Precisely what happened is not quite clear.[47] General Zyryanov said only that the Border Troops were "subordinated to the [regular] military forces." Shevchenko says the Border (and Internal) Troops were given the job of guarding the rear of the active fronts through an *NKVD* "Main Directorate of Troops for Guarding the Rear" and a "Directorate of Guard Troops" was formed under each front.[48] Another writer indicates rear security was handled by *NKVD* and "other units" through an "Institute of Chiefs of Security of the Rear of the Active Army."[49]

Many individual Border Troop soldiers and small groups of Border Troops, either overrun or bypassed in the initial fighting, escaped to link up with Soviet partisan bands. Several Border Troop officers commanded large partisan units (*soyedineniye*).[50]

Several non-Soviet sources, including some rather dated US official sources, throw further but still imprecise light on the Soviet Border Troop role in WWII. For example, the very comprehensive 1946 US *Handbook on USSR Military Forces* points out that the Soviet Border Troops (then *NKVD*) were designated as "Security Troops of the Rear Area of the Soviet Army" in active theater areas and that former Border Troop battalions were designated as security regiments subordinate to a "Chief of Security Troops of the Rear Area" of each front at a ratio of one regiment per army rear area and, in addition, five or six security regiments per front rear area. Regimental size was estimated at about 1650 men. The regiments were made up of three rifle battalions; organic machinegun, submachinegun, reconnaissance, communications, and antitank companies; and small engineer, transport, chemical, and maintenance elements.[51]

A 1953 US handbook generally corroborates the assignment of Border Troop units to the rear areas of the combat zones with the multiple tasks of sealing off the combat sectors, forestalling desertions, thwarting communication zone penetration by the enemy, conducting mop-up operations, aiding in evacuation, and guarding forward-moving supply columns.[52] A British source at the time also reports a security regiment per army area derived from Border Troop units and under the direction of a "special commander" at the "high command" of a "front."[53]

Only in the 1960s (in a spate of articles on their activities in WWII) were Border Troop actions against the Japanese in 1945 widely discussed by Soviet sources. The most informative articles indicate that Border Troops assigned to the three Soviet Asiatic border districts (Maritime, Transbaykal, and Khabarovsk) assaulted without warning Japanese border positions to kick off the Soviet Army's August 1945 offensive against the Japanese. According to the articles, the Soviet Border elements allegedly overran or destroyed between 250 and 280 border outposts, garrisons, and strong points along a 2,700–km front in a coordinated series of attacks. Some Border Troop naval craft were involved as well.

Border Troop activity during WWII also apparently included some participation in the mass evacuation of suspect minority populations to remote Central Asia. This apparently occurred in the Caucasus and later in the Ukraine and the newly acquired Baltic republics.[55]

Postwar Activity: Occupied Germany and the Chinese Border

Border (and probably other security) Troops played a role in occupied postwar Germany but the extent is unknown. Gregory Klimov refers to "soldiers in green caps: *MVD* Special Troops" sealing off the critical German atomic research areas, after their discovery, to even the highest ranking locally assigned Soviet officers.[56]

Other Soviet sources refer briefly to the Border Troops' having guarded "war criminals" and important installations, such as the site of the surrender negotiations.[57]

Border Troops—not forces under control of the Ministry of Defense—have been the Soviet participants in hundreds of incidents along the Sino–Soviet border since the end of World War II. One of the most publicized was the 1969 Battle of Damanskiy Island. It is widely known that only Border Troops were engaged on the Soviet side.[58]

Military Cooperation with Other Soviet Armed Forces: Future Military Implications

The rather thinly deployed Soviet Border Troops have the mission of absorbing and repelling small-scale armed intervention and, if possible, holding off large-scale penetration until help is forthcoming from the other elements of the armed forces—in particular, the Soviet Army. To this end, Border Troop commanders from the border *komendatura* on up have the responsibility of developing and maintaining with their Army and/or *MVD* Internal Troops opposite numbers a mutually agreed upon local defense plan which spells out actions to be taken in the event of an armed attack. It usually entails the dispatch of some Army or Internal Troops under the operational control of the local Border Troop commander concerned until relieved by a local major Army unit. At that time, the Border Troop unit assumes its classic rear security role of providing road, rail, and installation protection, as well as helping with antipartisan and antiairborne coverage. The overall plan is coordinated with the General Staff plan and an overall frontier defense plan is drawn up involving Army, Border, and Internal Troops when and where necessary (for example, at the outbreak of hostilities).[59]

It is believed that the future combat mission of the Soviet Border Troops will remain much the same as their World War II role: to absorb the first blow until relieved by Army forces, then basically to perform a mission of sealing off and protecting front and army rear areas in the combat zones. In noncombat areas, they will continue their normal border mission. However, it is assumed they will also be used in emergencies as shock troops and in other roles, also similar to their role in World War II.[60]

Other KGB Troops

The *KGB* has at least one and probably more bodies of troops under its jurisdiction in addition to the large and more publicized Directorate of Border Troops.

One purposely obscure but extremely important element of the Soviet security troops—almost never mentioned even obliquely in available open Soviet literature—is the body referred to as Government Signal Troops. Apparently these troops were organized as an *NKVD* element in WWII to improve military (and probably both government and party) communications and security and to carry out some signal intelligence duties.[61] They are believed to have been subordinate to the *KGB* since that body's creation in the mid–1950s.

Another very obscure aspect of *KGB* troop activity concerns the possible existence of a body of troops similar to those ascribed to the *MVD*, the *okhrana osobykh obyektov* (*OOO,*) or Special Facilities Guards. At present, there are not enough good data in open printed Western holdings to confirm their existence.

Function, Strength, and Organization of Government Signal Troops

The Government Signal Troops presumably are responsible for an unknown amount of communications facility installation, maintenance, operation, and security between the major civil government (and probably Party) echelons in Moscow and the various republic capitals. In addition, they are thought to be responsible for communications between the Defense Ministry and the various subordinate military districts as well as the groups of forces headquarters in Eastern Europe. They are also probably responsible for intra-*KGB* communications between the Moscow central headquarters and the major outlying *KGB* headquarters. They presumably monitor transmissions of Soviet (and possibly foreign) origin. It is assumed that their wartime role would be an extension—or possibly an expansion—of their peacetime role.[62]

The only open source Western strength figure ever postulated for this group is the WWII strength figure of 15,000 which appeared in a dated but very comprehensive 1946 US War Department manual based in large part on German WWII intelligence. The WWII version of the Government Signal Troops (*Gosudarstvennyye voyska svyazi*) was thought organized into about 15 independent regiments of about 1000 personnel each.[63]

Role in WWII

The only known Soviet reference to the possible existence of Government Signal Troops was in a 1965 *Pravda* article by then *KGB* Chairman, V. Semichastnyy, lauding the general role of Soviet intelligence and security personnel in WWII. In a 2,000–word article, Semichastnyy devotes one very brief paragraph to "special communications troops:"

> Special communications troops successfully operated on the fronts of the Great Fatherland War . . . the members of the state security communications organs insured reliable, covered communications for the leaders of the *Party* and the government and the staff of the Supreme Command with the *fronts and armies* and they successfully cut off the attempts of the enemy diversionists to interrupt communications.[64]

Semichastnyy's article could be interpreted to indicate these troops secured communications not only between Supreme Headquarters and fronts but between front and army echelons as well. It also indicates Party communications security, listed first, is considered even more important than government security. No more recent mention of the existence of these troops could be found in the Soviet press, but the fact *KGB* Chairman Semichastnyy listed them among the WWII *Chekists* tends to some degree to confirm both their current existence and subordination to the *KGB*.

Possible KGB Special Facility Guards

The most noticeable of the special guards are the very striking, beautifully uniformed young soldiers who guard Lenin's tomb and other Kremlin posts. These Kremlin Guards wear the characteristic royal blue flashing and piping of the *KGB* and may number from several hundred to several thousands. *KGB* generals have been identified as Kremlin commandants for years.

Western attaches in Moscow have seen similar *KGB* guards on duty inside the Kremlin buildings. For example, the commandant of the Presidium building is reportedly a KGB colonel. These guards are also reported at the Party Central Committee headquarters and other important Party and government buildings.

The same type of *KGB* guard arrangements have been reported in Kiev and Ryazan. During visits to the Smol'nyy Institute—which houses the Leningrad Central Committee and the City Executive Committee—a *KGB* officer, two or three enlisted men, and other uniformed guards have been seen. It is thought *KGB* uniformed guards provide security for Party headquarters buildings—at least at *oblast'* and republic level—and possibly for the government headquarters at the same echelons. Another activity which may be assigned to such *KGB* guard troops is the handling and storage of special and nuclear munitions. This is never mentioned in the Soviet press, of course, but it would seem logical to have these items in the hands of technically trained *KGB* troop units rather than, for example, within the purview of more civil-oriented *KGB* counterintelligence personnel. This may well be in the WWII tradition of the reported manning of the first highly secret Soviet multiple rocket launchers, called *Katyushas* and "Stalin organs," by specially trained *NKVD* troops.[65]

MVD Troops and Militarized Units

The Soviet Ministry of Internal Affairs (*MVD*) controls an elite body of regular troops (Internal Troops), the militarized police (militia) and firemen, and a great host of other civil employees. Some credible recent estimates (up 300 percent in the last 10 years) place the number of Internal Troops at least 250,000, although other experts think this figure should be still higher.

The Soviet civil police or militia are uniformed, armed, and have some mobile tactical units. The firemen are uniformed almost like the Internal Troops and are thought to have some firearms and basic riot control training. The various uniformed *MVD* components alone might possibly total one and one-half million personnel.[66]

All these elements—troops, police, and firemen—come under a Moscow–based ministry headed by an *MVD* four-star general (Army General). It is assumed that all constituent republics have ministers with ranks and staffs of appropriate size to supervise and direct the various autonomous or semiautonomous components of the *MVD*.

The system of *MVD* ministries probably has some other services and activities—e.g., political operatives, attached *KGB* counterintelligence, and schooling—common to all *MVD* components. A simplified diagram of the top level organization of the *MVD* is depicted in Figure 4.

Internal Troops

It is quite paradoxical that the element of the Soviet armed services whose personnel are most obvious to Western observers in the Soviet Union is also an element about which very little is known in the West. These are the Internal Troops of the *MVD*, and their members are seen on the streets of almost any large Soviet city in considerable numbers.

"Even before WWII, troops of the *NKVD* [which then included both Internal and Border troops] had the legal status of an armed force equivalent to the Red Army and Navy." This status has remained unchanged to the present day, although there have been a number of changes in the names of the ministries to whom these troops have been subordinate.[67]

MVD Troop
and other Security Elements

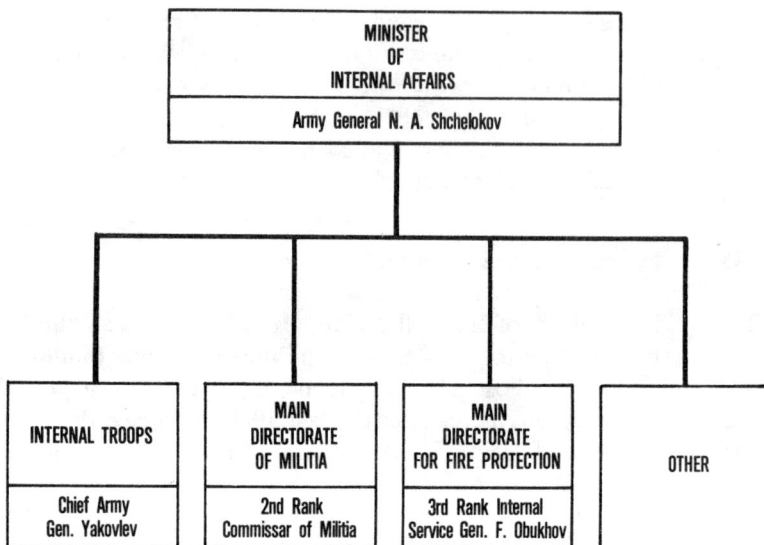

MINISTER OF INTERNAL AFFAIRS
Army General N. A. Shchelokov

INTERNAL TROOPS	MAIN DIRECTORATE OF MILITIA	MAIN DIRECTORATE FOR FIRE PROTECTION	OTHER
Chief Army Gen. Yakovlev	2nd Rank Commissar of Militia	3rd Rank Internal Service Gen. F. Obukhov	

- OPERATIONAL TROOPS
- SPECIAL DESIGNATION TROOPS (OSNAZ)
- SPECIAL FACILITIES GUARDS (OOO)
- CONVOY TROOPS
- OTHER

Figure 4

The current chief of the Internal Troops is Army General I. K. Yakovlev. When he was first identified in this position about 12 years ago, he was a lieutenant general of tank troops. (Whether this means he assumed this command from Army service is not known.) Yakovlev is also a deputy minister of the *MVD*. It is the Internal Troops, "the most significant element" of the *MVD*, which can act as a counterweight to the regular armed forces in the unlikely event that the latter should attempt to compete with the Party for power. Our understanding of the Internal Troops has been rather weakened by the fact these troops are generally lumped together with the highly trained individual soldiers of the Soviet *KGB* Border Guard and other armed *KGB* troop elements as "quasi-military" or "paramilitary" both in official US documents and other Western literature; they are even erroneously equated with young students taking premilitary training courses or with amateur civil defense buffs.[68]

Organization and Function

The exact post–WWII development and the present-day makeup, strength, and organization of the *MVD* Internal Troops remain unclear. There is general agreement the Internal Troops have included in their makeup, more or less continuously since WWII, the following troops:

- Operational troops
- Special designation troops (*OSNAZ*)
- Convoy troops
- Special facilities guards (*OOO*)
- Railway security troops (reported to be both in existence and abolished).

Operational Troops

These troops also appear to be referred to as "general purpose" or "regular" Internal Troops to distinguish them from the *OSNAZ* units. They are thought to have a fixed place of assignment in one or more key cities within a given home military district and to be organized into regimental and, in some cases, even separate battalion-sized units. Their mission appears to be the maintenance of local order within their given area when other *MVD* elements, namely the militia, are unable to do so alone.

Special Designation Troops (Voyska osobogo naznacheniya, or OSNAZ)

The *OSNAZ* are apparently a somewhat more elite body. The consensus is these troops are organized into units up to division size, they are a kind of national reserve without a permanent base assignment (outside the Moscow area), and they can be committed to internal trouble spots when local district operational troops cannot handle the situation.

As of the mid–1950s, there were believed to be one or more *OSNAZ* divisions in the Moscow area itself, organized in a similar fashion to an army motorized rifle division.[69]

Other later open sources (presumed to derive from former *MVD* officers) held there were possibly some separate tanks, artillery, and mortar regiments. Separate artillery battalions and cavalry squadrons, separate battalions of engineers, antiaircraft, and antitank artillery were also reported within the divisional makeup, as well as some separate aviation detachments and small numbers of light *OSNAZ* naval craft at key river ports. No estimates of overall *OSNAZ* strength were available.

Soviet sources are notably reticent about *MVD* troops units of any kind but do occasionally refer to the Independent Dzerzhinskiy Motorized Rifle Division as a *Chekist* division. A contingent of this division—apparently an *OSNAZ* division—reported to have existed since Civil War times, normally appears in the semiannual Moscow parades.[70]

Convoy Troops
These troops appear to have either a very flexible or a very obscure organization. At one time or another, convoy troops have been reported as being organized into separate divisions, separate regiments, separate battalions, and even separate companies. They reputedly have home stations but spend a fair amount of their time away, convoying prisoners as well as strategic shipments.[71] Convoy troops are rarely identified as such in the open Soviet press.

Special Facilities Guards [Okhrana osobykh ob'yektov]
The *OOO*, sometimes referred to as "sentry troops," act as full-time security guards for specially designated installations of strategic importance, apparently including some central depots of the Ministry of Defense.[72] Available official US literature does not indicate any organizational data, although some dated information from former *MVD* officers indicates that *OOO* units were organized into separate regiments, battalions, and even companies, depending on the size and importance of the guarded objective. Open Soviet literature on *OOO* troops is nearly nonexistent.

It is possible there is a special category of *MVD* troops or militarized guard personnel for the specific purpose of guarding places of confinement. Various US attaches, including the author, have seen numerous prison-like structures under the guard of *MVD* whose uniforms, even to the rust red shoulder boards, appeared no different from those of other *MVD* troops.[73]

Railroad Security and Other Troops
The current existence of some other types of *MVD* troops previously known to exist is very much in doubt. *MVD* railroad troop units—whose duties were to aid in convoying prisoners; transport designated segments of the population to resettlement areas; guard rail installations, rights of way, tunnels, defiles, bridges, rail centers, and manned armored trains; and convoy regular rail traffic through troubled areas—may well have been inactivated. *MVD* railroad troop units were last reported in the mid–1950s. There are other indications special duties formerly assigned to the railway troops may have been divided among other types of *MVD* troops, the civil police, or a special militarized guard of the Railway Ministry.[74]

Reports of small *MVD* air elements have persisted through the postwar years. Initially, these reportedly backed up both Internal and Border Troops, although the latter, now under the *KGB*, have their own organic aircraft. The *MVD* aircraft are reportedly used for liaison, reconnaissance, and VIP flights.

MVD also had jurisdiction prior to and throughout World War II over local civil defense. This control continued up to 1961 when the MOD assumed this function and centralized it under a deputy minister of defense.[75]

Schools and Training

MVD Internal Troop schooling and training are very rarely mentioned in the open Soviet press, military or otherwise. The contributors to *The Soviet Secret Police* maintained that, in the 1950s, Internal Troop officers were drawn from the Army's officer commissioning schools or from the Army as a result of straight transfer.[76]

Within the last five years, announcements soliciting *MVD* Internal Troop officer candidates have begun to appear in military journals at about the same time MOD officer candidate schools are advertised. Five such schools are now advertised:

- the Novosibirsk Higher Command School of the *MVD*;
- the Kirov Higher Command School of the *MVD* (located in Ordzhonikidze);
- the Dzerzhinskiy Higher Command School of the *MVD* (located in Saratov);
- the Higher Political School of the *MVD* named after the 60th Anniversary of the *Komsomol* (located in Leningrad);
- The Kharkov Higher Military School of the *MVD* for Rear Services.

Graduates from the Novosibirsk, Ordzhonikidze, and Saratov schools are commissioned as "lieutenants" and "motorized rifle unit" officers. The Kharkov school graduates are specialized in one of three fields: motor transport (either as motor transport officers or engineer/mechanics), artillery technical (or ordnance); and intendance (quartermaster) as food and material supply officers or engineer-economists. The Leningrad school turns out new officers "with a higher political education."[77]

Advanced education for *MVD* Internal Troop officers reportedly used to be given at MOD line or service branch academies, especially Frunze. At least some of this may now be given at the *MVD* Academy. (See Figure 5 for the locations of both *KGB* Border Troop and *MVD* Internal Troop officer commissioning schools.)

Basic training for enlisted Internal Troops is carried out at the parent unit to which the young conscript has been assigned. Convoy and guard troops receive tactical unit training up to battalion and perhaps regimental level, whereas operational and *OSNAZ* troops—particularly the latter—get division-level training and participate in large-scale troop maneuvers.

Locations of Known
KGB and OCS Schools

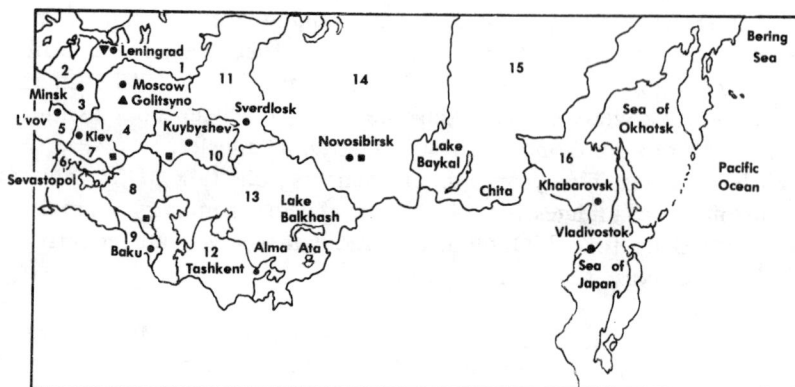

MILITARY DISTRICTS

1. LENINGRAD	9. TRANSCAUCASUS
2. BALTIC	10. VOLGA
3. BELORUSSIAN	11. URAL
4. MOSCOW	12. TURKESTAN
5. CARPATHIAN	13. CENTRAL ASIAN
6. ODESSA	14. SIBERIAN
7. KIEV	15. TRANSBAYKAL
8. NORTH CAUCASUS	16. FAR EASTERN

● 2 KGB Command Schools   ▲ 1 MVD Political School

■ 4 MVD Schools (3 Command, 1 Rear Services)   ▼ 1 KGB Political School

Figure 5

Each type of unit also receives operational service training in convoy duty; installation security; execution of raids, searches, and seizures; and sealing off small groups or even large inhabited areas. Specialist training is given to *MVD* Internal Troops assigned to artillery, armor, engineer, or signal duty.[78]

Other Personnel Matters

MVD Internal Troops are indistinguishable from Soviet Army troops except for their rust red shoulder boards and blue-topped service caps. Otherwise, rank and grade insignia appear to be identical to those of the Ground and Air Forces of the Ministry of Defense. *MVD*

specialists wear the same metallic insignia as Army specialists.

Call-ups

Annual recurring call-ups and discharge of *MVD* Internal Troop conscripts are accomplished through the countless local military commissariats throughout the country.[79] Long before the actual call-up, quotas for *MVD* (and *KGB*) troop unit conscripts have been furnished by the *MVD* (and the *KGB*) through Ministry of Defense channels, and the records of the young call-ups have been thoroughly reviewed. *MVD* and *KGB* representatives apparently sit temporarily on the call-up boards interviewing the young conscripts to ensure the *MVD–KGB* contingents are the pick of the local lot.

Article 99 of the Soviet Law on Universal Military Service stipulates the rights granted to the Minister of Defense in certain other articles are also granted to the Chairman of the *KGB* and to the USSR Minister of Internal Affairs with respect to the "troops, institutions, and educational establishments . . . of the *KGB*" or the USSR *MVD* Ministry.[80] Articles 39 to 41 and article 61 set up rank and grade structures and provide for promotion, reduction, transfer from one "branch (arm of service)" to another, "into the reserves," admission of conscripts or inactive reservists to career service establishments, the granting of reserve commissions, and the call-up of reserve officers.[81]

Possible MVD Troop Reservists

As in the case of the *KGB,* the status of *MVD* reservists is quite obscure. No available Soviet sources flatly state there are *MVD* troop reservists, but there are numerous intimations. Pre–WWII mobilization documents, for example, indicate reserve personnel were to be assigned to *NKVD* and *KGB* troop units, but whether these were from a special list of *NKVD* reservists or from general reserve manpower pools is unclear. When the 50–year medal was approved for awarding to regular Ministry of Defense, *KGB,* and *MVD* troops, it was stated that those who had already served 20 years on active duty and had been transferred to the reserves and/or were retired would also be awarded the medal. The specific reserve to which these inactive *KGB* or *MVD* military personnel had been transferred was not detailed.[82]

The military service law states both the *KGB* Chairman and *MVD* Minister can grant reserve commissions and discharge into the reserves. It is not stated there are specifically *KGB* or *MVD* reserves, but it is doubtful they would grant reserve commissions for forces other than their own.[83]

Contributors to *The Soviet Secret Police* state that local military commissariats of the Ministry of Defense kept separate *MVD* troop and Army reserve lists, as well as separate lists of active Army troops designated in advance of assignment to specific *MVD* units on mobilization. Such personnel were kept under constant surveillance and were

571

transferred immediately from the special security troop lists back to Army reserve lists should there be the slightest doubt as to their reliability.[84] (During the period in question, the *MVD* included what are now both *MVD* and *KGB* troops.)

Political Indoctrination and Surveillance

The Internal Troops also have a system of political officers and attached *KGB* counterintelligence agents who monitor all activities within the units.[85] Lieutenant General V. I. Kotov has been Chief of the Political Administration for Internal Troops for more than a decade.

As in the case of the KGB, the higher political reliability required for entry into these elite troops leads to the assumption that political training is stressed even more than in the Ministry of Defense forces and surveillance and security are even tighter than in the Army and Navy.

Role in WWII and Early Postwar Years

The exact WWII role of the *MVD* (then *NKVD*) Internal Troops is fuzzy and imprecise for at least two apparent reasons: (a) the limited amount of information given out by the Soviets on security troops and other security functions in general, and (b) a tendency to blur together as *NKVD* accomplishments the wartime achievements of Border and Internal Troop units and those of all the other Soviet security activities, including even counterintelligence work outside the comparatively small area specifically assigned to Army intelligence.

WWII *MVD* Internal Troops appear to have consisted of *OSNAZ* troops, operational troops, convoy troops, *OOO*, civil defense troops, and railway security troops (not to be confused with Army railway troops). Their specific organizational mix and overall strength remain undisclosed.

Wartime Functions

The activities of Internal Troops during and immediately following WWII—sometimes alone, sometimes in conjunction with Border and other troops and *MVD* elements—were as follows:

(a) Occasionally fought as elite shock troops in an emergency, sometimes to achieve breakthroughs or to cover Red Army retreats.

(b) Fought anti-Soviet partisans.

(c) Provided blocking detachments in front rear areas to prevent deep German penetration and actively discourage retreat by beleaguered Red Army forces.

(d) Guarded against enemy attack, sabotage, or penetration of especially strategic stockpiles; major government and

Party offices; and key transport facilities and choke points, including yards, bridges, tunnels, port facilities, and important transport right of way sections.

(e) Suppressed dissidence, revolts, uprisings, coups, and disorders among the populace and mutiny and insurrections within the armed forces.

(f) Convoyed important military and industrial supplies and raw materials in the interior zone and up through the rear areas of the fronts.

(g) Manned certain secret weaponry not yet entrusted to regular line units; e.g., the early multiple rocket launchers, *Katyushas,* were reportedly *MVD*–manned.

(h) Sent penetration or diversionist groups into German lines.

(i) Operated Red Army penal battalions used as shock troops.

(j) Operated as snipers and sharpshooters within the ranks of regular Army units.

(k) Evacuated or destroyed threatened Soviet industrial plants and government service installations.

(l) Disarmed and screened anti-German partisans and resettled those who were unassimilable.

(m) Guarded, convoyed, processed, and exploited the huge masses of German prisoners of war; have sometimes been accused of eliminating those whose liberation or escape seemed probable.

(n) Participated in pro–Soviet partisan activity in enemy-occupied areas.

(o) Reprocessed, screened, guarded, convoyed, and exploited the large masses of liberated Soviet PWs and slave labor freed from Axis hands.

(p) Screened, processed, and convoyed to places of resettlement huge numbers of politically suspect personnel from among the several indigenous national minorities forcibly resettled from European Russia deep into Soviet Asia.

(q) Under *NKGB* operational direction, supervised the screening, processing, guarding, and convoying to resettlement or imprisonment of large numbers of suspect personnel from the East European and formerly Japanese-occupied territories occupied or annexed by the Soviets.

(r) In some cases, supervised the operations of indigenous satellite elements who confined their prisoners in their own countries. Thousands of these political prisoners wound up in Soviet labor camps.

(s) Organized and participated in securing and sealing off various strategically important East European industrial and economic installations stripped as reparations—e.g., East German and Czechoslovak uranium sources.

(t) Guarded some of the more important special purpose concentration camps.[86]

Postwar Activity

As many as three Internal Troop Divisons along with Border and other Internal Troop units, some Army units, and militia reportedly were engaged in the Baltic area from 1944 to 1951 in putting down anti-Soviet partisan activity, according to a knowledgeable participant. Other half-confirmed stories, continuing up through the 1950s, tell of continuing *MVD* troop activity against Ukrainian, Lithuanian, and other Baltic insurgents.[87]

Future Military Implications

Allegedly, the *MVD* Internal Troops (as are the Border Troops of the *KGB*) are housed, clothed, fed, and equipped better than the armed forces of the Ministry of Defense and enjoy privileges not available to the country's Army and Navy. *MVD* and other security troop officers have received bonuses for services in special areas.[88] *MVD* and *KGB* troops have a long record of loyalty to the regime both in peacetime and wartime. These security troops, "whose reliability and fanatical devotion is without equal among the Soviet Armed Forces," provide a ready-made positive addition to the country's military muscle that must be reckoned with.[89] Why is it, then, that the security troops of the *KGB* and *MVD* have received comparatively little attention and have been held in fairly light regard?

The Generally Held Western Misperception of Soviet Security Troops

What we are discussing is a group conservatively two-thirds the size of the current US Army; taken together with similar and possibly low-side estimates of their East European security troop counterparts, they virtually equal the current size of the US Army. Soviet security troop strength is comparable to that of the Soviet Air Forces, the Soviet Air Defense Forces, and the Soviet Navy, and it exceeds that of the Strategic Rocket Forces. The Soviet security forces are larger than the armed forces of any East European satellite, including Poland. They are small only when compared to the Soviet Ground Forces.

There are a number of reasons which could be advanced for the continued light regard in which Soviet security forces are held in Western circles (and to my way of thinking none of them are very valid):

1) The lack of Soviet commentary on the strength and organization of the security forces. There is probably a good *internal* reason for this: the Soviet Party and government do not want, any more than necessary, to cram these troops—a counterweight against the MOD

forces and the populace in general—continuously down the latter's throats.

2) Western analytical circles apparently have a semantic block against using the words "troops" and "soldiers" in conjunction with the uniformed armed forces of the *KGB* and *MVD,* replete though they might be with armor and cannon. These gentry thus employ the word "militarized," or "paramilitary," "quasi-military," or worst of all, "police." This really is a professional insult to the *KGB* and *MVD* troops whose direct antecedents foughts as shock troops in division and army strength in many of the great battles of World War II. More important, it is a serious underestimate.

3) The redivision of the intelligence coverage pie in the US some years back has not helped matters any. In the early post–World War II days, the US Army's Office of the Assistant Chief of Staff for Intelligence had a "Special Projects Section" which specifically studied and analyzed Soviet and East European satellite security troops, then fully regarded as troops. With the repositioning of the study of the functions of the various Bloc security ministries under the purview of the newly organized Central Intelligence Agency, there was a growing reluctance on the part of the US military to delve too far into the workings of Bloc security troops which were lumped administratively with intelligence, counter-intelligence, and security elements under a common nondefense ministry. Nor did CIA seem to be enthusiastic about getting into the business of detailed "bean counting" of these smaller, somewhat exotic, non–MOD troop bodies.

Things have now proceeded to a wryly humorous point: the 1978 US Army *Soviet Operations Handbook* devotes more than 350 pages to the Soviet MOD ground forces and 1½ pages to Soviet security troops which are supposedly overseen by a "Ministry of Intelligence" (which, of course, does not exist).[90]

The 350,000 Soviet security troops carried in the otherwise fine 1978 US Army Handbook can be interestingly compared with the 500,000 figure for the same troops given in the US Air Force *Soviet Aerospace Handbook,* published in the very same year. This also otherwise fine publication devotes 222 pages to Soviet MOD forces and 1½ pages to the non–MOD Security Troops. It calls them a

. . . select group of militiarized security personnel . . . organized along military lines . . . and a highly effective police force. In wartime, the troops of both the *MVD* and *KGB* could be used to augment the forces under the control of MOD. These units would provide the Soviet Armed Forces with an additional half a million highly trained ground combat personnel.[91]

Who says you can't have it both ways? There it is—all on one page—"militarized security personnel," a "highly effective police force," and "a half million highly trained ground *combat* personnel." [Emphasis added.]

Those who find the half million estimate too high are given still another choice. On page 130 of the same publication, this appears:

> The Soviet Union also has about 330,000 militarized security personnel (border and internal troops) . . . half this number are in Soviet Border Troops (*KGB*). The Soviet Internal Troops (*MVD*) have the remainder.

The Defense Intelligence Agency also does some of this in its 1969 pamphlet devoted to the Soviet Armed Forces. The section on security troops is four and one-half pages (with pictures). The security troops are successively called "military security forces" and a "comprehensive police structure . . . ." It further states that in emergencies, they may be used as "front line troops."[92]

The worst offender is probably the Institute for Strategic Studies. Year after year, the august "Military Balance" of this organization carries the security troops as "paramilitary forces," lumping these elite units with the part-time Soviet military training organization *DOSAAF* which "takes part in athletics [and] shooting . . . and assists in premilitary training given those 15 and over."[93]

Maybe because the US has not found an efficient way to register its own people for possible induction, we continue to ignore this half-million-man body of registered, uniformed, trained full-time soldiery. In these days when our own Army has been described by its chief of staff as "hollow" and a large part of our Navy reportedly can't put to sea because of crew shortages, we are in a poor position to label Soviet security troops as "police" or "militarized" or otherwise to water down our perception. It's high time to get back to a humble but very pragmatic school of backwoods philosophy: "If it walks like a duck, swims like a duck, quacks like a duck, and has feathers—it's a duck."

I am suggesting that no rigorous, coordinated look has ever been taken at the Soviet (or East European) security troops either to establish more precisely their numbers and functions or to measure their capabilities and standards. This is one "duck" which cries out for identity and detailed study.

Notes

1. For example, David A. Smith, in "Soviet Military Manpower," *Air Force Magazine,* March 1977, lists the MOD forces at 4.4 million. The Department of the Air Force *Soviet Aerospace Handbook* (Washington, May 1978), on p. 120 lists their strength at about 4.8 million, but on p. 130 states, "The Soviet Union also has about 330,000 militarized security personnel." The *Military Balance, 1980–1981* on p. 9 lists Soviet Armed Forces' strength at 3,658 million, excluding some "500,000 railway,

construction, and security troops," the latter somehow not being part of the Armed Forces (London: International Institute for Strategic Studies, 1981).

2. Institute for Strategic Studies, *The Military Balance 1979–1980* (London: IISS, 1979).

3. Jean Pierre Brule, *Demain–L'Armee Sovietique* [The Soviet Army Tomorrow] (Paris: Copernic Press, 1978), pp. 145–150.

4. James T. Reitz, "An Overview of Manpower in the Soviet Military–Industrial Complex" in *Soviet Defense Manpower*, GE Tempo Report GE 77, TMP–18, 14 July 1977.

5. Harriet Fast Scott and William F. Scott, *The Armed Forces of the USSR* (Boulder: Westview Press, 1979), pp. 218–222, 376; Christina F. Shelton and James T. Reitz, "Soviet Security Troops," unpublished draft manuscript, November 1978 (Washington: GE Tempo); *Krasnaya zvezda*, hereinafter abbreviated as *KZ*, 27 May 1978 ("In Honor of the Border Troops," "On Guard of Our Active Ramparts," For Each Meter of the Border"), 27 May 1979 ("Always on Patrol"); and *Kommunist Vooruzhennykh Sil* [Communist of the Armed Forces], hereinafter abbreviated as *KVS;* No. 10, October 1978, "Sentries of the Border Patrol," and No. 10, October 1980, "On Unending Patrol."

6. "50th Anniversary of the USSR Border Troops—Always on Patrol," *Literaturnaya gazeta* [Literary Gazette], 29 May 1968; see also an interview in *Nedelya* [The Week], 6 May 1966 with Colonel General Zyrayanov. The interviewer states: "Our civilian imagination was instantly drawn to . . . the direct wires from all the furthest and nearest posts: the Chukotsk Islands, Turkmenia, the Far East, and the Kola Peninsula."

7. Simon Wolin and Robert N. Slusser, eds., *The Soviet Secret Police* (New York: Praeger, 1957).

8. Ibid., pp. 280–286.

9. V. P. Artem'yev and G. M. Viktorov, *Soviet Organs of State Security* (Garmisch: US Army School of Advanced Russian Studies, 1964), especially Chapter 18.

10. Department of the Army, *Handbook on the Soviet Army,* Army Pamphlet 30–50–1, Part I, 1953; and 1958 edition of the same publication, Appendix 1.

11. Artem'yev and Viktorov, op. cit.; B. H. Liddel Hart, ed., *The Red Army* (New York: Harcourt, Brace, and World, 1956).

12. Defense Intelligence Agency, *Handbook on the Soviet Armed Forces* (Washington: Government Printing Office, July 1969), Chapter 12.

13. Artem'yev and Viktorov, op. cit.

14. Department of the Army, *Soviet Army Operations,* Army Pamphlet PAM–IAG–13 U 78, April 1978, pp. 2–48.

15. Wolin and Slusser, op. cit., p. 268.

16. Scott and Scott, op. cit., p. 220.

17. Wolin and Slusser, op. cit., pp. 260–280; Artem'yev and Vikotorov, op. cit.; Liddel Hart, op. cit., p. 267; and Major General Yu. Neshumov, "On the Fatherland's Borders," *KZ,* 27 May 1977.

18. Wolin and Slusser, op. cit.; Department of the Army, op. cit.; Liddel Hart, op. cit.

19. V. A. Matrosov and V. K. Gaponenko, "The Border Troops," *Sovetskaya Voyennaya Entsiklopediya* [Soviet Military Encyclopedia], hereinafter abbreviated as *SVE* (Moscow: *Voyenizdat,* 1976), pp. 365–368.

20. Green is the characteristic color designation of the border troops of most, if not all, of the East European satellites. Most satellite internal troops wear an off-red similar to that worn by their Soviet counterparts or they wear the very bright blue characteristic of the *KGB* shoulder boards (not to be confused with Soviet KGB Border Troop green). Satellite army branch colors, on the other hand, differ widely from one another and from those of the Soviet Army.

21. Department of the Air Force, op. cit., pp 179–195.

22. Wolin and Slusser, op. cit., pp. 242–243.

23. Office of the Assistant Chief of Staff for Intelligence, United States Army, Translation G–6246, pp. 156–159.

24. "Watchmen of the State Borders," *Pravda,* 28 May 1968.

25. *TASS* English language broadcast, Radio Moscow, 26 December 1967; also, a greeting by Polish Defense Minister Marshal Spychaslki to "all Polish Border reservists" is another oblique indication that the Polish Border Troops, who have parroted faithfully their Soviet counterparts on mission, organization, and doctrine, may have followed Soviet custom in this as well. See *Zolinerz Wolnosci* [Soldier of Freedom], 10 June 1966.
26. Wolin and Slusser, op. cit., p. 243.
27. Ibid., pp. 300–306.
28. Ibid., p. 299.
29. Ibid., p. 303.
30. "Those Who Would Become Officers," *KZ,* 12 February 1980.
31. "Committee for State Security," *SVE,* Vol. 4 (Moscow: Voyenizdat, 1977), pp. 265–266; see also "Topical Tasks of Ideological Work," *KZ,* 13 April 1976 which describes a widely attended conference of political chiefs and workers of several armed forces branches as well as those of the Border and Internal Troops. Chief of the Main Political Administration of the Soviet Army and Navy Army General A. A. Yepishev chaired the meeting.
32. Address by Major General Kozovets, former Commanding General, Far East Military District, on Radio Khabarovsk, 27 May 1965.
33. See V. Igoshkin, *Formation Before the Banner* (Moscow: Young Guard Publishing House, 1968), p. 53 for illustrations of the "Young Friends of the Border Guards" uniforms; A. I. Getman, "A Truly All–Union Society," *Sovetskiy patriot* [Soviet Patriot], 30 June 1966. Getman was Chairman of *DOSAAF.* See also "Fighting Assistants of the Border Troops," *KZ,* 21 December 1967 for the story of awards to one such group of "hundreds" of young Komsomol Pioneer members.
34. Neshumov, op. cit.; James T. Reitz, "Selected Strategic Trends in the Communist World: Their Implications for Military Planning," Research Analysis Corporation Report RAC–T–458, Vol. I, December 1965, pp. 31–34; "Medal for Improving Combat Cooperation," *KZ,* May 1979.
35. P. Shankov, "Patrol of the Southern Border," *Pravda,* 28 May 1968.
36. "Outpost, to Your Weapons," *Sovetskaya Litva* [Soviet Lithuania], 25 May 1968.
37. General Kishentsev, "Our Frontiers Are Inviolable," *Sel'skaya zhizn'* [Rural Life], 28 May 1968.
38. "A Museum to the [Bulgarian] Border Guard," *Narodna Armiya* [The People's Army], 25 February 1966.
39. Interview with Zyrayanov, *Pravda,* 28 May 1968.
40. I. I. Petrov, "Party Solicitude in Strengthening the Border Troops, 1939–1941," *Voprosy istorii KPSS* [Problems of History of the CPSU], No. 5, May 1968, p. 95.
41. V. Shevchenko, "Soviet Border Troops in the Great Fatherland War," *Voyenno–istoricheskiy zhurnal* [Military–Historical Journal], hereinafter abbreviated as *VIZh,* No. 5, May 1968, p. 125.
42. Wolin and Slusser, op. cit., p. 264.
43. Petrov, op. cit.; Lieutenant General Zabolotnyy, "A Half Century on Guard on the Soviet Borders, *KVS,* No. 9, September 1968.
44. Zabolotnyy, op. cit.; Shevchenko, op. cit.; and Raymond L. Garthoff, *Soviet Military Doctrine* (Glencoe: Free Press, 1963).
45. *KZ,* 1 May 1965, 1968.
46. Shevchenko, op. cit.
47. Thus, Engineer Colonel G. Preobrazhenskiy was listed not as Deputy Chief of the Border Guard for Rear Services but simply as Chief of the Rear of the Border Troops. See "Always at the Combat Post," *Tyl i snabzheniye* [The Rear and Logistics], No. 5, May 1968; also see the following descriptions of additional pre–WWII Border Guard clashes, particularly with the Japanese: Colonel General P. I. Zyrayanov, "50 Years of Military Service," *Pravda,* 5 May 1968, and an interview with Zyryanov in *Neues Deutschland,* 22 June 1968.
48. Shevchenko, op. cit.

49. I. Boyko, "The Rear of the Western Front during the First Days of the Fatherland War," *VIZh,* No. 6, June 1966.
50. Zabolotnyy, op. cit.
51. United States War Department, *Handbook on the USSR Armed Forces,* TM 10–410 (Washington: Government Printing Office, 1946), Section IV.
52. Department of the Army, *Handbook* (1953).
53. Liddel Hart, op. cit.
54. A. Tsvetkov and L. Kozlov, "The Soviet Border Guard in the Great Fatherland War," *VIZh,* No. 6, June 1968; and Shevchenko, op. cit.
55. Robert Conquest, *Deportation of the Nationalities* (London: Macmillan, 1960); K. V. Taurus, *Guerillas of the Amber Coast* (New York: Voyages Press, 1962); Eugene Lyons, *Our Secret Allies* (New York: Duell, Sloan, and Pearce, 1954); James T. Reitz and Roman Redlich, *Major and Minor Uprisings in the Soviet Union,* 3 Vols. (Garmisch: US Army School of Advanced Russian and East European Studies, nd).
56. Gregory Klimov, *The Terror Machine: The Inside Story of the Soviet Administration in Berlin* (New York: Praeger, 1953). Klimov was a former Soviet Army major.
57. Ibid., p. 536.
58. Scott and Scott, op. cit., p. 220.
59. Wolin and Slusser, op. cit., pp. 268–292; Artem'yev and Viktorov, op. cit.; Petrov, op. cit.; Klimov, op. cit.
60. Department of the Army, *Handbook* (1958).
61. Wolin and Slusser, op. cit., p. 170; and War Department, op. cit.
62. Defense Intelligence Agency, op. cit.
63. War Department, op. cit.
64. "Soviet *Chekists* in the Great Fatherland War," *KZ,* 7 May 1963.
65. Department of the Army, *Soviet Army Operations;* Edgar O'Ballance, *The Red Army* (New York: Praeger, 1964).
66. Reitz, "Overview . . . ;" and ISS, op. cit.
67. *KZ,* 5 May 1965.
68. Garthoff, op. cit., pp. 414–415; Department of the Army, *Handbook* (1953 and 1958); Wolin and Slusser, op. cit., p. 414.
69. Defense Intelligence Agency, op. cit.
70. *KZ,* 1 May 1965, 1966, 1968.
71. "A Big Soviet Weakness," *The Intelligence Digest* (Cheltanham, UK), December 1965; Defense Intelligence Agency, op. cit.; Department of the Army, *Handbook* (1958); Brule, op. cit., Chapter 18.
72. Defense Intelligence Agency, op. cit.
73. Brule, op. cit.
74. Defense Intelligence Agency, op. cit.
75. Leon Goure, *Civil Defense in the Soviet Union* (Berkeley: University of California Press, 1962).
76. Wolin and Slusser, op. cit., p. 246.
77. Ibid., pp. 244–249.
78. Ibid.
79. Ibid.
80. "Law on Universal Military Service," *Izvestiya,* 13 October 1967.
81. Ibid.
82. *East Europe,* Vol. 78, No. 3 (April 1958); Richard F. Starr, "The East European Alliance System," United States Naval Institute *Proceedings,* September 1964.
83. "Law on Universal Military Service," *Izvestiya.*
84. Wolin and Slusser, op. cit., p. 243.
85. "Committee for State Security," *SVE,* Vol. 4 (1977), pp. 265–266.
86. Wolin and Slusser, op. cit., pp. 18–24, 129–189, 249, and 325–335; War Department, op. cit., pp. I–iv, IV–8, VII–73; Taurus; and Conquest.
87. Cf. Taurus; Conquest; and Reitz and Redlich.
88. Wolin and Slusser, op. cit., p. 249.

89. Two Western military writers, Louis Ely and E. Hinterhoff, referred to the Soviet security forces as being of the combat quality and morale of the German *Waffen-SS* formations of WW II. See Ely, The Red Army Today (Harrisburg: Military Publishing Company, 1951) and Hinterhoff, "The Warsaw Pact," *Wehr und Wirtschaft,* December 1961, p. 91.

90. Department of the Army, *Soviet Army Operations,* p. 2–47.

91. Department of the Air Force, op. cit., pp. 20–21.

92. Defense Intelligence Agency, op. cit., Chapter 12.

93. IISS, op. cit.

Soviet Strategic Reserves and the Soviet Navy

R. W. Barnett

Strategic Reserves

Although apparently a fundamental part of strategy, the concept of reserve forces and their impact on the way wars are fought has not always been evident. To take an early example, "the holding back of a powerful reserve force to be brought into play at a later, decisive, moment is very rare indeed in Greek warfare and rare in Macedonian strategy."[1] However desirable, national leaders for the most part simply did not have forces superfluous to the task at hand that might be maintained as a reservoir of power upon which to draw at the propitious time to turn the tide of battle. Such a situation was prevalent until the waning years of the 18th century when fighting men, previously an expensive commodity, became less expensive because of the widespread adoption of conscription. As a result, wars that had previously been fought for well-defined objectives with limited means became far less constrained in both. Subsequently, reserve forces played important roles in the major wars of the 19th and 20th centuries.

With the advent of nuclear weapons and attendant intercontinental means of delivery the question of wartime reserve forces—for American strategists, at least—centered implicitly on the residual strategic weapon force after a first strike had been absorbed. The theory was that if an "assured destruction force" were maintained that could threaten an enemy with unacceptable damage in retaliation, such a force would deter an initial strike. If both sides maintained such a residual force, moreover, deterrence would be deemed "stable." In this frame of reference, the question of a reserve force of intercontinental weapons simply never arose.

What was lacking in such thinking was the ability to work through the stages of a nuclear conflict and by doing so to gain an understanding of the value of strategic reserve forces. The tendency, rather, was to maintain such questions were moot because deterrence would not (could not!) fail. Far from the conviction of Enthoven and Smith that "once each side has enough nuclear forces virtually to eliminate the other's urban society in a second strike, the utility of extra forces is dubious at best,"[2] such strategic reserve forces may, in fact, be *crucial* to the determination of a victor in a war.

If it were the strategy of one adversary very carefully to plan and to take steps to ensure that it would possess manifestly more powerful forces than its enemy at every stage and through every phase of a war, the implications of such a strategy would be far-reaching indeed. They would influence heavily intrawar deterrence, escalation control, war termination, and negotiating leverage. If the more powerful of the antagonists were to threaten credibly to pursue a conflict until the point at which its residual superiority was acknowledged—that is, its opponent recognized that defeat was certain—it could conceivably claim the spoils of war without a fight. Put another way, the weaker side might as well succumb if it were to become clear that its opponent could always force and always win the *final* battle.

To dare to think that strategic nuclear war would be other than a spasmodic release of intercontinental weapons means to reach the understanding that there might be a concept of victory in such a war. A winner would be able to convince its adversary that the price of resistance or of continuation is too high. Whether a single round would be fired or not depends on a series of variables and unknowns. Deterrence of strategic nuclear war in this framework hinges not on capability and the will to destroy civilians and industrial targets but on preventing an opponent from believing that he would prevail at any level of conflict. Indeed, rather than fractions of population and industry that might be destroyed in an exchange of strategic weapons or in a series of exchanges, it would make better strategic sense to recognize the strategic reserve force as a yardstick for strategic superiority. Two conditions must obtain for the strategic reserve to assume a decisive character: it must be both superior and secure. And perceptions—not precise tallying—are what matter.

Strategic reserves encompass more than intercontinental weapons in the narrow sense that "strategic" is used in the United States. In a broader context, the term might include stockpiles of material and fuel; idle industrial or transportation capacity; manpower; the command, control, and communications system; and a variety of weapons. For the purposes of this essay, however, only the military component will be considered.

In the abstract, what might be the characteristics of an ideal strategic reserve force? Presuming the parties to a nuclear conflict did not empty their arsenals early in a war, strategic reserves would be employed to influence how a conflict was proceeding. Obviously, then, *quantity* would be an important characteristic. As in most military matters, more rather than less would clearly be preferable. And, as in most military matters, the subject of "how much" boils down ultimately to economic trade-offs and priorities.

Protection must be provided to strategic reserves so that they survive either to be used or to deter subsequent conflict. Protection can take many forms—concealment and active and passive forms of defense spring immediately to mind. A positive, reliable means of control must be provided also so that the strategic reserve might be employed effectively even in a nuclear warfighting environment. In the abstract, then, the ideal strategic reserve force would be large, well-protected, and it would have rapid and redundant means of control.

High quality would be desirable for a strategic reserve, but it seems less essential for a reserve force than the other characteristics. If the force were large, survivable, and controllable, high quality would be a bonus but not a requirement. More important, it would seem, might be *response time;* that is, how quickly the reserve could be committed once summoned. Response time involves a long list of desiderata, one of the most important being the level of readiness at which the capability is maintained in peacetime.

Soviet strategy, as revealed in the open literature, indicates that Soviet strategists—unlike the majority of their Western counterparts[3]— have thought about the question of nuclear warfighting and have integrated reserve forces into their strategy, taking account of a broad range of implications along the way. The next section of the article explores how Soviet authors envision the importance of strategic reserves, what they say about their composition, and what impact they expect reserves to have on a war. The characteristics postulated above for strategic reserves—quantity, protection, control, high quality, and responsiveness—provide a backdrop against which to assess the Soviet concepts. The third section of the article examines the evidence that the Kremlin plans to use naval forces as strategic reserves, and the final section contains conclusions and implications.

Strategic Reserves in Soviet Strategy

A logical starting point, the Soviet *Dictionary of Basic Military Terms,* offers only scant analytical assistance. "Strategic reserves," it states, are "reserves consisting of military-trained contingents and materiel stockpiles, under control of the Ministry of Defense or the Supreme High Command, and intended for use as supplementary resources in both peacetime and wartime."[4] This provides little enlightenment except to suggest a sharing of control of the reserves between the Ministry of Defense and the Supreme High Command. Exactly how this control is to be divided is not explicit, although the historical precedent of the State Committee of Defense acting as the *organizer* and *mobilizer* of the reserves and the *Stavka* of the Supreme High Command as the *employer* of the resources provided might be instructive.[5]

A review of the relevant tenets of Soviet strategy—as it is revealed in the open literature—will serve to illuminate better the position of the strategic reserves than will a definitional approach. The *course* and *out-come* of wars, for example, are subjects of particular interest to Soviet authors. In theorizing on the course of a war, the question of escalation inevitably must be addressed, and Soviet authors are not unwilling to tackle it—even if they are not always lucid. For example, they maintain:

> There exists no insurmountable barrier or solid wall between a limited war and a world war. Each local adventure contrived by the imperialists in some part of the world carries within itself the danger of escalation into a world conflagration, becoming as it were the detonator of a world war.[6]

This passage, of course, stands in direct opposition to the dominant strain of Western strategic thought which insists—and relies upon—a strong discontinuity between nuclear and non-nuclear war. To the Soviets, however, there is no "firebreak"; escalation may occur in a limited war, and the use of nuclear weapons merely increases the *risk* of escalation.[7]

In another context, the escalatory link is forged differently. If there is an "aggressive local war" and if it "infringes on the basic interests of the socialist countries and creates a threat to peace in the world," this will "obviously lead to a new world war . . . ."[8] The conditions here are more tightly drawn. Still, in a celebrated passage that has appeared unchanged in all three editions of *Military Strategy,* its authors assert:

> It should be emphasized that, with the international relations existing under present-day conditions and the present level of development of military equipment, any armed conflict will inevitably escalate into a general war if the nuclear powers are drawn into this conflict.[9]

This is obviously an attempt to plant a seed of uncertainty about escalation in local wars that do not directly affect the Soviet Union, its allies, or its "basic interests" and a concrete assurance that escalation will result if these core interests are violated.

The onset of a war may be by force of either nuclear or conventional weapons. This will in part depend upon the *correlation of forces* before the war begins. As a war progresses, moreover, a change in the correlation of forces can create conditions for a change in tactics or the application of various types of weapons. With regard to suggesting limits to conflict or interwar negotiating points, Soviet authors are very reticent—influenced undoubtedly by the fact that the entire concept of "limited" (vice "local") war is a criticized and unacceptable "bourgeois" theory.

In general, the limits of war are said to be determined solely by the nature of the political goals for which the war is being waged. There is a presumption throughout Soviet strategic thinking that if war occurs between capitalism and socialism, political goals will be essentially unlimited—it will be a war having no logical boundaries or discontinuities.

Warfighting depends strongly on the *correlation of forces,* an

584

appreciation for which is a major taproot of military thought. It may be conceived broadly as a comparison between two social systems, or it may be more narrow—an analysis of relative military strength on the battlefield, for example. Computing the correlation of forces necessitates first an evaluation of the social, military, economic, moral, and political capabilities and potentials of opposing forces and then a comparison of those evaluations. An appraisal of the relative strength of the sides is essentially a continuous process. At the macro level, this tends to be a subjective undertaking that includes estimates as a substantial ingredient; many of the factors that determine absolute strength and weakness are quantifiable, but the most important ones are not—at least in any verifiable way that would permit decisionmaking with low levels of inherent risk. Soviet strategists appear aware both of the importance of the correlation of forces and of its elusiveness and complexity:

> Relationship of forces is not something rigid and fatally predetermining the result of combat operations. It changes in relation to the economic, political, and ideological activity of the participants in the war and in relation to the course of military events.[10]

The correlation of forces occupies a central position in the Soviet formulation of the laws of war. Soviet military science contends that outcomes of wars depend directly on the correlation of forces as does the selection of weapons to be used in combat and the form a military engagement will assume.

At the system level, claims made for the shift in the world correlation of forces in favor of socialism indicate a conviction—totally at odds with Western thought—that military power confers political advantage. The claims most frequently encountered are that the change in relationships bears out the direction of history—namely, the inevitable victory of socialism; it has restrained imperialism from fomenting a new world war; it has thwarted "bourgeois adventurism" and its ability to intervene in national liberation movements of the "oppressed" people of the world; it has influenced the military doctrine of the imperialist countries; and it has created favorable conditions for political incentives.

This is by no means a Soviet drive for "parity"—a concept that is never espoused in Soviet literature—or for equality or "essential equivalence" but for *superiority*. *Superiority* in the military, technological, economic, and moral-political sphere is considered the sine qua non for *victory*. The shift in the correlation of forces to the socialist camp represents an assessment of socialist superiority. The quest is for superiority since "*the dialectics of modern world development are such that peace cannot be preserved if the military might of imperialism is not confronted by the superior military might of the socialist system.*"[11]

With regard to the anticipated *length* of a future war, ambiguity has long been a mainstay of Soviet military science.[12] This is a particularly difficult topic for Soviet writers to address, for an unequivocal determination one way or the other—that a strategic war could be terminated in a matter of hours or days or would stretch out over a period of time which permitted significant mobilization—has strong ramifications for force planning. In addition to affecting decisions on the size and structure of the armed forces the question of the duration of a future war has an impact on ideological positions, training and morale of active cadres, civil defense, and mobilization of the reserves. Geographical and historical considerations alone would argue that the Soviet Union must consider a long war to be a possibility and plan accordingly.

On balance, it should not be surprising that Soviet strategy exhibits ambivalence on the issue of the anticipated length of a war, especially because of the abstract way it must·be approached in the open literature in which specific scenarios of future wars are never broached. For obvious reasons, Soviet authors have no intention of detailing scenarios in their unclassified publications. Rather than stipulating "we just do not know how long a future will last," they are obliged to straddle the two stools, a not entirely disadvantageous posture.

By arguing the initial period of the war might well be decisive, they offer a persuasive rationale for superiority in the correlation of forces; at the same time, they cater to a visceral aversion toward a long, exhaustive conflict. By simultaneously maintaining the prolonged war possibility, they protect the mission of the ground forces, a mission that charges them not only with defending the soil of the Motherland from invaders but also with the occupation of the spoils of war. They are likewise faithful to the ideology in allowing for an intrawar revolutionary uprising in enemy countries; they support maintenance of large cadres of trained reservists; they provide the long-range planning basis for mobilization of the economy; and they avoid the notion that there can be no winners in a nuclear war—a notion derisively termed "nuclear fatalism."

Strategic reserves find their value in the overall scheme by their ability to influence the course and outcome of the armed struggle or the war. With regard to the Second World War, for example, Sokolovskiy lists the following ways strategic reserves were used:

— to create strategic groups in the course of the preparation
   for operations . . .
— to strengthen the fronts for counteroffensives . . .
— to increase the efforts in the development of an offensive
   in the direction of the main thrust . . .
— to protect the flank of a group delivering the main thrust
   by developing an offensive in the adjacent sector . . .
— to strengthen the fronts for the solution of new problems
   arising during a strategic offensive . . .

— to strengthen the troops operating in the outer encircling front . . .

— to strengthen the fronts for an offensive after stopping an enemy counteroffensive . . . .[13]

So important is the concept of the course and outcome of the war—and by extension the effect of the impress of strategic reserves—that in his highly regarded theoretical work, *The Basic Principles of Operational Art and Tactics,* Colonel V. Ye. Savkin sets forth four "Laws of War," *all* of which pivot on that concept. While disclaiming modestly that his efforts have exposed all the laws that can be derived, he nevertheless leaves his readers with an understanding that the laws he describes represent the extent to which military science has succeeded in elaborating them at present. Those laws are:

> . . . the course and outcome of war waged with unlimited employment of all means of conflict depends primarily on the correlation of available, strictly military forces at the beginning of the war, especially in nuclear weapons and means of delivery.
> . . . the course and outcome of war depends on the correlation of military potentials of the combatants.
> . . . the course and outcome of war depends on its political content.
> . . . the course and outcome of war depends on the correlation of moral-political and psychological capabilities of the people and armies of the combatants.[14]

It should be appreciated that these are the only laws of war suggested by Savkin; that they are wholly consistent with Soviet strategic writings; and that as "laws," they occupy a special place in Soviet military theory, for laws, by definition, are *scientific* and operate regardless of the actions of man. In this way *Laws* are distinguished from mutable *Principles.*

Important to this discussion is not that the place of strategic reserves in Soviet strategy has been proved, but that logic and evidence are not at odds with one another. But if the fit is good from a historical and theoretical perspective, what of an empirical, contemporary point of view? Is there evidence that strategic reserves can play a role in a future war? Lenin's oft-quoted assertion that "the victor in war is the one with the greater reserves, the greater sources of strength, and the greater staying power within the masses,"[15] might have been relevant 60 years ago, but what about today?

The words of Colonel General Lomov, in a major work, are informative:

> Military strategy proceeds from the necessity of creating the state and strategic manpower and material-technical

reserves even in peacetime, and with the use of them from the beginning of armed combat and the maintaining of them on the proper level in the course of the war. *The significance of these reserves under the conditions of modern war grows decisively.*[16]

This increasing emphasis on strategic reserves is said to be the result of the fact that nuclear weapons can be expected to exact large losses in terms of both manpower and material resources early in a war and also in great strategic depth. These two considerations in themselves would argue for large, dispersed, secure reserve forces. Moreover, the longer a war continued—and, as noted previously, long wars are accounted for in the theory—the greater the effect of strategic reserves.

Strategic reserves would be composed of

. . . operational *ob"yedineniya* of various branches of armed forces *soyedineniya* and *chasti* of arms, reserves of nuclear weapons and rockets, and other material and technical means which do not have a definite operational function and are at the disposal of the supreme command of the armed forces of a country.[17]

From this it appears that *all the branches of the Soviet Armed Forces would play a role* in forming the strategic reserves, that *both nuclear and conventional weapons would be part of the mix,* and that *missiles would be included in the weaponry.*

In the Soviet view, strategic reserves are to be established before the outbreak of war, deployed behind battle lines in a dispersed manner, and concealed and possibly protected so that they cannot be destroyed easily. The continuing large annual Soviet expeditures for air defense systems and civil defense might be understood, in part, as protection for strategic reserves.

Ground forces would certainly be relevant as strategic reserves in the event of a war in the European or Asiatic theaters. In a conflict with the United States, however, long-range missiles would be a more appropriate reserve force.

For land-based missile forces, it would seem that an ideal weapon to meet the requirements of a strategic reserve force would be a mobile intercontinental ballistic missile (ICBM). Such weapons were not included for limitation in the SALT I Interim Agreement, although the US delegation made a unilateral statement that their *operational deployment* would be inconsistent with the objectives of the Interim Agreement. As far as is known, neither side has operationally deployed mobile ICBMs. Since the launch silo is not destroyed by firing these weapons and reload missiles have not been controlled by SALT (either SALT I or the proposed SALT II treaty), the Soviets conceivably could reuse the launcher in a strategic reserve mode.

Naval forces are also considered to have a strategic reserve task.

Admiral Gorshkov writes in this regard about the US Navy:

> The attack carrier forces, which are the main means of attack by the Navy in local wars and are a highly trained reserve for the strategic strike forces in an all-out nuclear war, remain now as before the main element of the general-purpose naval forces.[18]

And, in a curious passage elsewhere, "based on materials from the foreign press" (a frequently employed technique of Soviet military writers), one finds:

> . . . experts in many countries believe that strategic naval forces, by having a narrow special mission, cannot undertake an active part in the execution of diverse operational and tactical missions. Moreover, they are incapable of realizing their own capabilities to a full degree in a nuclear war without appropriate support from other forces; in the case of a nonnuclear war, they will, on the whole, find themselves in the reserve.[19]

This latter excerpt captures one's attention for several reasons. In the first place, the context leaves no doubt the author is referring to ballistic missile submarines. That being the case, the first part of the statement—that they are not suited for a broad range of operational and tactical missions—appears reasonable. But the requirement for "support from other forces" is *not* one he gleaned from abroad. It is a product of *Soviet* interpretations of the history of submarine operations and has *not* been encountered in other than *Soviet* writings. Also, it seems important for Captain Aleshkin to tie the ballistic missile submarine to the reserve forces, even in a negative manner. The evidence for such a concept of employment for strategic submarines and the implications thereof must await expansion in the next section.

Soviet authors do not discuss *quantities* of their own forces except in very general ways. They say, for example, that the state provides for sufficient quantities to carry out the main tasks of the armed forces in time of war. They literally never reveal the size of their own force structures.

The Fiscal 1981 Report of the US Secretary of Defense places Soviet reserve ground force cadres with recent experience at a level of 4 million men, while William and Harriet Fast Scott claim that the Kremlin could have between 9 and 11 million men in uniform in 2 days.[20] Cold-launch capability currently exists in over 350 ICBM launchers of the SS–17 and –18 type, while the actual number of missiles (if any) stockpiled for the purpose of reloading these silos cannot be determined. If naval forces are to be used as strategic reserves, their numbers are 406 launchers installed in the DELTA–class (with long-range missile) and 544 launchers in the YANKEE–class (shorter-range missile). Whether or not these levels of reserves, in addition to whatever other forces are stockpiled or earmarked for reserve use, would be ample cannot be answered here. It should suffice to note that the US, in comparison, has a total of 832,000 reserve personnel, no ICBM cold-launch capability, and a total of 640 submarine-based ballistic missile launchers.

To say that modern-day problems of command and control in warfare have been recognized and taken under study by Soviet theoreticians would be to understate the case considerably. The "cybernetic revolution" represents the third stage in what the Soviets call the "revolution in military affairs." Owing to the increase in the destructive properties of weapons, the growth in the complexity of weapon systems, and the quantum decrease in the time available for decision-making and communications, demands have been placed on command, control, and communications that are acknowledged to be revolutionary in comparison to past wars. "Victory," according to a comtemporary work, "in the modern operation or engagement is *impossible* without well-organized troop coordination, coordination of their combat efforts in regard to objective, place, and time."[21]

There can be no gainsaying that the question of strategic reserves is one to which the Soviets have paid perhaps more attention than any other country in developing their strategy. From the foregoing discussion, the following conclusions can be drawn:

- Soviet military strategy addresses in some detail the difficult question of warfighting in the context of strategic nuclear warfare.
- Soviet military strategy takes the position that nuclear wars are possible, that there can be a winner in such a war, and that military superiority is required to secure victory.
- Soviet military strategy suggests that strategic reserve forces can have an effect on the course and outcome of war. It also notes that under conditions prevailing today:

  — Strategic reserves must be established and trained in peacetime.
  — Strategic reserves must be composed of nuclear rocket forces and of all branches of the services.
  — Strategic reserves must be secure, and they must be capable of being committed at the right time and place to be most influential on the progress and result of a conflict.
  — Strategic reserves will be controlled at the highest operational level (the *Stavka,* presumably), in wartime.

When longevity awards for service in high command are distributed, Fleet Admiral of the Soviet Union Sergey G. Gorshkov will take his place at the head of the line. Formally number one in the Soviet Navy since 1956, Gorshkov literally has transformed both Soviet naval strategy and the Soviet fleet in support of new initiatives. During his tenure, the world has witnessed several turns in Soviet naval policy, including the introduction of important new technologies—such as cruise and ballistic missiles, nuclear and gas turbine propulsion, sea-based air, and long-range replenishment capability—some of which the Soviet Navy was first in the world to deploy.[22] During his tenure, the Soviet Union has moved startlingly from a position of gross inferiority in strategic nuclear weapons to one of acknowledged parity and even arguable superiority.

Through decades of peace and rapid economic growth for the Soviet Union, the Soviet Navy under Gorshkov's tutelage has prospered. In fact, in comparison to the other branches of the Soviet Armed Forces, the Navy has fared extremely well indeed considering it would seem logically to have the lowest funding priority among the Soviet services. It is generally conceded that Gorshkov has been instrumental in securing for his navy what might appear to be a disproportionate fraction of fiscal support, given the Soviet Union's historical emphasis on land armies and its professed concern for homeland defense against *continental* enemies on two fronts, neither of which—in the absence of US support—can boast of strong maritime forces. For Gorshkov to succeed, it was no doubt necessary for him to act as the champion of the Soviet Navy in a way that was understandable—indeed reasonable—to his peers in the other branches of the Soviet Armed Forces.

Accordingly, one who has read extensively in Soviet military sources is struck by the consistency—and indeed the cleverness—with which Gorshkov relates naval warfare to the principles of military art with which the marshals and generals are so comfortable.[23] An excellent example of Gorshkov's care in ensuring that the principles of naval warfare (or naval *art* in Soviet terms) were argued in such a framework is his "Certain Questions Concerning the Development of Naval Art."[24] In that article, he divides the discussion into sections entitled "Scope of Conflict," "Battle," "Strike," "Maneuver," "Massing of Forms and Weapons," "Mutual Support," "Surprise," "Swiftness," "Tempo," "Control," and "Organization." *Seapower of the State* incorporated these ideas and further refined and extended them.

If *Seapower of the State* is read with the notion of filtering out the inconsistencies with military art as it applies to land (or air) battles, there is precious little that is set apart, no matter how fine the weave of the filter. That the major feature of the second edition of Gorshkov's *magnum opus* would be the incorporation of a new section devoted exclusively to the question of strategic coordination between the Soviet Navy and the other branches of the Soviet Armed Forces is completely in consonance with the suggestion that Gorshkov expends great efforts to ensure naval operations are described in a way to which others can relate. As another example, the literature routinely makes the assessment that victory in war is *impossible* without the "interworking" of the various services and their balances. The principle, moreover, enjoys great longevity in Soviet military thought: "Frunze's voice still speaks in Soviet doctrine when that doctrine says that war between first-rate opponents can only be decided by the employment of combined arms in a protracted struggle."[25]

The purpose of the preceding four paragraphs is to establish firmly the thought that if Soviet naval forces are to be suggested as fulfilling a strategic reserve mission, that suggestion must be wholly consistent with the overall fabric of Soviet military thought. Two other indicators would serve to anneal such a suggestion. A seabased Soviet strategic reserve should be supported by the literature, and such a reserve should enjoy at least a fairly good fit with the model characteristics for a strategic reserve force set forth earlier in this article.

Simply because ballistic missile submarines are not always on-station within range of what speculation might suggest to be their primary targets does not mean that they are being *purposefully* withheld or set aside for a reserve role. Premeditated withholding is not openly discussed in the literature.[26] From what is known about operating patterns, however, it would seem that because of their low ratio of time-on-patrol to time-at-home and the absence of Soviet bases in forward areas to service them, the YANKEE–class ballistic missile submarines equipped with the short-range (1600 nm) SS–N–6 would not be prime candidates for a strategic reserve role. Nevertheless, prior to a deliberate attack, or on perceived strategic warning of an attack by an adversary, these submarines could be scattered from their bases so that they would be within missile range of their targets. Alternatively, such submarines might be tasked to strike targets in less distant areas or even at sea.[27]

Some of the most powerful evidence Soviet ballistic missile submarines have a strategic reserve mission stems from argumentation about submarine protection. The theme appears frequently in Soviet writings, particularly in *Seapower of the State* where Gorshkov refers to the protection of submarines as affording them "combat stability." While the suggestion that submarines need protection—supplied by other submarines, surface ships, and aircraft—extends back at least as far as 1961[28] when the Soviet ballistic missile forces numbered fewer than 30 GOLF– and HOTEL–class ships, it is basically unaddressed in Western naval strategy. Gorshkov, however, does not equivocate:

> The new strategic orientation of the navies toward

warfare against the shore has also played a great role. All of this has to a great degree increased the need for the all-around support of the operations of forces prosecuting strategic missions. Therefore, the effort to establish favorable conditions in a certain area of a theater and for a certain time for the successful accomplishment by a major grouping of naval forces of the primary missions assigned to it and at the same time also to establish those conditions which would make it difficult for the enemy to carry out his own missions and would prevent him from disrupting the operations of the opposing side will apparently become widespread.[29]

In an article devoted exclusively to the subject of submarine protection, Captain First Rank V. Artamonov emphasized that all naval forces including naval aviation had a "most important task" of supporting the combat operations of submarines; that afloat and shore bases were also important; and that, in fact, "special groupings" of "antisubmarine submarines, ships, aircraft, and helicopters operate both independently and cooperatively in order to destroy or weaken and neutralize antisubmarine barriers and zones and to search for and destroy antisubmarine forces of the other side."[30]

Both Gorshkov and Artamonov allude to areas or zones where a relative preponderance of antisubmarine forces could be brought to bear. This has led to the concept of what James McConnell calls "sanctuaries" or what Michael MccGwire refers to as "bastions for strategic submarine deployment."[31] In this regard, the most detailed description of what are labeled "mobile zones of supremacy on the high seas"—although it does not even hint that they would be used to defend ballistic missile submarines—can be found in the article by Captain First Rank V'yunenko entitled "Some Trends in the Development of Naval Tactics."[32]

Antisubmarine warfare traditionally has been viewed in the West as a protective operation in which forces were deployed at sea to defend surface combatant groups, mercantile or military convoys, and amphibious or replenishment groups from attack by enemy submarines. Vigorous pursuit of antisubmarine technologies and tactics has often been a matter of some ambivalence, at least within the US Navy, because success in combating enemy submarines tends to make one's own submarines subject to the same techniques. Additionally, the necessity to detect and to attack Soviet ballistic missile submarines has been deemphasized both because of the ambivalence described above and because of US strategic policy concerns that considered antisubmarine warfare to be a counterforce capability and therefore destablizing.

The Soviets approach the problem differently. They list antisubmarine warfare as a basic mission of their navy, and they have built air, surface, and subsurface forces that give credibility to that emphasis. John Herzog observes, in fact, that, "Every class of major combatant laid down since the mid–1960s has been designated as ASW ship, with great emphasis on AAW as well."[33] The Soviets contend with the vulnerability of their own submarines to enemy countermeasures by means of pro-submarine operations.

Submarines derive a large measure of their survivability from covertness. Any requirement for a submarine to emit radiations—whether sonar, radar, radio, or identification signals—is resisted, for it tends to reduce the submarine's primary advantage—its stealth. Soviet authors acknowledge the point. According to Gorshkov:

> Seaborne strategic weapons platforms also lend themselves to deployment in depth, seeking shelter in the water and utilizing it not only for cover, but also for concealment, which to a great degree improves the viability of seaborne strategic weapons systems.[34]

As with combat operations in general, the importance of command and control for seaborne forces is also acknowledged in Soviet strategy. "Today," writes Gorshkov, "the ships, aircraft, and command posts of the Navy are equipped with powerful communications equipment which provide reliable control of naval forces over great areas."[35] As a basic rule, communications reliability varies almost directly with the distance between transmitter and receiver. Satellite communications capability has imposed a strong qualifier on such an assessment, but confidence in communications is still associated with range. One-way communications enjoy worldwide a high probability of receipt with modern communications equipment. For a covert—or, more simply, a concealed—military unit, a requirement to communicate a response—i.e., to establish two-way communications—severely complicates the security of the unit. If, in the case of strategic nuclear forces, a simple retaliatory, one-gasp strategy is in effect, then one-way communications should suffice. If, on the other hand, a strategic warfighting capability should be sought, one that would require the controlled modulation of attacks, then two-way communications assume additional importance.

For these reasons, keeping strategic submarines in areas adjacent to one's own territory should permit higher confidence and full-time—and, if required, two-way—communications with them. If those submarines are supported in defended bastions or sanctuaries, communications with the submarines can be carried out through intermediary surface or air units, restricting thereby the necessity for the submarine to risk exposure through long-distance electro-magnetic radiations. Thus, Engineering Captain Second Rank Yerofeyev wrote in 1972: "Arranging launch areas close to one's own shores considerably simplifies the organization of control and communications and cuts down on the expenditure of fuel and the time spent in transit."[36]

For nuclear-powered submarines, of course, the question of fuel savings is not germane, but the question of transit raises an additional argument that buttresses the appeal of the protected zone concept. Warfighting strategies assume from first principles the war will be prolonged. From a practical point of view, this means allowances must be made to provision naval ships, submarines included. Here, geography comes to the fore since Soviet ballistic missile submarines equipped with shorter range missiles would be obliged, in the absence of overseas bases, to transit geographic choke points to return to Soviet bases for logistic support in a long war. As they passed through those constrictions, they would be highly vulnerable to antisubmarine warfare action by the opponent.

The link between Soviet declaratory strategy and the concept of an at-sea strategic reserve force lies in the formulations set forth in Soviet writings concerning the *course and outcome* of the war. Michael MccGwire, in fact, claimed that the "dominant theme" of *Seapower of the State* "was the importance of naval forces as an instrument of state policy in peacetime and as a means of influencing the course and outcome of wars of all kinds. He also argued that "this importance was increasing."[37]

Precisely what effect the Soviet Navy would have on the course and outcome of war apparently continues to be an area of significant debate in Soviet military science. The strongest claim for the importance of naval forces to strategic warfighting would be that it would *decisively* affect *both* the *course* and the *outcome* of the *war*. Anything less would demonstrate an ambivalence about the impact of naval power, the reasons for which could be varied and quite subtle.

What one finds in the published efforts of naval authors on this score is a chaos which is wholly contrary to their usual careful selection of terms. For example, in the first edition of *Seapower of the State,* this statement appears in the foreword: "Today, through its strikes from the sea, the Navy is capable of altering the course and outcome of an armed conflict in the continental theaters of military operations."[38] The second edition deleted the words "and outcome" and attached the following phrase to the end of the sentence: "and of influencing its outcome."[39] This might appear to be low-level semantic tinkering, but it is far more than that. In the first place, *altering* the outcome of an armed struggle is distinguished from *influencing* it. Secondly, the magnitude of the alteration or influence is not included—a point that will be highlighted later. And, thirdly, *armed struggle* is not synonymous with *war* in the Soviet literature. Elsewhere in *Seapower of the State,* the Soviet Navy is described as having the capability to affect *directly* the course and even the outcome of a *war;* of having a direct influence on the course and even the outcome of a war; and of having a great, and at times decisive, influence on the outcome of a war.[40]

In fact, the literature contains about as many formulations as are possible in this regard, with no evident evolutionary progression. The "influence" has been said to be "decisive," "direct," "serious," "enormous," "substantial," "considerable," and "definite." The effect might in one instance be said to be on the course of a war, in another on the outcome of a war; alternatively, the effect might apply to the armed struggle, the armed struggle *as a whole,* the armed struggle in theaters of military action, or the armed struggle in ground theaters. This is undoubtedly an area of strong contention, and one that—from the most recent evidence in *Seapower of the State*—remains unresolved. It will bear watching.

What Soviet open-source publications have to offer with respect to the employment of the Soviet Navy as a strategic reserve force can be summarized as follows:

- Such a task is not discussed directly, nor is the question of withholding a fraction of sea-based strategic weapons discussed directly.
- Controlling sea areas for a discrete period of time for a particular purpose is well understood and developed.
- Providing for the "combat stability" of submarines, a concept not treated in Western literature, has received significant attention and rationalization.
- The advantages and importance of good command and control during a war are fully recognized.
- The employment of ballistic missile submarines in a strategic reserve role has great logical appeal but is very difficult to substantiate from Soviet military writings.
- Heavy emphasis on antisubmarine warfare in the Soviet Navy does not run counter to the at-sea strategic reserve argument; neither does it necessarily support it, however.

Compared to the abstract model for a strategic reserve force, the fit would seem to be good. *Quality,* always arguable, would seem to be sufficient. *Security* is achieved through the natural concealment submerged submarines enjoy and through their protection by other air, surface, and subsurface forces. *Control* is obviously important, and close-in operating areas enhance its effectiveness. The lesser attributes of a reserve force—quality and responsiveness—have more to do with its effectiveness than with its overall value and have not been emphasized.

All in all, the suggestion that some Soviet strategic submarines might be deployed into protected, secure zones in wartime and might act as a strategic reserve force finds stronger support in the logic of reserve forces and in day-to-day observables than in the theoretical underpinnings of Soviet strategy. Nevertheless, the concept is not at all at odds with Soviet strategy which has quite a bit to say about the subject of strategic reserves.

Conclusions and Implications

Warfighting strategies and strategic reserves go hand-in-hand. Western strategic concepts are only dimly perceiving either at present, while the indicators point to a strategy that has been under refinement for a long time in the Soviet Union. Geographical and political factors are tempered by history to make such a development understandable and even logical in the Soviet case.

The difficulty in panning the gold from the stream of available publications that ties together strategic reserves and sea-based strategic weapons could lie in the possibility that this touches upon a subject the Kremlin would prefer not to discuss. In strategic matters, it is sometimes important for deterrent purposes that the adversary know your strategy; on the other hand, it is sometimes preferable that an element of strategy be kept secret. In the first case, the importance of the knowledge of the existence of a Strangelovian "Doomsday Machine" or a launch-on-warning option is self-evident. In general, however, the US operates very openly. Only very sensitive topics such as the location of submarine patrol areas and the exact accuracy and yield of US strategic weapons retain high classifications. Most information about US strategic weapons receives no greater security than other forces; truly, a significant amount of detail is, for better or for worse, in the public domain.

In contradistinction, Soviet authors literally *never* discuss their own weapons systems or their capabilities in available publications. The penchant for secrecy in the first approximation might in this case be reinforced by the necessity for secrecy. That is, if the Soviet Union had a strategically significant weapon—or doctrine—the intention, the incentive, and the capability to keep that fact from the rest of the world might well be very strong.

If the specter of a secret, strategically significant weapon seems incredible, consider a single example. An effective area defense anti-ballistic missile (ABM) system could alter the strategic balance significantly. Given new technologies—lasers or charged particle beams—or even constructed around covertly produced and stored missile-type ABM launchers and weapons, the possibility for the Soviet Union (but not for the United States) is at least conceivable. The point is *not* that such a capability exists or is in the works, but that it is *possible* in view of the closed nature of the Soviet system. The premium on maintaining the secrecy of such a system would be large; most importantly, we should not be surprised that such a system and its possible impact on the strategic balance are not discussed in the open press. A strategy that emphasizes warfighting and a large, secure, controllable strategic reserve—especially one based at sea where it is not confidently secure from attack by hostile forces—would be subject to the same strictures. Ballyhooing such intent and capability would be tantamount to inviting offsetting actions by the adversary. In brief, the suggestion here is that one might expect direct evidence of such a plan to be scant indeed.

How powerfully a secure strategic reserve missile force might influence a war involving the Soviet Union and the United States was alluded to in the opening section of this article. Throughout the intervening discussion, the theme kept reappearing that US strategy had not adequately taken Soviet strategy into account. Indeed, knowledgeable observers in this country can come to remarkably different conclusions even though they theoretically have access to the same data. Thus, Richard Pipes can write:

> . . . ignoring or not taking seriously Soviet military doctrine may have detrimental effects on US security. There is something innately destabilizing in the very fact that we consider nuclear war unfeasible and suicidal for both, and our chief adversary views it as feasible and winnable for himself.[41]

On the other hand, Victor Utgoff of the National Security Council staff can stipulate:

> Even if the US could attain strategic superiority it would not be desirable because I suspect we would occasionally use it as a way of throwing our weight around in some very risky ways . . . . It is in the US interest to allow the few remaining areas of strategic advantage to fade away.[42]

The difference between the two viewpoints is that Pipes is saying what Utgoff is not appreciating: It is important, indeed crucial, to recognize that the Soviet leadership does not welcome the fact that US strategic nuclear forces have the capability to raze Soviet society as it exists today. The correlation of forces stands as a central concept in Soviet thought; we cannot wish that away.

A directly relevant allusion will serve to make the argument all the more powerful. In the matter of strategic submarine protection, the case has been made that the Soviet Navy claims such a mission, and observables support the claim. The US Navy has no comparable operational doctrine. The security of its submarines rests instead on superior quietness rendering them poor acoustic targets, the large ocean areas in which they can patrol—expanded by the deployment of the Trident submarine and the backfitting of the Trident missile into earlier model SSBNs—and on their sovereign immunity which ensures an attack against them would be treated as an attack against the territory of the United States. The last of this three-part thesis has been challenged in the past by asking, rhetorically, whether in fact the political will would exist to go to strategic nuclear war for the loss of a single (or two? or three? or how many?) submarines. Now appears this additional consideration, brought to light by Robert Bathhurst: "It is no longer obvious that a strike against one element of power of a country is necessarily a strike against the country itself."[43] He cites the *Pueblo* and *Mayaguez* cases, the Cuban missile crisis, and the Cod War between Britain and Iceland to support his assertion.

Soviet insensitivity to US strategic concerns has been noted on numerous occasions.[44] The candor with which the Soviets write on this point is noteworthy. Whereas the mainstream of US strategists would shrink from advocating attacks on Soviet strategic submarines in the name of stability, Gorshkov writes, emphatically:

> The new capabilities of a navy to operate against the shore and the enormous threat from seaward arising in connection with them have determined the character of the main efforts of the navy in the battle against the enemy fleet. The employment of naval forces against the enemy's seaborne strategic nuclear systems in order to disrupt or blunt the attacks against ground targets to the maximum degree has become the most important of these efforts.[45]

As a final observation in this brief look at the differences in the way the US and the Soviet Union approach military strategy, the question of economic constraints arises. In the abstract, it would seem that Soviet decisionmakers are forced to exercise many of the same types of guns-or-butter determinations as their Western counterparts. In fact, although they are not unconstrained by resources, the Soviets operate from a very different concept of how much is enough for defense. Claiming to have been forced to do so by the aggressive policies of imperialism, the Soviets acknowledge that "in order to ensure a high level of military strength," they are obliged "to proceed to the maintenance of a wartime economy in peacetime."[46] Yet, this is no recent policy, nor did it pass unobserved. In a work copyrighted in 1943, Edward Mead Earle wrote:

> A great many observers of the Russian scene during the years 1928–38 thought that the scarcity of consumer goods in the USSR was due to inefficiency in the administration of industry. As events proved, however, the primary cause was a war economy which sacrificed everything to the interests of the army and military preparedness.[47]

To bring the argument from the general to the specific and to demonstrate the priority given in Soviet thought to strategic reserves, this quotation is pertinent:

> Recognizing that war with Germany or Japan was a distinct possibility, the Party leadership gave special attention to plans for mobilization both of the Armed Forces and of the economy. At this time the Soviet Union was in turmoil

because of Stalin's forced collectivization of agriculture, and in many parts of the nation people were starving. Despite this widespread starvation and lack of consumer goods of all types, increases were made in the military's 'untouchable reserves' (*neprikosnovennyy zapas*), which were carefully stored and periodically renewed.[48]

The implications for US strategy of the Soviet pursuance of a warfighting strategy which pivots on large, secure, controllable strategic reserves would seem to fall into two classes. First, and most obvious, would be the understanding that thwarting such a strategy would require the kind and number of military forces that would be perceived as able to put the adversary's strategic reserves at risk. Stated another way, the correct strategic counter to such a strategy would be to take measures to ensure the adversary cannot perceive he holds a decisive correlation of forces at any stage in a conflict and *especially* not for what might be the final battle. A firm strategy of *victory denial* would be required.

The forces necessary to meet that kind of task must be both able and perceived to be able to prevent the application of strategic reserve power from dictating the outcome of a war. Conceivably, there are two ways of accomplishing that task: by amassing weaponry which can attack reserve forces—defeating their protective forces in the process if necessary—at any conceivable stage in a nuclear war, or by fielding programs that would provide for one's own secure reserve force. Either of these methods, or a combination of them, would seek to ensure the Soviets could not at any time during the course of a war be confident the correlation of forces would be strongly enough in their favor to ensure victory. Both methods would strengthen deterrence of the outbreak of war in the first instance; provisioning for one's own secure strategic reserve would have the additional benefit of intrawar deterrence—depending on the size, survivability, and controllability of the force.

The second class of implications extends into areas which demonstrate clearly the inseparability of military, foreign, and arms control policies as they impact on national security.

- A surge deployment of the Soviet Navy into open ocean areas or into heavily fortified at-sea bastions would be particularly ominous, for it would signal that not only was peace at great peril but also that the Soviets had decided the correlation of forces at the end of the conflict—vouchsafed by their strategic reserve forces—would favor them and ensure victory. What this says is that such a move could be much more ominous than Western strategists might consider today, resting comfortably as they have on a dogmatic conviction that deterrence cannot fail.

- Unconventional operating modes might be viewed from very different evaluation criteria. For example, operation of Soviet strategic submarines in Norwegian fjords can be judged as a method of attaining a degree of security for a strategic reserve.[49] It might not, in this context, be considered non-threatening, however. Likewise, if the option to place the strategic reserve at risk is to be taken seriously, then some additional thought necessarily must be given to other unusual deployment environments. In his previously cited article on supporting submarines, for example, Artamonov claimed that, "The ice cover in the Arctic reliably protects submarines from antisubmarine forces and, in many cases, from antisubmarine surface ships."[50] If the Barents Sea is an obvious deployment area for a strategic submarine reserve force, as MccGwire suggests,[51] then additional attention must be paid to shallow water ASW capability, for the Barents has an average depth of less than 600 feet.

- US policy with respect to Soviet naval bases in Cuba would be better informed if the question of strategic reserves were considered. The agreement on Cuba with the Soviet Union appears to preclude the stationing or staging of Soviet offensive weapons from that island, but this has been stretched and violated recently.[52] In the context of supporting nuclear ASW submarines capable of attacking US ballistic missile submarines that might be part of a strategic reserve, whether such a Soviet force based in Cuba is "offensive" or not becomes very contentious.

- With an altered perspective from acknowledging a Soviet strategy of warfighting and reserves, certain tenets of arms control take on a very different character. A strategic arms agreement, for example, might be appraised differently if reload missiles for the SS–17 and SS–18 cold-launch ICBM launchers were viewed as strategic reserve forces. It should be recognized, moreover, that *all* SLBM launchers are "cold-launch" capable and reloadable. Arms control might be controlling the wrong things, and verification, therefore, might be totally ineffective.

A policy of withholding SLBMs would, accordingly, make a travesty of the SALT I rationale for permitting the Soviet Union more submarine-launched missiles than the US. The justification—undoubtedly invented in Washington, not Moscow—was set forth by Henry Kissinger as follows: "Then there are such factors as deployment characteristics. For example, because of the difference in geography and basing, it has been estimated that the Soviet Union requires three submarines to two of ours to be able to keep an equal number on station."[53] This rationale seemed to have been persuasive, for the permitted totals of ballistic missile submarines in SALT I were three to two, as stipulated. Apart from the fact that the US was in effect giving the Soviets the base in Cuba from which to operate their strategic submarines by such a rationale (a forward base would have the same impact on on-station time as additional submarines), never had the Soviets deployed their submarines on strategic patrol in the *proportions* the US had. If the Soviet intent all along was to hold SLBMs back, the rationale—even though it has the veneer of arms control "equality"— fails abjectly.

The implications are quite weighty if we have misperceived the Soviet strategy, and the price to be paid for future miscalculation could be prohibitive. The question of the Soviet strategic reserve in general and of the sea-based reserve in particular offers an alternate perspective from which to view Soviet weapon programs and their anticipated employment.

The returns are not yet all in, so there is no way of knowing how much the US shall have to pay for forgetting strategy is a multiplayer game. US strategists often have acted as if they could take decisions about force sizing without reference—or at least strong links—*either* to Soviet capabilities *or* Soviet intentions. There are indicated policy directions that will help ensure the effect of that shortsightness not be disastrous.

Notes

1. F. E. Adcock, *The Greek and Macedonian Art of War* (Berkeley: University of California Press, 1967), p. 77.
2. Alain C. Enthoven and K. Wayne Smith, *How Much Is Enough: Shaping the Defense Program, 1961–1969* (New York: Harper and Row, 1971), p. 183.
3. The exceptions are noteworthy: James McConnell and N. Bradford Dismukes of the Center for Naval Analyses, who provided much of the inspiration for this effort, top a short list of those who have recognized the importance of strategic reserves to strategy.
4. A. I. Radziyevskiy, *Dictionary of Basic Military Terms,* trans. under the auspices of the US Air Force (Washington: Government Printing Office, 1976), p. 213.
5. V. D. Sokolovskiy, *Soviet Military Strategy,* ed. and trans. by Harriet Fast Scott, 3rd ed. (New York: Crane, Russak and Company, 1968) pp. 354–361.
6. Major General A. S. Milovidov and Colonel V. G. Kozlov, eds., *The Philosophical Heritage of V. I. Lenin and Problems of Contemporary War,* trans. under the auspices of the US Air Force (Washington: Government Printing Office, 1975), p. 48.
7. In the second edition of Sokolovskiy's *Military Strategy,* its authors flirted with the notion nuclear weapons might be introduced into a local war without its immediate escalation into a strategic war. Thomas W. Wolfe, in his *Soviet Strategy at the Crossroads* (Cambridge: Harvard University Press, 1964), analyzed the importance of "the possibility of limited war being fought on a rather large scale under theater

conditions." (pp. 121–122). The entire discussion was excised, however, in the third edition of Sokolovskiy.

8. Sokolovskiy, op. cit., p. 186.
9. Ibid., p. 195. The passage is "celebrated" because a translation of the first edition prompted a rejoinder by four Soviet strategists in the military newspaper *Krasnaya zvezda* [Red Star]. There was much resultant confusion, but the word "inevitably," the center of the storm, has remained in all three editions.
10. Milovidov and Kozlov, op. cit., p. 102. Whether the particular reference is to the "correlation of forces," the "relationship of forces," the "alignment of forces," or the "arrangement of forces" makes no difference. Each of these terms implies the same notion to the Soviet reader. For a discussion of these terms and their Russian equivalents, see Raymond L. Garthoff, *Soviet Military Policy: A Historical Analysis* (New York: Praeger, 1966), pp. 79–80.
11. Colonel B. Byely, Colonel Y. Dzyuba, Colonel G. Fydorov, Colonel Y. Khomenko, Colonel T. Kondratkov, Colonel Y. Medvedev, Colonel V. Morozov, Colonel K. Spirov, Major General Y. Sulimov, Major General N. Sushko, Colonel S. Tyushkevich, and Lieutenant Colonel D. Volkogonov, *Marxism–Leninism on War and Army*, 5th ed., trans. under the auspices of the US Air Force (Washington: Government Printing Office, 1974), p. 140–141. Emphasis in the original.
12. Thomas Wolfe devoted a chapter to debates of this subject in his *Soviet Strategy at the Crossroads*, pp. 130–138.
13. Sokolovskiy, op. cit., p. 149.
14. Colonel V. Ye. Savkin, *The Basic Principles of Operational Art and Tactics*, trans. under the auspices of the US Air Force (Washington: US Government Printing Office, 1976), pp. 89, 91, 92 and 93, respectively.
15. Colonel S. Taran, "Leninist Theoretical Principles of Soviet Military Strategy," *Voyennaya mysl'* [Military Thought], No. 6, June 1971, p. 52.
16. Colonel General N. A. Lomov, ed., *Scientific–Technical Progress and the Revolution in Military Affairs*, trans. under the auspices of the US Air Force (Washington: Government Printing Office, 1974), p. 138. Emphasis supplied.
17. Major General Kh. Dzhelaukhov, "Combatting Strategic Reserves in a Theater of Military Operations," *Voyennaya mysl'*, No. 11, November 1964, p. 2.
18. Admiral of the Fleet S. G. Gorshkov, *The Seapower of the State*, 2nd ed. (Moscow: Military Publishing House, 1979), p. 243.
19. Captain First Rank N. Aleshkin, "Some Trends in the Development of Naval Forces," *Morskoy Sbornik* [Naval Digest], No. 1, 1972, p. 25.
20. ". . . over 900,000 ground force personnel are released from active duty in the USSR each year, creating a pool of around 4 million men with recent military experience in the ground forces within the past 5 years." *Report of Secretary of Defense Harold Brown to the Congress on the FY 1981 Budget, FY 1982 Authorization Request and FY 1981–1985 Defense Programs* (Washington: Government Printing Office, January 29, 1980), p. 101. Cf. "The Soviet leadership should be able to mobilize 2 million to 3 million men in 24 hours. An equivalent number again could be called up within a 48–hour period, approximately doubling the regular peacetime force of between 4.5 million and 5 million men. This should give a total of between 9 million and 11 million men in uniform within 2 full days. Since in peacetime the Soviet Union has at least 9 million in the reserves who have had military service within a 5–year period, the Soviet Armed Forces probably could reach 13 million to 14 million in less than 10 days, if such numbers were needed." Harriet Fast Scott and William F. Scott, *The Armed Forces of the USSR* (Boulder: Westview Press, 1979), p. 326.
21. Milovidov and Kozlov, op. cit., p. 109. Emphasis supplied. See also Lomov, op. cit., Chapter VI.
22. Admiral Gorshkov even appears to take some credit in a passage in the first edition of *Seapower of the State*: "Already in the mid–50s it was planned to build in the first place powerful submarine forces and sea aviation, fit the fleet with nuclear missile weapons and use atomic power in submarine shipbuilding." (Annapolis: Naval

Institute Press, 1979), p. 281.

23. He understands the value of flattery also; *viz:* "The valiant land forces of the Soviet Army with the full support of other branches of the armed forces smashed the armed forces of reaction, the mightiest in the whole history of mankind." Ibid., pp. 282–283.
24. *Morskoy Sbornik,* No. 12, December 1974, pp. 24–32.
25. Walter Darnell Jacobs, *Frunze: The Soviet Clausewitz, 1885–1925* (The Hague: Martinus Nijhoff, 1969), p. 152.
26. Michael MccGwire, "Naval Power and Soviet Oceans Policy," in *Soviet Oceans Development,* Committee Print prepared at the request of the Honorable Warren G. Magnuson, Chairman, Committee on Commerce; and the Honorable Ernest G. Hollings, Chairman, National Oceans Policy Study, pursuant to Senate Resolution 222; 94th Congress, 2nd Session (Washington: Government Printing Office, 1976), p. 171.
27. For a recent discussion of the use of ballistic missile submarines to attack ships, see Lieutenant Commander Carl H. Clawson, Jr., "The Wartime Role of Soviet SSBNs—Round Two," US Naval Institute *Proceedings,* March 1980, pp. 64–71.
28. Captain First Rank Stepanov, "Protection for the Development of Submarines in the Course of Military Action," *Morskoy Sbornik,* No. 12, December, 1961. See also, Sokolovskiy, op. cit., p. 298.
29. Gorshkov, *Seapower of the State,* 1st ed., p. 233.
30. Captain First Rank V. Artamonov, "Supporting Combat Operations of Submarines," *Voyennaya mysl',* No. 9, September 1973, p. 47.
31. James M. McConnell, "Admiral Gorshkov and 'Navies in War and Peace,'" CNA Research Contribution, Monograph 257 (Alexandria: Center for Naval Analyses, September 1974), pp. 71–116. McConnell's monograph was summarized in R. G. Weinland, R. W. Herrick, M. MccGwire, and J. M. McConnell, "Admiral Gorshkov's 'Navies in War and Peace,' *Survival,* Vol. 18, No. 2 (March–April 1975), pp. 60–61. MccGwire, loc. cit.
32. *Morskoy Sbornik,* No. 10, October 1975.
33. "Perspectives on Soviet Naval Development: A Navy to Match National Purposes," in Paul J. Murphy, ed., *Naval Power in Soviet Policy* (Washington: Government Printing Office, 1978), p. 53.
34. Gorshkov, *Seapower of the State,* 1st ed., p. 279.
35. Ibid., p. 210.
36. Engineering Captain Second Rank V. Yerofeyev, "The Replacement of Polaris and Poseidon," *Morskoy Sbornik,* No. 1, January 1971, p. 89.
37. Michael MccGwire, "Naval Power and Soviet Global Strategy," *International Security,* Vol. 3, No. 4 (Spring 1979), p. 154.
38. Gorshkov, 1st ed., p. x.
39. Gorshkov, 2nd ed., p. vi.
40. Ibid., pp. 325, 327, and 405, respectively.
41. Richard Pipes, "Why the Soviet Union Thinks It Could Fight and Win a Nuclear War," *Commentary,* July 1977, p. 34.
42. Quoted by John Lehman in "A Strategic Symposium, SALT and US Defense Policy," *The Washington Quarterly,* Winter 1979, p. 39.
43. Robert Bathhurst, *Understanding the Soviet Navy: A Handbook* (Newport, Rhode Island: Naval War College Press, 1979), p. vii.
44. See, as a lone example, Arnold Horelick, "The Strategic Mindset of the Soviet Military: An Essay–Review," *Problems of Communism,* March–April 1977, pp. 80–85.
45. *Seapower of the State,* 1st ed., p. 221.
46. Milovidov and Kozlov, op. cit., p. 140.
47. "Lenin, Trotsky, Stalin: Soviet Concepts of War," in Edward Mead Earle, *Makers of Modern Strategy: Military Thought from Machiavelli to Hitler* (Princeton: Princeton University Press, 1943), p. 351.
48. Scott and Scott, op. cit., p. 230.
49. "To keep the Norwegians on edge, Soviet nuclear submarines have routinely

violated Norwegian waters—in fjords no less—where, it is believed, they have off-loaded spies and even tested submarine operations." W. Scott Thompson, *Power Projection: A Net Assessment of US and Soviet Capabilities* (New York: National Strategy Information Center, 1978), p. 57.

50. Artamonov, op. cit., p. 52.
51. "Naval Power and Soviet Global Strategy," loc. cit.
52. See Captain Leslie K. Fenlon, Jr., "The Umpteenth Cuban Confrontation," and Ensign Christopher A. Abel, "A Breach in the Ramparts," US Naval Institute *Proceedings,* July 1980, pp. 40–45 and 46–50, respectively.
53. US Senate, Committee on Armed Services, *Military Implications of the Treaty on the Limitations of Anti–Ballistic Missile Systems and the Interim Agreement on Limitation of Strategic Offensive Arms,* 92nd Congress, 2nd Session, 16–25 July 1972 (Washington: Government Printing Office, 1972), p. 123.

Soviet Paramilitary Training Programs

Leon Goure

Soviet paramilitary training programs and assessments of their effectiveness and contribution to Soviet defense and warfighting capabilities receive relatively little attention in the US. Yet, an examination of the variety and content of these programs and the enormous number of Soviet citizens involved in them suggests that Soviet society may be one of the most militarized in the world at the present time.

The scope of these programs is especially impressive. Their aim is to involve the vast majority of Soviet citizens from young children to retirees in one way or another in preparing for contributing to the defense of the Soviet Union and its use of the armed forces in support of Soviet foreign policy. The Soviets seek to achieve this aim through a complex of compulsory and voluntary training programs which involve many millions of persons—officials as well as volunteers, full or part-time—in their operations, including military personnel on active duty—among them marshals and general officers—and military reservists. The programs also involve the active participation of the Party and its youth organizations; governmental, economic, and administrative organizations and agencies at all levels; trade unions; USSR Civil Defense; the entire educational system; a variety of volunteer mass organizations such as the Voluntary Society for Assistance to the Army, Aviation and Navy (DOSAAF),* the Red Cross, the national sports program and its organizations, the war veterans organization; and also the mass media, literature, the arts, and so on.

The programs have received Brezhnev's personal public endorsement and have been promoted by resolutions of Party congresses as well as directives and decrees of the CPSU Central Committee and the USSR Council of Ministers. Furthermore, Soviet citizens are frequently reminded of Article 62 of the 1977 USSR Constitution which makes it a "sacred duty" of every Soviet citizen to "contribute" to the "strengthening" of the "might" and "defense" of the USSR.

The theoretical objective of the program is to prepare the entire population to contribute in one way or another to the defense of the Soviet Union. In particular, the programs seek to instill in the population, and especially the youth, loyalty to the system, patriotism, Soviet "internationalism," readiness to bear the hardships and sacrifices of a war, and the will to struggle on to victory. The programs also aim at promoting interest in military affairs and developing in youth physical

---

*DOSAAF—Dobrovol'noye obshchestvo sodeystviya armii, aviatsii, i flotu—Eds.

fitness, basic military knowledge, and technical skills so as to improve the quality of military conscripts and reservists and facilitate and expedite their assimilation by the armed forces and their effectiveness during military service. Another objective is to train the entire population in civil defense and on this basis develop a very large, effective, and ready national civil defense organization and system.

Overall, there is a program of "military-patriotic education" of the population. It is said to be an "integral part of communist education" intended to prepare the citizenry ideologically, psychologically, and practically for "carrying out the sacred duty of armed defense of the Motherland." Among other qualities, it seeks to instill in the population and especially the youth "love" for the Soviet Armed Forces and its "heroic" traditions and to make them "ready and able to defend their country, the achievements of the countries of the socialist fraternity, and also, to come to the aid of toilers struggling for their national and social liberation."

"Military-patriotic education" begins with preschool children and continues thereafter throughout the life of the Soviet citizen. History, literature, and the arts are used to emphasize his "heroic" heritage and to glorify martial values. In the secondary schools, students set up corners, rooms, or museums of "combat glory;" meet with war veterans, military servicemen, and cadets of military schools; visit battlefields; mount honor guards at war memorials; and so on.

Paramilitary training in the schools is both formal as well as voluntary. It begins in the first grade. In addition to patriotic and "heroic" education, it includes such paramilitary sports in the physical education program as grenade throwing, obstacle running, marksmanship (in 1977, 1.3 million school children received marksmanship rankings), and cross country skiing. Formal civil defense training is given in the second, fifth, and ninth grades of Soviet ten–year schools and in vocational schools as well as in institutions of higher learning where it is a part of an extensive ROTC–type compulsory instruction program.

In the schools, students are encouraged to organize voluntary paramilitary clubs and study circles such as "Young Soldiers," "Young Sailors," and "Young Border Guards." These groups have uniforms and rank insignia. They practice close order drill, map reading, camouflage, marksmanship, communications, civil defense, small unit tactics, medical first aid, and so on. Their instructors are teachers, veterans, cadets from nearby military schools, or servicemen from nearby units. Special programs are set up by military schools for those students in the eighth to tenth grades of secondary schools who indicate interest in a military career and in choosing the particular service branch represented by each military school. Paramilitary instruction and games are also conducted during the stay of youths in Pioneer summer camps which are attended by over eight million school children.

The "military-sports" games played by school children and youths are an important element of the paramilitary training program and are intended to develop physical fitness, endurance, courage, and military skills. A great variety of such games are designed to complement the abilities of various age groups. They include various forms of map exercises, cross country marches, use of communications equipment, defensive and offensive tactics, antitank and antihelicopter defense, crossing of "minefields" and "contaminated" areas, first aid and evacuation of casualties, firing military rifles, and so on.

There are two national "military-sports" games: *Zarnitsa* (Lightning) for students in the third through eighth grades and *Orlenok* (Eaglet) for youths 16 to 19 years of age. The *Zarnitsa* game program was instituted in 1967. Until 1974, it was headed by Marshal of the Soviet Union Bagramyan. Since then, it has been led by Army General Getman. Some 20 million school children organized into "Young Soldier" and other "battalions" with elected officers now participate annually in the game. Competitions culminate in a national contest among the best units. At times, armored personnel carriers, light planes, and helicopters participate in the tactical exercises.

Orlenok was initiated in 1972 by the *Komsomol* for older students and youths. The game program is led by Lieutenant General of Aviation Beregovoy. The Soviets claim that over nine million youths now participate annually in this program. Its objective is to prepare the participants to pass the norms of the national paramilitary physical fitness and sports program called "Ready for Labor and Defense" (*GTO*)* and to strengthen their military knowledge and technical skills in preparation for service in the Soviet Armed Forces.

A key role in paramilitary training is played by *DOSAAF* which provides a network of instruction programs and facilities for teaching militarily useful skills and is called "the reserve helper of the USSR armed forces." At present, *DOSAAF* is led by Marshal of Aviation Pokryshkin. Among its more than 90 million members are some 6.5 million "activists." Membership in *DOSAAF* begins at age 14. Through its clubs, schools, and facilities, *DOSAAF* trains its members in 32 militarily relevant skills such as truck, tractor, and armored vehicle driving; radar and radio operations; engine repair and maintenance of field power generators; scuba and deep sea diving; seamanship and navigation; marksmanship; gliding and aircraft piloting; parachute jumping; medical first aid; and so forth. The Soviets claim that at present, one conscript out of three has received basic technical training in *DOSAAF*.

One important reason for the paramilitary training programs in the schools and by *DOSAAF* is the Soviet Armed Forces' demand for compensation for the 1967 reduction of 1 year in the length of compulsory military service. In effect, the objective is to insure the majority of

---

GTO — "*Gotov k trudu i oborony*" — Ed.

new conscripts entering military service already have received a good deal of basic military training and large numbers of them possess basic technical knowledge and skills so as to shorten the time needed to train them and make them effective soldiers, thereby facilitating the maintenance of combat readiness of the units.

To further this objective, students in the ninth and tenth grades of secondary schools are given some 140 hours of compulsory military instruction, called "initial military preparation," which, as was noted, is supplemented by war games, *DOSAAF* training courses, and paramilitary sports programs. While the boys prepare for military service, the girls receive special instruction in medical and battlefield first aid. These students also receive 29 hours of civil defense instruction and are organized to carry out a number of pre- and poststrike civil defense measures.

As was noted, military and civil defense training comprise part of compulsory instruction at vocational and technical schools and institutions of higher learning. Graduates of the latter are usually given the rank of second lieutenant in the reserves.

The Soviets claim the national "military-technical" sports program for students and young adults has some 50 million participants. This program also emphasizes marksmanship, grenade throwing, cross-country running and skiing, swimming while fully clothed and carrying a rifle, running obstacle courses, activities while wearing gas masks, and so on.

Another aspect of Soviet paramilitary activities is the compulsory civil defense instruction program for the entire population. At the present time, in addition to the civil defense training of school children and students, every working adult is required to receive annually 20 hours of civil defense instruction. This may be supplemented by training exercises. In addition, over 20 million Soviet citizens—mainly professional and technical personnel, workers, and farmers—serve part-time in civil defense formations and units at their places of work or residence and are given additional training and practice in civil defense. Nonworking adults are given some civil defense instruction at their places of residence.

Undoubtedly, the paramilitary training programs signficantly benefit the capabilities of the Soviet Armed Forces and USSR Civil Defense. They create a large pool of citizens with basic military and military-technical skills and probably help generate a favorable attitude toward military service. They also appear to be effective in assuring an adequate supply of applicants to military schools.

At the same time, however, there are indications the programs are not without shortcomings. These include uneven implementation, inadequately qualified instructors and shortages of instructional and training equipment, failures to meet prescribed training standards, and the far from enthusiastic participation of the population in the compulsory training programs. It is also unclear how much of the indoctrination of martial values and "heroism" actually "takes" in an increasingly better educated and consumption-oriented Soviet society and as the "glorious victories" of World War II become ancient history. Yet, one cannot discount the effects of Soviet military-patriotic education, with its emphasis on patriotism, nationalism, martial virtues, and "hatred of the class enemy." It could become a significant factor in suppport of and a driving force behind an expansionistic and aggressive Soviet foreign policy.

The Soviet Military National University©

Gregory Lathrop

> . . . The process of communist education, begun at home, in school, and at the place of work, a process of all-round and harmonious development of the individual, continues during a person's service in the army. The latter, in fact, plays the role of 'nationwide university' which practically all the male citizens of the country 'finish.'[1]
>
> *Army General A. A. Yepishev, 1975*

When Leonoid Brezhnev and Aleksey Kosygin rose to power in 1964, they were faced with a dilemma of political socialization. This became increasingly evident as the regime established itself. Military authors in particular, but political leaders as well, spoke more and more often of the problem of the "generation gap."

The rising generation in the Soviet Union has experienced neither of the great heroic/sacrificial events of Soviet history: the October Revolution or the Great Patriotic War. Hence, they have been less susceptible to the patriotic appeal for self-sacrifice in the pursuit of a hazy vision of communism. This new generation is also the product of an increasingly complex and diverse economic and social system. Among the results of this fact has been a rising appetite for consumer goods. Confronted with increasing consumerism and ideological apathy, it is logical the new regime would be forced to reexamine the effectiveness of the old-style Stalinist "transmission belts." Apparently, those organizations have been found wanting, since the Brezhnev–Kosygin regime instituted a massive program keyed to the use of military and patriotic values, virtues, and activities in order to reinvigorate Soviet political socialization.

In casting about for agencies with which to promote the militarization campaign, it was only logical the new conservative leadership would turn to one of the most conservative agencies within the system to play the role of centerpiece—the armed forces. The military has acquired, therefore, a new political function. Based on its expertise in the intensive training of large numbers of civilians and the ideological commitment of the officer corps, the military has been put to the task of coping with the greater heterogeneity and ideological laxity of the complex civilian society. The army has become a "national university" of political socialization and mobilization. This involvement in a

---

predominantly civilian function—political socialization—has led the Soviet Armed Forces into a variety of domestic social activities which seem to contradict the Marxist notion that the military serves no further domestic purpose following the revolution.

Military-political socialization has in turn had several consequences for both the armed forces and the system at large. In select areas, it has meant a decrease in military effectiveness, altered training schedules, and more indoctrination work for the regular officer. Logically, increased military socialization would also indicate a long-term increase in the militarization of attitudes among the civilian population.

The integration of military and civilian political functions also has certain implications for the changed character of civil-military relations in general. For some time now, the discipline has continued to use the concept of "political control" of the Soviet Armed Forces with little regard for the fact that while this concept was developed to explain civil-military relations under Stalin, the Soviet system has changed and developed considerably. It would seem logical to argue, therefore, that the nature of civil-military relations within that system would also be altered considerably. It is quite possible this integration of civil-political functions within the military agency indicates the problem of "control" is no longer at issue.

This article will examine the intent of the Brezhnev regime in establishing the current program of military/political socialization.

The Armed Forces—A National University

The notion that the armed forces might serve as a very effective instrument of political socialization is not original with the present Soviet regime. The original Bolshevik concept of a military force involved the arming of the masses—a civilian militia. As early as 1923, Stalin saw the Red Army as a device to bind together the diverse groups and nationalities of the Russian Federation.[2] Voroshilov is similarly quoted as having pointed out that "the Red Army has become a unique university."[3] At the time, this unique university was applied principally to a peasantry which made up a large part of the ranks and was not wholeheartedly trusted by the Soviet regime. The virtues of army service as a "transmission belt" of ideological conformity were recognized early in Soviet history.

Today, the need to absorb and educate a petit bourgeois peasantry has passed, but the virtues of the military transmission belt have in no way been forgotten. Instead, the goals have been modified for use in a more complex and developed Soviet society. The modern Soviet system has seized upon these virtues of the national university with a vengeance. We are reminded of this by both Party and military spokesmen. In 1967, Brezhnev stated:

Probably nowhere are there such favorable opportunities for organizing Party-political work as in the Army and the Navy. Here are concentrated well-trained Communists who have passed through the school of Party upbringing and military tempering from among the commanders and engineering and technical cadre; here there has been established a harmonious system of the Party-political apparatus. Here are all the conditions for studying people comprehensively and for day-to-day political influence on each serviceman.[4]

One year later, the Party General Secretary noted:

In fulfilling military obligations almost the entire male population of the country serves for some period in the Armed Forces, and this takes place during the youthful years when the personality is taking shape and a world view and a politically conscious attitude toward life are being molded. The Army thereby becomes an important school of life for our young people and a component part of the whole system of Soviet upbringing.[5]

In 1975, Yepishev reiterated Brezhnev's themes by noting:

In our country, military service is not only a school of combat skill. It is also a good school of ideological and physical steeling, of discipline and organization.[6]

Theoretical Goals of the National University

Most Soviet sources use a standard formula for describing socialization goals of Party-political indoctrination in the armed forces. These publicly acclaimed goals fall into two, or possibly three, categories: political/ideological, military, and possibly social goals.

The most frequently cited political goals of armed forces training and indoctrination (Party-political work) include the fostering among draftees of several qualities: the spirit of proletarian internationalism; Soviet/socialist patriotism and dedication to the motherland and the people and their defense; dedication to the Party and its leading role and to the government; hatred of imperialist aggression, or, conversely, a positive world view—i.e., communist conviction; ideological stability/ vigilance; and the unity of the army and the people. Most practical among the political goals are labor discipline and personal responsibility for socialist property. In short, the army is to carry on the development of the "new Soviet man."[7]

Perhaps more important, at least to the professional soldier, are the military goals of armed forces training/indoctrination. Military indoctrination of the draftee should enhance combat readiness, strengthen military discipline, prepare the youth to withstand the psychological conditions of modern (nuclear) combat, and improve his general morale. The draftee should acquire the ability to work within a collective (here, the numerous crew-served weapons are often cited), a feature easily transferable to civilian life. In the same vein, the draftee should acquire the personal habits of maintaining labor discipline, caring for weapons and military property, maintaining a better physical condition, developing courage, and learning the value of the combat traditions of the armed forces and the "lofty meaning of military service."[8] Combat readiness is stressed with particular frequency.

Mixed in with these political/ideological and military goals are some which seem to be directed predominantly toward certain social ends. Proletarian internationalism, for instance, is a two-sided affair having both international and domestic connotations. The training should promote friendship toward the fraternal socialist states and the progressive peoples as well as the unity of the nationalities within the USSR. Similarly, learning to act as part of a collective, improving one's physical condition, and learning to accept military/labor discipline are all important virtues with a value for civil society. Lastly, the inculcation of a sense of history and the importance of the heroic "combat, revolutionary, and labor traditions" of the USSR (particularly concerning the Soviet victory in the Great Patriotic War) is designed to alleviate the problem of the Soviet generation gap and more generally to invest the children of a developed, complex society with a sense of ideological fervor and sacrifice. These goals are part of the experience of the national university of Soviet military service.

Training the Civilian Soldier

It is very difficult for the Western observer to analyze the practical realities of Soviet Party-political indoctrination in the armed forces. One is left to speculate on the basis of public Soviet claims as to the nature and quality of training. The accuracy and intent of these claims is open to debate. But at the very least, if one examines what military leaders say about Party-political work and Soviet military training in general, the intent of the leadership becomes clearer.

Soviet military training of the citizen soldier is divided into three principal elements: combat proficiency and battlefield skills, psychological preparation for the conditions of modern warfare, and moral-psychological preparation.[9] The first two topics refer to basic military skills. The last—the specific province of Party-political work—contains the essence of Soviet citizenship training.

The principal goal of Party-political work is the formation of a "communist world outlook" or "communist convictions".[10] The latter encompasses a basic knowledge of Marxism–Leninism augmented by the emotional attachments developed in part by military-patriotic

614

education. Army General Yepishev, Chief of the Main Political Administration (*GlavPU*) explains:

> It is on the basis of the scientific world outlook that man's communist convictions are formed. These concepts are similar, but not identical. Communist convictions are genuine, Marxist knowledge impregnated with feelings and emotions, a knowledge that has become man's immutable stand in life. Communist convictions are thus the same ideological knowledge, 'cemented' as it were by patriotic feelings, and this makes them still more effective.[11]

Thus, Yepishev makes an organic connection between the ideology and the Stalinist call to patriotic loyalty. Communist convictions combine both.

Communist convictions are established in the process of "ideological education" which is "the process of the purposeful formation of a person's character."[12] This idea involves a crucial notion. Party-political work is not simply the teaching of Marxism–Leninism during formal classroom sessions. Instead, it involves the all-round development of the personality. Therefore, ideological education includes three conjoint processes: general upbringing, specific education, and training—all of which are interdependent.[13]

In passing on communist conviction, military upbringing (*vospitaniye*) work performs a decisive function in furthering civilian political socialization. The Soviet soldier is trained in surroundings and from the viewpoint common to all of Soviet society. Hence, the frequent claims by Soviet military authors on the "unity of the army and the people" and its importance. Upbringing is a broad process designed to inculcate in the soldier a positive and socially useful outlook not only toward ideology but toward the basic institutions of civilian society and the solution of its problems.[14] This is essentially political socialization.

Ideological upbringing, for example, is said to include a positive attitude with regard to socially useful labor and military, or labor, discipline.

> Socially useful labor and practical work play a decisive role in the formation of an individual's personality and in the development of his qualities. V. I. Lenin repeatedly referred to the role of labor in the communist education of workers, especially the young . . . .
> Service, the combat training of Soviet servicemen, is socially useful work, the lofty and honorable duty of every citizen of the USSR.[15]

In doing military work, the 18–year-old acquires in a disciplined environment the labor habits so important in the civilian economy of later life.

Military labor takes place within the collective, a basic civilian socialization institution. In socializing citizens, the military collective is said to be superior to its civilian counterpart. The soldier joins the collective while still young and relatively impressionable. Military life is all-encompassing. The soldier eats, sleeps, works, studies, trains, and relaxes as part of a collective. He is never apart from the collective's influence during his term of service. Military work is also more rigorous and more disciplined than civilian labor, and, of course, the social value of military service—defending the homeland—is more readily apparent to the young soldier than is the value of digging potatoes on the collective farm or standing on the factory assembly line. Among collectives, the military variety is said to be uniquely effective by Soviet military authors: "Military activities, more than any other kind of activities, are of a collective nature."[16] Another military writer observed:

> A military collective, like any other socialist one, provides an opportunity for each person to play the most different social, practical-moral, and professional roles. However, in a military collective, these roles are defined with particular clarity and are precisely carried out . . . . The role of a citizen soldier is a particularly educating one.[17]

The military collective serves two purposes. First, it functions as the basic unit for ideological education. Second, the collective should serve to isolate and inhibit any negative, improper attitudes on the part of the individual soldier.[18]

As to the first function, "the core of this work is molding a communist world outlook in soldiers and instilling in them the ideas of Marxism–Leninism."[19] In practical terms, this work involves a variety of activities. The typical soldier receives four hours of political classes per week (two sessions of two hours each). This schedule varies from unit to unit and branch to branch. In some units and on some ships, it consists of one three-hour session each week. Construction units receive three hours in winter and two in summer "at the expense of training and working time."[20] "Mass propaganda work" or "political information classes" for draftees are held in addition to the above "political classes" and take place twice a week for 30 minutes on each morning when regular "political classes" are not held.[21] This formal political instruction may take the form of lectures, seminars, group discussions, or practical work, and it is supplemented by independent study.[22]

Practical work may involve any number of tasks. The "social duties" assigned to the personnel of an average company or battery include the following (for NCOs and draftees):

For purposes of indoctrination and organized beneficial leisure, each unit should have a "Lenin Room" as specified in the *Interior Service Regulations*.[24] Indoctrinational work should also include the use of unit (wall) newspapers (company level); the publication of occasional agitation leaflets; and the use of television, radio, and popular films. Instructional resources are derived from frequent articles in the military press and military libraries.[25]

Cultural work and sports—organized leisure activities—also form a major portion of Party indoctrinational work. The officer's text on *Military Pedagogy* points out that:

> Aesthetic education ensures the spiritual growth of the soldiers, raises their general educational and cultural level on the basis of the mastery of all achievements of science, literature, and art, and forms correct aesthetic views and feelings and the ability to understand the true beauty of life, labor, and military service.[26]

At the unit level, the emphasis is on structuring the leisure time of individuals. There are unit excursions to local museums, artistic performances, unit orchestras, dance ensembles, film showings, and discussions. The deputy company commander for political affairs is required by regulation to organize mass cultural and sports activities; manage the "company amateur artistic activities"; and use the "best literary works, as well as magazine articles on political, military, and cultural subjects.[27] *Komsomol* organizations also play a major role in organizing cultural and sports work such as volleyball, weightlifting, basketball, and boxing.[28] Thus, ideological work in the collective extends far beyond the area of formal educational work into seemingly distantly related activities. Indoctrinational work in the Soviet Armed Forces is designed not simply to enhance knowledge of the ideology but also to promote the all-round development of the personality of the new Soviet man.

The Unity of Combat and Political Training. Political work is not viewed simply as an addition to combat training. Rather, the relation-ship between the two is dialectical. Political work should penetrate all aspects of military life and combat training, and success in combat training and the achievement of a high state of readiness are seen as the surest proofs of the success of Party-political work.

In practical terms, the politcal officer is tasked to participate "in elab-oration of the calendar plan for the combat and political training of the battalion."[29] The regimental deputy commander for political affairs (*zampolit*) is to see to the creation among personnel of a sense of re-sponsibility for the maintenance of weapons and equipment. The company-level *zampolit* is further required to "explain the tasks of com-bat and political training . . .; cultivate outstanding trainees and dissem-inate their experience . . .; mobilize the soldiers, sergeants, and officers for the study and exemplary preservation of combat equipment, arma-ment, and other military and national property . . . ."[30]

In other words, the proper attitude toward an understanding of weapons and combat roles is also within the purview of the political officer and political training. This task, which developed during the 1960s in conjunction with the scientific-technical "revolution in military affairs," is part of the reasoning behind the establishment of a series of *GlavPU* schools designed to train political officers in military-technical specialties.[31] Aside from this, it is also the duty of the political officer to promote socialist competition as a moral incentive to the study of technically complex modern weaponry.

Political work in combat matters is indirect and varies according to the branch or service. The political officer cannot usurp the regular officer's role without some opposition. The *zampolit,* therefore, exerts his influence through his classes and his organizing and agitation work among Party and *Komsomol* bodies in the unit. Competition in a mis-sile unit, for example, will be in terms of reaction time to an alarm, while in the motor pool, it may concern the drive for economy in the use of fuel and lubricants.[32]

This theme of the unit of combat and political training is constantly reiterated in the military press:

> [T]he enhancement of the personnel's communist aware-ness, vigilance, and combat readiness has always been and is the basic aim of Party-political work in the Armed Forces. The enhancement of the combat readiness of the troops is the most important part of Party-political work, an indica-tion of its effectiveness. Therein lies the army's contribution to the common cause of communist construction.[33]
>
> Ideological education and training are inseparably linked, and there is a close interaction between them. The former imparts ideological direction to training and increases its effectiveness. In turn, both formal and ideological education

problems are resolved during the course of training.[34]

Party-political work is a decisive means of influencing the consciousness and hearts of the people. It increases by many times over the combat efficiency and morale of soldiers, facilitates the conversion of their spiritual strength into material strength, and multiplies the combat capabilities of the troops.[35]

In short, Party-political indoctrinational work is integral to the success of combat training and combat readiness . . . in theory. As General Yepishev noted above, successful combat training is the best indicator of successful indoctrination. Concealed within the dialectic is an interesting question: Is military training becoming the vehicle of the ideology and the soldier being molded into a new Soviet man, or is the ideology becoming a tool for the enhancement of Soviet military might and the new Soviet man being trained as a warrior? If the latter is true, it would imply a modification of the ideology in the direction of militarism.

However, the positing of this contrary relationship is founded upon the assumption military training and ideological indoctrination are hostile opposites; that by their natures, one must take precedence over the other. This has been the assumption of most Western analysts. It is fundamental to Kolkowicz's analysis—written in the 1960—and it is similarly fundamental to Warner's interest group/bureaucratic analysis—written in the mid–1970s.[36] Soviet authors, on the other hand, have vigorously protested this Western assumption and have actively posited a useful and different relationship between ideological and military training based on the integration of the two.[37] This can be seen in the content of military-political education.

The topics of indoctrination seem to fall into three general areas: 1) ideological/political topics; 2) social/economic topics; and 3) topics related to military effectiveness. There is some overlap between the second and third areas. Military effectiveness demands the solution of social problems which the draftee often brings with him into the service or which are not solely military in concern, such as drunkenness.

1) Ideological/political education is the core topic, and the core of the core is Marxism–Leninism. Other topics come under the political subheading, including current Party foreign and domestic policy and moral education:

> Military indoctrination is also closely connected with the moral education of servicemen—primarily through the category of morality known as military duty. The tasks of affirming in life and activity of soldiers the standards of communist society are carried out in moral education.[38]

"Soviet patriotism" and positive opposition to and vigilance against bourgeois and imperialist ideology come under this category as well:

When becoming familiar with the organization, equipment, and tactics of the armies of the imperialist states,
Soviet soldiers not only learn how best to employ their own
weapons . . . but also more concretely comprehend the reactionary essence of contemporary imperialism and the
plunderous character of wars unleashed by imperialist
states.[39]

In other words, ideological education in the military takes up where
civilian schools leave off. Military training provides important opportunities and useful examples for political instruction and conditioning.

2) Social topics of indoctrination are more varied in scope. They are
intended to keep the military man in tune with what is going on in
civilian society, thus developing the social implications of military service. The topics vary with the successes, failures, and drives going on
in the nonmilitary world and include current affairs, successes of the
economy, the modern achievements of the sciences, technical progress,
and plan fulfillment.[40] Aesthetic education—i.e., the "spiritual growth
. . . general educational and cultural level" of the soldier—falls into this
category. The armed forces are thus asked to produce not simply an
ideologically trained citizen but one with an appreciation of science,
literature, and the arts.

3) The third type of indoctrination subject is concerned primarily
with improving military effectiveness. The soldier is to be taught the
"requirements of the military oath," regulations, the importance of military discipline, the fulfillment of orders, and the mastery of weapons
and equipment, as well as the rules of military courtesy, respect for
superiors, and saluting. The draftee should also receive a modicum of
legal and economic education (the latter being more applicable to construction, trade, and similar personnel). Physical training is included
here as well.[41]

There are several implications to be drawn with regard to the intent
of the Soviet leadership. At the level of the draftee, the intent of the
current leadership has been to augment the political socialization effort
through the military experience and in the process to make military
training a vehicle for ideological training and the creation of the new
socialist man. This has required the integration of civilian values into
the military. More emphasis has been placed on creating a culturally
well-rounded man. The emphasis on aesthetic and moral education,
while having a limited influence on military effectiveness, no doubt
seemed designed primarily to create a model citizen. The emphasis the
Soviets place on discipline, respect for authority, and the maintenance
of socialist property is consistent with this idea. It has also led to the
assertion that the military collective is seemingly superior to the civilian collective in this role. Such an assertion would be necessary to justify the use of a traditional agency such as the military for socialization
purposes, particularly where such a domestic political function of the

military finds little ideological justification.

There are several results. First, the military becomes a vehicle for ideological training. This, incidentally, engenders a certain adaptation of the ideology to conform to military goals and methods. Second, the armed forces are increasingly politicized through their involvement in civilian political functions. The implication is that the notion of Soviet control of the military—based upon some "Bonapartist" threat to the Party—prevalent in Western analysis has little relevance to current Soviet civil-military relations. If the military still constituted a formidable threat to the political regime, how could Brezhnev justify its use as the centerpiece of a key civilian socialization program? If "control" is the proper term at all, it is accomplished through integration of the political function. Third, if the Soviet soldier is being politicized to a degree, it is reasonable to assume increased civilian contact with military affairs would lead to militarism among the civilian population. Though it may not have been intended, the new Soviet man is being raised as a soldier.

Military Collective II: Reeducation

The second function of the military collective is the isolation and reeducation of servicemen who have acquired negative habits or attitudes. Structured public opinion thus becomes an instrument of discipline and resocialization by providing organized feedback to the individual from his peers and immediate supervisors.

> Having common interests, the collective sees to it that the conduct of every soldier and sailor and their attitude to duty and training conform to Soviet laws and military regulations. Consequently, when a serviceman distinguishes himself, his act is appreciated by his comrades, and if he violates discipline, public opinion censures him, makes strict demands upon him, and sees to it that they are carried out.[42]

It is not unusual for a military collective to be asked to deal with attitude and discipline problems. All armies face this job. More to the point, in the Soviet case, this function of the military collective means the armed forces have become a surrogate solution for several unsolved social ills. The armed forces are asked to deal with problems of religious affiliation, drunkenness, dissidence, and delinquency and to assist in the socialization and education of rural youth and the national minorities.

Atheism. The military collective, particularly the *Komsomol* and the Party organization within it, should be concerned with the attitude of any religious believer and should actively conduct atheistic work in order to remove the "negative" influence. In 1971, *Krasnaya zvezda* cited the example of a young draftee and the wife of a sergeant who were both brought back to the path of atheism through the efforts of the military collective.[43] Such is the ideal. Whether or not all military commanders have the time or interest to delve into this problem is another matter entirely. The following year, *Krasnaya zvezda* described the situation in Lieutenant S. Martsinyuk's company. A Baptist group from a local village had somehow penetrated the unit. The wife of a sergeant had been persuaded "to attend prayer meetings." The correspondent found to his apparent horror that no atheistic propaganda was even planned! ". . . [A] small aluminum cross was found in the barracks, but Party members paid no attention, laughing it off as some inexplicable accident." The *Komsomol* was not conducting atheistic propaganda, and the unit library had only one book on religion. Two Moslems were even found among the company—one with a text from the Koran sewn into his clothes—and both were *Komsomol* members![44]

No doubt Lieutenant Martsinyuk's company was suitably chastized. The message is clear and two-fold. Party policy requires the military unit to carry on the antireligious struggle whenever required. And second, this type of work is apt to be forgotten or ignored in the press of daily business by the unit, its commander, and even the Party and *Komsomol* organizations.

Excessive drinking is another problem typical of civilian society which carries over into military life. It seems unlikely the *GlavPU* would assert any special ability on the part of the military collective in solving the problem of alcoholism. On the other hand, not solving the problem would have a serious deleterious impact upon military training effectiveness. Hence, the effort is demanded.[45]

Political Dissidence. The armed forces are also used as one of many devices by which the regime deals with political dissidence. In 1972, for example, Yevgeniy V. Levich, a Jewish physicist, applied for an emigration visa. He is the son of Venyamin G. Levich, a physical chemist and corresponding member of the Academy of Sciences, former professor at Moscow University, and Head of the Hydrodynamics Institute. The result of the younger Levich's visa application was the loss of his draft-exempt status as a scientist and his being drafted into the army. He was sent to a Siberian penal detachment. Remarkably, the young physicist, following his term of service, received permission in 1974 to leave the USSR, just prior to President Nixon's visit to Moscow. He finally left the USSR in 1976.[46]

In another instance, Andrey Sakharov's stepson, Aleksey Semenov, was expelled from the Moscow State Pedagogical Institute just seven months prior to the completion of his five years of study. He was expelled on the basis of having twice failed the examination at the end of his summer military training and for having "systematically broken military discipline."[47]

In both cases, the armed forces were used to apply indirect pressure on the dissidents involved through their relatives. The armed forces have not replaced the police-court-sanatorium-camp system which is the normal avenue of punishment for the political dissident, but these cases do point up the fact that the armed forces, as is the case with many other social institutions in the USSR, can and do play an integral role in such matters outside the military realm as domestic dissidence. This represents a further step in the politicization of the Soviet Armed Forces and their corresponding integration into the wider domestic system.

Delinquency. When all else fails—i.e., home, school, and *Komsomol*—the task of straightening out errant and delinquent youths is sometimes left to the "iron fist" of military discipline. Somehow, the armed forces are to remove not only the long hair and blue jeans but the underlying nonsocialist attitudes. The army must make "a new socialist man" out of the new Soviet boy.

A *Krasnaya zvezda* article reviewing a commentary in *Literaturnaya gazeta* described the transformation of a hippie into a soldier: "Tomorrow, they will go into the army, and the iron will of the solid collective, having torn them out of their environment for 2 years, will teach them to work and see the target, and some will be taken in hand to such an extent that they will dare not return to the old way."[48]

A 1964 *Krasnaya zvezda* poll described just such an occurrence. Petty Officer Second Class V. Vshivkin described his failure in school and his gradual loss of interest in his job. He began to drink and fight. But then he entered the service.

> Iron military discipline took me in hand on the first day. Everything was overturned and broken—my habits, my conduct, even the course of my thinking . . . . Not just the commander but the entire collective fought to turn me into a real man . . . . I fell in love with books. I began to take counsel with them. The bad was squeezed out of me drop by drop.
>
> Now, looking back, I shall say honestly, the years of service have fostered in me restraint, love for labor, independence, and respect for people. I have earned the great honor of being in the front ranks of the building of communism. I have been accepted as a candidate member of the CPSU . . . .[49]

These are, of course, ideals—ideals, by the way, which are also asserted in *DOSAAF* military training circles and are said to contribute similarly to the education of "difficult teenagers."[50]

Undoubtedly, military men would assert the social validity of the military way of life and the discipline which it imposes. Nonetheless, the officers seem a bit uncomfortable and resentful of this intrusion upon training them in which they are cast in the roles of surrogate parents for wayward boys. Lieutenant Colonel Khorev pointed out

623

that military service does not relieve family or the school of responsibility:

> 'Go into the Army,' they push their son and calm themselves; 'There they'll make a man of you' .... All of this, nevertheless, does not liberate either parents, school, or society, and, in particular, *Komsomol* organizations from concerns for the education of worthy reinforcements for the Army.[51]

Captain Orudzhev is quoted as complaining "some parents have avoided the education of their son, hoping that everything will be done for them by the Army. As if commanders and political workers have no concerns besides reeducation."[52]

Among the different branches of the Soviet Armed Forces, the ground forces—particularly the motorized rifle units—bear the brunt of this disciplinary reeducation task. The more specialized and technical units (practically all others) tend to send their disciplinary misfits to the "infantry" (motorized rifle troops). Generally, these people have a year of service remaining and are often reclusive and nonsocial in behavior.[53] This additional burden, concentrated in certain units, must lower military readiness and effectiveness. It may also explain the restiveness of army officers in regard to reeducation. But whether or not the motorized rifle commander and his *zampolit* can turn the draftee from jazz to Shostakovich, their doing so is certainly part of the picture which the leadership paints for the national/military university.

Proletarian Internationalism—National Minorities. The Soviet Armed Forces have long served as a road of upward and "urbanward" mobility for rural youth. The complaint that the army removes the youths from the farm village but fails to return them is often heard. This problem is itself in decline, however, as the Soviet population shifts toward an increasingly urban way of life. There is another problem, however, which shows few signs of an immediate solution—the minority nationality problem.

The socialization of minority nationalists is certainly not an effort unique to the Brezhnev regime. Nonetheless, it fits in well with the "national university" concept espoused by the regime since 1966. As Marshal Babadzhanyan commented:

> From the Soviet Army's very birth, V. I. Lenin and the Communist Party have constructed it on a multinational foundation. In this lies one of the special characteristics of our army: it is a new type of army. The military and political union of the Soviet Republics, forged in the years of the Civil War, appears as an indestructible fortress against [which] enemy hordes dash themselves.[54]

The problem and its import are no less salient today. Proletarian internationalism, national unity, and Soviet patriotism are among the most mentioned code words included in commentaries on military training and the social role of the Soviet Armed Forces. In this case, "proletarian internationalism" takes on a domestic connotation. The depth of national influences still presents a problem to be solved in military training.

> Here it must be considered that international indoctrination is more difficult and complicated than patriotic indoctrination. The problem is that a nation . . . has a strong and constant influence on the individual. From childhood a person is raised in a national linguistic environment, he is subjected to national traditions, and assimilates a national psychology and national feeling which have a strong emotional tint. This is why, in multinational collectives, the communist ideological effect on the awareness of the soldiers must be greater and stronger than anywhere else.[55]

As Goldhamer has noted, comments on the existence of a nationality problem rarely go beyond this level of vagueness.[56] Articles on nationality conflict do not appear at all. What one does find are descriptions of how the "friendship of the Soviet peoples" increases combat readiness. According to Marshal Babadzhanyan:

> Work among the troops has left one such episode in my memory. We had with us a leading tank crew in which two Russians, a Georgian, and an Armenian were serving. It was an exceptionally friendly and united military collective, and its soldiers were fully able to take each other's place. As a rule, the crew hit every target with the first shot, the first salvo.
>
> One time, Marshal of the Soviet Union A. A. Grechko was present at a firing practice. He asked them how they achieved such high scores in weapons training. Gun trainer Private Papyashvili answered for all of them: "Our crew is a friendly family. Each of us tries to serve the motherland honorably and conscientiously . . . ."[57]

Today, the Soviet Armed Forces include representatives of over 100 nationalities.[58] In the Turkestan Military District, it is not uncommon to find representatives of 12 to 15 nationalities in a company.[59] In dealing with this diversity, military-political indoctrination stresses the overriding concerns of class as opposed to national interests.

The armed forces must work to promote unity not only as a social goal valuable to civilian society but as military goal. The elimination of small group conflict within a subunit cannot fail to improve combat readiness. Also, the unit cannot perform credibly unless all of its members have a good command of the Russian language. Assimilation of the non-Russian speaker is facilitated by assigning the minority draftee to a unit stationed in a different area than the home nationality, thereby forcing him into contact with Russian speakers. Once assigned to his unit, the draftee will often be paired off with a Russian-speaking buddy so he can receive individual tutoring. Special study circles in the Russian language are organized in the subunit. Also, in conjunction with civilian authorities, the military promotes the teaching of the Russian language in civilian (non-Russian) schools and operates special language classes. Societies or circles for the study of the Russian language are organized at the unit and subunit level.[60]

Clearly, the Soviets regime's interest in using the armed forces to socialize minority nationalities has not disappeared. The armed forces offer a solution to the problem in two ways. First, and probably most important, the armed forces constitute a unique social institution: it is the only one which draws the vast majority of Soviet youth out of their home environment for a time and thrusts them into a uniform, ethnically heterogeneous society. The young Kazakh, Mongol, or Armenian is forced to live with his Russian comrades for two years, day and night. And this experience involves activities which are dedicated to Union-wide goals rather than republic, regional, or local goals. Whether or not the simple act of forcing people to live together reduces conflict, however, is open to question. In the short run, it is possible to speculate that minority conflict may increase through increased contact, but any such increase would be muted by the disciplinary stringency of military life. On the other hand, such internationality contact should tend, in the long run, to expand the horizons of all parties involved. The lack of available data makes more specific hypotheses problematic at best.[61]

Second, there is the matter of language training. Language proficiency is a natural prerequisite for a combat organization which must by nature be able to function swiftly and in a coordinated fashion. Language training must also take away significant hours from an already crowded training schedule. The degree of success is likely to be related not to formal classes but to the amount of time the non-Russian is forced to use the language in order to succeed in military life. Even this presumes a prior acquaintance with the Russian language. Military language training is, therefore, likely to have a limited value at best. Even if successful, linguistic homogeneity does not eliminate the possibility of conflict among ethnic groups: witness the US experience.

One further point ought to be made. Marshal Grechko pointed out that in the past, the armed forces provided "an important base for bringing up future cadres of Party and Soviet workers.[62] Today, the Party and *Komosol* apparat uses have been elaborated to such an extent, they have the capability to take care of their own recruitment needs. The armed forces do provide a 24–hour laboratory for the observation of individuals, however. Not even the Party can make claim. It is likely minority nationality leadership recruitment is still carried out in part through the instrument of the military.

Despite all these limitations, the defense leadership continues to extol the usefulness of national integration through military service. As Marshal Grechko stated:

> The utter devotion of all nations and nationalities to the socialist Motherland serves as a foundation for the might of our multinational Armed Forces. Their combat cooperation is an expression of the organic merging of key interests of all Soviet people with the noble national traditions of each nation and nationality. This inseparable unity has become a rich soil in which socialist patriotism of Soviet soldiers has grown and become strong.

Nonetheless, he adds a note of caution a bit further on:

> Particular attention is given to the fight against vestiges of nationalism. One cannot ignore the fact that a certain part of the people, albeit a very insignificant part, sometimes displays elements of national conceit and aloofness. There have been attempts to make a nationality issue out of various disagreements or personal affronts. The experience of progressive units and warships shows that an international upbringing has greatest results where a sensitive and attentive approach is taken to the needs of the soldiers.[63]

Reconsidering the Effectiveness of the National University

At this point, it is necessary to take a few moments to reevaluate the effectiveness of the Soviet Armed Forces as a "national university." The advantages and potentials of the institution have been discussed above. We must now examine the youth to be trained and several of the roadblocks in the path of effective socialization in the armed forces.

Perhaps the easiest way to get at the nature of the new Soviet citizen-soldier is to create a profile of the average draftee. The average soldier is 18 years old, just slightly younger than before the 1967 draft law. He is better educated than his predecessors: more than 60 percent of Soviet draftees have a secondary or higher education.[64] This is a fact much commented on in the military press, so much so that it probably indicates the military establishment is having difficulties in adjusting to this better educated soldier. Correspondingly, he is likely to demand more in the way of pedagogical excellence from his instructors. He has had a minimal introduction to the military way of life in his 140 hours of mandatory predraft education in secondary school. Also, the young soldier is likely to be a member of the *Komsomol*[65] and has acquired a military-technical specialty from the *DOSAAF*. Since he comes from an urban-academic as opposed to a rural-labor environment, he is less prepared physically than his counterpart of a generation ago but is better prepared in terms of technical knowledge. While he may have participated in mass sports activities, he does not have a sports rating.[66] Among his civilian friends and acquaintances, several—though, according to Soviet authors, only a minority—have a very negative attitude toward the armed forces and military service. (Keep in mind that most of these will be drafted as well.) They tend to see military service as a waste of time. One 17–year-old girl wrote to her soldier that his situation was not enviable. Colonel Kozhedub complained of the "snobbish attitude of some students towards youths in uniform, who tend to look down on soldiers, as 'people of lower rank.'"[67]

Perhaps the greatest single challenge presented by this draftee to the armed forces in his higher level of education. As Professor Erickson points out, this recruit is less inclined to accept ideology without question; he is more likely to question authority and may be less inclined to accept the values of the military way of life than the soldier of 1934. Thus, while his educational level may facilitate military-technical training, it may have the reverse effect on the modern Soviet draftee's acceptance of political training.[68]

The *GlavPu* has recognized this problem. In 1972 and 1973, respectively, textbooks on *Military Psychology* and *Military Pedagogy* were produced for the military-political officer's schools.[69] Officers are now instructed to follow a "personal approach" in training subordinates, deal with each man individually, and take account of the differences in each personality. This is a common theme in discussions on training.[70]

It is likely the other major problem presented by the new draftee is his attitude. No doubt, many fully accept the military-patriotic message. But this generation comes to the rigors of military life from an affluent society (relative to that of the ruling generation). The experience is, no doubt, distasteful to some. Also, the immediate threat to the security of the nation is less pressing than before. In Soviet parlance, the balance of forces has shifted in favor of the socialist camp, and Soviet power has preserved the peace since the Great Patriotic War. The justification for the call to arms is, therefore, rather vague to this affluent Soviet youth. This is what the Soviets intend when they refer to the problem of the "generation gap."

The military institution itself presents several complications for the operation of the national university. Service terms have been shortened by a year in order to increase the percentage of the 18–year-old cohort which will enter the national university, but the requisite training time has decreased even further since some useful service time must be included in addition to training during the 2 years. Erickson estimates the loss in training time at 50 percent.[71] In this sense, the 1967 draft law must have lowered the quality of the Soviet armed forces in favor of advantages gained in political socialization and is, therefore, militarily counterproductive.

Decreased service time also meant less time for the development of NCOs and therefore created a manpower crisis at the squad/platoon/company level. In the short run, this meant that junior officers were asked to perform NCO duty. In the long run, it required organizational restructuring to create the warrant officer ranks needed to fill the gap. Adding to the confusion is a semiannual call-up which requires simultaneous training for four different classes of first-term draftees during each two-year period.

Aside from these things, there are the typical problems. Indoctrination methods and topics are frequently poorly organized, boring, and held during those few precious hours of the soldier's free time. There are limits to the effectiveness of military socialization just as in other sectors of society.

The Soviet Armed Forces have been very conscious of the technical "revolution in military affairs." This revolution has meant that with the passage of time, the regular officer corps has come to be dominated by engineers and technicians. It is doubly difficult to involve the sterile technician in the grimy work of political education.

How successful is the "national university?"

The evaluation by the Western academic community has been mixed. Erickson, for example, pointed out that the USSR is unique among modern industrial societies in attempting to use its military establishment in this fashion, and he seems to feel its success is questionable.[72] He pointed out further "that the age of 'hurrah-patriotism' has passed and will never return."[73]

In fact, the Soviet Union is not as unique in this regard as Erickson asserts. More than one industrial state has adopted militaristic values to promote certain domestic as well as foreign goals. Such states have responded to a perceived or real threat by becoming nations-in-arms. Modern Israel is the most current example. Soviet ideology is certainly susceptible to this type of siege mentality.

Professor Erickson may be correct in asserting the end of "hurrah-patriotism" in the USSR, but the statement requires qualification. It is difficult to maintain a high state of emotional commitment to aroused patriotic sentiment over a long period of time. Certainly, the Soviets are struggling with this difficulty. On the other hand, neither human nature nor Soviet ideology have changed sufficiently to eliminate a new upsurge of belligerent patriotism, given the proper stimulus. "Hurrah-patriotism" is easily capable of resurgence.

Wesson asserts the military is "the most effective agent of russification."[74] This may indeed be true. It must be pointed out, however, that the military is not startlingly successful in this regard, as the above discussion has point out. If it is the most successful agency of russification, the others are in serious trouble.

Perhaps Herbert Goldhamer made the most telling evaluation of the Soviet national university. Claims of success are remarkably hard to find, he pointed out, but the Soviets have single-mindedly continued to pursue the militaristic policies involved.[75] If success is not indicated, certainly need is demonstrated. And in a general sense, one must note the USSR represents a very durable, institutionally successful political entity. Insofar as the military and its political indoctrination apparatus have contributed to Soviet civilian political socialization, they are responsible for Soviet stability.

The immediate apparent function of the Soviet military national university is to supplement the traditional socialization agencies—Stalin's transmission belts. That the Brezhnev regime would turn to a conservative agency to solve a socialization problem is logical, but it also points out the possibility of a crisis or partial failing of the old-style socialization agencies. This is not surprising, given the fact the current regime governs a much more developed system than the one which existed when the transmission belts were created, but it demands further investigation of the state of political socialization in general in recent years.

Another effect of this effort has been the politicization of the Soviet Armed Forces through civil-military integration and, no doubt, a corresponding decrease in military effectiveness.

Finally, if this phenomenon is typical of a developed communist system, the development of the Soviet military national university should have some implication for the development of similar agencies in other communist systems.

Notes

1. General of the Army A. A. Yepishev, *Some Aspects of Party–Political Work in the Soviet Armed Forces* (Moscow: Progress Publishers, 1975), p. 26.
2. This idea is discussed at greater length in William E. Odom, *The Soviet Volunteers: Modernization and Bureaucracy in a Mass Public Organization* (Princeton: Princeton University Press, 1973), pp. 26–30, and 49–52.
3. Ibid., p. 51.
4. L. I. Brezhnev, "Worthy Replenishment for the Armed Forces—Reception in the Kremlin in Honor of Graduates of Military Academies," *Pravda,* 6 July 1967, p. 1, in *Current Digest of the Soviet Press (CDSP)* Vol. 29, No. 27, p. 6.
5. L. I. Brezhnev, "Kremlin Reception in Honor of the Graduates of Military Academies: Loyalty to the Homeland, the Party and the People," *Pravda,* 9 July 1968, pp. 1–2, in *CDSP,* Vol. 20, No. 28, p. 10.
6. Yepishev, *Party–Political Work,* p. 25.
7. This is, obviously, a composite list of training or indoctrination goals from a variety of sources. Military and nonmilitary spokesmen are constantly enumerating such lists, with varying content. A sampling might include: Major General S. N. Kozlov, ed., *The Officer's Handbook* (Moscow: Voyenizdat, 1971), translated and published under the auspices of the United States Air Force (Washington: Government Printing Office, 1977), pp. 6, 32, 87–90, 93 and ff.; *Interior Service Regulations of the Armed*

Forces of the USSR, translated in Joint Publications Research Service, *Soviet Military Translations* (or *Translations on USSR Military Affairs*), (hereafter cited as JPRS–*SMT* or JPRS–*TMA*), No. 287, Chapter 3; Marshal of the Soviet Union R. Ya. Malinovskiy, "Soviet Defense Policy," *Military Review,* Vol. 46, No. 10 (October 1966), pp. 88–89; and *Pravda,* 6 July 1968, pp. 1–2.

8. Ibid.

9. John Erickson, "The Training of the Soviet Soldier: A Review of Recent Theory and Practice," *Journal of the Royal United Services Institute for Defence Studies,* Vol. 116, No. 664 (1971), p. 46.

10. This is an oft repeated idea. See, for example, Colonel A. Milovidov, "The Revolution in Military Affairs and the Spiritual Strength of Troops," *Kommunist Vooruzhennykh Sil,* No. 13, July 1965, pp. 8–17; "Toward a New Upsurge in Ideological Work Among the Troops," *Krasnaya zvezda,* 1 November 1972, p. 2, translated in the Foreign Broadcast Information Service—*Daily Report: Soviet Union* (hereafter cited as FBIS), 10 November 1972, p. M–3; and Yepishev, *Party–Political Work,* pp. 207–208.

11. Yepishev, op. cit., p. 220.

12. Kozlov, op. cit., p. 87.

13. Colonel A. M. Danchenko and Colonel I. F. Vydrin, eds., *Military Pedagogy* (Moscow: Voyenizdat, 1973), translated and published under the auspices of the United States Air Force (Washington: Government Printing Office, 1976), pp. 8–9, 113.

14. Ibid., p. 8.

15. Kozlov, op. cit., p. 98.

16. Ibid., p. 99.

17. Shelyag, V. V., et al., eds., *Military Psychology* (Moscow: Voyenizdat, 1972), translated and published under the auspices of the United States Air Force (Washington: Government Printing Office, 1976), pp. 218–2.

18. Ibid., p. 317–320.

19. *Krasnaya zvezda,* 1 November 1972, p. 2.

20. Mordasov states that "sailors have several hours of political science lessons a week," in *Life in the Soviet Navy* (Moscow: Novosti Press, 1975), p. 35. Jones cites a mandatory requirement of two hours per week in "The Revolution in Military Affairs," *Survey,* Vol. 20, No. 1, p. 92, plus supplementary conferences, thematic evenings, etc. In this case, one ought to err, if at all, on the conservative side. As John Erickson points out, the normal training day has only seven periods from 0840 to 1520 hours with rest breaks, plus one hour for private study. Doubtless, the schedule is crowded enough already for the unit commander without spending more than the minimum amount of time on noncombat activities. See John Erickson, op. cit., p. 48. Lieutenant General Khmel, however, states that political classes are three to four hours weekly. Group leaders attend 8 to 12 hours in seminars during working hours each month. Mass propaganda is in addition to these hours, as would be sports and cultural activities. See Lieutenant General A. Y. Khmel, *The Education of the Soviet Soldier: Party–Political Work in the Soviet Armed Forces* (Moscow: Progress Publishers, 1972), pp. 100–101, 106–107.

21. Khmel, op. cit., p. 107.

22. Kozlov, op. cit., pp. 954–96.

23. Ruban, *The Soviet School of Courage and Warcraft: The Main Principles and Methods of Training Soldiers in the Soviet Armed Forces* (Moscow: Progress Publishers, 1976), p. 129.

24. The Interior Service Regulations list the "Lenin Room" first among major space areas to be provided in the troop billets. *Interior Service Regulations of the Armed Forces of the USSR.,* Chapter 9, Article 139.

25. This list of basic indoctrinational methods is not all-inclusive, but gives some idea of the types of activities pursued. For more extensive discussions, see, Kozlov, op. cit., Chapters 1 and 4; Ruban, op. cit.; Danchenko and Vydrin, op. cit., p. 219; Yepishev, *Party–Political Work,* Chapter 4; and *Interior Service Regulations,* Chapters 3–6.

"Evening Universities of Marxism–Leninism" are not included here because they are directed toward permanent cadres rather than draftees.

26. Danchenko and Vydrin, op. cit., p. 207.
27. *Interior Service Regulations,*, Chapter 5, Article 119.
28. Ibid. See also Yepishev, *Party–Political Work,* pp. 160–161.
29. *Interior Service Regulations,* Chapter 6, Section 107.
30. Ibid., Chapter 3, Sections 71 and 119.
31. Jones, op. cit., p. 90–92.
32. Yepishev, *Party–Political Work,* pp. 164–170.
33. Ibid., p. 99.
34. Kozlov, op. cit., p. 87.
35. Marshal of the Soviet Union A. A. Grechko, *The Armed Forces of the Soviet State* (Moscow: Voyenizdat, 1975), published under the auspices of the United States Air Force (Washington: Government Printing Office, undated), pp. 292–293.
36. Roman Kolkowicz, *The Soviet Military and the Communist Party* (Princeton: Princeton University Press, 1967); and Edward L. Warner, III, *The Military in Comtemporary Soviet Politics: An Institutional Analysis* (New York: Praeger, 1977).
37. This theme is particularly well articulated in Yepsihev, *Party–Political Work,* Chapter 3.
38. Danchenko and Vydrin, op. cit., p. 207.
39. Ibid., p. 129. The same work also contains an interesting discussion of the other topics of ideological education. See pp. 205–208.
40. These topics are mentioned in numerous places, though not in the order in which they are placed here. See, for example, Danchenko and Vydrin, op. cit., pp. 205–208; *Interior Service Regulations,* Chapter 3; Khmel, *Education of the Soviet Soldier,* pp. 107–112.
41. Danchenko and Vydrin, op. cit., pp. 205–206.
42. Khmel, op. cit., p. 155
43. Lieutenant Colonel V. Devin, "Out of Step—When Anti–Religious Propaganda is Forgotten," *Krasnaya zvezda,* 22 August 1972, p. 2, in *CDSP,* Vol. 24, No. 37, p. 9.
44. Ibid., pp. 8–9.
45. *Krasnaya zvezda,* 1 November 1972, p. 2.
46. Christopher S. Wren, "Soviet Jews in Israel Express Concern Over Kin Left Behind," *New York Times,* 18 July 1978, p. A2; and Craig R. Whitney, "Levich Granted Soviet Exit Visa: Scientist to Leave Within Month," *New York Times,* 17 November 1978. The senior Levich received his exit visa in mid–November 1978.
47. "Sakharov's Stepson Ousted from Teacher's College," *New York Times,* 11 November 1972.
48. Cited by Herbert Goldhamer, *The Soviet Soldier: Soviet Military Management at the Troop Level* (New York: Crane, Russak and Company, 1975), p. 216.
49. *Krasnaya zvezda* Questionnaire: About Yourself and Your Friends and Comrades, *Krasnaya zvezda,* 7 July 1964, p. 4, in *CDSP,* Vol. 16, No. 46, p. 11.
50. M. Prokofiyev, "Rear Patriots," *Voyennyye znaniya* [Military Knowledge], No. 10, October 1967, p. 11., in JPRS–*SMT,* No. 411.
51. Lieutenant Colonel A. Khorev and Lieutenant R. Makushkin, "Belated Repentance," *Krasnaya zvezda,* 11 July 1970, p. 2, in JPRS–*TMA,* No. 631.
52. Ibid.
53. Major A. Kudryavtsev, "Into the Infantry for Correction," *Krasnaya zvezda,* 13 September 1973, p. 2, in JPRS–*TMA,* No. 974.
54. Marshal of Armor A. Kh. Babadzhanyan, "In Single Formation," *Krasnaya zvezda,* 18 February 1968, p. 2, in FBIS, *Special Supplement on the 50th Anniversary of the Armed Forces,* 1968, p. 25.
55. Lieutenant Colonel V. Samoylenko, "Multi–Nationality and the Moral Factor," *Kommunist Vooruzhennykh Sil,* No. 3, February 1970, pp. 18–25, in JPRS–*TMA,* No. 598.
56. Goldhamer, op. cit., p. 187.
57. Babadzhanyan, op. cit., p. 27.

58. This is a commonly cited figure. See Colonel V. Avrilov, "Friendship of the Peoples—The Source of the Might of the Soviet Armed Forces," *Kommunist Vooruzhennykh Sil*, No. 3, February 1972, pp. 177–24, in JPRS–*TMA*, No. 796; Moscow Domestic Service, 0600 GMT, 27 March 1973.

59. Goldhamer, op. cit., p. 187.

60. Samoylenko, op. cit., pp. 18–25; Avrilov, op. cit., pp. 17–24; Goldhamer, op. cit., pp. 195, 197; Mordasov, op. cit., p. 43.

61. C. C. Moskos, "Minority Groups in Military Organization," in Roger W. Little, ed., *Handbook of Military Institutions* (Beverly Hills: Sage Publications, 1971), pp. 277–284, points out that blacks in the US do tend to see military service as a road to social advancement and have a more favorable attitude toward service life than whites. Further, he states military separateness from society favors the integration of ethnic groups. Whether this is due to the nature of the armed forces per se or the nature of US military separateness is an open question. In the Soviet case, granted that US experience has a limited relevance, the integral relationship between military and society would in theory tend to decrease the army's ability to socialize and integrate minorities.

62. Grechko, *Armed Forces*, p. 107.

63. Ibid., pp. 112 and 122, respectively.

64. Erickson, op. cit., p. 45. The figures on educational levels of draftees vary widely, not so much from disagreement as from probable use of different reference points or base years. In 1967, Marshal Grechko gave a figure of 46 percent. See Grechko, "On Draft Law on Universal Military Service," *Izvestiya*, 13 October 1967, pp. 5–6. In 1969, General Major Mikhailovskiy cited a figure of 52.6 percent having a complete secondary education. See "Two Years of Surveys," *Krasnaya zvezda*, 10 October 1969, p. 2. And in 1974, Chief Marshal of Aviation P. Kutakhov cited a figure of 78 percent. See "The Motherland's Reliable Shield," *Sovetskaya kultura* [Soviet Culture], 22 February 1974, p. 1, in FBIS, 1 March 1974, p. V–7. Erickson's figure of 60 percent, adjusted upward slightly for the passage of time, seems a reasonable compromise.

65. Percentages are a bit vague on this point and tend to vary from author to author. Marshal Kutakhov states that approximately 80 percent are members of the Party or *Komsomol*, the majority being in the latter. Op. cit., p. V–7.

66. Mikhailovskiy, op. cit., p. 2.

67. Colonel General of Aviation I. Kozhedub, "Reflections About Letters: The Student and the Soldier," *Komsomolskaya pravda* [Komsomol Truth], 25 November 1970, p. 2, in *CDSP*, Vol. 22 No. 50, p. 25; Lieutenant Colonel F. Khalturin and Lieutenant Colonel A. Shchelokov, "Confessions of Men in Their Twenties," *Krasnaya zvezda*, 11 October 1964, p. 3 in *CDSP*, Vol. 16, No. 46, pp. 11–13; E. Losoto, "Letter to a Soldier," *Komsomolskaya pravda*, 10 June 1970, p. 4, in *CDSP*, Vol. 21, No. 50, p. 25.

68. John Erickson, "The Soviet Military, Soviet Policy, and Soviet Policies," *USSI Report* 73–3, reprinted from *Strategic Review*, p. 13, and "Soviet Military Manpower Policies," *Armed Forces and Society*, November 1974, p. 37.

69. Shelyag, loc. cit.; and Danchenko and Vydrin, loc. cit.

70. See, for example, Ruban, op. cit., pp. 99, 124.

71. Erickson, "Soviet Military Manpower Policies," op. cit., p. 36.

72. Erickson, "The Soviet Military, Soviet Policy, and Soviet Politics," p. 16.

73. Erickson, "Soviet Military Manpower Policies," p. 43.

74. Robert G. Wesson, "The Military in Soviet Society," *Russian Review*, Vol. 30, No. 2 (April 1971), p. 44.

75. Goldhamer, op. cit., pp. 249–251, 254.

Part VI

Soviet Military Strategy:
Its Development and Its Future

Part VI is concerned with an examination of issues which have generated intense—and perhaps the most—controversy within the United States and the rest of the Western alliance over Soviet strategic intentions: Do the Soviets share the Western concept of deterrence? How do the Soviets plan to employ their strategic nuclear forces in the event of war? Do the Soviets really believe they can attain the capability to achieve victory in a nuclear war? These issues are indeed contentious and likely will remain so, but their discussion is essential to the development of an understanding of Soviet military intentions.

John Baker describes the general continuity of Soviet military doctrine; a continuity that has been conditioned by historical factors, the Soviet Union's role as a continental land power, and the consequent dominance of the Soviet Ground Forces in Soviet military planning. As a result, he argues, even with the advent of nuclear weapons, the USSR still has a conservative approach toward modern military strategy. Baker probes the sources of Soviet military thought, the nature of its nuclear strategy, and the possibility for changes in that strategy during the 1980s.

Amoretta Hoeber urges a greater understanding of Soviet intentions and strategy in order to develop appropriate and effective counter-strategies. She contends that domination coupled with political and military victory appear to be serious, long-term Soviet aims. While the Soviets may not desire war, they will be prepared for its contingency. In order to do this, the Soviets emphasize surprise, force superiority, war survival measures, and specific plans for the occupation and control of enemy territory. The USSR's goal in war is the recovery of the USSR and its political domination of a defeated West.

Gregory Foster is concerned with Soviet perceptions of US strategic developments. He asserts that US policy has shown an insensitivity to Soviet perceptions; the result has been inconsistent, mixed, or even contradictory signals to Moscow. The US, he argues, must understand the impact of its words and actions upon the Soviets. The failure to do this will place the US at a considerable disadvantage in the global balance of power.

Paul Holman claims that standard methodologies, when applied to the study of Soviet military strategy, frequently degenerate into meaningless questions and inane answers because they ignore the context of

Soviet strategy. He prefers to examine Soviet military strategy from the standpoint of the concepts of deterrence versus warfighting—two concepts which as national objectives produce quite different results in terms of force posture and behavior. Holman's conclusion: the Soviets clearly prefer a warfighting strategy.

Tom Whitton explores the question of how the Soviets would control their military forces in the event of war. He examines the World War II role of the State Defense Committee (*GKO*) and the Supreme High Command (*Stavka*) and their control of the troops in the field through the General Staff and intermediate commands. Whitton forcefully argues that if war should occur, a portion of the present Party Politburo will constitute the new *GKO* and the current Defense Council will become the *Stavka*. The Soviets likely will also create High Commands in theaters where major military operations are being carried out.

Ken Stoehrmann focuses on the different perceptions of future war held by the likely participants and the probable impact of those perceptions upon policies and actions keyed to preventing such a war. He advocates the view that understanding these divergent perceptions is crucial to understanding the actions of the nations involved. Examining three different actors—the US, the USSR, and NATO—through the use of a perceptual scheme based on intensity and escalation scales, he attempts to show how the actions may well be related to perceptions of a future war. He argues that a better understanding by each actor of the others' perceptions may produce a synergistic effect of preventing a future war from ever occurring.

Richard Soll discusses the Soviet view of the possibility that future nuclear war may be a protracted rather than brief affair. To prepare for that contingency, Soll asserts, the Soviets feel they must acquire in peacetime the forces necessary to wage a prolonged conflict. Thus, the USSR must strive to create secure, well-hidden reserve forces as a hedge against the failure of its first echelon forces to achieve the desired goal: rapid defeat of the enemy.

Finally, David Twining, in an exceptionally detailed account of the April 1971 anthrax outbreak in Sverdlovsk, raises the specter of Soviet efforts to secure a biological warfare capability in contravention to international agreements. Although he argues that the evidence is insufficient to determine whether Soviet biological warfare agent research is for offensive or defensive purposes, the Soviet use of such weapons remains a very real possibility in light of the Sverdlovsk affair.

Continuity and Change
in Soviet Nuclear Strategy

John C. Baker*

The present character of Soviet nuclear strategy results from its historical roots as much as from the impact of the modern political-
military situation. While the advent of the long-range nuclear missile
fundamentally altered Soviet military doctrine and strategy, a traditional military approach to the nuclear weapons age is still strongly
exhibited in Soviet strategy. This influence undoubtedly stems from the
historical position of the USSR as a large continental power whose military traditions have been largely shaped by its ground forces. Today,
Soviet strategy in the event of nuclear war continues to reflect a mixture of traditional influences and contemporary requirements in the
form of its diverse wartime objectives and its distinctive operational
philosophy.

Influences on the Development of Soviet Strategy

Several underlying factors have fundamentally conditioned or shaped
the Soviet approach to seeking security in the nuclear age. Perhaps as
much as contemporary events, these more basic influences may account
for the distinctive nature of the Soviet strategic posture and the nuclear
strategy it supports. They include: (1) security requirements resulting
from the Soviet Union's geographic and political position; (2) the
USSR's military approach to the nuclear age; and (3) Soviet technological development and industrial capacity.

The most fundamental of these influences stems from the Soviet
Union's position as a large continental nation separated from powerful
neighbors by long and relatively accessible borders. The USSR's geographic and political position accounts for much of its preoccupation
with developments in areas contiguous to its borders. These unob-
structed borders often have provided passage for invasions and intru-
sions by foreign powers. The vulnerability of the USSR's western
border areas in particular has been impressed upon modern Soviet
thinking by the devastating German invasion of 1941. Furthermore,

*This is an edited text of a paper originally presented at the Assistant Chief of Staff/In-
telligence, USAF–sponsored conference in September 1980 on "The Soviet Union: What
Lies Ahead?" It is an adaptation of a chapter in the forthcoming study by Robert P. Berman and John C. Baker entitled, *Soviet Strategic Forces: Requirements and Responses*
(Washington: The Brookings Institution).

the presence of potential threats along both its eastern and western borders has fostered Soviet concern about the possibility of a "two-front" war. Only recently, with the fundamental political and military changes following the Second World War, have Soviet security interests significantly extended beyond the regions adjoining the Soviet borders.

The USSR's geographical and political positions have led it to develop a security perspective in which it attaches strategic importance to events occurring in regions adjacent to the USSR as well as in the United States and other areas beyond its borders.[1] The Soviet Union does not limit its characterization of "strategic" to weapon systems or operations involving long ranges or intercontinental capabilities.[2] Instead, the Soviets have developed a broader concept of what is strategically important which includes events in the regional as well as intercontinental theaters of military operations. Consequently, this combination is an important determinant of the general distinctiveness of the Soviet strategic posture as compared to those of Western nations.

Another effect of the Soviet Union's geographical and political situation is the premium it traditionally has placed on the maintenance of large ground forces. Historically, the USSR had to draw on its ample population to provide the numbers of troops required to defend its vast territory. Despite often uneven quality, its large army has made the Soviet Union a force to be reckoned with. Furthermore, large ground forces were appropriate since the major threat to the USSR had traditionally been that of land invasion by enemy armies. Alternatively, the development of Soviet air and sea power was inhibited by the subordination of the air and naval forces to the ground forces and the long-time absence of overseas bases capable of supporting Soviet air and naval operations. The latter factor also reinforced the Soviet predisposition to rely primarily on the military forces based within its own borders. It is therefore understandable that until the relatively recent establishment of the Strategic Rocket Forces in 1959, the Soviet Ground Forces had been the most important service of the USSR's military forces.[3]

The traditional primacy of the ground forces in Soviet military affairs helped produce another factor which has greatly influenced strategic thinking. This is the USSR's traditional military approach to the nuclear age. Soviet nuclear strategy reflects a more traditional approach to the advent of long-range nuclear weapons systems than is found in Western strategic doctrine by adhering to many objectives and a wartime approach which can be associated with traditional military thinking. Among these objectives is the high priority accorded to defeating the enemy's complete range of military forces and the occupation of important portions of the enemy's territory even in the event of nuclear warfare.[4] Such objectives also continue to ensure the importance of maintaining substantial nonnuclear forces.

Direct land combat with the enemy has traditionally received the highest priority in Soviet military planning since the USSR's accessibility to hostile neighbors precluded reliance on less direct methods for ensuring victory in wartime or conducting a successful defense. Reinforcing this trend is a conservatism in Soviet military tradition that is endemic to continental powers which lack the margin of error noncontiguous military powers enjoy.[5] This tendency is also reflected in the USSR's historical interest in creating a buffer zone of territorial acquisitions and allies along its borders to protect the Soviet heartland from intrusion. As discussed later, many of these more traditional political-military values continue to be embodied in contemporary Soviet military strategy concerning the use of strategic nuclear forces.

A third, perhaps less direct, influence on Soviet strategic policy and strategy is the USSR's capability for the technological development and industrial production of strategic weapons. The critical link in the chain of Soviet weapons acquisition is the design bureau which brings together weapon design and development.[6] The Soviet design bureau process also instills stability in weapons acquisition through its long-term focus upon steady improvements to existing systems and by constant planning for follow-up systems. Such a process probably gives the USSR more confidence to commit itself to achieving the long-term technical goals required by its strategic force objectives.

One of the major shortcomings of the Soviet weapons acquisition process has been its inability readily to exploit certain advanced technologies, such as advanced computer systems and micro-miniaturization.[7] Such technologies are critical to producing many sophisticated weapon systems, including passive sonar systems, airborne radars capable of filtering out ground clutter, and advanced guidance systems for missiles. The Soviet Union's inability to take advantage of these technologies restricts its capacity to solve certain military problems, particularly strategic defense. However, this limitation is offset to some degree by the Soviet military systems on a regular basis even during peacetime. In many cases, this limitation appears to arise not from a lack of knowledge and skill but from an economic system which encourages fulfillment of production targets at the expense of quality control, technological innovation, and exploitation of new technologies.[8]

The Role of Soviet Military Doctrine and Strategy

The Soviet Union's military doctrine and strategy reflect one nation's attempt to grapple with changes in the political-military situation and with the impact of modern technology. They also seek to set forth general principles about how to build a military posture in peacetime and how to use it in wartime.

In Soviet military writing, the terms "military doctrine" and "military strategy" are used more precisely than in the West and indicate the intricacy of Soviet political-military thought. Military doctrine is the highest level of military thinking and is presented by the Communist Party leadership as a set of official views about the types of warfare for which the Soviet military establishment must be prepared. Subordinate to Soviet military doctrine are various levels of military thought, including military strategy which develops the detailed organization, methods, and preparations for waging war.[9]

Although Soviet military doctrine and strategy are discussed in great detail in Soviet military writings, caution should be exercised in drawing conclusions from such works. Soviet doctrine and strategy do more than simply outline operational principles for the development and employment of military forces;[10] they also play an important internal role in shaping and reinforcing individual beliefs to correspond to official thinking. The state of the morale of the armed forces and the general population is an important concern to the Soviets even in the nuclear age. Earlier Soviet efforts in the 1950s to portray nuclear war as apocalyptic for its imperialistic enemies while rejecting the same possibility for the USSR may have been one manifestation of how the morale factor colors Soviet military doctrine.[11] Soviet military doctrine and strategy can be used to influence the adversary's perceptions. The negative statements made by the USSR concerning the American ability to wage limited war in Europe may be an example of this. Finally, many Soviet doctrinal precepts rationalize away intractable problems and appear to correspond to various institutional interests.[12]

Efforts to relate strategic force development to a nation's nuclear strategy also must take into account the fact that relationships among declaratory doctrine, employment options in wartime, and weapon acquisition choices are complex and often conflicting. In addition, not all aspects of these relationships are equally visible to the analyst. For instance, the details of how weapons actually would be employed in wartime often can only be assumed. Furthermore, decisionmakers are not strictly bound to preexisting doctrines or plans and may reject these during crises in favor of a more expedient course.

Consequently, Soviet military doctrine and strategy should not be viewed as binding blueprints for attaining Soviet political and military objectives; neither should they be dismissed as useless and unrevealing. When examined in the context of political-military requirements and strategic force development, Soviet doctrine and strategy can help shed light on the likely nature of Soviet military operations and mission priorities. Viewed over time, Soviet statements on military doctrine and strategy also can reveal the various ideological, institutional, and technological influences that have shaped the Soviet Union's strategic posture.

The Modernization of Soviet Doctrine and Strategy

Despite Stalin's interest in acquiring modern military systems such as nuclear weapons and ballistic missiles, Soviet military doctrine and strategy following the Second World War were constrained by military principles based solely on the experience of the prenuclear age.[13] After Stalin's death in 1953, Soviet military doctrine and strategy underwent a fundamental reevalution in light of the advent and availability of "weapons of mass destruction." This reevalution went on for several years and resulted in a major revision of military thinking . . . proclaimed in Soviet military writings as a "revolution in military affairs."

The basis of this transformation was the advent of long-range ballistic missiles armed with nuclear warheads. Acquisition of these missiles gave the USSR the unprecedented capability to destroy targets worldwide within a short time.[14] The political basis of the USSR's new doctrine was the belief that although war between socialism and capitalism was no longer inevitable, such a war would be a decisive clash between two opposing coalitions of states. Furthermore, regardless of the length of this war, inevitably—if the nuclear powers were involved—it would become a nuclear missile war of unprecedented destructiveness, and would result in the crushing defeat of the imperialists.[15]

The possibility of a nuclear world war had important implications for Soviet military organization, strategy, and operations. One of the most important of these was the envisioned change in the nature of war. The nuclear-armed ballistic missile not only was a new weapon, it also created the possibility of new forms of warfare. Massed nuclear strikes could accomplish strategic objectives at the outset of a war through the timely destruction of critical enemy targets.[16] This contrasted with the prenuclear experience in which the attainment of strategic wartime goals was a relatively slow and sequential process consisting of defeating the enemy's armed forces step-by-step and then seizing important enemy regions and political centers.[17]

Long-range nuclear weapons also helped to erase the traditional distinction in Soviet strategy between the frontline theaters of operation where the enemy's armed forces were directly engaged and the rear areas which contained the military, logistical, and administrative-economic structure which supported the war effort.[18] Previously, Soviet military efforts were directed almost exclusively toward military success along the front lines because it was believed attacks aimed at the enemy's rear would have a negligible impact on the course of the war. With the advent of nuclear-armed missiles, Soviet military strategy shifted to emphasize the importance of simultaneous attacks upon the enemy's front-line and rear areas—or throughout the depth of his military forces—as well as upon his economy and national control system.[19]

Soviet military writings also found the long-range ballistic missile far superior to the bomber for fulfilling military requirements. The missile's chief attributes were stated to be its high speed and ability—given the absence of effective defenses—to reach its target. By comparison, the strategic bomber was portrayed as slow and vulnerable to enemy air defenses.[20] The initial Soviet lead in the development of long-range ballistic missiles—as opposed to the prevailing American advantage in strategic air power—also provided the USSR with political and military incentives to belittle the bomber's continuing utility.

The Soviet military establishment may have found nuclear missiles more compatible with its military heritage and values than the concept of strategic bombardment. Unlike the strategic bomber, the ballistic missile could be conceived of as a modern extension of battlefield artillery, which the Russians historically have characterized as the "god of war" since it provided their main firepower in battle.[21] In fact, in many ways the artilleryman's mind-set seems to characterize best the Soviet approach to nuclear warfare since it reflects both general Soviet military values and the specific involvement of artillerymen in the development of the Soviet strategic missile forces.

Although official doctrine relegated the traditionally predominant ground forces to a secondary role of exploiting the nuclear strikes by the Strategic Rocket Forces, Soviet military writings continually have emphasized that final victory can be achieved only by the combined efforts of all branches of the Soviet Armed Forces.[22] The Soviet Ground Forces' unique ability to seize and occupy enemy regions and to defend the USSR against invasion is often cited as an example of the continuing importance of the traditional services.[23]

To some degree, this is a convenient intermingling of Soviet doctrinal assumptions and institutional interests. The continued importance of the ground forces in seizing and holding territory illustrates how traditional Soviet military forces manage to retain a significant wartime role despite Soviet doctrinal adherence to a concept of all-out nuclear war. Even in light of the "revolution in military affairs," Soviet military strategy envisages that regional military forces in a world war might simultaneously employ a full range of weaponry—including conventional, chemical, and nuclear weapons—to achieve their objectives.[24] Furthermore, the shift in Soviet military strategy in the mid–1960s toward a greater recognition that regional warfare could begin with an extended phase of nonnuclear warfare further ensured the continuing relevance of traditional Soviet forces.[25]

Accepting the possibility of nonnuclear warfare has renewed the importance of certain Soviet conventional forces including attack aircraft, conventional artillery, and airborne troops. Not suprisingly, then, the Soviet military posture is based on a compromise between the old and the new in terms of military strategy and force structure. Although this balance leans heavily toward the modern nuclear side of the equation, it carefully continues to retain an important role for traditional Soviet military forces.

Viewed from a broader perspective, this fundamental shift in Soviet military strategy can be interpreted as the difficult but essential step of a power with a traditional continental military perspective toward refashioning its military strategy in response to changes in the postwar political and military environment. Unlike earlier times, its major postwar adversary was a transoceanic power which could affect significantly Soviet security by means of its long-range strategic air and sea power and its secure military-industrial mobilization base. Equally important was the sudden growth of a nuclear threat (mostly in the form of nuclear-armed aircraft) in the regions surrounding the Soviet Union in the 1950s. Neither of these threats—intercontinental or regional—could be directly or effectively countered any longer by the traditional guardian of the USSR's military security, the Soviet Ground Forces.

Thus, the "revolution in military affairs" offered the USSR both a possible solution and further challenge to its defense plans. Long-range, nuclear-armed ballistic missiles could effectively counter the growing regional nuclear threat to the Soviet homeland and also could strike various targets deep in the enemy's homeland. While they also presented an increased strategic threat to the USSR as the United States deployed its own strategic missiles, the new weapons restored the USSR's ability to respond directly and decisively to all major military threats; but, unlike its regional objective in wartime of seeking the eventual occupation of important regions of Western Europe upon the defeat of the enemy's armed forces, Soviet intercontinental strategic forces would be tasked to destroy both the US military and administrative-economic capability, thereby totally neutralizing the US as a threat.[26] As such, Soviet intercontinental forces would serve to offset the American strategic capability by protecting the Soviet homeland and to ensure the success of its regional forces in wartime. Consequently, the acquisition of modern nuclear weapons enabled the USSR to create a strategic force posture and strategy more appropriate for responding to its intertwined regional and intercontinental security requirements.

Soviet Nuclear Strategy: Wartime Objectives

Soviet wartime objectives reflect not only the diverse security problems facing the USSR but also the fusing of a traditional military approach with the modern military requirements of the postwar era. Major Soviet military objectives in a world war can be characterized as: (1) defense of the homeland; (2) defeat and neutralization of military adversaries; and (3) seizure and occupation of vital contiguous areas.[27] Although these objectives probably always have been manifest in the Soviet security approach, the existence of modern strategic forces has altered both their nature and relative priority. In more specific terms, the USSR's strategy for a world war appears to envisage a need to occupy Western Europe while simultaneously relying on Soviet strategic forces to offset either politically or militarily the United States and certain regional threats to its security, such as China. In other words, contemporary Soviet military strategy consists of two different but complementary sets of military requirements in the event of a world war—regional and intercontinental.

Central Europe is undoubtedly the most important regional theater of military operations (*TVD*)* for the Soviet Union.[28] According to Soviet military writings, warfare in Europe could begin solely with conventional forces or with a combination of conventional and nuclear forces.[29] Similarly, such warfare might occur simultaneously with intercontinental nuclear strikes or only regionally at first. Defeat of the enemy's military forces and occupation of important territories would remain the wartime objectives regardless of circumstances. Soviet military strategy therefore sees the necessity to integrate nuclear and nonnuclear combat at the tactical, regional, and even intercontinental levels given the possibility that such multilevel conflict could occur simultaneously.

Soviet interest in occupying certain portions of Europe even in the event of intercontinental nuclear warfare probably results from two concerns: first, that a worldwide conflict might be prolonged and conventional warfare could be important in ending the conflict in regional theaters by denying forward bases for US reinforcement; and second, that the wartime acquisition of European industrial facilities and resources could help Soviet postwar economic recovery. The latter aspect may be rooted in the Soviet Union's experience during World War II when a large part of its industry was relocated successfully to avoid advancing German troops. After the war, the USSR also drew on the defeated German economy to revitalize its own.

Soviet plans for the wartime occupation of Europe provide evidence the USSR does not necessarily embrace a strategy aimed at devastating the European urban-industrial base. Instead, Soviet regional nuclear strikes might be discriminatingly targeted in order to avoid obstructing the operations of the Soviet Ground Forces.[30] Such targeting is consistent with the Soviet "all arms" approach to regional warfare in which the operations of tactical nonnuclear forces would be integrated with those of regional nuclear strike forces. In the event nuclear weapons are employed, Soviet military writings prescribe the use of nuclear strikes to destroy the enemy's military forces and other important targets. Soviet armored, motorized rifle, and airborne troops would then attempt to exploit these attacks by striking into the enemy's rear areas in order to destroy remaining enemy units and seize important territory.[31]

---

*TVD—*teatr voyennykh deystviy*—Ed.

If Soviet strategy sought to devastate Western Europe rather than occupy it, the wartime role of Soviet tactical forces would be reduced. In many respects, then, the Soviet all arms approach illustrates how Soviet security requirements and institutional interests may converge. The mission of defeating and occupying adversary nations around the periphery of the USSR is actually an extension of the traditional mission of the Soviet Ground Forces, and an emphasis on occupying contiguous areas—even in a worldwide nuclear conflict—assures their continued importance.

The eventual Soviet acceptance in the mid–1960s of the possibility of an extended phase of nonnuclear warfare further enhanced the importance of traditional military forces, but this modification did not require fundamental changes in the Soviet military posture since nonnuclear forces always had been required. Instead, the expansion in Soviet nonnuclear capabilities following this doctrinal decision was aimed at giving the USSR full flexibility to wage armed conflict effectively under any circumstances.[32] Consequently, improved nonnuclear forces are consistent with Soviet requirements for nuclear as well as nonnuclear warfare.

In a nonnuclear conflict, Soviet tactical forces—such as tanks, airborne units, and tactical aircraft—would be used to attack (to the degree possible) the same targets as in a nuclear conflict.[33] Soviet targeting priorities in regional theaters of military operations appear to be the same regardless of whether the conflict is nuclear or nonnuclear. In either case, the most important mission is to neutralize the enemy's nuclear delivery systems and other important enemy military forces.[34] In addition, the probability of sudden escalation to the nuclear level compels the USSR during nonnuclear warfare to deploy its tactical forces for the contingency of nuclear combat. The commonality of the goals, targeting priorities, and operational approaches of the Soviet tactical forces in nuclear and nonnuclear warfare reflects the integral relationship of these forces to the nuclear plans of the Soviet regional strategic forces.

The diversity of the Soviet Union's regional theaters of military operations necessitates a multifaced approach to regional wartime operations. Soviet wartime objectives in the continental European *TVDs*—defeating the enemy's military forces and occupying important areas—are much less applicable to other *TVDs*—China, the Persian Gulf, Britain, and Japan. Objectives in these regional theaters probably are tailored more to their priority and what is possible to accomplish. For instance, given the questionable feasibility and desirability of occupying large parts of China, the Soviet Union would probably attempt to neutralize the latter in the event of world war. Using nuclear strikes, the USSR might seek to destroy important military targets and major administrative-economic centers. Unlike the Western *TVD*s Soviet forces deployed along the Sino–Soviet border more likely would be tasked to provide a nuclear defense force capable of protecting against Chinese military incursions across the Soviet border.[35]

Regional powers such as Japan, Britain, and the Persian Gulf countries present special problems for Soviet wartime strategy. The great economic value of the Persian Gulf countries and Japan is countervailed by their limited defense capability. Consequently, Soviet wartime strategy may be oriented toward trying to remove these countries from a world nuclear conflict and bringing them under Soviet influence more by means of political intimidation than through full-scale invasions. The military strength of the United Kingdom, on the other hand, combined with its geographic insularity, probably would lead the USSR to devote enough nuclear force against it to neutralize it quickly as a potential political and military threat to Soviet regional operations.

The remaining Soviet strategic objectives in wartime would be fulfilled in intercontinental TVDs. The most important of these is in the northern hemisphere, where the main Soviet objective would be to neutralize the United States through nuclear strikes on a variety of targets. Alternatively, the USSR could use its intercontinental nuclear forces to offset politically the United States by deterring the latter from using nuclear forces even while the US and its allies were suffering a military defeat in the regional theaters.

Soviet military writings suggest that in the event of intercontinental exchanges, the American threat would be countered by means of a comprehensive nuclear targeting strategy.[36] Deep strikes aimed at various military and nonmilitary targets would attempt to devastate the US to a point at which it could no longer influence the course of the war. The success of the Soviet intercontinental forces' mission would greatly improve the Soviet Union's chances of achieving its regional military objectives and assuring the survival of its homeland.

A wide range of targets comprise Soviet targeting strategy.[37] They can be categorized as (1) counterforce (strategic nuclear targets), (2) counter command and control, (3) countermilitary (general purpose forces), and (4) countervalue (administrative-economic centers).

Despite its comprehensiveness, this strategy corresponds to the many specific Soviet requirements and priorities. Soviet emphasis on neutralizing the enemy's command and control centers, for example, takes into consideration not only the systems supporting strategic nuclear and conventional forces but also the national political control system. Effective nuclear strikes on such targets offer a way to disable and degrade the whole spectrum of enemy military forces as well as to destroy the enemy's political system.[38] This element of Soviet strategy reflects both the USSR's own high priority on a centralized command system and its view of nuclear war as a conflict waged between opposing political systems.

By comparison, the American economic base is much more of a potential threat to the USSR than are European administrative-economic centers since the latter eventually could be used to reconstitute the Soviet economy. In a prolonged world war, the American economic base could provide a continuing capability for the war effort and for support of tactical forces deployed overseas in the regions surrounding the USSR. Consequently, the destruction of the American defense industrial base is an important extension of Soviet regional requirements as well as a hedge against the postwar military and economic recovery of the United States. Such a strategy resembles the US nuclear targeting plans of the 1950s which were directed against the Soviet economic and transportation networks. This targeting was based on the idea of a prolonged "broken-back" war in which Western theater forces would be supported indirectly by such nuclear strikes.[39]

The targeting of administrative-economic centers frequently has been cited in Soviet military writings as an essential part of Soviet targeting doctrine. Indeed, the destruction of the enemy's administrative-economic base was proclaimed as a major new tenet of Soviet military doctrine following the USSR's acquisition of nuclear-armed strategic missiles. The availability of such weapons altered Soviet military doctrine to give priority for the first time to attacking the enemy's administrative-economic centers as well as his military forces.

Similarly, Soviet discussions of nuclear attacks against military targets (including strategic nuclear forces) deployed in the US mainland indicate the targets are broader in nature than usually thought in the West. Countermilitary targets—in terms of nonnuclear forces—could range from US Army, tactical fighter, and airlift bases to naval ports and conventional munitions depots.

The most important American military target which concerns the USSR is, of course, the US triad—intercontinental strategic forces composed of ICBMs, strategic missile submarines (SSBNs), and heavy bombers. Here again, Soviet targeting doctrine is not limited to attacking these forces directly through strikes against ICBM silos, SSBN ports, and bomber bases. Equal or even greater importance is given to destroying the supporting systems which enable these forces to perform effectively in wartime.[40] These systems include the national command and control system and its links to each major component of the US strategic forces, as well as early-warning sites and navigational aids. In some instances, such as for US strategic submarines on patrol, destruction of less survivable communications and navigation systems may be the only way available for the USSR to neutralize or degrade such weapons.

Soviet conceptions of intercontinental theaters of military operations are not confined to continental landmasses but may also include the ocean areas between them. In addition, the Soviets note there are maritime *TVD*s which together with the *TVD*s on land may comprise a theater of war. Soviet writings indicate the ocean *TVD*s contain both naval targets at sea and naval-related targets—such as ports and naval bases—in the enemy's coastal zones.[41] Although the Soviet Navy has an important role in these theaters, Soviet military writings note it is not an exclusive one. The Strategic Rocket Forces and Long Range Aviation may also be used to attack naval targets in the event of war.[42] The most important targets to be destroyed on the open oceans would include the forces capable of delivering nuclear strikes against the Soviet homeland: ballistic missile submarines and aircraft carriers armed with nuclear-capable aircraft.[43] Other missions—including disrupting the enemy's lines of communication at sea—could be accomplished through nuclear strikes on the enemy's coastal installations as well as on its forces at sea.

The Present Basis of Soviet Strategic Doctrine

Ultimately, the Soviet Union's strategic forces and nuclear strategy exist to support its fundamental political-military objectives of deterring nuclear war and, in the event deterrence fails, of enhancing the prospects for national survival. As with other aspects of the Soviet strategic posture, its strategic doctrine also has been shaped distinctively by its more traditional military perspective on questions in the nuclear age.[44] This more traditional military cast of Soviet strategic doctrine is reflected in its emphasis on militarily prevailing over the enemy in wartime as the best means for achieving national survival and, coincidentally, maintaining a credible deterrent in peacetime. While some Soviet military writings explicitly refer to victory as the goal in wartime, they often lack a statement of its definition in the context of an all-out nuclear war.[45]

Despite the ambiguity concerning the meaning of victory in a world war involving the massive use of nuclear weapons, Soviet strategy, as noted earlier, does continue to adhere to several wartime objectives traditionally associated with military victory during the prenuclear period. These include physically defending the homeland against enemy attack, decisively defeating the enemy's military forces, and occupying enemy territory. Aspiring to achieve such wartime goals has the benefit of creating relatively definable military requirements—although ones that are understandably difficult to fullfill in the nuclear age. The integration of strategic and tactical operations—and nuclear with nonnuclear forces—also is made easier by positing such clear-cut military aims. Finally, such an approach has definite implications for force structure choices. Among the latter is a clear predisposition for time-urgent means to deliver nuclear strikes (such as strategic missiles) and the encouragement of the integration of strategic defensive forces into the overall strategic posture.

The more traditional military character of Soviet strategic doctrine may be the result of several factors. Most important is the previously noted distinctive military heritage of the USSR. The Soviet Union's military tradition of direct, decisive battles against its enemies,[46] naturally fostered by its continental position, serves as an important historical link between its traditional military approach and its modern strategic doctrine. The influence of the traditional approach has been augmented by other, more contemporary factors. One of these is the prominent role of the Soviet military in formulating military strategy. With the exception of Khrushchev's short-lived attempt to dominate Soviet strategy and force planning, the USSR apparently has lacked the substantial civilian input which has characterized the development of Western postwar strategic thought.[47] Thus, in many respects, Soviet strategic thinking probably reflects more of a "pure" military perspective on the problems of modern strategy.

Another important condition has been the absence of a real Soviet requirement to extend a credible nuclear guarantee to its allies. Its geographic proximity to and political dominance of the neighboring Warsaw Pact countries obviates the necessity for a commitment similar to the one which exists between the US and its NATO allies. For the United States, this relationship has been a critical reason for embracing a less traditional strategic doctrine. For instance, such doctrinal concepts as limited nuclear war and selective strategic targeting were motivated, in part, by a need to enhance the credibility of the US commitment to the defense of NATO. By comparison, external alliance requirements have had relatively little impact on the postwar evolution of Soviet strategic doctrine.

Soviet strategic doctrine clearly contrasts with that of the United States and the other Western nuclear powers. Instead of seeking to rebuff the enemy physically—as in Soviet doctrine—Western doctrine relies more on persuading the enemy the costs of his actions (in terms of prospective losses) will far outweigh his gains. Thus, posing the threat of unacceptable losses in economic capacity, military power, and/or political cohesion, Western doctrine attempts to dissuade the enemy from initiating nuclear war. If war breaks out, national survival is pursued by means of intrawar deterrence, a process which seeks war termination through threats to escalate the conflict to increasingly higher levels of destruction. Consequently, because it has been less willing to entrust peacetime deterrence and wartime survival simply to the enemy's perception of the risks involved, the Soviet Union has attempted to obtain additional insurance by striving for the capability not only to devastate the enemy's homeland but also to prevail militarily in the event of a world war.

Finally, the underlying uncertainty of any analysis of Soviet strategic doctrine must be acknowledged. In part, this is due to the fact the great visibility of Soviet military writings on questions of strategy is generally unmatched by similar insights into the actual thinking of the top political leadership on the fundamental questions of war and peace. In absence of such information, conclusive analysis of the Soviet leadership's actual perceptions of deterrence and its likely actions in the event of world war must necessarily be based on speculation or—at best—inferred only in general terms from Soviet writings and force posture choices.

The Soviet Operational Philosophy

While the previous section reviewed the general nature of Soviet strategic doctrine and its wartime objectives, this section examines aspects of the USSR's operational philosophy for employing its strategic forces in the event of nuclear war. It is in this area that traditional military values and the continental heritage of Soviet nuclear strategy are most clearly manifested.

Among the most important factors in the Soviet operational philosophy is the skepticism expressed in Soviet writings concerning the real possibility (or desirability) of controlling escalation in a major conflict. Partly as a result of the USSR's continental position and its more traditional military approach to questions of nuclear warfare, Soviet military writings have tended to emphasize the greater likelihood that any direct conflict between the US and USSR would escalate into full-scale nuclear war.[48] Not surprisingly, the USSR's continental position naturally makes it less receptive to the idea of limiting conventional or nuclear warfare to the theaters surrounding (and possibly including) the USSR, since these "limited" conflicts could result in substantial destruction to it. Acceptance of the various thresholds of escalation based on limitations in weapons types or where they are used—as outlined in Western writings—is often absent or quite qualified in Soviet works.[49]

Soviet military writings in general tend to portray "decisiveness" as the highest operational value in wartime operations rather than an emphasis on limited measures which might keep the conflict from further escalation. Thus, Soviet writings reflect a greater propensity to engage the complete range of military resources available—once the threshold of war has been crossed—as the surest means of defeating the enemy and guaranteeing national survival. This strategic approach—in its unconstrained pursuit of military victory once war begins—is consistent with traditional military values.

Finally, Soviet emphasis on the inevitability of escalation also arises from its attempts to minimize US confidence in the possibility of limited warfare and to erode the political confidence of the US allies in American defense guarantees. Indeed, with the growth of Soviet limited war capabilities in the 1960s, Soviet military writings increasingly began to accept the possibility a major conflict directly involving the US and USSR might not escalate immediately into nuclear war. Despite greater acceptance of a conventional phase of combat, Soviet doctrine appears to see the paramount threshold as that between wartime and peacetime, unlike Western doctrine which foresees a number of thresholds to higher levels of conflict once war begins.

Another important question concerns the degree to which the Soviet Union would rely on the use of a preemptive nuclear strike in the event of war. It is impossible to know whether the USSR actually would depend on preemption in wartime since such an action—to be successful—would be contingent on the prevailing circumstances and timely decisionmaking by the Soviet leadership. However, an examination of Soviet doctrinal writings and operational patterns reveals to what degree the USSR is predisposed to employ its forces in a preemptive mode.

Soviet military writings have long emphasized the potential decisiveness of the initial phase of a world conflict on the course of the war and its final outcome.[50] This concern is not only a general recognition of the character of nuclear warfare; it may also be a legacy of the traumatic experience of Germany's surprise attack on the USSR in June 1941.[51] In general, explicit emphasis on preemption in Soviet military writing ended in the 1950s;[52] however, current Soviet writings do not rule out the possibility of preemption. To some degree, this is still another reflection of the traditional military character of the Soviet Union's nuclear strategy. Given the nature of modern warfare and the current absence of any effective defense against strategic weapons, a natural military solution is to look to a preemptive strike as the best way to neutralize the enemy's strategic force. In this regard, the use of a preemptive strike in wartime would certainly be consistent with the Soviet emphasis on decisiveness in warfare.

A Soviet decision to undertake a preemptive nuclear strike against the United States most likely would be made during an ongoing conventional conflict—probably one in the European theater and under the US threat of nuclear escalation. Soviet strategic values may hold that once the threshold of direct US–Soviet conflict has been crossed, restraint in the use of force would not be worth the risk of being exposed to an enemy surprise attack. In the case of a conflict in Europe, this consideration would be particularly important in light of the US commitment to use nuclear weapons first if necessary to defend Europe against a major Warsaw Pact attack.[53] Under the right circumstances, then, a preemptive strike could be seen as enhancing the Soviet Union's military position against the United States.

Because a preemptive strike is an employment option dependent on timely internal decisions and favorable external conditions (that is, the enemy has neither launched a first strike already nor is prepared to "launch-under-attack"),[54] it is unlikely Soviet military leaders count on achieving preemption in their strategic planning, nor could they rely on it to solve all their strategic problems since large numbers of US forces on alert could survive even a successful preemptive attack. The USSR more likely sees preemption as an option of last resort to be employed when the enemy's nuclear attack appears imminent.

Other operational possibilities available to the Soviet Union include "launch-under-attack" or "riding out" the attack and then responding in a second-strike attack of its own. Along this spectrum of options from preemption to "ride-out," the Soviet operational philosophy appears more predisposed toward the preemption and "launch-under-attack" end of the spectrum. In recent years, Soviet military writings have occasionally shown interest in the option of "launch-under-attack."[55] At about the same time, in the late 1960s, the USSR began deploying many of the weapon systems that were necessary for such a capability.

Finally, while the Soviet operational approach may be predisposed toward the early launch of its strategic weapons, it has not neglected the importance of maintaining strategic forces that can "ride out" an enemy first strike. The wide range of measures aimed at increasing Soviet strategic force survivability—such as highly hardened ICBM silos—probably reflects the Soviet desire to hedge against the possibility the USSR may be the victim of an enemy first strike. Such measures also would be consistent with the importance the USSR places on maintaining a strategic reserve force capable of surviving prolonged nuclear conflict.

A more tangible characteristic of the Soviet operational philosophy is manifested in the low alert rates of its strategic forces. Until recently, the USSR was known to keep only a small portion of its land-based missiles on full alert,[56] and its bomber forces apparently have never been maintained in a peacetime ground alert posture.[57] Soviet strategic missile submarine deployments also have consisted of only a small fraction of the total force available.[58] While initially constrained in part by various technical and geographical factors from higher alert rates, the continuation of this Soviet practice seems best explained by certain underlying judgments in the Soviet operational philosophy.

The most important of these judgments is the Soviet leadership's fundamental concern with "positive control" of nuclear weapon forces. The priority placed on the strict command and control of nuclear forces has been indicated in several ways: constrained alert rates, certain command arrangements, and associated operational practices.[59] This attitude toward the tight command and control of nuclear weapons probably accounts for the general Soviet predisposition against using changes in its nuclear weapon alert status as a means for sending political signals during crisis situations.[60] The Soviet tradition of a highly centralized system of political and military control seems to reinforce the natural disinclination of any political leadership to devolve its authority regarding the use of weapons capable of large-scale destruction. Soviet military writings also have noted that the advent of such weapons has increased substantially the role of the top leadership in directing wartime operations.

The paramount importance of such strict control of Soviet nuclear forces is evidenced by the fact it is bound to constrain the effectiveness of Soviet strategic forces in the event of war. This is particularly true given the great emphasis in Soviet writing on the necessity to take decisive counteraction during the initial phase of a major conflict. This limits Soviet options with regard to nuclear preemption.

The tension between the conflicting Soviet requirements for political control and military effectiveness is resolved (at least in theory) by the Soviet expectation that "strategic warning" will be available in a crisis.[61] Prior warning time—presumably on the order of several days or more—would give the USSR sufficient time to bring its strategic force levels to higher alert rates and to deploy more of its submarines to safer positions at sea. Furthermore, since the 1950s—as the USSR has accumulated more experience with the US in crisis situations and the survivability of Soviet strategic forces has improved—actual Soviet apprehensions concerning a surprise attack by the US probably have diminished, thereby enabling the USSR to rely more confidently on receiving adequate strategic warning.

Finally, the lower alert rates of the Soviet Union's strategic forces are also consistent with the Soviet preference for conserving military assets by limiting their peacetime operations and holding down the potentially high expense of maintaining a large military force. This desire to prolong the life of and reduce maintenance costs for military systems is reflected in the USSR's operation of its conventional forces as well.[62]

Issues in Soviet Nuclear Strategy for the 1980s

With the exception of the "revolution in military affairs" of the early 1960s, Soviet nuclear strategy is notable for how little it has changed in approach and objectives over the past 30 years. Indeed, this basic continuity in Soviet strategic thinking offers an interesting contrast to the dramatic evolution of the Soviet strategic force posture in structure and capability as it has attempted to meet the military requirements outlined by modern Soviet strategy. Looking to the next decade, it would seem likely only major changes in the strategic environment will result in significant alterations to current Soviet nuclear strategy. Conceivably, changes could result from shifts in such factors as Soviet political-military requirements or the advent of significant new weapon technologies.

One possibility receiving great attention in recent years concerns the likelihood the USSR may become interested in selective nuclear strikes against strategic targets in the United States as a result of its acquisition of increasingly effective counterforce weapons. In a scenario which has become quite familiar, the USSR undertakes selective nuclear strikes against a variety of strategic targets in the United States. The primary aim of the attack would be to destroy virtually the entire US ICBM force, thereby eliminating the American capability for effective counterstrikes against Soviet missile silos. This action supposedly would confront the US leadership with the difficult choice of either submitting to Soviet political demands or senselessly escalating the conflict to countercity exchanges. According to those who postulate this scenario, the Soviet military potential to engage in such an action could translate into a meaningful political edge in the event of a future US–USSR confrontation.

Thus, an important question exists as to the plausibility of this scenario; that is, is it supported by Soviet strategic thinking, or is it based purely on projections of a technical possibility? Given the essential nature of Soviet nuclear strategy as outlined in this paper, the consistency of such a planning scenario with the values historically exhibited in Soviet military writings on nuclear strategy raises serious questions. In many respects, attributing the USSR with a serious interest in selective nuclear strikes appears to be more a projection of American values and concerns than a probable evolution in Soviet nuclear strategy. As noted earlier, the acceptance of the concept of limited and selective nuclear warfare in American strategic thinking stems from both a distinctive political-military tradition and the requirement for a credible ability to extend deterrence to cover overseas allies—two important factors absent in the Soviet Union's case.

By contrast, the Soviet approach to nuclear warfare appears to be rooted in more conservative and traditional military thought. It does not tend naturally toward the limited application of military forces to achieve its wartime objectives. Furthermore, the USSR lacks the external political-military requirements which led the US to adopt the concept of selective nuclear strikes. Clearly, in the final analysis, a concept of selective strategic strikes which gives priority to limited political objectives in wartime through the constrained application of military force is essentially more compatible with the strategic doctrine adopted by the United States. A traditional strategy such as the USSR's derives its confidence from physically defeating the enemy rather than psychologically dissuading him from undertaking nuclear retaliation.

Most importantly, selective nuclear strikes appear to be at odds with the traditional military values which underlie Soviet nuclear strategy. As discussed in this paper, these values encourage the "decisive" appplication of military force against the enemy once the threshold between peace and war has been crossed. This Soviet emphasis upon shock power in its nuclear strategy is reflected in the priority Soviet military writings place on massed nuclear strikes, surprise in undertaking attacks, and the comprehensive targeting of the enemy's political, military, and economic system. Such an approach militates against embracing a selective use of strategic nuclear weapons which sacrifices certain warfighting advantages in exchange for an uncertain and high-risk political outcome. In particular, a selective strike scenario could compel the USSR to forego the opportunity to disable or degrade important components of the enemy's strategic force system such as its national command and control system and certain strategic forces deployed near highly populated centers. Strikes against these targets could undermine the feasibility of a selective strike by reducing the enemy's ability or desire to bargain for a political settlement.

To suggest conceptions of selective nuclear warfare do not naturally arise from Soviet strategic thinking is not to imply the USSR simply would use its nuclear forces in spasm strikes in the event of a world war. Even in an all-out nuclear conflict, it could be expected that certain forces would be withheld as a strategic reserve for traditional military considerations. Nor would it be surprising if target priorities did not require all targets to be struck simultaneously: the time-life value of different target sets would obviously vary. Yet, such considerations for the economical application of military power in wartime are still a long way from the type of political-military thinking which underlies Western conceptions of the role of selective nuclear strikes.

One source of potential change in Soviet nuclear strategy in the 1980s could be the availability of new, advanced technologies. Currently, the greatest potential for new technological advances in strategic weaponry appears to be in the area of strategic defenses. In part, this is due to the fact that past Soviet efforts to develop an effective "denial" capability in this area have been relatively inadequate compared to Soviet strategic offensive developments.

Entering the 1980s, there is evidence both the US and USSR may be able to deploy new strategic defensive forces which could improve significantly—if not dramatically—their capability against strategic offensive forces. These improvements could encompass all facets of the defensive mission—including strategic air defenses and antisubmarine warfare capabilities—although the greatest potential for improvement appears to be with the antiballistic missile (ABM) defenses. Both sides are reported to be developing advanced systems with potential ABM applications. These include developments in directed energy weapons as well as improvements to more conventional antiballistic missile systems. Consequently, a major issue in the 1980s will be the degree to which such advances in defensive technologies will reverse the long-standing balance between offensive and defensive weaponry in strategic nuclear warfare.

While the substantial improvements in the effectiveness of strategic defenses would be important for US as well as Soviet nuclear strategy, it is not clear the impact would be similar in each case. The nuclear strategy of the USSR long has held strategic defenses to be an integral element of an effective military capability, although in reality the strategic defense forces have been technically deficient in making a serious contribution toward this goal. Therefore, major advances in strategic defense effectiveness would continue to be compatible with both the basic approach and wartime objectives outlined in Soviet nuclear strategy.[63] By comparison, such advances could present a serious challenge to US strategic thinking. This arises from the fact the offensive-dominated doctrine of the United States has tended to view strategic defenses as basically infeasible and possibly undesirable for reasons of strategic stability. Consequently, while improvements in strategic defenses during the next decade primarily would serve to narrow the gap between doctrinal aspirations and reality in terms of Soviet nuclear strategy, they are likely to pose far more fundamental questions for American strategic doctrine.

Another factor which could lead to alterations in Soviet nuclear strategy over the next decade is a change in its political-military requirements. While Soviet military requirements will continue to evolve as the United States and its NATO allies engage in the modernization of their nuclear forces, such changes are not likely to be fundamentally different in terms of the problems they pose for Soviet strategic thinking. By comparison, one area where existing Soviet military priorities for the pursuit of modern warfare may be less well-suited is in the possibility of a major military conflict involving the People's Republic of China.

Although the significant expansion of Soviet nuclear and nonnuclear forces along the Sino–Soviet border in the late 1960s provided some indication of the USSR's increasing military concern over China, it has not been paralleled by any clear alterations in Soviet writings on nuclear strategy. This was probably due in part to certain ideological reservations as well as to the fact existing Soviet concepts were also applicable to some degree to its new situation with China. Consequently, despite changes in the Soviet military posture along the Sino–Soviet border in the 1960s, no evidence exists to suggest the basic Soviet perception concerning the nature of a world war and its wartime operational strategy had changed substantially. Instead, it appears likely the new requirements posed by hostilities with China were merely added to the existing Soviet force plans and operational approach.

During the last decade, in contrast, a number of developments have given rise to the possibility basic changes have occurred in Soviet planning regarding war with China. Some have involved changes to the Soviet force structure, such as the increasingly Chinese orientation of several first-line Soviet strategic force deployments and exercises.[64] Further indications the USSR is interested in creating a separate operational arrangement for the use of regional military force against China were reflected in modifications to the Soviet command structure for the Far East. During 1978, Party General Secretary Brezhnev and Defense Minister Ustinov undertook a noteworthy tour through the Far East which included stops at a Strategic Rocket Forces base, the Far East Military District headquarters, and the *Admiral Senyavin,* a command and control ship of the Soviet Pacific Fleet.[65] Quite possibly, these trips served to inaugurate the increasing command autonomy of Soviet forces in the Far East. Additional evidence of this interpretation was provided in subsequent reports that a major reorganization had occurred in the Far East by early 1979 and had resulted in the establishment of a new high command under the leadership of a senior Soviet military commander.[66]

The new high command appears aimed at reorganizing the military districts along the Sino-Soviet border into a special, more autonomous military command. In doing so, it may have set the basic framework for an independent Far Eastern *TVD* command which would exist in peacetime as well as wartime. Perhaps the first active indication of this command change occurred in March 1979 when the largest Soviet military exercises ever held in the Far East took place coincidentally with the final stages of the Sino–Vietnamese border conflict.[67] Such new command arrangements are noteworthy since even the Soviet-dominated Warsaw Pact always has been more of a peacetime administrative structure rather than the actual basis for a wartime operational command.[68] Thus, such changes in the nature of the Soviet command structure provide additional evidence the USSR has established a more autonomous high command in the Far East enabling it to prosecute more effectively operations in that *TVD* in the event of war. Furthermore, an increasing Soviet desire to "decouple" the use of its nuclear and nonnuclear forces deployed against China from its overall war plans also may be a possibility in the 1980s in light of the unabated Sino–Soviet hostility and the prospect of an increasingly powerful and externally active China. Given such a possibility, further alterations in Soviet concepts of military operations may be necessary during the 1980s in order to account effectively for the unique requirements created by this situation.

Summary

Soviet military doctrine and strategy provide not only the general principles concerning the wartime use of Soviet strategic forces but also serve as useful reflections of the Soviet Union's sensitivity to the various historical, institutional, and technological influences which have shaped its strategic force posture. Contemporary Soviet military thinking concerning strategic weapons has resulted from the efforts of a continental military power to refashion itself to respond effectively to the political and technological changes of the postwar world. Consequently, the Soviet Union's strategic doctrine continues to reflect a more conservative military approach to the nuclear age. This is especially true in terms of its emphasis on seeking an effective military capability for prevailing over the enemy as the best means for achieving both peacetime deterrence and the survival of the Soviet state in the event of war. The likely prospects for Soviet nuclear strategy in the 1980s are only modest alterations, probably to account for the availability of new technologies or to engage in the refinement of existing strategic options.

Notes

1. See Thomas W. Wolfe, *Soviet Power in Europe, 1945–1970* (Baltimore: The Johns Hopkins Press, 1970), pp. 32–42 and 195–199; Fritz W. Ermarth, "Contrasts in American and Soviet Thought," *International Security*, Fall 1978, pp. 146–148; and William T. Lee, "Soviet Targeting Strategy and SALT," *Air Force Magazine*, September 1978, p. 120.
2. V. D. Sokolovskiy, *Soviet Military Strategy*, ed. Harriet Fast Scott (New York: Crane, Russak, and Company, 1975), pp. 146 and 286–287.
3. Edward L. Warner, III, *The Military in Contemporary Soviet Politics: An Institutional Analysis* (New York: Praeger, 1977), p. 30.
4. Sokolovskiy, op. cit., pp. 13 and 284.
5. The author is indebted to his former colleague, Barry Posen, for drawing his attention to this and similar points.
6. Under Secretary of Defense for Research and Engineering William J. Perry, *The FY 1980 Department of Defense Program for Research, Development, and Acquisition* (Department of Defense, 1979), pp. II–4 to II–6; and Arthur J. Alexander, *Decision–Making in Soviet Weapons Procurement* (London: International Institute for Strategic Studies, Winter 1978/79) Adelphi Papers No. 47 and 48, pp. 21–24.
7. Under Secretary of Defense for Research and Engineering, *The FY 1979 Department of Defense Program for Research, Development, and Acquisition* (Department of Defense, 1978), p. II–8.
8. Ibid., pp. II–4 to II–7.
9. A. A. Grechko, *The Armed Forces of the Soviet State*, translated and published under the auspices of the United States Air Force (Washington: Government Printing Office, 1975), p. 84; and Benjamin S. Lambeth, "The Sources of Soviet Military Doctrine," in Frank B. Horton, III, Anthony C. Rogerson, and Edward L. Warner III, eds., *Comparative Defense Policy* (Baltimore: The Johns Hopkins University Press, 1974), pp. 200–204.
10. Lambeth, "The Sources of Soviet Military Doctrine," pp. 214–215.
11. Sokolovskiy, *Soviet Military Strategy*, pp. 208–209; and Ermarth, "Contrasts in American and Soviet Strategic Thought," p. 144.
12. Benjamin S. Lambeth, *How to Think About Soviet Military Doctrine*, Report P–5939 (Santa Monica: The Rand Corporation, 1978), pp. 15–16.
13. Raymond L. Garthoff, *Soviet Strategy in the Nuclear Age* (New York: Praeger, 1958), pp. 61–63.
14. Among the several sources, see Colonel General M. Povaliy, "Development of Soviet Military Strategy," *Voyennaya mysl'* [Military Thought], No. 2, 1967, pp. 67–71; and Sokolovskiy, *Soviet Military Strategy*, pp. xx and 191–194.
15. Sokolovskiy, *Soviet Military Strategy*, pp. 170–171 and 194–195. The Soviet view of the inevitability of escalation was firm through the early 1960s; see Wolfe, *Soviet Power and Europe, 1945–1970*, pp. 209–212.
16. Colonel General Nikolay A. Lomov, "The Influence of Soviet Military Doctrine on the Development of Military Art," in William R. Kintner and Harriet Fast Scott, trans. and eds., *The Nuclear Revolution in Soviet Military Affairs* (Norman: University of Oklahoma Press, 1968), pp. 160–161.
17. Sokolovskiy, *Soviet Military Strategy*, p. 242; and General N. A. Sbitov, "The Revolution in Military Affairs and Its Results," in Kintner and Scott, pp. 28–29.
18. Sokolovskiy, *Soviet Military Strategy*, pp. 11, 193–194, and 274; and Colonel M.

Skovorodkin, "Some Questions on Coordination of Branches of Armed Forces in Major Operations," *Voyennaya mysl',* No. 2, 1967, pp. 36–38.

19. Povaliy, "Development of Soviet Military Strategy," p. 71; and Marshal N. Krylov, "The Nuclear–Missile Shield of the Soviet State," *Voyennaya mysl',* No. 11, 1967, p. 17.

20. Sokolovskiy, *Soviet Military Strategy,* pp. 193 and 252.

21. Ibid., pp. 241–242.

22. Ibid., pp. 198–199 and 247.

23. Ibid., and see Army General I. Pavlovskiy, "The Ground Troops of the Soviet Armed Forces," *Voyennaya mysl',* No. 11, 1967, p. 35.

24. Sokolovskiy, *Soviet Military Strategy,* pp. 199 and 243.

25. Joseph D. Douglass, Jr., *The Soviet Theater Nuclear Offensive* (Washington: Government Printing Office, 1976), pp. 116–118; and Colonel B. Samorukov, "Combat Operations Involving Conventional Means of Destruction," *Voyennaya mysl',* No. 8, 1967, pp. 29–30.

26. Army General S. Ivanov, "Soviet Military Doctrine and Strategy," *Voyennaya mysl',* No. 5, 1969, p. 47.

27. Sokolovskiy, *Soviet Military Strategy,* pp. 282 and 285; Benjamin S. Lambeth, *Selective Nuclear Options in American and Soviet Strategic Policy,* Report R–2034–DDRE (Santa Monica: The Rand Corporation, 1976), pp. 34–37; William T. Lee, "Soviet Targeting Strategy and SALT," pp. 121–125; and Joseph D. Douglass, Jr. and Amoretta M. Hoeber, *Soviet Strategy for Nuclear War* (Stanford: Hoover Institution Press, 1979), pp. 14–33.

28. For recent discussions of the role of the *TVD* in Soviet military operations and planning, see Gregory C. Baird, "Glavnoye Komandovaniye: The Soviet Theater High Command," *Naval War College Review,* May/June 1980, pp. 40–48; and Phillip A. Petersen, "The Soviet Conceptual Framework for the Application of Military Power," *Naval War College Review,* May/June 1981, pp. 18–20.

29. Douglass, *The Soviet Theater Nuclear Offensive,* pp. 4, 45–53, and 99–121. Also see A. A. Sidorenko, *The Offensive,* translated and published under the auspices of the United States Air Force (Washington: Government Printing Office, 1976), pp. 40–70; Krylov, "The Nuclear–Missile Shield of the Soviet State," pp. 17–18; and Povaliy, "Development of Soviet Military Strategy," pp. 70–71.

30. Soviet interests in avoiding the nuclear devastation of large portions of Western Europe are said to arise from both its requirement for European industrial assets to aid in its own postwar recovery and the problem of prevailing westerly winds. See Lee, "Soviet Targeting Strategy and SALT," p. 124. Some analysts have concluded this facet of Soviet regional strategy should lead the West to reevaluate its perception that Soviet strike forces are necessarily armed with only high-yield nuclear warheads. See Joseph D. Douglass, Jr., "Soviet Nuclear Strategy in Europe: A Selective Targeting Doctrine?" *Strategic Review,* Fall 1977, pp. 19–32.

31. Sokolovskiy, *Soviet Military Strategy,* pp. 292–294.

32. Phillip A. Petersen, "Flexibility: A Driving Force in Soviet Strategy," *Air Force Magazine,* March 1980, pp. 94–96.

33. For instance, see Samorukov, "Combat Operations Involving Conventional Means of Destruction," pp. 29–32; and Major General Kh. Dzhelaukov, "The Infliction of Deep Strikes," *Voyennaya mysl',* No. 2, 1966, pp. 47–49.

34. Ibid., and A. A. Sidorenko, *The Offensive,* pp. 132–137.

35. S. T. Cohen and W. C. Lyons, "A Comparison of US–Allied and Soviet Tactical Nuclear Force Capabilities and Policies," *Orbis,* Spring 1975, pp. 79–80.

36. Sokolovskiy, *Soviet Military Strategy,* pp. 284 and 289–290; Povaliy, "Development of Soviet Military Strategy," p. 71; Krylov, "The Nuclear–Missile Shield of the Soviet State," pp. 17–18; and Major General V. Zemskov, "Characteristic Features of Modern Wars and Possible Methods of Conducting Them," *Voyennaya mysl,* No. 7, 1969, p. 20.

37. Ibid.

38. Skovorodkin, "Some Questions on Coordination of Branches of Armed Forces in Major Operations," pp. 36–37.

39. For instance, see Henry Rowen's account in "A Strategic Symposium: SALT and US Defense Policy," in *The Washington Quarterly*, Winter 1979, p. 52.

40. Along this line, see Lieutenant Commander Floyd D. Kennedy, USNR, "Attacking the Weakest Link: The Anti–Support Role of Soviet Naval Forces," *Naval War College Review*, September–October 1979, pp. 48–55.

41. Sokolovskiy, *Soviet Military Strategy*, pp. 299–302; and Rear Admiral V. Andreyev, "The Subdivision and Classification of Theaters of Military Operations," *Voyennaya mysl'*, No. 11, 1964, pp. 19–20.

42. Sokolovskiy, *Soviet Military Strategy*, p. 302.

43. Admiral S. G. Gorshkov, *The Navy*, JPRS–72286 (Joint Publications Research Service, 1978), p. 36. Also, see James M. McConnell, "Strategy and Missions of the Soviet Navy in the Year 2000," in James L. George, ed., *Problems of Sea Power as We Approach the Twenty–First Century* (Washington: American Enterprises Institute for Public Policy Research, 1978), pp. 47–50.

44. Benjamin S. Lambeth, *The Elements of Soviet Strategic Policy*, Report P–6389 (Santa Monica: The Rand Corporation, 1979), pp. 5–6; and John Erickson, "The Soviet Military System: Doctrine, Technology and 'Style,'" in John Erickson and E. J. Feuchtwanger, eds., *Soviet Military Power and Performance* (London: Archon Books, 1979), pp. 24–28.

45. For instance, see the recent statement by Marshal of the Soviet Union N. V. Ogarkov, Chief of the Soviet General Staff, reprinted in *Strategic Review*, Summer 1980, pp. 93–95.

46. Lambeth, *The Elements of Soviet Strategic Policy*, p. 5; and Erickson, "The Soviet Military System," pp. 25 and 28.

47. Stanley Sienkiewicz, "SALT and Soviet Nuclear Doctrine," *International Security*, Spring 1978, p. 92; and Dennis Ross, "Rethinking Soviet Strategic Policy: Inputs and Implications," *The Journal of Strategic Studies*, May 1978, p. 14.

48. Zemskov, "Characteristic Features of Modern Wars and Possible Methods of Conducting Them," p. 23; and Warner, *The Military in Contemporary Soviet Politics*, pp. 156–157.

49. Sokolovskiy, *Soviet Military Strategy*, p. 195; also, see Douglass, pp. 101–113.

50. Sokolovskiy, *Soviet Military Strategy*, pp. 204–205; and Colonel D. Samorukov and Colonel L. Semeyko, "The Increase of Effects in Nuclear Warfare Operations," *Voyennaya mysl'*, No. 10, 1968, p. 44.

51. Sokolovskiy, *Soviet Military Strategy*, pp. 226–286; and Lambeth, *How to Think About Soviet Military Doctrine*, p. 10. Also, note the continuing reflection of this Soviet concern in the reported pledge of General Secretary L. Brezhnev that the USSR is "taking into consideration the lessons of the past and [is] doing everything so that nobody catches us by surprise." Major General N. Vasendin and Colonel N. Kuznestov, "Modern Warfare and Suprise Attack," *Voyennaya mysl'*, No. 6, 1968, p. 48.

52. Warner, p. 151.

53. Secretary of Defense James R. Schlesinger, *The Theater Nuclear Force Posture in Europe: A Report to the United States Congress in Compliance with Public Law 93–365* (Washington: Department of Defense, 1975), p. 15; and Herbert Y. Schandler, *US Policy on the Use of Nuclear Weapons, 1945–1975* (Washington: Congressional Research Service, 1975), pp. 30–35.

54. In a "launch-under-attack" strategy, a country would seek to launch its vulnerable land-based strategic forces against their targets upon notification by tactical warning systems that an enemy attack is actually in progress.

55. Particularly, see Marshal Krylov's statement, "The Nuclear–Missile Shield of the Soviet State," p. 18. Also, see Major General N. Vasendin and Colonel N. Kuznetsov, "Modern Warfare and Surprise Attack," pp. 46–47; and Raymond L. Garthoff, "Mutual Deterrence and Strategic Arms Limitation in Soviet Policy,"

International Security, Summer 1978, pp. 129–132.

56. *Allocation of Resources in the Soviet Union and China—1978,* Part 4, pp. 67–68 and 117–118; Joseph J. Kruzel, "Military Alerts and Diplomatic Signals," in Ellen P. Stern, ed., *The Limits of Intervention* (Beverly Hills: Sage Publications, 1977), pp. 83 and 87–89; also, Secretary of Defense Harold Brown, *Department of Defense Annual Report for Fiscal Year 1980* (Washington: Government Printing Office, 1979), pp. 72–73.

57. Ibid., and US Congress, Senate Armed Services Committee, *Hearings: Department of Defense Appropriations for FY 1980* (Washington: Government Printing Office, 1979), Part 3, pp. 476–477.

58. Chairman of the Joint Chiefs of Staff, *United States Military Posture for FY 1979* (Washington: Government Printing Office, 1978), pp. 27–28; and US Congress, House Appropriations Committee, *Hearings: Department of Defense Appropriations for FY 1980* (Washington: Government Printing Office, 1979), Part 3, pp. 476–77.

59. Kruzel, "Military Alerts and Diplomatic Signals," pp. 87–89.

60. Lambeth, *Selective Nuclear Options in American and Soviet Strategic Policy,* p. 35.

61. *Allocation of Resources in the Soviet Union and China—1978,* Part 4, pp. 67–68 and 117–118.

62. Ibid., pp. 67–68

63. For a more detailed discussion of Soviet interest and efforts in ballistic missile defenses, see Sidney Graybeal and Daniel Goure, "Soviet Ballistic Missile Defense (BMD) Objectives: Past, Present, and Future," in *US Arms Control Objectives and the Implications for Ballistic Missile Defense,* Proceedings of a Symposium held at the Center for Science and International Affairs, Harvard University, November 1979, pp. 69–90.

64. This included both SS–N–6 SLBMs and SS–11 land-based ICBMs during the 1970s. See William Beecher, "Missile Shots in Soviet Asia Reported," *New York Times,* 17 February 1973; and Fred S. Hoffman, "Two Test Failures Reported for Soviet MIRV Missiles," *Washington Star,* 18 August 1975.

65. Foreign Broadcast Information Service (FBIS) *Daily Report: Soviet Union,* 31 March 1978, pp. R–2 and R–3; 5 April 1978, p. R–1; and 7 April 1978, pp. R–1 and R–2.

66. This was Army General V. I. Petrov, recently promoted to the position of Commander in Chief of the Soviet Ground Forces. William Beecher, "Soviet Staging War Games Near China," *Boston Globe,* 29 March 1979. Also see Gregory C. Baird, "The Soviet Theater Command: An Update," *Naval War College Review,* November/December 1981, pp. 90–93.

67. Ibid.

68. John Erickson, "The Ground Forces in Soviet Military Policy," *Strategic Review,* Winter 1978, p. 78.

Soviet Strategic Intentions

Amoretta M. Hoeber

It is time to worry not just about the disparity in military postures between the United States and the Soviet Union but, more seriously than has been the case in the past, about the disparity in strategic thought between the two superpowers. The United States' industrial potential, technical strength, and overwhelming nuclear superiority have been responsible for US security and, to a large extent, that of our allies for over three decades. Perhaps reflecting awareness that these factors provided the advantage, analyses of the Soviet threat have focused principally on determining the corresponding aspects of their capability—systems, RDT&E, production rates, performance characteristics, and deployments. In contrast, however, data on the so-called soft areas, such as Soviet strategy and intentions, have been relatively ignored. Analyses of Soviet thought are relatively sparse, and—even where they have existed—they often have been cast aside or deprecated. One reason for the dismissal of these types of analyses has been their basically unprovable conclusions. A second reason is the wide variations in interpretation of the underlying data. Further, aspersions are cast at these analyses because intentions are seen as highly nonstatic and subject to wide variations over time and from governing body to governing body within a country. (A former Director of Central Intelligence used this latter argument, saying "the adversary's intention is not necessarily the key to determining his future action. His intention can change, his intention may not yet be formed, his intention may be rather a hope than a commitment to action.") A final—although not necessarily articulated—rationale acknowledges that the perception of such intangibles as the intentions and strategy of one's opponent is probably the single most important factor which governs one's recommendations on what courses of action—systems deployment, employment strategies, and arms control measures—should or should not be pursued. Therefore, analyses of the adversary's intentions and strategy are sometimes dismissed because the message has been, or is feared to have been, inconsistent with desired policy recommendations.

When the United States had a preponderant military superiority, it was not wise but neither was it crucial that the adversary's strategy was largely ignored and in general assumed to be a mirror image of our own, albeit with a few years' lag. However, this ethnocentricity is no longer permissible if US security is to be preserved. The United States no longer has uncontested superiority at any level—strategic nuclear, naval, theater nuclear, or conventional. We can no longer correct inventory imbalances with technology leads, as these have largely evaporated over the past decade or exist only in the laboratory. Nor can we depend on our industrial potential, since future strategic nuclear war would preclude a long-term buildup such as occurred in WWII. Further, the realities of the US budget process dictate that a significant redressing of the imbalances is unlikely for the foreseeable future.

Therefore, to maintain US security interests here and abroad, to deter aggression against ourselves and our allies—up to and including nuclear aggression—and to survive—if not to come out ahead—in the event of war, it is essential to concentrate much more of our national attention upon understanding Soviet intentions and strategy in detail and developing countering strategies. Twenty-four centuries ago Sun Tzu said, "What is of supreme importance in war is to attack the enemy's strategy." This is especially valid today not only for war but for the continuing and unabating competition between ourselves and the Soviet Union. Critical aspects of Soviet strategic planning need to be thoroughly understood: their long-range political and military goals and implementing tactics; their perception of US intentions, strategy, and capabilities (both technical and leadership); their assessment of war outcomes and the possibility of victory; and, especially, their views on the value of surprise and superiority, on potential scenarios for war initiation, and on concepts of escalation.

Surprise and Superiority

The study of Soviet intentions and strategy faces two closely intertwined problems. First, there is a tendency on the part of the perceiver to see what he wants to see or to find that for which he is looking. For example, if one side clearly "understands" that nuclear warfighting is impossible, then the tendency is to believe the adversary must sooner or later also reach this conclusion. Secondly, if one side's policy and force development are based on such a belief, then it is difficult to conclude the other side is building a capability to threaten that which is viewed as impossible. The second problem exacerbates the first because, if the policy and force development of the first side— based on its view of the impossibility of war—are to the advantage of the adversary, then the adversary has a strong incentive to feed or substantiate the perception of the first side.

These two problems are acutely hampering US understanding of Soviet thought on nuclear war and the role and importance of nuclear forces in the absence of such war. To understand what is happening, it is essential to appreciate the importance the Soviet leadership attaches to lulling the West. When nuclear weapons became available to the Soviet Union in quantity, which the Soviets suggest happened in the mid–1950s, they undertook a searching reexamination of military

662

doctrine (which is similar in concept to national security policy in the West) and strategy. Of concern was the impact of nuclear weapons on the full range of military concepts.

The Soviet leadership reviewed the range of military concepts—laws, principles, tactics, strategy, and so on—to learn what changes would be required. They saw the driving characteristics to be the massive destructiveness of nuclear weapons, particularly thermonuclear weapons coupled with long-range missiles which could deliver the weapons to any target immediately at the start of the war. Given a sufficient quantity of these weapons, the Soviets concluded, it would be possible to achieve strategic results; namely, the destruction of the enemy's military capability and political (government) organization—the latter being an essential component of both the Soviet political philosophy and military strategy for achieving victory in war—right at the beginning of war.

Thus, postures and actions existent at the beginning of the war would be decisive and determine the eventual outcome. In effect, this possibility represented the most significant change from the past and had the most significant impact on the "revolution in military affairs." Unlike the past, there could be no strategic defense in a future war. That is, one could not afford to plan to absorb the first blow, fall back, and conduct a strategic defense while mustering the capability to mount a counteroffensive to regain the strategic initiative. It was viewed as essential in nuclear war to seize the strategic initiative right at the start of the war; that is, if war became inevitable, to strike first. Thus, the stark conclusion was that the revolution in all aspects of military affairs—equipment, training, tactics, doctrine, and strategy—necessitated by the advent of the nuclear weapon drastically increased the importance of prewar preparedness—of surprise and of superiority—strategically, operationally, and technically.

This was a real change in the perceived role of surprise. In the Stalin era, the Soviets regarded surprise as a temporary factor whose importance was more tactical than strategic. In the nuclear age, however, they decided this was no longer true; achieving both strategic (superiority in armaments) and operational (a successful first strike if war became inevitable) surprise were considered crucial. Surprise, in the Soviet view, is now seen as *"ensuring success"* both in military and political ventures. In the more restricted military sense, surprise ensures success because it makes it possible to inflict heavy losses in short periods of time, to paralyze the enemy's will, and to deprive him of the possibility of offering organized resistance. As repeatedly stated by the Soviets, these are all the immediate strategic objectives in nuclear war if it comes. "Any aggressor," the Soviets explain,

> . . . risks unleashing a nuclear war only with confidence of achieving victory. And confidence in the success of a nuclear attack can occur in conditions whereby there is a

sufficiently high guarantee that nuclear strikes will be delivered to the objectives of destruction, that a mass launch of ballistic missiles and takeoff of aircraft will occur for a relatively long time undetected by the country against which the attack is being carried out, and that the armed forces, and above all the strategic nuclear means of the enemy, will suffer such destruction that they will be incapable of carrying out a powerful retaliatory nuclear strike.

Misleading the West as to Soviet intentions is one of the means to be employed in achieving superiority and surprise. To achieve his goals, what the aggressor does regarding his own forces is only part of the story. Equally important is his ability to influence his opponent (for example, the United States) to be unprepared and unresponsive. All techniques—secrecy, cover, deception, disinformation—are to be employed actively to this end. Consequently, an important element of Soviet diplomacy, emphasized by all major Soviet leaders beginning with Khrushchev, is the attempt to convince the West that the USSR does not seek superiority and opposes the concept of the first strike. Two examples, 20 years apart, are as follows: Marshal R. Ya. Malinovskiy in the 9 May 1958 *Pravda* stated that "our peaceloving policy does not permit any kind of 'preventive war,' 'preemptive blows,' or 'surprise attack' about which some foreign slanderers are trumpeting;" on 18 January 1977, Marshal L. I. Brezhnev, General Secretary of the CPSU, described as "absurd and totally unfounded" the allegation that the Soviet Union "strives for superiority in armaments with the aim of delivering a 'first strike' . . . . The Soviet Union has always been and remains a convinced opponent of such concepts."

The tactics employed can be understood as a simple application of Lenin's initial guidance on deception to Dzerzhinskiy, the first chief of the Soviet secret police: "Tell them what they want to believe." Or, as explained by Marshal Stalin,

> Words must have no relations to actions—otherwise, what kind of diplomacy is it? Good words are but a mask for concealment of bad deeds. Sincere diplomacy is no more possible than dry water or wooden iron.

Such activity—the use of misinformation to forestall the enemy's preparation—is also referred to in the new authoritative *Soviet Military Encyclopedia* under the topic "Surprise."

However, the image conveyed by Soviet public statements regarding nuclear war, surprise, superiority, and first strike stand in stark contrast to the principles, objectives, and strategic goals set forth in the Soviet *internal* military and political literature. As reflected in their internal literature, and in contrast to the image put forth by the Malinovskiy and Brezhnev statements cited above, nuclear war is not a mere a theoretical abstraction. The Soviets are serious about preparing for the possibility of a global nuclear war. The common Western assumption, however, that the Soviet concern for preparation does not reflect an adequate appreciation of the consequences of such a war is not true. On the contrary, the Soviets clearly recognize the magnitude of damage which would accompany such a war. It is because of this recognition that they consider it crucial for the survival of the state to determine how best to fight such a war and then actually to prepare for that war.

As part of this preparation, quantitative and qualitative superiority in nuclear forces is a first goal. On the quantitative side, reserve nuclear missile forces—unaccounted for in Western perceptions of the Soviet threat—are considered extremely important. While presently there is insufficient public evidence to enable one to state with certainty that the Soviets have implemented their doctrine with respect to such forces, the principle and its logic are clearly present in authoritative internal Soviet literature, and implementation is certainly a possibility. This is an extremely important issue because of the political as well as the military implications. The possibility of such reserve missile forces challenges two major aspects of US strategic policy. The first is the validity of the Western discussions and calculations of force balance which simply may leave out what might be a significant component of the Soviet forces and a significant factor in the Soviet assessment of the balance. The second is the relevance of the US approach to arms control and verification in terms of strategic missile forces. The approach apparently has been to impose limitations on verifiable elements—silos in the case of ICBMs—even if they are relatively meaningless indices of force postures, rather than to attempt to limit, for example, total numbers of missiles. Because of the extent to which the Soviets focus on reserves, including nuclear missile reserves, the total size of the Soviet intercontinental missile force might well be (and we believe is) considerably larger than indicated by the conventional approach which just counts silos. Given that a consistent case can be made for the Soviets having an interest in concealing such reserves, one should observe considerable caution in relying on the assumption that what we do not see does not exist.

The Soviets consider qualitative superiority to be equally important; however, the Soviet assessment of quality differs from the Western. In calculating the qualitative force balance, the Soviets consider a number of factors in addition to the missile accuracy measure which appears to dominate Western assessments. The Soviets include command and control, reconnaissance, readiness, and survivability—the latter involving a combination of hardness, secrecy (including cover and deception), and recoverability. Command flexibility is considered an especially important qualitative aspect of Soviet nuclear force development objectives. This flexibility does not refer to options from which the Soviet leadership can select on the eve of the war but to the capability to shift efforts, redirect strikes, and alter the sequence of missions *during* the war. The most important explicit characteristic is the ability to execute a surprise first strike. In other words, flexibility means realtime nuclear battle management at the strategic level. Whether or not the Soviets have succeeded in achieving such a capability, it is clearly an objective which is being seriously pursued, and—among other things—it implies a Soviet concept of war far different from the retaliation and spasm exchange generally assumed in the West. The focus on battle management is a reason why not only command and control but also reconnaissance and technical support, including the generation of new strategic missile force armies from reserves, are so important in the Soviet calculation of the nuclear correlation of forces. Moreover, the battle management aspect is one reason why the Soviets regard the ability of the leadership on both sides to use their capabilities as a major factor in the war outcome. Superiority, while important, is not sufficient by itself. Rather, the Soviets emphasize the need not only to have superiority but *to use* it. The strategic leadership is judged according to its ability to use this power. In peace, the main political use of superiority is to help isolate the United States, demoralize the West generally, and "facilitate" worldwide the process of the transition to socialism through the deterrence of "counterrevolutionary forces." In war, it would be used to strike first if possible, both to limit damage to the Soviet homeland and to destroy capitalist governments in the process.

Other critical aspects of the Soviet preparation for global war include the development and implementation of war survival measures to ensure as rapid a recovery of the economic and military potential of the Soviet Union as possible and the establishment of specific plans for postwar occupation and control of continental and intercontinental theaters of military operations. Soviet planning encompasses all forces (military intelligence, espionage, civil defense, army, air force, navy, and strategic missile forces), all means (nuclear, chemical, conventional), all forms of warfare (diplomatic, economic, and military), and all phases of the conflict, including recovery of the Soviet Union and political domination of the West (first and foremost, of the United States).

Potential Scenarios of War Initiation and Concepts of Escalation

The Soviets emphasize the need to prepare for several variants of global nuclear war. These variants are distinguished mainly by perceptions of the way the war starts and, to a lesser extent, by the ordering of and the speed with which the various goals are pursued. The principal variants most often discussed in the Soviet literature are a surprise attack from the West and a Soviet surprise attack on the West. The Soviets view both of these variations as possible in a scenario in which the war begins as a local war and then escalates.

While Soviet plans encompass the variant of a surprise attack from the West, they consider this to be an unacceptable way for the war to begin. Accordingly, the Soviets direct considerable efforts—beginning with strategic espionage and continuing through analyses of enemy (US) capabilities, exercises, plans, doctrine (i.e., national security policy), and leadership personalities and abilities—toward countering this possibility. The Soviets also consider technical warning sensors to be important, but only to enable a launch-on-warning response which, while better than being completely surprised, is considered a poor second best way for the war to start.

If the Soviets consider war inevitable, they would clearly want to implement what is in their view the only acceptable variant—a Soviet first strike. The Soviet measure of success of the initial strike is a combination of the superiority gained (i.e., the anticipated nuclear correlation of forces *after* the exchange of nuclear strikes) and the level of the strike that the enemy (mainly the United States) is capable of returning. There are two important immediate objectives of a Soviet first strike: the disruption of the US capability to organize a response, thus preventing an immediate Western counterstrike, and—more importantly—the destruction of the total Western military capability beginning with the nuclear component but also including navy and army elements as well.

The first nuclear strikes, therefore, most likely would be directed against US command and control capabilities in order to maximize surprise and, in effect, to decapitate the US strategic nuclear capability. It might be accompanied, or slightly preceded by, highly selective acts of sabotage designed to achieve the same goals, if such actions can be coordinated successfully.

The Soviet literature views the war as beginning with several successive salvos which might extend over several hours. The principal targets, in addition to the enemy's immediate military potential—nuclear capabilities and reserves, all types of forces, command and control, and intelligence/reconnaissance—would be political and administrative control centers, communications, transportation centers, and electric power facilities. This latter group is considered the basis of military potential, and the Soviets may assess its destruction as likely to have the most major and immediate impact on the enemy's capability to resist and recover and on the morale of the population. Regarding command and control, the notion of leaving the strategic leadership and communications intact for negotiation purposes appears to be a Western concept wholly alien to the Soviets. More likely, the Soviets would strive first to destroy the government—"the aggressive leaders who unleashed the war"—so the realistic or progressive elements can rise to power.

While Soviet literature places considerable stress on the concept of the simultaneous, mass initial strike, it should not be inferred from this

667

that the Soviets think only or even principally in terms of one massive blow at the beginning of the war, or even one exchange, as constituting the entire conflict. Quite the contrary, the Soviets see the war as proceeding in a phased fashion in which one performs missions in accordance with specific priorities. The initial period of the war is even described as lasting only until the *short–term* strategic goals have been attained. The overall purpose of this initial period, as typically described in the Soviet literature, is to inflict sufficient casualties and destruction to ensure the collapse of the enemy's economic, moral, political, and military capabilities, thus making it impossible for the West to continue and thereby presenting the United States with *de facto* defeat.

This is not the end, however. The ultimate aim is to track down and destroy the remnants of US and other capitalist military capabilities and to consolidate Soviet military gains in other parts of the world, most notably Western Europe and the Middle East. For the Soviets, the war—if it occurs—will be global. Even the political competition which exists in the absence of such a war will be global. It will be a class conflict between communist and capitalist states. There are no neutrals, and domination—*total* political and military victory over the entire enemy coalition of which the most important member is the United States—appears to be a real and serious long-term objective of Soviet strategy. This goal is the most important for the Soviet military, the Party and state as a whole, and the satellite countries.

The Soviets treat the question of escalation, particularly escalation from conventional or theater war to intercontinental warfare, in an interesting fashion. Because of the strong possibility theater war might escalate to general war, the Soviets discuss the possibly advantageous use of theater war to cover preparations for general war; that is, its use as an opportunity better to prepare and achieve surprise. For example, Marshal Krylov, the head of the Strategic Missile Forces, wrote the following on this topic in 1967:

> . . . The variant is not excluded whereby military operations will begin and will be conducted for some time with the use of merely conventional means of armed conflict. In this case, the army, the state, and its economy will have some time to complete the strategic deployment of the armed forces, to take measures in mobilizing and concentrating the troops in theaters of military operations, and also to reorganize industry on a military footing.

Implications

The Soviets are achieving more and more of their aims without overt military activities. While some in the West believe allowing the

Soviets to "catch up" and even exceed the United States will lead to a more stable situation, this is not true from the Soviet point of view. The Soviets do not view their superiority per se as lessening the risk of war. They view their strength as providing them with many significant advantages (e.g., flexibility) but not security. Only disarming the West provides security, but the path is dangerous. The Soviets reason that as the West grows weaker, the risk of war and the possibility the West itself will initiate war can actually increase. This perception, of course, increases the risk of Soviet preemption. If we do not pay more heed to Soviet strategy and actions as they really are rather than as we wish them to be, the Soviets are extremely unlikely to have to do any more.

Soviet Perceptions of US Strategic Activities: A Realtime Retrospection

Gregory D. Foster

The story was once told by Chekhov about an inspector who is being driven by a peasant through a forest. Suspicious of the inspector, the peasant keeps turning his head, whereupon the inspector, who each time the peasant turns his head becomes more afraid of the driver, begins to boast how well-armed he is. The more the inspector boasts, the greater is the peasant's fear; as his fear grows, the more he glances over his shoulder. The more he glances over his shoulder, the louder grows the panicky inspector's boast about his sharpshooting. At last the peasant, unable to bear the suspense any longer, jumps down and flees into the winter wood, leaving the inspector alone in the snow. Stranded in the bitter weather because they were so afraid of each other, they grope through the forest until they chance to meet again, whereupon they confess their mutual fears, are reassured, and, full of goodwill, continue their journey.

There is, of course, more than merely the story of an inspector and a peasant in this parable. An obvious analogy can be drawn with the relations which exist among nations. Perhaps more than any other single factor, an inability or unwillingness to perceive "reality" in congruent terms has contributed to the conditions of tension and conflict so prevalent in nation-to-nation relationships today. As Dr. William Davidson of the Institute for Psychiatry and Foreign Affairs in Washington, DC, has observed:

> To a large extent, the foreign policy of a nation is determined by the nation's perceptions—and misperceptions—of itself and of other nations, its adversaries and its allies. It reflects the behavior of the nation generally and of its decisionmakers specifically.[1]

While an increasing appreciation of the perceptual dimension of foreign and military policy has evolved over the past three decades, such appreciation has been purchased only very slowly and even grudgingly. It is instructive in this regard to view international relations relative to other aspects of our daily lives from a perceptual standpoint. At the organic family or team level, where contact is both close and frequent, there exists essentially what phenomenologists term an intersubjective view of reality which allows us almost to *know* what another is thinking. At the national or subnational level, proximity is reduced, but a common cultural heritage, media saturation, and such devices as opinion polling allow us at least to *judge* what another is thinking. In contrast, at the supranational level, we are reduced to *guessing* underlying intent and meaning from surrogate indicators such as policy pronouncements emanating from foreign elites.

Whether at the organic, the subnational, or the supranational level, communication lies at the heart of this perceptual process. In fact, it has become something of a truism that all behavior, insofar as it is perceived by someone else and whether intended or not, is communicative. Our behavior is (potentially) informative—it carries information about us, the situation we are in, our relationship with others, and so forth.[2]

Behavior, to be meaningful, must be interpreted. Culture, conceived of as a code—a program, set of rules, or body of knowledge—provides the mechanism for guiding such interpretation.[3] When the members of one culture attempt to interpret the behavior of another culture, what typically results is a form of ethnocentrism or "centri-cultural bias"— the inherent difficulty of trying to understand the mental processes of another culture.[4] This in turn produces such common simplifying devices as mirror imaging or stereotyping.

The purpose of the present inquiry is to explore the perceptual relationship Richard Barnet has referred to as

> . . . the struggle of two elites with radically different backgrounds and perceptions to understand each other. The problem of communication is complicated because each elite wishes to reveal itself and to remain mysterious at the same time. Each wants to avoid miscalculation. Neither wants to telegraph important moves.[5]

The centrality of the communication process to such an investigation is self-evident. In any communicative act, there are five major elements: a sender, a receiver, a message, a medium, and the environment. Traditionally, because of the aforementioned difficulty of interpreting behavior across cultures, foreign perceptions have been treated primarily as being reflected in the message (words and actions) of a particular sender (the perceived party). The obvious difficulty of any such approach has been suggested by Soviet political analyst Aleksandr Bovin: "The verbal expression of policy can play a dual role: it either reflects real political interests and intentions, or, conversely, is called upon to conceal these interests and intentions."[6]

Rarely, if ever, is an attempt made to assume the perspective of the perceiving party (typically the receiver of the message) to discern how it might have interpreted and responded to the stimuli provided by the sender. The present inquiry therefore seeks to expand upon earlier research by the author which attempted to reconstruct the statements and actions of the United States (the perceived party) during a selected time frame—the year 1967—to determine what was there to be seen, irrespective of any subsequent interpretation. With the advantage of hindsight, it is possible to assess not only how closely our actions hewed to our words but what the Soviet Union *could* have seen as a basis for undertaking subsequent diplomatic, political, and military actions.

More specifically, it will be suggested that (1) there exists a relationship of mutual influence between the US and the USSR; (2) Soviet policymakers collectively manifest a particular set of personality traits which influence their interpretation of and response to US behavior; and, (3) if properly structured and transmitted, the words and actions of US policymakers can have a not insignificant impact on changing Soviet elite attitudes and opinions. The intent here is not to establish any causal link between what the US says (or does) and what the Soviet reaction will be. Given the virtually inestimable number of variables operative in the field of foreign affairs—attitudes, beliefs, and values; international and domestic conditions; capabilities; context; historical conditions; ideology; and so on—that is a near impossibility. It is difficult enough to draw correlations between the words and actions of a single state. Rather, the intent is twofold:

- to assess the extent to which US policymakers seem to evince sensitivity to and a recognition of the potential effects of their policy utterances (and actions) on Soviet behavior; and,
- to suggest tentatively how what we say and do may either prompt subsequent Soviet actions, contribute to those actions, or merely provide an *ex post facto* rationale for that which they otherwise would do anyway.

The US–Soviet Relationship

There tend to be two major—and diametrically opposite—views of the nature of the US–Soviet relationship and, more generally, of Soviet external behavior. The first is essentially deterministic in nature and reflects acceptance of the Soviet-espoused belief in objective factors and historical inevitability. According to this view, which typically is espoused by Americans of the conservative right, everything the Soviets currently are doing and have done over the past three decades can be traced directly to statements of purpose enunciated in the 1950s. The Soviets, they say, have not deviated materially from the course originally set at that time. Alexander Dallin has been among those, however, who have questioned the validity of such a rigorous interpretation:

> There has been too much stress on continuity, a "static bias" and a "monochromatic" approach toward the Soviet

system, and these deficiencies are connected with acceptance of the totalitarian model. Furthermore, students of Soviet society have tended to accept Soviet assertions that nothing is accidental in politics and history; this has led to what might be called an overintegrated perspective of the Soviet system, in which everything is purposeful, planned, or intentional. Such a view also attributes more control to the leadership and more cohesion to the social order than may be the case.[7]

The other perspective is best exemplified by the statement of then Secretary of Defense Robert McNamara in 1967:

> The Soviet Union and the United States mutually influence one another's strategic plans. Whatever be their intentions, actions—or even realistically potential actions— on either side relating to the buildup of nuclear forces, be they either offensive or defensive weapons, necessarily trigger reactions on the other side. It is precisely this action-reaction phenomenon that fuels an arms race.

This probably was the first formal statement of what has come to be known as the action-reaction model of strategic interaction. The model evolved at least partially as a function of dissatisfaction with the deterrence model of US–Soviet behavior. Focused specifically on weapon systems developments, the model sees the US as not merely meeting Soviet challenges but perhaps as inadvertently provoking them. Thus, every weapon innovation action taken by the technically superior United States is bound to be followed by a Soviet reaction, thereby driving weapons destructiveness up a theoretically endless spiral. Four distinctive types of responses have come to be associated with the action-reaction model:

- A "counterresponse," in which a given threat is directly opposed by a different type of weapon, as in the case of a surface-to-air missile against an aircraft.
- A "symmetrical response," in which a more or less equivalent capability to the original threat is sought— bomber for bomber, helicopter for helicopter, etc.
- A "conceptual duplication," a related but more extreme version of the symmetrical response in which significant aspects of the original threat are purposely duplicated.
- An "anticipatory response," a reaction fielded against a threat known or thought to be under development.

This is a fundamentally behavioralist, or Skinnerian, perspective which views all behavior as a response to some external environmental stimulus. Institution and experience would suggest the reality in all likelihood lies somewhere between these two views. The experience of

673

the past 30 years is sufficient to support the contention the Soviets have a "grand design" which they have pursued aggressively and relentlessly. On the other hand, intuition suggests the international environment is so fraught with complexity and uncertainty, the idea of any nation having sufficient foresight to map a strategy which adequately accommodates all unforeseen contingencies is inconceivable. Paul Hollander therefore has taken the following position: "If I had to choose between the extremes of designating the political style of the [Soviet] leaders as 'flexible and pragmatic improvisation' versus 'planned implementation of long-range objective,' I would prefer to err along the line of the latter."[8]

The Importance of Images and Beliefs

The central functions comprising foreign policy decisionmaking have been defined as (1) the cognitive interpretation of incoming information—what it is, and what its dimensions, characteristics, and properties are; (2) its affective evaluation—is it good or bad, supportive or threatening, and so on; (3) the formulation and explication of intention or policy; and (4) the affective ordering of preference.[9]

Obviously, the cognitive and affective functions of both interpretation and policy are inextricably linked. As Kenneth Boulding has noted, the individuals whose decisions determine the policies and actions of nations do not respond to the "objective" facts of a situation (whatever that may mean) but to their "image" of the situation. It is what we think the world is like, rather than what it is really like, that determines our behavior. The "image" must be thought of as "the total cognitive, affective, and evaluative structure of the behavior unit, or its internal view of itself and its universe."[10]

The relationship of these national images to international conflict has been suggested as a clear one: decisionmakers act upon the definition of the situation and their images of states—others as well as their own. These images in turn are dependent upon the decisionmakers' belief system and may or may not be accurate representations of "reality."[11]

The "belief system," in turn, is composed of a number of images of the past, present, and future and thus includes all the accumulated, organized knowledge the organism has about itself and the world. It may be thought of as a set of lenses through which information concerning the physical and social environment is received. It orients the individual to his environment, defining it for him and identifying for him its salient characteristics. National images may be denoted as a subpart of the belief system—"models" which order for the observer what otherwise would be an unmanageable amount of information.[12]

The structuring or delimiting nature of the belief system has been described by Alexander George in his discussion of the operational code construct:[13]

. . . [The operational code is] a prism or filter that influences the actor's perception and diagnosis of political situations, and that provides norms and standards to guide and channelize his choices of action in specific situations. The function of an operational code belief system in decision-making, then, is to provide the actor with "diagnostic propensities" and "choice propensities."[14]

The importance of these concepts lies in explicit recognition of the idea, empirically supported, that major differences in attitudes, beliefs, and values exist across cultures. In fact, it has been shown that belief content varies as a function of the frequency and type of contact between ethnic groups.[15] As intuitively obvious as this may seem, it nonetheless has not prevented policymakers and analysts from falling prey to what Robert Jervis has called the "trap of believing," where the actors involved assume their intentions, especially peaceful ones, are clear to others, thereby failing to realize they may be seen as a threat.[16]

Boulding has referred to the national image as the last great stronghold of unsophistication. He suggests the unsophisticated image, by contrast, portrays the world from many imagined viewpoints as a system in which the viewer is only a part.[17]

As a function of this lack of sophistication, and to the extent each side continues to adhere to original images by assimilating new perceptions to old, we see an almost inevitable tendency toward stereotyping and mirror imaging. In summarizing past stereotype research, Berrien has noted: "It has generally been held that the characteristics ascribed to persons or groups we dislike are not those of which we approve; and conversely we tend to ascribe favorable characteristics to persons or groups we admire."[18]

Bronfenbrenner has cited the mirror image in Soviet and American perceptions of each other, noting five major distortions of reality held by both sides: (1) "they" are aggressors; (2) "their" government exploits and deludes the people; (3) the mass of "their" people are not really sympathetic to the regime; (4) "they" cannot be trusted; and (5) "their" policy verges on madness.[19]

On the one hand, Gibert has identified four fundamental impediments to American understanding of Soviet motivations and intentions which lead to such oversimplification:

- First, Americans have created a false dichotomy between Marxist–Leninist ideology and Soviet national interest; this has resulted in countless sterile debates about which of these two concepts guides the actions of the Soviet state.
- Second, there is a belief that people are always "practical" or "pragmatic" in behavior and could not possibly

be swayed by such utopian visions as are embedded in Marxism–Leninism.

- Third, foreign policy analysts frequently do not accord sufficient weight to the legitimizing function of Marxism–Leninism, which requires Soviet leaders to give infinitely more lip service to their ideology.
- Finally, many Americans frequently misunderstand Soviet foreign policy because they stubbornly refuse to learn the meanings the Soviets attach to words. Soviet writers, for example, rarely use the term "detente"; rather, they employ a phrase connoting much less friendly relations, "peaceful coexistence." Similarly, when Soviet spokesmen use words like "liberation," "freedom," "justice," and "democracy," they mean very different things from the images such words conjure up in the minds of Americans.[20]

Though Gibert's emphasis on ideology is open to conjecture, he nonetheless underscores the extent of American appreciation of Soviet life. Schwartz similarly has pointed to Soviet misunderstanding of American life:

> . . . In their attempt to understand the American political system, Soviet analysts suffer from a variety of disabilities. They have been burdened . . . by the constraints of rigid ideological preconceptions and, until recently, limited personal contact with the United States. They also lack the benefit of useful historical guidance . . . . They are attempting to comprehend a democratic political system, one whose institutions and processes neither they nor their countrymen have even had any experience with . . . . There is virtually nothing to guide the Russians' efforts to make sense out of the Senate Foreign Relations Committee, the *Washington Post,* Senator Henry Jackson's public opinion polls and the American legal system.[21]

What the above characterizations do is to place in startling relief the fundamental difficulties which militate against cross-cultural understanding. This certainly is not to suggest, however, that such misconceptions are inevitable. Rather, in terms of the effective prosecution of foreign and military policy, one must use this recognition of misconception as a point of departure for defining the dimensions of the belief system of interest—in this case, that of Soviet officialdom. This in turn should serve as a dynamic, evolving framework for interpreting one's own words and actions from the standpoint of the other side—in other words, of emulating the recipient's perceptions.

Gibert has provided a useful depiction of the Soviet world view or belief system. He defines four key components:

- The belief that social development is a natural evolutionary process whereby mankind moves through historical stages until it reaches the final stage of communism.
- The organic view of society, whereby society is a "living organism" in its functioning and development.
- The Leninist injunction that imperialism is the highest stage of capitalism, and that capitalism is at its most dangerous in this phase.
- The theory of revolution. Revolution is said to occur in the wake of wars or severe depressions or other great crises. The Communist vanguard, recognizing that "objective factors" are favorable, successfully exploits the situation.[22]

A Strategy of Attitude Change

If one ascribes a degree of significance to the perceptual dimension of foreign and military policy, then a key (though perhaps implicit) objective in the formulation and prosecution of such policy becomes that of influencing the perceptions of the various actors of relevance. Where there is a natural inconsistency in beliefs, as between the US and USSR, this becomes an exercise in changing attitudes.

Kurt Lewin has identified three processes involved in attitude change: unfreezing, changing, and refreezing. Unfreezing is the induction of uncertainty in the belief structure, which makes the individual less confident about his existing opinions; in the changing phase, the new information and persuasive support are made available, and the attitude structure shifts to accommodate them; in refreezing, the new formation reaches stability and solidity.[23]

To accomplish such attitude change, one first must understand the major factors contributing to the derivation and solidification of a belief system. Heradstveit has identified three such factors:

- Centrality—the degree to which other beliefs in the belief system are dependent on the belief in question.
- Stability—the strength of beliefs across situations.
- Consistency—the "logical" linkage or connectedness between the beliefs in a belief system.[24]

Consistency assumes dominant importance in this scheme. At issue is the concept of cognitive dissonance. Cognitive dissonance theory predicts that inconsistency between cognitive elements will not be tolerated by an individual if the inconsistency exceeds a certain level. Festinger defines cognition as "any knowledge, opinion, or belief about the environment, about oneself, or about one's behavior." Two elements are dissonant if, "considering these two (elements) alone, the obverse of one element would follow from the other." Cognitive dissonance can be caused by a number of sources, such as exposure to new information, cultural values, conflicting past experiences, the withdrawal of previously existing social support, or change in a related opinion.[25]

Thus, a powerful strategy for changing attitudes is to point out to subjects—or bring about—a state of inconsistency in their beliefs, opinions, or behavior. The dominant schools of attitude theory assume such contradictions are unpleasant. Consequently, the individual is strongly motivated to avoid or eliminate them, often by changing one of the incompatible attitudes. This effect may be followed by substantial changes in behavior even over a long period of time.[26] In dealing with Soviet attitudes toward the United States, this strategy would operationalize itself by distinguishing between central or core beliefs on the one hand and peripheral beliefs on the other. These latter peripheral beliefs—perhaps manifested best by the mirror images alluded to by Bronfenbrenner—then would serve as the object of an intensive effort to engender dissonance. The underlying premise here is that by concentrating first on peripheral beliefs which are less subject to the centrality principle (and thus more amenable to change), a suitable foundation would be established for the eventual, longer term adjustment of core beliefs.

The Role of Personality

Any strategy for effecting the sort of permanent attitude change suggested above must reflect a thorough understanding of the personality characteristics of the Soviet elite. More importantly, the strategy itself must target specifically any personality sensitivities or vulnerabilities which can be identified. Though the argument has been made that susceptibility to attitude change is related directly to personality characteristics,[27] this susceptibility has not been exploited adequately to date. As suggested by one source:

> One approach that has not been sufficiently explored is the matching of [attitude change] procedures to the personality characteristics of the recipient. Thus, for example, one might construct different messages for audiences that differ in authoritarianism . . . . A few studies have shown that the appropriate tailoring of the message to relevant personality traits (including intelligence, conceptual complexity, and defensiveness) can in fact strengthen the impact of the presentation.[28]

There are, it has been suggested, triangular, bilateral, and reciprocal relationships among culture, behavior, and personality. Behavior influences personality and in turn is determined by it. "Culture shapes behavior and personality, and behavior rooted in individual

678

personalities produces cultural change—from infinitesimal to major and from imperceptibly gradual to dramatically sudden."[29]

Gordon Allport has been the foremost proponent of the trait theory of personality. According to this school of thought, personality structure is represented primarily in terms of traits, and, at the same time, behavior is motivated or driven by traits. In the words of Guilford, a trait is "any distinguishable, relatively enduring way in which one individual differs from another."[30]

A trait must (1) be a characteristic in which persons differ; (2) be sufficiently identifiable that different observers can agree reasonably well on how much (or how little) of the characteristic an individual has or displays; and (3) show some degree of consistency over time; that is, the relative amount of a characteristic must not change radically in a person from moment to moment or day to day.[31] Traits cannot be observed directly but must be inferred from behavior. In Allport's words:

> A specific act is always the product of many determinants, not only of lasting sets, but of momentary pressures in the person and in the situation. It is only the repeated occurrence of acts having the same significance (equivalence of response) following upon a definable range of stimuli having the same personal significance (equivalence of stimuli) that makes necessary the inference of traits and personal dispositions. These tendencies are not at all times active, but are persistent even when latent, and have relatively low thresholds of arousal.[32]

Because Soviet attitudes are of primary concern to us here, it is important to note the fundamental relationship which exists between traits and attitudes and yet to distinguish between the two concepts. Whereas the attitude is linked to a specific object or class of objects, the trait is not. Thus, the generality of the trait is almost always greater than that of the attitude. The attitude may vary in generality from the highly specific to the relatively general, while the trait must always be general. Furthermore, the attitude usually implies evaluation (acceptance or rejection) of the object toward which it is directed, while the trait does not.[33]

Without doubt, the most important—and most obvious—realization to be derived from the trait approach to personality is that no two individuals have the same personality. Somewhat ironically, however, it may be suggested that in the national policy arena, such individual differences become submerged or are winnowed away as decisions are made, so that the external observer is left with a more or less collective representation of the personalities involved. Sidney Verba has suggested that the more ambiguous the cognitive and evaluative aspects of a decisionmaking situation and the less a group context is used in decisionmaking—as in an authoritarian regime—the more likely are personality variables to assert themselves.[34]

In light of the fact that we are dealing with national policy, it therefore is not at all inappropriate to think in terms of a *collective* personality which produces such policy. This leads us to consideration of what has been termed "national character." National character is predicated, in its simplest form, upon the expectation of a single personality type within a larger cultural-political unit. What tends to distinguish national character as a concept is, first, its usual restriction to the citizens of modern, politically organized states and, second, its emphasis upon the articulation of a large number of components into a structure or pattern. It thus defines a "basic personality" of sorts.[35]

On the one hand, it must be noted that the obtrusive reality of intra-group, and even interpersonal, variabilities within all large-scale national cultures has done much to dampen enthusiasm for and to usher in disenchantment with the concept of national character.[36] This problem is exacerbated further when one is attempting to come to grips with a "closed" society, particularly in light of the quality of accepted methodological and analytical tools available: test instruments, questionnaires, and so on.

On the other hand, Hans Morgenthau has suggested that certain qualities of intellect and character occur more frequently and are more highly valued than others; moreover, they show a high degree of resiliency to change. As a consequence, such national character cannot fail to influence national power. The observer of the national scene who attempts to assess the relative strength of different nations, therefore, must take this factor into account, however difficult it may be to assess correctly.[37]

The Soviet Character

Our interest here, of course, is with the particular character of the Soviet ruling elite. To some, this investigative focus may seem obvious and natural. To others, particularly those who have studied the dynamics of governmental decisionmaking, it may not be so obvious. Edward Luttwak, in dealing with the question of perceptions in the international arena, has defined three generic classes of perceivers: (1) policymakers and inner elite members with access to privileged information (and technical advice) and with a strong professional interest in politico-military issues; (2) media operatives and other opinion makers with access to large information flows, not necessarily detailed, and with a less concentrated interest in politico-military issues; and (3) the general public with access only to the data conveyed by mass media, and whose level of attention to politico-military issues varies from the very intense (e.g., in countries at war) to the very low, the latter being the more common. Luttwak also distinguishes four categories of countries, of which the Soviet Union is a Type II system characterized by its highly centralized, totalitarian nature. In such systems, only the perceptions of the policymakers and inner elite are considered to have an impact on policy formation over the short and medium term.[38]

Actually, as numerous authorities have suggested, it cannot be said that the Soviet policymaking machinery is truly a monolithic body. Aspaturian has identified six interest groups which exert some degree of influence: (1) the Party apparatus, (2) the government bureaucracy, (3) the economic managers and technicians, (4) the cultural, professional, and scientific intelligentsia, (5) the police, and (6) the armed forces. Similarly, Gehlen has identified eight such groups: (1) the Party apparatus, (2) the state bureaucracy, (3) the military bureacracy, (4) the scientific elite, (5) the writers, (6) the trade unions, (7) the workers, and (8) the consumers.[39]

Though each of these groups may exert varying degrees of influence under particular circumstances, it nonetheless seems safe to accord predominant influence to the inner elite. Furthermore, as suggested earlier, divergent attitudes at this level tend to get submerged in final outcomes; consequently, to the external observer, final outcomes must be construed as the "consensual" representation of the whole. Some, such as former Deputy Secretary of Defense Paul Nitze, have gone so far as to suggest that there are, in fact, no meaningful internal differences among the Soviet leadership. Robert Conquest likewise has contended:

> The Soviet leaders . . . are the products of a history very different from our own, of a longstanding political psychology alien to ours in its motives, its judgements, and its intentions . . . . The basic point . . . is that it isn't a matter of their having "opinions" . . . . They are simply soaked in their tradition . . . . Brezhnev has enough ideology to get along and the rest is soaked into his bones.[40]

In contrast, others have argued that two general and distinct tendencies can be found in Soviet leadership circles: one aggressive, militaristic, mistrustful of the United States, and hostile to detente; the other sober, moderate, and concerned less about the danger of war than the benefits to be gained in specific areas from mutual collaboration.[41] In the final analysis, the issue is essentially moot, but, as Hedrick Smith has observed:

> It is undoubtedly true, as Russians and Western scholars assert, that the Soviet *nachalstvo,* the ruling bosses, are not a monolithic group. The elite has its fundamentalists and its modernizers, its hard-line police and security men, its strict ideologists, and its efficiency-oriented technocrats in industry and science. The cultural elite has conservatives and liberals. But in the Brezhnev-Kosygin years, whenever

frictions have appeared publicly the leadership has repeatedly made conservative compromises to preserve unity and set aside differences.[42]

The question confronting us, then, is one of which personality characteristics tend to drive attitudes and, thus, decisions within the Soviet policy elite. Gibert has acknowledged the potential contribution of personality characteristics to the Soviet world view but has accorded more significance to ideology:

> . . . Marxist–Leninist beliefs constitute the most coherent and organized components of the Soviet world view . . . . It is likely also that psychological characteristics of Soviet leaders affect their world view. Some of those characteristics may be peculiar to the personality of a given leader. Other psychological aspects, however, may be derived from the cultural heritage. This latter phenomenon, generally referred to as "national character," also undoubtedly influences the ways in which Soviet leaders view the world. However, being more inchoate, not institutionalized and lacking official sanction, these components of the world view may not have an impact upon Soviet perceptions to the same degree or constitute an established element of the political culture as does the Marxist–Leninist framework.[43]

William Jones has gone a step further in observing that Soviet scholars generally explain Soviet behavior as the product of a complex, interactive nexus of individual leadership personality traits, ideologically based codes of operation, bureaucratic institutional pressures, and a collection of attributed aspirations to a position of world power in the economic, industrial, and political spheres. Such sources, however, provide little agreement as to how such factors interact and which of them seem to dominate Soviet decisionmaking. Jones therefore defines four types of Soviets:

- The Oligarchic Leadership Soviet, which imputes a dominant influence to experienced Soviet bureaucrats.
- The Economic Aspirations Soviet, which imputes a dominant influence to major economic and industrial development.
- The Doctrinaire Soviet, which imputes a dominant influence to the Marxist–Leninist doctrine.
- The Institutional Soviet, which imputes a dominant influence to the functionally structured and highly institutionalized administrative organizations and agencies.[44]

Morgenthau has characterized the Russian national character as one of "elementary force and persistence." He notes that in Russia, the tradition of obedience to authority and fear of foreigners has made large permanent military establishments acceptable to the population. Thus, by being able to transform a greater peacetime portion of national resources to defense, Russia has gained an initial advantage in the struggle for power, due principally to its national character.[45]

The Soviets have been described variously as manifesting any or all of the following traits: cynicism, defensiveness, deviousness, inflexiblity, insecurity, mendacity, narrow-mindedness, opportunism, resilience, secretiveness, and suspiciousness. In 1966, one prominent pollster asked a cross-section of Americans to select three words which seemed best to describe the Russians. The results of that poll are as follows (percentages shown are based on 300 percent total): hard-working—45 percent; warlike—24 percent; intelligent—23 percent; progressive—19 percent; ordinary—16 percent; sly—15 percent; cruel—13 percent; good-tempered—13 percent; practical—13 percent; arrogant—11 percent; brave—10 percent; ignorant—10 percent; unimaginative—8 percent; conceited—7 percent; dull—7 percent; artistic—6 percent; honest—5 percent; and the balance as religious, aristocratic, lazy, or of no opinion.[46]

Ultimately, all of these descriptions can be traced to two dominant characteristics of the Soviet personality: authoritarianism and insecurity. The theoretical and empirical literature characterize the authoritarian personality in terms which coincide with most popular conceptions of Soviet behavior: submissiveness to authority, rigidity of opinions, concern with toughness and power, generalized hostility, conformance to conventional values, and projection of unconscious emotional impulses.[47]

As Schwartz has observed: "In contrast to the American tradition, where 'power is multiple, fragmented, temporary, limited and comprehensible,' the Soviet people share a 'notion of overarching power that is both absolute and legitimate.'"[48] Similarly, Smith has noted that, "The Russian obeys power, not the law. And if Power is looking the other way, or simply does not notice him, the Russian does what he thinks he can get away with."[49]

Concerning the insecurity of the Soviets, Richard Barnet has pointed to the "national inferiority complex" of the USSR, reflected in shame for her backwardness, fear for her vulnerability to foreign invasion, and self-pity for being bypassed by the main currents of European civilization.[50] This idea has been underscored further by Hedrick Smith:

> The Russians historically are a country with an enormous inferiority complex toward the West—I called it an Avis complex. They're constantly feeling as though they've got to catch up and they've got to be seen as equals and they want to be seen as equals. This creates an enormous dilemma for us, because if you're going to have an arms

agreement or something as important to you as that, you want to be sure that you can trust them, you want to be sure that you're strong enough to cope with any threat that they actually represent. But you have the trouble of trying to gauge what it is they're doing against their intentions. Are they trying to overtake you and surpass you? Or are they merely trying to catch up? And it seems to me we have this constant dilemma of having to be sufficiently powerful, sufficiently firm, and yet at the same time allowing them the national dignity of being seen globally as our equals so that they're no longer driven by this horrible insecurity complex.[51]

The Perceptual Efficacy of US Policy

It generally has come to be recognized that certain personality types are more receptive to particular kinds of messages than other personality types. In the present context, that is to say that if the US is able to diagnose the personality characteristics which dominate Soviet decisionmaking, then it should endeavor to counteract the natural attitudinal propensities of its major adversary by structuring its own behaviors (words and actions) accordingly. Given what we have suggested to be the dominant Soviet characteristics, this means essentially that what emanates from the United States as a reflection of national policy must, from a structural standpoint, appear authoritative, unambiguous, and consistent and reflect clear intent; from a substantive standpoint, it must evince sensitivity to the Soviet need for international recognition and stature, and it must appear nonthreatening yet firm.

In this latter regard, a major dilemma—noted above by Smith—presents itself. On the one hand, it has been argued convincingly by psychologists and anthropologists that the true key to the character of an authoritarian is the fact that he has a closed belief system and therefore changes his beliefs only when authorities to whom he is highly responsive advocate policies or perceptions at variance with his own beliefs.[52] Thus, change-inducing behaviors must be authoritative, irrespective of content.

On the other hand, to accomodate the innate insecurity of the Soviets, one must present an appearance of accepting the USSR as a full and equal partner on the world stage. To most Americans, it is inexplicable that the Soviets should continue to suffer from an inferiority complex; yet, given the Soviets' conception of the world correlation of forces, it seems obvious they have yet to "self-actualize." The critical dilemma, of course, is how at one and the same time to appear both authoritative—in raw power terms meaningful to the Soviets—and accommodative—i.e., not intruding into domains judged by the Soviets to be their inalienable prerogative.

Superficially at least, the only available alternative to some would seem to be to remain intentionally vague, noncommittal, and ambiguous. Uri Ra'anan for one has suggested the American government pursue a policy of "intentional unpredictability" in order to help discourage the USSR from assuming that, because of chronic domestic turmoil, American power on the world scene is becoming increasingly irrelevant. Only by occasional and somewhat unpredictable demonstrations of US determination and strength, he argues, will the Soviet leadership be dissuaded from pursuing a more assertive and more dangerous foreign policy course.[53]

Others have taken a contrary position. The obvious difficulty or weakness of an intentionally ambiguous approach lies in the unwitting misinterpretation of the signals transmitted. This point has been made quite forcefully by Robert Jervis:

> Certain perceptual tendencies increase the chances that the receiver will misinterpret ambiguous signals even if he realizes they are signals rather than noise. It is well-known that people interpret incoming information in the light of their pre-existing views. Furthermore, the greater the ambiguity of the information, the greater the impact of the established belief. There are several implications of this. First, since actors tend to perceive what they expect to perceive, a signal in accord with the receiver's expectations can be quite subtle and still have the desired impact. Indeed, such signals may be perceived even if they are not sent. The other side of this coin is that signals that go against the established view of the perceiver will have to be much clearer before they are noticed, let alone understood. Thus the screen that provides protection for an actor's image while he sends ambiguous signals may at times be too strong for everyone's good.[54]

The question which must be answered is the extent to which the United States, through its words and actions, evinces an adequate understanding of (1) the centrality, stability, and consistency of various Soviet beliefs; (2) the fundamental dominance of particular personality characteristics in framing such beliefs; and (3) the appropriate themes necessary to counteract those traits and produce lasting attitude change. In other words, is what we say and do—viewed in consonance—structurally authoritative, unambiguous, and consistent, while also being substantively accommodating and nonthreatening, yet firm? An historical example will suffice to provide an anecdotal answer to this question.

The original impetus for this inquiry, and the retrospective aspect implied in the title of the article, was an earlier investigation by the author to reconstruct the policy utterances emanating from the United

States during a recent historical period to determine what picture we might have been presenting to the outside world, particularly to the Soviet Union. It is not the intent here to recreate in detail the results of that analysis. Rather, a few examples will suffice to demonstrate the extent of US perceptual sensitivity (or insensitivity) during the period of interest.

The year 1967 was selected for the earlier inquiry because it marked the midpoint, as well as being probably the busiest year, in a period of considerable activity between the US and the USSR. Among other things, 1966 saw France withdraw from NATO, the first official US cognizance of a Soviet-deployed antiballistic missile defense system, and statements at the 23rd CPSU Congress concerning Soviet intentions relative to the deployment of mobile land-based strategic missiles, strategic bombers, and missile-launching submarines. 1968, in turn, marked the occurrence of the Pueblo crisis, the Tet Offensive, and the signing by the US, Britain, the Soviet Union, and 58 nonnuclear nations of the Nuclear Non-Proliferation Treaty. More importantly, in August of that year, the USSR and forces from four of its Warsaw Pact allies invaded Czechoslovakia.

During 1967 alone, the following constituted but a few of the many events which occurred:

- The six-day Arab Israeli War in the Mideast.
- The Chinese Cultural Revolution.
- The Chinese detonation of its first H-bomb at Lop Nor.
- The signing by the US, the USSR, and 60 other nations of a treaty to limit military activities in outer space.
- The summit meeting between President Johnson and Premier Kosygin in Glassboro, New Jersey, to discuss the Mideast, Vietnam, and the arms race.
- The 50th Anniversary of the Russian Revolution.
- The Soviet display of numerous new weapons systems, including the SS–9 ICBM, the GOLF–II diesel-powered submarine armed with the SS–N–5 SLBM, and the YANKEE–I nuclear-powered submarine carrying the SS–N–6 SLBM.
- The announcement by the US of plans to withdraw up to 38,000 troops and almost 100 planes from West Germany in 1968.
- The announcement by the US of a troop buildup in Vietnam, bringing the total to approximately 525,000.
- Major racial riots throughout the US, particularly in Newark and Detroit.

A brief look at the official statements emanating from the United States during that year paints a complex, if not confusing, picture. President Johnson, for example, in his State of the Union message, noted on the one hand that "our objective is not to continue the cold war but to end it," and that the USSR and the US share a "common interest in arms control and in disarmament." On the other hand, he indicated that "we have chosen to fight a limited war in Viet Nam [sic] in an attempt to prevent a larger war" and concluded by noting that "our test is not whether we shrink from our country's cause when the dangers to us are obvious and close at hand, but rather, whether we carry on when they seem obscure and distant—and some think it is safe to lay down our burdens."

At least twice during the year, Johnson tied our involvement in Vietnam to broader strategic concerns. In a 15 March address to a joint session of the Tennessee state legislature, he described as one of our basic objectives in Vietnam "a concrete demonstration that aggression across international frontiers or demarcation lines is no longer an acceptable means of political change." He followed this in a 17 November press conference by describing our threefold goals in Vietnam: to protect the security of the United States, to resist aggression, and "to do whatever it is necessary to do to see that the aggressor does not succeed."

In his speech before the Tennessee legislature, Johnson underscored what surfaced during the course of the year as the underlying theme of our foreign policy—concurrent resolve and restraint:

> We are succeeding, after a few short years, in developing an integrated and highly expert attack on the problem of arms control and disarmament. Our security has two faces—strength and restraint; arms and arms control . . . .

He reinforced our position vis-a-vis the Soviet Union in June before the National Foreign Policy Conference for Educators:

> We have tried hard to enlarge, and we think we have made great progress in improving the arena of common action with the Soviet Union.
>
> Our purpose is to narrow our differences where they can be narrowed and thus to help secure peace in the world for future generations. It will be a long slow task, we realize. There will be setbacks and discouragements. But it is, we think, the only rational policy for them and for us.

Reinforcing this somewhat dichotomous picture, Secretary of State Rusk on the one hand called repeatedly during the year for the creation of "a durable peace." At the same time, Vice President Humphrey was calling for the reunification of Germany and "matching deterrence with peaceful engagement." In a 5 March address, he remarked: "It is our hope that the Iron Curtain may one day, too, lie in ruins, its remnants a symbol of a time mercifully ended."

Secretary of Defense McNamara was, if not the Administration's foremost spokesman on overall foreign policy, at least its major source of key strategic and defense pronouncements. In his Fiscal Year 1968 posture statement before the Senate Armed Services and Appropriations Committees, McNamara outlined the key elements of US strategic doctrine:

- [Assured Destruction]: To deter deliberate nuclear attack upon the United States and its allies by maintaining, continuously, a highly reliable ability to inflict an unacceptable degree of damage upon any single aggressor, or combination of aggressors, at any time during the course of a strategic nuclear exchange, even after absorbing a surprise first strike.
- [Damage Limitation]: In the event such a war nevertheless occurred, to limit damage to our population and industrial capacity.

Without doubt, the single most significant policy statement emanating from the Johnson Administration in 1967 was McNamara's September 18 address before the annual convention of the United Press International editors and publishers in San Francisco. He began by suggesting the gravest problem the Secretary of Defense must face is the planning, preparation, and policy governing the possibility of thermonuclear war:

If, then, man is to have a future at all, it will have to be a future overshadowed with the permanent possibility of a thermonuclear holocaust.

About that fact, we are no longer free. Our freedom in this question consists rather in facing the matter rationally and realistically and discussing actions to minimize the danger . . . .

. . . We must understand the differences between actions which increase its risk, those which reduce it, and those which, while costly, have little influence one way or another.

In that same speech, though he subsequently minimized its importance, McNamara noted the US strategic superiority over the USSR:

. . . The most meaningful and realistic measurement of nuclear capability is neither gross megatonnage nor the number of available missile launchers, but rather the number of separate warheads that are capable of being delivered with accuracy on individual high-priority targets with sufficient power to destroy them . . . . The United States currently possesses a superiority over the Soviet Union of at least three or four to one.

Finally, in what must have appeared to be the most confusing and contradictory decision of the year, McNamara, who time and again had argued against the utility of an antiballistic missile system as "a profitless waste of resources," announced the decision to deploy a limited "Chinese-oriented" ABM system in the United States.

In the final analysis, it must be said that the official picture portrayed during the particular period analyzed—1967—was at best confusing and at times even contradictory. One rationally and uncompromisingly could have interpreted the signals provided in virtually whatever manner served to fill his needs and preconceptions. Given the Soviet mistrust, if not fear, of foreigners, his defensive-mindedness, his view of the media as an instrument of the State, and the ideological strictures imposed on the Soviet policymaking machinery by Marxist–Leninist thought, it is not hard to understand how our activities during 1967 might have been construed as either expansionist and inflammatory at one extreme to completely confused and impotent at the other. One can only speculate on the effect our "policy" may have had on subsequent Soviet behavior.

It would be fruitless to attempt to establish a rigorous causal link between US policy statements and subsequent Soviet behavior, even though some of the action-reaction relationship seems plausible. The point here, rather, is to suggest that US policy abroad has evidenced a general pattern of perceptual insensitivity over the years, manifested in inconsistent, mixed, and even contradictory signals. Given the continuity in both Soviet ruling personalities and US policy processes, the author does not hesitate to employ a 13–year-old analogue to support the argument. Others have spoken more directly to the confusing nature of our recent foreign policy.[55]

It remains for those who formulate US policy to acknowledge the impact our words and actions have on the outside world. Virtually everything we say and do constitutes a message of some significance to others. The meaning imputed to these messages is influenced materially by the images and beliefs, and, in turn, by the particular personality traits of its recipients.

Placed in the context of the US-Soviet relationship, therefore, it seems hardly adequate to accept the advice once offered by George Kennan:

> If we keep our distance and concede to them the privelege of their privacy and their differentness, as we would like to have it conceded to us, being prepared to reserve judgment on that which we cannot understand and which need not concern us, I see no reason why a satisfactory relationship should not be established.

The Soviets, no less than others, are subject to carefully orchestrated themes and symbols which reflect the peculiarities of their "collective personality" and thus, in the ultimate, are designed to alter established images and beliefs. To fail to recognize this is to disadvantage ourselves in the global balance of power. It is a lesson not lost on the Soviets. It should not be lost on us.

Notes

1. US Senate, Committee on Foreign Relations, *Perceptions: Relations Between the United States and the Soviet Union* (Washington: Government Printing Office, 1978), p. 303.
2. Jack Bilmes and Stephen T. Boggs, "Language and Communication: The Foundations of Culture," in A. Marsella, R. Tharp, and T. Ciborowski, eds., *Perspectives on Cross-Cultural Psychology* (New York: Academic Press, 1979), pp. 47–76.
3. Ibid.
4. Thomas J. Ciborowski, "Cross-Cultural Aspects of Cognitive Functioning: Culture Knowledge," in Marsella, Tharp, and Ciborowski, pp. 106–226.
5. Richard J. Barnet, *The Giants: Russia and America* (New York: Simon and Schuster, 1977), p. 74.
6. Quoted in Morton Schwartz, *Soviet Perceptions of the United States* (Berkeley: University of California Press, 1978), p. 6.
7. Alexander Dallin, "Bias and Blunder in American Studies on the USSR," *Slavic Review,* September 1973.
8. Paul Hollander, *Soviet and American Society: A Comparison,* 2nd ed. (Chicago: University of Chicago Press, 1978). p. xxv.
9. Robert C. North, Ole R. Holsti, M. George Zaninovich, and Dina A. Zinnes, *Content Analysis: A Handbook with Applications for the Study of International Crisis* (Evanston, Illinois: Northwestern University Press, 1963), pp. 9–10.
10. Kenneth E. Boulding, "National Images and International Systems," *Journal of Conflict Resolution,* June 1959, pp. 120–131.
11. Ole R. Holsti, "The Belief System and National Images: A Case Study," *Journal of Conflict Resolution,* Vol. 6, No. 3 (1962), pp. 244–252.
12. Ibid. Converse has defined a belief system as "a configuration of ideas and attitudes in which the elements are bound together by some form of constraint or functional interdependence." Philip E. Converse, "The Nature of Belief Systems in Mass Publics," in David Epter, ed., *Ideology and Discontent* (New York: Free Press, 1964), pp. 206–261.
13. The operational code construct originally was put forth by Nathan Leites, *The Operational Code of the Politburo* (New York: McGraw-Hill, 1951).
14. Alexander L. George, et al., "Toward a More Soundly Based Foreign Policy: Making Better Use of Information," *Report of the Commission on the Organization of the Conduct of Foreign Policy,* Appendix D, Vol. 2, 1975, p. 2.
15. Andrew R. Davidson, "Culture and Attitude Structure and Change," in Marsella, Tharp, and Ciborowski, pp. 137–157.
16. Robert Jervis, *Perception and Misperception in International Politics* (Princeton: Princeton University Press, 1976), pp. 409–410.
17. Boulding, op. cit.
18. F. Kenneth Berrien, "Familiarity, Mirror Imaging and Social Desirability in Sterotypes: Japanese Versus American," *International Journal of Psychology,* No. 4, 1969, pp. 207–215.
19. Urie Bronfenbrenner, "The Mirror Image in Soviet-American Relations," *Journal of Social Issues,* Vol. 27, No. 1 (1971), p. 46–51.
20. Stephen P. Gibert, *Soviet Images of America* (New York: Crane, Russak, 1977), pp. 19–21.
21. Schwartz, op. cit., pp. 33–34.
22. Gibert, op. cit., pp. 5–7.

23. Kurt Lewin, *Field Theory in Social Science* (New York: Harper and Row, 1951).

24. Daniel Heradstveit, *The Arab–Israeli Conflict: Psychological Obstacles to Peace* (Oslo: Universitetskorlaget, 1979), pp. 17–19.

25. Leon Festinger, *A Theory of Cognitive Dissonance* (Stanford: Stanford University Press, 1957).

26. B. B. Wolman, ed., *International Encyclopedia of Psychiatry, Psychology, Psychonalysis, and Neurology,* Vol. 8 (New York: Van Nostrand–Reinhold, 1977), pp. 339–341.

27. M. Margaret Conway and Frank F. Feigert, *Political Analysis: An Introduction,* 2nd ed. (Boston: Allyn and Bacon, 1976), p. 147.

28. B. B. Wolman, op. cit.

29. Juris G. Draguns, "Culture and Personality," in Marsella, Tharp, and Ciborowski, pp. 179–207.

30. Quoted in E. Lowell Kelly, *Assessment of Human Characteristics* (Belmont, California: Brooks/Cole, 1961), p. 374.

31. Ibid., p. 16.

32. Gordon W. Allport, *Pattern and Growth in Personality* (New York: Holt, Reinhart, and Winston, 1961), p. 374.

33. Ibid., p. 348.

34. Cited in Holsti, op. cit.

35. Anthony F. C. Wallace, *Culture and Personality,* 2nd ed. (New York: Random House, 1970), p. 149.

36. Draguns, op. cit.

37. Hans J. Morgenthau, *Politics Among Nations,* 5th ed. (New York: Alfred A. Knopf, 1973), pp. 129–132.

38. Edward N. Luttwak, *The Missing Dimension of US Defense Policy: Force, Perceptions and Power* (Alexandria, Virginia: Essex Corporation, 1976), pp. 27–28.

39. Both cited in Frederic Fleron, "Representation of Career Types in the Soviet Political Leadership," in R. B. Farrell, ed., *Political Leadership in Eastern Europe and the Soviet Union* (Chicago: Aldine, 1970), pp. 108–139.

40. Both Nitze and Conquest are cited in William B. Husband, "Soviet Perceptions of U.S. 'Positions-of-Strength' Diplomacy in the 1970s," *World Politics,* July 1979, p. 495.

41. Schwartz, op. cit., p. 164.

42. Hedrick Smith, *The Russians* (New York: Ballantine Books, 1977), p. 64.

43. Gibert, op. cit., p. 8.

44. William M. Jones, *Modeling Soviet Behavior and Deterrence: A Procedure for Evaluating Military Forces,* Report R–1065–PR (Santa Monica: The Rand Corporation, 1974), pp. 36–37.

45. Morgenthau, op. cit., pp. 133–134.

46. US Senate, Committee on Foreign Relations, *Perceptions: Relations Between the United States and the Soviet Union* (Washington: Government Printing Office, 1978), p. 132.

47. T. W. Adorno, Else Frenkel–Brunswik, Daniel J. Levinson, and R. Nevitt Stanford, *The Authoritarian Personality,* Part I (New York: Science Editions, 1964), p. 228.

48. Schwartz, op. cit., p. 52.

49. Smith, op. cit., p. 335.

50. Barnet, op. cit., p. 86.

51. Hedrick Smith, Interview with William F. Buckley, "Firing Line", Public Broadcasting System, 19 January 1976.

52. Conway and Feigert, op. cit., p. 119.

53. Uri Ra'anan, *The Changing American–Soviet Strategic Balance: Some Political Implications,* Memorandum prepared for the Subcommittee on National Security and International Operations, US Senate (Washington: Government Printing Office, 1972), p. 12.

54. Robert Jervis, *The Logic of Images in International Relations* (Princeton: Princeton University Press, 1970), p. 132.

55. See Charles William Maynes and Richard H. Ullman, "Ten Years of Foreign Policy," *Foreign Policy*, Fall 1980, pp. 3–32.

Deterrence vs Warfighting:
The View from Moscow

G. Paul Holman*

Moscow draws an indelible line between deterrence and warfighting: deterrence, for the Soviets, is primarily the province of the diplomat, the disinformer, and the propagandist,[1] while warfighting is now and always has been the primary pursuit, preoccupation, and passion of the Soviet military strategist. This distinction is deeply rooted in the very nature of the Soviet system and clearly reflected in the voluminous Soviet literature on modern warfare. The impact of this warfighting orientation is both heavy and omnipresent, with the result that it is most unlikely to vanish or even to lighten significantly over the 1980s.

American observers of Soviet affairs have been remarkably slow to appreciate Moscow's warfighting preferences. Although individual scholars and some research institutes have worked hard to correct this ignorance, Soviet military doctrine remains *terra incognita* for a surprising number of scholars, journalists, and analysts.[2]

As a result, the Soviet concept of strategic superiority often has been dismissed on the grounds that it concerns an allegedly elusive question. By the same logic, Soviet statements about victory in nuclear war regularly have been overlooked or excluded from consideration because they are supposedly vague, incomplete, or contradictory. The clear implication of such judgments is that Soviet military doctrine warrants no serious study. At most, the adherents of this persuasion seem to regard Soviet military doctrine as an expression of Soviet "bureaucratic politics" which owes its stridency to memories of suffering in World War II and to the Soviet predilection for morale-building propaganda.

No one would deny that Soviet military doctrine bears the scars of the Muscovite school of politics. Still less would anyone scoff at the impact of Russia's many wars or at the Communist Party's continuing need to preach and proselytize among the dubiously motivated masses.

Even so, such cultural and political factors should not distract Western attention from the single most important fact about Soviet military doctrine: its striking congruence with Soviet force posture. Indeed, on virtually every major issue, the written expression of Soviet strategic objectives has preceded its transmutation into physical reality by a number of years, and sometimes by decades.

*This article originally was prepared for and presented at the Assistant Chief of Staff/Intelligence, USAF–sponsored conference, "The Soviet Union: What Lies Ahead?" in September 1980, and later reprinted in *Air Force Magazine,* Vol. 64, No. 3 (March 1981).

Perhaps the best way to study Soviet strategy is to find an appropriate historical context in which procurement decisions could be evaluated in the light of their social background, technological limitations, and equivalents in rival countries. Hence, the title of this article, which examines Soviet nuclear strategy from the perspective of a dichotomy between two extreme goals: deterrence and warfighting. These two objecives may be hard or even impossible to distinguish at any given time; when they are pursued over decades, their impact on force posture and national behavior is starkly different.[3]

Like all other nuclear powers, the USSR began with nothing more than a very modest capability for deterrence. But, unlike all its rivals—and at the cost of much bluffing in the 1950s and early 1960s—Moscow has proclaimed a bold, warfighting strategy from the earliest days of the nuclear era down to the present. Even that sweeping generalization somewhat understates Soviet strategic consistency, inasmuch as the origins of the Soviet preference for warfighting lie much further back than the detonation of the first Soviet atomic bomb in 1949.

No single speech in all of Russian history better illustrates Moscow's view of the importance of military power than Stalin's defense of his brutal but effective program for industrialization in 1931:

> To slacken the tempo would mean falling behind. And those who fall behind get beaten. But we do not want to be beaten. No, we refuse to be beaten! One feature of the history of old Russia was the continual beatings she suffered because of her backwardness. She was beaten by the Mongol khans. She was beaten by the Turkish beys. She was beaten by the Swedish feudal lords. She was beaten by the Polish and Lithuanian gentry. She was beaten by the British and French capitalists. She was beaten by the Japanese barons. All beat her—because of her backwardness, because of her military backwardness, cultural backwardness, political backwardness, industrial backwardness, agricultural backwardness . . . .
>
> We are fifty or a hundred years behind the advanced countries. We must make good this distance in ten years. Either we do it, or we shall go under.[4]

This speech should correct some misapprehensions about Soviet national strategy. Above all, the Soviet military buildup was not initiated by Brezhnev as a political "payoff" to the General Staff in exchange for their helping him overthrow Khrushchev in 1964. On the contrary, the current strength of the Soviet Armed Forces is the direct and inevitable result of the socio-economic priorities which Lenin sketched and Stalin built irrevocably into the Soviet system. Notwithstanding such major events as the post-World War II demobilization, Khrushchev's reforms, and Brezhnev's erratic displays of concern for the Soviet consumer, little has changed with regard to the Soviet Armed Forces. Politically subservient to the Communist Party but physically fattened by the best materiel that Soviet industry can produce, the Soviet Armed Forces today are precisely what Stalin would have wanted them to be.

Stalin's speech of 1931 also sheds some light on whether we should characterize Soviet military doctrine and strategy as offensive or defensive. Such a morbidly fearful and hostile view of the world is not "defensive" in the usual sense (which conjures up images of the Swiss, Austrian, or Japanese attitudes toward current military problems). Nor does "offensive" quite capture the Soviet mentality, if such a characterization means that the Soviets are simply power-hungry militarists with a taste for occasional conquests of new land.

Abnormal psychology probably contains the richest lexicon for categorizing the Soviet view of military power. Recent travelers to Moscow describe an *obsession* with China which seems largely to have replaced the traditional preoccupation with the alleged threat from Germany. Indeed, Soviet officials are now explaining their "defense" of Afghanistan as a necessary response to the evil acts of Chinese spies, Pakistani guerrillas, and Egyptian saboteurs, all egged on by sensation-hunting American journalists and the CIA. Some of these claims may be dismissed as conscious lies by people who know better but need a propaganda facade to justify their invasion of a supposed ally. However, when ordinary Soviet citizens express such allegations with apparent sincerity—not to mention their general hostility toward foreigners—most Westerners sooner or later begin to decide that the Russian people suffer from *paranoia*. The definition of this much overused term in *Webster's New Collegiate Dictionary* is directly applicable to the Russian sickness: "A chronic mental disorder characterized by systematized delusions of persecution and of one's own greatness, sometimes with hallucinations." The result of all this, of course, is a *compulsion* to acquire military power, even at an economic cost which other countries would deem irrational.

Yet, in some respects, the Soviet attitude toward military power is intensely rational, coldly calculating, and even wise. As an old, continental power with historical enemies on all fronts, Russia has good reason to appreciate the direct link between a powerful armed force and an effective foreign policy. As a country which has often been beaten, Russia also knows the wisdom of overpreparing for combat—especially when neither the tactical conditions nor the level of opposition can be determined precisely in advance.

It is also likely that Moscow has a deep appreciation for the "rationality of irrationality" under certain international conditions. Soviet strategists seem to believe that Khrushchev's "rocket rattling" of 1956 frustrated the Anglo–French–Israeli attack on Egypt and disrupted the NATO alliance, even though the USSR was far from ready to fight World War III at the time.[5] The Soviets also have criticized the alleged "irrationality" of American strategic threats during the Cuban Missile Crisis of 1962 and the Middle East Crisis of 1973, but they know perfectly well that in both cases a display of American strategic readiness altered Soviet foreign policy quite drastically.[6]

The Soviets, of course, attribute irrationality solely to their opponents, whose behavior stands in supposedly stark contrast to their own wise use of military power. Explicit Soviet discussions of this theme increased noticeably in the early 1970s, both before and after the 24th CPSU Congress in 1971. The chief of the Main Political Admininstration took pride in Moscow's growing ability to alter imperialist foreign policy through its military strength:

> Thus, under modern conditions, the defense of socialism is closely associated with furnishing comprehensive assistance to national liberation movements and to young states struggling to gain their freedom and independence. Today, it is obvious that the revolutionary achievements of our Soviet nation and also those of other nations would be under threat were it not for the tremendous military power of the Soviet Union and other socialist bloc countries. If at times the imperialists show fear in carrying out particular actions, it is because they know the risk involved.[7]

However one balances the themes of rationality and irrationality in Moscow's attitude toward military power, there should be no doubt that the Soviet preference for warfighting influences every aspect of their strategy, force posture, and national economy. Nowhere is this attitude more clear than in the Soviet response to Western notions of deterrence. The word itself is rare in Soviet parlance and used primarily to describe foreign, "bourgeois" military doctrine.

Two different Russian words are used to translate "deterrence." *Sderzhivaniye*—meaning a halt, diminution, or restraint imposed upon forward movement—is usually applied to American policies of the Truman era. For the more recent past, the Soviets tend to prefer *ustrasheniye,* which connotes the halting of an opponent's behavior through the imposition of fear, fright, or terror. The Soviets are well aware that neither word quite captures what Americans mean by "deterrence." According to one article by a Soviet military scholar: "The English word 'deterrence' has two basic meanings: *ustrasheniye* and *sderzhivaniye.* 'Ustrasheniye' conveys more precisely the essence of the new strategy [of 'realistic deterrence']."[8]

Never have the Soviets subscribed to the Western concept of deterrence. Even in its most general sense, they use the word only rarely to characterize their own strategy.[9] More importantly, both doctrinal specialists and "Americanologists" have rejected deterrence as the basis for Soviet strategy. Georgiy Arbatov—Director of Moscow's Institute of the USA and Canada—was in total agreement with the Soviet General Staff when he wrote in 1974 that "the concept of deterrence itself cannot be defended—it is a concept of 'peace built on terror' which will always be an unstable and a bad peace."[10]

In part, the Soviets seem to have rejected a strategy of deterrence because of their own conservatism and reluctance to abandon the Stalinist emphasis on the open-ended acquisition of military power. They also seem to suspect that acceptance of the Western concept of deterrence would in some sense entrust Soviet national security to another and hostile power rather than exclusively to their own armed forces. But most importantly, by their own testimony, they disapprove of deterrence because it was propounded by their class enemies who allegedly sought military and political advantages unobtainable by other means.[11]

Colonel Belyy and his collective of authors summarized their view of Western military doctrine and strategy quite pungently in *Marxism–Leninism on War and Army:*

> Bourgeois sociological and philosophical thought is unable to resolve so complex a problem as the essence of the nuclear war. It distorts the essence of nuclear war in many ways and consequently distorts also its content and character.[12]

The Soviets perceive two extremes in American attitudes toward nuclear war: some Americans exaggerate the destructiveness of nuclear war and verge on pacifism; others hope to use nuclear weapons for their own, reactionary political purposes. In both cases, however, American rhetoric about deterrence allegedly masks the reality of unchanging imperialist aggression. According to the *Soviet Military Encyclopedia,* "The trend toward expanding the scope of local wars and aggravating the conflict in them increases the danger that a local war will escalate into a world war."[13]

Not to worry, however, for the *Encyclopedia* hastens to point out the historical solution to the problem of imperialist irrationality and aggression: "With the simultaneous growth of the economic and military might of the socialist community, there is an increased possibility of preventing local wars from escalating into a clash on a worldwide scale."[14] Although phrased in a propagandistic way, this allusion to the "peaceful" nature of socialist military power is of more than minor interest.

The fact that the Soviets have rejected a strategy of deterrence in favor of a strategy of warfighting does not necessarily mean the Soviets have no concept whatever of deterrence. On the contrary, they do have such a concept, but it differs radically from the American notion of deterrence.[15] To the Soviets, preventing war between the superpowers and managing the level of conflict in the Third World are very good things indeed, as long as two conditions are fulfilled: the trend of Third World conflict outcomes favors the USSR,[16] and the USSR continues its progress toward a superior warfighting and warwinning capability against the United States and all other possible rivals.[17]

When they review the evidence of the 1970s, Soviet strategists like what they see. That decade began with the official recognition of US-Soviet superpower equality at SALT I and then saw the most impressive succession of victories that Soviet proxies have ever won on Third World battlefields. Such displays of the physical and political utility of Soviet arms may explain why US and Soviet military doctrines diverged no less sharply than their capabilities throughout the past decade. Having rejected a strategy of deterrence, the Soviets quite inevitably favored a steadily rising military budget and constant, evolutionary improvements in their armed forces. Moscow denied itself no known opportunities to improve its position in the strategic balance while at the same time experimenting with increasingly ambitious acts of intervention in regional wars.

In force posture no less than political behavior, the strategies of deterrence and warfighting favor very different things. There was a time—perhaps a decade ago, at most—when it was still possible to see the differences between US and Soviet force postures as the result of Moscow's more primitive technology.[18] Surely those days are over. What explanation other than a strong strategic preference for warfighting do we have when we review such differences as the greater Soviet interest in high throwweight and megatonnage; the greater fraction of the Soviet arsenal to be delivered by ICBM (more vulnerable intrinsically, but the first-strike and warfighting system *par excellence*) and the lesser fraction allocated to SLBMs and bombers; the greater Soviet concern for passive and active defense; the keener Soviet interest in chemical and bacteriological warfare; the far more military orientation of the Soviet space program; the far higher Soviet priority on obtaining antisatellite capabilities; the vastly larger proportion of the Soviet gross national product allocated to defense; and a host of others?

The differences between deterrence and warfighting also pervade Soviet military doctrine. Warfighting maintains, stresses, and constantly tests the distinction between its goal—victory in war—and its means—military force. To obtain the former, the Soviets endlessly review their thinking about the latter. This attitude may explain why the tightly controlled and censored Soviet press periodically allows Soviet officers to air their differences of opinion over contested issues.[19] More importantly, the Soviets' preference for warfighting is also reflected in their concern for combat realism in most of their exercises; for the integration of civil defense into their overall doctrine for nuclear war; for their retention of a conscript army and a highly militarized society; and for the very considerable official prestige they bestow upon military practitioners and theorists.

698

From a strictly theoretical perspective, nothing symbolizes more clearly the difference between deterrence and warfighting than the Soviet description of "strategic missions." To most Americans, "strategic" equates to "intercontinental," both because of our geographic location and because of our implicit assumption that transoceanic attack is the only mission which really matters in central nuclear war.

To the Soviets—schooled in the Clausewitzian concept of war and surrounded by potential enemies on all fronts—"strategic missions" consist of all those diverse actions which the High Command must take to gain victory. The list is long. Marshal Sokolovskiy summarized these missions at great length in *Military Strategy*, which still stands as the single most important Soviet book on the subject.[20] The last edition of Sokolovskiy's book is now over a decade old, but more recent, albeit less prestigious, authors have not deviated from his views.

Colonel M. P. Skirdo, a former professor at two senior Soviet staff colleges, has outlined the Soviet concept of nuclear war quite concisely in *The People, the Army, the Commander.* He asserted that attainment of victory would require the destruction of enemy means of nuclear attack; disorganization of his rear areas; repelling attacks on one's own country and one's allies by enemy air, airborne, amphibious, and ground forces; safeguarding the homeland against enemy subversive activities; and using combined arms operations to rout the enemy's armed forces, crush his resistance, and seize control of strategically important regions, staging bases, and military, political, and economic centers.[21]

For any military planner, Skirdo's list of missions would seem fairly ambitious. But he left his readers in no doubt about the Soviet ability to win a nuclear war. Indeed, he claimed the Soviets would gain victory thanks to their superiority in a large number of measures of strategic power, ranging from the size of their national territory to their "indisputable advantage in the creation of the military-economic and scientific-technical potential necessary for victory in a modern war."[22]

It must be admitted, however, that neither Sokolovskiy, Skirdo, nor any other official spokesman has given very satisfactory answers to some political questions about war which many Westerners regard as critical. For example, what potential gains would be so important to the Soviets as to justify risking their national existence by fighting World War III? Would the Soviets attack the continental United States with airborne, amphibious, or ground troops? How would the Soviets provide for intrawar negotiations and bargaining, if at all? What would be the postwar military and political situations of their supposedly defeated rivals?

Soviet attention to such questions as these is non-existent at worst and propagandistic at best. War initiation--to which American arms control specialists have devoted astronomical numbers of analyses— interests them only as an aspect of "imperialist" foreign policy. As for

480-900 0 - 85 - 23

themselves, the Soviets assert they would never dream of starting a nuclear war, thanks to the very nature of their way of life. Soviet spokesmen are equally unready to discuss war termination save to note rather piously that, in the aftermath of a nuclear war, the peoples of the capitalist countries will carry out their own revolutions against the governments which led them into a disastrous and losing war.[23]

The Soviets do not seem to regard their evasion of such abstruse topics as a weakness in their military doctrine. They do provide in general terms for any possible mission which might be assigned to their armed forces, but they do not discuss subjects which might convey either intelligence information or political ammunition to their anti-Soviet rivals (or which simply may be unanswerable at the present time). In any event, it is apparently the business of spokesmen for the Soviet Armed Forces to plan for fighting and winning wars, while leaving to their political masters such questions as when, why, and how to begin or end their wars.[24]

Regardless of how one weighs the subtler points of Soviet military doctrine, a warfighting strategy seems historically inevitable for the USSR. It has many advantages: supporting the Soviet claim to super-power equality with the US, intimidating any possible revanchists or irredentists in China or Germany, winning global clients because of the spreading impression in many minds that the USSR can be counted on to provide more than a little help to its friends, maintaining domestic cohesion through a constant atmosphere of military danger, and keeping large military forces ready for use against unruly allies such as Poland.

Without a warfighting strategy, Moscow would rule a far smaller empire than it does. Its control over the Soviet and East European masses would be less secure, and its foreign policy in every corner of the globe would become less credible. To the extent that a strategy of deterrence would reverse some or all of these gains, it hardly seems surprising for men schooled in the Soviet tradition to cling tenaciously to their preference for warfighting.

On their southern border, the Soviets are now fighting a war which may serve as a test case for Soviet military doctrine and strategy. If the Soviets are beaten and withdraw ignominiously, Moscow's foreign policy will be badly discredited. The seeds may be sown for incremental changes in Soviet military strategy, although their effect on Soviet thinking about central nuclear war would probably be modest. But if the Soviets persevere and prevail, the blood they shed in Afghanistan will only increase global respect for Soviet decisiveness and thus reinforce Moscow's satisfaction with its military strategy.

As for Poland, its future social and economic situation may still be in doubt but not its vulnerability to Soviet armed attack. Indeed, it seems likely that the major reason why the Polish workers refrained from anti-Soviet sloganeering and anticommunist violence for so long was their intimate understanding of the Soviet proclivity for coercion. Whatever the level of violence which may be necessary to restore Polish orthodoxy, this most recent demonstration of East European instability only will exacerbate Moscow's distrust of all its neighbors.

From the American perspective, unrest in Afghanistan and Poland may appear supremely irrelevant to nuclear strategy. Not so for the Soviets. They claim to see class warfare *on their borders* which threatens Soviet interests, jeopardizes the security of other communist parties, calls Soviet decisiveness into question, and threatens to impact very unpleasantly on Moscow's control of its own masses, both Russian and (more poignantly) non-Russian.[25]

These are matters which cut to the very heart of the Soviet political system. When combined with what Moscow has described for the past several years as "intensified anti-Soviet tendencies" in America, the only possible result will be to strengthen still further Moscow's oldest and darkest fears. Given their distrust of large numbers of their own people and their supposed "allies," the Soviets will be less likely than ever before to model their nuclear strategy upon that of their most serious rival. The basis of their objection will not be deterrence's general objective of avoiding war—a goal which they have good reason to share—but rather the specific association of deterrence with roughly equal levels of destructive power on both sides. As retired Army Colonel D. M. Proyektor has observed:

> If one's goal . . . is to establish genuine peace and a lasting security system, one cannot recognize NATO's concept as constructive, for it counts upon armed strength, upon the 'deterrence' doctrine, according to which the threat of mutual destruction is the only way to ensure peace. Nevertheless, Western policy still attaches the utmost importance to the strength aspect.[26]

Over the coming decade, the Soviets will probably find increasing reason to agree with the comment of retired Army Colonel V. M. Kulish about the importance of military power in general and of strategic superiority in particular:

> . . . it must be borne in mind that even a relatively small and brief superiority by the United States over the Soviet Union in the development of certain "old" or "new" types and systems of armaments would increase significantly the strategic effectiveness of American military force, exert a destabilizing influence on the international-political situation throughout the entire world, and present extremely unfavorable consequences for the cause of peace and socialism. In such a case, the USA would be expected to intensify its aggression, employ military blackmail as a means for achieving its foreign policy on a more extensive scale, and thus

701

aggravate international tension on the whole.[27]

It remains to be seen whether the Soviets will enjoy a "relatively small and brief superiority" during the 1980s, let alone what impact this would have on their own international behavior. With or without such an advantage, however, deterrence seems likely to remain in the 1980s what it has always been for the Soviets—an alien strategy, wholly inadequate as the basis for their military doctrine and force posture. Warfighting will remain Moscow's nuclear strategy, and other nations will have to plan accordingly.

Notes

1. Over the past decade, there has been a significant increase in the quality of Soviet diplomacy, disinformation, and propaganda. For some examples—which use the rhethoric of deterrence to influence Western audiences—see Anthony Austin, "Moscow Expert says US Errs on Soviet War Aims," *New York Times,* 25 August 1980, p. 2 (summary of an interview with retired Lieutenant General Mikhail A. Mil'shteyn, Director of the Political-Military Department of Moscow's Institute of the United States of America and Canada); Radomir Bogdanov and Lev Semeyko, "Soviet Military Might: A Soviet View," *Fortune,* 26 February 1979, pp. 46–52; and the several statements to the American organization "Physicians for Social Responsibility" by Soviet Ambassador to the United States Anatoliy Dobrynin, President Leonid I. Brezhnev, and Academician Georgiy A. Arbatov (Director of the Institute of the United States of America and Canada), *Washington Post,* 23 March 1980, *Pravda,* 23 March 1981, and Radio Moscow, "International Observers Roundtable," Domestic Service in Russian, 29 March 1981.
2. Richard Pipes has probably done more than anyone else to correct this problem. No single article on Soviet strategy in the past three decades has evoked more commentary, praise, and rebuttal than his, "Why the Soviet Union Thinks it Could Fight and Win a Nuclear War," *Commentary,* Vol. 64, No. 1 (July 1977), pp. 21–34.
3. Surprisingly few Western scholars have taken this approach. For one who did—and whose conclusions have largely stood the test of time—see Carl G. Jacobsen, "Deterrence or War-fighting?: The Soviet Case; Soviet Military Posture, and its Relevance to Soviet Concepts of Strategy," *Canadian–American Slavic Studies,* Vol. 9, No. 1 (Spring 1975), pp. 18–29.
4. J. V. Stalin, "The Tasks of Business Executives. Speech Delivered at the First All–Union Conference of Leading Personnel of Socialist Industry, February 4, 1931," *J. V. Stalin. Works* (Moscow: Foreign Language Publishing House, 1952–1955), Vol. 13, pp. 40–41.
5. As Khrushchev said later, ". . . everybody knows that much of the credit for ending the war in Egypt goes to the Soviet Union." *Pravda,* 14 January 1957.
6. For a demonstration that urbane and well-documented studies of American defense policy have become an Arbatov family tradition, see Aleksey Georgiyevich Arbatov's discussion of the 1962 and 1973 crises in *Bezopasnost' v yadernyy vek i politika Vashingtona* [Security in the Nuclear Era and Washington's Policy] (Moscow: Izdatel'stvo politicheskoy literatury, 1980), pp. 37–47 and 50–157.
7. A. A. Yepishev, *Sovetskiy patriot* [Soviet Patriot], 9 June 1971.
8. N. Nikitin, "Evolyutsiya voyennoy doktriny i strategicheskikh kontseptsiy SShA posle vtoroy mirovoy voyny" [The Evolution of the Military Doctrine and Strategic Concepts of the USA after the Second World War], *Voyenno–istoricheskiy zhurnal* [Military-Historical Journal], No. 4, April 1977, p. 66. (For this citation and other suggestions, I am indebted to Dr. Michael C. Deane.) The Soviets have intensified

the ambiguity of their terminology by using *sderzhivaniye* as a translation for the political concept of containment (as in "the containment and rollback of Communism") as well as the military concept of deterrence. Ibid., p. 67.

9. For example, A. A. Yepishev attributes the creation of the Strategic Rocket Forces to the fact that "the nuclear-rocket weapon was considered the main means of deterrence [*sderzhivaniye*] of the aggressive intentions of imperialism." *Partiya i armiya* [Party and Army], 2nd ed. (Moscow: Izdatel'stvo politicheskoy literatury, 1980), p. 264.

10. G. Arbatov, "Tupiki politiki sili; k voprosu o bankrotstve filosofii 'Kholodnoy voyny'" [Impasses of the Policy of Force: On the Question About the Bankruptcy of the Philosophy of the 'Cold War'], *Problemy mira i sotsializma* [Problems of Peace and Socialism], No. 2, February 1974, p. 45. In this same article, Arbatov combined the two Russian words for deterrence into a single phrase referring to American views about *sderzhivaniye putem ustrasheniya* as a guarantee of peace. Clearly, he did not mean "deterrence through deterrence." "Deterrence through the use of threats (or terror)" would seem preferable.

11. A. Ye. Yefremov has devoted an entire book to this theme. *Yevropeyskaya bezopasnost' i krizis NATO. Bankrotstvo politiki "ustrasheniya"* [European Security and NATO's Crisis. The Bankruptcy of the "Deterrence" Policy] (Moscow: Izdatel'stvo politicheskoy literatury, 1975).

12. B. Belyy, et al, *Marxism–Leninism on War and Army* (Moscow: Progress Publishers, 1972), trans. under the auspices of the United States Air Force (Washington: Government Printing Office, 1974), p. 23.

13. "Lokal'naya voyna" [Local War], *Sovetskaya Voennaya Entsiklopediya* [Soviet Military Encyclopedia] (Moscow: Voyennoye izdatel'stvo Ministerstva Oborony, 1976–1980), Vol. 5, p. 22.

14. Ibid.

15. In one of their forays into the "bourgeois press," Radomir Bogdanov and Lev Semeyko made this point quite eloquently: "Too many Americans still assume that Soviet thinking about military and political matters is essentially similar to their own thinking." They argued that parity with the Soviet Union would endanger none of the political or economic interests of the US, "so long as those interests involve mutually advantageous cooperation, international stability, and a lasting peace. What parity *can* deter is 'atomic diplomacy,' American or NATO-staged acts of intervention, shows of force for the sake of political pressure, and military activity to bolster dictatorial, "racist," or militarist regimes in various parts of the world. But, to be objective, one must say that *this kind of deterrence* [emphasis added] is not a bad thing from the standpoint of those interested in peace and human progress." "Soviet Military Might: A Soviet View," *Fortune,* 26 February 1979, pp. 47 and 52.

16. For one of the most specific and detailed assessments of Third World conflicts ever published by a Soviet author, see I. Shavrov, "Lokal'nyye voyny i ikh mesto v global'noy strategii imperializma" [Local Wars and their Place in the Global Strategy of Imperialism], *Voyenno–istoricheskiy zhurnal* [Military–Historical Journal], No. 3, March 1975, p. 66, where he alleges that the "progressives" won 33 victories on Third World battlefields in 1970–1975, compared to 12 victories for the "reactionaries" during the same period.

17. Dimitri K. Simes rightly has pointed to a deemphasis in Soviet references to the winnability of nuclear war and to their once loudly proclaimed goal of strategic superiority, especially in statements emanating from the highest levels of the Soviet military-political system. "Deterrence and Coercion in Soviet Policy," *International Security,* Vol. 5, No. 3 (Winter 1980), p. 89. However, Simes notes that such statements still occur at lower levels of the Soviet hierarchy, above all from sources affiliated with the Main Political Administration.

18. For an especially well-documented version of this argument which describes Soviet military developments of the late 1970s as a response to an alleged American superiority in counterforce capabilities, see Raymond L. Garthoff, "Mutual

Deterrence and Strategic Arms Limitation in Soviet Policy," *International Security,* Vol. 3, No. 1 (Summer 1978), p. 135.

19. Garthoff interprets the real issue underlying at least some of these "debates" as "whether war is recognized as so unpromising and dangerous that it can never occur." Ibid., p. 114. For a persuasive rebuttal of such an approach to interpreting the Soviet press, see John J. Dziak, "The Institutional Foundations of Soviet Military Doctrine," *International Security Review,* Vol. 4, No. 4 (Winter 1979–1980), pp. 317–332.

20. V. D. Sokolovskiy, ed., *Voyennaya strategiya* [Military Strategy], 3rd ed. (Moscow: Voyennoye izdatel'stvo Ministerstva Oborony, 1968), pp. 207–256 and 403–456.

21. M. P. Skirdo, *The People, the Army, the Commander* (Moscow, 1970), trans. under the auspices of the United States Air Force (Washington: Government Printing Office, ND), p. 30.

22. Ibid., p. 13.

23. This formulation is enshrined in the current CPSU Program, *Programma Kommunisticheskoy partii Sovetskogo Soyuza. Prinyata XXII s"yezdom KPSS* [Program of the Communist Party of the Soviet Union. Adopted by the 22nd Congress of the CPSU] (Moscow: Izdatel'stvo politicheskoy literatury, 1976), p. 59. Although adopted in 1961, this Program still provides the standard language for Soviet statements on the "winnability" of nuclear war—sometimes with and sometimes without attribution.

• A. S. Milovidov and V. G. Kozlov paraphrase the 1961 Program, attributing the inevitable defeat of imperialism not merely to the Soviet offensive forces but also to "the fundamental, decisive superiority of the civil defense of the socialist state over the civil defense of bourgeois countries." *The Philosophical Heritage of V. I. Lenin and Problems of Contemporary War.* (Moscow, 1972), trans. under the auspices of the United States Air Force (Washington: Government Printing Office, 1975), pp. 17 and 250. Skirdo emphatically agrees, adding the intriguing point that nuclear war would also confront the imperialists with "a massive partisan movement and other forms of armed resistance in their rear." Op. cit,. p. 73.

24. M. P. Skirdo says succinctly, ". . . the answer to the most critical question of our day depends in large part on the political leadership: Is there or is there not to be a thermonuclear world war?" He also lists a number of other tasks which fall primarily or exclusively on the political leaders. They include: formulating Soviet military doctrine; determining war aims; duplicating, dispersing, and concealing important economic installations in peacetime; organizing civil defense; planning the national economy so as to achieve "military-technological superiority" over the enemy; stockpiling combat materiel before the war begins; discovering enemy intentions to attack and deciding to carry out a "retaliatory" strike; making the decision to employ nuclear weapons; assuring a flexible, powerful coalition with Soviet allies; using with maximum effectiveness all military, economic, and moral-political potential from the very start of the war; resolving unprecedented problems during the war itself; and instilling in Soviet citizens "faith in victory . . . under the most difficult conditions of a potential nuclear war." Ibid., pp. 97–109. The specific role of military leadership flows from the view that "the achievement of victory in war is dictated first and foremost by skilled leadership in military operations." Ibid., p. 109.

25. In his speech to the 26th CPSU Congress, General Secretary Brezhnev asserted that "imperialism unleashed a real undeclared . . . war against the Afghan revolution. This created a direct threat to the security of our southern border also." However, he obscured the problem of the Afghan situation's putative impact on Soviet Muslims. "We communists respect the religious convictions of people of the Islamic faith just as of other religions. The main issue is the aims pursued by the forces declaiming particular slogans. The liberation struggle can unfold under the banner of Islam. This is shown by the experience of history, including most recent history. But reaction also operates with Islamic slogans while raising counterrevolutionary mutinies. Therefore, the whole essence of the matter is the real content of a particular movement." Moscow *TASS* in English, 23 February 1981.

26. P. P. Cherkassov, et al., *European Security and Co–operation: Premises, Problems, Prospects,* trans. Galina Sdobnikova (Moscow: Progress Publishers, 1978). For an argument that deterrence (*ustrasheniye*) is inherently unstable and dangerous, especially when qualitative or quantitative changes violate the "balance of terror," see V. Basmanov, *Za voyennuyu razryadku v tsentral'noy Evrope* [For Military Detente in Central Europe] (Moscow: "Mezhdunarodnyye otnosheniya," 1978), p. 6.

27. V. M. Kulish, et al, *Voyennaya sila i mezhdunarodnyye otnosheniya. Voyennyye aspekty vneshnepoliticheskikh kontseptsiy SShA* [Military Forces and International Relations. Military Aspects of the Foreign Policy Concepts of the USA] (Moscow: "Mezhdunarodnyye otnosheniya," 1972), p. 226.

Soviet Strategic Wartime Leadership

Tommy L. Whitton

When Hitler's armies invaded the USSR on 22 June 1941, the Soviet military was caught unprepared. Even its first echelon forces had not been placed on a wartime footing organizationally and had not been fully equipped. Just as importantly, the structural framework necessary to manage the war at the strategic level had not been elaborated.

The present generation of military and political leaders in the Soviet Union, weaned on the lessons of the Great Patriotic War, have vowed not to make the same mistakes again. Recently, a number of Soviet military writers have openly and unequivocally expressed their concern that both an overall system of strategic wartime leadership and its various echelons must be set up ahead of time, before the outbreak of war, and must be structured precisely in accordance with the nature and scope of possible military operations.

Soviet literature provides us with a few concrete facts about the organs of strategic leadership which would control a future war effort and their wartime responsibilities and authority. In addition, much can be learned about current Soviet plans by studying the strategic control of Soviet forces in World War II, and more precisely by observing how Soviet military writers today assess the advantages and disadvantages of the various forms in which strategic leadership was exercised in the previous war. Finally, the status and prestige of certain officers in the Soviet military hierarchy can be used to develop hypotheses about the probable composition of each of these strategic organs.

Strategic Leadership versus Command and Control

The Soviets have two terms to express the system through which leaders exercise their will in directing a war—*upravleniye* and *rukovodstvo*—most frequently translated as command and control and leadership, respectively. [In the US, the terms "operational command and control" and "strategic command and control" are commonly used.] In WWII, the highest organ of "command and control" generally was the front command. Above this level, direction of the war effort became the task of organs of "strategic leadership." In certain instances, these functions were merged under one commander. The structure of these organs and the functions which they performed are of particular interest here, for the manner in which strategic leadership would be exercised in a future war depends to a great extent on

706

whether similar functions would need to be performed and on whether the types of organs created in WWII were, in retrospect, considered effective in achieving their objectives.

The term "strategic leadership" is used by the Soviets when referring to direction of the conduct of war by the highest state, Party, and military organs and when such direction has more of a coordinating and goal-setting purpose, combining military-strategic and sociopolitical functions. Hence, the supreme military command would lead (*rukovodit'*) the armed forces, while the front commander would control (*upravlyat'*) its armies. The determination of whether a particular organ exercises strategic leadership is important in that with such leadership comes a greater degree of authority over civilian, government, and Party organs, as well as military formations. The Soviets also distinguish between organs of strategic leadership of the country and strategic leadership of the armed forces, with the latter being a component of, and subordinate to, the former.

Soviet Strategic Leadership in World War II

The Initial Period

The first manifestations of strategic leadership by the Soviets, upon being informed of the German attack in 1941, were performed by the Main Military Council of the People's Commissariat of Defense. The Council issued orders to the first echelon of Soviet forces—the five western military districts (MDs); the Northern, Baltic, and Black Sea Fleets; and five air defense zones—to implement their war plans (such as they were) and to "drive back" the invaders. The operational war plans called for three fronts to be formed in the event of an attack in Europe: the Northwestern Front from the Baltic Special MD, the Western Front from the Western Special MD, and the Southwestern Front from the Kiev Special MD. The commanders of the three special MDs became the three front commanders.

In addition, representatives of the Commissariat of Defense were sent immediately to each of the fronts to assess the situation:

- to the Northwestern Front —
Deputy Chief of the General Staff Vatutin;

- to the Western Front —
Deputy Commissars of Defense Shaposhnikov and Kulik,
Deputy Chief of the General Staff Sokolovskiy, and
Chief of the Operations Directorate Malandin;

- to the Southwestern Front —
Chief of the General Staff Zhukov.

For the first week of the war, strategic leadership of the country was exercised by existing Party and state agencies—the CPSU Politburo and the Council of People's Commissars (CPC). One of their first acts was the creation on 23 June 1941 of the General Headquarters (*Stavka*) of the High Command (*Glavnoye komandovaniye*), whose membership consisted of the following:

- Commissar of Defense Timoshenko (Chairman) Stalin
- Commissar of Foreign Affairs Molotov
- Chairman of the CPC's Defense Committee Voroshilov
- Chief of the General Staff Zhukov
- First Deputy Commissar of Defense Budennyy
- Commissar of the Navy Kuznetsov.

Despite its swift creation, *Stavka* did not instantly assume control of the military situation and did not issue its first directive until 27 June. When the initial reports regarding German movements were assessed, it was determined the line of contact covered a greater distance than had been anticipated in the contingency plans, and it was necessary to create additional fronts on the left and right flanks of those which had already been formed. Timoshenko issued the directive to create the Northern and Southern Fronts not as Chairman of *Stavka* but as Commissar of Defense. The Northern Front was formed on 24 June from the Leningrad MD. The Southern Front was formed on the basis of the 9th Army from the Odessa MD and several divisions from the Southwestern Front, which became the 18th Army; the front command was formed from the Moscow MD command, which was flown hastily to Odessa.

Several important observations can be made from these initial measures taken at the outbreak of war. First, there were no prior arrangements as to how wartime strategic leadership of the country would be exercised. Also, the fact *Stavka* did not begin to function as a body until several days after the invasion suggests its composition and authority had not been elaborated in advance. Thus, the precious first week of the war at the highest level had to be devoted primarily to setting up the system for managing the wartime economy and determining how to respond militarily and organizationally to the rapidly advancing German forces.

Second, the designation of three of the five western MDs as "special" (*osobyye*) MDs and their immediate transformation into fronts indicate that contingency plans for command and control (*upravleniye*) had been developed (however incomplete and unrealistic). Greater numbers of forces, the most modern equipment and weapons, and larger supplies of munitions, fuel, and reserves were concentrated in special MDs.[1] The first special MDs—the Belorussian and Kiev Special MDs—were created in 1938, a full year before the Nazi–Soviet Nonaggression Pact, showing that some preparations for wartime command and control were made in anticipation of war as early as that time. In July 1940, the Belorussian Special MD became the Western Special MD; in August 1940, the Baltic Special MD was formed.

A third observation is that in all preparations for combat and, indeed, throughout the entire war, the Soviets viewed their European borders as being divided into three geographical areas, or strategic axes (*napravleniya*). For example, WWII fronts are indentified in Soviet literature. by locating them in either the northwestern, western, or southwestern axes, even when no single command element united forces in these axes. This is important to keep in mind because this historical perception of Europe as consisting of three distinct areas is still valid today and affects current Soviet planning.

The State Defense Committee

By 30 June 1941, the basic decisions regarding strategic leadership of the country had been made and the State Defense Committee (*Gosudarstvennyy komitet oborony—GKO*) was created by joint decree of the Politburo, the Council of People's Commissars, and the Presidium of the USSR Supreme Soviet. Its membership initially consisted of Stalin (Chairman), Molotov (Deputy Chairman), and Voroshilov—all of whom were Politburo members and also members of *Stavka*—as well as Central Committee Secretary for Personnel Malenkov and People's Commissar of Internal Affairs Beriya. The latter two were candidate members of the Politburo at the time. Stalin assigned each of the other members of the *GKO* responsibility for a major sector of strategic leadership:

Molotov—	diplomacy
Voroshilov—	military-party relations
Malenkov—	party relations
Beriya—	domestic policy

Within three weeks, however, the need arose for more members of the party leadership to be brought directly into the decisionmaking process. As a result, Deputy Chairman of the CPC for Trade Mikoyan, People's Commissar of Railroads Kaganovich—both full Politburo members—and Chairman of the State Planning Committee Voznesenskiy—a candidate Politburo member—were made members of the *GKO*. At this time, responsibility for managing the basic branches of the war economy was parceled out among the members:

Molotov—	tank production
Malenkov—	aircraft/aircraft engines production
Beriya—	relocation of industry

Mikoyan—	food, fuel, and clothing supply
Kaganovich—	transportation network
Voznesenskiy—	national planning and armaments and munitions production.

The composition of the *GKO* remained unchanged throughout the war with only one exception: in November 1944, Bulganin, who had served as the member of the Military Council (i.e., political officer) in several fronts, was appointed Deputy Commissar of Defense and a member of the *GKO*.

The *GKO* had total authority over all matters within the country, relying on the Council of People's Commissars and *Gosplan* for staff support. It was a decisionmaking body not an executive one. In exercising its control over the economy, it delegated to the CPC and the Politburo many of the responsibilities which they normally had in peacetime. For example, the CPC created the new Commissariats for Tank Production and for Mortar Production and made decisions on industrial production levels, the relocation of industry, construction projects, and the rights and authority of people's commissariats under wartime conditions. The Politburo handled directly all partisan movements and the establishment of Communist Party organs in "liberated areas." The Politburo and the CPC jointly approved the highest level military promotions and national economic development plans. The Politburo, along with the *GKO* and *Stavka,* also formally approved general plans on the conduct of the war and the specific plans for major military operations.

The *GKO,* while delegating to *Stavka* responsibility for conducting military operations, retained for itself many traditionally military functions. One of the most important of these was rear supply. The *GKO* directly ensured the flow of supplies to the fronts and to besieged areas and reorganized organs of the rear to carry out these duties. It controlled military research and development, the production of war materiel, and the supply of strategic resources. The Commissariat of the Navy was technically subordinate to the *GKO,* not to *Stavka.* When required to support ground operations, the Baltic, Northern, and Black Sea Fleets were placed under the operational control of *Stavka,* who then turned them over to the fronts. However, the *GKO* retained direct control over shipbuilding, the construction of naval bases, material-technical supply of fleets, and the assignment of naval personnel to ground fronts. Authorization of the *GKO* was required to create special military units not in the normal table of organization.

The military functions which were performed in the war by the *GKO* instead of *Stavka* are now, in peacetime, performed within the Ministry of Defense. It is interesting to note the current deputy ministers of defense are divided into two groups, with the lesser group (in terms of status and prestige) consisting of those deputy ministers in charge of functions performed by the *GKO* in World War II: rear supply, R&D, construction and billeting, and civil defense. The implications of this situation will be discussed later.

General Headquarters (Stavka)

In the early weeks of the war, *Stavka* attempted to exercise strategic leadership directly over each of the five fronts through its executive arms—the General Staff and the directorates of the Commissariat of Defense. However, the rapid movement of the German "blitzkrieg," frequent disruptions in communications, and a general lack of coordination among major formations quickly created what one Soviet historian so diplomatically called "a certain discrepancy between the system of strategic leadership and the scope and character of the war."[2]

As a result, on 10 July 1941, a major reorganization of strategic leadership of the armed forces was approved by the *GKO*. At the top, *Stavka* was renamed *Stavka* of the Supreme Command (*Stavka Verkhovnogo Komandovaniya*) and Stalin replaced Timoshenko as its chairman. Shaposhnikov, who three weeks later became Chief of the General Staff, was added as a member. *Stavka's* direct control over the navy was further limited, however, by removing Navy Commissar Kuznetsov from its membership.

On 19 July, with Timoshenko then in a field command (see below), Stalin also assumed the position of Commissar of Defense. He further enhanced the list of his titles on 8 August when *Stavka* once again underwent a name change, becoming *Stavka* of the Supreme High Command (*Stavka Verkhovnogo Glavnokomandovaniya*). Stalin became Supreme Commander in Chief (*Verkhovnyy Glavnokomanduyushchiy*). A year later, in August 1942, Zhukov was formally named Deputy Supreme Commander in Chief.

The most significant portion of the 10 July 1941 reorganization was the formation of a High Command (*Glavnoye komandovaniye* or *GK*) in each of the three European axes:

Northwestern Axis High Command—CinC—Voroshilov
    Member of the Military Council—Zhdanov
    Chief of Staff—Zakharov

    Area of Control: Northwestern Front, Northern Front, Baltic Fleet, Northern Fleet.

Western Axis High Command—CinC—Timoshenko
    Member of the Military Council—Shaposhnikov
    (until 30 July, then Sokolovskiy)

    Area of Control: Western Front (later also the Central Front, which subsequently became the Bryansk Front).

Southwestern Axis High Command—CinC—Budennyy
Member of the Military Council—Khrushchev
Chief of Staff—Pokrovskiy

Area of Control: Southwestern Front, Southern Front, Black Sea Fleet (control of the Black Sea Fleet was transferred to the newly created North Caucasus Axis High Command in April 1942).

The CinCs of these axis High Commands (*GK*s)—who were all members of *Stavka*—their chiefs of staff, and the Party overseers—who were all full members of the Politburo—formed the military councils of the *GK*s. Decisions were made by the CinC after the situation had been discussed by the military council. The *GK*s, which were located near the front, were to analyze the operational-strategic situation and report back to the *Stavka* in Moscow, which had been reduced to Stalin, Molotov, Shaposhnikov, and Zhukov. Upon orders from Moscow, the CinCs were to prepare operations and coordinate their execution with the front commands and the naval forces under their operational control. The CinC was assisted by a staff which consisted of departments for operations, intelligence, rear services, military transportation, and communications; and of the chiefs of tank troops, aviation, artillery, engineering troops, and the medical services, as well as the ever-present political department.

These three *GK*s—and one established later in the North Caucasus axis (CinC—Budennyy; Member of the Military Council—Seleznov; Chief of Staff—Zakharov; Deputy CinC for Naval Affairs—Isakov)—were all short-lived and their performance has been assessed by Soviet military historians as having been generally ineffective in exerting significant influence on the course of military operations.

Chronology of High Commands in Strategic Axes

10 Jul 41	Northwestern *GK* created—Voroshilov is CinC; Western *GK* created—Timoshenko is CinC; Southwestern *GK* created—Budennyy is CinC
29 Aug 41	Northwestern *GK* abolished
10 Sep 41	Western *GK* abolished
13 Sep 41	Timoshenko replaced Budennyy as CinC in the Southwestern *GK*
1 Feb 42	Western *GK* reestablished—Zhukov is CinC
26 Apr 42	North Caucasus *GK* created—Budennyy is CinC
5 May 42	Western abolished
20 May 42	North Caucasus *GK* abolished
21 Jun 42	Southwestern *GK* abolished (Soviet accounts differ on this date)[3]

There were a number of reasons, according to Soviet authors, why the axis *GK*s were unable to perform properly the function of strategic leadership. The citing of these problems by these authors can be "mirror imaged" to read as a list of "do's" for present-day planners. One of the most important errors was the fact these organs were not established (and not even planned for and exercised) prior to the outbreak of war. As a result, the optimum size of the staff, its internal relationships, and its functions vis-a-vis the front staffs were undetermined. Also, there were not enough qualified officers with sufficient experience in coordinating such large-scale operations.

Another major problem with the axis *GK*s was their lack of sufficiently broad authority, which is extremely surprising since they included a member of *Stavka* itself and a Politburo member. However, the problem here was not that the axis *GK* was incapable of handling such broad authority but that Stalin insisted on retaining ultimate control over all matters. From his Kremlin office, which had been converted into the main *Stavka* communications center, he maintained direct contact with each of the fronts as well as with the *GK*s. Frequently, orders were issued directly to the front commanders, bypassing the *GK*. Even when *Stavka* did communicate with the *GK*s, its instructions were often untimely. For example, the Southwestern *GK* did not receive its first *Stavka* directive regarding the missions of the fronts until 19 August—40 days after the *GK* had been established!

Stavka determined where the *GK* was to establish its headquarters, established the specific mission of each front, and sent requirements (usually unrealistic) as to the number of divisions which had to be kept in reserve. While the CinC could move divisions within armies and make personnel decisions regarding army commands, he had to get *Stavka* authority to resubordinate armies or corps or to assign newly formed ones.[4] He had no authority over the staffing of front commands.

In the final analysis, it can be concluded that in practice, the axis *GK*s were neither organs of command and control nor organs of strategic leadership but served primarily as intermediary links between *Stavka* and the fronts. The *GK* merely sanctioned the command and control decisions of the front commanders and executed the strategic coordination called for by *Stavka*. Had Stalin's confidence in his front commanders been greater and communications more reliable, this form of the axis *GK* would not have been required.

Stavka Representation

Following the abandonment of the axis *GK* as a means of controlling the fronts, day-to-day strategic leadership was again exercised directly by *Stavka*. However, when major counteroffensives were planned, *Stavka* sent representatives (*predstaviteli*) to coordinate operations in two or more fronts. These *Stavka* representatives, assisted by a small staff of officers from the General Staff and the central military apparatus, were given authority to make fundamental decisions on the spot. In the three largest operations—the Battle of Stalingrad, the Battle of Kursk, and the Belorussian Operation—both Zhukov and Vasilevskiy were sent as representatives, each having control over a specific portion of the overall operation.

Chronology of Stavka Representation

Nov 42-Feb 43	Battle of Stalingrad	Zhukov, Vasilevskiy
Jan 43	Leningrad Blockade	Voroshilov, Zhukov
Mar-Jun 43	Battle of Leningrad	Timoshenko
Jun-Nov 43	Novorossiysk-Taman' and Kerch' operations	Timoshenko
Jul-Aug 43	Battle of Kursk	Zhukov, Vasilevskiy
Autumn 43	Donbas and North Tavriya operations	Vasilevskiy
Aug-Dec 43	Battle of the Dnepr	Zhukov
Jan-Feb 44	Operations in the Ukraine	Vasilevskiy
Feb-Jun 44	Operations in the Baltic	Timoshenko
Apr 44	Operations in the Crimea	Vasilevskiy
Jun-Aug 44	Belorussian Operation	Zhukov, Vasilevskiy
Aug-Sep 44	Yassko-Kishinev Operation	Timoshenko
Sep-Nov 44	Baltic Operation	Vasilevskiy
Sep 44-May 45	Operations in the Ukraine	Timoshenko
Nov 44-May 45	Vistula-Oder and Berlin Operations	Zhukov
Jan-Apr 45	East Prussian Operation	Vasilevskiy

Beginning in late 1944, *Stavka* representation took on a new and, according to Soviet assessments, improved form. Zhukov and Vasilevskiy began not only to coordinate but personally to direct operations of groups of fronts. In this form, the *Stavka* representatives exercised both strategic leadership and command and control. In the Vistula–Oder and Berlin Operations, Zhukov assumed direct command of the most important front, the Belorussian Front. In February 1945, Vasilevskiy was released as Chief of the General Staff and became Commander of the Third Belorussian Front and *Stavka* representative for the East Prussian Operation.

Stavka representation was an effective means of exercising strategic leadership for basically two reasons. First, representatives were sent to the field on an ad hoc basis with the purpose of executing a specific operational plan which had already been approved by *Stavka* and generally also by the Politburo and the *GKO*. Second, the nature of the representation allowed Stalin's two most trusted and capable generals—Zhukov and Vasilevskiy—to assume most of the command responsibilities themselves. This is extremely important because it was only by virtue of Stalin's acquired confidence in them that they were granted sufficient authority to carry the operations through to a successful conclusion. Zhukov and Vasilevskiy had proved themselves so militarily wise, they were allowed to exercise their own judgment and were among the few who could safely insist upon doing things their own way.

Strategic Leadership in the Manchurian Campaign

The final form in which strategic leadership was manifested during the Great Patriotic War was the High Command in the Far Eastern theater of operations (*teatr voyennykh deystviy—TVD*) which existed for the Manchurian offensive against the Japanese Kwangtung Army in August 1945. The CinC of this *GK* was Vasilevskiy himself; in June 1945 he had been sent as the *Stavka* representative to assess the situation and to make initial preparations for the offensive. However, within two weeks of his arrival, he reported back to Moscow that he did not have sufficient authority over the civilian sector to carry through the massive and extremely secret concentration of forces. Also, his position vis-a-vis the Mongolian national forces and his ability to accept the surrender of Japanese troops were inadequate.[5]

Stavka immediately formed a High Command and named Vasilevskiy Commander in Chief of Soviet Forces in the Far East. This Soviet command controlled a much larger force than any previous command. It included 3 fronts, 80 divisions, 3 air armies, the Pacific Fleet, the Amur Flotilla, the North Pacific Flotilla, and the area border guards and their Amur River patrol vessels.[6] Since this was, in fact, all forces in the Far Eastern theater of operations, the command was considered by the Soviets to have been a High Command in a *TVD* and is distinguished in all contemporary Soviet literature from the axis *GK*s.

Vasilevskiy was assisted by a small combined arms staff. Commander of the Soviet Air Forces Novikov was sent as a *Stavka* representative for aviation, subordinate to Vasilevskiy, and exercised direct control over all air assets, including naval aircraft of the Pacific Fleet. Navy Commissar Kuznetsov, now officially a member of *Stavka* was sent to the Far East to coordinate ground and naval operations; he was subordinate not to Vasilevskiy directly but to *Stavka* for this campaign. That portion of naval assets which supported operations of the First and Second Far Eastern Fronts on the Asian continent, including the Pacific Fleet commander himself, was made operationally subordinate to Vasilevskiy and, in turn, to the front commanders. Kuznetsov personally controlled naval units assigned to interdict enemy lines of communication and those involved in supporting forces of the Second Far

715

Eastern Front in landing operations on the Kurile Islands and South Sakhalin.

The manner in which this *GK* functioned is unique in the extent to which it exercised strategic leadership independently of Moscow. Once the overall plan had been approved in June 1945 by the *GKO, Stavka,* and the General Staff—with the participation in Moscow of Vasilevskiy and his front commanders (Vasilevskiy acted relatively autonomously. He worked directly with local government and party organs to solve political, economic, and logistics problems both before and during the campaign.)

The strategic plan called for the Transbaykal Front to launch the major offensive into western Manchuria while the First Far Eastern Front launched a secondary attack into southeastern Manchuria. Vasilevskiy was given the authority to determine when the Second Far Eastern Front would begin its operations across the Amur River into northeastern Manchuria. Such authority to initiate frontal operations previously always had been retained by *Stavka.* In addition, Vasilevskiy was to decide if and when landing operations on Japanese–controlled islands would be launched. Thus, the extent of the *TVD* CinC's strategic leadership was nearly absolute. He lacked the authority only to order a cessation of hostilities.

The Manchurian campaign is praised by Soviet military writers, both historians and those presently in decisionmaking positions, as the almost perfect model of how an operation should be planned, coordinated, and executed. One of the most important aspects was that the entire command structure was worked out and set up prior to the initiation of hostilities. The ability to amass secretly such a large force provided the Soviets with the element of complete surprise. Deceptive measures concealed the area from which the major offensive was to be launched. Finally, the concentration of all aspects of strategic leadership in a field command permitted the most effective use of all assets. One author summarized the functioning of the *TVD* High Command by asserting that "the development of events confirmed the vitality of this system of strategic leadership of troops and forces in an independent *TVD* remote from the center."[7]

Soviet Strategic Leadership in a Future War

The experience of the Great Patriotic War has served for the past 35 years as the major rallying cry to the Soviet people and especially to military officers. With the last of the distinguished generals in that war rapidly dying off, the lessons of the war are coming more and more to be analyzed from the viewpoint of military effectiveness rather than as nostalgic reminiscences. Yet, even in this context, and despite the existence of vastly different circumstances brought about by the "revolution in military affairs" and the current correlation of world forces,

Soviet strategists still consider the experiences of 1941–1945 to be valuable in planning an effective system of strategic leadership for a future war.

In discussing the organs which would direct Soviet participation in a future armed conflict, the most essential thing to remember is that the actual organizational structure would correspond to the scope of the war and the type of weapons with which it would be fought. Strategic leadership in a limited nuclear war would differ significantly from that in a protracted, two-front conventional war. However, in preparing for a future war, the Soviets must develop plans for every contingency which, in their threat assessments, is believed to have a given level of probability. As a result, the organs of strategic leadership have to be able to respond appropriately to a worst-case scenario. The extent to which such preparations are made in advance is an indicator of Soviet perceptions of the likelihood of this worst case being realized and their assessment of relative probabilities of other situations arising. Once a total system of strategic leadership has been devised, any portion of it can be activated to cope with an actual conflict situation.

A general principle of Soviet strategic leadership in World War II, which from all indications is still operative today, is that central control should extend to the lowest link in the chain of command at which operational-tactical and strategic goals coincide. Separate organs of strategic leadership should exist in geographical areas where strategic objectives are identifiably distinct. As a hypothetical example, in a Sino–Soviet armed conflict, if the Soviet objectives were to subjugate the northeast provinces of China by attacking on two or more fronts, as they did in August 1945, strategic leadership would probably extend only to the echelon above the front; i.e., a High Command. However, if the objective were to make a surgical strike to control Xinjiang using only one front, strategic leadership would be exercised at the front level, and there would be no need to have a separate High Command. However, even in this latter situation, the commanding general could be designated a CinC if the authority commensurate with such a title were required.

Future Strategic Leadership of the Country

The discussion of specific forms of wartime leadership should, of course, begin at the highest level. According to Marshal Sokolovskiy's authoritative *Voyennaya strategiya* (Military Strategy), strategic leadership of the country and of the armed forces in a war would be exercised by the CPSU Central Committee, "with the possible organization of a higher agency of leadership of the country and of the armed forces. This higher agency of leadership may be given the same powers as the State Defense Committee during the war." No subsequent pronouncement by the Soviets has indicated any change in this intention, thereby making the *GKO* during the Great Patriotic War a valid model for the future. A number of Western analysts assume that what has been identified publicly since the mid–1970s as the USSR Defense Council would become the *GKO* equivalent in wartime. However, despite the linguistic similarity of the name of these two bodies, there is, I assert, sufficient information to reject this assumption. The question of what, then, would be the current Defense Council's wartime function will be addressed below.

In attempting to identify the probable composition of the highest organ of strategic leadership (which I shall call here the *GKO*, although the exact name may be somewhat different), it is necessary to identify distinctive subsets of the Politburo. The *GKO*, as a higher organ of the Central Committee responsible for the conduct of all aspects of the war effort, would almost assuredly consist of only Politburo members, as it did during the last war. Before the death of Kosygin and Suslov and the elevation of Tikhonov, three such groups of Politburo members could be distinguished from an analysis of public appearances reported in the Soviet press and the signing of obituaries of prominent personalities (see Table 1):

Group 1:   Brezhnev, Kosygin, and Suslov;

Group 2:   Brezhnev, Kirilenko, Kosygin, Suslov, Ustinov, and Chernenko; and

Group 3:   Brezhnev, Andropov, Gromyko, Kirilenko, Kosygin, Suslov, Ustinov, and Chernenko.

From an analysis of the responsibilities of these Politburo members, it can be seen that those members in Group 3 performed virtually all the major functions which the GKO in World War II performed.

Therefore, it is asserted that, prior to October 1980, the eight Politburo members in Group 3 would have formed the *GKO*. There is every reason to believe Tikhonov has replaced Kosygin as a potential *GKO* member should a war break out today. No one probably will replace Suslov, at least initially, in this capacity.

Future Strategic Leadership of the Armed Forces
The highest organ of strategic leadership of the armed forces in a future war would likely be somewhat different from the World War II *Stavka*. From its inception until February 1945, *Stavka*—headed by Stalin as Supreme CinC—consisted of 2 civilians and 5 professional military officers. Throughout much of the war, the military members of *Stavka*, however, were out in the field. The force of circumstances made the General Staff at least as important an actor as the Politburo, a situation with which the party was uncomfortable but to which there were no alternatives.

Table 1. Military Personalities Whose Obituaries Brezhnev and Other Full Politburo Members Signed

Date	Deceased	Highest Position	Signatories (in order of signing)
17 Jun 1972	Maryakhin	Chief, Rear Services	Brezhnev, Podgornyy, Kosygin
21 Nov 1973	Komarovskiy	Chief, Const/Billet	Brezhnev, Podgornyy,* Kosygin, Grechko, Kirilenko, Suslov, Ustinov*
3 Jan 1974	Vershinin	CinC, Air Forces	Brezhnev, Podgornyy, Kosygin, Suslov, Grechko, Ustinov*
18 Jul 1975	Khalipov	Chief, PVO Pol Date	Brezhnev, Podgornyy, Kosygin
19 Nov 1975	Vishnevskiy	Chief, Surgeon MoD	Brezhnev, Grechko, Kirilenko, Kosygin, Mazurov, Pelshe, Podgornyy, Suslov, Ustinov*
25 Apr 1976	Shtemenko	CoS, Warsaw Pact (was chief of GS)	Brezhnev, Grechko, Kirilenko, Kosygin, Podgornyy, Suslov, Ustinov
11 Jun 1976	Katukov	Chief Inspector, MoD	Brezhnev, Podgornyy, Koysgin, Kirilenko, Suslov, Ustinov
31 Aug 1976	Koshevoy	CinC, GSFG	Brezhnev, Kirilenko, Kosygin, Podgornyy, Suslov, Ustinov, Shcherbitskiy
17 Apr 1977	Rodimtsev	1st Deputy MD Cmdr	Brezhnev, Podgornyy, Kosygin, Suslov, Kirilenko, Ustinov
14 Jul 1977	Lobov	Asst Chief, GS (Navy)	Brezhnev, Kirilenko, Kosygin, Suslov, Ustinov
19 Jul 1977	Fedyuninskiy	MD Commander	Brezhnev, Kirilenko, Kosygin, Suslov, Ustinov
1 Nov 1977	Babadzhanyan	Chief, Tank Troops	Brezhnev, Kirilenko, Kosygin, Suslov, Ustinov
19 Feb 1978	Vinogradov	(GRU)	Brezhnev, Ustinov
18 Aug 1978	Tyulenev	MD Commander	Brezhnev, Kirilenko, Suslov, Ustinov
22 Aug 1978	Gelovani	Chief, Constr/Billet	Brezhnev, Kirilenko, Kosygin, Suslov, Ustinov
15 Oct 1978	Peresypkin	Chief, Signal Academy	Brezhnev, Kirilenko, Kosygin, Suslov, Ustinov
12 Dec 1978	Belonozhko	MD Commander	Brezhnev, Kirilenko, Kosygin, Suslov, Ustinov, Ryabov**
2 Sep 1979	Radziyevskiy	Chief, GS Academy	Brezhnev, Kirilenko, Kosygin, Suslov, Ustinov
28 Dec 1979	Kazakov	CoS, Warsaw Pact	Brezhnev, Kirilenko, Kosygin, Suslov, Ustinov
12 Mar 1980	Psurtsev	Chief of Comms (later Min of Comms)	Brezhnev, Kirilenko, Kosygin, Suslov, Ustinov, Chernenko
15 Jun 1980	Belik	MD Commander	Brezhnev, Kirilenko, Kosygin, Suslov, Ustinov, Chernenko
31 Jul 1980	Golikov	Chief, Main Pol Dte	Brezhnev, Kirilenko, Kosygin, Suslov, Ustinov, Chernenko
14 Nov 1980	Alekseyev	Dep MoD (Armaments)	Brezhnev, Kirilenko, Ustinov, Chernenko

*Ustinov was Central Committee Secretary for Defense Industries and was only a candidate member of the Politburo at this time.

**Ryabov was only the Central Committee Secretary for Defense Industries at this time.

719

Area	Responsible Person(s):	
	In WWII	In Future War
Chairman	Stalin	Brezhnev
Deputy Chairman	Molotov	Suslov
Wartime economy (overall planning)	Stalin and Voznesenskiy	Kosygin
Military production and R&D	Molotov, Malenkov, and Voznesenskiy	Kirilenko
Logistics support	Mikoyan and Kaganovich	Kirilenko
Party relations	Malenkov	Chernenko
Military-civilian relations	Voroshilov	Ustinov
International diplomacy	Molotov	Gromyko
Domestic security	Beriya	Andropov

In a future war, the *Stavka* equivalent (which I shall call here the Supreme High Command—VGK) most likely would be tightly controlled more by political/Party figures. This is due only not to the need to ensure Party supremacy; it is also a consequence of the nuclear aspects of future war. Such important military decisions as when to go nuclear and the extent of the use of nuclear weapons cannot be based solely on military requirements. In addition, the increased importance of the time factor in modern war would require the military members of the VGK to devote their whole attention to their central duties. It is highly unlikely that in a large-scale war, VGK members would be assigned field commands.

The peacetime Defense Council appears to be the organ which would be transformed into a wartime VGK. Brezhnev, on extremely rare occasions, has been identified in Soviet open sources as the Supreme Commander in Chief, which means head of the VGK. In these instances, his full title has been given as "General Secretary of the CPSU Central Committee, Chairman of the Presidium of the USSR Supreme Soviet, Supreme Commander in Chief Marshal of the Soviet Union L. I. Brezhnev."[8] Under much more common circumstances, instead of Supreme CinC, Brezhnev is referred to as "Chairman of the USSR Defense Council Marshal of the Soviet Union L. I. Brezhnev". His military rank is employed only when his position as the Chairman of the Defense Council is noted. Also, it can be assumed that his military rank was conferred in connection with the fact he would head the highest organ of strategic leadership of the armed forces in wartime— the VGK. All this taken together strongly suggests the Defense Council would become the the VGK and the title "Supreme CinC" is the wartime equivalent to the peacetime position of Chairman of the USSR Defense Council.

The next question is, what is the current membership of the Defense Council? It would consist of a combination of civilian and military figures. In looking for those nonmilitary members, we should again look for a subset of the Politburo, particularly one which has a special relationship to the military. Those Politburo members in Group 2 above—Brezhnev, Kirilenko, Kosygin (until October 1980), Suslov (until January 1982), Ustinov, and Chernenko—fit this criterion. These six consistently have signed the obituaries of prominent military personalities. Most Western analysts intuitively believe that Andropov and Gromyko also are on the Defense Council. However, they do not sign military obituaries and their areas of responsibility are among those which in wartime would be performed by the *GKO*, not the VGK. Consequently, they would be members of the inner circle of the Politburo which would form the *GKO* but would not be members of the VGK/Defense Council.

As is suggested from an analysis of military obituaries since 1972 (See Table 1), Chernenko probably only since 1978 has been a member of the Defense Council, filling a void created when Podgornyy lost all his positions in late 1977. Obituaries appearing since Kosygin's "resignation" from the Council of Ministers indicate Tikhonov has assumed Kosygin's seat on the Defense Council as well as head of the Council of Ministers.

Perhaps the most important clue with regard to the military members of the Defense Council is found in an interview which the London *Sunday Times* correspondent Henry Brandon had with Nikolay Inozemtsev, Director of the Soviet Institute of the World Economy and International Relations and Deputy Chairman of *Gosplan.*[9] In reference to a question on the military's role in decisionmaking, Inozemtsev responded that military representation on the Defense Council is greater than on the Politburo but the military are still "not in the majority." First, this contradicts those assertions by some Western analysts that the Defense Council is composed of only Politburo members; second, it suggests there are no more than three military officers, in addition to Ustinov, on the body. At the time of the interview, as reflected in military obituaries, there would have been only four civilians on the Defense Council. Therefore, it is most likely the three first deputy ministers of defense—Ogarkov, Kulikov, and Sokolov—are all members.

If this assessment of the composition of the Defense Council is accurate, an interesting fact appears with regard to the Soviet military intervention in Afghanistan in December 1979. At that time, the Defense Council—I allege—would have consisted of Brezhnev, Kirilenko, Suslov, Ustinov, Ogarkov, Kulikov, and Sokolov; Kosygin was incapacitated following a heart attack. This meant the military temporarily would have been in the majority. While this alone may not have been sufficient to have carried the decision to enter Afghanistan militarily, the military members would have had to convince only Kirilenko or Suslov to go along with them in order to have forced Brezhnev to acquiesce. As if to confirm the untenable position in which Kosygin's illness had left Brezhnev vis-a-vis the Defense Council, Chernenko shortly after the Afghanistan intervention began signing military obituaries, thus signaling his elevation to the Defense Council. His addition would have reduced the opportunity for the military to have as much influence in the future.

Other Central Organs

The General Staff would again serve as the primary executive arm of the Supreme High Command in wartime. However, the World War II model of General Staff operations would have to be revised significantly to deal with the addition of the arsenal of strategic nuclear weapons. Strategic nuclear offensive forces, in peacetime, are under the control of the Strategic Rocket Forces (SRF), the Navy, and the Air Forces. Yet, the CinCs of these force components would not be members of the VGK or part of the General Staff itself. It seems unlikely, however, that in planning and conducting intercontinental nuclear war, men like CinC of the SRF Tolubko and CinC of the Navy Gorshkov would be left out of the formal decisionmaking process. Therefore, it would seem that in a strategic nuclear war, the Soviets would have need for an additional body to determine how the *GKO's* orders regarding such a war could best be executed. This body might make such decisions as the proper mix of ICBMs, SLBMs, and strategic bombers to employ to achieve the objectives set by the *GKO*. The determination of which targeting options to employ and the preparations for a follow-on strike might also be appropriate functions for such a body. The General Staff, on the other hand, is best suited for planning and conducting continental war.

Admittedly, there are no real indications such a body would formally be constituted. However, if it were, it would probably include only military officers since its mission would be the efficient and most effective military execution of strategic decisions made by the highest organ of strategic leadership of the country. A subset of the Ministry of Defense (MOD) might constitute this body. Such a group suitable for this task can be identified from an analysis of Soviet open sources. The top ten officers in the MOD—the minister, the three first deputy ministers, the chief of the Main Political Directorate, and the CinCs of the five force components—collectively have been referred to as the Higher Command (*Vyssheye Komandovaniye*) of the Armed Forces.[10] In protocol listings and obituary signings, these officers quite obviously form a group separate from the rest of the deputy ministers of defense. It is worth noting that those deputy ministers outside this major group are those whose areas of responsibility most likely would fall under the direct purview of the *GKO;* e.g., rear services, civil defense, R&D, and construction and billeting. If the "Higher Command" is not to be a formally constituted decisionmaking body, the CinCs of the force components almost certainly would be brought into the process as "advisers" to *Stavka.*

Intermediary Links

Soviet historians assessing the High Commands and *Stavka* representation in the Great Patriotic War make it clear some form of intermediary strategic leadership between the central organs and the fronts would be activated in a future war. According to one source, it has become "practically impossible for a supreme high command to exercise direction of military operations of major groupings of armed forces without an intermediary echelon."[11] This echelon almost surely would take the form of a High Command, defined as an organ "exercising leadership of the armed forces on a strategic axis or within a theater of operations." Given that some intermediary organs of command and control would be activated, it is important to identify the number of such High Commands and to determine whether they would be axis or *TVD* High Commands.

In attempting to find clues as to where the Soviets would create *GK*s, the historical precedents in World War II and the current structure of NATO forces which any European HC would oppose are appropriate starting points. The NATO structure in Europe, as described by the Soviets using their own terminology, consists of the Supreme Command (*Verkhovnoye komandovaniye*) in Europe, headed by the Supreme Commander in Chief (*Verkhovnyy glavnokomanduyushchiy*), with subordinate HCs in the Northern European, the Central European, and the Southern European *TVDs,* each headed by a CinC (*Glavnokomanduyushchiy*). In addition, there is the *GK* (British) in the English Channel Zone. In World War II, as mentioned previously, the Soviets viewed their European borders as being divided into three geographical regions and initially established fronts, and later *GK*s, to control forces in these three axes. The entire area was referred to variously as the Russian *TVD,* the Western *TVD,* or the European *TVD.* All of this strongly suggests that in a major conflict with NATO, three *GK*s in Europe might be anticipated, each of which would correspond roughly to one of the geographical divisions of NATO.

The election of military officers to the CPSU Central Committee (CC) at Party congresses provides the best clues as to who the CinCs of these *GK*s would probably be. The use of this indicator is valid because, as Sokolovskiy stated, it is the CC, through its established organs, which would exercise all strategic leadership of the country and of the armed forces. Therefore, it is essential and expedient for those who would command organs of strategic leadership (e.g., High Commands) to have a place on the CC.

An analysis was made of the CC elections held at the four CPSU congresses convened since Brezhnev came to power—the 23rd in 1966, the 24th in 1971, the 25th in 1976, and the 26th in 1981. From this, several observations can be made. First, the Ministry of Defense is allocated a specific number of full CC seats. Second, most of these full memberships go to officers in the central hierarchy.[12] Finally, after all of the requirements for central apparatus personnel have been met, the remaining MD full CC seats are given to commanders of military districts (MDs) or the CinC of the Group of Soviet Forces in Germany (GSFG). There were 2 such full CC memberships available in 1966, 4 in 1971 and 1976, and 5 in 1981 (see Table 2).

The incumbent commanders of the Moscow MD, Leningrad MD, Kiev MD, and the CinC of GSFG were always represented on the CC, either as full or candidate members. Each of the latter three is the most prestigious (in terms of future career opportunities) position in each of the geographic areas opposite a NATO *GK*. Therefore, it is believed the Soviets would form as many as three *GK*s in Europe and the Commanders of the Leningrad and Kiev MDs and the CinC of GSFG would become the *GK* CinCs.

Thus far, nothing has been said about *GK*s for a Soviet war against China. However, the CC membership/HC linkage can be used to determine this as well. To do this, one additional element—military rank—has to be considered. With the limited number of full CC seats, not all those who would assume major field command positions[13] can be elected full members. Therefore, the determination of which are elected full members and which only candidates, is most always made on the basis of rank and time in rank (see Table 3). Thus, the entire linkage theory asserts that "those MD/group of forces commanders who are elected full CC members are the highest ranking of those who have been designated to assume major field commands in wartime." A corollary to this can help to identify those who would not assume any major command and, consequently, the areas where *GK*s would not be formed: "An MD/group of forces commander who is not elected a full CC member, but who outranks some who are, is not designated to assume a major wartime field command." This corollary is useful only infrequently because the designated major commanders generally are first in line for promotions.

With these tools, it is possible to develop a hypothesis tracing the development of plans for *GK*s in a war with China since 1966. This hypothesis leads to the conclusion that as of the 1976 CC elections, the Soviets planned to create *GK*s in the Central Asian MD area and in the Far East MD area. The transfer to the Transbaykal MD in 1979 of G. I. Salmanov, who was subsequently promoted to Army General, suggested the Soviets had begun to anticipate a third *GK* in this area. Salmanov was formerly the Commander of the Kiev MD and then Deputy CinC of the Ground Forces for Combat Training. His transfer to the Transbaykal would have been inappropriate unless the wartime responsibilities of the incumbent had been increased significantly. Confirmation of a potential Transbaykal *GK* came at the 26th Party Congress in February 1981 with Salmanov's election as a full member

Table 2. MD Officers Elected as Full Central Comittee Member at the 23rd, 24th, 25th, and 26th CPSU Congresses

Position	23rd Congress (April 1966)	24th Congress (April 1971)	25th Congress (March 1976)	26th Congress (March 1981)
Minister of Defense [MOD]	Malinovskiy	Grechko	Grechko	Ustinov
First Dep MOD (Warsaw Pact)	Grechko	Yakubovskiy	Yakubovskiy	Kulikov
First Dep MOD (General Staff)	Zakharov	Zakharov	Kulikov	Ogarkov
First Dep MOD	(1)	Sokolov	Sokolov	Sokolov
Chief, Main Polit. Dte.	Yepishev	Yepishev	Yepishev	Yepishev
Dep MOD (SRF)	Krylov	Krylov	Tolubko	Tolubko
Dep MOD (Ground Forces)	(1)	Pavlovskiy	Pavlovskiy	Petrov
Dep MOD (Air Defense)	(2)	Batitskiy	Batitskiy	Koldunov
Dep MOD (Air Forces)	Vershinin	Kutakhov	Kutakhov	Kutakhov
Dept MOD (Navy)	Gorshkov	Gorshkov	Gorshkov	Gorshkov
Dep MOD (Main Inspectorate)	Moskalenko	Moskalenko	Moskalenko	Moskalenko
Dept MOD (Rear Services)	Bagramyan	Maryakhin	Kurkotkin	Kurkotkin
Dep MOD (Civil Defense) (3)	Chuykov	Chuykov	Altunin	Altunin
Dep MOD (Unidentified duties)	(1)	(1)	Ogarkov	
Inspector-Generals (all Marshals of the Soviet Union)	Konev	Bagramyan Konev	Bagramyan Chuykov	Bagramyan Batitskiy
First Dep Chief, General Staff	Batitskiy(4)	Ogarkov	(5)	
Commander, Kiev MD	Yakubovskiy	(5)	(5)	(5)
Commander Moscow MD	Beloborodov	Ivanovskiy	(5)	Lushev
Commander in Chief, GSFG	(5)	Kulikov	Ivanovskiy	Zaytsev
Commander, Central Asian MD	(1)	Lyashchenko	Lyashchenko	(5)
Commander, Leningrad MD	(5)	Shavrov	(5)	(5)
Commander, Far East MD	(6)	(5)	Petrov	Tretyak(7)
Commander, Belorussian MD				Ivanovskiy

1. Position did not exist at the time of this congress.
2. Position was vacant at the time of this congress.
3. Position of Chief of Civil Defense received Deputy MOD status in 1972.
4. Batitskiy became Deputy Minister of Defense/Commander in Chief of Air Defense in July 1966.
5. Incumbent received only candidate Central Committee status at this congress.

725

6. Incumbent was elected to the Central Auditing Commission at this congress.

7. I. M. Tretyak was actually Commander of the Belorussian MD at the time of the 25th CPSU Congress; however, he became Commander of the Far East MD in Jun 1976 following V. I. Petrov's promotion to First Deputy Commander in Chief of the Ground Forces.

Table 3. Linkage of Central Committee Membership and Rank to Major Wartime Commands

Peacetime Command	Commander	Rank (Date of Rank)	CC Status	Area of Potential Major Command
23rd CPSU CONGRESS (1966) (2*)				
Kiev MD	Yakubovskiy	Army Gen (-62)	Full	Southwestern HC
Moscow MD	Belodorodov	Army Gen (-63)	Full	Moscow MD
GSFG	Koshevoy	Army Gen (04-64)	Cand	Western HC
Leningrad MD	Sokolov	Col Gen (11-64)	Cand	Northwestern HC
24th CPSU CONGRESS (1971) (4*)				
Central Asian	Lyaschenko	Army Gen (02-68)	Full	Central Asian HC
GSGF	Kulikov	Army Gen (04-70)	Full	Western HC
Leningrad MD	Shavrov	Col Gen (06-67)	Full	Northwestern HC
Moscow MD	Ivanosvskiy	Col Gen (11-67)	Full	Moscow MD
Kiev MD	Salmanov	Col Gen (12-69)	Cand	Southwestern MD
25th CPSU CONGRESS (1976) (4*)				
Central Asian MD	Lyaschchenko	Army Gen (02-68)	Full	Central Asian HC
GSFG	Ivanovskiy	Army Gen (11-72)	Full	Western HC
Far East MD	Petrov	Army Gen (12-72)	Full	Far Eastern HC
Far East MD	Tretyak**	Col Gen (11-67)	Full	Far Eastern HC
Moscow MD	Govorov	Col Gen (10-70)	Cand	Moscow MD
Leningrad MD	Gribkov	Col Gen (02-73)	Cand	Norwestern MD
Kiev MD	Gerasimov	Col Gen (11-73)	Cand	Southwestern MD

---

*Number of full seats after central apparatus requirements have been justified.

**Tretyak's replacement of Petrov was anticipated at the time of the Congress. Tretyak became Commander of the Far East MD officially in June 1976.

of the Central Committee.[14]

The 26th Congress, while generally consistent with the previous 3 congresses with regard to selection criteria for CC membership, produced some anomalies which demonstrate that Soviet plans for High Commands are flexible and are still undergoing refinements. In 1981, Army General V. L. Govorov was elected a full CC member. Govorov was commander of the Moscow MD until late 1980 and was subsequently identified as the Commander in Chief of Forces in the Far East, a new position apparently created between congresses, reviving the title Vasilevskiy held in August 1945. Govorov, as the superior to MD commanders in the Far East, who—as indicated above—are on the

CC, therefore warrants a full CC seat.

Army General Ye. F. Ivanovskiy's retention of his full CC status despite his transfer from the GSFG to the Belorussian MD indicated that his change of position was not considered to be a demotion. The reason for his transfer may be related to some further refinements in the strategic command structure for Europe, perhaps similar to what has occurred in the Far East.

The other anomaly in the 1981 CC elections was the failure of Army General I. A. Gerasimov, Commander of the Kiev MD, to be elevated to full CC status. Gerasimov is senior to three MD commanders who were given full CC memberships, but he was elected only as a candidate member of the Central Committee. The election of the Turkestan MD commander, Colonel General Yu. P. Maksimov, to the CC for the first time ever, even as a candidate member, may shed some light on Gerasimov's situation. The Turkestan MD, bordering on Afghanistan, has acquired additional importance since the invasion of Afghanistan in December 1979. Therefore, the Turkestan MD commander, by virtue of circumstances, may have acquired greater credentials than the Kiev MD commander as a potential CinC of a High Command.

Once again, it should be emphasized the activation of *GK*s in specific situations is distinct from the perception of a "potential" requirement for such intermediate organs of strategic leadership. The Soviets, like any prudent military establishment, must prepare for a wide range of possibilities. Only the specific set of circumstances encountered in a conflict situation will determine the actual form of strategic leadership necessary.

The scope of a future war will have a bearing also on whether the *GK*s which would be activated would be considered axis *GK*s or *TVD* *GK*s. In WWII, if the scale of operations against a given enemy (i.e., Germany or Japan) extended beyond the jurisdiction of one *GK*, then the *GK*s in existence were said to have controlled strategic axes. However, if the area of responsibility of a given *GK* subsumed all operations against an enemy, as it did in Manchuria, then the organ was referred to as a *GK* in a *TVD*. There is considerable confusion today as to whether the Soviets see Europe as one *TVD* divided into three axes, as was the case in World War II, or as three *TVDs* constituting the European theater of war (*teatr voyny—TV*), which is the way they describe the NATO forces in Europe. The Soviets, of course, have not commented on this publicly.

The key to this question is the Soviet perception of the extent to which strategic objectives in various areas are seen as distinct and independent. The Soviets tend to see things in the broader rather than the narrower context. Therefore, they probably would view operations throughout Europe as being very closely related with regard to strategic objectives. This suggests that the European *GK*s would again be considered axis *GK*s, although their authority certainly would be much more extensive than the axis *GK*s in World War II. Continuing with the same criteria and pattern of logic, then, if two or more HCs were activated against the Chinese, they would almost certainly be considered axis *GK*s.

What difference does all this make? A good question. For the most part, an axis *GK* and a *TVD GK* would look the same structurally and would operate similarly. However, the CinC of a *TVD* High Command—due to his control over relatively independent operations—probably would have a greater degree of authority and autonomy. The perceived mutual dependence of axis *GK*s, particularly if there were three of them operating against one enemy and if there were two separate enemies (i.e., NATO and China), creates a potential need for additional organs of strategic leadership to coordinate the operations of all of the axis *GK*s opposing a given enemy. Such an organ would resemble NATO's Supreme Allied Command in Europe. From the various names under which *Stavka* operated in World War II, it is apparent a supreme command (*verkhovnoye komandovaniye*) is the appropriate term for an organ between a high command (*glavnoye komandovaniye*) and the supreme high command (*verkhovnoye glavnokomandovaniye*). The commanding officer of such a wartime supreme command might have the title of "Supreme CinC" followed by a geographical designation. For example, in a war with the Chinese, there could be a "Supreme Commander in Chief of Forces in the Far East" (which would be an upgraded variation of the title Vasilevskiy had in August 1945 and Govorov has now) to whom might be subordinated commanders in chief in up to 3 separate strategic axes. The extent to which the Soviets believe an organ such as a supreme command might be required is not known.

Improving the overall system of strategic wartime leadership, as evidenced by the proliferation of Soviet writings about the WWII system, is of great current concern to the Soviets. It takes time for new suggestions to be analyzed and evaluated thoroughly. Also, as new weapons systems are introduced; as command, control and communications (C^3) and anti-C^3 equipment and measures are perfected; and as crises in international relations appear; coordination requirements and the urgency of implementing new measures are intensified. As a result, concepts of strategic leadership are always in a state of flux. However, the Soviet press does provide significant indications as to the orientation of current Soviet thinking. Such clues should be searched for actively and analyzed in depth.

Notes

1. In June 1941, the Baltic, Western, and Kiev Special MDs were responsible for 1600 kilometers (47 percent) of the western borders and included 74 percent (127 of 171) of all divisions, 73 percent of all artillery and mortars, 89 percent of all tanks, 68 percent of all aircraft and about 75 percent of all troops. *Istoriya vtoroy mirovoy voyny*

1939–1945 [History of World War II 1939–1945] (Moscow: Voyenizdat, 1975), Vol. 22.

2. Colonel I. Vyrodov, "O rukovodstve voyennymi deystviyami strategicheskikh gruppirovok voysk vo vtoroy mirovoy voyne" [On the Leadership of Military Operations of Strategic Troop Groupings in World War II], *Voyenno–istoricheskiy zhurnal* [Military Historical Journal], No. 4, 1979, p. 18, hereafter cited as Vyrodov.

3. The personal account of General Pokrovskiy (*Voyenno–istorciheskiy zhurnal*, No. 4, 1978), who was Chief of Staff of the Southwestern *GK* under both Budennyy and Timoshenko, differs from the official Soviet record regarding when this HC was abolished. Shortly after Timoshenko took over as CinC in September 1941, the entire command of the Southwestern Front, having been denied permission to withdraw, was killed. According to the official history, on 26 September, Timoshenko became both CinC of the *GK* and Commander of the Southwestern Front. However, according to Pokrovskiy, who as Chief of Staff should have known, the *GK* was abolished at this time. The truth probably lies technically in Pokrovskiy's account; but Timoshenko—as a front commander, member of *Stavka*, and former Commissar of Defense—certainly retained authority over the other front (the Southern Front) in this axis, even if informally.

4. Pokrovskiy asserts that in one instance, it took Budennyy 12 days to get permission from *Stavka* to resubordinate two armies.

5. There is no evidence that Vasilevskiy was ever officially made a member of *Stavka*; also, since he had relinquished his position of Chief of the General Staff for the East Prussian operation, he had no official position at this time.

6. The axis High Commands never controlled more than two fronts at any one time.

7. Vyrodov, p. 22.

8. *Voyennyy vestnik* [Military Herald], No. 10, 1977, p. 10.

9. *Washington Star*, 15 July 1979, p. D3.

10. *Voyennyye znaniya* [Military Knowledge], No. 5, 1977, center page. Interestingly, this term was also employed briefly in WWII by the Soviets. The military personnel who were immediately sent to the fronts when Hitler's armies invaded were said to have been representatives of the *vyssheye komandovaniye.*

11. Vyrodov, p. 23.

12. The specific criteria for these elections has been determined, but the issue is not pertinent to the discussion at hand.

13. A major field command is defined here as a High Command or the command of the Moscow MD, which has the status of a HC with respect to CC seats.

14. As of February 1982, the incumbent officers who, it is hypothesized, might have major field commands in the event of war, listed in rank order, were as follows:
    I. M. Tretyak, Army General (10/76) — Cmdr, Far East MD
    I. A. Gerasimov, Army General (10/77) — Cmdr, Kiev MD
    G. I. Salmanov, Army General (10/79) — Cmdr, Transbaykal MD
    M. M. Zaytsev, Army General (11/80) — CinC, GSFG
    M. I. Sorokin, Colonel General (1976) — Cmdr, Leningrad MD
    P. G. Lushev, Colonel General (1976) — Cmdr, Moscow MD
    D. T. Yazov, Colonel General (1978) — Cmdr, Central Asian MD.

Perceptual Differences in Thinking the Unthinkable: World War III

Kenneth C. Stoehrmann

Introduction

While the nations of the world try to avoid such an encounter, the simple truth remains that World War III could become a stark reality in the future. No matter how it begins or, for that matter, who brings it on, a world war and its consequences must be comtemplated. Furthermore, it is incumbent upon every nation, every world leader, and every individual citizen to discuss objectively and rationally the prospects for such a war. Not to think about it will not make the possibility disappear. On the contrary, a failure to approach and analyze the problem is, in effect, a gross disservice to mankind.

In any study of any given situation, a complete, unbiased, and objective analysis is impossible. Each nation and individual has some prejudices and opinions which, knowingly or not, creep into any attempt at rational analysis. These biases and opinions form perceptions; because of these perceptions, the results of any analysis of a particular subject can be markedly different from another analysis of the same subject. Furthermore, if rational courses of action or policy options are formulated from these analyses, it is quite obvious a single set of circumstances can produce more than one set of actions or policies.

This article deals with these differing perceptions in the context of the possibility of a third world war. This article will seek to show these differing perceptions can be used to explain many of the past and present actions (in the areas of military doctrine and strategy) of several nations. And, in wartime, these doctrines and strategies translate into military action.

To accomplish this goal, this study will analyze the possibility of a third world war from three distinct national perceptions—the United States, the Soviet Union, and the member states of the North Atlantic Treaty Organization (NATO),[1] respectively. The first two perceptions represent those of the world's superpowers and must be taken into account in any possible future world war. The final perception represents a regional view of a nation(s) in a region (Europe) where a war could begin. (This region could have been just as easily the Mideast with Saudi Arabia, for example, selected as the actor.) The NATO perception was chosen because the region it represents still remains the focal point of possible superpower conflict.

It is not the purpose of this article to recommend solutions to problems which might arise in an analysis of differing perceptions. Rather, this paper only attempts to focus on the *need for recognition* of the fact there *are* differing perceptions. Advocacy of appeasement toward any one of these divergent views also is not suggested. However, the simple realization divergent views do exist can:

1. Make each nation more aware of the perceptions of other nations, thus *partially* explaining their actions;
2. Increase a nation's awareness of its own biases and lack of total objectivity in the structuring of its analyses and policy options; and
3. Help create a synergistic effect among the above factors which hopefully can strengthen national strategies and prevent a world war from occurring.

After a brief look at the methodology of this study, each of the differing perceptions outlined above will be analyzed.

Methodology

The methodology used to analyze the perceptions of the three actors under consideration is based on a scenario of a world war in Europe. In this methodology, two specific scales (or levels) of intensity are used. The first deals with the *geographic scope* of the war and the second with the *types of military force employed.*

Geographically, this scenario has the war beginning as a European theater or regional conflict.[2] This implies the homelands of the two superpowers are not threatened or attacked.[3] At some point in the scenario, this theater conflict will spread to the much larger scale of a general war. In this case, the homelands of both the United States and the Soviet Union are under at least the threat of direct attack. Thus, this geographic scale of intensity is a continuum which runs from a small, limited geographic area through, ultimately, a much larger area encompassing the superpowers.

On the second intensity scale, the types of military force employed, the major distinction is between the use of conventional and nuclear weapons. Yet, this scale does not represent an "either/or" condition. Both conventional and nuclear weapons can be employed in a variety of ways, on a variety of targets, and at various levels of intensity. Thus, this intensity scale is one which begins with the minimal use of conventional weapons and increases through the greater use of conventional weapons, minimal use of nuclear weapons, and, finally, greater use of nuclear weapons.[4] In effect, this scale is also a continuum based on weapon type and use.

Each of these intensity scales can be related to the war's overall level of escalation. Figure 1 shows this relationship. However, any position on each intensity scale will not produce the same war escalation level value for each of the three nations under consideration. The reason— perceptions. Each nation will make its own analysis of intensity versus escalation levels based on its perceptions of the situation. The result is three different analyses based on three different perceptions. The following sections explore these perceptions and analyses in detail.

Basic Relationship of Intensity Scales to Escalation Scale

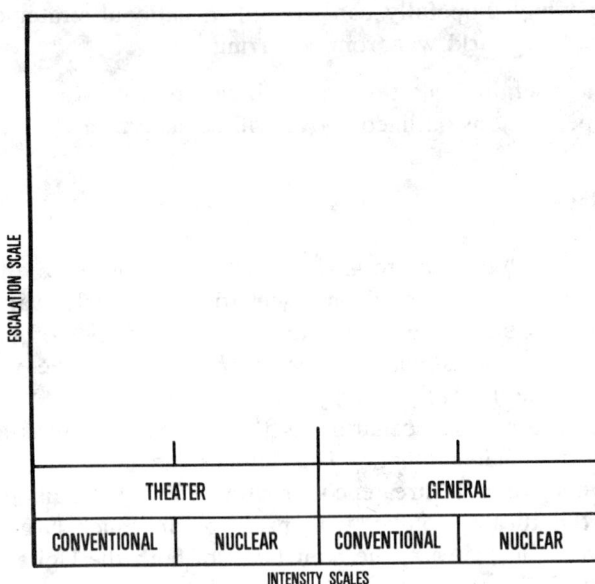

Figure 1.   Basic Relationship of Intensity Scales to Escalation Scale.

A final few words of caution are needed. It is important to remember each nation's perceptual analysis is separate and distinct from all others. Therefore, while it is correct to analyze relative differences in escalation levels (given certain values on the intensity scales) for each nation, it is incorrect to attempt to correlate different escalation levels for *different* nations (given definite values on the intensity scales). Each perceptual analysis is a complete product in and of itself. The only comparison which can (and most assuredly should) be made among the nations' perceptual analyses is a comparison of the policies and actions these analyses foster. For in the end, it is the policies and actions of each nation which affect the other nations in the arena of international politics.

The deterrence of aggression and the preservation of international stability remain the primary objectives of US military policy.[5]

The American perception of escalation levels versus intensity scales for a future world war is depicted in Figure 2. This perception is characterized by:

1. A gradual increase in the escalation level as the use of conventional weapons is increased in a theater conflict.
2. A sharp increase in the escalation level when the theater conflict moves into the use of nuclear weapons.
3. A slow but steady increase in the escalation level as the use of nuclear weapons in the theater conflict is expanded.
4. An ambiguous area of unknown or unidentifiable escalation in the arena of a general war with conventional weapons.
5. Another large and sharp increase in the escalation level as the general war moves into the use of nuclear weapons.
6. A gradual increase or possible leveling off of the escalation level as the use of nuclear weapons increases in the general war.

In a theater conventional war, the United States would respond by coming to the defense of its European allies. This has been American policy for decades:

There can be no doubt that Western Europe is of vital interest to the United States . . . . We are prepared, if necessary, to fight in defense of our European allies again.[6]
. . . The United States is committed to the integrity and security of Western Europe because it is in the vital interest of the United States to defend Europe. We followed that course in 1917 and again in 1941. Let no one think otherwise; we are fully prepared to follow it again.[7]

Initially, this defense would be concerned with stopping the onslaught of the Warsaw Pact (WP) forces. Because of the generally accepted belief that a massive amount of firepower will be needed to halt this advance, a variety of conventional weapons in varying (but probably large) quantities would be used. In addition, it is accepted that a WP thrust into central Europe would gain a certain amount of NATO territory before it is repulsed. Therefore, the required firepower (and commensurate destruction) will be applied in the NATO nations, especially West Germany. Thus, as more territory is lost to Pact forces and an increased amount of firepower is used to repel the attack, the escalation level most assuredly will increase.

United States Perceptions

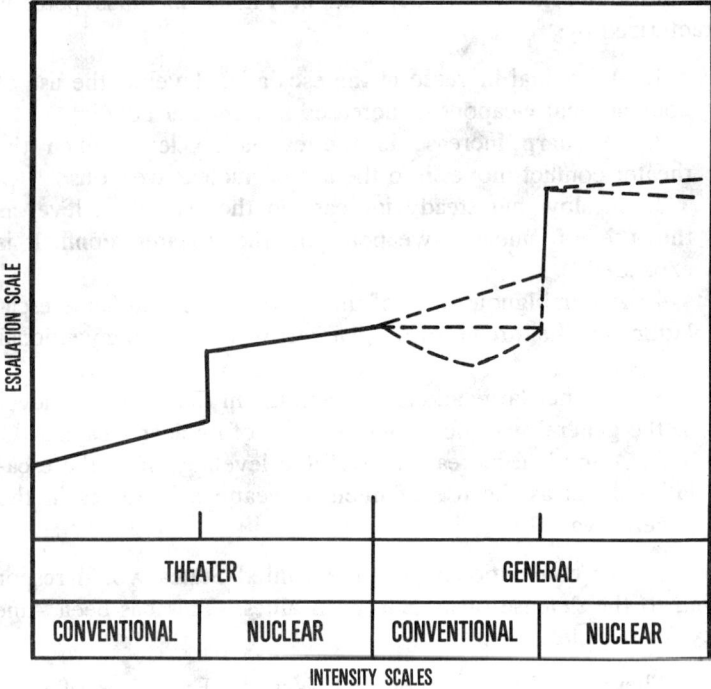

Figure 2.   The Perceptions of the United States.

However, this level of escalation will increase dramatically once nuclear weapons are employed. In keeping with the current American and NATO doctrine of flexible response, the employment of theater nuclear forces (TNF) represents a serious increase in escalation. Although many military and civilian scholars might argue to the contrary, the *stated* American policy on the use of TNF is that it is designed to impress upon the Pact nations the need to "cease and desist" immediately. As Defense Secretary Brown has stated, TNF capabilities

> . . . enhance our capability for forward defense and . . . create the risk of escalation to higher levels of conflict . . . . It remains essential . . . for NATO to maintain . . . the flexibility to leave the Soviets under no illusion that some way exists, by nuclear means, to gain military or political leverage on the Alliance.[8]

Indeed, America constantly refers to the "nuclear threshold" and the "selective employment of nuclear weapons" as distinct departures from the course of a theater nuclear conflict up to that point. This reasoning and this threshold can exist only if what is on one side of the threshold is, in some measurable form, different from what is on the other side. This can only be true if the perception of theater nuclear war is seen as a measurable increase in escalation over theater conventional war.

Once theater nuclear weapons are used, escalation will continue to increase as the employment of these weapons increases. The threshold has been crossed and no longer matters. What now becomes important are the answers to the employment questions of "how many?" and "where?" Yet, in the American perception, the war is still a regional conflict away from the American homeland. It is still of secondary importance to the survival of the US. As succinctly stated by General David C. Jones, Chairman of the Joint Chiefs of Staff: "The defense of Europe stands *second* in importance only to the defense of American territory."[9] Even though American forces and weapons are in use, the perception is still one of a distant conflict with gradual escalation. American doctrine mirrors this. Very little thought is given to nuclear weapon employment *after the initial use* of these weapons. For the reasons cited above, the threshold is what is important, not follow-on actions. This brings to mind the often-asked question: "Can the US fight a European theater nuclear war?" The answer is unclear. Indeed, the need to ask the question only recently has surfaced. Perceptions appear to have prevented it from surfacing sooner.

If the conflict were to spread to a general war, there is an ambiguous escalation region involving the use of conventional weapons on the American homeland. Not much thought has been given to this type of war for two main reasons: (1) the strategic arsenals of each superpower are not structured around conventional weapons, and (2) intercontinental delivery systems for conventional weapons would most assuredly be manned bombers. Besides being the weakest and (some maintain) most vulnerable part of a strategic delivery force, neither superpower appears to have enough aircraft to mount a sustained, effective, and widespread conventional bombing campaign against the other.[10] Therefore, it is difficult to ascertain what a general war with conventional weapons would do to escalation levels. Maybe it is a moot point since the issues raised above negate the possibility of a conventional general war. However, some escalation possibilities do exist. They are (with appropriate rationale):[11]

1. No change in escalation from the highest level in the theater conflict because the use of nuclear weapons is already taking place; as long as their use does not increase neither will the escalation level.

2. An initial increase in the escalation level due to the perception the use of nuclear weapons in the theater conflict

might decrease as resources are devoted to conventional attacks on the US. This would be followed by a gradual escalation level increase as these attacks on the US homeland became greater.

3. A continued increase in the escalation level (be it gradual or sharp) as the American homeland now comes under direct attack. This is based on the rationale that escalation is a function of the geographic area under attack; an attack on the US itself is at a higher escalation level than any attack on any ally.

It is impossible to determine which of these (or any other) possibilities is correct. This is mirrored in US strategic thought. Discussion and serious consideration of a manned conventional strategic bomber has fallen from favor since the advent of nuclear weapons. In addition, the slow yet steady decay of American air defense forces (aimed primarily at defending the US against an attack by manned Soviet aircraft) might be a further signal this type of war will never again be fought (or so it is believed). What little resurgent interest there is in these two areas, particularly the former, is in terms of a theater conflict.[12] Therefore, actions and thinking—or the lack thereof—reflect the nebulous and indiscernible perceptions of this level of conflict.

The same cannot be said for the next level of conflict, general nuclear war. The use of nuclear weapons on the American homeland represents the highest level of escalation imaginable. Accordingly, the bulk of US strategic thought and action has concentrated on this level. This effort is mainly directed at preventing an attack from ever occurring—deterrence. As espoused by President Carter:

> In all our actions, we have maintained two commitments: to be ready to meet any challenge by Soviet military power, and to develop ways to resolve disputes and keep the peace. Preventing nuclear war is the foremost responsibility of the two superpowers.[13]

Yet, efforts are also directed towards the possibility of failure; in other words, toward retaliation or warfighting. If this latter possibility does occur, it is difficult to say whether escalation will continue or not. It appears to be a function of the initial Soviet usage rates of nuclear weapons—i.e., a massive first strike designed to obliterate the US as a world power versus a selective use of strategic nuclear weapons to gain a political or military advantage—as well as the American perception of the relative importance of deterrence and warfighting strategies vis-a-vis each other. This second factor is the most important. No matter what type of attack the Soviets launch, if the US views this failure of deterrence as the final, supreme act of war (and thus ignores a warfighting strategy), then escalation can occur because its occurrence would have to be part of a warfighting strategy—a strategy to which the US does not, in this perception, subscribe.[14] However, if the opposite perception holds true—that no matter what type of attack the Soviets launch, the failure of deterrence only means a warfighting strategy is now paramount and, therefore, employed—escalation can increase as the warfighting strategy dictates a continued struggle on the nuclear war level.[15] But, in either perception, it is obvious that the escalation level of a general nuclear war is a quantum jump above any previous escalation level. Thus, there is a massive amount of thought, time, and money devoted to US strategic forces and doctrine designed to deter just such an attack.

Finally, in analyzing current American policies and actions, it is interesting to note that the escalation "jumps" where the US has concentrated its efforts. The current debates (and decisions) to modernize both the theater nuclear forces (e.g., Pershing II, GLCM) and the strategic nuclear forces (e.g., Minuteman III, MX, and the manned bomber) support this point. Virtual ignorance of general war with conventional weapons also supports this view.

Overall, American perceptions force American analyses to be focused on key points on the escalation scale and not spread out over the entire escalation spectrum. The result is a somewhat choppy policy that only appears to address the peaks and worries little about the valleys. Thus, American perceptions clearly dictate not only current policies and actions but serve as a basis for future efforts in specific areas deemed important by the national decisionmakers.

The Perceptions of the Soviet Union*

The most fundamental security objectives of the Soviet leaders are the defense of the Communist regime and the territorial integrity of the USSR.[16]

---

*The perceptions of the Soviet Union discussed in this chapter are from the viewpoint of the Soviets' wanting to prevent an invasion of their homeland as well as the buffer zone of the East European Warsaw Pact nations. It was suggested at the conference that this viewpoint does not analyze Soviet perceptions in the area of waging an offensive war in Western Europe. In other words, the following analysis is structured around Soviet measures to build a solid defense around their homeland and does not address the Soviet measures of building a strong offense against Western Europe. However, as was noted at the conference, the two viewpoints might be inexorably related in that by building a strong offensive force aimed at Europe, the NATO nations are forced to concentrate their efforts on defensive actions against the Soviet offense. This, then, precludes the NATO nations from building a strong offense which the Soviets would view as threatening. In effect, the Soviets might be using a variation of the standard American football cliche that the "best offense is the best defense." I am indebted to Mr. T. K. Jones of the Boeing Company, fellow panel members, and conference participants for bringing this crucial point to light.

737

The Soviet perception of escalation levels versus intensity scales for a future world war is depicted in Figure 3. It is characterized by:

1. A gradual increase in the escalation level throughout the theater conflict corresponding to the increased use of both conventional and nuclear weapons.

2. An ambiguous area of unknown or unidentifiable escalation in the arena of a general war with conventional weapons.

3. A large and sharp increase in the escalation level as the general conflict moves into the use of nuclear weapons.

4. A gradual increase in escalation with the expanded use of nuclear weapons in a general war.

Soviet perceptions in a theater conflict appear to be governed by the overriding belief it is best to fight a war away from the Soviet homeland. As history clearly shows, a string of devastating invasions of European Russia by a variety of foes has fostered a deep-seated obsession with territorial defense of the homeland.

> . . . The Soviets have a deep-seated and historically well-founded concern about foreign military invasion . . . . Soviet concern about foreign invasion is not based simply on bitter Russian historic experience at the hands of such aggressors as the Mongol hordes of Ghengis Khan and Napoleon's *Grande Armee*. Their wariness also reflects direct experience during the Soviet period.[17]

And these experiences of the Soviet period—especially World War II—are still vivid in the minds of most Soviet citizens and, more importantly, the Soviet leadership. The latter constantly fuels the invasion fears of the people by continually reminding them of their sacrifices for the Soviet homeland and promising such sacrifices will not have to be made again. In effect, this cleverly disguised use of domestic propaganda is the basis for the justification the Soviet leadership uses on its own people for the existence of the Warsaw Pact and the vast amounts of Soviet manpower and resources devoted to the alliance. Yet, there are also other forces at work which reinforce the Soviet desire for a strong territorial defense. Geography has also played a part:

> The Soviet Union occupies a central geographic position, straddling the continents of Europe and Asia . . . . Thus, Soviet interests and concerns range from their Scandinavian neighbors in Norway and Finland in the northwest, through the communist client regimes of Eastern Europe, on to Turkey, Iran and Afghanistan in the Near East, to Pakistan and

India in South Asia, and China and Japan in the Far East. The majority of these frontiers are marked by no significant geographic barriers, thus contributing to the historical perceptions and reality of Russian vulnerability to overland invasion.[18]

Soviet Perceptions

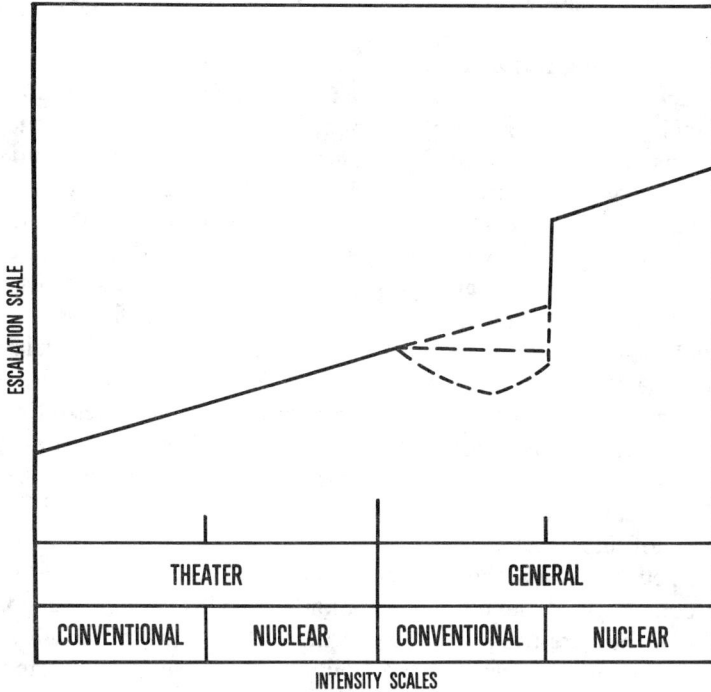

Figure 3. The Perceptions of the Soviet Union.

Indeed, one very logical rationale for the existence of the Warsaw Pact is that the non-Soviet Warsaw Pact (NSWP) member states act as a buffer against any future war being fought on Soviet territory.

The Soviet near obsession with defense has provided a powerful impetus for the accumulation of military power and for the steady expansion of Soviet political and military control beyond their political frontiers. Motivated by what some observers have called a quest for "absolute security," the Soviets have, for over forty years, accorded the highest investment priority to defense. In addition, they have sought to establish and enlarge a territorial buffer, particularly in Europe, between themselves and their prospective enemies. This drive to erect a *cordon sanitaire* lay behind the Soviet establishment of their first Communist satellite regime in Outer Mongolia in 1921 and their absorption of the Baltic states and eastern portions of Poland, Czechoslovakia, and Romania in 1939–1940. It also lay behind the subsequent westward expansion of "baggage train" communist regimes, that were imposed throughout most of Eastern Europe in the wake of advance of the Red Army at the end of World War II.

Retention of subservient communist governments throughout Eastern Europe has remained a high priority Soviet security objective throughout the post war period.[19]

Thus, strengthening this buffer zone to prevent attack is of great importance. And if a war should occur, an aggressive defense within (but not extending eastward beyond) this buffer zone is a necessity.

With this as a background, it is somewhat easier to understand the Soviet perception that any conflict in the buffer zone—at any weapon employment intensity level—is simply a theater conflict. The use of conventional or nuclear weapons does not bring the sharp escalation jump that is found in Western (particularly American) perceptions. To the Soviets, the use of nuclear weapons in a theater conflict is a graduated and logical (and possibly needed) upward extension of escalation. In effect, the Soviet perception appears to be one of making it more and more costly for any potential adversary to attempt to seize Soviet-allied territory, thereby deterring an attack on the Soviet Union proper. Whatever level of punishment is necessary to stop such aggression is used. The distinction as to whether that punishment is conventional or nuclear is not important.

Soviet actions follow these perceptions. Soviet units train to fight a theater conflict at all levels of escalation with all types of weaponry. In addition, they are trained to defend themselves against the full spectrum of weaponry. Overall, Soviet military doctrine is postulated on the belief that all available means of warfare must be used in any theater conflict if aggression cannot be halted:

> . . . The contemporary Soviet approach to theater war and, to a considerable extent, intercontinental conflict as well clearly reflects key elements that were already evident in the Soviet doctrine for massed, armored warfare called the theory of "operations in depth," developed almost fifty years ago . . . . At the same, Soviet doctrine calls for *all possible offensive and defensive efforts* to limit the damage that the Soviet Union itself would suffer in a war.[20]

A nuclear (or, for that matter, a chemical or biological) battlefield is not alien to the Soviets. It is simply fighting at an escalation level appropriate for the conditions at hand, conditions that must be manipulated into a Soviet advantage so as to prevent invasion of Soviet territory.

As the theater conflict spreads to an arena of a conventional general war there is—as with the US perception—an ambiguous area of unknown escalation. For many of the same reasons as cited in the US case, Soviet perceptions in this area appear to be based on the concept such a war will never occur; however, possibilities for escalation do exist.[21] Three potential perceptions of the situation are:

1. No escalation from the level attained in the theater conflict. This could be rationalized by believing the use of nuclear weapons in the theater conflict is a greater escalation than the use of conventional weapons on the Soviet homeland. However, given the Soviets' lack of distinction between theater conventional and theater nuclear war and the overriding Soviet obsession to protect their homeland, it is more likely a general conventional war would see

2. An increase in the level of conflict. This increase would vary in size depending on the type, location, and frequency of the conventional attacks on the Soviet Union.

3. An initial de-escalation could occur if the use of nuclear weapons in the theater conflict were reduced as resources were devoted to attacking the Soviet homeland. However, this initial reduction would have to be followed by an escalation as conventional attacks on the homeland became more numerous and destructive.

While no definitive answer concerning the Soviet perception in this area is possible, it appears that circumstances favor the second escalation perception. Soviet actions appear to confirm this. The Soviets' massive defensive system is designed to prevent any air-breathing or ballistic missile threat from reaching the Soviet Union. (This system is much more effective against the former than the latter.) No distinction seems to be made, especially in the case of the air-breathing threats, as to what type of weapon is being carried. Such a defensive network must be a reflection of the perception that even a conventional attack on the Soviet Union is unacceptable and, therefore, is in itself an increase in the level of escalation.

As the general war moves into the use of nuclear weapons, a sharp escalation rise does take place. The Soviet perception which accounts for this change is twofold. First, the homeland is under attack; second, the weapons being used are the most destructive imaginable. However, after the initial use of nuclear weapons in a general war, escalation can continue to increase no matter how severe and all-encompassing the first attack. This can be accounted for by the Soviet perception that a general nuclear war does not equate to the end of Soviet society. Rather, the expanded use of nuclear weapons in a general war represents only another increase in escalation.

To this end, Soviet actions mirror this perception. Probably the best example of this is the massive civil defense program in the Soviet Union designed to protect its people, industry, military production facilities, and leadership from repeated nuclear attack:

> Civil defense plays a major role in Soviet war survival strategy. The Soviets view civil defense as a strategic asset essential to ensure survival of the state and victory in war. For this reason, they have created an extensive civil defense organization.[22]

According to the Soviets, the basic goals of civil defense are:

> 1. protecting the population from weapons of mass destruction;
> 2. preparing national economic installations for work stability under conditions of enemy attack;
> 3. conducting urgent rescue and emergency restoration operations at sites of destruction.[23]

Soviet doctrinal writings which constantly discuss the warfighting capability of the USSR's strategic nuclear forces, rooted in a warfighting military doctrine at both the conventional and nuclear levels, reinforce this point:

> . . . Soviet doctrine . . . dwells little on such matters as deterrence-maintenance and pre-war crisis diplomacy and devotes by far the greatest amount of its attention to . . . the prosecution and successful termination of nuclear war in the event deterrence fails.[24]

Neither example above would appear to be useful if the Soviets perceived a general nuclear war (in its initial stages) as the highest level of escalation possible.

Overall, Soviet perceptions of escalation tend to represent a logical and steady increase as a conflict progresses through the two intensity scales. With the one noticeable exception of an escalation jump occurring at the onset of general nuclear war, the Soviets follow a smooth, incremental approach to escalation. Their actions on several fronts and their doctrinal approaches to theater and general war confirm these perceptions. In the final analysis, these Soviet perceptions provide the Soviet decisionmaking hierarchy with a solid basis for a thorough and complete analysis of escalation which appears to handle adequately all intensity levels.

The Perceptions of NATO

The perceived threats to security are almost exclusively those posed by the Soviet Union and its Warsaw Pact allies; and the response to them has been framed within an Atlantic Alliance setting, for national security is judged to be inseparable from that of the NATO area as a whole and capable of being safeguarded only by acknowledging interdependence.[25]

The NATO perception of escalation levels versus intensity scales for a future world war is depicted in Figure 4. It is characterized by:

1. A gradual increase in the escalation level as the use of conventional weapons is increased in the theater conflict.
2. A sharp increase in the escalation level when the theater conflict moves into the use of nuclear weapons.
3. A slow but steady increase in the escalation level as the use of nuclear weapons expands in the theater conflict.
4. A leveling off of the escalation level in all phases of a general war at all weapon employment levels.

The NATO perception differs markedly from either the Soviet or American perception in two very basic, yet crucial, ways. First of all, the war begins on NATO's territory. There is no "theater" or "regional" conflict which precedes an all-out attack on its member states.[26] As such, from the beginning of the war, the member nations of NATO are fighting for their basic survival. Such is not the case with the superpowers (at least until general war is reached). In addition, NATO is not a superpower. This colors its perception of its place in the international political arena. It is a unique outlook, singularly peculiar to NATO and the Europeans:

The European model of the cold war or of the East-West conflict with its two blocs, two armies, two types of regime, has never been reproduced in the rest of the world.[27]

These perceptions explain why at the initial level of conflict—theater conventional war—the escalation level is quite high, with a continued increase as the war consumes more and more NATO territory and more and more conventional weaponry is employed by both sides. In essence, NATO's perceptions dictate that it must try to avoid war. If that fails, a successful and decisive repulsion of invading Warsaw Pact forces must occur swiftly. NATO's actions and doctrines tend to reinforce this belief since the alliance stresses:

The Perceptions of NATO

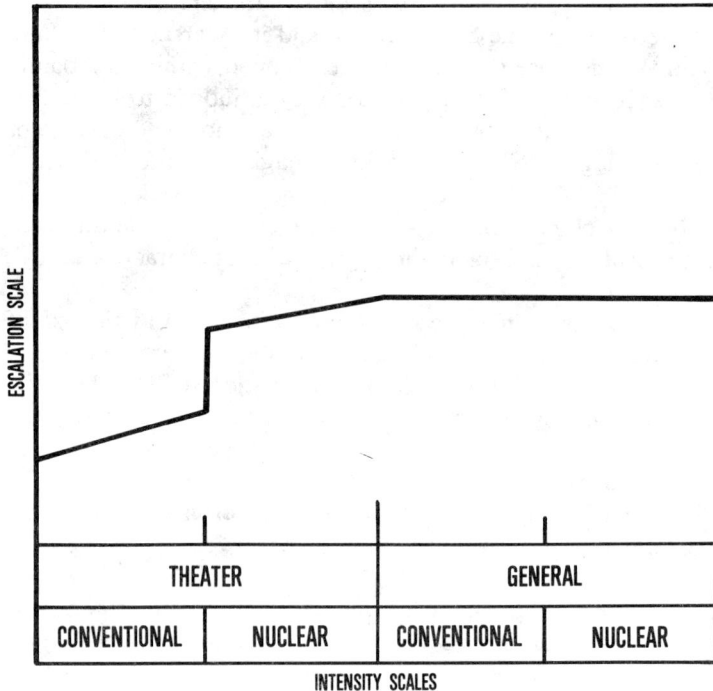

Figure 4.   The Perceptions of NATO.

1. A strong conventional defense using the concept of "forward defense;"[28]
2. An ability to mobilize and deploy forces rapidly;
3. An adequate supply of weaponry;
4. A "nuclear guarantee" from the United States;[29]
5. Strong support for the doctrine of "flexible response."

However, should these policies fail and a conventional theater conflict expand, a much worse fate awaits NATO. That fate is, quite obviously, a theater nuclear conflict. Escalation takes a large jump as this type of conflict erupts, simply because the weapons now being used by and on the NATO nations are much more detrimental to their continued existence as functioning nation-states. As with the American perception, the move from theater conventional to theater nuclear weapons is the crossing of a threshold with all the attendant implications. But, in addition—in NATO's eyes—this threshold crossing to a theater nuclear war equates to a general nuclear war for the superpowers. It is no wonder then that this escalation level is significantly higher than the theater conventional escalation level.

The policies and actions followed by NATO as regards this level of conflict clearly show NATO's concern for preserving its individual member states while at the same time maintaining a strong deterrent force to prevent war and a strong defensive force to fight a war. This presents NATO with an interesting paradox, no more obvious than in the area of theater nuclear forces (TNF). On the one hand, most NATO nations believe that strong TNF are needed to deter aggression and prevent war. However, the actual use of TNF (and the corresponding Warsaw Pact response) means that the nuclear threshold has been crossed, the escalation level has increased dramatically, and the very survival of the NATO nations is in question. Thus, the NATO TNF policy has been a shifting and nebulous one, accurately reflected in the ongoing debates within NATO over the utility of upgrading the TNF. Overall, the NATO (and, in a sense, the European) case has been perceptively stated by Henry Kissinger:

> Europeans dreaded at one and the same time the devastation of a nuclear war on their densely populated continent and our [US] apparently growing reluctance to resort to nuclear weapons. They wanted to make the Soviet Union believe that any attack would unleash America's nuclear arsenal. If the bluff failed, however, they were not eager to have us implement the threat on their soil. Their secret hope, which they never dared to articulate, was that the defense of Europe would be conducted as an intercontinental nuclear exchange over their heads; to defend their own countries, America was invited to run the risk of nuclear devastation from which they were shying away.[30]

Finally, once the regional conflict expands into a general war (of either conventional or nuclear proportions), the escalation level has a tendency to drop off. This is because the main emphasis has shifted away from the theater conflict to the superpowers' homelands. It is still probably true that fighting will continue in Europe for some time, but the majority of the resources and weaponry will now be devoted to the superpowers, leaving Europe to wait for the outcome. The theater war fought in Europe already has decimated many European nations. Further escalation seems unimaginable since the war is now being fought elsewhere and Europe is in partial or total ruin.

This perception is also evident in current NATO policies. Very little thought has been given to NATO's place or role in a general war.[31] Quite the contrary; most of the NATO nations link their security to the security of Europe[32] and structure their policies accordingly. Britain's stated defense policy stresses this point:

Of the nation's actual policy objectives, the central one is: to help deter aggression against either the United Kingdom itself or its European allies. National and regional secruity are regarded as inseparable.[33]

Even non-NATO West European nations such as France believe in this perception (although France still participates in NATO's non-military activities):

The fate of France cannot be separated from that of the rest of Europe. Clearly France's sovereignty, at the very least, would be greatly impaired by the loss of one of her neighbor's freedom . . . . Therefore, one of the critical missions of the French armed forces, directly connected to national security, is to take part in the defense of Europe.[34]

In addition, this lack of concern for a general war might also be due to two other perceptions. First, there is the belief among some that NATO will no longer exist when the war moves from a theater to a general conflict because, as previously mentioned, a theater conflict for NATO is tantamount to general war. Secondly, for NATO, a general war would seem to be the result of a theater war which failed to resolve the issue at hand. Thus, this theater war is what is of greatest importance (so the issue can be resolved, ideally in NATO's favor) and, therefore, where NATO's analysis, time, and money should be directed.

In conclusion, it appears that, based on NATO's perceptions, escalation has two very definite, specific levels, both occurring in the theater conflict setting. To NATO, a general war, by definition, has meant its efforts in the theater conflict have failed. NATO's policies and actions, from deterrence to warfighting, are structured accordingly.

Conclusions

Any conclusions drawn from this study must be built on the realization that the perceptions of one nation cannot be used either to predict future actions of another nation or to analyze and find reasons for that nation's current actions. A truly meaningful appraisal of "the other side" can only come about by viewing the situation (in this case, a possible future world war) from the other side's perception. This can then logically lead to the formulation of new policies based on the perceptions of *both* nations. Anything less could result in policies not in the best interests of each nation's national objectives.

Failure to use this technique has been perceived by some scholars as presently occurring in several instances in the United States. One instance is the attempt to explain Soviet strategic "doctrine" using American perceptions, even though there might be fundamental differences between the two countries:

> The predisposition of the American strategic community is to shrug off this fundamental doctrinal discrepancy [between the United States and the Soviet Union]. American doctrine has been and continues to be formulated and implemented by and large without reference to its Soviet counterpart . . . it is high time to start paying heed to Soviet strategic doctrine, lest we end up deterring no one but ourselves.[35]

> There is something innately destablizing in the very fact we consider nuclear war unfeasible and suicidal for both, and our chief adversary views it as feasible and winnable for himself.[36]

A second instance is in the realm of strategic arms limitation negotiations with the Soviets:

> By projecting our views onto the Soviets, and failing to appreciate their real motives and perceptions, we have underestimated the difficulties to achieving genuine strategic stability through SALT and over-sold the value of what we have achieved.[37]

From the analysis presented in this article, it appears clear differing perceptions do exist. In terms of geographic intensity, there is the obvious dichotomy between NATO fighting for its survival in a theater war while the two superpowers see the fighting as not penetrating their respective homelands. In addition, there is a further differentiation in terms of how the United States views a theater war (a conflict in a region allied to America) and how it is viewed by the Soviet Union (a theater conflict on the "doorstep" of the nation). Each of these differing perceptions translates into different views of escalation. Therefore, each nation's methods of controlling this escalation and keeping it at an acceptable level differ. This can be a partial explanation of the current defense and foreign policies of these nations, to wit:

1. A NATO policy of a strong deterrent coupled with the forward defense of its territory.
2. An American policy of the maintenance of flexible response, capable of responding in kind (i.e., not letting the theater conflict expand) to Soviet aggression.
3. A Soviet policy of military might which uses its East European buffer zone as a strong wall to prevent any conflict from spreading onto Soviet soil.

In terms of weapons employment intensity, perceptual differences are also present. The Soviets clearly view any theater conflict as a war which can, and most assuredly will, see the employment of the full range of conventional and nuclear weapons. Soviet doctrine stresses this, and Soviet field training confirms it. For the United States, a theater conflict is one which should be kept at conventional levels as long as possible with the use of nuclear weapons being a last resort. Furthermore, the Soviets regard the use of nuclear weapons as a logical continuation of warfare in the theater context. Americans view the use of nuclear weapons as a quantum jump in the level of escalation which should be avoided. NATO countries view any type of weapons employment—conventional or nuclear—as detrimental to their continued existence. Thus, while the Soviet Union trains for a theater war of any magnitude, America shies away from an early . . . or possibly first . . . use of nuclear weapons, and NATO takes measures to avoid any type of war at just about any cost.

Once a theater conflict spreads to general war, both superpowers see a nuclear attack on their respective homelands as a significant increase in escalation. Here again, there are differences, however. The Soviet Union sees further escalation occurring after the initial exchange of nuclear weapons. This is reflected in its belief it can fight and win this type of conflict. The United States, on the other hand, tends to view such an exchange as cataclysmic and probably sees no further escalation occurring.[38] Thus, the latter sees the need to avoid general nuclear war at all costs; the former is not so definitive in such pronouncements. Finally, the NATO nations view a general war of any magnitude as an indication their efforts to save Europe have failed. In effect, NATO watches a general war from the ruins of its continent. Therefore, to plan for and participate in a general nuclear or conventional war is of minimal, if any, importance. The defense policies of the NATO nations are structured accordingly.

These differing perceptions at all intensity levels mean that each nation has different priorities. Policies reflecting these priorities are part and parcel of the present defense programs of these nations and form the basis for the different deterrent, defensive, and (presumably) offensive strategies each employs. Without due regard for these perceptions and priorities, one-sided or uninformed criticism or condemnation of a specific policy or strategy is most probably incorrect and, more important, detrimental to world peace. Likewise, an attempt by one nation to force its policies upon other nations without considering these factors could be equally disastrous.

In conclusion, it is worth repeating that these differing perceptions point to the need for nations to come to grips with the realization that:

1. Differing perceptions do exist;
2. A nation's own perceptions cannot be used to analyze

another nation's actions;

    3. A nation has its own set of perceptions, and they must be critically analyzed to insure objectivity in that nation's own analyses.

The product of these realizations can only be a synergistic one which results in better national policies and hopefully prevents a future world war from ever occurring.

Often one hears the expression: "You wouldn't feel that way if you were in my shoes!" As it applies to the varying perceptions of nations in the international arena involved in preventing a future world war, it could not ring more truly.

Notes

1. It can be argued that the NATO perception applies equally to the non-Soviet Warsaw Pact nations. This is based on the fact the issue dominating each perception—the levels of escalation—is viewed in the same light by all European nations, be they members of NATO or the Warsaw Pact. Equally important, this perception can be shared by other European nations which do not belong to either alliance, such as Austria and Sweden.

2. Once again, it is worth repeating the selection of Europe as the region where a future world war could occur was arbitrary. It just as easily could have been (and many scholars maintain that it more likely will be) the Mideast.

3. The case can be made this definition is fallacious because any European theater conflict must involve both the European nations themselves and that portion of the Soviet Union in Europe. However, this study assumes a European theater war to be essentially a war fought either in the NATO nations, the NSWP nations, or in both, rather than in the Soviet Union proper. The Soviets see a European war as being fought in this manner, too. See Edward L. Warner, III, "Defense Policy of the Soviet Union," in *Comparative Defense Policy*, 2nd ed., Douglas J. Murray and Paul R. Viotti, eds., (Baltimore: The Johns Hopkins University Press, 1981), p. 14.

4. It can be argued persuasively that the amount of damage done by the high-level use of conventional weapons is comparable to, if not greater than, the selective, minimal use of low-yield nuclear weapons. The fire bombings of Tokyo in World War II versus modern nuclear artillery shells are a good example of this. However, as defined in this study, the intensity scale for the employment of force is *not* a measure of damage inflicted, but rather a measure of the usage rates and types of weapons used.

5. David C. Jones, *United States Military Posture for FY 1981* (Washington: Government Printing Office, 1980), p. 7.

6. Harold Brown, *Department of Defense Annual Report, Fiscal Year 1981* (Washington: Government Printing Office, 1980), p. 45.

7. Ibid., p. 96.

8. Ibid., pp. 91 and 94.

9. Jones, *Military Posture*, p. 2. Emphasis added.

10. The case can be made that the United States does have enough B–52 and FB–111 bombers to launch a massive conventional air attack on the Soviet Union. However, the excellent Soviet air defenses and the questionable penetrability of the American bombers would probably mean a fairly high attrition rate. Thus, the United States would appear to be unable to maintain a *sustained* conventional bombing program against the Soviet Union.

11. Neither the possibilities listed nor the rationale for each are all-inclusive. This discussion is only meant to show possibilities. There is plenty of room for healthy disagreement in each area.

12. It is a well-known fact B–52D aircraft were used in the closing stages of the Vietnam conflict and, advocates of heavy bombers argue, helped bring the war to a close. There is a substantial body of disagreement over this contention. However, the point is the use of bombers in a conventional role seems myopically limited to a theater conflict scenario without due regard for possible strategic uses.

13. "Excerpts from 'State of the Union' Address by President Carter, 23 January 1980" *Survival*, May–June 1980, p. 120.

14. Many critics of current American strategic doctrine lament this ignorance of such a warfighting strategy in favor of total reliance on deterrence. As Benjamin Lambeth puts it, "The emphasis on 'mutual assured destruction' rather than 'improved war outcome' capabilities in U.S. force planning provides a standing confirmation of this American strategic orientation, as does the virtual absence of discussion in American strategic writings of how one might effectively cope with (and terminate) a crisis which devolved into strategic nuclear exchanges. Whether out of a genuine belief in the efficacy of mutual deterrence or out of a reluctance to 'think about the unthinkable,' American strategic thinking by and large seems to grind to a screeching halt at the point where deterrence gets bowled over by war." Benjamin S. Lambeth, "The Sources of Soviet Military Doctrine," in *Comparative Defense Policy*, 1st ed., Frank B. Horton III, Anthony C. Rogerson, and Edward L. Warner III, eds. (Baltimore: The Johns Hopkins University Press, 1974), p. 210.

15. There are indications the United States is moving towards a strategy which takes into account some of the precepts of a warfighting strategy. However, deterrence is still of primary importance. Secretary Brown: "The most fundamental objective of our strategic policy is nuclear deterrence." Brown, *DOD Annual Report*, p. 65. Changes are occurring in targeting doctrine, however. See "Carter Policy Avoids Nuclear 'Apocalypse,'" *Denver Post*, 10 August 1980, p. 10.

16. Edward L. Warner III, "Defense Policy of the Soviet Union," p. 14.

17. Ibid., p. 4. Warner continues, "The Soviet assiduously kept alive the memory of several foreign incursions. These include: the invasion by Imperial Germany just weeks after the Bolsheviks seized power in November 1917; the military interventions of Britain, France, the United States and Japan on behalf of the rival "White" forces who battled the Bolsheviks during the Russian Civil War, 1918–1920; their border clashes with Imperial Japan in 1938 and 1939; and, most significantly, the devasting effects of the Nazi invasion and brutal occupation in 1941–44."

18. Ibid., p. 35.

19. Ibid., p. 14. Warner continues on p. 15, "This unrelenting Soviet determination has been visibly demonstrated in the Soviet Army's brutal suppression of would-be defector regimes in Hungary in 1956 and Czechoslovakia in 1968. The Soviets demonstrated a similar willingness to employ armed forces to maintain a 'friendly' communist regime in power in neigbboring states in Asia as well in their 1979 invasion of Afghanistan."

20. Ibid., p. 40. Emphasis added.

21. See note 16.

22. *Soviet Aerospace Handbook* (Washington: Government Printing Office, 1978), p. 22.

23. P. T. Yegorov, I. A. Shlyakov, and N. I. Alabin, *Civil Defense* (Moscow: Izdatel'stvon "Vysshaya Shkola," 1970) translated under the auspices of the United States Air Force (Washington: Government Printing Office, 1976), p. 6.

24. Benjamin S. Lambeth, "The Sources of Soviet Military Doctrine," in *Comparative Defense Policy*, 1st ed., p. 210.

25. David Greenwood, "British Defense Policy," in *Comparative Defense Policy*, 2nd ed.

26. This statement is not entirely true, especially in the case of Britain and France. If a Warsaw Pact attack were to occur, the immediate *land battle* would be fought, most probably, in West Germany. However, air strikes would probably occur in all

NATO nations and the relatively short distances (when measured against the distances between the two superpowers) between NATO and the Warsaw Pact nations would seem to dictate an early involvement by every European nation in a European theater conflict.

27. Raymond Aron, "The 1978 Alistar Buchan Memorial Lecture," *Survival,* January–February 1979, p. 5.

28. "West German White Paper on Defence," *Survival,* November–December 1979, p. 276. This document spells out the concept of "forward defense" quite well. In the West Germans' perception, "An essential element of NATO's strategy is the principle of forward defense. Forward defense is defined as a coherent defense conducted close to the intra-German border with the aim of losing as little ground as possible and confining damage to a minimum. This includes the recapture of lost territory. For the Federal Republic of Germany there can be no alternative to forward defense: in view of her geostrategic situation, her population density near the border to the Warsaw Pact and the structure of her economy, any conceptual model of defence involving the surrender of territory is unacceptable."

29. This guarantee is being seriously questioned by some nations. "At the same time, the credibility of America's military capability is being questioned. At the point of nuclear parity, the old Gaullist suspicion that the United States would not risk its cities for the defense of Berlin or Hamburg has taken on new plausibility." Fritz Stern, "Germany in a Semi-Gaullist Europe," *Foreign Affairs,* Spring 1980, p. 870. However, on p. 884 Stern stresses that not all nations feel this way: "For all the temptations of detente and for all the apprehensions of an eastward drift, the Germans know that the Western alliance and the American nuclear shield are the sole guarantee of German security . . . ."

30. Henry A. Kissinger, *White House Years* (Boston: Little, Brown and Company, 1979), p. 83.

31. The one major exception to this might be the British and French independent nuclear forces. Britain's recent decision to buy the Trident system certainly attests to the interest of that nation in maintaining modern strategic systems. Improvements in French nuclear forces also point in this direction. However, it is unrealistic to assume either nation has or will have the necessarily large strategic systems to fight a general war for any length of time. Both nations see their present strategic systems as one-use "punishment" systems aimed at deterrence. Thus, not much thought is given to strategic planning for a protracted general war.

32. "It is only in alliance with the North American countries that the security of Europe and the Federal Republic of Germany is assured. At the same time, Europe is an important factor in American security." "West German White Paper," p. 273.

33. Greenwood, "British Defense Policy," p. 21.

34. "Speech by Yvon Bourges (Excerpts), 27 August 1979," *Survival,* January–February 1980, p. 39. French policy was not always this way: "At the strategic and doctrinal level, two principal changes occurred. First, the idea of France as a 'total sanctuary' was discarded, and replaced by the concept of the *sanctuarisation elargie* (enlarged sanctuary or enlarged security area). This meant that French forces would now be expected to engage an opponent in areas approaching France—the classic *bataille de l'avant* (forward battle) . . . . Second, the nuclear heavy doctrine of 'massive retaliation' was replaced by a doctrine of 'flexible response', remarkably similar to that of NATO . . . ." Alan Ned Sabrosky, "The Defense Policy of France," *Comparative Defense Policy,* 2nd ed.

35. Richard Pipes, "Why the Soviet Union Thinks It Could Fight and Win a Nuclear War," *Commentary,* July 1977, p. 1.

36. Ibid., p. 14.

37. Fritz W. Ermarth, "Contrasts in American and Soviet Strategic Thought," *International Security,* Fall 1978, p. 154.

38. This conclusion could possibly change.

The Soviet Union and Protracted Nuclear War©

Richard S. Soll

In early August 1980, reports in the US press of a so-called Presidential Directive 59, signed by President Carter in July, prompted some gusts of controversy both within the United States and in reactions from Moscow. According to the reports, the Presidential Directive approved a revised US strategic nuclear doctrine featuring a priority on targeting military installations in the Soviet Union in the event of a nuclear war—e.g., Soviet missile bases and political headquarters—rather than on destroying Soviet cities in a mass attack.

The ostensible rationale behind the directive was that the nuclear prowess of the Soviet Union had grown so significantly since the 1960s, the threat of destroying Soviet urban centers no longer was deemed a sufficient US deterrent to Soviet attack. American defense officials now felt that the best way to prevent a major conflict with the Soviet Union was to acquire the capability to knock out selected portions of the Soviet nuclear arsenal in a prolonged but precisely focused war.

The Soviet response to this announcement was immediate and vehement . . . but hardly surprising. Thus, Anatoliy Krasikov, a *TASS* commentator, charged on 8 August:

> The White House is trying to instill in Americans and people of other countries the idea that it is possible to wage a nuclear-missile war dealing blows only against troops and command posts while the civilian population escapes suffering only minimally. This is a very dangerous doctrine whose aim is to lull people's vigilance and to bring closer the destruction of civilization.

Krasikov went on to issue dire warnings about an intensification of the arms race. The US strategy, he averred, would require a new generation of more precise missiles, and "it would be naive to think that the Soviet Union would be idle" if such new weapons were produced.[1]

There was nothing really startling in the Soviet reaction, given not only its obvious propaganda content but also the fact the Soviets have for a long time accused the United States of harboring designs of a "counterforce" posture. Indeed, in a commentary on the announced US strategy in *Krasnaya zvezda* [Red Star] on 8 August, L. Semeyko contended that "one wonders what is new about it."

Nevertheless, even if the harsh Soviet reaction was predictable, it was tainted by a certain irony. For what the Soviets are accusing the United States of is the latter's ostensible movement toward the nuclear "warfighting" doctrine which has animated Soviet military strategy and weapons procurement for two decades. Put differently, what Moscow is excoriating is in effect its own mirror image.

Victory As The Central Soviet Criterion

By its very nature, the Soviet view of the feasibility of fighting and winning a nuclear war is an exercise in thinking about what most Americans still regard as unthinkable. The initial gesture toward a US "countervailing strategy," implicit in Presidential Directive 59, testifies to the budding awareness in Washington that the US strategic posture no longer should be steeped exclusively in the concept of assured destruction and, concomitantly that US and Soviet political-military perceptions and values are dissimilar. Nevertheless, with few exceptions, authoritative US thinking in the realm of deterrence continues to focus on the massive nuclear exchange (as well as lower levels of violence) and fails to look beyond this contingency. There are occasional allusions to a "secure US strategic reserve force," but the failure to consider nuclear warfighting and warwinning places this reserve force into a vague no-man's land of strategy.

Soviet military leaders and analysts, in contrast, evince belief in the attainability of victory in a nuclear war; they have contended over the past two decades that victory can be assured only if the Soviet Union prepares for every nuclear war contingency. They reason that although the destructiveness of nuclear weapons might point to the likelihood that a general war's outcome will be shaped within a relatively short period of time, the possibility of a more protracted engagement needs serious consideration. Since in the Soviet view, victory—not "war termination" in the US understanding—is the ultimate (and only acceptable) outcome, the temporal dimension is driven by the need to achieve decisive conditions for victory rather than by reliance upon the initial objectives achieved in the massive exchange.

This view of the possible prolongation of general nuclear warfare clearly imposes requirements in the areas of military force planning and acquisition; economic recovery; civil defense; political control; and military strategy, operational art, and tactics. Moreover, it is undoubtedly recognized in the Soviet Union that the satisfaction of these requirements promotes a certain self-fulfilling prophecy; namely, the combatants, having planned for a long-war contingency, are able to deny each other victory for an indefinite length of time. The Soviet image of protracted warfare thus also implies a Soviet view of the United States as possibly being prepared to conduct military operations in an extended time frame.

Since the early 1970s, beginning with the SALT I agreements and other accords heralding the so-called era of detente, a controversy has been swirling among US analysts of Soviet military-strategic beliefs and objectives. The assertions of the 1960s, which explicitly spelled out the requirements for military superiority and a preemptive nuclear strike strategy vis-a-vis the United States, have given way to a body of literature in which Soviet interests and intentions are much less sharply silhouetted. In some cases, Soviet spokesmen appear to deny or contradict the earlier formulations. Some US analysts—most notably Raymond L. Garthoff—have seen in this a real shift in Soviet military perceptions and expectations; according to this view, a convergence has taken place in Soviet and US thinking about mutual deterrence and strategic parity.[2]

There is a contrary view shared by this writer: Soviet military doctrine and strategy publicized throughout the 1960s remain in place and continue to guide all facets of Soviet military actions; the "modified" (and obfuscated) public line adopted by the Soviets on military doctrine and strategy has mirrored the attempt to influence US arms limitation and weapons procurement policies; a careful analysis of Soviet writings, particularly when correlated with observable force posture phenomena on the Soviet side, can demonstrate the consistency of the Soviet strategic doctrine which has spanned two decades. The unclassified Soviet military literature upon which the present analysis principally is based offers sufficient insight into the Soviet view of protracted nuclear warfare.

Clear evidence emerges from those writings that Soviet military thinkers continue to reject the concepts of mutual deterrence and assured destruction. Although explicit references to preemption and military superiority are often deleted—and, in some cases, Soviet adherence to these concepts is denied outright—the basic precepts of nuclear warfighting and warwinning clearly remain the centerpieces of Soviet military doctrine and strategy.

Thus, in the entry on "Military Strategy" in the authoritative *Soviet Military Encyclopedia,* Marshal of the Soviet Union N. V. Ogarkov, Chief of the General Staff and First Deputy Minister of Defense, asserts that the Soviet Union, in keeping with its defensive character, does not envisage "preemptive strikes or premeditated attacks."[3] In order not to deceive the Soviet reader, however, Ogarkov reverses this formulation two pages later with the statement that Soviet military strategy stresses "the aim of frustrating or repelling the aggressor's attack" (the former term long being used as a euphemism for preemption).[4] The reader is signaled further by the bibliography which immediately precedes Ogarkov's signature: included is the definitive text on Soviet military thought published in the 1960s, the third edition of *Voyennaya strategiya* [Military Strategy], edited by Marshal of the Soviet Union V. D. Sokolovskiy.[5]

With respect to protracted nuclear warfare and victory, Ogarkov's commentary in the *Encyclopedia* is unequivocal:

> It is considered that, with the contemporary means of destruction, world nuclear war will be comparatively short. However, considering the enormous potential military and economic resources of the coalitions of belligerent states, *it cannot be excluded that it may also be prolonged.* Soviet military strategy proceeds from the view that should the Soviet Union be thrust into a nuclear war then *the Soviet people and their Armed Forces need to be prepared for the most severe and protracted trial.* The Soviet Union and the fraternal Socialist states will be in this case, in comparison to the imperialist states, in possession of definite advantages: the established just goals of the war, and the advanced nature of their social and state systems. This creates for them the *objective possibility of achieving victory.* However, for the realization of this possibility there is the necessity for timely and comprehensive preparation of the country and the armed forces.[6]

Although Ogarkov does not offer any details regarding the force posture procurement and employment implications of this strategy of preparing for a protracted nuclear warfare contingency, these can be gleaned from the Soviet military literature of the 1960s and early 1970s. This body of literature which is comprised of a number of works, including the Ministry of Defense journal *Voyennaya mysl'* [Military Thought] and Sokolovskiy's authoritative book, largely antedates the start of the deliberate effort by the Soviets to obfuscate their strategic intent. In light of the continuity in Soviet military doctrine and strategy over the past two decades, these earlier works still are highly germane to current Soviet thinking.

The term "protracted nuclear warfare" may be somewhat misleading in that the discussion here is about Soviet views of warfare beyond the initial use of nuclear weapons. Soviet spokesmen also discuss the possibility of waging conventional (as well as nuclear) operations for some time after an initial nuclear exchange. The central point in any case is that Soviet military thinkers do not consider the massive nuclear exchange between the superpowers as necessarily ending the war and appear to have planned for the contingency of extended military conflict.

Stated Soviet Wartime Objectives

The Soviet image of protracted general warfare is a logical outgrowth of fundamental Soviet perceptions and objectives of war. War,

755

in the Soviet view, is a manifestation of political phenomena; a global nuclear war, specifically, would be the decisive clash between capitalism (i.e., imperialism) and socialism. According to an authoritative Soviet military theoretician, a war waged by imperialism against the Socialist countries would have certain characteristics:

> The first of these is that this war would inevitably become worldwide in scale and, in terms of its political content, would be a struggle between the two opposed systems—socialist and capitalist—and a struggle with most clear-cut objectives. The second most important feature of a possible world war would be in the coalition nature of both sides. A third characteristic of such a war would be that, as regards the means of armed struggle, it would be a thermonuclear war. Finally, this war would undoubtedly be on an intercontinental scale, which modifies our concepts of front and rear, the main targets for strategic strikes, reserves, and so forth.[7]

While in the US conception, a future thermonuclear war would constitute an aberration from—indeed, a virtual abandonment of—politics, Soviet spokesmen assert not only that politics guide military strategy but that "success in war can be achieved *only when* politics and strategy are in total conformity with one another."[8] According to this formulation, the class struggle will rage throughout the course of the war, and victory will be achieved by the socialist countries as assuredly in war as it would be by the preferred alternative of peaceful means. Soviet authors explicitly reject the Western view of war, which they label "bourgeois pacifism" or "bourgeois pessimism." In the words of the Editor in Chief of *Voyennaya mysl'*:

> If international imperialism unleashes a war, then the people of the Socialist countries and their Marxist–Leninist parties will not cringe in terror and will not lose heart, as the monopolists would like. The peoples of the world of socialism will engage the enemy decisively, filled with confidence in the triumph of their cause.[9]

Consequently, the broader political goals of socialism (and the Soviet union in particular) will determine Soviet wartime objectives and the military means by which they are realized.

As Zavyalov has articulated, the Soviet objectives in a future world war will be "most clear-cut." Generally these objectives entail: (1) defeat of the enemy's armed forces; (2) disruption and destruction of the enemy's administrative-political centers; (3) disruption and destruction of the enemy's military-industrial centers; and (4) total disorganization of the enemy's rear areas.[10] Moreover, some Soviet military spokesmen contend that although initial wartime aims can be fulfilled via nuclear missile strikes, these may not suffice in the attainment of the overall political-military objective: "Combat operations will continue for the purpose of the final defeat of the enemy on his own territory."[11]

It is clear, too, that with respect at least to Europe this means the seizure and occupation of territory for the purpose of facilitating the reconstitution of Soviet military forces and the recovery of the war-torn Soviet economy. As one Soviet military writer puts it:

> . . . it is very important to determine which targets and enemy economic regions should be left intact or rapidly reconstructed and used in the interests of strengthening the economic potential of our own country and for supplying the troops. It is important also to determine which, what, where, and in what quantity the local resources can be stored and used in the interests of the troops. It is important also to determine what are the conditions for acquiring or using local resources (the presence of electric-power and transportation means, manpower resources, transport capability, etc.).[12]

These objectives can be mastered, according to the same author in a subsequent article, by determining the effects which nuclear strikes will exert at a specific time in the course of the war and the impact the elimination of a given target will have on the continued military, economic, and political functioning of the enemy.[13] "Critical links" in the economy should therefore be identified and targeted; in addition to military industry, these are said to include in particular the chemical and petroleum industries, power-generating facilities, and transportation.[14]

It appears, in addition, that Soviet military planners are sensitive to the problem of imposing a level of firepower which is adequate to knock out a target but permits its subsequent reconstruction and use by Soviet troops and the Soviet economy. In line with this, Soviet spokesmen preach a careful matching of the appropriate combination of weapon and yield to the given target. The following passage is an example:

> Initial attention is given to the selection of those enemy targets against which strategic nuclear means could be best used. Depending on the features of the strike targets, a selection is made of the nuclear weapons carriers (strategic missiles, missile-armed aircraft, submarines, or surface craft) which could best and most rapidly execute the assigned

757

mission with minimum expenditure of explosive power.[15]

This principle of addressing the minimum necessary explosive power to the target should not be confused with the Western concept of collateral damage avoidance. Soviet military planners are concerned *solely* with the fulfillment of a given military-political mission. They do not appear inhibited by the prospect that the destruction of a given objective will spill undesired damage beyond the target. For example, although the populations of enemy countries apparently are not Soviet targets themselves, projected civilian casualties incidental to the attack of a political, military, or economic target would not restrain the target decision. The Soviet Union appears resigned to the prospect that large numbers of people would be killed (and even entire countries annihilated) in a future world war. The achievement of victory, however, remains the sole political-military (as well as moral) imperative.

Survival of the Homeland

The Soviet concept of victory does not equate simply to a cessation of hostilities but encompasses both the "final defeat" of the enemy (by means of the coordinated application of combined arms) and the continued functioning of Soviet political, military, and economic institutions. With regard to the "final defeat" of the imperialist enemy (i.e., the United States, the NATO countries in Western Europe, Japan, and the People's Republic of China), Sokolovskiy stated in all three editions of *Voyennaya strategiya:*

> In order to achieve victory in war, it is still not sufficient to destroy the military potential of the aggressor, his strategic combat weapons, and his government and military leadership. For final victory, it is absolutely necessary to defeat the armed forces of the enemy, capture his military bases, if for some reason they cannot be destroyed, and to seize strategically important regions. In addition, it is also necessary to defend one's own country from invasion by land, air, and naval forces. These tasks and a number of others can be performed only by modern ground troops . . . .[16]

As will be discussed below, this concept of the conditions and requirements for achieving victory has contributed significantly to the Soviet perception of war's possible duration.

The principal assumption behind the tenet of "victory" in a nuclear war—namely, the survival of the Soviet national entity and its vital institutions—does not seem linked to unrealistically low expectations of likely damage to the Soviet homeland. In fact, Soviet spokesmen assert that one precondition for victory is the peacetime manufacture and storage of material, since the range of nuclear weapons and their destructive potential have wiped out the old military distinction between the front and rear. The homeland, in the words of one author, must be organized "as a theater of military operations."[17]

Nonetheless, the objective of limiting damage to the Soviet homeland is a key element in Soviet military doctrine and strategy and is to be satisfied by both offensive operations (e.g., preemptive counterforce strategy, antisubmarine warfare, anticarrier warfare) and defensive means (e.g., air defense, ballistic missile defense, civil defense). The apparent improvements in Soviet damage-limiting capabilities, most notably civil defense,[18] seem to have created a shift in Soviet thinking about the prospects of the continued functioning of the economy in *wartime.*

In a 1968 aritcle published in *Voyennaya mysl',* two leading Soviet military theoreticians wrote:

> . . . nuclear war may be conducted only with means existing at its beginning, since it will not be possible to count on mobilizational development of the economy in these conditions. The possibilities of production functioning in a period when nuclear strikes are exchanged and during a lengthy period after them are wholly problematical.[19]

By the mid–1970s, however, then Minister of Defense Grechko proposed that the Soviet economy could continue to function during the war if appropriate measures were taken:

> If one does not carry out timely measures for raising the steadiness of the work of the national economy and for the protection of the population, then from the start of the war, this can lead to a sharp decline in industrial production, the disruption of economic ties among individual regions, the disabling of tranportation, of means of control and of electrical power systems, the destruction of cities, and enormous human and material losses. And as is well known, war cannot be waged without a reliable and functioning rear.[20]

Although Grechko's statement could be interpreted as more urging measures still to be implemented rather than acknowledging current Soviet capabilities, the implicit optimism contrasts sharply with the formulation a decade earlier.

In either case, Soviet spokesmen proclaim that the Soviet economy, based upon the principles of socialist management and organization, is inherently better equipped to cope with the trials of nuclear warfare than are the economies of the capitalist countries. It is argued that the ability of the economy to achieve intrawar or postwar recovery, and especially the prewar amassing of state reserves, are preconditions for victory. According to Sokolovskiy:

> There can be no doubt about the fact that the enormous exertion of a future war is going to be able to be borne only by states having a stable social and governmental system, enjoying the support of the whole of the people and possessing a highly developed economy . . . . In a word, a modern economy must be able, in the shortest possible time, to provide the armed forces with the maximum number of modern means of warfare and to provide them completely and regularly with everything necessary in case the duration of the war is extended. The economy must be prepared for this in peacetime.[21]

The importance of economic recovery was similarly emphasized by a Soviet civil defense official in 1972:

> The immeasurably increased dependence of the Soviet Armed Forces on economic bases makes it incumbent on our civil defense to consider its highest priority responsibility to be that of participating in the restoration of the vital activities of those industrial and agricultural production facilities damaged by the enemy.[22]

Given the primacy of politics in the Soviet view of war, the survival of the national political-military (i.e., "strategic") leadership inheres in the concept of nuclear warfighting and war-winning. Indeed, some Soviet military spokesmen have maintained that "if nuclear war becomes fact, the importance of political leadership in such a war will increase to an exceptional degree."[23]

Soviet writers envisage the Soviet national leadership in a future world war being organized as it was during World War II:[24] a select agency of the Party's Central Committee, corresponding to the current Council of Defense and the World War II State Committee of Defense, will manage the country and the armed forces. As in World War II, direct control over the armed forces will be accomplished by the *Stavka* [Headquarters] of the Supreme High Command, a collegial body of leadership under the chairmanship of the Supreme Commander in Chief and the major nexus of political and military control.[25]

This national leadership—and, beyond it, the Party and governmental leaders at various levels throughout the USSR—apparently are given priority by the civil defense organization. It is estimated that some of the leaders' shelters are harder than those provided for the general population. Moreover, while fixed leadership shelters would be vulnerable to direct nuclear attack, the national leadership most likely has recourse to alternate (e.g., mobile) means of protection.[26] The requirement for ensuring the wartime survival and uninterrupted functioning of the Soviet national leadership is stated explicitly in all three editions of *Voyennaya strategiya:*

> Concentration of the leadership of the country and its Armed Forces in the hands of the highest political agency of governmental control, as during the years of the last war, is *a decisive condition of the victorious waging of a war,* in case one should be unleashed by imperialist aggressors. Only an organic relation between the leadership of the country and the Armed Forces can provide the most efficient utilization of the economy and all the scientific and technological achievements of the country, the complete mobilization of the material and moral and political forces of the state, and the utilization of the Armed Forces *in order to achieve victory.*[27]

To iterate, several elements fundamental to the Soviet concept of general nuclear warfare have shaped Soviet views and expectations with regard to the possible duration of a war:

- War is a manifestation of political phenomena, as defined by the class struggle; therefore, the belligerents wage war for clear-cut objectives.
- The global triumph of communism, through either war or peace, is inevitable.
- The Soviet wartime objective of achieving decisive victory requires the final defeat of the enemy by means of conducting combined arms operations subsequent to nuclear missile strikes. This entails the seizure and occupation of enemy territory and facilities in order to enable Soviet recovery during and subsequent to the war.
- The continued functioning of Soviet political-military and economic institutions is a vital condition for wartime victory.

The Evolution of Soviet Concepts of Extended War

The notion articulated by Ogarkov in 1979 and cited earlier—that while the destructive potential of nuclear weapons suggests that a future world war will be comparatively short, "it cannot be excluded that it may also prolonged"—has been a consistent theme in Soviet military thought for over 20 years, even though the emphasis has shifted somewhat over that time frame. In the early post-Stalin period, the view gained currency among Soviet military theoreticians that the initial nuclear exchanges of a war could (but not necessarily would) determine the outcome of the war.[28] The effect of the initial exchange was (and still is) believed to depend upon the ability of the Soviet forces-in-being at the start of the war either to achieve a surprise first strike against the enemy and destroy the bulk of his forces-in-being at the start of the war or, alternatively, to blunt an enemy first strike. In either case, but particularly the latter, it was thought the role of mobilized reserves in the subsequent phase of the war might be decisive. The greatest significance was attached, however, to forces-in-being of both sides since their success in achieving a surprise attack or blunting an enemy attack would condition the efficacy of the reserves in the later phases.[29]

This view contrasts sharply with that which was prevalent prior to the mid–1950s and which put the major emphasis on the forces that could be mustered after the outbreak of hostilities. Nevertheless, the supreme value of victory in war dissuaded Soviet military thinkers from the other extreme; namely, the nature of the new type of weaponry determined *a priori* that the next conflict would be a lightning war which would be over in a matter of hours. Soviet military doctrine was forced to make provisions for the case of the US first strike against the USSR, or a less-than-disarming Soviet strike against the United States, and thus allow for Soviet victory in the subsequent period.

In his speech to the 22nd Congress of the Communist Party of the Soviet Union (CPSU) in 1961, then Minister of Defense Malinovskiy repeated the position that the Soviet Union would:

> . . . devote special attention to the initial part of a possible war. The importance of this period lies in the fact that the very first mass nuclear strikes are capable, to a vast extent, of predetermining the whole subsequent course of the war and could lead to such losses in the rear and among the troops as would put the people and the country in an exceptionally difficult position.[30]

Malinovskiy, like the military theoreticians of the 1950s, admits to the possibility of the war continuing subsequent to the initial strategic strikes, although the duration of this subsequent phase is not described.

By 1962, however, the notion that this subsequent period might be protracted began to be reflected in authoritative Soviet doctrinal and strategic writings. The "possibility of a protracted war" was raised in a few places throughout the first edition of *Voyennaya strategiya* (1962),[31] as it was later that year in a monograph authored by Minister of Defense Malinovskiy. According to the latter:

> At the present time, no one can deny the possibility of a

short-lived war . . . . However, it is quite obvious that depending on the conditions of origin of the war (for example, who strikes first), the armed struggle to the finish will not be limited only to attacks with nuclear weapons. It may be dragged out and may require long and maximum effort of all forces of the army and of the country as a whole.[32]

Within a year, with the publication of the second edition of *Voyennaya strategiya,* references to the possibility of a extended nuclear conflict multiplied. This might have been in response to the gradual realization that with improving weapon accuracies and concomitantly lower nuclear yields, the damage which would ensue from the initial strikes might not be as great as formerly had been believed. In addition, the notion advanced by US Secretary of Defense McNamara of a city-advoidance targeting strategy in June 1962—an event which received considerable attention from Soviet military analysts[33]—as well as increasing prospects for successful combined arms exploitation of the results of the massive nuclear exhange may have enhanced, in the Soviet view, the possibility and feasibility of conducting protracted operations.

The following passage from *Voyennaya strategiya* documents this trend in Soviet thinking. The first part of the paragraph appeared in both the first (1962) and second (1963) editions of *Voyennaya strategiya;* the second part, identified by italics by the present author, first appeared in the 1963 edition. The entire paragraph was carried over into the third edition (1968).

The enormous possibilities of nuclear-rocket weapons and other means of combat enable the goals of war to be attained within a relatively short time. Therefore, in order to ensure the interests of our country and all the Socialist camp, it is necessary to develop and perfect the ways and means of armed combat, anticipating the attainment of victory over the aggressor first of all within the shortest possible time, in the course of a rapidly moving war. *But the war may drag on and this will demand protracted and all–out exertion of army and people. Therefore, we must also be ready for a protracted war and get the human and material resources into a state of preparedness for this eventuality.*[34]

A further addition to the 1962 text, linked to the protracted warfare issue, is a statement found in the second edition: "We should particularly note the ever increasing need to utilize the local resources within enemy territory, something for which our rear units must be prepared."[35] It should be noted that the addition of these and similar statements to *Voyennaya strategiya* probably reflected the accretion of a consensus among leading Soviet military theoreticians rather than an actual shift in Soviet thinking, inasmuch as they mark a change in emphasis rather than in substance.

Soviet military spokesmen seem to envisage a combination of nuclear and conventional weapons being invoked in the so-called subsequent period of war. For example, in the 1962 statement cited above, Malinovskiy alluded to the case in which military operations to secure final victory would entail such a mixture of forces; that is, the campaigns "will not be limited only to attacks with nuclear weapons."[36] Some Soviet writers, particularly in the 1960s, opined that the belligerents' nuclear stockpiles would be depleted (or destroyed) in the initial phase of the war and extended operations, therefore, would be primarily conventional in nature. The following statement, made in 1969, was representative of this theme:

> The possibility is not excluded that a war can assume a relatively prolonged nature. The combatants, quickly expending the supplies of nuclear weapons created during peacetime and unable to produce them during the war, especially in its final stages, will carry out operational-strategic missions mainly by conventional means.[37]

One may speculate that substantial refinements in Soviet (as well as US) capabilities since the 1960s—by such advances as MIRVing and improved reconnaissance systems—may have dampened such earlier notions regarding the rapid expenditure of opposing nuclear arsenals in the initial phases of conflict. Nonetheless, the operational requirements of the *final* Soviet endeavor to achieve victory—i.e., the seizure and occupation of European territory and facilities and the countering of local resistance—implies a continuing emphasis on nonnuclear warfare in the protracted engagement.

A Phased Approach to General War

One of the most coherent depictions of protracted general warfare appeared in a 1969 article by General Major V. Zemskov, Editor in Chief of *Voyennaya mysl'*. Zemskov attributes to unnamed "military theoreticians of the United States" the view that a strategic nuclear war will feature two periods: "the first, which lasts for several days, and the next, which lasts for an undetermined time."[38] Zemskov tends to mix these alleged US views—the sources of which are not cited—with Soviet concepts in such a way that the reader must infer that these were Soviet views from the beginning. (The Soviet literature is rife with examples of Soviet concepts being advanced under the guise of "foreign points of view.") Furthermore, Zemskov takes the position that if the United States wants to wage war in this manner, the Soviet

Union had better be prepared and plan its forces accordingly.

Zemskov describes the initial period of the war as comprising, for the most part, a global nuclear attack conducted by both intercontinental and theater weapons systems. During this period, "the main military-political goals will be achieved."[39] The subsequent (or possibly protracted) period is characterized as follows:

In the course of the subsequent period, it is planned to implement also the regrouping of the forces, means and resources retained, the creation of new groupings of troops, restoration of the control and support system, and carrying out of operations for the purpose of achieving the goals of war [i.e., final victory].[40]

Additionally, in Zemskov's view, attention might shift back to the theaters of military operations (e.g., Europe and the naval domains) in the period subsequent to the initial exchanges, with "continuation of an extremely active nuclear conflict" in these theaters. This possible shift occurs, according to Zemskov, because the respective target sets in the United States and USSR presumably have been satisfied in the initial period. He suggests, nonetheless, that specific objectives in both the "deep regions" (that is the United States) and other theaters will continue to be targeted by nuclear means:

At this time, individual strikes can be inflicted by the surviving strategic forces (aircraft and nuclear submarines which did not succeed previously in entering the regions of fire positions), as well as the massed group and single strikes by operational-tactical means.[41]

In Zemskov's view, "the role of conventional means of destruction" will increase in the wake of these nuclear strikes in pursuit of exploiting the results of the latter. He further states that lengthy operational intervals, or lulls, may occur in particular zones or in entire theaters, with fighting subsequently breaking out anew.[42] These intervals are presumably driven by the requirement on both sides for force reconstitution, damage assessment, retargeting, and possibly some degree of economic recovery. According to the *Soviet Military Encyclopedia* (1977), protracted warfare in the generic and historical sense is characterized by these intervals:

The belligerents generally have utilized these intervals for diplomatic negotiations, for preparing and accumulating reserves and material means, and for gradual seizure of the initiative. Sometimes after the first battles (strikes), the belligerents, not having achieved strategic results, temporarily have discontinued combat activities.[43]

Incidentally, the role of diplomatic negotiations in the Soviet image of protracted nuclear warfare appears quite minimal, in light of the frequent emphasis on the "uncompromising nature of military operations."[44] Furthermore, as was indicated previously, the elimination of the political leadership of the enemy is consistently claimed as an objective that will be satisfied in the initial period of the war. The reference to diplomatic negotiations in the above-cited passage of the *Encyclopedia* therefore should be regarded as pertaining to a broad spectrum of conflicts and not necessarily to the specific context of general nuclear war.

Soviet spokesmen do not spell out the contemplated duration of the subsequent phase of the war. Although Zemskov states that "in comparison with previous wars, a nuclear war, in regard to time, has the tendency of sharply decreasing its duration," he is drawing a comparison with past wars (e.g., World Wars I and II) which raged over periods of several years. The factor of damage wreaked by nuclear weapons, particularly in the massive exchanges in the initial period, is believed to militate against future world wars of such lengths. Nevertheless, it is not unreasonable to assume that Soviet military theoreticians and planners look to the possibility of a general nuclear war of several months' duration, given the survivability of certain weapons systems and the expectation that the belligerents will be able to draw upon certain strategic reserves as well as limited economic recovery assets.[45]

Soviet Organization and Planning for Protracted Warfare

Soviet military leaders have long articulated the belief that in the event a future world war breaks out, "its initial period [will be] . . . of decisive significance."[46] What this denotes is an obvious Soviet preference for rapid victory. In the Soviet view, the optimal approach to planning for a protracted war is to prevent the war from becoming protracted in the first place—that is, by seizing the strategic initiative at the beginning of the war so that the enemy's ability to continue military operations will be throttled. Soviet military leaders understand, however, that this may not be accomplished, and that they must plan for a longer struggle. In Sokolovskiy's words:

> Planned preparation of a country for war should assure: the possibility of repelling the aggressor at any moment and of inflicting upon him a shattering retaliatory nuclear strike for the purpose of seizing the strategic initiative; the attaining of victory in the shortest possible time; the possibility, *if need be*, of waging war for a protracted period of time; *the*

ability to "hold out" against the massive nuclear strikes of the enemy with the fewest possible losses; and maintaining a high moral-political state of the population and bolstering its determination to achieve victory.[47]

Although, as was discussed previously, Soviet military leaders may believe that wartime production of materiel is possible (or will prove to be in the future), the emphasis is on peacetime production and protected storage of reserves. The assertion by one Soviet writer that in order for current peacetime production to meet future wartime requirements for the armed forces, "it is necessary to have an exact idea of the probable duration of the war"[48] is indicative of this position.

Major emphasis is devoted, therefore, to strategic reserves said to be at the disposal of the Supreme High Command (i.e., the State Committee of Defense and the *Stavka*) and intended primarily for employment in the so-called subsequent phase of the war. Sokolovskiy distinguishes between emergency and mobilization reserves on the one hand and strategic reserves on the other.[49] Emergency reserves are defined as those which are located with the combat units and commands in peacetime and thus are available at the inception of the war for early replenishment needs; mobilization reserves are distributed to units and commands as necessary after the outbreak of hostilities for the purpose of fulfilling missions in the initial period of the war. Strategic reserves, however, are to be used only when mandated by the Supreme High Command. The implication is clear that ideally they are to be withheld in the initial period of the war.

Soviet military spokesmen discuss the concept of "sequence of mobilization" which corresponds to the echeloned organization of the military forces of the country.[50] According to one commentator, the major task entrusted to the forces-in-being (that is, the first echelon) at the beginning of the war is the repulsion of an enemy surprise attack and the conduct of operations which are required immediately thereafter.[51] This principle of sequential mobilization is said to be essential since the complete mobilization and deployment of all echelons at the start of the war, "as was done in previous wars," is viewed as impossible in the throes of a rapidly moving nuclear conflict. The fact, too, that modern nuclear delivery systems blot out the former distinction between the front and rear puts, in the Soviet view, a further premium on the echeloned organization of the armed forces. The allegation is, therefore, that the Soviet Union maintains in a prepared condition in peacetime only "those armed forces which would be able to ensure the achievement of the most important strategic goals of war [i.e., in the initial period] until the time that the strategic reserves are mobilized and go into operation [i.e., in the subsequent period]."[52] In addition, the strategic reserves are required to correspond to all branches of the armed forces[53]—Strategic Rocket Forces, Air Defense Forces, Ground

Forces, Navy, and Air Forces—and include weapons, combat and support equipment, and associated manpower.

The obvious benefit of echeloned deployment is the protection of the strategic reserves during the period of large-scale nuclear missile exchanges as well as in the concomitant capability to achieve surprise and seize or retain the strategic initiative during the war. According to Major General Kruchinin: "The dispersal and covered displacement of the reserves, their concealment, especially against enemy aerial and space strikes, and their prompt and purposeful employment will ensure the successful execution of the missions."[54]

First echelon forces cannot be dispersed prudently and concealed to the extent that (1) their being mustered to alert status tips off an imminent preemptive or first strike or (2) their ability to respond or retaliate in a time-urgent manner is curtailed; yet, the forces intended mainly for employment in the subsequent period of the war can be protected without running similar risks of compromising the mission. A further consideration is the likelihood that the probability of the reserve forces' being detected will dwindle with the attrition of enemy reconnaissance systems as the war rages on.

Soviet military planners regard the employment of deceptive forms of concealment—particularly camouflage of actual troops and materiel or display of "dummy" or "decoy" equipment and installations—as essential, especially in the case of the reserves. According to an East German article reprinted in *Voyennaya mysl'*, operational camouflage includes "keeping operations preparations secret (radio silence, concealed control, dissemination of false information to the enemy); concealment of troop regroupings; camouflage of assembly areas of support echelons (reserves and supply bases); creation of dummy troop concentrations, command posts, defensive installations, structures, etc.[55] Strategic camouflage, additionally, is defined as "a component of defense of home territory and includes camouflage of important installations *from the moment of their construction.*"[56]

Submarines armed with ballistic or cruise missiles are vaunted by Soviet military spokesmen for their attributes of survivability, concealment, mobility; and dispersal—qualities that will stand them in good stead in a protracted war. Thus, one Soviet naval writer has attributed to nuclear-powered submarines "practically unlimited range and duration of autonomous cruising."[57] In the words of another author:

> It is sufficient to say that a nuclear-powered missile carrier is capable of delivering an accurate and powerful attack on strategically important targets at very long range. Naturally, the success of this attack will largely depend on whether the missile carrier can remain undetected until the moment its weapons are used and, more precisely, whether the ship's commander and the entire crew can maintain

secrecy *for a long time* under the complex situation of the antisubmarine struggle.[58]

Soviet naval planners recognize that, notwithstanding these inherent advantages, in a protracted war the submarine forces may have to be reconstituted.[59] The deployment of submarine support capabilities such as the *Amga*-class of missile support vessels which can reload submarine launch tubes with ballistic missiles while at sea is a salient example of the Soviet commitment to the principle of continious combat beyond the initial phase of conflict.

The reserve echelonment, or "duplication," of land-based missile forces is said to provide an additional strand of protracted war preparations. Although we do not know the extent of Soviet plans and capabilities for reloading cold-launch-equipped silos or for bringing older missile systems back into service, if need be, in the subsequent period of a war,[60] the concept of "duplication" appears in the open Soviet literature:

> In our press it has been noted that we place our rocket equipment so that double and triple duplication are ensured. The territory of our country is huge, and we are capable of dispersing rocket equipment and concealing it well. We create such a system that if some means intended for striking a counterblow were taken out of commission, it is always possible to place into operation duplicative equipment and to strike the target from reserve positions.[61]

This suggests echeloned *deployment* rather than simply *employment.* The implications of this for arms control agreements such as SALT, in which the total extent of each party's inventory is supposedly known to the other, is significant.

Concealment, therefore, is regarded by Soviet military planners as an essential feature of strategic reserve forces since it provides the forces with not only the requisite endurance (that is, protection from missile strikes in the initial period of the war) but also the cover under which they may have to be amassed in peacetime. Barring US development and deployment of a counter-silo capability against the Soviet Union—such as the MX—it could be argued that the Soviet leadership may feel comfortable in assigning a reserve role, beyond the submarine-based missile force, to a component of their land-based ICBMs—specifically, the SS–17 force as well as some of the SS–18s and SS–19s which might be left behind in a Soviet preemptive counterforce strike.

Lingering Uncertainties

The belief that a general nuclear war can be extended beyond the initial massive exchanges for an indefinite period of time is an important facet of Soviet military thinking and almost certainly affects Soviet force planning and deployments. The vitality of this belief can be demonstrated both deductively—from the logical context of Soviet reasoning on the requirements for nuclear war victory and national recovery—as well as inductively—from the body of authoritative military writings which explicitly discuss the subject. Nevertheless, a number of questions remain unanswered:

- What is the probable duration of protracted nuclear warfare envisaged in Soviet discussions? Is it thought of in terms of weeks, months, or years?
- Although final victory is claimed to be the only acceptable outcome of a future world war, and notwithstanding the fact that the Soviets play down the potential role of diplomatic initiatives in the midst of a nuclear conflict, are there nevertheless circumstances in which negotiated settlement (i.e., war termination without establishment of conditions for decisive victory) would be a tenable option to Soviet leaders?
- Have the Soviet military planners drawn up specific missions and scenarios with regard to protracted warfare?
- What do Soviet military thinkers perceive as the US assets which might deny the Soviet Union victory in the initial period of the war, thus causing the war to become protracted?
- What forces do Soviet planners deem required by protracted warfare? Are they now in the Soviet inventory? Do they represent excesses with regard to the ceilings established in SALT II?
- Is a specific proportion of Soviet strategic forces to be withheld from the initial period of the war in deference to considerations of protracted warfare? How much reliance do Soviet planners place on economic recovery in projecting force reconstitution prospects?

Perhaps not even Soviet military leaders and theoreticians can answer all of the foregoing, given the uncertainties that loom in the period beyond an initial nuclear exchange. It is evident, nonetheless, that they have long pondered these as well as other issues germane to the concept of protracted general nuclear warfare. While Soviet strategic thought has been exploring distant and uncharted waters, US military thinking is only beginning to venture forth from the comfortable harbor of beliefs about mutual deterrence and assured destruction.

Notes

1. Anthony Austin, "Reported U.S. Change in its Nuclear Strategy Condemned by Soviets," *New York Times,* 9 August 1980.
2. Raymond L. Garthoff, "Mutual Deterrence and Strategic Arms Limitation in Soviet Policy," *International Security,* Summer 1978, pp. 112–147.
3. Marshal of the Soviet Union N. V. Ogarkov, "Strategy," *Sovetskaya Voyennaya Entsiklopediya* [Soviet Military Encyclopedia] (Moscow: Voyenizdat, 1979), Vol. 7, p. 563.
4. Ibid., p. 565.
5. Ibid. Given the Soviet proclivity to purge impertinent material from bibliographies and libraries as part of the general exercise of rewriting history, the presence of a title in a listing of this nature affirms the current validity of this work.
6. Ibid., p. 564, emphasis added.
7. Lieutenant General I. Zavyalov, "The Creative Character of Soviet Military Doctrine," *Krasnaya zvezda* [Red Star], 19 April 1973.
8. Colonel S. Taran, "Leninist Theoretical Principles of Soviet Military Strategy," *Voyennaya mysl'* [Military Thought], No. 6, June 1971, trans. in Foreign Broadcast Information Service, *Foreign Press Digest* (hereafter referred to as *FPD*), No. 0015/74, 12 March 1974, p. 47, emphasis added.
9. Major General V. Zemskov, "Characteristic Features of Modern Wars and Possible Methods of Conducting Them," *Voyennaya mysl',* No. 7, July 1969, trans. in *FPD,* No. 0022/70, 6 April 1970, p. 22. See also Major General K. Bochkarev, "Nuclear Arms and the Fate of Social Progress," *Sovetskaya Kirgiziya* [Soviet Kirgizia], 25 August 1970; Rear Admiral V. Shelyag, "Two Ideologies—Two Views of War," *Soviet Military Review,* No. 11, November 1974, pp. 9–10.
10. Taran, op. cit., p. 46.
11. Colonel A. Gurov, "Economics and War," *Voyennaya mysl',* No. 7, July 1965, trans. in Central Intelligence Agency, *Foreign Documents Division* (hereafter referred to as *FDD*), No. 692, 25 May 1966, p. 5.
12. Colonel M. Shirokov, "Military Geography at the Present Stage," *Voyennaya mysl',* No. 11, November 1966, trans. in *FPD,* No. 0730/67, 27 July 1967, p. 60.
13. Colonel M. Shirokov, "The Question of Influences on the Military and Economic Potential of Warring States," *Voyennaya mysl',* No. 4, April 1968, trans. in *FPD,* No. 0052/69, 27 May 1969, p. 36.
14. Ibid., pp. 37–38.
15. Major General V. Kruchinin, "Contemporary Strategic Theory of the Goals and Missions of Armed Conflict," *Voyennaya mysl',* No. 10, October 1963, trans. in *FDD,* No. 965, 20 July 1966, p. 16.
16. Marshal of the Soviet Union V. D. Sokolovskiy, *Voyennaya strategiya* [Military Strategy] (Moscow: Voyenizdat, 1962, 1963 and 1968) trans. by Harriet Fast Scott as *Soviet Military Strategy* (New York: Crane, Russak and Company, 1975), p. 247.
17. General of the Army S. Ivanov, "Soviet Military Doctrine and Strategy," *Voyennaya mysl',* No. 5, May 1969, trans. in *FPD,* No. 0116/69, 18 December 1969, p. 50.
18. See Leon Goure, *War Survival in Soviet Strategy: Soviet Civil Defense* (Coral Gables, Florida: Center for Advanced International Studies, University of Miami, 1976), for a detailed analysis of Soviet civil defense capabilities.
19. Marshal of the Soviet Union V. D. Sokolovskiy and Major General M. Cherednichenko, "Military Strategy and Its Problems," *Voyennaya mysl',* No. 10, October 1968, trans. in *FPD,* No. 0084/69, 4 September 1969, p. 39.
20. Marshal of the Soviet Union A. A. Grechko, *Vooruzhennyye Sily Sovetskogo gosudarstva* [The Armed Forces of the Soviet State], 2nd ed. (Moscow: Voyenizdat, 1975), p. 114.
21. Sokolovskiy, op cit, p. 226. See also, Colonel V. Vasin, "Commentary 'On the Question of the Role of Economics in Nuclear Warfare,'" *Voyennaya mysl',* No. 11,

November 1965, trans. in *FDD*, No. 953, 8 March 1966, p. 33.

22. Colonel General V. Grekov, "Civil Defense—A Nationwide Matter," *Kommunist Vooruzhennykh Sil* [Communist of the Armed Forces], No. 19, October 1972, p. 21.
23. Taran, op. cit., p. 47, cites M. Povaliy, "Politics and Military Strategy," *Voyennaya mysl'*, No. 7, July 1970, on this point. The latter article is unavailable in the United States.
24. Sokolovskiy, op. cit., p. 361.
25. See N. A. Sbytov, "*Stavka* of the Supreme High Command," *Sovetskaya Voyennaya Entsiklopediya* (Moscow: Voyenizdat, 1979), Vol. 7, pp. 511–512.
26. Director of Central Intelligence, *Soviet Civil Defense*, NI78–10003, July 1978, pp. 8–9.
27. Sokolovskiy, op. cit., p. 361, emphasis added.
28. See the discussion in Herbert S. Dinerstein, *War and the Soviet Union* (New York: Frederick A. Praeger, 1959, pp. 215–222.
29. Colonel V. Petrov, "On the Essence of War Potential. An Aid to Students of the Marxist–Leninist Theory of War and the Army," *Sovetskaya aviatsiya* [Soviet Aviation], 20 May 1958, cited in ibid., pp. 220–221.
30. Marshal of the Soviet Union R. Ya. Malinovskiy, speech to the 22nd CPSU Congress, Moscow Domestic Service in Russian, 1030 GMT, 24 October 1961, reported in Foreign Broadcast Information Service, *22nd CPSU Congress*, Vol. 9, p. 20.
31. Sokolovskiy, op. cit., pp. 226, 306, 385.
32. Marshal of the Soviet Union R. Ya. Malinovskiy, *Bditel'no stoyat' na strazhe mira* [Vigilantly Stand Guard Over the Peace] (Moscow: Voyenizdat, 1962), p. 26.
33. Sokolovskiy, op. cit., pp. 56–61.
34. Ibid., p. 211.
35. Ibid., p. 317.
36. Malinovskiy, op. cit., p. 26.
37. Major General N. Vasendin and Colonel N. Kuznetsov, "Modern Warfare and Surprise Attack," *Voyennaya mysl'*, No. 6, June 1968, trans. in *FPD*, No. 0005/69, 16 January 1969, p. 48.
38. Zemskov, op. cit., p. 19.
39. Ibid.
40. Ibid.
41. Ibid., p. 21.
42. Ibid.
43. "Zatyazhnaya voyna" [Protracted Warfare], *Sovetskaya Voyennaya Entsiklopediya* (Moscow: Voyenizdat, 1977), Vol. 3, p. 416.
44. Zemskov, op. cit., p. 19.
45. Sokolovskiy, op. cit., p. 279, describes a Western conception of a general nuclear war of up to 2–months' duration.
46. Ibid., p. 384.
47. Ibid., p. 306, emphasis added.
48. Vasin, op. cit., p. 33.
49. Sokolovskiy, op. cit., p. 313–314.
50. See Sokolovskiy and Cherednichenko, op. cit., p. 40.
51. Lieutenant Colonel G. Lukava, "Some Theoretical Aspects of the Combat Readiness of Troops," *Voyennaya mysl'*, No. 6, June 1968, trans. in *FPD*, No. 0005/69, 16 January 1969, p. 50.
52. Ibid.
53. Kruchinin, op. cit., p. 20; Colonel I. Zhernosek, "On Theoretical Bases for the Development of Principles and Systems of Rear Support," *Voyennaya mysl'*, No. 4, April 1965, trans. in *FDD*, No. 957, 6 April 1966, p. 3.
54. Kruchinin, op. cit., p. 21.
55. Engineer–Lieutenant Colonel Kh. Adam and Lieutenant Colonel R. Gebel', "Military Camouflage," *Voyennaya mysl'*, No. 11, November 1971, trans. in *FPD*, No. 0004/74, 22 January 1974, p. 79.

56. Ibid., p. 82, emphasis added.
57. Captain 1st Rank B. Bannikov, "Characteristic Features of Contemporary Naval Operations," *Voyennaya mysl',* No. 2, February 1973, trans. in *FPD,* No. 0045, 20 November 1973, p. 37.
58. Rear Admiral A. Mikhaylovskiy, "The Tactical Aspects of Secrecy," *Krasnaya zvezda,* 9 June 1974, emphasis added.
59. Captain 1st Rank V. Artamonov, "Supporting Combat Operations of Submarines," *Voyennaya mysl',* No. 9, September 1973, trans. in *FPD,* No. 0055, 3 October 1974, pp. 47–48.
60. See David S. Sullivan, "The Legacy of SALT I: Soviet Deception and U.S. Retreat," *Strategic Review,* No. 1, Winter 1979, pp. 26–41.
61. P. T. Astashenkov, *Sovetskiye raketnyye voyska* [Soviet Rocket Troops] (Moscow: Voyenizdat, 1967), p. 65, cited in Harriet Fast Scott and William F. Scott, *The Armed Forces of the U.S.S.R.* (Boulder: Westview Press, 1979), p. 139.

Message from Sverdlovsk:
The April 1979 Anthrax Incident[*]

David T. Twining

Introduction

In early April 1979, a serious outbreak of anthrax took place in Sverdlovsk, a city of 1.2 million people located 875 miles east of Moscow. According to Western press reports, late one night between 3 and 6 April anthrax bacteria escaped into the air from a Soviet military facility, an accident which ultimately led to the deaths of as many as 1,000 Soviet citizens.

This article will assess the message of Sverdlovsk by reviewing the incident, tracing the Soviet reaction to the ensuing controversy, and examining the possible implications of this development for World War III—should uncertain destinies lead to this end. The task of objective intelligence analysis requires we think the unthinkable when disturbing events such as the Sverdlovsk incident occur. While answers to such investigations may prove less than satisfactory, failure to pursue these footnotes of contemporary life may ultimately prove more cataclysmic than the message such inquiries may reveal. The April 1979 anthrax incident is such a footnote, with a message for the present and for the future.

In viewing the totality of modern military means being pursued by the Soviet Union, one should not become preoccupied with new weaponry of an exotic nature at the expense of existing or supposedly antiquated systems. A Soviet scientist who defected recently to the West reported that 80 percent of the research in the USSR involves military-related subjects. He said genetics is receiving renewed attention in the USSR because of its military role in biological warfare. The defector, a molecular biologist, cited the case of a student attached to his staff to complete his doctoral degree. The student scientist, from a top secret military installation near Moscow, told the defector the purpose of his education was to prepare him for working at the biological warfare facility to which he was assigned.[1]

Biological warfare is the use of biological agents to cause casualties in man or animals as well as damage to plants or materiel. It also includes defensive measures taken to prevent the use of biological

---

[*]Orignally prepared for and presented at the Assistant Chief of Staff/Intelligence, USAF-sponsored conference "The Soviet Union: What Lies Ahead?" in September 1980 and reprinted in *Air Force Magazine*, Vol. 64, No. 3 (March 1981).

agents.[2] While biological warfare may not be a new or particularly exciting field of weaponry, the Sverdlovsk incident has reminded us we can ill afford to ignore the possibility of its future use.

The Sverdlovsk Incident

Available information on the incident in open publications is incomplete and largely drawn from secondary sources of unknown reliability. Thus, it is difficult to be certain what actually happened, particularly since Sverdlovsk is a closed city. Any analysis based on open sources alone must be considered highly speculative. The following section summarizes the reports which have appeared in open sources.

Sometime between 3 and 6 April 1979, an accidental explosion at a secret biological warfare facility in Sverdlovsk reportedly released a cloud of lethal anthrax spores. According to Mark Popovskiy, a Russian science journalist who emigrated from the USSR last year, the explosion took place at Military Compound 19, located in the southern outskirts of the city. Biological weapons research and production were reportedly being carried out at the installation which is under the command of Colonel General Yefim Ivanovich Smirnov, chief of a USSR Ministry of Defense biological warfare research directorate.[3] The poisonous cloud drifted away from the center of the large industrial city and headed towards the village of Kashino, 18 miles southeast of its origin.[4]

The first casualties were said to be military scientists and technicians on duty at Military Compound 19 at the time of the explosion. A number of people at a nearby ceramics factory, "possibly the entire work shift," became ill, and the residents of Kashino were particularly hard hit. Several hundred people died during the first days following the explosion, and deaths continued at the rate of 30 to 40 per day through the middle of May.[5]

The illness was called "Siberian ulcer," the Russian expression for anthrax. Some Soviet citizens developed rashes and boils typical of this virulent bacterial disease which can also result in lung congestion, paralysis of the larynx and lungs, and, ultimately, death. Others collapsed at home and died before they could be taken to a hospital. An emergency immunization program was initiated, and the city's main newspaper, *Vecherniy Sverdlovsk,* published three articles on Siberian ulcer at the time of the accident.[6] The editor of the newspaper later denied the articles were motivated by a health epidemic.[7]

Soviet military authorities reacted quickly by distributing large amounts of antibiotics, and medical personnel were sent from Moscow to assist with the developing situation.[8] A special section of the Sverdlovsk hospital manned by military doctors and nurses was established to treat the casualties. The bodies of those who died were returned to their families but were said to have been cremated

775

following a brief funeral ceremony.[9]

A mass inoculation program was initiated which included the several hundred thousand residents of Chkalov borough, the southern region of Sverlovsk where the explosion occurred. They received vaccinations of an unknown serum both in mid and late April. This program was apparently unsuccessful, as many inoculated persons also died. As the epidemic subsided, city residents were mobilized to clean the streets, topsoil was removed in the vicinity of the path of the cloud, and the streets of Kashino were covered with fresh asphalt.[10]

Hundreds or perhaps as many as a thousand Soviet citizens reportedly perished from the epidemic. Had the winds blown toward the center of Sverdlovsk instead of away from it, the death toll would have been much greater.[11] Autopsies of the dead revealed that the victims' lungs were filled with fluid, a possible indication of pulmonary anthrax caused by the inhalation of airborne anthrax spores.[12]

The incidence of anthrax in humans is rare, even in underdeveloped countries. Long a dreaded disease affecting cattle and sheep, it was a common cause of animal deaths until 1881 when Louis Pasteur developed a vaccine to protect livestock.[13] Humans can contract anthrax in three forms: gastric, cutaneous, and inhalation or pulmonary. Gastric anthrax is caused by eating contaminated meat, while cutaneous anthrax is caused by anthrax spores touching the skin; both gastric and cutaneous anthrax rarely cause death. Inhalation anthrax is nearly always fatal, but it is found in nature only under especially unusual circumstances and not in proportions sufficient to cause epidemics. Inhalation anthrax is the form most likely to be used in biological warfare attacks involving aerosols. The Subcommittee on Oversight of the House Permanent Select Committee on Intelligence reported that US government information indicates the Sverdlovsk victims had the symptoms of inhalation anthrax.[14]

Following the incident, rumors of the anthrax epidemic began to reach Moscow.[15] The first published report of a biological warfare-related accident appeared in the British news magazine *Now* on 26 October 1979, and it was reprinted by the Hamburg *Bild Zeitung* the following day. This account said several thousand people had died from an unknown virus or agent at a bacteriological weapons facility in the Soviet city of Novosibirsk.[16] On 13 February 1980, *Bild Zeitung* reported the deaths in Sverdlovsk of more than 1,000 people who had become infected through inhalation. According to this account, the incident was caused by an explosion at a Military Installation 19 factory for bacteriological bombs.[17]

Russian science journalist Mark Popovskiy said he became aware of the Sverdlovsk incident in January from underground communications with friends in Sverdlovsk. Although his information was not revealed until after the incident became public in March, Popovskiy said his sources reported a shift in the wind away from the city saved it from a much greater disaster and a similar accident took place in 1958, with fatalities again limited by a shift in wind. The writer, who now lives in the US, said, "They ask me until what time will God continue to save the city by changing the wind."[18]

In response to rising concern that a biological warfare related accident had taken place, US Ambassador Thomas J. Watson, Jr. met with Georgiy M. Korniyenko, Soviet First Deputy Foreign Minister, on 17 March 1980 to inquire about the Sverdlovsk incident. Mr. Korniyenko reportedly replied he knew nothing about the epidemic but would examine the matter.[19] On 18 March, State Department spokesman David Passage provided the first official indication to the public that an epidemic had occurred. On that date, Passage said, "There have been some disturbing indications that an outbreak of disease in the Soviet city of Sverdlovsk in the spring of 1979 may have resulted from inadvertent exposure of large numbers of people to some sort of lethal biological agent."[20] Passage noted the US had expressed its concern to Soviet authorities about these reports, and he revealed the subject was being discussed at the 3–21 March conference in Geneva reviewing compliance with the 1972 Biological Weapons Convention.[21]

A major concern surfaced at this time over whether the reports, if true, constituted a violation of the 1972 Convention. This agreement had been ratified by the US, the USSR, and 85 other nations, and it came into effect on 26 March 1975.[22] While the actual use of biological means of warfare was unilaterally renounced by the US on 25 November 1969[23] and further codified by the 1975 US ratification of the Geneva Protocol of 1925,[24] the 1972 Convention prohibited

> . . . *development, production, stockpiling, acquisition or reten–tion* of biological agents or toxins, of *types and in quantities that have no justification for peaceful purposes,* as well as weapons, equipment and means of delivery designed to use such agents or toxins for hostile purposes or in armed conflict.[25]

In response to questions that the incident may have violated the 1972 convention, Passage said, "We are not necessarily charging a violation."[26]

The public airing of US concern over the Sverdlovsk incident brought a quick response from the Soviet government. On the day following the State Department's startling revelation, a Soviet Foreign Ministry spokesman strongly denounced the US claim, terming it the "latest fabrication of American propaganda" for which there was no basis and "obviously slander."[27] Also on 19 March, *Krasnaya zvezda* charged the British and the US with cooperating in the development of chemical and bacteriological weapons.[28] On 20 March, the Soviet news service *TASS* accused NATO of the illegal production and storage of bacteriological weapons and the CIA of planting the Sverdlovsk story in *Bild Zietung* in an effort to justify funds for further "new billions" for bacteriological weapons.[29]

The official Soviet response to Ambassador Watson's inquiry of 17 March was given on 20 March to American diplomats at the Soviet Foreign Ministry. The Soviet reply stated that an outbreak of gastric anthrax had occurred in Sverdlovsk and its source was contaminated meat which had been handled improperly.[30] This explanation was followed by phone calls to Western correspondents in Moscow by Foreign Ministry personnel. In what was considered to be an unusual step, the newsmen were read a statement which rejected efforts designed to raise doubts about the USSR's good faith in fulfilling the 1972 Biological Warfare Convention as well as all other agreements to which the Soviet Union had acceded. The statement reiterated that the USSR had announced in 1975 it no longer possessed "bacteriological agents and poisons, arms, equipment or delivery means" covered by the convention.[31]

The anthrax issue was also raised at the Geneva conference mandated by the 1972 convention after the first 5 years to review the agreement's operation. Prior to the conference's adjournment on 21 March, Ambassador Charles Flowerree, the US representative, said the US had initiated consultations with the Soviet Union about whether a lethal biological agent had been present in 1979 in the USSR in quantities inconsistent with the provisions of the convention. Soviet Ambassador V. I. Issrayelyan responded to the charge by asserting the USSR was complying strictly with the provisions of the convention. He said the anthrax outbreak was a natural occurrence in which people had contracted the disease when meat from sick animals was used as food. Ambassador Issrayelyan did not give any indication of the number of fatilities from the incident, and he termed the controversy an "epidemic of anti-Soviet hysteria."[32]

Soviet media continued to deny anything but a natural outbreak of an animal disease passed to humans had taken place. Radio Moscow, in an English-language broadcast, reported some Soviet citizens had become infected by cutaneous and intestinal (or gastric) anthrax due to the handling and consumption of animal meat processed in violation of Soviet veterinary standards. The broadcast stated that no quarantine had been imposed on Sverdlovsk or its environs but said the population had been warned to adhere to hygienic norms and to avoid buying unauthorized meat.[33] One Soviet publication accused the CIA of creating an inflammatory incident from what actually had been an outbreak of foot-and-mouth disease in the Urals.[34] Other Soviet media continued to accuse the US of preparing for chemical and biological war,[35] including the cultivation of anthrax.[36]

As the incident received further attention, Western correspondents in Moscow continued to hear stories that a leak from a secret military research installation, known as a "post office box" to conceal its identity, was responsible for the outbreak. According to sources in Moscow, Sverdlovsk residents heard within hours of the incident that the secret installation had been working on bacteriological weapons and a fatal disease was spreading from it. Some citizens fled the city, while those who remained were subjected to an extensive vaccination program. At the time of the outbreak, the official Soviet version of the incident, which attributed the illness to contaminated meat, reportedly had not been heard in the city.[37]

In September 1980, a USSR legal journal provided the first indication two Soviet citizens had been tried in connection with the incident. According to this account, a man reportedly had thrown a diseased cow carcass into an abandoned mine shaft. The cow was later determined to have died from anthrax, and the illegal disposal allegedly contaminated ground water supplies. A second person was said to have given some lamb to relatives and sold the rest following the deaths of two anthrax-infected sheep. Both were convicted and received minor penalties.[38]

An epidemic of gastric anthrax is a possibility which deserves consideration. According to a 1961 Soviet epidemiology text, 6 outbreaks of the gastric form involving 64 people took place in the Soviet Union between 1923 and 1940. The largest number of deaths in a single outbreak was 27. These cases had as their cause the consumption of diseased meat, often sausage, which had not been thoroughly cooked. Soviet case data indicated outbreaks of gastric anthrax occurred approximately every three years, and Sverdlovsk reportedly has been an area long associated with the disease.[39]

Although *Soviet* medical literature indicates that in the USSR gastric anthrax is usually fatal in humans,[40] if meat alone had been the cause of the Sverdlovsk incident and open source reports about the number of deaths are correct, hundreds of people would have to have contracted the disease by eating improperly cooked meat since thorough cooking destroys the bacilli.[41] Additionally, it is highly unlikely the contamination of a water source by one diseased animal would cause a concentration of organisms sufficient to induce widespread anthrax illness.

A May 1980 article on the Sverdlovsk incident by two Soviet medical officials asserted the actual form of anthrax can become complicated once the bacteria enters the bloodstream. This development, the doctors suggest, would promote the accumulation of fluid in the lungs and other symptoms of pulmonary anthrax.[42] According to a standard pathology reference, however, all forms of anthrax conceivably could lead to fluid in the lungs as a secondary result of the organism's toxic effect.[43] From a clinical point of view, however, a properly conducted autopsy would clearly indicate the cause of the illness due to the location and age progression of lesions found on or within a victim's body.[44]

Until more details about the incident are obtained—particularly on the number of victims, their location, as well as on signs and symptoms—definitive conclusions are premature. In particular, it is the judgment of the Subcommittee on Oversight of the House Permanent Select Committee on Intelligence that the official explanation failed to meet the requirements of Article 5 of the 1972 Biological Warfare Convention. The article obligates signatories to "undertake to consult one another and to cooperate in solving any problems which may arise in relation to the objective of, or in the application of the provisions of, the Convention."[45]

The US. House of Representatives, in House Resolution 644 of 22 April 1980, expressed its displeasure with the Soviet response and requested the President seek to determine Moscow's compliance with the convention.[46] On 14 May, the US Senate unanimously passed a resolution requesting the Soviet Union furnish a satisfactory explanation of the incident or debate the issue in the United Nations Security Council.[47]

Congressional concern over Soviet compliance with the 1972 Biological Warfare Convention also has led to some expressions of dissatisfaction with the Convention itself. A major provision of the Convention charges signatories to:

> Never in any circumstances to develop, produce, stockpile, acquire or retain microbial or other biological agents, or toxins whatever their origin or method of production, of types and in *quantities that have no justification for pro–phylactic, protective, or other peaceful purposes,* as well as weapons, equipment and means of delivery designed to use such agents or toxins for hostile purposes or in armed conflict.[48]

Some believe this provision contains a significant loophole because it fails to specify what quantities of a substance beyond those required for "prophylactic, protective, or other peaceful purposes" would constitute a violation. As noted by the report of the Subcommittee on Oversight of the House Permanent Select Committee on Intelligence, "A very large supply would be convincing evidence of a violation, but a relatively small quantity released into the air could cause an epidemic."[49] This loophole, in essence, means biological warfare research is not banned by the convention.[50]

Additionally, some consider the provisions for investigating complaints regarding possible violations as less than satisfactory. A party suspecting a violation must first consult and cooperate with the suspected party, either directly or through procedures of the United Nations, to obtain clarifying information. Should this step prove to be inadequate, the only other recourse is for the party suspecting a violation to bring the matter to the UN Security Council.[51] According to Ambassador Curt Lidgard, Sweden's representative to the Geneva review conference:

> It seems doubtful that any decision to investigate a complaint could ever be taken against the interest of a permanent member of the Security Council. It is equally doubtful that the present procedures could ever lead to ascertainment that violation has occurred.[52]

In its report on the Sverdlovsk incident, the Subcommittee on Oversight of the House Permanent Select Committee on Intelligence acknowledged that verification of compliance with the 1972 convention primarily rests with its provisions for consultation and cooperation. It also notes it is

> disturbing that the USSR may have built military facilities at microbiological plants since the negotiation and signing of the Convention, while the United States—in keeping with the letter and spirit of the Convention—has closed or converted its former military biological facilities to peaceful use.[53]

According to the report, such Soviet military facilities would not represent a violation of the letter of the convention, but they raise as yet unanswered questions regarding their purpose. The report concluded an epidemic of pulmonary anthrax occurred—"almost certainly" the result of a man-made bacterial strain—at a military facility long suspected as a site for biological warfare-related activities. Whether a violation of the 1972 convention took place cannot be ascertained, in the subcommittee's view, since the convention failed to specify the quantity of a substance constituting a violation.[54]

Possible Soviet Motivations

Broadly speaking, there are two possible motivations for pursuing biological warfare activities. The first could be purely defensive—the desire to conduct research involving biological agents in order to develop measures and equipment to protect a country's population and armed forces from their possible use. The second motivation is far more serious: to develop biological agents and the means for their delivery for offensive, warfighting purposes. Both possibilities, defensive and offensive, deserve further examination.

Biological research for prophylactic and protective purposes is continually underway in virtually all countries of the world, including neutral ones. This scientific vigilance is necessary to insure basic national survival in case prohibited biological weapons are ever used against a country's population.[55] It is also necessary because many microbial or other biological agents which could be used for hostile purposes also constitute threats in their natural state to human, animal, and plant health. As previously noted, the 1972 Biological Warfare Convention specifically permits biological research programs for prevention, protective, and other such peaceful purposes; therefore, the cultivation and possession of laboratory quantities of bacteria such as anthrax is of itself not unusual.

Most countries of the world conduct research and immunization programs to control the incidence of anthrax in animal populations. The disease is caused by *Bacillus anthracis,* a virulent organism which is spread by sporebearing germs in the air, on contaminated material, or in contaminated meat. Anthrax was one of the first recorded diseases, and it was discussed by Moses in the Old Testament (Exodus 9:9) and by Homer, Hippocrates, Pliny, Virgil, and other classical authors. It was the first disease for which the cause was determined to be a specific microorganism, thus laying the groundwork for the scientific fields of modern bacteriology and immunology.[56] Although anthrax is now controlled largely through the vaccine developed by Pasteur in 1881, its continued incidence in nature would warrant an ongoing Soviet research effort.

The second possible motivation for biological warfare-related activities is to employ its considerable capabilities for offensive, warfighting purposes. The use of microorganisms for military purposes is not new, and an ideal biological agent should be highly infectious, capable of being produced in large amounts, stable both in storage and after release, and suitable for dissemination by aerosol.[57]

Bacillus anthracis possesses characteristics which have caused anthrax to be considered a potential biological warfare agent since the inception of research on biological weapons. In its pulmonary form, anthrax has a mortality rate approaching 100 percent. It is ideally suited for aerosol dispersal because it forms spores which provide a protective layer for the genetic material, enable it to withstand most methods of aerosolization, and have a long life after dispersal. Anthrax spores can survive in soil for decades and can be stored for years. Anthrax's incubation period in man ranges from less than a day for an extreme exposure to up to four days. It is usually considered the most hardy, the most easily produced, and the most easily disseminated disease-producing organism for use against humans.[58]

In recent years, the attractiveness of biological agents as weapons has decreased in the view of Western observers. Studies of natural outbreaks of infectious diseases have revealed their effectiveness depends upon so many uncontrollable factors that the final result of their use is often unpredictable. Biological agents are affected by such things as the living conditions and levels of protection of the human target, and the state of the atmosphere, wind, and topography. Additionally, their persistence for varying periods of time can make decontamination a significant problem.[59] It is for just such reasons the US unilaterally renounced biological weapons in 1969.

Biological agents, however, continue to possess some unique advantages. Biological weapons destroy only personnel while leaving materiel intact, penetrate closed spaces, and are cheaply and easily produced and disseminated. Biological warfare materials can be developed at ordinary laboratories, and deadly amounts of agents can be produced even in private residences for clandestine purposes. Because small quantities can be very lethal, biological agents such as anthrax spores can be dispersed by rifle-fired explosive shells or small powder disseminators which release inconspicuous aerosols.[60]

In view of the advantages and disadvantages inherent in biological weapons, perhaps their most likely use is for strategic purposes against key command and communication centers, weapons storage sites, and missile silos, particularly where their persistence does not pose a problem. Because large-scale attacks against major cities and large geographic areas subject the agent to the unpredictable vagaries of weather and terrain, local attacks against strategic targets are likely to be much more effective. Such attacks can be executed covertly during peacetime when deliberate contamination and the responsible party can be concealed or during wartime as part of a larger attack plan. Lethal agents may be concealed in hair spray containers, fountain pens, and insecticide bombs activated by automatic timers which permit the perpetrators to escape prior to agent release and incubation. Strategic facilities of limited size are prime targets for such covert attacks.[61]

Considering the possible utility of biological weapons applied selectively and covertly against strategic targets, it is possible Military Compound 19 in Sverdlovsk was engaged in biological weapons research and production. Mark Popovskiy has asserted the USSR has actively pursued bacteriological weapon research since signing the Geneva Protocol of 1925. According to Popovskiy, a secret institute outside Moscow conducted such research in the 1920s and 1930s. The institute was later moved to an island where it was concealed as a cattle disease research facility. When World War II began, Stalin reportedly had the institute moved to Kirov and later established a chain of similar installations for germ warfare research. As of early 1979, Popovskiy said he had definite information two of the institutes were located in Kirov and Sverdlovsk.[62]

It also should be noted the Soviet Union was accused of having used biological warfare against the Japanese in the Soviet Far East before and during World War II. In one case, a Japanese colonel told a US interrogator following the war that in 1935 the Kwantung Army apprehended 5 Soviet spies carrying glass bottles and ampules which contained dysentery organisms and mixtures of anthrax and cholera spores. The Japanese officer claimed he personally observed the anthrax bacteria.[63] In 1950, another Japanese officer accused the USSR of using biological warfare against Japanese forces. The officer reported he had been told anthrax organisms were released in 1944 at Shenho, a location in Manchuria occupied by the Japanese.[64] These accusations have not been substantiated.

Soviet writings on military science and military doctrine support the possibility that the exigencies of military preparedness for the next war demand attention be given biological warfare. According to V. I. Lenin, "the most dangerous thing is to underestimate the enemy and to rest on the belief that we are stronger."[65] What is termed "scientific prediction" of military affairs requires Soviet planners to anticipate the nature of future warfare, potential weaponry, and the organization of enemy armed forces.[66] Additionally, it requires the potential enemy be studied assiduously:

> Lenin also pointed to the necessity of studying everything which the enemy possesses or may possess. One's attention is drawn precisely by the latter part of this statement; that is, study of that which the enemy may possess. In this case we emphasize the importance of prediction and taking into account the possible development of military theory and practice on the part of the probable adversary as well as his acquisition of new weapons.[67]

Ideological considerations might also lead Soviet military planners to invest in biological warfare programs. The Leninist revolutionary ethic must be influential: morality should be judged in terms of the extent to which a specific act or decision assists the revolutionary cause of world communism. Furthermore, the Leninist view of the world is dialectical; that is, the greater Soviet strength becomes, the stronger peace becomes and the greater the chances of preventing war.[68]

Earlier Soviet writings on future warfare predicted it would be characterized by the use of weapons of mass destruction such as nuclear, chemical, and biological weapons. Since 1972, however, Soviet officials have stated the USSR does not possess biological weapons. The 1925 Geneva Protocol officially prohibits the USSR from *using* biological weapons and the 1972 Biological Warfare Convention prohibits the *development, production, and stockpiling* of biological weapons, but Soviet media clearly ascribe this capability to NATO nations. It is possible Soviet authorities, though in compliance with the letter of the biological warfare accords, have maintained limited amounts of biological warfare materials so as not to deny themselves the advantages of these weapons in specific strategic operations, particularly if they perceive a potential adversary may choose to do the same.

Conclusion

This review of open source reports of the Sverdlovsk incident has suggested two possible explanations for its occurrence. First, the USSR may maintain small quantities of biological warfare materials for preventive, protective, and other peaceful purposes in compliance with the 1972 Biological Warfare Convention. There is substantial reason to believe this is correct; virtually all nations are believed to engage in biological research for defense programs and public health purposes.

The second possibility—that the Soviet Union is conducting biological warfare research and production for offensive, warfighting purposes—simply cannot be proved. While a scenario may be envisioned in which small quantities of lethal biological agents are covertly deployed against strategic targets of great importance either before or during a war by agents and *Spetsnaznacheniya* (Special Designation) units controlled by the KGB,[69] there is no evidence the Soviets are planning such uses of biological weapons.

The truth may also lie somewhere between these two possibilities. The nature of biological weapons research is such that defensive efforts inevitably provide information and materials which can be used for weapons purposes. Quantities of biological agents are routinely tested in laboratories, and some of the procedures undertaken for biological warfare defensive purposes are identical with those required for offensive preparations.[70] For this reason, a defensive program could be used to conceal a program undertaken for offensive purposes.

Although it is difficult to judge what actually happened at Sverdlovsk, the message to the West is that Soviet use of biological weapons in future warfare remains a possibility. Despite the moral imperatives which have led most people to reject biological weapons as too reprehensible for man to use against man, the incident at Sverdlovsk serves to remind us that we can never be sure. The reality of Sverdlovsk requires that we think the unthinkable about World War III—and be alert to insure it never occurs.

Notes

1. Malcolm W. Browne, "Soviet Science Assessed as Flawed But Powerful," *The New York Times,* 20 May 1980, p. C3.
2. US Department of Defense, *Dictionary of Military and Associated Terms,* Joint Chiefs of Staff Pub. 1 (Washington: Government Printing Office, 1 June 1979), p. 50.
3. US Congress, House Subcommittee on Oversight, House Permanent Select Committee on Intelligence, *Soviet Biological Warfare Activities,* Subcommittee Report, 96th Congress, 2nd Session (Washington: Government Printing Office, 30 June 1980), p. 2.
4. "1,000 Are Said to Die in Soviet Accident," *The New York Times,* 16 July 1980, p. A7. This article reported an account published in Paris on 3 July by the Russian emigre newspaper *Russkaya mysl'* [Russian Thought] which identified the bacterial strain as I–21.
5. Ibid.

6. "A Case of Siberian Ulcer," *Newsweek,* 31 March 1980, p. 37.
7. "Sverdlovsk Editor's Comment," *The New York Times,* 21 March 1980, p. A6.
8. New Reports on Soviet Anthrax Convince US of Germ–War Tie," *The New York Times,* 29 March 1980, p. 21.
9. "'Bacteriological' Explosion Near Kashino Reported," *Bild* (Hamburg), 13 February 1980, page unknown, in *Soviet Union: Daily Report,* Foreign Broadcast Information Service, 14 March 1980, p. AA 2.
10. "1,000 Are Said to Die in Soviet Accident," loc. cit.
11. US Congress, House Subcommittee on Oversight, House Permanent Select Committee on Intelligence, loc. cit.
12. "Anthrax Caused Deaths in USSR, US Asserts," *Philadelphia Inquirer,* 4 April 1980, p. 8C.
13. "Soviet Victims of Own Germ Warfare?" *US News and World Report,* 31 March 1980, p. 12.
14. US Congress, House Subcommittee on Oversight, House Permanent Select Committee on Intelligence, loc. cit.
15. "A Case of Siberian Ulcer," loc. cit.
16. "British Magazine Cited on Bacterial Catastrophe," *Bild* (Hamburg), 27 October 1979, page unknown, in *Soviet Union: Daily Report,* Foreign Broadcast Information Service, 14 March 1980, p. AA 1.
17. "'Bacteriological' Explosion Near Kashino Reported," loc. cit.
18. Constance Holden, "What is Siberian Ulcer Doing in Sverdlovsk?," *Science,* 4 April 1980, p. 37.
19. "US Hints of Germ–Weapon Ban Violations Called 'Anti–Soviet Hysteria,'" *The Baltimore Sun,* 22 March 1980, p. A4.
20. "Soviet City Exposed to Lethal Germs," *The Kansas City Times,* 19 March 1980, p. A6.
21. Ibid.
22. Ibid. The convention was signed simultaneously in Washington, London, and Moscow on 10 April 1972; ratification was recommended by the US Senate on 16 December 1974; and it took effect on 26 March 1975. US Department of State, *United States Treaties and Other International Agreements,* Vol. 26, Part 1, 1975 (Washington: Government Printing Office, 1976), p. 583.
23. US Congress, Senate Committee on Foreign Relations, *Convention on the Prohibition of Bacteriological and Toxin Weapons,* 93rd Congress, 2nd Session, Executive Report No. 93–36 (Washington: Government Printing Office, 1974), p. 1.
24. US Department of State, op. cit., p. 571.
25. US Congress, Senate Committee on Foreign Relations, *Convention,* loc. cit., emphasis added.
26. "Soviet City Exposed to Lethal Germs," loc. cit.
27. "Soviets Deny Germs Killed Any Russians," *The Baltimore Evening Sun,* 19 March 1980, p. A2.
28. "Poisoners Share Experience," *Krasnaya zvezda* [Red Star], 19 March 1980, p. 3.
29. "From a Position of Liars," Moscow *TASS* International Service, 20 March 1980, in *Soviet Union: Daily Report,* Foreign Broadcast Information Service, 20 March 1980, p. AA1.
30. US Congress, House Subcommittee on Oversight, House Permanent Select Committee on Intelligence, op. cit., p. 4; "Soviet Ties Epidemic to Anthrax," *The Baltimore Sun,* 21 March 1980, p. A1.
31. "Doubts About Adhering to 1972 Germ Warfare Accord Rejected," Reuters, 20 March 1980, in *Soviet Union: Daily Report,* Foreign Broadcast Information Service, 21 March 1980, p. AA1; see also "Soviet Ties Epidemic to Anthrax," loc. cit.
32. "US Hints of Germ–Weapon Ban Violations Called 'Anti–Soviet Hysteria,'" loc. cit.
33. "Anthrax Propaganda Used to Poison World Situation," Moscow *TASS* in English, 24 March 1980, in *Soviet Union: Daily Report,* Foreign Broadcast Information Service, 25 March 1980, pp. AA1–AA2.

34. "Another VOA False Report," *Literaturnaya gazeta* [Literary Gazette], 26 March 1980, p. 9, in *Soviet Union: Daily Report*, Foreign Broadcast Information Service, 28 March 1980, p. AA1.

35. "US Supports Chemical Warfare," Moscow Domestic Service, 28 March 1980, in *Soviet Union: Daily Report*, Foreign Broadcast Information Service, 28 March 1980, p. AA2.

36. "US Plans to Increase Chemical, Germ Warfare Capability," Moscow *TASS* in English, 20 March 1980, in *Soviet Union: Daily Report*, Foreign Broadcast Information Service, 21 March 1980, p. AA2.

37. "Reports from Soviet Town Link Anthrax, Military Site," *The Baltimore Sun*, 27 March 1980, p. A4.

38. "Soviet Journal Sheds Light on 1979 Anthrax Outbreak," *The New York Times*, 26 September 1980, p. A5.

39. Nicholas Wade, "Death at Sverdlovsk: A Critical Diagnosis," *Science*, 26 September 1980, pp. 1501–1502.

40. P. N. Burgasov, B. L. Cherkasskiy, L. M. Marchuk and Yu. F. Shcherbak, *Sibirskaya yazva* [Siberian Ulcer] (Moscow: Meditsina, 1970), p. 62.

41. US Insists Anthrax Cases Came from Germ Weapons," *The Baltimore Sun*, 29 March 1980, p. A4.

42. Nicholas Wade, "Death at Sverdlovsk: A Critical Diagnosis," op. cit., p. 1502.

43. Frederick G. Dalldorf and Francis A. Beall, "Capillary Thrombosis as a Cause of Death in Experimental Anthrax," in *Archives of Pathology*, Vol. 83, 1967, pp. 154–161.

44. Daniel P. Perl and John R. Dooley, "Anthrax," in Chapman H. Binford and Daniel H. Connor, eds., *Pathology of Tropical and Extraordinary Diseases*, Vol. 1 (Washington: Armed Forces Institute of Pathology, 1976), pp. 118–123.

45. US Congress, House Subcommittee on Oversight, House Permanent Select Committee on Intelligence, op. cit., p. 4.

46. Ibid.

47. "Gas Warfare: Russia Steals a March on US," *US News and World Report*, 16 June 1980, p. 37.

48. US Congress, Senate Committee on Foreign Relations, *Convention*, op. cit., p. 2, emphasis added.

49. US Congress, House Subcommittee on Oversight, House Permanent Select Committee on Intelligence, op. cit., p. 3. US intelligence officials have said that if the actual number of fatalities were as many as 1,000, this would mean the USSR possessed more anthrax than needed for laboratory purposes alone. "Soviets May Have Violated 1975 Germ Warfare Pact," *Washington Post*, 29 June 1980, p. 2.

50. Frank Barnaby, "CBW—An Unresolved Horror," *Bulletin of the Atomic Scientists*, Vol. 36. No. 6 (June 1980), p. 9.

51. US Department of State, op. cit., p. 588.

52. Barnaby, loc. cit.

53. US Congress, House Subcommittee on Oversight, House Permanent Select Committee on Intelligence, op. cit., p. 5.

54. Ibid., pp. 6–7.

55. E. Barrairon, "Biological Weapons—Myth or Reality," *Zivilverteidigung* (West Germany), No. 4, 1975, pp. 25–30, trans. by D. A. Fraser (Orpington, England: Defence Research Information Centre, 1978), p. 8.

56. "Anthrax," *Encyclopedia Britannica*, Micropaedia, 15th ed., Vol. I, pp. 412–13.

57. Dan Crozier, "The Biological Warfare Problem," *Journal of Occupational Medicine*, No. 11, 1969; p. 509.

58. Julian Perry Robinson with Carl–Goran Heden and Hans von Schreeb, *CB Weapons Today* (Vol. II of *The Problem of Chemical and Biological Warfare: A Study of the Historical, Technical, Military, Legal and Political Aspects of CBW, and Possible Disarmament Measures*), 6 Vols. (New York: Humanities Press, 1973), pp. 65–66. For a study of the effects of anthrax on primates due to an intradermal injection of anthrax spores, see Frederick Klein, et al, "Neurological and Physiological Responses of the

787

Primate to Anthrax Infection," *Journal of Infectious Disease,* No. 118, 1968; pp. 97–103. For a study of the effects of inhalation of anthrax spores by primates, see Wilhelm S. Albrink and Robert J. Goodlow, "Experimental Inhalation Anthrax in the Chimpanzee," *American Journal of Pathology,* No. 35, 1959; pp. 1055–1065.

59. United Nations, *Chemical and Bacteriological (Biological) Weapons and the Effects of Their Possible Use* (New York: United Nations, 1969), pp. 52–60.

60. Julian Perry Robinson, *The Rise of CB Weapons: The Problem of Chemical and Biological Warfare: A Study of the Historical, Technical, Military, Legal and Political Aspects of CBW and Possible Disarmament Measures,* Vol. 1 of 6 Vols. (New York: Humanities Press, 1971), p. 111.

61. S. Jacksen, H. Markkula, and L. E. Tammelin, *B–Protection in Swedish Security Politics* (Sundbyberg, Sweden: The Armed Forces Research Institute, 1967), trans. by US Army Foreign Science and Technology Center, August 1974, pp. 7–16.

62. Holden, loc. cit. Popovskiy identified Kalinin and Novosibirsk (the location of the germ warfare accident reported by *Now* on 26 October 1979 and *Bild Zeitung* on 27 October 1979) as two sites where he had tentative information similar institutes were located. According to Popovskiy, "Everything I have said gives me a basis to believe that what the American press is reporting is true." See also, Mark Popovskiy, *Manipulated Science: The Crisis of Science and Scientists in the Soviet Union Today,* trans. by Paul S. Falla (Garden City: Doubleday and Company, 1979).

63. Robinson, *The Rise of CB Weapons,* op. cit., p. 222, citing Scientific and Technical Advisory Section, GHQ, AFPAC. Report on scientific intelligence survey in Japan, September and October 1945, Vol. 5, Biological Warfare (BIOS/JAP/PR/746).

64. Ibid., citing "Germ Warfare Laid to Russia," *The New York Times,* 23 February 1950, p. 10. It should be noted the Japanese were also accused of using biological warfare in the Far East against the USSR, the Peoples Republic of Mongolia, and China. Ibid., pp. 217–220, 342–347.

65. V. I. Lenin, *Complete Collected Works,* Vol. 41 (Moscow: Political Literature Publishing House, 1963), p. 144.

66. General Major A. S. Milovidov and Colonel V. G. Kozlov, eds., *The Philosophical Heritage of V. I. Lenin and Problems of Contemporary War,* translated and published under the auspices of the US Air Force (Washington: Government Printing Office, 1976), p. 261.

67. Ibid., p. 266.

68. Ibid., p. 262.

69. Robert Moss, "Spetsnaz—The Special Forces of the KGB," *The London Daily Telegraph,* 27 May 1980, p. 6.

70. Barnaby, loc. cit., and I. Malek, "Biological Weapons," in Steven Ross, ed., *CBW: Chemical and Biological Warfare (Boston: Beacon Press, 1968), pp. 55–56.*

Part VII

A Soviet Emigre's View of the US–Soviet Strategic Relationship

In his celebrated *Will the USSR Survive Until 1984?* Andrei Amalrik forecast the collapse of the Soviet political system as the result, among other things, of a conflict with China. Amalrik grew increasingly pessimistic about his prediction in later years, primarily as a result of what he saw as the failure of the West to understand and react to Soviet international designs. In one of his last public appearances before his most untimely and tragic death, he spoke to the conference attendees about the Soviet danger to the West. Amalrik urged the West to develop a new, coherent strategy for dealing with the USSR—a strategy that recognizes the realities of the Soviet threat.

Three Western Approaches to the USSR*

Remarks Delivered by Andrei Amalrik
at Concluding Banquet on 27 September

Ladies and gentlemen, first of all, forgive my poor English. Even though I'm reading, I will be stumbling and making mistakes, but nonetheless I will read my speech in English no worse than our great leader Leonid Ilyich Brezhnev reads his speeches in Russian.

As you know, this summer the Olympic Games were held in Moscow, and a story circulated about Brezhnev reading his speech at the opening. First he looks at his paper—just as I'm doing right now—and dramatically begins: "O! O! O! O! O!" Lord Killanin nervously whispers to him, "President Brezhnev, that isn't your speech there, that's only the Olympic emblem."

American self-sufficiency and isolation, on the one hand, have provided the US a higher level of security than Europe, but on the other hand have weakened your ability to understand other peoples and cultures. This is dangerous for a country that shapes world policy, as one may see by the events in Vietnam or Iran.

The same could be said about US relations with the Soviet Union. I would single out four dangerous points in your approach:

1. A belief that the USSR is seeking the same reasonable compromise as the US, and as soon as compromise is achieved, maintenance of the status quo and tranquility will be insured for a long time.

But the word "compromise" is a dirty word in the Russian language, and if the USSR sometimes makes a compromise, it looks upon the established position as a springboard for new pressure and for achieving a new "compromise" which is even more advantageous for the Soviet Union.

2. A belief that if pressure on the USSR does not bring quick results, it must be abandoned.

For example, when the Jackson–Vanik Amendment did not bring about an immediate increase in Jewish emigration, or when the embargo on grain sales did not lead to an immediate withdrawal of Soviet troops from Afghanistan, voices immediately were raised that the pressure was not working and therefore must be abandoned.

But pressure can be effective only if it is applied for a long period of

---

*Portions of this speech first appeared in *Soviet Analyst,* Vol. 9, No. 14 (9 July 1980), pp. 3–7. Reprinted by permission.

time. We Russians are patient and whatever pressure the US is ready to apply for 10 months, the USSR can endure for 10 years.

3. A belief that in general the USSR has the same intentions as the US; that is, to strengthen its influence in the world while preserving world stability at the same time.

However, the USSR seeks world destabilization.

4. You ascribe to the USSR your own values and seek to explain its actions from an American perspective, primarily from the point of view of American gain. Even the Russian revolution is explained by the need to rapidly industrialize the country, or the urge to establish control over Iran by the Soviets' desire to obtain oil for themselves or deny it to the West.

As it was, the revolution did not hasten but, in fact, retarded the industrialization of Russia. Actually, the USSR had tried to get control of Iran before oil began to play its current role. The USSR is richer than the US in natural resources; the level of education there—especially technical education—is at least as high as the US. Russians are no more stupid than Americans. And if the USSR lags behind the US in the field of economics, technology, and standard of living, then it is precisely because it is not its primary objective.

If the US considers economics as the main instrument for exerting its influence in the world and as the main weapon in its self-defense, and uses economics as the chief measure of its successes and failures, then it is in for a disappointment. For the role it gives to economics is really no more than a kind of escapism from political and ideological problems.

It is not just that the Soviet Union is capable in the event of nuclear war of destroying the West or of being destroyed by it. The USSR is the country in which totalitarian socialism first triumphed and which is both geographically and mentally located half-way between Europe and Asia. It is possible that the confrontation between the "developed" and "underdeveloped" strata of society which took place in the terrifying revolution of 1917–1921 in Russia is in fact a harbinger of what is to happen on a world scale.

The US can respond in three ways, depending on how it assesses Soviet intentions and on what moral, political, economic, and military forces it has at its disposal.

The first possible response is a policy of enmeshing the USSR in relations which are sufficiently advantageous for it to want to maintain the existing world order and not seek to destroy it. This policy assumes the *de facto* and *de jure* recognition of the external acquisitions and the internal political structure of the USSR and also that the West will support it economically by means of technology credits, grain, etc. At the root of such a policy clearly lies the undeclared idea of buying the USSR, and it reminds one of the historical model of relations between a trading power and a military one. Such a policy is being conducted

791

now and carries the label "detente."

The second is a policy of containment—that is, the *de facto* recognition of what the USSR controls and what it is but accompanied by an attempt to prevent any further ideological, political, or military expansion, while at the same time avoiding an exaggerated response. Such a policy was conducted during the Cold War and also had the aim of preserving the status quo but involved greated international tension.

The third possible response to the USSR is a "forward" policy, an attempt to squeeze it out of its spheres of influence and to compel it to alter its external and internal policies. Such an approach has never been tried in its pure form—but there were elements of it during the Cold War and detente periods such as, for instance, radio broadcasts to the USSR or pressure on it to permit freer emigration—and the policy undoubtly had an effect, albeit not a very great one, on the internal situation in the USSR. It is obvious that a policy of detente requires that the interests of the USSR coincide at least partially with those of the US so that the USSR will prefer peace to war, economic development to stagnation, a rise in living standards to the pauperization of the population, cooperation between countries to isolation. Such a partial sharing of interests does indeed exist and this makes detente possible, but not as a long-term policy.

The regime has its own priorities, and the fact that, for example, it is anxious for the standard of living to rise does not mean that it will not sacrifice this secondary goal to achieve its principal one.

Although the USSR both acts and speaks quite openly about its ultimate aims, these remain somewhat unclear to the West. As far as Soviet statements are concerned, reflections on the "international revolutionary movement" and the "worldwide victory of communism" are assigned by the West to the ritualistic side of the regime, the more so that in that verbal propaganda porridge you can discover anything you like from "merciless struggle" to "peaceful coexistence". As for Soviet actions, they are explained within the framework of traditional Russian imperialist policy: Stalin divided Poland with Hitler, just as Catherine the Great divided it with Frederick the Great of Prussia; Khrushchev suppressed the Hungarian rising of 1956, but after all Nicholas I did just the same; Brezhnev, with the help of the Cubans, established communist regimes in Africa, but then Nicholas II considered a plea for arming the blacks to fight against the English.

In this way many US observers see the USSR as heir to the Russian Empire pursuing national goals, certainly anxious to snatch up anything at all insecure, but basically interested in the existence of a balance of forces in the world and recognizing the interests of others. Even when taking such a narrow view, it should not be forgotten that Imperial Russia did not consider itself a European power but a Eurasian one— heir to two world empires, the Mongol and the Byzantine. It is from this that Russian dreams derive, dreams of uniting all the Slavs, of gaining access to the Southern seas, of taking Constantinople, of the mission of the Russian people, of the Russians as the Chosen People. The Marxist legend of the proletariat-as-Messiah, world revolution, and a world state found fertile ground in Russia. It is this combination of nationalist and state interests with Russian messianism and Marxist messianism that makes the Soviet policy so straightforward in its aggressiveness and at the same time so difficult to explain from the rationalist point of view of the West.

No one ever makes for a distant goal by taking a straight line to it. For all of this, however, the general strategy of the USSR is quite clear: whenever in the old world a crack appears, hammer in a wedge; whenever a fire breaks out, pour on petrol. What is more, it is immaterial whether those who are doing the work of destruction are Marxists or not, even whether they are "for" the Soviet Union: the main thing is that they should be "against" the West. Further developments are to follow three basic stages: old order—disorder—new order.

In the first years after the 1917 revolution the Bolsheviks argued about where to direct their main efforts—towards a revolution in Europe which, in theory at least, was about to begin; or towards anti-colonialist movements which were only in an embryonic form. History resolved this debate for them: European revolution failed to materialize, whereas the Afro–Asian nationalist movement became a powerful force. The USSR could not symphathize with nationalism as such, not even with national-communism, but it saw in it a weapon against Western democracies.

The democracies—in full flower, rich, free, arrogant, taking what they wanted by skill and not by force—were that "old world," that Carthage which had to be destroyed to its foundations, as Castro put it and as the words of the *Internationale* have it. Relations between the USSR and the West, in simplified form, also proceed according to a triple pattern: pressure—isolation—detente.

First the USSR exerts pressure on the West, either directly or in some indirect fashion; then the West starts to resist, breaking established ties with the USSR; or the USSR isolates itself in order to digest what it has just gobbled up. Ultimately, isolation begins to cause tensions within the USSR, and the West begins to get nervous, not knowing Soviet intentions and detente begins. The USSR begins to absorb the scientific and economic achievements of the West, receives the West's recognition of what it has seized during the period of tension, and eases off the internal pressure. This allows the USSR to gather new strength and begin a new period of outward pushing.

Thus, the postwar years were a period of pressure when the USSR was making Eastern Europe communist and was supporting the communization of Asia. The Berlin blockade and the beginning of the Korean War were the culmination of this period. The resistance of the West and the isolation of the USSR so increased internal tensions that

Stalin's heirs immediately undertook internal reforms and the easing of relations with the West. The period of so-called "peaceful coexistence" began. The strength that was gathered during this period permitted the USSR to embark on new forms of pressure on the West, culminating in the construction of the Berlin Wall and the Cuban crisis.

The response of the US once more obliged the USSR to retreat into isolation, renewed internal tension—which began with economic difficulties and ended with the phenomenon of dissidence—and forced the USSR to embark on detente. Since these periods do not have a clear dividing line but ripen, as it were, within the preceding one, at the height of detente the USSR began to tighten its grip on Angola and Ethiopia and has now taken its troops into Afghanistan. Soviet pressure has produced a response from the West, albeit not a very strong one, and it is not yet clear how long the USSR can keep up this pressure before it again enters a period of isolation.

For this reason, I think that it is impossible for the West to reach a long-term agreement with the USSR, and I also believe that in this confrontation the West is not only on the defensive but is being forced back onto lines of defense that are even closer to its heart. No agreement with the USSR can give the West a feeling of security; talks on the limitation of nuclear arms, should they succeed, can only alleviate slightly the economic burden of armaments but cannot remove the threat of nuclear strike which has held back the USSR for so long and, indeed, still holds it back from a likely invasion of Europe.

But the USSR may not need to invade militarily in order to establish its control over Western Europe. One can envisage the following sequence of events: the death of Khomeini produces a collapse of authority in Iran, Soviet troops enter the country—at someone's request of course. The US will not drop a nuclear bomb because of Iran and partial bombardment or the sending in of paratroopers—who would in any case probably be unwelcome to the Iranians—would not stop the Soviet forces. It follows from this that left-wing radical regimes would be established in the countries of the Persian Gulf; the trend for the majority of the feudal regimes of the Afro-Asian "underbelly" of Europe to become leftwing is already apparent. Such regimes, at least to begin with, would enter the Soviet orbit.

In this situation, the Soviet Union offers France, Germany, and Italy a choice: either do without oil or declare themselves neutral, breaking the alliances with the United States. If some Western European countries adopted the second course as being preferable to economic catastrophe, the next step would be for the USSR to demand that communists be allowed to take part in government, then that they be given key posts. Innumerable Soviet "advisers" would appear and also Soviet garrisons. In short, what would happen would be the "East Europeanization" of Western Europe. The USSR would be sensible enough not to allow the mixing of Russians and Europeans but would redraw the map of Europe by creating a new system of vassalage.

All this could happen, but I am not saying that it is bound to happen. In the first place, the USSR itself is not invincible: it is in danger of being drawn into a long and exhausting Asian war; it could encounter the resistance of Eastern European countries or of a firm Western alliance; it could equally get bogged down in internal problems—the nationalities question, economic difficulties, and also the dilemma of the gulf that divides the changing structure of Soviet society and the unchanging structure of power.

It seems to me that the most sensible course for the US to follow is to make careful use of these difficulties in order to lead to a small crisis, with the aim of avoiding a greater one. A small crisis, such as there was at the death of Stalin, could bring reforms in the USSR—and more fundamental ones this time—and the democratization of the USSR would be the best guarantee of its own security that the West could have. In other words I have in mind the "third approach" to the USSR—neither its enmeshing in ties with the West nor its isolation from the West, but the attempt to change its internal system.

This is possible to the extent that the Soviet system contains within itself the capacity for change. As Russian and Soviet history has shown, this capacity does exist. Each step in the direction of dictatorship left behind an unrealized democratic alternative, and the idea of ruling themselves is no way foreign to Russians.

The best strategy the West can follow towards the USSR, it seems to me, is to work out a common approach so that the actions of some countries do not undermine the actions of others and so that the long-term security of the West is not threatened for the sake of short-term national gain. With some common organ to work out the policy of pressure on the USSR to change, the risk and losses associated with such a policy would not rest on certain Western countries or groups alone to the advantage of others.

To give an example, I approve of the boycott of the Moscow Olympics and the restrictions on the sale of grain to the USSR, but at the same time I feel it is unjust that the whole burden of the boycott fall only on sportsmen and grain producers while some Western businessmen continue to get fat on trade with the USSR. The prior condition for the USSR to be granted credits, technology, and grain should be changes in its internal and external policies—just a little each time but gradually leading to change within the whole system.

One final point: the USSR does not only have missiles and tanks in its armory. It also has its ideology, and ideology can only be opposed by ideology. Just as the idea of social equality is the moral foundation of the communist world and the idea of national rights of the foundation of the Third World, the idea of universal human rights can become the moral basis of the policies of the West. It is not just a question of offering help to a few dissidents or would-be emigrants, it is the whole problem of what values will gain the dominant position in the world order that is even now in the making.

Contributors

John C. Baker is a National Security Analyst with the Pacific-Sierra Research Corporation, Arlington, Virgina.

Richard E. Bissell is Associate Director of the Foreign Policy Research Institute. He was formerly the Managing Editor of *Orbis.*

Michael M. Boll Professor of Soviet and East European History and Government at San Jose State University.

Roger W. Barnett, Captain, USN, is Deputy Head, Extended Planning Branch, Systems Analysis Division of the Office of the Chief of Naval Operations.

Ray S. Cline is Executive Director of World Power Studies, the Center for Strategic and International Studies, Georgetown University.

Robert S. Clute is Professor of Political Science and Graduate Coordinator, Department of Political Science, the University of Georgia.

Kenneth M. Currie, Major, USAF, is a Soviet Specialist with the Assistant Chief of Staff, Intelligence, currently engaged in research at George Washington University.

Robert H. Donaldson is Provost and Dean of Faculties, Herbert H. Lehman College, City University of New York.

Gregory D. Foster is Associate Director (Research) and Manager, Washington Operations, of the Foreign Policy Research Institute.

Howard E. Frost, III, is a Soviet Affairs Analyst with the Central Intelligence Agency.

Stuart D. Goldman is a Soviet Affairs Analyst with the Congressional Research Service of the Library of Congress.

Leon Goure is Director of Soviet Studies, Science Applications, Incorporated, McLean, Virgina.

Gary L. Guertner is Henry Stimson Professor of Political Science, US Army War College, Carlisle Barracks, Pennsylvania.

Daniel M. Hannaway, Lieutenant Colonel, USAF, is Professor and Head of Department of Foreign Languages, United States Air Force Academy.

Lynn M. Hansen, Colonel, USAF, is Chief, Regional Negotiating Division, Arms Control and Disarmament Agency.

Amoretta M. Hoeber is Principal Deputy Assistant Secretary of the Army (Research, Development, and Acquisition).

G. Paul Holman is a Soviet Specialist with the Defense Intelligence Agency.

David R. Jones is Editor, *Soviet Armed Forces Review Annual* (SAFRA) and is associated with the Russian Micro project, Killiam Library, Dalhousie University, Nova Scotia.

Robert Kennedy is a Strategic Research Analyst with the Strategic Studies Institute, United States Army War College.

Stanley H. Kober is Senior Advisory Consultant of the Strategic Studies Center, SRI International, Arlington, Virgina.

George Kolt, Colonel, USAF, is currently serving on the National Intelligence Council.

Lincoln Landis is a Consultant of Soviet Affairs.

Gregory Lathrop is Associate Professor of Political Science, Northern Illinois University.

Vojtech Mastny, Professor of History at the University of Illinois, Urbana–Champaign, is currently Visiting Professor of Soviet Studies, the School of Advanced International Studies, Johns Hopkins University.

M. Rajan Menon is Assistant Professor of Political Science, Vanderbilt University.

Norbert Michaud is Chief of the Strategic Defense Economics Branch, Resources and Installations Division, Directorate for Research, Defense Intelligence Agency.

H. Lyman Miller is an Analyst with the Foreign Broadcast Information Service.

Mark E. Miller is a Senior Analyst with the Advanced International Studies Institute, Washington, DC.

W. L. Morgan is an Analyst with the Advanced Systems Resources and Management Branch, Foreign Technology Division, United States Air Force Systems Command.

Robert L. O'Connell is an Intelligence Research Specialist with the United States Army Foreign Science and Technology Center.

Martha Brill Olcott is Assistant Professor of Political Science, Colgate University.

Eugenia V. Osgood is an Analyst with the Federal Research Division of the Library of Congress.

Bruce D. Porter is an Analyst with Radio Free Europe/Radio Liberty.

Richard E. Porter, Lieutenant Colonel, USAF, is assigned to special warfare matters in the Office of the Assistant Director for Special Plans, Deputy Chief of Staff for Plans and Operations, Headquarters United States Air Force.

Carl W. Reddel, Colonel, USAF, is Professor and Head of the Department of History, United States Air Force Academy.

James T. Reitz is a Senior Staff Member of the BDM Corporation, McLean, Virginia.

Edward L. Rowny, Lieutenant General, USA (Ret.), was Co-Chairman, Reagan for President Defense Advisory Committee.

Haskell R. Scheimberg is an Analyst with the Future Systems Division, Directorate of Technology and Threat, Foreign Technology Division, United States Air Force Systems Command.

John W. Skipper is an Analyst with Ketron, Incorporated, Arlington, Virginia.

Alan B. Smith is an Analyst of Soviet Affairs with the Central Intelligence Agency.

Richard S. Soll is a Senior Scientist with Science Applications, Incorporated, McLean, Virginia.

Kenneth C. Stoehrmann is a Staff Member at the BDM Corporation.

Rebecca V. Strode is a Soviet Analyst with the National Institute for Public Policy.

Richard E. Thomas is Director of the Center for Strategic Technology, Texas A&M University.

David T. Twining, Lieutenant Colonel, USA, is a Member of the Strategic Studies Committee, Department of Strategy and Theater Operations, United States Army Command and General Staff College.

Gregory Varhall, Lieutenant Colonel, USAF, is a Soviet Specialist currently engaged in postdoctoral research at the University of Edinburgh.

Tommy L. Whitton is a Senior Research Specialist with the Long Range Estimates Branch, General Threat Division, Headquarters United States Air Force.

800

GPO : 1985 0 - 480-900